CLEAR SERENITY, QUIET INSIGHT – VOL. 2

NANZAN LIBRARY
OF ASIAN RELIGION
AND CULTURE

EDITORIAL ADVISORY BOARD

James W. Heisig
Kim Seung Chul
Okuyama Michiaki
Paul L. Swanson
Nanzan Institute for Religion and Culture

Hayashi Makoto
Aichi Gakuin University

Thomas Kasulis
Ohio State University

James W. Heisig and John C. Maraldo, eds., *Rude Awakenings: Zen, the Kyoto School, and the Question of Nationalism* (1995)

Jamie Hubbard and Paul L. Swanson, eds., *Pruning the Bodhi Tree: The Storm over Critical Buddhism* (1997)

Mark R. Mullins, *Christianity Made in Japan: A Study of Indigenous Movements* (1998)

Jamie Hubbard, *Absolute Delusion, Perfect Buddhahood: The Rise and Fall of a Chinese Heresy* (2001)

James W. Heisig, *Philosophers of Nothingness: An Essay on the Kyoto School* (2001)

Victor Sōgen Hori, *Zen Sand: The Book of Capping Phrases for Kōan Practice* (2003)

Robert J. J. Wargo, *The Logic of Nothingness: A Study of Nishida Kitarō* (2005)

Paul L. Swanson and Clark Chilson, eds., *Nanzan Guide to Japanese Religions* (2006)

Ruth Fuller Sasaki, trans. and commentator, and Thomas Yūhō Kirchner, ed., *The Record of Linji* (2009)

James W. Heisig, Thomas P. Kasulis, and John C. Maraldo, eds., *Japanese Philosophy: A Sourcebook* (2011)

Benjamin Dorman, *Celebrity Gods: New Religions, Media, and Authority in Occupied Japan* (2012)

James W. Heisig, *Nothingness and Desire: An East-West Philosophical Antiphony* (2013)

Clark Chilson, *Secrecy's Power: Covert Shin Buddhism in Japan and Contradictions of Concealment* (2014)

Paul L. Swanson, trans. and commentary, *Clear Serenity, Quiet Insight: T'ien-t'ai Chih-i's Mo-ho chih-kuan* (2017)

Clear Serenity, Quiet Insight

T'ien-t'ai Chih-i's *Mo-ho chih-kuan*

VOLUME 2

Translation and commentary
by
Paul L. Swanson

University of Hawai'i Press
HONOLULU

Printed in China
Second printing, 2023

Library of Congress Cataloging-in-Publication Data
Names: Zhiyi, 538–597, author. | Swanson, Paul L.
Title: Clear serenity, quiet insight : T'ien-t'ai Chih-i's Mo-ho chih-kuan / translation and commentary by Paul L. Swanson.
Other titles: Mo he zhi guan. English
Description: Honolulu : University of Hawaiʻi Press, [2017] Includes bibliographical references and index.
Identifiers: LCCN 2017017425 | ISBN 9780824873776 (pbk. ; alk. paper)
Subjects: LCSH: Zhiyi, 538-597. Mo he zhi guan. | Tiantai Buddhism—Doctrines—Early works to 1800. | Meditation—Buddhism—Early works to 1800. | Śamatha (Buddhism)—Early works to 1800. | Vipaśyanā (Buddhism)—Early works to 1800.
Classification: LCC BQ9149.C454 M613 2017 | DDC 294.3/92—dc23
LC record available at https://lccn.loc.gov/2017017425

Publication of the book has been assisted by a grant from the Tendaishū Kyōgaku Shinkō Jigyōdan 天台宗教学振興事業団.

The design and typesetting for this book were prepared by the Nanzan Institute for Religion and Culture.

University of Hawaiʻi Press books are printed on acid-free paper and meet the guidelines for permanence and durability of the Council on Library Resources.

Contents of vol. 2

The Great Cessation-and-Contemplation

VII. Contemplation Proper [48c25–140]

An Outline of the Ten Objects of Correct or Proper Contemplation . . . 747
Introduction . . . 747
1. Advice for Proficient Practice of Cessation-and-Contemplation . . . 747
2. Those Who Are Not Proficient in Cessation-and-Contemplation . . . 751
The Ten Objects of Contemplation . . . 754
1. Explanation of the Ten Objects of Contemplation . . . 755
2. Ten Ways the Ten Objects of Contemplation Arise: Nine Pairs and a Single Sevenfold Category . . . 760
3. Questions and Answers . . . 771
4. Sixteen Questions and Answers [fielded by Kuan-ting] . . . 772
1. Contemplating the Sense Fields . . . 786
1. Introduction . . . 786
2. Contemplating the Sense Fields While Sitting Properly in Meditation: The Ten Modes of Contemplation . . . 795
1. Contemplating Objects as Inconceivable . . . 795
2. Arousing a Compassionate Mind: Arousing True *Bodhicitta* . . . 837
3. Skillful Means for a Peaceful Mind . . . 842
4. The Universal Deconstruction of Dharmas . . . 869
5. Knowing What Penetrates and What Obstructs the Path . . . 1121
6. Cultivating the Steps on the Path . . . 1135
7. Controlling and Healing through Auxiliary Methods . . . 1173
8. Knowing the Graded Levels of Attainment . . . 1244
9. Resting in Patient Forbearance . . . 1263
10. No Passionate Attachments to Dharmas . . . 1269
11. Summary of the Ten Modes of Contemplation: The Parable of the Great Cart . . . 1271
3. Contemplating the Sense Realms while Responding to Objects as Conditions Arise . . . 1275
2. Contemplating the Objects of Passionate Afflictions . . . 1291
1. Clarifying the Marks of Passionate Afflictions . . . 1292

2. Clarifying the Causes and Conditions for the Arising of Passionate Afflictions 1296
3. The Methods for Controlling the Passionate Afflictions 1298
4. Cultivating Contemplation 1300
3. Contemplating the Objects of Disease 1322
1. The Marks of Disease 1326
2. The Causes and Conditions that Give Rise to Disease 1329
3. Clarification of the Methods for Healing Disease 1336
4. Clarification of Losses and Benefits 1348
5. Clarification of Cessation-and-Contemplation 1351
4. Contemplating the Objects of Karma 1364
1. The Causes and Conditions for the Arising of the Marks of Karma. 1365
2. The Proper Arising of the Marks of Karma 1366
3. Commentary with Questions and Answers 1373
4. Cultivating Cessation-and-Contemplation 1377
5. Contemplating the Objects of Demonic Forces 1387
1. Distinctions concerning Similarities and Differences 1388
2. Clarifying the Marks of the Arising of Māra 1390
3. Clarifying Their Obstructions and Disturbances 1396
4. Clarifying Ways to Control Demonic Influences 1399
5. Cessation-and-Contemplation 1401
6. Contemplating the Objects of Dhyāna Meditation 1410
1. Clarifying the Presentation of Dhyāna 1411
2. The Causes and Conditions of the Arising of Dhyāna 1421
3. The Marks of the Arising of Dhyāna 1422
4. Cessation-and-Contemplation 1517
7. Contemplating the Objects of Mistaken Views 1529
1. The People and Teachings of Mistaken Views 1531
2. The Causes and Conditions for the Arising of Mistaken Views. 1541
3. The Faults of Mistaken Views 1556
4. Cultivating Cessation-and-Contemplation 1583

The Great Cessation-and-Contemplation

VII. Contemplation Proper

VII. Contemplation Proper [48c28–140c]

AN OUTLINE OF THE TEN OBJECTS OF CORRECT OR PROPER CONTEMPLATION [48C28–51C20]

SEVENTH IS the correct, proper cultivation of cessation-and-contemplation. In the first six levels [or chapters] I relied on the sūtras to reveal the sublime understanding [of cessation-and-contemplation]. Now I will rely on this sublime understanding to establish the correct practice [of cessation-and-contemplation].

INTRODUCTION [48C29]

1. Advice for Proficient Practice of Cessation-and-Contemplation [48c29]

Oil and fire are mutually dependent [in order for a lamp to give light], and the eyes and feet help each other [for a person to advance]. If you are diligent in both practice and understanding, then the three obstacles and four demonic forces [that hinder contemplation] will confusedly contend with each other and arise [in your thoughts]; this will multiply your darkness and magnify your distractions, thus shading and disturbing the light of your con-

Contemplation proper 正觀: or, "correct contemplation." The rest of the *Mo-ho chih-kuan*, almost two-thirds of the whole, consists of the exposition on this topic.

The first six levels 前六重: the six chapters already expounded above, that is, 1. Synopsis (or Great Intent), 2. Explanation of Terms, 3. Features of the Essence [of Cessation-and-Contemplation], 4. Encompassing All Dharmas, 5. Incomplete and Perfect [Cessation-and-Contemplation], and 6. Clarification of Means.

Reveal the sublime understanding 開妙解: or, "to bring forth sublime understanding."

Rely on this sublime understanding to establish the correct practice 依妙解以立正行: it is not that Chih-i ceases to rely on Buddhist scriptures as a source of authority and as "proof texts"; he continues to quote them at about the same rate as before. Rather, he is claiming that the interpretations that follow are based as much on his own practice and experiential insight (or, in more technical terms, his "contemplation of the mind" 觀心) as on scriptural authority. This is a remarkable claim, and a forthright admission to the creative reinterpretation being undertaken by Chih-i in his presentation and molding of the Buddhist tradition.

Three obstacles 三障: these are 1. the obstacles of passionate afflictions 煩惱 such as greed, anger, and ignorance; 2. evil karmic deeds 業, such as the five or ten evil deeds; and 3. the karmic retribution 報 that comes from past evil deeds.

Four demonic forces 四魔: these are the "demons" of the 1. passionate afflictions 煩惱, 2. the five aggregates or skandhas 陰, 3. death 死, and 4. supernatural demons 天.

Shading and disturbing the light of

centration. You should not follow after, nor be afraid of [these phenomena]. If you follow after them, they will lead you to the evil destinies; if you fear them, they will hinder your cultivation of the correct Dharma practice. You should utilize [the practice of] contemplation to contemplate the darkness, and thus brighten the darkness. You should utilize [the practice of] cessation to stop the distractions, and thus the distractions will be quiescent.

This [practice of both cessation and contemplation] is like a wild boar polishing and wiping a mountain of gold [and thus revealing its treasures]; like all streams flowing into the sea [and yet the sea remaining the same]; like firewood causing the fire to flame up; and like the wind causing the locusts to increase.

your concentration 翳動定明: or, "shading your light (= insight) and disturbing your concentration (= cessation); 定 corresponds to the calming or cessation of dhyāna meditation, or samādhic concentration, and 明 corresponds to the bright insight of contemplation.

Like a wild boar polishing and wiping a mountain of gold 猪揩金山: perhaps this refers to a wild boar digging in the ground and revealing the gold hidden on a mountainside? This analogy is from a section expounding the perfection of patience in the *Ta chih tu lun*, T 25.281a6–7. The context is ambiguous (280c29–281a8):

> Patience is a power of all home-departed ones that allows them to conquer all evil and to manifest special deeds in the assembly. Patience allows one to uphold and keep [the perfections of] charity and the precepts, so that they will not be broken.... Patience is like a great ship, with which one is able to cross from this shore of samsara to the other shore of nirvana. Patience is a whetstone that can bring out the luster of various good qualities; [for example,] if a person is associated with evil, *this is like a wild boar polishing or wiping off a mountain of gold: the benefits are illuminated thereby.*"

Lamotte, *La Traité* 4, 1962, translates:

> La patience est une lime qui fait reluire les qualités *(guṇa)*: en effet l'homme qui vous fait du mal est pareil au cochon qui, se frottant contre le Mont d'or, en augmente encore l'éclat." Lamotte notes that this "traduction proposée sous toutes réserves.

All streams flow into the sea 衆流入海: a common image used in Mahāyāna Buddhism to refer to the unity of truth, or of the Buddha Dharma. See, for example, the *Mahāparinirvāṇa Sūtra*, T 12.621b8–19 and 625a1.

Firewood causing the fire to flame up 薪熾於火: see the *Mahāparinirvāṇa Sūtra* at T 12.798c28–799a4:

> If you are not able to contemplate in this way, this is called "not cultivating the precepts" and "not cultivating the mind [of enlightenment]." If you are not able to contemplate, your thoughts are easily provoked and agitated, difficult to control and difficult to regulate. They charge around like a mad elephant. The thoughts are quick as lightning, appearing quickly yet not dwelling, like monkeys, and like an illusion or flame. This is the root of all evil. The desires of the five senses are difficult to satisfy, *as fire consumes firewood, and as the great sea swallows the flow of all the rivers.*

Wind causing the locusts to increase 風益求羅: see the *Ta chih tu lun*, T 25.113b3–4. The context reads:

> The light of this body [of the Buddha]

This vajra-like contemplation can split the array of passionate afflictions, and these hard and strong feet [of cessation] can take you beyond the field of birth-and-death *(samsara)*. Wisdom purifies practice, and practice brings forth the progress of wisdom—[together] they illuminate, "moisten" [and enrich], guide, and accomplish, and thus adorn each other with brightness, as the two hands of a single body wipe and clean each other.

It is not that you should merely clear away the obstacles and inwardly progress on your own path, but you should also be diligent in mastering the sūtras and treatises and reveal them to outsiders who have not yet heard them. Heal yourself and heal others, and thus be endowed with [the good qualities of] benefiting both [yourself and others]. Who else can be considered a teacher of people and treasure of the nation?

Again, learn from the Buddha's compassion, which has no hint of stinginess, and be of service to others by expounding cessation-and-contemplation. Open the gate and tilt the store [of the Dharma] to "cast out" the [wish-fulfilling] *maṇi* jewel. The jewel then radiates light, causes jewels to

> is the source of all light. From this light there branches out immeasurable and innumerable rays of light. It is like the *k'ie lo k'icou lo* 迦羅求羅 insect, whose body is very small but expands with the wind, and is able to eat everything. The rays of light [from the Buddha's body] are also like this. They are able to save sentient beings and expand infinitely.

Does this refer to a swarm of locusts that seems to grow with the blowing of the wind? Ikeda (*Kenkyūchūshaku*, 341) identifies this insect as the 迦羅求羅蟲, but points only to this passage in the *Ta chih tu lun* to describe it. Lamotte, *La Traité* 1, 443–44, translates:

> Les rayons du corps [du Buddha] sont une source de lumière *(ālokamūla)* et les courants secondaires issus de cette source sont innombrables *(apramāṇa)* et incalculables *(asaṃkhyeya)*. De même que l'insecte *K'ie lo k'icou lo* (?), dont le corps est minuscule *(paramāṇu)*, s'agrandit au contact du vent au point de pouvoir dévorer tout, ainsi les rayons du Buddha, au contact des êtres à convertir *(vineyasattva)*, se développent à l'infini.

Teacher of people and treasure of the nation 人師國寶: this phrase is one of the sources for Saichō's famous saying:

> What is the treasure of the nation? It is our religious nature [道心; *bodhicitta*]. Thus those who have this religious nature are the treasures of the nation. Long ago a man said, "Ten large pearls do not constitute the nation's treasure, but he who sheds his light over a corner of the country is the nation's treasure."

For a full translation and discussion of this passage by Saichō see Paul Groner, *Saichō: The Establishment of the Japanese Tendai School* (1984), 116–17.

Be of service to others by expounding cessation-and-contemplation 説於心[止]觀施於彼者: the Taishō text (49a11) has "the mind of contemplation" 心觀, but variant editions of the *Mo-ho chih-kuan* have "cessation-and-contemplation" 止觀, and I follow this reading. A translation of the Taishō text would read, "Be of service to others by expounding the mind of contemplation."

"Cast out" the *maṇi* jewel 捨如意珠: in other words, "gain" the Dharma by giving it away.

rain [from the sky], illuminates the darkness, enriches the poor, brightens the night, and saves the destitute.

You can go a far distance by driving [a vehicle] with two wheels, and a bird can fly high by flapping both wings. You cannot speak too highly of the moisturizing jewel [of cessation] and the clear brilliance of the jasper [of contemplation]. Can it be said that even the pulverizing of [Sadāprarudita's] bones at Pāṭaliputta, and the physical sacrifice from the cliffs [of the saintly

You can go a far distance by driving with two wheels, and a bird can fly high by flapping both wings 馳二輪而致遠翥兩翅以高飛: see the *Mahāparinirvāṇa Sūtra*, T 12.691c29–692a1:

> *It is like a cart that has two wheels, and thus is able to carry things, or like a bird that has two wings, and thus is able to fly.* An ascetic is also like this. I can see that he is rigorous in upholding the negative precepts, but I do not know if he has profound wisdom or not. If he has profound wisdom, then it should be known that he is able to carry the heavy burden of supreme enlightenment.

Presumably one can go even faster and further with four wheels (and a powerful engine), but the point here is the importance of balancimg two factors compared to relying on one. The two wheels or the two wings are representative of the two aspects of cessation and contemplation, of practice and wisdom, of meditative concentration and intellectual study cum understanding.

See also the famous opening section of the *Hsiao chih-kuan* (T 46.462b10–14):

> Therefore it says in the *Lotus Sutra,*
>
> The Buddha himself dwells in the Mahāyāna,
> And in accordance with his attainments
> Is adorned with the power of concentration and wisdom,
> With which he saves sentient beings.
>
> It should be known that these two aspects are like *the two wheels of a cart, or the two wings of a bird*; if one side is cultivated disproportionately, then one falls prey to mistaken excess. Therefore it says in a sutra,
>
> One who disproportionately cultivates the blessings and virtues of dhyānic concentration and does not study wisdom is called "stupid" 愚.
> One who disproportionately studies wisdom and does not cultivate the blessings and virtues of dhyānic concentration is called "crazy" 狂.

Clear brilliance of the jasper [of contemplation] 玉潤碧鮮: following the interpretation of Chan-jan; see BT–III, 124. The phrase is from the classical text of the *Wu tu fu* 呉都賦.

The pulverizing of [Sadāprarudita's] bones at Pāṭaliputta 香城粉骨: the story of Sadāprarudita and his various sacrifices for the sake of the Dharma were referred to by Chih-i in the previous passage of the *Mo-ho chih-kuan*, T 46.48b29–c9, to illustrate the five supplemental preparatory virtues of yearning, diligence, mindfulness, skillful discernment, and single-mindedness. See the *Pañcaviṃśati Sūtra*, T 8.418c–420 (*Ta chih tu lun*, T 25.745c–748) where it tells how Sadāprarudita offers to sell his body in order to get an offering that he could present to the bodhisattva Dharmodgata. No one took him up on his offer until Indra, disguised as a Brahman in order to test Sadāprarudita's sincerity, approached him with a request for some material to use in a sacrifice. Sadāprarudita proceeded to cut open his left arm for some blood, and broke open

ascetic] of the Himālayas are sufficiently rewarded with merit [in recompense for the sacrifice and compared to the greater rewards of cessation-and-contemplation]?

2. Those Who Are Not Proficient in Cessation-and-Contemplation [49a15]

A nimble horse takes to the right road just by seeing the shadow of a whip. [On the other hand,] those who are stupid and dull [are in a state wherein] "poisonous vapors have entered deeply, and they have lost their normal mind." As long as they do not have faith, they cannot receive [the Buddha Dharma]. Since they do not have the hook of hearing the Dharma, they are

his right thigh for some flesh, and started to break open his bones to get at the marrow. He was stopped by a woman who was watching the scene from afar and provided donations for the offering.

Physical sacrifice from the cliffs of the Himālayas 雪嶺投身: see the story of the Buddha's experience in a former life as an ascetic in the Himālayas where he threw himself off a cliff in order to learn the second part of a verse on transiency. See the *Mahāparinirvāṇa Sūtra*, T 12.692a–693b; see also the note at *Mo-ho chih-kuan* 45b28 for a full telling of the tale.

Sufficiently rewarded: the implied answer is, "of course not." In other words, the practice of cessation-and-contemplation is much more efficacious and beneficial than ascetic sacrifices, even the offering of one's own body or life.

A nimble horse takes to the right road just by seeing the shadow of a whip 快馬見鞭影卽著正路: in other words, those who have the talent for it will take to cessation-and-contemplation naturally. There are people, however, who are not naturally inclined to such practice, and Chih-i considers their situation in this section.

On the "nimble horse," see the analogy of the four kinds of horses in the *Saṃyuktāgama*, T 2.234a16–b20; 429b15–c10. Chih-i has used this example before; see notes at *Mo-ho chih-kuan* 19a23 and 34c5–6.

Poisonous vapors have entered deeply, and they have lost their normal mind 毒氣深入失本心故: a phrase from the analogy of the good physician whose sons would not take their medicine, in the chapter on "The Life-span of the Tathāgata" of the *Lotus Sūtra*, T 9.43a21–22. Hurvitz (*Lotus Sūtra*, 241 [222]) has: "It is that through the deep entry of the poisonous vapors they had lost their sanity." Burton Watson (*The Lotus Sutra*, 228) has: "Because of the poison in them, their minds are completely befuddled." *The Threefold Lotus Sutra*, 253, has: "the poison has entered deeply, they have lost their senses."

The hook of hearing the Dharma 聞法鉤: a phrase from the *Mahāparinirvāṇa Sūtra*, T 12.756a26. The context (756a23–28) says,

> [The causes for hearing the Dharma and thus approaching nirvana] are analogous to when a drunk elephant goes crazy and tries to cause much damage, and the elephant trainer has a great iron hook with which he gets a hold of the elephant and controls it until its evil thoughts are stilled. It is the same for all sentient beings. They are drunk with greed, anger, and ignorance, and wish to perform much evil. The bodhisattvas use *the hook of hearing the Dharma* to control them and make it so that they cannot perform evil. This is the meaning of saying that the causes for hearing the Dharma allow one to approach great nirvana.

not able to understand what they hear. Their eyes of wisdom are deficient, so they are not able to distinguish between the true and the false. Their bodies are numb, so that even if they act or walk they do not go forward. They have neither perception nor knowledge, and bring about great transgressions against the community. How should we endeavor to teach [cessation-and-contemplation] to such people [who have no religious spirit or capacity]?

There are those who demonstrate a weariness with the world, but delight in an inferior vehicle. They climb up to the branches and leaves [and ignore the roots], and are like a dog that associates with a menial worker [instead of a rich patron]. They pay respect to a monkey thinking it is Indra, and

Their eyes of wisdom are deficient, so they are not able to distinguish between the true and the false 乏智慧眼不別眞僞: the classical commentaries state that these phrases are from the *Pañcaviṃśati Sūtra* and *Ta chih tu lun*, but the *Inyō* admits that the phrase cannot be located in these texts. Ikeda (*Kenkyūchūshaku*, 341) links the phrase with one in the *Ta chih tu lun*, T 25.161a15: "by means of the eye of wisdom one can perceive and know the reality of all dharmas." Lamotte (*La Traité* 2, 843) has:

> Par l'oeil de la sagesse *(prajñācakṣus)*,
> Il contemple le Vrai [caractère] des Dharma.

Delight in an inferior vehicle 翫下劣乘: this must refer to "Hīnayāna" home-departed ones.

They climb up to the branches and leaves 攀附枝葉: they miss the forest for the trees? The phrase is from the *Pañcaviṃśati Sūtra*, T 8.319a12. The context reads:

> A bodhisattva who learns other sūtras but discards the Prajñāpāramitā [sūtras] will finally be unable to attain *sarvajñā*. Good sons and good daughters, [this is like] rejecting the roots *and climbing up to the branches and leaves*.

Like a dog that associates with a menial worker 狗狎作務: again, from the same section of the *Pañcaviṃśati*, T 8.319a24. The context reads:

> Subhūti, when a bodhisattva-mahāsattva learns *prajñāpāramitā*, he also learns [other] worldly and trans-worldly dharmas. Subhūti, suppose there is *a dog that does not seek for food from a great householder but instead follows after and seeks [grub] from a menial worker*. Like this, Subhūti, in the ages to come there will be good sons and good daughters who reject the profound Prajñāpāramitā [sūtras] and *climb up to the branches and leaves* [and ignore the roots].

Pay respect to a monkey thinking it is Indra 敬獮猴爲帝釋: see the story in the *Sūtra of the Buddha Treasury* 佛藏經 (T no. 653, translation attributed to Kumārajīva), T 15.787a23–b3:

> Śāriputra. In the past there was an ignorant man who did not know about monkeys. When he entered a great grove of trees and saw a group of monkeys assembled in one place, and remembered what he had heard about the Trāyastriṃśa heaven [where Indra dwells], he thought that this was the Trāyastriṃśa heaven. After emerging from the forest and returning to his village he asked many people, "Have you not seen the Trāyastriṃśa heaven?" The people replied that they had not seen it. Then the man said, "I have already seen it. Don't you want to see it?" Everyone replied that they would like to see it. So the man led a great assembly of people to the forest and showed them the group of monkeys, saying, "Look. This is the Trāyastriṃśa heaven." But all the people said, "This is not the Trāyastriṃśa heaven. These

mistake broken tiles for a luminous jewel. How can the Buddhist path be expounded to people in such darkness?

Again, there is a type of [Zen] meditator who does not have penetrating understanding into other people's [various] basic natures, and merely teaches [the same thing to everyone, like an incompetent doctor prescribing] milk as medicine [for every disease]. [There are various types of meditation being taught, such as] "essential mind," "to tread the mind," "harmonious merging," "seeking perception," and "either quiescence or completing"; these are all [stuck] in a single rut. There are a myriad ways of having [your

are just monkeys playing in the forest. Because of your perverted ignorance you do not know about monkeys, and you do not know about the Trāyastriṃśa heaven either."

Mistake broken tiles for a luminous jewel 瓦礫是明珠: see the story in the *Mahāparinirvāṇa Sūtra*, T 12.617c3–10, where a jewel is dropped from a boat into a muddy lake, and people try to find it again, mistaking various stones and tiles for the jewel. Chih-i has referred to this story previously in the *Mo-ho chih-kuan*; see notes at 20b15 and 43a3 for a full translation of the context.

Merely teaches milk as medicine 純教乳藥: see the story of the incompetent and competent doctors in the *Mahāparinirvāṇa Sūtra*, T 12.618a–b. This story also has been referred to previously in the *Mo-ho chih-kuan*; see the notes under 19a29 and 36a22.

"Essential mind" 體心, **"to tread the mind"** 踏心, **"harmonious merging"** 和融, **"seeking perception"** 覺覓, **and "either quiescence or completing"** 泯了: this appears to be a list of various terms associated with *dhyāna* practice, or perhaps schools of meditative practice in Chih-i's time, or terms from *dhyāna* texts. Very little or nothing is known about them, except for some commentary by Chan-jan. Kanno, *Ichinen-sanzen to wa nanika*, 87–88, points out that Chan-jan uses some of these terms in describing a "lineage of nine teachers" 九師相承. There is no mention of "essential mind."

As for "treading the mind," the sixth lineage [out of nine] is "called 'wisdom' and uses 'treading the mind' [for meditation]. [They claim that] the mind is unobtainable—internally, externally, and in between. [The mind is] quiescent and pure, and rests on the five sense objects."

As for "harmonious merging," the second lineage is "called 'greatest' and uses 'merging of the thoughts' [for meditation]. Natures are merged and marks are merged; there is no obstruction among phenomena."

As for "seeking perception," the seventh lineage "is called 'verbal' and uses perceptions of the mind [for meditation, using] the samādhi of various contemplations, the samādhi of extinction, and the samādhi of immediacy. [It teaches that] the mind cannot discriminate phenomena."

As for "either quiescence or completing," the fourth lineage "is called 'fulfillment' and uses 'quieting the mind' [for meditation]" and the fifth lineage "is called 'control' and uses 'completing the mind' [for meditation], thus perceiving thusness."

None of this makes much sense, being too terse, and more sources are needed to identify these terms accurately. In any case, Chih-i makes short work of and dismisses these types of meditative practices.

practice and insight] obstructed and made difficult, and [these people] are confused and do not know [the various options]. They have a slight insight into different aspects [that are unlike ordinary, mundane experience] and conclude that they have therefore attained the path [of the Buddha]. But they are not themselves vessels [worthy] of the [Buddha] Dharma, and they lack [the ability to] teach others. This is like a teacher and disciple both being blind and lame, and falling together. It is indeed pitiful to see the blind stumbling around in the darkness.

This cessation-and-contemplation [as expounded below in the *Mo-ho chih-kuan*] should not be taught to the above [types of] people. When it comes to cessation-and-contemplation, there is an advanced [way] for advanced people, and an inferior [way] for inferior people.

2. THE TEN OBJECTS OF CONTEMPLATION [49A27]

I will expound ten [objects of] contemplation.

1. the sense fields 陰入界 [that is, the five aggregates (*skandha*), twelve sense entrances *(āyatana)*, and eighteen sense realms *(dhātu)*]
2. the passionate afflictions 煩惱 *(kleśa)*
3. disease 病患
4. karmic marks 業相
5. demonic forces 魔事
6. dhyāna concentration 禪定
7. mistaken views 諸見
8. overweening pride or arrogance 增上慢
9. the two vehicles 二乘 [of śrāvaka and pratyekabuddha] **[49b]**
10. bodhisattvahood 菩薩

These ten objects have in common [the characteristic] that they can obstruct [your contemplation].

Teacher and disciple both being blind and lame, and falling together 盲跛師徒二俱墮落: the proverbial "blind leading the blind." The *Kōgi* (BT–III, 129) says that this phrase is from the **Śata*[*ka*]*-śāstra*, perhaps at T 30.173b21–23. This passage does contain the phrase "being like the blind and the lame because of [experiencing] different aspects 異相," but otherwise does not seem to be a very good candidate for the source of this saying. Ikeda (*Kenkyūchūshaku*, 342) points to an earlier section of this text at 172b.

Ten [objects of] contemplation 止觀爲十: Chih-i explains below the rationale behind this list. For details, see Sekiguchi's extensive note in *Makashikan* 1, 381–82.

Mistaken views 諸見: this is the last section actually covered in the *Mo-ho chih-kuan*. The rest is left unexplained.

Have in common [the characteristic] that they can obstruct 此十境通能覆障: or, "The penetration of these ten allows one

1. Explanation of the Ten Objects of Contemplation [49b1]

[1. The sense fields] There are two reasons why skandhas [and the sense fields] come at the beginning: first because they are readily manifest, and second because this follows [the teaching of] the sūtras. The *Pañcaviṃśati Sūtra* says, "The śrāvakas practice the path in accordance with mindfulness concerning four objects [of body, sensation, mind, and dharmas], and bodhisattvas first contemplate visible form *(rūpa)* and so forth until [they attain] universal wisdom." The chapters [of the sūtras] all [teach] this, and therefore it is not contrary to [the teachings of] the sūtras.

Again, one who practices has bodily experiences; who does not have the heavy burden of directly experiencing the [five] skandhas and the sense organs and objects? Therefore these are the first to be contemplated. If later the different marks [of the other nine categories] appear, then you can [contemplate] them each separately.

[2. The passionate afflictions] Now, the five skandhas are intermingled with the four categories [of passionate afflictions]. If you do not clearly examine these [passionate afflictions], you cannot be aware of how they gallop out of control. This would be like shutting yourself in the hold of a boat and floating down a river; it would be better to know about the splashing currents [and thus be able to control the boat]. It is when you go against the flow that you realize and get to know the swift galloping current. By contemplating the results of the skandhas, you can affect the causes of pas-

to overcome hindrances." Thus one must control or master them through contemplating them.

Readily manifest 現前: right in front of one's eyes, as it were.

The śrāvakas practice … universal wisdom 聲聞人依四念處行道菩薩初觀色乃至一切種智: the *Kōgi* (BT–III, 132) identifies this phrase as coming from the *Ta chih tu lun*, section "32-7" (around T 25.324–325), but the *Inyō* admits that the phrase cannot be located. Ikeda (*Kenkyūchūshaku,* 342) proposes a section from 328b20–26, which contains the phrases "mindfulness concerning four objects" and "universal wisdom," and how the bodhisattva perceives the ways of śrāvakas and pratyekabuddhas and uses them to save sentient beings.

Four categories [of passionate afflictions] 四分: I follow Chan-jan (BT–III, 134) in substituting "four parts" 四分 for the "four great [elements]" 四大 in the Taishō text. The four great elements are earth, water, fire, and wind, and makes no sense in the current context—instead, it appears in the next paragraph. The four types of passionate afflictions is a classification Chih-i uses later in the *Mo-ho chih-kuan* under the section on contemplating *kleśa* (T 46.102b), that is, the three poisons (of greed, anger, and ignorance) individually make the first three categories, and the three poisons collectively make the fourth category.

Following the Taishō text would read: "the five skandhas are intermingled with the four great elements."

sionate afflictions. Therefore the four categories [of passionate afflictions] are expounded next, after [the contemplation of] the five skandhas [and the sense fields].

[3. Disease] The four great [elements of earth, water, fire, and wind] are [the basis for] physical disease; the three poisons [of greed, anger, and delusion] are [the basis for] mental disease. It is due to these factors that you do not attain realization from within the passions. [Be aware that] if you contemplate the great [elements] and the categories [of passionate afflictions] together, this can be a great shock to your physical body, thus causing [the four physical elements to be like] four "serpents," and thus provoke disease. [Therefore the objects of "disease" are contemplated next.]

Four serpents 四蛇: see, for example, the *Ta chih tu lun*, T 25.145b9–22, where the four elements are compared to four poisonous snakes. Lamotte, *La Traité* 2, 702–707, translates:

> Ainsi, dans le *Āsīviṣopamasūtra*, on raconte ce qui suit:
>
> Un homme s'étant rendu coupable envers le *roi*, ce dernier lui ordonna de prendre en main unne *malle*. Dans cetta malle, il y avait *quatre serpents venimeux*, et le roi donna l'ordre au coupable de les garder et de les élever. L'homme se dit, "Il est dangereux de s'approcher de ces quatre serpents; ils tuent celui qui s'approche d'eux. Il est impossible de nourrir un seul de ces serpents et, à fortiori, tous les quatre à la fois." Alors il jeta la malle et s'enguit. Le roi ordonna à *cinq hommes* de tirer l'épèe et de le poursuivre. Sur ce, *un personnage*, de paroles engageantes mais animé intérieurement de dispositions hostiles, dit à l'homme: "Il serait raisonable de nourrir ces serpents, cela ne te causerait aucun tort." Norte homme, qui l'avait deviné, prit sa course et sauva sa vie par la fuite. Il arriva à un village vide, oú un *brave homme* lui dit adroitement *(upāyena)*: "Bien que ce village soit vide, il sert de halte aux voleurs. Si tu restes ici, tu devras prendre garde aux voleurs. Ne reste donc pas." Alors notre homme arriva près d'une *grande rivière*; sur l'autre rive *(pāra)* de la rivière, il y avait un *pays étrange*, pays bienheureux *(sukhāvati)*, apaisé, pur et exempt de tourments. Aussitôt l'homme réunit des matériaux et des cordes et se fabrique un *radeau*. Des *mains et des pieds*, il se dépensa pour traverser la rivière et parvint enfin à l'autre rive, à la Sukhāvatī exempte de tourments.
>
> Le *roi*, c'est le roi Māra; la *malle* c'est le corps humain; les *quatre serpents venimeux*, ce sont les quatre grands éléments *(catur-mahābhūta)*.

Chodron (2, 562–63) translates:

> In the *Āsīviṣopamasūtra*, it is said:
>
> A man who had committed an offence against the king was commanded by the latter to take a chest containing four venomous snakes and to guard them and take care of them. The man said: "It is dangerous to come near these four snakes; they kill anyone who approaches them. It is impossible to feed even one of these snakes, let alone four at once." Then he threw away the chest and fled. The king ordered five men to take their swords and pursue him. Thereupon, an individual, of attractive speech but inwardly hostile, said to the man: "It would be reasonable to feed these snakes; that would not cause any harm." Smelling a rat, our man went his own way and saved his life by fleeing. He came to an empty village where an honest man skillfully said to him: "Although this village is empty, it serves as a stopping-place for thieves. If you stay here, you should watch out for the rob-

[4. Karmic marks] The immeasurable [marks] of karma cannot be calculated. The good that is done while you are distracted is very weak and can hardly move [the effects of karmic retribution]. If you cultivate cessation-and-contemplation and recuperate from these diseases without any deficiency, you can "move" the wheel of birth-and-death. Or, you can move it by sprouting good [karma], or move it by destroying evil [karma], or move it by experiencing the recompense from the display of goodness, or move it by rebuking the retribution that comes from evil [karma]. Thus the explanation of [the contemplation of the object of] "karma" comes after that of "disease."

[5. Demonic forces] By "moving" evil [karmic retribution], you extinguish evil desires; by moving good [karma], you arouse good desires. [In such a situation] demonic forces quickly emerge from the sense objects and bring forth various impediments or destructive [barriers] to the path. Therefore "demonic forces" are explained after "karma."

[6. Dhyāna concentration] If you get past the demonic forces, then meritorious qualities arise. Then, either because of the associated causes of the past, or your current powers to practice, various dhyāna meditations are aroused, such as [enjoying the] flavor [of dhyāna], or pure [dhyāna], or [experiencing dhyāna] horizontally or vertically. Therefore dhyāna is explained after "demonic forces."

[7. Mistaken views] "[Cognitive] reflection" is one of the [five] constituents of [the first] dhyāna, and causes false "wisdom" to arise. [This involves] deviant reflection on dharmas, so that you become warped, arouse various perversions, and indulge in furious and specious arguments. Therefore "mistaken views" are explained after dhyāna.

bers. So don't stay here." Then our man came to a great river; on the other shore of the river, there was a foreign land, a very happy country, peaceful, pure and free of torment. Immediately, our man gathered materials and ropes and built himself a raft. Using his hands and feet, he paddled across the river and reached the other shore, Sukhāvatī, free of torment.

The king is king Māra; the chest is the human body; the four poisonous snakes are the four great elements; the five soldiers with drawn swords are the five aggregates,...

[Enjoying the] flavor 味 **[of dhyāna]**: a low level of dhyāna meditation in which the practitioner enjoys the bliss of his dhyāna attainment and becomes overly attached to it. This is discussed further in the *Mo-ho chih-kuan* from 118a16.

[Cognitive] reflection is one of the [five] constituents of dhyāna 禪有觀支: as explained in the notes above to *Mo-ho chih-kuan* 48a27–b2, the *Ta chih tu lun* explains the Abhidharma teaching of the five constituents of dhyāna as conceptual examination *(vitarka)*, reflection/contemplation *(vicāra)*, joy *(prīti)*, bliss *(sukha)*, and concentration *(cittāikāgratā)*. Here Chih-i uses the character *kuan*, but this refers to *vicāra*, not *vipaśyanā*.

[8. Arrogance] If you are conscious of [such] mistaken views and reject them, this will stop the deluded attachment [that derives from mistaken views], and neither the sharp nor dull [passionate afflictions such as] covetousness and anger will arise. Those who are not wise think that they have already attained nirvana. Those of the Hīnayāna perversely surmise that [the attainment of] the four dhyānas constitute the four fruits [of stream-enterer, once-returner, non-returner, and arhat]. Those of the Mahāyāna also experience visions of Māra who proclaims [their Buddhahood]. These people have not yet attained [enlightenment], but are arrogant [in thinking that they have]. Therefore "arrogance" is explained after "false views."

[9. The two vehicles] When mistaken views and arrogance have sub-

Sharp nor dull 利鈍: this probably refers to the "five sharp afflictions" 五利使 and the "five dull afflictions" 五頓使. The former are also called the "five [false] views" 五見:

1. *satkāya-dṛṣṭi*: the false view that the physical body possesses a substantial self,
2. *antaparigraha-dṛṣṭi*: the false extreme views of nihilism and eternalism,
3. *mithyā-dṛṣṭi*: the false view that denies cause and effect,
4. *dṛṣṭi-parāmarśa-dṛṣṭi*: the false arrogance than ones own views are superior to all others,
5. *śīla-vrata-parāmarśa-dṛṣṭi*: the false view that the only way to liberation is by keeping non-Buddhist precepts.

The "five dull afflictions" are covetousness, anger, ignorance, pride, and doubt.

Visions of Māra who proclaims [their Buddhahood] 魔來與記: see, for example, the *Pañcaviṃśati Sūtra*, T 8.352b22–c26, where it warns how Māra can appear to those who have practiced insufficiently and fool them into thinking they have attained enlightenment:

> [Māra appears before] a bodhisattva who has not practiced the six perfections for very long and does not have the power of means *(upāya)*. Subhūti. You should know that this is a demonic experience for a bodhisattva. Subhūti. What are these evil demonic [experiences] of a bodhisattva-mahāsattva who has not practiced the six perfections for very long and have not yet realized the bodhisattva stages? Subhūti. *Māra will transform himself into various bodies [and appear in front of] and say to the bodhi-sattva, you have already attained anuttarasaṃyaksaṃbodhi among the Buddhas.* Your name was so-and-so, your father's name was so-and-so, your mother's name was so-and-so, your brothers' and sisters' names were so-and-so,… you lived in such-and-such and country in such-and-such a village, [and so forth]."

These people have not yet attained, but are arrogant 未得謂得增上慢人: the phrase is from the second chapter on "Skillful Means" in the *Lotus Sūtra*, where those who think they have already attained enlightenment stand up and leave upon hearing the Buddha preach the *Lotus Sūtra*. Hurvitz (29 [28]) translates:

> While he was speaking these words, in the assembly bhikṣus, bhikṣuṇīs, upāsakas, upāsikās to the number of five thousand straightway rose from their seats and, doing obeisance to the Buddha, withdrew. For what reason? *This group had deep and grave roots of sin and overweening pride, imagining themselves to have attained and to have borne witness to what in fact they had not.*

sided, then, due to this subsiding [of mistaken views and arrogance, Hīnayāna habits] arise from having learned Hīnayāna in past lives. An example of this is when Śāriputra discarded his eyes. The *Pañcaviṃśati Sūtra* says, "Bodhisattvas as numerous as the sands of the Ganges River arouse great thoughts, but only one or two realize the [upper] levels of bodhisattvahood, and most lapse into that of the two vehicles [of the śrāvaka and pratyekabuddha]." Therefore [the contemplation of] "the two vehicles" is explained after "arrogance."

[10. Bodhisattvahood] Those who, because they keep in mind the original vow [to save all beings] and thus do not lapse into [a mistaken attachment to] emptiness, will thereby arouse the path of [skillful] means in the realm of bodhisattvahood. The *Pañcaviṃśati Sūtra* says, "There are bodhisattvas who do not practice the six *pāramitā* for a long time;... if they hear the profound Dharma they give rise to abuse [against the Dharma] and

From having learned Hīnayāna in past lives 先世小習因靜而生: in other words, as long as faults such as mistaken views and arrogance get in the way, good (though limited) Hīnayāna habits do not come to the fore, but when such faults subside, these limited virtues come to the surface.

Śāriputra discarded his eyes 身子捨眼: see the story of Śāriputra, who abandons the altruistic bodhisattva path and returns to the Hīnayāna after he donates one of his eyes to a beggar, who proceeds to stomp on and destroy the eye. Thus Śāriputra becomes disillusioned with the possibility of saving such people; see the *Ta chih tu lun*, T 25.145a12–b2. The story illustrates the virtue of giving and the meaning of *pāramitā* as "crossing to the other side." The full quote from Lamotte, *La Traité* 2, 701–2, and Chodron (2, 560) is given in the note to *Mo-ho chih-kuan* 35b14.

Bodhisattvas as numerous ... lapse into that of the two vehicles 恒沙菩薩發大心若一若二入菩薩位多墮二乘: see the *Pañcaviṃśati Sūtra* at T 8.284c5–9:

> I, with my Buddha eye, looked to the east and saw immeasurable, incalculable sentient beings that have aroused the aspiration [for Buddhahood] and practice *anuttarasaṃyaksaṃbodhi* and practice the bodhisattva way. But because these sentient beings are far and isolated from the power of means *(upāya)* and *prajñāpāramitā*, only one or two abide at the stage of non-retrogression *(avaivartyabhūmi)*, and most lapse into the stage of the śrāvaka and pratyekabuddha.

The path of [skillful] means in the realm of bodhisattvahood 諸方便道菩薩境界: in Chih-i's classification scheme, the bodhisattvas at the levels of the Tripitaka, Shared, and some of the Distinct Teachings are treading the "path of [skillful] means]" 方便道, whereas the advanced bodhisattvas of the Distinct Teachings and those of the Perfect teaching tread the "true path" (or "the path of true reality") 眞實道.

There are bodhisattvas who do not practice the six *pāramitā* for a long time; ... if they hear the profound Dharma they give rise to abuse and thus fall into hell 有菩薩不久行六波羅蜜。若聞深法卽起誹謗墮泥犁中: this is a conflation of two passages in the *Pañcaviṃśati Sūtra*. T 8.298a17–18 and 304c10–12. The contexts read:

> If bodhisattva-mahāsattvas do not, for a long time, practice the six perfections, do not pay homage often to the Buddhas, do not plant good roots, do not approach and

thus fall into hell *(niraya)*." This refers to bodhisattvas of the six perfections. Those of the Shared Teachings **[49c]** at the level of [skillful] means still sometimes abuse [the profound Dharma], but those who realize the true way do not abuse [the profound Dharma]. Even the beginners of the Distinct Teachings know the profound Dharma and thus do not abuse it. These are all beings with tentative good roots. Therefore this [kind of bodhisattvahood] is explained after [that of the contemplation of] "the two vehicles."

2. Ten Ways the Ten Objects of Contemplation Arise: Nine Pairs and a Single Sevenfold Category 九雙七隻 [49c3]

These ten types of objects [of contemplation] apply [to the whole gamut of Buddhist practice,] from the situation of the ordinary, ignorant person to the [skillful] means of the Noble One. [At least] one object, that of the sense fields, is constantly manifested right before our eyes; whether or not [the sense objects] actually "arise" or "do not arise," you are always able to contemplate them. As for the other nine types of objects, they can be contemplated if they arise. But how can they be contemplated if they do not arise? Also, eight of the objects [of contemplation] are far removed from the right path, but if you deeply restrain and guard against [the defects therein], then you can return to the right track. The [last] two objects [of the two vehicles

associate with good friends, do not learn well that the marks of dharmas are empty, this will be the conditions and activities of these bodhisattvas. [298a17–20] There are bodhisattvas who are sitting in the midst of the assembly and hear the profound perfection of wisdom *(prajñāpāramitā)* but are not pleased with it and so they reject it. Why is this? These are goods sons and good daughters who had rejected the profound perfection of wisdom in previous lives when they heard it, and so when they hear the profound perfection of wisdom in the present life, they reject it [again].... These people reject the universal wisdom of the Buddhas of the past, present, and future, and therefore they arouse the karma of destroying dharmas. Because of having assembled karma from destroying dharmas, they will fall into hell for immeasurable hundreds of thousands of millions of years. [304c2–12]

Bodhisattvas of the six perfections 六度菩薩: that is, bodhisattvas of the Tripitaka Teachings.

Beings with tentative good roots 諸權善根: in contrast to those with "real" 實 good roots.

How can they be contemplated if they do not arise 不發何所觀: therefore the first category of the sense fields as the objects of contemplation is the most "convenient" or accessible object for contemplation. The passionate afflictions are pretty steady and pervasive, too, but one cannot deny Chih-i's point that the skandhas and the sense fields are always a part of any human experience.

Eight of the objects 八境 **[of contemplation]**: one presumes that Chih-i is referring to the first eight categories, since the last two are the realms of the two vehicles and the bodhisattvas.

and bodhisattvas] are near to the right way, so if you reach this level you need not be concerned about a lack of contemplation—even a cursory cultivation will result in [attaining] the correct [path and attainment].

Again, if you do not have understanding, then the various objects arise mutually and arouse a great web of doubt; it will be as if you are standing at the crossroads and do not know which way to go. If you are forewarned [by this explanation], your mind will be peaceful like space no matter how arbitrary and bizarre [the distractions and afflictions appear and are manifested].

There are ten ways in which [the ten objects of contemplation] arise mutually:

1. Successively or not successively (random)	次第不次第
2. Mixed or not mixed (one-by-one)	雜不雜
3. Completely or incompletely (all together or not)	具不具
4. Cultivated or not cultivated (consciously or spontaneously)	作意不作意
5. Perfectly or imperfectly	成不成
6. For benefit or harm	益不益
7. For a long or short time	久不久
8. Difficult or easy	難不難
9. Repeatedly or just once	更不更
10. The three obstacles and four demonic forces	三障四魔

Thus there are nine pairs (#1–#9) and one seven-fold category (#10).

1. Successively or Not Successively [49c13]

There are three meanings to [arising in] succession: dharmas 法, cultivating 修, and arousing 發.

[Successive] dharmas refers to progressing in succession from shallow to profound dharmas [such as teachings and practice].

[Successive] "cultivating" refers to having successively studied and practiced [the Buddha Dharma] already in previous lives, or to successively cultivating [the Buddha Dharma] in this life.

[Successive] "arousing" refers to relying on successive cultivation to successively arouse [progress toward enlightenment].

There are three meanings to [arising] randomly: dharmas, cultivating, and arousing.

[Random or non-successive] "arousing" refers to being indeterminate, so that perhaps first you arouse the objects of bodhisattvahood, and later arouse [the objects of] the sense fields. Although they are not successive [from the first to the last], still there are only ten categories.

[Random or non-successive] "cultivating" refers to first cultivating [the contemplation of the objects of] disease if you [suffer from] imbalance of the four elements, or first cultivating [the contemplation of the objects of] passionate afflictions if you are faced with increases in the four types of passionate afflictions. In this way, each person should first cultivate [the type of contemplation] in accordance with the strengths [of their individual experiences and capacities].

"Dharmas" refers to [1] the fact that the sense fields of the eyes, ears, nose, tongue, and so forth are all the gates to quiescence; they are the *dharmadhātu*. Why should we then abandon this [phenomenal world] and depart for that [world of enlightenment]? So it says in the *Jewel Trunk Sūtra*. You should know that there are no dharmas outside the *dharmadhātu*, and which are [really] successive [or hierarchical].

[2] The passionate afflictions are [indivisible from] the *dharmadhātu* 煩惱卽法界. As it says in the *Sūtra of Non-actvity*, "covetous desires are indivisible from the path." The *Vimalakīrti Sūtra* says, "by practicing the anti-path, [the bodhisattva] penetrates and achieves the Buddhist path." Since the Buddhist path is already penetrated, there is no further "succession."

[3] Disease is the *dharmadhātu* 病患是法界. The *Vimalakīrti Sūtra* says, "[Just as] now my [that is, Vimalakīrti's] sickness is neither real nor sub-

The sense fields of the eyes, ears, nose, tongue, and so forth are all the gates to quiescence; they are the *dharmadhātu* 眼耳鼻舌陰入界等皆是寂靜門亦是法界: under the topic here of the non-successive or non-gradual dharmas, Chih-i discusses the indivisibility of each of the ten objects of contemplation with the whole of reality, the *dharmadhātu*. This section is reflected in the famous opening by Kuan-ting in terms of the indivisibility of samsara and nirvana, and so forth (see 1c–2a).

Also, in this case "non-successive" seems to connote more the meaning of "immediate" rather than "random" in the case of "arousing" and "cultivating."

So it says in the Jewel Trunk Sūtra 出寶篋經云云: see the **Ratnakāraṇḍa-[kavyūha]-sūtra* 大方廣寶篋經, T no. 462. The passage at 14.470c22–23 reads: "Manjuśrī said to the Buddha, 'World Honored One. All dharmas are the gates to quiescence. All words and expressions are the gate to quiescence, because they signify or point to quiescence."

Covetous desires are indivisible from the path 貪欲卽是道: see the *Sūtra of Non-activity*, T 15.752a7 and 759c13–19. This phrase has been quoted by Chih-i earlier; see the notes at *Mo-ho chih-kuan* 39a1, and the discussion of this topic earlier in the *Mo-ho chih-kuan*, 18a–b.

By practicing the anti-path, [the bodhisattva] penetrates and achieves the Buddhist path 行於非道通達佛道: see the *Vimalakīrti Sūtra*, T 14.549a27. This phrase also has been quoted previously by Chih-i in the *Mo-ho chih-kuan*; see 17b29, 18b3, and 47c9–10. See particularly the discussion at 18b–19b where Chih-i takes pains to deny the possible antinomian implications of this statement.

My sickness is neither real nor substantial, the sickness of sentient beings

stantial, the sickness of sentient beings is neither real nor substantial." Thus [a bodhisattva] regulates himself and also saves [other] sentient beings. [Vimalakīrti conventionally] consigned himself to being ill in a ten-feet square room, and [the Buddha at the time of his *parinirvāṇa*] became "ill" at the Śāla Grove. This is the meaning here.

[4] The marks of karma are the *dharmadhātu* 業相爲法界. Karma is [the result of] the aggregate of volition *(saṃskāra)*. The *Lotus Sūtra* says, "Having profoundly mastered the marks of [both] offences and goodness, and universally illuminated the ten directions, [the Buddha's] extremely subtle and pure Dharma body is endowed with the thirty-two marks." If you realize that karma arises from conditions, and does not exist on its own and is

is neither real nor substantial 今我病者非眞非有衆生病亦非眞非有: from the famous scene in the *Vimalakīrti Sūtra* where Vimalakīrti "pretends" to be sick in order to provide an occasion for sharing the Buddha Dharma. See T 14.545a26–27. Boin (*Vimalakīrti Sūtra*, 125) translates:

> A sick Bodhisattva should make the following considerations *(evam upalakṣitavyam)*: Just as my sickness is unreal *(abhūta)* and nonexistent *(asat)*, so the sicknesses of beings are also unreal and nonexistent.

Consigned himself to being ill in a ten-feet square room 方丈託疾: the *Vimalakīrti Sūtra* itself does not mention a "ten-feet square room," but the term derives from its use in classical Chinese commentaries on the sūtra. The context (T 14.539b10–13) has Vimalakīrti feigning illness as a skillful means so that people will come to question him about the Buddha Dharma. Boin (*Vimalakīrti Sūtra*, 32–33) translates:

> Through skill in means, Vimalakīrti made it known that he was ill *(glāna)*. In order to ask him about his illness, the king, ministers, the governors, the young people, the brahmans, the householders, the guildsmen, the citizens, the country folk, and several thousands of other people left the great town of Vaiśālī and went to ask him about his illness. Then Vimalakīrti addressed them at length with a discourse on bodily diseases *(kāyavyādhi)*.

For further discussion by Chih-i on this topic of "disease as skillful means" see later in the *Mo-ho chih-kuan*, 110c–111a.

Became "ill" at the Śāla Grove 雙林病行: legend has it that the Buddha "passed away" after becoming ill and, facing north, lay down on his right side among the trees in the Śāla Grove at Kuśinagara. See the description of Śākyamuni's "death" and the discussion on "disease" in the *Mahāparinirvāṇa Sūtra*, T 12, 669c–673b. The *Mahāparinirvāṇa Sūtra* accepts the conceit that the Buddha "feigned" death for the sake of helping sentient beings; see the passage in T 12.669c14–16:

> At that time when the Tathāgata finished his speaking, for the sake of helping sentient beings overcome their craving, he manifested his body as being sick and lay down on his right side like a sick person.

Having profoundly mastered … endowed with the thirty-two marks 深深達罪福相遍照於十方微妙淨法身具相三十二: or, more literally, "profoundly penetrated." See the *Lotus Sūtra*, T 9.35b28–29. This verse has been quoted many times already in the *Mo-ho chih-kuan*; see the note at 6c2–3.

Realize that karma … is thus empty, then karma can destroy karma 達業從緣

thus empty, then [you realize that] karma can destroy karma. If sentient beings are to attain [the liberation of] "crossing over" through karma, then various [types of] karma should be manifested [conventionally] to establish karma through this [conventional] karma. [But you should realize that] both the bonds of [conventional] karma and the liberation of [empty] non-karma are "unobtainable." The manifestations of the "Universal Gate" [of Avalokiteśvara] illumine both bondage and liberation, and therefore it is called "profound accomplishment." How can it be said that such a figure is [merely] a Vaipulya (Mahāyāna) master? [Surely such a figure is even greater than that.]

[5] Demonic forces are the *dharmadhātu* 魔事爲法界. The *Śūraṅgama [Samādhi] Sūtra* says, "The thusness of the demonic realm of Māra and the thusness of the Buddha realm are a single thusness and not two [different] thusnesses." In reality we cannot perceive [the substantial existence of] a Buddha, much less can we perceive the [substantial] existence of demons.

生不自在故空 此業能破業: that is, the realization of the emptiness of karma destroys the power of karma; if karma is "empty," how can it affect you?

Both the bonds of karma and the liberation of non-karma are "unobtainable" 業與不業縛脱叵得: Chih-i seems to be applying the threefold pattern of emptiness, conventionality, and the Middle to karma and how to overcome karma. Karma is "empty" of substantial being, and yet it affects us conventionally. If so, then this phrase concerning the "unobtainability" of both the emptiness and conventional aspects of karma, and the next phrase concerning the power of Avalokiteśvara over both of these aspects, would represent the position of the Middle.

Manifestations of the "Universal Gate" [of Avalokiteśvara] 普門示現: a phrase from the very end of the twenty-fifth chapter of the *Lotus Sūtra*, T 9.58b4–5, the chapter on the manifestations of Avalokiteśvara (the full translated title being "The Gateway to Everywhere of the Bodhisattva He Who Observes the Sounds of the World"). Hurvitz (*Lotus Sūtra*, 319 [294]) translates:

If there is a living being who shall hear the Chapter of the Bodhisattva He Who Observes the Sounds of the World, the deeds of self-mastery, *the manifestation of the gateway to everywhere*, the powers of supernatural penetrations, be it known that that person's merit shall not be slight.

The thusness of the demonic realm of Māra and the thusness of the Buddha realm are a single thusness and not two [different] thusnesses 魔界如佛界如一如無二如: see the *Śūraṅgama Samādhi Sūtra*, T 15.639c14–15:

The thusness of the demonic realm of Māra is indivisible from the thusness of the Buddha realm. The thusness of the demonic realm of Māra and the thusness of the Buddha realm are neither two nor distinct. We are not independent of this thusness. The marks of the demonic realm of Māra are indivisible from the marks of the Buddha realm. The dharmas of the demonic realm of Māra and the dharmas of the Buddha realm are neither two nor distinct. We can neither transcend nor go beyond these dharmas and marks.

Even if there "are" demons, you can endure and control them "by applying good medicine to your sandals."

[6] Dhyāna is the *dharmadhātu* 禪爲法界. Being able to contemplate the nature of the mind is called "superior concentration." This is the Śūraṅgama [Samādhi], which involves neither darkness nor distraction, but is a realization of the King of Samādhis that includes all samādhis within it.

[7] [Mistaken] views are the *dharmadhātu* 見爲法界. The *Vimalakīrti Sūtra* says, "One realizes correct marks by means of deviant marks." and "One is unmoved by the various false views and cultivates the thirty-seven auxiliary practices [of the path]." Also, [it is possible] to cultivate the thirty-seven steps [on the path] while being moved [by mistaken views], to cultivate while not being moved, to cultivate while both being moved and not being moved, and to cultivate while neither being moved nor not being moved. Thus, [mistaken] views are the gate [for entering the path], and [mistaken views are] the attendants [for realizing enlightenment].

[8] Arrogance is the *dharmadhātu* 慢爲法界. Upon reflection [you see

Applying good medicine to your sandals 良藥塗屣: this is an example of a short quote that serves as a kind of metanym; it does not make much sense in itself, but is clear when its entire context is understood. The phrase is from the *Mahāparinirvāṇa Sūtra*, T 12.661a12, where the Buddha teaching how the sūtras serve as a means to gain wisdom and to avoid being an *icchantika*. The context (lines 9–15) reads:

> In this way the scriptures serve people as a cause for gaining *bodhi*-wisdom and to avoid being an *icchantika*. Again, good sons. It is analogous to a good doctor and a good doctor's son. Suppose you know that you are going deep [into the forest] away from any doctors. You know well the supreme spells for removing poison. If you wish to have good spells and medicine [to guard against] poisonous snakes, dragons, and vipers, you should *use this good medicine and apply it to your leather sandals*. Even if you step on poisonous vermin, the poison will be neutralized by this [medicine].... The Mahāyāna scripture, the *Mahāparinirvāṇa Sūtra*, is also like this.

Śūraṅgama 首楞嚴 **[Samādhi]**: for Chih-i, this samādhi is the state wherein one has a full realization of the Middle Way; see the discussion of the Dharma body earlier in the *Mo-ho chih-kuan*, 20c13–21.

Darkness 昧: a play on words with the character that is used in the transliteration of samādhi 三昧.

One realizes correct marks by means of deviant marks 以邪相入正相: see the *Vimalakīrti Sūtra*, T 14.540b6–7:

> If you are able, realize the eight liberations *(vimokṣa)* without abandoning the eight depravities *(mithyātvasamatā)*; thus *by means of mistaken marks one realizes the correct marks*.

One is unmoved by the various false views and cultivates the thirty-seven steps [on the path] 於諸見不動而修三十七品: see the *Vimalakīrti Sūtra*, T 14.539c24. Boin, 44, translates Vimalakīrti's advice to Śāriputra:

> Not avoiding false views *(dṛṣṭigata)*, but basing oneself on the thirty-seven auxiliaries of enlightenment *(bodhipākṣikadharma)*, this is how to meditate.

that arrogance is] passionate affliction. [You should] contemplate arrogance as non-arrogance, arrogance as great arrogance, and as neither arrogance nor non-arrogance, thus perfecting the secret treasury and entering great nirvana.

[9] The two vehicles are the *dharmadhātu* 二乘爲法界. [The *Mahāparinirvāṇa Sūtra* says that] "If you perceive only emptiness and do not perceive non-emptiness, [this is not the Middle Way]" and so forth, and "A wise person perceives emptiness and also non-emptiness." If you "reach a definite consummation of the śrāvaka teachings [through] the king of all sūtras [i.e., the *Lotus Sūtra*], and clearly consider it upon hearing it, you can approach near to the supreme way."

Contemplate arrogance as non-arrogance, arrogance as great arrogance, and as neither arrogance nor non-arrogance 觀慢無慢慢大慢非慢非不慢: that is, utilize the threefold pattern to contemplate arrogance first as empty and without substantial existence, then in its aspect as conventionally existent and greatly influential, and finally as the Middle Way.

Perfecting the secret treasury and entering great nirvana 成祕密藏入大涅槃: in a passage quoted many times before in the *Mo-ho chih-kuan* (and will be used many more times below), the *Mahāparinirvāṇa Sūtra* (T 12.616b9–10) speaks of the Buddha leading all sentient beings to dwell peacefully in "the secret treasury" and then "entering nirvana." For a full translation of the context see the note at *Mo-ho chih-kuan* 20c1.

If you perceive only emptiness and do not perceive non-emptiness 若但見於空不見不空: see the *Mahāparinirvāṇa Sūtra*, T 12.767c23. for a full translation and discussion of this passage see the note at *Mo-ho chih-kuan*, 28a6–8.

A wise person perceives emptiness and also non-emptiness 智者見空及與不空: see the *Mahāparinirvāṇa Sūtra*, T 12.767c20; see previous note; the passage continues: "... [perceives] permanence and transience, suffering and bliss, selfhood and non-selfhood."

Reach a definite consummation of the śrāvaka teachings [through] the king of all sūtras, and clearly consider it upon hearing it, you can approach near to the supreme way 決了聲聞法是諸經之王聞已諦思惟得近無上道: an almost direct quote from the *Lotus Sūtra*, T 9.32a15–17. Hurvitz (180–81 [165]), translates:

O Medicine King, you are to know
That, in this way, men
Who do not hear the Scripture of the Dharma Blossom
Are very far removed from Buddha-knowledge.
If they hear this profound scripture
Which determines precisely the dharma of the voice-hearer,
This king of scriptures,
And, having heard it, think on it with understanding,
Let it be known that these persons
Are close to Buddha-wisdom.

Chih-i seems to take the "śrāvaka teachings" as that which one should consider after hearing it, which allows śrāvakas to approach the supreme way, but in the *Lotus Sūtra* it is the *Lotus Sūtra* itself, the "king of scriptures," that the śrāvakas are supposed to consider after they hear it, and it is attention to the *Lotus Sūtra* that will lead them to approach the supreme wisdom of a Buddha. This phrase and quote

[10] The objects of the bodhisattva are the *dharmadhātu* 菩薩境爲法界. Even the lowest and evil [forms of existence in] samsara, and the inferior [followers of] Hīnayāna, are indivisible from the *dharmadhātu*; how can it be said that the bodhisattva Dharma is not the path of the Buddha? Also, the tentativeness of the [skillful] means of the bodhisattva is a tentativeness that is indivisible from the real, and yet is neither tentative nor real; thus [the bodhisattva] perfects the secret treasury and enters great nirvana. Each and every dharma is indivisible from the dharmadhātu. This is the mark of dharmas as "not successive."

2. Mixed or Not Mixed [50a21]

The mixed or not mixed [arising of the ten objects of contemplation] is as follows. "Not mixed" (i.e., one-by-one) is for one object to arise, and then another object to arise, in a sequential and clearly distinguished way. "Mixed" arising is when it happens that [the objects of] the sense fields are aroused, and then also passionate afflictions arise, and before the passionate afflictions are released 謝, karma and demonic forces and dhyāna and false views and arrogance and so forth also spring up one after the other or along side each other. Though [the objects are] called "mixed," they do not go beyond these ten categories.

3. Completely or Incompletely [50a25]

For the ten [objects of contemplation to arise] together is called "complete," and for nine or fewer [to arise together] is called "incomplete." This [category of] "complete or incomplete" applies [to the above two types of] "successive or not successive (random)" and "mixed or non-mixed."

Also, there is a comprehensive completeness, and comprehensive incompleteness, a distinct completeness, and a distinct incompleteness. For the ten [objects of contemplation to arise] together [comprehensively] is called "comprehensive completeness." For the ten [objects to arise together] yet without some individual aspects is called "comprehensive incompleteness." For there to be nine [or fewer] and [also] missing [some individual

has appeared in the *Mo-ho chih-kuan* previously; see 33b11 and 34c3.

Comprehensive incompleteness 総不具: or, "incomplete though comprehensive. Chan-jan (BT–III, 153) explains this as meaning that "although all ten arise together, each of the individual categories may have some aspect missing." For example, even though all ten objects arise together, not all of the dhyāna stages included in the sixth object of "dhyāna concentration" may be present, or, not all possible demonic temptations within the fifth object of "demonic forces" may be present.

aspects within the categories] is called "distinct incompleteness." For there to be nine [or fewer] and yet [comprehensively including] all the individual [aspects] within [those categories] is called "distinct completeness."

Also, there is horizontal completeness, horizontal incompleteness, vertical completeness, and vertical incompleteness. For example, suppose you arouse the four dhyāna meditations [50b] and you reach [the dhyāna concentration that is] beyond conceptualization, this is "vertical completeness." If you reach only the abode of no function, this is "vertical incompleteness." If you attain [the six] penetrating [supranormal powers] and [three] illuminating insights, the [eight] liberations, and so forth, this is "horizontal completeness." Stopping at arousing only seven liberations is [an example of] "horizontal incompleteness." Also, arousing from the first dhyāna stage and reaching the fourth dhyāna stage is "vertical completeness." To attain [only] up to the third dhyāna stage [or below] is "vertical incompletion." To reach the ninth level of the first dhyāna stage is [an example of] "vertical completion." Reaching the eighth level would be [an example of] "vertical incompletion." For one level to include all five [preliminary] constituents [of meditation] is "horizontal completion." To achieve only four [or fewer] components is "horizontal incompletion." You should know that other examples could be given in the same pattern, ad infinitum.

4. Cultivated or Not Cultivated (Consciously or Spontaneously) [50b6]

Conscious cultivation of the sense fields [as objects of contemplation] and thus reaching an understanding of these sense fields is "the arising of (conscious) cultivation. To unconsciously [contemplate] the sense fields

Arouse the four dhyāna meditations and you reach beyond conceptualization (*naivasaṃjñā-saṃjñāyatana*) 發四禪至非想: the highest of the four stages of formlessness that are beyond the four dhyāna stages. See Hurvitz, *Chih-i*, 340–42.

Abode of no function 不用處 **(*ākiṃcanyā*)**: the third of the four stages of formlessness.

[The six] penetrating [supranormal powers] and [three] illuminating insights 通明: the supranormal powers attained by an arhat: three illuminating "insights" 三明 (knowing past actions, knowing future results, and knowing present conditions) and the more well-known six supranormal powers 六(神)通. For details, see the *Tz'u-ti ch'an-men*, T 46.529a.

The ninth level of the first dhyāna stage 初禪九品: in the *Tz'u-ti ch'an-men* (T 46.512c3–5) Chih-i explains that in cultivating dhyāna there are three "levels" of superior, middling, and inferior abilities. Each of these three are also divided into superior, middling, and inferior, thus giving nine levels or abilities in cultivating dhyāna. Hence the ninth level of dhyāna would be the "superior superior" level.

All five constituents 五支: these are the five qualities of examination, reflection, joy, bliss, and singlemindedness.

and thus spontaneously arouse penetrating understanding of mental and physical objects is "the arising of (unconscious) non-cultivation." The same is true [for the other nine objects of contemplation] up to the objects of bodhisattvahood. You should know that the four options of the tetralemma is the basic pattern, and the weaving of these options gives thirty-six options. Details are given in the section on the objects of passionate afflictions.

5. Perfectly or Imperfectly [50b10]

If you arouse one of the objects [of contemplation] and utterly fulfill it, and after fulfilling it let it go, and then arouse the other objects [of contemplation], and then fulfill the other objects[, this is called "perfectly" (contemplating the ten objects)]. If you arouse one category so that it suddenly arises and suddenly perishes, so that you not only miss some of the categories, but also some of the individual parts are vague and unclear[, this is called "imperfect" (contemplation of the objects)]. The above category of "complete and incomplete" involved only clarifying the number of items, but this category involves discussing the essential parts from beginning to end.

6. For Benefit or Harm [50b14]

Even if you arouse evil dharmas, this can bring about enormous benefit in cessation-and-contemplation, deepening the quiescence [of cessation] and luminosity [of contemplation]. On the other hand, arousing good dharmas can [ironically] bring about great loss in cessation-and-contemplation. This may involve loss in quiescence and illumination, or increase in quiescence and loss in illumination, or loss in quiescence and increase in illumination, or both increase [in some sense] and loss [in another sense].

8. Difficult or Easy [50b17]

Sometimes evil dharmas have a difficult or easy [arising], and sometimes good dharmas have a difficult or easy [arising], or both are difficult or both easy.

Thirty-six options 三十六句: each option of the tetralemma (a, non-a, both, and neither) is applied to all four, giving sixteen options. When you include the original four options, this gives twenty options. There is a further sixteen options that are applied to nirvana. All added together (four plus sixteen plus sixteen) give thiry-six logical possibilities.

Details are given in the section on the objects of passionate afflictions: see the explanation in *Mo-ho chih-kuan*, 104c–106a.

8. Difficult or easy 難易: for some unknown reason, items 7 and 8 are reversed from their sequence in the original list.

7. For a Long or Short Time [50b18]

Sometimes there is an object [of contemplation] that does not pass away for a long time, or there is an object that passes away immediately upon arising, and so forth.

9. Repeatedly or Just Once [50b19]

Sometimes there is an object [that appears] again and again many times, or there is an object that arises once and then goes to rest and does not arise again, and so forth.

In these ways [the arising of the objects of contemplation] are various and dissimilar; you should know this meaning well and not be mistakenly detached or attached [to these various forms of arising]. Refine them all through [the practice of] cessation-and-contemplation, and you will not stagnate [at a lower level of achievement].

10. The Three Obstacles and Four Demonic Forces [50b23]

The Contemplation of Samantabhadra says, "People in Jambudvīpa have three heavy obstacles." [1] The sense fields and [3] disease are obstacles of [karmic] retribution. [2] Passionate afflictions, [7] mistaken views, and [8] arrogance are obstacles of passionate affliction. [4] Karma, [5] demonic forces, [6] dhyāna, [9] the two vehicles, and [10] bodhisattvahood are obstacles of karmic deeds. These obstruct cessation-and-contemplation so that it is not clear and quiescent, block the path of *bodhi*-wisdom, and lead the practitioner to not penetrate and attain the five (preliminary) grades (of the disciple) and the level of the purification of the six senses; therefore they are called "obstacles."

People in Jambudvīpa have three heavy obstacles 閻浮提人三障重: from the opening section of "the sūtra of meditation on the bodhisattva Universal Virtue" 佛說觀普賢菩薩行法經, T 9.389c28–29. *The Threefold Lotus Sutra*, 348–49, translates:

> The Bodhisattva Universal Virtue is boundless in the size of his body, boundless in the sound of his voice, and boundless in the form of his image. Desiring to come to this world, he makes us of his free transcendent powers and shrinks his stature to the small size [of a human being]. *Because the people in Jambudvīpa have the three heavy hindrances,* by his wisdom-power he appears transformed as mounted on a white elephant.

In this text the "three hindrances" seem to refer to the three poisons of greed, anger, and delusion, but Chih-i gives these categories a new spin.

Five grades and the level of the purification of the six senses 五品六根清淨位: the five preliminary grades is the level Chih-i claims on his deathbed to have reached during his life. The "purification of the six senses" is equivalent to the level of the "identity of resemblance," the fourth of the levels of Six Identities.

The four demonic forces are as follows. [The sense fields of] the skandhas and sense entrances *(āyatana)* are properly the "demons of the skandhas," and [the objects of] karma, dhyāna, the two vehicles, and bodhisattvahood are also called "demons of the skandhas" because they are involved in the skandha of volition. [The objects of] the passionate afflictions, mistaken views, and arrogance are included in the "demons of the passionate afflictions." Disease is a cause of death, and thus is included in the "demon of death." Demonic forces [as the object of contemplation] [50c] are included in [the category of] the "supernatural demons."

Māra [the personification of demonic forces] is also called "the plunderer." The destroying of contemplation is called "plundering life" and the destroying of cessation is called "plundering the body." Māra is also called "deceitful grinder," because he grinds down contemplation and deceitfully leads to darkness, and grinds down cessation and deceitfully leads to distraction and licentiousness. Therefore these are called "demons."

3. Questions and Answers [50c3]

Question: What is the meaning of "arising mutually"?

Answer: [These arisings of the objects of contemplation] all depend on causes and conditions from the two realms [of the past and the present].

If in the past you planted the seed of [cultivating] gradual contemplation, now by obtaining the rain of practice you can arouse successive arising [of the objects of contemplation].

If in the past you cultivated undetermined or variable seeds, then you will experience "mixed" arising.

If in the past you cultivated numerous Dharmas completely, then you will experience "complete" arising. If in the past you cultivated numerous Dharmas incompletely, then you will experience "incomplete" arising.

If in the past you encountered the attainment of illumination, now you will experience arising "perfectly." If in the past you only cultivated without [attaining] illumination, now your arising will be "imperfect."

If the causes from the past are strong, then there will be arising even without cultivation in the present. If in the present the conditions are strong, then by proceeding to cultivation there will be arising.

If both the causes in the past and the conditions in the present are good and skillful and faced toward the supreme path, then benefits will arise in the present. If there is poison mixed in with the causes and conditions of the past, then you will suffer loss.

If the causes for arising are weak, they will not last long; if the causes for arising are strong, they will last a long time.

You should judge the strength and weakness [of the causes and conditions of your meditation] step by step from the crude and minute stages to the [highest] fourth dhyāna, and so forth.

The ease with which good can arise is related to lightness of the impediments, and the difficulty with which good can arise depends on the heaviness of the impediments. The difficulty with which evil can arise depends on the sharpness of your faculties, and the ease with which evil can arise depends on the dullness of your faculties.

If evil desires are extinguished, they will take their leave; if good desires arise they will make themselves known—this happens once and not repeatedly. If good desires are extinguished and you seek assistance, or if you seek relief from the emergence of evil desires, these [experiences will arise] repeatedly over and over again.

These matters should all be taught orally [directly from master to disciple], using wisdom in good measure. You should not rely on your own heart and mind as your teacher, or you will make mistaken judgements as to what is right and wrong. You should accept this humbly, and [practice cessation-and-contemplation] diligently and seriously.

4. Sixteen Questions and Answers [fielded by Kuan-ting] [50c18]

Some private speculations are as follows.

[1.] Dharmas are [as numerous as] dust; why are the objects [of contemplation] set at ten?

Answer: This is analogous to the great earth, which is one and yet is able to give birth to various plants. As a number, [ten] is neither too broad nor too brief, and its meaning is easily comprehended. Therefore [Chih-i] speaks of ten [categories].

[2.] Question: What features do the ten objects [of contemplation] share in common, and [which features are] distinct?

Answer: No one is without a [physical] body when one [is born and] begins to have physical experiences, and so when the sūtras teach contemplation, they often begin with [expounding on] the arising of sensual forms.

Some private speculations 私料簡: here follows sixteen questions and answers on the above subject that seem to have been fielded by Kuan-ting and were not part of Chih-i's original lectures. The purport of the questions and answers is often obtuse, and one is left wondering what is the point of many of the issues, other than scholastic elaboration.

The great earth, which is one and yet is able to give birth to various plants 大地一能生種種芽: a phrase from verses in the *Avataṃsaka Sūtra*, T 9.428a16.

Therefore [Chih-i] speaks of ten 故言十: a similar explanation is given at the beginning of the *Mo-ho chih-kuan* (3b) to explain why it has ten chapters, no more and no less.

Therefore [1] the skandhas [and sense fields] are the first [of the objects of contemplation]. With the skandhas as the basis [for the rest of the objects of contemplation, the passionate afflictions and karmic marks are] causes of skandhas, [disease is] the disease of skandhas, [demonic forces are] the lords of the skandhas, [dhyāna concentration results in] good skandhas, [mistaken views and arrogance are also] causes of skandhas, and [those of the two vehicles and bodhisattvas have] distinct skandhas, and so forth.

[2] Features [that are shared] with that of passionate afflictions: [mistaken] views and arrogance are the same as passionate afflictions; the skandhas and sense fields and disease are the results of passionate afflictions; karma is the cause of passionate afflictions; through dhyāna one remains unmoved by karmic forces; karma is the functioning of passionate afflictions; demonic forces control this realm of desires and are the lords of passionate affliction; and the two vehicles and bodhisattvahood are distinct from the constraints of passionate afflictions.

[3] Features shared with [the objects of] disease: the skandhas and the sense fields are the basis of disease; passionate afflictions, [mistaken] views, and arrogance are the disease of passionate afflictions. The *Vimalakīrti Sūtra* says, "Now, my disease is something that arises from delusions in the past and passionate afflictions." Karma is the same as for disease. The *Mahāparinirvāṇa Sūtra* says, "The King's disease is now serious." This points to the fact that the five heinous offences are diseases. Demonic forces are able to produce disease. [For example,] the three kinds of disasters [brought

With the skandhas as the basis … distinct skandhas, and so forth 以陰本陰因陰患陰主善陰又陰因別陰等: this passage is a good example of the extreme brevity or terseness of some of the explanations in the *Mo-ho chih-kuan*. I have followed the interpretation by Chan-jan (BT–III, 169), and the expanded translation by Kanno (*Ichinen sanzen*, 111) and Ikeda (*Gendaigoyaku*, 264ff.).

Now, my disease is something that arises from delusions in the past and passionate afflictions 今我病者皆從前世妄想諸煩惱生: see the *Vimalakīrti Sūtra*, T 14.544c27–28, where Vimalakīrti is explaining the causes of his illness. Boin (*Vimalakīrti Sūtra*, 121) translates:

> *My sickness arises from the actions produced by the radically perverted views (pūrvāntābhūtaviparyāsa), imaginations (parikalpa) and passions (kleśa).* In the body, there does not really exist any dharma that can undergo this sickness.

The King's disease is now serious 王今病重: see the *Mahāparinirvāṇa Sūtra*, T 12.720b13. The context is part of a statement by King Ajātaśatru Vaidehiputra, a contemporary of Śākyamuni, who killed his own father Bimbisāra (the king of Magadha) and, together with Devadatta, conspired unsuccessfully against the Buddhist Sangha:

> Jaya [the great doctor], *I am now seriously ill.* I have aroused evil and grave harm against the king of the good Dharma. All good medicine, wonderful herbs, magical spells, and skillful means with regard to disease are not capable of healing me.

about by fire, water, and wind] are external disorders, and shortness of breath and ecstasy are internal disorders [brought about by demonic forces]. Dhyāna is sometimes accompanied by a kind of ecstasy that is an internal disease. Those of the two vehicles and bodhisattvas may suffer from the disease of [attachment to] emptiness, but [you should know that] the disease of [attachment to] emptiness is also empty.

[4] Features shared with [the objects of] karma: the skandhas and the sense fields are the results of karma; passionate afflictions, false views, and arrogance are the basis for karma; disease is karmic retribution; demonic forces are demonic karma; through dhyāna you remain unmoved by karma; and those of the two vehicles and bodhisattvas have undefiled karma.

[5] Features shared with [the objects of] demonic forces: the skandhas and sense fields are the demons of the skandhas; passionate afflictions, mistaken views, and arrogance are the demons of passionate afflictions; disease is the demon of death; demonic forces are the supernatural demons; the rest are all encompassed by the demonic forces of the skandha of volition.

[6] Features shared with [the objects of] dhyāna concentration: dhyāna itself is the object; skandha and the sense fields, passionate afflictions, mistaken views, arrogance, and karma are all encompassed within the ten great [mental] domains of concentration on mental activity; demonic forces are the results of pre-dhyāna preparations when you have not yet [attained higher levels of] contemplative insight, and these are also encompassed within [or happen during the practice of] concentration on mental activity; those of the two vehicles and the bodhisattvas are encompassed within [the

A kind of ecstasy that is an internal disease 喜樂是内過患: "ecstasy" (or "joy and bliss") are two aspects of earlier stages of the four dhyāna stages that are transcended in later and higher stages, because ecstasy from dhyāna can become an obstacle to higher enlightenment.

The disease of emptiness is also empty 空病亦空: a phrase from the *Vimalakīrti Sūtra*, T 14.545a13, where Vimalakīrti is discussing the "emptiness" of his apparant disease. Boin, 123, translates the context:

> From the point of view of sameness *(samatādarśana)*, there is no separate sickness, there is only an empty sickness. Emptiness and sickness should be considered as equally empty. Any why? Because this emptiness and this sickness are absolutely empty *(atyantaśūnya)*.

Ten great [mental] domains 十大地 **(*mahā-bhūmikā*) of concentration on mental activity** 心數定: all of the various types of mental activity. The *Abhidharmakośa* lists the ten as sensation 受, perception 想, volition 思, contact 觸, desire 欲, wisdom 慧, remembrance 念, attention 作意, determination 勝解, and concentration 三摩地.

You have not yet [attained higher levels of] contemplative insight 未到(至)地定 **(*anāgamya*)**: a term referring to preliminary dhyāna practices where one has not yet entered into the four dhyāna stages proper.

realm of] pure dhyāna [concentration], and are encompassed in the three types of [superior, middling, and inferior] concentrations. The superior concentration encompasses the bodhisattvas and those of the two vehicles, the two middling and inferior concentrations encompass the other eight realms [of the objects of contemplation].

[7] Features shared with [mistaken] views: [the objects of] the skandhas and sense fields correspond to the [mistaken] views of self and of sentient beings, [the objects of] passionate afflictions encompass the five [mistaken] views, [the objects of] disease [correspond to] the [mistaken] views of things with life and the life force, karma and dhyāna [correspond to] [mistaken]

Three types of [superior, middling, and inferior] concentrations 三定: see the *Mahāparinirvāṇa Sūtra*, T 12.769b12–20:

> Good sons. All sentient being are endowed with three types of concentrations: superior 上, middling 中, and inferior 下. The superior [concentration] is Buddha-nature. Therefore it is said that all sentient beings without exception have the Buddha-nature. The middling [concentration] is that all sentient beings are endowed with [the potential to attain] the first dhyāna stage. When there are [proper] causes and conditions, then one is able to cultivate it. If there are no [proper] causes and conditions, then one is not able to cultivate it. There are two types of causes and conditions: first are disasters, and second are the breaking of the bonds of this realm of desires. Therefore it is said that all sentient beings without exception are endowed with the middling concentration. The inferior concentration is the concentration on mental activity within the ten great [mental] domains. Therefore it is said that all sentient beings without exception are endowed with the inferior concentration.

Features shared with [mistaken] views 通稱見: as Chan-jan (BT–III, 174–75) points out, the terms in this section seem to be based on a passage in the *Pañcaviṃśati Sūtra*, T 8.221c12–19, and the commentary on this passage in the *Ta chih tu lun*, T 25.319b–c.

The passage from the *Pañcaviṃśati Sūtra* and *Ta chih tu lun* reads:

> The Buddha said to Śāriputra: "When the Bodhisattva-mahāsattva practices *prajñāpāramitā* he should consider this, that bodhisattvas have only nominal existence, Buddhas have only nominal existence, *prajñāpāramitā* has only nominal existence,... Śāriputra, in this way the self has only nominal existence. The eternal existence of all *selves* is unobtainable. Things with the *life-force* of *sentient beings*, things with *life*, things that are born, things that are cultivated and *produced* by many people, things that are produced through afflictions, things that arise, things that *arise through afflictions*, things that are experienced, things that are *experienced as afflictions*, things that are known, and things that are viewed; these are all unobtainable. They are unobtainable because they are empty. They are only given names. Bodhisattva-mahāsattvas, when they practice *prajñāpāramitā*, should not perceive the self or sentient beings [as substantially existing].

Five [mistaken] views 五見: these are mistaken views concerning the body 身見 (that it has selfhood 我見), extreme views 邊見, deviant views 邪見, attachment to false views 見取見, and attachment to the precepts 戒禁取見.

views on things that are produced, and also the [mistaken] views from being attached to the precepts; demonic forces are encompassed by the false views of the production of afflictions, the experiencing of afflictions, and the arising of afflictions, and also samsara is encompassed by the extreme views; arrogance is encompassed by the [mistaken] view of the self; the two vehicles and the bodhisattvas of skillful means are all encompassed by twisted views.

[8] Features shared with [the objects of] arrogance: the skandhas and the sense fields are encompassed by self-arrogance; passionate afflictions are encompassed by arrogant pride; disease is encompassed by incomparable arrogance; karma is encompassed by haughty arrogance, because haughtiness creates karma; demonic forces are encompassed by great arrogance; dhyāna is encompassed by haughty arrogance; false views are also encompassed by great arrogance; those of the two vehicles and bodhisattvas are encompassed by overweening arrogance.

[9] Features shared with those of the two vehicles: the four mindfulnesses [concerning the objects of body, sensation, mind, and dharmas] and the four truths encompass the other nine objects [of contemplation].

[10] Features shared with the objects of bodhisattvahood: the other nine objects are encompassed by the Four Universal [bodhisattva] Vows.

[3.] Question: these [categories] share in common the fact that they are called dharmas of these objects [of contemplation]. Do those who practice also share something [such as their name], or not?

Answer: The *Mahāparinirvāṇa Sūtra* says, "Why is it that those who

The two vehicles and the bodhisattvas of skillful means 二乘方便菩薩: the bodhisattvas of the Tripitaka and Shared Teachings, and some of the bodhisattvas of the Distinct Teachings.

Encompassed by twisted views 曲見: Chan-jan (BT–III, 175) explains this term by referring to a passage in the *Mahāparinirvāṇa Sūtra*, T 12.731a13–b6:

> What is that called the mistaken *twisted view* of the śrāvaka and pratyekabuddha? They perceive the bodhisattva to have [literally] descended from the Tuṣita heaven riding on a white elephant and entering the noble womb of his mother, with his father's name being Suddhodana and his mother's name Maya,… [and so forth through the major events of Śākyamuni's life] … until he entered parinirvāṇa at Kuśinagara. Such a view is called the "twisted view" of the śrāvaka and pratyekabuddha.

Features shared with arrogance 通稱慢: in this section Kuan-ting seems to be following the list of various kinds of arrogance given in the *Mahāparinirvāṇa Sūtra*, T 12.670a14–15, though there is some difference: arrogance 慢, arrogant pride 慢慢, incomparable arrogance 不如慢, overweening arrogance 增上慢, self-arrogance 我慢, mistaken arrogance 邪慢, and haughty arrogance 憍慢.

Encompassed by self-arrogance 我慢攝: or, arrogance based on the belief that there is a substantial "self."

Four Universal Vows 四弘誓: see the earlier section of the *Mo-ho chih-kuan*, 8a7–10b7, on the Four Universal Vows.

have not yet aroused aspiration for enlightenment … are also called 'bodhisattvas'?" Thus, people who [contemplate] the first nine objects are also called bodhisattvas. As for sharing the features of those of the two vehicles, there are the categories of the four types of śrāvaka. The people [who contemplate] the bottom eight objects are encompassed by [the category of] "śrāvakas of overweening arrogance." The bodhisattvas are encompassed by [the category of] the śrāvaka of the Buddha path [i.e., the transformed śrāvaka].

[4.] Question: Are [the ten objects of contemplation] all transient, or not?

Answer: The *Ratnagotravibhāga* says, "Bodhisattvas dwell in an undefiled realm, but have the perverted view that it is transient."

[5.] Question: Are they all defiled, or not?

Answer: They all share [the experience of] being defiled, but there are slight differences in the meaning of the existence [of defilements].

[6.] Question: Do they share the feature of partial truth, or not?

Answer: They all share the feature of being partial, but there are slight differences in their "truth."

Why is it that those who have not yet aroused aspiration for enlightenment … are also called "bodhisattvas" 云何未發心而名爲菩薩: an extract from a longer passage in the *Mahāparinirvāṇa Sūtra*, T 12.658c23–659a1:

> Kāśyapa said to the Buddha, "World Honored One. *How do those who have not yet aroused aspiration to enlightenment* obtain the cause for *bodhi*-wisdom?"
>
> The Buddha said to Kāśyapa, "If they hear the *Mahāparinirvāṇa Sūtra* and say 'I do not need to arouse aspiration for enlightenment,' they slander the good Dharma.… When those people come to the end of their lives, and if they then dwell in the three [evil] destinies or as human or divine being and then again are mindful of [attaining] the mind of *bodhi*-wisdom, then these people *should be known as great bodhisattva-mahāsattvas*."

This passage does not seem to say what Kuan-ting has in his truncated version.

Four types of śrāvaka 四種声聞: the *Treatise on the Lotus Sūtra* (**Saddharmapuṇḍarīkopadeśa*, T no. 1519, 26.9a15–17), attributed to Vasubandhu, includes a list of four types of śrāvaka: "determined" śrāvakas 决定声聞, śrāvakas of overweening arrogance 増上慢声聞, śrāvakas who have retrogressed from aspiration to enlightenment 退菩提心声聞, and transformed śrāvakas 應化声聞 (bodhisattvas and Buddhas who have taken on the form of a śrāvaka in order to save sentient beings).

Bodhisattvas dwell in an undefiled realm, but have the perverted view that it is transient 菩薩住無漏界中有無常倒: the *Kōgi* (BT–III, p. 182) identifies this phrase as coming from "section 3-9" of the *Ratnagotravibhāga*, and Ikeda (*Kenkyū-chūshaku*, 346–47) tentatively identifies a passage from T 31.830a–b, but this passage in the *Ratnagotravibhāga* discusses four kinds of obstacles for bodhisattvas to become Tathāgatas, and does not contain the phrases "quoted" here. It is not clear what point Kuan-ting is trying to make.

Partial truth 偏眞: in contrast to being "perfectly" or "completely" 圓 true.

[7.] Question: The shared features are now understood; how about the distinct features?

Answer: The ten objects [of contemplation] are not the same, and therefore they have distinct meanings. Some features are both shared and distinct. The skandhas [and sense fields] **[51b]** are the basis for physical experience, and are also the beginning for contemplating wisdom; therefore [this category] is distinct [from the other nine objects] and comes first. This one [category of] the objects [of skandhas and the sense fields] has both shared and distinct features. The later nine objects [of contemplation] get their names from the various marks from which they arise; thus they either have shared or distinct features, and they cannot have both shared and distinct features.

[8. Question:] If so, then [the objects of] passionate afflictions are also the basis of all phenomena, and are also the beginning for contemplating [wisdom] and the ground for curing delusions. The four elements of a diseased body are also the basis [of all phenomena], and are the beginning for contemplating [wisdom] and the grounds for curing disease. What is the meaning of saying that [these other objects] cannot have both shared and distinct features?

Answer: If the body [that is, the skandhas and sense fields] is caused by passionate afflictions, then [these passionate afflictions] are those of a previous life. Passionate afflictions in this life depend on the existence of a physical body. Disease is not everlasting, and is thus too weak to be a basic phenomenon. The sūtras and treatises do not treat the contemplation of disease as primary, and therefore it cannot have both shared and distinct features. Having neither shared nor distinct features is beyond conceptual understanding; one skandha is all skandhas, and is neither one nor all.

[9.] Question: The nine objects [of contemplation] arise one after the other, and each has a distinct name. As you arouse an understanding of the skandha and sense fields, then should you establish distinct names [for the various phenomena]?

Answer: When you arouse an understanding of the skandhas and sense fields, you should not necessarily make distinctions, but [realize that] all are encompassed in "the skandhas and sense fields." If you are attached to this understanding, this corresponds to a mistaken view. If in accordance with

... and they cannot have both shared and distinct features 不得是亦通亦別: the logic of this passage escapes me. I do not understand the significance of why these objects cannot have "both shared and distinct" features. Perhaps rhetorically this category needs to be reserved for the highest level of "inconceivability."

Neither one nor all 非一非一切: see the discussion below (*Mo-ho chih-kuan,* 55b) on the interpenetration of "the one and the all."

this understanding you arouse passion and anger, this is encompassed in the passionate afflictions. If you solicit disease or the coming of demonic forces, you must judge distinctly in accordance with the situation. If understanding is aroused clearly without any of the features of the [other] nine objects, this is the disposition of cessation-and-contemplation. However, though there are shared and distinct features, this does not mean that they obtain both shared and distinct features [simultaneously].

[10.] Question: Can the ten objects [of contemplation] be clearly distinguished, or not?

Answer: The four mindfulnesses are a distinct feature of [contemplating the objects of] the skandhas, contemplating the empty village is a distinct feature of [contemplating the objects of the twelve] sense entrances *(āyatana)*, and [contemplating] non-selfhood is a distinctive feature of [contemplating the objects of the eighteen] sense fields *(dhātu)*. The five [meditations for] putting the mind at rest are a distinctive feature of [contemplating the objects of] the passionate afflictions. The eight mindfulnesses are a distinctive feature of [contemplating the objects of] disease. The ten good deeds are a distinctive feature of [contemplating the objects of] karma. The "five fetters" are a distinctive feature of [contemplating the objects of] demonic

Disposition of cessation-and-contemplation 止觀氣分: Chan-jan (BT–III, 187) explains that this is the stage or attitude of one ready to practice the Buddhist path, before entering even that of the five preliminary grades of the disciple.

Contemplating the empty village 空聚: a phrase from the *Vimalakīrti Sūtra*, T 14.543b2. Boin (*Vimalakīrti Sūtra*, 103) translates the context:

> The daughters of the gods asked: What is this pleasure that has as its object the garden of the Law?
>
> Vimalakīrti replied: It is the pleasure which consists in believing firmly in the Buddha, in desiring to hear the Law, attending to the community, driving away pride and respecting the teachers,... unerringly considering the (twelve) bases of consciousness like *an empty village*, protecting the thought of enlightenment,...

Eight mindfulnesses 八念: to be mindful of the Buddha 佛, Dharma 法, sangha 僧, the precepts 戒, equanimity 捨, divine matters 天, the inhaling and exhaling of one's breath 出入息, and death 死. See the *Ta chih tu lun*, T 25.218c–228c.

Ten good deeds 十善: the opposite of the ten evil deeds: to avoid killing, stealing, lustful acts, lying, slandering, harsh language, frivolous language, greed, anger, and false views.

Five fetters 五繫: Chan-jan (BT–III, 189) points to a passage in the *Mahāparinirvāṇa Sūtra*, T 12.637c21–24, which has the Buddha giving advice to Kāśyapa:

> You should, from now on, overcome Pāpīyas [the evil one]. You should say, "Pāpīyas, you should not appear in such a form. If you do [appear in such a form], we will bind and fetter you with the *five fetters.*" When Māra hears this he will depart and, like a rogue dog, will not return.

This passage does not explain the content of the "five fetters," but in his commentary to the *Mahāparinirvāṇa Sūtra* (T no. 1767, 38.95b23–24), Kuan-ting explains:

forces. The six subtle gates [of contemplation] are a distinct feature of [contemplating the objects of] dhyāna. The [thirty-seven] steps on the path are a distinct feature of [contemplating the objects of] mistaken views. Transiency, suffering, and emptiness are distinct features of arrogance. The Four Noble Truths and twelvefold [causes and] conditions are distinct features of the two vehicles. The six perfections are a distinct feature of bodhisattvas.

[11.] Question: If the five [ordinary] skandhas include [all] the objects [of contemplation], then are there things to be contemplated outside of and distinct from [the realm of] name-and-form *(nāma-rūpa)* [that is, the skandhas]?

Answer: From the perspective of the wisdom of the realm of the inconceivable, the skandhas themselves are the objects of contemplation, but further distinctions should be made. Non-good (i.e., evil) and neutral skandhas are the objects [of contemplation], and the good five skandhas [of those who practice dhyāna] are that which contemplates. Since that which contem-

There are two interpretations for the "five fetters": One is the fetters of "the five corpses" 五尸, and the second is the fetters of "the five limbs 五處 [of the two arms, two legs, and neck]. The "five corpses" refers to the demons of desires that are conquered through the five types of contemplations of impurity 不淨觀 [which involve contemplating corpses in their various stages of decay].

Six subtle gates 六妙門: there are two categories within T'ien-t'ai texts that this term can refer to, both characterized as a "progressive" or "graded" form of practice:

1. The six contemplative practices 六行觀: to contemplate progressively the dust of passions 麁, suffering 苦, obstacles 障, quietude 静, subtlety 妙, and liberation 離.

2. More commonly this refers to the six subtle "gates" of contemplation through which one can pass to nirvana. These six gates are the specific theme of Chih-i's *Liu-miao fa-men* 六妙法門 (T no. 1917, 549–555), which in the T'ien-t'ai scheme teaches the "undetermined" or "variable" type of contemplation (see also the *Mo-ho chih-kuan*, 108a):

1. the gate of counting one's breaths 數息門: to calm one's mind by counting one's breaths from one to ten.
2. the gate of following after one's breaths 隨息門: to calm one's mind not by counting one's breaths but by breathing freely and spontaneously.
3. the gate of stopping *(sthāna)* 止門: to calm and quiet one's mind by focusing through concentration on a single object.
4. the gate of contemplation 觀門: to contemplate the object of concentration.
5. the gate of "returning," "restoring," or reflection 還門: to reflect on the mind of contemplation and realize its emptiness, and "restore" the original mind.
6. the gate of purity 淨門: for the mind to be pure and unattached to anything.

[Thirty-seven] steps on the path 道品: the four mindfulnesses 四念處, four proper endeavors 四正勤, four supranormal powers 四如意足, five good roots/faculties 五根, five powers 五力, seven components of perceptions 七覺支, and eightfold noble path 八正道. See Hurvitz, *Chih-i*, 344–46.

Wisdom of the realm of the inconceivable 不思議境智: this is the subject of the next section; see *Mo-ho chih-kuan*, 52b2–55b26.

plates is pure and mature, there is no [substantial] evil nor neutral [objects]; there are only the good skandhas. The [fundamentally] good skandhas turn into the skandhas of means, the skandhas of means turn into the undefiled skandhas, the undefiled skandhas turn into the skandhas of Dharma-nature which are the skandhas that are incomparable and equivalent 無等等陰 [to enlightenment]. How, then, can it be said that there is nothing to be contemplated outside of and distinct from [ordinary] skandhas? This is so even in the Hīnayāna; how much more so for [the Mahāyāna practice of the contemplation of] the inconceivable [realm]?

[12.] Question: If the skandhas are turned into [the fundamentally good subject of the] contemplator, then are the retributive [elements of the] skandhas also transformed?

Answer: [Yes.] The *Pañcaviṃśati Sūtra* says, "Since visible form *(rūpa)* is pure, therefore [the other four skandhas of] feeling, perceptions, impulses, and consciousness are pure ... and *prajñā*-wisdom is [also] pure." The *Lotus Sūtra* says [of one who practices the Buddha Dharma], "The color of his face is clear and white ... and the six senses are pure." This is the meaning, that

The good skandhas turn into the skandhas of means 善陰轉成方便陰: this is beginning to sound suspiciously like a substantialist, "fundamental purity" type analysis. Chan-jan (BT–III, 191) explains this passage by saying that the categories of "evil, neutral, good" skandhas apply to people who are still ignorant and at the earliest stages of practice where one must cultivate the "five meditations for putting the mind at rest," and the category of "skandhas of means" applies to those who have just begun Buddhist practice ("insiders") who practice at the levels of the "four good roots."

Skandhas of means turn into the undefiled skandhas 方便陰轉成無漏陰: according to Chan-jan, this applies to the level of the arhat.

Undefiled skandhas turn into the skandhas of Dharma-nature 無漏陰轉成法性陰: according to Chan-jan, these are the skandhas of one who dwells in the "land of means" 方便土, one of the "four [Buddha] lands" 四土.

Since visible form is pure, therefore feeling, perceptions, impulses, and consciousness are pure ... and *prajñā*-wisdom is [also] pure 色淨故受想行識淨般若亦淨: from the *Pañcaviṃśati Sūtra*, T 8.306a7–10.

The color of his face is clear and white ... and the six senses are pure 顏色鮮白六根清淨: the first phrase is from verses in the fourteenth chapter of the *Lotus Sūtra* on "Peaceful Practices" (T 9.39b15). Hurvitz (*Lotus Sūtra*,221 [203]) translates the context:

One who reads this scripture
  Shall ever be without care or agony,
Also without sickness or pain,
  His color a fresh white,
Nor shall he be born into poverty, want,
  Lowliness, degradation, ugliness, or restriction.
Living beings shall desire to see him
  As they would aspire to see a sage or a saint.
The children of the gods
  Shall be his servants and messengers ...
[and so forth].

though the skandhas are transformed, the [subject of] contemplation and the objects [of contemplation] remain as they are.

[13.] Question: What is the relationship between the ten [types of the arising of the] objects [of contemplation] and the five parts [of the practice of dhyāna]?

Answer: The "five parts" are an analysis of [the practice of] dhyāna, and the ten types of arising are in reference to the objects [of contemplation]. Let us now [51c] show where they meet. Whether [the objects of contemplation arise] successively or not successively, one [object] from its arising to its end corresponds to the part of "progressing." [For the first] along with the other nine to have already come corresponds to the part of "abiding." To consciously intend to keep [your concentration] firm corresponds to the part of "guarding." To arouse one [object of contemplation] and then lose it corresponds to "retreating." The part of "accomplishing" should [already] be known [without having to be explained]. If each and every object [of contemplation involves] performing the five parts [of dhyānic practice], they can be consciously analyzed, and it is not necessary to outline the distinctions [any further]. However, the five parts [of dhyāna practice] and ten objects [of contemplation] are all phenomena [or, "dharma-marks"], so they mutually reflect the significance of the others. [On the other hand,] the graded levels of the Six Identities and the ten stages are shallow or profound, and so are not of the same type [as the five parts and the ten objects of contemplation, which are interpenetrating and not graded stages].

[14.] Question: Thoughts and the nature [of reality, that is, one who contemplates and that which is contemplated] are separate, as conditions and the nature [of reality] are also separate. If there are no conditions and no thoughts, then there is nothing to be measured. How, then, can you [speak of] the inclusiveness of the ten dharma realms?

Answer: [The ten dharma realms are] inconceivable. They are without marks yet with marks; contemplative wisdom [perceives them] as such.

The second phrase is found in verses from chapter 20 of the *Lotus Sūtra* on "The Bodhisattva Never Disparaging" (T 9.51b19, again describing one of many ideal forms of a practitioner of the Buddha Dharma:

But the bodhisattva Never Disparaging
Was able to bear this [abuse] with equanimity.
He was able to hear this scripture,
And his six senses were purified.

The ten objects and the five parts 十境與五分: Chan-jan (BT–III, 194–95) refers to a passage in the *Tz'u-ti ch'an-men* (T 46.512b20–c12) which makes a distinction between four aspects of progressing or retreating in the practice of dhyāna: 1. retreating 退分, 2. dwelling 住分, 3. progressing 進分, and 4. accomplishing 達分. The fifth aspect, "keeping/guarding" 護分, is not included in the *Tz'u-ti ch'an-men* passage.

Others have expressed this by saying "Mount Sumeru absorbs a mustard seed, and a mustard seed absorbs Mount Sumeru," "a lotus emerging from the fire," and "a person being able to cross the sea." Mysterious matters are understood as "inconceivable." Now we understand [these matters] as "without mind" 無心, "without thoughts" 無念, not able to go and not able to arrive; this is the principle of inconceivability. This principle is superior to the phenomena.

[15.] Question: Is the interinclusiveness of the ten dharma realms present at the level of cause or result [of attaining enlightenment]?

Answer: At both levels. However, the "results" are distant [for ordinary people] and difficult to manifest, though the causes are common and easy to know. [As for causes,] it is like the story of Maitrakanyaka, who aroused [an altruistic] Buddha mind while in hell, or like a bodhisattva who has not

Mount Sumeru absorbs a mustard seed, and a mustard seed absorbs Mount Sumeru 須彌容芥芥容須彌: a common phrase; see the *Mahāparinirvāṇa Sūtra*, T 12.628a19–20:

> If a bodhisattva-mahāsattva dwells in great nirvana, [this is like] Mount Sumeru, king [of the mountains] in its height and expanse, to be completely taken in by a mustard seed." See also the *Vimalakīrti Sūtra*, T 15.546b25–27: "If a bodhisattva dwells in liberation, [this is like] the height and expanse of Mount Sumeru being within a mustard seed without any increase or decrease."

Lotus emerging from the fire 火出蓮華: see the many explanations of "liberation" in the *Mahāparinirvāṇa Sūtra*, which includes the following (T 12.633b16–17):

> Again, liberation is called "mysterious." For example, it is not mysterious if a lotus emerged out of the water, but if it emerges out of the fire, then this is mysterious.

A person being able to cross the sea 人能渡海: again, see the *Mahāparinirvāṇa Sūtra*, T 12.714a17–20:

> Good son. Suppose there is a person who says, "I can float and cross the waters of the great sea [by myself]." Would such a statement be conceivable?
>
> World Honored One. Such a statement would be conceivable [in some sense] but inconceivable [in another sense]. Why? It is inconceivable that an [ordinary] person could cross [the sea by himself], but it is conceivable that an asura would cross.
>
> Good son. I am not speaking of an asura. I am speaking of a human being.
>
> World Honored One. It is conceivable or inconceivable even with regard to human beings. There are two types of human beings: first is the sage, and second is the ordinary ignorant person. [Crossing the sea] would be inconceivable for the ordinary person, but conceivable for the sage.

Maitrakanyaka, who aroused Buddha mind while in hell 慈童女以地獄界發佛心: see the *Sūtra of the Store of Various Treasures* 雜寶藏經, the seventh section on the story of Maitrakanyaka (T 4.450c18–451c8). This sūtra is a miscellaneous collection of stories, Jātaka tales, parables, and moral lessons. See the English translation in the Numata series #10–I, *The Storehouse of Sundry Valuables* (1994, 23–25). The story is that of a boy [? though the name in Chinese means "girl of compassion"] named Maitrakanyaka who suffered

yet received the prophecy [of future Buddhahood] disdaining one who has received the prophecy. If they do not feel remorse, they cannot transcend [the results of] their offences.

Let me give some examples [of the results]: Both sages and ordinary people are all endowed with the five skandhas, but it cannot be said that the skandhas of the sages are like the skandhas of ordinary people. Again, the Buddha is endowed with five [types of] eyes [and their insights], but why should [the insight of] the Buddha eye be interpreted in terms of the results gained from the [physical] human eyes or divine eyes? [Also,] the Buddha is endowed with five practices: [though strictly speaking] the practice of disease is that of the four evil destinies [of hell, hungry ghosts, beasts, and asura], parental practices are that of the human and divine realms, noble practices are those of the realm of the two vehicles, noble conduct [that is, altruistic practices] are those of the realm of bodhisattvas, and divine practice is that of the realm of Buddhas.

[16.] Question: One thought includes the ten dharma realms, but does this inclusion occur deliberately and consciously, or spontaneously and naturally?

much from acting unfilially toward his mother. Finally, he came to a city where an irremovable burning iron wheel was placed on his head. Then,

> Maitrakanyaka asked the jailer, "When can I get rid of this wheel I am carrying?" The jailer answered, "When there is someone in the world who has done evil as well as meritorious acts, as you have done … only then will he come here and experience this evil instead of you. This iron wheel will never fall to the ground."…
>
> [Maitrakanyaka] further asked, "Are there now in this prison some who experience their own evil the way I do?" The jailer replied, "Countless hundreds and thousands. Their number is incalculable!" Having heard these words, he thought, "I shall never escape! *I wish that all who have to experience suffering would put their entire burden on myself!*; When he had this thought, the iron wheel fell to the ground.

Like a bodhisattva who has not yet received the prophecy disdaining one who has received the prophecy 如未得記菩薩輕得記: see the *Pañcaviṃśati Sūtra*, T 8.352b–353c, a long section on bodhisattvas receiving the prophecy that they will attain *anuttarasaṃyaksaṃbodhi*. See especially 353a4–7:

> Those who I have described as having the features of non-retrogression *(avaivartika, avinivartanīya)* will not remain that way for long. They merely have an empty name, and make light of and despise other people; therefore they are far removed from *anuttarasaṃyaksaṃbodhi*.

Five [types of] eyes 五眼: the physical eye, divine eye, eye of wisdom, Dharma eye, and Buddha eye.

Five practices 五行: a list based on the chapters on "noble practices" in the *Mahāparinirvāṇa Sūtra*, T 12.673b–729b: practice of disease 病行, parental practices (toward their children) 嬰兒行, noble practices 聖行, noble conduct [that is, altruistic practices] 梵行, and divine practice 天行.

Answer: The nature of dharmas is spontaneous and natural, and not produced through actions, as a minute speck of dust [naturally] includes parts from the whole universe [lit., the ten directions].

[end of Kuan-ting's Questions and Answers]

1. CONTEMPLATING THE SENSE FIELDS [51C20–101C23]

1. Introduction [51C20]

First, contemplating the objects of the skandhas and the sense fields 觀陰入界境 refers to [the contemplation of] the five aggregates *(skandha)*, the twelve [sense] entrances *(āyatana)*, and the eighteen [sense] realms *(dhātu)*.

The skandhas are called "overshadowing darkness" because they obscure and cover good dharmas; this terminology is based on [the role of the skandhas as] cause [for the arising of evil dharmas]. Again, the skandhas are an "accumulation," the recurrent alternation of [the cycle of] birth and death; this terminology is based on [the role of the aggregates as] the results [of your actions].

The [twelve sense] "entrances" that is, the six sense organs and their objects] are so-called because [of their role in] "stepping or passing into" [sense experience]; they are also called the "gates for turning [in and out]" [of experience].

The [eighteen] "realms" [that is, the six sense organs, their six objects, and their six consciousnesses] are so-called [because they are each] distinct realms. They are also called "the individual nature." The *[Abhidharma-] vibhāṣā[-śāstra]* clarifies the relationship between these three topics.

The five aggregates *(skandha)*, the twelve [sense] entrances *(āyatana)*, and the eighteen [sense] realms *(dhātu)* 五陰十二入十八界: that is, all the components of a human being and your experience—the five "aggregates" that make up a human being (form, sensations, perceptions or conceptions, impulses or volitions, and consciousness); and the six senses of sight, sound, taste, smell, touch, and consciousness, the six respective sense organs, and their respective six types of sense objects.

Skandhas are called "overshadowing darkness" because they obscure and cover good dharmas 陰者陰蓋善法: this appears to be a gloss based on the meaning of the Chinese character 陰.

Skandhas are an "accumulation," the recurrent alternation of birth and death 陰是積聚生死重沓: see, for example, the explanation in the *Abhidharma-vibhāṣā-śāstra* 阿毘曇毘婆沙論, T 28.288a11–16, where the aggregates are explained in terms of the "accumulation" of various things. Chih-i quotes this Abhidharma text directly a few lines below, so he probably had this passage in mind when defining the aggregates in terms of "accumulation."

"Stepping or passing into" [sense experience]; they are also called the "gates for turning [in and out]" 涉入亦名輸門: see again the *Abhidharma-vibhāṣā-śāstra*, e.g., T 28.279a21–22 and 285a16–21, where this term is used to define the sense entrances, or *āyatana*.

Individual nature" 性分: that is, their specific combination gives each person his or her individual character. This is one of the three terms used by Chih-i below [53a23] to define the meaning of "nature."

Clarifies the relationship between these three topics 毘婆沙明三科開合: see the *Abhidharma-vibhāṣā-śāstra*, T 28.278b–290a, esp. 279a14–29.

If you are confused, then concentrate on a single skandha of visible form (*rūpa*) and let go of the [other] four skandhas. If you are confused by [the great variety of objects included in] "visible form," let go of the ten sense entrances [of objects and sense organs] and their individual sense entrances, and concentrate your thoughts on the single sense of consciousness [itself] or on the sense objects of the phenomena [that are the objects of consciousness]. If you are confused about both [form and mind], let go [all] the eighteen [sense] realms.

Abhidharma scholastics explain that the five skandhas are simultaneous; that consciousness is the "king of the mind," and that the [other] four skandhas are functions of the mind. They clarify the meaning [of the five skandhas] from the perspective of "existence"; thus [they teach that] the mind and its functions are mutually supportive and arise simultaneously.

Scholars of the [*Satyasiddhi*-]*śāstra* explain [that the process of the five skandhas goes as follows:] first consciousness **[52a]** makes distinctions, followed by the acceptance of sensations, the making of distinctions through conceptualization, the arising of aversive or receptive impulses or volitions, and [finally] the experience of form through the impulses. They clarify the meaning [of the five skandhas] from the perspective of "emptiness"; thus [they teach that the skandhas] arise mutually but progressively.

[My view is as follows.] If [the skandhas are analyzed] from the perspective of that which gives birth and that to which birth is given, you go from

If you are confused 若迷心: lit., "have a deluded mind." Given the context, this probably refers to being confused by having so many possible "objects" to contemplate.

Ten sense objects and sense organs 十入: that is, the five sense objects of sight, sound, smell, taste, and touch, and the sense organs of the eyes, ears, nose, tongue, and body.

Individual sense entrances 一入少分: or "the partial individual sense entrance."

Abhidharma scholastics 數人: literally the term means "number people" or "counters" (or "number crunchers"), perhaps referring to the penchant of Abhidharma scholarship for numerical lists. The the character 數 is also a technical term for functions of the mind or consciousness, thus this could be translated as "idealists" to match Chih-i's explanation. NAKAMURA (802) explains that the term can refer to followers of the Sāṃkhya school, but in this context Chih-i is referring to fellow Buddhists. Chan-jan and the *Kōgi* (BT–III, 214) claim that this refers to the position of the Sarvāstivāda school. Thus the term could be translated as "[Abhidharma] scholastics" or "scholars concerned with numbers." "Idealist" in this context may be misleading, since it probably does not refer to the Yogācāra or "mind only" tradition, let alone Western-style idealism. See also the use of this compound at *Mo-ho chih-kuan* 70a16, 74a21, and 127c16.

Scholars of the *śāstra* 論人: the *Kōgi* (BT–III, 214) indicates that this is the position of the *Ch'eng-shih lun (Satyasiddhi-śāstra)* scholars.

the fine [that is, mind or consciousness] to the crude [that is, form]; therefore [it must be said that] consciousness comes first. If [analyzed] from [the perspective of] practice, you go from the crude to the fine, and therefore form comes first. In any case, you cannot separate the mind from its functions. If, for example, you discuss the "mindfulness concerning four objects" [of body, sensation, mind, and dharmas], the "mind" comes in the middle, but this is merely a verbal convenience.

1. Nine Levels of People in Terms of the Five Skandhas and the Centrality of the Mind [52a5]

Again, there are nine types of distinctions [that are made concerning the five skandhas to describe different types of people and their attainments].

1. Your mind and [physical] form during a single lifetime are the "five skandhas of resultant retribution" 果報五陰.
2. Tranquil and impartial perceptions and feelings are "the neutral five skandhas" 無記五陰.
3.–4. Those who arouse false views and those who arouse passions are both "defiled five skandhas" 污穢五陰.
5.–6. Both "the five skandhas of good" and "the five skandhas of evil" 善惡五陰 [refer to those who] mobilize their physical and verbal actions [to produce karmic results].
7. Those who transform [themselves] and manifest [attainment of the Buddhist path] are "the skillful five skandhas" 工巧五陰.
8. People with the five good roots 五善根人 [of faith, diligence, mindfulness, concentration, and wisdom] are "the five skandhas of [skillful] means" 方便五陰.
9. Those who realize the fourth fruit [of arhatship] are "the undefiled five skandhas" [or, "the five skandha with no outflows of passions] 無漏五陰.

These various types [of five skandhas] all have their basis in the mind. The *Sūtra on Contemplating the Correct Dharma* says that [the mind is] like

Merely a verbal convenience 言說為便: because in fact the "mind" (mental function) or "consciousness" is always present, even though it may not be the specific object of mindfulness that is being practiced at the moment.

Nine types of distinctions 分別九種: the following list starts with the basic five aggregates as the fundamental existence of human beings, moves on to the five aggregates in terms of human defilement and imperfection, and gradually moves on to the existence of those who realize enlightenment and become arhats, thus being of "undefiled five skandhas." There is a similar detailed discussion of nine types of "five skandhas" in the *Ta ch'eng i chang*, T 44.623c. Though some of the terms differ, the content is basically the same.

a painter whose hands use the five colors—black, blue, red, yellow, white, and [also] the whitest white. The hand that paints is an analogy for the mind. The color black is an analogy for the dark skandhas of hell, the color blue is an analogy for hungry ghosts, red is an analogy for beasts, yellow is an analogy for asura, white is an analogy for humans, and the whitest white is an analogy for the gods. These six types of skandhas are limited to those within this world. If we refer to [the passage in] the *Avataṃsaka Sūtra*, "The mind is like an artist; it draws with the five skandhas," this shows that in all realms [of experience], both within this world and transcending this world [of delusions], there is no [sense experience] that is not created through the mind. Even the mind and form [that is, mental and material aspects] of this world cannot be completely exhausted; how much more so for that which is transworldly! How can you comprehend this with an ordinary mind? Ordinary eyes are blurred and cannot see even that which is up close; how can it see things that are far away? Even if you live for a long time in a more auspicious time in the distant past 彌生廣刧 *(anādikāla?)*, you cannot properly perceive even a corner of this world [of delusions], let alone disclose the limits of the realm beyond delusions. [One who tries to do so] is like a thirsty deer that chases after fire, or a rabid dog that attacks and bites the snow.

Like a painter whose hands use the five colors ... 如畫師手畫出五彩黑青赤黃白白白畫手譬心黑色譬地獄陰青色譬鬼赤譬畜黃譬脩羅白譬人白白譬天: see various passages in the *Sūtra on Contemplating the Correct Dharma*, T no. 721, 17.19a4–16, 23b18–c25, and 135a17–b10. None of these passages fit precisely with Chih-i's "quote," though taken together they fit quite nicely.

Note that Chih-i lists six colors while talking of the "five colors," though strictly speaking "white" and "whitest white" are one color. A passage in the sūtra (19a) identifies black with hell, blue with the cycle of birth and death (samsara), yellow with hungry ghosts, red with blood, and white with humans and gods.

A later passage (135a17–b10) contains the analogy of the mind as a painter, which is similar to the analogy found in the *Avataṃsaka Sūtra*. The passage reads:

> As a single artist produces many decorations, so a single mind produces various kinds of karma. Things are manifested in five colors: the perception of these arouses passions and pleasures. The [images] painted by the five sense organs are also like this.... Attractive and ugly forms are drawn ... the activity of the mind is also like this. It is able to produce good and evil results.

Chih-i considers this sūtra to be a Mahāyāna meditation text. The contents are generally closer to Hīnayāna teachings, though it contains "Mahāyāna" elements such as the analogy of the mind as a painter.

The mind is like an artist; it draws with the five skandhas 心如工畫師畫種種五陰: see the *Avataṃsaka Sūtra*, T 9.465c26. For a full translation of the context, see the note under *Mo-ho chih-kuan* 8b23.

A thirsty deer that chases after fire, or a rabid dog that attacks and bites the snow 如渴鹿逐炎狂狗齧雷: are these images from the *Mahāparinirvāṇa Sūtra* or *Ta chih tu lun*? The classical commentaries do not say. They appear to reflect

What meaning is there in it? Even if it leads to some understanding and enlightenment, it is of the Hīnayāna and is not the great way [of Mahāyāna].

Therefore *The Great Collection of Sūtras* says, "People with the mistaken view of eternalism teach the severance [of passions and attachments] through different thoughts; people with the false view of annihilationism teach the severance [of passions and attachments] in one thought." Thus they fall into two extremes and do not attain the Middle Way. Especially after the [historical] Buddha leaves this world, people's faculties become increasingly dull; they become attached to verbal distinctions and start fighting, criticizing each other, and falling into false evil views. Therefore Nāgārjuna attacked [all the interpretations of] the five skandhas as one, different, simultaneous, or consecutive. [The skandhas are] all like a flame, an illusion, an echo, a

a broader story behind each saying, but I was unable to find any explanation. Perhaps it just means what it says, that fire will not quence thirts, and snow will not satisfy hunger.

People with the mistaken view of eternalism teach the severance through different thoughts; people with the false view of annihilationism teach the severance in one thought 常見之人説異念斷。斷見之人説一念斷: this phrase could also be translated "To people with the mistaken view of eternalism, teach the severance [of passions and attachments] by different thoughts; to people with the false view of annihilationism, teach the severance [of passions and attachments] in one thought." This interpretation would be closer to the original in the *The Great Collection of Sūtras (Saṃnipāta-sūtra)*, T 13.158c2–4, which reads:

> To people with the mistaken view of annihilationism say that one thought severs [delusions]. To people with the mistaken view of eternalism, say that the eight kinds of forbearance [that lead to wisdom] severs [delusions]. Then both of these two types of people will attain the goal and later be separate from passionate afflictions, as well as become unhindered [by passions and delusions].

However, Chih-i's discussion that follows indicates that he understood the phrase as I have translated it.

Five skandhas as one, different, simultaneous, or consecutive 五陰一異同時前後: it is not clear if Chih-i is referring to the general thrust of Nāgārjuna's works here, or if he is referring to a specific textual passage. See, for example, the opening verses and their commentary in the *Middle Treatise* (T 30.1b–c), which claims that people's faculties are dulled in the second 500 years after the Buddha's decease (see Bocking's translation in *Nāgārjuna in China*, 103–5). See also the opening section of chapter 18 in the *Middle Treatise*, T 30.23c16–24a14. The first verse reads, "If the individual self *(ātma)* were [identical to] the skandhas, then it would partake of origination and destruction. If [the individual self] were different from the skandhas, then it would be without the characteristics of the skandhas." (adapted from Streng, *Emptiness*, 204.)

A flame, an illusion, an echo, a magical transformation 炎幻響化: part of a standard list of analogies for the emptiness of things. See, e.g., the opening section of the *Pañcaviṃśati Sūtra*, T 8.217a19–21, which gives the ten images of an illusion, a flame, the reflection of the moon in the water,

magical transformation; they cannot be obtained. Why, then, be attached to whether the mind and its functions [and the interplay with the other skandhas] are simultaneous or not?

In any case, all skandhas and sense entrances—whether part of this world [of delusions] or the realm beyond delusions—all arise dependent on the mind. The Buddha once said to a monk, "One dharma encompasses all dharmas; this ['one dharma'] is the mind." The *Treatise* says, "In the entire world there is only name-and-form. If you wish to contemplate reality as it is, then you should merely contemplate name-and-form." The mind is the basis of delusions, and this is the meaning. If you wish to contemplate, you must sunder the roots [of delusion], like applying moxa to the right points in order to heal disease. As you abandon yards to measure feet, and abandon feet to measure inches, so you should leave behind the other **[52b]** four skandhas such as form (and feelings, perceptions, and impulses), and only contemplate the skandha of consciousness. The skandha of consciousness is the mind.

empty space, an echo, a magical castle, a dream, a shadow, a reflection in a mirror, and a magical transformation.

They cannot be obtained 悉不可得: that is, they are empty of substantial Being.

One dharma encompasses all dharmas; this [one dharma] is the mind 一法攝一切法所謂心是: the *Kōgi* identifies this quote as from "section 4-6" of the *Expanded Āgama (Ekottarāgama)* 增一阿含經, T 2.539–540, but the closest phrase I could find in this section is that "the *tathāgata-garbha* is the most superior of all dharmas" (540a4).

In the entire world there is only name-and-form. If you wish to contemplate reality as it is, then you should merely contemplate name-and-form 一切世間中但有名與色。若欲如實觀但當觀名色: see the verses from the *Artha-vargīyāṇī sūtrāṇi* quoted in the section of name-and-form in the *Ta chih tu lun*, T 25.259b25–28. Lamotte, *Le Traité* 4, 1749, translates the context as follows:

> En outre "tous les dharma" sont les noms et formes *(nāmarūpa)*. Ainsi dans les *Arthavargīyāṇī sūtrāṇi*, le Buddha dit ces stances:
>
> Pour qui recherche la vision correcte,
> Il n'y a que les noms et formes.
> Celui qui veut juger et connaître en vérité
> Ne connaîtra lui aussi que les noms et formes.
> Qu'un esprit imbécile multiplie les notions
> Et s'attache à distinguer quantité de dharma,
> Il n'y aura jamais autre chose
> Que les noms et formes.

Chodron (4, 1436–37) translates:

> Furthermore, 'all dharmas' are names and forms. Thus in the *Arthavargīyāṇi sūtrāṇi*) the Buddha spoke these stanzas:
>
> For the person who seeks right seeing
> There are only names and forms.
> The person who wants to consider and know truly
> He too will know only names and forms.
> When a foolish mind multiplies notions
> And is attached to distinguishing many dharmas,
> He will never have anything
> But names and forms.

2. The Ten Modes of Cessation-and-Contemplation [52b1]

Contemplating thoughts [or, "the mind of contemplation" 觀心] includes ten modes of practice [or "Dharma gates"]:

1. Contemplating objects as inconceivable	觀不可思議境
2. Arousing compassionate thoughts	起慈悲心
[or, arousing true *bodhicitta]*	發眞正菩提心
3. Skillful means for a peaceful mind through cessation-and-contemplation	巧安止觀
4. The universal deconstruction of dharmas	破法遍
5. Knowing what penetrates and what obstructs	識通塞
6. Cultivating the steps on the path	修道品
7. Controlling and healing through auxiliary methods	對治助開
8. Knowing the stages [of attainment]	知次位
9. Resting in patient forbearance	能安忍
10. Avoiding passionate attachment to dharmas	無法愛

If you have attained realization of [1] the subtle objects [through contemplation of inconceivable objects], then you arouse a vow [2] to have compassion for others. Next you [3] take action to realize your vow. If you skillfully perform this vow and practice, there are [4] no limits to [the evil dharmas] that can be destroyed or deconstructed. While destroying or deconstructing [evil dharmas] everywhere, you [5] come to know minutely what penetrates and what obstructs [contemplation and the attainment of enlightenment]. This leads to progress on [6] [cultivating] the steps on the path, and is useful as [7] auxiliary aids for opening up the path. [8] The stages along the path are already known both for yourself and others, and you are [9] internally and externally peaceful and patient with regard to what is honorable and what is humiliating, and you are [10] not attached to the Middle Way nor passionately attached to dharmas. Therefore you can reach attainment quickly and realize the level of a bodhisattva. It is like having Viśvakarman build a

Viśvakarman build a victory tower 毘首羯磨造得勝堂: the Indian god of building or construction. See, for example, the *Ta chih tu lun*, T 25.88a5, where Viśvakarman is described as "a skillful master of transformations" (un métamorphoseur habile [*dakṣa nirmātṛ*], Lamotte, *Le Traité* 1, 256).

See the story concerning the "victory tower" built by Indra in the *Long Āgama (Dīrghāgama)*, T 1.142c21–29:

The Buddha said to the monks: In the past there was a time when the gods and asura fought against each other. At one time the gods were able to attain victory, and the asura retreated. When Indra had won the battle he returned to his palace and built a tower, calling it "supreme victory" 最勝. It was a hundred yojanas long from east to west, and sixty yojanas long from north to south.... This tower was built because of the joy and happiness from victory in battle over the asura, and therefore it was called "supreme victory."

victory tower; it would be neither rough nor closed, with cracks only large enough for a thin thread, soaring high and towering to the sky. This is not something that a clumsy [ordinary] artisan can plan or accomplish. Again, it is like a good artist painting the walls [of a room] with images near and true [to the original subjects], with fine and marvelous brush strokes so that they seem alive and vibrant. How, then, could an [ordinary] designer be able to decorate or enhance it further?

These ten modes of contemplation are comprehensive both vertically and horizontally, are fine and subtle, and are minutely applicable. The first [mode, that is, contemplating the inconceivable] involves examining the truth and falsity of objects, the middle [modes, from the second mode of arousing compassion and *bodhicitta* to the eighth mode of knowing the stages] involves applying the proper and auxiliary practices [of the Buddhist path], and the final involves "resting in patient recognition" and "[avoiding passionate] attachment" [that is, the ninth and tenth modes]. When your will is perfect and the modes are applicable, everything is well organized and ready. These [modes] serve as a model for beginners and act as incentives for the practitioner to reach omniscience *(sarvajña)*. However, this is not something that can be known by meditation masters with an enlightenment that is darkened [by lack of learning], or by masters who merely read or chant the texts [and do not practice meditation and have insight into the meaning]. Generally speaking, [the accomplishment of this practice] is based on a Tathāgata's accumulation over the eons of diligent seeking [after the Buddhist path], culminating in a sublime awakening at the place of enlight-

How could an [ordinary] interior designer 豈填彩人所能點綴: lit, "one who fills in the colors" or "ordinary painter."

... applying the proper and auxiliary practices [of the Buddhist path] 正助相添: according to Chan-jan (BT–III, p. 231–32), the seventh method involves the auxiliary aids to the path, and the second, third, fourth, fifth, sixth, and eighth method involves "proper" practices of the path.

Meditation masters with an enlightenment that is darkened [by lack of learning] 闇證禪師: that is, people who only practice meditation without reading the scriptures and/or learning about the Buddhist teachings.

Masters who merely read or chant the texts 誦文法師: the emphasis on a balance between learning and meditation, teaching and practice, is a prominent characteristic of Chih-i's system. See, for example, the opening section of the *T'ien-t'ai hsiao chih-kuan*, T 46.462b11–16, where these two aspects are compared to the two wings of a bird or the two wheels of a cart.

Based on a Tathāgata's accumulation over the eons of diligent seeking, culminating in a sublime awakening at the place of enlightenment 蓋由如來積劫之所勤求 道場之所妙悟: these phrases reflect the contents of the chapter on "The Life-Span of the Tathāgata" in the *Lotus Sūtra* (T 9.42c), which teaches that the Buddha has attained enlightenment from the immeasurably distant past.

enment. That which Śāriputra requested three times, and the content of the threefold teachings of the doctrine and parables [and stories of the *Lotus Sūtra*], are truly contained in this [set of the ten modes of contemplation].

Śāriputra requested three times 身子之所三請: at the opening of the second chapter of the *Lotus Sūtra* (T 6c7–7a5), Śāriputra beseeched the Buddha three times to preach the wonderful Dharma of the *Lotus Sūtra*. Finally the Buddha relented, saying, "Since you have now thrice earnestly besought me, how can I not preach? Now listen with understanding and with careful thought, for I will state it to you explicitly" (tr. by Hurvitz, *Lotus Sūtra*, 29 [28]).

Threefold teachings of the doctrine and parables [and stories 因緣 **of the *Lotus Sūtra*]** 法譬之所三說: in T'ien-ta'i parlance, these three refer to the Dharma teachings or doctrine found 1. in the second chapter of the *Lotus Sūtra* on "Means"; 2. in parables such as that of the poor son found in the third chapter on "Parables"; and 3. in "stories" (explaining the causes and conditions, or history, of certain matters), such as in the story of the "conjured city" (or the sixteen sons of the Buddha Great Universal Wisdom) as found in the seventh chapter of the *Lotus Sūtra*. This can be described as a threefold exegetical division (三周説法) of the first half of the *Lotus Sūtra*: In other words, this refers to the Buddha's three different iterations of the message of the "one vehicle." In the "Skillful Means" chapter, Śākyamuni reveals the teaching of "opening the three vehicles to reveal the one" (開三顯一) in doctrinal terms (法説周) as the true aspect of all phenomena, and thus Śāriputra, the śrāvaka of the most superior capacity, achieves realization. Then, through the Buddha's teaching of the parables of the burning house and the medicinal herbs (譬喻周), the "four great śrāvakas"— Subhūti, Mahākātyāyana, Maudgalyāyana, and Mahākāśyapa—who are of median capacity, reach understanding. Then, finally, in the "Conjured City" chapter, Śākyamuni succeeds in conveying the message to the śrāvakas of inferior capacity by telling of his past connection to them from the remote time of the Buddha Victorious through Great Penetrating Wisdom (因緣周).

Or, this could merely refer in general to the whole of the *Lotus Sūtra*, represented through three types of "teachings": in doctrines, parables, and stories?

1. Contemplating the Sense Fields While Sitting Properly in Meditation [52b18–100b16]

1. Contemplating Objects as Inconceivable [52b18–55c26]

The first [mode of] "contemplating thoughts" 觀心 is [to contemplate] objects as inconceivable. It is very difficult to explain these objects [as incon-

Contemplating objects as inconceivable 觀不可思議境: this section is one of the most important and influential of all of Chih-i's work, especially his analysis of (what Chan-jan identifies as) the "three thousand realms in a single thought or moment of consciousness" 一念三千 (Jpn. *ichinen-sanzen*). There is room for debate as to whether or not Chih-i meant the exact term of the "three thousand realms in a single thought" to be taken as *the most essential* phrase that exemplifies his thought. I will argue below that the presentation of the "three thousand realms in a single thought" is the expression of objects as inconceivable on the level of the contemplation of conventionality, one aspect of "threefold contemplation," and that Chih-i goes on to expound "objects as inconceivable" at the other levels, namely of the contemplation of emptiness and the contemplation of the Middle. Thus it may not be appropriate to take this phrase as the final and highest expression of Chih-i's thought. Admitting this is not to deny the influence of this phrase, especially in the Japanese Tendai and Nichiren traditions. Hurvitz focuses on this section in his work on Chih-i (see *Chih-i*, 271–318); Kanno Hiroshi's book based on a translation of this section is entitled *Ichinen sanzen to wa nani ka* [What is "the three thousand realms in a single thought"](1992).

The first [mode of] "contemplating thoughts" 觀心 is [to contemplate] objects as inconceivable 一觀心是不可思議境: or, to give a more traditional reading, "the first [mode of contemplation] is to contemplate thoughts (or, "the mind") as inconceivable object[s]." However, it is the "skandhas, sense entrances, and sense realms" (which includes "consciousness" or "mind") that are "inconceivable objects," not just "mind" or "thoughts." The question is this: is it the mind itself (or "thoughts") that is/are the inconceivable object(s), or is it that one contemplates all phenomenal objects (including the "skandhas, sense entrances, and sense realms," including the mind, or thoughts) as inconceivable—that is, as beyond conceptual understanding, and incapable of being "apprehended" or "obtained"? Does Chih-i mean that the mind contemplates only itself or its own thoughts as "objects" (a position that involves the danger of a mistaken reification of a "mind" independent of mental functions, e.g., "a mind and its thoughts"), or does he intend to say that the "objects" are the wider phenomena "beyond" (though only apprehended and experienced through) the mind or mental functions (a more "realist" position). I believe that the second position more closely approximates Chih-i's intention.

Grammatically speaking, one can take the two characters 觀心 as a compound, or one can take "contemplating" 觀 to modify the whole phrase. The second reading is the traditional one, giving the interpretation "contemplating the mind (or 'thoughts') as an inconceivable object." See the readings of Sekiguchi, *Makashikan* 1, 279; Kanno, *Ichinen sanzen*, 143; and the *kaeriten* of the standard *Mo-ho chih-kuan* texts (see BT–III, 235), as well as in the Taishō canon (T 46.52b18–19). Hurvitz (*Chih-i*, 302–303) avoids the problem by

ceivable], so first I will clarify [the meaning of] objects as conceivable. Then it will be easy to manifest [the meaning of] objects as inconceivable.

1. Contemplating the Conceivable [52b20]

Conceivable dharmas are as follows. The Hīnayāna also teaches that all

translating as "the contemplation of the 'realm of the inconceivable.'" Actually this is an accurate translation by Hurvtiz of the first entry of the ten objects of contemplation (52b1), not of the phrase that appears here on 52b18.

Perhaps such a distinction is not important, and the dilemma only appears when trying to translate the phrase into a Latin language. In the section above and in what follows, Chih-i is careful to point out that in any case there are no actions that we do or phenomena we can experience outside of our thoughts, or the workings of our "mind," and that there is no radical separation between a mind, thoughts, and the world that is experienced (see line 52b26: "The mind that contemplates also does not remain or abide from thought to thought"). The important factor is what we do to contemplate, comprehend, interpret, and utilize the experience of these phenomena.

More important is the meaning here of "mind" or "thoughts," and the interpretation of these terms has traditionally been controversial. Chih-li, for example, criticized the interpretation of "the mind of contemplation" as referring to a Buddha-nature-like "pure" or "real" mind, and argued that "mind" or "thoughts" here refers to ordinary, ignorant thoughts (see Ikeda, *Makashikan kenkyū josetsu*, 1986, 230–52). This was a crucial point in the debate between the "on-mountain" and "off-mountain" T'ien-t'ai interpreters of Chih-li's time.

I have chosen the interpretation and translation of "contemplating objects as inconceivable" because I think that it better reflects the context. This is the opening phrase for explaining the first of the ten modes of contemplation, which is part of the first of "the ten objects of contemplation." It makes sense to understand "inconceivable objects" as the focus of the "contemplating thoughts," and not just mind or thoughts as inconceivable, though of course "mind" and "thoughts" are included in the objects of contemplation and Chih-i focuses on contemplating thoughts as the most accessible of "objects." A few lines earlier (52b1) where the ten methods of contemplation are listed, the two characters "contemplating thoughts" are clearly taken as a compound. Thus, the first "type" or "mode" of "contemplating thoughts" is "*contemplating* objects as inconceivable."

Finally, the closing sentence of this section (54a18) describes the relationship between thoughts and their objects ("all phenomena" *[sarva-dharma]*) as "beyond conceptual understanding and verbalization," and thus "the inconceivable objects." It seems likely that in this section Chih-i is teaching that both thoughts and external phenomena—all mental functions and their objects—are inconceivable, and not just "the mind."

Objects as inconceivable 不思議境: or, "this inconceivability of objects."

Conceivable dharmas 思議法: this phrase is very ambiguous, depending on how you interpret "dharma"—as phenomenal object, as teaching, as method or way, as the practice of contemplation?—and whether or not the term "object" 境 is implied following the term "conceivable"

dharmas arise through the mind, that is, [in terms of the teaching of the cycle of] cause and effect in the six destinies [from hell to gods] and transmigration in the triple world [of desire, form, and no-form]. [According to this teaching,] if you wish to depart from the ordinary [realm of deluded beings] and seek the noble [realm of the sages], you should abandon what is below and reach what is above, that is, the wisdom of extinction [of consciousness] and the reduction of the body to ashes. This includes [the understanding of] the Four [Noble] Truths as "created" [that is, as "arising-and-perishing"]; these are dharmas that are conceivable.

The Mahāyāna also clarifies [the teaching that] all dharmas arise through the mind, that is, [in terms of the teaching of] the ten dharma realms [from hell to Buddhahood]. [According to this teaching,] if in contemplating thoughts [you contemplate objects] as existing, [you realize that] there are

思議. Thus, this phrase could be translated as, "phenomena that can be conceived," "the way or method to conceive (objects)," "the way or method [to contemplate the mind or objects] as conceivable," or, "the conceivable teachings." I have chosen to leave it ambiguous.

Wisdom of extinction and the reduction of the body to ashes 灰身滅智: one of the four phrases used in T'ien-t'ai to express the ("inferior") Hīnayāna understanding of nirvana: "warped" in understanding, "clumsy" in their means of salvation, and involving the belief that nirvana means a reduction of the body to "ashes" and the extinction of consciousness, and is analogous to the travelers in the parable of the conjured city who tarry "near" the city rather than advancing further on the way to the final goal. See "warped, clumsy, ashes, and near" in the Glossary. See also the use of this term in the *Mo-ho chih-kuan* above at 23c29–24a1.

Four [Noble] Truths as "created" 有作四諦: or, "involving action"; the first of the four kinds of understanding of the Four Noble Truths, at the level of those of the Tripitaka Teachings, which emphasizes the constant arising and perishing of the interdependent web of causes and conditions that are phenomena. For an analysis of these four types see Swanson, *Foundations*, 9–11, and the translation of Chih-i's analysis of these four types in the *Fa-hua hsüan-i* (T 33.700c–702a) in Swanson, 226–34. See also the discussion of these four categories earlier in the *Mo-ho chih-kuan* at 5b13–6a6.

Following the pattern of the threefold truth and the *Middle Treatise* verse 24:18, this interpretation corresponds to the first level of "the dependent arising of all dharmas."

These are dharmas that are conceivable 思議法: in this case it is fairly clear that "dharma" refers to "phenomena," namely phenomena as the causes and effects of the arising and perishing of things. Phenomena in this sense can be conceptually understood. Still, it is not impossible to interpret "dharma" here as "teaching," that is, the Hīnayāna teachings that can be conceptually understood.

If in contemplating thoughts [you contemplate objects] as existing 觀心是有: "If you contemplate thoughts as existing" would be a more natural reading of the Chinese, but the discussion that follows clearly is discussing types of "existences" or "destinies," not just good and evil thoughts; though for Chih-i there is no hard separation between "thoughts"

good and there are evil [existences]. There are three kinds of evil [thoughts and existences]: the causes and results of the three [evil] destinies [of hell, hungry ghosts, and beasts]; and there are three kinds of good [existences]—the causes and results of asuras, human beings, and gods. If you contemplate these six kinds [of existences] as transient and as arising-and-perishing, then [you realize that] the mind that contemplates also does not remain or abide from thought to thought.

Both that which contemplates and that which is contemplated arise through conditions. Because they arise through conditions they are empty. Both are the causes and results of phenomena [as understood] by those of the two vehicles [of the śrāvaka and pratyekabuddha].

If through contemplating this emptiness of existence you fall into the two extremes [of eternalism or annihilationism]—by drowning in emptiness or stagnating in [delusions concerning] Being—you should arouse great compassion and "re-enter" conventional existence to save and transform [other] beings. Although you do not really have a [physical] body, you conventionally create a body; though in reality there is no [substantial] emptiness, **[52c]** you conventionally teach emptiness and thus guide and transform [other beings]. This is [the understanding of] the causes and results of phenomena by the bodhisattva.

In contemplating these phenomena [in this way]—those who save and

and the "realm of existence"; what one is thinking is the realm within one dwells. Thus in this case also I take "contemplating thoughts" 觀心 as a compound.

There are three kinds of good: the causes and results of asuras, human beings, and gods 善則三品脩羅人天因果: these phrases are found in the *Ta chih tu lun*, T 25.280a22–23, though it is not clear whether or not Chih-i was consciously "quoting" the *Ta chih tu lun*.

The mind that contemplates also does not remain or abide from thought to thought 能觀之心亦念念不住: perhaps a reference to a passage in the *Ta chih tu lun*, T 25.372b19–21:

> There are two types of "transience." First is the extinction from thought to thought. All conditioned phenomena do not last or abide for even one momentary thought. Second is the transience that is so-named because of the destruction of all dharmas that continue [one after the other].

Note that this passage denies an ongoing, fundamental ("pure") mind.

Both that which contemplates … by those of the two vehicles: following the pattern of the threefold truth and the *Middle Treatise* verse 24:18, this interpretation corresponds to the second level of "emptiness" and the Shared Teachings.

If through contemplating this emptiness … by the bodhisattva: following the pattern of the threefold truth and the *Middle Treatise* verse 24:18, this interpretation corresponds to the third level of "conventionality," the Distinct Teachings.

In contemplating these phenomena … by the Buddha: following the pattern of the threefold truth and the *Middle Treatise* verse 24:18, this interpretation corre-

those who are saved—[you realize that] all phenomena have the true aspect of the Middle Way and are ultimately pure. What is good and what is evil? What exists and what does not? Who is saved and who is not saved? [These distinctions are not ultimately real.] All dharmas are just like this—this is [the understanding of] the causes and results of phenomena by a Buddha.

These ten dharma[-realms from hell to Buddhahood] are adjoined and wind from the shallow to the profound; [in any case] they all arise through the mind. [This understanding] is included in the Mahāyāna [interpretation of] the Four [Noble] Truths as "immeasurable." This still concerns objects as conceivable, and this is not what is contemplated in the current [practice of] cessation-and-contemplation [as taught in the *Mo-ho chih-kuan*].

2. Contemplating the Inconceivable [52c6]

[The contemplation of] objects as inconceivable is as follows. As it says in the *Avataṃsaka Sūtra*: "The mind is like an artist that creates the various five skandhas [like a painter creates images with various colors]; But in all the world there is nothing that is not created through the mind." "The various five skandhas [or aggregates]" refers to the five skandhas of the ten dharma realms as explained above.

1. The Ten Dharma Realms [52c9]

"Dharma realm" has three meanings. The number "ten" refers to that which

sponds to the fourth level of "the Middle" and the Perfect Teaching.

Four [Noble] Truths as "immeasurable" 無量四諦: the third of the four types of understanding the Four Noble Truths which emphasizes the "immeasurable" aspects of conventional existence. See note above on the four types of Four Noble Truths.

The mind is like an artist that creates the various five skandhas; But in all the world there is nothing that is not created through the mind 心如工畫師造種種五陰。一切世間中莫不從心造: see the *Avataṃsaka Sūtra*, T 9.465c26–27. The *Avataṃsaka Sūtra* text is slightly different: "The mind is like an artist; it draws with the various five skandhas. But in all the world there is no dharma that is not so produced." For a full translation of the context, see the note under *Mo-ho chih-kuan* 8b23.

"Dharma realm" has three meanings 法界者三義: corresponding to the pattern of the threefold truth and similar to the threefold reading of the phrase "ten suchlikes" as explained below and in the *Fa-hua hsüan-i* (T 33.693b5–694a8); see Swanson, *Foundations*, 179–84. In short, emphasizing the individual and specific aspects of the *ten* dharma realms is to emphasize the aspect of their conventionality, emphasizing the common essence of the ten *dharma realms* is to emphasize their emptiness, and to take the "ten dharma realms" as a whole is to emphasize the aspect of the Middle. This reading

depends 能依 [that is, their multifarious conventionality]; the "dharma realms" refers to that which is depended upon 所依 [that is, their emptiness], and since they are merged together they are called "ten dharma realms" [which corresponds to the Middle].

Again, each of the ten dharma [realms] has its own causes and own results that are not mixed or confused with the others; therefore they are called "*ten* dharma realms." Again, these ten dharma [realms] are each in themselves and in essence all the Dharma realm *(dharmadhātu)*, therefore they are called "ten *dharma realms*," and so forth.

The "ten dharma realms" are also known as [various amalgamations of] the [five] aggregates *(skandha)*, the [twelve] sense entrances *(āyatana)* and the [eighteen] sense realms *(dhātu)*, but in reality they are [each] not quite the same. The three [evil] destinies consist of defiled and evil skandhas, sense realms, and sense entrances. The three good [destinies] consist of defiled yet good skandhas, sense realms, and sense entrances. Those of the two vehicles [of the śrāvakas and pratyekabuddhas] consist of undefiled skandhas, sense realms, and sense entrances. The bodhisattvas consist of both defiled and undefiled skandhas, sense realms, and sense entrances. A Buddha consists of neither defiled nor undefiled skandhas, sense realms, and sense entrances. The *Treatise* says, "The supreme dharma is nirvana"; thus this dharma is nei-

seems more forced than the similar interpretation of the threefold readings of "ten suchlikes."

Ten **dharma realms** 十法界: this is the aspect of the immeasurable variety of existence as conventionally existent.

Each in themselves and in essence all the Dharma realm 十法一一當體皆是法界: or, each dharma realm has its own individual identity and character, but all are in the same way empty yet in essence part of the Dharma realm that is *dharmadhātu*. Chih-i is playing with words here, first using the term "dharma realm" 法界 to refer to each of the individual destinies or realms of existence from hell to Buddhahood, and then using the same term "Dharma realm" 法界 as the translation of *dharma-dhātu* to convey the participation of each phenomenon in the totality of reality.

Therefore they are called "ten ***dharma realms*****"** 故言十時[法]界: this is the aspect of the dharma realms as universally empty of substantial existence. Note that the Taishō text (T 46.52c12) has "ten time realms" 十時界 here, but this does not make any sense and later editions (see BT–III, 243) correct this to "ten dharma realms." Perhaps it was a copyist's error, as the term "ten times" appears below.

And so forth: Chih-i skips repeating the third aspect of the ten dharma realms as the Middle.

Skandhas, sense realms, and sense entrances 陰界入: for some unknown reason, the usual order of the *āyatana* and *dhātu* is reversed in this section.

Both defiled and undefiled 亦有漏亦無漏: they are "defiled" (that is, still involve "outflows" of passions] because they choose to remain in this defiled world to help others.

The supreme dharma is nirvana 法無上者涅槃是: the *Ta chih tu lun* says "Among

ther defiled nor undefiled. The *Sūtra of Immeasurable Meanings* says, "The Buddha does not have any of the [five] elements [of earth and so forth] or skandhas or sense realms," but this means that [the Buddha] has none of the skandhas, sense entrances, or sense realms of the first nine destinies. Now, to say that [the Buddha] does have [skandhas and so forth] means that he has the constantly dwelling skandhas, sense realms, and sense entrances of nirvana. The *Mahāparinirvāṇa Sūtra* says, "By extinguishing transient form *(rūpa)* you attain permanent form, and the same is the case with [the other skandhas of] sensation, conception, volition, and consciousness." For bliss and eternity to overlap is the meaning of "accumulation," and to be covered with compassion is the meaning of "overshadowing." Since the types of skandhas in the ten realms are not the same, they are called the "world of the five skandhas."

all the dharmas, nirvana is the supreme dharma, just as the Buddha is supreme among all sentient beings" (T 25.72b3–4). There is no mention of being "neither defiled nor undefiled."

The Buddha does not have any of the elements or skandhas or sense realms 佛無諸大陰界入: see the verses in the *Sūtra of Immeasurable Meanings*, T 9.384c29–385a3, which read:

> Great is the great awakened one, the great noble Lord;
> Who is without defilement, without contamination, and without attachment.
> He is the master of gods, men, elephants and horses,
> His moral breeze and fragrance of virtue permeates all.
> Serene is his wisdom, calm his emotion, and stable his prudence.
> His thought is settled, his consciousness extinct, and his mind quiescent.
> Long since he has severed dreamlike and deluded thoughts;
> *Neither does he have any of the [five] elements or the skandhas, sense entrances, or sense realms....*

See also *The Threefold Lotus Sutra*, 6.

By extinguishing transient form you attain permanent form, and the same is the case with sensation, conception, volition, and consciousness 因滅無常色獲得常色。受想行識亦復如是: this phrase from the *Mahāparinirvāṇa Sūtra* (T 12.838b16–18) has been quoted before in the *Mo-ho chih-kuan*, at 23b29. The full context reads:

> Form is transient. By extinguishing form you attain liberation and the form of constant dwelling. It is the same for sensations, conceptions, volitions, and consciousness. By extinguishing consciousness you attain the consciousness of constant dwelling.

For bliss and eternity to overlap is the meaning of "accumulation," and to be covered with compassion is the meaning of "overshadowing" 常樂重沓卽積聚義。慈悲覆蓋卽陰義: hence the connection with "the skandhas" (the "aggregates"). These two terms— "accumulation" and "overshadowing darkness"—are used at the beginning of this section as synonyms of the five skandhas; see *Mo-ho chih-kuan* above at 51c22–23.

World of the five skandhas 五陰世間: one of three categories 三種世間 (as expounded in the *Ta chih tu lun*, T 25.402a) into which the world is divided, that is, the world of the five skandhas, the world of sentient beings 衆生世間, and various lands 国土世間.

[The accumulation of various factors that are made of] the mixture of the five skandhas is customarily called "a sentient being," but sentient beings are not all the same. The mixture of the five skandhas of the three evil destinies is sentient beings full of offence and suffering. The mixture of the skandhas of human beings and gods is sentient beings who experience bliss. The mixture of undefiled skandhas is a true and noble sentient being [such as a śrāvaka or pratyekabuddha]. The mixture of skandhas of compassion is a sentient being that is a [bodhisattva-]mahāsattva. The mixture of the skandhas of constant dwelling [of nirvana] is a sentient being of ultimate honor [that is, a Buddha]. The *Ta chih tu lun* says, "The supreme sentient being is the Buddha." How can it be said that [the Buddha is] the same as the ordinary and inferior [being]? The *Mahāparinirvāṇa Sūtra* [also] says, "From the time of *kalala* [the first week of a fetus in the womb] the names [for a sentient being] are different, until at the time of old age the names are different [and yet it is the 'same' human being]. At the stage of a sprout the names are different, up to the time of becoming a fruit the names are different." When examined from the perspective of a complete life [from conception to death], you can distinguish ten periods. [in a single human being];

[Bodhisattva-]mahāsattva 大士: lit. "great being," or *mahāsattva*; one of the synonyms for a bodhisattva.

The supreme sentient being is the Buddha 衆生無上者佛是: another paraphrase from the *Ta chih tu lun* passage quoted above, T 25.72b3–4.

From the time of *kalala* … the names are different 歌羅邏時名字異乃至老時名字異。芽時名字異: a considerably abbreviated version of a longer exposition illustrating the transiency of physical form *(rūpa)* in the *Mahāparinirvāṇa Sūtra*, T 12.688a8–29:

> Form is transient; fundamentally [that is, substantially] it does not arise, because as it arises it is already perishing. [When a fetus is] in the womb within the body, at the time of *kalala* [the first week after conception] fundamentally it does not arise, because as it arises it is already perishing. Outside, all sprouts and stems [of plants] fundamentally do not arise, because as they arise they are already perishing. Therefore it should be known that all phenomenal dharmas of form are transient.
>
> Good sons. Forms that exist within [the body] change over time. At the time of *kalala* it is different; at the time of *arbuda* [the second week] it is different; at the time of *ghana* [the fourth week] it is different; at the time of *peśī* [the third week] it is different; at the time of *praśākhā* [the fifth week] it is different; at the time of birth it is different; at the time of infancy it is different; at the time of childhood it is different; and so forth, up to at the time of old age and so forth, each stage [in the development of a human being] is different and involves change. Outer forms [such as plants] are also likewise. A sprout is different, a stem is different, a branch is different, a leaf is different, a flower is different, and a fruit is different.
>
> Again, good sons, the flavors are different,… the powers are different,… the appearances are different,… *the names are different* … [and so forth].

Ten periods 十時: see the *Mahāparinirvāṇa Sūtra*, T 12.836a21–24. The ten

how can you not see differences between sentient beings of the ten realms? [53a] Therefore these are called the "world of sentient beings."

The places where the ten types [of sentient beings] dwell is commonly called "various lands" and are as follows: hell, in which beings dwell in red[-hot] iron; [the land of] beasts, which dwell in the earth, water, and sky; the asura, who dwell near the seashore and under the sea; human beings dwell on the earth; and gods dwell in [heavenly] palaces. The bodhisattvas of the six perfections dwell on the earth, the same as human beings. As for the bodhisattvas of the Shared Teachings, those who still have not yet extinguished their delusions dwell the same as human beings or gods, and those who have severed and extinguished their delusions dwell in the land where skillful means [remain]. As for bodhisattvas of the Distinct and Perfect Teachings, those who have not yet extinguished all delusions dwell the same as human beings or gods, or in the land where skillful means [remain], and those who have severed and extinguished their delusions dwell in the land of true recompense. Tathāgatas dwell in the land of eternal quiescent light. As it says in the *Jen-wang ching*, "Those in the three levels of erudition and the ten

periods are: 1. membrane 膜; 2. foam 泡; 3. in the placenta 胞; 4. ball of flesh 肉團; 5. growth of limbs 身支; 6. infancy 嬰孩; 7. childhood 童子; 8. youth 少年; 9. mature adult 盛壯; and 10. decrepit old age 衰老.

The "world of sentient beings" 衆生世間: the second of the three types of worlds into which the realm of experience is divided.

"Various lands" 國土世間: the third of the three types of worlds into which the realm of experience is divided.

Red[-hot] iron 赤鐵: the use of the compound "hot iron" is more common, so I have translated this as "red-hot iron." See, for example, the description of hell in the *Ta chih tu lun*, T 25.175c–176c.

Dwell near the seashore and under the sea 海畔海底住;: see, for example, the *Long Āgama*, T 1.129c2–3: "The Buddha said to the monks, 'At the bottom of the sea to the north of Mount Sumeru, there is a city of the asura.'"

Bodhisattvas of the six perfections 六度菩薩: that is, bodhisattvas of the Tripitaka Teachings.

Land where skillful means [remain] 方便土: one of the "four [Buddha] lands" as taught in the T'ien-t'ai system.

Dwell the same as human beings or gods 同人依地住: perhaps the "land where ordinary people, divine beings, sages, and so forth dwell together," one of the "four [Buddha] lands."

Land of true recompense 實報土: another one of the "four [Buddha] lands," a state wherein a bodhisattva enjoys the well-deserved rewards of his good karma.

Land of eternal quiescent light 常寂光土: another one of the "four [Buddha] lands." The phrase is from the *Contemplation of Samantabhadra*, T 9.392c16.

Three levels of erudition 三賢: in this case referring to the three groups of ten abodes, ten levels of practice, and ten levels of merit transference, not the three levels of practice prior to attaining arhatship.

Those in the three levels of erudition and the ten noble stages dwell with the fruit of their reward, and only the Buddha

noble [bodhisattva] stages dwell with the fruit of their reward, and only the Buddha alone dwells in the Pure Land." Each of these lands is not the same; [as the others]; therefore they are called "various lands."

These thirty types of worlds are all created through the mind.

2. *The Ten Suchlikes* [53a10]

Again, each and every one of the ten types of five skandhas [from the beings of hell to Buddhahood] is endowed with ten characteristics: suchlike 1. appearance, 2. nature, 3. essence, 4. power, 5. activity, 6. causes, 7. conditions, 8. results, 9. recompense, and 10. the beginning and end ultimately equal. First I will give a general interpretation, and then an interpretation according to type [of dharma realm].

1. General interpretation of the ten suchlikes [53a12]

1. "Appearance" [or "marks"] has its point of reference externally. As the *Ta chih tu lun* says, "It is called 'appearance' because it is easily known, as the

alone dwells in the Pure Land 三賢十聖住果報唯佛一人居淨土: verbatim from the *Jen-wang ching*, T 8.828a1.

Thirty types of worlds 三十種世間: that is, the ten destinies each contain the three types of worlds, giving thirty types of experiential realms.

Suchlike 如是: "suchlike" is an awkward phrase, but implies "just as [things truly are]." See the following note.

Suchlike appearance 相, **nature** 性, **essence** 體, **power** 力, **activity** 作, **causes** 因, **conditions** 緣, **results** 果, **recompense** 報, **and the beginning and end ultimately equal** 本末究竟等: this list is based on a passage from the second chapter on "Means" of the *Lotus Sūtra* (T 9.5c11–13) as translated by Kumārajīva, which, as Hurvitz points out, is so different from the extant Sanskrit that he devotes a long note to discussing the differences (see Hurvitz, *Lotus Sūtra*, 349–50 [317–18]). Hurvitz translates the Chinese as follows:

> Concerning the prime, hard-to-understand dharmas, which the Buddha has perfected, only a Buddha and a Buddha can exhaust their reality, namely, the suchness of the dharmas, the suchness of their marks, the suchness of their nature, the suchness of their substance, the suchness of their powers, the suchness of their functions, the suchness of their causes, the suchness of their conditions, the suchness of their effects, the suchness of their retributions, and the absolute identity of their beginning and end.

This is a prime example of the importance and influence of Kumārajīva's translations for the development of T'ien-t'ai and Chinese Buddhist thought. See Hurvitz's lengthy discussion of this issue in his *Chih-i*, 271–318.

For a discussion of Chih-i's analysis of the same topic in the *Fa-hua hsüan-i* see my *Foundations*, 131–35; for a fully annotated translation of the section of the *Fa-hua hsüan-i* (T 33.694a10–696a3), see 184–96. See also Kanno 1992.

It is called 'appearance' because it is easily known, as the difference between water and fire is known by their appearance 易知故名爲相如水火相異則易可知: from the *Ta chih tu lun*, T 25.91a25, in

difference between water and fire is known by their [different] appearance." This is like people [revealing] all their happiness [and sorrow, good and] evil through the visible form of their faces; you can know [what they are like] internally by observing their external appearance or marks.

In the [distant] past the "marks" of Sun and Liu were manifest, and the "marks" of Ts'ao were hidden, so that the diviner cried out in a great voice, "[The land between] the four seas will be divided into three, and the people will suffer greatly." Thus, even if there are marks, people who are in the dark

answer to the question "What is that called 'appearance or mark' *(lakṣaṇa)*," in the context of a discussion of the Buddha's thirty-two major physical "marks." Lamotte, *Le Traité* 1, 280, translates:

> Question. Pourquoi les appelle-t-on marques *(lakṣaṇa)*?
> Résponse. Parce qu'elles sont faciles à reconnaître. Ainsi l'eau, qui diffère du feu, se reconnaît à ses marques.

Chodron (1, 234) translates:

> Question. Why are they called marks (*lakṣaṇa*)?
> Answer. Because they are easy to recognize. Thus water, which is different from fire, is recognized by its marks.

As can be seen in this example, 相 is the Chinese translation of *lakṣaṇa*. Although usually translated as "marks," "characteristics," "signs," or "features," I have chosen to translate it usually as "appearance" in this context, though sometimes "marks" is more appropriate. For Chih-i it is a single term that he uses in various senses that cannot be conveyed with a single consistent English translation.

Happiness [and sorrow, good and] evil 休否: this translation follows the explanation given by Chan-jan (BT–III, 256).

In the [distant] past the "marks" 相: that is, the evidence that allows a person who can "read the signs" to predict the future, or "read" someone's personality.

Sun 孫, **Liu** 劉, **and Ts'ao** 曹: famous generals who occupied a prominent place during the wars of the Three Kingdoms in the third century AD. See note below for details.

The diviner 相者: lit., "one [who can interpret] the marks," that is, a soothsayer or fortune teller.

The four seas will be divided into three, and the people will suffer greatly 四海三分百姓荼毒: Chan-jan (BT–III, 256–57) explains: This example is given to illustrate how physical "marks" indicate or foretell the future. According to the opening section of the Chinese classic tale of *The Three Kingdoms*, at the end of the Han period (third century, just before the period of the "Three Kingdoms"), these three people together visited a diviner. The "marks" were apparent that Sun and Liu would reign over a kingdom, and they were told so. Ts'ao's marks were first concealed from the diviner. But Ts'ao knew that the diviner's [predictions?] were unavoidable and so he lifted up his robes and exposed [what formerly he had hidden?]. *When the diviner finished his examination he cried out in a loud voice that the land under heaven and between the four seas would be divided into three and that there would be much suffering.* By the end of the Later Han the fruits [of the labors] of these three people was such that they divided and took possession of the three areas of China. Sun (182–252) took possession of the Wu, Liu (161–223) took possession of the Minor Han, and Ts'ao (155–220) took possession of the Wei.

[and don't know how to interpret them] do not know [what they mean]; [on the other hand,] even if there are no [clear] marks, a diviner can reach a penetrating understanding [of them]. You should follow a good diviner (or reader of signs), and believe that people's external faces embody all the marks [that indicate their inner nature and true self].

The mind is also like this; it includes all marks. The marks of sentient beings [as to their future potential or Buddhahood] are hidden, the marks of Maitreya [that reveal his enlightenment] are manifest. The Tathāgata knows these [marks] well, and therefore can predict the near and distant [future]. Those who cannot perceive [these things] well and do not believe that the mind includes all marks should follow one who can perceive accurately and truly, and believe that the mind includes all marks.

2. Suchlike nature: nature has its point of reference internally. Generally speaking, this has three meanings:

1. "Nature" is also called "that which does not change." The *Sūtra of Non-activity* uses the term "unmoving nature."
2. Again, "nature" is called "individual nature." This is the meaning [of the characteristics] of specific types, which are not the same from one to the other [divisions or individuals], and each do not change.
3. Again, "nature" is "true nature," that is, [it participates in] the nature of reality, the ultimate reality that is without deficiency; this is another name for the Buddha-nature.

The "unmoving nature" corresponds to emptiness, the specific [indi-

Unmoving nature 不動性: see the *Sūtra on the non-activity of all dharmas*" 諸法無行經, T no. 650. This text contains many references to "unmoving" or "immobile" marks, but not to "unmoving nature." See, for example T 15.756b21–29:

> All sentient beings realize the nature of *bodhi*-wisdom; therefore it is said that all sentient beings attain *bodhi*. However, this *bodhi* is not a mark that is attained. Why? Because the nature of sentient beings is that of *bodhi*. Therefore for all sentient beings to attain *bodhi* is called "the unmoving mark (or characteristic)" [of sentient beings].
>
> The World Honored One said: All sentient beings fulfill all wisdom; this is called an "unmoving mark (or characteristic)."
>
> Manjuśrī said: Why is this called an "unmoving mark (or characteristic)"?
>
> The World Honored One said: All sentient beings are without a [substantial] nature. Because they are without a [substantial] nature, they can realize the Tathāgata's state of equanimity. From the beginning they have this nature of all wisdom. Because this nature is the same [whether one is an ordinary ignorant being or an enlightened one], it is called an "unmoving mark (or characteristic)."

Individual nature" 性分: that is, the individual or personal characteristics with which one is born.

vidual] nature corresponds to conventionality, and the "true nature" corresponds to the Middle.

Now I will clarify [only the first meaning, that of] the inner nature as unchanging. Take, for example, the nature of fire [existing as a potential] within bamboo. Although [this nature] cannot be seen, it cannot be said to be nothing, for if dried grass is kindled, all will be burned away. The mind is also like this; it includes the natures of all of the five skandhas. Although these cannot be seen, they cannot be said to be nothing. If you contemplate this with the eye of wisdom **[53b]**, [you can realize that] all natures are included therein.

[The misconceptions of] the people of the world [concerning the idea of "unchanging"] are laughable. They evaluate [the teachings of] the perfect sūtras on the basis of a one-sided hearing. Because the *Mahāparinirvāṇa Sūtra* clarifies that the Buddha knows that sentient beings have Buddha-nature, they conclude that this means an "ultimate permanence." Because the *Lotus Sūtra* clarifies that the Buddha knows the suchlike nature of all phenomena, they conclude that [everything is] transient. Why should it be concluded that [the teaching of] permanent [nirvana] is of little wisdom, and [the teaching of] transiency is of much wisdom [when both perspectives should be taken into account]? The *Lotus Sūtra* also says that the Buddha knows all phenomena, that all are of "one type and one nature." These words,

Now I will clarify ...: actually Chih-i launches into a discussion of the need for a balanced understanding of "permanence" and "transiency," presumably as the correct way to understand the meaning of "unchanging."

It cannot be said to be nothing for if there is a kindlier with dried grass, all will be burned away 不得言無燧人乾草遍燒一切: Chan-jan (BT–III, 259) and the classical commentaries link this analogy to the *Mahāparinirvāṇa Sūtra*; see the passage at T 12.689b2–6:

> Good sons. Take, for example, the arousing of fire by means of tinder, or by rubbing sticks, or by hand, or with dried cow's dung. The tinder does not say, "I am able to arouse fire," nor do the sticks, hands, or cow's dung say "I am able to arouse fire." The fire does not say, "I am able to arouse fire." The Tathāgata is also like this.

The Buddha knows that sentient beings have Buddha-nature 佛知衆生有佛性: see, for example, the *Mahāparinirvāṇa Sūtra*, T 12.643b7–8, 648b, and 767b.

The Buddha knows the suchlike nature of all phenomena 佛知一切法如是性: see the passage of the *Lotus Sūtra* quoted above, T 9.5c11–12.

The Buddha knows all phenomena, that all are of one type and one nature 佛知一切法皆是一種一性: supposedly from the same passage in the *Lotus Sūtra*, T 9.5c, though Chih-i seems to be rephrasing the passage in his own way. See also a later passage in the *Lotus Sūtra*, T 9.13c7–10, at the end of the parable of the burning house; Hurvitz (*Lotus Sūtra*, 63–64 [59–60]) translates:

> Then he gives the Great Vehicle equally to all, not allowing any of them to gain passage into extinction for himself alone,

then, should also be of "little [wisdom]"; how, then, can they [one-sidedly] evaluate [the *Mahāparinirvāṇa Sūtra* as teaching merely the idea of permanence and the *Lotus Sūtra* as teaching merely the idea of] transiency?

Again, there are teachers who assess the ten suchnesses in the *Lotus Sūtra* and say that the first five are tentative and belong to ordinary people, and that the last five are real and belong to the sages. If we rely on this interpretation, then ordinary people have no [relation to] the real, and will forever be unable to attain sagehood, and the noble sages have no [relation to] the tentative and thus cannot have true universal knowledge. This is truly a capricious attitude; it slanders the Buddha and ridicules ordinary people.

> but conveying them all to the extinction of the Thus Come One. To all these living beings who have escaped the three worlds he gives the Buddhas' dhyāna-concentration, their deliverance, and other devices of enjoyment, *all of one appearance, of one kind,* all praised by the saints, all able to bring about the prime, pure, and subtle joy.

Little [wisdom] 亦少: like above, where people conclude that the teaching of the *Mahāparinirvāṇa Sūtra* is of "little wisdom" because it speaks of a permanent and "constant" nirvana.

How, then, can they evaluate transiency 何故判爲無常: in other words, the "perfect" teaching includes a balance of the ideas of permanent or constant abiding and transiency, which is beyond adequate verbal expression.

First five are tentative and belong to ordinary people, and that the last five are real and belong to the sages 前五如屬凡是權後五屬聖爲實: in the *Fa-hua hsüan-i* this theory is attributed to "teachers from the northern lands" in an extension of his criticism of Fa-yün's position. The passage (T 33.693b26–c5) reads:

> Next, in classifying the tentative and the real, Fa-yün classified the first five suchlikes as the tentative that belong to ordinary ignorant people. The next four sucklikes were classified as the real that belong to sages. The last suchlike is a general one that brings together the tentative and the real. This verse [from the *Lotus Sūtra*] is quoted as proof: "the suchlike great results and recompense" Because they are "great," therefore you can know the real. Because of "various meanings of nature and appearance" you can know the tentative.
>
> I think that this [interpretation by Fa-yün] is mistaken. There are three meanings to the word "great": large, many, and superior. If you accept "large" to be the meaning of the real, then you should also accept the meanings of "many" and "superior." But is not the fact of having various names [which is the defining characteristic of conventional existence] the meaning of many? If you say that the tentative belongs to ordinary ignorant people, does that mean that ordinary people lack [participation in] the real? If the real belongs to the sages, then does that mean that sages lack [participation in] the tentative? If you examine this position, you can see that it is unreliable.
>
> Also, the northern Masters say that the first five are the tentative and the later five are the real. This [interpretation is based on] human emotions [and not on wisdom, and so is unacceptable.]

For details, see the annotated translation in my *Foundations*, 181–82.

A capricious attitude 專輒: lit., "concerned only with the side of the chariot where the weapons are carried."

Again, the *Mahāparinirvāṇa Sūtra* clarifies that "all sentient beings without exception have Buddha-nature," and this is taken to imply "permanence." The *Vimalakīrti Sūtra* says that "all sentient beings have the marks of *bodhi*-wisdom," and this is taken to imply "transiency." If the marks of Buddha-nature and *bodhi*-wisdom are different, then you could say that one is permanent and the other is transient. If they are not different [as it surely is the case], then this assessment [that one represents permanence and the other transiency] is a great error. It is like a diviner perceiving the marks and nature of a king and concluding that he will rise to the highest position; [in the same way] how can it be said that the marks of Buddha-nature and *bodhi*-wisdom are not the same?

3. Suchlike essence: that which is the central quality [of something] is called its "essence." The skandhas of these ten dharma realms have the [respective] functioning of their form and mind as their essential quality.

4. Suchlike power: this is the enduring [potential] power to function. It is like a king's champion who has thousands of myriads of skills; when he is sick none of them are any good, but when the disease is healed he recovers these functions. The mind is also likewise; it includes [the potential for] all powers, but because of the passionate afflictions one is not able bring them into play. If observed as it truly is, then [you will realize that the mind] includes all powers.

5. Suchlike activity: that which activates and constructs is called "activity." There is nothing that is activated independently of the mind. Therefore know that the mind includes all activity.

6. Suchlike causes: that which solicits results are "causes"; they are also called "karmic deeds." The karmic deeds of the ten dharma realms arise from

All sentient beings without exception have Buddha-nature" 一切衆生悉有佛性: see, for example, the *Mahāparinirvāṇa Sūtra*, T 12.767a29.

All sentient beings have the marks of *bodhi*-wisdom 一切衆生即菩提相: see the *Vimalakīrti Sūtra*, T 14.542b16. This passage has been quoted before in the *Mo-ho chih-kuan*; for a full translation of the context see the notes at 18b4.

This is taken to imply "transiency" 判是無常: it is not clear to me how this passage implies "transiency." It strikes me more as implying a "permanent" nature, unless "marks" here refer to the "transient" thirty-two major and eighty minor physical marks of a Buddha. Or is it because *bodhi*-wisdom implies insight into the true nature of emptiness and transiency?

The mind includes all activity 心具一切作: thus "power" is the potential for activity, and "activity" is the actual functioning of activity.

Suchlike causes 如是因: in the *Fa-hua hsüan-i*, "causes" are defined as "repetitive causes" *(vipākahetu)*, and "conditions" are defined as "auxiliary causes." It is not clear why Chih-i leaves this explanation out in

the mind; if only there is mental activity, then all karmic deeds are included therein. Therefore it is called "suchlike causes."

7. Suchlike conditions: "conditions" gets its names from [the term] "conditioned origination." Auxiliary karmic conditions all have the sense of "conditions." Ignorance, passions, and so forth are able to stimulate karmic deeds; hence mental activity becomes a condition.

8. Suchlike results: bringing in a harvest is called a "fruit" or "result." The "repetitive causes" *(vipākahetu)* come first repeatedly, and then the "repetitive results" *(niṣyandaphala)* are harvested. Therefore these are called "suchlike results."

9. Suchlike recompense: "retributive causes" are called "recompense." Repetitive causes and repetitive results are together called causes for recompense in the future. This recompense is punishment [which naturally arises] from such causes.

10. Suchlike beginning and the end ultimately equal: "Appearance is the "beginning" and "recompense" is the "end." The "beginning" and "end" all arise from conditions. Because they arise from conditions they are empty. The beginning and end are all empty; because of this emptiness they are all "equal."

Again, "appearance" is only a word and "recompense" is also only a word. These are all conventional [verbal] constructions; because they are merely conventional terms, they are all "equal." Again, the beginning and end mutually reflect each other. You first perceive appearances, then later recompense is manifested; by later perceiving the recompense, you can know the original appearances. It is like knowing wealth by perceiving [the act of] charity, and knowing charity by seeing wealth. The beginning and the end exist together. This is the presentation of "equality" from the perspective of conventionality.

Again, [the fourfold possibilities of] appearance, non-appearance, both-non-appearance-and-appearance, and neither-appearance-nor-non-appearance; recompense, non-recompense, both-recompense-and-non-recompense, and neither-recompense-nor-non-recompense—each one of these are included in the limits of reality. This is the presentation of "equality" from the perspective of the Middle.

the *Mo-ho chih-kuan*, since he uses the phrases in his definition below of results and recompense.

Repetitive causes 習因: causes that bring about a result similar to the cause, such as a good deed bringing about good results. A "habitual" cause.

Repetitive results 習果: results that are the same as its cause, such as an evil thought resulting in more evil thoughts. A "habitual" result.

This recompense is punishment 報酬: that is, for evil karmic deeds performed in the past.

2. Interpretation of the ten suchlikes according to type of dharma realm [53c6]

Second, interpreting [the ten suchlikes] according to type involves bundling the ten dharma [realms] into four types.

[1.] Suffering is the "appearance" or "mark" made manifest by those in the three evil destinies. Their "nature" is to accumulate certain set evil [characteristics, deeds, recompense, and so forth]. Their "essence" is the pounding and breaking of body and mind *(rūpa-citta)*. Their power is to tread on blades and enter [boiling] cauldrons. Their "activity" is to arouse the ten evil deeds [from killing to having false views]. Their "causes" are their defiled and evil karmic deeds. Their "conditions" are passions, attachments, and so forth. Their "results" are the evil repetitive results. Their "recompense" is [to be reborn in] the three evil destinies. These [three realms] are the same in that ignorance is both their beginning and end.

[2.] The [three] good [destinies are as follows.] Their appearance or

Ten suchlikes according to type of dharma realm: compare the discussion of this topic in the *Fa-hua hsüan-i*, T 33.694a19–696a3, which contains a more detailed analysis; for an annotated translation see my *Foundations*, 184–96. For Hurvitz's analysis of this passage in the *Fa-hua hsüan-i*, see his *Chih-i*, 289–302.

Bundling the ten dharma [realms] into four types 束十法爲四類: that is, into the four categories of 1. the three evil destinies or dharma realms (hell, hungry ghosts, beasts), 2. the three good destinies (asura, human beings, gods), 3. the realms of the two vehicles (śrāvaka and pratyekabuddha), and 4. the two realms of the bodhisattva and Buddha. Note that in the *Fa-hua hsüan-i* the first category includes the *four* evil destinies (including the asura), and the second category consists of the two "good" destinies of human and divine beings. This categorization makes more sense to me than the one found here in the *Mo-ho chih-kuan*.

Pounding and breaking of body and mind 摧折色心: the *Fa-hua hsüan-i* (694b1–4) elaborates: First in this life they abuse their minds, and so in the next life their material body is abused. Also, the results and retributions from this world in which the mind and body is abused are such that in the next world the results and retributions will consist of the abuse of mind and body. Therefore the abuse of body and mind is the essence of those in the four evil destinies.

Tread on blades and enter [boiling] cauldrons 登刀入鑊: Hurvitz (*Chih-i*, 309), interprets this as referring to "being carved and cooked, whether in Hell by demons or [as beasts] on earth by men for food." It could also refer to the propensity of beings to abuse themselves, even up to "climbing over the blades of swords or entering cauldrons of boiling water," in futile attempts to satisfy their appetites.

Defiled and evil karmic deeds 有漏惡業: that is, since they actively commit evil deeds, these serve as karmic causes and lead to "evil repetitive results."

Evil repetitive results 惡習果: That is, the "evil" results that come from evil deeds as causes.

marks is the manifestation of bliss. Their nature is to accumulate certain set good [characteristics, results, and so forth]. Their essence is a mind and body that ascends [toward enlightenment]. Their power is [their potential] to experience bliss. Their causes are good deeds. Their conditions are a passion and attachment for good. Their results are good repetitive results. Their recompense is [to be reborn] as humans and gods. Their equality, from the perspective of their conventional designation, is that the beginning and end mutually exist in each other.

[3.] The two vehicles [are as follows.] Their appearance or mark is the manifestation of nirvana. Their nature is that of liberation. Their essence is to be endowed with five [virtuous] qualities [of keeping the precepts, concentration, wisdom, liberation, and the knowledge-insight of liberation]. Their power is [the potential] to be free from bondage [to passionate afflictions and so forth]. Their activity is the [thirty-seven] steps on the path. Their causes are the undefiled practice of [intellectual] wisdom. Their conditions are the practice of [experiential] practice. Their results are the four

Accumulate certain set good 定善聚: In the *Fa-hua hsüan-i* Chih-i uses the terms "white" *(śukla-dharma)* and "black" to describe the natures, respectively, of the "good" and "evil" destinies.

A mind and body that ascends 升出色心: in the *Fa-hua hsüan-i* (694b29) Chih-i uses the term "peaceful mind and body."

[Their potential] to experience bliss 樂受: in the *Fa-hua hsüan-i* (694b29) Chih-i uses the term "enduring potential for good."

Good deeds 白業: lit, "white karmic actions."

Good repetitive results 善習果: in the *Fa-hua hsüan-i* (694c1) Chih-i uses the phrase "the spontaneous arising of the results of a good mind."

Humans and gods 人天: here Chih-i does not include the asura as a "good" rebirth, thus reverting to the categorization of two good destinies in the *Fa-hua hsüan-i*.

Five [virtuous] qualities 五分[法身]: or, the fivefold qualities of the Dharma body; in T'ien-t'ai, the highest attainment possible by those of the Hīnayāna.

Free from bondage 無繫: the *Fa-hua hsüan-i* (694c5) has "the ability to appear and move about [in this triple world] and the potential capacity to attain the path."

Steps on the path 道品: the *Fa-hua hsüan-i* (694c6) has "to strive diligently."

[Experiential] practice 行行: lit., "the practice of practice." This compound is used in contrast to the above "practice of wisdom" 慧行. In the *T'zu-ti ch'an-men*, T 46.535b13–17, Chih-i defines these terms as follows:

> There are two types of practice. The first is the practice of wisdom, and the second in the practice of practice.... The practice of [experiential] practice is so-called because through this practice one conquers and destroys all passions. The second practice of [intellectual] wisdom consists of severing delusions concerning reality through correct contemplation of the four noble truths, twelvefold conditioned arising, and true emptiness.

See also the extensive explanation of these terms earlier in the *Mo-ho chih-kuan* at 30b13–28.

fruits [of the stream winner, once-returner, no-more-returner, and arhat]. As they will have no more rebirth in the fields [of this triple world], they have no recompense. And so forth [with regard to all being "equal."]

[4.] That of the bodhisattvas and Buddhas is as follows. Their appearance or marks are the conditions and causes [that bring about wisdom]. Their nature is the complete cause [for realizing Buddhahood]. Their essence is the direct cause. Their power is the Four Universal Vows. Their activities are the myriad practices of the six perfections. Their cause is the "adornment of wisdom." Their condition is the "adornment of virtue." Their result is perfect wisdom *(saṃbodhi)*. Their recompense and reward is great nirvana. And so forth [with regard to all being "equal"].

[There is a] contrary and regular 逆順 [flow of] causes and conditions.

As they will have no more rebirth in the fields [of this triple world], they have no recompense 既後有田中不生故無報: the *Fa-hua hsüan-i* (694c7–15) provides a more detailed analysis:

> [According to Hīnayāna teachings, there is no recompense for śrāvakas and pratyekabuddhas, for three reasons.] First, since śrāvakas and pratyekabuddhas are without further rebirth, they have no recompense. The reason is that when the [understanding] of the real is aroused, this is the [ultimate] result and there is no need to discuss any further recompense. Second, if undefiled dharmas arise as the recompense for repetitive causes, then repetitive results will be attained. Since the lack of further birth from having no defilements [a characteristic of arhats] is not a condition wherein one is shackled by further birth, there is no later recompense. Third, the first three [i.e., the stream-enterers, once-returners, and non-returners] have recompense, because they have remaining [mistaken] conceptions which have not been severed. Therefore the stream-enterers, once-returners, or those reborn in the realm of form, do not share in the [lack of] recompense [gained from total] non-defilement. Therefore [according to Hīnayāna teachings] these beings have nine and not ten [suchlike characteristics].
>
> According to Mahāyāna doctrine, even this [so-called] non-defilement [of śrāvakas and pratyekabuddhas] contains some defilement. The *Mahāparinirvāṇa Sūtra* (T 12.767b21–29) says, "The adornment of virtue" means being conditioned and defiled. This refers to the śrāvakas. They are not completely undefiled. They have not gotten rid of all delusions and they still experience rebirth in the world of transmigrations. If complete non-defilement is the cause and ignorance the condition, then they are reborn in the realm of transformations. Therefore they do have recompense.

See Hurvitz's note on 297–99 for a different interpretation and lengthy discussion of this section. Chih-i picks up on some of these points a few lines below.

Bodhisattvas and Buddhas: in contrast to the terse analysis that follows, the *Fa-hua hsüan-i* (694c15–696a3) gives a long analysis of this classification in terms of the bodhisattvas of the Tripitaka, Shared, and Distinct Teachings, and a long discussion of the ten characteristics of the Buddha realm in terms of the Middle Way. See *Foundations*, 189–196.

Conditions and causes 緣因, **complete cause** 了因, **direct cause** 正因: these are the three aspects of threefold Buddha nature.

The "regular" [flow of] birth and death consists of defiled karmic actions as the causes and passions and attachments as the conditions. The "contrary" [flow of] birth and death consists of undefiled wisdom as the cause and the practice of [experiential] practice as the conditions; together these [causes and conditions] prevent rebirth [in unwelcome destinies] and destroy delusions. Even when one is in the cycle of birth and death in the realm beyond delusions, undefiled wisdom is still the cause, and [the still unsevered propensity toward] ignorance is the condition. If you go contrary to the [ordinary flow of] life-and-death (samsara), then the wisdom of the Middle Way is the cause, and the myriad practices [of the six perfections] are the conditions; together these prevent (the continued cycle of) birth and death that is a transformation beyond conceptual understanding. Since this is the case for causes and conditions, the contrary and regular [flow] of the other [characteristics] can be surmised and known [in the same way].

If we depend on [the Hīnayāna teaching of] the śrāvaka, then they only have nine [suchlike characteristics] and not ten [because they have no "recompense"]. But if we depend on the Mahāyāna teaching of the threefold Buddha, then [even] the Buddha has a "body of recompense." If you depend on [only] the meaning of extinction through the severing of delusions [to understand this issue], then [you must conclude that] there is no later reward or retribution. The issue of nine or ten [characteristics for śrāvakas and pratyekabuddhas] should be understood in this context.

The world of sentient beings is that of conventional designation and lack of [substantial] essence that can be distinguished; [it is just that] real phenomena are taken and established conventionally. So [it includes] the appearances, nature, essence, **[54a]** power,... and ultimate equality of sentient beings of the evil destinies, and so forth [also for sentient being of the good destinies]. So also for the appearances, nature, essence, power,...

Birth and death that is a transformation beyond conceptual understanding 變易生死: in contrast to the "ordinary" cycle of birth and death of people in samsara. This distinction is based on a passage in the *Śrīmālādevī Sūtra*, T 12.219c, to account for differences (from the Mahāyāna perspective) between ordinary people and the "rebirth" of those who have supposedly severed all delusions.

Mahāyāna teaching of the threefold Buddha 大乘三佛義: that is, that the Buddha consists of three "bodies": the Dharma body (*dharmakāya* 法身); the body of enjoyment 報身, in which the Buddha enjoys the "fruits" (rewards or recompense) of his enlightenment; and the body of transformation 應身, that is, the historical manifestation of the Buddha.

Should be understood: for details, see the section of the *Fa-hua hsüan-i* quoted in the note above.

Real phenomena 實法: that is, our actual experience of the objects of our senses as interpreted through our mind.

and ultimate equality of undefiled sentient beings [such as the śrāvaka and pratyekabuddha], and for the appearances, nature, essence, power,… and ultimate equality of the Dharma realm of bodhisattvas and Buddhas. This can all be understood in accordance with the examples given above.

The world of various lands also includes the ten dharma realms, that is the appearances, nature, essence, power and so forth of the evil lands; of the good lands; of the undefiled lands; the appearances, nature, essence, power and so forth of the lands of the bodhisattvas and Buddhas.

3. Three thousand realms in a single thought: The contemplation of the conventional [54a5]

[Thus] a single thought includes the ten dharma realms. A single dharma realm includes the [other] ten dharma realms, so there are one hundred dharma realms. One realm includes thirty types of worlds [that is, each of the ten dharma realms are included in each of the three types of worlds: the world of sentient beings, the world of the five skandhas, and various lands], multiplied by one hundred dharma realms. This results in the inclusion of three thousand types of worlds. These three thousand [worlds] exist in a single momentary thought.

If there is no thought, that is the end of the matter. If there is even an ephemeral thought, this includes three thousand [realms]. But we cannot say that the single thought has prior existence, and that all phenomena *(sarva-dharma)* exist later, nor can we say that all phenomena have prior existence, and that the single thought exists later. For example, it is like a thing that changes through eight aspects [of arising, abiding, changing, and perish-

A single thought 一心: lit., "one mind," but I have chosen to translate this compound as a "single thought" to avoid the implication of a reified "mind" as separate from mental functioning and "objects" that are experienced. Chih-i also uses the phrase "one thought-moment" 一念, sometimes interchangeably with "one mind." In any case, it refers to the almost instantaneous occurrence of a single mental function.

A single momentary thought 一念心: as Chih-i has explained earlier in the *Mo-ho chih-kuan*, a "single momentary (thought)" refers to an extremely short amount of time. For example, "A sūtra says that a single thought-moment has six hundred arisings and perishings. *Satyasiddhi* masters say that there are sixty moments in a single thought-moment" (see notes at *Mo-ho chih-kuan* 27c23–24); and "even an ephemeral thought 介爾 surely arises through the senses, and there is not one dharma that does not arise through conditions. To arise through conditions means that each and every phenomenon is transient. It is said that one thought lasts for sixty moments *(kṣaṇa)*, and others say for three hundred trillion moments. A *kṣaṇa* does not abide, and thoughts do not remain from one to the other" (see the *Mo-ho chih-kuan*, 32b2–7).

Eight aspects 八相: the "original" and "following" aspects of arising, abiding,

ing]; it is not that things exist prior to these aspects and are caused to change through them, nor do the aspects exist prior to things and are caused to change through them [but things and their passing through arising, abiding, and so forth occur together]. There can be no priority nor posteriority [since it occurs simultaneously]. It is just that things are said to change by passing through these aspects, and these aspects are said to occur to things.

Thoughts are also like this. If all phenomena arise from a single thought, this is a horizontal [relationship]; if a thought in one moment encompasses all phenomena, this is a vertical [relationship]. But these are neither [merely] vertical nor [merely] horizontal. It is just that thought is all phenomena, and all phenomena is thought. Therefore [the relationship of thought and phenomena, the mind and objects] is neither [merely] vertical nor horizontal; they are neither the same nor different. This is mysterious and sublime, profound in the extreme, cannot be grasped conceptually, and cannot be verbalized. This is what is called [contemplating] "objects as inconceivable." This is the meaning here [in terms of conventionality].

changing, and perishing, giving eight aspects. See Paramārtha's translation of the *Abhidharmakośa*, T 29.185c11–13.

This is the meaning here [in terms of conventionality] 意在於此: many commentators have identified "the three thousand realms in a single thought" as the ultimate expression of Chih-i's thought and the content of contemplating objects as "inconceivable." However, in this section (54a5 [or earlier?]–54a19) Chih-i is speaking in terms of "contemplating conventionality," one of the three types of threefold contemplation. If so, then understanding the "three thousand realms in a single thought" is not the fullest or final expression of objects as inconceivable. In the next section (54a19–55a15), Chih-i discusses the inconceivable in terms of contemplating emptiness, and finally (55a15–b10) in terms of contemplating the Middle. Thus the ultimate expression of objects as inconceivable is this last passage, which speaks not only about the inclusion (and exclusion) of all thoughts in one thought, but also the inclusion (and exclusion) of all senses in one sense experience, all sentient beings in one sentient being, all lands in one land, and so forth, that one is all, all is one, and things are neither "one" nor "all." It is the threefold truth, not the expression "three thousand realms in a single thought" that is the more fundamental insight. What prompted Chan-jan to identify the "three thousand realms in a single thought" as the key to Chih-i's thought, thus making this a central idea in the history of T'ien-t'ai Buddhism in China and Korea—and in Tendai and Nichiren Buddhism in Japan—is an important topic for further research.

Note also the curious order of this discussion. In almost all other cases in the *Mo-ho chih-kuan*, a subject is interpreted in the threefold pattern, first as empty, then as conventional, and finally as the Middle. Here the interpretation in terms of the conventional (as the "three thousand realms in a a single thought") comes first, followed by the empty and the Middle. One may argue that this reflects the importance of "contemplating conventionality" over the more abstract contemplation of emptiness and the Middle.

4. "Objects as inconceivable" from the perspective of emptiness and in terms of the tetralemma [54a18]

Question: The arising of thoughts is necessarily dependent on certain [objective] conditions. If so, are the three thousand dharmas included in the thoughts, included in the conditions [that is, the objects], included in both [thoughts and their objects], or included separate from [thoughts and their objects]? If they are included in the thoughts [themselves], then thoughts arise [by themselves] and do not need [objective] conditions[, which is obviously impossible]. If they are included in the [objective] conditions, then, being included in the objects themselves, there is no involvement with mental activity[, which is also impossible]. If they are included together, that means that when they are not yet together then neither side has [the three thousand dharmas], but then how can [thoughts and their objects] have [the three thousand dharmas] when they are together? If they are included separate from [thoughts and their objects,] then [the three thousand dharmas] are already separate from thoughts and their objects; but then how can they suddenly be included in thoughts [as in the teaching of the three thousand realms in a single thought]? None of the four options is obtainable. What does it mean, then, to say that the three thousand dharmas are included [in one momentary thought]?

Answer: Scholars of the *Treatise on the Ten Stages (Ti-lun)* say that all understanding and ignorance, truth and delusion are dependent on the support of the nature of dharmas *(dharmatā)*. The nature of dharmas sup-

[Objective] conditions 緣: generally this term refers to "indirect causes" in contrast to "direct causes" 因, but here it refers specifically to "conditions" in the sense of the objects of our thoughts. Earlier in the *Mo-ho chih-kuan* (8a14–15) Chih-i says, "Mental activity does not arise by itself, but necessarily depends on conditioned arising 緣起. The mental sense organ is the cause [of thoughts], the multifarious objects [of mental activity] are the conditions, and the mental thoughts which thus arise are the dharmas that are thus produced."

Are the three thousand dharmas included in the thoughts, included in the conditions, both, or separate 爲心具三千法爲縁具爲共具爲離具: thus the relation of thoughts and their objects are considered with the four options of the tetralemma: a, b, both, or neither. To put it another way, do thoughts arise from themselves, from responding to or with objective conditions, both, or neither? Earlier in the *Mo-ho chih-kuan* (8a29–c1) Chih-i says, "Though we say in a deluded [provisional] way that thoughts 'arise', in this arising there is actually no own-being, nor other-being, nor both together, nor an absence of causes."

Note that in the T'ien-t'ai system the use of the tetralemma represents the level of the Distinct Teachings, which emphasizes the perspective of emptiness.

All understanding and ignorance, truth and delusion are dependent on the support of the nature of dharmas. The nature of dharmas supports truth and

ports truth and delusion, and truth and delusion depend on the nature of dharmas. The *Summary of the Great Vehicle (She-lun)* says that the nature of dharmas is not defiled by delusion, nor purified by truth. Therefore the nature of dharmas neither supports [delusion] nor is dependent [on the truth]. The *ālaya*-consciousness is that which supports and that on which things are dependent, and which gathers and supports all the seeds of undying ignorance. If we follow the scholars of the *Ti-lun*, we would say that all dharmas are included in the mind; if we follow the scholars of the *She-lun*, we would say that all dharmas are included in [objective] conditions.

These two kinds of scholars each represent one extreme. If [following the Ti-lun scholars] we say that the nature of dharmas gives birth to all dharmas, then this "nature of dharmas" [is something that] is neither mind nor [objective] conditions[, but this is impossible because there is nothing outside of thoughts and their objects]. **[54b]** If we say that all dharmas arise from the mind because [the nature of dharmas] is not thoughts, then it follows also that all dharmas arise from [objective] conditions because [the nature of dharmas] is not [objective] conditions[, but this does not make any sense]. How, then, can you arbitrarily say that the nature of dharmas is the support of truth and delusion? If [following the She-lun scholars] we say that the nature of dharmas is not the support [of thoughts and their objects], but that the *ālaya*-consciousness is, then this implies that there is an *ālaya*-consciousness that supports [thoughts and their objects] but is outside of and separate from the nature of dharmas, that is, has no relation with the nature of dharmas. [But this is impossible.] If it is said that the nature of dharmas is not separate from the *ālaya*-consciousness, then what is supported by the *ālaya*-consciousness is also supported by the nature of

delusion, and truth and delusion depend on the nature of dharmas 一切解惑眞妄依持法性。法性持眞妄眞妄依法性也: the *Kōgi* (BT–III, 295) says that this is from "section 10/2" of the *Treatise on the Ten Stages*, but I could not locate a corresponding passage (see T 26.179–180?). It is not clear if Chih-i is actually quoting the *Treatise on the Ten Stages*, or is only summarizing a teaching of the Ti-lun scholars.

The nature of dharmas is not defiled by delusion, nor purified by truth. Therefore the nature of dharmas neither support nor is dependent 法性不為惑所染不為真所淨故法性非依持: once again, it seems that Chih-i is summarizing a teaching of the *Summary of the Great Vehicle*, or a teaching of the She-lun scholars, rather than quoting a specific passage of the treatise itself.

***Ālaya*-consciousness** 阿黎耶: the *ālaya-vijñāna,* the "store consciousness." A concept of the Yogācāra school, which taught the existence of an underlying consciousness, a "pre-consciousness," that unifies into one experiential whole all the diverse operations of conscious activity.

Undying ignorance 無沒無明: lit., "ignorance that does not sink (become extinct)." A Chinese translation of *ālaya* which interprets the term as *a-laya.*

dharmas. How, then, can you arbitrarily say that the *ālaya*-consciousness is the support [of mind and its objects]? This is contrary to what is in the sūtras. A sūtra says, "Neither internal, nor external, nor somewhere in between, nor always existing on its own." It is also [different from the teaching of] Nāgārjuna. Nāgārjuna says, "Dharmas do not arise from themselves, and they do not arise from another, nor together, nor without causes."

Let us examine the issue by using an analogy. Do you have a dream because of mental functions, or have a dream by sleeping, or have a dream by the coming together of sleep and mental functions, or have a dream by being separate from mental functions and sleeping? [None of these options are acceptable.] If you say that you have a dream because of mental functions, then you could have a dream without sleeping[, but in fact you cannot]. If

Neither internal, nor external, nor somewhere in between, nor always existing on its own 非内非外亦非中間亦不常自有: a summary of a passage in the *Pañcaviṃśati Sūtra*, T 8.272a14–28:

> Śāriputra said to Subhūti: Why do you say that dharmas have nothing on which they depend?
>
> Subhūti said: The nature of form is always empty. It does not rely on something internal, nor rely on something external, nor rely on something in between these two. The nature of sensation, conception, volition, and consciousness is always empty. It does not rely on something internal, nor rely on something external, nor rely on something in between these two. The nature of seeing, hearing, smelling, tasting, touching, and thinking is always empty. It does not rely on something internal, nor rely on something external, nor rely on something in between these two. The nature of form is always empty, and the nature of dharmas is always empty. It does not rely on something internal, nor rely on something external, nor rely on something in between these two. The nature of the perfection of giving is always empty, [and so forth for the six perfections] through the nature of the perfection of wisdom is always empty. It does not rely on something internal, nor rely on something external, nor rely on something in between these two. The nature of internal emptiness is always empty, and the nature of emptiness of both existing and non-existing dharmas is alway empty. It does not rely on something internal, nor rely on something external, nor rely on something in between these two. Śāriputra, the nature of the four mindfulnesses is always empty, [and so forth] through the nature of universal wisdom is always empty. It does not rely on something internal, nor rely on something external, nor rely on something in between these two. What is the reason? Śāriputra, all dharmas are without dependence, because their nature is empty. Śāriputra, when the Bodhisattva-mahāsattvas practice the six perfections they should in this way purify their form, sensations, conceptions, volitions, and consciousness, and purify their universal wisdom.

Dharmas do not arise from themselves, and they do not arise from another, nor together, nor without causes 諸法不自生亦不從他生不共不無因: a famous verse from the opening of the *Middle Treatise* (T 30.2b6–7) which concludes with the phrase "therefore know that there is no [substantial] arising." This verse has been quoted previously in the *Mo-ho chih-kuan*; see at 22a1–2 and 29a27–29.

you say that you have a dream by sleeping, then a dead person is "sleeping" and should have a dream[, but this is not the case]. If you say that you have a dream by the coming together of sleep and mental functions, then why is it that some people do not dream even when they are sleeping? Also, if having a dream is part of both sleep and mental functions, and you have a dream when the two factors come together, then in fact each factor does not include dreaming, and you cannot [dream] when they come together. If you say that you have a dream separate from mental functions and separate from sleep, then since empty space is separate from these two factors [of mental functions and sleep], it should always involve dreaming.

By examining dreams with the tetralemma we see that none [of the options] are obtainable. How, then, do we see all sorts of things in a dream when we sleep? Here "mental functions" are analogous to the nature of dharmas and "sleep" is analogous to the *ālaya*-consciousness. How can you lean to one side and say that either "the nature of dharmas" or "the *ālaya*-consciousness" gives rise to all dharmas? You should know that the mental functions are unobtainable through the four options [of the tetralemma]; by examining the three thousand dharmas [with the tetralemma we see that they] also are unobtainable. We thus see that horizontally, through the tetralemma, the arising of the three thousand dharmas is unobtainable.

Then [to examine the matter in a vertical fashion], do the three thousand dharmas arise from the extinction of one momentary thought? The extinction of a thought cannot give rise to one dharma, so how can it give rise to three thousand dharmas? Do the three thousand dharmas arise from both the extinction and non-extinction of a thought? But the nature of extinction and non-extinction are different, like water and fire; the two cannot stand together. Then how can this give rise to three thousand dharmas? Do the three thousand dharmas arise from neither the extinction nor the non-extinction of a thought? But [the option of] "neither extinction nor non-extinction" does not provide the power nor the place 非能非所 [to give rise

Empty space 虚空: an example of an "unconditioned" dharma.

"Mental functions" are analogous to the nature of dharmas and "sleep" is analogous to the *ālaya*-consciousness 心喻法性夢喻黎耶: the *Mo-ho chih-kuan* text has "dreams" instead of "sleep," but the flow of the argument suggests that "sleep" is what is really meant. Chan-jan (BT–III, 298) adds: "It is likely that this is a copyist's error. In the analogy the contrast is always between sleep and mental functions, so here it should be the case that mental functions are analogous to the nature of dharmas and sleep is analogous to the *ālaya*-consciousness. The activity of dreaming would be analogous to the arising of dharmas."

to even one dharma], so how can there be the power or place to give rise to three thousand dharmas?

Thus we see that the three thousand dharmas are unobtainable if we seek them both in a horizontal and vertical fashion. The three thousand dharmas are also unobtainable if we seek them in a neither horizontal nor vertical fashion. This is beyond words; discursive thought is inadequate. Therefore they are called "inconceivable objects."

The *Mahāparinirvāṇa Sūtra* says, "the arising of arising is unexplainable; the non-arising of arising is unexplainable; the arising of non-arising is unexplainable; the non-arising of non-arising is unexplainable." **[54c]** This is the meaning [of what I am trying to say] here. You should know from the perspective of the supreme [truth], that even a single dharma cannot be obtained, how much less so three thousand dharmas. From the perspective of the mundane truth, one thought contains immeasurable dharmas, not to mention three thousand dharmas. As the Buddha said to the nun when she asked, "Is ignorance internal?" [he answered,] "No." "Is it external?" "No." "Is it both internal and external?" "No." "Is it neither internal nor external?" "No?" Then the Buddha said, "This is the way it is...." Nāgārjuna said,

This is beyond words 言語道斷; **discursive thought is inadequate** 心行處滅: lit., "the way of words and discourse is severed" *(sarva-vāda-caryā-uccheda)* and "the locus of discursive thought is annihilated *(citta-pravṛtti-sthīti-nirodha)*. These phrases have been used before by Chih-i to express that one has come to a point where one can only admit the inadequacy of verbal expression and conceptual understanding. See especially the note at *Mo-ho chih-kuan* 21b7.

Therefore they are called "inconceivable objects" 故名不可思議境: or, "this is called the inconceivable realm."

The arising of arising is unexplainable; the non-arising of arising is unexplainable; the arising of non-arising is unexplainable; the non-arising of non-arising is unexplainable 生生不可說。生不生不可說。不生生不可說。不生不生不可說: see the *Mahāparinirvāṇa Sūtra*, T 12.733c9–20. This passage also has been quoted by Chih-i previously; see the note at 3a12–14. For Chih-i, these four phrases represent the Fourfold Teachings respectively of the Tripitaka, Shared, Distinct, and Perfect. See Chart 1 in Swanson, *Foundations*, 358–59. These phrases are discussed in detail at 60a10–62a14.

As the Buddha said to the nun ... "This is the way it is" 如佛告德女。無明内有不。不也。外有不。不也。内外有不。不也。非内非外有不。不也。佛言。如是有: a summary of a story in the *Ta chih tu lun*, T 25.101c20–102a8. Lamotte (*Le Traité* 1, 361–62) has:

> Ainsi, dans le *Therīsūtra*, la Terī demande au Buddha, "Bhagavat! L'ignorance *(avidyā)* est-elle interne *(ādhyātmika)*?
> —Non.
> —Est-elle externe *(bahīrdhā)*?
> —Non.
> —Est-elle interne et externe à la fois?
> —Non.
> —-Bhagavat! Cette ignorance provient-elle de la génération précédente *(pūrvajanma)*?
> —Non.
> —Cette ignorance a-t-elle une naissance *(utpāda)* et une destruction *(nirodha)*?
> —Non.

"[dharmas] arise not from themselves, nor from others, nor together, nor without cause." The *Mahāparinirvāṇa Sūtra* says, "The arising of arising is unexplainable, and so forth, to the non-arising of non-arising is unexplainable. [Arising] due to causes and conditions is also unexplainable—this

—Y a-t-il un Dharma existant vraiment qui soit nommé ignorance?

—Non.

Alors la Therī dit au Buddha:

—Si l'ignorance n'est ni interne, ni externe, ni interne et externe à la fois, si elle ne passe pas de la génératon précédente à la génération actuelle et de la génération actuelle à la génération suivante, si elle ne possède pas une vraie nature, comment l'ignorance *(avidyā)* est-elle la condition *(pratyaya)* des formations *(saṃskāra)* et ainsi de suite [pour les douze membres du *pratītyasamutpāda*] jusqu'à cette accumulation de la masse des douleurs *(duḥkhaskandhasyotpādaḥ)*? Bhagavat, c'est comme si un arbre *(vṛkṣa)* n'avait pas de racine *(mūla)*: comment pourrait-il produire un tronc *(skandha)*, de noeuds *(granthi)*, des branches *(śākhā)*, des feuilles *(dala)*, des fleurs *(puṣpa)* et des fruits *(phala)*?

Le Buddha répondit:

—Le caractère des Dharma, c'est le vide *(śūnya)*. Néanmoins, le profane *(pṛthagjana)*, ignorant *(aśrutavat)* et sans savoir *(ajñānavat)*, produit à leur endroit toutes espèces de passions *(kleśa)*, [dont la principale est l'ignorance]. Cette passion est la cause et condition *(hetupratyaya)* d'actes corporels, vocaux et mentaux *(kāyavāgmanaskarman)*, lesquels sont la cause d'une nouvelle existence *(punarjanma)*. En raison de cette existence, on éprouve de la douleur *(duḥkha)* ou du plaisir *(sukha)*.

Chodron (1, 296) translates;

Thus, in the *Therīsūtra* the therī asks the Buddha: "O Bhagavat, is ignorance internal?"

"No."

"Is it external?"

"No."

"Is it both internal and external?"

"No."

"O Bhagavat, does this ignorance come from the previous lifetime?"

"No."

"Does it come from the present lifetime and does it pass to the next one?"

"No."

"Does this ignorance have an arising and a cessation?"

"No."

"Is there a truly existent dharma that could be called ignorance?"

"No."

Then the therī said to the Buddha: "If ignorance is not internal, not external, neither internal nor external, if it does not pass from the previous lifetime to the present lifetime and from the present lifetime to the following lifetime, if it does not have a true nature, how can ignorance be the condition for the formations and so on [for the twelve members of *pratītyasamutpāda*] up to this accumulation of this mass of suffering? O Bhagavat, it is as if a tree has no root: how could it produce a trunk, knots, branches, leaves, flowers and fruit?"

The Buddha replied: "The nature of dharmas is emptiness. However, worldly people, ignorant and without knowledge, produce all kinds of afflictions in regard to dharmas, [of which the main one is ignorance]. This affliction is the cause and condition for actions of body, speech and mind which are the cause of a new existence. As a result of this existence we experience suffering or pleasure.

Nāgārjuna said: see note above, where Chih-i quotes the same phrase.

The *Mahāparinirvāṇa Sūtra* says: this passage also has just been quoted above.

refers to the causes and conditions of the four *siddhānta*. Although the four options of the tetralemma are hidden [from comprehension] and quiescent, [the Buddha,] with compassion and sympathy, teaches about that which has no name or form by using conventional words and forms.

5. "Objects as inconceivable" from the perspective of emptiness and in terms of the four *siddhāntas* [54c9]

If you use the worldly [method] to teach the inclusion of all dharmas in a thought, those who hear will rejoice. For example, to say that "there are no separate dharmas in the triple world which are apart from those created by the mind" is this kind of text. Or, if you teach that all dharmas arise from [objective] conditions, those who hear will rejoice. For example, sayings such as "the five [sensual] desires lead people to fall into evil destinies" or "a

Four *siddhānta* 四悉檀: or, "the four methods of instruction" used by the Buddha to teach sentient beings: the worldly, the individual, the therapeutic, and the supreme methods. In terms of the twofold truth, the first three *siddhāntas* are variations of the mundane truth, and the fourth corresponds to the supreme or real truth *(paramārtha-satya)*; see my discussion in Swanson, *Foundations*, 23–30. The four *siddhāntas* is the theme of the following section, *Mo-ho chih-kuan* 54c9–55a15.

With compassion and sympathy, teaches about that which has no name or form by using conventional words and forms 慈悲憐愍於無名相中假名相說: Chih-i does not indicate that he intends to quote a sūtra here, but see the opening of the *Sūtra of the Buddha Treasury* 佛藏經, T 15.782c24–25: "The World Honored One teaches with names and forms that which has no name and form, and teaches with words Dharmas that are beyond words." This sūtra was quoted by Chih-i at 49a20.

The worldly [method] 世界說: the first of the four *siddhāntas*; to explain the Dharma in conventional terms so that worldly people will understand; presumably, this is why these sayings make those who hear rejoice.

There are no separate dharmas in the triple world which are apart from those created by the mind 三界無別法唯是一心造: see, for example, the *Avataṃsaka Sūtra*, T 9.558c10: "The triple world is an empty delusion; it is only made by the mind." See also the *Ta chih tu lun*, T 25.276b10: "The existences of the triple world are all creations of the mind."

The five desires lead people to fall into evil destinies 五欲令人墮惡道: it is not clear whether this is intended to refer to a specific sūtra passage. The *Kōgi* (BT–III, 306) identifies it as from the *I chiao ching*, but there is no exactly corresponding passage; the closest is on T 12.1111a12:

> If you allow *the five senses to run free*, then not only will the five sensual desires become boundless and out of control, but this [situation] will be like a bad horse that is not reined in, causing the rider to fall into the gutter.

Ikeda (*Kenkyūchūshaku*, 354) points to a latter passage at 1111c5–10:

> You bhikṣus, if you wish to be free from all suffering, should contemplate knowing sufficiency 知足. The dharma of knowing sufficiency is the place of abundant bliss and peaceful calm. People who know sufficiency experience peaceful bliss even though they sleep on the

good friend is a great cause and condition; that is, such a person can transform and guide you to attain the insight of a Buddha" are this kind of text. Or, if you say that all dharmas arise together along with their causes [that is, thoughts] and [objective] conditions, those who hear will rejoice. For example, to say "If mercury is blended with true gold, you are able to mold images of various forms" is such a text. Or, if you say that all dharmas arise separate from [objective] conditions, those who hear will rejoice. For example, to say that "the arising of twelvefold causes and conditions is not created by the Buddha, nor created by gods, people, or asura, but through its own nature" is such a text. Such are the four options of the tetralemma for the "worldly *siddhānta*" in teaching that the three thousand dharmas arise in the mind.

What about the "individual method"? Sayings [on the role of the mind] such as "The Buddha Dharma is like the sea; only those who have faith are

ground; those who do not know sufficiency are not satisfied even though they live in a heavenly mansion. Those who do not know sufficiency are poor even if they are rich; people who know sufficiency are rich even if they are poor. *Those who do not know sufficiency are constantly bound by the five [sensual] passions*, and are to be pitied by those who know sufficiency. This is what is called "knowing sufficiency."

A good friend is a great cause and condition; that is, such a person can transform and guide you to attain the insight of a Buddha 善知識者是大因緣所謂化導令得見佛: a direct quote from the *Lotus Sūtra*, T 9.60c9–10, quoted previously by Chih-i. See notes at 3a28–b1 and 43a18–19. Hurvitz (329–30 [303]) has: "Let it be known that a good friend is a great cause and condition. This means that he converts and guides, making possible the vision of a Buddha and the opening up of the thought to anuttarasaṃyaksaṃbodhi."

If mercury is blended with true gold, you are able to mold images of various forms 水銀和眞金能塗諸色像: the *Kōgi* (BT–III, 306) identifies this quote as from a "Treatise on the Nature of the Dharma Realm" 法界性論, but this is not extant in the current Chinese Buddhist canon.

The arising of twelvefold causes and conditions is not created by the Buddha, nor created by gods, people, or asura, but through its own nature 十二因縁非佛作。非天人修羅作其性自爾: see the *Miscellaneous Āgama*, T 2.85b23–25. This passage has been quoted by Chih-i previously in the *Mo-ho chih-kuan* at 7a17.

The "individual method" 爲人悉檀: the second of the four *siddhānta*s; to explain the Dharma in accordance with the mental or spiritual capacity of the individual, which presumably is why it gives rise to faith.

The Buddha Dharma is like the sea; only those who have faith are able to enter 佛法如海唯信能入: see the first section of the *Ta chih tu lun*, T 25.63a14–15, which discusses the opening phrase *evaṃ mayā śrutam ekasmin samaye*: "*The person who does not have faith is not able to enter into the sea of my Dharma*; as a parched tree cannot give forth flowers, such people cannot attain the fruits of the monk. Even though such persons shave their head, wear the dyed robe [of a monk], and read various sūtras and śāstras, it will be difficult for them to find answers." Lamotte (*Le Traité* 1, 57) translates:

S'il n'a pas la foi, il ne peut pas entrer dans

able to enter," "faith is the source of the way and the mother of virtue; all good dharmas arise from it," and "you should arouse only the thoughts of *(anuttarasamyak) saṃbodhi*, and then you will be endowed with [the upholding of] all the precepts of prohibition of the home-departed-one," are texts that arouse faith in those [individuals] who hear them. Or, there is the teaching that all dharmas arise through conditional objects. The saying that "if you do not meet a Buddha, then you will fall into a hell of suffering

la mer de ma loi. Comme un arbre pourri qui ne produit ni fleurs ni fruits, il ne gagne pas le fruit de la vie religieuse, Il peut se raser la tête, teindres ses vêtements, étudier toutes espèces de sūtra et de śāstra, il ne tire aucun profit de la loi bouddhique.

Faith is the source of the way and the mother of virtue; all good dharmas arise from it 信則道源功德母一切善法由之生: a phrase from a section in the *Avataṃsaka Sūtra* (T 9.433a26) on faith. The context [433a22–28] reads:

> A profound mind and pure faith are indestructible.
> Respect and pay homage to all Buddhas,
> Honor the true Dharma and the noble monks,
> Have faith in the three treasures, and as a result you will arouse *bodhicitta*.
> Deeply believe in the Buddhas and the true Dharma,
> And also believe in the path followed by bodhisattvas.
> A true mind trusts in the Buddhas and his *bodhi*-wisdom;
> Due to this the bodhisattvas arouse their first aspiration for enlightenment.
> *Faith is the basis of the way* 道元 *and the mother of virtue;*
> *It increases all good dharmas.*
> Remove and extinguish all doubt and delusion,
> And manifest and arouse the supreme Way.

You should arouse only the thoughts of *saṃbodhi*, and then you will be endowed with all the precepts of prohibition of the home-departed-one 汝但發三菩提心是則出家禁戒具足: the *Kōgi* (BT–III, 307) identifies this quote as coming from the *Śrīmālādevī Sūtra*, section 9, and Ikeda (*Kenkyūchūshaku*, 355) points to a section at T 12.219b, but such a phrase does not appear in the Taishō edition of the *Śrīmālādevī Sūtra* (T no. 353). It is not clear which, if any, text Chih-i was citing here.

If you do not meet a Buddha, then you will fall into a hell of suffering for immeasurable eons; by seeing a Buddha you can attain a rootless faith, like an *eraṇḍa* plant giving rise to sandalwood 若不值佛當於無量劫墮地獄苦。以見佛故得無根信如從伊蘭出生栴檀: see the *Mahāparinirvāṇa Sūtra*, T 12.727c28–728a7, where King Ajātaśatru responds to the teachings of the Buddha:

> World Honored One. I look at the world and see that an *eraṇḍa* seed gives birth to an *eraṇḍa* tree. I have not seen an *eraṇḍa* [seed] giving birth to a sandalwood tree. I now see for the first time an *eraṇḍa* seed giving birth to a sandalwood tree. [That is to say,] my body is the "*eraṇḍa* seed," and my mind, with no roots of faith, is the "sandalwood tree." To say "no roots" [of faith] means that at first I did not know or respect the Tathāgata, and did not have faith in the Dharma and Sangha. This is the meaning of "no roots." World Honored One. If I did not meet the Tathāgata, the World Honored One, then I would have to dwell in a great hell for immeasurable, incalculable eons, and experience immeasurable suffering. But now I have seen the Buddha, and by seeing the Buddha

for immeasurable eons; by seeing a Buddha you can attain a rootless faith, like an *eraṇḍa* plant giving rise to sandalwood," this gives birth to faith for those [individuals] who hear it. Or, there is the teaching that all dharmas arise through the merging [of thoughts and their conditions]. The sayings that "when the waters of the mind are clear and pure, the form of the jewel manifests itself" and "with the fundamental power of compassionate goodness, you can see things as they are," are texts that arouse faith in those who hear them. Or, there is the teaching that all dharmas arise separate from [thoughts and their conditional objects]. The saying that "it is not through internal contemplation that you attain this wisdom, and so forth through [the idea that] it is not through either internal or external contemplation that you attain this wisdom; if you have any attachments, then you cannot attain even the small faith of Śrenika, much less abandon mistaken [views] and realize the right," is a text that arouses faith in those who hear it. Such are the four options of the tetralemma for the "individual *siddhānta*" in teaching that the three thousand dharmas arise in the mind.

I have attained virtuous qualities, and have destroyed entirely the evil mind of passionate afflictions that belongs to sentient beings.

A rootless faith 無根信: lit., a faith "without roots." This does not imply "invalid" or "baseless," but refers to receiving faith from or through the power or grace of the Buddha, and not based on one's own deeds or power. It refers to one "without roots" in one's own deeds or attitudes—such as taking refuge in and honoring the three treasures—but nevertheless gives rise to faith in the Buddha.

***Eraṇḍa* plant** 伊蘭: a type of plant whose seeds are toxic and is famous (in contrast to sandalwood) for its foul smell; used to make castor oil.

When the waters of the mind are clear and pure, the form of the jewel manifests itself 心水澄清珠相自現: see the story of the people on a boat who drop a jewel in the pond and cannot find it until the water settles and becomes pure, in the *Mahāparinirvāṇa Sūtra*, T 12.617c3–10. Chih-i has referred to this parable numerous times already; see the detailed note at *Mo-ho chih-kuan* 43a3.

With the fundamental power of compassionate goodness, you can see things as they are 慈善根力見如此事: perhaps this refers to the same passage of the *Mahāparinirvāṇa Sūtra* (see previous note), in which a wise person uses "skillful means" to see and recover the jewel.

...then you cannot attain even the small faith of Śrenika, much less abandon mistaken [views] and realize the right 若有住著先尼梵志小信尚不可得況捨邪入正: see the story of Śrenika and his attainment of universal wisdom through faith, in the *Pañcaviṃśati Sūtra*, T 8.236a11ff., especially lines 17–19. Śrenika is given as an example of one who attains wisdom by means of the perfection of faith, and that this attainment is "not through internal contemplation, nor through external contemplation, nor both internal and external contemplation, nor by no contemplation." It concludes, "Śrenika attained universal wisdom through having faith in his mind. Therefore Śrenika had faith in the true aspects of all dharmas" (236a25–27). See also the note at *Mo-ho chih-kuan* 48c18.

[55a] What about the "therapeutic method"? [First, there is] the teaching that all evil is healed by the mind. The saying that "the attainment of single-mindedness extinguishes a myriad of mistaken [views]" is such a text. Or, there is the teaching that all evil is healed by objective conditions. The saying "By hearing of the great, supreme light of wisdom, the mind becomes concentrated and is immobile like the earth," is such a text. Or, there is the teaching that all evil is healed by a combination of causes [thoughts] and [objective] conditions. The saying "part arises from your own conceptual thinking, and part comes from your teacher" is such a text. Or, there is the teaching that all evil is healed separate from [thoughts and their objects]. [The saying] "I did not [actually] attain all dharmas when I sat on the seat of enlightenment, but I lured and saved all [as if] deceiving a small child with an empty fist" is such a text. Such are [the four options of the tetralemma

The "therapeutic method" 對治悉檀: the third of the four *siddhānta*; the teaching as a remedy for the maladies that afflict sentient beings, which presumably is why it heals or destroys evil.

The attainment of single-mindedness extinguishes a myriad of mistaken [views] 得一心者萬邪滅: verbatim from the *Sūtra on the Auspicious Appearances and Origins of the Prince Siddhārtha*, T 3.475a25. The phrase is followed by the explanation that "'The way of single-mindedness' refers to the arhat. The arhat is a true person. He is not corrupted by [the sensual desires] of sound or sight."

By hearing of the great, supreme light of wisdom, the mind becomes concentrated and is immobile like the earth 聞無上大慧明。心定如地不可動: the *Kōgi* (BT–III, 307) admits that the source of this phrase is unknown.

Part arises from your own conceptual thinking, and part comes from your teacher 一分從思生一分從師得: the *Kōgi* (BT–III, 307) admits that the source of this phrase is unknown.

I did not attain all dharmas when I sat on the seat of enlightenment, but I lured and saved all [as if] deceiving a small child with an empty fist 我坐道場時不得一切法。空拳誑小兒誘度於一切: that is, the Buddha taught as if he had "attained" all dharmas under the Bodhi tree (when there are no substantial dharmas to attain), as if fooling a child by making it think he had something in his fist when he did not? This phrase as given in the *Mo-ho chih-kuan* is confusing and unclear. Its source in the *Ta chih tu lun*, T 25.211a4–5, is much clearer. The context consists of verses that illustrate the teaching that "since all dharmas arise through the merging of causes and conditions, therefore there is no self-sufficiency *(svabhāva)*." Lamotte (*Le Traité* 3, 1262–63) translates:

> Enfin les dharma étant issus du complexe des causes et des conditions *(hetupratyayasāmagrī)*, n'ont pas de nature propre *(niḥsvabhāva)*. Leur nature propre n'existant pas, ils sont éternellement vides *(śūnya)* et, dans cet éternellement vide, l'être n'existe pas *(sattvo nopalabhyate)*. C'est ainsi que le Buddha a dit:
>
> Lorsque j'étais assis sur l'aire de l'illumination,
> *Ma sagesse était inexistante.*
> *Comme le poing vide trompant les petits enfants,*
> *J'ai sauvé tout le monde.*
> Vrai caractère *(bhūtalakṣaṇa)* des choses,

for] the "therapeutic *siddhānta*" for the teaching that all evil is destroyed by the mind.

What about the "supreme method"? [First, the teaching that] you attain insight into the principle [of the truth] with the mind is like the saying that "When the mind is opened and you understand, then you attain the way immediately." Or, the teaching that you attain insight into the truth through conditional objects is like the saying "Anyone who hears this will attain ultimate and perfect wisdom." Or, the teaching that you attain the path by a merging of causes [thoughts] and [objective] conditionals is like [the analogy of] the nimble horse that advances on the right road just by catching a glimpse of the whip. Or, the teaching that you are able to attain insight into the truth separate from [thoughts and their objects] is like the saying "Not attaining is attaining, and having attained is not attaining." Such are the four

> C'est la marque des êtres *(sattvanimitta)*.
> Mais saisir la marque des êtres,
> C'est s'écarter loin du vrai Chemin.

Chodron (3, 1036) translates;

> Finally, dharmas, coming from causes and conditions, have no intrinsic nature. Since their intrinsic nature does not exist, they are eternally empty and, in this eternal emptiness, the being does not exist. Thus the Buddha said:
> When I was seated on the sphere of enlightenment,
> My wisdom was non-existent.
> Like the empty fist that deceives little children,
> I have saved the entire world.
> The true nature of things
> Is the mark of beings.
> But to seize the mark of beings
> Is to stray far from the true Path.

The "supreme method" 第一義悉檀: the fourth of the four *siddānta*; teaching the Dharma directly, the supreme truth just as it is; presumably this is why those who hear it attain insight into the principle of the truth.

When the mind is opened and you understand, then you attain the way immediately 心開意解豁然得道: the *Kōgi* (BT–III, 308) attributes this phrase to "section 42/18" of the *Ta chih tu lun*, (T 25.369a–b), but I could not locate a corresponding passage.

Anyone who hears this will attain ultimate and perfect wisdom 須臾聞之即得究竟三菩提: from the tenth chapter of the *Lotus Sūtra*, T 9.31a10–11. Hurvitz (*Lotus Sūtra*, 176 [161]) translates:

> When this man preaches Dharma with joy, *anyone who hears it for a moment shall straightway achieve ultimate anuttarasaṃyaksaṃbodhi.*

The nimble horse that advances on the right road just by catching a glimpse of the whip 快馬見鞭影即得正路: see the analogy of the four types of good horses in the *Miscellaneous Āgama*, T 2.234a16–b20. Chih-i has referred to this analogy many times before; see note at 19a23. See also the appearance of this analogy in the *Ta chih tu lun*, T 25.62a7–8.

Not attaining is attaining, and having attained is not attaining 無所得即是得。已是得無所得: the *Kōgi* (BT–III, p. 308) attributes this phrase to "section 1-13" of the *Viśeṣacintibrahma-paripṛcchā*; the phrase is close to the teachings of this sūtra, but I could not locate a corresponding passage in this section of the text (T 15.36–37).

options of the "supreme *(siddhānta)*" for insight into truth [as emptiness]. How much more so for [the idea of] three thousand dharmas that arise in a [single] thought?

6. "Objects as inconceivable" from the perspective of contemplating the Middle: Beyond all dualities (including "non-duality") [55a15]

The gist of the Buddha's [teaching] is to exhaust and purify, and does not involve [merely the four options of] cause [thought], conditional objects, both, or neither; the worldly truth is [taught on the basis of] the supreme truth.

Again, any and all of the four options can [and should] be taught [in terms of the mundane truth]: you could assert cause [thought], conditional objects, both, or neither. If you attempt to explain [the whiteness of] milk to a blind person, saying it is like [the whiteness of] a shell, or like rice powder, or like snow, or like a [white] crane, the blind person will hear this explanation and reach [a certain] understanding of milk. [This illustrates that] the worldly truth is indivisible from the supreme truth [and vice versa].

How much more so for three thousand dharmas that arise in a thought 何況心生三千法耶: or, to translate more plainly: "What need is there to speak of three thousand dharmas that arise in a [single] thought? [Answer: none.]" Here Chih-i shifts to the perspective of the Middle. That is, from the perspective of the Middle, even the conventional spelling out of the idea of three thousand realms in a single thought is superfluous, or "unobtainable." Ikeda's interpretation (*Gendai-goyaku*, 287) goes so far as to translate this phrase: "Here we do not need the idea of the three thousand [dharmas] arising in a thought" [or, "in the mind"]. Kanno (*Ichinen sanzen*, 185), however, follows the opposite interpretation, opting for the importance of the idea of "three thousand in a single thought." He translates: "It goes without saying that three thousand dharmas arise in a thought" [or, "in the mind"], reiterating the importance of the "three thousand dharmas." The phrase is open to either interpretation, depending on one's perspective; the tradition that emphasizes the centrality of the idea of the "three thousand realms in a single thought" 一念三千 would naturally opt for the second interpretation. I prefer the former interpretation, that at the level of the Middle, even the idea of the "three thousand realms in a single thought" is "unobtainable," perhaps even an "extreme view."

The worldly truth is [taught on the basis of] the supreme truth 即世諦是第一義也: or simply, "the worldly truth is the supreme truth [and the supreme truth is the mundane truth]." This is the "positionless position," the "inexpressible expression," the "non-dualistic dualism," the positive expression of ultimate negation, of the Middle. For similar expressions see *Mahāparinirvāṇa Sūtra*, T 12.684c10–18.

Explain milk to a blind person 盲人說乳 ...: see the parable of the blind man in the *Mahāparinirvāṇa Sūtra*, T 12.688c, which has been quoted frequently by Chih-i already. Note that, contrary to the interpretation given by Chih-i, the sūtra says that no matter how many examples are given (a shell, rice powder, snow, and a white crane), a blind person cannot know the true meaning of "white."

Thus it should be known that "expounding throughout the day is [the same as] not expounding throughout the day, and not expounding throughout the day is [the same as] expounding throughout the day." At all times both extremes are covered, and at all times both extremes are illumined, establishing while deconstructing, and deconstructing while establishing. [The teachings of] the sūtras and treatises are all like this.

Vasubandhu and Nāgārjuna internally had insight and were enlightened, and externally each responded appropriately to the needs of their times on the basis of tentative means. However, some [Buddhist] teachers have a one-sided understanding, and some scholars are carelessly attached [to their own limited interpretation], so that they [argue and fight uselessly,] like shooting arrows at a rock. They each maintain one extreme, and thus pervert

Expounding throughout the day is not expounding the day, and not expounding throughout the day is expounding throughout the day 終日説終日不說。終日不說終日說: this is reminiscent of the teachings of Chuang-tzu; see the twenty-seventh chapter of the *Chuang-tzu* on "Imputed Words." Burton Watson (*The Complete Works of Chuang-tzu*, 304–305) translates the context:

> With these goblet words that come forth day after day, I harmonize all things in the Heavenly Equality, leave them to their endless changes, and so live out my years. As long as I do not say anything about them, they are a unity. But the unity and what I say about it have ceased to be a unity; what I say and the unity have ceased to be a unity. Therefore I say, we must have no-words! *With words that are no-words, you may speak all your life long and you will never have said anything. Or you may go through your whole life without speaking them, in which case you will never have stopped speaking.*

At all times both extremes are covered, and at all times both extremes are illumined 終日雙遮終日雙照: the first phrase indicating the denial of the four options of the tetralemma and the possibility of explaining anything in words or with concepts, and the second phrase indicating the affirmation of the four options of the tetralemma and the possibility of explaining things in words and with concepts.

Vasubandhu and Nāgārjuna internally had insight and were enlightened 天親龍樹内鑒冷然: lit., "internally [they reflected truth] like a mirror and had pure and spontaneous [enlightenment]." The first compound 内鑒 implies an internal insight that reflects reality clearly like a mirror. The second compound 冷然 is a variant of 泠然: 冷 means "cool" and 泠 means "pure and enlightened"; as a compound it implies pure, clear enlightenment. The compound was used to modify the pure sound of flowing water. Kanno (*Ichinen sanzen*, 195) points out that in the classical *Issaikyō ongi* 一切經音義 (T 54.73a), this compound is defined as meaning "awakened understanding" 解悟.

Each responded appropriately to the needs of their times on the basis of tentative means 外適時宜各權所據: I have translated rather freely here. Literally the text reads "externally, as appropriate to the demands of the times, each depended on tentative means."

Like shooting arrows at a rock 矢石: my translation is rather free, but follows the interpretation given by Chan-jan (BT-III, 310): "'Arrow-rock' refers to shooting an arrow at a rock. The meaning does not penetrate, because each [of those who

the noble path. If you obtain this meaning, then you comprehend both the impossibility of verbal expression and the necessity of verbal expression.

If you were to respond appropriately [in accordance with tentative expressions], you should say that when ignorance shapes the dharmas according to Dharma-nature *(dharmatā)*, then all dharmas arise as all things that happen in a dream are a result of the mind in a state of sleep. The merging of the mind with external conditions results in the three types of worlds [of the five skandhas, sentient beings, and various lands], and thus the three thousand [internal and external] features [of the three thousand realms] arise from the mind. A single internal feature is small or few, but it is not nothing; ignorance is multitudinous, but has no [substantial] Being. Why? If we focus on one thing as [an example of] many, the many are not many; if we focus on many as one, this one is not a few. Therefore these thoughts are called inconceivable objects.

[The gist of the Middle:] If **[55b]** it is understood that one thought is all thoughts, all thoughts are one thought, and these are neither one nor all, one skandha is all skandhas, all skandhas are one skandha, and these are neither one nor all; one sense entrance *(āyatana)* is all sense entrances, all sense entrances are one sense entrance, and these are neither one nor all; one sense realm (*dhātu*) is all sense realms, all sense realms is one sense realm, and these are neither one nor all; one sentient being is all sentient beings, all

argue their own limited understanding] rely on their own speculation, and does not realize the principle of the perfect [truth]. Thus this is like [shooting] arrows at a rock." Kanno (*Ichinen sanzen*, 196) points out a different interpretation. He argues that arrows and stones are representative weapons and the compound merely indicates that the scholars argue and fight with each other. My translation incorporates both possibilities.

A single internal feature is small or few, but it is not nothing 一性雖少而不無: or, the compound "one nature" 一性 could be interpreted as "the one [dharma-] nature" 一[法]性. Chan-jan [BT-III, 312] says "'one-nature/feature, though small, is not nothing' is because all dharmas arise through conditions 緣成法生." The *Kōgi* more clearly interprets this phrase in terms of the Dharma-nature 法性. However, I take this 性 to refer back to the same character in the previous phrase, the "three thousand [internal and external] features [of the three thousand realms]" 三千相性.

One thought is all thoughts, all thoughts are one thought, and these are neither one nor all 一心一切心。一切心一心。非一非一切: "one is all" is the perspective of conventionality, "all are one" is the perspective of emptiness, and "neither one nor all"—that is, neither a simple unity nor a diversity—is the perspective of the Middle.

One skandha is all skandhas ... neither one nor all 一陰一切陰。一切陰一陰。非一非一切 ...: note that this section is on "contemplation of the objects of the skandhas and sense fields *(skandha-āyatana-dhāta)*."

sentient beings are one sentient being, and these are neither one nor all; one land is all lands, all lands are one land, and these are neither one nor all; one mark is all marks, all marks are one mark, and these are neither one nor all; [and so forth for the other categories of the ten suchlike characteristics] up to and including one ultimate is all ultimates, all ultimates are one ultimate, and these are neither one nor all. Everything and anything that we experience; all are inconceivable objects. [This is the perspective of the Middle.]

7. Recapitulation in terms of the two truths, threefold truth, threefold contemplation, and threefold wisdom [55b9]

If we say that the merging of ignorance and the Dharma-nature results in all phenomena, the skandhas and sense fields, and so forth, this is [to speak in terms of] the mundane truth [of conventionality]. If we say that all sense fields are one dharma realm, this is [to speak in terms of] the real truth [of emptiness]. [To say that] these are neither one nor all is [to speak in terms of] the supreme truth of the Middle Way. In this way, in everything and anything that we experience, there is nothing that does not involve the inconceivable threefold truth.

To say that one dharma is all dharmas is [an expression of the phrase from the *Middle Treatise*, verse 24:18, that] "things arise through causes and conditions" 因緣所生法. This refers to conventional designation 假名 and the contemplation of conventionality 假觀. To say that all dharmas are one dharma is [an expression of the phrase] "this I explain as emptiness" 我說即是空, which is the contemplation of emptiness 空觀. To say "neither one nor all" is the contemplation of the Middle Way 中道觀.

The emptiness of one [thing] is the emptiness of all; just because there are the meanings of conventional existence and the Middle does not mean that they are not empty. This is the general contemplation of emptiness. The conventionality of one [thing] is the conventionality of all; just because there are the meanings of emptiness and the Middle does not mean that they do not have conventionality. This is the general contemplation of conventionality. The Middle of one is the Middle of all; just because there are the meanings of emptiness and conventionality does not mean that they do not have Middleness. This is the general contemplation of the Middle. Thus, as the *Middle Treatise* explains, this is the threefold contemplation of a single thought [or, "the single-minded threefold contemplation (of objects)"] as inconceivable 不可思議一心三觀. All phenomena that we experience are also likewise.

If we say that all phenomena arise through [the interplay of] causes and conditions, this is [the perspective of] [skillful] means *(upāya)*, "in accordance with feelings" [of sentient beings] 隨情, and the tentative wisdom of the path 道種權智. If we say that all dharmas are one dharma, this is [the perspective of] "this I explain as emptiness," "in accordance with wisdom" 隨智, and [the wisdom of] omniscience 一切智. If we say "neither one nor all," again this is called the meaning of the Middle Way, that is, neither tentative nor real 非權非實, and universal wisdom 一切種智. Following this pattern, one tentative matter is all tentative matters, one real matter is all real matters, and all is neither tentative nor real; everything and anything that we experience involves the inconceivable three wisdoms.

"In accordance with feelings" is another way to say "in accordance with the thoughts of others," and "in accordance with wisdom" is another way to say "in accordance with [the Buddha's] own thoughts." To say "neither tentative nor real" is another way to say "neither [in accordance with merely] the thoughts of others or [the Buddha's] own thoughts." Thus everything and anything that we experience is not unrelated to the inconceivable teaching of [the three types of] gradual, sudden, and variable [contemplations]. If you understand the sudden [teachings and contemplation], you understand [the workings of] the mind [or thoughts]. But the mind and its thoughts are unobtainable; how can it be said that they "incline" or "do not incline"? If you understand the gradual [teachings and contemplation], you understand that all dharmas are "inclined" to [or based on] the mind. If you understand the variable [teachings and contemplation], you understand that [all dharmas] do not transcend their inclination toward [or reliance on] the mind.

[55c] All of these are different terms but their meaning is the same. As a guiding track for practitioners, these are threefold teachings. That which

The inconceivable three wisdoms 不思議三智: Chih-i has already explained the three wisdoms; see the *Mo-ho chih-kuan* at 26b–c.

In accordance with the thoughts of others 隨他意 **and "in accordance with [the Buddha's] own thoughts"** 隨自意: Chih-i has discussed these terms previously; see the glossary. For a long exposition on these terms see the *Mahāparinirvāṇa Sūtra*, T 12.820b2–821c3.

"Incline" 趣 **or "do not incline"** 非趣: that is, there is a "place" that is "the mind," or that there is no "place" for mental functions; neither option obtains. See the *Pañcaviṃśati Sūtra*, T 8.333a–c; for details, see note at *Mo-ho chih-kuan* 46c2–4. See also the note in Kanno, *Ichinen sanzen*, 197–98, which provides the Sanskrit for this passage (from P. L. Vaidya, ed., *Aṣṭasāhasrikā Prajñāpāramitā*, Buddhist Sanskrit Texts No. 4, 1960, 148): "*tat kasya hetoḥ śūnyatāgatikā he Subhūte sarvadharmāḥ / te tāṃ gatiṃ na vyativartante/*." This indicates that the Sanskrit for 趣 is *gati*, "place of refuge" or "that which is relied on."

As a guiding track for practitioners, these are threefold Dharma teachings 軌則行人呼爲三法: this could refer to the threefold pattern in Chih-i's teachings in general (the threefold truth, three wisdoms, threefold Buddha-nature, and so forth; see charts in Swanson, *Foundations*, 358–59). Or, it could refer specifically to Chih-i's categories of the "three tracks

is illuminated is the threefold truth. That which is aroused is threefold contemplation. [The content of] the perfection of contemplation are the three wisdoms. Teaching others involves threefold words. "Returning to the gist" involves three [meanings of] "inclination." With this meaning, all types of teachings can arise. There are various flavors, and you should not disdain this because of its complexity.

[The analogy of the *maṇi* jewel:] This is like the wish-fulfilling *(maṇi)* jewel, which is the most supreme and heavenly treasure. It has a [small and round] shape like a mustard seed or grain of millet, but it has great and effective powers. Pure and sublime [objects] of the five desires, and the seven jewels and other gems [which can be provided magically by the wish-fulfilling jewel] are neither contained within it, nor do they come from the outside. [They appear] without being planned before or after, without a choice of many or few, without a crude or subtle production, but [the wish-fulfilling jewel] provides bountifully and carefully as it intends. [The wish-fulfilling jewel is like] the rain that falls abundantly, without [the need for] augmentation and without being exhausted. Even such a mundane object can act in this way; how much more so is the mind mysterious and sublime. How can it not include all dharmas?

[The analogy of the three poisons:] Again, the deluded thoughts of the

[of reality]" 三軌, that is, the true nature of reality itself 眞性軌, the wisdom that illumines this true nature 觀照軌, and the practice that perfects one's inherent disposition for wisdom 資成軌; see Chart 7 in Swanson, *Foundations*, 364. Chih-i outlines these categories in the *Fa-hua hsüan-i*, T 33.741b.

Teaching others involves threefold words 教他呼爲三語: that is, words that are in accordance with the thoughts of others, words that are in accordance with the thought of the Buddha himself, and words that are neither of the above. See the use of these terms a few lines above.

"Returning to the gist" involves three [meanings of] "inclination" 歸宗呼爲三趣: that is, 1. "inclining"—admitting the conventional existence of a mind; a "place" for thoughts to function and arise; this corresponds to the mundane truth or the truth of conventionality; 2. "not inclining"—denying any substantial mind or ground for thoughts or objective reality, that the mind "cannot be obtained"; this corresponds to the truth of emptiness or the real truth; 3. "neither"—corresponding to the Middle.

This is like the wish-fulfilling jewel, which is the most supreme and heavenly treasure 如如意珠天上勝寶: see, for example, the *Pañcaviṃśati Sūtra*, T 8. 291c–292a; at 291c27–28 it says, "The *maṇi* jewel is the most supreme divine treasure, the treasure of Jambudvīpa."

It has great and effective powers 有大功能: see also the *Ta chih tu lun*, T 25.134a, where it lists the seven types of jewels and then adds (134a24):

> [the wish-fulfilling jewel is] the most supreme in the world, and even the gods cannot obtain it. Why? Because it produces great and effective merits.

three poisons [of greed, anger, and ignorance] arise in the single thought of the mind, as well as eighty-eight passions, including the sharp passions, such as [the mistaken view of a substantial] body and extreme [views], and dull passions, up to eighty-four thousand passionate afflictions. If we say that these have previous existence, then why do they wait for certain conditions [before appearing]? If we say that they are originally nothing [or non-existent], why do they become manifest in response to certain conditions? They neither exist [as substantial Being] nor not exist [as nothingness] 不有不無. If we settle on [viewing them as] "existing," this is a mistaken view. If we settle on [viewing them as] "not existing," this is a delusion. You should know that they exist [conventionally], yet do not exist [as substantial Being]; they do not exist, yet they do exist. Deluded thoughts are likewise. How much more so the inconceivable single mind [or, "a single thought as inconceivable"]?

[The analogy of a dream:] Again, even if you see hundreds of thousands of millions of things in a dream while sleeping, when you are wide awake not even one remains, not to mention the other hundreds of thousands [or so things]. When you are not quite asleep, you neither dream nor are awake, and there is neither many [events in a dream] nor one [experience of being wide awake]. You experience many things through the power of sleep; you experience a few things through the power of being awake. Chuang-tzu dreamt that he was a butterfly, flittering here and there for a hundred years, but when he awoke he knew that he was not a butterfly, and that he

Eighty-eight passions, including the sharp passions, such as [the mistaken view of a substantial] body and extreme [views], and dull passions 身邊利鈍八十八使: the "eighty-eight passions" is a general term for all the passions. There are five "sharp passions": 1. the false view that the body is substantial (身見 *satkāya-dṛṣṭi*), 2. extreme views (邊見 *antagrāha-dṛṣṭi*), 3. mistaken views (邪見 *mithyā-dṛṣṭi*), 4. attachment to false views (見取見; *dṛṣṭi-parāmarśa*), and 5. excessive attachment to the precepts (lit., "morality and vows"; 戒[禁] 取見; *śīlavrata-parāmarśa*). There are also five "dull passions": covetousness/greed, anger, stupidity/ignorance, arrogance, and doubt.

Chuang-tzu dreamt that he was a butterfly, flittering here and there for a hundred years, but when he awoke he knew that he was not a butterfly, and that he had not lived for all those years 莊周夢爲蝴蝶翾翔百年寤知非蝶亦非積歲: among other things, Chih-i here is illustrating how "a hundred years" can be incorporated in a moment's dream. Actually, the famous story of Chuang-tzu dreaming he is a butterfly goes like this:

> Once Chuang Chou dreamt he was a butterfly, a butterfly flitting and fluttering around, happy with himself and doing as he pleased. He didn't know he was Chuang Chou. Suddenly he woke up and there he was, solid and unmistakably Chuang Chou. But he didn't know if he was Chuang Chou who had dreamt he was a butterfly, or a butterfly dreaming he was Chuan Chou. Between Chuang Chou and a butterfly there must be *some* distinction! This is called the Transformation of Things.

had not lived for all those years. [To perceive] ignorance [arising] on the basis of dharma-nature and for one thought to be all thoughts is like falling into a deep sleep. To have penetrating understanding of the indivisibility of ignorance and dharma-nature, and that all thoughts are one thought is like being wide awake. Again, suppose those who practice the practices of peaceful bliss are asleep and dreaming. First they arouse the aspiration [for enlightenment] and so forth until they becomes Buddhas and sit on the seat of enlightenment, turn the wheel of the Dharma, save sentient beings, and enter nirvana. Then they awaken and realize that this was all an event in a dream.

If you believe in [the meaning of] these three analogies [of the *maṇi* jewel, the three poisons, and the dream], you can believe in single-mindedness. This cannot be [adequately] expressed verbally, nor can it be measured through [human] feelings.

What (Dharma) teaching can contain [the idea of] objects as inconceivable? [Understanding] these objects [in this way] arouses wisdom; what wisdom is not aroused? On the basis of [understanding] objects [as inconceivable], the vow [of aspiration for enlightenment] is aroused, and so forth to [the tenth mode of avoiding] passionate attachment to dharmas. What vow is not included herein, and what practice is not completed? When explaining it we follow the above order, but when practicing it, all thoughts are included within one thought.

See the last section of the second chapter of the *Chuang-tzu*; translated by Burton Watson, *Complete Works of Chuang Tzu*, 49.

Suppose those who practice the practices of peaceful bliss are asleep and dreaming 行安樂行人一眠夢: the set of four practices based on chapter 14 of the *Lotus Sūtra*: the 1. physical, 2. verbal, and 3. mental practices to 4. realize the vow to attain peaceful bliss.

Then they awaken and realize that this was all an event in a dream 豁寤秖是一夢事: once again, this illustrates how a whole life of practice and experience can take place in a single thought.

You can believe in single-mindedness 信一心: or, "you can believe in [the inclusion of all dharmas in] a single thought," or "you can trust singlemindedly"?

The vow [of aspiration for enlightenment] is aroused 依此境發誓: this is the theme of the next of the ten modes of contemplation of the mind. See below, at *Mo-ho chih-kuan* 55c26–56b13.

[The tenth mode] of [avoiding] passionate attachment to dharmas: see below at *Mo-ho chih-kuan* 99c–100a.

2. Arousing a Compassionate Mind: Arousing True *Bodhicitta* [55c26–56b12]

THE SECOND [mode of contemplation] is to arouse true and correct aspiration for enlightenment *(bodhicitta)* [due to arousing a compassionate mind]. We have already deeply considered [the contemplation of] objects as inconceivable, and know that one suffering is all suffering. We should reflect on and commiserate over [the reasons for] our past suffering. Delusions are aroused through being engrossed in the coarse impediments of the sights and sounds [of mundane experiences], and we indulge in physical, verbal, and mental [activities] that produce karmic deeds that are not good. We thus transmigrate in evil destinies and are encoiled in scorching passions, so that we suffer both physically and mentally and thus abuse and injure ourselves. Nevertheless we turn back again and bind ourselves in the cocoon of passions [**56a**], and burn with the flames of deluded ignorance for a hundred million kalpas. How painful this all is!

Suppose that, wishing to abandon the three [evil] destinies, you take delight in the five [basic] moral precepts and the ten good deeds. But to cultivate goodness only formally is like lightly bartering and exchanging goods at the market; [the effects or awareness of] your offences will only increase. It is similar to a fish entering the mouth of a basket trap, or a moth flying into

Arouse true and correct aspiration for enlightenment (*bodhicitta*) 発眞正菩提心: or, more literally, "arousing the thought of *bodhi*-wisdom." The list of the ten modes of contemplation given above (52b2) has "arousing compassionate thoughts" 起慈悲心 as the title for this section, the reason for which is plain from the contents.

One suffering is all suffering 一苦一切苦: or, "the suffering of one is the suffering of all." See section above at 55bff.

The cocoon of passions 愛繭: see the *Mahāparinirāṇa Sūtra*, T 12.768c5–8:

> Good sons, all sentient beings are unable to perceive [the truth of] twelvefold causes and conditions, and therefore they transmigrate in the cycle of birth and death. It is like a silkworm that builds a cocoon for its own birth and death. All sentient beings are also like this. They do not perceive Buddha-nature, so they create their own bonds of karmic deeds and flow through the cycle of birth and death.

Five moral precepts 五戒 **(*pañca-śīla*) and the ten good deeds** 十善: that is, try to follow the minimum moral standards for a Buddhist lay life.

To cultivate goodness only formally is like lightly bartering and exchanging goods at the market 相心修福如市易博換翻更益罪: because monks are not supposed to be involved in business affairs? Or, in line with what follows, being taken advantage of because of your inexperience? Perhaps your "offences" will increase because merely "formally cultivating goodness" only makes you more aware of your own inadequacies?

Similar to a fish entering the mouth of a basket trap 似魚入筍口: this phrase is found in the *Sūtra on the Auspicious Appearances and Origins of the Prince Siddhārtha*, T 3.475c4, as one of many analogies for passionate attachments:

a flame, and by reacting confusedly making things worse by furthering the delusions and becoming even further [from the goal of enlightenment]. This is like drinking saltwater when you are thirsty, or like becoming entangled in a dragon's beard and suffering injury when it enters the water, or like wrapping a cow's hide around your body which hardens when exposed to the light of the sun, or like a blind person who enters a thorny thicket and falls into a whirlpool and drowns. It is like grasping a sharp sword or embracing a flaming torch. It must be admitted that this is painful. It can be compared to stepping on a tiger's tail or on a snake's head; how frightening and grievous this all is!

If you reflect in this way concerning yourself, you should in the same way have pity [and feel compassion] for others. Suppose someone rebels and uses a narrow path to escape to enemy territory. He must still be ready for a painful process, sometimes losing consciousness and then reviving, arriving at a poor village and being hired to work for a day, sleeping in a grass hut, never being able to make any progress, and finding pleasure only in rustic activities. [Such a person] does not believe in or know [any better way]. This is a matter of pity and astonishment. Thus should you consider [the situation of] both yourself and others, as fish bones stuck in the throat.

Therefore arouse great pity, and animate two vows: "though sentient beings are unlimited I vow to save them [all]," and "though passionate afflictions are innumerable, I vow to sever them [all]." Although sentient beings

"One hinders oneself with the net of desires, and burdens oneself with the covering of passions, thus binding oneself in a dungeon, *like fish entering the mouth of a basket trap*." This general context was also quoted earlier by Chih-i at 8a23–24, and just above at 55a2–3.

Becoming entangled in a dragon's beard and suffering injury when it enters the water 龍須縛身入水轉痛: perhaps from the *Ta chih tu lun*, T 25.98b29, which uses an analogy of "like beings *bound with ropes of hair* that cut the skin and break the bones," but does not mention dragons. The *Kōgi* (BT-III, 326) also gives a reference to the *Udānavarga* (section 3-25); chapter 3 does contain a passage comparing people and their passions to a fish caught in a trap (T 4.632c–633a), but I did not locate any reference to a dragon.

Uses a narrow path to escape to enemy territory 假令隘路叛出怨國: this phrase appears in the *Mahāparinirvāṇa Sūtra*, T 12.635a3: "It is like *a narrow path* that does not allow two people to pass side by side. Liberation is not like this."

He must still be ready for a painful process … finding pleasure only in rustic activities 備歷辛苦絕而復穌往至貧里傭賃一日止宿草庵不肯前進樂為鄙事: these phrases are reminiscent of the trials and tribulations suffered by the "ignorant son" in the parable in the fourth chapter of the *Lotus Sūtra*, T 9.17a–18a.

Animate two vows 誓願: the first two of the famous "four universal bodhisattva vows," which find their classical formulation in Chih-i's work. See notes under *Mo-ho chih-kuan* 5b13 and 8a7–10b.

are [unlimited] like empty space [and without substantial Selfhood], vow to save sentient beings that are like empty space. Although you know that passionate afflictions are without [substantial] Being, vow to sever passionate afflictions that are without [substantial] Being. Although you know that sentient beings are exceedingly numerous, you should save these exceedingly numerous sentient beings. Although you know that passionate afflictions have no limit and no end, you should sever these limitless and endless passionate afflictions. Although you know that the thusness of sentient beings is like the thusness of a Buddha, you should save these sentient beings that have the thusness of a Buddha. Although you know that passionate afflictions have the thusness of the true aspect [of reality] 如實相, you should sever these passionate afflictions that have the thusness of this true aspect.

What should be done? If you extract only the causes of suffering and do not extract the results of suffering, [the performance of] this vow is mixed with poison. Therefore you must contemplate emptiness. But if you contemplate emptiness one-sidedly, and do not perceive sentient beings [in their conventional and multitudinous being], how can you save them? Such a person is called "one who is attached to emptiness." This is not what the Buddhas have taught. [On the other hand,] if you one-sidedly perceive sentient beings [as substantial beings] to be saved, you will fall into the [mistaken] view of great compassion based on passionate [mistaken] views, which is not the way of liberation.

Now [the Middle Way of compassion I advocate here] is neither [mixed with] poison nor false, and therefore it is called "true." It is neither the extreme of [one-sided emphasis on] emptiness nor the extreme of [substantial] Being; therefore it is called "correct." It is like a bird that flies through the empty sky 空 but does not abide in this emptiness. Although [the bird] does not abide in this emptiness, it follows the tracks [in the sky] without fathoming it.

The thusness of sentient beings is like the thusness of a Buddha … 衆生如如佛如: note that in this string of statements Chih-i uses the character 如 both as a comparative connector ("x is like y") and in its technical sense of "thusness" *(tathatā)*.

Also, note that these statements follow the pattern of the threefold truth: the first set of two statements point out the "emptiness" of sentient beings and passionate afflictions, the second set of statements concern their conventional aspect as multitudinous, and the third set concerns their "thusness" (the Middle).

Neither poison nor false 非毒非僞: an extreme and mistaken emphasis on emptiness is a stance that is "mixed with poison"; Nāgārjuna compares it to grasping a poisonous snake. An overemphasis on conventional reality involves the danger of becoming attached to false "realities" and mistaking merely provisional existence for ultimate reality.

Follows the tracks [in the sky] without fathoming it 跡不可尋: the *Inyō* refers to

Although [sentient beings are] empty, they are to be saved; although they are to be saved, they are empty. Therefore it is said that such a vow involves "locking horns with emptiness." Therefore this is called "arousing true and correct aspiration for enlightenment" 眞正発菩提心. This is the meaning here.

Again, know that [contemplating] thoughts as inconceivable [means perceiving that] one blissful thought involves all blissful thoughts. Your own self and [other] sentient beings have in the past sought bliss, though without knowing the causes for [true] bliss, like those who grasp tiles and stones thinking they are wish-fulfilling jewels, or who ignorantly point at the light of a firefly and call it the sun or the moon.

Now, however, as you begin to understand [correctly], you should arouse great compassion and animate two vows: "though Dharma [teachings] are immeasurable, I vow to know them [all]," and "though the Buddhist path is supreme, I vow to perfect it." Although you know that Dharma teachings are forever quiescent, like emptiness, you vow to cultivate and practice them [all] as forever quiescent. Although you know that *bodhi*-wisdom has no [substantial] Being, you seek yourself within this lack of Being. Although you know that Dharmas are like emptiness and without Being, you vow to "paint" and adorn the emptiness [with provisional "colors"]. Although you

a passage in the *Mahāparinirāṇa Sūtra*, T 12.656c11–12; although many of the same words are used, the meaning is quite different:

> As people who dwell on the earth gaze up at the sky but cannot see *the tracks [of the flight] of the birds*, so, good sons, sentient beings do not have divine eyesight. They dwell within passionate afflictions and do not perceive that they themselves have the nature of the Tathāgata. Therefore I teach the secret teaching of nonselfhood. Why? Because those without divine eyesight cannot know the true self.

Locking horns with emptiness 虛空共鬪: this phrase is found in the *Pancaviṃśati Sūtra*, T 8.360c4–5: "A person who makes a vow for the sake of sentient beings wishes *to lock horns with emptiness*."

One blissful thought involves all blissful thoughts 一樂心一切樂心: or, "blissful thoughts for one involves blissful thoughts for all."

Grasp tiles and stones thinking they are wish-fulfilling jewels 如執瓦礫謂如意珠: this analogy from the *Mahāparinirvāṇa Sūtra* (T 12.617c3–10) has been used many times already in the *Mo-ho chih-kuan*; see notes under 20b15 and 43a3.

Two vows: the third and fourth of the four universal bodhisattva vows. See note above.

Like emptiness 如空: or, "with the thusness of emptiness."

Vow to "paint" and adorn the emptiness 誓願畫續莊嚴虛空: the *Kōgi* claims that this phrase is from the *Viśeṣacintibrahmaparipṛcchā* (T no. 586, section 2-8), but I could not locate the phrase in this sūtra. A SAT search revealed that the entire phrase appears in the Taishō canon only at this point in the *Mo-ho chih-kuan*, though the second phrase "adorn the emptiness" 莊嚴虛空 appears frequently in the *Avataṃsaka Sūtra*.

know that the Buddhist path is not something to be perfected, you can attain flowers and fruits, like "planting a tree in empty space." Although you know that Dharmas and the fruit of Buddhahood are neither cultivated nor not cultivated, neither illumined nor attained, nevertheless you illumine and attain them in their lack of being illumined and attained. This is called "neither false nor [mixed with] poison," and thus it is true. It is neither [extreme] emptiness nor the mistaken view of passions [for the conventional world]; thus it is called "correct."

In this way the vows of compassion come neither before nor after the wisdom of [contemplating] objects as inconceivable, but both arise simultaneously. Compassion is [indivisible from] wisdom, and wisdom is [indivisible from] compassion. [Ideally,] you universally cover all, without conditions and without deliberation, naturally 任運 extracting suffering and spontaneously 自然 granting bliss. This is not the same as harmful poison, nor [the extreme of] merely emptiness, nor the [mistaken] view of passions [for the conventional world]. This is the meaning of [the Middle Way] called "true and correct aspiration for enlightenment." It means that you have pity on yourself and have pity on [other] sentient beings, as explained above. Contemplating thoughts should be understood [in this way].

Planting a tree in empty space 如虛空中種樹: a phrase from the *Viśeṣacintibrahmaparipṛcchā*, T 12.42c12–13:

> It is analogous to a tree that does not rely on the ground but is in space, and yet has extraordinary roots, trunk, branches, leaves, flowers, and fruit.

Neither cultivated nor not cultivated, neither illumined nor attained, nevertheless you illumine and attain them in their lack of being illumined and attained 非修非不修而修非證非得以無所證得而證而得: as above, the first set of two statements reflects the aspect of emptiness, the next set reflects the aspect of conventional existence, and the last set reflects the Middle Way.

Have pity on yourself and have pity on sentient beings, as explained above 自悲己悲衆生義皆如上說: see the section in the *Mo-ho chih-kuan* above on "Arousing the Great Thought" of *bodhicitta* and compassion, especially the section on the four universal bodhisattva vows at 8a7–10b7.

3. Skillful Means for a Peaceful Mind [56b12–59b7]

The third [mode of contemplation] is skillful means [practiced] for [attaining] a peaceful mind. This refers to the good use of cessation-and-contemplation to peacefully rest in Dharma-nature. [In the sections] above [we have examined] the profound fulfillment of [contemplating] objects as inconceivable in depth and subtle mystery [in section 1], and the broad exercise of compassion [in section 2]. If both of these have been covered, you should make good on the vows [discussed in the previous section] through practice. The practice [to be done] is cessation-and-contemplation.

1. Cessation and Contemplation [56b16]

[Cessation] The basis for ignorance and fatuous delusion is none other than Dharma-nature (or, "the nature of reality") 法性. Due to fatuous delusion, Dharma-nature changes, producing [the state of] ignorance and arousing perverted views and [the dualities of] good and not-good and so forth. This is like when the cold comes and water changes and hardens into ice. Also, it is like when sleep comes and the mind changes and you have various dreams.

Now, you should realize that perverted views are indivisible from Dharma-nature; they are neither one nor different 不一不異. Although [it is said that] perverted views arise and perish, they are [empty] like a spinning wheel of fire. Do not believe that perverted views [substantially] arise and perish. Only believe that these thoughts are the Dharma-nature alone. What arises is the arising of Dharma-nature, and what perishes is the perishing of Dharma-nature. There is no true arising and perishing of an essence, and we speak of arising and perishing in a deluded sense. However, when

Due to fatuous delusion, Dharma-nature changes, producing ignorance and arousing perverted views and [the dualities of] good and not-good and so forth 以癡迷故法性變作無明起諸顛倒善不善等: this is a significant, yet ambiguous, phrase. What is meant by the character 變 (alter, change, transform)? How is Dharma-nature "transformed" by fatuous delusion? What is involved in this "transformation," so that ignorance arises? In what sense is the Dharma-nature the "basis" of ignorance and delusion? Does this imply a radical and total identity of Dharma-nature and ignorance, so that (as later Tendai commentators claim), ignorance (just as it is) is Dharma-nature and delusion (just as it is) is enlightenment? Chih-i himself does not go that far; as he points out a few lines later, these are "neither one nor different." Ignorance shares the same "thusness" as Dharma-nature, but it is not exactly the same as (does not completely overlap) Dharma-nature. When there is ignorance, there is Dharma-nature, but there are ways in which ignorance is not the same as Dharma-nature, and delusion is not the same as enlightenment.

These [also] are all Dharma-nature 悉是法性: or, they all partake in or share the same "thusness" of Dharma-nature.

we indicate "deluded conceptions," these [also] are all Dharma-nature. Fix [your concentration] to Dharma-nature by means of Dharma-nature, and be mindful of Dharma-nature by means of Dharma-nature. Dharma-nature is constant; there is nothing that is not Dharma-nature.

The essence is already accomplished; deluded conceptions are not obtainable. Dharma-nature also is unobtainable. Returning to the source and turning back to the basis 還源反本, the Dharma-realm is fully quiescent. This is called "cessation." When cessation [is practiced and accomplished] in this way, all of the flowing and turning [of passions in samsara] ceases.

[Contemplation] Contemplation involves thoroughly contemplating the thoughts of ignorance. On the one hand these [ignorant thoughts] are equal with Dharma-nature as fundamentally and originally empty, and on the other hand equal with all deluded conceptions, [the dualities of] good and evil [and so forth]. All are like empty space; [ignorance and Dharma-nature are] neither two nor separate 無二無別. This [equal emptiness of all things] is like at the end of a kalpa when [the entire universe] from here on earth to the [heavenly realm of] the first dhyāna stage is engulfed in flames so that there is no place that is not on fire. Again, it is like the bodhisattva Ākāśagarbha manifesting features [of the world] as "all empty." It is like [the bodhisattva] Sea of Wisdom manifesting the first place he appears as "all water" [to illustrate the unity of Dharma-nature and the mundane world].

The end of a kalpa 劫盡: a kalpa consists of various stages: the arising of the world, the lengthy continuation of the world, the annihilation of the world, and an intervening period of chaos. Thus the "end of a kalpa" refers to the stage of annihilation, when the entire universe is engulfed in three kinds of disaster: that caused by water, fire, and wind.

The bodhisattva Ākāśagarbha manifesting features [of the world] as "all empty" 虛空藏菩薩所現之相一切皆空: see the "Section on Ākāśagarbha" in *The Great Collection of Sūtras*, T 13.93b–94b, especially 93c18–94a18, which explains the reason why this bodhisattva is named Ākāśagarbha ("store of empty space"): he teaches that all dharmas are like empty space 虛空 because they have no place of abiding, no form, are pure and undefiled, have the nature of quiescence, and so forth.

Sea of Wisdom manifesting the first place he appears as "all water" 如海慧初來所現一切皆水: see the "Section on the Bodhisattva Sea of Wisdom" in *The Great Collection of Sūtras*, T 13.46b26–47c14, especially 47a3–28:

> At that time there was a Brahman named Cultivator of Wisdom who had the thought, "For what reason is there this great expanse of water which fills the trichiliocosm, yet there is no flood damage. I should now ask the World Honored One about this." Accompanied by 68,000 other Brahmans he visited the World Honored One. They bowed their heads in respect, circumambulated him to the right three times, kneeled, pressed their palms together, and said, "World Honored One. For what reason is the trichiliochosm filled with an adornment of seven-jeweled lotus flowers, on which immeasurable bodhisattvas sit, each individually on a flower; and why are the

At the momentary arising of an ephemeral thought, both the thinker and the thought are empty. "Emptiness" is also unobtainable. It is like a piece of wood used as kindling to start a fire, which is itself consumed in the fire. When the Dharma realm is penetratingly illumined, then everything is very clear. This is called "contemplation."

[Cessation-and-contemplation] Cessation is wisdom; wisdom is cessation. Immovable cessation is immovable wisdom. Immovable wisdom is immovable cessation. When Dharma-nature is illumined by immovable wisdom, this is the wisdom of contemplation and you attain peace. This is also the peace of cessation. The immovability corresponds to that of the Dharma-nature; therefore this is the peace of cessation, and also the peace of contemplation. These are neither two nor separate.

What should be done if you are not able to attain the peace of both [cessation and contemplation] together? Now, mental activity is mysteriously dark [the opposite of illuminated contemplation] and swift in effect [the opposite of calm cessation], and without form or essence. As soon as it arises, it perishes; it is impossible to grasp and hold. It quickly comes and quickly goes, and is not easy to restrain. Even if you attain cessation of this [mental activity], it again quickly drives on, like a shimmering flame fanned by the wind. Even if you attain insight [concerning this mental activity], [the thoughts] are darker than jet black lacquer. Even though you take pains to attain success, the scattered delusions seem to redouble in intensity. "The enemy is strong and our strength is weak; a sandpiper and frog clutch each other so that neither can advance nor retreat." Be willing to give up your life

three-thousand worlds filled with great [expanses of] waters?"

The Buddha said to the Brahman, "Good son. This is due to the supranormal powers of the bodhisattva-mahāsattva Sea of Wisdom."

Mental activity is mysteriously dark and swift in effect, and without form or essence 心神冥昧儚利怳惘: the meaning of the characters here is not clear; I base my translation on the interpretation given in the *Kōgi* (BT–III, 345).

The enemy is strong and our strength is weak; a sandpiper and frog clutch each other so that neither can advance nor retreat 敵強力弱鷸蚌相扼: Ikeda (*Kenkyū-chūshaku*, 357) explains that "this is a traditional image illustrating the idea of running off with a prize while others are fighting for it, or taking advantage of two opposing forces that are concerned only with each other. The story goes that once upon a time a sandpiper was pecking at a frog when the frog grabbed the bird's beak in its mouth and would not let go. [As both had neutralized the other,] a fisherman came along and was able to capture both." Chan-jan (BT–III, 345) comments that this phrase is used only to illustrate the idea of mutual opposition or obstruction, and is not concerned with the details of the image; thus Ikeda (*Gendaigoyaku*, 295) freely translates this passage, "one is stuck without advancing nor retrogressing, without having attained cessation-and-contemplation." The story is found in the 戦國策 (*Inyō*, 42).

in dedication to the path; sacrifice your flesh and bones [in wholehearted pursuit of cessation-and-contemplation]. Vow to skillfully attain a peaceful mind. Use various means in turn to attain a mutual correspondence [of cessation-and-contemplation], and thus perfect the level of contemplative practice.

2. A Peaceful Mind by Teaching Others and Practicing Oneself [56c14–59a8]

There are two [ways of attaining a] peaceful mind. The first is by teaching others, and the second is by practicing for oneself.

1. *A Peaceful Mind by Teaching Others* [56c15]

There are also two types of "teaching others." The first is that by a noble teacher [such as an arhat], and the second is that by an ordinary teacher.

A noble teacher has the power of the eye of wisdom and thus can clearly [apply the proper] Dharma medicine. He has the power of the Dharma eye, and thus is aware of the obstacles of diseases. He has the power of converting people to the path, and so bestows medicine in accordance with the disease and in ways that people can accept. It is like Upagupta who knew [the capacities of] his disciples, using [one disciple's] faith to awaken him by causing him to climb a tree, and using [another disciple's appetite for] food to lead him to drink [scalding] coagulated milk, and assuming the form of a woman to scold [another disciple] into awakening. One by one they unveiled their

Level of contemplative practice 觀行位: the third level of the "six identities"; see chart 1 on the "Levels of Attainment" in Volume 3.

Like Upagupta knew his disciples ... 如毱多知弟子: these three examples are from *The Transmission*, T 50.311b–312a. The first example, of Upagupta ordering his disciple to climb a tree in order to test his faith and lead him to rid himself of attachment to his own body, has been referred to by Chih-i above in the *Mo-ho chih-kuan* at 45c10. The other two examples go as follows:

[311b7–16] There was a monk who by nature had an [excessive] taste for food and drink, and because of these desires could not attain the path. Upagupta invited this man into his room and offered him scalding milk, saying that he should wait until it cooled before drinking it. The monk blew on the scalding milk, trying to cool it, saying to the noble man [Upagupta] that the scalding milk was already cool. The noble man pointed out that "although the scalding milk is cool, you wish for it to be blazing hot. You should extinguish your mental fires with the water of contemplation. Also, vomit your food out into an empty vessel; after vomiting out the food you should turn around and use this food." The monk replied, "This [regurgitated food] is mixed with saliva; how can it be eaten!?" The noble [Upagupta] said, "All food and drink are no different than this. You should thoroughly contemplate

dawn [of awakening], without a fine hair's difference between them. Without missing any opportune time, [a teacher who knows when and what to do] will offer words that lead to awakening. After the Buddha has departed from this world, these kinds of [noble] teachers are exceedingly difficult to find, [as much as] the odds of a blind turtle [in the vast expanse of the ocean] coming up accidentally into the eye of a buoy, or [the difficult odds] of dropping a mustard seed [from a great height] and having it pierce the head of a needle.

Second, an ordinary teacher, though not possessing the above three powers, can also help convert people. [Such teachers are] analogous to a good doctor, who carefully discriminates the medicine according to the disease. By interpreting the color [of the face], the voice, and the pulse [of the patient], [the doctor] applies medicine with discrimination so that even one whose life span seems to be exhausted will not die. If he cannot interpret the pulse, the doctor will question [the patient] concerning his symptoms and take measures in accordance with what he is told, sometimes fortuitously attaining [good results]. But even one of noble virtue such as Śāriputra

the deluded arising of passionate attachments. You should now contemplate food in its impurity." After hearing this explanation [the monk] attained the way of an arhat.

[312a18–29] There was a female householder who said to a bhikṣu, "I wish to go with you, oh you of great virtue." The bhikṣu replied, "The Buddha does not allow me to be accompanied by a woman." The woman said, "I look up to you of great virtue, and thus will follow after you." The bhikṣu had pity on her desires and allowed her to accompany [him]. Then the Honored One made a [magical] transformation and created a great river. The woman said to the one of great virtue, "I will cross along with you." But the monk [attempted to cross] at a lower point, and the woman went upstream [to cross the river]. Later the woman [in attempting to cross] fell into the river and began to drown, and called out to [the monk of] great virtue saying, "Help me to cross [and save me from] this tragedy!" At that time the monk pulled her out [of the water] but feeling her soft and smooth, aroused thoughts of passionate desires, and realized that he was not a non-returner (*anāgāmin*). He felt a great passionate attachment for this woman, and wished to go to a hidden place to have [sexual] relations. In the distance he saw Upagupta, and hung his head in shame. The Honored One said, "In the past you were that arhat. How can you desire evil things like this?"...

Blind turtle coming up accidentally into the eye of a buoy, or dropping a mustard seed and having it pierce the head of a needle 盲龜何由上值浮孔墜芥豈得下貫針鋒難難: these examples of extreme odds are from a passage in the *Mahāparinirvāṇa Sūtra*, T 12.612b13 and 18, which illustrate the difficulty and extreme odds against the opportunity to meet a historical Buddha.

The doctor will question ... sometimes fortuitously attaining 醫問病相依語作方亦挑脫得差: the wording here is vague; I follow the interpretation of Chan-jan (BT–III, 350). See also the description of how a doctor makes a diagnosis later in the *Mo-ho chih-kuan* in the section on "The Marks of Disease" at 106b15ff.

makes a misdiagnosis; ordinary people with their bonds [of passions] can be called "doctors who promote disease" 病導師.

Now [here in the *Mo-ho chih-kuan*] I am not discussing the noble teacher, but the proper exposition by ordinary teachers in teaching others to have a peaceful mind. There are [again] two types of "[teaching] others." The first is practice based on faith [which involves a focus on learning or study], and the second is practiced based on Dharma[-meditation] [which involves a focus on meditative practice]. The *Abhidharma-vibhāṣa-śāstra* clarifies that the level of these two [types of] people is that of "insight into the path [of the Four Noble Truths]." Those who enter [the path] by hearing [the Dharma] **[57a]** are ones who "practice based on faith"; those who enter [the path] by pondering [the Dharma through meditation] are ones who "practice based

Śāriputra makes a misdiagnosis 身子聖德亦復差機: perhaps a reference to a passage in the *Mahāparinirvāṇa Sūtra*, T 12.764a21–b5:

> At one time Śāriputra was teaching two disciples; one to whom he recommended the contemplation of white bones, and another he led in [the meditation of] counting breaths. Even after many years of practice, these people did not attain samādhi, and as a result gave rise to false views, saying "There is no such thing as a nirvana, a dharma of no-outflows. If there were, we would have attained it. Why? Because we have been good in keeping the precepts." When I (the Buddha) saw these monks with their depraved thoughts, I scolded Śāriputra saying, "You did not teach them well. Why do these two disciples proclaim perverted views. You did not properly differentiate the natures of these two disciples.... [The first should practice counting breaths, because he is a goldsmith working with a bellows and thus familiar with counting breaths; the second should practice the contemplation of white bones, because he is a cleaner used to working with impurities.]" Then I taught the Dharma in accordance with [the natures of] the two disciples, and after the two heard [the Buddha's exposition], they attained the fruit of an arhat. Therefore I am the true good friend of sentient beings, and not Śāriputra or Maudgalyāyana.

First is practice based on faith, and the second is practice based on Dharma[-meditation] 一信行二法行: this first, "practice based on faith," is practice based on faith or trust in what one hears or learns from Dharma masters, and thus is focused on the teachings or doctrines and what one studies and learns; "practice based on Dharma[-meditation]" refers to practice based on your own experience of meditation or "pondering" the Dharma. The terms may be misleading or counter-intuitive, with "faith" 信 taken as the experiential side of practice and "Dharma" 法 taken as the doctrinal side, but here there is no simple dichotomy between "teaching" and "practice" or "doctrine" vs "experience." See the explanation that follows in the *Mo-ho chih-kuan*.

The level of these two [types of] people is that of "insight into the path." Those who enter by hearing are ones who "practice based on faith"; those who enter by pondering are ones who "practice based on Dharma[-meditation]" 此二人位在見道。因聞入者是爲信行。因思入者是爲法行: a summary of a longer passage in the *Abhidharma-vibhāṣa-śāstra*, T 28.216b–217b; see especially 216c13–17, which speaks of "people who are firm in

on Dharma[-meditation]." [In the *Ch'eng-shih lun* it is explained that] the Dharmagupta [school] says that these [two types of people] are at the level of "[skillful] means." [Of the first type,] there are few who can perceive [the Dharma] on their own. For those with the power to hear [the Dharma], they will certainly hear the Dharma and attain awakening at a later time. These people are called [those who] practice based on faith. [Of the second type,] there are few with the power to hear [the Dharma]; there are many who perceive the Dharma on their own. [For those with the power to perceive the Dharma on their own,] at a later time they will certainly ponder [the Dharma] and attain awakening. These people are called [those who] practice based on Dharma[-meditation]. [However,] if these people are on the level of "insight into the path [of the Four Noble Truths]," they should be proficient in the mental state of non-conceptualization, which, when once experienced, is true [enlightenment]. In this case there is no clear distinction between [the categories of practice based on] faith and Dharma. [The analysis of] the *Abhidharma-vibhāṣa-śāstra* is based on the perfection of practice, while the *Ch'eng-shih lun* is based on capacity for understanding [or spiritual potential]. They each have their rationale, and do not necessarily contradict each other.

faith" and "people who are firm in the Dharma" who "attain the path by abandoning the path."

The Dharmagupta [school] says that these [two types of people] are at the level of "means" 曇無德云位在方便.... These people are called [those who] practice based on Dharma[-meditation] 名為法行: see the *Ch'eng-shih lun*, T 32.245c3–246c18, a section on "Discriminating [the Four Levels of] the Wise and the Noble."

[245c4] Question: For what reason are people called "monks" (bhikṣu) 僧.

Answer: They are called "monks" because they are pure in virtues such as keeping the precepts, concentration, and wisdom due to four practices and four attainments. The four practices are those of the stream-enterer, once-returner, non-returner, and arhat. The four attainments are those of the stream-enterer, once-returner, non-returner, and arhat.

There are three types of stream-enterer: first, those who practice according to faith; second, those who practice according to Dharma [methods]; and third, those who practice according to no set form 無相.

Those who practice according to faith are as follows. Suppose a person has not yet realized the wisdom of emptiness and no-self, but since he has faith in the Buddha Dharma he practices according to the words of the Buddha. Therefore this is called "practice according to faith."...

[245c27] Those who practice according to Dharma are as follows. Such a person attains the wisdom of emptiness and no-self through gradually passing through the practices of the levels [of the four good roots] of "heat," "summit," "patience," and "supreme in the world." Since [one attains insight into] emptiness and no-self, this is called "practice according to Dharma."

These two types of practice involve realizing insight into the truth of the path. Insight into the truth of extinction is called "practice according to no set form."

As for the teacher [we are discussing] now [that is, ordinary teachers], let us examine their long-term background. Those who have attended to studies for a long time attain the seeds of "[practice based on] faith," and those who have sat in (dhyāna) meditation for a long time attain the seeds of "[practice based on] Dharma[-meditation]." Those who, from one life to the next, have become perfumed [with the Buddhist Way] will attain spiritual capacity. Each of them realize awakening by hearing and pondering [the Dharma]. If we speak in terms of sharp and dull capacities, those who practice based on Dharma[-meditation] are "sharp" in the sense that they contemplate [and have insight into] the Dharma internally on their own; those who practice based on faith are "dull" in the sense that they rely on hearing [the Dharma] from others. Again, those who practice based on faith are "sharp" in the sense that they are awakened after one hearing [of the Dharma]; those who practice based on Dharma[-meditation] are "dull" in the sense that they thoroughly contemplate the Dharma[-teachings] one-by-one over time. Or, it can be said that they are both "sharp" and "dull" in that those who practice based on faith are "sharp" in their wisdom for hearing, but "dull" in their wisdom for cultivating practice, and those who practice based on Dharma[-meditation] are "sharp" in their wisdom for cultivating practice, but "dull" in their wisdom for hearing.

We have thus finished explaining the spiritual capacities among people. How [do they attain] "a peaceful mind"? A teacher should ask [the practitioners] saying, "Which do you seek to attain, concentration or wisdom?" If the person should say, "I have heard that the Buddha says [that the method of] a good teacher is like the shape and light of the moon that gradually turns full, or is like the steps of a ladder that gradually reach the top. He skillfully teaches [step by step] and thus converts people's minds to have all the causes and conditions for attaining the path. My aspiration is like a burning thirst, like a baby calf seeking its mother." You should know that such a person is one who should practice based on faith. Or, if the person should say, "I have heard that the Buddha says a mirror distinctly and clearly reflects visible forms if it is unmoved, and the pure water [of a lake] undisturbed by waves spontaneously reveals the fishes and stones within. I joyfully forsake [all negative] notions and perceptions, as if abandoning a heavy burden." You should know that such a person is one who should practice based on Dharma[-meditation]. Once you know their spiritual capacities, there are eight ways for leading individual people to attain a peaceful mind.

For a long time 久劫: lit., "for a long eon" or kalpa; many millions of billions of years (Skt. *kalpa-sahasra-koṭi*). That's a long time to be studying the Dharma.

1. Eight ways for leading those who practice based on faith to attain a peaceful mind

1. A peaceful mind by cessation through arousing a desire for bliss [57a20]

[One could say,] "Listen, good son. For immeasurable kalpas you have drunk the poison of crazed distraction, chased after the objects of the five senses, risen and fallen in the triple world, and gone from suffering to afflictions and from afflictions to suffering, like a raging wind blowing the flowers (Skt. *tūla*) off of trees, or like the rising and falling of beans boiled in a great scorching cauldron. Why do you not still your thoughts and penetrate to the basis [of understanding], and thus unify your thoughts [and attain concentrated awareness]. If your thoughts are unified, how can you not discern suffering and the causes of suffering? If your thoughts are unified [and you attain concentrated awareness], you will no longer transmigrate [in this samsaric existence]. If your thoughts are unified, then ignorance will not come into play, and so forth [for the rest of the twelve links of conditioned arising] up to and including old-age-and-death. If you can split the great tree [of passionate afflictions] and bring them to an end and not create any more new ones; if you attain unity [of concentrated thought] then the six obscurations [will be put to an end] and you can cross to the other shore [of enlightenment]. This alone is bliss." With good and skillful means, with various causes and conditions, with various parables and analogies, expansively praise [the attainment of] cessation and arouse a feeling for this joy. This is called [attaining] a peaceful mind by cessation through arousing a desire for bliss.

2. A peaceful mind by cessation through the use of skillful means [57a29]

Again [you could say], "Good son. Suppose the heavens are always clear so that the rivers and lakes all dry up, all the grass is burnt and withered, and the hundred grains dwindle to nothing. If the Dragon King Sāgara devises clouds for seven days **[57b]** and pours forth rain in the four directions, the great earth will be drenched and all the seeds will bring forth sprouts, all

Eight ways for leading individual people to attain a peaceful mind 於一人所八番安心: these "eight ways" consist of the use of the four *siddhānta* with regard to the two methods of cessation and contemplation.

Six obscurations 六蔽: of avarice/covetousness, immorality/breaking the precepts, anger, indolence/sloth, distractedness/lack of concentration, and stupidity/ignorance; see the *Mo-ho chih-kuan* 17b17.

Dragon King Sāgara 娑伽羅: one of the eight Dragon Kings; Sāgara is capable of bringing forth rain.

Devises clouds for seven days and pours forth rain in the four directions 七日構雲四方注雨大地霑洽: for verses describing the rain-making activities of the Dragon Kings and comparing this to the activity of the Tathāgata, see the *Avataṃsaka Sūtra*, T 9.622b9–c11.

roots and stumps will flourish, all branches and leaves will grow luxuriantly, and all flowers and fruits will blossom. People are the same. Because they are distracted and dissipated, the good that they should arouse does not arise, and the good that has already arisen is in turn lost. The river of meditative concentration is dry, and the tree of the "steps on the path" perishes. Myriad goodness is burnt and withered, and the hundred blessings are all emaciated. The flower of practice [which is the cause,] and the fruit of [the attainment of] the path [which is the result] does not reach maturation. However, if you are able to unify your thoughts within a quiet forest, so that nothing goes out from within, and nothing comes in from outside, a quiet "cloud" ensues and various meditative concentrations are aroused; this is like the falling of rain. The forest of merit—the levels of "[skillful] means" such as that of "heat" and "the summit," the eye of wisdom, clear awakening, [various kinds of patience such as] the forbearance that comes from faith, the forbearance from [pliantly] following [the path], [the forbearance that comes from realizing] non-arising, and [the forbearance of] quiescent extinction, up to [the attainment of] unsurpassed *bodhi*-wisdom; all of this is mastered and acquired." Thus good and skillful means, and various [causes and] conditions and [various parables and] analogies, are used to expansively praise [the attainment of] cessation and to give rise to good roots. This is called [attaining] a peaceful mind by cessation through the use of expedients.

3. A peaceful mind by cessation through therapeutic means [57b12]

Again [you could say,] "Good son. A distracted mind is the most pernicious

"Heat" 煖 and "the summit" 頂: these are the first two of the four "levels of means" (or "four good roots"), early stages on the path to enlightenment for those of the Tripitaka Teachings.

Forbearance that comes from faith 信忍, the forbearance from [pliantly] following [柔]順忍, [the forbearance of] non-arising 無生[忍], and [the forbearance of] quiescent extinction 寂滅[忍]: these are perhaps parts of the stage of the eight kinds of forbearance, wherein you attain the patience or recognition of insight into the Four Noble Truths, or one of the sub-levels of attainment for those in the Tripitaka Teachings (the third of the "four good roots"), or the third of the ten *bhūmi* stages for those in the Shared Teachings. These four (though slightly different, e.g. "forbearance from overcoming passions" instead of "forbearance from faith") appear again at *Mo-ho chih kuan* 92b7–9, specifically applying them to the Fourfold Teachings:

> "Right mindfulness" and so forth for the Tripitaka Teachings means forbearance from overcoming [passions] 伏忍. "Right mindfulness" and so forth for the Shared Teachings means the "forbearance from pliantly following [the path]" 柔順忍. "Right mindfulness" and so forth for the Distinct Teachings means "the forbearance of the non-arising [of dharmas]" 無生(法)忍. "Right mindfulness" and so forth for the Perfect Teaching means "the forbearance of quiescent extinction" 寂滅忍.

of all evils. It is like a drunken unshackled elephant which stomps on and destroys a lotus pond, or a camel [without a bridle in its] nose-holes overturning and dropping its load. It is quicker than lightning, stronger than the poison on a snake's tongue. [It obstructs understanding and insight,] like the five [overlapping] shades such as dust and mist that block the light of the sun, so that both the eyelashes that are up close and the sky that is far away cannot be seen. If you are able to cultivate concentration, this is like a flame

A distracted mind is the most pernicious of all evils. It is like a drunken unshackled elephant which stomps on and destroys a lotus pond, or a camel [without a bridle in its] nose-holes overturning and dropping its load 散心者惡中之惡。如無鉤醉象踏壞華池。穴鼻駱駝翻倒負䭾: these images are from the *Ta chih tu lun*, T 25.184c7–8, in a section concerning "the obstacle of restlessness and remorse." This is the section of the *Ta chih tu lun* that is used also in the *Hsiao chih-kuan* (see T 46.464c1–7) as the basis for its exposition of "rejecting restlessness and remorse" as one of the twenty-five preparations for entering meditation. The *Ta chih tu lun* passage reads: "A person who is distracted and restless is like an unshackled drunken elephant or a camel without 決/缺 [a bridle in its] nose; they cannot be restrained." The *Ta chih tu lun* lists "hole" 穴 as a variant for 決/缺.

Since "hole-nose" 穴鼻 means "rabbit," a possible variant reading for this passage in the *Ta chih tu lun* is "like an unbridled drunk elephant, rabbit, or camel," an interpretation followed by Charles Luk in his translation of the *Hsiao chih-kuan* (*The Secrets of Chinese Meditation*, 120). Chih-i uses the character 穴, but adds phrases which make it clear that there is a parallelism between "elephant" and "camel" and their unbridled, destructive actions. The phrase appears again later in the *Mo-ho chih-kuan* at 92c3–4, where it clearly means "a crazy drunk elephant running wild without a hook/bridle in its nose-holes."

Five shades such as dust and mist that block the light of the sun 重沓五翳埃靄曜靈: the "five shades" that block the light (lit., "the spirit") of the sun or moon are smoke, clouds, dust, fog, and the asura Rāhu (the mythological figure who causes eclipses). In the *Hsiao chih-kuan* (T 46.465b1–3) these illustrate five obstacles that need to be removed in preparation for practicing meditation. The "five shades" appear in many sources; see a passage in the *Ta chih tu lun* (T 25.185a9–11) which follows shortly after the passage on elephants and camels (see note above), reads:

> A practitioner [of meditation] is also like this. He removes five impediments so that his mind is peaceful, pure, and blissful. This is like the sun and moon having five things that cover and obstruct them: smoke, clouds, *dust, fog,* and the hand of the asura Rāhu [who causes an eclipse] hinder [the sun and moon] so that they are not able to shine. The minds of people are also like this. What is obstructed by the five obstacles is of no use, and is not able to benefit people.

The *Mahāparinirvāṇa Sūtra* (T 12.761a7–10) contains a similar passage, using the same compound 五翳.

The eyelashes that are up close and the sky that is far away cannot be seen 睫近霄遠俱皆不見: this phrase is perhaps from the *Mahāparinirvāṇa Sūtra* (T 12.777a20–21):

> There are some things in the world that, for some reason, cannot be seen. What are these reasons? For example, things that are *far away* cannot be seen, like the tracks of birds in *the sky*. Things that are

in a closed room that is able to destroy a great darkness. When the membrane [covering a blind person's eyes] is removed with a scalpel, then the color of the sky is translucently clear, and you can fully [see] whether there is one finger or two fingers or three fingers [held up in front of your face]. As a great rain is able to settle the billowing dust, great concentration is able to quiet crazed idleness. Cessation is able to destroy distraction and extinguish vacuous delusions." Thus good and skillful means, and various conditions and analogies, are used to expansively praise [the attainment of] cessation and to destroy lethargy and distraction. This is called [attaining] a peaceful mind by cessation through therapeutic means.

4. A peaceful mind by cessation through the supreme meaning [57b19]

Again [you could say,] "Good son, 'a mind that dwells in [a samādhi of] concentration is able to know the features of the arising and perishing of dharmas in this world,' and is also able to know the features of the non-arising and non-perishing of dharmas of the transcendent realm. The Tathāgata enjoyed samādhi even after attaining the path; how much more should ordinary beings [enjoy the bliss of samādhi]. One who is in meditative concentration, 'like catching sight of the path by a flash of lightning in the night,'

close cannot be seen, *like the eyelashes* of a person's [own] eyes. Some things cannot be seen because of something being broken, like one whose eyes are disabled.…

The quote is not exact, and does not quite fit the context, so Chan-jan speculates that the reference is from the *Middle Treatise*, and the *Kōgi* says that the source cannot be identified (BT–III, 360–62).

When the membrane is removed with a scalpel, then the color of the sky is translucently clear, and you can fully [see] whether there is one finger or two fingers or three fingers 金錍抉膜空色朗然。一指二指三指皆了: this image is from the *Mahāparinirvāṇa Sūtra*, T 12.652c4–7:

The bodhisattva Kāśyapa said to the Buddha, "World Honored One. How exceedingly profound and difficult to see and difficult to realize is the Buddha-nature."

The Buddha said, "Good son. It is like a hundred blind men visited a good doctor in order to receive treatment for their eyes. At that time the good doctor used *a scalpel to remove the membrane over their eyes*. Holding up *one finger* he asked, 'Can you see?' The blind person answered, 'I cannot see yet.' He then held up *two fingers and then three fingers*, and [the blind person] said he could see a little. Good son, this profound scripture of great nirvana which the Tathāgata has not yet preached is also like this. Immeasurable bodhisattvas, though they complete the practices of all the perfections up to the stage of the tenth abode, still are not able to see that they have the Buddha-nature."

A mind that dwells in concentration is able to know the features of the arising and perishing of dharmas in this world 心若在定能知世間生滅法相: a phrase from the *I chiao ching*, T 12.1111c26–27. This passage has been quoted in the *Mo-ho chih-kuan* before; see note under 24c26.

Catching sight of the path by a flash of lightning in the night 夜見電光卽得見道:

destroys innumerable billions of penetratingly burning evil factors, and eventually attains and perfects universal wisdom." Thus good and skillful means, and various conditions and analogies, are used to expansively praise [the attainment of] cessation and to encounter thusness 眞如. This is called [attaining] a peaceful mind by cessation through the supreme meaning.]

5. *A peaceful mind by contemplation through arousing a desire for bliss* [57b25]

If a person says, "I have heard of quiescence, but it does not arouse any yearning [on my part]. However, if I can hear an explanation, I will listen and not be bored." Then you should explain as follows, "[The sufferings of] the three evil destinies—burning [in hell], the heavy burdens of the beasts, the hunger and thirst of the hungry ghosts—these are not called [true] suffering. For one to be in the darkness of ignorance without being able to hear or know about the direction you should take; this is great suffering. [On the other hand,] this is blissful: to hear much and enjoy [the bliss of] discernment; to perceive the Dharma and enjoy the joy of the Dharma; to overcome evil with good. [57c] An arhat who has no attachments is called one who enjoys the greatest bliss. Hear about the ambrosia-like bliss [of awakening] from one who has heard [and learned] much; contemplate thoroughly according to these teachings and know what is the path and what is not the path; avoid the pitfalls and go directly [on the path] without wandering." Thus good and skillful means, and various conditions and analogies, are used to expansively praise [the attainment of] contemplation and arouse a feeling for this joy. This is called [attaining] a peaceful mind by contemplation through arousing a desire for bliss.

6. *A peaceful mind by contemplation through skillful means* [57c4]

Again, [you may say,] "Good son. The lotus flowers blossom with the moon [in the night], work is done with the sun [during the day], someone in busi-

another phrase from the *I chiao ching*, T 12.1112a26–27:

> If there are people who are beginners in entering the Dharma, they will all attain deliverance upon hearing the preaching of the Buddha. This is analogous *to catching sight of the path by a flash of lighting in the night.*

Destroys innumerable billions of penetratingly burning evil factors 破無數億洞然之惡: I have interpreted the character 然 to stand for "burning" 燃.

The lotus flowers blossom with the moon 月開蓮華: an image from the *Mahāparinirvāṇa Sūtra*, T 12.724b5–7:

> It is analogous to the light of the *moon* being able to induce the Utpala *flower to bloom* in all its glory. The Moon Passion Samādhi is also like this.

Work is done with the sun 日興作務: another image from the *Mahāparinirvāṇa Sūtra*, T 12.661a28–29:

ness should follow his boss, painting requires glue, ceramic goods are of no use unless they are passed through fire, the blind cannot advance even one step without guidance—the same is true for practicing without the wisdom of contemplation. Universal wisdom has contemplation as its fundamental basis, and is adorned by immeasurable virtues." Thus good and skillful means, and various conditions and analogies, are used to expansively praise [the attainment of] contemplation, which arouses virtue. This is called [attaining] a peaceful mind by contemplation through the use of expedients.

7. A peaceful mind by contemplation through therapeutic means [57c10]

Again, [you could say,] "Good son. A wise person knows malice, so malice is unable to harm him. [It is like] a general who has a plan that is able to destroy his powerful enemy. If not the wind, what could twirl the clouds? If not the clouds, what could screen the heat [of the sun]? If not water, what could extinguish fire? If not fire, what could remove the darkness? An axe is used to split firewood, and a sword is used to sunder bonds. What surpasses wisdom [for healing ignorance]?" Thus good and skillful means, and various conditions and analogies, are used to expansively praise [the attainment of] contemplation, which leads to the destruction of evil. This is called [attaining] a peaceful mind by contemplation through the use of therapeutic means.

8. A peaceful mind by contemplation through the use of the supreme meaning [57c15]

Again, [you could say,] "Good son. [A collection of] the seven types of jewels in a well, and bottles and trays [of food and drink?] in a dark room, must wait for the light of day. When the sun rises, then all will be seen clearly

It is analogous to the fact that in the dark night all places of business stop all their *activity*; those who are looking for something should wait for *the light of day*. [In this way] those of the Mahāyana, though they cultivate all the samādhis in the sūtras, must wait for the sun of the *Mahāyāna Nirvāṇa Sūtra*.

Seven types of jewels in a well, and bottles and trays in a dark room, must wait for the light of day. When the sun rises, then all will be seen clearly and fully 井中七寶闇室瓶盆要待日明: this analogy seems to be from the *Mahāparinirvāṇa Sūtra*, T 12. 735b13–17, illustrating the "hiddeness" of nirvana:

> Good son. It is like a collection of *the seven jewels in a well in a dark room*. People know it is there, but cannot see it because of the darkness. A wise person who knows well about skillful means lights a great torch, brings it, and illuminates [the room] so [the jewels] can be seen. This person does not arouse the thought that the water and seven types of jewels are originally nothing but now exist [just because it can be seen now]. Nirvana is also likewise. It exists originally, and not just suitably for now.

and fully. You should, with the eye of wisdom, contemplate and know the true marks of all dharmas. You realize all dharmas through the contemplation of equality. *Prajñā-pāramitā*, the perfection of wisdom, is the greatest illumination." Thus good and skillful means, and various conditions and analogies, are used to expansively praise [the attainment of] contemplation, which leads to attaining awakened understanding. This is called [attaining] a peaceful mind by contemplation through the supreme meaning.

In this way there are eight ways to explain [the attainment of] a peaceful mind for those whose practice is based on faith.

2. Eight ways for leading those who practice based on Dharma-meditation to attain a peaceful mind [57c20–58b14]

If a person says, "I yearn for a mind that is still, for silence again after silence, 'relinquishing this and relinquishing that until I reach [the state of] non-activity.' I find no pleasure in [detailed] discriminating [learning], and find no benefit from 'sitting while pursuing' [scholastic learning]," this kind of person has the spiritual capacity of one who practices based on Dharma[-

Attaining awakened understanding 得悟解: note that the corresponding variety [4. "A peaceful mind by cessation through the supreme meaning"] uses the term "encounter thusness" 眞如; here it is "attaining awakened understanding." Until now, the same terms have been used for corresponding varieties.

I yearn for a mind that is still, for silence again after silence, relinquishing this and relinquishing that until I reach [the state of] non-activity 我樂息心默已復默損之又損之遂至於無爲: a phrase found in the forty-eighth chapter of Lao-tzu. Chan (*A Source Book on Chinese Philosophy*, 162) translates:

> The pursuit of Tao is to decrease day after day.
> *It is to decrease and further decrease until one reaches the point of taking no action.*
> No action is undertaken, and yet nothing is left undone.

The phrase also appears in the "Knowledge Wandered North" chapter of the *Chuang-tzu*. Watson (*Complete Works of Chuang-tzu*, 235) translates:

> He who practices the Way does less every day, *does less and goes on doing less, until he reaches the point where he does nothing,* does nothing and yet there is nothing that is not done.

Find no benefit from 'sitting while pursuing' 坐馳無益: a phrase from the "In the World of Men" chapter of the *Chuang-tzu*. My translation follows the interpretation given in the *Kōgi* (BT–III, 367), that "even though one is sitting, one is mentally distracted by the pursuit of verbal learning," connecting the phrase specifically to the pursuit of learning rather than to a distracted and "racing" mind in general. Watson (*Complete Works of Chuang-tzu*, 58) translates:

> Fortune and blessing gather where there is stillness. But if you do not keep still—this is what is called *sitting but racing around.* Let your ears and eyes communicate with what is inside, and put mind and knowledge on the outside.

Watson adds a note to this phrase: "The body sits but the mind continues to race."

meditation]. [As above, there are eight ways to lead those who practice based on Dharma(-meditation) to attain a peaceful mind.]

1. A peaceful mind by cessation through arousing a desire for bliss [57c23]

[For such a person,] you should explain [the practice of] cessation. [You could say,] "You should focus on internally maintaining equilibrium and not be concerned with external matters. The flow of conceptual notions that arise from contact with external objects all arise out of delusion, like a spinning wheel of fire that vanishes when the movement of the hand [holding the torch] is brought to an end. The great waves stirred up by an angry wind beat like a drum, but settle down when [the winds are] quiet. As it says in the *Vimalakīrti Sūtra*, 'Whence comes the flourishing of conditions [whereby delusions and so forth arise]? Through association with the triple world. How do you put an end to these "flourishing conditions"? Through the mind not obtaining [conditions that lead to their arising].' The *Sūtra on the Auspicious Appearances* says, 'One who attains single-mindedness has extinguished the myriad mistaken views.' Nāgārjuna says [in the *Ta chih tu lun*], 'True dharma[-teaching]s are not perverted views. When conceptual thoughts have been removed, verbal dharmas are extinguished; when all the immeasurable offences are removed, the pure mind [remains] in its constant oneness. A noble and wonderful person such as [one who has attained] this is able to perceive *prajñā*-wisdom.' The mysterious quiet 幽寂 of the

Great waves stirred up by an angry wind beat like a drum, but settle down when [the winds are] quiet 洪波鼓怒風靜則澄: although the traditional commentaries do not attribute as such, this image of "great waves stirred up by an angry wind and beating like a drum" is found in the *Laṅkāratāra Sūtra*; see the variants in T 16 484b9–11, 523b19–20, and 594c10–11.

Whence comes the flourishing of conditions? Through association with the triple world. How does one put an end to these 'flourishing conditions'? Through the mind not obtaining 何謂攀緣。謂緣三界何謂息攀緣。謂心無所得: a phrase from the *Vimalakīrti Sūtra*, T 13.a18–20. This passage has been quoted in the *Mo-ho chih-kuan* before; see the long note at 21b17–18.

One who attains single-mindedness has extinguished the myriad mistaken views 其得一心者則萬邪滅矣: almost exactly from a phrase in the *Sūtra on the Auspicious Appearances and Origins of the Prince Siddhārtha*, T 3.475a25. The context reads:

> What is that called a "monk"? The answer: a monk is one who follows the path. He abandons home and wife and children, rejects the passionate desires, severs the emotions of the six senses, maintains the precepts with inaction; this is the pure path. *One who has attained single-mindedness has extinguished the myriad mistaken views.*

This passage has been referred to above in the *Mo-ho chih-kuan*; see note at 55a2–3

True dharma[-teaching]s are not perverted views.... A noble and wonderful person such as this is able to perceive

mountains [58a] is praised by the Taoist hermits 神仙. How much more so should the wise and noble ones honor and adore the clear purity of nirvana. The *Sūtra of Stories of the Buddha* says, 'When monks are in the village, the Buddhas worry about them even if they are diligently disciplined both physically and verbally. But when monks are in the mountains, having put an end to [mundane] matters and resting in peace, the Buddhas all rejoice.' How much more so when they sit in the lotus position, fold their hands, purse their lips, hold their tongues, quietly ponder the marks [of reality], and [attain] the equilibrium and cessation at the basis of the mind and the same quiescence as the Dharma realm. Is this not what is required for the path? This alone is noble; other [ways] are unable to match it." Thus good and skillful means, and various causes and conditions and various parables and analogies, are used to expansively praise [the attainment of] cessation, which arouses a joyful mind. This is called [attaining] a peaceful mind by cessation through arousing a desire for bliss.

2. *A peaceful mind by cessation through the use of skillful means* [58a7]

If a person says, "I contemplate the marks of dharmas, but this only increases my confusion, and nothing good comes from it," you should explain cessation [to this person, as follows]. "Cessation is the plain, proper, and good field of the Dharma realm; there is no dharma that is not provided therein. Cessation is to abandon the 'flourishing conditions' [of delusion], which is [the perfection] of giving. The essence of cessation is 'non-evil'; this is [the perfection of observing the] precepts. The essence of cessation is immobile; this is [the perfection of] patience. Cessation does not involve any [distracting] mixture [of miscellaneous activity], which is [the perfection of] diligence. Cessation is determination (or "firm concentration" 決定), which is [the perfection of] dhyāna meditation. Cessation has no 'method', and there is no [substantial] 'person' who does cessation; this is [the perfection of *prajñā*] wisdom. Cessation as the cause [of enlightenment] [is to know that] there is neither cessation nor is there the lack of cessation; this is [the perfection of skillful] means. One cessation is all cessation; this is [the per-

***prajñā*-wisdom**: from verses in the *Ta chih tu lun*, T 25.190b20–23, already quoted previously by Chih-i at *Mo-ho chih-kuan* 16c15 and 21c11–12; see note under *Mo-ho chih-kuan* 16c15 for Lamotte's French translation of these verses.

Wise and noble ones 賢聖: that is, those on the three levels of erudition and ten noble stages; see Chart 1 in Volume 3.

Sūtra of Stories of the Buddha 佛話經: the *Kōgi* (BT–III, 369) points out that this text is "no longer extant in the canon."

I contemplate the marks of dharmas 我觀法相: Ikeda (*Gendaigoyaku*, 301) translates, "I contemplate according to the teachings ..."

Nothing good comes from it 善法不明: lit., "good dharmas are not clarified."

fection of] vows. Cessation as the cessation of passions and cessation as the cessation of [mistaken] views is [the perfection of] power. This cessation is neither different nor distinct from the cessation of the Buddha; this is [the perfection of] wisdom. Cessation includes all dharmas; it is the secret treasury [of the Buddhas]. Just rest peacefully in cessation; why use other methods of cultivation?" Thus good and skillful means, and various conditions and analogies, are used to give rise to good roots. This is [attaining] a peaceful mind by cessation through the use of expedients.

3. A peaceful mind by cessation through the use of therapeutic means [58a17]

If [a person] says, "I contemplate the marks of dharmas, but am distracted and lethargic, and cannot remove [the passions and delusions]," you should explain cessation [to this person as follows]. "Cessation has much power. Cessation is a wall-like concentration: the eight winds of evil notions cannot enter therein. Cessation is like pure water: it washes away the eight perversions such as covetousness and lust. It is like the sun, whose rising dissipates the morning dew. Cessation is great compassion; like an angry parent who also has pity, it is able to overcome angry bitterness. Cessation is a great spell; it can remove all ignorance and doubt. Cessation is Buddhahood; it is the path for destroying and removing all obstacles [to enlightenment]. Like the *agada* panacea it universally heals all [disease], and it is like a wonderful and good doctor who can magically charm a withered [person] and raise the dead." Thus good and skillful means, and various conditions and analogies,

... this is [the perfection of *prajñā*] wisdom: this completes an analysis of cessation in terms of the ten perfections *(pāramitā)*, from *dāna* to *jñāna*.

Wall-like concentration 壁定: this compound brings to mind the ambiguous binome "wall-gazing" 壁觀 associated with Bodhidharma, but is unrelated. See my article on "Daruma to 'hekigan' to bonkan gōseigo" 「ダルマと『壁観』と梵漢合成語 [Bodhidharma, wall-contemplation, and Sanskrit-Chinese mixed binomes], in 駒澤大學仏教学部論集 35 (2004): 53–68.

Eight winds of evil notions cannot enter therein 八風惡覺所不能入: the "eight winds" are the eight happy and unhappy conditions that agitate the human mind: benefit 利, decline 衰, ruin 毀, honor 誉, praise 稱, slander 譏, suffering 苦, and pleasure 樂.

Eight perversions such as covetousness and lust 貪婬八倒: usually there are four "perversions"—the four perverted views that the world is permanent, blissful, having selfhood, and pure—but here this seems to be just a general number for the "many" passions and delusions.

Wonderful and good doctor who can magically charm a withered [person] and raise the dead 妙良醫呪枯起死: I am not sure if Chih-i really means there is a doctor who can raise the dead, or if this is just hyperbole, but there you have it.

are used to lead people to destroy evil. This is [attaining] a peaceful mind by cessation through the use of therapeutic means.

4. A peaceful mind by cessation through the use of the supreme meaning [58a24]

If a person says, "Even when I contemplate thoroughly, I do not attain awakening," you should explain cessation [to this person as follows]: "Cessation is the essence of truth; even when illuminating [something] it is constantly quiescent. Cessation [happens] in accordance with conditions; it constantly illumines even though it is quiescent. Cessation is a cessation that is not cessation; it both hinders [passions] and illumines [delusions]. Cessation is the mother of Buddhas; it is father and mother. Cessation is the teacher of Buddhas, the body of the Buddhas, the eye of the Buddha, the physical marks of the Buddha, the treasury of the Buddha, the dwelling place of the Buddha. There is nothing it does not include." This **[58b]** refers to [attaining] a peaceful mind by cessation through the supreme meaning.

5. A peaceful mind by contemplation through arousing a desire for bliss [58b1]

If a person says, "Cessation makes me depressed, and does not please me," you should explain contemplation and the pondering of the principles of the path [to this person as follows]: "The seven components of awakening include the faculty for discernment 擇覺支, the eightfold Path includes 'correct views' 正見, and the six perfections includes *prajñā*-wisdom; so [contemplation] is the main and guiding center of Dharma teachings. Furthermore, 'correct awakening' 正覺, 'great awakening' 大覺, and 'universal awakening' 遍覺, are all synonymous with the wisdom of contemplation 觀慧. It should be known that the wisdom of contemplation is the greatest of noble and sublime [wisdom]. Thus, this is expansively praised." This refers to [attaining] a peaceful mind by contemplation through the arousing a desire for bliss.

6. A peaceful mind by contemplation through the use of skillful means [58b6]

Suppose you explain, "The diligent cultivation of contemplation is able to

Cessation is the essence of truth; even when illuminating it is constantly quiescent 止即體眞照而常寂: this is the perspective of emptiness; see the discussion of threefold cessation earlier in the *Mo-ho chih-kuan*, 24a2–b5.

Cessation in accordance with conditions; it constantly illumines even though it is quiescent 止即隨緣寂而常照: this is the perspective of conventional existence.

Cessation is a cessation that is not cessation; it both hinders and illumines 止即不止止雙遮雙照: this is the perspective of the Middle.

give rise to faith, [keeping of] the precepts, concentration, wisdom, liberation, and the knowledge and insight of liberation. If you know the disease and are aware of the medicine, then you can proceed boldly with teaching and saving others. Even if you encounter all good [practices], there is none that surpasses contemplation." This refers to [attaining] a peaceful mind by contemplation through the use of expedients.

7. A peaceful mind by contemplation through the use of therapeutic means [58b9]

[Suppose you explain,] "Contemplation is able to destroy the darkness, and is able to illuminate the path. It is able to remove malice, and allows you to attain [Dharma] treasure. It tilts over a mountain of deviant views, and depletes a sea of passions. Such is the power of concentration." This refers to [attaining] a peaceful mind by contemplation through the use of therapeutic means.

8. A peaceful mind by contemplation through the use of the supreme meaning [58b11]

[Suppose you explain,] "When you contemplate with the method of contemplation, there is nothing that is attained. If you wish to have your thoughts emptied and reveal that which is obscure, you should simply and diligently practice contemplation, thus exposing, signifying, awakening to, and entering [the path]." This refers to using the supreme meaning to [attain] a peaceful mind by contemplation.

In this way there are eight ways to expound [the attainment of] a peaceful mind for those whose practice is based on Dharma[-meditation].

Again, there are people whose capacity is variable, revolving from time to time. The *Abhidharma-vibhāṣa-śāstra* clarifies turning the dull into the sharp, and the *Ch'eng-shih lun* clarifies that as one repeatedly practices, one becomes sharp. These texts discuss being dull or sharp at the beginning or

If you wish to have your thoughts emptied and reveal that which is obscure, you should simply and diligently practice contemplation, thus exposing, signifying, awakening to, and entering [the path] 心慮虛豁朦朧欲開但當勤觀開示悟入: the last phrase is a famous one from the *Lotus Sūtra*, T 9.7a22–28, which speaks of "exposing, signifying, awakening, and entering the knowledge and insight of the Buddha."

Turning the dull into the sharp 轉鈍爲利: the traditional commentaries do not identify any specific passages in the *Abhidharma-vibhāṣa-śāstra* or the *Ch'eng-shih lun* for this idea; perhaps it just indicates a general teaching (see BT–III, 373).

As one repeatedly practices, one becomes sharp 數習則利: as with the previous phrase, the traditional commentaries do not identify any specific passages in the *Ch'eng-shih lun* (see BT–III, 373).

end [of practice], and explain how this is not attained [in the same way] at one time.

Now I will clarify how the mental activities of sentient beings are variable. [Sometimes] at one moment they are dull, and at another moment they are sharp. This happens spontaneously and naturally, and not because of a change in [innate] capability or because of repeated practice. At times you practice contemplation but do not become adept, [but at other times] attain awakening [just] by hearing [the Dharma]. Or at times you hear for a long time but do not understand, and [at other times] you reach an assurance [or determination] after pondering for some time. Therefore you should discuss [attaining] a peaceful mind in terms of these turnings of capabilities.

If one whose practice is based on Dharma[-meditation] turns into one whose practice is based on faith, you should use eight variations on the *siddhāntas* [as explained above] in accordance with these turnings of capabilities to impart a peaceful mind. If one whose practice is based on faith turns into one whose practice is based on Dharma[-meditation], you should use eight variations on the *siddhāntas* [as explained above] in accordance with these turnings of capabilities to impart a peaceful mind. If this meaning is understood, you can explain both broadly and in detail. If you include both the variable and non-variable cases, there are all together thirty-two ways of [explaining cessation and contemplation for the sake of attaining] a peaceful mind.

2. *Attaining a Peaceful Mind by Practicing Oneself* [58b23]

[Attaining] a peaceful mind by practicing by oneself means that you should thoroughly contemplate your own thoughts.

1. Practice based on Dharma-meditation [58b24]

What do you seek? If you wish to still delusions and quiet your thoughts and conceptions, you should try the practice based on Dharma[-meditation]. [1] If you seek to hear the exposition [of the Dharma teachings] and wish to become adept at getting to the bottom of your ignorance, you should try the practice based on faith. Seeking quiescence, you come [to know] that delusions arise from your thoughts, and by stilling your thoughts all delusions are quieted. [2] If you wish to illuminate and know, you should get to know the basis of the mind. The basis of the mind is not dualistic; that is, just like

How this is not attained [in the same way] at one time 不得一時: the context is ambiguous, and I have taken liberties with my translation in an attempt to make some sense of the passage.

all phenomena, all are empty. This is [attaining] a peaceful mind by self-practice through arousing the desire for bliss.

[3] If you broadly differentiate [the immeasurable] thoughts and phenomena in your mind [**58c**], [you can see that] there is no arising of even a thin hair's worth of good, such as faith, mindfulness, or diligence. However, if you arrest and halt [mental activity] so that there is no movement, good and meritorious factors will arise out of the tranquility. [4] If when you arrest and halt [mental activity] you gradually sink into the tranquility without making any progress in [attaining insight or virtue such as] patience, you should make deliberate calculations and discursive evaluations to whip yourself into arousing [contemplation].

[5] If you cannot concentrate from thought to thought, like a sweaty horse running wild, you should use [the practice of] cessation to heal and control the galloping [thoughts]. [6] If the quietude and silence is futile and you just feel sleepy, then you should cultivate contemplation to break through the dark confines [of your mental block].

[7] If you cultivate cessation for a long time without achieving anything, then you should cultivate contemplation. Contemplate all dharmas as unobstructed and undifferentiated, calmly clarify and sharpen [your understanding], and gradually attain an awakening that is like emptiness. [8] If the dark obstacles are not removed even after cultivating contemplation for a long time, then switch to cultivating cessation. Stop all conditioned thoughts 緣念 [or, "thoughts focused on objects"], for there is no one who does [the thinking] and no object [corresponding to the thought]; the thinker and the thought are quiescent. This gives rise to the wisdom of emptiness.

Such are the eight varieties of cultivating practice by oneself for those whose practice is based on Dharma[-meditation], the good and skillful means which lead to the attainment of a peaceful mind.

2. Practice based on faith [58c10]

[The attainment of] a peaceful mind by those whose practice is based on faith [is as follows]. [1] If you wish to hear of a quiescence that is like Mt. Sumeru, which does not quiver at the winds from the eight directions, then you should attend to cessation. [2] If you wish to hear of the benefits of

Contemplate all dharmas as unobstructed and undifferentiated 觀一切法無礙無異: or, "in contemplating all dharmas, be unobstructed and without making differentiations."

Calmly clarify and sharpen 怗怗明利: the meaning is ambiguous; I follow the interpretation of the *Kōgi*, BT–III, 375.

Does not quiver at the winds from the eight directions 不畏八動: lit., "eight movements"; my translation is based on the interpretation in the *Kōgi*, BT–III, 376, that this phrase means "not afraid of the violent winds from the eight directions."

contemplation, which destroys all passionate afflictions like the sun removes the darkness, then you should attend to contemplation. [3] If you attend to contemplation too much, like the sun scorching young sprouts, then you should attend to cessation, which moisturizes with the water of concentration. [4] Or, if you attend to concentrated meditation [cessation] for too long, like when sprouts overgrow and do not allow [new sprouts] to arise, then you should attend to contemplation and let the wind and the sun [of insight] arouse movement and lead good dharmas to appear. [5] Or, when your conceptual notions [and perceptions] are running amuck, and even a single thought does not remain steady, then you should attend to cessation and subdue your distracted thoughts. [6] Or, if you sink into a dark and obscure mist of seated [meditation], then you should attend to contemplation that destroys a deep lethargy. [7] Or, if you attend to cessation and it is amply successful, then you should attend exclusively to cessation. [8] Or, if you attend to contemplation and it resonates, then you should attend exclusively to contemplation.

Such are the eight varieties of cultivating practice by oneself for those whose practice is based on faith, the skillful means [which lead to the attainment] of a peaceful mind.

3. Summary [58c19]

If we take into account those who turn from one whose practice is based on Dharma[-meditation] to one whose practice is based on faith, plus those who turn from practice based on faith to practice based on Dharma[-meditation], plus all the expedient and skillful applications [of cessation and/or contemplation] for all appropriate situations [to attain a peaceful mind], there are thirty-two varieties for those who practice themselves. [As outlined above, the category of] saving others also has thirty-two [varieties]. Together that makes sixty-four [varieties of ways to attain a] peaceful mind.

3. Attaining a Peaceful Mind in Terms of Mutual Support [58c22]

Again, [practice based on] faith and Dharma[-meditation] are not independent of each other. "Hearing" and "pondering" [that is, learning and meditation] mutually support each other.

[1] Those whose practice is based on Dharma[-meditation] can, through hearing one phrase [of the Buddhist teachings] accomplish a profoundly peaceful quiescence, remove all their dream-like delusions, and return to their sitting and pondering with joy in their hearts. [2] Again, upon hearing of cessation, they can return to further pondering and give rise to meditative concentration. [3] Again, upon hearing of cessation, they can return to pondering and destroy all deluded thoughts. [4] Again, upon hearing of

cessation, they can return to further pondering and attain [full] translucent awareness of their desired awakening. [5] Again, upon hearing of contemplation, they can return to further pondering with joy in their hearts. [6–8] Again, upon hearing of contemplation, they can return to further pondering and give rise to good [dharmas], destroy evil [dharmas], and attain their desired awakening, as outlined above. This is "practice based on Dharma[-meditation]" that consists of little hearing [that is, learning or studying] and much pondering [that is, meditative practice], but that does not mean that it does not involve any hearing [and learning] at all.

Those whose practice is based on faith [with a focus on hearing, learning, or studying], though sitting erect [in meditation], may not experience delight while pondering the quiescence of extinction, **[59a]** but after arising [from meditation] and hearing of cessation, may enjoy the sweet bliss [of awakening]. Or, when sitting erect, they may not be able to arouse good [dharmas] even though pondering good thoughts, but after arising and hearing of cessation, their faith in the precepts and diligence doubles or increases even further. Or, when sitting erect and [attempting to] subdue evil [dharmas] they may not be able to remove the evil [dharmas], but after arising and hearing of cessation they destroy and extinguish such distractions. Or, when sitting erect and [pondering] the true [emptiness] they may not be able to realize the true, but after arising and hearing of cessation they fully attain the quiescence of awakening. This is practice based on faith, which consists of little sitting [in meditation] and much hearing [and studying], but that does not mean that it does not involve any pondering [in meditation] at all.

The earlier analysis was focused exclusively on spiritual capacities. Now we have analyzed the mutual support among these spiritual capacities. We could also discuss variations with regard to turning or not turning [from one type of practice to another] with regard to the mutual support between them. This would result in thirty-two varieties of [ways to attain] a peaceful mind. Since there are also thirty-two varieties [if we analyzed the category of] saving others in terms of their mutual support, this gives a total of sixty-four. Along with [the sixty-four varieties] discussed above, there are one hundred and twenty-eight varieties of [ways to attain] a peaceful mind.

3. Final Summary [59a8]

The mind 心地 [or, "the basis of the mind"] is difficult to pacify; if inimical you will suffer, and if congenial you will have bliss. Now, let us discuss the pacification [of the mind] in accordance with its tendencies. For example it is like nourishment—we eat and drink appropriate to our physical bodies in order to maintain our lives. Nourishing the Dharma body is also like this—

cessation is drink and contemplation is food. Medicine is also like this. There are round pills and there is powdered medication 散; some is used to get rid of a fever and some is used to remedy the chills. [It is the same] for healing the disease of ignorance—cessation is like a round pill [for subduing the heat of passions], and contemplation cures distraction 散 [like powdered medication]. Again, it is like the teaching of Yin and Yang. Yang corresponds to the wind and the sun; Yin corresponds to the clouds and the rain. If there is too much rain, vegetation becomes overly ripe; if there is too much sunlight, the vegetation is scorched. Yin is like concentration [meditation or cessation], and Yang is like wisdom [contemplation]. Those who are one-sidedly unbalanced with regard to wisdom or concentration cannot perceive Buddha nature. That is why it is important to harmonize the eight varieties [of ways to attain a peaceful mind].

There is a type of meditation master 禪師 who exclusively utilizes cessation-type practice and does not allow for the practice of contemplation. Such a person quotes a verse that says, "Thinking and thinking, one follows one's own thoughts. Thinking and thinking, one brings suffering to oneself. To still this [conceptual] thinking is the path. As long as there are [conceptual] thoughts, one cannot perceive [the path]." There is also a type of meditation master who exclusively utilizes the practice of contemplation and does not allow for the practice of cessation. Such a person quotes a verse that says, "Stopping and stopping, one brings about cessation; this is darkness without any support. The stopping of cessation is the path. One encounters the principle [of reality] through the insight of contemplation." Both of these types of teachers follow only one of the methods for realizing [enlightenment], and teach other people on the basis of the benefit they have received from [their one-sided practice]. Those who study [under them] are not aware of their [one-sided] intentions. [It is like the story in the *Mahāparinirvāṇa Sūtra*,] "one who exclusively drinks milk will have difficulty getting a drink

Perceiving the Buddha nature 見佛性: this a quality of the Buddha alone, and not even of bodhisattvas. See the *Mahāparinirvāṇa Sūtra*, T 12.767b8–15, which has been quoted frequently by Chih-i above in the *Mo-ho chih-kuan*.

Thinking and thinking, one follows one's own thoughts. Thinking and thinking, one brings suffering to oneself. To still this [conceptual] thinking is the path. As long as there are [conceptual] thoughts, one cannot perceive [the path] 思思徒自思。思思徒自苦。息思即是道。有思終不覩: the source of this quote is unknown, but it sounds similar to some modern Zen stereotypes and sayings.

Stopping and stopping, one brings about cessation; this is darkness without any support. The stopping of cessation is the path. One encounters the principle [of reality] through the insight of contemplation 止止徒自止。昏闇無所以。止止即是道。觀觀得會理: again, the source of this phrase is unknown. See the traditional commentaries in BT–III, 382–83.

[of cream], not to mention ghee." If people rely exclusively [on either cessation or contemplation, or on only one teaching or practice] to attain understanding, then what why did the Buddha offer such a variety of teachings? The heavens are not always clear; a doctor does not rely exclusively on powdered medicine; you do not always eat rice. The mundane world is not [exclusivistic] like that, how much less so the transmundane world! In this way there are sixty-four varieties [of ways to attain a peaceful mind]—in accordance with capabilities, in accordance with the disease—for each of [the categories of] self-practice and saving others [for a total of one hundred and twenty-eight]. If you add the three types of cessation and contemplation, this gives us three hundred and eighty-four [varieties]. Also, the single-minded practice of cessation and contemplation each have sixty-four varieties [for another one hundred and twenty-eight varieties], for a total of five hundred and twelve [varieties for attaining a peaceful mind].

The [first] three types of *siddhāntas* involve [ways to attain] a peaceful mind in this world. Since it is like being cured by a doctor of this world, [the disease,] though healed, may recur. The one [final] *siddhānta* [of supreme meaning] involves a peaceful mind that transcends the mundane world. Since the Tathāgata does the healing, it is final and ultimate, and [the disease] does not recur. In this way the ways of the worldly and the transworldly are mutually perfected and manifested together.

There is no peaceful mind apart from the threefold truth. There is no way [to attain] a peaceful mind **[59b]** apart from cessation-and-contemplation. If your mind finds peace in the [threefold] truth [through the practice of cessation-and-contemplation], then one phrase is sufficient [for realizing

One who exclusively drinks milk will have difficulty getting a drink [of cream], not to mention ghee 一向服乳。漿猶難得況復醍醐: Chan-jan (BT–III, 382–83) refers to a story in the *Mahāparinirvāṇa Sūtra*, T 12.621c12–24. Although the story contains the same phrase that Chih-i uses, the point of the story seems quite different:

> The Buddha said to Kāśyapa, it is like a rich man who had many cows. Though they were of many colors, they were of the same herd.... This great rich man raised these cows, and did not seek to have any milk and curds but only ghee. He said, "I will now establish my holdings in all directions to attain this [ghee]. Ghee is called the greatest flavor in the world. But I have no vessels or facilities or a place to keep the milk." He discussed it with others, saying, "There are skins for keeping [the milk], and though there is thus a way to keep it, we do not know how to stir it [in order to make ghee]. *It will be difficult to attain a drink [of cream], not to mention the next stage* of curds." Then the hoodlums, in order to obtain ghee, added water [to the milk]. Because they added so much water, the milk, curds, and ghee was all lost. Ordinary [ignorant] people are like this....

The [first] three types of *siddhāntas* 三悉檀: that is, the worldly, individual, and therapeutic *siddhāntas* or methods of teaching.

this attainment]. If you do not find peace in this way, then skillfully utilize various means [as explained above] to lead your thoughts to attain peace. You cannot catch a bird with a net that has only one "eye" or "mesh," but it is one "eye" or "mesh" of the net that catches the bird. The mental activities of sentient beings are varied and not the same; at times many people have the same thoughts, and at times one person has many various thoughts. As it is for one person, so it is for many, and as it is for many people, so it is for one. Therefore we should spread the mesh of the Dharma net widely, so that the bird of mental activities can be caught [and controlled].

[end of fascicle five, part one]

You cannot catch a bird with a net that has only one "eye" or "mesh," but it is one "eye" or "mesh" of the net that catches the bird 一目之羅不能得鳥得鳥者羅之一目: this may be a classical saying or reference, but I was not able to identify it as such. A general Google search gave the *Mo-ho chih-kuan* as the source of the saying.

4. The Universal Deconstruction of Dharmas [59b14–86a9]

THE FOURTH [MODE OF CONTEMPLATION] is the universal deconstruction [or destruction] of dharmas.

[As for dharmas,] Dharma-nature is pure, neither merged nor scattered, beyond words [and conceptions], and beyond discursive thought. [Dharmas and Dharma-nature] are neither destroyed nor not destroyed. How can we speak, then, of their "destruction" [or "deconstruction"]?

Sentient beings have many perversions, and little that is not perversion. Destroying perversions leads to [attaining] that which is not perverted. Therefore we speak of [and aim to attain] the universal deconstruction of [undesirable] dharmas.

In the above [section we expounded on] the good and skillful means for a peaceful mind for the disclosing and arousing of concentration and wisdom. [If these instructions were successfully applied,] there should be no need for further [practice involving] destruction or deconstruction [of dharmas]. If, however, you have not yet achieved rapport [with the previous mode of contemplation and its resultant attainment of concentration and wisdom], you should use the wisdom based on the meditative concentration that you have achieved to exhaustively purify yourself. Therefore we speak of "destroying" [or "deconstructing" undesirable dharmas].

The universal deconstruction (destruction) of dharmas 破法遍: or, "the complete deconstruction of dharmas." Although the term "deconstruction" fits well in many cases, there are many places in this section and others where a more literal "destroying" is fitting. The character 破 implies more of a "grinding down," not a total annihilation or destruction. Another advantage of the term "deconstruction" is that it implies the possibility, even the necessity, of "reconstruction," an implication also emphasized in T'ien-t'ai teachings of the role of reaffirming "conventionality" after the deconstructive process of realizing emptiness.

Here "dharma" is used in lowercase as it refers to the phenomena of worldly experiences.

Note also that this is the longest and most complicated section in the *Mo-ho chih-kuan*, taking up 27 pages in the Taishō canon, though one can debate whether or not it is the most "important" section. As Chih-i himself notes later, this section focuses on the method of the Shared Teachings, with an emphasis on the idea of emptiness and non-arising.

Beyond words [and conceptions] 言語道斷, **and beyond discursive thought** 心行處滅: these last two phrases have been quoted by Chih-i many times in the *Mo-ho chih-kuan* above; see Glossary for details.

Destroying perversions leads to that which is not perverted 破顛倒令不顛倒: that is, virtue, enlightenment, awakening, correct views, and so forth; technically speaking, the four correct (non-perverted) perceptions of the world as transient, full of pain, lacking selfhood, and impure, instead of the four perverted views that the world of phenomenal things is permanent, full of pleasure, having Selfhood, and pure.

The destruction of [undesirable] dharmas requires a dependence on many methods, or "gates" 門. The explanation of these gates is not the same in all sūtras. [1] Some use "words and letters" as the gate. The *Pañcaviṃśati Sūtra*, for example, clarifies the "gate of forty-two letters" [of the alphabet]. [2] Some use "contemplative practice" as the gate. The *Ta chih tu lun*, for example, clarifies that bodhisattvas cultivate three kinds of samādhi as the condition to realize the true aspect of all dharmas. [3] Some use "wisdom" as the gate. The *Lotus Sūtra* refers to "This gate of wisdom." [4] Some use "prin-

The explanation of these gates is not the same in all sūtras 經說門不同: or, "sūtras explain that these gates or methods are not all the same." Chih-i proceeds to identify four "gates" or methods—1, verbal teachings, 2. contemplative practice, 3. wisdom, and 4. principle—that correspond to other fourfold T'ien-t'ai categories: the Fourfold Teachings (Tripitaka, Shared, Distinct, Perfect); the fourfold categories of arising-and-perishing, non-arising, immeasurable, and actionless; the four possibilities of the tetralemma (a, b, both, and neither); the four lines of the *Middle Treatise* verse (conditioned arising, emptiness, conventional, Middle); the four possibilities of existence [naïve realism], emptiness [nihilism], both, and neither; and so forth. See Chart 1 in Swanson, *Foundations*, 358–59, and Chart 3 in Volume 3.

Gate of forty-two letters 四十二字門: see the *Pañcaviṃśati Sūtra*, T 8.256a–b, and the *Ta chih tu lun*, T 25.684b–687c, where the wisdom of realizing "formlessness" is expressed symbolically in terms of the forty-two letters or syllables of the Siddham alphabet, from *a* 阿 to *ḍha* 荼. See Ikeda (*Kenkyūchūshaku*, 504–5) for a complete list of the syllables and their corresponding Chinese characters.

Bodhisattvas cultivate three kinds of samādhi as the condition to realize the true aspect of all dharmas 菩薩修三三昧緣諸法實相: see the long section in the *Ta chih tu lun*, T 25.206c–208a (Lamotte, *Le Traité* 3, 1220–32), which contains a discussion of the three types of liberation, wisdom, and samādhi in terms of emptiness 空, formlessness 無相, and actionlessness 無作. Part of this section (207c4–18) reads:

> In the Mahāyāna, a single dharma is explained in three ways because it functions due to causes and conditions. [1] To contemplate all dharmas as empty is called "emptiness." [2] There are no marks to grasp within this emptiness; thus this emptiness is called "formlessness." [3] There is no [substantial] activity occurring within the formlessness of this triple world; thus this formlessness is called "actionlessness." It is like a walled city that has three gates. A person cannot physically enter through all three gates at the same time. But if a person enters through one gate, one [realizes] the true aspect of all dharmas and [enters] the city of nirvana. This "city" has three gates: emptiness, formlessness, and actionlessness.

This gate of wisdom" 其智慧門: a phrase from the opening chapter on "Means" in the *Lotus Sūtra*, T 9.5b26. Hurvtiz (*Lotus Sūtra*, 22) translates the context:

> At that time, the World-Honored One rose serenely from his samādhi and proclaimed to Śāriputra, "The Buddhas' wisdom is profound and incalculable. *The gateways of their wisdom* are hard to understand and hard to enter, so that no voice-hearer or pratyekabuddha can know them."

ciple" as the gate. The *Pañcaviṃśati Sūtra* clarifies that non-arising dharmas neither come nor go; [realizing] this is Buddhahood.

It is through [depending on] the gate of the [verbal] teachings that you penetrate [the gate of] contemplative [practice]. It is through the gate of contemplative [practice] that you penetrate [the gate of] wisdom. It is through the gate of wisdom that you penetrate [the gate of] the principle [of reality]. To what do you penetrate through the gate of the principle [of reality]? Teaching, contemplation, and wisdom all depend on the principle [of reality], so if that which depends [on principle] are "gates," then how can it be that [the principle] on which they depend is not a "gate"? Even though there is no place to which one penetrates [beyond the gate of "principle"], it ultimately penetrates [everything] universally. Therefore [the principle of reality] is the sublime and subtle "gate."

1. General Exposition of the Universal Destruction of Dharmas in Terms of "Non-Arising" [59b27–62a22]

1. Exposition of Non-Arising in Terms of the Teachings of Various Sūtras [59b27]

Here I will expound only on the [first] gate of [verbal] "teaching" [of non-arising] and will leave aside the other three gates.

The four gates in terms of the Tripitaka Teachings involves first

It is curious that a quote from the *Lotus Sūtra* is used to illustrate this third gate, which corresponds to the Distinct Teachings, whereas a quote from the *Pañcaviṃśati Sūtra* is used to illustrate the fourth "gate," which corresponds to the Perfect Teaching.

Non-arising dharmas neither come nor go; [realizing] this is Buddhahood 無生法無來無去即是佛: an almost exact quote from the *Pañcaviṃśati Sūtra*, T 8.421b29. This section is included in the *Ta chih tu lun* at T 25.744c18–19, The full context reads:

> The Buddhas do not come nor go, nor is there any place to which they arrive. Why? The suchness of all dharmas is to be immobile. The suchness of all dharmas is Buddhahood. Good son. *The non-arising of dharmas neither comes nor goes. The non-arising of dharmas is Buddhahood.*

… therefore [the principle of reality] is the sublime and subtle gate 是妙門也: the "gates" of teaching, contemplative practice, and wisdom are all means to attain the realization of the principle of reality, and in turn are dependent on the principle of reality for their meaning. In a sense realizing the principle is the "goal" and is thus different from the first three "gates," but as the basis of the first three, "the principle of reality" is also a "gate" or "method," part of the process of realizing Buddhahood. The difficulty of translating this passage is compounded by Chih-i's multivalent use of the terms such as "gate" 門, "dependence" 依, and "penetrating" 通, which play on both the literal meaning "gate" or "passing through these gates," and its extended meaning of "method" or "teaching."

[deconstructing or] destroying mistaken views, and then destroying deluded attitudes, and then destroying both [mistaken views and deluded attitudes].

The four gates in terms of the Shared Teachings also first involves destroying mistaken views, and then destroying **[59c]** deluded attitudes, and then destroying both. However, this involves destroying [only] the four categories of delusions, so one cannot say that it is "universal."

The four gates in terms of the Distinct Teachings is the gradual severance of the five levels of delusions. This is universal in vertical or lineal terms, but not universal in horizontal or lateral terms.

These [first three of the Fourfold Teachings] are not the content of what I am expounding now [in the *Mo-ho chih-kuan*]. Now [I am expounding the Perfect Teaching, which concerns] that which is inconceivable: [the teaching that] one object includes all objects, and one thought includes all thoughts. All dharmas, whether viewed horizontally or vertically, are all included in the workings of the mind. By destroying [undesirable] thoughts, all [undesirable dharmas] are destroyed. Therefore this can be called "universal." The destruction by other gates [and Teachings] is not universal, so I will not expound on them here.

The four gates of the Perfect Teaching are able to destroy [undesirable dharmas] universally, that is, [the four possibilities of] Being, nothingness, both Being and nothingness, and neither Being nor nothingness. Now I will set aside three of the possibilities and depend [for my discussion] on the [second] approach of "emptiness" or "non-arising" [that is, the Shared Teachings]. One is able to penetrate cessation-and-contemplation through the gate of "non-arising," and attain both the causes and result [of Buddhahood].

1. The causes of Buddhahood [59c8]

Again, one is able to manifest [the truth of] non-arising, and employ the light [of the true way to its full extent]. Why? Cessation-and-contemplation is the

Four gates 四門: here, as we shall see below, the "four gates" refers to the four possibilities of the tetralemma, though by extension these four possibilities correspond to the various meanings of "four gates" outlined above.

This is universal in vertical or lineal terms, but not universal in horizontal or lateral terms 斯乃竪遍横不遍: that is, it covers all the vertical levels of attainment, but not necessarily all of the delusions or problems contained horizontally in these levels.

All included in the workings of the mind 悉趣於心: or, "always tend toward mental activity."

Being, nothingness, both Being and nothingness, and neither Being nor nothingness 有門無門。亦有亦無門。非有非無門: again, these four possibilities correspond to the four categories of arising-and-perishing, non-arising, immeasurable, and actionless. See Chart 1 in Swanson, *Foundations*, 358–59.

practice and "non-arising" is the teaching; cultivating this practice by depending on this teaching allows one to penetrate and attain the "forbearance [from realizing] the non-arising of dharmas" (*anutpattika-dharma-kṣānti*), which includes all the levels of the causes [for attaining Buddhahood].

The *Vimalakīrti Sūtra* speaks of thirty-two bodhisattvas who each explain [their interpretation of] the "gate of non-duality." All of these bodhisattvas realized their level [of understanding] through the gate [of the teaching of emptiness], with "non-arising" as the primary focus.

The *Pañcaviṃśati Sūtra* clarifies the teaching of the letter *a* [which symbolizes emptiness], that is, that all phenomena from the beginning do not [substantially] arise. This shows that the gate of non-arising penetrates [the practice of] cessation-and-contemplation and leads to the attainment of the causes [of Buddhahood]. This meaning should be perceived here. Cessation-and-contemplation enlightens the gate of non-arising. The Dharma does not manifest itself; it must be disseminated by people. It is when people undertake practice that the Dharma teachings are made manifest, the teaching of non-arising is made [clear and] unobstructed both horizontally and vertically, you have penetrating understanding of everything you touch, and you perfect the meaning of the teaching. [This process or attainment] is analogous to a person in this world who goes in and out of a gate; the gate evinces splendor in accordance with the status of that person. The subject of the analogy [that is, the teaching of non-arising] should be understood in terms of the object of the analogy.

2. The fruit of Buddhahood [59c17]

[Scriptural evidence for] penetrating the gate [of non-arising] in terms of the fruit [of Buddhahood is as follows:] The *Mahāparinirvāṇa Sūtra* says that "*nir* means 'not' and *vāṇa* means 'arise.' Thus 'non-arising' is the meaning of great nirvana."

Thirty-two bodhisattvas who each explain [their interpretation of] the "gate of non-duality": see the famous section in the chapter on "The Gate of Non-Duality" in the *Vimalakīrti Sūtra*, T 14.550b29–551c27, where various bodhisattvas give their interpretation of "non-duality," finishing with Mañjuśrī and leading up to Vimalakīrti's dramatic answer where he responds with a deafening silence.

Teaching of the letter a 阿字門: see the section of the *Pañcaviṃśati Sūtra*, T 8.256a, mentioned in the note above on the forty-two letters of the Siddham alphabet.

The subject of the analogy should be understood in terms of the object of the analogy 能譬既然所譬可解: that is, as Ikeda (*Gendaigoyakuhen*, 311) paraphrases, the true stature and meaning of the teaching of "non-arising" is made clear in proportion to the level and understanding of the one who practices, thus creating causes for attaining Buddhahood.

"*Nir* means 'not' and *vāṇa* means

It also says that "the two dharmas of concentration and wisdom are able to bring great benefit, up to [the attainment of] *bodhi*-wisdom."

The *Pañcaviṃśati Sūtra* says that "non-arising dharmas neither come nor go. [Realizing] the non-arising of dharmas is Buddhahood."

The *Lotus Sūtra* says,

> The Buddha himself dwells in Mahāyāna,
> And in accordance with his attainments
> Is adorned with the power of concentration and wisdom,
> With which he saves sentient beings.

Thus I have quoted from three scriptures in order to show that [the teaching of non-arising contains] the meaning of the fruit [of Buddhahood].

Cessation-and-contemplation also is able to manifest the fruit [of Buddhahood]. The fruit does not manifest itself [spontaneously]; rather, the fruit [of Buddhahood] is completed through practice. The completion of the fruit [of Buddhahood] means the completion of all things. "Lofty and majestic, like the brightness of the moon in the midst of the stars" "illuminating

'arise.' Thus 'non-arising' is the meaning of great nirvana 般涅言不。槃者言生。不生之義名大涅槃: a rather free paraphrase of a passage from the *Mahāparinirvāṇa Sūtra*, T 12.758c18–23:

> *Nir* means "not" and *vāṇa* means extinction, so non-extinction is the meaning of nirvana. *Vana* also means "covering," so "uncovered" is the meaning of nirvana. *Vāṇa* also means "coming and going," so nirvana means "neither coming nor going."…

I have my doubts about the validity of this etymological explanation.

The two dharmas of concentration and wisdom are able to bring great benefit, up to *bodhi*-wisdom 定慧二法能大利益乃至菩提: see the *Mahāparinirvāṇa Sūtra*, T 12.793c–794a, which lists a number of bodhisattvas who are characterized by both concentration and wisdom. See especially line 793c24: "Bodhisattva-mahāsattvas are endowed with two characteristics that enable them to have great benefit: one is concentration and the second is wisdom." The context also refers to the "samādhi of emptiness."

Non-arising dharmas neither come nor go. [Realizing] the non-arising of dharmas is Buddhahood 無生法無來無去無生法即是佛: see the *Pañcaviṃśati Sūtra*, T 8.421b29; the same passage was quoted a few lines above (59b24).

The Buddha himself … saves sentient beings: from the second chapter of the *Lotus Sūtra*, T 9.8a23–24. Hurvitz (*Lotus Sūtra*, 34 [33]) translates the context:

> Only this one cause is true,
> For the other two are unreal.
> To the very end he does not resort to the Lesser Vehicle;
> To ferry the beings across.
> *The Buddha himself dwells in the Greater Vehicle;*
> *Whatever dharmas he acquires,*
> *Adorned with the strength of concentration and wisdom,*
> *Through them does he rescue the beings.*

Lofty and majestic, like the brightness of the moon in the midst of the stars 巍巍堂堂如星中月: a phrase from the *Abhiṣeka Sūtra*, T 21.532c12–13. This is the only place in the *Mo-ho chih-kuan* that this *Sūtra* is quoted by Chih-i; perhaps it was a famous

the mountains of the ten treasures," its effect ruling over the four seas;... the fruit [of Buddhahood] is also like this—the most supreme of the most supreme. Its merits are higher than those of the ten *bhūmi* stages, and it is able to scoop up and entice all those of the four types of capabilities. The *Suvarṇaprabhāsa Sūtra* speaks of [the whole assembly being amazed at] the Buddha paying homage to the bones in a stupa. This is the meaning here.

The teaching of non-arising vertically includes both the causes and results [of Buddhahood]. This meaning has already been clarified. Now I will explain how both are included in a horizontal sense.

The *Pañcaviṃśati Sūtra* says, "If you hear [and understand] the teaching of non-arising, you will understand the meaning of all [things], as the first letter *a* includes the other forty-one letters and the other forty-one letters include the letter *a*, **[60a]** and the same is true for [all the letters] in between. Both the horizontal and vertical meanings are completely included [in the teaching of non-arising], as shown in this text.

This meaning is difficult to perceive. I will quote further from the *Sūtra of the Buddha Treasury* to illustrate these features. Next I will quote the *Mahāparinirvāṇa Sūtra*, and then comment on its meaning. Later I will explain the teaching of non-arising and the destruction of [undesirable] dharmas.

phrase and Chih-i did not intend this specifically as a quote from a sūtra.

Illuminating the mountains of the ten treasures 照十寶山: an analogy for the ten *bhūmi* stages from the *Avataṃsaka Sūtra*, T 9.574c–575a.

Four types of capabilities 四機: Chan-jan (BT–III, 399) interprets this to refer to those of the varying capacities of the Fourfold Teachings.

The Buddha paying homage to the bones in a stupa 佛禮骨塔: see the *Suvarṇaprabhāsa Sūtra*, T 16.353c22–29. The context—the beginning of the seventeenth chapter of the sūtra, on "abandoning the body"—reads:

> At that time the god of the Bodhi tree said to the Buddha, "World Honored One. I have heard that when the World Honored One cultivated the bodhisattva path in the past, he experienced immeasurable hundreds and thousands of ascetic practices, sacrificing his body, life-force, flesh, blood, bones, and marrow. I appeal to the World Honored One to share a little about his experiences of this ascetic practice in the past, so that this may benefit sentient beings and bring them bliss."
>
> Then the World Honored One manifested supranormal powers, and through these supranormal powers caused the great earth to tremble in six ways. Then in the midst of the assembly in the great hall there arose out of the earth a seven-jeweled stupa, covered on top with many jewels. When the great assembly saw this event they were filled with awe. Then the World Honored One arose from his seat and *paid homage to the stupa*....

The first letter *a* includes the other forty-one letters: see the *Pañcaviṃśati Sūtra*, T 8.256a–b, as already quoted above.

Sūtra of the Buddha Treasury 佛藏: translation attributed to Kumārajīva in 405 (T no. 653, 15.782–804); this text expounds on the non-arising, non-perishing, no-marks, and unconditionedness of dharmas.

The *Sūtra of the Buddha Treasury* says, "When [the world is] aflame at the end of a kalpa, a bodhisattva will be able to extinguish it with one spewing [of saliva], and can get the world going again with one breath." [The point is,] it is not that first [the world] perishes, and then later it is recreated. Both the perishing and the arising happen in the midst of the single spewing [of saliva]. This sūtra clarifies the external functions, but internally it includes the teaching of non-arising. Destroying universally and establishing universally are simultaneous and indivisible 即破遍即立遍; "destroying" and "establishing" do not require two [separate] thoughts. If the potential was not already present internally, then there would be no point to great efforts being made externally. That which is internal is manifested through external display, thus it is expressed in this way.

If we were to interpret this in terms of cessation-and-contemplation, the impending close of one person's life is like the time of the perishing of a kalpa, and the three poisons are like the three disasters [of fire, water, and wind at the end of a great kalpa], which is expressed verbally as "fire." Cessation is used to stop [these delusions and passions], like spitting extinguishes [the fire]. Contemplation is used to contemplate this, like having [the world] arise again through blowing, and so forth.

2. *The Non-arising of Dharmas according to the Mahāparinirvāṇa Sūtra* [60a10]

Interpreting the meaning [of the non-arising of dharmas according to] the *Mahāparinirvāṇa Sūtra* [is as follows]. The phrase "hearing of non-hearing" has many meanings. First it says, "the non-arising of arising, the non-arising

When [the world is] aflame at the end of a kalpa, a bodhisattva will be able to extinguish it with one spewing, and can get the world going again with one breath 劫火起時菩薩一唾火即滅一吹世界即成: see the *Sūtra of the Buddha Treasury*. T 15.783b3–4, which is more precise:

> It is like *the great fire that burns* [the whole world] *when a kalpa is exhausted.* Such a person *(a bodhisattva) will be able to extinguish that fire with one spew [of saliva], and then again reform the world and all the heavens with one breath.*

The three disasters 三災 **[at the end of a great kalpa]**: the end of a great kalpa is marked by universal destruction through fire, water, and wind.

The phrase "hearing of non-hearing" has many meanings 不聞聞一句有種種義: this is the first phrase of a tetralemma of phrases on "hearing" and "non-hearing," followed by a similar tetralemma on "arising" and "non-arising" in the *Mahāparinirvāṇa Sūtra*, T 12.733b13–16:

> Good son. In this way you are able to sincerely listen to the dharma; this is a hearing of that which cannot be heard. Good son. There is the *hearing of non-hearing*; there is the non-hearing of non-hearing; there is the non- hearing of hearing; and there is the hearing of hearing. Good son. It is like the arising of non-arising, the non-arising of non-arising, the non-arising of arising, and the arising of arising. It

of non-arising, the arising of non-arising, and the arising of arising." The gate of non-arising is considered with respect to these four phrases, which encompass the causes and result [of Buddhahood] through one's own practice and the ability to save others, thus universally including all dharmas.

[Distinct Teachings. First,] the arising of non-arising. [The *Mahāparinirvāṇa Sūtra* says,] "[The arising of non-arising refers to] peacefully abiding in the worldly truth, as when one first emerges from the womb; this is called the non-arising of arising." Now, to interpret [this passage]. [In this context] "worldly truth" refers to the shared reality of ignorance and Dharma-nature, which gives rise to all discriminative distinctions and differentiation; therefore this is called the "worldly truth." "Peacefully abiding" refers to attaining peace concerning the worldly truth through cessation-and-contemplation by realizing that the objects [of one's experiences in this world] are inconceivable. Since you attain the level of "contemplative practice," this is called "peacefully abiding." Since it is a "peaceful abiding," this is called "being entrusted to a noble womb" [of the bodhisattva stages]. Upon first realizing a Buddha's knowledge and insight, you attain the forbearance [from realizing] the non-arising of dharmas *(anutpattika-dharma-kṣānti)*. This is called "emerging from the noble womb." [The delusions of] the worldly truth of ignorance are not perceived; therefore this is called "non-arising." You achieve a Buddha's knowledge and insight; therefore this is called "arising." The *Ta chih tu lun* says, "Dharmas do not arise, yet *prajña*-wisdom arises";

> is like the attainment of non-attainment, the non-attainment of non-attainment, the non-attainment of attainment, and the attainment of attainment....

This section has been quoted by Chih-i in the *Mo-ho chih-kuan* above; see notes at 3a12–14.

The non-arising of arising ... 不生生。不生不生。生不生。生生: see the *Mahāparinirvāṇa Sūtra*, T 12.733b15; see previous note.

Arising of non-arising 不生生: the "arising of non-arising" reflects the Distinct Teachings, with its reaffirmation of conventional reality, since it affirms "arising" in a conventional sense on the basis of realizing emptiness ("non-arising").

Peacefully abiding in the worldly truth, as when one first emerges from the womb; this is called the non-arising of arising 安住世諦初出胎時名不生生: or, in the context of a womb, the "birth of non-birth." This phrase comes at T 12.733b17, immediately after the passage quoted above.

Level of contemplative practice 觀行位: the third level of the "six identities."

Being entrusted to a noble womb" 託聖胎: the "noble womb" refers to the bodhisattva stages of the ten abodes, the ten levels of practice, and the ten levels of merit transference, because they are the "womb" from which Buddhahood is born.

Dharmas do not arise, yet *prajña*-wisdom arises: a phrase from the *Ta chih tu lun*, T 25.496c28–29; the full context (496c22–29) reads:

> Śāriputra said to the Buddha, "World Honored One. How can one give rise to the perfection of wisdom?"

this is the meaning here. This is the explanation of the level of "the forbearance of the non-arising of dharmas" attained through your own practice; this refers to [the process of] attaining the causes [of Buddhahood through practice].

[Perfect Teaching: Second,] the non-arising of non-arising. The *Sūtra* says, "The non-arising of non-arising is called Great Nirvana, because it is the extinction of the arising of marks," and is attained through cultivating the path. Now, to interpret [this passage]. Results [that is, the "fruit" of Buddhahood] are obtained through causes [that is, the causal stages]; therefore it says "attained through cultivating the path." If the virtues that sever [passions and delusions] are already perfected, then ignorance does not arise; if the virtue of wisdom is already perfected, then *prajña*-wisdom does not arise. Therefore this is called the "non-arising of non-arising." This is "the forbearance of quiescent extinction through one's own practice"; this refers to attaining the result [of the fruit of Buddhahood through practice]. If both the causes and results [of Buddhahood] are perfected, then this is the meaning of what is clarified in the *Sūtra of the Buddha Treasury* where it says that "the extinction and establishment [of the world] are realized in one spewing of spit."

[Shared Teachings: Third,] the non-arising of arising. The *Sūtra* says, "The time of the death of the worldly truth is called the non-arising of arising."

> The Buddha said to Śāriputra, " Forms do not arise; therefore the perfection of wisdom arises. Sensations, conceptions, volitions, and consciousness do not arise; therefore the perfection of wisdom arises. The perfection of giving does not arise; therefore the perfection of wisdom arises. [The rest of the perfections] up to the perfection of meditation does not arise; therefore the perfection of wisdom arises. Internal emptiness, the emptiness of the dharmas of being and nothingness, the four mindfulnesses [of body, sensation, mind, and dharma], the eightfold path, the ten powers of a Buddha, omniscience, and universal wisdom do not arise; therefore the perfection of wisdom arises. In this way, all dharmas do not arise, and therefore the perfection of wisdom arises.

Note that this passage is from the *Pañcaviṃśati Sūtra* itself, and not from the *Ta chih tu lun* commentary.

The non-arising of non-arising is called Great Nirvana, because it is the extinction of the arising of marks, and is attained through cultivating the path 不生不生名大涅槃生相盡故修道得故: from the *Mahāparinirvāṇa Sūtra*, T 12.733b18–19, right after the passage quoted above. However, the last phrase on "attaining through cultivating the path" is not in the sūtra.

The extinction and establishment [of the world] are realized in one spewing of spit: see note above on the *Sūtra of the Buddha Treasury*. T 15.783b3–4.

Non-arising of arising 生不生: this phrase reflects the Shared Teachings and its emphasis on emptiness in the sense that phenomenal things are "empty" of substantial Being and thus do not "arise."

The time of the death of the worldly truth is called the non-arising of arising

Now, to interpret [this passage]. [In this context] "worldly truth" refers to the foundation of ignorance. That is, the "death of the worldly [phenomena]" refers to destroying ignorance. Since it is the death of worldly [phenomena], it is called "the non-arising of arising." Comparing [this phrase] with the first phrase [which appears to be the same except for a reverse in order]: the first phrase is "the arising of non-arising" because it refers to perfecting [and "arising" of] the virtue of wisdom with regard to the principle [of reality]; **[60b]** this phrase is "the non-arising of arising" because it refers to perfecting the virtue of severing [ignorance and passions] and destroying delusions. Although the same phrase "non-arising" is used, there is a great difference [in terms of referent] of "phenomena" 事 and "principle" 理. The first phrase uses the term "arising" to refer to the opening and arousing of wisdom; this [second] phrase uses the term "arising" to refer to the arising and movement of binding karmic activity. Although the same term "arising" is used, there is a great difference [in terms of referent] of "shackles" and "liberating understanding." You should not be confused by the [use of the same] terminology and confuse the gist of the matter. You should think about it and consider it very carefully. The first phrase is like the "spewing out" being included in the "blowing," and this phrase is like the "blowing" being included in the "spewing out." The spewing and the blowing are simultaneous; there is no before and after.

Another interpretation of this sūtra is that "the bodhisattvas who [overcome] the four categories [of delusions]" are described as the "non-arising of arising," because they have a mastery over arising. Now, to interpret [this passage]. The previous [interpretation of] "the non-arising of arising" was an explanation in terms of self-practice for extinguishing delusions. This [current] interpretation is [an explanation of] "the non-arising of arising" for clarifying the way to save others. Why? When bodhisattvas sever the four categories of delusions, they destroy the arising of karmic bonds, and thus are able to have mastery over this arising. The same is true with regard to severing the five levels of delusions. What is true for the inferior [four categories of delusions] is so for the superior [five levels of delusions], thus

世諦死時名生不生: from the *Mahāparinirvāṇa Sūtra*, T 12.733b19–20, right after the passage quoted above.

Liberating understanding 解: this single character can be taken to mean "understanding" or as the first character of the compound 解脱, "liberation." Chih-i plays with both senses in the passage that follows, so I have translated the single character with the awkward but more comprehensive "liberating understanding."

Because they have a mastery over arising 生自在故: from the *Mahāparinirvāṇa Sūtra*, T 12.733b22–23, shortly after the passage quoted above.

this clarifies [the inclusion of] "saving others." Those of the two vehicles sever delusions but become mired in [a negative] emptiness, and are not able to do this [saving of others]. Thus this refers to bodhisattvas. Extinguishing delusions is like clarifying "spitting"; arousing [the way of] saving others is like clarifying "blowing."

[Tripitaka Teachings: Fourth,] the *Sūtra* says "the arising of arising because of the momentary arising of all defiled thoughts." Now, to interpret [this passage]. This phrase clarifies the objects [that is, the people] to be saved. The reason why it is said that bodhisattvas are "non-arising yet arise" is that, since all defiled sentient beings continuously lack the severance [of passions and delusions and are bound by passionate afflictions], bodhisattvas must arouse great compassion and show their mastery of arising by saving and liberating them.

Thus this is the gate of non-arising that encompasses the causes and result [of Buddhahood] through one's own practice, and the ability to save others; all is included herein.

[Further details and explanation:] As for "the bodhisattvas of the four abodes," the *Bodhisattva-bhūmi* says, "From the stage of the first aspiration for enlightenment through the ten *bhūmi* stages, these are contained in six [categories of] abodes 六住: 1. the abode of one's nature *(gotra)* 種性住; 2. the abode of practicing liberating understanding 解行住, 3. the abode of a pure mind 淨心住, 4. the abode of the tracks of practicing the path 行道迹住, 5. the abode of determination 決定住, and 6. the ultimate abode 究竟住. Among those at [the level of] the "abode of one's nature," there are people without any nature [or potential for doing good and realizing Buddhahood]. Even though they give rise to [practicing] the good path, they will repeatedly make progress and repeatedly retrogress, and will not

This clarifies [the inclusion of] "saving others" 彌彰化道: presumably because overcoming the four categories of delusions is still in the realm of "saving oneself," the lower attainment of pre-bodhisattva figures, whereas overcoming the five levels of delusions means that one has attained the level of a bodhisattva and Buddha, whose activity must include saving others.

The arising of arising because of the momentary arising of all defiled thoughts 生生者一切有漏念念生故: from the *Mahāparinirvāṇa Sūtra*, T 12.733b21–22, just before the passage quoted above.

The bodhisattvas of the four abodes 四住菩薩: translated and interpreted above as "the bodhisattvas who [overcome] the four categories [of delusions]."

From the stage of the first aspiration … they continuously increase and progress: based on a passage in the *Bodhisattva-bhūmi*, T 30.901a7–13, although the order and some of the terms are different, some of the sentences are convoluted, and the "six types" are not clear:

> The maturation of people consists of six types of bodhisattva abodes and six stages of maturation for sentient beings. That is, abiding at the stage of practic-

gain the attainment that would allow them to be counted among the six types of bodhisattvas. If people have realized their nature [for doing good and realizing Buddhahood], then there is no retrogressing or loss, and they continuously increase and progress [on the path]" and can become one [of the bodhisattvas or Buddhas].

People who practice liberating understanding are at the level of preparation for the first *bhūmi*-stage. Those at the abode of a pure mind have entered the first *bhūmi*-stage. Those who have attained a mind that transcends this [mundane] world are free from the obstacle of an ordinary view of the self; therefore this is called "abiding with a pure mind." Those at the abode of the tracks of practicing the path abide at the stage of cultivating the path from the second to the seventh *bhūmi*-stage. Those at the abode of determination are at the eighth and ninth *bhūmi*-stage. They have already attained the recompense for their practice, and will never return or retrogress [to a lower stage]. Therefore it is called "determined." Those at the ultimate abode have finally completed their learning and practice for attaining the tenth *bhūmi*-stage [of Buddhahood]. Therefore this is called the ultimate abode.

The *[Mahāparinirvāṇa] Sūtra* phrase "the four abodes are called the non-arising of arising" surely refers to the "abode of the tracks of practicing the path" [in the *Bodhisattva-bhūmi*]. From the second *bhūmi*-stage and above, these are properly the levels wherein people "reenter the conventional world" to save others. They are manifested as arising ["being born"] in various places,

ing liberation/understanding 住解行地, the bodhisattva practices understanding. Abiding at the stage of a pure mind 住淨心地, the bodhisattva practices a pure mind. Abiding at the stage of the tracks of practicing the path 住行道跡地, the bodhisattva practices the tracks of the path. Abiding at the stage of determination 住決定地, the bodhisattva abides in determination; the bodhisattva who abides in the practice of determination practices the practice of determination. Abiding at the ultimate stage 住究竟地, the bodhisattva reaches the ultimate [attainment]. Those who have no nature to bring the good destinies to maturation will repeatedly progress and retrogress. Those who do have this nature will attain maturation, and continuously increase and progress without any retrogression or loss.

There is some similarity between these six categories and Chih-i's classification of the Six Identities.

... Therefore this is called the ultimate abode: it is not clear to me how this analysis based on the *Bodhisattva-bhūmi* explains the term "bodhisattva of the four abodes" or how it fits into Chih-i's scheme and analysis of the *Mahāparinirvāṇa Sūtra*. If I were editing the text, I would recommend leaving out this section.

The four abodes are called the non-arising of arising 四住名生不生: see the *Mahāparinirvāṇa Sūtra*, T 12.733b22–23, which actually reads, "The bodhisattvas of the four abodes [or, the bodhisattvas who overcome the four categories of delusions] are described as the non-arising of arising."

[60c] but this is not a substantial arising [and thus is a "non-arising of arising"]. This is an example of [a text of] the Distinct [Teachings, that is, the *Bodhisattva-bhūmi*] manifesting a Perfect [Teaching]. The idea that one is able to benefit others and have a mastery over saving sentient beings from the time one emerges from the womb is surely a meaning corresponding to the "Perfect" [Teaching], and it is not a mistake to apply it in that way.

The *[Mahāparinirvāṇa] Sūtra* also contains six phrases: "The arising of non-arising is unexplainable. The arising of arising is unexplainable. The non-arising of arising is unexplainable. The non-arising of non-arising is also unexplainable. Arising is also unexplainable. Non-arising is also unexplainable." Now I will use these six phrases to clarify the gate [or teaching] of non-arising to universally destroy [and deconstruct undesirable] dharmas.

If you wish to destroy the conceivable delusions, you should use the first four phrases. If you wish to destroy inconceivable delusions, you should use the last two phrases. Why? Conceivable delusions are abundant, but there are none outside of those of the [triple] world [of desires, form, and no-form] and those beyond [the triple world]. The delusions of the realm beyond [the triple world] [that is, the roots of fundamental ignorance] arise as part of the essence [of reality], and therefore this is called "the arising of non-arising." The delusions of this [triple] realm are like the branches; therefore this is called "the arising of arising." If these delusions [arise] chaotically, it presents a realm of objects in need of salvation. For the sake of these objects, [a bodhisattva] will masterfully present the arising of [appearances in this realm to save these beings from their delusions]. But that which is to be saved [or, "transformed"] is unobtainable, as well as the one who does the saving [or "makes the transformations"]. Both the subject and object, the actor and that acted upon, are lost 亡. Therefore both "the non-arising of arising" and "the arising of arising" are unexplainable.

Have a mastery over saving sentient beings 他化生自在: or, "a mastery over the arising of transformations."

The *[Mahāparinirvāṇa] Sūtra* also contains six phrases: at T 12. 733c10–12, This passage has been quoted and discussed above; see *Mo-ho chih-kuan* 3a12–14 and 54b28–29.

Part of the essence [of reality] 附體: in Chih-i's system the "essence [of reality]" is a term implying emptiness.

Delusions of this [triple] realm are like the branches 界内惑是枝末: that is, the phenomenal ignorance that appears in this triple world (the first four of the five levels of delusions), in contrast to "fundamental" root ignorance (the fifth of the five levels of delusions), the habitual tendencies that must be removed even after the "explicit" delusions are severed.

That which is to be saved is unobtainable, as well as the one who does the saving 所化既不可得何處有能化: that is, in the paradoxical language of Mahāyāna, there are no substantial beings to be saved, and no substantial entity that does the saving, yet the saving must be done.

Suppose you are to destroy [delusions through] conceivable liberating understanding. Although such types of [conceivable] liberating understanding are abundant, there are none that go beyond the [triple] world [of desires, form, and no-form] or what transcends it. Liberating understanding within this [triple] realm stops at removing [the delusions and passions of] [ordinary] constituent [samsara], so it is referred to as "the arising of non-arising." The liberating understanding of those [practitioners] who have transcended the [triple] world involves removing [the passions and delusions of] both constituent [samsara] and the realm of transformation [that is beyond conceptual understanding], so it is referred to as "the non-arising of non-arising." There are shallow and profound liberating understandings, so there are various types of self-practice for attaining the causes and results [of Buddhahood]. There is not just one principle [for attaining liberating understanding]; rather, there are many types.

Now we seek to universally spew out and destroy [undesirable dharmas], so we say that the non-arising of arising is unexplainable, and that the non-arising of non-arising is also unexplainable.

Suppose we are to destroy inconceivable delusions. This refers to [fundamental] ignorance. It arises because it is ignorance; it is ignorance because it arises. Ignorance is unexplainable. Arising is unexplainable. Now all are to be spewed out and destroyed, so we say that arising is unexplainable.

Suppose we are to destroy inconceivable liberating understanding. This refers to perfect liberating understanding. Perfect liberating understanding, from beginning to end, involves extricating the causes and result [of Buddhahood]. But the principle [guiding this action] is neither one-sided nor perfect, and has neither beginning nor end; how can it have a cause or result? Now all are to be spewed out and destroyed, so we say that non-arising is unexplainable.

If we interpret the gate of non-arising for the universal destruction of dharmas according to the intent of this sūtra [in this way], the meaning should be clear.

The Buddha himself interprets these six phrases, saying "Why is the arising of non-arising unexplainable? Non-arising is called arising; therefore

None that go beyond the [triple] world [of desires, form, and no-form] or what transcends it 不出界内外: or, "nothing transcends [the delusions of] the triple world."

Perfect liberating understanding 圓解: that is, the liberating understanding of the Perfect Teaching.

The principle is neither one-sided nor perfect, and has neither beginning nor end; how can it have a cause or result 理不遍圓亦非始終那有因果: or, "how can it involve the process of cultivating practice, or the result of attaining enlightenment."

Why is the arising of non-arising unexplainable? Non-arising is called

it is unexplainable. . . .” Now, to interpret [this passage]. “Non-arising” refers to Dharma-nature. “Arising” refers to ignorance. Those of the two vehicles realize “non-arising” [that is, the emptiness of dharmas], and yet they still accept the “arising” of Dharma-nature, so it is said that “non-arising” is called “arising.” Based on the point made by the Buddha, we can know that the delusions of the transmundane realm that are part of the essence [of reality] are “non-arising” and yet are called “arising.” “Arising” involves perverted views, but perversions and non-perversions are indivisible. This is beyond discursive thought and beyond words [and conceptions]; therefore it is unexplainable.

[The *Mahāparinirvāṇa Sūtra* also says] “Why is the arising of arising unexplainable? Arising arises, therefore it arises. Arising arises, therefore it is non-arising. Therefore it is unexplainable.” **[61a]** Now, to interpret [this passage]. To say “arising arises, therefore it arises” refers to a great arising giving rise to a smaller arising, such as the progression of the eight phases [of a Buddha’s historical life] in this world of defiled dharmas. Based on the point made by the Buddha, we can know that this refers to [the arising of] the defiled dharmas of this [triple] world. “Arising arises, therefore it is non-arising” means that “dharmas that arise through causes and conditions” are simultaneously empty and the Middle; this is beyond discursive thought and beyond words, and therefore it is unexplainable.

[The *Mahāparinirvāṇa Sūtra* also says,] “Why is the non-arising of arising unexplainable? Although arising is called arising, in arising there is no arising by itself. Therefore it is unexplainable.” Now, to interpret [this passage]. “Arising is called arising” means that phenomenal dharmas do not arise [substantially], but *prajñā*-wisdom does arise. “Arising does not involve arising by itself” means that this arising of *prajñā*-wisdom does not

arising; therefore it is unexplainable . . . 云何不生生不可説。不生名爲生故不可説: see the explanation of these six phrases in the *Mahāparinirvāṇa Sūtra*, T 12.733c12ff.

Why is the arising of arising unexplainable? Arising arises, therefore it arises. Arising arises, therefore it is non-arising. Therefore it is unexplainable 云何生生不可説。生生故生。生生故不生。故不可説: from the *Mahāparinirvāṇa Sūtra*, T 12.733c13–15.

“Dharmas that arise through causes and conditions” are simultaneously empty and the Middle 因縁生法即空即中: see the Middle Treatise, chapter 24, verse 18, T 30.33b11–12.

Why is the non-arising of arising unexplainable? Although arising is called arising, in arising there is no arising by itself. Therefore it is unexplainable 云何生不生不可説。生即名爲生。生不自生故不可説: from the *Mahāparinirvāṇa Sūtra*, T 12.733c15–16.

Phenomenal dharmas do not arise, but *prajñā*-wisdom does arise 諸法不生般若生: see the *Ta chih tu lun*, T 25.496c28–29.

This arising of *prajñā*-wisdom does not follow the four options 此般若生不從

follow the four options [of the tetralemma]. "Arising does not involve arising by itself" refers to the first of the possibilities [of the tetralemma], which includes saying [the other three options] that "arising does not involve arising from another," "arising does not involve arising together," and "arising does not involve arising without a cause." Also, when *prajñā*-wisdom has arisen, the worldly [phenomena] have already perished, and will not come into being again; [for a bodhisattva] to arise and be born in the triple world happens through certain conditions [such as his desire to save beings] and not because of karmic retribution. Therefore it is said that "this arising is not arising by itself." If *prajñā*-wisdom arises, or something arises on its own, this is all beyond words [and conceptualization] and thus is unexplainable. On the basis of this meaning we can know that this concerns liberating understanding within this triple world.

[The *Mahāparinirvāṇa Sūtra* also says,] "Why is the non-arising of non-arising unexplainable?… Because it is attained by cultivating the path." Now, to interpret [this passage]. "Attainment through cultivation of the path" refers to the ultimate fruit of enlightenment. It is not something that can be known in the lower of the ten *bhūmi* stages. How, then, can it possibly be explained? On the basis of this meaning we can know that this concerns the liberating understanding of the realm beyond [the triple world].

The *[Mahāparinirvāṇa] Sūtra* says, "Arising is also unexplainable, because nothing [substantial] arises." Now, to interpret [this passage]. This refers to the destruction of inconceivable delusions. The arising of arising within the triple world certainly arises, and the non-arising of arising in the realm beyond [the triple world] also arises. However, when ignorance arises, this arising is surely an arising based on conditions. Arising [based on] conditions is simultaneously empty and the Middle, beyond discursive thought and beyond words. Therefore it is unexplainable.

The *[Mahāparinirvāṇa] Sūtra* says, "Non-arising is unexplainable, because it involves attainment." Now, to interpret [this passage]. This refers to destruction through inconceivable liberating understanding. Liberating

四句: that is, it is "unexplainable" because the four possibilities are all unobtainable.

Why is the non-arising of non-arising unexplainable?… Because it is attained by cultivating the path 云何不生不生不可說。以修道得故: an abbreviation of the section in the *Mahāparinirvāṇa Sūtra*, T 12.733c16–18. The full content reads:

> Why is the non-arising of non-arising unexplainable? "Non-arising" is the name of nirvana. Nirvana does not arise; therefore it is unexplainable. Why? Because it is attained by cultivating the path.

Arising is also unexplainable, because nothing arises 生亦不可說以生無故: see the *Mahāparinirvāṇa Sūtra*, T 12.733c18–19.

Non-arising is unexplainable, because it involves attainment 不生不可說以有得故: see the *Mahāparinirvāṇa Sūtra*, T 12.733c19.

understanding within this [triple] world involves attainment through cultivation of the path, and liberating understanding beyond this [triple] world also involves attainment through cultivation of the path. Attainment involves coming to grips with the principle [of reality], and the principle [of reality] transcends mental or verbal [expression]. Therefore it is unexplainable.

[In this way] the Buddha used six phrases to deconstruct the dharmas of liberating understanding and delusion. All are said to be unexplainable. Surely this manifests the universal destruction [or deconstruction] of dharmas by the gate of non-arising. In terms of the *Sūtra of the Buddha Treasury*, the first four phrases correspond to "both blowing and spewing out," and the last two phrases summarize the previous "blowing" and "spewing." The six phrases [as a whole] are concerned exclusively with [the negative thrust of] "spewing out."

The *Laṅkāvatāra Sūtra* says, "I, from the night in which I started on the path to attainment, until the night in which I entered nirvana, did not express a single word. The Buddha used two methods for preaching in this way, that is, the Dharma of one's own conditions 緣自法, and the Dharma of the fundamental abode 本住法. The Dharma of one's own [conditions] refers to my attainment of the attainments of a Tathāgata, which neither increase nor decrease, and are separate from verbal expression and deluded conceptions, **[61b]** from words and letters, and from dualistic tendencies."

Sūtra of the Buddha Treasury: see T 15.783b3–4 quoted above.

The six phrases are concerned exclusively with "spewing out" 此六句專論於唾也: that is, with the negative "unexplainability" of non-arising, rather that the positive "re-creative" aspect of "blowing."

I, from the night in which I started ... from dualistic tendencies: a paraphrase of a famous passage from the *Laṅkāvatāra Sūtra*, T 541c2–29. This passage—and the *Sūtra* in general—was very important in the Ch'an tradition. Chih-i, however, does not quote this *sūtra* often, and his paraphrase is quite loose. The full text reads:

> The Bodhisattva Great Compassion again said to the Buddha, "World Honored One. The Tathāgata has said that 'I, from the night of my awakening to great *bodhi*-wisdom to the night I entered *parinirvāṇa*, have not spoken a single word. The Buddha spoke but did not speak.' On what meaning does the World Honored One depend in order to say such words?"
>
> The Buddha said to Great Compassion, "Great Compassion. The Tathāgata depends on two Dharmas to say such things. What are these two? I teach in these ways: first, by depending on the Dharma that I myself have internally awakened to; and second, I depend on the Dharma of the fundamental abode [of truth and reality]. I depend on these two dharmas to say such things.
>
> "Great Compassion, what does it mean to depend on the Dharma that I myself have internally awakened to? This is the Dharma attained by and which is the content of the enlightenment of all Buddhas and Tathāgatas in the past. This enlightenment and attainment neither increases nor decreases. This enlightenment that I myself have internally awakened to

To interpret this passage, "the Dharma of one's own conditions" refers to [the Buddha's] enlightenment concerning the noble and real truth of the real [Dharma-]nature 聖眞諦實性. "To be separate from verbal expression and deluded conceptions" is to be inconceivable [that is, empty]. "To be separate from words and letters" refers to being free from conventional designation. "To be separate from dual tendencies" is to be free from [the duality of] speech and what is spoken of, concepts and what is conceptualized, designations and what is designated. The "Dharma of the fundamental abode" refers to the constantly-abiding Dharma realm that is the noble path trod by the noble ones in the past. It is like the castle town found at the end of the road. The road on which people go [to the castle town] is not made by the people who go on it. The road leads to the castle town; it is not that the people who arrive build the castle town. The *[Laṅkāvatāra] Sūtra* says, "A wise person sees the wide and level road and follows it to the castle town, and there experiences many pleasures. I and all Buddhas before me [have

involved practice within this objective realm, but it is separate from the two types of verbal expression, of words and discriminative thinking.

"Great Compassion, what is the Dharma of the fundamental abode? Great Compassion, it is the wide and level path on which one goes; it is like the place where there are treasures such as gold, silver, and pearls. Great Compassion, it is that called the fundamental abiding place of the Dharma-nature. Great Compassion, all Buddhas and Tathāgatas transcend the world but do not transcend the world. The Dharma-nature of the Dharma realm, the abiding of dharmas, the marks of dharmas, and the dharmas of enlightenment are constantly abiding, like the castle town at the end of the main road. Great Compassion; it is like a person who goes in the midst of a vast field, but sees and then faces toward the castle town on the wide and level road, and thus is able to enter the castle town. By entering the castle town he can experience various pleasures, perform various works.

"Great Compassion, what does this mean? Does it mean that this person is the first to make this road that enters into the castle town? Does it mean he is the first to have various adornments?"

Great Compassion said to the Buddha, "No, World Honored One."

[The Buddha said,] "Great Compassion, I and all the Buddhas before me [have relied on and become awakened to] the Dharma-nature of the Dharma realm, the abiding of dharmas, the marks of dharmas, and the dharmas of enlightenment that are constantly abiding in this way. That is why I spoke not a word between the night I attained great *bodhi*-wisdom and the night I entered *parinirvāṇa*. Also, it is not that I have already spoken what should be spoken and manifested."

Then the World Honored One expressed this again in a verse:

I, from the night I attained the path,
To the night I entered nirvana,
In this period of time
I did not express anything.
Internally I realized Dharma-nature
And expressed it on this basis.
For myself and the Buddhas of the ten directions,
There is no distinction among all the dharmas.

A wise person sees … not spoken even one word between the two nights: see the

realized] the constantly abiding Dharma realm in this way. Therefore I have not spoken even one word between the two nights [from the time of enlightenment to entering final *parinirvāṇa*]." Thus it should be known that the determination of these two Dharmas is not something that can be verbalized or discriminated [conceptually], or is subject to change and differentiation. The "Dharma basis" 本法 is the principle of reality itself 如理; the "Dharma of one's own [conditions]" 自法 refers to true enlightenment [attained through one's practice].

The meaning [of this passage from the *Laṅkāvatāra Sūtra*] and the passage of the *Mahāparinirvāṇa Sūtra* on the four unexplainables has the same intent. "The arising of arising is unexplainable" corresponds to the unexplainability of the Dharma basis. "Arising as arising based on conditions" corresponds to the unexplainability of the Dharma basis. "The non-arising of arising is unexplainable" corresponds to the unexplainability of severing dharmas by oneself. "The non-arising of arising is unexplainable" corresponds to the unexplainability of the dharmas of wisdom [realized] by oneself. "The non-arising of non-arising is unexplainable" corresponds to the unexplainability of the dharmas of ultimately realizing enlightenment by oneself. Of the final two phrases, one phrase corresponds to "arising is unexplainable" and the unexplainability of the Dharma basis, and one phrase corresponds to "non-arising is unexplainable" and the unexplainability of the Dharma of one's own enlightenment.

The *Mahāparinirvāṇa Sūtra* says, "Ten types of causes and conditions provide causes for the arising of arising; this can be explained." Now, to interpret [this passage]. This refers to the meaning of non-arising that can be established universally. In terms of the *Sūtra of the Buddha Treasury*, it is like the [positive] establishing [or "re-creation" of the world at the end of a kalpa] through universal "blowing." The "ten types of causes and conditions" are those [in the twelve-link chain of conditioned arising] from the link of "ignorance" to the link of "existence." Here "establish" 立 has three meanings. First, to establish sentient beings; second, to establish opportunities; and third, to establish a hearing of the [Buddha's] teachings.

[1.] "Establishing sentient beings" means that the two causes of the past [ignorance and volitional activity] and the five results in the present [consciousness, name-and-form, the six senses, contact, experience] interact as

translation of the *Laṅkāvatāra Sūtra*, T 16.541c13–24, in the note above.

Ten types of causes and conditions provide causes for the arising of arising; this can be explained 十因縁法爲生作因亦可得說: see the *Mahāparinirvāṇa Sūtra*, T 12.733c20–21, immediately after the passage quoted above.

causes and conditions to establish [the accumulation of] the five aggregates that is conventionally designated "a sentient being."

[2.] "Establishing opportunities" means that in the past one has cultivated the practice of the analytical method [of the Tripitaka Teachings], the practice [of the Shared Teachings of realizing the emptiness] of essence, the gradual practice [of the Distinct Teachings], or the sudden practice [of the Perfect Teaching], and through this practice has accumulated [good] karma that is dampened by ignorance, resulting in [a human life with] consciousness, name-and-form, the six senses, contact, and experience. The working of the aggregates, and the effect of what one has accomplished in the past, gives rise to passions, attachments, and existence in line with analytical [skills], or gives rise to passions, attachments, and existence in line with [the realization of the emptiness of] essence, or gives rise to passions, attachments, and existence in line with gradual [attainments], or gives rise to passions, attachments, and existence in line with sudden [attainments]. Because attachments and existence arise, thus one gains opportunities [for further advancement toward Buddhahood].

[3.] "Establishing the hearing of [the Buddha's] teachings" means that when one has the passions, attachments, and existence in line with analytical [skills], one has empathy for the Tripitaka Teachings. This corresponds to [the phrase] "the arising of arising is unexplainable." These ten types of causes and conditions provide causes for the arising of arising which can be explained. This is the explanation of the arising of arising.

When you have the passions, attachments, and existence in line with [the realization of the emptiness of] essence, **[61c]** you have empathy for the Shared Teachings. This corresponds to "the non-arising of arising is unexplainable." These ten types of causes and conditions provide causes for the non-arising of arising that can be explained. This is the explanation of the non-arising of arising.

When you have the passions, attachments, and existence in line with gradual [attainment], you have empathy for the Distinct Teachings. This corresponds to "the arising of non-arising is unexplainable." These ten types of causes and conditions provide causes for the arising of non-arising that can be explained. This is the explanation of the arising of non-arising.

When you have the passions, attachments, and existence in line with sudden [attainment], you have empathy for the Perfect Teaching. These ten types of causes and conditions provide causes for the non-arising of non-arising that can be explained. This is the explanation of the non-arising of non-arising.

When sentient beings are established, all the causes and results of delusions are established, all things to be saved are established. When the opportunities and teachings are established, all causes and results of practices and liberating understanding are established, and all potential power for saving beings is established. This is the gate of non-arising, that all are established in the establishment of one. Thus it says in the *Pañcaviṃśati Sūtra* that "if you hear [and understand] the gate of the letter *a*, you understand all meanings." The *Sūtra of the Buddha Treasury* says, "One blow establishes all [the world]."

As it says in the *Bodhisattva-bhūmi*, there are four types of maturation, "that of those with the nature *(gotra)* of the śrāvaka, that of those with the nature of the pratyekabuddha, that of those with the nature of the Buddha, and that of those with the nature of the bodhisattva. Those who do not have these [specific] four natures can reach maturation in one of the good destinies [of the human or divine realms]." Those with the nature of the Buddha have the capacity [and opportunity] of the Perfect [Teaching]. Those with the nature of the bodhisattva have the capacity [and opportunity] of the Distinct [Teachings]. This text says, "Those with the 'seed' of the bodhisattva are able to gradually sever both the obstacles of passionate afflictions *(kleṣāvaraṇa)* and the wisdom obstacle *(jñeyāvaraṇa)*, whether there is or is not a Buddha

If you hear the gate of the letter *a*, you understand all meanings 若聞阿字門則解一切義: see the *Pañcaviṃśati Sūtra*, T 8.256a–b, as quoted above.

One blow establishes all 一吹一切悉成: see the *Sūtra of the Buddha Treasury*, T 15.783b4–5, as quoted above.

Those with the nature of the śrāvaka, that of those with the nature of the pratyekabuddha, that of those with the nature of the Buddha, and that of those with the nature of the bodhisattva. Those who do not have these four natures can bring them to maturation in one of the good destinies 聲聞種性緣覺種性佛種性菩薩種性。無此四性以善趣熟之: a rephrasing of a passage in the *Bodhisattva-bhūmi*, T 30.900a16–21. Note that for Chih-i the fourth type is that of the bodhisattva, whereas in the *Bodhisattva-bhūmi* the fourth type is "those with no nature." It is not clear in this context whether this refers to an *icchantika*-type being who has no hope of attaining any of these achievements, or whether this "no-nature" type can attain any of the various possible attainments, depending on his/her actions in their current life. The context reads:

> [2] The maturation of people can be briefly summarized into four types. There are those with the nature of the śrāvaka, who come to maturation in the śrāvaka vehicle. There are those with the nature of the pratyekabuddha, who come to maturation in the pratyekabuddha vehicle. There are those with the nature of the Buddha, who come to maturation in the supreme, great vehicle [of Mahāyāna]. There are those with no [specific] nature, who can reach maturation in the good destinies.

The obstacles of passionate afflictions 煩惱障 **and the wisdom obstacle** 智障: on these two terms see the note at *Mo-ho chih-kuan* 16c12 and Swanson 1983.

Those with the 'seed' … whether there is a Buddha or is not a Buddha: the section of the *Bodhisattva-bhūmi* quoted above opens as follows (T 30.900a7–12):

> What is "maturation"? Briefly, there are

[in their world]." How can this not be referring to the capacity of the Distinct [Teachings]? Those with the nature of the śrāvaka must be disclosed as of distinct types. Those who [attain the stages of the four] good roots [an inferior nirvana of extinction] have the capacity [and opportunity] of the Tripitaka [Teachings]. Those who have the nature of retrogressing from the Mahāyāna and taking the way of the Hīnayāna have the capacity [and opportunity] of the Shared [Teachings]. Thus these four types of maturation correspond to the meaning of the four types of capacities [and opportunities of the Fourfold Teachings].

Question: The above passage on the six phrases illustrates that the gate of non-arising involves the destruction of all in the destruction of one, and [the passage on] the ten types of causes and conditions illustrates that the gate of non-arising involves the establishment of all in the establishment of one. The passage above on the four phrases illustrates that the gate of non-arising involves both destruction and establishment. But how about the fourth possibility of "neither destruction nor establishment"?

Answer: The opening section of the nineteenth fascicle of the *Mahāparinirvāṇa Sūtra* says that "there are ten virtues that are inconceivable, and people who hear of them are amazed; they are neither difficult nor easy, neither internal nor external, neither marked nor unmarked, neither square nor round, neither pointed nor slanting, and so forth." The meaning of this passage corresponds to the fourth possibility of "neither destroyed nor established."

six types: First, the maturation of one's nature; second, the maturation of persons; third, the maturation of distinct types; fourth, the maturation of means; fifth, the maturation sentient beings; and sixth, the maturation of human marks. [1] The maturation of one's nature refers to there being good dharmas and seeds. By cultivating this good dharma one gradually [overcomes] the two obstacles [of *kleṣāvaraṇa* and *jñeyāvaraṇa*], has the physical and mental power to be pure and liberated, and with true means is endowed with the ultimate [enlightenment]. *Whether or not there is a Buddha [in this world], one is able to gradually sever both kleṣāvaraṇa and jñeyāvaraṇa.*

The passage above on the four phrases 上四句: see note above at 60a10.

There are ten virtues that are inconceivable, and people who hear of them are amazed; they are neither difficult nor easy, neither internal nor external, neither marked nor unmarked, neither square nor round, neither pointed nor slanting, and so forth 十事功德不可思議聞者驚怪。非難非易非内非外非相非非相非方非圓非尖非斜等: this is the opening of the section which contains the "four phrases" and "six unexplainables" discussed by Chih-i above; see *Mahāparinirvāṇa Sūtra*, T 12.731a7–27:

> Then the World Honored One said to the bodhisattva-mahāsattva,... "Good son. If there are bodhisattva-mahāsattvas who cultivates great Nirvana in this way, they will *attain ten virtues* that are not shared by śrāvakas and pratyekabuddhas. *These are inconceivable, and people who hear of them are amazed. They are neither internal nor external, neither difficult nor easy, neither marks nor non-marks.* They are

Question. If the gate of non-arising embraces all Dharma teachings, then are all the other gates and teachings not [needed]?

Answer. The gate of non-arising embraces all gates. But it is also the case that all the [other] gates embrace the gate of non-arising. Here we speak in terms of the gate of non-arising, since [in the current discussion] we are taking the perspective of the virtue of wisdom, but we could speak in terms of four possibilities: the gate of arising, the gate of non-arising, the gate of both arising and non-arising, and the gate of neither arising nor non-arising. Each of these gates includes these four gates or possibilities, so four times four gives sixteen gates. If we were to take the perspective of the virtue of severance [of passions and delusions], we would have the gate of perishing, [62a] the gate of non-perishing, the gate of both perishing and non-perishing, and the gate of neither perishing nor non-perishing. Each single gate has four gates, so four times four gives sixteen gates. Together we have thirty-two gates. The *Mahāparinirvāṇa Sūtra* points out that "the light of the moon increases for fifteen days. This is analogous to [the increase of] the virtue of wisdom. From the sixteenth day the light of the moon decreases. This is analogous to [decrease in passions and delusions due to] the virtue of severance. [However,] the moon itself does not increase or decrease." Rather,

not worldly dharmas, nor do they have conventional appearances, nor are they of this world.

What are these ten? First, there are five. What are these five? One, to be able to hear what cannot be heard; two, to be able to benefit from what is heard; third, a mind that is able to sever doubt and delusions; fourth, a mind of wisdom that is direct and not warped; and fifth, the ability to know the secret treasury of the Tathāgata. These are five matters.

What does it mean to "be able to hear what cannot be heard"? This refers to the profound and secret treasury, that all sentient beings without exception have the Buddha-nature. There is no distinction between Buddha, Dharma, and Sangha; the nature and characteristics of these three treasures is that of constancy, bliss, selfhood, and purity. Buddhas do not ultimately enter nirvana, but abide constantly without changing. The Tathāgata's nirvana is neither Being nor nothingness, neither conditioned nor unconditioned, neither defiled nor undefiled, neither form nor non-form, neither named nor unnamed, neither marked nor unmarked, neither existence nor non-existence, neither matter nor non-matter, neither cause nor effect, neither relative nor non-relative, neither clear nor dark, neither transcendent nor non-transcendent, neither permanent nor transient, neither severed nor non-severed, neither beginning nor end, neither past nor future nor present, neither aggregates nor non-aggregates, neither realization nor non-realization, neither worldly nor non-worldly, neither of the twelvefold links of causation nor not of the twelvefold links of causation. In this way this Dharma is exceedingly profound and minutely secret; it was not heard of in the past, but one is able [now] to hear of it.

... the moon itself does not increase or decrease: see the *Mahāparinirvāṇa Sūtra*, T 12.724b11–17; this passage has been quoted above in the *Mo-ho chih-kuan* at 10c14 and 31a10–11.

there can be said to be increase in terms of the "white" area, and there can be said to be decrease in terms of the "dark" area [during the waxing of the moon, and the opposite during the waning of the moon]. The true aspect [of reality] is not [fully taken care of] by either wisdom nor severance—wisdom is taught with regard to illumination, and severance is taught with regard to quiescence. If you attain a high level of realization with regard to the gate of non-arising embracing all dharmas, this is a vertical embracing of all dharmas. If you attain a wide and universal realization with regard to the gate of non-arising embracing all dharmas, this is a horizontal embracing of all dharmas.

Question. The gate of non-arising is a "gate" called "non-arising" which has its objects, delusions, wisdom, severance, and so forth, all of which should be modified by "non-arising." Why, then, do you speak of the non-arising of arising, the arising of arising, and the mastery over arising?

Answer. These topics assist in clarifying the gate of non-arising. The "patience from realizing non-arising" is called the arising of non-arising. We speak of the "arising of arising" in order to clarify that which must be saved [that is, sentient beings in this world of samsaric existence]. We speak of "mastery over arising" to clarify the application [of that saving action]. [Instead of presenting problems,] rather, these topics are [part of the meaning of] non-arising. "Spewing out" corresponds to non-arising, and "blowing" corresponds to the arising of non-arising and so forth; all the more we have manifested the idea that the gate of non-arising embracing all dharmas universally. Here the meaning of this gate has been interpreted in terms of the *Mahāparinirvāṇa Sūtra*.

3. *Three Ways to Discuss the Deconstruction of Dharmas in Terms of Non-arising* [62a14]

Next I will clarify the "deconstruction of dharmas universally" in three parts.

First is to completely exhaust the foundations of the gate of non-arising from beginning to end in a vertical deconstruction of dharmas universally. [62a22–83b17]

Second is to completely exhaust the foundations all of the dharma gates [of teaching and practice] from beginning to end in a lateral [or horizontal] deconstruction of dharmas universally. [83b17–84b24]

"Spewing out" and "blowing": see the reference to the *Sūtra of the Buddha Treasury* above.

The "deconstruction of dharmas universally" in three parts 破法遍者為三: as one can see from the page numbers, these three parts contain the most detailed subsections of the *Mo-ho chih-kuan*, covering twenty-two Taishō pages, from 64a to 86a, almost half of fascicle 5 and all of fascicle 6.

Third is to completely exhaust the foundations of the non-duality of the vertical and horizontal from beginning to end in a universal deconstruction of dharmas that is neither vertical nor horizontal. [84b24–86a9]

The "vertical" involves [attainment] in terms of high [stages], and the "horizontal" involves [attainments] in terms of expansive [achievements]. If you achieve [a high stage] vertically and then attempt [expansive] horizontal [achievements], the horizontal [achievements] will also be high; if you achieve [expansive] horizontal [achievements and then attempt vertical [advancement], the vertical [achievements] will also be expansive. The *Lotus Sūtra* says, "The vehicle is tall and wide." The vertical and the horizontal [attainments] are non-dual, and therefore are neither vertical nor horizontal. Therefore it says [in the *Lotus Sūtra*], "This Dharma is undifferentiating and equal; it does not involve higher or lower."

2. Deconstructing Dharmas Vertically in Terms of Non-Arising [62a22–83b17]

The universal deconstruction of dharma in terms of the gate of non-arising has another three parts:

1. the universal deconstruction of dharmas by entering or realizing emptiness from conventionality 從假入空;
2. the universal deconstruction of dharmas by entering or realizing conventionality from emptiness 從空入假; and
3. both contemplations [of emptiness and conventionality] as means for the universal deconstruction of dharmas for attaining and realizing the supreme truth of the Middle Way 中道第一義諦.

The vehicle is tall and wide 其車高廣: a phrase from the parable of the burning house with regard to the one great vehicle given to all the children, T 9.12c18–19. Hurvitz (*The Lotus Sūtra*, 60 [56]) translates the context: "Śāriputra, at that time the great man gives to each child one great carriage. *The carriage is high and wide*, adorned with a multitude of jewels...."

This Dharma is undifferentiating and equal; it does not involve higher or lower 是法平等無有高下: a paraphrase from the *Lotus Sūtra*, T 9.20c4–5. Hurvitz (*Lotus Sūtra*, 120 [111]) translates: "The territories of this land shall be well adorned, having no filth or evil, no tiles or pebbles, no thorns or thistles, no excrement or other impurities. Its soil *shall be flat and even, having no high or low*, no hills or crevices...."

Deconstructing dharmas vertically in terms of non-arising 無生門破法遍: note that this sub-section alone covers 21 pages of the Taishō text, by far the longest in the *Mo-ho chih-kuan*.

Entering or realizing 入: this character literally means "entering" but implies "realizing." I usually use "realize," but shift between the two terms depending on the context, because sometimes a more literal "entering" is implied.

This threefold contemplation is truly present in a single thought 一心. This Dharma is sublime and difficult to understand, so I will rely on "three" to manifest "one." The *Ta chih tu lun* says, "The three wisdoms are truly present in a single thought." [The three] are divided according to three types of people in order to make it easy for each type of person to understand. The *Avataṃsaka Sūtra* also indicates two intentions: [the passage] "he proclaimed [the gradual-and-successive] practice for bodhisattvas over the span of kalpas" indicates [a type of gradual and progressive practice and

The three wisdoms are truly present in a single thought 三智實在一心: a rephrasing of text from the *Ta chih tu lun*, T 25.260b17–18: "*In a single thought one attains omniscience* 一切智 *and universal wisdom* 一切種智, and severs all habits of passionate afflictions." Lamotte (1758–59) translates the passage, "C'est en un même et unique moment de pensée que le Bodhisattva obtient l'omniscience *(sarvajñatā)*, la science de tous les aspects *(sarvākārajñatā)* et détruit tous les relents de passion *(sarvakleśavāsanā)*. See note at *Mo-ho chih-kuan* 26a26.

Divided according to three types of people in order to make it easy for each type of person to understand 爲向人説令易解故分屬三人: see the *Ta chih tu lun*, T 25.649a2–6:

> Again it was asked, "The Buddha constantly speaks of three types of wisdom. What are the differences between the three types of wisdom?"
>
> The Buddha answered, "*Sarvajñā* is the wisdom of the śrāvaka and the pratyekabuddha. Why? Because the śrāvakas and pratyekabuddhas know all the characteristics of the twelve internal sense organs and external sense objects, that they are all transient, involve suffering, and are empty and without selfhood. The wisdom of the path is the wisdom of the bodhisattva-mahāsattvas. . . .
>
> [649b16] "Universal wisdom is the wisdom of a Buddha."

He proclaimed practice for bodhisattvas over the span of kalpas 宣説菩薩歴劫修行: the quote is actually from the *Sūtra of Immeasurable Meanings*, which indicates the role or place of the *Avataṃsaka Sūtra* in the preaching career of the Buddha. See the full context in T 9.386b21–28:

> Good sons, first [the Buddha] taught the four [noble] truths for those who sought to be śrāvakas, and the eight billion heavenly beings descended [to earth] to hear the Dharma, and an aspiration [for enlightenment]. In the middle, he preached here and there about the profound twelvefold [links of] causation for those who sought to be pratyekabuddhas, and immeasurable sentient beings aroused the aspiration [for enlightenment] or remained on the stage of the śrāvaka. Next [he preached] the twelvefold scriptures such as the Vaipulya sūtras, the *Mahā-prajñāpāramitā Sūtras*, and the sea of emptiness of *the Avataṃsaka, in which he propounded the cultivation of a progressive practice over the span of kalpas for bodhisattvas*, and hundreds of thousands of monks and immeasurable ten of thousands time hundreds of millions of people and divine beings became stream-enterers, once-returner, non-returners, and arhats, or remained within the conditions of the pratyekabuddha. Good son, from this you should know that the preaching is the same but the meaning is distinct and different [according to the hearer].

The translation in *The Threefold Lotus Sutra*, 15–16, reads:

> Good sons! At the beginning, though I preached the Four Truths for those

contemplation] for those of dull faculties. "At the time of his first aspiration [for enlightenment] he had already perfected correct awakening,… possessed the body of wisdom, and this enlightenment did not rely on others"; this indicates [the sudden type of practice and contemplation] for those with sharp faculties. The *Lotus Sūtra* has only one intention, "to directly abandon [conventional] means and preach only the supreme path." Now I wish to use distinctions [between the three types of contemplations] **[62b]** to manifest them generally, and through this gradual progression to discuss that which is without gradual progression [that is, perfect and sudden contemplation]. Therefore, first I will interpret and discuss the three [distinct] meanings [of the three contemplations].

1. *The Contemplation of Entering or Realizing Emptiness from Conventionality* [62b1–75b27]

The universal deconstruction [or destruction] of dharmas by entering or realizing emptiness from conventionality also has three parts. First, entering or realizing emptiness from conventionality in terms of [mistaken] views; next, entering or realizing emptiness from conventionality in terms of conceptual attitudes; and finally, in terms of the fourfold teachings. Thus entering or realizing emptiness from conventionality also has two parts: first is the clarification of conventionality in terms of [mistaken] views, and second is the clarification of the contemplation of emptiness.

who sought to be śrāvakas, eight koṭis of heavenly beings came down to hear the Law and raised the desire for enlightenment. In the middle, though I preached in various places the profound Twelve Causes for those who sought to be pratyekabuddhas, innumerable living beings raised the aspiration for enlightenment or remained in the stage of śrāvaka. Next, *though I explained the longterm practice of bodhisattvas*, through preaching the twelve types of sutras of Great Extent, the Mahā-Prajñā, and *the voidness of the Garland Sea*, a hundred thousand bhikshus, myriad koṭis of men and gods, and innumerable living beings could remain in the merits of srota-āpanna, sakṛdāgāmin, anāgāmin, and arhat or in the law appropriate to the pratyekabuddha. Good sons! For this reason, it is known that the preaching is the same, but the meaning varies.

At the time of his first aspiration he had already perfected correct awakening,… possessed the body of wisdom, and this enlightenment did not rely on others 初發心時便成正覺所有慧身不由他悟: almost word for word from the *Avataṃsaka Sūtra*, T 9.449c14–15: "*At the time of his first aspiration he had already perfected correct awakening*, knew the true nature of all dharmas, *was fully endowed with the body of wisdom, and this enlightenment did not rely on others*."

To directly abandon means and preach only the supreme path 正直捨方便但説無上道: a famous phrase from the second chapter of the *Lotus Sūtra* on "Skillful Means"; T 9.10a19. This has been quoted already in the *Mo-ho chih-kuan* at 2c9 and 33a21–22, and will be quoted many more times.

1. The Contemplation of Entering or Realizing Emptiness from Conventionality with Regard to Mistaken Views [62b4–69c27]

1. The conventionality of mistaken views [62b4]

The delusions of [mistaken] views arise associated with the essence [of reality as empty], and yet in turn are able to obstruct [realization of] the essence [of reality]. It is like a flame that depends on empty space 空 yet agitates that empty space; like a dream that is caused by sleep, and yet that dream can befuddle your sleep. If the dream does not come to an end, you will never awaken from your sleep, and if these delusions are not removed, the essence [of reality, that is, its emptiness] will not be made manifest. However, [correct] insight 見 is to perceive the principle [of reality]; such an insight is truly non-delusional. When you perceive the principle [of reality], you are able to sever these delusions. The name is given from the perspective of understanding; therefore they are called "the delusions of [mistaken] views."

There are four types of deluded views: 1. the individual fourfold views, 2. the multiple fourfold views, 3. the integrated or combined fourfold views, and 4. the fourfold views that are beyond words.

1. **The individual fourfold views** 單四見 refers to attachment to being [or Being], attachment to non-being [or "nothingness"], attachment to both being and non-being, and attachment to neither being nor non-being. With regard to one view of "being," there are those who are sharp and those who are dull. For example, with regard to there being a self, if you take the self as something that has [substantial] Being and always arouse self-centered

Associated with the essence [of reality] 附體: or, "in addition to, adhesions to, connected to" the essence of reality, that is, emptiness.

Like a dream that is caused by sleep 似夢因眠: in the sense that one must fall asleep in order to dream. Daydreaming does not count.

Four types of deluded views 四見惑: as will be seen in the discussion, in this context the "fourfold [mistaken] views" refer to views with regard to the four possibilities of the tetralemma.

Being and non-being 有無: in this section I usually use the terms "being" and "non-being" for 有無 (*yu-wu*) instead of "Being" and "nothingness," or "existence and non-existence [or non-Being]," for the sake of consistency and in order to facilitate the interplay of the two poles. However, there are times when I use "Being" or "nothingness" when the terms are used in the sense of the two extremes to be avoided. Thus, depending on the context, in this section I use "Being," "being," "exist," or "existence" for 有, and "non-being," "nothingness," "do not exist," or "non-existence" for 無. See my discussion of these terms and the importance of these distinctions—that *yu* can be used negatively as substantial Being or positively as conventional existence, and *wu* can be used positively in the sense of a denial of substantial Being and negatively as nihilistic nothingness—in Swanson, *Foundations*, especially Chart 2 on page 360.

thoughts, then the "self" that corresponds to this [view] is [1] *the [mistaken] view of the self*. Since you make calculations based on this [mistaken view of the] self, you arouse [2] *extreme views*. Because of these extreme [views of the] self, you destroy the causes and fruits [of enlightenment] in this realm and in the transcendent realm. These are called [3] *deviant views*. If you seek to penetrate to nirvana with attachment to these [mistaken views] as your path, this is called [4] *the attachment to precepts*. To take these [views] as real, slander all other [views], and not accept any other views is called [5] *attachment to [mistaken] views*. [One-sidedly] affirming your own dharma [teaching] is called [6] *passion*. Against those who deny your own dharma [teaching], you feel [7] *anger*. Thinking that you understand what others do not understand arouses [8] *arrogance*. Not knowing that within the view of "Being" lies suffering and the causes of suffering is [9] *ignorance*. Drifting with uncertainty is [10] *doubt*.

These ten types of afflictions coincide with the four truths of the realm of desires as follows: [1. the truth of] suffering involves all ten [afflictions]; [2. the truth of] the causes [of suffering] involves seven—it does not include the views of the self, extreme views, and attachment to precepts; [3. the truth of] the path involves eight—it does not include the views of the self and extreme views; and [4. the truth of] extinction involves seven—it does not include the views of the self, extreme views, and attachment to the precepts. All together this gives thirty-two [varieties of] afflictions. There are twenty-eight afflictions that coincide with the four truths of the realm of form, and the same for the realm of no-form—neither of these [two] realms includes "anger" [for each of the four truths]. This gives a total of eighty-eight afflictions. Each of the other three [of the fourfold views] also includes eighty-eight afflictions. Each of the sixty-two kinds of [mistaken] views also includes each of the eighty-eight afflictions. Thus there are wave after wave of overflowing [passionate afflictions], such that they cannot be counted. The net of mistaken views becomes ever more minute, so that [insight into and perception of] the essence of the principle [of reality as empty] is obstructed.

The Great Collection of Sūtras says, "If an eye sees a favorable visible form, therein are [the passions] of the skandhas and the accumulation [of suffering]. If it sees evil visible forms, therein are [the passions] of the skandhas and the accumulation [of suffering]. If it sees neutral visible forms, therein

Views of the self 身見: lit. "view of the body," but this corresponds to the first mistaken view of a substantial self 我見.

If an eye ... one hundred and eight afflictions: this is supposed to be a summary of a passage in *The Great Collection of Sūtras*, T 13.395a–b, and many of the same terms appear, but in a very different order. It is not clear how far Chih-i intends the quote to continue.

are [the passions] of the skandhas and the accumulation [of suffering]. It is this way whenever there is the intent to come in contact with a phenomenon. Each sense faculty has three types [that is, favorable, evil, and neutral views, for a total of eighteen], and there are six [sense faculties] with three types [of experiences, that is, suffering, pleasure, and abandonment, for another eighteen], so the six sense faculties include thirty-six [views]. This multiplied by the three times [of the past, present, and future] gives a total of one hundred and eight. The sixty-two views and the eighty-eight afflictions also each include the one hundred and eight afflictions." It should be known that if a thought [with a mistaken view] is aroused for even a moment, immediately an unlimited wave [of passionate views] washes over you and darkens your sight so that you cannot see [properly] or be awake.

There are those who lecture in the world saying, "Being" **[62c]** is a [mistaken] view, but "non-being" is not a [mistaken] view, or "both being and non-being" is a [mistaken] view, but "neither being nor non-being" is not a [mistaken] view. These words are not in accord with the sūtras, and are a burden to [correct] thinking. A sūtra says, "reckoning for all the views involves sixty-two [mistaken] views." If we understood the views in this way [that "non-being" was not a mistaken view], however, they would not add up [to sixty-two]. The *Middle Treatise* deconstructs both notions of [arising through] self and others.[The view of] Being is [the notion of a] self-nature 自性. If we submit [the idea of] non-being in contrast to Being, this non-being refers to the "other-nature" 他性. Whether Being or non-being, both involve a nature [that needs to be denied]. How, then, can one say that "non-being" is not a [mistaken] view?

Again, this "non-being" [that is, nothingness in contrast to Being] is not the "non-being" [conventional existence] understood from the perspective of enlightenment concerning the principle [of reality]; how can it not be a [mistaken] view? The non-Buddhist paths [propose various theories concerning] the current kalpa and current views, and the kalpa yet to come and views yet to come. If for even a moment you believe that these theories are

Those who lecture in the world 世講者: the traditional commentaries do not identify these people.

Reckoning for all the views involves sixty-two [mistaken] views 依止此諸見具足六十二: the *Kōgi* (BT–III, 462) says that this is not from any specific sūtra.

The *Middle Treatise* deconstructs both notions of self and others 中論破自他性: see the arguments, for example, in the beginning of the *Middle Treatise* at T 30.2b.

The current kalpa and current views, and the kalpa yet to come and views yet to come 本劫本見末劫末見: see the *Long Āgama*, T 1.89c23–28:

> Some monks and brahmans propose numerous varieties of theories concerning the current kalpa and current views, and the kalpa to come and the views to come, exhausting the sixty-two [mistaken]

right and the other [Buddhist theories] are deceptive, then your [mistaken] views will expand and your errors be prolonged, the poison [of a mistaken view] of the self will increase, you will "grab their heads and pull out their hair" [while arguing over the various views], and produce further rebirth in samsara. Take the case of Dīrghanakha who, although he did not accept all Dharma teachings, did accept [some] that should not be accepted, and thus did not realize [the two truths of] suffering and its causes; when the Buddha admonished him with a single [word or question], he was defeated for the second time. Even such an adept non-Buddhist has yet to elude all [mistaken] views; how much more so is this true for those inferior [lecturers] who say that errors are correct [such as saying that "non-being" (or nothingness) is not a mistaken view].

Now, I conclude that all these [mistaken views listed above] correspond to and are included in the individual fourfold views.

[2.] **The multiple fourfold views** 複四見: [The mistaken views of] the being of being, the being of non-being, the non-being of being, the non-being of non-being, both being and the being of non-being, both non-being and the being of non-being, neither being nor the being of non-being, and neither non-being nor the being of non-being; these are multiple fourfold views. Each individual view includes the eighty-eight afflictions. Also, each view of the sixty-two views also include the eighty-eight afflictions, the one hundred and eight afflictions, and so forth, [giving innumerable combinations of views and afflictions] as explained above.

[3.] **The integrated or combined fourfold views** 具足四見: The view of "Being" includes four [mistaken views]: the being of being, the being of non-

> views. The numerous varieties of theories concerning the current kalpa and current views, and the kalpa to come and views to come, do not go beyond the sixty-two [mistaken] views.

These themes are discussed exhaustively in the pages of the *Long Āgama* sūtra that follow; see T 1.89c–94a.

Grab their heads and pull out their hair 捉頭拔髮: a phrase from the *Mahāparinirvāṇa Sūtra*, T 12.725a5.

The case of Dīrghanakha 長爪: see the story of Dīrghanakha ("long nails") in the prologue to the *Ta chih tu lun*, T 25.61b18–62a28 (Lamotte, *Le Traité* 1, 46–51), where Dīrghanakha does not agree with the teachings of the Buddha as expounded by Śāriputra; see especially 62a2–10. Chih-i has referred to this story above in the *Mo-ho chih-kuan*; see note at 40c13.

The being of being, the being of non-being … neither non-being nor the being of non-being 有有。有無。無有。無無。亦有有無。亦無有無。非有有無。非無有無。: or, "the being of being, the being of nothingness, the nothingness of being, the nothingness of nothingness, both being and the being of nothingness, both nothingness and the being of nothingness, neither being nor the being of nothingness, and neither nothingness nor the being of nothingness"; or, "the existence of existence, the existence of non-existence, the non-existence of existence,…" and so forth.

being, the being of both being and non-being, and the being of neither being nor non-being. [The view of] "non-being" includes four [mistaken views]: the non-being of being, the non-being of non-being, the non-being of both being and non-being, and the non-being of neither being nor non-being. [The view of] "both being and non-being" includes four [mistaken views]: being as both being and non-being, non-being as both being and non-being, both being and non-being as both being and non-being, and neither being nor non-being as both being and non-being. [The view of] "neither being nor non-being" includes four [mistaken views]: being as neither being nor non-being, non-being as neither being nor non-being, both being and non-being as neither being nor non-being, and neither being nor non-being as neither being nor non-being. This is called the integrated or combined fourfold views. One phrase includes the eighty-eight afflictions. In this way each view of the sixty-two views include the eighty-eight afflictions, the one hundred and eight afflictions, and so forth, [giving innumerable combinations of views and afflictions] as explained above.

[4.] **The fourfold views that are beyond words** 無言四見: Beyond the individual fourfold views there is one view that is beyond words. Beyond the multiple fourfold views there is one view that is beyond words. Beyond the integrated or combined fourfold views there is one view that is beyond words. Each one of these views arouses the eighty-eight afflictions, the sixty-two views, the one hundred and eight afflictions, and so forth, as explained above.

These various views arise in response to the various non-Buddhist teachings.

There are also views that arise in response to the Buddha Dharma. There are fourfold views that arise with regard to the four gates of the Tripitaka [Teachings], fourfold views that arise with regard to the four gates of the Shared [Teachings], fourfold views that arise with regard to the Distinct [Teachings], and fourfold views that arise with regard to the Perfect [Teaching]. Again, beyond each type **[63a]** of the four gates, there is for each a view that is beyond words. In this way, within each individual view, each one arouses delusions such as the eighty-eight afflictions, the sixty-two views, the one hundred and eight afflictions, and so forth, as explained above.

[Discussion in terms of conventionality.] Again, [the realm of] the delusions of [mistaken] views does not get its name merely as [the opposite of] understanding, but is also referred to as "conventionality" because of a relation with the essence [of reality as empty]. That which is conventional or provisional is so-called because [it belongs to the realm of] empty delusion and perverted views. Following the previous example, I can say that there is also individual fourfold conventionality, multiple fourfold conventionality, integrated or combined fourfold conventionality, and each of these having a conventionality that is beyond words. With regard to the Buddha Dharma, again, there are sixteen types of conventionality, each one as explained above.

Again, each individual conventionality contains three types of conventionality, that is, conventional existence as causally arising, conventional existence as continuity, and relative conventional existence. When a phenomenal object reacts with a sense organ and consciousness, a single thought arises; this is "conventional existence as causally arising." When a previous thought and a later thought succeed each other without interruption, this is "conventional existence as continuity." To know that this thought exists, in contrast to the non-existence of other thoughts, is "relative conventional existence." [Conventionality as] causal arising is explained in terms of external objects and internal senses; [conventionality as] continuity is [explained] only in terms of internal senses; [conventionality as] relative refers vertically to non-Being [which is a correct view] in contrast to nihilistic nothingness 滅無, and horizontally to [the state of] no-thought 無心 of the three types of unconditioned nothingness. K'ai-shan spoke of "a 'concurrence of causes' of two conventionalities, or again, to 'continue beyond.'" This clarifies [the idea that] when the third conventionality [as relative] arises, the first two [types of] conventionalities are the cause. Therefore [Chih-tsang] speaks of "a concurrence of causes." If a later conventionality arises before the former

Three types of conventionality 三假, **that is, conventional existence as causally arising** 因成假, **conventional existence as continuity** 相續假, **and relative conventional existence** 相待假: this is a summary of the meaning of "conventionality" used by many pre-Chih-i Buddhist scholars, based for a great part on the *Ch'eng-shih lun* (see T 32.327c29–328c23). The terms also appear in Hui-yüan's *Ta ch'eng i chang* (T 44.477c25–481b22). For details, see Swanson, *Foundations*, chapters 5 and 6, esp. 73–74, 87, and 94.

Three types of unconditioned [nothingness] 三無爲: an Abhidharma category of three "things" that are unchanging and unconditioned: unconditioned empty space *(ākāśa)*, unconditioned chosen extinction [that is, nirvana] *(pratisaṃkhyā-nirodha)*, and unconditioned unchosen extinction *(apratisaṃkhyā-nirodha)*.

K'ai-shan spoke of "a 'concurrence of causes' of two conventionalities, or again, to 'continue beyond' 開善云因兼二假或亦過之: that is, "a concurrence of causes" refers to "conventionality as causally arisen," and "to continue beyond" refers to "conventionality as continuity." This no doubt refers to Chih-tsang 智藏 (458–522) of the K'ai-shan ssu 開善寺, a prominent scholar of the *Ch'eng-shih lun* and *Mahāparinirvāṇa Sūtra*. His original writings do not survive, but some of his analysis of conventional existence and so forth are quoted (and criticized) by later scholars such as Chi-tsang. For details, see Swanson, *Foundations*, 89–95.

"A concurrence of causes" 因兼 **and to "continue beyond"** 過之: these two phrases of Chih-tsang, illustrating conventionality as causal arising and as continuity, appear again below at *Mo-ho chih-kuan* 65a2–7.

conventionality is removed[, this is "continuity"]; therefore [Chih-tsang] uses the phrase "to continue beyond." This clarifies the three [meanings of] conventionality in terms of the mind.

Next is to clarify three conventionalities in terms of [material] visible form *(rūpa)*. The karmic deeds from past lives are entrusted for birth through a mother and father, and thus you attain a physical body. This is conventional existence as causal arising. From the time you are in the womb to when you are a white-headed [elderly person], this is conventional existence as continuity. To have a body in contrast to not having a body is relative conventional existence.

Again, the world in which we dwell also involves three conventionalities. For example, a pillar is made of the four aspects of sensual perception [of sight, scent, taste, and touch], it changes as it passes through time and yet the continuity [as a "pillar"] is not interrupted, and it is a pillar in contrast to that which is not a pillar, as well as [having characteristics such as] long and short, large and small, and so forth. These are the three [meanings of] conventionality in accordance with the contents of the Tripitaka sūtras, as interpreted by the treatise masters. However, these terms are common [to the Mahāyāna] and not limited only to the Hīnayāna. [The *Ta chih tu lun* explains that] the Mahāyāna also speaks of three conventionalities. Things that arise though ignorance are like an apparition or magical illusion; these things have conventional designations but no [substantive] reality. The four aspects of sensual perception [of a pillar] reflected in a mirror are unobtainable, much less the image of a pillar. The pillar itself is unobtainable, so that even if there is continuity through time, and there is relative length or shortness of the illusory apparition; these are also unobtainable. In order to simplify this difficult matter, there are ten analogies [for emptiness]. Visible form itself is empty; it is not that form is extinguished to obtain emptiness. This is the meaning here; this is the principle of the three conventionalities from the perspective of the Mahāyāna.

Again, the *Ta chih tu lun* clarifies three kinds of existence: relative existence 相待有, existence as conventional designation 假名有 [or "nominal existence"], and the existence of [phenomenal] dharmas 法有. [1] Relative [existence] refers to the idea that something that is "long" is caused by the existence of something that is "short." Something that is "short" is caused

Treatise masters 論師: Chih-i is probably thinking in particular of the scholars of the *Ch'eng-shih lun*.

The Mahāyāna also speaks of three conventionalities … ten analogies 大乘亦名三假 … 明十喻: a summary of a lengthy passage from the *Ta chih tu lun*, T 25.357a1–358c8. See the glossary for details on the ten analogies, such as an echo, apparition, or magical illusion.

by the existence of something that is "long." All such comparisons are the same. There is something in the east, so there is something in the west. There is west, so there is east. There is no thing **[63b]** which is an exception [to this rule], and it is from this [relative contrast] that we have the distinction between east and west. These are names, and not [substantive] realities. This is "relative existence." [2] As for "existence as conventional designation," let us take cream [as an example]. The four aspects of the color, odor, flavor, and touch [of cream] combine in a confluence of causes and conditions to form that which is called "cream." Although it exists, it is not the same as its [constituent] causes and conditions. Although it has no [substantial] Being, it is not the same as the nothingness of the horns of a rabbit or the hair of a tortoise. It is just that it exists [provisionally] as a result of the combination of causes and conditions. This is called "existence as conventional designation." [3. The "existence of dharmas":] again, let us take the minute particles of form, scent, flavor, and touch which make up hair. Because of the hairs, there is down. Because of the down there is cloth. Because of the cloth there is a robe. This is the "existence of dharmas," that is, the merging of the minute particles of form, scent, flavor, and touch. Therefore we speak of "the existence of dharmas."

This is called "existence as conventional designation 是爲假名有: this sentence actually appears a couple of lines later in the Chinese text, but I think belongs here.

Again, ... Therefore we speak of "the existence of dharmas.": this whole paragraph is a summary from the *Ta chih tu lun*, T 147c6–21; see Lamotte, *La Traité* 2, 727–28, It is the second part of an argument against the realist position, in a section on "the non-existence of external objects":

> *Réfutation du 2e argument.*—En outre, il y a trois sortes d'existences *(bhāva)*: 1. l'existence relative *(prasparā-pekṣikabhāva)*, 2. l'existence nominale *(prajñāptibhāva)*, 3. l'existence réelle *(dharmabhāva)*.
>
> 1. Ont une existence relative, par exemple la longueur *(dīrghatva)* et la petitesse *(hrastva)*, la qualité d'être "celui-là," etc. En réalité, il n'y a ni longueur ni petitesse, ni objet éloigné, ni objet rapproché; c'est à cause d'une mutuelle relation qu'il est parlé de tout cela. La longueur existe à cause de la petitesse, et la petitesse existe à cause de la langueur; "celui-là" existe à cause de "celui-là." Si je me trouve à l'est d'un objet, il passera pour "occidental"; si je me trouve à l'ouest, il passera pour "oriental"; par rapport à un même et unique objet, existent des distinctions *(bheda)* entre est et ouest; mais, bien qu'elles portent un nom, elles n'ont pas de réalité. Voilà ce qu'on entend par existences relatives; il ne s'y trouve aucune réalité vraie, et elles ne sont pas comparables aux couleurs *(rūpa)*, odeurs *(gandha)*, saveurs *(rasa)*, tangibles *(sparṣṭavya)*, etc.
>
> 2. l'existence nominale *(prajñāptibhāva)*, par exemple, le lait *(kṣīra)* qui possède quatre facteurs: couleur *(rūpa)*, odeur *(gandha)*, saveur *(rasa)*, tangible *(sparṣṭavya)*. Quand ces causes et conditions *(hetupratyaya)* sont réunies, on parle vulgairement *(prajñaptitas)* de lait. Le lait existe, mais non pas de la façon dont la corne du lièvre *(śaśaviṣāṇa)* et le poil de la tortue *(kūrmaroma)* sont

[Question:] The *Ta chih tu lun* speaks of "provisionally establishing three [types of] conventionality." What do these "three [types of] conventionality" mean here?

> inexistants. C'est seulement en raison du complexe des causes et conditions *(hetupratyayasāmagrī)* qu'on dit vulgairement que le lait existe. Il en va de même pour l'étoffe.
>
> 3. En outre, c'est à cause des couleur, odeur, saveur et tangible à l'état d'atomes ultimes *(paramāṇu)* qu'il y a des particules de poils *(romabhāga)*: à cause des particules de poils, il y a des poils *(roman)*: à cuase des poils, il y a du duvet; à cause du duvet, il y a des fils *(tantu)*; à cause des fils, il y a une étoffe *(paṭa)*; à cause de l'étoffe, il y a un vêtement *(vastra)*.— Si les causes et conditions, à savoir la couleur, l'odeur, la saveur et le tangible à l'état d'atomes ultimes faisaient défaut, il n'y aurait pas de particules de poils; les particules de poils n'existant pas, il n'y aurait pas de poils; le poils n'existant pas, il n'y aurait pas de duvet; le duvet n'existant pas; il n'y aurait pas de fils; le fils n'existant pas, il n'y aurait pas d'étoffe; l'étoffe n'existant pas, il n'y aurait pas de vêtement.

Chodron (2, 577) has:

> Refutation of the 2nd argument. – Furthermore, there are three kinds of existence: 1. relative existence, 2. nominal existence, 3. real existence.
>
> 1. For example, length and shortness, the qualty of being "this" or "that," etc., have relative existence. In reality, there is neither length nor shortness, neither distance nor closeness; it is because of mutual relationship that we speak thus. Length exists as a result of shortness, and shortness exists as a result of length; "that" exists as a result of "this" and "this" exists as a result of "that." If I am east of an object, it will be looked upon as "western"; if I am west of an object, it will be looked upon as "eastern"; distinctions between east and west exist in relationship to one and the same object; but even though they have a name, they are not reality. That is what is meant by relative existences; no true reality is found there and they are not comparable to colors, smells, tastes, tangibles, etc.
>
> 2. Nominal existence, milk, for example, which has four factors: color, smell, taste, and touchable. When these causes and conditions come together, we commonly speak of milk. The milk exists, but not in the way dharmas coming from causes and conditions exist; the milk does not exist, but not in the way that the horns of a rabbit or the hair of a tortoise are non-existent. It is only as a result of the complex of causes and conditions that we commonly say that milk exists. It is the same for the cloth.
>
> 3. Moreover, it is as a result of color, smell, taste and tangible in the state of ultimate atoms that particles of hair exist; as a result of the particles of hair, there are hairs; as a result of hairs, there is fluff; as a result of fluff, there is thread; as a result of thread, there is cloth; as a result of cloth, there is a garment. - If the causes and conditions, namely, color, smell, taste and tangible in the state of ultimate atoms were lacking, there would be no hair particles; the hair particles not existing, there would be no hair; the hairs not existing, there would be no fluff; the fluff not existing, there would be no thread; the thread not existing, there would be no cloth; the cloth not existing, there would be no garment.

Provisionally establishing three [types of] conventionality 三假施説: a rephrasing from the *Ta chih tu lun*, T 25.357c2; however, the phrase is in the *Pañcaviṃśati Sūtra*, not the commentary section of the *Ta chih tu lun*:

> Bodhisattva-mahāsattvas practice the perfection of wisdom by provisionally

Answer: This is not a discussion of a different meaning; it matches what I am saying here. The provisional establishment of conventionality as phenomenal dharmas 法假施説 corresponds to causally arising 因成; the provisional establishment of conventionality as sensations 受假施説 corresponds to continuity 相續; the provisional establishment of conventionality as designation 名假施説 corresponds to relative [conventional existence] 相待. The *Ta chih tu lun* says, "The dharmas such as the five aggregates and so forth are 'conventionality as dharmas,' because the combining and merging of the five aggregates [and so forth] are called 'sentient beings.' It is from the roots, trunks, branches, and leaves that a tree gets its name; this is 'conventionality as sensations.' By using words to grasp the marks of two dharmas and explain them as two types; this is 'conventionality as designation.'" Thus we know that the meaning of these three conventionalities are the same [as the ones discussed above].

The *Ying-lo ching* also has a passage on three conventionalities. The *Pañcaviṃśati Sūtra* says, "Conceptions arise due to conditions; if there are no conditions, there would be no arising of conceptions"; this refers to the meaning of [conventionality as] causal arising.

The *Mahāparinirvāṇa Sūtra* says, "It is like when chanting the Dharma

establishing conventional existence as designation 名, provisionally establishing conventional existence as sensations *(vedanā)* 受, and provisionally establishing conventional existence as phenomenal dharmas 法.

The dharmas such as ... this is 'conventionality as designation': a summary of a passage in the *Ta chih tu lun*, T 25.358b21–26, which is the commentary on the passage identified in the previous note:

> Bodhisattvas should in this way learn of three types of conventionality 波羅聶提*(prajñapti)*: the dharmas such as the five aggregates are "conventionality as dharmas," because the five aggregates combining and merging through causes and conditions are called 'sentient beings'; the various bones combining and merging are called the skull, like roots, trunks, branches, and leaves combining and merging to be called a tree—this is called "conventionality as sensation" [or, (with the variant reading), as "taking" 取 (on characteristics)]; to use words to grasp the marks of two dharmas and explain them as two types is "conventionality as designation."

A passage on three conventionalities 三假之文: see the *Ying-lo ching*, T 24.1019c7–8:

> All phenomena arise through conditions. Conventional dharmas are without selfhood. The dharmas of existence are relative. Everything is marked with emptiness. That which has continuity is called one; emptiness is unobtainable.

Conceptions arise due to conditions; if there are no conditions, there would be no arising of conceptions 有縁思生無縁思不生: see the *Pañcaviṃśati Sūtra*, T 8.347a18–20:

> Śāriputra said, "Karmic deeds without conditions do not arise; conceptions without conditions do not arise; karmic deeds with conditions do arise; conceptions with conditions do arise."

[from a sūtra]—even though each succeeding thought perishes, nevertheless one is able to advance from one Āgama to another Āgama." It is like drinking and eating; though [the food and liquid] perishes from moment to moment, nevertheless one is able to [advance] from a state of hunger to that of satiety. This refers to the meaning of [conventionality as] continuity.

The *Vimalakīrti Sūtra* teaches that "Dharmas are without mutual relations, and not even a single thought abides [forever]." [This refers to the meaning of conventionality as relative.]

Thus you should know that the term "three types of conventionality" is in common use by both the Mahāyāna and Hīnayāna. It is not just the Hīnayāna that refers to samsaric dharmas as "views" and "conventional existence." As explained above, the Mahāyāna also refers to samsara in terms of "views" and "conventional existence."

In other words, the four gates of the Tripitaka [Teachings] gives rise to four views, and each of these views incorporates the three types of conventionality, the sixty-two views, the one hundred and eight afflictions, and so forth. The four gates of the Shared Teachings give rise to four views, and each of these views incorporates the three types of conventionality, the sixty-two views, the one hundred and eight afflictions, and so forth. The four gates of the Distinct Teachings give rise to four views, and each of these views incorporate the three types of conventionality, the sixty-two views, the one hundred and eight afflictions, and so forth. The four gates of the Perfect Teaching give rise to four views, and each of these views incorporates the three types of conventionality, the sixty-two views, the one hundred and eight afflictions, and so forth. The teachings of the Tathāgata attests to people an indisputable Dharma. For those who can assimilate [the teachings], it is like ambrosia; for those who cannot assimilate [the teachings], it is like poisonous herbs, and true words become vain words and give rise to [mistaken] verbal views, and the sixteen possibilities of the four gates give rise to [mistaken] views and conventionality [instead of to enlightenment].

It is like when chanting the Dharma . . . to advance from one Āgama to another Āgama 如讀誦法雖念念滅亦能從一阿含至一阿含: see the *Mahāparinirvāṇa Sūtra*, T 12.686a27–29:

> World Honored One. It is like chanting the Dharma [sūtras]; you chant from one Āgama to the second Āgama, up to the third and fourth Āgama. In this way, what you are chanting is transcient 無常, and finally you cannot reach the fourth [level]. However, as a result of increasing and lengthening the causes and conditions of this chanting, it is called "constant" 常.

Dharmas are without mutual relations, and not even a single thought abides 說法不相待一念不住: a phrase from the *Vimalakīrti Sūtra*, T 14.541b26. This passage has been quoted by Chih-i in the *Mo-ho chih-kuan* previously; see the note at 22b17.

2. The contemplation of emptiness [63b29–69c27]

Second, clarifying the contemplation for deconstructing the conventional consists of three parts: 1. the contemplation of deconstructing the conventional 破假觀; 2. clarification of **[63c]** gain and loss 得失; and 3. clarification of levels [of attainment] 位.

1. The contemplation of deconstructing the conventional [63c1–69a29]

The contemplation [of deconstructing the conventional] also consist of four topics: 1. deconstructing the individual [views]; 2. deconstructing the multiple [views]; 3. deconstructing the integrated or combined [views], and 4. deconstructing the [views that are] beyond words.

1. Deconstructing the individual views:
The mistaken views of Being and non-being [63c2–65b11]

Destroying the individual [mistaken] views consists of two parts: first a summary, and then a detailed exposition.

1. Summary [63c3]

To briefly summarize: when one momentary thought arises in the mind 一念心, this [thought] necessarily corresponds to one view from among the four individual types of views. A view involves the three types of conventionality; it consist of empty delusion and is without reality, and overflows with the eighty-eight afflictions as explained above. It manifests and exhibits all manner of evil, as explained fully below. One must have penetrating insight on the matter. Sparks fanned by the wind depend on [or originate from] a flame, the flame depends on [empty] space, and [empty] space does not depend on anything. [Empty] space is not empty [nothingness] 空尚無空. Where, then, do the flame and windblown sparks exist? Again, it is like experiencing hundreds of thousands of joys and sorrows in a dream while sleeping; originally both [these joys and sorrows] are quiescent and ultimately pure. [Realizing] this is "cessation."

Contemplation of deconstructing the conventional 破假觀: the following long discussion [to the end of page 69c] proceeds in terms of the tetralemma of existence and non-existence; being, non-being, both, and neither. Following the above pattern (see 62c) the first two options are discussed as the "individual views" [63c2–66a6], "both" as the "multiple" views [66a6–b4], and "neither" as the "integrated" views [66b4–c16], closing with a discussion of the views as beyond verbalization [66c17–69c29]. It is tempting to use the terms "existence" and "non-existence" here (instead of the usual "being and non-being") since the context below calls for using the verbs "exist" and "do not exist," but I use the terms "being and non-being" to maintain consistency with the previous section.

Again, contemplate ignorance as indivisible from Dharma-nature, non-dual and not different. Dharma-nature is originally pure, neither arising nor perishing. Ignorant, deluded thoughts are also pure. What arises, and what perishes? If we say that these thoughts arise and perish, then, horizontally speaking, Dharma-nature also arises and perishes. But the Dharma-nature does not arise, so how can it give rise to sorrow? Dharma-nature does not perish, so how can it give rise to joy? If there is no [arising of] joy and sorrow, how can we discriminate, saying, "this is Dharma-nature" and "this is ignorance"? Both the contemplator and that which is contemplated are like empty space. When you contemplate in this way, [you realize that everything is] ultimately pure. This is the contemplation of entering or realizing emptiness from conventionality.

2. Detailed Exposition [63c14]

Those with sharp faculties in practice based on faith [in the teachings] realize awakening with one hearing [of the Dharma]. Those whose practice is based on dharmas [of meditation] can attain understanding after pondering [the matter]. Those with dull faculties cannot realize awakening even if they hear [the Dharma] or ponder, but instead their flaws increase. Therefore the *Middle Treatise* says, "In the future, people in this world will turn increasingly dull, and produce various evils. They will not know for what reason [the teaching of] ultimate emptiness was taught. Therefore we have expansively produced methods of contemplation, and taught this *Middle Treatise*." Now, in the same way, for the sake of those with dull faculties, we must [explain] in detail the deconstruction of individual [views], multiple [views],

Originally both are quiescent and ultimately pure 本末雙寂畢竟清淨: that is, they are part of the dream, and "disappear" when one awakens. "Purity" is another expression for "empty."

In the future, people in this world will turn inceasingly dull,… taught this *Middle Treatise* 將來世中人根轉鈍造作諸惡。不知何因緣故說畢竟空。是故廣作觀法說於中論: a summary of the commentary on the opening verses of the *Middle Treatise*, T 30.1b29–c4 (see also the translation by Bocking, *Nāgārjuna in China*, 104–5):

> After the death of the Buddha, in the latter five hundred years, in the age of the shadow Dharma, *people's faculties will turn dull and they will become deeply attached to various dharmas*, and will seek the definitive marks of the twelvefold links of causation, the five aggregates, the twelve senses and sense organs, the eighteen sense fields, and so forth. *They will not know the intent of the Buddha* and merely cling to the verbal [explanations]. When they hear the Mahāyāna Dharma that teaches ultimate emptiness, *they will not know the reasons for this emptiness*, and give rise to doubt and [mistaken] views, [saying] "If everything is ultimately empty, then how do we distinguish between retribution or recompense for offences or virtue?" In this way they will not recognize [the difference between] the worldly truth and the supreme truth; they will grasp the

and so forth up to the views that cannot be verbalized. Generally I will use Nāgārjuna's tetralemma to deconstruct [mistaken views] and exhaust their purity.

1. The non-arising of Being [63c20]

If one momentary thought arises in the mind, this includes the three conventionalities. The three conventionalities are as explained above. You should contemplate this single thought [as follows]: [1] do thoughts arise in the mind on their own, or [2] do these thoughts arise in response to [external] objects, or [3] do these thoughts arise from both mental functions [the mind] and objects, or [4] do these thoughts arise apart from mental functions and objects?

[1.] If thoughts arise on their own, and the "pre-thought" is the sense faculty and the "after-thought" is consciousness, then do thoughts arise from sense faculties, or do thoughts arise from consciousness? If it is the case that sense faculties are able to arouse consciousness, then is it that they can arouse consciousness because consciousness exists in the sense faculty, or is it that they can arouse consciousness because consciousness does not exist in the sense faculty? If consciousness exists in the sense faculty, then the sense faculty and consciousness exist together, and there is neither that which does the arousing or that which is aroused [that is, one cannot give rise to the other]. Suppose consciousness does not exist in the sense faculty; however, [the sense faculty] is able to give rise to consciousness, but things without consciousness cannot give rise to consciousness. If consciousness does not already exist in the sense faculty, then how can it give rise to consciousness?

marks of emptiness and arouse covetous attachments. They will arouse various faults with regard to ultimate emptiness. It is for this reason that the bodhisattva Nāgārjuna produced this *Middle Treatise*.

Use Nāgārjuna's tetralemma to deconstruct and exhaust their purity 通用龍樹四句破令盡淨: the basic pattern for this logic is presented early in the *Middle Treatise*; see verse 3 of Chapter 1, T 30.2b6–10. Bocking (*Nāgārjuna in China*, 109–10) translates:

Dharmas are not self-produced,
Nor do they arise from others,
Nor from both, nor without a cause,
Therefore we know there is no arising.

As to "not self-produced": things do not exist by arising from their own substance but invariably depend upon a host of causes. Moreover, if they did arise from their own substance then each single dharma would have two substances. One would be the produced and the other would be the producer. If things were produced from their own substance without extraneous causes, then they would have neither causes nor conditions. Furthermore, arising would in turn have an arising, and there would be an endless regression of arising.

Chih-i's logic and presentation in what follows (63c20–66a6) is an almost endless variation on this basic pattern.

Suppose consciousness does not exist in the sense faculty but that there is a "consciousness-nature," and therefore [the sense faculty] can arouse consciousness. However, does this "consciousness nature" exist or not exist? If it exists, it is already consciousness [and not just its "nature"] and it exists in the sense faculty. **[64a]** Why, then, call it a "nature"? If a "consciousness-nature" does not exist in the sense faculty, then it cannot arouse consciousness. Again, are this "consciousness-nature" and consciousness [itself] one or different? If one, then it is already consciousness, and they can neither act on nor be acted upon [each other, since they are the same thing]. If different, this means that this involves "arising from another," and is no longer a thought arising on its own. In this way, by following the inferences [of the tetralemma] to their logical conclusions, we can ultimately know that a thought does not arise on its own.

[2.] Suppose we say that thoughts do not arise on their own, and that thoughts arise when an external object comes and arouses the thoughts, quoting the *[Pañcaviṃśati] Sūtra* that "Conceptions arise due to conditions; if there are no conditions, there would be no arising of conceptions." If this is so, then it means that the objects exist outside the mental functions, and come and arouse the internal consciousness, and therefore thoughts

Does this "consciousness nature" exist or not exist? If it exists, it is already consciousness and it exists in the sense faculty 此之識性是有是無。有已是識並在於根: or, "is this 'consciousness-nature' Being or nothingness? If it is Being, then the consciousness already exists in the sense faculty."

If a "consciousness-nature" does not exist in the sense faculty, then it cannot arouse consciousness 根無識性不能生識: or, "if the sense faculty does not possess the nature of consciousness ..."

... we can ultimately know that a thought does not arise on its own 如是推求畢竟知心不從自生: I must admit that I cannot follow the logical necessity of these conclusions, but it is clear that here and below Chih-i is attempting to follow Nāgārjuna's argumentation and the logic of the tetralemma. See also the discussion of "Coming and Going" in the second chapter of the *Middle Treatise* (T 30.3c5–5c15; Bocking, *Nāgārjuna in China*, 119–31), which opens:

> In the already-gone there is no going
> And in the not-yet-gone there is no going
> Apart from the already-gone and the not-yet-gone
> The moment of going also has no going.
>
> In the already-gone there is no going, since it is already gone. If there existed an "action of going" separate from "going" this would not be right. The not-yet-gone similarly has no going, since there is not yet any dharma of going. "The moment of going" means half gone and half not-yet-gone, because it is not separate from the already-gone and the not-yet-gone.

See also Richard Robinson's essay "Did Nāgārjuna Really Refute All Philosophical Views?" (1972).

Conceptions arise due to conditions; if there are no conditions, there would

depend on something else to arise. Now, if we analyze or make inferences concerning these external objects, is it that they are already thoughts and thus give rise to thoughts, or that they are not thoughts and thus give rise to thoughts? If [external] objects are [already] thoughts, then they cannot be called objects; Again, if they are not external to the mental functions, then this is a case of something arising from itself [which is not logically acceptable, as shown above]. Again, if two thoughts are lined up together, then there is neither "actor" nor that "acted upon." If the object is not [the same as] the thought, how is it able to give rise to thought? This [position] is deconstructed as shown above. If we say that there is a "nature for arousing" within the objects for giving rise to thoughts, then does this nature exist or not exist? If this "nature" exists, then the objects and this nature are lined up together, and there is neither "the actor" nor that "acted upon." If it does not exist, something that does not exist cannot give rise [to anything]. In this way, by following the inferences to their logical conclusions, we can know that thoughts ultimately do not arise from [external] objects.

[3.] Suppose we say that thoughts arise from a combination of the senses and their objects. Is it that the thoughts exist in each of the senses and their objects, and thoughts arise from their combination, or is it that the thoughts do not exist in each and then thoughts arise from their combination? If it is so that [thoughts] exist in each, then their combination should result in the arising of two thoughts; this falls into the contradiction of both [arising from] self and others [which was refuted and deconstructed above]. If it is so that [thoughts] do not exist in each, then there will be none even if they combine. This is analogous to saying that a mirror and a face each have an image so the image arises from combining them, or that neither has an image so an image arises from combining them. If [the mirror and a face] each have an image, then the result [of their combination] would be two images. If neither has an image, then their combination would not give rise [to an image]. Suppose you say that the combination of a face and a mirror results in one — an arising of an image. However, [the face and mirror] are not truly combined, and if they really are combined, there is no image. Suppose you say that the mirror and the face are separate, and therefore this gives rise to an image. However, this implies that each has one side and that therefore there is an image, but surely this cannot be. The combination and separation of the senses and their objects are also like this [that is, they are

be no arising of conceptions 有緣思生無緣思不生: from the *Pañcaviṃśati Sūtra*, T 8.347a18–20, as quoted above under *Mo-ho chih-kuan* 63b14–15.

Combination of the senses and their objects 根塵: lit. "sense organs and sense objects" but "the senses and their objects" make more sense in this context.

logically unobtainable]. In this way, by following the inferences to their logical conclusions, we can know that ultimately thoughts do not arise from a combination [of two factors].

Again, suppose that the "nature" of thoughts exists in the senses and their objects, and thoughts arise through their combination. One should consider, then, whether this "nature" exists or does not exist, and this position is deconstructed as shown above.

[4.] Suppose that senses and their objects give rise to thoughts while separate from each other. This is an arising of conditions without cause [which is impossible]. Does this "separation" exist or does this "separation" not exist? If we say that this separation exists, then when we say that [thoughts] arise through conditions, what does it mean to say that they are "separate"? If this separation does not exist, then what can arise from nothing? If we say that there is a "nature" [of arising] that exists in this separation, then does this "nature" exist or not exist? If this nature exists, then when [thoughts] arise through conditions, we cannot call this a "separation." If this nature does not exist, then what can arise from nothing? In this way, by following the inferences to their logical conclusions, we can know that thoughts ultimately do not arise from the separation [of two factors].

The *Middle Treatise* says, "dharmas do not arise from themselves, nor do they arise from others, nor do they arise together, nor **[64b]** without a cause. Therefore they are said to be 'non-arising.'" This is the meaning here.

1. Conventionality as causally arising [64b1]

If we follow the logical inferences of the tetralemma with regard to "conventionality as causally arising" to discover that arising is "unobtainable," then our attachment to the nature [of mistake views] is weakened. There is only verbal designation, which [in this case] is the name "the arising of thoughts." This "designation" does not exist internally nor externally, nor somewhere in between. Neither does it have permanent self-existence. The words are "non-abiding." That is, they do not abide in the sense of the four possibilities of

Dharmas do not arise from themselves, nor do they arise from others, nor do they arise together, nor without a cause. Therefore they are said to be 'non-arising'. 諸法不自生。亦不從他生。不共不無因。是故説無生: see the third verse in the first chapter of the *Middle Treatise*, T 30, 2b6–7. See note above and the translation by Bocking, *Nāgārjuna in China*, 109:

Dharmas are not self-produced,
Nor do they arise from others,
Nor from both, nor without a cause,
Therefore we know there is no arising.

Arising is "unobtainable" 不得: that is, there is no way it can be logically explained or "obtained."

This "designation" does not exist internally nor externally, nor somewhere in between 名不在内外中間: a phrase from

being, nor is it that they do not abide at all (that is, are nothing), nor is it that they do not abide in the sense of the four possibilities of non-being or nothingness; therefore thoughts do not abide. Thoughts "exist" [conventionally] as verbal designation; verbal designations are empty [of substantial Being]. If we use the tetralemma [in this way] to make inferences concerning the nature [of views] and realize that there is no [substantial] "nature" of views, this is the worldly truth, the deconstruction of the nature [of views]; this is called the "the nature of emptiness [of views]." If we use the tetralemma to make inferences concerning designations and realize that there is no [substantial] "designation" of views, this is the real truth, the deconstruction of the conventional; this is called the "emptiness of marks." The nature and marks [of views] are both empty; this is the general [analysis of] the contemplation of entering or realizing emptiness from conventionality. Therefore the *Middle Treatise* says that dharmas do not arise from themselves. To use contemplation in this way is the same as the intent of the *Middle Treatise*.

[Eighteen Kinds of Emptiness] [The arising of] thoughts cannot be obtained if we examine the senses [themselves]; this is "internal emptiness." There are no thoughts if we examine [sense] objects; this is "external emptiness." It cannot be obtained if we examine the senses and their objects merged together; this is "internal and external emptiness." It cannot be obtained if we examine them separately [from each other]; this is the "emptiness of emptiness." It cannot be obtained if we examine the four natures; this is the "emptiness of natures." It cannot be obtained if we examine the four possibilities [of the tetralemma]; this is the "emptiness of marks." If we examine external objects, we realize that they have no Being anywhere in the ten directions; this is "great emptiness." It cannot be obtained even by seeking through the greatest vehicle; this is "emptiness as the supreme meaning." It cannot be obtained through analyzing causes and conditions with the tetralemma; this is the "emptiness of the conditioned." If we explain the unconditioned as caused by the conditioned, then the conditioned is unobtainable and the unconditioned is unobtainable; this is the "emptiness of the unconditioned." If we seek the basis of the arising of thoughts through

the *Pañcaviṃśati Sūtra*, T 8.230c8–9: "The term 'bodhisattva' is *also only a verbal designation. This verbal designation does not exist internally, nor does it exist externally, nor does it exist somewhere in between.*"

Words are "non-abiding" 字不住: the "non-abiding" of verbal designation or words is discussed at length in the *Pañcaviṃśati Sūtra*, T 8.234a–235a.

Dharmas do not arise from themselves: see the *Middle Treatise*, T 30, 2b6, quoted a few lines above.

Four natures 四性: that is, things do not arise from themselves, from others, from a merging of these two, or separate from these two 自他共離.

the tetralemma, it is unobtainable; this is the "emptiness of that without beginning." If we seek the perishing of thoughts through the tetralemma, it is unobtainable; this is the "emptiness of that which is dispersed." If we seek the arising and perishing of thoughts through the tetralemma, it is unobtainable. The non-arising and non-perishing of thoughts is also unobtainable. This is the "emptiness of the ultimate." "There are no separate dharmas in the triple world apart from those created by the mind," but if we examine these thoughts, they are unobtainable. This is the "emptiness of all." In contemplating thoughts or the mind, there is no "mind"; in contemplating emptiness, there is no "emptiness"; this is the "emptiness of that which cannot be obtained." If we contemplate the three conventionalities of views as existing, they cannot be obtained; this is the "emptiness of dharmas that exist." If we contemplate the three conventionalities of views as not existing, they cannot be obtained; this is the "emptiness of dharmas that do not exist." If we contemplate the three conventionalities as both existing and not existing, they cannot be obtained; this is the "emptiness of dharmas that exist and do not exist." To contemplate in this way is the same as the intent of the *Pañcaviṃśati Sūtra*; these are eighteen types of contemplation of entering or realizing emptiness from conventionality.

2. Conventionality as continuity [64b25]

If you cannot become awakened [through the above logical analysis of conventionality as causally arising], then turn your attention to "conventionality as continuity" to deconstruct [mistaken views]. Why? Because even though, by means of the fourfold deconstruction [of views] from the perspective of conventionality as causally arising [you should see that] the arising of thoughts cannot be obtained, if you observe the thoughts [and views] that manifest themselves now, the arising and perishing of these thoughts is continuous and unending. How can one say [simply] that they are "non-arising"? As for these thoughts, is it that first one thought perishes and a later thought arises? Or is it that a prior thought does not perish before the later thought arises? Or is it that a prior thought both perishes and [64c] does not

There are no separate dharmas in the triple world apart from those created by the mind 三界無別法唯是一心作: see, for example, the *Avataṃsaka Sūtra*, T 9.558c10: "The triple world is an empty delusion; it is only made by the mind." See also the *Ta chih tu lun*, T 25.276b10: "The existences of the triple world are all creations of the mind."

To contemplate in this way is the same as the intent of the *Pañcaviṃśati Sūtra*: see the list of "eighteen kinds of emptiness" in the *Pañcaviṃśati Sūtra*, T 8219c9–12 or 250b–c; see also the *Ta chih tu lun*, T 25.285c7–10. This list has been referred to already in the *Mo-ho chih-kuan*, 13b29.

perish, and then the later thought arises? Or does a prior thought neither perish nor not perish before the later thought arises?

If a prior thought does not perish before another thought arises, this means that a thought gives rise to a thought by itself, that both arisings appear together, so that there is no [distinct] "actor" and "acted upon." If the "nature" of arising exists in the prior thought, which arises as the later thought, does this "nature" exist or not exist? If it exists, it is not [merely] a nature, and if it does not exist, then it cannot arise, as explained previously. What if the later thought arises after the prior thought perishes? [In the previous example we said that] an arising while the prior [thought] had not yet perished is called [having] "selfness" [or "own-being"] 自性*(svabhāva)*, that is, the arising of a later thought [on its own]. Now [in this case] the arising depends on the perishing; non-perishing [that is, "arising"] aspires for perishing. What is this if not an "other-nature"? As for this "other-nature" within perishing, is there arising because the arising exists, or is there arising because the arising does not exist? Suppose we say that arising exists for this arising; however, arising and perishing are mutually exclusive. This is the arising of arising; how can it be said that arising perishes? Suppose we say that arising does not exist in perishing; but how is nothing able to result in arising? Suppose the "nature" of arising exists in perishing, but we can deconstruct [this idea of] nature as explained above. Suppose the prior thought both perishes and does not perish for the arising of the later thought? If perishing is already associated with perishing, and if non-perishing is already associated with non-perishing, or if non-perishing is merged or combined with perishing to result in arising, then these are examples of arising together. But "arising together" is itself contradictory [and mutually exclusive]. How can mutually exclusive factors result in arising? Again, suppose that each arises individually? This contains two faults. Each cannot arise individually [and independently], and neither can they arise merged together. Suppose the "nature" of arising exists within perishing and non-perishing. Does this [nature] exist or not exist? If the nature has a fixed existence, how can it be called "perishing" or "non-perishing"? If this [nature] does not have a fixed existence, then again how can it be called "perishing" or "non-perishing"? This cannot avoid the mistake of [the two extremes] of annihilationism and eternalism, which cause people to fall into the mistake of [thinking that things arise] together. Suppose that the prior thought neither perishes nor does not perish, and yet the later thought arises in the mind. Does this "neither-arising-nor-not-arising" exist, or does this "neither-arising-nor-not-arising" not exist? If it exists, then it does not

"Other-nature" 他性: that is, depending on something else, or an "other," in order to arise.

lack a cause. If it does not exist, the lack of a cause cannot result in arising. Suppose that the "nature" of arising exists in the lack of a cause; but then this "nature" would be a "cause." How could you say that there is lack of cause? If it does not exist, then what can arise from nothing?

In this way, if we follow the inferences of the tetralemma with regard to conventionality as continuity, we discover that thoughts [and views] are unobtainable and the four natures [of arising from one's self, from another, from both, or from neither] have no reality, then mental attachments will weaken. Thoughts exist only as verbal designations; these words do not abide [eternally or substantially], neither internally nor externally nor somewhere in between. Again, they have no eternal self-existence. Their continuity is without [essential] nature; this is the deconstruction of [the concept of] nature from the perspective of the worldly truth. These designations are empty in nature. Their continuity is without designation; this is the deconstruction of the conventional from the perspective of the real truth. "Designations" imply the "emptiness of marks"; "nature" and "marks" are both empty, and so forth as explained previously with regard to the eighteen types of emptiness. This is called the contemplation of entering or realizing emptiness from conventionality.

3. Conventionality as relativity [64c25]

If realization was not obtained [through the above analysis], you should conjecture by comparing thoughts as existing with thoughts as not existing. This is different from the above [analysis of conventionality as causally arising and as continuity] in that the delusions of relativity arise. [The perspective of] causally arising involves taking and merging the two dharmas of senses and their objects for the sake of [speaking of] causal arising. [The perspective of] continuity involves vertically grappling with the intentional [mental] faculty from the prior to later [thoughts] for the sake of [speaking of] continuity. Approaching arising and perishing from a vertical perspective is to consider [arising and] perishing with distinct [individual characteristics]. A distinct [individual perspective of arising and] perishing is narrow. Now, "conventionality as relativity" is a comparison of general [or shared characteristics of] [arising and] perishing. This meaning is vast.

The general or common [characteristics of arising and] perishing is as follows. It is like the three types of unconditioned [nothingness]; these do not involve "perishing" per se **[65a]**, but they warrant being referred to as "non-arising." To speak of the arising of thoughts in relative comparison to

Three types of unconditioned 三無為: see above at 63a12, which contains these terms in the context of a similar discussion; Chih-i is building on these above arguments.

the non-arising of empty space; this is "conventionality as relativity." If you do not attain awakening through the above [analysis], but instead this causes the above delusions [associated with conventionality as causal arising and continuity], so that this [later] delusion [associated with conventionality as relativity] arises together [with the above delusions]; this is called a "concurrence of causes." Or if the above delusions already exist, and again arise with this [later] delusion, it is referred to as "continuing beyond." Again, "concurrence of causes" refers to the arising of the root of consciousness in response to the objects of non-arising phenomena; this refers to [conventional reality as] causally arisen. The relativity of continuity is caused by the above conventional thoughts; this refers to [conventional reality as] continuity. Therefore we speak of "concurrent causes." "Continuing beyond" refers the arising of delusions that are not of the general or common [characteristics of arising and] perishing with regard to the above two kinds of conventionality. Now [delusions] do arise in terms of the general or common [characteristics of arising and] perishing; how can this not be [the meaning of] "continuing beyond"? This interpretation is different from the old ones, but I have borrowed these terms to signify the characteristics of conventionality as relativity.

Now, if we examine these thoughts, is it [1] that thoughts arise in [relative] relation to the non-arising of thoughts, or is it that [2] thoughts arise in relation to the existence of thoughts, or is it [3] that thoughts arise in relation to both the arising and non-arising of thoughts, or is it that [4] thoughts arise in relation to neither arising nor non-arising?

[1] If thoughts arise in relation to non-arising, does this "non-arising" exist or does this "non-arising" not exist? [2] If they arise in relation to existence, this is a relative existence. [If they arise in relation to non-existence,] how can there be a relative non-existence? [3] If this is a mutual relationship between existences, then this is an arising from itself [which is untenable]. If

Non-arising of empty space 虚空: that is, thoughts exist, relatively speaking, compared to the non-existence or nothingness of empty space.

"Concurrence of causes" 因兼: this is a phrase quoted above from the work of Chih-tsang 智蔵, to illustrate "conventionality as causally arisen." See the discussion above at 63a12–15.

"Continuing beyond" 過之: another phrase of Chih-tsang, illustrating "conventionality as continuity." See previous note.

I have borrowed these terms to signify the characteristics of conventionality as relativity: Chih-i admits that he has taken Chih-tsang's terms ("concurrent causes" and "continuing beyond") and given them a new twist or interpretation. Perhaps among the Cheng-lun scholars these were important technical terms with specific meaning, but Chih-i reinterprets them for his own system.

the non-arising does not exist, then how can there be a relationship [between anything]? [4] If it is just that this is a relationship between non-existences that yet gives rise to thoughts, then all is non-existent [nothingness], and yet this non-existence gives rise to thoughts. Non-existence yearns for existence; this non-existence would involve "arising from another" [which is untenable].

Again, suppose that although non-arising does not exist, yet it has the "nature" of existence, and that in relation to this nature we can know that there are thoughts. Is this "nature" "former arising" or "pre-arising"? If it is "former arising," then the thought has already arisen. How can it be called a "nature"? If the nature is "pre-arising," then how can this pre-arising give rise [to anything]? If thoughts arise in relation to arising, then arising is in turn related to arising; but how can "long" be in relation to "long"? This has no meaning. How, then, can one obtain the arising of thoughts? Suppose non-arising is related to arising, and therefore there is the arising of thoughts. But this is like obtaining the existence of "long" through the relation of "long" and "short." This falls into two faults. Suppose each exists, but then two arisings are together [which is untenable]. Suppose each do not exist; but this is completely untenable, as explained above. Suppose the arising of thoughts involves a relation between neither arising nor non-arising? The *Middle Treatise* says, "Arising is not possible through causes and conditions; how can it be possible through no causes and conditions?"

Again, does this "lack of cause" exist or not exist? If it exists it in turn is related to existence. If it does not exist then it is related to non-existence. How, then, can it be said to lack a cause? Suppose we say that there is a "nature"? Does this nature exist or not exist? If the nature exists, does it arise

Non-existence yearns for existence 無望於有: or, "nothingness seeks being," or "nature abhors a vacuum"?

Two faults 二過: the two logical inconsistencies of "arising from itself" and "arising from another"?

Arising is not possible through causes and conditions; how can it be possible through no causes and conditions? 從因緣生尚不可何況無因緣: a paraphrase of the *Middle Treatise*, T 30.2c18–19. The context reads (Bocking, 105–106):

> As to "no arising," the commentators expound the characteristic of "arising" in various ways. Some say that cause and effect are identical, some say that cause and effect are different, some say that the effect pre-exists in the cause, some say that the effect does not pre-exist in the cause, some say that things arise from themselves, and some say that they arise from other things, while some say that they arise from both together. Some say that arising exists, while others say that arising is non-existent. Such ways of expounding the characteristic of arising are entirely wrong, and these matters will be enlarged upon later. Since no fixed characteristic of arising is tenable, there is no arising. As for "no ceasing"; if there is no arising, how can there be ceasing? Since there is no arising and no ceasing, the remaining six are also negated.

or not arise? If it arises, then how can it be said to be [just] a "nature"? If it does not arise, then how is it able to arise?

If you follow the tetralemma in this way, you discover that the arising of thoughts as relative conventionality is unobtainable. Your thoughts that are attached [to mistaken views] are thus weakened, and you do not give rise to [the idea of a substantial] nature or reality, but [realize] that they have existence merely as conventional designations. The arising of conventional designations is not an arising [of substantial being]; these words do not exist [substantially] either internally nor externally nor in between, nor do they have eternal self-existence. These words have no [substantial] existence [as their referents]; if you seek **[65b]** their "nature," it is unobtainable. [To realize] this is the destruction or deconstruction of "nature" as the worldly truth. This is called "the emptiness of nature." If you seek the name, you find that it is unobtainable; this is the deconstruction of conventionality as the real truth. This is called "the emptiness of marks." Again, if you seek the sense realms in terms of [essential] natures or marks, you find that they are unobtainable. This is called the "emptiness of dharmas." And so forth for the eighteen types of emptiness as explained above.

This is called "entering emptiness from conventionality," opening the eye of wisdom, and perceiving the supreme meaning. It is not merely that the delusions of the [mistaken] views of the three types of conventionality are removed, but that all the delusions and [mistaken] views will be purified, and correct wisdom made manifest. This is called "penetrating the gate of non-arising through cessation-and-contemplation." Again, [the practice of] cessation-and-contemplation perfects the gate of non-arising.

If you still do not realize awakening [through the above analysis], then you should utilize cessation-and-contemplation to skillfully deconstruct the [mistaken] views of conventionality. Alternate between [practice based on] faith and [practice based on] the dharmas [of meditation] to perfect and realize the way of [preparatory] means and thus overcome the mistaken views of being. Immeasurable afflictions can all be overcome. Because they are overcome, this is called [a state of] good yet [still] defiled five aggregates. Since these are overcome, [mistaken] views of being do not arise. However, this time [mistaken] views of non-being [or nothingness] will enter your calculations, and should be deconstructed as [I will explain] below.

2. *The non-arising of non-Being [or nothingness]* [65b11]

The deconstruction of these [mistaken] views [of nothingness] varies depending on [those whose practice is based on faith through] hearing 聞

Eighteen types of emptiness: see the discussion above at *Mo-ho chih-kuan* 64b.

or [those whose practice is based on the dharma of meditation or] pondering 思. People with superior faculties will come to know both arising and non-arising through hearing of the contemplation of arising, and thus destroy attachments and attain awakening. People with middling faculties have light attachments, so they can realize the overcoming of [mistaken] views through [skillful] means and a good [state] of the defiled five aggregates. Those of inferior faculties have heavy attachments, and so they grasp hard onto these attachments and, hearing that arising is deconstructed and unobtainable, they then take "non-arising" as the truth, thus giving rise to [mistaken] views concerning non-arising.

Again, one should make a general and distinct detailed analysis of the destruction of this [mistaken view of nothingness].

1. General analysis [65b16]

The general analysis is as follows. As it says in the *Pañcaviṃśati Sūtra*, "The non-arising of consciousness is unobtainable; how much more so the arising of consciousness. Again, the arising of consciousness is unobtainable; how much more so the non-arising of consciousness. Arising and non-arising are both unobtainable." In the *Laṅkāvatāra Sūtra* there is an extensive discussion of the deconstruction of the [mistaken] views of non-arising. However, the principle of non-arising is not something that can be known through conscious [deliberation]; how much less so through emotions. If you abandon [the mistaken view of substantial] being but then take on [the mistaken

General 總 and distinct 別 detailed analysis: Chan-jan (BT–III, 508) points out that the "general" analysis concerns destroying or deconstructing views directly through the cultivation of contemplation, and that the "distinct" detailed analysis involves an analysis of the three types of conventionality and the tetralemma.

The non-arising of consciousness ... are both unobtainable 識無生尚不可得何況識生。又識生尚不可得何況識無生。生與無生俱不可得: the source of this quote is not certain. The *Kōgi* (BT–III, 509) identifies it as from "section 43-3" in the *Ta chih tu lun*, and Ikeda (*Kenkyūchūshaku*, 367) identifies a passage in the *Ta chih tu lun*, T 25.369c–370a. This section in the *Ta chih tu lun* is a actually a passage from the *Pañcaviṃśati Sūtra* and contains the following similar phrasing:

> Form is empty; the arising and culmination of this form is unobtainable. Sensations, conceptions, volitions, and consciousness are empty; the arising and culmination of this consciousness [and so forth] is unobtainable. And so forth up to ultimate reality is empty; the arising and culmination of this ultimate reality is unobtainable.

An extensive discussion of the deconstruction of the [mistaken] views of non-arising 廣破無生見: see the *Laṅkāvatāra Sūtra*, e.g. T 16.542a5–13:

> People in the world fall into two [mistaken] views. What are these two? The first is the view of [substantial] existence

view of] non-being [or nothingness], you are like an inchworm [which can only make a little progress]. Again, this is like a monkey. One should not, with vain delusion, grasp onto these attachments of [mistaken] views.

This is the general [analysis of] the deconstruction [of mistaken views].

2. Distinct detailed analysis [65b21]

The distinctive [detailed] analysis is as follows. If practitioners use cessation-and-contemplation to deconstruct the three [types of] conventionality [such as that of] causally arising, they realize that "natures" and "marks" [and so forth] are unobtainable. Having put an end to [mistaken views], they enter meditative concentration wherein there are no relative forms such as "internal and external" or "before and after." They dwell in quiescent concentration, awake yet oblivious of body and mind, wherein all is pure. They arouse thoughts of nothingness, and spontaneously attain the cessation-and-contemplation of non-arising, thus [prematurely thinking that] they have perfected both concentration and wisdom. However, they arouse attachment

[or Being]. The second is the view of non-being [or nothingness]. Therefore they perceive all phenomena as existing, or perceive all phenomena as non-existing.... Why do people in the world fall into the [mistaken] view of nothingness? They speak of greed, anger, and ignorance as substantially-existing greed, anger, and ignorance, and also speak of the non-existence of greed, anger, and ignorance. They thus discriminate between being and non-being.

See also the translation by D.T. Suzuki (*The Laṅkāvatāra Sūtra*, 125):

> Then the Blessed One said: People of this world are dependent on two things, Mahāmati, that is, they are dependent on the idea of being and on that of non-being, and they fall into the views whereby they take pleasure either in nihilism or realism. They imagine emancipation where there is no emancipation.... Now, Mahāmati, what is meant by being dependent upon the idea of non-being? It means, Mahāmati, admitting greed, anger, folly, and yet discriminating as regards the non-reality of what makes up greed, anger, and folly; and, Mahāmati, there is one who does not admit the reality of things because of their being devoid of individual marks; and there is another who, seeing that the Buddhas, Śrāvakas, and Pratyekabuddhas are free from greed, anger, and folly, because of all things being devoid of individual marks, [think that greed, anger, and folly] do not exist.

Like an inchworm 歩屈蟲: or, 屈歩蟲. See the earlier reference to an inchworm at *Mo-ho chih-kuan* 41b5: "You realize [the extreme of] nothingness by getting rid of [lit., "moving" the notion of] Being, like an inchworm who can attain [some] movement but is not able to cultivate the practices of the path," a reference to a passage in the *Mahāparinirvāṇa Sūtra*, T 12.410b22–24.

Like a monkey 似獼猴: it is not clear in what sense Chih-i is comparing those who shift from a mistaken view of Being to a mistaken view of nothingness to a monkey. The *Kōgi* (BT–III, 510) takes a stab at interpretation by pointing out that monkeys swing from branch to branch as they play in the trees.

to the [mistaken] view [of non-being], and become attached to this empty concept. This is not what the Buddhas have taught. Why is this not what they have taught? If you contemplate thoughts and speculate thereupon, you will arouse a minute part of meditative concentration, and give rise to a partial understanding of emptiness. This then becomes a [mistaken] view of emptiness; how can the correspondence of your thoughts with such [an understanding of] phenomenal objects be equated with [a full understanding of] non-arising? The *Ta chih tu lun* explains briefly that there are two types of contemplations of emptiness: Buddhist and non-Buddhist. How are they different? "The non-Buddhist [contemplation] involves becoming passionately attached to the wisdom that comes from contemplating emptiness." Thus those who face in this direction arouse a sense of the emptiness of sense objects **[65c]** and think that this is [the attainment of] nirvana. There are people who perceive [emptiness] in this way. Those who perceive in this way give rise to the [mistaken] view [of the substantial existence of] the body. Because of this view of the body, they have the ten afflictions, both sharp and dull, up to and including the eighty-eight [types of passionate afflictions], and their activity in the cycle of birth and death is as explained above. Such offences and faults are all based on and arise from [the one-sided view of] the emptiness of sense objects. They obstruct the true [realization of emptiness] and thus the path is lost; how can this be an encounter with nirvana! This is called a heretical non-Buddhist perception of emptiness. When

Thoughts of nothingness 無心: or, "they arouse [the state of] no-thoughts (*mushin*)."

The non-Buddhist [contemplation] involves becoming passionately attached to the wisdom that comes from contemplating emptiness 外道愛著觀空智慧: from a section in the *Ta chih tu lun* on "the *prajña*-wisdom of non-Buddhists"; see Lamotte, *Le Traité* 2, 1070–74, esp. 1071 (T 25.191c15–19):

> Question.—Vous disiez ci-dessus que les hérétiques contemplant le vide. En contemplant le vide, ils rejettent tous les Dharma; pourquoi dites-vous donc qu'ils ne rejettent pas tous les Dharma et qu'en conséquence ils n'ont pas le vraie sagesse?
>
> Réponse.—En contemplant le vide, les hérétiques saisissent les caractères du vide (*śūnyanimittāny udgṛhṇanti*); bien qu'ils connaissent la vacuité des Dharma (*dharmaśūnyatā*), ils n'admettent pas la vacuité du Moi (*ātmaśūnyatā*), car ils s'attachment à la sagesse contemplant le vide.

Chodron (2, 831) has:

> Question. You said that heretics contemplate emptiness. In contemplating emptiness, they do reject all dharmas; why do you say then that they do not reject all dharmas and consequently do not have true wisdom?
>
> Answer. In contemplating emptiness, heretics grasp at the characteristic of emptiness; they do not accept the emptiness of self for they are attached to the wisdom contemplating emptiness.

Ten afflictions, both sharp and dull 利鈍十使: these ten afflictions (from "a mistaken view of the self" to "doubt") are listed by Chih-i above at *Mo-ho chih-kuan* 62b10–18, and again below at 66a19–23.

disciples of the Buddha contemplate non-arising, if they arouse thoughts of emptiness—or when they arouse thoughts of emptiness—they know that this is a passionate [attachment]. Why? Because what arises is a passionate [attachment] to dharmas. A phenomenon of passionate attachment is a matter of ignorance. Ignorance gives rise to the eighty-eight passionate afflictions such as the [mistaken] view of a [substantial] self. Each and every one of these includes the delusions of the three types of conventionality. Finally, [the disciples of the Buddha] are not attached [to these mistaken views] as true non-arising.

What are the three types of conventionality [with regard to the mistaken view of non-being or nothingness]? Suppose that, as outlined above, the [mistaken] views of being of the three types conventionality are overcome and you realize the view of non-being. The non-arising phenomenal object presents itself to the [intentional] mental faculty, and this gives rise in the mind to a thought of emptiness; this is conventionality as causal arising. The mental process that arises thus perishes, and therefore there is the arising of a non-arising thought; this is conventionality as continuity. Suddenly there is a "non-arising" in contrast to an "arising" of an existence; this is conventionality as relativity.

If we were to speculate concerning the arising of this non-arising thought, is it [1] that the arising comes from the mind, or that [2] the arising comes from the phenomenal object, or [3] from both, or [4] separate from them?

[1] If it arises from the mind, does it arise from the [mental] sense faculty or does it arise from consciousness? If it arises from the organ, does consciousness arise because consciousness exists in the organ, or does consciousness arise because consciousness does not exist [in the organ]? If consciousness exists in the organ, that organ is not [just] an organ. If the consciousness exists in the organ, then it cannot be the place of its activity. But if the consciousness does not exist in the organ, how can consciousness arise there? Suppose the "nature" of arising consciousness exists in the organ. Does this "nature" exist or not exist? If the nature exists, then the nature of consciousness and consciousness itself are both one and different. If one, then the nature is the consciousness. If different, then how can something different give rise to it? If we examine the thoughts as arising from themselves, this also is unobtainable. It is all as explained in detail above.

[2] Suppose non-arising thoughts arise on the basis of phenomenal objects. Do these objects exist in the thoughts or not exist in the thoughts? If they exist in the thoughts, then they cannot be the place [of activity]. If they do not exist, they are not able to give rise [to thoughts]. Again, are these objects one or different from [thoughts]? If one, then they cannot act

as the place [of activity]. If different, then they are not able to give rise [to thoughts]. If we examine the possibility of different thoughts, this also is unobtainable. This is all as explained in detail above.

[3] Suppose there is the arising of non-arising thoughts due to the combination of the [mental] organ and phenomenal objects. This [supposition] has two faults, as explained previously.

[4] Again, suppose there is the arising of non-arising thoughts apart from the [mental] organ and apart from phenomenal objects. This is unobtainable due to the interplay of causes and conditions. Why? [The idea that nothing arises] without a cause is as explained above.

It should be known that non-arising thoughts come neither from themselves nor from others nor from a merging [of the two] nor separate from [the two] 不自不他不共不離, so they do not have these four natures. Since they do not have these four natures, this is called "the emptiness of [essential] natures." The emptiness of natures means that though there are no [substantial] thoughts, it is [conventionally] said that there are thoughts. "There is only verbal designation; this verbal designation does not exist either internally nor externally." This is called the "emptiness of marks," and so forth for the eighteen kinds of emptiness, as explained above. This is to realize emptiness from conventionality and perceive the supreme meaning. It means that you do not merely deconstruct **[66a]** [the delusions of] conventionality with regard to the [mistaken] view of non-existence, but you remove all [delusions and mistaken views] from the higher delusions to the lower obstructions, and attain correct wisdom. If there are some [faults] that are not yet extracted, diligently use cessation-and-contemplation to skillfully cultivate [their removal]. If you alternate between [the practices based on] faith and dharma[-meditation] to perfect the way of [skillful preparatory] means, you can overcome suffering and the causes of suffering, and overcome all the eighty-eight afflictions of the sense fields. Since these can be overcome, this is called a defiled yet good [mental state]. Through the power [gained] from such diligent cultivation, the [mistaken] view of nothingness within [the delusions of] conventionality will not arise again. Instead, this time you will face the [mistaken] views of both being and non-being within [the delusions of] conventionality. These are to be deconstructed next [as explained below].

There is only verbal designation; this verbal designation does not exist either internally nor externally: this passage from the *Pañcaviṃśati Sūtra*, T 8.230c7–9, has already been quoted above at *Mo-ho chih-kuan* 64b2–3; see note above.

2. *Destroying the multiple views: Deconstructing the mistaken views of both-being-and-non-being* [66a6]

Next, the deconstruction of the three conventionalities of the [mistaken] views of both-being-and-non-being 亦有亦無 is as follows. When a practitioner utilizes cessation-and-contemplation well and overcomes the delusions of the [mistaken] views of nothingness, then the conventionalities of [the mistaken views of] nothingness do not arise. This may represent progress that is [an attainment of] a partial concentration and wisdom, in which you arouse mental correspondence with [the idea of] both-being-and-non-being. Then you can say, "If thoughts do not exist, who is it who knows this non-arising? 'Non-arising' does not exist, but the one who knows this does exist." When these thoughts arise, you experience the [mistaken] view of both-being-and-non-being. If you take this as the real truth and become firmly attached to it so that you cannot get rid of it, you will not realize its faultiness. This is like Dīrghanakha, who thought he had [attained] the way, but actually had realized [only the first two truths of] suffering and the causes of suffering, and was not able to realize [his shortcomings]. The Buddha pointed this out, and he was finally able to attain awakening. People who arouse [mistaken] thoughts are the same as this. Made delusory by the poison of these views, they cannot know the correct truth. If they hear [a teaching] that points out [their faulty views], then their thoughts of attachment are quickly resolved, as if blown away by the wind. How can this be pointed out? The *Pañcaviṃśati Sūtra* says, "the five aggregates [of receiving sensual experience] all do not receive experience [substantially]." How, then, can you [substantially] accept or experience 受 phenomenal objects as both existing and not existing? How can this not be the aggregate of sensation?

'Non-arising' does not exist, but the one who knows this does exist 無生是無。知卽是有: or, "Non-arising is non-Being, and the knowing of this is existence."

Dīrghanakha 長爪: the figure of "long nails" has been referred to previously in the *Mo-ho chih-kuan*; for details, see the notes under 40c13 and 62c8–10; see the *Ta chih tu lun*, T 25.61b18–62a28 (Lamotte, *Le Traité* 1, 46–51).

The five aggregates (*pañca-upādāna-skandha*) all do not receive experience 五受皆不: see the *Pañcaviṃśati Sūtra*, T 8.237c7–10:

Śāriputra. Therefore, for the Bodhisattva-mahāsattva who practices *prajñā-pāramitā, the practice does not involve receiving experience [substantially];* non-practice does not involve receiving experience [substantially]; both practice and non-practice does not involve receiving experience [substantially]; and neither practice nor non-practice does not involve receiving experience [substantially]. The lack of receiving experience does not involve receiving experience [substantially].

The aggregate of sensation 受陰: the context has forced me to translate 受 in a variety of ways (aggregate, experience, receive, sensation [the skandha]), but it

Through coming in contact with these images and forms [produced through sensations], and through the functioning of these phenomena (dharmas), these phenomena are fully discriminated; the [other] four aggregates arise as a matter of course. In this way [the aggregates such as] sensations and conceptions all are called "defiled and impure" [because they involve mistaken views]. These [mistaken] views rely on the aggregate of visible form. Again, the mental organ receives the sensation of both being and non-being from sense objects, and this is a sense field (*dhātu*). The mutual crossover of sense faculty and object is called "entering" [experience; *āyatana*]; this is called "suffering."

Again, if [the concept of] a "self" is active and experienced 能行能受, and you are able to know that this dharma is a conventional designation, then the [mistaken] view of a self arises. If you arouse a view of the self [as substantial], then you have an extreme view, and if you reject causality, this is a deviant view. If you take this for the way, this is [the mistaken view of] attachment to precepts. If you take this for nirvana, this is an attachment to [a mistaken] view. If [others] disagree, you are angry; if they agree you are happy; you [are attached to] your own understanding and slander others. Not knowing [the truths of] suffering and the causes of suffering, you are ignorant, and later this will lead to great doubt. In this way, these ten kinds of afflictions also include the eighty-eight [afflictions] as one passes through the three realms. This is contrary to the true way, but in accordance with samsara, and arise in the thoughts [based on] the [mistaken] views of non-existence of both-existence-and-non-existence.

Again, these thoughts of [mistaken] views include the three conventionalities, which can be known as explained above. Now, destroying or deconstructing the views of the three conventionalities by using the four possibilities [of the tetralemma] should be understood as individually listed above. After destroying or deconstructing them in this way, [you should know that] the aggregates and the sense fields [as understood through] the four possibilities of the three conventionalities are all without a true [substantial] nature. This is the "emptiness of natures." They have merely verbal designation, and this verbal designation is empty; this is the "emptiness of marks." "Nature" and "marks" are empty, and so forth for the eighteen types of emptiness as explained above. This is to realize the supreme meaning and **[66b]** to manifest correct wisdom. If you still do not realize this, you should

should be pointed out that Chih-i is using the same character throughout, giving a continuity (and perhaps ambiguity) to the Chinese text that I have failed to reproduce in English translation.

The mistaken view of a self 我見: this is the first of the "ten afflictions"; see the full list above at 62b10–18.

use the [four] siddhānta and alternate [practices based on] faith and the dharma [of meditation] to skillfully cultivate cessation-and-contemplation, overcome all the [mistaken] views, and realize the expedient and good yet [still] defiled dharma. Although you have now overcome [the mistaken views of] both-being-and-non-being so that they no longer arise, next you must deal with the views of neither-existence-nor-non-existence. Their deconstruction is as explained below [in the next section].

4. *Destroying the integrated or combined views: Deconstructing the mistaken views of neither-being-nor-non-being* [66b4]

Next, the deconstruction of [mistaken] views of neither-being-nor-non-being 非有非無 is as follows. Above we have [discussed] diligently utilized means to overcome the views of being and non-being. Now, in addition, we [will discuss mistaken views from the perspective of] arousing thoughts that are apart from being and non-being. What does this refer to? If thoughts are determined to exist, then they cannot be nothing. If thoughts are determined to be nothing, then they cannot exist. How can they be both-being-and-non-being? If they are not determined to exist, then they do not exist. If they are not determined to be nothing, then they are not nothing. "Non-being" means they do not arise. "Not non-being" means they do not perish. To transcend the polarity of "being" and "non-being" is the Middle Way. This is the same as [the teaching of] the *Middle Treatise*. Why is this so? The view of being [explained] above corresponds to [the first line in the verse], "dharmas that arise through conditioned arising." The view of non-being corresponds to "emptiness." both-being-and-non-being corresponds to "conventionality." "Neither-being-nor-non-being" corresponds to the Middle.

If you are firmly attached to these thoughts and think that they are true, then you will arouse immeasurable faults and mistakes. Why is this so? Those who take these thoughts [of mistaken views] as true take empty words to be true words, and thus give rise to the [mistaken] view of [attachment to] words. Therefore they are not true. If they were true, then these thoughts should be permanent, blissful, having selfhood, and pure. However, these thoughts arise and perish, so they are not permanent. These thoughts involve receiving sensations [which necessarily involve suffering], so they are not blissful. They do not involve full mastery, so they are not a [self-sufficient] self. They are defiled, and so they are not pure. They give rise to thoughts of [substantial] selfhood, and so this is the [mistaken] view of a [substantial] body. With the [mistaken] view of a [substantial] body, the question of being

The same as the *Middle Treatise* 與中論同: see the contents of Chapter 24 in the *Middle Treatise*, T 30.33b, which contains the verse (18) on the threefold truth.

or non-being cannot avoid [affirming the mistaken view of] neither-being-nor-non-being, like an inchworm [which can only make a little progress]; this is called an extreme view. If we say that the view of neither-being-nor-non-being is the Middle Way, this is common to all samsaric views, and thus is a deluded and ignorant thesis. To say that something that is not the Way is the Way, and something that is not a letter is a letter, is called [the mistaken view] of attachment to precepts. To say that [realizing] the thoughts of neither-being-nor-non-being is nirvana is to be endowed with all the sharp and dull afflictions of the sense fields; this is called attachment to views, and to [mistakenly] say that "neither-being-nor-non-being" is the correct Dharma. Or, to say that the destruction of all worldly causes and conditions is called "non-being," and the destruction of all transworldly causes and conditions is called "non-being,"—[such an unacceptable logic] destroys the dignity of right views and is not accepted even by worldly [non-Buddhist] principles. How could it be accepted as a transworldly principle? These [mistaken views] are aroused by the [mistaken] view of the self, [which leads to the accumulation of mistaken views as large] as Mount Sumeru; by not taking evil to be empty, one accepts that which is incorrect as correct. This is called a "deviant view." If you follow and approve [these mistaken views], this is called [the poison of] "passionate craving." To slander those who disagree is [the poison of] "anger." If you are not conscious of [the difference between] these thoughts as [like unto] poisonous weeds and medicinal herbs [lit., the "medicine king"], this is [the poison of] "ignorance." To act presumptuously for oneself and insultingly toward others is "arrogance." This will all lead to great doubt. In short, there are ten types of faults [that is, the ten afflictions], which, if explained in detail, cannot be exhausted. These types of faults all emerge from the [mistaken] view of "neither-being-nor-non-being."

Again, each and every one of these faults all include the three types of

Inchworm 屈步蟲: see the above reference to inchworm at 65b11.

An extreme view ...: here again Chih-i lists the ten afflictions, though not in the same order as in the above sections.

... by not taking evil to be empty, one accepts that which is incorrect as correct 不惡取空不正爲正: a similar phrase appears in the *Laṅkāvatāra Sūtra*, T 16.542b2–3 (near the passage in this sūtra quoted above), but with quite a different context:

They arouse the view of the self [as much] as Mount Sumeru, and thus arouse great pride and do not say that all dharmas are empty nothingness.

Poisonous weeds 毒草 **and medicinal herbs** 藥王: the *Mahāparinirvāṇa Sūtra* has a passage (T 12.831b2) that says, "In the Himālaya mountains there are *poisonous weeds with minute yet wondrous medicinal* [qualities]" to illustrate that, just as sentient beings are indivisible from passionate afflictions, so also all sentient beings are endowed with the "wondrous medicine king" [of enlightenment].

conventionality, as explained above. **[66c]** If you are to destroy these [mistaken] views of conventionality, you should use the method of cessation-and-contemplation of the tetralemma as [described] above. Gradually [mistaken views] will be destroyed or deconstructed, as explained above.

Again, the disclosure of various [mistaken] views of the five aggregates signifies [the truth of] suffering; the disclosure of [the mistaken views of] the ten types of afflictions signifies [the truth of] the causes [of suffering]; utilizing cessation-and-contemplation for destroying [undesirable dharmas] signifies [the truth of] the path; the overcoming and negating of various [mistaken] views signifies [the truth of] extinction. All non-Buddhist paths and mistaken understandings, and the immeasurable faults and mistakes that come from perverted assessments of the Buddha Dharma, can all be destroyed through utilizing the Four [Noble] Truths. It is not impossible for an ordinary [ignorant person] to reform and become a noble [sage]. This was possible even with the power [of the teachings] when the Tathāgata first preached the Four Truths of the Āgamas [of the Tripitaka Teachings]. How much more so [is it true] for the threefold [types of] the Four Truths of the Mahāyāna, and what [undesirable dharmas] cannot be destroyed? If you destroy the [mistaken] views [associated with the idea] of neither-being-nor-non-being, then all delusions are also severed and obliterated, and you arouse true wisdom. This is called insight into the supreme meaning by entering or realizing emptiness from conventionality. If you are not able to enter or realize [in this way], you should utilize cessation-and-contemplation, alternating between [practices of] faith [that rely on the teachings] and [practices of] dharma[-meditations], skillfully cultivating the means of the four appropriate methods. If you overcome the various [mistaken] views and delusions, and your grasping thoughts weaken, you can dwell on the path of [preparatory] means and perfect the dharmas that are still defiled. When the [mistaken] views no longer arise, you can cross and enter into [the realm wherein one is faced with mistaken views that are] beyond words. These are to be destroyed or deconstructed as explained below.

The reason I have explained the [mistaken] views and faults point by point [in the above sections] is so that those who practice diligently can, through contemplation of the mind, be conscious of the poisonous weeds and clearly understand the medicinal herbs. If you understand this intent, finally you will not make false assessments. The sections and points are complicated and vexing, but if they are taken in order and not confused, you will be able to fully understand, and can discuss the path. But for those who insist on being like the blind, how can they know [the color of] milk?

Know [the color of] milk 識乳: an allusion again to the analogy in the *Mahā-*

5. Destroying the views of conventionality that are beyond words [66c17]

Next is the destruction or deconstruction of [mistaken] views of conventionality that are beyond words. If you are able to destroy [mistaken views and so forth] as discussed above, and progress to where you arouse meditative concentration and wisdom, you will be fully awake with luminous quiescence. Next you will arouse a different understanding, saying, "Things exist in this way [that is, empty of substantial Being and with only conventional existence], and this is the way samsara is. In terms of the tetralemma, everything is conventional, empty, delusionary, and without [substantial] reality. The principle [of reality] is beyond words, and transcends the tetralemma. This is [the true meaning of] non-arising." However, although you think that this [understanding] goes beyond the tetralemma, it does not go beyond it [in all ways].

In brief, there are three types of [mistaken views as understood through] the tetralemma that this does go beyond: first, the individual; second, the multiple; and third, the integrated or combined [types of mistaken views]. If we say that the principle of reality is beyond words, this does go beyond the tetralemma of the individual type, but does not go beyond the second phrase of the multiple [mistaken] views and does not go beyond the first phrase of the integrated or combined [mistaken] views. Thus you should realize how

parinirvāṇa Sūtra, T 12.688c15–20, where the blind person cannot know the white color of milk except by seeing it, even if he is told "it is like the snow, like rice powder" and so forth, as a person cannot know the Buddha Dharma expect by "seeing" it and experiencing it directly (see note above at *Mo-ho chih-kuan* 3a21–22 and 4a14–15).

Fully awake 豁然 with luminous quiescence 明靜: note that these are the characters which open the *Mo-ho chih-kuan*, that is, the clear insight and peaceful quiescence of cessation-and-contemplation 止觀明靜. See note at *Mo-ho chih-kuan* 1a6.

Individual, multiple, integrated: see the *Mo-ho chih-kuan* at the beginning of this section, 62b9–10, which lists four types of mistaken views: the individual, multiple, integrated, and those beyond verbalization, which are then analyzed in terms of the tetralemma. As we have seen in the sections above, the "individual" type refers to the first two possibilities of the tetralemma, that of "being" and "non-being"; the "multiple" type refers to the possibility of "both-being-and-non-being"; and the "integrated" type refers to the possibility of "neither-being-nor-non-being." This seems to exhaust the tetralemma, but Chih-i argues that it does not, and that there is still the category of that which is "beyond words."

Does not go beyond the second phrase of the multiple [mistaken] views and does not go beyond the first phrase of the integrated or combined [mistaken] views 不出複見第二句亦不出具足見初句: Chan-jan (BT-III, 523–24) "explains" that the "second phrase of the multiple views" refers to the "non-being of nothingness" 無無, which is beyond verbalization, and that

[deeply] the web of [mistaken] views is concealed and intertwined [within our existence], and how difficult it is to escape it. The *Lotus Sūtra* says, "There are ghosts and demons here and there and all about."

All of the various [mistaken] views of the multiple and combined [type] each incorporate the three conventionalities of [the truths of] suffering and the causes [of suffering]. The contemplation to deconstruct these conventionalities is all as explained above. All who are able to cultivate the steps on the path, with regard to the various [mistaken] views, should attain awakening point-by-point, enter or realize emptiness from conventionality, and perceive the supreme meaning. If there are those who have not yet attained [awakening] even though they have overcome all the individual, multiple, and combined types of various [mistaken] views, and have perfected the good yet defiled five aggregates, the [mistaken] views will no longer arise and they will make progress in arousing meditative understanding. Again, they will say, "We have gone beyond and transcended the individual, multiple, **[67a1]** and integrated or combined types of [mistaken views as understood through] the tetralemma. This is beyond verbalization and [beyond] discursive thought. Things are utterly clear and pure. This is [the meaning of] non-arising, the path that is absolutely beyond words." One who conjectures in this way in turn [embraces] the [mistaken] "view of unexplainability and beyond words." How can this be regarded as the correct path? So you say that this is [absolutely] beyond words, but in the final [analysis] it is not beyond words. Why? Because if you are calling "absolute" or "beyond" 絕 that which is in relative [contrast] 待 to that which is not absolute 不絕, then it is [relatively] absolute only in contrast to that to which it is relative, and if it is relative in contrast to something, it cannot be called "absolute" or "beyond." This is like trying to avoid space without being exempt from the principle [of space].

the "first phrase of the integrated views" refers to the fourth phrase of the first type of the tetralemma, that is, existence as "neither-being-nor-non-being"; or as the fourth type of understanding the first phrase of the tetralemma, that is, "neither-being-nor-non-being" as existence. What more can one say, except to hope for relief in the quietude "beyond words"? After a list of such verbose options, one longs for a cessation of words.

There are ghosts and demons here and there and all about 魑魅魍魎處處皆有: a phrase from the verses on the parable of the burning house in the *Lotus Sūtra*, T 9.14a3, though the two phrases are in opposite order. Hurvitz (*Lotus Sūtra*, 65 [61]) translates:

> Here and there and all about
> Were ghosts and demons.

Calling "absolute" or "beyond" 云何稱絕: here Chih-i shifts his argument to play on the word "absolute" 絕 (or, literally, "to sever, cut short"), which he has used in this section as part of the compound 絕言 (lit. "cut off words"), translated as "beyond words." Here he is contrasting the character 絕 with 待 ("relative").

Next I will vertically deconstruct [the idea of] "not absolute" or "not beyond" 不絶. Since the thoughts [of mistaken views] do not end, the non-verbal [mistaken] views are included in the arising of all the causes and conditions of samsara. How can these be said to be "absolute" or "beyond" or "cut off" 絶?

As [explained] point-by-point above, all [mistaken views] are to be deconstructed both horizontally and vertically: the single [individual] views are to be deconstructed horizontally, and the layered [multiple and combined] views are to be deconstructed vertically. [The mistaken views based on] conventionality as causal arising are to be deconstructed horizontally; those [based on] conventionality as continuity are to be deconstructed vertically; those [based on] conventionality as relativity are to be deconstructed both horizontally and vertically; and the general deconstruction [of all mistaken views] is neither horizontal nor vertical.

Ordinarily [the mistaken views are] deconstructed horizontally, but now I will discuss their vertical deconstruction. If you have thoughts of attachment [to views that are beyond words], something will [be caused to] arise. What will arise? The five [contemplations for] putting the mind at rest? The general and distinct [states of mindfulness]? [The "four good roots" of] heat, summit, patience, and supreme in the world? The arising of true clarity and

Thoughts [of mistaken views] do not end 心不絶: here Chih-i seems to be using the term 不絶 in the sense of "not severed, not cut off, not coming to an end" rather than "not absolute, relative" or "not beyond." There is "continuity" in the Chinese, since he is using the same character, but the shift in meaning requires use of different translation terms, making it difficult to maintain continuity and logical consistency in the English.

Conventionality as causal arising: the Taishō edition of the *Mo-ho chih-kuan* has 因戒假, but the context suggests that this is a misprint for 因成假, as corrected in BT–III, 527.

Five [contemplations for] putting the mind at rest 五停心: this and the following terms have appeared previously in the *Mo-ho chih-kuan*. For details, see the Glossary and Chart 1 on the levels of attainment. Note the gradual progression from the lower to higher levels of attainment.

Four good roots 四善根: the preparatory practices for attaining Arhatship:

1. "heat" 煖 *(uṣma-gata)*, to burn away the passions with the fire of wisdom, to contemplate the Four Noble Truths and cultivate its sixteen aspects;
2. the "summit," "peak," or "crossroads" 頂 *(mūrdha-avasthā)* between regressing to the previous stage or advancing to the next; where one perfects the good roots;
3. patience 忍 *(kṣānti)*, where one patiently accepts the truth of the Four Noble Truths, the stage before Arhatship where merit is irreplaceably attained; and
4. "supreme in the world" 世第一, the stage just before that of the arhat.

In T'ien-t'ai, four early levels of attainment (beyond the five contemplations for putting the mind at rest, distinct states of mindfulness, and general states of mindfulness) for overcoming deluded views and attitudes in the Tripitaka Teachings.

patience with regard to suffering [that is, the eight kinds of forbearance]? The arising of deep consideration and pondering? The arising of the path through "thirst for wisdom"? The arising of insight into truth by those on [the stage of] the eighth person? The arising of supremacy in supranormal powers and vows to support [the overcoming of] latent habitual tendencies? The arising of understanding like that of the enlightenment of the three levels of erudition for overcoming [delusions]? The arising of the true understanding like those of the ten noble [*bhūmi*] stages ? The arising of enlightenment like that of [the stage of] the iron *cakravartin*? The arising of enlightenment like that of [the stage of] the copper *cakravartin*? The arising of mastery to pervade the universe *(dharmadhātu)* [like a Buddha]? If we look at these various arisings and examine your thoughts of attachment [that accompany them], how can you say that they involve no disposition [towards delusion or cessation-and-contemplation] and that they are not "views"? They are all "views."

If you suppose that thoughts do not arise, that "non-being" [or "nothingness"] and "non-arising" are the same, then what do you mean by "non-arising"? Do you mean that views do not arise, that [deluded] attitudes do not arise, that latent habitual tendencies do not arise, that the dust-like [delusions] do not arise, that ignorance does not arise, that karmic deeds do not arise, that [karmic] retribution does not arise, that volitions do not arise, and that the principle [of reality] does not arise?

Some people in the world say, "Non-arising means that the Buddha is non-arising. Enlightenment is the Dharma-Buddha." Now I will explain these words. Buddhahood is threefold. The non-arising of the principle [of reality] is the Dharma-Buddha 法佛. The non-arising of ignorance is the Buddha of recompense 報佛. The non-arising of dust-like [delusions] and [mistaken] views and attitudes is the Buddha of transformation 應佛. Again, the non-arising of ignorance is the Dharma-Buddha, the non-

Insight into truth by those on [the stage of] the eighth person 八人見諦: the third of the ten *bhūmi* bodhisattva stages (*aṣṭa-maka-bhūmi*), equivalent to the "eight types of forbearance." It is not clear why this is repeated if it is equivalent to the eight types of forbearance.

Three levels of erudition 三賢: here this probably refers to the three groups of stages of the ten abodes, the ten levels of practice, and the ten levels of merit transference. See Glossary under "three levels of erudition and ten noble stages."

The iron *cakravartin* 鐵輪: the "wheel-turning king" who rules over the southern continent of Jambudvīpa; symbolic of which stage to that of "resemblance," the fourth of the stages of the Six Identities.

The copper *cakravartin* 銅輪: the second of six "wheel-turning kings"; symbolic of the stage corresponding (in terms of the six identities) to the level of "partial realization of the real truth," just prior to Buddhahood.

Dharma-Buddha 法佛: or, "the Buddha as *dharmakāya*"?

arising of [mistaken] views and attitudes is the Buddha of recompense, and the non-arising of dust-like [delusions] is the Buddha of transformation. Again, the non-arising of the levels of karmic and volitional activity is the Buddha of transformation, the non-arising of the karmic [recompense of] wisdom is the Buddha of recompense, and the non-arising of the nature of reality is the Dharma-Buddha. Again, the Buddha of transformation arises from [Buddha-nature as the practices of] conditional causes, the Buddha of recompense arises from [the Buddha-nature of wisdom as] the "complete cause" [of Buddhahood], and the Dharma-Buddha arises from [Buddha-nature as] the "direct cause" [of Buddhahood]. Thus the "arising" of threefold Buddhahood is "non-arising," and "non-arising" is the "arising" of threefold Buddhahood. If you hear the letter 'a,' **[67b]** you understand [and interpret] all meanings. So it is also with a single understanding. [As the *Mahāparinirvāṇa Sūtra* says,] "A sharp hoe hacks into the earth, [removing] rocks and gravel, until it reaches the diamonds [buried therein]." By hearing of one non-arising, you can universally understand the non-arising of the universe *(dharmadhātu)*. By understanding all non-arising [in this way], you can examine your thoughts of attachment [to the idea of non-arising as beyond words] and see that it is unacceptable. How can you say that it is not a [mistaken] view?

Some person has criticized the *Middle Treatise* saying, "[The idea of] non-arising and non-perishing is not the profound truth. Why? Passionate afflictions are dharmas that arise. After twirling through the three phases [of arising, changing, and perishing], these dharmas perish. All you are saying is that 'non-arising and non-perishing' is not this kind of arising and perishing. This is merely a realization of emptiness, and not an insight into the meaning of the Middle." The teachers of the *Middle Treatise* understand this as follows: "Neither-arising-nor-perishing means that it is neither non-arising nor non-perishing that manifests the Middle Way." This interpretation may

If you hear the letter 'a,' you understand [and interpret] all meanings 若聞阿字門卽解一切義: perhaps a reference to the *Ta chih tu lun*, T 25.408b15–16: "A bodhisattva hears the letter 'a' in all words and then knows the meaning [of the rest], that is, that all dharmas from the beginning have the mark of non-arising." The first letter of the Sanskrit syllabary is often presented in Buddhist teachings as symbolic of emptiness and non-arising, and the key to understanding all things.

A sharp hoe hacks into the earth, [removing] rocks and gravel, until it reaches the diamonds 利钁斲地徹至金剛: from the *Mahāparinirvāṇa Sūtra*, T 12.649c17–20. This passage has been quoted above; see the note under *Mo-ho chih-kuan* 21c7–8.

Some person has criticized the *Middle Treatise*: source unknown, but this is a criticism of the opening verse of the *Middle Treatise*, T 30.1b14–15.

help [to understand the idea of] the Middle, but it is a disservice to the text and misses the meaning. Why? Nāgārjuna's intent is to combine the Shared [Teachings of emptiness with that of the Tripitaka Teachings] and include the Distinct [Teachings of conventionality], and thus says "neither-arising-nor-perishing." "Non-arising" refers to [the idea that] the twenty-five realms of existence do not [substantially] arise [because they are empty], and that after twirling through the three phases [of arising, changing, and perishing] they do not [substantially] perish. [If you realize this,] you are able to destroy the twenty types of [mistaken] views of the body and perfect the ways of those from the stream-enterer to the [arhat] who has nothing more to learn. Thus this combines the intent of the Shared [Teachings of emptiness], and also includes the intent of the Tripitaka [Teachings]. The idea "both-arising-and-perishing" is the same position as that of "arising," taking nirvana as merely emptiness and quiescent extinction. [The idea that] things do not arise in this way and do not perish in this way avoids both extremes [of eternalism and annihilationism], and thus includes the intent of the Distinct [Teachings]. Arising and perishing [should be understood in terms of the threefold truth of the *Middle Treatise* that] "dharmas that arise through conditioned arising are simultaneously empty, conventional, and the Middle." Things do not arise because they are "simultaneously empty." They do not perish because they are "simultaneously conventional." They neither-arise-nor-perish" because they are the Middle Way. If we understand and interpret [non-arising] according to this text, it combines two [Tripitaka and Shared Teachings], includes the Distinct [Teachings], and manifests the Middle [Perfect Teaching]. The four meanings are there. Nāgārjuna's ingenuity was in broadly including all Dharma teachings in the single phrase "neither-arising-nor-perishing" and thereby disclosing the Mahāyāna [Dharma]. [His critics, however,] even if they open their lips and move their tongues, they just repeatedly stammer [like a madman] "calling on a phoenix"; or even if

The teachers of the *Middle Treatise* 中論師: perhaps scholars of the San-lun tradition?

Twenty types of [mistaken] views of the body 二十種身見: Chan-jan (BT–III, 535) points out that different texts give various interpretations for this category. Ikeda (*Kenkyūchūshaku*, 368) says that there are four mistaken views associated with each of the five skandhas, that is, 1. the self is smaller yet included in the skandhas, 2. the self is larger yet within the skandhas, 3. the self and the skandhas are overlapping and the same, and 4. the self exists outside the skandhas.

Even if they open their lips and move their tongues, they just repeatedly stammer [like a madman] "calling on a phoenix" 若開脣動舌重吃鳳兮之聲: a reference to a story in the *Analects* that is used to illustrate the ravings of a madman, or the mimicking of sounds without understanding the meaning. Waley (*The Analects*, 219) translates the context:

they take up a brush and dip it in ink, they merely smear characters. They are only able to obtain a single meaning and lose the other three, thus are [worse than useless, like] swelling tumors and protruding wens. Wishing to helpfully add [to understanding], they end up losing what they have.

Chieh Yü, the madman of Ch'u, came past Master K'ung, singing as he went:

Oh phoenix, phoenix
How dwindled is your power!
As to the past, reproof is idle,
But the future may yet be remedied.
Desist, desist!
Great in these days is the peril of those who fill office.

Master K'ung got down, desiring to speak with him; but the madman hastened his step and got away, so that Master K'ung did not suceed in speaking to him.

The story also appears at the end of the fourth chapter in *Chuang-tzu* where the madman is presented in a more positive light; Watson (66–67) translates:

When Confucius visited Ch'u, Chieh Yü, the madman of Ch'u, wandered by his gate crying, "*Phoenix, phoenix*, how his virtue failed! The future you cannot wait for; the past you cannot pursue. When the world has the Way, the sage succeeds; when the world is without the Way, the sage survives. In times like the present, we do well to escape penalty. Good fortune is light as a feather, but nobody knows how to hold it up. Misfortune is heavy as the earth, but nobody knows how to stay out of its way. Leave off, leave off—this teaching men virtue! Dangerous, dangerous—to mark off the ground and run! Fool, fool—don't spoil my walking! I walk a crooked way—don't step on my feet. The mountain trees do themselves harm; the grease in the torch burns itself up. The cinnamon can be eaten and so it gets cut down; the lacquer tree can be used and so it gets hacked apart. All men know the use of the useful, but nobody knows the use of the useless!"

Even if they take up a brush and dip it in ink, they merely smear characters 抽筆染毫加於點涂之字: according to the *Kōgi* (BT–III, 537), these last characters refer to smearing or dirtying something with black ink, as with a clumsy calligrapher. Apparently Chih-i is comparing our clumsy attempts (or that of the anonymous interpreter referred to at the beginning of the paragraph) to understand "non-arising" with the skillful and profound handling by Nāgārjuna.

Swelling tumors and protruding wens 懸疣附贅: a phrase that appears at the beginning of the eighth chapter (on "Webbed Toes") of the *Chuang-tzu* to illustrate things that are extraneous—not just useless but actually harmful. Watson (*Chuang-tzu*, 99) translates:

Two toes webbed together, a sixth finger forking off—these come from the inborn nature but are excretions as far as Virtue is concerned. *Swelling tumors and protruding wens*—these come from the body but are excretions as far as the inborn nature is concerned. Men overnice in the ways of benevolence and righteousness try to put these into practice, even to line them up with the five vital organs! This is not the right approach to the Way and its Virtue. Therefore he who has two toes webbed together has grown a flap of useless flesh; he who has a sixth finger forking out of his hand has sprouted a useless digit; and he who imposes overnice ways, webs, and forked fingers, upon the original form of the five vital organs will become deluded and perverse in the practice of benevolence and righteousness and overnice in the use of his hearing and sight....

1. Ten interpretations of non-arising in terms of the Fourfold Teachings [67b21]

Now let me interpret [further] the single phrase "non-arising [and non-perishing]." Why include only four meanings? There are still further [meanings] that can be summarized in ten meanings of non-arising and neither-arising-nor-perishing.

[1] The first is that all dharmas should be deconstructed, and all words should be transformed. They are neither being nor nothingness, they are beyond words and separate from expression, and not one dharma enters your thoughts. This is one [interpretation] of non-arising [as beyond verbalization]. This "non-arising" also does not arise, and therefore it is called "neither-arising-nor-perishing." Ordinary emotional beings think that [the dharmas] are non-arising, but actually they do arise [conventionally]. It is like saying that [the samādhi of] "non-conceptualization consists of no concepts at all," while, in fact, minute conceptions are being made. This is a mistaken view, a heterodox interpretation of "neither-arising-nor-perishing."

[2] Second, followers of Vātsīputrīya conjectured that a "self" existed

Therefore it is called "neither-arising-nor-perishing" 不不生: lit. "not non-arising" but Ikeda (*Gendaigoyaku*, 348–50) translates the phrase as "neither-arising-nor-perishing," and I follow his lead because it is the only way to make any sense out of the following passage.

Like saying that non-conceptualization consists of no concepts at all 如非想謂言無想: see the last few pages of the *Mahāparinirvāṇa Sūtra*, T 12.850c–852b, which discusses the "concentration of non-conceptualization and not-non-conceptualization" 非想非非想定, especially 851c20–23:

> Good son. You have first renounced the crude conceptions. Now why should you passionately cling to the minute conceptions? Since you do not know to renounce in this way the subjects of non-conceptualization and not-non-conceptualization, therefore these are called conceptualizations, like an ulcer, a boil, poison, or an arrow.

In fact, minute conceptions are being made 而成就細想: or, "[the level of] non-conceptualization [in the formless realm] is like saying 'there are no conceptualizations,' but in fact [by saying so,] minute conceptualizations are being made."

See the section in *The Great Collection of Sūtras*, T 13.161b23–26, which says that those who overcome the crude afflictions through the "concentration of non-conceptualization and not-non-conceptualization" still face "minute" afflictions that accompany ten dharmas: sensations, conceptions, volitions or actions, contact, pondering, desires, understanding, mindfulness, concentration, and wisdom.

Followers of Vātsīputrīya conjectured that a "self" existed as the fifth inexpressible category 犢子道人計我在第五不可説藏中: see the opening section of the *Ta chih tu lun*, T 25.61a21–25. Lamotte (*Le Traité* 1, 43) translates:

> Dans le système bouddhique également, il y a des Bhikṣu *Tou tseu* (Vātsīputrīya) qui disent: "De même que, par la réunion des cinq agrégats *(pañcaskandha-*

as the fifth inexpressible category. This is one [example of] "non-arising." Since this non-arising also does not arise, therefore it is "neither-arising-nor-perishing."

[3] Those of the two vehicles (śrāvaka and pratyekabuddha) of the Tripitaka [Teachings] sever the [mistaken] views and attitudes of the triple world. Thus one "non[-arising]" is that views do not [arise]; another "non[-arising]" is that [deluded] attitudes do not [arise]; therefore this is called **[67c]** "neither-arising-nor-perishing," except that latent habitual [delusions] still arise.

[4] The Buddhas of the Tripitaka [Teachings] have completely exhausted both the explicit and latent [afflictions], so this is called "neither-arising-nor-perishing." Thus one "non[-arising]" is that the explicit [afflictions] do not [arise]; another "non[-arising]" is that the latent [habitual afflictions] do not [arise]. Therefore this is called "neither-arising-nor-perishing." This is the "neither-arising-nor-perishing" of the analytical method [for realizing emptiness and non-arising].

[5] As for the Shared Teachings, [emptiness] is embodied by the [mistaken] views that are originally non-arising, and [emptiness] is embodied by the [deluded] attitudes that are originally non-arising. Therefore this is called "neither-arising-nor-perishing." The *Viśeṣacintibrahma-paripṛcchā* says, "I attained enlightenment through non-arising and actionlessness."

> *saṃyoga)*, il y a un Dharma 'individu' *(pudgala)*." Dans le *Tou tseu a pi t'an* (Vātsī-putrīyābhidharma), il est dit: "Les cinq agrégats *(skandha)* ne sont pas à part du Pudgala et le Pudgala n'est pas à part des cinq agrégats. On ne peut pas dire que les cinq agrégats soient le Pudgala ni qu'à part des cinq agrégats il y ait un Pudgala. Le Pudgala est une cinquième catégorie, un Dharma ineffable *(avaktavya)*, contenu dans la corbeille des textes *(piṭaka)*.

Chodron (1, 55–56) has:

> In the Buddhist system as well, there are bhikṣus (Vātsīputrīya) who say: "Just as there is a dharma 'eye' by the coming together of the four great elements, so there is a dharma 'individual' (pudgala) from the coming together of the five aggregates."
>
> In the *Vātsīputrīyābhidharma* it is said: "The five aggregates (skandha) are not separate from the pudgala and the pudgala is not separate from the five aggregates. It cannot be said that the five aggregates are the pudgala nor that there is a pudgala apart from the five aggregates. The pudgala is a fifth category, an ineffable dharma, contained in the piṭaka."

For more details on this figure see the discussion in the section on mistaken views at *Mo-ho chih-kuan* 132b22ff.

I attained enlightenment through non-arising and actionlessness 我於無生無作而得作證: the closest passage I could find in the *Viśeṣacintabrahma-paripṛcchā* was at T 15.37a3–4: "World Honored One, one who correctly practices the path, with regard to dharmas does not produce any arising and does not produce any perishing; there is no attainment and no fruit."

Those of the two vehicles may realize the non-arising [emptiness] of [mistaken] views and attitudes, but the latent habitual tendencies still arise.

[6] As for the Buddhas of the Shared Teachings who sit on the seat of enlightenment and completely exhaust both explicit and latent [afflictions of views and attitudes], this is "neither-arising-nor-perishing." This is the "neither-arising-nor-perishing" of [ordinary] constituent [samsara].

[7] As for the people of the Distinct Teachings, they sever both the shared and distinct delusions. One non[-arising] is the non[-arising] of the shared [delusions], and the other non[-arising] is the non[-arising] of the distinct [delusions]. Therefore this is called "neither-arising-nor-perishing." This is called the "neither-arising-nor-perishing" of [severing] one [lower] degree [of delusions] and [attaining] one part [of wisdom], and [severing] a second [middling] degree [of delusions] and [attaining] a second part [of wisdom]. But the higher parts [of delusions] still arise.

[8] As for the Buddhas of the Distinct Teachings who exhaust the higher part [of delusions], this is called "neither-arising-nor-perishing." But this is still the "neither-arising-nor-perishing" of conventional means.

[9] As for the people of the Perfect Teaching, one non[-arising] is the non[-arising] of the shared [delusions], and the oth non[-arising] is the non[-arising] of the distinct [delusions]. Therefore this is called "neither-arising-nor-perishing." However, since they still dwell in the causal stages, the practices, wisdom, recompense, and so forth of the higher stages still arise.

[10] As for [one who has attained] sublime awakening and complete wisdom, this wisdom is non-arising. Ignorance is completely exhausted, so the delusions are non-arising. Practices, wisdom, recompense, and so forth are ultimately completed, so they "neither-arise-nor-perish." Again, since this is the ultimate truth, there is only one "neither-arising-nor-perishing." Since it is the ultimate perfect principle [of reality], there is only one "neither-arising-nor-perishing." Again, this is the basis of the principle [of reality], and the basis is non-arising, so this is "neither-arising-nor-perishing."

[Thus we can see that diverse] teachings are included and exhausted in the single phrase "non-arising," as explained above. [Diverse] teachings are included and exhausted in the single phrase "neither-arising-nor-perishing." When you use [the phrase] "non-arising," which [meaning of] "non-arising" do you intend? When you use [the phrase] "neither-arising-nor-perishing," which [meaning of] "neither-arising-nor-perishing" do you intend? Some

This wisdom is non-arising 其智更不生: that is, the wisdom no longer arises because it is complete?

When you use [the phrase] "non-arising" 汝作不生: that is, the above critic of the *Middle Treatise*?

others are not aware even of the [first] heterodox [meaning of] "neither-arising-nor-perishing." How can they be aware of the last [Perfect meaning of] "neither-arising-nor-perishing"? How can these mistaken views not be recognized as unpleasant? They are painful and should be deconstructed.

The vertical deconstruction of views as both existence and non-existence, or neither existence nor non-existence, is as explained above [in the section] on *bodhicitta*, and on absolute [cessation-and-contemplation] in the section on "The Explanation of Terms." If you say thoughts "both arise and do not arise," then what is it that arises or does not arise? Does it mean that [mistaken] views do not arise but true ones do arise? Does it mean that [mistaken] conceptions do not arise but true ones do arise? Does it mean that the latent habitual [afflictions] do not arise, but true [wisdom] does arise? Does it mean that the dust-like [afflictions] do not arise, but that the functioning of [supernormal] powers do arise? Does it mean that ignorance does not arise but the Middle Way does arise? Does it mean that internal karmic activity does not arise, but external karmic activity does arise? Does it mean that internal retribution does not arise, but external retribution does arise? Does it mean that small [Hīnayāna] activity or practice does not arise, but that large [Mahāyāna] practice does arise? Does it mean that one-sided principles do not arise, but that the perfect principle [of reality] does arise? [What does it mean] to say "both-arising-and-non-arising"? If it is not these meanings of "both-arising-and-non-arising," then it is a [mistaken] view.

If you say that thoughts "neither arise nor do not arise," then in what sense do things neither arise nor not arise? **[68a]** Does it mean the neither-arising-nor-non-arising [that is realized] through analysis of [the two extremes of] annihilationism and eternalism, or the neither-arising-nor-non-arising [that is realized] through realizing the essential [emptiness that is the middle way between the two extremes] of annihilationism and eternalism? Does it mean the neither-arising-nor-non-arising [that is realized] with the double flow of enlightenment and insight at the eighth *bhūmi* stage [of the Tripitaka Teachings]? Does it mean the neither-arising-nor-non-arising that is the attainment of nirvana when samsara is destroyed or deconstructed at the first *bhūmi* stage [of the Shared Teachings]? Does it mean the neither-arising-nor-non-arising that is the result after [attaining] the ten *bhūmi* stages [of the Shared Teachings]? Does it mean the neither-arising-nor-non-arising that is realized from [overcoming] the obstacles

Explained above on *bodhicitta*: see the *Mo-ho chih-kuan* above at 4a20–c13.

The section on "The Explanation of Terms": see the section (Chapter 2) of the *Mo-ho chih-kuan* above at 21c21-22b20.

What is it that arises or does not arise 爲是何等亦生亦不生: or, "what does it mean to arise or not arise"?

of the two extremes at the first stage of abodes [of the Distinct Teachings]? Does it mean the neither-arising-nor-non-arising that is realized from progress on the Middle Way at the stages of the ten levels of practice [of the Perfect Teaching]? Does it mean the neither-arising-nor-perishing that is realized at the stages of the ten levels of merit transference? Does it mean the neither-arising-nor-non-arising that is realized at the ten *bhūmi* stages [of the Perfect Teaching]? Does it mean the neither-arising-nor-non-arising that is realized at the ultimate stage of sublime awakening? If it is not these meanings of "neither-arising-nor-non-arising," then it is a [mistaken] view.

If you say "beyond words," there are many meanings to the term "beyond words"; what do you mean by "beyond words"? There are meanings for "beyond words" outside the individual four phrases [of the tetralemma]. There are meanings for "beyond words" outside the multiple four phrases [of the tetralemma]. The brahman practice of maintaining silence is also called "beyond words" [or to "cut off words"]. Again, Dīrghanakha did not accept all the teachings; this also is a kind of "cutting off of words." Vātsīputrīya said that there is a self in [terms of] the worldly truth; the self is in the category of the inexpressible. "Inexpressible" also means "beyond words." In the Tripitaka [Teachings], realizing the true and illuminating the real is said also to be inexpressible. Therefore Śāriputra said, "I have heard that liberation is inexpressible." "Liberation" in the Tripitaka [Teachings] consists of four gates or methods for entering or realizing the true, so there are four types of inexpressibility. The people of the three vehicles of the Shared Teachings in the same way use the way of inexpressibility for severing passionate afflictions, so this also involves four gates of inexpressibility. People of the Distinct Teachings contemplate the non-verbal and inexpressible nature of the

Dīrghanakha did not accept all the teachings 長爪一切法不受: see the story in the *Ta chih tu lun*, T 25.61b18–62a28 (Lamotte, *Le Traité* 1, 46–51). Chih-i has referred to this figure before; see the note at *Mo-ho chih-kuan* 40c13.

Vātsīputrīya 犢子: see note above at *Mo-ho chih-kuan* 67b27 on this reference to *Ta chih tu lun* 25.61a21–25.

Therefore Śāriputra said, "I have heard that liberation is inexpressible" 故身子云吾聞解脱之中無有言説: see the story of Śāriputra's response to the devī in the *Vimalakīrti Sūtra*, T 14.548a8–13; for a full translation of this context see the note at *Mo-ho chih-kuan* 29b4. Note that, unlike Vimalakīrti's more famous silence earlier in the text, Śāriputra's silence is criticized as based in ignorance.

"Liberation" in the Tripitaka consists of four gates for entering or realizing the true 三藏解脱凡有四門入實: that of the stream-winner, once-returner, no-returner, and arhat; [or of the tetralemma; or the four types based on the *Mahāparinirvāṇa Sūtra*?]?

Four types [gates] of inexpressibility 四門不可説: that of śrāvaka, pratyekabuddha, bodhisattva, and Buddha [or of the tetralemma]?

constantly abiding principle [of reality], and so this also involves four gates of inexpressibility. The Perfect Teaching cannot be asserted or signified; Vimalakīrti kept his mouth closed, and Mañjuśrī recognized [his wisdom]. This also involves four gates of inexpressibility. Thus there are many types of inexpressibility. Which meaning of inexpressibility do you mean? Your type of inexpressibility does not approach even the level of Vātsīputrīya, let alone the level of the four inexpressibilities of the Tripitaka [Teachings]. Why is this so? Vātsīputrīya speaks of inexpressibility in the context of the worldly truth, and he does not conjecture concerning [the real truth of] nirvana. You are conjecturing concerning the real [truth], and therefore your knowledge does not approach that of Vātsīputrīya. Vātsīputrīya's is definitely a [mistaken] view; how can yours not be a [mistaken] view? It is clear that this kind of [mistaken] view broadly arouses passionate afflictions, as explained above.

2. Ten types of the tetralemma [68a24]

Let me deconstruct [the idea of] "beyond words" even further. You say that which is "beyond words" exists outside the tetralemma. I will now clarify ten

Vimalakīrti kept his mouth closed, and Mañjuśrī recognized 淨名杜口文殊印之: see the famous story of Vimalakīrti's silence that was "like a lion's roar" in response to Mañjuśrī's query on the meaning of non-duality in the *Vimalakīrti Sūtra*, T 14.551c. Boin (*Vimalakīrti*, 202–3) translates:

> When the Bodhisattvas present in the assembly had each had their say as they understood it, they together asked Mañjuśrī the crown prince: Mañjuśrī, what really is the entry of the Bodhisattvas into non-duality?
>
> Mañjuśri replied, Worthy sirs (*satpuruṣa*), you have all spoken well; however, in my opinion, all that you have said still implies duality.
>
> If Bodhisattvas do not say anything, do not speak of anything, do not designate anything and do not teach anything regarding any dharma, they avoid all idle chatter (*prapañca*) and cut off every ideation (*vikalpa*), then they penetrate the doctrine of non-duality.
>
> Then Mañjuśrī the crown prince said to the Licchavi Vimalakīrti: Son of good family (*kulaputra*), now that each of us has had his say, it is your turn to expound to us what the doctrine of the entry into non-duality (*advayadharmamukha*) is.
>
> The Licchavi Vimalakirti remained silent (*tūṣṇībhūto 'bhūt*).
>
> Mañjuśrī the crown prince gave his assent (*sādhukāraṃ adāt*) to the Licchavi Vimalakīrti and said to him, Excellent, excellent, son of good family: this is the entry of the Bodhisattva into non-duality. In this way, syllables (*akṣara*), sounds (*svara*) and concepts (*vijñapti*) are worthless (*asamudācāra*).
>
> These words having been spoken, five thousand Bodhisattvas, having penetrated the doctrine of non-duality, obtained the certainty concerning the non-arising of dharmas (*anutpattika-dharmakṣānti*).

Ten types of the tetralemma 十種四句: this could be read to mean "the fourth phrase [of the tetralemma, that is, nei-

types of [understanding] the tetralemma. Which of these four types of the tetralemma do you say that [your meaning of] "beyond words" is outside of?

The ten types are:

[1.] the ordinary 一往 [meaning of the] tetralemma;
[2.] the inexhaustible 無窮 tetralemma;
[3.] the tetralemma as "binding the levels together" 結位;
[4.] the tetralemma as "covering all [four] corners" 褶[or 攝]牒;
[5.] the tetralemma as attaining awakening 得悟;
[6.] the tetralemma of comprehensive classification 攝屬;
[7.] the tentative and real 權實 tetralemma;
[8.] exposing and manifesting 開顯 the tetralemma;
[9.] losing the intent 失意 of the tetralemma, and
[10.] attaining the intent 得意 of the tetralemma.

[1] The "ordinary" [meaning of the] tetralemma is the way the tetralemma is commonly expounded to both ordinary and noble people. **[68b]** The meaning should [already] be known.

[2] The "inexhaustible" tetralemma refers to the tetralemma as including other [meanings of the] tetralemma and thus overflowing incalculably. These features were expressed above [in the discussion] on forty-eight types.

[3] The tetralemma as "binding the levels together" refers to discriminating among [the meanings of] the tetralemma and judging what is right and wrong, as with the individual, multiple, and combined types [of the tetralemma as discussed above]. Being attached to it without end is [the understanding] of the tetralemma by ordinary [ignorant] people; if not [being attached to] the meaning of the tetralemma is taken as the meaning of the tetralemma, this is [the understanding of] the tetralemma by noble ones.

[4] The tetralemma as "covering all [four] corners" refers to binding together and subsuming [the understanding of] ordinary people under the

ther-arising-nor perishing], which would fit the context. However, the explanation of the list indicates that it refers to the tetralemma as a whole. In the following list and explanation, the term "tetralemma" could be substituted with the term "fourth phrase."

Covering all [four] corners 褶牒: in a previous appearance in the *Mo-ho chih-kuan* I have translated this compound as "applying [the various forms of practice] as needed"; see note at 18c9. The *Kōgi* (BT–III, 547) explains this term as referring to "pasting down mats." Given the explanation below, this seems to refer to something like "nailing down all four corners," or the English expression "covering all your bases."

Above [in the discussion] on forty-eight types 如四十八番中示其相: as far as I could ascertain, there is no discussion of forty-eight types of anything prior to this in the *Mo-ho chih-kuan*, but there is a mention later in the text of "forty-eight variations of the siddhāntas" (76b16).

phrase of "being"; subsuming that of the two vehicles under the phrase of "non-being"; subsuming that of the bodhisattvas under the phrase of "both-being-and-non-being"; and subsuming that of the Buddha under the phrase of "neither-being-nor-non-being."

[5] The tetralemma as "attaining awakening" refers to attaining awakening and realization through the tetralemma, so that the tetralemma perfects the four gates.

[6] The tetralemma as "comprehensive classification" refers to [classifying] which Dharma teaching you have awakened to and realized according to the various possibilities of the tetralemma. If you distinguish according to Dharma teaching, then all Dharma gates can be classified.

[7] The tetralemma as "tentative and real" refers to the idea that, of the various Dharma teachings of the gate of the tetralemma, three of the four are tentative and one of the four is real.

[8] "Exposing and manifesting" the tetralemma refers to the idea that if all types of the tetralemma are exposed [as to their ultimate meaning], they "enter" the one real [meaning] of the tetralemma; if you "enter" and realize the real [meaning] of the tetralemma, [you realize that] all is inexpressible. This is the culmination of the Buddha's teaching of the tetralemma.

[9] "Losing the intent" of the tetralemma refers to becoming attached to the Buddha's [teaching of the] tetralemma and arousing arguments and conflict, thus being as faulty as ordinary people.

[10] "Attaining the intent" of the tetralemma refers to when a bodhisattva perceives the flaw of losing the intent [of the tetralemma], writes Hīnayāna or Mahāyāna treatises [like Nāgārjuna] to express the various [meanings] of the tetralemma of the Buddha, and thus destroys attachments and removes delusions so that people can attain the [real and true] intent of the tetralemma, and there is no longer a need to produce treatises or arguments.

If you are not satisfied with these interpretations of "beyond words," then [in light of] the various meanings of the tetralemma outlined above, in what sense of "outside the tetralemma" do you mean by saying that the truth is beyond words?

Three of the four are tentative and one of the four is real 三四爲權一四爲實: the first three possibilities are "tentative," and only the fourth (neither a nor b) is "real." This interpretation clearly refers to all four phrases (of the tetralemma) and not just the fourth phrase.

No longer a need to produce treatises or arguments 作論之功息矣: this phrase is ambiguous and I have translated it rather freely. Ikeda (*Gendaigoyaku*, 353) translates to the effect that "the end or purpose of producing treatises has been accomplished."

3. Deconstructing the tetralemma vertically to show the superiority of Buddhism over Taoism [68b18]

Previously we have deconstructed the tetralemma horizontally. Now I will vertically deconstruct the tetralemma as "beyond words."

There are many evil demonic bhikṣus in our time. They discard the precepts and return home [to lay life] and, afraid of being punished, go so far as imitating Taoists. Or they seek fame and profit and arrogantly discuss [the works of] Chuang-tzu and Lao-tzu. They pilfer ideas from the Buddha Dharma to settle [their own] heterodox scriptures. They push away what is elevated and adhere to what is base; they shirk from what is noble and associate with what is ignoble, assuming that [all teachings] are equal. They quote [the saying of *Lao-tzu* that] "the way that can be spoken of is not the eternal Way, and the name that can be named is not the eternal Name," claiming that this is the same as the Buddhist teaching of inexpressibility. However, [the similarity between these two ideas] is like insects chewing wood and [accidentally] producing [intelligible] characters. If we closely examine these principles 道理 [of Taoism], there is a chasm between their deviance and Buddhist correctness. Things that the foolish believe in are laughed at by those who are wise. Why? As I explained above, there are various [meanings of] "arising," various [meanings of] "non-arising," various [meanings of the] tetralemma, and various [meanings of] unexplainability. Your

In our time 今世: or "in this world." Chan-jan (BT–III, 549) gives many examples of evil monks. He refers specifically to the monks of the Northern Chou dynasty who conspired with the authorities in carrying out policies that were detrimental to the Buddhist Sangha.

The way that is [called] the way is not the eternal Way, and the name that can be named is not the eternal Name 以道可道非常道。名可名非常名: the famous opening phrase of the *Lao-tzu* or *Tao-te ching*; Wing-Tsit Chan (*The Way of Lao Tzu*, 985, 97) translates:

> *The Tao that can be told is not the eternal Tao,*
> *The name that can be named is not the eternal name.*
> The Nameless is the origin of Heaven and Earth;
> The Named is the mother of all things.

Robert Hendricks, based on the recently-discovered Ma-Wang-Tui texts (*Lao Tzu Te-tao ching*, 1989, 53) translates:

> *As for the Way, the Way that can be spoken of is not the constant Way;*
> *As for names, the name that can be named is not the constant name.*

Insects chewing wood and producing characters 如蟲食木偶得成字: a phrase from the *Mahāparinirvāṇa Sūtra*, T 12.618b2–4. Chih-i has quoted this phrase many times already in the *Mo-ho chih-kuan*; for a full translation of the context see the note under 10b27. This image is also used frequently in Taoist polemics. I suppose a modern Western equivalent would be the frequently cited but misguided idea that if enough monkeys typed on a word processor long enough, they will produce the plays of Shakespeare.

[meaning of "beyond words"] is not [even at the level of the meaning of] unexplainability that is beyond the individual [phrases of the] tetralemma, let alone beyond the multiple or the combined [type of tetralemma], or even that of Vātsīputrīya. How can it be [at the level of] the Tripitaka, Shared, Distinct, or Perfect [Teachings]?

[Reasons why Taoism and Buddhism are not comparable or on a par] From the perspective of the basic principles of the [Buddha] Dharma, how can the terms "eternal name" 常名 and "eternal way" 常道 mean the same [in both Buddhism and Taoism], and how can they be considered the same from the perspective of the features of their teachings? Even more so, **[68c]** how can they be considered to be on a par when you compare the [Buddhist] truths of suffering and the causes of suffering to [the Taoist teaching of] "revealing past transgressions and afflictions"? And even more so, how can they be considered to be on a par when one considers [the Buddhist teaching of] the steps on the path [compared to the practices of Taoism]? As for the essentials of the true Dharma, the basis 本 is not the same [as Taoism], and the [extended] traces 迹 [of the two] are not the same either. The [phenomenal, historical] traces of the Buddha extend from [world to world and] age to age; he was truly a ruler *(kṣatriya)* of the golden ring [underlying] India. As for Lao-tzu and Chuang-tzu, one [Lao-tzu] was only "the scribe at the base of a pillar" at the periphery of a small country in China 眞丹, and [the other, Chuang-tzu] was [merely] a servant in the lacquer[-tree] groves of the country of the Sung. How can these be compared as being on a par!

Revealing past transgressions and afflictions 過患彰露: that is, the Taoist belief in possible evil influences from former lives or the ancestors.

How can they be considered to be on a par when one considers the steps on the path 云何得齊況將道品: Ikeda (*Gendaigoyaku*, 353) extrapolates from the previous phrase—on the first and second of the Four Noble Truths—to take this phrase to refer to the third and fourth Truths, thus translating: "There is nothing [in Taoism] that is on a par with the basic teachings of Buddhism with regard to the truth of the path and the truth of extinction."

... he was truly a ruler of the golden ring [underlying] India 佛迹世世是正天竺金輪刹利: in Buddhist cosmology, the earth is supported by four layers or "rings": from the bottom, that of wind, water, earth, and gold (or metal). Thus the golden ring is the layer immediately below the four continents, including Jambudvīpa (India), the realm in which human beings dwell. Thus a universal ruler of the world is referred to as a "ruler of the golden ring." See Sadakata Akira, *Buddhist Cosmology* (1997), 24–27.

The scribe at the base of a pillar 柱下書史: a common title for Lao-tzu; not very noble, compared to the awe-inspiring titles of the Buddha. As described in the *Shih-chi* (see next note), he was merely "an official of the archives in Chou."

A servant in the lacquer groves of the country of the Sung 宋國漆園吏: the earliest records of the life of Lao-tzu

The Buddha has thirty-two [major] marks and eighty [minor] characteristics associated with his physical body, but Chuang-tzu and Lao-tzu were physically just ordinary, with ordinary forms that were small and stunted, ugly and worthless. A sūtra says that the human form in [this world of] Jambudvīpa is like that of a demon. How can it be on a par with that of the Buddha!

When the Buddha preached the Dharma he emitted [rays of] light and the earth shook; all divine and human beings gathered, pressed their palms together, and listened to the Dharma. He preached in accordance with the capacities [of his audience], [his words] flowed forth like noble reverberations, his eloquence was inexhaustible. Those who heard his words did not experience them in vain, and all attained the path. [On the other hand,] Lao-tzu lived during the Chou 周 dynasty; the ruler did not know him, and the masses did not recognize him. He did not presume to put forth even

and Chuang-tzu are found in the *Shih-chi (Records of the Historian)* of Ssu-ma Ch'ien, whose account Chih-i seems to follow here. With regard to Lao-tzu Burton Watson (*The Way of the Tao*, 37–38) translates the relevant section from the beginning of chapter 63 of the *Shih-chi*:

> Lao Tzu was a native of Ch'ü-jen hamlet in Li county, in the K'u district of the state of Ch'u. His surname was Li, private name Erh, courtesy name Po-yang, and posthumous name Tan. *He was an official of the archives in Chou* [the capital]....
>
> Lao Tzu practiced the Way and its virtue. His learning aims at self-effacement and possessing no fame. Having lived in Chou for a long time, he realized that it was in decline and left. As he reached the pass, the pass-keeper, Yin-hsi, said, "You are about to retire. Please try your best to write a book for me." Thereupon Lao Tzu wrote a book in two parts, expounding the ideas of the Way and its virtue in over five thousand words and then departed. None knew how he ended.

With regard to Chuang-tzu, Burton Watson (*The Complete Works of Chuang Tzu*, 1) writes:

> All we know about the identity of Chuang Tzu, or Master Chuang, are the few facts recorded in the brief notice given him in the *Shih chi* or Records of the Historian (ch. 63) by Ssu-ma Ch'ien (145?–89? B.C.). According to this account, his personal name was Chou, he was a native of a place called Meng, and he once served as "an official in the lacquer garden" in Meng. Ssu-ma Ch'ien adds that he lived at the same time as King Hui (370–319 B.C.) of Liang and King Hsüan (319–301 B.C.) of Ch'i which would make him a contemporary of Mencius, and that he wrote a work in 100,000 words or more which was "mostly in the nature of fable."...
>
> Scholars disagree as to whether "lacquer garden" is the name of a specific location, or simply means lacquer groves in general, and the location of Meng is uncertain, though it was probably in present-day Honan, south of the Yellow River. If this last supposition is correct, it means that Chuang Chou was a native of the state of Sung, a fact which may have important implications.

A sūtra says that the human form in Jambudvīpa is like that of a demon 閻浮提人形状如鬼: the *Kōgi* (BT–III, 555) admits that this source cannot be identified.

The masses did not recognize him 群下不識: Ikeda (*Gendaigoyaku*, 353) takes this

one word of admonition [to the ruler], and was not able to save even one person [among the masses]. He departed through the western barrier riding on a decrepit cart, speaking stealthily to Yin-hsi 伊喜 [before he disappeared forever]. Where is the public prominence in this [compared to the glory of the Buddha's preaching]? Again, [Chuang-tzu worked] in the lacquer[-tree] garden; he stained his brush to compose a document, adjusting the phrasing and adding corrections, but [the results] creaked with abstraction. He produced "inner" and "outer" sections [of the *Chuang-tzu*] and sought [the approval of] those who have achieved insight, but who listened sympathetically, and who attained the way [because of him]? [Nobody.] How can these [activities and accomplishments] be considered on a par with [those of the Buddha]?

Such differences are immeasurable, such that they cannot be expounded, and [attempting to do so would be] tiresome. How can one take the deviant and oppose it to the correct?

Again, when the Buddha went forth, Indra was on his right, Brahmā was on his left, Vajrapāni (guardian spirits) led the way, and the four assemblies followed after, flying through the sky. Lao-tzu drove himself to the western barrier on a cart of thin planks [pulled by] a blue-black bull, and worked in a field. Chuang-tzu was a servant in another's employ as a guard for the lacquer trees. How can these activities be considered on a par [with those of the Buddha]?

It was destiny that the Tathāgata would become a world ruler (*cakravartin*) and [the people of] the four seas waited in reverent awe for him to attain the divine jewel [of royal accession]. But he disregarded this glorious rank and left home to become the Buddha. [On the other hand] when Lao-tzu was east of the barrier he served parsimoniously as a minor official, and when he was west of the barrier he tilled a field and cherished a few *mou* [of land instead of cherishing and serving people]. He was never able to abandon

to refer to the "courtiers," but I believe the passage that follows makes more sense if it is taken to refer to the general masses of people. I believe the contrast being made is that Lao-tzu had no influence either with the rulers above or the general people below (at least during his lifetime).

Creaked with abstraction 軋軋若抽: or, "he spoke in metaphors"?

Blue-black bull 青牛: lit., "bluish-green"; this refers to the bluish-black sheen of a bull or horse's fur.

Worked in a field 作田: this phrase about "working in a field" is not part of the standard legend surrounding Lao-tzu. Perhaps it reflects the Buddhist attempt to counter the Taoist legends that Lao-tzu went to India and became the Buddha after he went west of the barrier and disappeared?

A few *mou* 畝 [of land]: a measure of land; about 6.6 *mou* make up one acre.

the bustle of his public and private activities. How can [the lives of] these be considered on a par [with that of the Buddha]!?

Blind people with no sight may believe what you are saying, but those who have [the insight of] wisdom will be suspicious and feel pity. Therefore it should be known that your [interpretation of] inexpressible is a [mistaken] view of [the meaning of] "beyond words"; it embodies [the mistaken views based on] the three conventionalities, brings about suffering and the causes of suffering, and involves samsara as a matter of course. It is like embracing a torch—you will burn yourself and suffer injury. But if you destroy and deconstruct these [mistaken] views, [the result will be] as explained above.

Again, non-Buddhists sometimes use [the saying] "The way that can be spoken of is not the eternal Way" to define [the meaning of] "beyond words." They criticize [the teaching of] "neither-arising-nor-perishing" in the *Middle Treatise* and say that [the meaning of] "beyond words" transcends this phrase of the tetralemma. Ordinarily, hearing this assertion may indeed seem to indicate a transcendence [this phrase of the tetralemma], but in truth it is not so. What is meant by "non-arising" [in the *Middle Treatise*] is that thoughts of [mistaken] views do not arise. **[69a]** Since there is no arising, there is no perishing. Therefore it says "neither-arising-nor-perishing." However, thoughts of [mistaken] views [based on the idea] of "beyond words" give rise to all types of passions, [mistaken] views, doubt, and self-centeredness. How can such arising and perishing be used to destroy the non-arising-and-perishing of others? Such ignorant and frivolous argument should not be accepted.

4. Questions and answers [69a3]

Question: Will not this [interpretation] arouse [mistaken] views of non-arising-and-non-perishing?

Answer: There are six possibilities. [1] "Beyond words" destroys "neither-arising-nor-perishing." [2] "Neither-arising-nor-perishing" destroys "beyond words." [3] "Beyond words" nurtures "neither-arising-nor-perishing." [4] "Neither-arising-nor-perishing" nurtures "beyond words." [5] "Beyond words" is indivisible from "neither-arising-nor-perishing." [6] "Neither-arising-nor-perishing" is indivisible from "beyond words."

No ordinary ignorant people can ascend the noble path. Even their arousing of ephemeral notions in all cases involves [the arousing of mistaken] views. Because they have these views, the passionate afflictions of suffering and the causes [of suffering] based on the three conventionalities [as explained above] follow accordingly. The king of the fish and the mother of shellfish are endowed with a multitude of followers; the bonds of karma grow vigorously like weeds in an overwhelming [sea of] samsara. [The passionate afflictions and mistaken views] experienced in the life of one single person are without limit or boundary; how much more so for many people. It should be known that [mistaken] views and attitudes are greatly to be feared. Diligently practice cessation-and-contemplation in order to break and overcome them. If you arouse an individual [mistaken] view, use [the practice of] cessation-and-contemplation of the tetralemma to destroy their essence one by one. If you avoid the individual but experience the multiple [views], or avoid the multiple but experience the integrated or combined [views], or avoid the integrated or combined but experience [the views] "beyond words," they arise like weeds without end. Deal with them one by one through cessation-and-contemplation, and there are none that cannot finally be defeated. Be constantly quiescent [through cessation] and constantly illuminated [through the insight of wisdom], and control [the mistaken views] without ceasing. Sever all [views] you encounter as with a vajra sword, and seize awakening as your destiny. If you are able to contemplate in this way, but still do not arouse [a full awareness of] the truth [of emptiness], the [mistaken] views will be overcome and you will attain [the state of] the five skandhas of [skillful] means. If you attain the realization of emptiness, all [mistaken] views will be erased and eradicated. Therefore [it is said that] "what is destroyed at [the stage of] the first fruit [of the stream-enterer] is like crossing waters of forty *li*; its merit is exceedingly great. I am afraid that those who hear this will arouse doubt but, in brief, three [types of passionate] bonds are severed. The [insignificant] remainder that are not exhausted are like a drop of water. Although the [deluded] attitudes are not yet exhausted, there are no longer any remaining [explicit mistaken] views. I

The king of the fish and the mother of shellfish are endowed with a multitude of followers ... 魚王貝母衆使具足: a summary of a passage from the *Mahāparinirvāṇa Sūtra*, T 12.678b21–25. The context reads:

> Good son. In this way people also become sick and die. Again, Kāśyapa, it is like a *cakravartin* who is master over soldiers, and has ministers who are constantly before him giving advice to the kind, and following after him. Again, it is like when *the king of the fish*, the king of the ants, *the king of the shellfish*, the king of the bulls, and the master merchant go forth in front of them, the multitude all follow, without abandoning [their leader].

What is destroyed at the first fruit is like crossing waters of forty *li* 初果所破如竭四十里水: see the *Mahāparinirvāṇa Sūtra*, T 12.824c16–18:

> As the Buddha explained previously, the passionate afflictions severed by a *srotāpanna* (stream-enterer) are like an expanse of water whose length and breadth is forty *li*, and what remains is like a drop of water.

Three bonds are severed 略斷三結: the *Abhidharma-kośa*, for example, teaches that one who attains the fruit of the stream-enterer severs three types of passionate afflictions: the bonds of mistaken views 見結 (namely, the view of a Self), the bonds of attachment to the precepts 戒取結, and the bonds of doubt 疑結.

have spoken in order from that of the more numerous, so that you can attain enlightenment concerning the universal destruction or deconstruction of [undesirable] dharmas.

Question: Realizing emptiness from conventionality deconstructs immeasurable [mistaken] views. What is [left to be] deconstructed by the two [remaining types of] contemplations?

Answer: The contemplation of realizing emptiness destroys [mistaken] views and attitudes, and [the two types of contemplation] together can be said to involve the deconstruction of "being." The next contemplation [of realizing conventionality from emptiness] involves the deconstruction of "non-being." That which is deconstructed by the contemplation of the Middle is both [being and non-being] so that it is not either extreme, but correctly manifests the Middle Way. Therefore the *Ta chih tu lun* says, "The two [mistaken] views of being and non-being are extinguished without remainder; we bow our heads to the Dharma teaching venerated by the Buddha." Thus you should know that all [mistaken] views, both vertical and horizontal, are not yet [fully] deconstructed through the second contemplation [of realizing conventionality from emptiness], so do not mistake it for the true [and final] Dharma.

Question: You have identified [the Tripitaka teaching of] samsara as "being" and identified [the Shared teaching of] the two vehicles as "non-being." The vertical and horizontal ramifications of the [mistaken] views of being are immeasurable; is it the same for non-being?

Answer: Ordinary ignorant beings have deluded notions and arouse attachments to things they come in contact with; therefore there are many [mistaken views related to] being. Those of the two vehicles have already severed [the explicit] views and attitudes, so in a horizontal sense they do not [have such immeasurable afflictions]. However, they are enlightened [only] about emptiness. The Mahāyāna involves destroying or deconstructing that which is called "the [mistaken] view of emptiness."

The two views of being and non-being are extinguished without remainder; we bow our heads to the Dharma teaching venerated by the Buddha 有無二見滅無餘稽首佛所尊重法: from the opening verses of the *Ta chih tu lun*, T 25.57c13–14. Lamotte (*Le Traité* 1, 3) translates:

> *Destruction sans reste des deux vues d'existence et de non-existence,*
> Vrai Caractère des choses prêché par le Buddha,
> Éternelle, stable, immuable, purifiant les passions:
> *Je m'incline devant la Loi vénérable du Buddha.*

Chodron (1, 28) has:

> Ceaseless destruction of the two views of existence and non-existence,
> The true nature of the things preached by the Buddha,
> Eternal, stable, immutable, purifying the passions:
> I prostrate to the venerable Dharma of the Buddha.

2. Clarification of gain and loss [69a29]

The second subject concerns **[69b]** gain and loss.

Question: What is to be gained or lost from practicing the cessation-and-contemplation of [mistaken] views one by one in this way?

Answer: This can be answered with four phrases: 1. old delusions are not removed and new delusions also arise; 2. old delusions are removed and new delusions also arise; 3. old delusions are not removed and new delusions do not arise; and 4. old delusions are removed and new delusions do not arise.

First, this can be compared to taking medicine. [The first situation is like when] an old disease is not healed and the medicine is causing yet another disease to arise. The second [situation is like when] the disease is healed but the medicine causes another disease [as a side effect]. The third [situation is like when] the disease is not healed but the medicine does not cause any harmful side effects. The fourth [situation is like when] the old disease is healed and the effects of the medicine also wear off.

The first two types are characteristics of gain and loss for non-Buddhist ways [of practice], and the latter two types are characteristics of gain and loss for Buddhist disciples.

What does this mean? [As for the first phrase, suppose that] basically you utilize cessation-and-contemplation to heal the delusions of samsara, but you have thoughts of covetous desires, and not all [passionate afflictions] are put to rest. As a result of [the practice of] cessation-and-contemplation, further [mistaken] views are aroused, destroying the causes and results [of enlightenment] without exception. This is [the situation wherein] old delusions are not removed and new delusions also arise.

Second, [suppose that] when you cultivate cessation-and-contemplation, the crude passionate afflictions, such as covetous desire for food and clothing, are stilled and no longer arise. You put up with the cold and patiently bear suffering, and do not arouse hate when [your body is] cut with a sword or passion when [your body is] smeared with perfume, and you maintain equanimity with regard to gaining or losing material riches. However, you should be very wary of thoughts of attachment and [mistaken] views. They are like thirsty horses who guard their water; they are impudent

Do not arouse hate when cut with a sword or passion when smeared with perfume, and you maintain equanimity with regard to gaining or losing material riches 刀割香塗不生憎愛財物得失其心平等: see the *Mahāparinirvāṇa Sūtra*, T 12. 644b19–21:

Again, the Tathāgata *maintains equanimity* among both enemies and friends. Whether his body is *cut with a sword* [by enemies] *or smeared with perfume* [by friends], he does not arouse thoughts of *enriching or taking revenge* against these two types of people.

and destructive, and can make the causes and results [of enlightenment] come to naught. This is [the situation wherein] old delusions are gone but new delusions arise.

These [first] two types [of situations] correspond to non-Buddhist [practices]. Objects of passion arouse passion, and objects of anger arouse anger. If there are those who learn cessation-and-contemplation yet succumb to these things, they are the same as the non-Buddhists.

Third, the disciples of the Buddha cultivate cessation-and-contemplation and practice the way of [skillful] means. They are profoundly aware of the causes and conditions of [mistaken] views, passions, and ignorance. When an ephemeral thought arises, they know its three conventionalities, and one by one they deconstruct the nature and marks [of mistaken views and so forth] through cessation-and-contemplation. Even though [some vestiges of] greed and anger remain, they are devoid of the attachments of [mistaken] views, and the sixty-two [kinds of mistaken views] have been overcome and do not arise. This is [the situation wherein] old delusions are not removed and new delusions do not arise. These are people who are on the path of [skillful] means.

Fourth, if you are able in this way to examine and reproach and be mindful one by one [of the mistaken views] through the four types of contemplation of the three conventionalities, to penetrate delusions and the emptiness of their nature and marks, become fully awake and arouse [insight into] the truth [of emptiness], and attain the insight of the principle [of reality], then you have not merely removed the old disease forever, but new disease will not be aroused. This is to realize the path of insight into the truth, and to become a Noble One.

3. Clarification of levels [69b24]

Third is to clarify the levels of the destruction or deconstruction of [mistaken] views.

If you cultivate these methods and are clearly aware of the Four Truths, and skillfully use the wisdom of contemplation to overcome [mistaken] views, this is to rely on the method of the Tripitaka [Teachings], that is, [to practice] the general and distinct states of mindfulness. This overcomes the four warped views; if the four warped views do not arise, you arouse the level of "heat," and perfect the various preparatory levels of means. Progressing to the destruction of [mistaken] views, you arouse [insight into] the truth [of emptiness] and become a noble [arhat]. This is the level of the first fruit.

General and distinct states of mindfulness 總別念處: see the Glossary for details on these terms, and Chart 1 on the levels of attainment in Volume 3.

If you rely on the Shared Teachings, the level for overcoming [mistaken] views is the stage of "parched wisdom." If you attain [and drink] the water of the principle [of reality], the mind is moistened and you attain the stage of [realizing your] potential. If you advance further **[69c]** and destroy the [mistaken] views, you realize the stages of the "eighth person" and of "insight."

If you rely on the Distinct Teachings and overcome [mistaken] views, this is [the stage of] the iron *cakravartin*, the ten levels of faith. If you destroy [all] mistaken views, this is [the stage of] the copper *cakarvartin*, the levels of the ten abodes.

If you rely on the Perfect Teaching and overcome [mistaken views], this is the level of the five preliminary grades. If you destroy [and sever all mistaken] views, this is the level of purifying the six senses.

"Sever" 斷 and "overcome" 伏 are similar terms, but the contemplative wisdom [that they respectively imply] is very different. The contemplative wisdom of severing and overcoming [mistaken views and so forth] in the Tripitaka Teachings involve contemplating the conceivable truth [of emptiness] through the analytical method. The contemplative wisdom of severing and overcoming in the Shared Teachings involve contemplating the conceivable truth [of emptiness] through realizing the essential [emptiness of all things]. The contemplative wisdom of severing and overcoming in the Distinct Teachings involve knowing the Middle Way, though gradually and progressively. The contemplative wisdom of severing and overcoming in the Perfect Teaching involves [realizing] the Middle [Way] in a single thought. Thus you should not confuse their meanings by hearing [the similarity of] the terms [and thinking they are the same].

Question: If one can enter the level of the wise person by overcoming the [mistaken] views of conventionality, then even if one has not yet gotten rid of [all] old delusions, new delusions should no longer arise. When such people cultivate cessation-and-contemplation, do they arouse the objects of various [mistaken] views or not?

Answer: This situation involves arousing karmic influences from past lives. The [mistaken] views [that arise based on] karmic influences from past lives are "old delusions." This is like when people take medicine and the medicine attacks the latent disease so that the latent disease is affected [lit., "moved"] to heal itself in an instant. Therefore this medicine does not cause any new disease.

Question: Why do you not directly clarify the levels of realizing emptiness by destroying and deconstructing the conventional for the Distinct and Perfect [Teachings], instead of clarifying the levels for realizing emptiness for the Tripitaka and Shared Teachings?

Answer: In the above (section at the beginning of the fifth fascicle), I have clarified the cultivation of arousing and non-cultivation of arousing the ten objective realms, their interpenetration, and so forth, wishing to point out the shallow and profound methods for those who practice, and to discuss the various levels [of attainment]. Also, I directed the practitioner's awareness concerning this things, wishing to clarify the partial and complete levels. Again, the partial methods for realizing and entering emptiness are all means and auxiliary practices of the path for the Distinct and Perfect [Teachings]. Again, this is the meaning of the phrase "There are many attendants who serve and guard." Again, there is no true reality separate and apart from [the conventional reality of] means, so [realizing] the partial is [to realize] the complete. Therefore it says [in the *Pañcaviṃśati Sūtra*], "The wisdom and severance of those of the two vehicles is [equivalent to] the bodhisattva's forbearance of the non-arising of dharmas."

To summarize the meaning of cessation-and-contemplation with regard to [penetrating] the essence of conventionality by realizing emptiness [is as follows]. The wheel of [mistaken] views is stilled, and "once you experience [the stage of] non-retrogression, you are forever quiescent"; this is called "cessation." To penetrate [the realization that] views have no [substantial] nature, and that both nature and marks are empty, is called "contemplation." To perceive the principle of the real truth is called "non-arising." The principle itself does not arise, and the principle also does not perish. This "non-arising-and-non-perishing" is also called "the forbearance from realizing the non-arising [of dharmas]." Also, [mistaken] views and delusions do

There are many attendants who serve and guard 多僕從而侍衞之: the traditional commentaries give no explanation of this phrase or where it is from, but it is a phrase from the parable of the burning house in the *Lotus Sūtra*, T 9.13c23–24. Hurvitz (60 [56]) translates:

> At that time the great man gives to each child one great carriage. The carriage is high and wide adorned with a multitude of jewels,… it is yoked to a white ox, whose skin is pure white, whose bodily form is lovely, whose muscular strength is great, whose tread is even and fleet like the wind. [This ox] *also has many attendants serving and guarding it.*

The wisdom and severance of those of the two vehicles is [equivalent to] the bodhisattva's forbearance of the non-arising of dharmas 二乘若智若斷卽是菩薩無生法忍: see the *Pañcaviṃśati Sūtra*, T 8.381b23–26:

> Subhūti, the wisdom and severance of those [at the level of] "the eighth person," corresponding to the attainment of the "first fruit"] *is [equivalent to] the bodhisattva's forbearance of the non-arising of dharmas.* The wisdom and severance of the stream-enterer, the wisdom and severance of the once-returner, the wisdom and severance of the non-returner, and the wisdom and severance of the arhat, are all [equivalent to] the bodhisattva's forbearance of the non-arising of dharmas.

Once you experience non-retrogression, you are forever quiescent 一受不退永寂: a phrase from the opening section of the *Vimalakīrti Sūtra*, T 15.537c21.

not arise; this is called the "non-arising of causes." There is no [substantial self who] experiences retribution in the three evil destinies; this is called the "non-arising of results." Causes and results neither arise, nor do they perish. This "non-arising-and-non-perishing" is also called "the forbearance of the non-arising [of dharmas]." This teaching of non-arising is common to [all forms of] cessation-and-contemplation. Again, it is through [the practice of] cessation-and-contemplation that one perfects the gate of non-arising. Thus ends [the exposition of] the universal destruction or deconstruction of [mistaken] views and delusions by realizing and entering emptiness through conventionality. [end of fascicle five]

2. The contemplation of realizing emptiness from the conventional in terms of conceptual attitudes [70a6–73b25]

Second is [to penetrate] the essence of conceptual attitudes by realizing emptiness and deconstructing dharmas universally. This consists of three parts: 1. to clarify conceptual attitudes as conventional; 2. to clarify the contemplation of the essence [of the emptiness of conceptual attitudes], and 3. to clarify the levels [of attainment].

1. Conceptual attitudes as conventional [70a7]

"Conceptual attitudes as conventional" refers to [attitudes such as] [greed or] covetousness, anger, ignorance [or delusion], and [selfish and arrogant] pride. These are called the "dull [obvious passionate] afflictions," and properly speaking are also called the "three poisons." As we traverse through the triple world (of desire, form, and no-form), we experience ten [destinies, from hell to Buddhahood]. These three realms each include nine stages, and each of these stages include nine levels, giving a total of eighty-one levels. All of these involve the generation of karma [with its concomitant recompense], which leads to experiencing rebirth in the triple world. These [karmic retributions and conceptual attitudes] are not exhausted even at [the level of attaining] the first fruit [of the stream-enterer], [at which one must still experience rebirth] seven times. [One who has attained the first fruit and

The three poisons 三毒: for reasons unclear, here Chih-i uses the terms covetousness 貪 or passions 愛, pride 慢, and ignorance 癡, rather than greed, anger, and delusion (or ignorance), the terms more common for the "three poisons."

These three realms each include nine stages, and each of these stages include nine levels, giving a total of eighty-one levels 三界凡九地。地地有九品。合八十一品: the *Abhidharma-kośa* (fascicle 6, sec 5–8; see T 29.32a–b) divides the triple realm as a whole into nine stages: one for the realm of desires, four for the realm of form (the four dhyāna stages), and four for the realm of no-form. Chih-i, however, claims that there are nine stages (each with nine levels) for each of the three realms, resulting in eighty-one levels. This is turn serves as the basis for counting the delusions of "eighty-one types of conceptual attitudes" that make up, in addition to all the delusions of mistaken views, the first of the three categories of delusions. I could not identify the source for this numerical classification.

Not exhausted even at the first fruit [of the stream-enterer], [at which one must still experience rebirth] seven times 初果猶七反未盡: see, for example, the *Abhidharma-vibhāṣa-śāstra*, T 28.183b25–27:

> The Buddhist sūtras explain that if you sever the three [types of the] bonds [of passionate afflictions], you are called a *śrotāpanna* (stream-enterer), will not fall back into the evil destinies, and will certainly realize the ultimate path. However, you will still experience seven existences and seven births in the human and divine realms.

overcome many delusions and passionate afflictions] is like a lamp, which burns more brightly just before [the fuel is] exhausted. [At this stage] you still have [passionate sexual] desires, but you do not lust after those who are not your spouse; you experience anger, but you "cultivate the stages without calamity"; you have delusions, but you do not conceptualize the nature of reality [as substantial]; you naturally [keep] the precepts that accompany the path; therefore these are called "passionate afflictions proper." This [situation] is not the same as with the delusions of [mistaken] views, which overflow without direction and give rise to attachments whenever there is contact with [sense] objects.

That which is called "conceptualization" gets its name from reliance on [conceptual] understanding. At the early [stages], the contemplation of the true [that is, emptiness] is shallow, and still involves matters that are obstacles [to realization]. These delusions are removed at later [stages] after repeated reflection on emptiness. Therefore these are called "the delusions of conceptual attitudes." The [Abhidharma] scholastics say that "[The afflictions of] the realm of desires are called 'greed or covetousness'; [the afflictions of] the higher realms are called 'passions.'" The scholars of the *Ch'eng-shih lun* criticize this statement, saying that those in the upper realms still covet the flavor of dhyāna meditation [and thus are guilty of covetousness], and those in the lower realms also have passionate desires. Thus passions and

Cultivate the stages without calamity 墾地不夭: this phrase is ambiguous; I have taken 地 to refer to the "stages" (as in *bhūmi*) with regard to the "nine stages" of the triple world. Ikeda (*Gendaigoyaku*, 361) translates the phrase literally: "you cultivate the land for a living so you do not die young." It seems to me that the context would be better served by understanding 地 as "stages" rather than "land." Again, the phrase strikes me as a classical or popular saying, but the traditional commentaries do not identify it as such.

Passionate afflictions proper 正煩惱: that is, the explicit afflictions of conceptual attitudes, not the habitual traces.

Scholastics 數人: lit., "those concerned with numbers." Perhaps referring specifically to scholars who were concerned with compiling lists and categorizing Buddhist teachings in terms of their numerical content, e.g., three realms, nine liberations, ten stages, and so forth, which Chih-i may identify generally as "Abhidharma."

[The afflictions of] the realm of desires are called 'greed or covetousness'; [the afflictions of] the higher realms are called 'passions' 欲界爲貪上界名愛: the *Shiki* (BT–IV, 6) points out that in the beginning of the fourth fascicle of the *Abhidharmahṛdaya-śāstra*, (T 28.899c13ff.), there is a distinction made between the afflictions of covetousness and passions. The context does claim that of the ninety-eight types of afflictions, five are of "covetous desires" and ten are of "passions," but there is no mention of the distinction between which afflictions belong to which realm.

The scholars of the *Ch'eng-shih lun* … no greed or covetousness: the source of this position attributed to the *Ch'eng-shih lun* scholars is unknown.

covetousness are common to both [those in the lower and higher realms]; in what sense can they be fixed as belonging to one side [or the other]? If it is said that greed or covetousness is heavier for those in the lower realms, and greed or covetousness is lighter for those in the higher realms, then does this mean that those whose greed or covetousness is "light" have no greed or covetousness? This is just one [tentative] explanation. When the Buddha was in the world he gave various explanations in accordance with various conditions; these are conventional verbal [explanations], and not fixed [for all situations at all times]. Thus you should not rely on just one interpretation [among many possibilities]. When you are faced with passionate afflictions, you should just destroy and remove them, and not be bothered with arguing whether they are [to be called] "covetousness" or "passion." This is analogous to removing dung [from toilets]: the primary purpose is to remove the impurities, and it is not crucial to make fine distinctions [concerning the types of excrement being handled]. There are means that are essential to entering the path, but verbal [scholastic] distinctions are secondary. If you wish to know the fine points [concerning such scholastic matters], you should consult [texts such as] the Abhidharma and *Ch'eng-shih lun*, where they are clarified and discussed in detail. What I am going to discuss here is the [practical] contemplation of emptiness and conventionality [for the deconstruction and destruction of conceptual attitudes].

2. *Contemplation of the conventionality of concepts* [70a25–71b29]

Second is to clarify the contemplation of the essence [of emptiness, for the sake of deconstructing and destroying conceptual attitudes].

Those of the teaching of arising-and-perishing [of the Tripitaka Teachings], use analytical wisdom to sever [mistaken] views in the first [stages],

Not be bothered with arguing whether they are "covetousness" or "passion" 何勞諍於貪愛: this point is reminiscent of the famous analogy of the poisoned arrow, in which the Buddha teaches that—as one who is shot by a poisoned arrow should not be concerned with such details as who shot the arrow and where the poison came from but should be concerned with pulling the arrow out and being healed—people in this world should not be concerned with metaphysical questions (such as if the world has a beginning or not) but with removing passionate afflictions and realizing enlightenment.

Analogous to removing dung: the primary purpose is to remove the impurities, and it is not crucial to make fine distinctions 譬如除糞唯以却穢爲先分別非急: the classical commentaries do not give a source for this analogy; perhaps it is Chih-i's variation on the "poisoned arrow" theme. Or, perhaps, it is also a reflection of the work done in the parable of the "poor son" in the *Lotus Sūtra*.

Consult the Abhidharma and *Ch'eng-shih lun* 委知毘曇成論: see, for example, sections 122–125 of the *Ch'eng-shih lun* (T 32.309b–311b) on the features, causes, faults, and severance of covetousness.

and then they again use analytical wisdom to deeply reflect on and sever conceptual attitudes in the later [stages]. Those of the teaching of neither-arising-nor-perishing [Shared Teachings] use insight into the essence [of reality] to realize emptiness in the first [stages], and then in the later [stages] they again use [contemplation of] the essence of conceptual attitudes to deeply reflect on [their emptiness], without relying on other ways. We are now concerned with realizing emptiness through [contemplating] the essence of covetous desires as conventional. When the nine levels of desires and delusions arise one after the other, they each involve the three kinds of conventionality, just as a woman has six desires, that is, 1. desire for "color-

A woman has six desires 女有六欲: these are six kinds of desires felt by human beings with regard to members of the opposite sex. See, for example, the discussion of the "nine considerations [of the decay of a corpse]" and "rejecting the seven types of passions" in the *Ta chih tu lun*, T 25.218a13–24; Lamotte (*Le Traité* 3, 1322–23) translates:

> 1. Rejet des sept sortes d'amour
>
> Ces Neuf Notions [des horreurs] écartent chez l'homme les sept sortes d'amour *(saptavidha rāga)*.
>
> 1. Il y a des hommes qui s'attachent aux couleurs *(varṇa)*: rouge *(lohita)*, blanc *(avadāta)*, rouge-blanc *(śvetarakta)*, jaune *(pīta)*, noir *(kṛṣṇa)*.
>
> 2. Il y a des hommes qui ne s'attachment pas aux couleurs, mais qui s'attachent seulement aux figures *(saṃsthāna)*: peau fine, doigts effilés, yeux expressifs, hauts sourcils.
>
> 3. Il y a des hommes qui ne s'attachent ni aux figures ni aux couleurs, mais qui s'attachent seulement aux attitudes *(īryāpatha)*: manières d'entrer, de s'arrêter, de s'asseoir, de se lever, de marcher, de stationner, de saluer, de lever ou de baisser la tête, de hausser les sourcils, de cligner des yeux, de s'approcher, de presser un objet en main.
>
> 4. Il y a des hommes qui ne s'attachent ni aux figures, ni aux couleurs, ni aux attitudes, mais qui s'attachent seulement au langage: sons doux termes élégants, discours appropriés aux circonstances, répondant à la pensée, respectant des ordres, capables d'émouvoir le coeur des hommes.
>
> 5. Il y a des hommes qui ne s'attachent ni aux figures, ni aux couleurs, ni aux attitudes, ni aux sons doux, mais qui s'attachent seulement [aux fourrures] fines, lisses, adoucissant la peau, assouplissant la chair, rafraichissant le corps par temps chaud et l'attièdissant par temp froid.
>
> 6. Il y a des hommes qui s'attachent simultanément aux cinq choses mentionnées ci-dessus.
>
> 7. Il ya des hommes qui ne s'attachent pas à ces cinq choses, mais qui s'attachent seulement à l'apparence humaine, homme ou femme. Jouiraient-ils même des six amours *(kāma)* submentionnés, s'ils viennent à perdre la personne aimée, ils refusent encore de s'en séparer et ils renoncent aux cinq objets de la jouissance *(pañcakāmaguṇa)* si estimés du monde, pour la suivre dans la mort.

Chodron (3, 1082–83) has:

> These nine notions [of the horrible] eliminate the seven types of lust in people.
>
> 1. There are people who are attached to colors, red, white, reddish-white, yellow, black.
> 2. There are people who are not attached to colors but who are attached only to shapes, delicate skin, tapered fingers, expressive eyes, arched eyebrows.
> 3. There are people who are not attached to either colors or shapes, but who are attached only to postures, ways

fulness" [or "sexiness"] 色欲, 2. desire for [good] appearance [or "a comely face"] 形貌欲, [70b] 3. desire for a noble demeanor 威儀姿態欲, 4. desire for [beautiful] words and sounds 言語音聲欲, 5. desire for delicacy 細滑欲, and 6. a desire for [attractive] physical marks 人相欲. Various distinctions can be made [concerning these desires]. If an ascetic comes into contact with these six desires, they can defile his sense faculties; his blood will pound in his veins, and the appearance of covetousness will be manifested externally. These [six desires] are not severed even at the level of the first fruit [of the stream-enterer]. How much less so [can they be avoided] by ordinary beings. Ānanda still had habitual traces [of these desires], so when he saw women within the assembly he would speak with them first. His [sensual] desires were aroused by these remaining habitual traces; how much more [would desires be aroused] by the passionate afflictions themselves. The *Lotus Sūtra* says, "One should not preach the Dharma with reference to a

of entering, of stopping, sitting, rising, walking, standing, bowing, raising or lowering the head, raising the eyebrows, winking the eye, approaching, holding an object in the hand.

4. There are people who are not attached to colors or shapes or postures, but who are only attached to language, soft sounds, elegant words, speech appropriate to the circumstance, replying to a thought, honoring orders, capable of moving people's hearts.
5. There are people who are not attached to colors or shapes or positions or soft sounds, but who are only attached to fine smooth [furs], gentle to the skin, softening the flesh, refreshing the body in the heat and warming it in the cold.
6. There are people who are attached to all five things listed above at once.
7. There are people who are not attached to these five things but who are only attached to the human appearance, male or female. Even if they were to enjoy the five lusts mentioned above, when they come to lose the loved person, they refuse to separate from them and they renounce the five objects of enjoyment so esteemed by the world so as to follow their loved one in death.

Ānanda still had habitual traces, so when he saw women within the assembly he would speak with them first 難陀餘習衆中見女先共言談: or, "he would speak to them first [before being addressed by them]," breaking the rule that monks should not speak to women unless first being addressed by them? See the reference to Ānanda in the *Ta chih tu lun*, T 25.260c9–12:

> In this way the other wise and noble ones, though they are able to sever passionate afflictions *(kleśa),* are not able to sever their habitual traces. Ānanda, for example, had habitual traces of lustful desires, and though he had attained the path of the arhat, when he sat in the midst of an assembly of men and women his eyes would first look at the assembly of women and he would talk and preach to them.

This section in the *Ta chih tu lun* contains many examples of the results of "latent habitual traces" of passionate afflictions suffered by many of the Buddha's main disciples.

Also, the *Inyō* points to the biography of Ānanda in the *Great Collection of Jewels*, T 11.326b–327c.

One should not preach the Dharma with reference to a female body and

female body and become attached to those forms that arouse attitudes of [sensual] desire." If you become attached to these forms, these sense objects will agitate your mental faculties and arouse thoughts of [sensuous] desires; this is conventionality as causal arising. Thoughts [of sensual desires] will arise continuously [one after the other] without a break, finally leading you to actually perform the deed; this is conventionality as continuity. The features of thoughts with [sensual] desires are different from those that have no [sensual] desires; this is conventionality as relativity. [If you realize the conventionality of conceptual attitudes in this way, that] conventional things are empty and have no [substantial] reality, you will not become conceptually [attached] to these [afflictions], and will take this [realization] as the principle of the path.

Contemplate these thoughts of [sensual] desires. Do they arise from the sense faculties, or do they arise from the sense objects, or do they arise from both [the faculties and objects], or do they arise apart from [the faculties and objects]? If [we say that] they arise from the sense faculties, this means that thoughts arise on their own before coming in contact with sense objects [but this is impossible]. Do they arise from the sense objects? But sense objects are an "other" [existence outside the senses]; how can they be responsible for [the arising of sensual desires] in oneself? Do they arise from both? But that would require the arising of dual mental functions. Do they arise without a cause? But it is impossible [for something to occur] without a cause. If we examine [the arising of sensual] desires with the tetralemma, [we can see that] desires do not "come" from anywhere. Since they do not come from

become attached to those forms that arouse attitudes of desire 不於女人身取能生欲想相而爲説法: a phrase from the opening of chapter 14 on "The Practice of Peace" in the *Lotus Sūtra*, T 9.37b3–4. The phrase is ambiguous, especially since Chih-i's quote leaves out the closing phrase, that "one should not take pleasure in seeing [a woman]." Hurvitz (*Lotus Sūtra*, 209 [192]) translates:

> Nor should a bodhisattva-mahāsattva *take a woman's body as the mark of something that can produce thoughts of desire; but even when preaching the Dharma to her*, he should have no desire to see her. If he enters another's house, he does not talk with little girls, or maidens, or widows.

The Threefold Lotus Sūtra (222) translates:

> Again a bodhisattva-mahāsattva *should not preach the Law to women, displaying an appearance capable of arousing passionate thoughts*, nor have pleasure in seeing them; if he enters the home of others, he does not converse with any girl, virgin, widow, and so forth.

The BDK translation of the *Lotus Sūtra* (Kubo and Yuyama, 206) has:

> The bodhisattva, a great being, *should expound the teaching without any thought of or desire for*, or wish to see, *a woman's body*.

Ikeda (*Gendaigoyaku*, 363) translates:

> One should not preach the Dharma using topics that would arouse desirous attitudes with regard to the female body.

anywhere, they do not go anywhere. They are ultimately empty and quiescent. When people with sharp faculties contemplate in this way, one level of conceptual attitudes as conventional is removed, and one part of true clear [wisdom] is manifested. If you do not yet feel a rapport [with this conclusion], use the four *siddhāntas*, alternate between study and meditation, and properly regulate your practice of cessation-and-contemplation in order to attain rapport [with the emptiness and conventionality of conceptual attitudes], thus severing one level of conceptual attitudes and manifesting a part of the truth [of emptiness].

If people of dull faculties contemplate [the conventionality of conceptual attitudes] as "causally arisen" [as explained in the previous paragraph] but are not able to remove even the first level [of afflictions], they should contemplate [the conventionality of conceptual attitudes] as "continuity." Do they arise upon the perishing of the previous thought, or do they arise when [the previous thought] has not perished, or do they arise from both the perishing and not perishing [of the previous thought], or do they arise from neither the perishing nor not perishing [of the previous thought]? Suppose we say that they arise upon the perishing [of the previous thought], but then the perishing is not able to arise. Suppose we say that they arise when [the previous thought] has not perished, but [this cannot be because] there is no arising without perishing. Suppose we say that they arise from [both] perishing and not perishing, but [this cannot be because] their natures are mutually exclusive. Suppose we say that they arise apart [from each other], but this is impossible [because they are mutually dependent]. Thus through the tetralemma [we can realize that] desires do not exist [substantially], and the four [possibilities of the tetralemma] do not [obtain]. When you contemplate in this way you should realize both that which arises [such as covetousness and other afflictions of conceptual attitudes] and the objects (dharmas) are both empty. If you still do not realize this, you should skillfully cultivate the four *siddhāntas*.

If you still do not realize this through such cultivation [of the *siddhāntas*], you should next contemplate [the conventionality of conceptual attitudes] as "relative" in order to reach an understanding as outlined above. This is how it should be done for the first level [of afflictions], and the same should be done for the later eight levels, thus destroying or deconstructing nine levels of covetous desires. It is the same for destroying or deconstructing nine levels

They do not come from anywhere, they do not go anywhere 既無來處亦無去處: or, "they have no basis for coming, and no basis for going."

Alternate between study and meditation 信法迴轉: lit., "between faith [from hearing the teachings] and [the contemplative practices based on] the Dharma."

of greed, ignorance, and selfish pride. This should be understood as outlined above, so I will not repeat the explanation here. Thus the true [emptiness] of the nine levels [of afflictions] is made manifest; this is the principle of non-arising. The delusions of nine levels are exhausted; this is the cause for their non-arising. The results of the realm of desires do not arise; this is the result of non-arising. Since there is no arising, there is no perishing; this is the forbearance of the non-arising of dharmas, and so forth.

[70c] Question: Must the passionate afflictions of the realm of desires be fixed at nine levels [or types]?

Answer: The *Ch'eng-shih lun* says that [there are differences between the afflictions] overcome on the unobstructed path and those severed on the path of liberation, but just teaches nine levels [of afflictions]. The Abhidharma teaches that [afflictions are] overcome on the [first] "path of means" 方便道 and on the "path of supreme progress" 神進道, they are severed on the "unobstructed path," and enlightenment is realized on the "path of liberation," which shows that there is a state without delusions [but there

The unobstructed path 無礙道 ***(ānantarta-marga)***: one of the "four paths" 四道 that lead to nirvana, as taught in the Abhidharma. 1. The path of practice 加行道 (also translated as the "path of means" 方便道) wherein one severs afflictions by attaining the three levels of erudition and the four good roots; 2. the "unobstructed" path 無礙道 (also translated as 無間道), wherein one severs afflictions through the attainment of wisdom; 3. the path of liberation 解脱道, wherein one attains true wisdom beyond the previous level; and 4. the path of supreme progress 神進道, wherein one progresses even further to attain the results of both meditation and wisdom. See the *Abhidharma-kośa*, fascicle 25 (T 29.129aff.).

The path of liberation 解脱道: one of the "four paths" as taught in the Abhidharma. See previous note.

Just teaches nine levels 唯論九品: the *Shiki* says that this teaching of the difference between the two paths is not found in the *Ch'eng-shih lun*, and the *Kōgi* adds that this is a teaching of the *Ch'eng-shih lun* scholars and is not in the treatise itself (see BT–IV, 15–16). The category of "nine types of afflictions" is found in the treatise in chapter 139 at T 32.324b3ff.:

> Some people say that there are nine types of passionate afflictions, [three each of] the superior 上, middling 中, and inferior 下: the inferior inferior, the middling inferior, the superior inferior, the inferior middling, the middling middling, the superior middling, the inferior superior, the middling superior, and the superior superior. There are also nine types of wisdom [with the same combinations of superior, middling, and inferior]. The first afflictions to be severed are the superior superior ones, and the inferior inferior ones are [severed] last. The inferior inferior wisdom severs the superior superior afflictions, and so forth until the superior superior wisdom severs the inferior inferior afflictions....

Abhidharma teaches that ... enlightenment is realized on the "path of liberation" 阿毘曇有方便道勝進道兩道伏無礙道斷解脱道證: see, for example, the opening section of the *Abhidharma-vibhāṣā-śāstra*, where these terms appear at T 28.3c13–15.

are still nine types of afflictions]. There are many examples in the sūtras [that say there are nine types of afflictions], so we will rely on these for now. If you enter contemplation [and realize emptiness] through the conventionality of [mistaken] views, with such an undefiled mind you are quick to sever [afflictions] without emerging from contemplation, and there is no need to discuss levels and such distinctions. The path of cultivation 修道 *(bhāvana-marga)* is slow and gradual, and requires various means for attainment. It must be carefully cultivated with skill, alternating between study with faith and dharma-meditation. In order to turn and enter the [fourth and highest] path of supreme progress, there are numerous [means required to attain this] superior progress, and you should know that there are many levels and distinctions. [In this sense] there are not only nine [levels of afflictions]. "Nine" is used just as a general division.

1. The realm of forms [70c8]

Next, destroying or deconstructing the nine levels [of afflictions] of the realm of form involves using worldly wisdom or using undefiled wisdom. For example, there are those who attain liberation through wisdom and have not experienced worldly dhyāna meditation 世禪, but they have attained [the level of] one who has no more to learn by using undefiled [wisdom]. People who have attained the first fruit [of the stream-enterer] and have not experienced dhyāna meditation must progress in their cultivation by serious reflection on the principle [of reality] by using undefiled [wisdom]. A person who has attained liberation through both can use either undefiled wisdom or worldly wisdom. Let us, for now, look at the situation with regard to one who relies on worldly wisdom to attain dhyāna meditation.

If, upon first practicing dhyāna meditation you destroy the obstacles of actual deeds, you can thus arouse concentration (samādhi) within the realm of desires, and by destroying [the deeper] obstacles of the nature [of reality], you can arouse concentration (samādhi) within [the realm of] form. There-

Arouse concentration within the realm of desires 發欲界定: see the passage just quoted above from the *Ch'eng-shih lun*, where the "concentration within the realm of desires" is mentioned at T 32.324b17.

Destroying [the deeper] obstacles of the nature [of reality] 破於性障: usually "phenomenal or actual obstacles" 事障 (that is, actual, phenomenal matters, deeds, or experiences that serve as obstacles to attaining the path) are contrasted with "obstacles of principle" 理障 (that is, more deeper, habitual aspects of the way things are that serve as obstacles to attaining the path). In this context "obstacles of nature" [or should this be "obstacles to (Buddha-)nature?] probably corresponds to "obstacles of principle," and to the latent habitual tendencies of the afflictions remaining after one has severed the blatant, "active" passionate afflictions.

fore it is said that the obstacles of phenomenal or actual deeds [obstruct] what is to come [if one had progressed on the path], and the obstacles of nature [obstruct] the [four] basic [dhyāna]. If you remove the obstacles of nature, the dharmas of the first dhyāna [stage] will arise. The marks of the first dhyāna stage are that the body will be sensitive to the eight tactile senses and give birth to the meritorious qualities of the five constituents (of examination, reflection, joy, bliss, and concentration). [At this level,] "savoring" [the experience or "taste" of meditation] is called "covetousness"; making light of those who have not yet attained [this level] is called "pride"; and not knowing that suffering and the causes of suffering still exist within dhyāna meditation is called "ignorance." In this way there are also nine levels [of afflictions] within these three delusions, and each level involves the three kinds of conventionality. For the eight tactile feelings in the realm of form to come into contact with the mental sense organ and so forth of the realm of desires is [the conventionality of] "causal arising." To make distinctions within your contemplation without severing them from thought to thought is [the conventionality of] "continuity." For the mind that arouses dhyāna meditation to be different from the mind that does not arouse this is [the conventionality of] "relativity." If you do not destroy [the afflictions] through this contemplation, you will experience further rebirth in accordance with [the afflictions associated with one-sided] dhyāna meditation. How can this be called "non-arising"?

To use the tetralemma [in conjunction with] cessation-and-contemplation [in this way] is a good and skillful cultivation of practice, [this practice is the content of the paths of] "means" and "superior progress." If you sever one level of delusions, this is called "the unobstructed path." If you realize a state of no delusions, this is "the path of liberation." If you remove even one part of the delusions, then both the cause and the result are non-arising, so this is called "realizing emptiness from conventionality." Using the tetralemma [in conjunction with] cessation-and-contemplation [to contemplate conventionality] as "continuity" and as "relativity" is in the same way to realize emptiness through the contemplation of conventionality. The destruction of

[Four] basic 根本 **[dhyāna]**: for details on the four dhyāna stages in T'ien-t'ai thought see Ikeda, *Kenkyūchūshaku*, 479–81. Ikeda's note is based on the entry on in Chih-i's *Introduction to Graded Terms of the Dharma Realm*, T 46.671a–672b.

Eight tactile senses 八觸: the eight tactile sensations of heavy 重, light 軽, cold 冷, hot 熱, rough 渋(澁), smooth 滑, soft 軟, and coarse 麁. Or, eight sensations that hinder meditation in its early stages: movement/restlessness 動, itchiness 痒, lightness 輕, heaviness 重, cold 冷, heat 煖, roughness 澁, and smoothness 滑.

Five constituents 五支: see Chih-i's previous use of this term at *Mo-ho chih-kuan* 48a25–29. These are the five constituents of the first dhyāna stage.

the first level [of afflictions] is already [to destroy] the remaining eight levels in a like manner. The destruction of covetousness is already, in a like matter, the destruction of the nine levels of pride and ignorance.

1. The first dhyāna stage [70c26]

If you deconstruct and destroy the obstacles of actual deeds at the first dhyāna stage and arouse a median [state of concentration and attainment] and your life ends at this stage, you will not give birth to the second dhyāna stage. This is, for example, like not giving birth to the first dhyāna stage because you have not escaped from the obstacles of nature in the realm of desires. The second dhyāna stage is aroused when you destroy the [obstacles of] nature of the first dhyāna stage, along with joy, so it is accompanied by the four constituents of [inner purity,] concentration, joy and bliss. Within this [stage] there is the savoring [of the bliss of meditation], there is covetousness, [71a] there is pride, and there is ignorance, each with nine levels [of afflictions], and each level involving the three conventionalities. When the inner purity of sense objects [in the meditator's mind] combines with the mental sense organ, this is [conventionality as] "causal arising." The internally pure thoughts continue [one after the other; this is conventionality as "continuity"]. Internal [thoughts] that are pure are in contrast to internal [thoughts] that are not pure[; this is conventionality as "relative"]. These are the three kinds of conventionality [for this level]. If these are not examined through contemplation, you will experience rebirth in accordance with this dhyāna [because it still involves the above afflictions]. You should now use cessation-and-contemplation to cultivate practice and perfect [the paths of] "means" and "superior progress," sever delusions [through the] unobstructed [path], become enlightened to the truth [of emptiness through the path of] liberation, and realize the non-arising of both phenomena and principle. If you have not realized this yet [through the contemplation of conventionality as causal arising], you should contemplate [conventionality as] continuity and relativity in a similar manner, remove the [other] eight levels in a like manner, and [get rid of] ignorance and pride and so forth in a like manner.

2. The second dhyāna stage [71a7]

The second dhyāna stage also has obstacles of phenomena and obstacles of nature. When [the obstacles of] actual deeds are gone, you arouse a median state [of concentration], and when those of nature are gone you arouse the third dhyāna stage. This [third dhyāna] is aroused along with bliss, and

Four constituents 四支: these are the constituents of the second dhyāna stage.

this bliss is profoundly sublime. A Noble One is able to abandon [these obstacles], but it is difficult for an ordinary person to abandon them. Within this [stage] there are passions and pride and ignorance, each with nine levels, and each level involving the three types of conventionality. Bliss [arises] in response to the mental sense organ[; this is conventionality as "causal arising"]. Blissful thoughts continue [one after the other; this is conventionality as "continuity"]. There is bliss in contrast to non-bliss[; this is conventionality as "relativity"]. If you do not contemplate thoroughly, you will experience rebirth in accordance with this dhyāna. You should now use the contemplative wisdom of the tetralemma to deconstruct and destroy these [afflictions]. Sever delusions through [the paths of] means, superior progress, and non-obstruction, and realize the truth [of emptiness] through [the path of] liberation, thus realizing the non-arising of both phenomena and principle [since you realize that they are merely causally arisen]. If they still are not removed, then cultivate [the contemplation of covetousness in terms of their conventionality] as continuity and relativity, and approach the remaining eight levels in a like manner. Approach the nine levels of [the afflictions of] ignorance and pride in a like manner.

3. *The third dhyāna stage* [71a14]

The third dhyāna stage also has the dual obstacles of actual phenomena and of nature. If you destroy the obstacles of nature [at this stage, you arouse the fourth dhyāna stage]. This arising is accompanied by equanimity or abandonment, but also involves passions, pride, and ignorance, which each have nine levels and [involve] the three types of conventionality. When the immobile dharmas 不動法 come in contact with the mental sense organ, this is [conventionality as] causally arising; and so forth [for conventionality as continuity and relativity]. If you do not contemplate thoroughly, you will experience rebirth in accordance with this dhyāna. You should now use cessation-and-contemplation [to realize the causal arising of afflictions, and to cultivate the paths of] means, superior progress, non-obstruction, and liberation, and thus realize the non-arising of both phenomena and principle. If they are still not removed, then contemplate [their conventionality in terms of] continuity and relativity in a like manner. Approach the remaining eight levels [of covetousness] and [the nine levels of] ignorance and pride in a like manner.

This bliss is profoundly sublime 此樂深妙: with the five constituents of equanimity or abandonment 捨, mindfulness, wisdom, bliss, and single-mindedness.

4. *The fourth dhyāna stage* [71a20]

Suppose you attain the [so-called] "non-conceptual heavenly state" [within the fourth dhyāna stage]—this is called "non-conceptual" because thoughts are extinguished but form remains—[ordinary] sentient beings consider this as "non-conceptual," but actually this state still involves conceptions. For example, even though the phenomenal obstacles are severed, the [latent habitual] obstacles of nature still remain. Since this does not involve liberation from form, it is called a non-Buddhist heavenly state. If you have previously destroyed the thoughts of [mistaken] views, and these thoughts of [mistaken] views are gone forever, then there is no reason to be born in this heavenly state. If, for some reason your mind arouses this state of concentration, you should realize that this [state] also involves the three types of conventionality, and you should use the four contemplations [of the tetralemma?] to deconstruct it [as causally arisen]. The same goes for [contemplating it in terms of the conventionality of] continuity and relativity.

[The five realms of the non-returner *(anāgāmin)*] Suppose you attain the five divine realms of the non-returner and further refine the fourth dhyāna stage. If you use the undefiled to affect the defiled, so that your concentration [within the realm] of form turns clear, your resultant reward becomes superior. When this superior concentration arises, it also involves the delusions of nine levels of passions, pride, and ignorance with their three types of conventionality. Use the four contemplations to realize penetrating insight into the essence [of emptiness and conventionality as causal arising], and realize the non-arising of phenomena and principle through unobstructed wisdom and liberation. If [the afflictions] still are not removed, then cultivate [real-

Non-conceptual heavenly state 無想天: the fourth of the "divine realms" within the fourth dhyāna stage. In the T'ien-t'ai scheme, there are nine such levels; for details, see Hurvitz, *Chih-i*, 341–42. It is also identified as one of the twenty-five realms of existence. Hurvitz (342) adds:

> We have already encountered this as the name of the fourth world of the fourth dhyāna stage. Chih-i understood the first three of these worlds to be within the reach even of ordinary persons, if they but kept the Buddhist ten commandments and performed dhyāna, and the fourth, which is characterized by sensation but lack of thought, to be within the reach of practitioners of religions other than Buddhism. Because of the ease of slipping into this state and, through error, remaining in it, Chih-i gave it a category of its own in addition to including it in the fourth dhyāna stage.

For some reason 或爲因縁: lit., "the confluence of causes and conditions."

Five divine realms of the non-returner (*anāgāmin*) 五那含天: the "five divine realms of the non-returner" are equivalent to the fifth through ninth levels of the fourth dhyāna stage. One who reaches this level is considered to have no more retrogression into the lower stages. For details, see Hurvitz, *Chih-i*, 341–42.

ization of their conventionality as] continuity and relativity in a like manner. Remove the other eight levels in a like manner, and [sever the afflictions of] ignorance and pride in a like manner. [Thus you realize that] the thirty-six levels [of afflictions]—that is, the nine [levels each] of four [dhyāna stages]—[**71b**] are ultimately non-arising.

2. The realm of no-form [71b1]

Next is deconstructing and destroying the nine levels [of afflictions] of the realm of no-form 無色界. Suppose you wish to extinguish "the three types of matter [that is, 'visible form' *(rūpa)*] with regard to resistance and so forth." At that time if you destroy the phenomenal obstacles, you will arouse [the concentration of] pre-dhyāna preparations, and if you destroy the obstacle of nature you will realize [the concentration of] the place of emptiness. The

The three types of matter with regard to resistance and so forth 若欲滅有對等三種之色: these are 1. that which is visible and has resistance 可見有對, 2. that which is invisible yet has resistance 不可見有對, and 3. that which is invisible and has no resistance 不可見無對. This is based on a passage from a section on the four *samāpattis* in the *Ta chih tu lun*, T 25.212a21–23. Lamotte (*Le Traité* 3, 1276–77) translates:

> C'est pourquoi le yogin "dépasse la notion de matières *(rūpasaṃjñāmataikrāmati)*, détruit la notion de résistance *(prati-ghasaṃjñāṃ nirodhyati)* et ne songe plus à la notion de multiplicité *(nanātva-saṃjñāṃ na manasikaroti)*."
>
> Le Buddha a parlé de trois sortes de matières *(rūpa)*: "1. il y a une matière visible et résistante *(asti rūpāṃ sanidarśanaṃ sapratigham)*; 2. Il y a une matière invisible et résistante *(asti rūpāṃ anidarśanaṃ sapratigham)*; 3. Il y a une matière invisible et non-résistante *(asti rūpāṃ anidarśanaṃ asapratigham)*."

Chodron (3, 1048) has:

> This is why the yogin "transcends the notion of matter, destroys the notion of resistance and no longer thinks about the notion of multiplicity."
>
> The Buddha spoke of three kinds of form: "1. There is form that is visible and resistant; 2. There is invisible resistant form; 3. There is invisible non-resistant form."
>
> When the yogin "transcends the notion of matter," this concerns visible resistant form; when he "destroys the notion of resistance," this concerns invisible resistant form; when he "no longer thinks about the notion of multiplicity" this concerns invisible non-resistant form.
>
> Furthermore, by the destruction of visibles seen by the eye, the yogin "transcends matter"; by the destruction of the ear and sounds, the nose and smells, the tongue and tastes, the body and tangibles, he "transcends the notion of resistance." In regard to other forms and many varieties not described as form, we speak of "the notion of multiplicity."

Pre-dhyāna preparations 未到[定]: also written 未至 (or 到地) 定, "incompletely attained concentration."

The place of emptiness 空處: short for "the samādhi (concentration) which is the realization of the inexhaustibility of emptiness" 空無邊處定 *(ākāśa-ānantya-āyatana-samādhi)*, the first level of the realm of no-form. See Chih-i's treatment of these terms in his *Introduction to Graded Terms of the Dharma Realm*, T 46.675a18–b14; see also the Glossary on the "four concentrations on emptiness."

concentration that realizes the place of emptiness also involves passions, pride, and ignorance. You should use the four contemplations [to cultivate the paths of] means and superior progress to realize the non-arising of the phenomenal and principle. If [the afflictions are] not removed, then cultivate [realizing their conventionality as] continuity and relativity, in a like manner. Approach the [other] eight levels and [the nine levels of the afflictions] of ignorance and pride in a like manner.

[In the formless realm] you first come in contact with emptiness, but if there is a excess of emptiness [which causes] distraction, then you should abandon emptiness and come in contact with [the concentration of the inexhaustibility of] consciousness, that is, you attain the concentration of [the inexhaustibility of] consciousness, and your thoughts attain mutual rapport [with the formless realm]. This [state] also involves the delusions of passions, pride, and ignorance. Again, use the four contemplations [to cultivate the paths of] means and superior progress and so forth to realize the non-arising of the phenomenal and principle. The other matters should be known [as outlined above].

If you first come in contact with [the realm of the inexhaustibility of] consciousness and have a excess of a concentrated mind so that you are distracted, you should abandon your excessive [reliance on samādhic] consciousness and come in contact with the consciousness of the place of non-existence. But if you come in contact with even a little consciousness, how can this be referred to as "non-existence"? If you use even a little consciousness, how can this be referred to as "the place where nothing is used"? [Nevertheless at this level] you now realize concentration by coming in contact with non-existence. If your thoughts are in rapport with this dharma, [you should know that this realm] also involves the three types of conventionalities and so forth, and you should use the four contemplations, and so forth; the other matters should be known [as outlined above].

First, the realm of [inexhaustible] consciousness is like an ulcer, and the realm of non-existence is like a boil. There is a further, superior [realm

First come in contact with emptiness 先縁空: or, as Ikeda extrapolates (*Gendaigoyaku*, 367), "you experience the samādhi of the place [of inexhaustible] emptiness."

Come in contact with [the concentration of the inexhaustibility of] consciousness 捨空縁識: or, experience the concentration (samādhi) of the inexhaustibility of consciousness 識無邊處定, the second level of the realm of no-form.

Come in contact with the consciousness of the place of non-existence 縁無所有識: that is, the third level of the realm of no-form. Also called the "lesser place" 少處 by Chih-i, since it involves "neither consciousness nor no-consciousness"; see the *Graded Terms*, T 46.675a24–28.

An ulcer 癰 **and a boil** 瘡: that is, they are situations that must be healed in order to reach a higher state?

of] concentration called that of "neither conceptions nor no-conceptions." The *Abhidharma-vibhāṣā-śāstra* says "this is neither the non-conceptuality of the non-conceptual heavenly state, nor the conceptuality of the three kinds of emptiness, and therefore it is called 'neither conceptions nor no-conceptions.'" A teacher of people has said, "[The realm of] no-form is a variant realm of the heavens of form, but the terms should not be used in the same way. If we interpret the terms with regard to the realm itself, [we should say that] conceptions were already removed by the previous realm [or concentration] of non-existence, and here one removes [the conceptual attitude of] no-conceptions. Both [attitudes of] 'concepts' and 'no-concepts' are abandoned; therefore this [realm] is called 'neither conceptions nor no-conceptions.'" The *Ta chih tu lun* says, "[There are four (levels of) formlessness.] One is constantly defiled, and distinctions need to be made concerning [the other] three." The

Concentration called that of "neither conceptions nor no-conceptions" 非有想非無想: this is the fourth and highest realm of formlessness.

This is neither the non-conceptuality of the non-conceptual heavenly state, nor the conceptuality of the three kinds of emptiness, and therefore it is called 'neither conceptions nor no-conceptions' 非無想天之無想非三空之有想故言非有想非無想: see the *Abhidharma-vibhāṣā-śāstra*, T 28.326c24–28:

> Question: Why is this called "the place of neither conceptions nor no-conceptions"? Answer: It is not characterized as fully conceptual, and it is not characterized as fully non-conceptual. "Not characterized as fully conceptual" means it is not characterized [as involving conscious conceptualization] like the samādhi of the ten conceptualizations [of a decaying corpse], and "not characterized as fully non-conceptual" means it is not characterized [as fully lacking in conception] like the samādhi of complete extinction or the samādhi of non-conceptualization.... Therefore it is called "neither conceptions nor no-conceptions."

A teacher of people 人師: the identity of this teacher and the source of this quote is unknown.

[There are four (levels of) formlessness.] One is constantly defiled, and distinctions need to be made concerning three 一常有漏三當分別: see the *Ta chih tu lun*, T 25.212a29–b1, following the section quoted above on the "three types of *rūpa*." Lamotte (*Le Traité* 3, 1278) translates:

> Parmi ces quatre [recueillements] immatériels *(ārūpya)*, *un* [à savoir le Naivasaṃjñānāsaṃjñāyatana] *est toujours impur (sāsrava). Pour les trois autres ils faut distinguer.*
>
> L'Ākāśānantryāyatana est tantôt impur *(sāsrava)* et tantôt pur *(anāsrava)*. S'il est impur, cet Ākāśāyatana contient quatre agrégats impurs *(anāsravaskandha)*; s'il est pur, il contient quatre agrégats purs. Pour le Vijñānānantryāyatana et l'Ākiṃcanyāyatana, il en va de même.
>
> Tous ces recueillements sont conditionnés *(saṃskṛta)* et bons *(kuśala)*. S'il est impur l'Ākāśāyatana comporte rétribution *(savipāka)* et est indéterminé moralement *(avyākṛta)*; s'il est pur, il ne comporte pas rétribution. Pour le Vijñānāyatana et l'Ākiṃcanyāyatana, il en va de même.
>
> S'il est bon, le Naivasaṃjñānā-saṃ-jñāyatana comporte rétribution et est indéterminé moralement, mais [en soi] il ne comporte pas rétribution.

first three [realms of emptiness, consciousness, and non-existence] are both defiled and undefiled. If one is able to arouse transworldly wisdom [in or through these realms], then it can be called undefiled; if one does not arouse [transworldly wisdom] in or through this [realm of] concentration, then it is defiled. Teachings are given in response to the needs and capacities [of the listeners], so they are sometimes obscure and sometimes clear; thus I have given this explanation. There are, in fact, some people who arouse [the attainment of] non-defilement from within this [fourth realm of] concentration[, despite the quote from the *Ta chih tu lun*]. What should we make of this? For now I will just rely on the teaching [and leave it at that].

Although there are no crude passionate afflictions within this [formless realm of] concentration, there are ten types of minute dharmas [of passionate afflictions], as [explained] in the *(Tz'u-ti) ch'an-men*. You should know that [even] this [realm of] concentration involves the three types of conventionality. Now you should singlemindedly utilize undefiled wisdom to deconstruct [the paths of] means, superior progress, non-obstruction, and liberation and realize the non-arising of phenomena and principle. The nine levels [of afflictions of this and other types of conventionality should be deconstructed] in a like manner, and should be known as outlined previously. If you use worldly wisdom to sever all the delusions of conceptual attitudes, this is called the wisdom of exhaustion [of afflictions]. If you sever them with undefiled wisdom, this is called the wisdom of non-arising. This is called the contemplation of the essence of conceptual attitudes [as empty]. This exhaustively destroys the nine times nine [types of afflictions] in the triple world, or eighty-one levels of the delusions of conceptual attitudes. This is to deconstruct and destroy dharmas universally.

Chodron (3, 1049) has:

> Of the four formless [absorptions], one, namely, the naivasaṃjñānā-saṃjñāyatana, is always impure. For the other three, one can single out: the ākāśasnantyāyatana is sometimes impure and sometimes pure. If it is impure, this ākāśāyatana contains four impure aggregates; if it is pure, it contains four pure aggregates. It is the same for the vijñānā-nantyāyatana and the ākiṃcanyāyatana. All these absorptions are conditioned and good. If it is impure, the ākāśāyatana involves retribution and is morally indeterminate; if it is pure, it does not involve retribution. It is the same for the vijñānāyatana and the ākiṃcanyāyatana. If it is good, the naivasaṃjñānā-saṃjñā-yatana involves retribution and is morally indeterminate, but [in itself] it does not involve retribution.

Ten types of minute dharmas 十種細法: see the *Tz'u-ti ch'an-men*, T 46.523c3–4. Chan-jan (BT–IV, 30) identifies these as subtle afflictions associated with sensation 受, conceptions 想, volitions 行, contact 触, attitudes 思, desires 欲, understanding 解, mindfulness 念, concentration 定, and wisdom 慧.

3. *Clarification of the levels of attainment* [71b29–73b25]

Third, clarifying the levels of entering or realizing emptiness through conventionality by deconstructing or destroying [the afflictions of] conceptual attitudes consists of four parts: 1. the levels of deconstructing or destroying conceptual attitudes [71c] for those of the Tripitaka [Teachings]; 2. the levels of deconstructing or destroying conceptual attitudes for those of the Shared [Teachings]; 3. the Distinct [Teachings] with names in common with the levels of the Shared [Teachings]; and 4. the Distinct [Teachings], in terms of the levels of bodhisattvas of the Shared [Teachings].

1. Tripitaka Teachings [71c2]

The levels of deconstructing or destroying [the afflictions of] conceptual attitudes in the Tripitaka [Teachings] are as follows. The *Ch'eng-shih lun* clarifies that [the realization of] the sixteen mental [contemplations of the Four Noble Truths] is properly the level of the first fruit [of the stream-enterer]. Other traditions claim that [realizing] these sixteen mental [contemplations] is the level of insight into the way (*darśana-mārga*).

Levels of realizing emptiness from conventionality by deconstructing conceptual attitudes 破思假入空位: for some help in following the detailed levels outlined below, see Chart 1 on the levels of attainment and the Fourfold Teachings in Volume 3. My translations of the names of the stages follow the Chinese and (when given) Chih-i's explanation of their content, and do not necessarily reflect their "original" meaning or their Sanskrit equivalent. A full explanation of the names of the stages in terms of their original Sanskrit, their variations in numerous sources, and their transmission and interpretation in China is beyond the scope of this current translation.

The *Ch'eng-shih lun* clarifies ...: the Kōgi (BT–IV, 32) says that "This is a teaching of the [*Ch'eng-shih lun*] scholars, and not a text that is clarified in the treatise."

Sixteen mental 十六心 **[contemplations of the Four Noble Truths]**: or, "having attained insight into the sixteen aspects of the Four Noble Truths."

Other traditions claim that these sixteen mental [contemplations] is the level of insight into the way (*darśana-mārga*) 異部明十六心是見道位: Chan-jan (BT–IV, 32) points out that the term "other traditions" refer to Buddhist traditions other than that of the *Ch'eng-shih lun*. However, he hastens to add, the Abhidharma tradition claims that there are only fifteen such mental contemplations realized at the attainment of the level of "insight into the way [of the Four Noble Truths]." See, for example, the *Abhidharma-hṛdaya-śāstra*, T 28.911a2, where it is claimed that one who had attained the sixteenth mental contemplation already dwells in the "fruit" or "result" of the stream-enterer. Thus, the *Kōgi* adds, this text claims that only the first fifteen such contemplations correspond to the level of insight into the way (見道, *darśana-mārga*), and the sixteenth corresponds to the higher "path of cultivation" (修道, *bhāvanā-mārga*). In any case, for Chih-i, in the Tripitaka Teachings the highest attainment of the stream-enterer is to have full insight into the way (見道,

If, for now, we consider only the path of cultivation (*bhāvanā-mārga*) [beyond the attainments of a stream-enterer], those who sever the first level of the desirous delusions [of conceptual attitudes] and gradually reach the fifth level of exhausting [conceptual attitudes] are all called those facing [the way of] the once-returner *(sakṛdāgāmin)*. If they go beyond this severance and attain the exhaustion of the fifth level, all of these are called "wandering sages." Next, those who exhaustively sever the six levels are called [those who have attained] the fruit of the once-returner, and those who go beyond severance to attain the [full] exhaustion of the sixth level are called "once-returners."

Next, those who sever the seventh level and reach the eighth level are called those facing [the way of] the non-returner *(anāgāmin)*. Those who go beyond this severance and attain the eighth level are called "sons with seeds for only one life." Next, those who exhaustively sever the ninth level are called [those who have attained] the fruit of the non-returner, and finally they do not return again to the realm of desires.

Next, those who sever the first level of the first dhyāna [stage] attain the eighth level of [the realm of] non-conceptuality, and [exhaust] all of seventy-one levels [of conceptual delusions]. These are called those facing [the way of] the arhat. This [level] includes within it six levels of the non-returner. Those who [attain] the ninth [degree of conceptual delusions] through the unobstructed path, exhaustively sever the ninth [level of] delusions through [the concentration of] non-conceptualization, and realize the ninth [and top level] of the path of liberation are called those who have attained the fruit of the arhat. Those who exhaust the conceptual [attitudes and delusions] of the triple world and attain the wisdom of exhaustion [of delusions] and the wisdom of non-arising are called those who do not give birth to passionate afflictions. Those who realize the true emptiness of even a part of the eighty-one [delusions and afflictions] are called those who [realize] the non-arising of the principle [of reality, that is, the emptiness of all things]; for true wisdom [that is, the realization of emptiness] to be sufficient is called the wisdom of non-arising. Not experiencing [any further rebirth in] samsara is

darśana-mārga) of the Four Noble Truths, which consists of sixteen insights or contemplations.

Once-returner 一往來: up to this point Chih-i has been using the transliteration for *sakṛdāgāmin*, but here he uses the Chinese translation.

Wandering sages 家家: lit. "[those who go from] house to house," or from this world to a heavenly realm and back.

Sons with seeds for only one life 一種子: that is, those who will not be reborn again after this life, or "non-returners." Once again Chih-i first uses the transliteration and then the translation, in this case, of *anāgāmin*.

called the resultant reward [or, "fruit and recompense" 果報] of [realizing] non-arising.

If we were to discuss [the level and attainments of] the pratyekabuddha, this involves further subjugation of minute habitual traces [of delusions]. They are different [from śrāvakas] in that they do not give birth [to even these habitual traces].

This is a short summary of the classification of levels of severing [deluded] conceptual attitudes of conventionality in terms of analytical [destruction or deconstruction as used in the Tripitaka Teachings].

2. Shared Teachings [71c17]

Second is with regard to those of the Shared [Teachings], to examine the essence [that is, emptiness] of conceptual attitudes in terms of levels that are in common with that of the Tripitaka [Teachings]. As it is clarified in the *Pañcaviṃśati Sūtra*, the [first of the ten *bhūmi*] stages of "parched wisdom" and "potential" up to the sixth stage [of "freedom from desire"] are shared with the śrāvakas [that is, those of the Tripitaka Teachings], those up to the seventh stages [of "completion"] are shared with pratyekabuddhas, those up to the eighth stage [of pratyekabuddhahood] and ninth stage [of bodhisattvahood] are shared with bodhisattvas, and when those on the stage of bodhisattvahood convert, they enter the tenth stage, called the stage of Buddhahood. As for the stages that are said to be "shared," there are higher and lower [attainments within the stages]. But, as the *Ta chih tu lun* says, the three people [śrāvaka, pratyekabuddha, and bodhisattva] are the same in severing the afflictions proper, and the same in entering nirvana with and without remainder. Therefore it is said that they are "shared." It is like when

Stages of "parched wisdom" and "potential" up to the sixth stage 乾慧地性地乃至第六地 ... they enter the tenth stage, called the stage of Buddhahood 轉入第十名佛地: see the *Pañcaviṃśati Sūtra*, T 8.346b2–7, which gives a list of the ten *bhūmi* stages:

> Subhūti spoke to the Buddha, saying, "World Honored One. What are the ten *bhūmi* stages, wherein bodhisattvas are endowed with and have attained supreme wisdom *(anuttara-saṃyak-saṃbodhi)*? "
>
> The Buddha said, "Bodhisattva-mahāsattvas are endowed with the stages of parched wisdom, potential, the eighth person, insight, weakening [delusions], freedom from desires, completion, pratyekabuddhahood, bodhisattvahood, and Buddhahood. Being endowed with these stages, they attain supreme wisdom."

See also the *Ta chih tu lun* at T 25.584c–586a, which gives an interpretation of this passage similar to that given by Chih-i here. Probably, as is often the case, Chih-i is reading the *Pañcaviṃśati Sūtra* through the grid of the *Ta chih tu lun* commentary.

The three people are the same in severing the afflictions proper, and the same in entering nirvana with and without remainder 三人同斷正使同入有餘無餘涅槃: see the discussion of the ten *bhūmi* stages in the *Ta chih tu lun*, T 25.320c–322b.

you burn wood, some becomes charcoal [leaving something left to burn] and some becomes ash; in this way there are higher and lower [attainments by different people].

The stage of "parched wisdom" corresponds to the three levels of acquiring erudition 三賢位: first, the five contemplations for putting the mind at rest 五停心[觀], the distinct states of mindfulness 別相念處, and the general states of mindfulness 總相念處. Generally these are still levels of an ordinary outsider, and therefore it is called the stage of "parched wisdom." [The second stage of] "potential" corresponds to the levels of the four good roots. Through the power of the general states of mindfulness, one arouses good from within the defiled five skandhas; this is called "heat" [the first of the four good roots]. By advancing further to the preliminary, middling, and later [advanced] states of mind, one attains and realizes [the other three good roots of] the "summit," "patience," and "the dharma supreme in the world." Generally this is called [the levels of those who are] (low-level) insiders; therefore this is called the stage of "potential." These two levels share [the activity of] overcoming mistaken views and delusions.

[The third stage of] "the eighth person" is that of "eight kinds of forbearance." Here one advances from [the level of the fourth good root of]

See also Lamotte's extensive note on the ten *bhūmi* stages appended to volume 5 of his translation of the *Ta chih tu lun* (*Le Traité* 5, 2373–2445, which includes a translation of the Sanskrit text that is commented on in chapter XX of the *Ta chih tu lun* (T 25.409c–419c), though this list is different than the list of ten *bhūmi*s followed by Chih-i here.

Like when you burn wood, some becomes charcoal and some becomes ash 如燒木有炭有灰等: this image is from the *Ta chih tu lun*, T 25.260c23–27. Lamotte (*Le Traité* 4, 1761) translates:

> De tels saints, tout en ayant détruit leurs impuretés *(kṣiṇāsrava)*, avaient encore des relents de passion. *Ainsi quand le feu [ordinaire] a brûlé le combustible, il reste encore des cendres et des charbons*, car la force de ce feu est si faible qu'elle ne peut les consumer.

Chodron (4, 1447) has:

> While having destroyed their impurities, saints such as these still have the traces of passion. Thus when [ordinary] fire has burned the fuel, there remain the ashes and charcoal, for the strength of the fire is so weak that it cannot consume them.
>
> At the end of the kalpa, the [cosmic] fire consumes the *trisāhasramahāsāhasralokadhātu* of which nothing remains, for the strength of this fire is very great. The fire of the Buddha's omniscience is also very great: it consumes the passions without leaving any trace.

Generally 通: or, "for those of the Shared Teachings."

[The third stage of] "the eighth person" is that of "eight kinds of forbearance" 八人者八忍也: the mixing or identifying of the terms "eighth person" and "eight forbearances" seems common in the Chinese context, and I am not sure of its origin or significance, though there is a phonetic and visual resemblance. The original Sanskrit (*aṣṭamaka-bhūmi*; see, e.g. *Pañcaviṃśatisāhasrikā Prajñāpāramitā*, ed. N. Dutt, 1934, 225) suggests that "eighth per-

"supreme in the world" and turns to realize or enter the Uninterrupted Samādhi. Therefore it is called [the stage of] "the eighth person."

[The fourth stage of] "insight" **[72a]** involves insight into the true [emptiness], the severance of the mistaken views and conceptual attitudes of the triple world, and the complete exhaustion of the eighty-eight passionate afflictions. Therefore this is called the stage of insight.

[The fifth stage of] "weakening [delusions]" involves removing six levels of conceptualizations in the realm of desires. Therefore this is called the stage of "weakening delusions."

[The sixth stage of] "freedom from desires" involves exhaustively removing nine levels [of conceptual delusions] in the realm of desires. Therefore this is called the stage of "freedom from desires."

[The seventh stage of] "completion" involves exhaustively removing seventy-two levels [of conceptual delusions] in the form and formless realms. [Up to this stage] this is like a fire that burns wood to leave charcoal. Therefore this is called the stage of "completion."

[The eighth stage of] "pratyekabuddhahood" involves a deepening and sharpening of one's goodness and wisdom so that one overcomes and removes the habitual traces [of passionate afflictions and delusions], as when in burning wood only ash remains.

[The ninth stage of] "bodhisattvahood" involves a deepening and sharpening of one's goodness and wisdom, proficiency in both the path and contemplation, severance of the habitual traces as well as mental and physical ignorance, and attainment of the Dharma eye and the wisdom of the path, with supremacy in supranormal powers to purify a Buddha land, masters

son" is the original meaning, though it is not certain what this "eighth person" refers to. Tilman Vetter (following Edgerton) proposes that this refers to the eighth stage of the śrāvaka where one will no longer regress to a lower stage (see the discussion in *T'oung Pao* LXXXIV, 1998, 181). Chih-i makes this connection again in the *Mo-ho chih-kuan* (72c14) and in the *Fa-hua hsüan-i* (T 33.730c27), where he identifies the stage of the "eighth person" with a bodhisattva's attainment of *anutpattika-dharma-kṣānti*. See also *The Great Collection of Sūtras*, T 13.158c2, where this claim is made explicitly; on this passage see the note at *Mo-ho chih-kuan* 74a13–14.

Uninterrupted Samādhi 無間三昧: a state of concentration achieved within the level of "supreme in the world"; to contemplate non-arising and understand that both inner self and outer objects are empty.

Proficiency in both the path and contemplation 道觀雙流: or, more literally, "one flows in both the path and contemplation."

Supremacy in supranormal powers 遊戲神通: this phrase appears in the *Ta chih tu lun*, T 25.342a14, in a passage quoting the *Pañcaviṃśati Sūtra*, which speaks of "supremacy in supranormal powers to go from one Buddha land to another Buddha land."

the dharmas of the Buddha's [ten] powers and the [four] fearlessnesses, and exhausts all remaining traces [of passionate afflictions and delusions], as [an intense fire] leaves only a little ash.

[The tenth stage of] "Buddhahood" involves great virtue, the accumulation of sharp wisdom, the attainment of all wisdom contained in a single thought, and the eternal exhaustion of habitual traces [of passionate afflictions and delusions], as the fire at the end of a kalpa leaves no charcoal and no ash.

These are the ten *bhūmi* stages—the levels of the severance of conceptual delusions—that are shared by those of the three vehicles.

3. Distinct Teachings with names in common with the Shared Teachings [72a11]

Third is the names of the levels [of severing conceptual delusions] in the Distinct Teachings that are shared with those of the Shared Teachings. Formerly it has been said that mistaken views are severed at the third stage, or it has been said that mistaken views are severed at the fourth stage, or it has been said that conceptual [delusions] are exhaustively severed at the sixth stage, or it has been said that conceptual [delusions] are exhaustively severed at the seventh stage. If we consider these words, [it can be said that] the masters who say that all mistaken views are severed at the third stage or the fourth stage do not understand the meaning of the Shared Teachings. Why? Because at the levels that those of the three vehicles share, they are the same in that they enter the Uninterrupted Samādhi; they sever mistaken views without going in and out [of their concentrated state] of contemplation. Why abruptly conclude that conceptual attitudes are severed at either the third stage or fourth stage? If you take the position that mistaken views are severed on the third stage, then [it must follow that] conceptual attitudes should be severed at the fourth stage. If you take the position that mistaken views are severed at the fourth stage, then this means that mistaken views are not yet severed at the third stage. If you take the position that mistaken views are severed at both stages, is this achieved by going in and out of contemplation, or by not going in and out of contemplation? If it is achieved by not going in and out of contemplation, then [the severing of mistaken views] does not occur at both stages [since it would have to occur at one or the other]. If it is achieved by going in and out of contemplation, this cannot be the level at which mistaken views are severed [because the severance of views involved Uninterrupted Samādhi]. The human masters [who teach

Formerly it has been said 舊云 …: it is not known where or by whom these claims were made.

this] justify their position by saying that the sūtras teach it, but these masters do not understand the intent of the sūtras. Now I say that these sūtras are borrowing the meaning of the Distinct [Teachings] to manifest the Shared [Teachings]. The meaning of "mistaken views" in the Distinct [Teachings] is very extensive [lit., "long"], and so it is taught that [it covers both] the third stage and the fourth stage; the meaning of "mistaken views" in the Shared [Teachings] is more limited [lit., "short"], and so [their severance] is not by going in and out of contemplation. Thus the names are borrowed from the Distinct [Teachings] but the meaning is certainly taken from the Shared [Teachings]. Let us interpret [the issue of the severance of mistaken views at the third or fourth stage] in terms of not going in and out of contemplation: if we speak of the third stage, this refers to the early severance of mistaken views, and if we speak of the fourth stage, this refers to the later severance of mistaken views, all done without going [in and] out of contemplation. This is like saying that the sixteen mental [contemplations of the Four Noble Truths] are sometimes called "the path [for severing mistaken] views" and sometimes called "the path [for severing] conceptual attitudes."

[Next,] naming the Shared levels by borrowing names from the Distinct [Teachings] is as follows. The three levels of acquiring erudition by "outsiders" corresponds to the stage of "parched wisdom," but [in the Distinct Teachings] this is called the "ten levels of faith." The levels of the four good roots of "insiders" corresponds to the stage of "potential," which [in the Distinct Teachings] is called the "ten abodes," the "ten levels of practice," and the ten levels of merit transference." The [third and fourth] stages of the "eighth person" and "insight" correspond to the stream-enterer, **[72b]** which [in the Distinct Teachings] is called the first *[bhūmi]* stage of "joy" 歡喜.

Sometimes called "the path [for severing mistaken] views" and sometimes called "the path [for severing] conceptual attitudes" 或言是見道或言是思道: here Chih-i seems to be playing with the term 見道 ("insight into the way," *darśana-mārga*, in Abhidharma coupled with the higher "path of cultivation" 修道, *bhāvanā-mārga*) to contrast it with the compound 思道 (which, as far as I know, has no Sanskrit equivalent). The meaning of the terms, however, have been shifted from their Indian Abhidharma context to Chih-i's Chinese context to fit his scheme of first severing "mistaken views" 見 and then severing "conceptual attitudes" 思. The meaning of 見, then, has shifted from the positive meaning of "insight" *(darśana)* to the negative meaning of "mistaken views" *(dṛṣṭi)*, with Chih-i giving no indication that such a shift has occurred.

Ten levels of faith 十信 ...: once again, see Chart 1 in Volume 3.

Ten levels of merit transference" 十回向: this stage doesn't seem to match other explanations of the stages by Chih-i, as reflected in Chart 1.

First stage of "joy" 歡: here Chih-i begins to draw from a different list of

The stage of "weakening [delusions]" corresponds to the once-returner. The once-returner includes [the phases of] facing toward [the goal] and [achieving] the fruit. Facing toward [the goal] corresponds to the stage of "freedom from defilements" 離垢, and establishing the fruit corresponds to the stage of "clarity" 明. The stage of "freedom from desires" corresponds to the non-returner. The non-returner includes [the phases of] facing towards [the goal] and [achieving] the fruit. Facing toward [the goal] corresponds to the stage of "flame" 炎, and establishing the fruit corresponds to the stage of "difficult victory" 難勝. The stage of "completion" corresponds to the arhat. The arhat includes [the phases of] facing towards [the goal] and [achieving] the fruit. Facing toward [the goal] corresponds to the stage of "manifestation" 現前, and establishing the fruit corresponds to the stage of "far practice" 遠行. The establishment of the level of the pratyekabuddha corresponds to the stage of the "immovable" 不動. The establishment of the stage of bodhisattvahood corresponds to the stage of "good wisdom" 善慧. Or, the later [advanced] mental stage of one who has achieved the stage of bodhisattvahood corresponds to the stage of the "Dharma cloud." Or[, in another section of the *Ta chih tu lun*], the stage of Buddhahood corresponds to the stage of the Dharma cloud. The *Pañcaviṃśati Sūtra* says, "The bodhisattva on the tenth *bhūmi* stage is like a Buddha," so this interpretation is possible.

If we borrow the names [of stages] from the Distinct [Teachings] to

the ten *bhūmi* stages than the one he used above, this one apparently based on the list in the *Sūtra on the Ten Stages (Daśabhūmika)*. The original Sanskrit for this list is: *pramuditā, vimalā, pravākarī, arciṣmatī, sudurjayā, abhimukhī, dūraṅgamā, acalā, sādhamatī*, and *dharmameghā*.

Stage of the "Dharma cloud" 法雲: the *Kōgi* (BT–IV, 58) indicates that this phrase refers to a passage in the *Ta chih tu lun* at T 25.586a21–22. Chih-i may have been relying on this context of the *Ta chih tu lun* for his discussion in this section (see note below under 72c18 for a translation of this section from the *Ta chih tu lun*).

The *Kōgi* refers to a number of texts in discussing this section: the *Ta chih tu lun*, *Pañcaviṃśati Sūtra*, *Jen-wang ching*, and *Daśabhūmi-vyākhyāna*. It seems that a concerted effort would be required to straighten out the various lists of stages, and to figure out how and why Chih-i organized and interpreted them in the way he does.

The stage of Buddhahood corresponds to the stage of the Dharma cloud 佛地爲法雲: see the *Ta chih tu lun*, T 25.419b23–26:

> You should know that, like a Buddha, when a bodhisattva sits in this way under the [Bodhi] tree, he enters the tenth *bhūmi* stage called the stage of "Dharma cloud." It is as if a great cloud rains on the tree steadily without interruption. A mind spontaneously arises that has immeasurable, unlimited, and pure Buddha Dharmas, and whose thoughts are immeasurable.

The bodhisattva on the tenth *bhūmi* stage is like a Buddha 十地菩薩爲如佛: the exact phrase is found in the *Pañcaviṃśati Sūtra* at T 8.257c7.

classify the levels of those of the three vehicles of the Shared [Teachings], then those on the first stage sever the delusions of mistaken views, those on the second stage sever the first and second levels of conceptual attitudes in the realm of desires; those on the third stage sever [up to] the sixth level of conceptual attitudes; those on the fourth stage sever the seventh and eighth levels of conceptual attitudes; those on the fifth stage sever [up to] the ninth level of conceptual attitudes; those on the sixth stage sever up to the seventy-first level of conceptual attitudes; those on the seventh level sever up to the seventy-second level of conceptual attitudes; those on the eighth stage and above conquer the habitual traces [of afflictions and delusions] and sever ignorance and so forth. This should be known as outlined previously.

4. Distinct Teachings in terms of the levels of the Shared Teachings [72b14]

Fourth is borrowing names [of stages] from the Distinct [Teachings] to name the bodhisattva levels of those of the Shared [Teachings]. [The stage of] "parched wisdom" corresponds to the "outsiders." The stage of "potential" corresponds to the "insiders." "Eighth person" corresponds to the first *bhūmi* stage [of "joy"?]. [The first] fifteen mental [contemplations] corresponds to the second stage. The sixteenth mental [contemplation] corresponds to the third stage. These three stages all involve severing the delusions of mistaken views without going out of contemplation.

[Also, attaining] the four forbearances corresponds to the first stage; [attaining] the four wisdoms corresponds to the second stage; the four comparable recognitions correspond to the third stage; and the four comparable wisdoms correspond to the fourth stage. These four stages all involve severing the delusions of mistaken views without going out of contemplation. How can these be said to be the same as the former interpretations [of old masters]?

[The first] fifteen mental [contemplations] 十五心: according to Chan-jen (BT–IV, 61), this refers to attaining the "eight kinds of forbearance or recognition" and the first seven of the eight kinds of wisdom.

The four forbearances 四忍[認]: four levels of "forbearance" or "recognition": recognition or forbearance from overcoming [delusions]; from attaining faith; from pliantly following [the path]; and the forbearance of the non-arising of dharmas.

[Attaining] the four wisdoms correspond to the second stage, the four comparable recognitions correspond to the third stage, and the four comparable wisdoms correspond to the fourth stage 四智爲二地。四比忍爲三地。四比智爲四地: it is not clear which "four wisdoms" are meant here, and what is meant by the "comparable" recognitions and wisdoms. The classical commentaries (see BT–IV, 61–62) attempt some explanation, but I had difficulty making any sense of it.

[Further, the stage of] "weakening [delusions]" is the fifth stage, at which [up to] the sixth level of conceptual attitudes are severed. "Freedom from desires" is the sixth stage, at which [up to] the ninth level of conceptual attitudes are severed. "Completion" is the seventh stage, at which the conceptual attitudes of the form and formless realms are exhaustively severed. "Pratyekabuddhahood" is the eighth stage and, up to the stage of "Buddhahood," these involve the severance of habitual traces [of afflictions and delusions] and ignorance, as outlined previously.

It was formerly said [by old masters] that conceptual attitudes were exhaustively severed at the sixth stage, so one becomes an arhat [at this stage]. Or they refer to the *Jen-wang ching* that claims that one becomes an arhat at the seventh stage. However, the sixth stage is called "freedom from desires," where one stops at becoming free from [up to] the ninth level of [conceptual delusions] in the realm of desires, which should be equivalent to a non-returner [and not an arhat]. Even if you wrap up the fruit [of a non-returner] and practice [that which involves] facing [toward the goal of an arhat], [at this stage] you still have the nine levels [of delusions] of non-conceptuality, so this cannot be the attainment of an arhat. If you attain the seventh stage of "completion," this can be said to be the fruit [of an arhat]. In the sense that "facing" [toward the goal] coincides with the [final] fruit, [it can be said that] completing the levels of the first dhyāna stage coincides with the seventh stage, but it is at this time [at the seventh stage] that it is worthy of the name "completion."

Let us now interpret this and clarify the meaning in terms of the ten perfections. One realizes the wisdom of emptiness with the sixth [perfection] of *prajñā*-wisdom, thus exhaustively severing delusions and becoming an arhat. **[72c]** With the seventh [perfection] of means *(upāya)*, one goes beyond *prajñā*-wisdom [for oneself] and utilizes conventional transformations [to save other beings]. This is called "utilitarian service" 便. If one becomes an arhat on attaining the seventh stage, then in terms of matching the stages with the "facing" and "fruits" [of the four levels from stream-enterer to arhat], it is appropriate that the seventh stage matches the fourth fruit [of the arhat]. These are all tentative and subjective correspondences, and the sūtras and treatises are not all the same [with regard to their lists and definitions

It was formerly said 舊云: it is not known to whom this refers.

***Jen-wang ching* that claims that one becomes an arhat on the seventh stage** 仁王經七地齊羅漢: it is not known to what passage of the *Jen-wang ching* this refers.

It is at this time [on the seventh stage] that it is worthy of the name "completion" 爾時得名已辦: so it cannot be said that one becomes an arhat previous to this stage?

The sūtras and treatises are not all the

of the stages]; it is necessary to consider these matters, but one should not become attached to the petty details.

5. Questions and answers concerning the stages [72c4]

Question: [You say that] those of the three vehicles share the severance [of views and conceptual attitudes. This meaning is not yet clear. Why do you comment only on the bodhisattva stages?

Answer: The *Ta chih tu lun* uses the classification of three stages of a "burning wick" to illustrate that there are three "places" [or stages] of sever-

same; it is necessary to consider these matters, but one should not become attached to the petty details 經論不定復須斟酌不可苟執: this is an understatement, to say the least. The lists of various stages of practice and attainment in the traditional Buddhist texts are quite complex and varied. Chih-i seems to be attempting here to bring some sort of order to these varied lists by subsuming them under his scheme of the Fourfold Teachings. The details do not quite work [without a stretch of the imagination], but this schematization allowed the T'ien-t'ai tradition, and other Chinese Buddhists, to accept the appearance of order and ignore the varied details. Perhaps this is one of Chih-i's greatest contributions to East Asian Buddhism: the appearance of an ordered acceptance of the details and contradictions of the imported scholastic Buddhist tradition so that the Chinese Buddhists could focus and develop other aspects of Buddhist practice and teachings.

Three stages of a "burning wick" 焦火主: see the *Ta chih tu lun* section from 584c–586a which discusses the ten *bhūmi* stages and uses the analogy of burning a candle to illustrate how different afflictions and delusions are removed ("burned away") by bodhisattvas at different stages. First, the text from the *Pañcaviṃśati Sūtra*:

> The Buddha said to Subhūti, "I will explain to you through an analogy. The attainment of wisdom is easily understood if we use an analogy. Subhūti, it is like a burning flame or candle. First a flame is used to light a candle's wick, and later a flame burns on the wick. [Are these flames the same or different?]"
>
> Subhūti said to the World Honored One, "[The later flame] is not the original flame that lights the wick, nor is it completely separate from the original flame. World Honored One. "[The original flame] is not the later flame that burns on the wick, nor is it completely separate from the later flame."
>
> "Subhūti, what do you mean? That the wick does not burn?"
>
> "World Honored One. The wick truly burns."
>
> The Buddha then said to Subhūti, "[The attainment of wisdom by] bodhisattva-mahāsattvas is also like this. It does not use the first aspiration for supreme wisdom, nor is it separate from the first aspiration for supreme wisdom, nor does it use the later attainment of supreme wisdom, nor is it separate from the later attainment of supreme wisdom." [T 25.584c19–28]

Next, the interpretation of the *Ta chih tu lun* commentary:

> [The attainment of wisdom] is like the flame on a wick, which is neither the original flame [with which the candle was lit] alone, nor is it separate from the original flame, nor is it separate from the later flame [which burns on the candle], for the wick burns. The Buddha says to Subhūti, "You yourself see the burning wick; [the flame is] neither the original

ing delusions by bodhisattvas. [The stage of] parched wisdom involves overcoming delusions; this is like the original flame with which you light [the candle]. Now, [the delusions are] truly severed at [the stage of] the "eighth person"; why can we not say that this involves the original flame?

Again, the *Pañcaviṃśati Sūtra* says that "the bodhisattva of the tenth *bhūmi* stage is like a Buddha." This already clarifies the fact that the last stage is proximate to the ultimate [stage or attainment of Buddhahood]; why cannot the same claim be made that there are no "middling stages" or the "early stages" [since they are "included" in the final stage]? On this basis we can further speculate concerning individuals by revealing the ten *bhūmi* stages of bodhisattvas; where is the fault [in this]? [On the other hand] if there were no stages [of progressive attainment], the sūtras would not speak of bodhisattvas cultivating the practices of the stages from the first stage to the tenth stage and of the various Dharma gates that correspond to each stage.

Again, the *Ta chih tu lun* says, "The stage of parched wisdom, with regard to the dharma of the bodhisattva, consists of 'the forbearance from overcoming [delusions].' The stage of 'potential,' with regard to the dharma of the bodhisattva, consists of 'forbearance pliantly following [the path].' The stage

[flame] nor [merely] the later flame, and yet the wick burns. I, also, with my Buddha eye, see that bodhisattvas attain the supreme path; this is attained neither with [merely] their original aspiration nor is it [attained] separate from their original aspiration, nor is it attained [merely] with their later mind, nor it is attained apart from their later mind, and yet they do attain the supreme path. The burning [candle] is like the bodhisattva path. The [candle] wick is like the afflictions such as ignorance and so forth. The flames are like the wisdom corresponding to the first stage through the wisdom corresponding to the Vajra Samādhi [at the highest stage?]. The burning is like the burning up of afflictions such as ignorance and so forth, which, when they are exhaustively burnt up, one attains the supreme path. [T 25.585c18–25]

The bodhisattva of the tenth *bhūmi* stage is like a Buddha: this phrase was just quoted above; see the *Pañcaviṃśati Sūtra*, T 8.257c7.

The sūtras would not speak of bodhisattvas cultivating ...: As in, for example, the passage in the *Pañcaviṃśati Sūtra*, T 8.256c–257c.

The stage of parched wisdom ... but with regard to the bodhisattva is 'forbearance of the non-arising of dharmas: a summary of the *Ta chih tu lun*, T 25.586a1–22, a section which Chih-i has referred to previously (33c25, 72b7), and which immediately follows the passage on the "burning candle" quoted above:

> Sometimes cultivate the samādhi of contemplating the Buddha or the contemplation of impurity, or sometimes practice the contemplation of compassion or transience, and thus discriminate and accumulate good dharmas and abandon non-good dharmas. [At this stage] one has only wisdom, and has not attained the water of dhyāna meditation. Therefore one is [yet] not able to attain the path, and thus this is called the stage of "parched wisdom." Here a bodhisattva has experienced the aspiration for

of the 'eighth person,' with regard to the bodhisattva, corresponds to the 'forbearance of [realizing]the non-arising of dharmas.' The stage of 'insight,' with regard to the bodhisattva, corresponds to the fruit of the forbearance of the non-arising of dharmas. The stage of 'weakening [delusions]', with regard to the bodhisattva, corresponds to freedom from desires and purity. The stage of 'freedom from desires,' with regard to the bodhisattva, corresponds to supremacy in supranormal powers. The stage of 'completion,' with regard to the śrāvaka, is called the stage of Buddhahood, but with regard to the bodhisattva is [the attainment of] 'forbearance of the non-arising of

enlightenment, but has not yet attained the forbearance of following [the path].

The stage of "potential" is, for śrāvakas, [the attainment of the four good roots] from "heat" to "Dharma supreme in the world." For bodhisattvas, they attain the forbearance of following [the path] and are passionately attached to the true marks of reality; also, they do not give rise to mistaken views, and attain the water of dhyāna meditation.

The stage of the "eighth person" involves[, for the śrāvaka, attaining] the [first] fifteen [of the sixteen] mental [contemplations], from the forbearance of the dharma of suffering to the forbearance of wisdom that is comparable to the path. For a bodhisattva, this involves the forbearance of the non-arising of dharmas and realizing the level of a bodhisattva.

The stage of "insight" is [for the śrāvaka] the first attainment of the fruit of a noble sage, that is, the fruit of a stream-enterer. For a bodhisattva, this involves attaining the stage of non-retrogression.

The stage of "weakening [delusions]" is [for the śrāvaka the level of] the stream-enterer and once-returner, because of the severance of nine types of passionate afflictions of the realm of desires. For the bodhisattva, this involves going beyond the stage of non-retrogression to [the stage] where one has not [quite] yet attained Buddhahood, because it involves severing all [active] passionate afflictions and removing, though "weakly," their residual traces.

The stage of "freedom from desires" is [for the śrāvaka the level of] freedom from the covetous desires and all passionate afflictions of the realm of desires, and is called [that of the] non-returner. For the bodhisattva, one attains the five supranormal powers due to the effect of becoming free from desires.

The stage of "completion" is, for the śrāvakas, the attainment of wisdom from exhausting [the passionate afflictions] and the wisdom of [realizing] the non-arising [of all things], and [corresponds to] the attainment of an arhat. For a bodhisattva, this is the fulfillment of the stage of Buddhahood.

The stage of pratyekabuddhahood [is attained by those who] in their previous life [planted] the seed of the causes and conditions for the path of a pratyekabuddha, so in this life they attain it with only minor causes and conditions upon becoming a home-departed one. Or, they deeply contemplate the truth of causes and conditions *(pratītya-samutpāda)* and thus fulfil the path of a pratyekabuddha. [The term] "pratyeka" is [translated] into Chinese as 因緣 ("causes and conditions") or 覺 "awakening."

The stage of bodhisattvahood is as explained above for the stages from "parched wisdom" to "freedom from desires." There is also the bodhisattva stages from the stage of "joy" to the stage of "Dharma cloud." These are all called "bodhisattva stages."

dharmas.'" Therefore it says in the *Pañcaviṃśati Sūtra*, "The wisdom and severance of a stream-enterer are, for a bodhisattva, [the realization of] the forbearance of the non-arising of dharmas, and so forth up to the wisdom and severance of a pratyekabuddha are, for a bodhisattva, the forbearance of the non-arising of dharmas." These [sūtras and] treatises make such distinctions in terms of the bodhisattva. Hence I follow their example in giving my interpretation. Where is the fault in that?

Question: [You point out that] nine levels [of afflictions and delusions] in the realm of desires are severed. What is the meaning of making so many categories of fruits?

Answer: If a dangerous place presents many hazards, many protective walls are necessary. In the same way the realm [of desires] presents many hazards, and so many [levels of] "fruits" [are necessary] to reassure [the practitioner].

[Question:] If so, as there are many distractions in this realm [of desires], you should establish [or insist on the practice of] many dhyāna meditations.

Answer: The realm of desires is not [a stage] for practicing concentrative meditation, so it is not [appropriate] for establishing dhyāna meditations. [On the other hand,] conditions are appropriate for [attaining] non-defilement, so one can establish [various] fruits [such as that from stream-enterer to arhat].

Question: Those of the three vehicles equally realize wisdom and severance. Why is this called "wisdom and severance" for those of the two vehicles [of śrāvaka and pratyekabuddha] and called "the forbearance of [the non-arising of] dharmas" for bodhisattvas?

Answer: "Forbearance" 忍 is the cause and "wisdom" is the fruit; therefore the [first] fifteen mental [contemplations] are called "forbearances," and the sixteenth mental [contemplation] is called "wisdom." Again, those of the two vehicles have [in a manner of speaking] already reached [their] "enlightenment," so it is more convenient to classify them in terms of "wisdom and severance"; bodhisattvas still anticipate Buddhahood, and so are

The wisdom and severance of a stream-enterer are, for a bodhisattva, the forbearance of the non-arising of dharmas, and so forth up to the wisdom and severance of a pratyekabuddha are, for a bodhisattva, the forbearance of the non-arising of dharmas 須陀洹若智若斷是菩薩無生法忍乃至支佛若智若斷是菩薩無生法忍: see the *Pañcaviṃśati Sūtra*, T 8.380a29–b1.

If a dangerous place presents many hazards, many protective walls are necessary 如險處多難多須城壁: as with a fortified city in hostile territory.

Many "fruits" [are necessary] to reassure 從界多難多果休息: or, "to put [the desires] to rest"? Or, a difficult journey requires many places to rest, like in the parable of the conjured city?

still in a "causal" state [leading to Buddhahood], and thus we use the term "forbearance." Again, bodhisattvas give rise to one part of mastery for each level of conceptual attitudes that are exhausted. Therefore, as each level [of delusions] passes away, another level [of mastery] arises—the bodhisattva bears 忍 the strenuous suffering [of this samsaric world] of arising and passing away and [72c] does not enter [final] nirvana; therefore this is called "forbearance."

If we were to clarify the levels of the deconstruction or destruction of the conventionality of conceptual attitudes with regard to the Distinct Teachings, first, by deconstructing [mistaken] views you properly realize the first abode [of "aspiration"]. From the second abode [of "maintenance"] to the seventh abode [of "non-retrogression"] you deconstruct the conventionality of conceptual attitudes. If you wish to minutely divide the ordered levels and classify the levels of the abodes [from the second to the seventh], this can be known and inferred from the above [explanations]. From the eighth, ninth, and tenth abode you properly overcome the habitual traces [of afflictions and delusions]. The ten levels of practice is where you properly go beyond the levels of conventionality, so it is not related to what was explained above.

If we were to clarify the levels of the deconstruction or destruction of the conventionality of conceptual attitudes with regard to the Perfect Teaching, first you deconstruct the conventionality of [mistaken] views properly at the first level of [the ten levels of] "faith." From the second level of faith to the seventh level of faith, you deconstruct the conventionality of conceptual attitudes. If you wish to minutely divide the ordered levels, you should compare the various levels of faith, and this can be known and inferred from the above [explanations]. From the eighth to the tenth level of faith you exhaustively sever the habitual traces [of afflictions and delusions]. The *Avataṃsaka Sūtra* says that at the time of the first aspiration [for enlightenment], [both the afflictions] proper and their [latent] habitual traces are exhausted in a moment, without any remainder. The habitual traces of the supramundane realm are not yet exhausted, even though the habitual traces of this realm are exhausted. The *Avataṃsaka Sūtra* also says that "the first aspiration [for

... Therefore this is called "forbearance" 忍: Chih-i here seems to be is playing with the nuances of the Chinese terms: the meanings of "patience" and "forbearance" for 忍, and the dying and coming to birth 生死 of samsara.

At the time of the first aspiration, [both the afflictions] proper and their habitual traces are exhausted in a moment, without any remainder 初發心時正習一時俱盡無有餘: the *Shiki* (BT–IV, 76) traces this quote to a passage in the *Avataṃsaka Sūtra* at T 9.456b2–6, but the context is quite different. Perhaps this is an example of Chih-i's creative interpretive quoting?

The first aspiration exceeds that of [Śākya]muni 初發心已過於牟尼: once again the *Shiki* points to a passage in the

enlightenment] exceeds that of [Śākya]muni." This is the meaning here. What does it mean to "exceed" [the attainment of Śākyamuni]? If [the afflictions] proper and their habitual traces are both exhausted, one is able [to attain] the eight phases in the life of a Buddha, which means one is equal [to a Buddha such as Śākyamuni]. If you further perfectly cultivate the threefold contemplation [of emptiness, conventionality, and the Middle], you will exceed and surpass [the attainment of the historical Śākyamuni].

[Question:] If this is so, then can there be śrāvakas whose [attainments] exceed that of a bodhisattva?

[Answer:] Yes. The śrāvakas of the Buddha path clearly exceed the bodhisattvas [of the Tripitaka and Shared Teachings]. Again, they use the same terms with regard to deconstructing conventionality at the earlier levels, but they are different in the wisdom used to realize the principle [of reality]. When those of the two vehicles of the Tripitaka and Shared Teachings deconstruct conventionality and destroy the mundane truth, they are not able to transcend conventionality and do not give rise to [supranormal] masteries. When the bodhisattvas of the Shared Teachings deconstruct conventionality and destroy the mundane truth, they in turn are able to transcend conventionality and do give rise to [supranormal] masteries, and when their transformed conditions are consumed, their bodies become ash and they realize emptiness. When those of the Distinct Teachings deconstruct conventionality, they also are able to transcend conventionality and give rise to [supranormal] masteries; they manifest the Middle Way and do not ultimately dwell in emptiness. When those of the Perfect Teaching deconstruct conventionality, they already perceive emptiness, already realize conventionality, and already realize the Middle, and perfectly overcome ignorance. If we say that those of the two vehicles and bodhisattvas are all the same in their wisdom and severance [of delusions], but different in teaching and saving others, this is to compare them from the perspective of the Shared Teachings. If we say that those of the two vehicles and the bodhisattvas are different in their wisdom but the same in their severance [of delusions], this is to compare them from the perspective of the Distinct and Perfect Teachings.

Question: To deconstruct the conventionality of conceptual attitudes

Avataṃsaka Sūtra at T 9.472c16, but again the context and the terms used in the sūtra are quite different. The line reads, "[The person for whom] all dharmas are unobstructed; the practice of this person is superior to that of [Śākya]muni."

The śrāvakas of the Buddha path 佛道聲聞: that is, the śrāvakas who follow the teachings and practices of the Distinct and Perfect Teachings.

Destroy the mundane truth 世諦死時: lit. "when the mundane truth dies."

and realize emptiness, one deconstructs nine times nine, or eighty-one levels [of conceptual attitudes]. Is it possible to go beyond even this result?

Answer: If we differentiate [the levels] sequentially, we come up with the number as [explained] previously. But one who practices does not necessarily unidimensionally follow these levels in order. [For example,] after [a follower of] the Tripitaka [Teachings] attains the last of the sixteen mental concentrations, he can go beyond this fruit in a single thought-moment and attain [the level of] a non-returner, or go beyond that and become an arhat, without advancing gradually and sequentially as explained in detail above. One exhausts the delusions of all the levels and arouses the concentrations of all the levels even if one does not sequentially go through all the levels. Again, take the example of the Tripitaka Buddha: in the twinkling of an eye all [mistaken] views and conceptual attitudes are immediately exhausted, and the virtues **[73b]** of a Buddha are made manifest in a single moment. Such a person has sharp faculties and so does not need to pass sequentially through various levels. But just because one with sharp faculties transcends the levels does not make the levels meaningless. Why? Because they are explained in this way [with various levels] in the Dharma teachings of the Buddhas.

Question: One with sharp faculties is able to transcend [the details of the levels]. But Śāriputra was the sharpest of them all. Why did he [remain a śrāvaka and] not transcend [the levels]?

Answer: The Hīnayāna is for guiding those of dull [faculties], and so they rely on these levels for attaining tranquility 蘇息 *(śānti)* and cannot transcend them. [As it says in the *Ta chih tu lun*,] Śāriputra was of great wisdom, and was a leader in turning the wheel of the Dharma and making distinctions concerning the structure of the levels, and [required] seven days or fifteen days [to attain enlightenment], and thus did not transcend

In the twinkling of an eye 一念相應: lit., "[in the time span] corresponding to a single thought-moment," or, "contained in one single thought."

Śāriputra was of great wisdom, and was a leader in turning the wheel of the Dharma and making distinctions concerning the structure of the levels, and [required] seven days or fifteen days, and thus did not transcend … 身子大智應作轉法輪將分別品秩故七日或云十五日不超: see the section in the *Ta chih tu lun* which discusses the conversion of Śāriputra and Maudgalyāyana, T 25.136c18–23. Lamotte (*Le Traité* 2, 633) translates:

… Śāriputra obtint l'état d'Arhat. Or celuiu qui trouve le Chemin au bout d'une quinzaine doit, à la suite du Buddha, faire tourner la roue de la loi *(dharmacakra)* et, dans le stade des aspirants *(śaikṣabhūmi)*, pénétrer en face *(abhimukham)* tous les Dharma et les connaître sous leurs divers aspects *(nānākāraṃ). C'est pourquoi Śāriputra obtint l'état d'Arhat au bout d'une quinzaine.* Ses qualités *(guṇa)* de tous genres étaient très nombreuses. Aussi, bien que Śāriputra soit un Arhat [et non pas un Bodhisattva], c'est à lui que le Buddha prêche la doctrine très profonde *(gambhīradharma)* de la Prajñāpāramitā.

[the sequential practice of the levels]. Ānanda worked as a servant [of the Buddha], and thus did not transcend [the practice of the levels]. It is not that they did not have sufficient power of wisdom. The bodhisattvas of the Shared Teachings are sharper in wisdom than those of the two vehicles, and are able to transcend [the levels], but when they carry the responsibility of other beings and serve as their guides, they must depend to a great extent on the distinctions [of the levels] and therefore do not teach about transcending [them]. Those of the other two Teachings of the Distinct and the Perfect are also like this. Although they can transcend or not transcend [the levels], the final goal is to universally deconstruct the conventionalities of conceptual attitudes.

"Transcending the fruit" [of the levels] consists of four [types]: 1. a transcendence that is a basic severance; 2. a minor transcendence; 3. a major transcendence; and 4. a great major transcendence. [1] Suppose that fundamentally you are at the stage of an ordinary person and attain the con-

Chodron (2, 507) has:

> ... Śāriputra attained arhathood. Now he who finds the Path at the end of a fortnight should, following the Buddha, turn the wheel of the Dharma, and in the stage of aspirant, penetrate directly all dharmas and cognize them in all their various aspects). This is why Śāriputra attained arhathood at the end of a fortnight. His qualities of all kinds were very numerous. And so, although Śāriputra was an arhat [and not a bodhisattva], it is to him that that the Buddha preached the profound doctrine of the Prajñāpāramitā.

Note that the *Ta chih tu lun* says it took Śāriputra a "half-month" to attain "the path"; there is no mention of "seven days."

Ānanda worked as a servant, and thus did not transcend [the practice of the levels] 阿難爲作侍者故不超: see the story of Ānanda in the *Mahāparinirvāṇa Sūtra*, T 12.849b23–c7:

> At that time Ājñāta-Kauṇḍinya and five hundred arhats went to Ānanda and said, "Ānanda, you should now wait on the Tathāgata and receive his [dying] requests." Ānanda said, "Virtuous Ones, I truly am not worthy to wait on the Tathāgata. Why? Because the Tathāgata is noble and to be respected, like the lion king, like a dragon, and like fire. I am defiled and weak; how would I be able to accomplish this?" The bhikṣus said to Ānanda, "If you accept our request and wait on the Tathāgata, you will gain great benefits," and thus asked him a second and a third time. Ānanda said, "Virtuous Ones, I do not seek great benefits. I truly am not worthy to wait on the Tathāgata, at his right and his left. Then Mahāmaudgalyāyana said, "Ānanda, there is something you do not know." Ānanda said, "Virtuous One, please explain this to me." Mahāmaudgalyāyana said, "Recently the Tathāgata sought a servant from among the assembly. The five hundred arhats all sought to do this for the Tathāgata, but he would not hear of it. I entered samādhi and perceived that the Tathāgata wishes for you [to serve him]. Why do you reject this and not accept it?" When Ānanda heard this he put his palms together and knelt on one knee and said, "Virtuous Ones, if this is so, then, in accordance with the wishes of the Tathāgata and your triple requests, I will follow the wishes of the assembly and serve [the Tathāgata] in all things [lit., "on the right and on the left"]."

centration of no-conceptions, and now arouse [the state of] non-defilement and consummate the sixteen mental contemplations, thus becoming a non-returner. Suppose that fundamentally you are at the stage of an ordinary person and attain the first dhyāna and the second, third, and fourth dhyāna, now consummating the sixteen mental contemplations; again you become a non-returner. Suppose that fundamentally you are at the stage of an ordinary person and sever the nine levels [of delusions] of the realm of desires by means of worldly wisdom, and, depending on whether many or few [severances], consummate the sixteen mental contemplations, and transcend the fruit in accordance with these fundamental severances. These are all called "transcendence that is a severance of fundamentals." [2] If you are at the stage of an ordinary person and have not yet achieved dhyāna, but consummate the sixteen mental contemplations, you can transcend [the earlier levels] while removing the delusions of the various levels of the realm of desires. Or, there are those who [sever] two or three levels and become "wandering sages" (once-returners) and "sons with seeds for only one life" (non-returners), and so forth. This is a "minor transcendence." [3] Suppose that fundamentally you are at the stage of an ordinary person and hear the Dharma, and receive the invitation "Well come" [from the Buddha], and become an arhat. This is a "great transcendence." [4] Suppose you completely exhaust both [the afflictions] proper and their habitual traces in a single thought-moment, like the Buddha; this is a "great major transcendence."

The people of the Perfect [Teaching] have the sharpest [faculties], and they teach what is truly real, and are not involved in the structure of levels [of attainment]. This is the greatest transcendence. The *Ying-lo ching* clarifies the "sudden [or immediate] awakening of the Tathāgata." The *Lotus Sūtra*

"Wandering sages" 家家 and "sons with seeds for only one life" 一種子: Ikeda (*Gendaigoyaku*, 376) interprets this to refer to "those on the path and having attained the fruit of the arhat."

You are at the stage of an ordinary person and hear the Dharma, and receive the invitation "Well come," and become an arhat 本在凡地聽法聞唱善來成羅漢: the *Kōgi* (BT–IV, 87) points to a number of texts, including the *Mahāparinirvāṇa Sūtra*, as the source for this phrase, but none of them are compelling.

Sudden [or immediate] awakening 頓悟 of the Tathāgata 頓悟如來: a phrase from the *Ying-lo ching*, T 24.1018c, though it uses the character 覺 instead of 悟.

In an instant attained awakening 一刹那便成正覺: phrases from the story of the enlightenment of the young daughter of the dragon king in the *Lotus Sūtra*, T 9.35b25–26, where "in the space of a *kṣaṇa* [moment] she produced bodhi-thought" *(bodhicitta)* (Hurvitz, *Lotus Sūtra*, 199). Later Mañjuśrī says that "I do not believe that this girl in the space of a moment directly and immediately achieved right, enlightened intuition," but later the girl "in the space of an instant turned into a man" and then attained enlightenment.

says, "In an instant [the daughter of the dragon king] attained awakening," so this is an example of transcendence [of sequential levels]. The vow of compassion [to save all beings in this world] is a heavy responsibility, so it does not involve transcending [the levels]. The *Vimalakīrti Sūtra* says "Although one has attained the path of the Buddha, in order to save sentient beings one practices the path of the bodhisattva." This involves both transcendence and non-transcendence. The principle of true reality is neither transcendent nor non-transcendent. All is fluid when one teaches in accordance with people's capacities, but in regard to the principle [of reality these distinctions] are always "quiescent."

Although one has attained the path of the Buddha, in order to save sentient beings one practices the path of the bodhisattva 雖成佛道度衆生而行菩薩道: see the *Vimalakīrti Sūtra*, T 14.545b26–c3, which includes the phrase, "although one contemplates all dharmas as non-arising, one does not enter the proper level [of Buddhahood]; this is the practice of a bodhisattva."

Quiescent 常寂: Ikeda (*Gendaigoyaku*, 376) interprets "quiescent" here to mean "without function; meaningless."

3. The Four Gates of the Fourfold Teachings [73b25–75b27]

Third is to consider the matter [of the deconstruction of dharmas] from the perspective of four gates.

1. Tripitaka Teachings

1. The Gate of Being [73b26]

Both the delusions of [mistaken] views and conceptual attitudes are obstacles to the two principles of the Shared and Distinct [Teachings][that is, "emptiness" and "conventionality"]. If you destroy the obstacles and manifest the principle[s], the gate [of realization] is not impenetrable. The Abhidharma clarifies that "I and various people seek what is unobtainable, like the hair of a tortoise or the horns of a rabbit." Real dharmas [as causally co-arising and

Four gates 四門: See the explanation of this pattern at the beginning of this section at 59b and 60a–62b, and the summary of the fourfold pattern with regard to "non-arising" in Chart IV. In general the term "four gates" reflects the fourfold pattern that forms the structure of Chih-i's thought and can refer to the tetralemma—specifically to the four options of being 有 (or Being, existence, naïve realism), non-being 無 (or non-existence, nothingness, emptiness, nihilism), both 亦有亦無, or neither 非有非無; these options also correspond to the four teachings of conditions co-arising, emptiness, conventionality, and the Middle, which are the basic positions of the Fourfold Teachings of Tripitaka, Shared, Distinct, and Perfect (though in the passage below, a further interpretation of the "four gates" within each of the Fourfold Teachings is presented). Ikeda (*Gendaigoyaku*, 377ff.) consistently translates this as "teaching" 教, but I have chosen the more literal "gate" because of the ambiguity and multivalence of the term; in various contexts it can be translated "teaching," "option," "interpretation," "gate," "approach," or "entrance." Chih-i uses it in many senses, including the literal image of a gate that one "passes through" or "enters" on the way to destroying delusions and attaining wisdom.

Hair of a tortoise and horns of a rabbit 龜毛兎角: see the opening section of the *Ta chih tu lun*, T 25.61a25–c6, which brings up these images for the non-substantial existence of things. Lamotte (*Le Traité* 1, 43–45) translates:

> Les adeptes du Sarvāstivāda disent: "En aucune manière, en aucun temps, en aucun texte *(dharmaparyāya)*, le Pudgala n'est établi. Il est inexistant comme le corne de lièvre *(śaṣaviṣāṇa)* ou le poil de la tortue *(kūrmaroman)*. De plus, les dix-huit éléments *(dhātu)*, les douze bases de la connaissance *(āyatana)* et les cinq agrégats *(skandha)* existent réellement, mais parmi eux ne se trouve pas de Pudgala." Par contre, dans le système bouddhique, les adeptes du Fang kouang *(Vaipulya)* disent: "Tous les Dharma sont non-nés *(anutpanna)*, non-détruits *(aniruddha)*, vides *(śūnya)*, et inexistants *(akiṃcana)*. Ils sont inexistants comme la corne du lièvre ou le poil de la tortue. Tous ces maîtres *(upadeśācārya)* vantent leur propre système, mais rejettent celui d'autrui: "Ceci dissent-ils, est vrai; le rest est faux *(idam eva saccaṃ mogham aññam)*." C'est leur système qu'ils acceptent, c'est leur système qu'ils honorent *(pūjayanti)*, c'est leur système qu'ils pratiquent *(bhāva-yanti)*. Quant au système d'autrui, ils ne l'acceptent pas, ne l'honorent pas: ils le critiquent.

empty] are all that exist. People are deluded concerning these real dharmas [or, the "true Dharma"] and perversely arouse [mistaken] views and conceptual attitudes. These [mistaken] views and conceptual attitudes are transient, and do not abide from thought to thought; they twirl [through the three phases of arising, changing, and perishing] as real dharmas, arising and perishing in turn [73c]. If you contemplate [things] in this way, you are able to deconstruct all the individual, multiple, and combined [mistaken] views, and destroy the eighty-one levels of conceptual attitudes in the triple world and realize the non-arising of causes and results and delusion and wisdom. This is the meaning of deconstructing dharmas with the teaching or "gate" of being [or naïve realism] by those of the Tripitaka [Teachings]. This [teaching] was first revealed [when the Buddha preached] at the Deer Park, where first [Ājñāta-]Kauṇḍinya and the five mendicants *(pañcavargika)* [were converted by Śākyamuni and] acquired purity; when Aśvajit taught the three truths, Śāriputra destroyed his [own mistaken] views in a period of seven days and later became an arhat [upon hearing the Dharma from the Buddha]. A

For an English translation, see note at *Mo-ho chih-kuan* 132b24–25.

Note also that the section just previous to this in the *Ta chih tu lun* was quoted above in the *Mo-ho chih-kuan* at 67b27.

Real (or true) dharmas 實法: that is, within the context of all things as empty and causally co-arising?

Kaundinya and the five mendicants 拘隣拘隣五人: according to Buddhist legend, these are the five mendicants in the company of which Śākyamuni devoted himself to strenuous ascetic practice for six years, and who deserted him when he renounced such extreme ascetic ways. After Śākyamuni's enlightenment, they were the first people to whom he preached the sermon on the Four Noble Truths at Deer Park in Vārāṇasī, the so-called "first turning of the wheel of the Dharma."

Aśvajit 頞鞞説三諦: more accurately, Aśvajit taught the truth of causality (which Chih-i extrapolates as the threefold truth). See note below.

Śāriputra destroyed his views 身子破見經七日後得阿羅漢: see the story of Śāriputra's conversion as related in the *Ta chih tu lun*, T 25.136b–137a, part of which has been referred to above (see note at 73b4–5). Also, the text says that Śāriputra gained insight in "half a month," not seven days. Lamotte (*Le Traité* 2, 630–33) translates:

> En ce temps-là, le Buddha, ayant converti les frère Kāśyapa et leurs mille disciples, circulait dans les diverses contrées et arriva à la ville de Rājagṛha où il se fixa dans la Veṇuvana. Les deux maîtres brahmacārin [Śāriputra et Maudgalyāyana], apprenant qu'un Buddha était apparu dans le monde, se rendirent ensemble à Rājagṛha pour recueillir des nouvelles. A ce moment, un bhikṣu, nommé *A chouo che* (Aśvajit), [un des cinq premiers disciples], revêtu de ses vêtements *(cīvara)* et tenant le bol aux aumônes *(pātra)*, entrait dans la ville pour y mendier sa nourriture. Śāriputra, remarquant sa bonne tenue et le recueillement de ses sens, s'approche de lui et lui demanda, "De qui es-tu le disciple? Qui est ton maître?" Aśvajit répondit: "Le prince héritier *(kumāra)* du clan des Śākya, dégoûté des souffrances de la vieillesse *(jarā)*, de la maladie *(vyādhi)* et de la

mort *(maraṇa)*, a quitté le monde *(pravrajita)*, s'est exercé dans le Chemin et a obtenu la suprême et parfaite illumination *(anuttarasaṃyaksaṃbodhi)*. C'est lui mon maître." Śāriputra lui dit: "Dis moi quelle est la doctrine qu'enseigne ton maître?" Il répondit par cette stance:

Je suis encore jeune,
Mon instructions en est à ses débuts.
Comment pourrais-je parler en véritê
Et exposer la pensée du Tathāgata?

Śāriputra lui dit: "Dis-moi l'essential en résumé *(saṃkṣiptena)*":
Alors le bhikṣu Aśvajit dit cette stance:

Les Dharma naissent des causes;
De ces Dharma il a dit la cause.
Les Dharma périssent par les causes;
Le grand maître en a parlé en véérité.

Lorsque Śāriputra eut entendu cette stance, il obtimt le premier fruit du Chemin [l'état de Srota-āpanna]....
Une quinzaine après, lorsque le Buddha eut prêché la Loi au brahmacārin *Tch'ang tchao* (Dīrghanakha), Śāriputra obtint l'état d'Arhat.

Chodron (2, 505–8) translates the full context:

At that time the Buddha, having converted the Kaśyapa brothers and their thousand disciples, was traveling about in various countries and came to the city of Rājagṛha where he stayed at the Veṇuvana. The two brahmacarin masters (Śāriputra and Maudgalyāyana), hearing that a Buddha had appeared in the world, went to Rājagṛha together to welcome the news. At this time, a bhikṣu named Aśvajit, [one of the first five disciples], wearing his robes and carrying his begging bowl, entered the city to beg for his food. Śāriputra, noting his fine manner and his meditative faculties, came to him and asked: "Whose disciple are you? Who is your teacher?" Aśvajit answered: "The crown prince of the Śākya clan, disgusted by the sufferings of old age, sickness and death, has left the world, exerted himself on the Path and has attained complete perfect enlightenment. He is my teacher." Śāriputra said: "Tell me what is your teacher's doctrine?" He replied with this stanza:

I am still young,
My instruction in it is still at its beginning
How could I speak truthfully
And explain the mind of the Tathāgata?

Śāriputra said to him: "Tell me its essence in summary."

Then the bhikṣu Aśvajit spoke this stanza:

All dharmas arise from causes;
He has taught the cause of these dharmas.
Dharmas cease due to causes;
The great teacher has taught the truth of them.

When Śāriputra heard this stanza, he attained the first fruit of the Path [the state of srotāpanna]. He went back to Maudgalyāyana who, noticing the color of his complexion and his cheerfulness, asked him: "Have you found the taste of the Immortal? Share it with me." Śāriputra communicated to him the stanza he had just heard. Maudgalyāyana said to him: "Repeat it again," and when he had heard it again he also attained the first fruit of the Path.

The two teachers, [each] accompanied by 250 disciples went together to the Buddha. Seeing these two men coming with their disciples, the Buddha said to the bhikṣus: "Do you see these two men at the head of these brahmacārins?" The bhikṣus answered that they saw them. The Buddha continued: "These two men will be foremost among my disciples by their wisdom and by the bases of miraculous powers." Arriving in the crowd, the disciples approached the Buddha, bowed their head and stood to one side. Together they asked the Buddha: "We wish to receive, in the Buddha-dharma, the leaving of the world and higher ordination." The Buddha said to them: "Come, O bhikṣu." At once their beards and hair fell off, they were clothed in

thousand and two hundred and more people came to perceive the supreme meaning [of the Dharma] through this "gate of being." The *Ta chih tu lun* says, "If you attain the [skillful] means of *prajñā*-wisdom, you realize [the true meaning of] the Abhidharma and yet do not succumb to [a naïve view of] being [that is, the deluded idea of substantial Being or 'realism']." *The Great Collection of Sūtras* says, "For the people with the [extreme] view of eternalism, teach that there is a severance between [different] thoughts." This

> monks' robes, furnished with the robe and begging bowl, and they received ordination. A fortnight later, when the Buddha had preached the Dharma to the brahmacārin (Dīrghanakha), Śāriputra attained arhathood.

A thousand and two hundred and more people came to perceive the supreme meaning [of the Dharma] through this "gate of being" 千二百等多於有門見第一義: the classical commentaries refer to the story of the "first turning of the wheel of the Dharma" in the first chapter of the 中本起經, T no. 196, 4.147c–149a.

If you attain the [skillful] means of *prajñā*-wisdom, you realize the Abhidharma and yet do not succumb to being 若得般若方便入阿毘曇不墮有中: a rewording of a phrase from the *Ta chih tu lun*, T 25.194a28–b1: "If you do not attain the dharma of *prajñā-pāramitā*, you will enter the gate of Abhidharma and will succumb to [the idea of] being." Note that the negative is in a different place in the *Mo-ho chih-kuan* quote, giving a quite different meaning to the phrase. Lamotte (*Le Traité* 2, 1095) translates the context:

> L'homme qui pénètre les trois enseignements [du Piṭaka, de l'Abhidharma et du vide] sait que les enseignements du Buddha ne se contredissent pas les uns les autres. Comprendre cela, c'est la force de la Prajñāpāramitā qui, en face de tous les enseignements du Buddha, ne rencontre aucun obstacle *(āvaraṇa)*. *Quiconque n'a point saisi la règle de la Prajñāpāramitā* [se heurtera dans l'interprétation de la Loi à des contradictions sans nombre]: *s'il aborde l'enseignement de l'Abhidharma, il tombe dans le réalisme*; s'il aborde l'enseignement du vide, il tombe dans le nihilisme; s'il aborde l'enseignement du Piṭaka, il tombe [tantôt] dans le réalisme et [tantôt] dans le nihilisme.

Chodron (2, 848) translates:

> The person who enters into the three teachings [of the Piṭaka, the Abhidharma and Emptiness] knows that the teachings of the Buddha do not contradict one another. Understanding that is the power of the Prajñāpāramitā which encounters no obstacles to any of the Buddha's teachings. Whoever has not understood the Prajñāpāramitā [will come up against innumerable contradictions in interpreting the Dharma]: *if he approaches the Abhidharma teaching, he falls into realism.* If he approaches the teaching on emptiness, he falls into nihilism; if he approaches the Piṭaka teaching, [sometimes] he falls into realism and [sometimes] into nihilism.

For the people with the [extreme] view of eternalism, teach that there is a severance between thoughts 常見之人説異念斷: see *The Great Collection of Sūtras:* see T 13.158c2, where the terms are similar but not quite the same:

> To people with the mistaken view of annihilationism say that one thought severs [delusions]. To people with the mistaken view of eternalism, say that the eight kinds of forbearance [that lead to wisdom] severs [delusions].

This passage was referred to previously; see note at *Mo-ho chih-kuan* 52a19–20.

refers to the severance of the bonds [of *kleśa*s] by the stream-enterer. Is this not [an example of] the deconstruction of conventionality by [those of] the "gate of being"? Why do the people of the *Ch'eng-shih lun* reject this and say that this is merely a means for controlling the mind and is not an attainment of the path?

2. The gate of emptiness (or non-Being) [73c9]

According to the *Ch'eng-shih lun*, "Both myself and other people are originally non-existent; [it appears that] there are 'real dharmas,' but they are vacuous and do not exist [substantially]." If you are deluded concerning this vacuous [existence], you will perversely arouse [mistaken] views and conceptual attitudes and flow in the cycle of birth-and-death. Contemplate these [mistaken] views and conceptual attitudes as all [endowed with] the three kinds of conventionality and as vacuous [emptiness], and that conventional realities have no [substantial] being; this is called the equality of emptiness. If you cultivate contemplation in this way, you will deconstruct the immeasurable individual, multiple, and combined [mistaken] views, deconstruct the eighty-one levels of conceptual attitudes, and realize the non-arising of delusions and wisdom and causes and results. This is what is referred to by the meaning of "deconstructing dharmas through the gate of emptiness in the Tripitaka [Teachings]." Therefore this *[Ch'eng-shih lun]* says, "I now wish to clarify the true meaning of the Tripitaka." Here the "true meaning" refers to "emptiness." The Āgama sūtras say, "[We speak of] this [or 'my'] old age

People of the *Ch'eng-shih lun* 成論人: The source of this claim is unknown.

Both myself and other people are originally non-existent; [it appears that] there are "real dharmas," but they are vacuous and do not exist 我人本無雖有實法浮虛非有: see the *Ch'eng-shih lun* chapter 32 on "nonself " at T 32.259a–c, especially 259a9–13:

> Question: what is truly real 實? Answer: truly there is no dharma of the self. Why? It is as in the sūtras where the Buddha says to the bhikṣus, "There are only designations, only conventional constructions, only being as function; this is given the name "self." Since these are only designations and so forth, we know that [the "self"] is not truly real.

The equality of emptiness 平等空: that is, all phenomena are "equal" in that they are empty of substantial Being.

I now wish to clarify the true meaning of the Tripitaka 我今正欲明三藏中實義: a phrase from the opening verses of the *Ch'eng-shih lun*, T 32.239b2, stating the intent of the treatise.

The Āgama sūtras say "This old age and death ... the emptiness of sentient beings 阿含經云。是老死誰老死二俱邪見。是老死即是法空。誰老死即衆生空: see the *Ta chih tu lun*, T 25.192c26–193a1, in a section on the teaching of emptiness in the Hīnayāna. Lamotte (*Le Traité* 2, 1079–80) translates:

> Le Buddha a dit dans le *Mahāśūnyatāsūtra*; Les douze causes *(dvādaśa nidāna)* vont de l'ignorance *(avidyā)* à la vieillesse-mort *(jarāmaraṇa)*. L'homme qui

and death, or another's old age and death; both of these are deviant views. This [or 'my'] old age and death is nothing but the dharma of emptiness [of the self]; the old age and death of others is the emptiness of [other] sentient beings." Again, it says [in the *Ta chih tu lun*], "The body of the Buddha Dharma is emptiness.... Subhūti was clear in his wisdom of emptiness and was able, while in a stone cavern, to perceive this body of the Buddha

> demande ce qu'est la vieillesse-mort est dans la vue fausse *(mithyādṛṣṭi)*. Et il en va de même [pour les autres causes, à savoir]: la naissance *(jāti)*, l'acte d'existence *(bhava)*, l'attachement *(upādāna)*, la soif *(tṛṣṇā)*, la sensation *(vedanā)*, le contact *(sparśa)*, les six bases internes de la connaissance *(ṣaḍāyatana)*, le nons-et-forme *(nāmarūpa)*, la connaissance *(vijñāna)*, les formations *(saṃskāra)* et l'ignorance *(avidyā)*. Si on est d'avis que le principe vital est la même chose que le corps *(sa jīvas tac charīram)* ou si on est d'avis que le principe vital est différent du corps *(anyo jīvo 'nyac charīram)*, les duex avis, quoique différents, sont pareillement vue fausse.

Chodron (2, 838) translates:

> In the *Mahāśūnyatāsūtra*, the Buddha said: "The twelve causes go from ignorance to old age and death. The person who asks what is old age and death or to whom does old age and death belong has erroneous views. And it is the same [for the other causes, namely]: birth, the act of becoming, attachment, thirst, sensation, contact, the six internal bases of consciousness, name and form, consciousness, the formations, and ignorance. If someone thinks that the vital principle is the same thing as the body, or if someone thinks that the vital principle is different from the body, the two opinions, although different, are both wrong view. The Buddha said: "That the vital principle is the same as the body, that is wrong view, unworthy of my disciples; that the vital principle is different from the body, that also is wrong view, unworthy of my disciples." In this sūtra, the Buddha proclaims the emptiness of dharmas. If someone asks "To whom does old age and death belong?," they should know that this question is wrong and that there is 'emptiness of beings'. If someone asks "What is old age and death?," they should know that this question is wrong and that there is 'emptiness of dharmas.' And it is the same for the other [members of the causal chain] up to and including ignorance.

The body of the Buddha Dharma is emptiness.... Subhūti was clear in his wisdom of emptiness and was able, while in a stone cavern, to perceive this body of the Buddha Dharma 佛法身者卽是空也。須菩提空智偏明能於石室見佛法身: a summary from T 25.137a1–21, after the section on Śāriputra quoted above. Lamotte (*Le Traité*, 2, 634–36) translates:

> En outre, Subhūti pratique excellemment la concentration de la vacuité *(śūnyatāsamādhi)*. Lorsque le Buddha, après avoir passé la retraite, d'été *(varṣa)* chez les dieux Tao li *(Trāyastriṃśa)*, redescendit dans le Jambudvīpa, *Subhūti, qui se trouvait alors dans une grotte de pierre (śailaguhā)*, se dit en lui-même: "Le Buddha descend du ciel des Trāyastriṃśa; irai-je auprès de lui ou n'irai-je pas auprès de lui?" Il se disait encore: "Le Buddha a toujours dit: Si quel-qu'un contemple par l'oeil de la sagesse *(prajñācakṣus) le Corps de la Loi (dharmakāya) du Buddha, c'est la meilleure façon de voir le Buddha.*" Puis, lorsque le Buddha descendit du ciel des Trāyastriṃśa, les quartre assemblées de Jambudvīpa étaient réunies; les dieux voyaient les hommes et les hommes voyaient les dieux; sur l'estrade, se trouvaient le Buddha, un noble roi cakravartin et la grande assemblée

des dieux: la réunion *(samāja)* était plus ornée *(alaṃkṛta)* qu'elle ne l'avait jamais été. Mais Subhūti se disait: "Bien qu'aujourd'hui cette grande assemblée soit toute spéciale *(viśiṣṭa)*, son pouvoir *(prabhāva)* ne durera pas longtemps. Les Dharma périssables *(nirodhadharma)* font tous retour à l'impermanence *(anityatā)*." Grâce à cette considération de l'impermanence *(anityatyaparīkṣā)*, qui est la première porte [du Chemin], il connut que tous les Dharma sont vides *(śūnya)* et sans réalité *(asadbhūta)*. Ayant fait cette considération, il obtint aussitôt l'intuition du Chemin *(mārgasākṣātkāra)*. En ce moment tous les êtres voulaient être les premiers à voir le Buddha et à lui rendre respects *(satkāra)* et hommages *(pūja)*.

La bhikṣuṇī *Houa sö* (Utpalavarṇā), pour dissimuler son sexe mal famé, se transforma en un noble roi cadravartin avec ses sept joyaux et ses mille fils. Lorsque les êtres le voyaient, ils quittaient leurs sièges et s'écartaient [pour lui faire place]. Quand ce roi fictif fut arrivé auprès du Buddha, il reprit sa forme première et redevint la bhikṣuṇī. Elle fut la toute première à saluer le Buddha. Cependant le Buddha dit à la bhikṣuṇī: "Ce n'est pas toi qui m'a salué la première; c'est Subhūti. Comment cela? *Subhūti, en contemplant le vide de tous les Dharma, a vu le Corps de la Loi (dharmakāya) du Buddha*; il a trouvé le véritable hommage *(pūja)*, l'hommage par excellence. Venir saluer mon Corps de naissance *(jan-makāya)*, ce n'est pas me rendre hommage."

C'est pourquoi nous disions que Subhūti, qui pratique sans cesse la concentration de la vacuité, est associé *(saṃprayukta)* à la Prajñāpāramitā, vide par caractère. Pour cette raison, le Buddha lui ordonne de prêcher la Prajñāpāramitā.

Chodron (2, 508–10) translates:

Furthermore, Subhūti excels in practicing the concentration of emptiness. Having spent the summer retreat among the Trāyastriṃśa) gods, the Buddha came down into Jambudvīpa. Subhūti, who was then in a rock cave, said to himself: "The Buddha is descending from the Trāyastriṃśa heaven; should I or should I not go to him?" Again he said to himself: "The Buddha has always said: 'If someone contemplates the dharmakāya of the Buddha with the eye of wisdom, that is the best way of seeing the Buddha.'" Then when the Buddha descended from the Trāyastriṃśa heaven, the four assemblies of Jambudvīpa had gathered; the gods saw the people and the people saw the gods; on the platform were the Buddha, a noble cakravartin king and the great assembly of the gods: the gathering was more embellished than ever before. But Subhūti said to himself: "Even though today's great assembly is quite special, its power will not last for a long time. Perishable dharmas all return to impermanence." Thanks to this consideration of impermanence, he understood that all dharmas are empty and without reality. Having made this consideration, he at once obtained the realization of the Path. At that moment, everyone wanted to be the first to see the Buddha and to pay their respect and homage to him.

In order to disguise her disreputable sex, the bhikṣuṇī Utpalavarṇa) transformed herself into a noble cakravartin king with his seven jewels and his thousand sons. When people saw him, they left their seats and moved away [to give him place]. When this fictive king came near the Buddha, he resumed his former shape and became the bhikṣuṇī again. She was the first to greet the Buddha. However, the Buddha said to the bhikṣuṇī: "It is not you who has greeted me first; it is Subhūti. How is that? By contemplating the emptiness of all dharmas, Subhūti has seen the dharmakāya of the Buddha; he has paid the true homage, the excellent homage. To come to salute my birth-body is not to pay homage to me."

This is why we said that Subhūti, who ceaselessly practices the concen-

Dharma." Therefore in the *Pañcaviṃśati Sūtra* this person [Subhūti] teaches about emptiness, and Śāriputra teaches about *prajñā*-wisdom. The Buddha wishes to compare "great" emptiness [or the emptiness of Mahāyāna] with "small" emptiness [or the emptiness of Hīnayāna], and great wisdom [or *prajñā*, the wisdom of Mahāyāna] with small wisdom [of the Hīnayāna]; therefore he has two people present the teachings. The *Ta chih tu lun* says, "If you do not attain the [skillful] means of *prajñā*-wisdom and yet realize emptiness, you will succumb to [the mistaken view of] nothingness or nihilism." *The Great Collection of Sūtras* says, "For the people with the [extreme, mistaken] view of annihilationism, teach that there is a severance of [each] individual thought." Thus you should know that the Tripitaka [Teachings] also teach the gate of emptiness. Why do the Abhidharmists capriciously say that this is [only] a Mahāyāna meaning of emptiness?

3. The gate of both Being and emptiness [73c26]

Take, for example, Kātyāyana who, on the basis of what he had realized, composed the Peṭaka [or Piṭaka] treatise and transmitted it to southern

tration on emptiness, is associated with the Prajñāpāramitā, empty by nature. For this reason, the Buddha entrusted Subhūti to preach the Prajñāpāramitā.

Subhūti and Śāriputra: see the sections of the *Ta chih tu lun* quoted above, T 25.136b–137a, and the *Pañcaviṃśati Sūtra*, T 8.230b21–c.

Two people present the teachings 令二人轉教: see the *Ta chih tu lun*, T 25.137a, quoted in the note above.

If you do not attain the [skillful] means of *prajñā*-wisdom and yet realize emptiness, you will succumb to nothingness or nihilism 若不得般若方便入空墮無中: see the *Ta chih tu lun*: T 25.194a26–c1, quoted above.

For the people with the view of annihilationism, teach that there is a severance of [each] individual thought 斷見之人説一念斷: see *The Great Collection of Sūtras* at T 13.158c2, noted above.

Kātyāyana 迦旃延: one of the chief disciples of the Buddha; known as foremost in debating skills. See Lamotte, *History of Indian Buddhism*, 325 [356–57]:

> Mahā Kātyāyana, the Buddha's great disciple, not to be confused with Mahākātyāyanīputra, the author of the *Jñānaprasthāna*, who lived in the third century after the Nirvāṇa. It seems that Mahākātyāyana had composed a *Pi lê* (Piṭaka) during the Buddha's lifetime in order to explain the Āgamas of his Master, and the work was still in use in southern India.

For details on Kātyāyana, see Lamotte, *History of Indian Buddhism*, 189–90 [207–208]; see also the notes below.

Peṭaka [or Piṭaka] treatise 毘勒論: on this text see Lamotte, *History of Indian Buddhism*, 188–89 [207]:

> In 1949, the Pali Text Society published the complete text of a *Peṭaopadesa* "Teaching on the Piṭaka(s)" in eight chapters. The text is obscure and presents insurmountable difficulties. In its present form it is not especially old since it contains numerous quotations not only from the Vinaya and Suttapiṭaka (*Dīgha, Majjhima, Saṃyutta,...*), but also from the *Nettipakaraṇa*. Nevertheless, it was

India. [This text teaches] "nothingness" as conventionality, as explained previously, so that "real dharmas" both exist and do not exist. If you arouse a fixed affinity [for this view], you will perversely arouse [mistaken] views and conceptual attitudes. Contemplate these real dharmas as an appearance of being and non-being, and thus deconstruct the single, multiple and so forth [mistaken] views and eighty-one [levels of] conceptual attitudes, and realize the non-arising of delusions and wisdom and causes and results. This is called the meaning of deconstructing dharmas with the gate of both emptiness and being in the Tripitaka [Teachings]. Therefore it says in the *Ta chih tu lun*, "If you attain the [skillful] means of *prajñā*-wisdom, you realize [**74a**] [the real meaning of] the teachings of the Peṭaka [treatise] and do not succumb to [the mistaken views of] being and non-being."

4. The gate of neither Being nor emptiness [74a1]

The gate of neither emptiness nor Being is as follows. As the *Ta chih tu lun* clarifies that when Chandaka controls his thoughts and becomes forbearing,

used, seemingly as a canonical authority, by Buddhaghosa in his *Atthasālinī* (165) and *Visuddhimagga* (ed. Warren, 114).

The work itself claims to be written by the Thera Mahācaccāyana when living at the Jambudvana, and this attribution is confirmed by the *Gandhavaṃsa* (p. 59) and the Burmese Buddhists who incorporated the *Peṭakopadesa* in their *Khuddhakanikāya*.

There is no reason why we should not see in this text a distant echo of the Abhidharmic work carried out in Ujjayinī by the Buddha's great disciple Mahākātyāyana, the missionary from Avanti.

Transmitted to southern India 傳南天竺: see also the *Ta chih tu lun*, T 25.70a20–22. Lamotte (*Le Traité* 1, 113) translates:

> Mahākātyāyana, du vivant du Buddha, expliqua les paroles du Buddha, et fit un *Pi lê* (Peṭaka) [en langue des Ts'in, Boîte-Collection]. Jusqu'à ce jour il est en usage dans l'Inde du Sud.

Chodron (1, 106) translates:

> During the lifetime of the Buddha, Mahākātyāyana explained the words of the Buddha and composed a *Pi le* (*peṭaka*), 'box-collection' in the language of the Ts'in. It is used even today in southern India.

If you attain the means of *prajñā*-wisdom, you realize the teachings of the Peṭaka and do not succumb to [the mistaken views of] being and non-being 若得般若方便入毘勒門不墮有無中: see the long section of the *Ta chih tu lun* quoted above, T 25.194a–b. The phrase in the *Ta chih tu lun* (194b1) reads: "if you realize the teaching of the Piṭaka, you will fall into [the mistaken idea of both] Being (naïve realism) and nothingness (nihilism)." Lamotte (*Le Traité* 2, 1095) translates: "s'il aborde l'enseignement du Piṭaka, il tombe [tantôt] dans la réalisme et [tantôt] dans le nihilisme."

Chandaka 車匿: Śākyamuni's servant and charioteer before he left home to seek the path. Chandaka accompanied Gautama (before he became Śākyamuni) on the night of his "great departure" as he rode his horse out of the palace at Kapilavastu; Chandaka stayed behind with the horse as Gautama cut off his hair and left for the forest. After Śākyamuni's enlightenment, Chandaka joined the Buddhist

then you should preach the *Saṃthakātyāyana Sūtra* to him. By becoming free of both [extreme views of] Being and nothingness he will be able to attain the path. By this contemplation you are able to deconstruct the individual, multiple, and so forth [mistaken] views and the eighty-one [levels of] conceptual attitudes, realize emptiness from conventionality, and realize the non-arising of delusions and wisdom and causes and results. This is what is meant by "deconstructing conventionality with the gate of neither Being nor nothingness in the Tripitaka [Teachings]." [However,] you should know that Chandaka attained the Hīnayāna path, but you should not exaggerate and say that he attained the Middle Way of Mahāyāna.

These "four gates" are all ways for the stream-enterer to attain the path, because the stream-enterer is the "first fruit" [of the "four fruits" culminating with that of the arhat]. Those who are superior [in ability or insight] are worthy of this name in a distinct way; there is a distinct or specific [attainment of the stream-enterer] for each of the [first] three gates, and a general or shared [attainment of the] stream-enterer. That of the "gate of Being" is the stream-enterer [who realizes] transience. That of the "gate of nothingness" is the stream-enterer [who realizes] the equality of emptiness. That of the gate of "both Being and non-Being" is the stream-enterer [who realizes conventional] appearance. That of the "gate of neither Being nor non-Being" is the stream-enterer [who realizes] the denial of both [extremes]. These [various types of] stream-enterers are all the first fruit of these four gates. They are distinct in the way they contemplate the four gates or teachings,

Sangha, though he was known for his arrogance and pride for being a member of the Śākya clan.

Saṃthakātyāyana Sūtra 那陀迦旃延經: a short text on Kātyāyana's meditation on ineffable reality and the Tathāgata. Chinese translations in the Taishō include text no. 926 of the *Miscellaneous Āgama* (T #99, 2.235c–236b) and text no. 151 of another translation of the *Miscellaneous Āgama* (T #100, 2.430c–431b). For details, including the Sanskrit text, see Lamotte, *Le Traité* 1, 86.

By becoming free of both Being and nothingness, he will be able to attain the path 離有離無乃可得道 …: See the phrase in the *Ta chih tu lun* at T 25. 66c11–13, which explains the phrase *evam mayā śrutam* (thus have I heard) by giving examples of how the Buddha preached the Dharma to different people in various ways; see Lamotte, *Le Traité* 1, 86:

> Voire conducteur *(chaṇḍaka),* ô Bhikṣu, après mon Nirvāṇa, sera le châtimont selon la loi de Brahmā *(brahmadaṇḍa).*— Si quelqu'un a l'esprit frappé *(abhihatacitta),* il faudra lui enseigner le *Chan t'o kia tchan yen king* (Saṃthakātyāyanasūtra); alors il pourra obtenir le Chemin.

Lamotte gives a long note explaining the content and significance of this sūtra. Chodron (1, 86–87) translates:

> After my Nirvana, your guide, O bhikṣu, will be the punishment according to the rule of Brahmā. - If someone is in a state of mind of panic, he should be taught the *Saṃthakātyāyanasūtra*; then *he will be able to obtain the Path.*

but are the same in their perception of the real truth. It is like a city that has four gates; they are not different in the sense that they all offer a passageway to [meet and] assemble [in the city]. Therefore *The Great Collection of Sūtras* says, "For the people with the [extreme] view of eternalism, teach that there is a severance between thoughts. For the people with the [extreme] view of annihilationism, teach that there is a severance of [each] individual thought. These two [types of] people are different [in their assumptions], but there is no distinction with regard to their attainment of the path." The *Mahāparinirvāṇa Sūtra* says, "The five hundred bhikṣus each gave an individual explanation for the causes of the body; it is not the case that these explanations are incorrect [just because each is different]." Guṇavarman

For the people with the view of eternalism,... no distinction with regard to their attainment of the path 常見之人說異念斷。斷見之人説一念斷。二人雖殊論其得道更無差別: see *The Great Collection of Sūtras* at T 13.158c2. The first phrases have already been quoted above at 73c8 and 73c22. The context (T 13.158c1–4) reads:

> Ājñāta-Kauṇḍinya, what is the "eighth person" 八人? What does it mean to be fixed 決定 [in your attainment]? Ājñāta-Kauṇḍinya, to the people with the [extreme] view of annihilationism, teach that [each] individual thought is severed; to the people with the [extreme] view of eternalism, teach the severance [which is the realization] of the eight recognitions. These two types of people both attain a fixed [attainment], are later freed from passionate afflictions, and are both unhindered. Ājñāta-Kauṇḍinya, one who is able to attain the eight recognitions is called the "eighth person"; one who attains the sixteen mental [contemplations] is called "fixed." This is called "in accordance with the Dharma" 如法. Ājñāta-Kauṇḍinya, if there is a bhikṣu who perfects the inhalation and exhalation of breath, this one has attained that [stage] of the "eighth person."

The five hundred bhikṣus each gave an individual explanation for the causes of the body; it is not the case that these explanations are incorrect 五百比丘各説身因無非正説: see the *Mahāparinirvāṇa Sūtra* at T 12.820b12–18:

> What is that called "teaching in accordance with the thoughts of others? It is like when five hundred bhikṣus asked Śāriputra, "O Śāriputra, Virtuous One [Bhagavat], what is the meaning of the "causes of the body"? [Śāriputra gives his answer.] At that time five hundred bhikṣus each gave an explanation of their individual understanding. Together [yet one by one] they came up to the Buddha, bowed their heads at the Buddha's feet, circumambulated to the right three times, and when they were done paying their respects they sat facing him. Each in this way gave his own explanation, facing the Buddha to give the explanation. Then Śāriputra said to the Buddha, "World Honored One. Of these, which is the correct explanation, and which explanation is incorrect?" The Buddha said to Śāriputra, "Well done, well done. *It is not the case that the explanation is incorrect for any of these bhikṣus.*"

This passage is from an extended section of the *Mahāparinirvāṇa Sūtra* (T 12.820b2–821c3) that explains the idea of the Buddha preaching appropriately, "in accordance with the thoughts of others" 隨他意 and "in accordance with his [the Buddha's] own thoughts" 隨自意. Chih-i has discussed these terms previously; see *Mo-ho chih-kuan* 55b20–27.

said, "Various treatises each provide different teachings, but the principle that is practiced is not different. There is [debate as to] right and wrong when people cling to sides, but for those who have realized [awakening] there is no disagreement or disputation." At the time of the Sung (420–479?) the *Ch'eng-shih lun* was popular among scholars, and disputes arose concerning various interpretations. Therefore this verse was presented [by Guṇavarman] as a reproach. The real truth is quiescent and solitary; it is neither one nor four. Śāriputra said, "I have heard that there is no verbalization in liberation." Why, then, should the four gates be [verbally] recorded? If you become attached to [the extreme view] of arising [= being, naïve realism], you will never be able to attain the path; why say that this is so only for the gate of being? If you remove [mistaken] views and conceptual attitudes, you will attain [the path]; why say that this is so only for the gate of emptiness? It is not the case that the words of only one treatise [that is, the *Ch'eng-shih lun*] constitute the meaning for attaining [the path], and that of the scholastics [of the Abhidharma] constitute destruction [through analyzing dharmas]. If you realize the intent of the four *siddhāntas*, then [you will realize that the teaching of] both the *Ch'eng-shih lun* and the Abhidharma are valid. If you cannot realize this intent, then both the *Ch'eng-shih lun* and the Abhidharma will be [limited to the] destruction [of analyzing dharmas]. It is the same also for [the other aspects of the four gates] up through [the teaching of] "neither being nor non-being." If you use the gate of being to clarify the features of phenomena [or, the Dharma], this is "crude." If you use the gate of emptiness to clarify dharmas [or, the Dharma], this is "fine." If you judge that one is skillful and the other is crude for attaining or destroying [the path], then [you must conclude that the first] three gates are all inferior [to the fourth]. But one gate alone is not [in all ways superior to the rest].Why is it popular to argue about the four gates [or teachings] in this manner? This is based on the idea that those of the two vehicles save only themselves, and that there is only one path that must be followed strictly, depending only on this and not allowing any compromise. People who came along later and studied this [way of thinking] gave rise to error for this reason.

Guṇavarman [求那]跋摩: a royal prince of Kashmir [?] who was born in 367 and traveled to Ceylon, Java, and Canton, arriving in Nanking in 431. He translated a number of texts on the precepts into Chinese.

Various treatises each provide … no disagreement or disputation 諸論各異端修行理無二。偏執有是非達者無違諍: phrases from the biography of Guṇavarman in the *Biographies of Eminent Monks*, T 50.342a21–22.

Śāriputra said "I have heard that there is no verbalization in liberation." 吾聞解脱之中無有言說: see the *Vimalakīrti Sūtra*, T 14. 548a10–11. This phrase has already been quoted by Chih-i; see the note and explanation at *Mo-ho chih-kuan* 3a14–15.

The bodhisattvas of the Tripitaka [Teachings] are not like this. They overcome delusions through an analytical [realization of] emptiness, and thus learn the four gates one-sidedly, but have extensive knowledge of the features of dharmas in order to save others, and when they become Buddhas they are called "those with true universal knowledge." Therefore the *Ta chih tu lun* quotes Kātyāyanīputra's [**74b**] clarification of the meaning of a bodhisattva, saying that "the bodhisattva Śākyamuni first met [the possibility of becoming] the Buddha Śākyamuni and aroused his first aspiration for enlightenment; [from then] until the time of the Buddha Khāṇuśikhin was the first immeasurable kalpa, when in his mind [Śākyamuni] did not yet know that he would become a Buddha, nor did he say anything about it. Next, up to the time of the Buddha Dīpaṃkara was the second [immeasurable kalpa]. The Buddha Vipaśyin was in the third [immeasurable kalpa].

One-sidedly 偏: Ikeda (*Gendaigoyaku*, 380) substitutes 遍 for 偏, thus reading "learn the four gates universally or extensively."

True universal knowledge 正徧知: here this refers to 正遍知, *samyaksaṃbuddha*, one of the titles of a Buddha or Tathāgata.

Kātyāyanīputra 迦旃延子: an Abhidharma master of the third century after the death of the Buddha and the author of the Sarvāstivādin *Jñānaprasthāna* (translated into Chinese as T #1543 and T #1544). Not to be confused with Kātyāyana, the great disciple of the Buddha, mentioned briefly above.

Here Chih-i is referring to the section of the *Ta chih tu lun* at T 25.86c–87a on "The Bodhisattva in the Abhidharma System"; see notes below.

The first immeasurable kalpa 初阿僧祇: a more useful summary is found in the *Outline of the Fourfold Teachings (T'ien-t'ai ssu-chiao-i)*, T 46.776a. Chappell (*T'ien-t'ai Buddhism*, 104) translates:

> Since [the bodhisattva] has developed the mind [dedicated to enlightenment], he must cultivate the practices in order to fulfill the vows. For three *asaṃkhya kalpas* [the bodhisattva] cultivates the practice of the Six Perfections. For a hundred *kalpas* he plants [conditions for the 32 Primary] Marks and the [80 secondary] Signs [of Buddhahood]. Speaking of the three *asaṃkhya* (innumerable) *kalpas*, I shall discuss the divisions in terms of the time when Śākyamuni was cultivating the bodhisattva path.
>
> [1] [The period during which Śākyamuni] met 75,000 Buddhas, starting with the Ancient Śākya and on up to Śikhin Buddha, is called the First *asaṃkhya kalpa*. From then on, he always avoided the female form, and avoided the Four Evil Rebirths while constantly cultivating the Six Perfections. However, he himself did not know that he would become a Buddha.

The second immeasurable kalpa: the summary in Chappell (*T'ien-t'ai Buddhism*, 104–5) continues:

> [2] Next, [the period during which Śākyamuni] met 76,000 Buddhas, starting with Śikhin Buddha and on up to Dīpaṃkara 然(燃)燈 Buddha, is called the Second *asaṃkhya kalpa*. At this time, using the seven stalks of the lotus flower as offerings, he spread his hair, covered it with mud, and then received the predictions [that he would become a Buddha], and was given the name of Śākyamuni. From that time on he knew that he would become a Buddha, and yet he could not say so aloud.

[Śākyamuni] practiced the six perfections and consummated them during each of these time periods. He consummated the perfection of giving, like Śivi giving [his body as an offering] in substitution for a pigeon, and so forth up to consummating the perfection of wisdom like the minister Govinda,

The third immeasurable kalpa: the summary in Chappell (*T'ien-t'ai Buddhism*, 105) continues:

> [3] Next, [the period during which Śākyamuni] met 77,000 Buddhas, starting with Dīpaṃkara Buddha and on up to Vipaśyin 毘婆尸 Buddha, is called the completion of the Third *asaṃkhya kalpa*. At this time, he himself knew and he let others know that he must become a Buddha. Neither he himself nor others had any doubt.

Practiced the six perfections and consummated them ... like the minister Govinda 行六度滿各有時節。如尸毘代鴿是檀滿乃至劬嬪大臣分閻浮提是般若滿: Śivi and Govinda are the first and the sixth of the examples given in the *Ta chih tu lun* (T 25.87c–89b) to illustrate the practice of the six perfections. Chappell (*T'ien-t'ai Buddhism*, 106) translates the summary given in the *Outline of the Fourfold Teachings*:

> In cultivating the Six Perfections, each has a given moment for fulfillment. For example:
>
> [1] To fulfill the Perfection of Giving, the King Śivi [offered his body to a hungry eagle] to save a pigeon.
>
> [2] To fulfill the Perfection of Discipline, King Śrutasoma [was willing to] sacrifice [his life and] his country.
>
> [3] To fulfill the Perfection of Forbearance, Kṣāntivādi-ṛṣi endured mutilation by King Kali without giving in to hatred.
>
> [4] To fulfill the Perfection of Exertion, Prince Mahādāna scooped up the sea water [to recover his wish-granting gem]. In another story, [Śākyamuni Bodhisattva was so engrossed] in worshipping Puṣya Buddha he kept his foot raised for seven days.
>
> [5] To fulfill the Perfection of Meditation, Jāliya-ṛṣi [continued in meditation in order not to disturb] the nest of a magpie on his head.
>
> [6] To fulfill the Perfection of Wisdom, Prime Minister Gobinda [Govinda] divided the country of Jambudvīpa into seven parts, [one each for the seven kings,] which put an end to their fighting.

These examples are also used to illustrate the six perfections in the *Hokke-shū gishū* (Collected Teachings of the Tendai Lotus School; see the BDK English Tripitaka 97–II, 26–27):

> Q: In cultivating the Six Perfections, is there a specific time when this practice is perfected?
>
> A: There is a time of perfection when one has no obstacles in giving alms. For example, charity was perfected when King Sivi gave his body [to be eaten by a hawk] on behalf of a dove. The keeping of the precepts was perfected when King Sutasoma, though losing his throne, still wrote a verse praising the moral life and did not indulge in slander. Patience was perfected when the hermit Kṣānti bore no resentment as his limbs were severed by King Kali, and his body was restored. Diligence was perfected when Prince Mahātyāgavat entered the sea to search for a [wish-fulfilling] jewel for the sake of all the people. He finally obtained the jewel [from the hair of the Dragon King] to help the poor. However, the sea god hid the treasure while he was sleeping. When the Prince awoke he vowed to scoop out the entire ocean with his own body. Indra was moved by this sight and all the heavenly deities helped him until it was half done. Also, for seven days Śākyamuni stood on one foot and praised

who [wisely] divided up Jambudvīpa [to avert conflict]. Over the course of a hundred kalpas he planted the seeds of the thirty-two marks [of a Buddha]."

> the Buddha Puṣya. Concentration was perfected when a bird built a nest in the hair of the hermit Śaṅkhācārya while he was in a concentrative state. He did not emerge from his concentrative state until the chicks could fly away. Wisdom was perfected when the Prime Minister Govinda divided the land of Jambudvīpa into seven parts, which put an end to the bitter fighting between [the seven] countries.

On the three immeasurable kalpas and the Buddhas of these times, see the *Ta chih tu lun* 87a12–19; Lamotte (*Le Traité* 1, 248–49) translates:

> Pour le Buddha Śākyamuni, le premier Asaṃkhyeya va de l'ancien Budddha Śākyamuni au Buddha *La na che k'i* (Ratnaśikhin). Dès ce moment, le Bodhisattva était exempt de toute existence féminine.—Le deuxième Asaṃkhyeya va du Buddha Ratnaśikhin au Buddha Dīpaṃkara. C'est alors que le Bodhisattva offrit au Buddha Dīpaṃkara sept lotus bleus *(nīlotpala),* étala son vêtement en peau d'antilope *(ajinavāsa)* et disposa sa chevelure *(keśa)* pour en couvrir la boue *(kardama).* A cette occasion, le Buddha Dīpaṃkara lui fit la prédiction *(vyākaraṇa)* suivante: "Plus tard, tu sera Buddha sous le nom de Śākyamuni."—Le troisième Asaṃkhyeya va du Buddha Dīpaṃkara au Buddha Vipaśyin.—Après ces trois Asaṃkhyeyakalpa, le Bodhisattva accomplit les actes producteurs des trente-deux marques.

On Śivi giving his body as a substitute for a pigeon, see T 25.87c27–88a5; Lamotte (*Le Traité* 1, 245–46) translates:

> Question.—Comment le Bodhisattva remplit-il *(paripiparti)* le vertu du don?
> Réponse.—Il donne tout sans restriction et, quand il a donné jusqu'à son corps, son cœur n'éprouve aucun regret: par exemple le roi Śibi qui donna sons corps au pigeon *(kapota).*
> Le Buddha Śākyamuni, dans une ses existences antérieures *(jātaka),* était un roi nommé Śibi; ce roi possédait hommage *(namas),* refuge *(śaraṇa)* et dhāraṇī; il était très énergique *(vīryavat)* et rempli de bienveillance *(maitrī)* et de compassion *(karuṇā)*: il considérait tous les êtres avec l'amour d'une mère pour son fils.

On the minister Govinda see the *Ta chih tu lun*, T 25.89b22–24; Lamotte (*Le Traité* 1, 266) translates:

> Lorsque son grand esprit réfléchit *(manasikaroti)* et analyse *(vibhanakti).* Ainsi le brâhmane Govinda, grand ministre *(mahāmātya),* divisa la grande terre *(mahāpṛthivī)* du Jambudvīpa et en fit sept parts; il divisa également en sept parts un nombre déterminé de grandes et de petites villes *(nagara),* de villages *(nigama)* et de hameaux *(antarāpaṇa).* Telle était sa vertu de sagesse.

... planted the seeds of the thirty-two marks 種三十二相: A very brief summary of a long passage from the *Ta chih tu lun* (T 25.86b–89b) discussing the definition of a "bodhisattva." Lamotte (*Le Traité* 1, 245–46) translates the opening section (T 25.86c4–16):

> Dans l'Abhidharma, les disciples de Kātyāyanīputra, disent: Qu'appelle-t-on Bodhisattva? Est nommé Bodhisattva celui qui s'est illuminé lui-même et a ensuite illuminé les autres; est nommé Bodhisattva celui qui doit nécessairement devenir Buddha. La Bodhi est la sagesse *(prajñā)* du saint qui a détruit les impuretés *(kṣīṇāsrava).* L'homme né de cette sagesse, protégé par les sages et servi par les sages est nommé Bodhisattva.
>
> Ils disent encore qu'il est nommé Bodhisattva dès qu'il a émis la pensée sans régression *(avaivartikacitta).*
>
> Ils dissent encore qu'il faut avoir éli-

[In this context,] when we discuss the causes [for Buddhahood], we refer to Śākyamuni; when we discuss the fruit [of Buddhahood] we point to Maitreya; this involves universally practicing the four gates [or teachings] and the methods of the path to overcome and weaken the passionate afflictions. [In the *Ta chih tu lun*] Nāgārjuna criticized this [approach] saying that "'weakening' means 'severing.' As a once-returner conquers six levels of con-

> miné cinq Dharma et gagné cinq Dharma pour être nommé Bodhisattva. Quels sont ces cinq Dharma? 1. Il est affranchi des trois mauvaises destinées *(durgati)* et renaît toujours parmi les dieux *(deva)* et les hommes *(manuṣya)*; 2. Il échappe à la pauvreté *(dāridrya)*, à la roture *(nīcakula)*, et appartient toujours à une famille noble *(uccakula)*; 3. Il n'est jamais du sexe féminin *(strībhava)*, mais toujours de sexe masculin *(puṃbhāva)*; 4. Il est exempt de défauts physiques et d'infirmités *(vaikalya)*; ses organes sont au complet *(avikalendriya)*; 5. Il n'a pas d'oublis *(saṃpramoṣa)*, mais se souvient de ses existences passées *(jātismara)*.—Possédant la sagesse de ses existences passées *(pūrvanivāsa)*, écartant toujours tous les mauvais Dharma *(akuśaladharma)*, se tenant éloigné des mauvaises gens, recherchant toujours la loi du Chemin *(mārgadharma)*, s'attachant des disciples, il est nommé Bodhisattva....

Chodron (1, 208–9) translates:

> In the Abhidharma, the disciples of Kātyāyanīputra say: Who is called bodhisattva? He who has awakened himself and then awakens others is called bodhisattva; he who necessarily will become Buddha is called bodhisattva. Bodhi is the wisdom of the saint who has destroyed the impurities. The person born from this wisdom, protected by the sages and served by the sages, is called bodhisattva.
>
> They also say that he is called bodhisattva as soon as he has produced the non-regressing mind.
>
> They also say that he must have eliminated five dharmas and gained five dharmas in order to be called bodhisattva. What are these five dharmas? 1. He is freed from the three unfortunate destinies and is always reborn among gods and men. 2. He escapes from poverty, from commoners, and always belongs to a noble family. 3. He is never a female but always a male. 4. He is free of physical defects and weaknesses; his organs are complete. 5. He never has lapses of memory but remembers his past existences. — Possessing the wisdom of his past lives, staying away from evil people, always searching for the path of Dharma, drawing disciples to himself, he is called bodhisattva....

***Ta chih tu lun* on "weakening"** 薄, see T 25. 262a11–17; Lamotte (*Le Traité* 4, 1782–83) translates:

> De plus, il y a atténuation [du triple poison] chez l'homme détaché du désir *(vītarāga)* qui a détruit les entraves relatives à la terre inférieure *(avarabhāgīya saṃyojana)*, mais conserve encore les entraves relatives aux terres supérieures *(ūrdhvabhāgīya saṃyojana)*. Il y a aussi atténuation [du triple poison] chez le Srota-āpanna qui a supprimé les entraves à détruire par la vision des vérités *(satyadarśanaheya saṃyojana)* mais n'a pas supprimé les entraves à détruire par la méditation *(bhāvanāheya saṃyojana)*. Enfin, comme le Buddha l'a dit: "Par la destruction de trois entraves *(trayāṇāṃ saṃyojanānāṃ prahāṇāt)* et par l'atténuation de l'amour, de la haine et de l'aberration *(rāgadveṣamohānāṃ ca tanutvā)* on est Sakṛdāgāmin." Mais [pour accumuler les attributs de Buddha, il ne suffit pas] d'atténuer comme vous le dites [le triple poison], il faut le détruire.

Chodron (4, 1464–65) translates:

ceptual attitudes, this is called the stage of weakening [delusions]. But they have not yet severed [the delusions]; how can this be the attainment of [the stage of] weakening [delusions]?" Therefore you should know that is a discussion of "weakening" [delusions] only in terms of overcoming [them, and not "severing" them]. [The attainment of] the thirty-four enlightened mental states is called "severing." Even if we are able to explain [severing] in this way, this is still an explanation that is a [skillful] means of an early teaching [that is, of the Tripitaka Teachings]. The *Mahāparinirvāṇa Sūtra* calls this a "partial" [teaching]. The *Lotus Sūtra* uses the illustration that for twenty years [the ignorant son] "constantly removed dung." The *Ta chih tu lun* calls it "clumsy medicine." The *Vimalakīrti Sūtra* speaks of "the poor way to attain

> By weakening the three poisons, he could only obtain an existence as a noble chakravartin king or king of the gods, but that would be insuffucient to acquire the mass of Buddha qualities. It is necessary to destroy the three poisons but not to have eliminated the traces, in order to be able to accumulate the qualities.
> Moreover, there is a weakening [of the three poisons] in the person detached from desire who has destroyed the fetters related to the lower level but who still keeps the fetters relative to the higher levels. There is also weakening [of the three poisons] in the srota-āpanna who has suppressed the fetters to be destroyed by the seeing of the truths, but has not suppressed the fetters to be destroyed by meditation. Finally, as the Buddha said: "One is sakṛdāgāmin by means of the destruction of three fetters, desire, hatred and delusion." But [in order to accumulate the Buddha attributes, it is not enough] to weaken [the three poisons] as you have said; they must be destroyed.

Partial teaching 半字: see the *Mahāparinirvāṇa Sūtra*, T 12. 631a11. Chih-i has used this illustration before; see the note at *Mo-ho chih-kuan* 32c23.

Constantly removed dung 常令除糞: a reference to the work accepted by the ignorant son, in the parable in the *Lotus Sūtra*; he was not aware of the fact that he was working for his true father, so he was given this lowly job until he was ready for a higher station. See the *Lotus Sūtra*, T 9.17a12–13. Hurvitz (*Lotus Sūtra*, 87) translates the context:

> At that time the great man, wishing to entice his son, devised an expedient: he secretly dispatched two men, whose appearance was miserable and who had no dignity of bearing, saying to them, "You may go to that place and say gently to that poor fellow, 'There is a work place here, to which we will accompany you.'" If the poor fellow agrees, bring him along and put him to work. If he asks what you wish him to do, then you may say to him, "You are being hired to sweep away dung. We two shall also work with you." At that time the two messengers sought out the poor son directly. When they had found him, they told him the above in detail. The poor son first took his pay, then *swept the dung* with them.

Clumsy medicine 拙醫: See the *Ta chih tu lun*, T 25.107a17–28 on skillful means *(yāthātmyāvatāraṇakuśala)*. Lamotte (*Le Traité* 1, 397–98) translates:

> *Sūtra*: Ils excellaient à sauver convenablement *(yāthātmyāvatāraṇakuśalaiḥ)*.
> *Śāstra*: Les systèmes des hérétiques *(tīrthikadharma)*, tout en sauvant les êtres, ne les sauvent pas convenablement, car il y reste toutes espèces de vues fausses *(mithyādṛṣṭi)* et d'entraves *(saṃyojana)*.— Les duex Véhicules [celui des

bliss [for sentient beings]." Vasubandhu calls it "the inferior vehicle." These all refer to these four gates [of the Tripitaka Teachings], and this [interpretation] is not what I intend to use here [in the *Mo-ho chih-kuan*].

Śrāvaka et des Pratyekabuddha], tout en possédant des moyens de salut, ne sauvent pas comme il faudrait *(yathāyogam),* car leurs adeptes n'étant pas omniscients *(sarvajña)* ne disposent que d'artifices salvifiques *(upāyacitta)* assez rudimentaires. Il n'y a que les Bodhisattva qui puissent sauver convenablement.

[Il y a une bonne et une mauvaise façon de sauver les êtres, comme il y a une bonne et une mauvaise façon de faire traverser un fleuve ou de guérir une maladie]. Ainsi, pour passer quelqu'un à l'autre bord, le maître passeur *(taraṇāvārya)* peut employer un radeau de paille de pêcheur *(kaivartatṛṇakola)* ou un grand vaisseau *(nau-)*; entre ces deux modes de passage, il y a des différences notables. De même [les Śrāvaka et les Pratyekabuddha mènent les êtres l'autre rive du salut, en utilisant le radeau de paille du Petit Véhiclue, tandis que les Bodhisattva les transportent sur le vaisseau du Grand Véhicle]. Ou encore, pour guérir les maladies *(vyādhi)*, il y a divers remédes tels que herbes médicinales *(oṣadhi)* ou cautérisations à l'aiguille; mais il y a encore une herbe plus marveilleuse nommée *Sou t'o chan t'o* (Śuddhaśāntā?) qu'il suffit que le malade regarde pour que tous ses maux soient guéris. Bien que les remèdes soient semblables, leur qualité diffère. Il en va de même pour les Śrāvaka et les Bodhisattva dans leurs méthodes pour convertir les êtres: ascèse *(tapas), dhūtāṅga*, pratique des trois nuits *(prathama-madhyama-pañcima-yāma)*, énergie *(vīrya-citta)* et extase *(dhyāna)*. Selon la doctrine des Śrāvaka, on trouve le Chemin en considérant la douleur *(duḥkha);* selon la doctrine des Bodhisattva, la pensée trouve la puretê *(viśuddhi)* en considérant les Dharma comme exempts de lien *(bandhana)* et exempts de délivrance *(mokṣa)*.

Chodron (1, 322–23) translates:

Sūtra: They excelled in saving appropriately.

Śāstra: The systems of the heretics, while saving beings, do not save them appropriately, because all kinds of wrong views and fetters remain.

The two vehicles, [that of the śrāvakas and that of the pratyekabuddhas], while possessing the means of salvation, do not save as they should, for their adepts, not being omniscient, use only rather rudimentary skillful means. It is only bodhisattvas who can save appropriately.

[There is a good and a bad way of saving beings, just as there is a good way and a bad way to cross a river or to cure a sickness.] Thus, to take someone across to the other shore, the master ferryman is able to use a fisherman's straw raft or a big boat; there are notable differences between these two ways of crossing. In the same way, [the śrāvakas and pratyekabuddhas lead beings to the other shore of salvation by using the straw raft of the Lesser Vehicle, whereas the bodhisattvas take them across in the ship of the Greater Vehicle]. Or again, there are different remedies for curing sicknesses, such as medicinal herbs or cauterization with a needle; but there is a still more wonderful herb called Śuddhaśāntā which it suffices that the sick person looks at it and all his ills are cured. Although these remedies seem similar, their quality differs. It is the same for the śrāvakas and pratyekabuddhas in their methods of converting beings: asceticism, dhūtaṅga, practice of the three nights, exertion and ecstasy. According to the śrāvaka doctrine, one finds the Path by considering suffering; according to the bodhisattva doctrine, the mind finds purity by considering the dharmas as free of bonds and free of deliverance....

2. *Shared Teachings* [74b14]

Next is the differences in the four gates of the Shared Teachings.

1. The gate of Being [74b14]

If you clarify that all conventional realities arise from ignorance, and that this ignorance is like an illusion, then all that arises is also like an illusion. To be "like an illusion" is to be like vacuous space; nevertheless this illusion needs to be contemplated and deconstructed as conventional. Although it is "like vacuous space," it nevertheless arises as vacuous space. Therefore it says [in the *Ta chih tu lun*], "Dharmas do not arise, and yet *prajña*-wisdom arises." In this way contemplative wisdom is able to deconstruct all [mistaken] views and conceptual attitudes, and you realize that delusions and wisdom and causes and results do not arise. This is what is called "the intent of contemplating the gate of being [in the Shared Teachings]."

2. The gate of emptiness (or non-Being) [74b18]

If we say that the essence of all dharmas of conventional realities are like an illusion or transformation, and so forth up to nirvana also being like an illusion or transformation, this is an easy way to understand these transformations as emptiness, but a difficult way to understand nirvana as emptiness. The easy is taken up to understand the difficult; both the easy and the difficult are empty. Again, this is like a illusory person fighting with emptiness; both that which contemplates and that which is contemplated are quiescent in nature. In this way, through the wisdom of emptiness you realize the

Poor way to attain bliss 貧所樂法: A phrase from the *Vimalakīrti Sūtra*, T 14.553a17–18. It seems that the phrase in the *Vimalakīrti Sūtra* can be taken quite differently, that is, it is the "poor" who are being helped, not the way itself that is "poor." Boin (*Vimalakīrti Sūtra*, 215) translates, "… he ripens base and wretched beings *(hīnadaridrasattvān paripācayati)* and resorts to all kinds of means to subdue and captivate them."

The inferior vehicle 下劣乘: The source of this attribution to Vasubandhu is unknown.

All conventional realities 假實: or, "the conventional appearance of reality."

Like an illusion 如幻: this phrase is found in the *Pañcaviṃśati Sūtra*, T 8.276b7. The context reads:

> I teach that the Buddha path is like an illusion and like a dream. *I teach that nirvana is also like an illusion and like a dream.* If nirvana is the most superior of all dharmas, I teach again that it is like an illusion and like a dream.

Dharmas do not arise … 貧所樂法生而般若生: see the *Ta chih tu lun*, T 25.496c28–29. This phrase has been quoted above in the *Mo-ho chih-kuan* at 60a20 and 61a6–7.

An illusory person fighting with emptiness 如幻人與空共鬪: A phrase from the *Pañcaviṃśati Sūtra*, T 8.360c5. Or, as translated above (56a24), this involves "locking horns with emptiness."

essence of [mistaken] views and conceptual attitudes as illusory and truly [empty], and you are able to realize the non-arising of delusions and wisdom and causes and results. This is what is called "the intent of deconstructing conventionality with the gate of emptiness."

3. The gate of both Being and emptiness [74b25]

If you clarify that all dharmas are like an image in a mirror which can be seen yet not seen, this "seeing" is its "being" and the "not seeing" is its "nothingness" [or emptiness]. It is non-existent [in lacking substantial Being] yet existent [conventionally]; it exists [conventionally] yet has no Being. If you contemplate in this way, you are able to deconstruct all the dharmas of [mistaken] views and conceptual attitudes, and realize the non-arising of delusions and wisdom and causes and results. This is what is called "the intent of the contemplation of deconstructing conventionality with the gate of both emptiness and being."

4. The gate of neither Being nor emptiness [74b28]

We have already said that these [phenomena] are [like] an illusion and transformation; how can they be described as "existing" or "nothingness"? Since they do not exist, it is not proper to say they have being 有有; since they are not nothingness, it is not proper to say that the nothingness does not exist 無無. In this way contemplative wisdom is able to deconstruct all dharmas of [mistaken] views and conceptual attitudes, and you can realize the non-arising of delusions and wisdom and causes and results. This is what is called "the intent of the contemplation of deconstructing conventionality with the gate of neither being nor nothingness."

If those of the Tripitaka [Teachings] arouse [mistaken] views by regarding [phenomena] as real, stream-enterers can avoid both of the two extremes [of eternalism and annihilationism] through analytical contemplation, by deconstructing the reality of[, for example,] a pillar just as it is. Those of the Shared Teachings arouse [mistaken] views by regarding forms as illusory, and by contemplating their essential emptiness they can avoid both of the two extremes, like viewing a pillar as [an image] in a mirror. Since this involves deconstruction in terms of essential [emptiness], this is called "neither being nor non-being." Although this is not the Middle Way, the method of [realizing emptiness in] essence is an "adapted vacuousness" which purifies attachment to [mistaken] views. Therefore the *Ta chih tu lun* says [in a

Nothingness does not exist 無無: or, "there is no nothingness."

Like a pillar in a mirror 如鏡中柱: These examples of "images" have appeared previously; see above at *Mo-ho chih-kuan* 63a18–26.

verse], "*Prajñā-pāramitā* is like a great fire, whose flames in all four directions make it unapproachable." This verse includes the meaning of the four gates; if you consider it carefully and minutely, this should become clear. The *Ta chih tu lun* also says, "*Prajñā*-wisdom has four types." Again it says, "The four gates are the entrance to the pure and cool pond [of wisdom]." These are all veritable witnesses to the four gates. If you do not become attached [to any single gate], they are all potential ways for you to pass through and realize [the path]. If you become attached to them, you will get burned by them. The Buddha taught the contemplation of these four gates in order to show people the way to avoid disputes.

Question: Where does the Buddha show people the way to dispute?

Answer: The Buddha does not show people the way to dispute. Disputes arise because sentient beings do not understand [correctly] and they become attached [to their one-sided views]. The Tripitaka Teachings are a shallow and proximate [interpretation] of the four gates, and it appears that they conflict [with each other]; therefore it is easy to become attached [to one side] and dispute [concerning which side is correct]. The *Ch'eng-shih lun* scholars

***Prajñā-pāramitā* is like a great fire, whose flames in all four directions make it unapproachable** 般若波羅蜜譬如大火焔四邊不可取: see the *Ta chih tu lun*, T 25.190c23–24; Lamotte (*Le Traité* 2, 1065) translates:

> La Prajñāpāramitā
> Est pareille à la flamme d'un grand feu:
> Insaisissable des quatre côtés,
> Sans prise ni non-prise.

***Prajñā*-wisdom has four types** 般若有四種相: see the *Ta chih tu lun*, T 25.517b20–28, in the context of a discussion of "turning the wheel of the Dharma":

> Question: Subhūti, why do you ask this question? Because of the emptiness of the dharmas of being and the dharmas of non-being. *Prajñā-pāramitā* neither "turns" nor "returns"; therefore it is transcendent. However, the Buddha "returns" [to the world to preach the Dharma?] with [the teaching of] emptiness.
>
> Answer: Some people say that there are four types of dharmas: the first is being, the second is non-being, the third is both being and non-being, and the fourth is neither being nor non-being. Since you arouse erroneous thoughts [on the basis of these four views], thus you perform four types of erroneous actions. Because you are attached to these four [types of] dharmas, this is called an erroneous path. If you have correct thoughts, and arouse four types of correct actions and are not attached to them, this is called the correct path. If you deconstruct [the position of] "neither being nor non-being," this is called the emptiness of the dharmas of non-being and the dharmas of being. The teachings of the Buddha deconstruct [the position of] "neither being nor non-being," and therefore it is taught that there is no [substantive] "turning" and no [substantive] "returning."

The four gates are the entrance to the pure and cool pond 四門入清涼池: a phrase from the *Ta chih tu lun*, T 25.640c10. This section has been quoted previously in the *Mo-ho chih-kuan*; see note and translation of the context at 13c14.

***Ch'eng-shih lun* scholars and Abhidharma scholars**: The source of these claims is unknown.

denounce the Abhidharma position, saying that it is merely a convenient method for regulating the mind, and does not allow at all for attaining the path. The Abhidharma scholars say that this [Tripitaka Teachings] is merely a way to attain the path by gaining insight into being, and that [the idea of] emptiness belongs to Mahāyāna. These two types of scholars have lost sight of the intent of the four gates. They denounce and oppose each other, and are resolutely attached to their own views; thus it is easy for disputes to arise among them. This is called [teachings that] show people the way to dispute. In the Shared Teachings, the essence of dharmas is [seen to be] like an illusion or transformation, with form having no [substantial] reality but only verbal designation [lit., "names and words"]. It is easy [to perceive that things that are only] names and words are vacuous [and empty] and to follow this [insight] without opposition; thus it gives rise to only a few disputes. The *Ta chih tu lun* criticizes the Tripitaka [Teachings] saying that other sūtras show many ways for people to dispute, but the Prajñāpāramitā Sūtras show the way for people to avoid dispute. This is also called "skill-

***Ta chih tu lun* criticizes the Tripitaka saying that other sūtras show many ways for people to dispute, but the Prajñāpāramitā Sūtras show the way for people to avoid dispute** 大論形斥三藏云餘經多示人諍法般若示人無諍法: the wording is different, but perhaps Chih-i is referring to the passage at the beginning of the *Ta chih tu lun* at T 25.60c7–61a2. Lamotte (*Le Traité* 1, 38–40) translates:

> Le point de vue absolu *(pramārthika-siddhānta)*.—Toutes les essences *(dharmatā)*, toutes les catégories du discours *(upadeśābhidhāna)*, tous les Dharma et Adharma, peuvent être divisés *(vibhakta)*, déchirés *(bhinna)* et éparpillés *(prakīrṇa)* les uns après les autres, mais le Dharma véritable *(bhūtadharma)*, domaine *(gocara)* des Buddha, des Pratyekabuddha et des Arhat, ne peut être ni déchiré ni éparpillé. Ce qui n'est pas compris dans les trois points de vue précédents est ici entièrement compris. Qu'en-tend-on par compris? Par compris on entend l'absence de tout défaut *(sarvadoṣavisaṃyoga)*, l'inaltérabilité *(apariṇāmatva)*, l'invincibilité *(ajeyatva)*. Pourquoi? Parce que, si on écarte le point de vue absolu, les autres enseignements *(upadeśa)*, les autres points de vue *(siddhārta)* sont tous détruits. Dans le *Tchong yi king* (Arthavargīya sūtra), des stances disent:
>
> Chacun, se basant sur des vues fausses *(dṛṣṭi)*,
> Et de vains bavardages *(prapañca)*, suscitent des querelles *(vivāda)*.
> Voir le néant de tout cela,
> C'est la vue correcte du savoir.
>
> Si refuser d'admettre le système d'autrui *(paradharma)*
> Est le fait d'un sot *(bāla)*,
> Alors tous les maîtres *(upadeśin)*,
> En vérité, sont des sots.
>
> Se baser sur des vues personnelles,
> Pour produire de vains bavardages,
> Constituait le pur savoir,
> Il n'y aurait personne de savoir impur.

Chodron (1, 52–54) translates:

> The absolute point of view. — Every essence, every category of speech, every dharma and adharma, may be subdivided, broken into pieces and scattered, one after the other; but the true Dharma, the domain of the buddhas, pratyekabuddhas and arhats can neither

ful saving in accordance with reality." The *Middle Treatise* says, "The three people [śrāvaka, pratyekabuddha, bodhisattva] share in attaining [insight into] the true marks of reality." The *Pañcaviṃśati Sūtra* says that the people of the three vehicles are the same in teaching the path without words, in severing passionate afflictions, and perceiving the supreme meaning." This

be broken apart nor scattered. That which has not been understood in the preceding points of view is completely understood here. What is meant by 'understood'? By 'understood' is meant the absence of any defect, unchangeability, invincibility. Why? Because if one deviates from the absolute point of view, the other teachings, the other points of view are all destroyed. Some stanzas in the *Arthavargīya sūtra* say:

> Being based on wrong views
> And on futile nonsense, each one gives rise to quarrels.
> Seeing the arising of all that
> Is the correct view of knowledge.
>
> If the refusal to accept the system of another
> Is the action of a fool,
> Then all the teachers
> Are, in truth, fools.
> If being based on personal views
> In order to produce futile nonsense
> Constituted pure knowledge,
> There would be no-one of impure knowledge.

Skillful saving in accordance with reality 如實巧度 *(yāthātmyāvatāraṇakuśala)*: this phrase is found in the opening section of the *Pañcaviṃśati Sūtra* and commented on in the *Ta chih tu lun* at T 25.107a–108a; see note at *Mo-ho chih-kuan* 74b12, with Lamotte's translation of this section.

The three people share in attaining the true marks of reality 諸法實相三人共得: see the closing comments of Chapter 18 on "Dharmas" in the *Middle Treatise*, T 30.25b23–29. Bocking (*Middle Treatise*, 285–86) translates:

> The true character taught by the Buddha is threefold. To attain the true character of all dharmas and end all the afflictions is terms the śrāvaka-dharma. To produce great compassion and arouse the unexcelled mind is called the great vehicle (Mahāyāna). If a Buddha does not enter the world and there is a time when there is no Buddha-dharma, pratyekabuddhas, because of their isolation, develop insight independently, for even if a Buddha after saving living beings enters nirvana without residue, and the Dharma he left behind completely dies out, if there are any who from a previous world are supposed to attain the Way, then if they meditate a little on the causes for despising and leaving samsara and go alone into the mountains and forests remote from any bustle and confusion, they will attain the Way. These are called pratyekabuddhas.

Three vehicles are the same in teaching the path without words, in severing passionate afflictions, and perceiving the supreme meaning 三乘之人同以無言說道斷煩惱見第一義: see the *Pañcaviṃśati Sūtra*, T 8.234a15–21:

> Subhūti, good sons and good daughters who wish to learn the stage of the śrāvaka also should listen to the Prajñāpāramitā [texts] and uphold it, recite it, read it, truly keep it in mind, and practice as it teaches. Those who wish to learn the stage of the pratyekabuddha also should listen to the Prajñāpāramitā [texts] and uphold it, recite it, read it, truly keep it in mind, and practice as it teaches. Those who wish to learn the stage of the bodhisattva also should listen to the Prajñāpāramitā [texts] and uphold it, recite it, read it, truly keep it in mind, and practice as it teaches. Why? Because the three vehicles are taught

is also called the "common *prajñā*-wisdom." The *Mahāparinirvāṇa Sūtra* calls this the "three animals crossing a river." All of these refer to the intent of the contemplation of the four gates in the Shared Teachings. Again, this [interpretation] is not what I intend to use here [in the *Mo-ho chih-kuan*].

3. Distinct Teachings [74c25]

Next is the four gates of the Distinct Teachings. This refers to contemplating a distinct principle 別理 and distinct delusions 別惑, and so is not the same as the content of the above [on the Tripitaka and Shared Teachings]. It is cultivated gradually and successively, and its enlightenment is gradual and successive, so in this way it is not the same as the next [Perfect Teaching]. The *Mahāparinirvāṇa Sūtra* says, "When they hear that the *Mahāparinirvāṇa Sūtra* has the highest path, the great assembly [of bodhisattvas] will practice it correctly," that is, they will arouse the aspiration for enlightenment, leave

extensively in these Prajñāpāramitā [texts]. Bodhisattva-mahāsattvas, śrāvakas, and pratyekabuddhas should study and learn from it.

Common *prajñā*-wisdom 共般若: see the *Ta chih tu lun*, T 25.357c13–16. The term "common *prajñā*-wisdom" itself does not appear; rather, it speaks of *prajñāpāramitā* that is "shared by" or "common to" śrāvakas and bodhisattvas:

> Again, there are two types of *prajñā-pāramitā*: the first is that taught and shared 共 by śrāvakas and bodhisattvas, and the second is that which is taught only by the Dharma bodies of the bodhisattvas.

Three animals crossing a river 三獸渡河: an analogy comparing the varying abilities of the śrāvaka, pratyekabuddha, and Buddha to that of a rabbit, horse, and elephant in their attempts to cross a river. The analogy appears in the *Mahāparinirvāṇa Sūtra* (T 12.746b1–5 and 768b6–11), but also appears more completely in the *Upāsaka-śīla Sūtra*, T 24.1038b8–13. See note at *Mo-ho chih-kuan* 7b7 for a translation of the full analogy.

When they hear … the great assembly will practice it correctly 聞大涅槃有無上道大衆正行: a summary of the section on "Noble Practice" in the *Mahāparinirvāṇa Sūtra* (T 12.673b28–c10ff.):

> Bodhisattva-mahāsattvas, when they hear in this way the *Mahāparinirvāṇa Sūtra*—whether from a śrāvaka or a Tathāgata—will arouse faith. After they arouse faith, they will ponder in the following way: "All Buddhas and World Honored Ones have the highest path, and have the great correct Dharma, and the great assembly practices it correctly. Again, there is the extensive Mahāyāna sūtras. I should crave for and seek the Mahāyāna sūtras, and abandon my beloved wife and children, my retinue, my dwelling and home; my money and treasures and wonderful jewelry; perfumed flowers, dancers, male and female servants; my elephant and horse-drawn carts; my bulls, sheep, chickens, dogs, and pigs." Again they will think, "My home is oppressive and like a prison. All sorts of passionate afflictions arise here. If I leave home I will be free like the empty sky. All good dharmas will be caused and increase. If I stay at home, I will exhaust my lifespan without attaining a pure cultivation of noble conduct. I should now cut off my hair, leave home, and learn the path," [and so forth] …

home, keep the precepts, cultivate concentrated meditation, contemplate the wisdom of the Four [Noble] Truths, and attain the twenty-five samādhis. This is not different from the Tripitaka Teachings in that the activities are performed gradually and progressively, but it is done with the spirit of the *Mahāparinirvāṇa Sūtra* [75a] in guiding [people] concerning all the dharmas. In this sense it is different from the previous [Tripitaka and Shared Teachings]. One gradually cultivates the five practices; in this sense it is different from the next [Perfect Teaching].

1. The gate of Being [75a2]

The four gates [in the Distinct Teachings] involve contemplating [mistaken] views and conceptual attitudes as illusions and transformations, and exhaustively [realizing] that visible forms *(rūpa)* are vacuous [empty] delusions but that there is a distinct form of sublime reality 妙色 that is called "Buddha-nature." The *Mahāparinirvāṇa Sūtra* says, "The emptiness of emptiness is a non-Buddhist path. Liberation is not emptiness, but is true, good, and sublime form. The secret treasury of the Tathāgata is not obtainable and not

Twenty-five samādhi 二十五三昧: a list of samādhis from the *Mahāparinirvāṇa Sūtra*; each samādhi allows one to overcome one of the twenty-five states of samsaric existence. See the *Mahāparinirvāṇa Sūtra*, T 12.690b2–23.

Spirit 心: This "spirit" [or "heart"] of the *Mahāparinirvāṇa Sūtra* is, presumably, the emphasis on the importance of recognizing conventional reality (including the idea of Buddha-nature), and altruistic bodhisattva practice in this world.

Five practices 五行: That is, noble practice, altruistic practice, divine practices, parental practices, and the practice of disease as expounded at length in the *Mahāparinirvāṇa Sūtra*, T 12.673b–729b.

Buddha-nature 佛性: Note that the idea of Buddha-nature corresponds here to the level of the Distinct Teachings, not the Perfect Teaching.

The emptiness of emptiness is a non-Buddhist path. Liberation is not emptiness, but is true, good, and sublime form. The secret treasury of the Tathāgata is not obtainable as Being 空空者卽是外道。解脱者卽是不空。卽是眞善妙 色。如來祕藏不得不有: Part of a passage discussing the meaning of "liberation" in the *Mahāparinirvāṇa Sūtra*, T 12.635c8–26, which paradoxically affirms such non-Buddhist views as the "self" with a choppy form of logic that is typical of the *Mahāparinirvāṇa Sūtra*:

> However, severing attachments is not to sever the view of the self. The view of the self is called Buddha-nature. Buddha-nature is true liberation. True liberation is the Tathāgata.
>
> Again, liberation is called non-empty emptiness 不空空. The emptiness of emptiness is called non-being. *Non-being is the non-Buddhist path* of the Nirgranthas, which is a calculated liberation. [This liberation of] the Nirgranthas is truly not a liberation; therefore it is called the emptiness of emptiness. The non-emptiness of emptiness is true liberation. True liberation is not like this; therefore it is non-empty emptiness. Non-empty emptiness is true liberation. True liberation is the Tathāgata.
>
> Again, liberation is called the emptiness of the non-empty. It is like a bottle

Being,"... "Selfhood is the treasury of the Tathāgata *(tathāgata-garbha)*. The *tathāgata-garbha* is Buddha-nature." The *Tathāgata-garbha Sūtra* gives ten analogies [for the *tathāgata-garbha,* like] gold wrapped and covered with rags, and a statue [concealed] within its mold of clay. This is the gate of being [for the Distinct Teachings].

2. The gate of emptiness (or non-Being) [75a7]

The gate of emptiness is as follows. The *Mahāparinirvāṇa Sūtra* says, "Kapilavastu is empty. The *tathāgata-garbha* is empty. Great nirvana

for water, liquor, milk, cream, honey, and so forth. Even when there is no water, liquor, cream, or honey, it is still called a bottle for water and so forth. This bottle [itself] is not said to be empty, therefore it is non-empty. If we say that it is empty, then it cannot be said to have any color or shape, smell, flavor, or feel. If we say that it is non-empty, then there is not reality to the water, liquor, and so forth [inside the bottle]. Liberation is likewise. It cannot be described either as "form" or as "without form." It cannot be described as "empty"; therefore it is non-empty. If we say that it is empty, then [the qualities of] "constant, blissful, selfhood, and pure" 常樂我淨 cannot be obtained. If we say that it is non-empty, then we can accept it as having the meaning of constant, blissful, selfhood, and pure. It cannot be described as empty, so it is non-empty.

"Empty" refers to the lack of the twenty-five types of existences with all its passionate afflictions, sufferings, marks, and conditioned activities, as a bottle without cream is called empty. *"Non-empty" refers to true, real, and good forms* that are constant, blissful, selfhood, pure, immovable, and unchanging, as a bottle has color and form, scent, flavor, and feel; therefore it is called "non-empty."

Selfhood is the treasury of the Tathāgata. The *tathāgata-garbha* is Buddha-nature 我者卽如來藏。如來藏者卽是佛性: phrases from the opening sentences of chapter 12 on "The Nature of the Tathāgata" in the *Mahāparinirvāṇa Sūtra*, T 12.648b6–9:

Kāśyapa said to the Buddha, "World Honored One. Do the twenty-five realms of existence have selfhood or not?"

The Buddha said, "Good son. *Selfhood is the meaning or essence* 義 *of the tathāgata-garbha*. All sentient beings have Buddha-nature. This is the meaning of "self." In this way the meaning or essence of the self is there from the beginning [or "basis"] 本. It is always covered with immeasurable afflictions; therefore sentient beings are not able to perceive it [or "attain insight"].

Ten analogies in the *Tathāgata-garbha Sūtra*: see the analogies at T 16.457b–459b; the two analogies mentioned here are the seventh (458c15–459a6) and ninth (459a26–b12) given in the sūtra. Chih-i has referred to these analogies before; see note (and expanded endnote) at *Mo-ho chih-kuan* 6a26. As pointed out previously, there are actually only nine analogies given in the sūtra.

Kapilavastu 迦毘城: Śākyamuni's birthplace and native land, at the foot of the Himalaya mountains.

Kapilavastu is empty. The *tathāgata-garbha* is empty. Great nirvana is empty 迦毘城空。如來藏空。大涅槃空: see the *Mahāparinirvāṇa Sūtra* at T 12.765c19–28; the context reads:

The perfection of giving is also empty; form is also empty; sight is also empty; consciousness is also empty, *the Tathāgata is also empty, mahāparinirvāṇa*

(mahāparinirvāṇa) is empty." It also says, "This leads all sentient beings to attain the great *parinirvāṇa* of no form." Nirvana is not "being." We speak of the "existence" of nirvana in worldly terms [or, lit., "due to worldly, mundane (concerns)], but nirvana has neither form nor sound [nor the other characteristics of experiential objects], so how can it be said to be seen or heard? This is the gate of emptiness [for the Distinct Teachings].

3. The gate of both Being and emptiness [75a11]

The gate of "both emptiness and being" is as follows. [The *Mahāparinirvāṇa Sūtra* says,] "A wise person perceives both emptiness and non-emptiness." [It also says that] if we affirm [merely] emptiness, then there is no permanence, bliss, selfhood, or purity. If we affirm non-emptiness, then again we can accept the permanence, bliss, selfhood, and purity [of great *parinirvāṇa*]. It is like a bottle that is filled with water, liquor, or cream that cannot be said to be empty, because it is not empty." This is called the gate of both emptiness and being [for the Distinct Teachings].

4. The gate of neither Being nor emptiness [75a15]

The gate of neither being nor nothingness transcends the four [options] and

> *is also empty*. Therefore bodhisattvas perceive that all dharmas are without exception empty. Therefore, when I was at Kapilavastu [after this homeland of the Buddha had been destroyed and his family wiped out] I said to Ānanda,... "You perceive Kapilavastu as having truly real existence; I perceive it as empty and quiescent, completely without [substantial] existence."

For a full translation of the context, see note at *Mo-ho chih-kuan* 13b29.

This leads all sentient beings to attain the great *parinirvāṇa* of no form: a paraphrase of a passage in the *Mahāparinirvāṇa Sūtra*, T 12.766a3–8, a few lines after the passage quoted in the previous note.

> Good sons. Bodhisattvas who cultivate the thirty-seven parts of the path realize Great Parinirvāṇa that is constant, blissful, selfhood, and pure. For the sake of sentient beings they differentiate and explain the *Mahāparinirvāṇa Sūtra* and manifest Buddha-nature. If stream-enterers, once-returners, non-returners, arhats, pratyekabuddhas, and bodhisattvas believe these words, they will all attain and realize Great Parinirvāṇa. If they do not believe, they will transmigrate in the cycle of birth-and-death (samsara).

Nirvana is not "being" 有: or, "Nirvana does not exist" [in a substantial sense].

A wise person perceives both emptiness and non-emptiness 智者見空及與不空: see the *Mahāparinirvāṇa Sūtra*, T 12.767c20. This passage has been quoted above; see the notes at *Mo-ho chih-kuan* 28a6–8 and 50a15. However, at the earlier passage (28a6–8), this passage is quoted in support of the Shared Teachings.

Cannot be said to be empty, because it is not empty 不可説空及以不空: or, "cannot be said to be either empty or non-empty"? See the passage in the *Mahāparinirvāṇa Sūtra*, T 12.635c8–26, quoted above.

is free from a hundred [negations]. This is beyond words and inexpressible. The *Mahāparinirvāṇa Sūtra* says, "Neither eternal nor severed; this is called the Middle Way." This is this gate [of neither being nor emptiness (or nothingness) for the Distinct Teachings].

If you realize the intent of these four gates, you will penetrate and realize the true aspect [of reality]. If you do not realize this intent, [you will realize only] the intent of overcoming delusions gradually and [at the level of skillful] means. The *Mahāparinirvāṇa Sūtra* calls this the "noble activity of the bodhisattva." The *Pañcaviṃśati Sūtra* calls it the "unique *prajñā*-wisdom [of the bodhisattvas]." This is the intent of the four gates of the Distinct Teachings, and is not what I will use here [in the *Mo-ho chih-kuan*].

4. Perfect Teaching [75a20]

Next is the four gates of the Perfect Teaching, which in its teaching of the sublime principle [of reality] and of sudden [practice] is different from the two previous [Shared and Distinct Teachings]. It is perfectly integrated and unhindered; in this way different from the step-by-step method of the Distinct [Teachings]. What are the four gates [for the Perfect Teaching]?

1. The gate of Being [75a22]

Contemplate the conventionality of [mistaken] views and conceptual attitudes as the Dharma realm 法界 and integrated with the Buddha Dharma 具足佛法. Again, [contemplate] all dharmas as [the result of] the causes and conditions of the nature of dharmas [or, Dharma-nature] 法性, and that the supreme meaning [of reality] is also [an aspect of] such causes and conditions. The *Mahāparinirvāṇa Sūtra* says, "the extinction of ignorance is the cause for attaining the burning flame of the torch of *bodhi*-wisdom *(saṃbodhi)*." This is called the gate of being [for the Perfect Teaching].

Neither eternal nor severed; this is called the Middle Way 非常非斷名爲中道: see the *Mahāparinirvāṇa Sūtra*, T 12.768b3–4:

> Next, good sons: sentient beings arouse two types of [extreme] views. The first is the view of eternalism, and the second is the view of annihilationism [lit. "severance"]. These two views are not that called the Middle Way.

Noble activity of the bodhisattva 菩薩聖行: see, for example, the section on "Noble Practice" in the *Mahāparinirvāṇa Sūtra*, T 12.673b28–c10ff. The exact phrase appears at 673b27–28.

Unique *prajñā*-wisdom 不共般若: see the *Ta chih tu lun*, T 25.357c13–15, quoted above at *Mo-ho chih-kuan* 74c23. The term "unique (or "unshared") *prajñā*-wisdom" itself does not appear; rather, it speaks of *prajñāpāramitā* that is "shared" by śrāvakas and bodhisattvas, and that which is unique to bodhisattvas.

The extinction of ignorance is the cause for attaining the burning flame of the torch of *bodhi*-wisdom 因滅無明即得熾然三菩提燈: a slight paraphrase from the

2. The gate of emptiness (or non-Being) [75a24]

The gate of emptiness is as follows. Contemplate the illusory transformations of [mistaken] views and conceptual attitudes and all dharmas as having no [substantial] causes or conditions. The self and nirvana are both empty. However, when there is [conventionally] an empty disease, this empty disease is also empty. Thus the three truths [of emptiness, conventionality, and the Middle] are all empty.

3. The gate of both Being and emptiness [75a27]

How about the gate of both-emptiness-and-being? [Contemplate] the illusory transformations of [mistaken] views and conceptual attitudes as [things that], though not truly real, can be differentiated as conventional designations and cannot be exhausted. This is like "thousands of sūtra scrolls existing within one minute particle of dust," or "being immovable in the supreme sense, [**75b**] yet able to distinguish all aspects of phenomena." Again, it is "like the great earth, which is one and yet is able to give rise to various sprouts," and "that which cannot be [fully expressed] with names and forms is spoken of conventionally with names and forms," and "The Buddha also is

Mahāparinirvāṇa Sūtra, T 12.732a23–24. This phrase has been quoted already in the *Mo-ho chih-kuan*; see note at 8a2–3 for full text.

Empty disease 空病: a phrase from the *Vimalakīrti Sūtra*, T 14.545a13, to indicate the Vimalakīrti's disease was not "real." This phrase has been quoted already in the *Mo-ho chih-kuan*; see note at 51a3.

Thousands of scrolls existing within one minute particle of dust 一微塵中有大千經卷: A phrase from the *Avataṃsaka Sūtra*, T 9.624a6. This has been quoted already in the *Mo-ho chih-kuan*; for a full translation of the context see notes and endnote at 9a16 and 20b7–8.

Being immovable in the supreme sense yet able to distinguish all aspects of phenomena 第一義而不動善能分別諸法相: a phrase from the *Vimalakīrti Sūtra*, T 14.537c13. This phrase has been quoted already in the *Mo-ho chih-kuan* at 25c8. In the sūtra the two phrase are reversed and read: "to be well able to discriminate the features of phenomena—this is to be immovable in the supreme sense."

Like the great earth, which is one and yet is able to give rise to various sprouts 如大地一能生種種芽: from the *Avataṃsaka Sūtra*, T 9.428a16, repeated at 428b1. The phrase has been quoted already in the *Mo-ho chih-kuan*, 50c19.

That which cannot be [fully expressed] with names and forms is spoken of conventionally with names and forms 無名相中假名相説: see the *Sūtra of the Buddha Treasury*, T 15.782c27–28:

> Śāriputra said to the Buddha, "World Honored One. Whenever I dwell in quietude I have the following thought. World Honored One, dharmas that are without name and form are expressed with names and forms. Dharmas that have no verbal [expression] are expressed with words. Pondering these things give rise to extraordinary thoughts 希有心.

This passage has been quoted previously; see note at *Mo-ho chih-kuan* 49a20 and 54c8–9.

merely a verbal designation." This is the gate of both being and nothingness [for the Perfect Teaching].

4. The gate of neither Being nor emptiness [75b3]

What is the gate of neither-being-nor-nothingness [for the Perfect Teaching]? Contemplate the illusory transformations of [mistaken] views and conceptual attitudes as Dharma-nature itself. Dharma-nature is inconceivable. It is not mundane, so it is not existent Being. It is not transworldly, so it is not nothing. There is not a single color nor scent that is not the Middle Way, and the middleness of one is the middleness of all. [The Buddha] Vairocana pervades all places. How can there be [mistaken] views and conceptual attitudes that are not real dharmas? This is called the gate of neither-being-nor-non-being [for the Perfect Teaching].

What does it mean for one gate to be indivisible from the [other] three gates? One gate includes all gates; why limit [this inclusiveness] to three? What does this mean? To contemplate "all things that arise through causes and conditions" is the first gate. All is included in the first gate. The first gate "is empty." One is empty and all is empty; this is the second gate. The first gate "is conventionality." One is conventional and all is conventional; this is the third gate. The first gate is the "Middle." One is Middle and all is Middle; this is the fourth gate. Thus the first gate is indivisible from the [other] three gates, and the three gates are indivisible from the one [other] gate. This is to take up one gate as nominally representative [of the others]; even though there are four names [for the four gates], their principle is not distinct.

The Buddha also is merely a verbal designation 佛亦但有名字: the *Kōgi* (BT–IV, 126) attributes this quote to the *Sūtra of the Buddha Treasury*, section 17, and Ikeda (*Kenkyūchūshaku*, 380) points out that the phrase is also found in the *Ta chih tu lun*, T 25.358b18–19.

Not a single color nor scent that is not the Middle Way 一色一香無非中道: this is the same phrase found in the opening passage of the *Mo-ho chih-kuan* at 1c24–25.

Vairocana pervades all places 毘盧遮那遍一切處: see *The Contemplation of Samantabhadra*, T 9.392c16–17. This has been quoted already in the *Mo-ho chih-kuan*; see note at 9a12. The full phrase in the sūtra reads, "Śākyamuni Buddha is called Vairocana Who Pervades All Places, and his dwelling place is called Eternally Tranquil Light."

All things that arise through causes and conditions 因縁所生法: the first phrase of the famous verse 24:18 of the *Middle Treatise*, as explained already; see *Mo-ho chih-kuan* 3b8–9.

Is empty 即空: short for the second phrase of the verse, "I explain as emptiness."

Is conventional 即假: short for the third phrase of the verse, "Again, this is a conventional designation."

Is the Middle 即中: short for the fourth phrase of the verse, "Again, this is the meaning of the Middle Way."

Take up: the Taishō text has 奉, but I follow the variant 擧.

To deconstruct [mistaken] views and conceptual attitudes on the basis of the gate of non-arising as explained above is the [second] gate of emptiness. One gate is all gates, and it is not that non-arising is completed by [one gate] alone. The deconstruction of one is the deconstruction of all, and it is not that [the process] stops and is completed with the deconstruction of [mistaken] views and conceptual attitudes. To realize emptiness from conventionality is [to realize] that the emptiness of one is the emptiness of all, and it is not that [the process] is completed [by realizing] merely emptiness, that is, the emptiness of life-and-death (samsara). This is the meaning of the four gates of the Perfect Teaching, and this is the proper [focus] to be used here [in the *Mo-ho chih-kuan*].

If this is so, then why was it necessary to bring up the various distinctions explained above? [It is necessary] because ordinary beings are benighted and dull, and they cannot [come to] know [fully] without such explanations. First they must be enticed to have this disclosed [slowly and gradually], and then later they will realize the correct path. The *Lotus Sūtra* says, "Although I preach various paths, truly there is only one vehicle." If you follow this meaning, then even if one makes distinctions all day, there is [ultimately] no place for making distinctions. The *Mahāparinirvāṇa Sūtra* says "There is the single practice which is the practice of the Tathāgata." The *Lotus Sūtra* calls it "directly abandoning means *(upāya)* and preaching only the supreme path." The *Pañcaviṃśati Sūtra* calls it "universal wisdom with

Although I preach various paths, truly there is only one vehicle 雖說種種道其實爲一乘: see the *Lotus Sūtra*, T 9.9b7–8 and 16; Chih-i's paraphrase seems to be a combination of these two phrases, though the entire context is a discussion of this idea. Hurvitz (*Lotus Sūtra*, 41 [38]) translates:

> The Buddhas of ages to come,
> Though they shall preach hundreds of thousands of millions
> Of numberless gateways to the Dharma,
> Shall, in fact, be doing it *for the sake of the One Vehicle*....
> They may demonstrate various paths, but
> *They do so, in fact, for the sake of* the Buddha Vehicle.

There is the single practice which is the practice of the Tathāfata 一行是如來行: A phrase from the opening of the chapter on "Noble Practice" in the *Mahāparinirvāṇa Sūtra*, T 12.673b26. This section has just been referred to above at 74c28 and 75a18. The context reads:

> Bodhisattva-mahāsattvas constantly cultivate these five practices [of noble practice, altruistic practice, divine practices, parental practices, and the practice of disease]. Again, *there is a single practice which is the practice of the Tathāgata*, that is, the Mahāyāna *Mahāparinirvāṇa Sūtra.*

For the text that continues after this passage, see the translation in the note at *Mo-ho chih-kuan* 74c28.

Directly abandoning means and preaching only the supreme path 正直捨方便但說無上道: see the *Lotus Sūtra*, T 9.10a19. This phrase has been quoted many times already in the *Mo-ho chih-kuan*; see the note at 2c9.

Universal wisdom with which you

which you know all dharmas." The *Vimalakīrti Sūtra* speaks of "entering a *campaka* grove and not smelling any other scent." The *Avataṃsaka Sūtra* speaks of the "Dharma realm" *(dharmadhātu)*. This is the meaning of the four gates [for the Perfect Teaching].

This above [explanation] is the gate of non-arising for deconstructing conventionality. If you realize this intent, this is the gate of the Perfect Teaching and not the gate of [provisional or conventional] means. This is called deconstructing dharmas universally [with regard to the Perfect Teaching].

know all dharmas 一切種智知一切法: perhaps a summary of a passage in the *Pañcaviṃśati Sūtra*, T 8.397c–398a, which discusses a bodhisattva being able to "fully penetrate all dharmas" (397b19) and attaining "universal wisdom," but does not contain this phrase as is. The *Kōgi* (BT–IV, 132) attributes it to "section 27/11" of the *Pañcaviṃśati Sūtra*.

This phrase also appears in the introduction of the *Mo-ho chih-kuan*; see note at 2c22–23, where it is attributed to a different section of the *Pañcaviṃśati Sūtra*, T 8.218c18–19, by pointing to "section 11/8 of the *Ta chih tu lun*" (see *Kōgi*, BT–I, 145).

Entering a *campaka* grove and not smelling any other scent 入薝蔔林不嗅餘香: see the *Vimalakīrti Sūtra*, T 14.548a25–26; this phrase also appears in the same section of the *Mo-ho chih-kuan* introduction as the above phrases from the *Lotus Sūtra* and *Pañcaviṃśati Sūtra*; see note at 2c19–22.

Dharma realm 法界: this term appears innumerable times in the *Avataṃsaka Sūtra*; see especially the last chapter on "entering the Dharma realm," T 9.676–788.

2. The Contemplation of Realizing Conventionality from Emptiness [75b27–80b16]

Second, deconstructing dharmas universally by entering or realizing conventionality from emptiness 從空入假 consists of four [parts]. First is the intent of "entering or realizing conventionality." Second is clarifying the causes and conditions for entering or realizing conventionality. Third is clarifying the contemplation of entering or realizing conventionality. Fourth is clarifying the levels of entering or realizing conventionality.

1. The intent of realizing conventionality (that is, to benefit others) [75b29]

The intent of entering or realizing conventionality is as follows. There is [the type of] merely [75c] entering or realizing conventionality from emptiness, and there is [the type of] knowing that emptiness is not empty and entering or realizing conventionality by deconstructing emptiness [as not nihilistic nothingness]. The wisdom and severance of those of the two vehicles are both the same [as that of bodhisattvas and Buddhas] with regard to attesting to the truth [of emptiness], but they are not called bodhisattvas because they do not have great compassion. The *Avataṃsaka Sūtra* says that those of the two vehicles also attain realization of the true nature and marks of all dharmas, but they are not called Buddhas. If you practice for yourself you can realize emptiness partially, but when it comes to saving [other] beings, you cannot accomplish it outside of conventionality. Bodhisattvas realize emptiness from conventionality and destroy their own bonds of attachments, so [in this sense] they are not the same as ordinary ignorant people.

***Avataṃsaka Sūtra* says that ...** : see T 9.566c19–20. These phrases have been quoted already in the *Mo-ho chih-kuan*; see note at 35a28. The original text reads "The true nature and mark of all dharmas is that of eternal abiding and no change or difference. Those of the two vehicles can realize this, but we do not call it [ultimate] Buddhahood."

If you practice for yourself you can realize emptiness partially, but when it comes to saving beings, you cannot accomplish it outside of conventionality 若論自行入空有分若論化物出假則無; this sentence is ambiguous. It could also be translated: "If we speak of practicing for self [benefit], realizing emptiness is 'part of the deal' 分有; but if we speak of saving [other] beings, this cannot be done without 'emerging in conventionality' 出假." "Emerging in conventionality" could also be translated, "transcending [mere emptiness by realizing] conventionality. The idea is that one must go beyond a one-sided, overly negative emptiness and reaffirm the mundane, conventional world, and "reemerge" in it in order to save other beings. Or, the fullness of Buddhahood cannot be accomplished without a compassionate involvement in saving other beings, and this necessitates activity in the mundane world.

They enter or realize conventionality from emptiness and destroy the bonds of others, so [in this sense] they are not the same as those of the two vehicles. Though abiding in [conventional, worldly] existence, they are not defiled [by it]; they discern [the proper] medicine [for various diseases] with their Dharma eyes; they put a halt to disease with their compassion; their vast love is unlimited; they never tire [in striving for] the concurrent salvation [of both oneself and others to "cross over" to the other shore]; they have complete mastery with their mind; their good and skillful means are "like trees planted in the empty sky" or "like shooting arrows into the sky, one after the

Vast love 博愛: Usually this character has negative connotations in the Buddhist context and is translated as "passions" or "craving." Here, however, the term is used in a positive sense, as in "compassion," so I have used the word "love" in the sense of *agapé*—selfless giving and a total concern for the wellbeing of others, the opposite of selfish egoism.

Trees planted in the empty sky 空中種樹: A phrase which reflects a passage from the *Ta chih tu lun*, T 25.267a19–24. Lamotte (*Le Traité* 4, 1849) translates:

> O Bhagavat, *si un homme plantait un arbre (vṛkṣa) sans l'enfoncer en terre* et que cet arbre produisait des racines *(mūla)*, un tronc *(skandha)*, des brances *(śākhā)*, des feuilles *(parṇa)* et donnait même des fruits *(phala)*, ce serait chose rare *(durlabha)*. Eh bien l'action *(caryālakṣaṇa)* de ces Bodhisattva est tout aussi extraordinaire. En effet, sans s'appuyer sur aucun dharma, ils manifestent des naissances *(jāti)* et des morts *(maraṇa)* dans les champs de Buddha *(buddhakṣetra)*, et là déploient à leur guise les talents de leur éloquence *(pratibhāna)* et de leur sagesse *(prajñā)*. Qui donc, entendant ces grands sages déployer en se jouant et à leur guise ce talent d'éloquence, ne produirait pas la pensée de la suprême et parfaite illumination *(anuttarasamyaksaṃbodhicitta)*?

Chodron (4, 1518) translates:

> O Bhagavat, if a man were to plant a tree without stamping down the ground around it and this tree produced roots, a trunk, branches, leaves), and even gave fruit, that would be a rare thing. Well, the activity of these bodhisattvas is just as extraordinary. Indeed, without relying on any dharma whatsoever, they manifest births and deaths in the buddha fields and there, as if at play, they display at will the talents of their eloquence and their wisdom. Then, hearing these great sages displaying this talent of eloquence playfully and at will, who would not produce the mind of supreme complete enlightenment?

Shooting arrows into the sky 仰射空中: see the *Ta chih tu lun*, T 25.197c17–20, where this analogy is given as part of a response to a question concerning the thirty-seven parts of the path. Lamotte (*Le Traité* 3, 1140) translates:

> Par ce dharma vrai *(bhūtadharma)*, le Bodhisattva qui pratique les perfections peut arriver à la Bodhi des Buddha. Mais bien qu'il exerce et qu'il connaisse ce dharma, il n'a pas encore rempli les six perfections, et c'est pourquoi il n'atteste pas *(na sākṣātkaroti)* immédiatement ce dharma vrai.
>
> Ainsi le Buddha a dit: *"C'est comme [un archer] qui, levant la tête, tire des flèches en l'air (ūrdhvaṃ kāṇḍaṃ kṣipati): les flèches successives se soutiennent mutueelement de façon à ne pas tomber à terre.* De même le Bodhisattva prenant la flèche de la Prajñāpāramitā la décoche en l'air contre les trois portes de la délive-

other so that they do not fall back to the ground." If you abide [always] in emptiness you can never benefit sentient beings. Striving to benefit others—this is the intent of "entering or realizing conventionality."

2. The causes and conditions for realizing conventionality [75c11]

The causes and conditions for entering or realizing conventionality can be summarized in five [aspects].

First is the overlapping of compassionate thoughts. When you first deconstruct conventionality, you perceive that sentient beings are perverted and bound in the prison [of their passionate afflictions] and are not able to escape, so you arouse great compassion [toward them], as [parents] love all their children equally. At this point you have already severed your delusions and realized emptiness, and so you feel pity and pain [toward the suffering sentient beings] as if you are one [with them and you feel the pain] doubling and multiplying. You put [the needs of other] people first, and yourself later, and your [desire to] grant [bliss] and extract [suffering] grows all the more fervent.

Second is the remembrance of your original [bodhisattva] vows. First [at the beginning of your spiritual life] you aroused the universal vows [of a bodhisattva] to extract suffering and grant bliss [for all sentient beings] and lead them to attain a calm peace. Sentient beings have much suffering, and they are not yet able to attain salvation. If you alone [are delivered and] become exempt [from such a situation], this would contradict your primary aspiration. You should not forget your original purpose [that is, your original vow]; how can you abandon [other] conscious beings? You "enter" [the mundane world of] conventionality and share their activity, and thus guide

> rance *(vimokṣamukha)*; ensuite, prenant le flêche des moyens salvifique *(upāya)*, il la décoche contre la flèche de la Prajñā de façon à ce qu'elle ne tombe pas sur le sol du Nirvāṇa."

Chodron (3, 939–40) translates:

> Although the bodhisattva remains in samsara for a long time, he must know the True Path and the false paths, the world and nirvana. Knowing that, he makes his great vow: "Beings are worthy of compassion; I must save them and bring them to unconditioned safety." The bodhisattva who practices the perfections is able, by means of this true dharma, to reach the Bodhi of the Buddhas. But although he practices and understands this dharma, he has not yet fulfilled the six perfections and this is why he does not immediately realize this true dharma.
>
> Thus the Buddha said: "It is like [an archer] who, raising his head, shoots his arrows into the air: the arrows support each other so that they do not fall to earth. In the same way, the bodhisattva, taking the arrow of the Prajñāpāramitā, shoots it into the air at the three gates of deliverance then, taking the arrow of skillful means, he shoots it at the arrow of Prajñā so that it does not fall on the ground of nirvana.

You are one 同體 : lit., "of one essence."

Share their activity 同事:or, "help through affinity"; one of the "four inducements" or methods used to induce people to enter the Buddhist path.

them [toward enlightenment]. "The first deeds [or practices on the path] of those of the two vehicles are not foolish methods"; [those of the two vehicles] also make the great vow [to save all beings], but as they pass through their lives they forget [this vow], retreat from the Mahāyāna and embrace the Hīnayāna, and must be reproached by the noble ones [to remember it again]. Bodhisattvas are not like this; they are like a mother who, upon gaining food, always brings to mind her children.

Third is the fierce sharpness of wisdom. When you realize emptiness, you come to know that within [the realization of] emptiness there is a excessive tendency to reject all other [things]. Why? Because when you abide [always] in emptiness, you do not purify a Buddha land or teach and transform sentient beings, nor are you completely endowed with the Buddha Dharma, nor are you able to accomplish it. After you realize this excessive tendency, you will deny [a one-sided] emptiness and enter and realize conventionality.

Fourth is [the power of] good and skillful means as you enter the [mundane] world. The passionate afflictions of [this samsaric world of] life-and-death are not able to impair wisdom. If you run into various impediments and difficulties, these [in turn] act to encourage you on the path of transformation [that is, of teaching, guiding, and saving others].

Fifth is the power of great diligence. Although the Buddha path is long and far, you should not consider it so remote [as to be out of reach]; although the number of sentient beings is numerous, you should have courage. Fortify your mind and do not retreat; diligently pursue your [original] aspiration for the path, and from the beginning do not grow weary or be lazy.

These are called the "five conditions" [for realizing conventionality]. These five meanings are the same as that found in the *Vimalakīrti Sūtra*. This text contains three types of consoling analogies [with regard to convention-

Foolish methods 愚法: or, "they were not ignorant of the Dharma." See the *Śrīmālādevī Sūtra*, T 12.222a29; note that the sūtra has "those of the three vehicles" instead of "those of the two vehicles." This phrase has been quoted previously in the *Mo-ho chih-kuan*, see note at 35b10, where I translate "those of the three vehicles were not ignorant of the Dharma [even at the level] of their 'first deeds' [on the path leading to Buddhahood]."

Accomplish it 辦 : or, given variant readings, "able to discriminate it" 辨 or "eloquently transmit it" 辯.

The Buddha path is long and far 佛道長遠: or, "is a long and winding road"?

Although the number of sentient beings is numerous, you should have courage 衆生數多而意有勇: note that these are two of the Four Universal Vows, though in a different form than is generally repeated today.

Consoling analogies 慰喩: see the *Vimalakīrti Sūtra*, T 14.544c17–26, where Vimalakīrti speaks of the "conventionality" of his sickness and how to console a "sick" person. Boin (*Vimalakīrti Sūtra*, 120–21) translates the context:

ality]. First it clarifies that the [physical] body that is contemplated is impermanent and so forth. This is the analogy for [**76a**] "realizing emptiness." At the end it says, "I am the king of physicians." This is the analogy for "realizing the Middle." Between these are the analogies for "realizing conventionality," which involve the five meanings [outlined above]. The phrase "through my own disease I have pity toward the disease of others" is the [first meaning of] "compassion of being one" [with others]. [The next phrase] "You should know the fate of suffering [by others] through innumerable kalpas" can be nothing other than [the second meaning, that is] "original vows." [The next phrase] "you should be mindful of benefiting all sentient beings" can be nothing other than [the third meaning, that is] "knowing the excessive [negativity] of emptiness." [The next phrase] "in your thoughts cultivate blessings, and be mindful of a pure life" is [the fourth meaning, that is] good and skillful means. [The next phrase] "do not give rise to discouragement, but always arouse diligence" is the fifth meaning. Thus the meaning [of these five "causes and conditions"] matches that of this text [of the *Vimalakīrti Sūtra*].

"Entering or realizing conventionality from emptiness" involves four aspects without which you would never be able to go beyond ["mere" emptiness to "emerge in conventionality"]. Now I will differentiate them in terms

Mañjuśrī: How does a Bodhisattva console *(saṃmodana)* a sick bodhisattva so as to gladden him?
Vimalakīrti: He tells him that the body is impermanent *(anitya),* but does not prompt him to feel for it any disgust *(nirveda)* or repugnance *(virāga)*. He tells him that the body is painful (*duḥkha*), but does not exhort him to delight in Nirvāṇa. He tells him that the body is without self (*anātman*), but prompts him to ripen being *(sattvaparipācana)*. He tells him that the body is calm *(śānta)*, but does not exhort him to seek the definitive calm *(atyantaśānti)*.

He exhorts him to repent of previous misdeeds *(pūrvaduścarita),* but does not say that these misdeeds are past *(saṃkrānta)*. He exhorts him to **use his own sickness to have pity on sick beings** and drive away their sickness. He **exhorts him to recall** *(anusmaraṇa)* **sufferings previously undergone** *(pūrvakoṭyanubhūtaduḥkha)* **to promote the welfare of beings** *(sattvārthakriyā)*. He exhorts him to **recall** *(anusmaraṇa)* **the countless good roots** *(kuśalamūla)* **already nurtured for practising a pure life** *(viśuddhājiva)*. He exhorts him **not to fear, but to give himself over to vigor** *(vīryārambha)*. He exhorts him to pronounce the great vow *(mahāpraṇidhāna)* to become the great king-physician *(mahāvaidhyarāja)* who heals all beings and definitively appeases the sicknesses of body and mind *(kāyacittavyādhi)*. It is thus that a bodhisattva should console a sick bodhisattva, so as to gladden him.

King of physicians 醫王: See the *Vimalakīrti Sūtra*, T 14.544c24. Boin has "the great king-physician."

Through my own disease 已之疾 ...: this and the following four phrases are in this passage of the *Vimalakīrti Sūtra*, T 14.544c22–24. I have given my own renderings; compare these phrases with the translation by Boin in the note above (in bold type).

of the single type of those with sharp faculties. Śrāvakas who abide in "mere emptiness" do not necessarily have dull faculties. Bodhisattvas who enter or realize conventionality do not necessarily have sharp faculties. Śāriputra, for example, was sharp in his wisdom, but did not advance beyond [the realization of emptiness] to [realize] conventionality. We should use a [fourfold] tetralemma in order to interpret this matter: either your faculties are sharp faculties and you abide in emptiness, or your faculties are dull and you abide in emptiness, or your faculties are sharp and you enter or realize conventionality, or your faculties are dull and you enter or realize conventionality. This is analogous to [four possible situations]: [1] Suppose your body is emaciated and you have no strength, but you are full of courage so that you can enter into danger and destroy the enemy, and there is no adversary left in front of you. [2] Suppose that your body's power is magnificent and you also have powerful courage, so that you can thrust to the left and strike to the right with no one to oppose you. [3] Suppose that your body is powerful but you are cowardly and fearful; even though you have [physical] power in your favor, you will lose your courage when faced with the ranks [of the enemy]. [4] Suppose you have no [physical] power and no courage, and are thus lacking in both areas; how would you be able to prevail? The person who abides in emptiness also is of two types [like the two types who are lacking in courage], and [the person who] [goes beyond emptiness to] "emerge in conventionality" is also likewise [like the two types who have courage and can thus prevail]. One who is endowed with the [above] five conditions is like someone who has parents 親 [or "intimate friends" who care for them], has the promise 約 [of a vow], has a strategy 策 [to go beyond emptiness], has the power 力 [of good and skillful means], and has the courage 膽 [to diligently persevere]; therefore such a person is able to enter or realize conventionality. Even if the root of wisdom is dull, such a person is able to enter or realize conventionality due to [the power of] the other four conditions. Even if a śrāvaka is [endowed with] sharp wisdom, he is not able to enter or realize conventionality because he does not have the [other] four conditions.

3. The contemplation of realizing conventionality [76a19]

Third is to clarify the contemplation of entering or realizing conventionality, which consists of three parts. First is knowing the disease, second is differentiating the medicine, and third is applying the medicine.

Four possible situations: see the *Kōgi* (BT–IV, 140) for a chart showing the correspondences between these categories.

Knowing the disease 知病, **differentiating the medicine** 識藥, **applying the medicine** 授藥: see the *Mahāparinirvāṇa Sūtra*, T 12.755b13–15:

Next, good sons, the Buddha and

1. Knowing the disease [76a20]

"Knowing the disease" refers to knowing the diseases of [mistaken] views and conceptual attitudes.

1. Knowing mistaken views [76a21]

[First is knowing mistaken views. This involves] knowing the fundamental roots 根本 of [mistaken] views, knowing the causes and conditions 因縁 that arouse [mistaken] views, knowing the far and near 久近 [that is, the past, present, and future] of [mistaken] views, and knowing the overlapping numbers 重數 of the delusions of [mistaken] views.

1. Knowing the fundamental roots of views [76a22]

What is it to know the fundamental roots of [mistaken] views? The [mistaken] view of the self is the basic root of all [mistaken] views. The mind of a single deluded thought is the basic root of the [mistaken] view of the self. Immeasurable [mistaken] views arise from this deluded mind, proliferating vertically and horizontally [in all directions] such that they cannot be calculated. The various karmic bonds are created through these [mistaken] views, so that one falls into the three [evil] destinies and floats and spins through them without end. As with a spinning wheel of fire, if you wish to make them cease you must stop the hand [that spins the wheel]. [You should] know that thoughts are not [substantial] thoughts, but that thoughts arise due to deluded conceptions. Again, know that the "self" is not a [substantial] self, and that the "self" arises due to perversions. If such perversions and deluded conceptions cease, the fundamental roots cease [to function], so naturally the branches and leaves [of mistaken views and conceptual attitudes] will pass away.

2. Knowing the causes and conditions that arouse views [76a28]

What is it to know the causes and conditions that arouse [mistaken] views? Causes and conditions are various, and so also the [mistaken] views that arise are different. How can we know them? We can know them through their internal [**76b**] and external marks. The internal and external marks are as follows. The environmental circumstances [lit., "dwelling places" 居處] of sentient beings are various and different. The time or season is hot or cold; the land is high or low; their upbringing is sophisticated or crude, their

bodhisattvas are "great physicians"; therefore they are called "good friends." Why? They know the diseases, they know the medicines, and they apply the medicine according to the disease. Therefore they are like a good physician …

Not [substantial] thoughts 無心: or, "the mind is not a [substantial] mind."

food is rich or meager [lit., "dark or pale" 濃淡]. Since their circumstances are different, so the results and retributions are various and different. Even those who come from the same climate 土風 [are different]: some are thrifty 蓄 and some are profligate 散, some are generous 豊 and some frugal 儉, some have [possessions] and some do not have [possessions], some gain 得 and some lose 失; there is poverty 貧 and wealth 富, hunger 飢 and satiety 飽, and so forth. Physical appearances are also different: [people are] short 矬 or tall 長, comely 端 or ugly 醜, grand 偉 or lean 瘠, healthy 健 or sickly 病, and so forth. Their personalities [or "fundamental natures" 根性] are various and different, and can be joyful or evil. Some are indifferent to fame and abandon high [social] status to enjoy themselves by cutting wood or fishing. Some "rein in a bull to attain [the rank of] prime minister" or "carry a kettle to become a cabinet minister." Some specialize in the literary arts, and some specialize in the martial arts. Some are absorbed in wine, and some have a fondness for tasty [food]. There is much greed, much extravagance, much anger, much [seeking after] pleasure, much ignorance, much frailty. In this way there are hundreds of thousands of millions of variations. These many various distinctions apply just to the human condition; how much more unspeakable variety is there among other kinds of beings? In this way there is a great variety and difference among sentient beings and the world in which they dwell, so you should know that their karmic deeds are also different. Because their karmic deeds are different, they arouse different [mistaken] views. Thus by perceiving the end results you can know the basic roots, and by perceiving the external [marks] you can distinguish and know the internal [features].

Indifferent to fame and abandon status to enjoy themselves by cutting wood or fishing 忽榮棄位樵漁自樂: this is followed by classical examples of people who will do anything, including putting themselves in danger or degrading themselves, in order to attain high rank or social status.

Rein in a bull to attain [the rank of] prime minister 扣牛干[宰]相: a classical reference to Ning-chi 甯戚. The *Huai-nan tzu* 淮南子 tells the story of how Ning-chi "reined in" or "knocked on" 扣 the horns of a bull and sang a song; the emperor heard of this and promoted Ning-chi to the rank of "prime minister" 宰相.

Carry a kettle to become a cabinet minister 負鼎邀卿[相]: a reference to I Yin 伊尹, famous minister of the ancient T'ang (Mathews has "1766 BC"). In the *Shih-chi* it says, "In ancient times Emperor Shun was caught in a burning granary and trapped in a well; I Yin was obliged to carry tripods and sacrificial stands;..." (Burton Watson, tr., *Records of the Grand Historian* 2, 453). Ikeda (*Kenkyūchushaku*, 381), based on Chan-jan's commentary (BT–IV, 144), explains that I Yin always carried around a kettle, proclaiming that if he was promoted to the rank of a cabinet minister, he would govern the way a chef prepares savorous food in a kettle.

3. Knowing the far and near (past, present, and future) of views [76b11]

What is it to know the "far and near" arising of [mistaken] views? It is to know that [the effects of] the accumulation and multiple layers of such [mistaken] views are not limited to one lifetime; to know that such-and-such views arose in a recent lifetime [in the past]; to know that such-and-such views happen to have arisen in this life [in the present]; and to know that such-and-such views will flourish in a future life.

4. Knowing the overlapping numbers of views [76b14]

What is it to know the many or few overlapping numbers of [mistaken] views? Three [types of] conventionalities emerge from one [mistaken] view of existence. Again, four options [of the tetralemma] emerge from the three conventionalities. These three conventionalities combine to involve twelve options. Again, the four methods of instruction *(siddhānta)* emerge from the four options [of the tetralemma]; combining with the twelve options to give forty-eight [variations on the] *siddhānta*s. Again, the nature of emptiness 性空 and the marks of emptiness 相空 emerge from one *siddhānta*, so the forty-eight [variations of] *siddhānta*s combine to give ninety-six [types of] the nature and marks of emptiness. Each and every option involves cessation and contemplation, combining to give one hundred and ninety-two options of cessation-and-contemplation. These combined with the previous fundamental [mistaken views] gives a total of three hundred and forty-eight options. This applies to those who practice [the path] based on faith [from hearing and learning the Buddha Dharma]; the same can be applied to those who practice [the path] based on Dharma[-meditation]. The same can be applied to those who turn from practice based on faith to practice based on Dharma[-meditation], and the same can be applied to those who change from practice based on Dharma[-meditation] to practice based on faith. If we combine [all the options from] these four [types of] people, there are one thousand three hundred and ninety-two (1,392) options. This applies to one [mistaken] view of existence. The same is true for one [mistaken] view of non-existence. The same is true for one [mistaken] view of "both existence and non-existence." The same is true for one [mistaken] view of "neither existence nor non-existence." Together these four [types of] views give five thousand five hundred and sixty-eight (5,568) options. It is thus for the individual fourfold views. It is also thus for the multiple fourfold views. It is also thus for the integrated or combined fourfold views. Together these three types of the four [mistaken] views give sixteen thousand seven hundred and four (16,704) options. The [fourfold] views that are beyond words are like the first view of existence; that is, it involves only one thousand three hundred and ninety-two options. Thus the combined total [for the four types of fourfold views] is eighteen thousand and ninety-six (18,096) options. These are objects to be destroyed or deconstructed; it is also the same for [the subject that] does the destroying or deconstructing. Combining the objects and subjects gives [76c] thirty six thousand one hundred and ninety-two (36,192). The practice for [saving] oneself is also like this, and [the activity of] saving others is also like this. Combining that of saving oneself and others gives a total of seventy two thousand three hundred and eighty-four (72,384). If we were to continue in this fashion with regard to all sixty-two [mistaken views] and eighty-eight [passionate] afflictions, discussing them in terms of the three conventionalities, four options, and so forth, we would come up with an immeasurable, unlimited, and inexhaustible [number of overlapping options and varieties of mistaken views].

The various aspects of disease are thus immeasurable, but the bodhisattva knows them all. [A bodhisattva] knows what and how the options combined to make this view, and knows what and how the options combined to make that view, whether it is deep or shallow or light or heavy. [The bodhisattva] skillfully distinguishes [concerning these views], without making any errors. This is called "knowing [the second Noble Truth of] the causes [of suffering]." When you already know the causes [of suffering], then you are able to know [the first Noble Truth of] suffering, that sufferings and their causes flow in the cycle [of samsara]; this involves a minute elucidation of the "root and branches," the origin and results [of mistaken views].

Again, if before you realize emptiness you universally contemplate the [mistaken] views and conceptual attitudes and thoroughly know the marks of disease, this is a [skillful] means for emerging in conventionality, and can later be used as one gate for severing delusions and entering or realizing emptiness. When you emerge in conventionality, it will be easy for you to discriminate among the [mistaken] views and conceptual attitudes and illuminate them, and even a light cultivation of cessation-and-contemplation will make the Dharma eye clear. When those of the two vehicles realize emptiness, they rely exclusively on one gate or method, so they do not have these "preliminary inducements" 弄引. It is a mistaken application of medicine [to use these methods as] the teaching for the two [types of Mahāyāna] disciples. Also, [those of the two vehicles] are lacking in the five intentional meanings [for realizing conventionality]; how can they enter or realize conventionality? Bodhisattvas, on the other hand, have the power of good and

Two disciples 二弟子: that is, those who practice based on faith and on Dharma-meditation? This may be a reference to a passage in the *Mahāparinirvāṇa Sūtra* (T 12.766a–b) which speaks of mixing the ambrosia of the true Dharma with the poisonous "medicine" of evil bhikṣus, but the context is not very applicable here.

skillful means, great compassion, their original vows, and great diligence. Or, by silencing all conceptual attitudes [bodhisattvas] arouse the Dharma eye, thus differentiating and knowing the diseases of [mistaken] views. Or, by penetrating contemplation of the phenomena of the [mistaken] views [bodhisattvas] arouse the wisdom of the path and clearly and fully know the phenomena of the delusions. If you do not realize this, then merely with the power of diligence you should strive to polish [the practice of] cessation-and-contemplation. When the internal causes mature, you will externally receive the support of the Buddha 佛加. Whether this is hidden or manifested, you will become fully awake and disclose awakening, and will clearly and fully know the diseases of [mistaken] views. You will know yourself and know others, as in seeing various colors and forms in a mirror, and your judgement of the truth will be unhindered.

2. Knowing conceptual attitudes [76c18]

Next is to clarify [four parts]: [1] knowing the fundamental root of the disease of conceptual attitudes, [2] knowing the causes and conditions for the arising of conceptual attitudes, [3] knowing the "far and near" of the arising of conceptual attitudes, and [4] knowing the overlapping numbers of the diseases of conceptual attitudes. The [first] three parts should be known from the discussion of the diseases of [mistaken] views [as discussed above], that is, the conventionality of conceptual attitudes has ignorance as its root, and so forth.

The overlapping numbers [of the conceptual attitudes] is as follows. The nine stages include eighty-one levels. The first level involves three conventionalities, and there are four options of cessation-and-contemplation, so the three conventionalities combine [with the four options] to give twelve options. One option includes the faith and understanding [of those who practice the path based on faith] and the insight and attainment [of those who practice the path based on Dharma-meditation], and each of these involves the use of the four *siddhānta*s; thus [the practices based on] faith and Dharma[-meditation] each involve eight [aspects], combining to give sixteen aspects. [The practices based on] faith and Dharma[-meditation]

Great compassion, their original vows 大悲本願: or, "their original vows of great compassion."

Sixteen aspects 十六番: as with the mistaken views, there are those who practice based on faith in the teachings they have heard and learned, those who practice based on Dharma-meditation, those who change from practice based on faith to that based on meditation, and those who change from practice based on meditation to that of practice based on faith. Each of these options contain eight variations: the four *siddhānta*s, multiplied by the two aspects of "faith and understanding" or "insight and attainment."

each involves changing to the other practice, giving an additional sixteen [aspects], combining with the previous [sixteen aspects] to give thirty-two options. Thus one option already contains thirty-two options. These thirty-two combined with the twelve options of the three conventionalities gives three hundred and eighty-four options. Each option also includes the two aspects of emptiness, that is, the nature and marks 性相 [of emptiness], combining for seven hundred and sixty-eight (768) options. If we combine this with the previous total, there are one thousand one hundred and fifty-two (1152) options. [The twelve options of] the fundamental root [of conceptual attitudes] gives one thousand one hundred and sixty-four (1164) options. [77a] This is so for one level, so the nine levels together give a total of ten thousand four hundred and seventy-six (10,476) options. This is so for the nine levels of the realm of desires; combining the nine levels of the triple world gives ninety-four thousand two hundred and eighty-four (94,284) options. This is so for the objects to be destroyed or deconstructed; it is the same for the subject who does the destroying or deconstructing. Combining [the options for] the objects and subjects gives one hundred eighty-eight thousand five hundred and sixty-eight (188,568) options. The practice for [saving] oneself is also like this, and [the activity of] saving others is also like this. Combining these gives a total of three hundred seventy-seven-thousand one hundred and thirty-six (377,136) options for cessation-and-contemplation [of conceptual attitudes]. If we would discuss this minutely, each and every one of these levels includes immeasurable levels; each and every dhyāna meditation includes immeasurable dhyāna meditations, [six] supranormal powers [three illuminating] insights, [eight] liberations or renunciations and so forth. Thus by the time one arouses just the various dhyāna meditations [there are so many variations that] they cannot be described, not to mention [the immeasurable conceptual attitudes that are destroyed or deconstructed at] the various levels of the various dhyāna meditations. [The conceptual attitudes that are destroyed] within the various levels also include the options of the three conventionalities, the [four] contemplations, and so forth. Their numbers are difficult to comprehend. If we say that the delusions of [mistaken] views are [a vast expanse like] forty *li* of water, these [delusions of conceptual attitudes are like] coming

94,284 options 九萬四千二百八十四句: it seems to me that the previous number should be multiplied by three (the triple world) instead of nine, but whose counting?

[Six] supranormal powers [three illuminating] insights, [eight] liberations or renunciations 通明背捨: basically the six supranormal powers, the three illuminating insights and the eight liberations/renunciations, as explained previously.

Forty *li* of water 四十里水 ...: these terms, if not the interpretation, come from

in contact with one drop of water, which is equivalent to ten *li* of water [of mistaken views]. Since these [conceptual attitudes] do not arise along side [each other], they are compared to drops of water which, if a large number are multiplied and overlaid together, would become [an expanse of] ten *li* [of water].

Those of the two vehicles directly realize emptiness, so they do not make these distinctions. Bodhisattvas first destroy or deconstruct the conventionality of conceptual attitudes as [skillful] means. First they get to know them in general [that is, realize their emptiness], then they emerge in conventionality and cultivate its contemplation, which helps to open the Dharma eye. In general 通 they use both cessation and contemplation, and this is their gate or method for knowing conventionality. There are various methods for cultivating them distinctly 別. Putting an end to conditioned thoughts 緣念 is called "cessation." [A bodhisattva cultivating] a relation 緣 to the delusions of conceptual attitudes is called "contemplation." With the power of great compassion, great vows, and great diligence, and with the majestic support 威加 of the Buddha, [bodhisattvas] become fully awake and disclose understanding, attain the insight of the Dharma eye and the knowledge of the wisdom of the path, and can clearly discriminate and distinguish the features of the diseases of the conventionality of conceptual attitudes.

As we have seen above, the overlapping numbers of [mistaken] views and conceptual attitudes are very complicated, but if they are known in this way, what can obstruct [your practice of cessation-and-contemplation]? [Teachings such as those found in] the five collections of precepts are not particularly heartwarming [or inspiring], but if you respond to these phenomena as you come in contact with them 對緣行事, you will be able to correct yourself and correct others. If you learn these various options, practicing and using them, you can practice [for] yourself and teach others, unhindered and in accordance with your will.

2. *Differentiating the medicine* [77a19]

Second is entering or realizing conventionality and differentiating the medicine. The marks of diseases are immeasurable, so the medicines [to treat the

the *Mahāparinirvāṇa Sūtra*, T 12.824c15–17:

> The passionate afflictions severed by a stream-enterer are equivalent to an expanse of waters whose length and breath is forty *li*. That which remains is like a single hair or drop of water.

This has been quoted above, for a different purpose, at *Mo-ho chih-kuan* 69a17.

Five collections of precepts 五部律 : the Vinaya collections associated with five of the traditional Indian sects: Theravādin, Mahīśāsakas, Dharma-guptakas, Sarvāstivādins, and Mūlasarvāstivādins; see Lamotte, *History*, 593–94 [657].

diseases] are also immeasurable. We can summarize them in three parts: first, the medicine of worldly teachings 世間法藥; second, the medicine of transworldly teachings 出世間法藥; and third, the medicine of the supreme transworldly teachings 出世間上上法藥. The *Pancaviṃaśati Sūtra* presents three kinds of "giving the Dharma [teachings]": "The triple refuge 三歸 [in the Buddha, Dharma, and Sangha], the five precepts 五戒 *(pañca-śīla)*, the path of the ten good deeds 十善, the four dhyānas 四禪, the [four] boundless demeanors 無量心, and so forth is called the 'giving of worldly teachings.' The second is the giving of transworldly teachings. The third is the giving of the supreme transworldly teachings." These should be known [as the three types of "giving the Dharma teachings"].

Three kinds of giving the Dharma 三種法施: see the *Pañcaviṃśati Sūtra*, T 8.394a18–b14, which actually presents only two types of "giving the Dharma teachings": worldly and transworldly. Chih-i takes an earlier section of this passage to be the content of his "worldly teachings," the "worldly" teachings in the sūtra become the content of Chih-i's "transworldly teachings," and the "transworldly" teachings in the sūtra become the content of Chih-i's "supreme transworldly teachings":

> [394a18] The bodhisattva finishes the offering and teaches the triple refuge—taking refuge in the Buddha, taking refuge in the Dharma, taking refuge in the Sangha; or teaches receiving the five precepts; or teaches the one-day precepts; or teaches the first dhyāna and so forth up to the concentration of neither conceptions nor non-conceptions; or teaches [the four boundless demeanors of] friendliness, compassion, joy, and equanimity; or teaches mindfulness of the Buddha, mindfulness of the Dharma, mindfulness of the Sangha, mindfulness of the precepts, mindfulness of liberation, and mindfulness of the heavens [?]; or teaches the contemplation of impurity; or teaches the contemplation of counting breaths *(anāpanna)*;...
>
> [394b3] In what ways does the bodhisattva "give the Dharma [teachings]" to assist sentient beings? Subhūti, there are two types of "giving the Dharma [teachings]": the first is worldly and the second is transworldly. What is the giving of the worldly Dharma teachings? It is to preach and make manifest the worldly Dharma teachings, that is, the contemplation of impurity, the mindfulness of your breaths, the four dhyānas, the four boundless demeanors, the four concentrations of non-form. These are the worldly Dharma teachings, which are dharmas that ordinary people can practice. This is called the giving of the worldly Dharma teachings. When the bodhisattva finishes giving these worldly Dharma teachings, with various causes and conditions he teaches and transforms [sentient beings], he leads them far away from the worldly teachings. After they are far away from the worldly teachings, he uses the power of skillful means to lead them to attain the noble and undefiled Dharma and the fruits of the noble and undefiled Dharma. What is this "noble and undefiled Dharma"? The noble and undefiled Dharma are the thirty-seven auxiliary parts of the way and the gates of three liberations. The fruits of the noble and undefiled Dharma are the fruits of the stream-enterer through that of the arhat, the path of the pratyekabuddha, and supreme enlightenment *(anuttarasaṃyaksambodhi)*.

1. The medicine of worldly teachings [77a24]

The *Ta chih tu lun* says, "What does it mean to utilize the giving of the worldly Dharma teachings? It is analogous to when a prince falls from a high place and his father the king, with loving thoughts, places silk on the ground where he falls to deliver him from pain and harm. It is the same for sentient beings. If they should fall into the three [evil] destinies, the Noble One, with compassionate thoughts, tentatively entices 權接引 them with good worldly teachings, to deliver them from the evil realms." However, ordinary deluded beings cannot know by themselves even this medicine of worldly teachings. All of them [depend on] the Noble One to "entrust his traces" 託迹 to the same [world] as ordinary beings, guiding and teaching 誘誨 them as ignorant children as long as there is no Buddha in the world. The *Mahāparinirvāṇa Sūtra* says, "All of the worldly, non-Buddhist scriptures are [actually] [77**b**] the teachings of the Buddha, and are not non-Buddhist teachings." The *Suvarṇaprabhāsa Sūtra* says, "All the good discussions in the world are all based on this sūtra." If you have a profound knowledge of the worldly teachings, [you realize that] this is the Buddha Dharma [itself].

What does it mean to utilize the giving of the worldly Dharma teachings? 何惠用世間法施 ...: the *Inyō* attributes this passage to the *Ta chih tu lun*, T 25.682c, where there is an extended discussion of the "giving of Dharma teachings." As Ikeda (*Kenkyūchūshaku*, 381) points out, however, this passage does not contain the analogy used by Chih-i.

All of the worldly, non-Buddhist scriptures are the teachings of the Buddha, and are not non-Buddhist teachings 一切世間外道經書皆是佛說非外道說: see the *Mahāparinirvāṇa Sūtra*, T 12.653c17–22:

> The Buddha said to Kāśyapa, "All the various discussions, spells, words, and texts are the teachings of the Buddha, and are not non-Buddhist teachings." The bodhisattva Kāśyapa said to the Buddha, "World Honored One, what are the fundamental teachings of the Tathāgata?" The Buddha said, "Good son. First I taught the partial teachings [lit., "half-words"] as my fundamental [teachings], using various discussions, spells, texts and such as the real Dharma teachings. Ordinary beings learned these words as basic [teachings], but later when they were able, they knew that this Dharma was not the [real, complete] Dharma."

All the good discussion in the world are all based on this sūtra 一切世間所有善論皆因此經: see the *Suvarṇaprabhāsa Sūtra*, T 16.344a8–10:

> Therefore the Tathāgata, for the sake of sentient beings, preaches the *Suvarṇaprabhāsa Sūtra* in this way. The worldly and transworldly matters of state and discussions produced by sentient beings and human kings in Jambudvīpa—these are all based on this sūtra. Wishing to lead sentient beings to attain peaceful bliss, the Tathāgata Śākyamuni proclaimed this sūtra and disseminated it broadly 廣宣流布.

If you have a profound knowledge of the worldly teachings, this is the Buddha Dharma 深識世法即是佛法: these statements go even further than the famous claim in the *Ta chih tu lun* that "all good and beautiful words are the words of the Buddha" (T 25.66b2–3), and Chih-i is

Why? The ten good deeds bundled together are [equivalent to, correspond to] the five precepts. If you profoundly know the meaning of the five constant (virtues) 五常 [of humaneness, duty, propriety, wisdom, and trust] and the five elements 五行 [of wood, fire, earth, metal, and water], [you will see that] they resemble the five precepts. Treating people with benevolent humaneness 仁慈 and nurturing others without bringing them harm corresponds to the [first] precept of not taking life. Yielding to what is dutiful 義 and honest 廉, and sacrificing yourself to favor others, corresponds to the precept of not stealing [or, "not taking what is not offered"]. Keeping propriety 禮 and behaving according to social custom 規矩, such as binding up your hair [in preparation] for marriage, corresponds to the precept to abstain from sexual misconduct. To have clear and sharp wisdom like a mirror, to be straightforward in your actions, and to act in accordance with the principles of the path, corresponds to the precept of not indulging in intoxicating beverages. To keep tokens of trust, to record things truthfully, and to act sincerely without taking advantage [of others] corresponds to the precept of avoiding false speech. These five constant (virtues) were established by [the Duke of] Chou and Confucius to be the medicine of worldly teachings that can save people and heal disease.

Again, [the characteristics of] the five elements resemble the five precepts. "Not taking life" resembles wood, "not stealing" resembles metal,

making quite a broad claim here. But does he really mean to go as far as he does? How about other passages where he criticizes non-Buddhist teachings, comparing them to the light of a firefly in contrast to the light of the sun for the Buddhist teachings (see *Mo-ho chih-kuan*, 32c17-22)? How about non-Buddhist teachings that blatantly contradict Buddhist teachings? Would he not want to qualify it more, such as "good" or "correct" non-Buddhist teachings, or the "real" or "deeper" meaning of non-Buddhist teachings? Or does he really mean that all non-Buddhist teachings per se in some way contain, or are potential "means" for realizing, the Buddha Dharma?

Binding up your hair 結髮: in contrast, perhaps, to "letting your hair down," is symbolic of chastity and propriety. Ikeda (*Kenkyūchūshaku*, 382) points out that this refers to a classical phrase from Chinese poetry of "binding the hair to become man and wife" (see fascicle 29 of the *Wen-hsüan* 文選).

Tokens of trust 信契: lit., "receipts," "promissory notes," or "bills of sale," that is, tokens or notes that record transactions or IOUs. The implication is that you honor your commitments and are honest in your dealings.

Resemble 防: the character means "to impede, protect, ward off, guard against, protect," but the literal meaning does not make sense here. Perhaps the character is used here as a homonym for 仿, meaning "resemble, imitate," thus implying "is tantamount to, is parallel to"?

Wood 木: in the symbolic system of the five elements, "wood" stands for the east, spring, new life, birth, and so forth. Thus

"abstaining from sexual misconduct" resembles water, "avoiding false speech" resembles earth, and "not indulging in intoxicating beverages" resembles fire.

Again, [the teachings of] the five classics [of the *Book of Changes, Books of History, Music, Rites,* and *Odes*] resemble the five precepts. The *Rites* 禮[記] clarify "restraint," which resembles [the precept against] indulging in intoxicating beverages. *[The Book of] Music* 樂 assuages the heart and mind, which resembles [the precept against] lasciviousness. The *Odes* 詩 use persuasion, which resembles [the precept against] taking life. The *Books of History* 尚書 clarify duty and yielding [to authority and what is right], which resembles [the precept against] stealing. The *Book of Changes* 易 deciphers the yin and the yang 陰陽, which resembles [the precept against] false speech.

If you carefully penetrate to the acme [lit. "extreme"] of these teachings of worldly wisdom, there is nothing that excels them and nothing that surpasses them; they lead all to be convinced [of the right way] and they act as a guide [for human beings]. Bodhisattvas who emerge in conventionality and who wish to know these teachings should distinctly set their mind to cultivate [the worldly teachings] within the contemplations of the [six] supranormal powers. If they, with the vows of great compassion, cultivate [these practices] diligently without neglect, they will receive the majestic support of the Buddhas, become fully awake and have clear understanding, and will never become entangled with doubts concerning the worldly teachings.

However, the medicine of worldly teachings is not the ultimate cure. Even if an inchworm moves its feet [quickly] and tries to pass across the entire world of triple existence, it will certainly fall back and revert [to its original state]. Therefore it must be said that even though ordinary people

it suggests the precept against taking life.

Metal 金: or "gold," stands for money, thus implying the precept against stealing.

Water 水: stands for north, darkness, fluidity, and the reproductive organs (or the lower part of the body), suggesting the precept against sexual misconduct.

Earth 土: stands for the center, the color yellow, the mediator for the other four elements, the axis, and proper communication. Thus it suggests the precept against false speech.

Fire 火: stands for the heart and for alcoholic beverages.

Teachings of the five classics 五經: some of these parallels are not very convincing, but Chih-i is in a position where he must fill in all the categories.

Restraint 撙節: a phrase from the book of *Rites* (part 1): "The gentleman respects restraint, and shows his propriety by holding back" 君子恭敬撙節退讓以明禮.

Contemplation of supranormal powers 通明觀: these practices are expounded in detail later in the *Mo-ho chih-kuan*, 121a–c.

World of triple existence 三有: that is, the triple world of desires, form, and no-form.

cultivate dhyāna with defilements, the aptness of their mental activity is like a leaky vessel; even though they give rise to [a state of] non-conceptuality, they will again fall back and revert [to their former state]. This is like when it rains on a dyed robe and the color washes out. Even though a physician of this world can provide some healing, this healing [does not last] and there is a recurrence [of the disease].

2. The medicine of transworldly teachings [77b21]

Next is the clarification of knowing the medicine of transworldly Dharma teachings. As it says in the *Mahāparinirvāṇa Sūtra*, "At times [the Buddha] preaches 'faith' as the path; or he teaches 'according to their pleasure or needs'; or he teaches non-indolence; or he teaches diligence; or he teaches the meditation on [the impurity of] the body; or he teaches concentration proper; or he teaches the cultivation of impermanence; or he teaches going to the forest [for ascetic practice; *araṇya*]; or he teaches the teachings for the sake of others; or he teaches upholding the precepts; or he teaches [the importance of] becoming intimate with a 'good friend'; or he teaches the cultivation of compassion, and so forth." Again, as it says in various sūtras,

At times ... and so forth 或說信為道。或說樂欲。或說不放逸。或說精進。或說身念處。或說正定。或說修無常。或說蘭若處。或說為他說法。或說持戒。或說親近善友。或說修慈等也: an accurate summary of a much longer passage from the *Mahāparinirvāṇa Sūtra*, T 12.683a4–b1. The context reads:

> The bodhisattva Kāśyapa said to the Buddha, "World Honored One. The meaning of the eightfold path and the Noble Truth of the path do not correspond. Why is this so?" The Tathāgata sometimes teaches *faith* as the path to be saved from defilements. Sometimes he teaches the path of *non-indolence*, that is, the Buddhas, World Honored Ones, attain *anuttarasaṃyaksaṃbodhi* due to non-indolence, and that for bodhisattvas this is a way to assist in practicing the path. Sometimes he teaches that diligence is the path. As he said to Ānanda, if there is a person who is able to persistently cultivate *diligence*, he will attain *anuttarasaṃyaksaṃbodhi*. Sometimes he teaches the contemplation of *meditating on [the impurity of] the body*, that if you are attached [to physical pleasures] you should diligently cultivate the meditation on [the impurity of] the body, and thus attain *anuttarasaṃyaksaṃbodhi*. Sometimes he teaches the path of *samādhi proper*, saying to Mahākāśyapa that samādhi proper is the true path, and that improper concentrations are not the path, and that if you enter proper samādhi and are able to ponder the arising and perishing of the five skandhas [you can attain *anuttarasaṃyaksaṃbodhi*], and not if you do not enter samādhi and ponder [these things]. Sometimes he teaches the one Dharma, that if people cultivate this they can purify sentient beings, extinguish and remove all suffering and passionate afflictions, and attain the true Dharma, that is, the samādhi of contemplating the Buddha. Or again he teaches *cultivating the consideration of impermanence* as the path; as he said to the bhikṣus, those who are able to cultivate much the consideration of impermanence are able to attain *anuttarasaṃyaksaṃbodhi*. Or he teaches sitting alone and *pondering in the empty quiet of the forest*, where one is able to

sometimes one single path is the medicine, as in the single-practice samādhi. As the Buddha said to the bhikṣus, you should not take things that belong to others. All dharmas are things that belong to others. If you do not "accept" 受 any of these dharmas, you can become an arhat. You should not "accept" [as final] any of the individual and multiple [mistaken] views, as clarified above. Or [sometimes] two paths is your medicine: cherishing [the practice of] concentration and encouraging [the development of] wisdom. These two "wheels" [77c] [of concentration and wisdom] should be equal [and balanced]. Or, three Dharma teachings are your medicine, that is, precepts,

quickly attain *anuttarasaṃyaksaṃbodhi*. Sometimes he teaches that *preaching for the sake of people* is the path, and that if people hear the dharma they can sever the chains of doubt, and if the chains of doubt are severed they can attain *anuttarasaṃyaksaṃbodhi*. Sometimes he teaches the upholding of the precepts as the path; as he said to Ānanda, if people diligently cultivate the upholding of the precepts of prohibition, these people can be saved from the great suffering of saṃsāra. Sometimes he teaches [the importance of *becoming intimate with a 'good friend'* and calls this the path; as he said to Ānanda, "If you approach and become intimate with a good friend, then you can rest assured in the pure precepts; if sentient beings can approach and become intimate with me, they can attain the mind of *anuttarasaṃyaksaṃbodhi*." Sometimes he teaches the *cultivation of compassion* as the path, and that those who cultivate compassion sever all passionate afflictions and are unmovable. Sometimes he teaches wisdom as the path;... [and so forth].

[683b10] Then the World Honored One praised the bodhisattva Kāśyapa saying, "Well done, well done. Good son, you now wish to know the secrets in the sublime bodhisattva scriptures of the Mahāyāna, and therefore you have framed this question. Good son. These [teachings] in the various sūtras are all ways to realize the [Noble] Truth of the path. Good son. As I have taught previously, if there are those who have faith in the path, this faith is fundamental and it is able to assist people on the path of *bodhi*-wisdom. Therefore what I teach is not mistaken. Good son, the Tathāgata is well aware of immeasurable means and, wishing to save sentient beings, uses various teachings in this way. Good son, this is *like a good physician who knows the various sources of the diseases of sentient beings, and applies medicine in accordance with their maladies.*

Single-practice samādhi 一行三昧: see Chih-i's presentation of this samādhi earlier in the *Mo-ho chih-kuan*, 11a28–12a19.

These two wheels should be equal 二輪平等: for a classic exposition of this idea see the introduction to the *Hsiao chih-kuan*, T 46.462b7–18:

> There are many ways to enter the true reality of nirvana, but none that is more essential or goes beyond the twofold method of cessation-and-contemplation 止觀. The reason is that "cessation" is the preliminary gate for overcoming the bonds [of passionate afflictions] 伏結; "contemplation" is the proper requisite for severing delusions 斷惑. "Cessation" provides good nourishment for nurturing the mind; "contemplation" is the sublime technique for arousing spiritual understanding 神解. "Cessation" is the preeminent cause 勝因 for [attaining] dhyāna concentration 禪定; "contemplation" is the basis [for the accumulation of] 由籍 of wisdom 智慧. If one perfects

concentration, and wisdom 戒定慧. Or, four Dharma teachings are your medicine, that is, the four mindfulnesses 四念處. Or, five Dharma teachings

the twofold aspects of concentration (samādhi 定) and wisdom 慧, then one is fully endowed with the aspects of both benefiting oneself 自利 and benefiting others 利他.

Therefore it says in the *Lotus Sutra*,

> The Buddha himself dwells in the Mahāyāna,
> And in accordance with his attainments
> Is adorned with the power of concentration and wisdom,
> With which he saves sentient beings.

It should be known that these two aspects are like the two wheels of a cart, or the two wings of a bird; if one side is cultivated disproportionately, then one falls prey to mistaken excess. Therefore it says in a sūtra,

> One who disproportionately cultivates the blessings and virtues of dhyanic concentration and does not study wisdom is called "stupid" 愚. One who disproportionately studies wisdom and does not cultivate the blessings and virtues of dhyāna concentration is called "crazy" 狂.

The excessive faults of stupidity and craziness are different only in a minor way, and there is no difference between them in the sense that [they contribute to] mistaken views and [encourage further] transmigration. Unless they are balanced and equal, then your practice is not perfect and complete. How, then, can one quickly ascend to the ultimate fruit [of Buddhahood]?

One, two, three, four Dharmas: for the categories of one to four dharmas, Chih-i seems to be following a passage from the *Ta chih tu lun*, T 25. 198a23–b1. Lamotte (*Le Traité* 3, 1144–45) translates:

> C'est comme un maître de médicaments *(bhaiṣajyaguru)* qui ne peut pas guérir toutes les maladies *(vhādhi)* par *un même et unique médicament (bhaṣajya)*: les maladies étant dissemblables, le remède à appliquer n'est pas unique. De même le Buddha s'adapte aux diverses formes de maladies mentales *(cittavyādhi)* [dont souffrent] les êtres et les guérit par des remèdes divers.
>
> *Tantôt le Buddha sauve les êtres en ne prêchant qu'une seule chose. C'est ainsi que le Buddha dit à un bhikṣu: "Ce n'est pas tien, ne le prends pas (na tāvakaṃ, tan mā gṛhāṇa)."* — Le bhikṣu dit: "Je le sais déjà, ô Bhagavat." — Le Buddha reprit: "Que sais-tu?" — Le bhikṣu répondit: "Les dharma ne sont pas miens *(ātmīya)*: il ne faut pas les prendre."
>
> *Tantôt le Buddha sauve les êtres par deux choses: la concentration (samādhi) et la sagesse (prajñā). Tantôt, c'est par trois choses: la moralité (śīla), la concentration (samādhi) et la sagesse (prajñā). Tantôt, c'est par quatre choses: les quatre fixations-de-l'attention (smṛtyupasthāna).*
>
> Ainsi donc, bien que les quatre fixations-de-l'attention suffisent pour obtenir le Chemin, il est encore d'autres dharma qui en diffèrent par l'exercice *(ācāra)*, les conceptions *(vikalpa)*, la quantité et le point de vue. C'est pourquoi il faut aussi prêcher les quatre efforts corrects *(samyakpradhāna)* et les autres dharma [auxiliaires].

Chodron (3, 943) translates:

> It is like a master physician who cannot cure all sickness with a single drug: sicknesses are dissimilar and the remedy to be applied is not single. In the same way, the Buddha adapts himself to the various types of mental illnesses from which beings suffer and cures them with different remedies.
>
> Sometimes the Buddha saves beings by preaching only one thing. Thus the Buddha said to a bhikṣu: "This is not yours, do not grasp it." – The bhikṣu said: "I know it already, O Bhagavat." – The

are your medicine, that is, the five powers 五力. Or, six Dharma teachings [are your medicine], that is, the six mindfulnesses 六念; or the seven components of awakening 七覺; or the eightfold right path 八正道; or the nine considerations 九想 [of decaying corpses]; or the ten wisdoms 十智. In this way you can increase the numbers and clarify [the practices of] the path, up to eighty-four thousand, or even as many as cannot be counted. Or, there could be many of a single Dharma teaching, or even an immeasurable amount of a single Dharma teaching, or a single Dharma teaching that cannot be expressed. Or, there could be many of ten Dharma teachings, or even an immeasurable amount of ten Dharma teachings, or ten Dharma teachings that cannot be expressed. Each and every single Dharma teaching has various names, various features, and various healing [powers]. All bodhisattvas who emerge in conventionality [that is, who go beyond emptiness to realize conventionality, and appears in the mundane world to save beings] should know these matters, and for the sake of sentient beings accumulate various medicines of Dharma teachings. This is like a pilot [of a boat] on the sea—if you do not know [what is necessary] you cannot benefit beings [and ferry them to the other shore]. Those who wish to know these matters [should] single-mindedly cultivate cessation-and-contemplation, and with the powers of great compassion, vows, and diligence, they receive the majestic support of the Buddhas, arouse and open the Dharma eye, and all are able to know fully, as in taking a fruit in your palm and contemplating it.

> Bhagavat replied: "What do you know?" – The bhikṣu answered: "Dharmas are not 'mine'; they should not be grasped."
>
> Sometimes the Buddha saves beings by means of two things, concentration and wisdom. Sometimes, by three things, morality, concentration and wisdom. Sometimes by four things, the four foundations of mindfulness.
>
> Thus, although the four foundations of mindfulness are enough to attain the Path, there are other dharmas that differ in practice, concepts, quantity and point of view. This is why the four right efforts and the other [auxiliary] dharmas must also be preached.

Six mindfulnesses 六念: these are spelled out by Chih-i below; see 77c25–78a1 (see also Ikeda [*Kenkyūchūshaku*, 488]). The six types of mindfulness are: 1. mindfulness of the Buddha 念佛, to be mindful of and want to become a Buddha; 2. mindfulness of the Dharma 念法, to be mindful of the Buddha's teachings and be committed to it; 3. mindfulness of the Sangha 念僧, to be mindful of cultivating the path of a home-departed one; 4. mindfulness of the precepts 念戒, to be mindful of keeping the precepts; 5. mindfulness of giving 念施, to be mindful of giving to others; and 6. mindfulness of the divine realms 念天, to be mindful of the possibility of being reborn in the divine realms due to the merit accumulated from practicing the Buddhist path.

... ten wisdoms 十智: see Ikeda's list (*Kenkyūchūshaku*, 497), which is somewhat different from the list Chih-i provides; see the discussion and notes below at 78a8–14.

3. The medicine of supreme transworldly teachings [77c11]

Again, [the third part is] to know the medicine of the supreme transworldly teachings. Medicine as one single Dharma teaching in terms of cessation-and-contemplation refers to the one real truth. The merging of ignorant thoughts and the Dharma-nature results in all the appearances of disease. If you contemplate this Dharma-nature, [you realize that] there is no [substantial] Dharma-nature; how much more so for ignorance and all phenomena [or Dharma teachings].

Or, two Dharma teachings are the medicine; this is [the two practices of] cessation and contemplation, to realize the essence of the nature of mind or thoughts [as empty] and to put the empty delusions to rest.

Or, three Dharma teachings are the medicine—cessation, contemplation, and the precepts that are in accordance with the path so that you naturally keep [the precepts]. Again, there are the three kinds of samādhi, of which "realizing emptiness from conventionality" is called the "samādhi of emptiness" 空三昧, not perceiving any features in emptiness is called the "samādhi of formlessness" 無相三昧, and to put an end to the karmic deeds of saṃsāra is called the "samādhi of actionlessness" 無作三昧.

Or, four Dharma teachings are the medicine, that is, the four mindfulnesses. [The first mindfulness is that the physical body is impure, but mistaken] views all depend on visible forms *(rūpa)* and that these forms are neither defiled nor undefiled. [The second mindfulness is to know that sensations are ultimately painful, but] the sensations 受 *(vedanā)* of various [mistaken] views and conceptual attitudes are neither painful nor blissful. [The fourth mindfulness is to know that phenomena are without substantial reality, that is, without selfhood, but you should realize that] the conceptions 想 *(saṃjñā)* and volitions 行 *(saṃskāra)* of [mistaken] views] have neither selfhood nor are lacking in selfhood. [The third mindfulness is to know that thoughts are impermanent, but] the mind 心 of [mistaken] views and conceptual attitudes does not consist of a [substantial] mind, not to mention neither permanent nor impermanent.

Or, five Dharma teachings are the medicine, that is, the five [good] roots 五[善]根. If you have no doubts when you cultivate cessation-and-contemplation, this is the root of faith. If you are constantly mindful of your cessation-and-contemplation and are not mindful of other matters, this is the root of mindfulness 念. If your cessation-and-contemplation never ceases, this is the root of diligence 精. If you single-mindedly stay concentrated, this is the

Precepts that are in accordance with the path 道戒隨; perhaps the same as 道共戒?

The mind 心: here this must refer to "consciousness" 識 *(vijñāna)*, if this follows the above pattern and this refers to the fifth skandha.

root of concentration 定. If through the tetralemma you realize penetrating insight into the essence of [emptiness as] lack of self-being *(asvabhāva)*, this is the root of wisdom 慧. When the five [good] roots grow and expand, they are called the "five powers."

Or, six Dharma teachings are the medicine, that is, the six mindfulnesses 六念處. To become aware, through cessation-and-contemplation, that [mistaken] views and conceptual attitudes are the Dharma-realm of the Buddha, without destroying the Dharma body, is called "mindfulness of the Buddha" 念佛. To constantly bear in mind cessation-and-contemplation without making distinctions between [and becoming attached to] the unitary and different features of cessation-and-contemplation is called "mindfulness of the Dharma 念法. To find rapport with the principle of cessation-and-contemplation, that it has the mark of the unconditioned, is called the "mindfulness of the Sangha" 念僧. **[78a]** [To realize that] the precepts that are in accordance with the path are included in cessation-and-contemplation is called the "mindfulness of the precepts" 念戒. [To realize that] cessation-and-contemplation is the supreme meaning is called "mindfulness of the divine realms" 念天. [To realize that] cessation-and-contemplation is to abandon the delusions of [mistaken] views and conceptual attitudes is called the "mindfulness of abandonment" 念捨.

Or, seven Dharma teachings are the medicine[, that is, the seven components of awakening 七覺支]. Cessation includes three components of awakening: [serenity from] removing [delusions] 除, equanimity or renunciation 捨, and concentration 定. Contemplation includes the components of awakening of discernment 擇, joy 喜, and diligence 精進. [The seventh component of] mindfulness 念 is common to both [cessation and contemplation].

Or, eight Dharma teachings are the medicine[, that is, the eightfold path]. To deconstruct conventionality with the tetralemma is to have "right views" 正見. To arouse and act on right views is called "[right] discrimination" 思惟. To cultivate practices on this basis is called "right deeds" 正業. To express this as cessation-and-contemplation is "right words" 正語. To nurture the body without allowing for improper behavior is called the "right way of life" 正命. To neither be detached from nor forget [your practice and purpose] is called "right mindfulness" 正念. Cessation is called "right concentration" 正定. Uninterrupted mindfulness is called "[right] diligence" 精進.

Or, nine Dharma teachings are the medicine[, that is, the nine consider-

Mindfulness of abandonment 念捨: according to some lists, the "mindfulness of giving" 念施. Chih-i often substitutes the character "abandon" 捨 for "giving" 施.

[Serenity from] removing 除 **[delusions]**: since all the other components are accounted for, this must refer to the fifth component of "serenity" 輕.

ations of decaying corpses]. Four views involve [considering] the impurity of the five skandhas; viewing the change and destruction of the five skandhas [upon the death of a human being] is called "considering the change in color" [of the corpse], and so forth up to ninth [consideration].

Or, ten Dharma teachings are the medicine, that is, the ten wisdoms 十智. [Realizing the truth about] the two conventionalities of [mistaken] views and conceptual attitudes are the "wisdoms of [the Noble Truths of] suffering and their causes" 集苦智. Cessation-and-contemplation is the "wisdom of [the Noble Truth of] the path" 道智. [To realize that] the twenty-five types of existence do not arise is the "wisdom of [the Noble Truth of] extinction" 滅智. To know the triple world just like this is the "wisdom of thisness" 比智. To teach in accordance with worldly names and words is called "worldly wisdom" 世智. To know that other sentient beings are also like this is called "the wisdom of [knowing] the mind of others" 他心智. To know how to discriminate or distinguish among all phenomena is called the "wisdom of equality" 等智. To know the exhaustion of suffering and its causes is called the "wisdom of exhaustion" 盡智. Undefiled wisdom is called the "wisdom of non-arising 無生智.

You should know that, in order to benefit sentient beings, [the practice of] cessation-and-contemplation should be increased or decreased in accordance with those people's capacities. Therefore up to ten [types of medicine or teachings] have been provided, but there are actually Buddha Dharmas as numerous as the sands of the Ganges River. This is analogous to Shen Nung tasting grasses and establishing prescriptions; one medicine or two medicines and so forth up to ten medicines can be the prescription, or many medicines can be the prescription. A prescription is established in accordance with the disease; it is not unrelated to the causes and conditions [of the disease]. Bodhisattvas who [re-]emerge in conventionality are also like this. They know the various Dharma teachings, from one teaching to two teachings up to immeasurable teachings; [they consider] whether there is a single disease or manifold diseases. Again, [they know that] there are various medicines—[made from] skins, meat, juice, fruit, roots, stems, branches, leaves—each individual in this way. Some are from the sea, mountains, lakes, or land; places in the four directions each provide their own [type of medi-

Wisdom of thisness 比智: perhaps this refers to the "wisdom of dharmas" in Ikeda's list (497)?

Wisdom of [knowing] the mind or thoughts of others 他心智: perhaps this is the "wisdom of types" 類 in Ikeda's list?

Shen Nung 神農: a legendary "emperor" dating back to 2838 BC, a supposed teacher of husbandry (MATHEWS, 792). The compiler of the *Catalogue of Herbs* 本草綱目 that set the standard in China for herbal prescriptions.

cine]. Some are plucked, dug out, dried, or steamed, each at the appropriate time. Again, they know that various medicines each have their own specific healing powers. Bodhisattvas who emerge in conventionality know the faculties of sentient beings and can discriminate the appropriate teaching for them in this way. They know which of this or that individual teaching, or which of the many teachings, fits their aspirations. They know whether this one teaching or two teachings [and so forth] do not fit their aspirations. They know whether this one teaching or two teachings [and so forth] are appropriate, and which are not appropriate, to heal or not heal [their diseases]. They can judge and discriminate whether [beings] can realize the supreme meaning or cannot realize the supreme meaning.

If you wish to heal only one disease, then one medicine is sufficient, but if you wish to be a great physician [and heal many diseases], you must have a universal expertise in various medicines. Those of the two vehicles [merely] heal their own delusions, and so [for them] one teaching is sufficient. Bodhisattvas, with their great vows [to save all sentient beings], must know all [medicines and their applications]. Again, consider that the great earth brings forth herbs, but [different] portions 分劑 [or doses] are produced in [different] places; or consider that the water [level] of a great river neither increases when a portion is scooped out, nor decreases when some is added. The medicine of Dharma teachings is also like this. [**78b**] Whether immeasurable cessations are disclosed in one quiescent [act of] concentration, or immeasurable contemplations are disclosed in one great [act of] compassion, they are all true and not vacuous. Again, as the conditions for the diseases of sentient beings are various and not the same, so also the sufferings and pains of various diseases are multifarious and not the same, the efficacy of various medicines are multifarious and not the same, and the conditions for healing disease are multifarious and not the same. Sometimes you should drink hot liquid, or vomit and purge, or use [acupuncture] needles or heat, or [ingest] pills 丸 or powdered 散 [medicine].The circumstances for healing are also not unitary. Bodhisattvas who emerge in conventionality are also like this. They know that the accumulation [or causes] of [mistaken] views, conceptual attitudes, and passionate afflictions is not the same [for various beings]; this is to know [the Noble Truth of] the causes [of suffering]. They know that good and evil, and the results of suffering, are not the same for all sentient beings; this is to know [the Noble Truth of] suffering. They know all

Heat 炙: or, "moxa" 灸 treatment?

Accumulation 集: a variant reading adds the character for "suffering" 苦, which would bring to mind the Four Noble Truths and give the rendering, "know that the causes of suffering from [mistaken] views, conceptual attitudes, and passionate afflictions are not the same."

Dharma teachings; this is to know [the Noble Truth of] the path. They know that all sentient beings are not the same in realizing enlightenment; this is to know [the Noble Truth of] extinction. The bodhisattvas who emerge in conventionality [beyond emptiness] know the various [permutations of] the Four [Noble] Truths universally, without lacking anything.

[end of fascicle 6, part 1]

Next, even if Shen Nung's basic prescriptions are used to heal people in later times, these are not necessarily efficacious. Hua T'o and P'ien Ch'üeh contemplated [and considered] the times and the [available] medicines in implementing further prescriptions. Why did they do this? The lands were [different according to] north and south; people were healthy or sickly; food was salty or bland; medicine was thick or diluted, diseases were light or serious; it was not enough to depend on the basic prescriptions [of Shen Nung] to efficaciously heal [these diseases]. They had to implement [their prescriptions] in accordance with their times [and circumstances] in order to obtain cures and healing. [It is the same with the Buddha and the Dharma teachings.] When the Buddha first appeared in the world, the sentient beings [of that time] had mature capabilities. [The Buddha] taught the Dharma within the limits of their faculties, and there were none who could not attain awakening. In later periods the seepage of emotional delusions took a turn for the worse, so there was no benefit in directly applying the Buddhist sūtras. Bodhisattvas considered peoples' capacities and prepared discourses on the common [intent] of the sūtras, thus leading sentient beings to attain awakening. Their sole intent was to awaken and thus benefit them. This is the proper intent of "entering or realizing conventionality." Why should we obstruct the path of transformation in order to protect the archaic [teachings]? The *Ta chih tu lun* says, "To widely establish various verbal [teachings] on the basis

Shen Nung's basic prescriptions 神農本方: see note above on Shen Nung.

Hua T'o 華他: a famous physician of the 3rd century AD; usually written 華陀.

P'ien Ch'üeh 偏鵲 A famous physician of antiquity. See, for example, the *Shih Chi* (Watson, *Records of the Grand Historian* 1, 116):

> When Kao-tsu was fighting against Ch'ing Pu, he was wounded by a stray arrow and on the way back he fell ill. When his illness continued to grow worse, Empress Lü sent for a skilled doctor. The doctor examined Kao-tsu and, in answer to his question, replied, "This illness can be cured." With this, Kao-tsu began to berate and curse him, saying, "I began as a commoner and with my three-foot sword conquered the world. Was this not the will of Heaven? My fate lies with Heaven. *Even P'ien Ch'üeh, the most famous doctor of antiquity, could do nothing for me!*" In the end he would not let the doctor treat his illness, but gave him fifty catties of gold and sent him away.

To depend on the basic prescriptions to heal 依本方治: as found in the *Catalogue of Herbs* 本草綱目; see notes above.

To widely establish various verbal

of the sūtra teachings, in order to present their meaning; this is called 'giving the Dharma teachings.'" Thus bodhisattvas, in order to cultivate this kind of wisdom, arouse great compassion and universal vows, bolster the power of diligence, and steadily cultivate cessation-and-contemplation. The Buddhas lend their majestic support, and [the bodhisattvas] become fully awakened, [with wisdom] as clear as a mirror. With the wisdom of realizing and entering conventionality, they attain mastery [in benefiting others].

3. Applying the medicine [78b28]

Third is applying the medicine that corresponds to the disease. You already know about the diseases [of the Noble Truths] of suffering and their causes, and you distinguish the medicines [of the Noble Truths] of the path and extinction. If sentient beings do not have the capability for **[78c]** transcending worldly matters, their spiritual capacities are weak, and they cannot endure a profound transformation, you should apply only worldly medicine. Confucius (K'ung Ch'iu 孔丘) and the Duke of Chou (Chi Tan 姬旦) established the categories of lords and ministers, fathers and sons [and so forth]; therefore [people] respect those above and cherish those below, and the world is in a proper order. There is moderation in the rules of propriety, and a proper order of the noble and ignoble; these matters help you keep the [Buddhist] precepts. Music assuages the mind and heart, and modifies manners and deportment; this helps your [practice of] concentration. The former rulers [established] the highest virtues 至德 and the essential way 要道; this helps you with wisdom. The primeval times 元古 were chaotic 混沌, and it was not appropriate for the Buddha to appear in the world. [People with] limited and superficial spiritual capabilities cannot respond to 感 the appearance of a Buddha. [*The Sūtra of Pure Dharma Practices* says,] "I [the Buddha] dispatched the three sages [Confucius, Lao-tzu, and Yen Yüan] to teach and transform the Chinese." Thus propriety is revealed first, and faith

[teachings] on the basis of the sūtra teachings, in order to present their meaning; this is called "giving the Dharma teachings" 依隨經法廣立名字而爲作義名爲法施: see the *Ta chih tu lun* at T 25.227a18–b22ff.; the wording of Chih-i's statement is quite different, but this passage in the *Ta chih tu lun* provides numerous examples of "giving the Dharma," including the comparison to "applying medicine according to the disease." This passage was referred to above in the *Mo-ho chih-kuan*; see note at 24a16–17.

Great compassion and universal vows 大悲誓願: or, "the universal vows of great compassion."

I [the Buddha] dispatched the three sages to teach and transform the Chinese 我遣三聖化彼眞丹: *The Sūtra of Pure Dharma Practices* 清淨法行經 is an apocryphal Chinese text that was believed lost, but was recently rediscovered among the texts of Nanatsu-dera 七寺 in Nagoya,

in the Mahāyāna and Hīnayāna sūtras should come later. This is already the case here in China, and the same applies to [lands and people in] the ten directions. Thus the worldly teachings should be utilized first, and then this [Buddha Dharma] can be applied.

Next, applying the transworldly medicine is as follows. There are ten types of causes and conditions for sentient beings to arise; their spiritual capacities are not the same, and so their diseases are different. Since [they need to be treated] in accordance with their diseases, the medicine to be applied is also different. [Their faculties are] inferior, middling, superior, or most superior.

There are four meanings to "inferior faculties." First is those who seek after that which is narrow and inferior; second is those who are ineffectual in their practice; third is those who are heavily impeded by the five impurities; and fourth is those who are extremely dull with regard to wisdom. For those who seek the "inferior" (Hīnayāna) Dharma, teach the Dharma of arising-and-perishing. For those who are ineffectual in their practice, have them cultivate the six perfections in deed. For those who are heavily impeded by the five impurities, have them work diligently to control them. For those who are dull in wisdom, have them sever their lustful covetousness, anger, and ignorance. This is called "liberation" [for these people]. This is to apply

Japan (see Ochiai Toshinori, *The Manuscripts of Nanatsudera*, 1991). The newly rediscovered texts are currently being edited and published. *The Sūtra of Pure Dharma Practices* is included in volume 2; see *Nanatsu-dera Koitsu Kyōten Kenkyū Sōsho Daini-kan Chūgoku Senjutsu Kyōten*, 1996, 13:

> I will now dispatch as disciples the three sages; they are all good conventional manifestations of bodhisattvas. Mahākāśyapa is here called Lao-tzu; the servant *(kumāra)* Pure Light 光淨童子 is here named Chun Ni 仲尼 [Confucius?]; the Moon Light Confucian/learned child 月明儒童 is here given the title Yen Yüan 顏淵 [a disciple of Confucius]. Thus they will proclaim my Dharma teachings. Lao-tzu produced the *Tao-te [ching]* and Confucius the *Analects*; these texts each have five thousand [characters]. The two sages of Confucius and Yen are the teachers. Together they have given lectures and discourses on the five works of the past 五住: [the books of] poetry 詞, traditions 傅, the changes (yin and yang) 易, rites 禮, and the laws of demeanor 威儀法則. Through these [worldly teachings] the people are gradually directed and taught, and these people [of China] are led to taste the flavor of the Dharma. In this way [the teachings in] the sūtras of the Buddha should pass on to China.

Ten types of causes and conditions 十種因縁: as explained below, four variations for those of inferior faculties, four variations for those of middling faculties, and those of superior and most superior faculties?

Those who seek after that which is narrow and inferior 志樂狹劣: or, "whose incentive or initiative is feeble."

Five impurities 五濁: the impurities of this kalpa, of mistaken views, of passionate afflictions, of sentient beings, and of your lifespan.

the medicine of the teaching of the causes and conditions of arising, which heals the diseases of those of inferior faculties. Although these are all of inferior faculties, they are not the same in the bliss that they seek. The sages [or "bodhisattvas"] have composed discourses that reveal four [teachings, that is, the four "gates" of existence, non-existence, both, and neither]. The Abhidharma is taught for those who seek to hear of existence. This gives rise to a little good and to the destruction of the five impurities, and through this means these people can perceive the real truth *(paramārtha-satya)*. The *Ch'eng-shih lun* is taught for those who seek to hear of non-existence. This gives rise to good, to the destruction of evil, and to a realization of the real [truth of emptiness]. The *Peṭaka Treatise* is taught for those who seek to hear of both existence and non-existence. This gives rise to good, to the destruction of evil, and to a realization of the real. The sūtras that teach freedom from both existence and non-existence are taught for those who seek to hear of neither existence nor non-existence. This gives rise to good, to the destruction of evil, and to a realization of the real. Thus bodhisattvas who emerge in conventionality produce these four [types of] discourses to express the four gates or teachings [of existence, non-existence, both, and neither], apply four [types of] medicine, and heal various diseases.

Next, applying medicine for people of middling faculties is as follows. These are people whose initiative is a little stronger, and whose ability to practice is a little better [than those of inferior faculties], so it is easier for them to give rise to good [insight into] reality. Their impediments from the five impurities are light, and they are a little sharp in their wisdom. In accordance with their inclinations, teach them that "causes and conditions are empty." If they hear this they will give rise to good [insight into] reality, destroy the causes of evil, and have insight into the supreme meaning. This is to apply the medicine of emptiness, which heals those with middling faculties. These people are also of four types: that is, inferior, middling, superior, and most superior; they "enter the [pure and cool] pond" [of wisdom] through the four gates [of existence, non-existence, both, and neither], as explained previously.

Next, to contemplate the applying of medicine for people of superior faculties is as follows. These people have a broad aspiration [to hear the Dharma], their good roots are ripe, they have already removed the five **[79a]** impurities, and have great wisdom. The teaching of the Four [Noble] Truths

The *Peṭaka Treatise* 毘勒論: the first character is different, but this surely refers to the *Peṭaka* (or *Piṭaka*) 毘勒論 of Kātyāyana, which provides the teaching of "both existence and non-existence." See detailed note at *Mo-ho chih-kuan* 73c26.

Good reality 理善: or, "good in principle" in contrast to "good in deed" 事善?

as immeasurable applies to them, and they give rise to the goodness of the realm beyond [delusions]. They gradually sever the five levels [of delusions] and realize the Middle Way. This is to apply the medicine of conventionality, which heals those with superior faculties. These people also are of four types, corresponding to the application of medicine according to the four gates, which should be known as explained above.

Next, to contemplate the applying of medicine for people of the most superior faculties is as follows. In everything, from their aspirations to their wisdom, they are incomparably [highest], and therefore they are called "most superior." The principle [of reality] should be taught to them directly, good arises [without hindrance] like emptiness, obstacles perish like emptiness, and they realize and enter the ultimate path. This is called applying the medicine of the Middle, which heals those with the most superior faculties. This also consists of four gates of applying medicine and healing disease and so forth [as explained above].

If you realize the contemplation of emptiness, [you realize that] there is not even one dharma, so how could there be many dharmas? But now we [go beyond "mere emptiness" and] apply sixteen [variations of the Noble Truths] of the path and extinction for the healing of sixteen [variations of the Noble Truths] of suffering and their causes. This is to realize conventionality. The sublime voices [of the Dharma teachings] should be universally proclaimed in accordance with the appropriate sounds [that can be heard by people according to their capabilities]. Through this their hearing consciousness will be aroused, and eventually [the Dharma teachings] will reach their minds and hearts, leading them to put them into practice, each gaining benefits from them. [As it says in the *Lotus Sūtra*,] "As one cloud causes rain to fall, yet all the grasses and trees each grow [according to their capacities]."

One cloud causes rain to fall 一雲所雨: see the analogy in the chapter on "Medicinal Herbs" in the *Lotus Sūtra*, T 9.19aff. Hurvitz (101–2 [95–96]) translates:

> Kāśyapa, consider the grasses, trees, shrubs, and forests, as well as the medicinal herbs, in their several varieties, and their different names and colors, that the mountains and rivers, the dales and vales of the thousand-millionfold world produce. A thick cloud spreads out, covering the whole thousand-millionfold world and raining down on every part of it equally at the same time, its infusions reaching everywhere. The grass and trees, the shrubs and forests, and the medicinal herbs—whether of small roots, stalks, branches, and leaves, or of middle-sized roots, stalks, branches, and leaves, or or large roots, stalks, branches, and leaves—and also all trees, great and small, whether high, intermediate, or low, all receive some of it. Everything rained on by the same cloud in keeping with its nature gains in size, and its blossoms and fruit spread out and bloom. Though produced by the same earth, and moistened by the same rain, yet the grasses and trees all have their differences. Kāśyapa, know that the Thus Come One is also like this:...

4. The levels of realizing conventionality [79a10]

Fourth is to clarify the levels of entering or realizing conventionality. First is to list the teachings and classify the levels; second is to clarify the benefits; and third is to summarize the universal destruction and deconstruction of dharmas.

1. Listing the teachings and classifying the levels [79a12]

Everyone is probably thinking, "First we should remove the conventionalities of [mistaken] views, and later eliminate those of conceptualization; the fruit of realizing emptiness is far too remote, and [the ideal of] emerging in conventionality and saving [other] beings is not within our capabilities," as in gazing over a cliff and losing all self-confidence. [In order to deal with this objection] I should now differentiate the levels of conventionality.

[As it says in the *Śrīmālādevī Sūtra*,] "those of the three vehicles were not ignorant of the Dharma [even at the level] of their 'first deeds' [on the path leading to Buddhahood]." Everyone wishes to seek Buddhahood, but being weary and sick of samsara, they prefer to retrogress [to a nirvana of extinction]. [As it says in the *Mahāparinirvāṇa Sūtra*,] "[such people are] like the person who heard that in another direction there is a mountain of the seven jewels; he became excited and made preparations [to go there], but when he considered that the road was difficult and dangerous, he abandoned his plans and did not proceed." The people who practice [the Buddhist path] are also like this. If they are fearful of samsara and retreat to become mired in

Those of the three vehicles were not ignorant of the Dharma [even at the level] of their 'first deeds' 夫三乘之初不愚於法: see the *Śrīmālādevī Sūtra* at T 12.222a29. This phrase has been quoted previously in the *Mo-ho chih-kuan*; see note at 35b10. It was also quoted at the beginning of this section at 75c18, though it is quoted more accurately here.

Like the person who heard … and did not proceed 有人俱聞他方有七寶山翹心束脚若念路艱險便退: a summary of a long analogy in the *Mahāparinirvāṇa Sūtra* at T 12.779b7–c4:

> Good son, you should not say that sentient beings do not have Buddha-nature just because you have a mind of retrogression. *It is as if there were two people who heard that in another direction there is a mountain of the seven jewels.* The mountain has a pure spring, whose taste is beautiful, and those who are able to reach it will forever get rid of their poverty, and those who drink this water will increase their lifespan to ten thousand years. However, *the road to this place is far and dangerous, and involves many difficulties.* At the time both of these people wished to dwell there together. One of them amassed various utensils [for the journey], and the other went empty-handed and did not carry anything. Together they proceeded on the road until they met a person who had many coins and the seven types of jewels. The two people asked him, "Is this the land where the seven-jeweled mountain exists?" The man answered "Truly this is it. I have already obtained the jewels

emptiness, when they later hear of the supreme and sublime qualities of a bodhisattva they will think "what a failure I am," and the great chiliochosm will shake with their tears [of regret]. Such a person does not wait upon [the practices that are] the causes [of Buddhahood], but indulges in melancholic regret. If people rely on this sort of thinking, they will merely realize emptiness, and not advance further to enter and realize the matters of conventionality.

1. Tripitaka Teachings [79a20]

If the Tripitaka bodhisattvas first cultivate the wolf of emptiness and overcome the sheep of passionate afflictions, they still do not sever the bonds [of passionate afflictions]. If they sever these bonds, they cannot nourish the body of the virtuous qualities of the six perfections. This is the level of the first incalculable 阿僧祇 [eon] *(asaṃkhyeya [kalpa])*. In the second incalculable eon the fat of passionate afflictions is eradicated, and instead virtues are nurtured. In the third incalculable eon they properly enter the level of conventionality to benefit [other] sentient beings. These [levels] are those

and drunk the water. However, the road is dangerous and there are many bandits…." *Upon hearing this one [of the travelers] regretfully said, "The road is too far and dangerous….* If I continue on this road I will lose my life, and without my physical wellbeing I cannot live in peace for long." The other person said, "If other people were able to pass, I also can pass…." Thus at that time, of the two people one retreated and one advanced until he reached the mountain and obtained many jewels and, as he wished, drank the water.… The seven-jeweled mountain is great nirvana, and the sweet and beautiful water is an analogy for Buddha-nature. These two people are like two bodhisattvas who arouse the aspiration [for Buddhahood], and the dangerous and evil road is an analogy for samsara.… *The person who retreats is like a bodhisattva of retrogression*, and the person who stays directly on the path is like a bodhisattva of non-retrogression.

What a failure I am 敗種 : lit., "I have seeds that have failed" or "defeated seeds"; see the next note.

The great chiliochosm will shake with their tears 泣動大千: the last part of this sentence is a quote from the *Vimalakīrti Sūtra*, T 14.547a3–14. Boin (*Vimalakīrti Sūtra*, 149) translates:

> Where then is the intelligent son or daughter of good family who, hearing this inconceivable liberation spoken of, would not produce the thought of supreme and perfect enlightenment?
>
> As for ourselves, men with ruined faculties *(praṇaṣṭendriya)* and who, *like a burnt and rotten seed (dagdhapūtikabīja)*, have no part in the Great Vehicle *(mahāyāne na bhājanibhūtāḥ)*, what should we do? We ourselves, śrāvakas and pratyekabuddhas, having heard this teaching of the Law *(dharmanirdeśa)*, *should give a cry of pain (ārtasvara) which would shatter the trichiliomegachiliocosm (trisāhasramahasā)*.

The fat of passionate afflictions is eradicated and instead virtues are nurtured 煩惱脂消功德轉肥: these themes and vocabulary are taken from a passage in the *Ta chih tu lun*, T 25.169b5–11. Lamotte (*Le Traité* 2, 908–909) translates:

> [*Le mouton corpulent, mais sans graisse*]. — Un roi possédait un grand ministre

of the people of inferior faculties. Those of middling faculties overcome the passionate afflictions and nourish the body of the six perfections, and so they are able to save [other] beings without waiting until the third incalculable era. Those of superior faculties, from the time of their first aspiration, make a vow to become a Buddha and save all [beings]. By hearing the teaching [of the Dharma] by another [that is, the Buddha], their minds attain clear understanding, and they profoundly know the truth. Therefore, in order that they may be able to save others, they do not seek an "enlightenment [that consists] of severance." Their minds turn [even more determined], thinking, "I should save others." They cannot endure not saving others, and strive diligently to discriminate [and know] all medicines and diseases. Why is this so? Because there are five matters that are to be taken seriously. [**79b**] It is like a person who guides a child through danger; that person

> *(mahāmātya)* dont il couvrait lui-même les fautes pour qu'elles demeurent ignorées. Il lui dit un jour: "Va me chercher un mouton qui soit gros, mais qui n'ait point de graisse; si tu n'en trouves point, je t'infligerai ton châtiment." *Le grand ministre avait du savoir: il mit à la chaîne un grand mouton, le gava d'herbes et de céréales, mais, trois fois par jour, il l'effrayait avec un loup. Ainsi le mouton, malgré toute la nourriture qu'il recevait, était gros, mais n'avait point de graisse.* Le ministre amena le mouton et le présenta au roi; celui-ci ordonna à ses gens de le tuer; il était gros mais n'avait point de graisse. Le roi demanda comment cela se faisait, et le ministre lui donna la raison qu'on vient de dire. Le Bodhisattva agit de même: il contemple *(samanupaśyati)* le loup de l'impermanence *(anityatā)*, de la douleur *(duḥkha)* et du vide *(śunya)* *de telle sorte que la graisse des passions (saṃyojanameda) fonde tandis que la chair des qualités (guṇamāṃsa) prend consistance.*

Chodron (2, 708) translates:

> [*The corpulent sheep without fat*]. A king had a prime minister whose faults he himself concealed so that they remained unknown. He said to him one day: "Go and find me a big sheep but that has no fat; if you don't find one, I will inflict punishment on you." The prime minister was learned: he chained up a big sheep, fed it with grass and grains; but three times each day, he frightened it with a wolf. Thus the sheep, in spite of all the food that it received, was big but had no fat. The minister brought the sheep and presented it to the king who commanded his people to kill it; it was big but had no fat. The king asked how that was done, and the minister gave him the reason we have just described. The bodhisattva acts in the same way: he contemplates the wolf of impermanence, suffering, and emptiness in such a way that the fat of the passions melts while the flesh of the qualities becomes solid.

Part of this passage has been quoted already in the *Mo-ho chih-kuan* as "trying to extinguish the glut of passionate afflictions"; see note at 27c18–19.

An enlightenment of severance 斷證: that is, they do not seek to attain a nirvana of complete extinction in which they will no longer be involved in this world of passionate defilements.

Five matters 五事: the five aspects of the causes and conditions of realizing conventionality summarized above at 75c11ff.: compassion, vows, wisdom, means, and diligence.

cannot be concerned only with his or her own peace and assurance and thus forsake the child. Even if you know emptiness yourself, you cannot abandon [this mundane, conventional world]. This is [what it means] to be able to enter and realize conventionality from the time of your first aspiration, without waiting until [the end of] the second incalculable eon.

2. Shared Teachings [79b3]

The levels of the Shared Teachings are as follows. People often become attached to [the literal teaching of] the sūtras and say that you cultivate "emerging in conventionality" at the eighth *bhūmi* stage, or that you sever the bonds [of passionate afflictions] at the sixth or seventh *bhūmi* stage and, becoming equivalent to an arhat you cultivate "emerging in conventionality" [at this level]. This is one possible interpretation, but is not necessarily applicable in all cases. The Buddha distinguishes between three [different] faculties [that is, inferior, middling, and superior]. Those of inferior faculties sever delusions exhaustively [to attain a nirvana of extinction for themselves] and then they are able to emerge in conventionality. In the *Lotus Sūtra* the Buddha demolished the mental attitude that is attached to this kind of nirvana, and encouraged people to arouse the aspiration for the supreme path [to Buddhahood], and to arouse the wisdom of [skillful] means. This is already so for those of the two vehicles, and the extremely dull bodhisattvas should also follow this teaching. This applies to classifying those of inferior faculties. Those of middling faculties have [by the sixth, seventh, or eight stage?] already severed the [active] delusions of [mistaken] views, have become somewhat unencumbered by samsara, and spontaneously sever conceptual attitudes. For them the second *bhūmi* stage is where they attain the supranormal powers of a bodhisattva, and it is after these [levels] that they are able to enter and realize conventionality.

Those of superior faculties realize (penetrating) insight into the essence of the emptiness of [mistaken] views and conceptual attitudes when they hear of the wisdom [of the Buddha Dharma] at the time of their first aspiration, so [at this earliest stage] they are already a steady support on which sentient beings can rely. Why should we insist that people "emerge in conventionality" only at the seventh *bhūmi* stage? The *Pancaviṃśati Sūtra* denounces the idea that the seventh *bhūmi* stage [is the level where everyone attains "emerging in conventionality." It says,] "There was a great bird whose body was three hundred *yojana*s in length, but since it did not have both

There was a great bird whose body was three hundred *yojana*s in length, but since it did not have both wings it fell from the sky and died or suffered like unto death. Bodhisattvas are also like this 有大鳥身長三百由旬而無兩翅從天而墮若死若死等苦。菩

wings it fell from the sky and died or suffered like unto death. Bodhisattvas are also like this." Those who exclusively cultivate only emptiness from the very beginning [of their practice] until they reach the sixth *bhūmi* stage will be glutted with the three emptinesses [empty 空, markless 無相, and uncreated 無作] and will not give rise to the wings of conventionality. If they fall into the path of the means of the two vehicles, this is called "suffering like unto death." If they fall down to [the level of] the first fruit [of the stream-enterer], this is called "death." If they exhaust their [mistaken] views, this is "like unto death." If they become "those who have nothing more to learn," this is "death." The bird may wish to return to the heavens, but cannot do so. Those who fall into the stage of "those who have nothing more to

薩亦如是: see the *Pañcaviṃśati Sūtra* at T 8.336a–c, which speaks of bodhisattvas obtaining different levels of attainment:

> [336a27] When Śāriputra taught in this way, two hundred bhikṣus exhausted their defilements by not experiencing any phenomenal dharmas, thus becoming arhats; five hundred bhikuṇis became free of their defilements, attained the Dharma eye, and were reborn as divine beings; five thousand bodhisattva-mahāsattvas attained the patient recognition that dharmas do not arise, and sixty bodhisattvas exhausted their defilements by not accepting/experiencing any phenomenal dharmas, thus attaining liberation and becoming arhats.…
>
> [336b20] "Śāriputra, again there are bodhisattva-mahāsattvas who are not freed by thoughts of *sarvajñā* and cultivate the dharmas of emptiness, marklessness, and uncreatedness; they realize the levels of a bodhisattva through the power of [provisional] means and attain *anuttarasamyaksaṃbodhi*. *Śāriputra, suppose there is a bird whose body is a hundred yojanas in length, or two hundred or three hundred yojanas [in length], but it has no wings and throws itself from the Trāyastrīṃśā heaven [and falls] to Jambudvīpa.* Śāriputra, what do you think? If the bird, while falling [lit. "in the middle of the path"], thinks that he would like to return to the Trāyastrīṃśā heaven, would it be able to return, or not?"
>
> "He would not be able, World Honored One."
>
> "Śāriputra, suppose this bird made a vow that when he reaches Jambudvīpa his body would not suffer or be hurt. Śāriputra, what do you think? Would this bird be able to attain his vow of not suffering or being hurt?"
>
> "He would not be able, World Honored One. *When the bird reaches the ground it will be hurt, or will suffer, or will die, or will feel pain like unto death.* Why, World Honored One? Because this bird's body is very large and does not have wings."
>
> "Śāriputra, *bodhisattvas are also like this.* Even though they cultivate giving, keeping the precepts, patience, diligence, and concentration for as many kalpas as the sands of the Ganges River, perform great deeds, are arouse the great thought [of aspiration for awakening], attain *anuttarasamyaksaṃbodhi*, and thus experience immeasurable vows, because these bodhisattvas are detached from the power of the means of *prajñāpāramitā*, they fall into being an arhat, or fall into being a pratyekabuddha. Why? Such bodhisattvas are detached from the mind of *sarvajñā*, giving, keeping the precepts, patience, diligence, and concentration, because they do not have the power of the means of *prajñāpāramitā*, and they fall to the stages of the śrāvaka or pratyekabuddha while on the path.

learn" may wish to arouse the aspiration for *bodhi*-wisdom, but they will not be able to do so for a long time. They are like a man who has been castrated and cannot feel the five kinds of sensual desires. The *Avataṃsaka Sūtra* and *Pañcaviṃśati Sūtra* teach that these people can never be healed. Only the *Lotus Sūtra* is able to lead "those who have nothing more to learn" to revive their good roots and attain the path of Buddhahood. That is why it is called "sublime" 妙. Again, [the *Mahāparinirvāṇa Sūtra* says that] if an *icchantika* has mental faculties, he can become a Buddha. Those of the two vehicles have extinguished their wisdom [along with the passionate afflictions and so forth] and so they cannot give rise to the mind [of *bodhi*-wisdom]. However, the *Lotus Sūtra* is able to heal [even those in this situation]; therefore it is called "sublime."

3. Distinct Teachings [79b24]

People of the Distinct Teachings cultivate the means of conventionality at the ten levels of practice beyond the ten abodes. Why? [The level of] the abodes is where they realize the principle of *prajñā*-wisdom [that is, emptiness], and these abodes give rise to virtuous qualities that are put into practice [at the levels of practice]. This refers to those of inferior faculties. There are those who have their first aspiration at the level of the ten abodes, and are already able to realize conventionality and attain [the state of] non-defilement [at these stages]. Once they experience this they do not retrogress, and are able to put it to good use, so why should they wait until they reach the ten levels of practice before they arouse great compassion? This refers to those of middling faculties. Again there are those of the Distinct Teachings who are not ignorant of the Dharma even at the level of their first aspiration. They penetratingly understand that all virtuous qualities are like a magical apparition and that they are verbal designations, and so they do not [**79c**] become entangled in them, and yet they cultivate [skillful] means [within the con-

If an *icchantika* has mental faculties, it can become a Buddha 闡提有心猶可作佛: see the ***Mahāparinirvāṇa Sūtra*** at T 12.737a25–b4:

> Good son. [The fate of] the *icchantika* is not fixed. If it was fixed, then the *icchantika* would never be able to attain *anuttarasaṃyaksaṃbodhi*. Since it is not fixed, they can attain it. As you say, the Buddha-nature cannot be severed. How, then can *icchantika* sever their good roots? Good son, there are two types of good roots. The first is internal, and the second is external. Buddha-nature is neither internal nor external. Because of this, Buddha-nature cannot be severed. Again, there are another two types. The first is defiled, and the second is undefiled. Buddha-nature is neither defiled nor undefiled. Therefore it cannot be severed. Again, there are another two types. The first is eternal, and the second is transient. Buddha-nature is neither eternal nor transient. Therefore it cannot be severed.

ventional world] and are endowed with the five causes and conditions [of realizing conventionality] and thus benefit sentient beings. These are those of superior faculties.

4. Perfect Teaching [79c2]

Those of the Perfect Teaching purify the six senses at the ten levels of faith, and thus can universally perceive [lit., "see and hear" 見聞] the activity of the ten dharma realms. If they realize [only] emptiness, there is not a single thing to be perceived, but since the six sense faculties are utilized, this is the level of entering or realizing conventionality. [This refers to those of inferior faculties.] Again, those at the five preliminary grades of the disciple properly practice the six perfections, and widely teach the Dharma; thus this also refers to the level of realizing conventionality — why is it necessary to wait until the six senses are purified [to say that one realizes conventionality]? [This refers to those of middling faculties.] Again, those who have their first aspiration [for *bodhi*-wisdom] are able to know the secret treasury of the Tathāgata, and can perfectly contemplate the threefold truth as indivisible from the Middle. How can this not include being indivisible from conventionality? The *Pañcaviṃśati Sūtra* says, "From when they first sit on the seat of enlightenment *(bodhimaṇḍa)* they have already attained correct awakening *(anuttarasaṃyaksaṃbodhi),* turned the wheel of the Dharma, and saved sentient beings." Again, if we were to examine this in terms of the Six Identities, there are further meanings of "emerging in conventionality"; why should such people wait until they reach the levels of the disciples? [This refers to those of superior faculties.]

Thus, as I have explained above, each of the teachings involve three levels [of inferior, middling, and superior]. If we were to focus on the classifications, we should pick that of inferior faculties and clarify its levels. There are two reasons for this: first is because we rely on the teachings [of the sūtras?], and the second is because you can enter or realize conventionality and perfect your practices with the certainty that you will not retrogress. Those of middling and superior faculties progress and retrogress, and therefore I do not base my discussion of the levels on them.

From when they first sit on the seat of enlightenment they have already attained correct awakening, turned the wheel of the Dharma, and saved sentient beings 初坐道場尚便成正覺轉法輪度衆生: see the *Pañcaviṃśati Sūtra* at T 8.226a9–10; also in the *Ta chih tu lun*, T 25.342b22–23. However, the original text does not contain the phrase "sit on the seat of enlightenment." This passage has been quoted above in the *Mo-ho chih-kuan* at 2c5–6.

5. Questions and Answers [79c12]

[Question:] [It has been explained that] there are three faculties [or capabilities] for emerging in conventionality. By precedent there should be three faculties [or capabilities] for realizing emptiness.

[Response:] [This is so; the three capabilities for realizing emptiness are] those who realize [at the level of] feelings, those who realize [at the level of] resemblance, and those who realize [at the level of insight into] the truth. To realize [while still at the level of] feelings refers to those people [of superior faculties] who are able to realize [emptiness] through coming in contact [with the four mindfulnesses of body, sensation, mind, and dharma], without being distracted by feelings. They contemplate and come in contact with the [Four Noble] Truths before they reach [the levels of] resemblance and true [emptiness] that correspond to the mental objects of emptiness.

[Question:] What benefit is there in this [realization at the level of feelings]?

[Answer:] There is the benefit of [realizing emptiness early on at the level of] feelings.

[Question:] If there is such a benefit, then is there no retrogression?

[Answer:] There is no retrogression [for these people]. Even if there is some retrogression, they are able to remember, and after cultivating [the Buddhist path] many times they will attain great benefit [of Buddhahood].

Question: Those of superior faculties of the Shared and Distinct [Teachings] are able to enter and realize emptiness and emerge in conventionality. How are they different from those of the Perfect [Teaching]?

Answer: People of the Shared [Teaching] realize [emptiness] and emerge [in conventionality], but not in the sense of indivisibility with the Middle. Those of the Distinct [Teachings] gradually and progressively realize [emptiness] and emerge [in conventionality], but are not able to do so in a single thought 一心 [or, "single-mindedly"]. People of the Perfect [Teaching] realize [emptiness] and emerge [in conventionality] in a single thought, and are also able to realize [emptiness] and emerge [in conventionality] distinctly [or, in separate thoughts]; that is, they often realize the Middle and seldom real-

Realize feelings ... distracted by feelings 謂情入。似入。眞入。情入者觸人能入非謂散情: following Chan-jan's interpretation (BT–IV, 208): Those who "realize through feeling" refers to people of superior faculties who realize emptiness while still at the level of the five contemplations 五停心觀; those who "realize through resemblance" refers to people of middling faculties who realize emptiness while at the level of the four good roots; those who "realize through the true" refers to people of inferior faculties who realize emptiness at a level at or beyond "insight into the Four Noble Truths" *(darśana-mārga)* 見道, that is, the stage of the stream-enterer.

ize the duality [of emptiness and conventionality], or they often realize the duality [of emptiness and conventionality] and seldom realize the Middle, or they often realize emptiness and the Middle and seldom realize conventionality, or they often realize conventionality and seldom realize emptiness and the Middle, or they often realize conventionality and the Middle and seldom realize emptiness, or they often realize emptiness and seldom realize conventionality and the Middle. Although this involves increase and decrease as with those of the Distinct [Teachings], it never lacks [the symmetry of] the threefold truth [of emptiness, conventionality, and the Middle]. Thus it is not the gradual and progressive [process] of the Distinct [Teachings]. We could say that it is superior to the Distinct [Teachings], and it is certainly not inferior.

2. *Clarifying the benefits* [79c24]

Second is to clarify the benefits of realizing conventionality. Bodhisattvas do not originally cultivate emptiness because they esteem emptiness; they originally cultivate emptiness because they want to benefit sentient beings. Because they do not esteem emptiness [excessively], they do not abide in it [forever]; they must emerge [into the mundane world of conventionality] in order to benefit sentient beings. Thus through [realizing] true [emptiness] they arouse the Dharma eye according to their capabilities. If they can save [sentient beings] through the body of a Buddha, they produce a body of the Buddha to teach the Dharma and apply the medicine. If they can save through [taking on] the forms of a bodhisattva, those of the two vehicles, devas, *nāga*-dragons, or the other eight types of beings, they manifest themselves accordingly. Thus they perfect sentient beings and purify Buddha lands; this is called "benefiting" [sentient beings by entering or realizing conventionality].

1. Tripitaka Teachings [79c29]

The Tripitaka [**80a**] bodhisattvas do emerge in conventionality, but with defiled supranormal powers and without arousing true manifestations.

Although this involves ... certainly not inferior 雖別增減而三諦不缺。若爾。則非次第之別。然尚能爲勝別。況不能爲劣耶: Ikeda (*Gendaigoyaku*, 406) translates this section rather liberally. He takes the last two phrases to be another "question and answer":

Question: If this is so, then how is this [Perfect Teaching] different from the gradual and progressive Distinct Teachings?

Answer: It is similar, but the Perfect Teaching involves many superior features, and thus is clearly different from the gradual and progressive [method] of the Distinct Teachings.

Without arousing true manifestations 非眞起應: that is, not the "manifestation

They discriminate with worldly wisdom, so their Dharma eye is not clear. Although they do benefit sentient beings, this is not perfectly fulfilled. Although they perform the deeds of a Buddha, they do not purify a Buddha land. They merely teach a small portion [of the Dharma], and the benefit [they provide] is very miniscule.

2. Shared Teachings [80a4]

When those of the Shared Teachings enter or realize conventionality, they can distinguish medicines and diseases, but rely only on the two truths, so their diagnosis is not profound. Their knowledge of medicine does not reach very far, and they have only deliberate supranormal powers, and do not arouse true manifestations. These manifestations have a beginning and an end. They become a father, mother, teacher, or leader; they form connections with the mundane world and gradually overcome it. They move through immeasurable kalpas until their good roots mature and they are born in a palace [like Śākyamuni], become a Buddha under a Bodhi tree, save people gradually or suddenly, and finally enter nirvana. The relics stay in this world to benefit people for a long time. This is called a manifestation that has a beginning and an end. What did not exist suddenly exists, appears temporarily, and then perishes again; therefore these are not true manifestations. Partial benefits [that last only] for a while are not called "perfect fulfillment." Reducing the body to ashes and entering [a nirvana of] extinction 灰身入滅 is not [the same as] the purifying of a Buddha land.

3. Distinct Teachings [80a11]

The content of the benefits of entering or realizing conventionality at the ten levels of practice by [the bodhisattvas of] the Distinct Teachings is the same as [the highest level] of the Shared Teachings. When they ascend the [first] *bhūmi* stage, they attain the Tathāgata's single body and immeasurable bodies, and they can profoundly respond to all [according to their needs]. At that time they know [all] disease and exhaust the deep source of the diseases. At that time they are conscious of the medicines and know all about the available medicines. At that time they can apply the medicines [appropriately], like a seal matches its imprint 如印不差. They realize the true wisdom of the path and the most supreme Dharma eye. They appear spontaneously everywhere that such transformations should appear. They "soften their light and join with the dust" [of this world]; this begins their relationship

body" 應身 of a Buddha wherein he enjoys the results of his enlightenment?

Soften their light and join with the dust 和光同塵: a famous phrase from the *Tao-te ching* of Lao-tzu, part 4. Chih-i has used this phrase at *Mo-ho chih-kuan* at 19b26.

[with this mundane world]. They experience the eight phases [in the life of a Buddha] to perfect the path; this brings it to an end. Sometimes this is called a "transformation" 化 [for the purpose of teaching 教化], and sometimes this is called a "manifestation" 應. Those who see or hear [these manifestations] cannot help but receive benefit. Their charitable actions purify Buddha lands. Thus the benefits from entering and realizing conventionality are all truly real and not vacuous. It is already this way when they ascend the [first] *bhūmi* stage; it is also like this at the later *bhūmi* stages.

4. Perfect Teaching [80a19]

As for [the bodhisattvas of] the Perfect Teaching, they enter and realize conventionality at the first stage of abodes, and provide truly real benefits. This continues through the later [higher stages of] mental states, again in the same way [as explained above].

If you understand this meaning and examine all varieties of changes and transformations [among sentient beings], you will be able to distinguish between the true and the false. Why? Demonic forces are also able to create undefiled forms with defiled intentions, and change into images of the Buddha. *Lao-tzu's Advance to the West* also says that "he [Lao-tzu] became the Buddha to save barbarians." Various non-Buddhist teachings attempt to change Śākyamuni into a sheep, or a river is dammed up into your ear, or

First stage of abodes: corresponding to the ten *bhūmi* stages for those of the Distinct Teachings.

Demonic forces are also able to create undefiled forms with defiled intentions, and change into images of the Buddha 魔亦能以有漏心作無漏形變爲佛像: see *Mahāparinirvāṇa Sūtra*, T 12.637c4–24:

> Kāśyapa said to the Buddha, "World Honored One. I will not rely on these four types of people. Why? As the Buddha explained to *Kuśila in the *Kuśila Sūtra*, if the heavenly and demonic beings wish to be destructive, they transform into the form of a Buddha, endowed and adorned with the thirty-two major and eighty minor marks,.... You should carefully examine those who approach you with such adornments, and decide whether they are false or real. If you recognize them [for what they are], you should overcome them....
>
> You should, from now on, overcome Pāpīyas [the evil one]. You should say, "Pāpīyas, you should not appear in such a form. If you do [appear in such a form], we will bind and fetter you with the five fetters." When Māra hears this he will depart and, like a rogue dog, will not return.

The last part of this section was referred to in the *Mo-ho chih-kuan* at 51b17.

He [Lao-tzu] became the Buddha to save barbarians 作佛化胡: see ***Lao-tzu's Advance to the West*** 老子西升: considered to be one of many apocryphal Taoist scriptures in which it is claimed that Lao-tzu, after passing through the Western barrier, ended up in India and became the Buddha. The text is not extant, though parts of it are quoted in other Buddhist texts; see, e.g., T 52.139c.

Change Śākyamuni into a sheep 變

the supranormal powers based on worldly wisdom are performed in various ways. In this way there are immeasurable and unlimited evil transformations [and methods of teaching]. These are not even the five kinds of supranormal transformations of the Tripitaka [Teachings], much less the spontaneous and true transformations [and teachings] of the Distinct and Perfect [Teachings]. There are kinds of verbal teachings and transformations, and those people without eyes [to see properly] will mistakenly believe and accept them. You must contemplate thoroughly and deeply, so that you will not be [a blind follower of false teachings,] like the echo of thunder. Thus you should know that one who manifests his traces from the Dharma body of the *bhūmi* stages to the ten dharma realms in order to save sentient beings [is a true beneficiary]; this way of entering or realizing conventionality [to help sentient beings] is a true benefit.

3. *Summarizing the universal deconstruction of dharmas* [80a28]

Third, summarizing the universal deconstruction of dharmas is as follows. Those who have not yet aroused true [insight into emptiness] are induced by their conceptual attachments to have hundreds of thousands of millions of [mistaken] views. **[80b]** This is like blind people who ask about [the color of] milk but are not able to know the true color of milk, or [they touch various

釋爲羊: that is, change Śākyamuni and his teachings into a passive reflection of other, superior teachings, rather than the "wolf" who overcomes passions and delusions? Or, see the *Mahāparinirvāṇa Sūtra*, T 12.839b8–16, which tells of a Nigrantha who had magical powers to turn himself "into the image of a man or woman, bull, sheep, elephant, or horse."

River dammed up into your ear 停河在耳: see the *Mahāparinirvāṇa Sūtra*, T 12.840b3–5:

> Great King, have you not heard of the sage Agastya, who for twelve years stopped up the waters of the Ganges River in his ear? Great King, have you not heard of the sage Gautama who manifested supranormal powers and for twelve years changed into the body of Śākyamuni?

Blind people who ask about milk but are not able to know the true color of milk 盲問乳非乳眞色: these phrases bring to mind the analogy of a person with healthy sight trying to explain the color "white" to a blind person; see the *Mahāparinirvāṇa Sūtra*, T 12.688c15–23.

> They are like a person blind from birth who does not know the color of milk. He asks another man, "What is the color of milk like?" The other person says, "The color white is like a shell." The blind man again asks, "Then, the color of milk is like the sound of a shell?" The man answers, "No." Again he asks, "What is the color of a shell like?" He answers, "It is like rice powder." The blind man again asks, "Is the color of milk soft like rice powder? What is [the color of] rice powder like?" He answers, "It is like snow." The blind man again asks, "Is this rice powder cold like the snow? What is [the color of] snow like?" He answers, "It is like a white crane." This man blind from birth, although he hears four analogies [for the color of white], finally is not able to know

parts of an elephant and say] "it is like a rope" or "it is like a baton" and completely miss what an elephant really is. [Mistaken] views are like talking in your sleep; [mistaken] views are conventional. Therefore you should gradually progress through the individual, multiple, and combined [mistaken views] and deconstruct them through [the practice of] contemplation [as explained above]. If this deconstruction is not universal, you cannot attain the realization of emptiness. If the [mistaken] views and conceptual attitudes are [thoroughly] exhausted, this is called the universal deconstruction of dharmas.

A literal interpretation [of deconstructing dharmas] would be as I have just explained, but the intent [here in the *Mo-ho chih-kuan*] is not like this

> the color of milk. All the non-Buddhists are like this; finally they are not able to know [that nirvana is] constant, blissful, selfhood, and pure.

This analogy is used frequently in the *Mo-ho chih-kuan*; see the note at 3a21–22.

Like a rope or baton 若繩若杵: see the famous analogy of blind men feeling different parts of an elephant and making mistaken generalizations about it in the *Mahāparinirvāṇa Sūtra*, T 12.802a. For example, some feel the head and say that the elephant is like a rock, some feel the trunk and say that it is like a baton, some feel the tail and say that it is like a rope, and so forth:

> Good son. Suppose there is a king who tells his grand minister to take an elephant and present it to some blind people. The minister does as the king commanded. He assembled many blind people and presented an elephant to them. Each of the blind people touched the elephant with his hands. The minister then returned to the king and reported that he had done as was commanded. Then the king called the group of blind people and asked each of them if they had perceived the elephant. Each of the blind people said that he had perceived the elephant. The king asked what the elephant was like. The one who had touched the tusk said that the elephant was shaped like the trunk of a tree. The one who had touched the ear said that the elephant was like a winnowing fan. The one who touched the head said that the elephant was like a rock. The one who touched the nose said that the elephant was like a pestle. The one who touched the feet said that the elephant was like a wooden mortar. The one who touched the back said that the elephant was like a bed. The one who touched the belly said that the elephant was like a large jar. The one who touched his tail said that the elephant was like a rope. Good son, in this way the blind people could not explain the essence of the elephant, nor can it be said that they did not explain [in part]. All of these aspects [in their individuality alone] are not the elephant, and yet there is no elephant apart from these aspects. Good son, the king is analogous to the Tathāgata's supreme and universal knowledge. The minister is analogous to the *Mahāparinirvāṇa Sūtra*. The elephant is analogous to Buddha-nature. The blind people are analogous to all ignorant sentient beings. Sentient beings hear this teaching of the Buddha and say, "Form *(rūpa)* is Buddha-nature." Why? Because although form perishes, it progressively continues. Therefore one is able to attain the thirty-two marks of the supreme Tathāgata. The Tathāgata's form is eternal. Since the Tathāgata's form is eternal, it is not severed. Therefore it is taught that form is Buddha-nature.

[explanation in the previous paragraph]. [The intent of the teaching here in the *Mo-ho chih-kuan* is as follows.] [Mistaken] views and conceptual attitudes are ignorance. Ignorance is indivisible from Dharma-nature [or, the nature of dharmas]. To destroy [mistaken] views and conceptual attitudes is to destroy ignorance. To destroy ignorance is to perceive the nature of dharmas [as empty] and realize the emptiness of the true aspect [of reality]. This is called the [true, real] universal deconstruction of dharmas. The universal deconstruction of dharmas by entering or realizing conventionality from emptiness is also like this. Conventionality involves immeasurable dharmas of diseases, medicines, and the application of medicine. If there is any part of these three separate aspects that you do not accomplish, then it cannot be said that you have universally destroyed all dharmas. If you have not yet aroused the Dharma eye, then even if you have some discrimination concerning [mistaken] views, this cannot be called a "universal deconstruction." When the six sense faculties are purified, you should [be able to] discriminate a single disease [to know] the many types, and by understanding one phrase of the Dharma [teachings] you can comprehend immeasurable phrases, and at once embrace the Dharma taught by the Buddhas of the ten directions. This is to attain the disposition [of cessation-and-contemplation] [at the level] of Resemblance. When you destroy the non-cognizance that obstructs supranormal powers, both of the two truths are illuminated; this is called the universal deconstruction of dharmas. If I were to speak only the essentials, [it can be said that] a gradual-and-successive deconstruction cannot be called "universal"; a deconstruction that is not gradual and successive is called "universal." Since the previous [discussion of the] methods of contemplation was very complex and intricate, I fear that some people might have been confused. Therefore after [the long discussion on] the two contemplations [of emptiness and conventionality], I have summarized the universal deconstruction of dharmas [in this way].

Level of Resemblance 相似: the fourth level of the Six Identities.

3. The Contemplation of the Middle Way [80b16–83b17]

Third is to clarify the universal deconstruction of dharmas through the correct contemplation of the Middle Way. The universal deconstruction of dharmas through the cessation-and-contemplation of the non-arising of arising [that is, emptiness] [discussed] above is focused on practice for oneself. The universal deconstruction of dharmas through the cessation-and-contemplation of the arising of non-arising [that is, conventionality] [discussed] next is focused on saving others. The universal deconstruction of dharmas through the cessation-and-contemplation of the non-arising of non-arising [the Middle] [discussed] now is focused on the mutual negation of both self and others, and on the illumination of [practice] for both self and others. The arising of non-arising [emptiness] is indivisible from the non-arising of arising [conventionality], and these again are indivisible from the non-arising of non-arising [the Middle]. [Practice for] the self is indivisible from [practice] not for the self, and again with [practice that is] neither for the self nor not for the self. The arising of non-arising [conventionality] is indivisible from the non-arising of arising [emptiness], and these again are [indivisible from] the non-arising of non-arising [the Middle]. [Saving] others is indivisible from [the saving of] "not-others," and also with [saving] neither others nor [saving] "not-others." The non-arising of non-arising [the Middle] is indivisible from the non-arising of arising [emptiness], and with the arising of non-arising [conventionality], and with neither the denial of both, and with the illumination of both. I have made these various distinctions as [explained] above in order to make it easier to understand.

This [contemplation of the Middle] consists of four parts: first, the intent of cultivating the contemplation of the Middle; second, the conditions for cultivating the contemplation of the Middle; third, the correct cultivation of the contemplation of the Middle; and fourth, clarifying the levels [of attainment] and their benefits.

1. Cultivating the contemplation of the Middle [80b26]

The intent of [cultivating the contemplation of the Middle] is as follows.

1. Tripitaka Teachings [80b26]

The bodhisattvas of the Tripitaka [Teachings] one-sidedly utilize worldly wisdom to illuminate the mundane [world]. Those of the two vehicles

Correct contemplation 正觀: the Taishō edition has "cessation-and-contemplation" 止觀, and offers "correct contemplation" 正観 as a variant. I have chosen to use the variant reading since it fits better with the title of this section 7 on "Proper/ Correct Contemplation." The *Bukkyō Taikei* (BT-IV, 223) also follows this variant.

[srāvakas and pratyekabuddhas] one-sidedly utilize an analytical [destruction of] conventionality to realize the truth [that is, emptiness]. The Buddha differs from the disciples in that he fully consummates the two truths [of the mundane truth and the real truth, conventionality and emptiness, the positions of the bodhisattvas and Buddhas], and provisionally establishes the third contemplation [of the Middle beyond the duality of Being and nothingness]. But, if we were to establish [merely] a denial of both Being and nothingness [or "being and non-being"], this would merely liberate us from the [one-sided, mistaken] views of Being and nothingness. Truly [80c] there is no distinct principle [of truth] 別理 [apart from the mundane and real, existence and non-existence] to be contemplated [by those of the Tripitaka Teachings]. Therefore it is not necessary [to mention] a "third contemplation" [of the Middle for those of the Tripitaka Teachings].

2. *Shared Teachings* [80c1]

Those of the two vehicles of the Shared Teachings one-sidedly utilize the method of [direct insight into] the essence [of everything as empty] to realize the truth [that is, emptiness]. Bodhisattvas enter and realize conventionality with compassion. Only a Buddha fully illuminates both [the wisdom of emptiness and compassion for the mundane world]. [The Buddha] is different from the disciples in that he is proficient in both the path [of wisdom and compassion] and contemplation, and provisionally establishes the third contemplation [of the Middle]. Again, there is no distinct principle [of truth] that is different from the real truth. The claim of [Chih-tsang of] K'ai-shan [ssu] that the fruit of Buddhahood does not transcend the two truths is in line with this meaning. Although there is no distinct principle [of

Fully consummates the two truths 二諦周足: the mundane truth *(saṃvṛti-satya)* and real truth *(paramārtha-satya)*, which correspond to the first two parts—conventionality and emptiness—of the threefold truth and threefold contemplation; see Chart 1 in Swanson, *Foundations*, 358–59.

The duality of Being and nothingness 有無二見: see my discussion of this issue throughout Swanson, *Foundations* (especially Chart 2, 360).

Provisionally establishes the third contemplation 假設第三觀: see Chih-i's analysis of the "Seven Levels [or Types] of the Two Truths" in the *Fa hua hsüan i*, T 33.702b6–c9, translated in Swanson, *Foundations*, 238–45.

The claim of [Chih-tsang of] K'ai-shan [ssu]... 開善所執佛果不出二諦外: Chih-tsang was a prominent scholar of the *Ch'eng shih lun* and *Mahāparinirvāṇa Sūtra* one generation before Chih-i and traditionally considered one of the "three great Dharma masters of the Liang Period"; see note above under *Mo-ho chih-kuan* 28a18. For details, see Swanson, *Foundations*, 89–95.

In line with this meaning 卽此義也: Chih-tsang's works are not extant and so we do not know the original source of this attribution.

truth], nevertheless you can attain the term "Middle Way" in which the truth [of emptiness] is [understood as] like an illusion or like a transformation, which can be called the "Middle Way that neither arises nor perishes." Also, attaining the meaning of the Middle Way—that is, the gate of the complete teachings of the Buddha—permeates [both] the Shared and the Distinct [Teachings]. Those of dull faculties stop at being able to penetrate the Shared [Teachings], and are not able to penetrate the Distinct [Teachings]; thus [it is recognized that some of] those of those of the [Shared] Teachings contain the meaning of "approaching" the Distinct [Teachings]. Those who are sharp can approach even further to utilize the Middle Way. Those who do not approach [in this way], for them the third contemplation [of the Middle] is not necessary. The meaning of "approaching [from the Shared] to the Distinct" is as explained earlier in [section III on] "manifesting the essence [of cessation-and-contemplation."

3. Distinct Teachings [80c10]

Those of the Distinct Teachings all basically know the Middle Way whether it is expressed as two truths or the threefold truth. In the case of the threefold truth, [the Middle Way] should already be understood[, since the term is included in this formulation]. In the case of the two truths, the Middle Way is the real [truth], and [the duality of conventional] existence and non-Being [emptiness] is the mundane [truth]. People are led to accept the Middle Way by illuminating [or becoming enlightened concerning] [the sublime meaning of] the two truths; this is called the Middle Way [for those of the Distinct Teachings]. Not being biased toward either of the two sides [of the two truths] is to be enlightened concerning both; although there are two names, the principle of the Middle is manifested in both. This principle is mysterious and profound; those with dull faculties and heavy obstacles are like blind people futilely trying to sew with a needle. How can they sew? Since the principle is constant, first you must destroy attachment to [phenomenal] marks and perceive emptiness with the eye of wisdom. Next you destroy ignorance and perceive conventionality with the Dharma eye. Then you progress to cultivate the Middle Way, whereby you destroy one part of ignorance, expose one part of the Buddha eye, and perceive one part of the Middle. These are "the real causes" [or "the causes for realizing the true" 眞因], and when the causes and fruits are perfect and complete, this is called "becoming a Buddha." The two truths [in themselves] are not the [ultimate] true intent [of the Middle], and therefore they are not called the cause [of

Manifesting the essence 顯體中說: see *Mo-ho chih-kuan* 29a7–12 in Chapter III, "Features of the Essence [of Cessation-and-Contemplation]."

Buddhahood]. For example, [those with] the [conventional] means of the Hīnayāna do overcome delusions but do not perceive the truth [of emptiness]; this is not called the [true or ultimate] cultivation of the path. You are endowed with the true cultivation of the path after arousing insight into the [Four Noble] Truths; only then is this the real cause 眞因 [for realizing Buddhahood], and becoming "one with nothing more to learn" is a real fruit 眞果. It is the same for the Distinct Teachings. The two [individual] contemplations [of emptiness and conventionality] are [provisional skillful] means that certainly require the Middle. [On the other hand,] although [the Middle] is required, first the two [individual] contemplations are necessary. If the two [individual] contemplations are not accomplished, then there is no opportunity for the third contemplation [of the Middle].

4. *Perfect Teaching* [80c23]

In the Perfect Teaching, the Middle is known from the very beginning. Also, the destruction of both delusions [of mistaken views and conceptual attitudes] in the previous [Distinct Teachings] involved extravagant and hurried [aspects], and therefore it is different [from the Perfect]. Why? In the Distinct [Teachings] both delusions are removed by traversing through thirty mental states, moving through numerous eons and then finally destroying ignorance for the first time. The Perfect [Teaching] is not like this. Here you immediately destroy both [types of] delusions within this very body, thus realizing the Middle Way and accomplishing it within one lifetime. It is analogous to three levels of bandits [who are threatening you]. Suppose there is a person who is clumsy at using weapons, weak in physical strength, and has few discerning strategies. First he will try to destroy two levels, and then when he is more prepared as a person, will go on to destroy the third. This takes the slow passing of many days and months. Suppose there is a person who is physically impressive, sharp in military prowess, and has many [superb] strategies. Within one day he can destroy all three **[81a]** levels, without the passing of much time. Through this analogy it is possible to understand this meaning [of the difference between the Distinct and Perfect Teachings]. Again, it is like two types of iron. One type needs to be tempered in the fire repeatedly before it becomes useful. Another type is of high quality and is useful immediately after firing it [once]. This illustrates the meaning [of the difference between the Distinct and Perfect Teachings].

Cultivation of the path 修道: or, "the path of cultivation" *(bhāvanā-mārga)*.

Accomplished 辦: a variant reading has "distinguished" 辨, which clearly does not fit the context.

Thirty mental states 三十心: that is, the stages of the ten levels of faith, the ten abodes, and the ten levels of practice?

In the Perfect Teaching you cultivate the threefold contemplation [of emptiness, conventionality, and the Middle] from the very beginning, not waiting to perfect the two [individual] contemplations. Because of this, it is necessary to clarify the third contemplation [of the Middle] [from the beginning].

2. The conditions for cultivating contemplation of the Middle [81a4]

The reasons, or "causes and conditions," for cultivating the contemplation of the middle are summarized in five parts: first, unconditioned compassion 無緣慈悲; second, to complete the universal vows 滿弘誓願; third, to seek the Buddha's wisdom 求佛智慧; fourth, to learn the great means 學大方便; and fifth, to cultivate a firm and strong diligence 牢強精進.

1. *Unconditioned compassion* [81a7]

First, unconditioned compassion refers to the compassion of the Tathāgata. This compassion is of the same essence as the true aspect [of reality]. It does not involve attachment to the [phenomenal] marks of sentient beings, and therefore it does not involve the [mistaken] views of passionate attachments. It does not involve attachment to the marks of nirvana, and therefore it is not [merely] empty quiescence. Since is not [merely] empty quiescence, it is not a compassion that is conditioned by the Dharma teachings. Since it does not involve the [mistaken] views of passionate attachments, it is not conditioned by sentient beings [as the objects of compassion]. Since it does not depend on either of these two extremes, it is called "unconditioned compassion." The *Mahāparinirvāṇa Sūtra* says, "The conditions of the Tathāgata are called 'unconditioned.'" [The Tathāgata] universally covers the Dharma

The conditions of the Tathāgata are called 'unconditioned' 緣如來者名曰無緣: see the passage in the *Mahāparinirvāṇa Sūtra* at T 12.694c5–10, which contains an explanation also for the statements just made by Chih-i:

> World Honored One. There are three [kinds of] conditions for friendliness 慈. First is the conditions of sentient beings [as the objects of compassion]. Second is the conditions of the Dharma [teachings]. Third is no conditions. It is also the same for [the other of the four boundless demeanors] of pity, joy, and equanimity 悲喜捨.... The conditions of sentient beings refers to the five skandhas and the desire to attain bliss therein. This is called the "conditions of sentient beings." The conditions of the Dharma refers to the conditions or things that are necessary for sentient beings and providing for them. This is called the "conditions of the Dharma." *"No conditions" refers to the conditions of the Tathāgata; this is called "unconditioned."*... The conditional objects of friendliness [and pity] are all sentient beings, as father and mother and wife and child and relatives are conditions [for a person?]. This is the meaning of the "conditions of sentient beings." The conditions of the Dharma refers to not perceiving father and mother and wife and child and relatives [as substantially real] and to perceive that all phenomena arise through conditions; this is called

realm, extracts and removes the basis of suffering, and grants ultimate bliss. There are limits to the compassion of both of the above [individual] contemplations [of emptiness and conventionality], but the Tathāgata's compassion [that is, of the contemplation of the Middle] is limitless. The compassion of the above two contemplations is shared by bodhisattvas, but unconditioned compassion is that of the Tathāgata alone. The compassion of the above two [contemplations] is not all-inclusive, but the compassion of the Tathāgata is endowed with all Buddha Dharmas such as the ten powers and fearlessness. This is the treasury of the Tathāgata *(tathāgata-garbha)*, the place to which all dharmas proceed [as all rivers flow to the sea]. Therefore the *Mahāparinirvāṇa Sūtra* says, "This compassion [of the Tathāgata]—whether it exists, or does not exist, or neither exists nor does not exist—such compassion is the realm of the Buddhas and Tathāgatas." You should know that [such] compassion is endowed with the threefold truth. Kāśyapa praised [such compassion] saying, "Now I wish to praise one dharma, that is, a compassionate mind engaged in the world. Such compassion is great nirvana. Such compassion is true liberation. Liberation is great nirvana." The above compassion [based on the contemplations of emptiness and conventionality] is brought about through conscious intent; this compassion [of the Tathāgata] is naturally spontaneous 任運 and does not depend on petitioning [an outside power]. This is accomplished spontaneously [or without conceptual thought 無心], as "in overcoming something by [magically] producing

the "conditions of the Dharma." "Unconditioned" refers to not abiding in either the marks of the Dharma or the marks of sentient beings; this is called "unconditioned." It is the same for [the other of the four boundless demeanors of] pity, joy, and equanimity.

This compassion—whether it exists, or does not exist, or neither exists nor does not exist—such compassion is the realm of the Buddhas and Tathāgatas 慈若有若無非有非無如是之慈乃是諸佛如來境界: a rephrasing of a passage in the *Mahāparinirvāṇa Sūtra* at T 12.699a18–21:

> Good son. Compassion—whether it exists, or does not exist, or neither exists nor does not exist—such compassion is not that of śrāvakas or pratyekabuddhas, which can be conceptualized. Such compassion is beyond conceptualization. Dharmas are beyond conceptualization. Buddha-nature is beyond conceptualization. The Tathāgata is also beyond conceptualization.

Kāśyapa praised ... "Liberation is great nirvana" 迦葉讚云。今我欲以一法讚所謂慈心遊世間。是慈卽是大法聚。是慈卽是眞解脫。解脫卽是大涅槃: the closing verses of a chapter from the *Mahāparinirvāṇa Sūtra*, T 12. 838b8–10, in which Kāśyapa praises the Buddha and his teachings:

> I now praise one dharma,
> That is, a compassionate mind engaged in the world.
> The Tathāgata's compassion is a great accumulation of dharmas.
> With this compassion he is able to save sentient beings.
> This is supreme and true liberation,
> And liberation is great nirvana.

Overcoming something by producing a lion from your hands 手出師子令

a lion from your hands," or "as a magnet attracts iron." [However,] if the iron is obstructed by something external, the magnet cannot absorb it. The mental nature of sentient beings [is also like this]; [even if they are offered] unconditioned compassion, they are hindered by the obstacle of ignorance and it is not possible to spontaneously absorb all of them [to experience their liberation]. Now, [through the contemplation of the Middle] you wish to destroy the obstacle of ignorance, manifest the magnet of the Buddha's compassion, and spontaneously absorb immeasurable Buddha Dharmas and immeasurable sentient beings. If you wish to cultivate this compassion, how are you able to disclose and develop it if not through the contemplation of the Middle Way? It is as fire that arises from water cannot be extinguished by water, but must be extinguished by fire. This obstacle of [fundamental] ignorance arises through dependence on the two [individual] contemplations, and it cannot be removed by the two [individual] contemplations; it can be destroyed only with the contemplation of the Middle Way. You should cultivate the third contemplation [of the Middle] for the sake of [attaining] these causes and conditions.

2. *Complete the universal vows* [81a28]

Second, completing the original universal vows is as follows. When you have the first aspiration [for attaining Buddhahood], you arouse the Four

彼調伏: see the *Mahāparinirvāṇa Sūtra*, T 12.699b28–c5, shortly after the passage on compassion quoted above:

> Good son. At that time, wishing to overcome and protect the valuable elephant, I [the Buddha] entered the samādhi of compassion and put forth my hand, and five lions emerged from my five fingers. The elephant saw this and, being filled with fright, defecated and fell to the ground, and paid homage at my feet. Good son. At this time there were truly no lions in my hand or at the tips of my fingers, but by cultivating the power of the good roots of compassion I was able to overcome [this elephant].

Magnet attracts iron 慈石吸鐵: this may refer to a passage in the *Mahāparinirvāṇa Sūtra*, T 12.801b3–c26 which compares the power of Buddha-nature to lead one to attain supreme wisdom to a magnet.

Fire that arises from water cannot be extinguished by water, but must be extinguished by fire 如水生火水不能滅還用火滅: see the *Ta chih tu lun*, T 25.395c21–396a10, which does not contain this statement *per se* but includes the following statements:

> If you are attached to emptiness you will arouse regret and in turn lose the path. This is analogous to grass catching on fire, and extinguishing it with water. If this is water from which fire arises [such as oil], this cannot extinguish the fire. When bodhisattvas first cultivate [the path], they are attached to forms, so they cultivate virtuous qualities [to extinguish these attachments], like burning grass can be extinguished [by water]. If they realize the essence of reality and bodhisattvas practice all practices with great compassion, it will be difficult for them to attain the destruction [of these attachments]. This is like fire arising in water; one cannot extinguish [this fire] with it.

Universal Vows [with an aspiration] that is commensurate with [realizing] emptiness as a void 虚空. **[81b]** Through the two [individual] contemplations of emptiness and conventionality you come to know suffering and to sever the causes of suffering, but these are only like the branches and leaves. That [fundamental ignorance] which you cannot yet sever is like the basic roots [that are left in the ground after cutting down a tree]. Through the two [individual] contemplations of emptiness and conventionality you cultivate the path and illuminate extinction; these are like a flame or a torch that is not powerful enough to illuminate the deep darkness of the mountains. Even though you cultivate both [individual] contemplations, the vows are not yet completed; this is analogous to a hundred rivers not being able to fill the sea. But when the Dragon King Sāgara brings forth rain, the springs and lakes are filled in one downpour. The correct contemplation of the Middle Way is also like this. [In one fell swoop, in one instant,] you know all suffering, sever all the causes [of suffering] in the Dharma realm, cultivate the supreme path, and illuminate the ultimate extinction. You must cultivate the third contemplation [of the Middle] to complete your original vow.

3. Seek the Buddha's wisdom [81b7]

Third, seeking the Buddha's wisdom refers to the universal wisdom and knowledge 一切種智知 of the Tathāgata. The Buddha eye sees broadly, greatly, deeply, and far, provides full awareness of both the vertical and horizontal [aspects of reality], and endows ultimate [insight into all things]. Compared to this Buddha Dharma [of the Middle], the insight and wisdom gained from the above two contemplations [of emptiness and conventionality individually] is as blind people attempting to conceptualize forms in the dark but not being able to perceive anything, so they fall into a pit; how then can they progress forward? Cultivating the Middle Way is like a person who has [healthy] eyes and feet and can thus reach the pure and cool pond [of enlightenment], remove the scorching agony of [passionate afflictions that come from] the two extremes, and become fully awake 醒覺 and still 休息. Drinking this water is cool, smooth, aromatic, and sweet. This is called the Buddha's wisdom and knowledge. Those who wish to attain the Tathāgata's eye of wisdom concerning the true aspect [of reality] cannot perfect it with-

Dragon King Sāgara 娑伽羅龍王: see the notes at *Mo-ho chih-kuan* 57b1–2, where Sāgara makes its appearance.

Know all suffering … and illuminate the ultimate extinction 知一切苦斷法界集修無上道證究竟滅: this implies a correspondence between the Four Universal Vows and the Four Noble Truths. For details on the relationship between these categories see Robert Rhodes on "The four extensive vows and four noble truths in T'ien-t'ai Buddhism" (1984, 53–91).

out the cessation-and-contemplation [of the Middle]. Therefore they cultivate the third contemplation [of the Middle].

4. *Learn the great means* [81b15]

Fourth, learning the great [skillful] means refers to [learning] the Tathāgata's non-scheming good tentative [means], the great functioning of his non-deliberate activity. By dwelling in the Śūraṅgama [Samādhi] and making various manifestations with the inconceivable power of skillful means, you can signify to all sentient beings the wind that is within the void of emptiness [or, "the empty sky" 虛空], and even the fires at the end of a kalpa will not burn or harm one who is entrusted with this grass [of wisdom?]. This is very difficult, and so it requires good and skillful means. It is like [in the *Vimalakīrti Sūtra* where] Maitreya first teaches the practice of non-retrogression for the sake of divine beings and Vimalakīrti scolds him, saying, "From which birth have they attained *bodhi*-wisdom?… This insight cannot be aroused without *bodhi*-wisdom. You [should] teach the quiescent extinction of *bodhi*-wisdom after [mistaken] views have already been destroyed, that is, [the realization that] non-duality is *bodhi*-wisdom, all

Non-scheming 無謀: Chan-jan (BT–IV, 238) adds that "'non-scheming' refers to 'great wisdom.' The thoughts come first [spontaneously] without any conventionality; therefore it is called 'non-scheming.'"

Will not burn or harm one who is entrusted with this grass 負草令無燒害: the significance of this "grass" is unclear. Perhaps it refers to some unidentified analogy in the *Mahāparinirvāṇa Sūtra* or *Ta chih tu lun*? The *Kōgi* (BT–IV, 238), in reference to the "fire," says,

> Chuang-tzu says that "the sage enters fire but is not burned, and enters water but does not drown. He goes beyond the thoughts of water and fire." Although the principle is not the same here, [the meaning] is similar. The nature of fire is empty; who can say what is burned or not burned?

This refers to a passage at the beginning of the 6th chapter of the *Chuang Tzu* ("The Great and Venerable Teacher") describing the characteristics of the ideal person. Watson (*Chuang Tzu*, 77) translates:

> What do I mean by a True Man? The True Man of ancient times did not rebel against want, did not grow proud in plenty, and did not plan his affairs. A man like this could meet with success and not make a show. A man like this could climb the high places and not be frightened, could *enter the water and not get wet, could enter the fire and not get burned*. His knowledge was able to climb all the way to the Way like this.

Still, the meaning here is unclear, and it seems that the traditional commentaries didn't know what to make of it either. Ikeda (*Gendaigoyaku*, 413) attempts: "This signifies that people who carry grass on their back will not be burned to death by the fires at the end of the kalpa."

Maitreya first teaches the practice of non-retrogression … and so forth 如彌勒先為天子說不退行。淨名卽彈云從如生得菩提耶云云。無菩提勿起此見。既破見已卽說寂滅是菩提。不二是菩提。一切衆生卽是菩提云云: a reference in the *Vimalakīrti Sūtra*

sentient beings are indivisible from *bodhi*-wisdom [and so forth]...." The divine beings heard this profound [teaching] and were awakened to the forbearance [from realizing] the non-arising of dharmas. These two great masters were like a hammer and block pounding [together]; they led to awakening those for whom it was difficult to be awakened, and awakened them to the Dharma that is difficult to be awakened to. If there are no [skillful] means, then how can you benefit others?

Again, when the Tathāgata first emerged [in this world], he did not immediately teach the Mahāyāna, but used "various means, parables, and explanations" "to guide sentient beings and lead them to be free of their attachments," and later revealed the Buddha's knowledge and insight and signified [the teaching of] the one vehicle. Therefore [it is said that] he "carefully and diligently praises [skillful] means." [The Buddha] was able to manifest

to where Vimalakīrti challenges the teachings and practices of Maitreya. See the long passage at T 14.542a27–b12.

Forbearance [from realizing] the non-arising of dharmas 無生法忍: see the *Vimalakīrti Sūtra*, T 14.542c8–9. Boin (*Vimalakīrti Sūtra*, 93) translates:

> Blessed One, when Vimalakīrti had pronounced this address, within the gathering of the gods *(devamaṇḍala),* two hundred sons of the gods obtained the certainty concerning the non-arising of dharmas *(dviśatānāṃ devaputrāṇāṃ anu tpattikadharmakṣāntipratilābho 'bhūt).* As for myself, I was reduced to silence *(niṣpratibhāna)* and could not answer at all.

Various means, parables, explanations 種種方便譬類言辭: from a famous and oft-quoted passage in the second chapter on "Skillful Means" in the *Lotus Sūtra*, T 9.7a19; Hurvitz (*Lotus Sūtra*, 29 [29]) translates the context:

> Śāriputra, the Buddhas preach the Dharma appropriately; their purport is hard to understand. What is the reason? By resort to numberless devices and to *various means, parables, and phrases* do I proclaim the dharmas. This Dharma is not a thing that discursive or discriminatory reasoning can understand. Only Buddhas can know it.

To guide sentient beings and lead them to be free of their attachments 引導衆生令離諸著: another phrase from the opening of the second chapter of the *Lotus Sūtra*, T 9.5c3; Hurvitz (22 [22]) translates the context:

> What he preaches accords with what is appropriate, but the end point of its meaning is hard to understand. Śāriputra, since achieving Buddhahood I have, by a variety of means and by resort to a variety of parables, broadly set forth the spoken doctrine, by countless devices *leading the living beings and enabling them to abandon their encumbrances.*

Revealed the Buddha's knowledge and insight and signified the one vehicle 開佛知見示以一乘: these phrases are also from the second chapter of the *Lotus Sūtra*, T 9.7a24–27, immediately following the phrase quoted above. This section has been quoted frequently in the *Mo-ho chih-kuan*; see, for example, the note at 26b27.

Carefully and diligently praises means 殷勤稱歎方便: another phrase from the second chapter of the *Lotus Sūtra*, T 9.6b11; Hurvitz (25–26 [25]) translates the context:

> Now, why has the World Honored One made this speech *earnestly praising expe-*

the real truth because of his use of good tentative [means]. Therefore it is said that "although he teaches various paths, there is truly only one vehicle," "in addition, various means are used to complement and manifest the [truth of] supreme meaning," "the Buddha's wisdom cannot be conceived; he uses means to teach according to people's capacities," [81c] "the intent of the Buddha is difficult to calculate," and "they are not able to understand." Therefore hundreds of thousands of means are used to lead those of dull faculties to have an affinity within the boundaries of the sublime [Middle Way] 妙契寰中.

The power and function of the wisdom [gained] from the above two contemplations [of emptiness and conventionality] are light and slight; for example, when Pūrṇa tried to convert the non-Buddhists [with his limited abilities and insight], they reacted by despising and mocking him, but when Mañjuśrī went to them, the teachers [of the non-Buddhist schools] were

> *dient devices*? The Dharma which the Buddha has gained is very hard to understand.... Why have you earnestly praised this profound and subtle Dharma, so hard to understand?

Although he teaches various paths, there is truly only one vehicle 雖說種種道其實爲一乘: another famous phrase from the second chapter of the *Lotus Sūtra*, T 9.9b16; Hurvitz (*Lotus Sūtra*, 41 [39]) translates:

> They may demonstrate various paths, but
> They do so, in fact, for the sake of the Buddha Vehicle.

Note that the phrase "Buddha Vehicle" is used here instead of "one vehicle." The term "one vehicle" occurs in a similar context a few lines earlier at 9b8, which Hurvitz translates:

> The Buddhas of ages to come,
> Though they preach hundreds of millions
> Of numberless gateways to the Dharma,
> Shall, in fact, be doing it for the sake of the One Vehicle.

Various means are used to complement and manifest the supreme meaning 異方便助顯第一義: another phrase from the second chapter of the *Lotus Sūtra*, T 9.8c10; Hurvitz (37 [35]) has:

> By resort to yet other devices
> [The Buddhas] help to clarify the Prime Meaning.

See also the note at *Mo-ho chih-kuan* 28b11.

The Buddha's wisdom cannot be conceived; he uses means to teach according to people's capacities 佛智叵思議方便隨宜說: a phrase from the third chapter of the *Lotus Sūtra*, T 9.12a28, except note that the sūtra uses the phrase "Buddha path" instead of "Buddha's wisdom." Hurvitz (*Lotus Sūtra*, 57 [54]) translates:

> The Buddha Path, beyond reckoning and discussion,
> We shall preach by resort to expedient devices and in accord with what is particularly appropriate.

The intent of the Buddha is difficult to calculate 佛意難可測: a phrase from the second chapter of the *Lotus Sūtra*, T 9.6b18; Hurvitz (*Lotus Sūtra*, 26 [26]) translates:

> *My mind [says the Buddha] is difficult to fathom,*
> Nor is anyone able to question it.

They are not able to understand 無有能得解: a summary of verses in the second chapter of the *Lotus Sūtra*, T 9.6a, which expounds on how people cannot understand the great wisdom of the Buddha.

[vanquished, like dust] scattered by the wind. If you wish to attain these means of the Tathāgata, how can they be perfected if not through the contemplation of the Middle? Therefore cultivate the third contemplation [of the Middle].

5. *Cultivate a firm and strong diligence* [81c5]

Fifth is "great diligence." If you wish to perform great deeds, you must act with great effort 大用功力. The *Lotus Sūtra* says, "Suppose there is a brave and robust person, who is able to do difficult things...." [As the *Ta chih tu lun* says,] one who is immovable and does not regress—such a person is called a [great] being *([Mahā]sattva)*. [Such people] do not mull over their physical life, not to mention [mundane] wealth. Even though they attain *bodhi*-wisdom, they still do not cease [in their quest for] what they have not yet attained. The results are few and the rewards small for [practicing and attaining] the above two contemplations [of emptiness and conventionality alone], but for the contemplation of the Middle the meritorious results cover the heavens and earth, and the reward is as great as [the pearl] from the [king's] top-knot. One cultivates the third contemplation [of the Middle] for the sake of great diligence.

Thus there are very many reasons, or "causes and conditions," for cultivating the contemplation of the Middle. I have summarized and explained

Scattered by the wind 靡風: see the story of Pūrṇa 富樓那 (one of the main disciples of the Buddha, known for his eloquence in preaching the Dharma) and Mañjuśrī (the bodhisattva of wisdom) in the *Jewel Trunk Sūtra*, T 14.476b–477c.

A brave and robust person, who is able to do difficult things 勇健能爲難事: a phrase from the verses in the fourteenth chapter of the *Lotus Sūtra*, T 9.39b2; Hurvitz (220 [202]) has:

> *If there is a brave and stout fellow*
> *Able to do difficult things,*
> The king separates from his top-knot
> A bright pearl, which he gives to him.

One who is immovable and does not regress—such a person is called a [great] being 不動不退方名薩埵: ***Ta chih tu lun***: see T 25.94a16–19; Lamotte (*Le Traité* 1, 309) translates:

> Le Sūtra dit: Mahāsattva. Qu'est-ce qu'un Mahāsattva?
> Réponse. — 1. *Mahā* signifie grand, et sattva, être ou bravoure. Est nommé Mahāsattva l'homme qui peut accomplir une grand oeuvre 大事, sans régression ni retour dans sa bravoure....

Chodron (1, 254) translates:

> The Sūtra says: Mahāsattva. What is a mahāsattva?
> Answer. - 1. *Mahā* means great, and *sattva* means being or bravery. The person who is able to accomplish a great work without regressing or turning back in his bravery is called mahāsattva.

Reward is as great as [the pearl] from the king's top-knot 賞窮解髻: see the phrases in the *Lotus Sūtra*, T 9.39b3, immediately following the phrases quoted above about the "brave and stout fellow." Hurvitz (220 [202) has, "The king separates from his top-knot/ A bright pearl, which he gives to him."

them in five parts in order to contrast them with the contemplation for emerging in conventionality.

3. Correct cultivation of the contemplation of the Middle [81c11]

Third is the correct cultivation of the contemplation of the Middle. This contemplation properly destroys [fundamental] ignorance. [Fundamental] ignorance persists and endures [despite the insights gained from the contemplation of emptiness and conventionality], and cannot be seen or known by the [four] eyes and [two] discernments [of the levels discussed above]. How, then, should [ignorance] be contemplated?

For example, it is like the first contemplation [of emptiness] wherein you contemplate the true[, that is, emptiness]. The true[, that is, emptiness] has no visible form nor any extension. You merely contemplate the thoughts of the aggregates (*skandha*), sense entrances *(āyatana)*, and sense fields *(dhātu)*, and analyze the delusions of the three conventionalities with the tetralemma, skillfully cultivate contemplation, and attain the arousing of undefiled [thoughts or wisdom]; this is called insight into the true[, that is, emptiness]. The next contemplation is the contemplation of conventionality. What is [the contemplation of] conventionality? Merely contemplate the wisdom of emptiness and realize non-emptiness. Examine one by one all activity [of the mind] in a single thought 一心 [or, "single-mindedly"], and thus arouse the Dharma eye and come to universally know [all] diseases and their medicinal remedies or antidotes; this is called the contemplation of conventionality.

The contemplation of ignorance is also like this. Through contemplating [and attaining] the wisdoms of the two contemplations [of emptiness and conventionality], you should destroy their respective delusions; this is called [a kind of] wisdom. But now you are aspiring for the Middle Way, so these wisdoms [based on the insights of emptiness and conventionality] become delusions. [Although a kind of "wisdom,"] these delusions are an obstacle to those [who seek] the wisdom of the Middle; therefore this is called an obstacle *of* wisdom [or, "wisdom obstacle" *(jñeyāvaraṇa)*]. Also, this "wisdom" [of

[Four] eyes and [two] discernments 眼慮: or, more simply, "Ignorance is hidden and cannot be seen with the eyes nor known through intellectual speculation"?

The "four" eyes and "two" discernments are glosses added by Ikeda (see *Gendaigoyaku*, 415). Presumably the four eyes are the "five eyes" minus the Buddha eye (since this "eye" is attained only at a higher level), that is, the physical eye, the divine eye, the eye of wisdom, and the Dharma eye; and the "two discernments" are those of the wisdom gained from the previous two contemplations, that is, of emptiness and conventionality.

Wisdom obstacle 智障: see my article on "Chih-i's interpretation of *jñeyāvaraṇa*: An application of the threefold truth

one-sided emptiness or conventionality] is an obstacle to the wisdom of the Middle, so that the wisdom of the Middle is not aroused; therefore it is called an obstacle *to* wisdom 智障. The first is wisdom as an active obstacle, and the second is wisdom that is being [passively] obstructed.

For example, it is like the sixty-two kinds of [mistaken] views—these views have a certain sapience, but this sapience is a worldly wisdom. If you aspire for the undefiled [pure wisdom of a Buddha, with no "outflows" of passions], then this [mundane] sapience, along with [mistaken] views and conceptual attitudes, is an obstacle to the true [realization of emptiness]. In the same way, the wisdom of the two truths, along with [fundamental] ignorance, obstructs the wisdom of the Middle. Again, "delusion" is that which obstructs 能障, and the wisdom of the Middle is that which is obstructed 所障. Thus "wisdom obstacle" refers to a combination of the active and passive, the subject and object 能所[, that is, both that which obstructs and that which is obstructed].

How, then, can the two wisdoms [of emptiness and conventionality] be contemplated as ignorance 無明? If this [wisdom] is enlightenment 明, then the universal wisdom [of a Buddha] would be readily manifested, and you would have penetrating knowledge of all the Buddha dharmas such as fearlessness and the ten powers, would be perfectly endowed with full awakening, and would have attained enlightenment. But the situation now [with only the wisdom from the contemplations of emptiness and conventionality] is not like this [since you have not yet attained Buddhahood]; how can it not be [a kind of] "ignorance" 無明 [instead of "enlightenment" 明].

This contemplation of ignorance consists of three parts: first, the contemplation of ignorance; second, the contemplation of Dharma-nature; and third, the contemplation of true [emptiness] and [conventional] conditions.

concept" (1983) for a discussion of how Chih-i uses the threefold truth structure to interpret this term *jñeyāvaraṇa* from the Indian tradition as both "obstacle *of* wisdom" (a tentative kind of wisdom that obstructs the attainment of a higher wisdom) and "obstacle *to* wisdom" (the higher wisdom that is being obstructed). I will use the ambiguous term "wisdom obstacle" to translate this term 智障 in order to include both of these meanings. This term is discussed again in more detail below; see *Mo-ho chih-kuan* at 85b22–c29.

The first is wisdom as an active obstacle 智能障, and the second is wisdom that is being obstructed 智被障: or, "The first is wisdom as the subject of obstruction, and the second is wisdom as the object of obstruction." The *Shiki* (BT–IV, 246) raises the question of whether or not fundamental ignorance and the wisdom of emptiness and conventionality are the same if they are both the content of the wisdom obstacle. The answer is that of course the two are not the same, yet they are both obstacles to higher wisdom. Chih-i deals with this question later.

1. The contemplation of ignorance [82a1]

[82a] The contemplation of ignorance is as follows. [First] bring your thoughts into conformity with the wisdom of emptiness and conventionality. Contemplate these two wisdoms [and ask yourself], would [the wisdom of the Middle] arise from Dharma-nature or would it arise from ignorance, or would it arise from a merging of Dharma-nature and ignorance? Suppose it arises from Dharma-nature, but [this cannot be so because] Dharma-nature is non-arising. Suppose it arises from ignorance, but [this cannot be so because] ignorance has no [ultimate] reality and thus has no connections with the Middle Way. Suppose it arises from a combination of them together, but this option involves the flaws of both. Suppose it arises apart from [these options], but this would involve [arising] without any cause or condition[, which is impossible]. The *Middle Treatise* says, "Dharmas do not arise from themselves, and so forth." Expansively deconstruct [dharmas] in this way, as I explained above in the section on [conventionality as] causally arising. When you perform this contemplation, [all delusions] are put to rest and purified, your thoughts are not dependent [on anything], and there is nothing to be attached to, awakened concerning, or know [because all dharmas are empty]. That which contemplates and that which is contemplated are both empty, and cannot be expressed. Even if you do not advance as far as arousing [insight into] the true [emptiness], by means of the tetralemma you can certainly attain [a state of] non-attachment. This is analogous to viewing a tree stump, in the dark and from afar, and wondering if it is a person or just a stump. [As you contemplate this image, you may think,] a person has

The flaws of both 則有二過: that is, Chih-i has just pointed out that wisdom cannot arise from either Dharma-nature or ignorance individually; the implication is, how could it arise from a combination of these insufficient options?

Dharmas do not arise from themselves 諸法不自生: see the famous phrases from the opening of the Middle Treatise, T 30.2b6–7, already quoted many times in the *Mo-ho chih-kuan*, that "dharmas do not arise from themselves, nor do they arise from others, nor do they arise together, nor without a cause; therefore they are said to be non-arising."

Section on causal arising 因成中説: see the *Mo-ho chih-kuan* at 64a29–b25.

Viewing a tree stump. in the dark and from afar, and wondering if it is a person or a just a stump 闇中遙望株杌不審人杌人: this image appears in the *Ta chih tu lun*, T 25.147c1; Lamotte (*Le Traité* 2, 727) translates the context:

> Pour la naissance d'une notion, il peut y avoir deux sortes de causes et conditions: certaines notions dérivent d'une réalité, d'autres, d'une non-réalité 不實, telles que les visions du rêve *(svapnadṛṣṭa)*, la lune réfléchie sur l'eau *(udakacandra) ou la souche, vue dans l'obscurité et qu'on prend pour un homme.*

Chodron (2, 576) translates:

> There can be two kinds of causes and conditions for the arising of a concept:

six types of the features of movement, and a tree stump does not have these six types [of movement]; the object does not move, so after contemplating it for a while you may [correctly] conclude that it is a tree stump [and not a person], though it is still not clear. Arousing attachment to the tetralemma is analogous to the features of movement 動相, "movement" 動 is analogous to transience 無常, and "no movement" 不動 is analogous to constancy 常; after contemplating this for a long time without ceasing, and certainly coming to know its constancy, attachment to the four [options] does not arise, but since you have not yet destroyed ignorance, you still do not fully comprehend. Even though you do not fully comprehend, you certainly know that the constancy of one is the constancy of all, because you practice the great and direct path 直道 [to Buddhahood] without adversity.

The previous [two contemplations of emptiness and conventionality] involve a piercing and thorough [deconstruction of] [mistaken] views, conceptual attitudes, and the minute dust-like [delusions]; however, the wisdom of these two contemplations is [insufficient to penetrate] the diamond-like [solidity of fundamental ignorance]. The contemplation that destroys and deconstructs the wisdom obstacle is called contemplation that is a piercing contemplation. Resting in this principle is called contemplation as penetrating insight. [To realize that] this principle is inconceivable is called the supreme meaning of emptiness. This is called wisdom in relative contrast to the obstinate emptiness of the two vehicles, but [the realization of] the Dharma-realm is neither [simply] wisdom nor non-wisdom. In this way the contemplation of the Middle involves three meanings.

some concepts stem from a reality, others from a non-reality, such as the visions in a dream, the moon reflected in water, or the tree-stump seen in the darkness and mistaken for a man. Such names come from non-realities but are able to provoke the arising of a concept.

Six types of the features of movement 六分動相: the activities of the six senses?

You practice the great and direct path without adversity 行大直道無留難: this phrase is from the *Sūtra of Immeasurable Meanings*, T 9.387b11. *The Threefold Lotus Sutra* (19) translates this as "there is no suffering in practicing the great direct way."

Diamond-like 金剛: see the analogy in the *Mahāparinirvāṇa Sūtra*, T 12.649c17–20, that of digging through the ground until one reaches a "diamond stratum" that cannot be pierced by even a sword or hatchet. This analogy has been used in the *Mo-ho chih-kuan* before; see notes at 21c7–8, and the discussion of the meaning of contemplation as a "piercing" 貫穿 of obstacles.

Piercing contemplation [貫]穿觀 **and penetrating insight** 觀達 **and emptiness**: compare these three meanings and terms with the "three relative meanings of contemplation" discussed in Chapter II on the "Explanation of Terms" in the *Mo-ho chih-kuan* at 21c5–21. The first two use the same terms, but in Chapter II the third meaning is that of "contemplation in [relative] contrast to non-contemplation."

Three meanings 三義: that is, wisdom,

Again, realizing (penetrating) insight into the essence of the wisdom obstacle of ignorance [means to realize that the arising of dharmas through] self, others, both, and without cause are all unobtainable. [As the *Mahāparinirvāṇa Sūtra* says,] it is like a precept-upholding bhikṣu who perceives that there is no bug on the water, and wonders if that which is moving [on the water] is a bug or some dust. A bug would show some sign of life, but dust would show no sign of life. After contemplating it precisely without ceasing, he would know that it is dust, though not clearly and fully. If you say that ignorance has the four natures, then it has the nature of arising and moving; if you say that [ignorance] does not have these four natures, then without these natures it does not arise nor move. Although you know that it does not move, this is not for certain; although it is not for certain, you certainly contemplate it as constantly abiding and unmovable. The flow and movement of the two extremes of samsara and nirvana have already been put to an end by the above two contemplations; however, ignorance still remains, so the rolling and turning [of transmigration] is not yet stilled. Now [with the contemplation of the Middle] the penetrating insight into the basis of the mind and the quieting and purification of ignorance is called "cessation as stilling." Resting in this principle is "cessation as stopping." [To realize] the constant abiding of this principle, that it is neither cessation nor non-cessation [is the meaning of "cessation" as the Middle]. This is called "cessation" in relative contrast to that which is transient and moving. **[82b]** Thus that which is neither cessation nor non-cessation is called the "cessation of the Middle," and this includes [these] three meanings.

Again, as for [overcoming] the thoughts [that form] the wisdom

non-wisdom, and neither wisdom nor non-wisdom; or the three meanings of piercing, penetrating insight, and inconceivable?

Precept-upholding bhikṣu who perceives that there is no bug on the water, and wonders if that which is moving is a bug or dust 如持戒比丘觀無蟲水此中動者蟲耶塵耶: see the *Mahāparinirvā Sūtra*, T 12.653a6–9, in a passage on the attainments of bodhisattvas of ten abodes:

> Again, they are like a precept-upholding bhikṣu who perceives no bug in the water, but only the signs of a bug [moving in the water], and has this thought, "I wonder if this movement [in the water] is that of a bug, or that of some dust?" After observing it for a while without ceasing, he would know that it is dust, though not clearly and fully. The bodhisattvas of the ten abodes perceives the nature of the Tathāgata within his own body, but also in this way and not clearly and fully.

Four natures 四性: of arising from self, others, both and without cause?

Rolling and turning 迴轉: or "switching back and forth between [the two contemplations]," as in the next paragraph.

Cessation as stilling 息止, **stopping** 停止, **and neither** 非止非不止: compare these three definitions to the three meanings of "relative cessation" discussed in Chapter II, 21b16–c5.

obstacle, there is the cessation-and-contemplation of the four options of the three types of conventionality, [the practices of] faith [in the Dharma teachings] and Dharma [meditation] and switching between them, and the skillful cultivation of the *siddhānta*s, all as explained previously. Thus [the practice of contemplating] the four options [of the tetralemma] is a gate of contemplation [of the Middle Way]. There is no place to cultivate contemplation apart from [the contemplation of] these four options, and through [the practice of] skillful means you can penetrate this gate and attain insight into the Middle Way, but once [you attain this insight of the Middle Way] there is no [longer any need for the] contemplation of the four [options]. If you attain realization [of the Middle] through one contemplation, there is no need to cultivate [the contemplations] any further since the other options are included therein. If you have not yet penetrated and realized [the Middle], you should diligently cultivate the four options, and with these means acquire awakening. If you are attached to these four [options], you will be burned and hindered and obstructed and will not be able to penetrate [the Middle]. If you are not entangled in attachments, then as you contemplate ignorance through the four options you can attain awakening.

2. *The contemplation of Dharma-nature* [82b9]

Second is the destruction of ignorance in terms of Dharma-nature. In the above [we discussed] the four options [of the tetralemma] to contemplate the wisdom obstacle, that even if we seek [to discover] the arising of ignorance it cannot be obtained with certainty. Although this gives rise to a type of understanding and to the arousing of one [type of] concentration, it certainly leads to the conclusion that ignorance is indivisible from Dharma-nature. But this sort of deliberate conceptualization is not the mind of awakening, but only arouses a contemplative understanding. This is like seeing dust [on the water] or a stump in the dark and knowing certainly that it is dust, or a stump. Now you should shift your contemplation to contemplate the Dharma-nature [as follows]: is it that the thoughts of ignorance should be extinguished and the thoughts of Dharma-nature arise, or is it that [the thoughts of ignorance] are not extinguished and the thoughts of Dharma-nature arise, or is it that they are both extinguished and not extinguished and the thoughts of Dharma-nature arise, or is it that they are neither extin-

As explained previously 皆例如前說: see earlier at *Mo-ho chih-kuan* at 65b.

Like seeing dust or a stump in the dark and certainly knowing that it is dust, or a stump 如闇見塵杌決謂塵杌: rather than an insect on the water or a human being; see the example of the dust on the water mistaken for an insect, above at *Mo-ho chih-kuan* 82b20–23, and the example of the tree stump at *Mo-ho chih-kuan* 81a10.

guished nor not extinguished and the thoughts of Dharma-nature arise? If ignorance is extinguished and the thoughts of Dharma-nature arise, how is it that extinguishing is able to result in arising? If it arises from not extinguishing, then enlightenment 明 [Dharma-nature] and ignorance 無明 are parallel 並 [and this is logically unacceptable]. If it is said that they arise together, this option involves the flaws of both [of the first two options]. And it is impossible for them to be considered apart [because nothing happens without a cause]. [All things arise] neither from themselves, nor from others, nor together, nor without a cause. In this way [you should consider] each of the four options within each individual option, [practice] faith [in the Dharma teachings] and Dharma [meditation] and switching between them, skillfully cultivate the four *siddhāntas*, and you will be able to attain awakening and, with these four gates, penetrate to the [cool and pure] pool [of wisdom]. Even if you do not yet attain awakening, you will have a certainty that you can destroy ignorance through the wisdom of the contemplation of the Middle Way. Constantly learn in this way, and do not cultivate other methods.

3. *The contemplation of the true emptiness and conventional conditions* [82b21]

Third is the destruction and deconstruction of ignorance in terms of the true [= emptiness] and the conditions [= conventionality].

In relative contrast to what does the contemplation of this contemplative wisdom [of the Middle] derive its names? Is it wisdom, or is it not wisdom? In terms of horizontal contrasts 橫待, the Buddhas of the ten directions have wisdom and enlightenment, and in contrast to them I do not have wisdom and enlightenment. In terms of vertical contrasts 竪待, I will in the future destroy and remove my blind dark [ignorance] and attain great enlightenment, and in contrast to this, now I do not have wisdom and I am not enlightened. In this way, are wisdom and enlightenment cultivated

Contemplation of the true and of conditions 觀眞緣: The *Kōgi* (BT–IV, 258) points out that these terms are found in the *Daśabhūmi-vyākhyāna* and discussed by the *Ti-lun* scholars, to whom "the cultivation of the real" referred to cultivation based on an unchanging substance, and "the cultivation of conditions" referred to cultivation based on the functioning of conditions. The *Kōgi* adds that, in terms of the three contemplations, "cultivation of conditions" refers to the contemplations of emptiness and conventionality, and the "cultivation of the true" refers to the contemplation of the Middle. "Cultivation of conditions" is a deliberative type of contemplation; "cultivation of the true" refers to a spontaneous, natural cultivation. However, as Chih-i points out below, the Middle is "neither the true nor conditions," so I prefer to interpret "true" [as is often the case with Chih-i] to refer to emptiness, and "conditions" to refer to conventionality.

according to [conventional] conditions, or cultivated according to the truth [of emptiness], or cultivated according to a combination of conditions and the truth, or [cultivated] apart from the truth and conditions? If we say that they are cultivated according to conditions, [this does not obtain because] conditions are transient 無常; how can they give rise to that which is constant or permanent 常? If we say that they are cultivated according to the truth, [this does not obtain because] the truth [of emptiness or the Middle] cannot be cultivated. There are two traditional interpretations of this. The first is that the cultivation of conditions manifests the cultivation of the true. The second is that the cultivation of conditions is extinguished and the true is spontaneously manifested. "The spontaneous manifestation of the true" means that it arises on its own. **[82c]** For [the true] to be manifested through [the cultivation of] conditions means that it arises through another. The combination of [the cultivation of] the true and conditions means that they arise together [but this is not possible]. [For wisdom and enlightenment to arise] apart from conditions and the true means that they arise without a cause [which again is not possible]. Thus, seeking wisdom through the four options, we find that it is unobtainable. Again, non-wisdom is also unobtainable. Why is this so? Because wisdom is explained in relative contrast to non-wisdom. If there is no wisdom, that which is in contrast to it is unobtainable. It is the same for non-wisdom. If you are attached to [conventional] conditions or the true [emptiness], and affirm one or the other, you cannot arouse the Middle [Way], and so both are "wisdom obstacles" [in the sense of obstacles to the wisdom of the Middle]. If you are not attached [to these options], this is the four gates [of teaching that lead to the attainment of the Middle]. If you attain an affinity with the principle [of reality, of the Middle], [you realize that] this principle is neither the truth [of merely emptiness], nor the conditions [of merely conventionality], nor both, not apart from them; it cannot be [fully] expressed or signified.

Nor should you be attached to a [specific] *siddhānta* or skillful means. The explanations are different according to conditions, and hearing them can lead to the attainment of the path. For example, you can give rise to the constant through [teaching about] the transient. The *Mahāparinirvāṇa Sūtra* says, "The causes are transient, but the fruit is constant," and "from a [foul-

Two traditional interpretations 釋此有兩家: the source of these interpretations is unknown. The *Kōgi* (BT–IV, 259) refers to the *Text on the Meaning of the Ten Stages* 十地義記, a *Ti-lun* text compiled by Hui-yuan towards the end of the 6th century, around the time of Chih-i.

The causes are transient, but the fruit is constant 因是無常而果是常: see the *Mahāparinirvāṇa Sūtra*, T 12.840c29–841a1:

> Brahman, in your Dharma teachings the cause is constant, and the results are

smelling] castor oil *(eraṇḍa)* seed arises a sandalwood tree." [This is arising from another.] At times it is said that this [insight of the Middle] arises from the seed-nature *(gotra)* of the Dharma King; this is [arising from itself and] the cultivation of the true. Or it is said that "the attainment of the light of *bodhi*-wisdom is caused by the extinction of ignorance." [This is arising from both.] Or it is said that "it is neither from internal contemplation nor external contemplation that you attain this wisdom." [This is arising from neither, or without a cause.] It is an attainment that is not an attainment; and thus there is no attainment that is attained; this is to realize the meaning of emptiness 入空意. [Realizing] that there is no attainment is an attainment; this is to realize the meaning of conventionality 入假意. Attainment and the lack of attainment are all unattainable; the illumination of both attainment and no attainment is the meaning of the Middle.

Bodhisattvas unilaterally give instruction from [the perspective of] one [of these four] gates. For example, Vasubandhu clarified [the idea of] the *ālaya* consciousness as the worldly truth, and that thusness is distinct [from this defiled consciousness]. This [idea] was the main point of his discourse, and meditative concentration *(dhyāna)* [was considered] an auxiliary practice of

> transient, but in my Dharma teachings, although the cause is transient, the result is constant. Where is the error?

From a castor oil seed arises a sandalwood tree 從伊蘭子生栴檀樹: a phrase from the *Mahāparinirvāṇa Sūtra* at T 12.728c1; a king, speaking to the Buddha, says:

> I now see for the first time an *eraṇḍa* seed giving birth to a sandalwood tree. [That is to say,] my body is the "*eraṇḍa* seed," and my mind, with no roots of faith, is the "sandalwood tree."

This simile has been used previously in the *Mo-ho chih-kuan*; see 10b3–4 and especially the numerous notes at 54c22–24.

Arises from the seed-nature of the Dharma King 從法王種性中生: the source for this phrase unknown.

Attainment of the light of *bodhi*-wisdom is caused by the extinction of ignorance 因滅無明則得菩提燈: see the *Mahāparinirvāṇa Sūtra*, T 12.732a23–24. This phrase has been quoted already in the *Mo-ho chih-kuan*; see note at 8a2–3.

It is neither from internal contemplation nor external contemplation that you attain wisdom 非內觀非外觀而得是智慧: see the *Pañcaviṃśati Sūtra*, T 8.236a16–19:

> The Brahman Senika [or Śrenika] attained the contemplation of the non-internal contemplation, and thus had insight into this wisdom. He attained the contemplation of the non-external contemplation, and thus had insight into this wisdom. He attained the contemplation of neither internal nor external contemplation, and thus had insight into this wisdom. He also attained the contemplation of that which is not non-wisdom, and thus had insight into this wisdom.

See also the notes at *Mo-ho chih-kuan* 48c18 and 54c27–29.

Vasubandhu clarified the *ālaya* consciousness as the worldly truth, and that thusness is distinct 天親明阿梨耶識爲世諦別有眞如: Ikeda (*Kenkyūchūshaku*, 389) cites the *Daśabhūmi-vyākhyāna* at T 26.179b–c as an example of this kind of thinking by Vasubandhu.

the path and a secondary adornment. For [another] example, the *Middle Treatise* [of Nāgārjuna] gives instruction concerning ultimate emptiness, so "emptiness" is the main point, and the rest [of the contents] are relegated to the status of auxiliary practices of the path. The other gates or teachings are also found in the treatises written by the bodhisattvas; these treatises present various different teachings, but they do not go beyond the four gates. Although there is a variety of teachings [and practices] as causes [for attaining wisdom], once you have encountered an affinity [with them and attained wisdom], [you realize that the teachings and practices] are not different [in their goal and results]. If you realize this intent, why should there be sharp disputations and painful debate of their [so-called] contradictions?

If you utilize the four gates to cultivate contemplation, at times this involves bliss [or "following one's desires"], at times it involves [using] skillful means, at times it involves regulating [or "healing, therapeutics" 對治], and at times involves realization [of the supreme truth]. It is this way for one gate, and is also the same for the other gates. Although the practices of contemplation [for each gate] are distinct, there is no difference with regard to the path that is attained. The sūtras and treatises are not the same because they are responding to [various] conditions; the ancient disputes, with their difficulties that cannot be penetrated, should be understood in this way, and [the difficulties will be resolved] like the melting of ice and the dissipation of clouds. Such a practice of contemplation will result in an affinity of the teachings [of the Buddha] and the faculties [of sentient beings] with the principle [of reality]. When these come together in harmony, how can there be [any argument over] affirmation or negation [of this or that position]? People with clear eyesight "rely on the meaning and do not rely on the words." People with wisdom will certainly not arouse doubt. Those without eyesight and without understanding will go to great trouble [to dispute over these matters] and should be pitied; of what benefit is it to them?

Ultimate emptiness 畢竟空: see, for example, the opening section of the *Middle Treatise*, T 30.1a–b; the phrase "ultimate emptiness" appears at 1c4.

Bliss 樂, **means** 宜, **regulating** 對, **realization** 入: these four possibilities parallel the four siddhāntas, though the terminology is a bit different.

Rely on the meaning and do not rely on the words 依義不依語: see, e.g., the *Mahāparinirvāṇa Sūtra*, T 12.642a21–24:

> The bhikṣus should rely on four [hermeneutical] methods. What are these four? [They should] rely on the Dharma and not rely on people; *rely on the meaning and not the words*; rely on wisdom and not rely on knowledge; rely on the sūtras of complete meaning and not rely on sūtras of incomplete meaning.

On these "four hermeneutical methods" see the article by Étienne Lamotte on "Assessment of Textual Interpretation in Buddhism" in Donald S. Lopez, ed., *Buddhist Hermeneutics*, 1988, 11–28.

Question: [You say that] ignorance is indivisible from Dharma-nature, and Dharma-nature is indivisible from ignorance. When ignorance is destroyed, is not Dharma-nature [also] destroyed? When Dharma-nature is manifested, is not ignorance manifested?

Answer: That is so. The principle [of reality] truly cannot be named [or expressed in words], but it is called "Dharma-nature" in relative contrast to ignorance. When Dharma-nature is manifested, ignorance turns and changes **[83a]** to enlightened clarity. When ignorance is destroyed there is no ignorance; in contrast to what does one still discuss a "Dharma-nature"?

Question: If ignorance is indivisible from Dharma-nature, and there is no ignorance, then with what is [Dharma-nature] indivisible 相即?

Answer: It is like pointing out to a person who is not familiar with ice that water is ice and ice is water, and that these are just names. How can you say that there are two [different] things that are indivisible? It is like a jewel that gives forth water[-like light] when facing the moon, and gives forth fire[-like light] when facing the sun, and [gives forth] neither water nor fire when not facing [the sun or moon]. These [ignorance and Dharma-nature] are one, and not two; as there is [one] jewel that [gives forth] water and fire.

4. Clarifying the levels of attainment and their benefits [83a6]

Fourth is the levels [of attainment] from cultivating the contemplation of the Middle. The previous two cessations [of emptiness and conventionality] are means for [removing] the dual impediments to the Middle Way. The two contemplations [of emptiness and conventionality] are means for the dual illumination [of emptiness and conventionality, and thus the Middle Way]. By means of this [removal of] impediments and [attainment of] illumination, you attain realization of the Middle Way. The dual currents flow naturally, and the dual illuminations [arise] naturally. The cultivation of these dual currents involves three contexts.

[1] First is the "Shared advancing to the Distinct" 別接通, which involves teaching the cultivation [of the path] up to the seventh *bhūmi* stage, and the teaching of enlightenment at the eighth stage. For the Distinct Teachings, [up through] the ten levels of merit transference involves teaching cultivation

Jewel and water and fire 如一珠向月生水向日生火不向則無水火: the source of this analogy is unknown. Although it sounds like it could be from the *Mahāparinirvāṇa Sūtra* or *Ta chih tu lun*, a digital search of the SAT database turned up only this *Mo-ho chih-kuan* passage and a quote from a later commentary on the *Laṅkāvatāra Sūtra* (T no. 1791).

Dual currents 雙流: of both emptiness and conventionality, that is, the Middle?

Three contexts 三處: that is, that of the Shared Teachings advancing to the Distinct Teachings, that of the Perfect Teaching, and that of the Tripitaka Teachings? See the discussion that follows below.

[of the path], and ascending to the *bhūmi* stages involves teaching enlightenment. In this way the cultivation [of the path] and [the attainment of] enlightenment is higher and farther and faster [in the Distinct Teachings]. Beginners cannot attain even the cultivation of [the first *bhūmi* stage of] "parched wisdom," so how are they able to have the enlightenment of the eighth stage? This contemplation of the Middle Way thus has no benefit for ordinary people. Again, beginners are not yet able to enter the stages from that of the ten levels of faith to the ten levels of merit transference. If they cannot [attain even] the levels of merit transference, how can they attain the cultivation of the Middle? If there is no cultivation, there is no enlightenment. For ordinary people, this contemplation of the Middle Way is like facing a cliff, and of no benefit.

[2] Now I will clarify [the levels of] the Perfect Teaching. The beginning at the five preliminary grades is a very ordinary stage, yet [those of the Perfect Teaching] are able to perfectly contemplate the three truths and thus cultivate emptiness[, conventionality,] and the Middle—"sit on the seat of the Tathāgata" and cultivate the forbearance of quiescent extinction [that is, emptiness], "don the robe of the Tathāgata" and cultivate the concentration and wisdom of a Buddha and be adorned oneself with the adornments of a Tathāgata [Middle], and cultivate unconditioned compassion and "enter the room of the Tathāgata" [conventionality]. At the beginning they start at the first level [of "joy," the first of the five preliminary grades], and then progress to enter the fifth [grade of "properly keeping the six perfections"], where they arouse the dharma [of the next level] of [identity in] resemblance. "When you see a crane, [you know] there is a lake; when you observe

Five preliminary grades 五品: the first and lowest stages for those of the Perfect Teaching. See Chart I in Volume 3.

Sit on the seat 坐如來座, **don the robe** 著如來衣, **enter the room** 入如來室 **of the Tathāgata**: phrases are from the *Lotus Sūtra*, T 9.31c23–26, referred to many times in the *Mo-ho chih-kuan*. Hurvitz (*Lotus Sūtra*, 179–80 [164]) has:

> If a good man or good woman after the extinction of the Thus Come One wishes to preach this Scripture of the Dharma Blossom to the fourfold assembly, how is he or she to preach it? This good man or good woman is to enter the room of the Thus Come One, don the cloak of the Thus Come One, sit on the throne of the Thus Come One, and only then preach this scripture broadly to the fourfold assembly. The room of the Thus Come One is the thought of great compassion toward all living beings. The cloak of the Thus Come One is the thought of tender forbearance and the bearing of insult with equanimity. The throne of the Thus Come One is the emptiness of all dharmas.

Level of resemblance 相似: the fourth of the "six perfections," corresponding to the "ten levels of faith" in the Perfect Teaching; see Chart 1.

When you see a crane, there is a lake; when you observe smoke, there is fire 見鵠知池望煙驗火: see the *Mahāparinirvāṇa*

smoke, [you know] there is fire," so people of the level of resemblance realize the purity of the six senses. For example, if non-Buddhists do not cultivate mindfulness, they can never attain the stage of "heat." It is the same for the two contemplations [of emptiness and conventionality]; unless you cultivate the Middle Way, you cannot arouse [true] understanding [of emptiness and conventionality]. Now [those of the Perfect Teaching] cultivate the Middle Way [at the level of] the five preliminary grades and are able to give birth to [true] understanding [of emptiness and conventionality], turn and enter [the stage of] the first abode, and thus destroy ignorance. Therefore the *Avataṃsaka Sūtra* explains the stage of the first abode as "undefiled like emptiness, the pure and wondrous Dharma body, profoundly responds to all [sentient beings]; the afflictions proper and their habitual proclivities are

Sūtra, T 12.708b18–c1:

> Good son, there are two types of seeing. First, there is the seeing of appearances 相貌見, and second, there is full and complete seeing 了了見. What is the "seeing of appearances"? It is like when you *see smoke from afar, and say that you have seen fire* even though you have not really seen fire. Although you have not actually seen fire, it is not a delusion [to conclude that there is fire]. Or, [it is like] *seeing a crane in the sky you say that you have seen [lake-]water*. Although you have not actually seen water, it is not a delusion [to conclude that water is near]. It is like a person who sees from afar a fence broken open by the horns of a bull, and says that he has seen a bull. Although this person has not actually seen a bull, it is not a delusion [to conclude that a bull was there]. It is like seeing a pregnant woman and saying that you have seen [sexual] desires. Although you have not actually seen [the playing out of] sexual desires, again it is not a delusion [to conclude that sexual intercourse took place]. It is like seeing a tree put forth leaves, and saying that you have seen water. Although you did not actually see water, again it is not a delusion [to conclude that water is nearby and available for the tree]. Again, it is like seeing clouds and saying that you have see rain. Although you did not actually see rain, again it is not a delusion [to conclude that rain may fall from the clouds]. It is like seeing physical and verbal deeds and saying that you have seen the mind. Although you have not actually seen the mind, again it is not a delusion [to conclude that mental functions are behind the physical and verbal deeds]. This is called the "seeing of appearances."
>
> What is "full and complete seeing"? It is as an eye sees visible form *(rūpa)*. Good son, it is as a person whose eyes are clear and pure can see what is in the palm of his hand without any longing.

The stage of heat 煖: the first of the four good roots, the levels of attainment just beyond that of the various states of mindfulness; see the stages under the Tripitaka Teachings in Chart 1. The traditional commentaries point to the section discussing the stage of "heat" in the *Mahāparinirvāṇa Sūtra*, T 12.824a–c, which includes the phrase "All non-Buddhist followers contemplate only six practices, but my disciples are involved in sixteen practice" (824b6–8), but the connection of this text with Chih-i's argument is tenuous.

Undefiled like emptiness, the pure and wondrous Dharma body, profoundly responds to all; the afflictions proper and their habitual proclivities are

all exhausted in a moment, with none left behind," and "Their first aspiration [for enlightenment] exceeds that of [Śākya]muni." This is the meaning here [of the levels of attainment for those of the Perfect Teaching]. From the beginning, at the first grade [of "joy"], until finally arriving at the first stage of abodes, can be cultivated in one life, and can be attested to in one life. It is not [like those of the Shared Teachings who must] wait to practice [the Middle Way] until they ascend to the seventh *bhūmi* stage, or [like those of the Distinct Teachings who must] wait until [the first *bhūmi* stage of] "joy" before they realize the "dual currents" [of the Middle Way that brings together both emptiness and conventionality]. The levels of the previous [Shared and Distinct] Teachings are set high; this is a teaching of means. The levels of the Perfect Teaching begin low; this is a truly real teaching. The *Lotus Sūtra* says, "Such things are my [skillful] means, and all the Buddhas **[83b]** do likewise. Now I should teach for you that which is most real." This is the meaning here [for the Perfect Teaching].

[3] Next, the bodhisattvas of the Tripitaka Teachings sit on the seat of enlightenment while they still embrace some delusions; therefore they do not have the dual currents [of the Middle, incorporating both emptiness and conventionality]. The level of the "dual currents" belongs only to [the final stage of] a Buddha. As for those who are able to advance to the Distinct from the Shared, the level of "dual currents" [of the Middle] is at the eighth *bhūmi* stage. For those of the Distinct Teachings, the level of "dual currents" [of the Middle] is at the first *bhūmi* stage. Thus these [Teachings] involve a gradual

all exhausted in a moment, with none left behind 無染如虛空清淨妙法身湛然應一切。正使及習一時皆盡無有遺餘: see the *Avataṃsaka Sūtra* at T 9.455a25–28 and c7:

> The pure Dharma body of bodhisattvas
> Is immeasurable yet empty.
> In accordance with the wishes and pleasure [of sentient beings]
> It does not fail to be manifested to all.
> This mind is undefiled,
> Truly real, and not a delusion.
> It purifies the passionate afflictions
> So that all of them no longer exist. . . .
> Removing and extinguishing all passionate afflictions,
> Forever exhausting them, with none remaining.

Their first aspiration exceeds that of [Śākya]muni 初發過牟尼: see the *Avataṃsaka Sūtra*, T 9.472c16. This phrase has been quoted by Chih-i previously in the *Mo-ho chih-kuan*; see at 73a10–11.

Such things are my means, and all the Buddhas do likewise. Now I should teach for you that which is most real 如此之事是我方便諸佛亦然。今當爲汝說最實事: a famous phrase from the *Lotus Sūtra*, T 9.20b20–22. Hurvitz (109 [102]) translates the context:

> Kāśyapa, let it be known
> That, when by invoking causes and conditions
> And a variety of parables
> I demonstrate the Buddha Path,
> *This is my expedient device.*
> *The other Buddhas are also this way.*
> *Now, for your sakes,*
> *I preach the most true Reality.*

guidance, and as the levels diminish to a lower level, the true intent becomes manifest. Thus although it is said that [in the Perfect Teaching] it is at [the stage of] the first abode that ignorance is partially destroyed and that this is the level of "dual currents" [of the Middle], this is only a summary statement, like hoisting a sail and traveling three thousand [miles] in one day and summarizing this by saying "one day's [travel]." Again, it is like [the statement that] dhyāna meditation has nine degrees being a great simplification. It is like when the Buddha attained the four dhyānas and Śāriputra did not know, Śāriputra realized the four dhyānas and Maudgalyāyana did not know, Maudgalyāyana realized the four dhyānas and the [other] bhikṣus did not know. In this way we can surmise that dhyāna meditation does not consist of merely nine degrees. It is the same for [the stage of] the first abode. [The destruction of] one degree [of passions or delusions] is [the destruction of] immeasurable degrees. At this level [those of the Perfect Teaching] are able to pervade the Dharma realm and perform the activities of a Buddha in an immeasurable fashion. This is as expounded extensively in the *Śūraṅgama*

Hoisting a sail and traveling three thousand [miles] in one day and summarizing this by saying "one day's travel" 擧帆一日三千略言一日耳: the classical commentaries do not identify the source of this analogy.

Śāriputra and Maudgalyāyana: see the biographical accounts in *The Transmission*, T 50.304b–c, which includes the phrase, "Mahāmaudgalyāyana and Śāriputra entered samādhi, and the rest of the arhats were not able to reckon it."

Expounded extensively ... 首楞嚴華嚴中廣說: the Kogi (BT–IV, 281) admits that such content is not found in the *Śūraṅgama Samādhi Sūtra*. As for the *Avataṃsaka Sūtra*, see the immeasurable activities and merits listed at in the chapter on "The Merit of the Initial Determination for Enlightenment" at T 9.449c–450b; Cleary (*The Flower Ornament Scripture*, 404–5) translates:

> "O Child of Buddha, suppose someone were to provide all comforts for all the beings of incalculable worlds in the eastern direction for a whole eon, and after that teach them to keep the five precepts with purity, and were to do the same thing in the southern, western, and northern directions, the four intermediate directions, and the zenith and nadir as well — do you think this person's merit would be much?"
>
> Indra said, "Only a Buddha could know this person's merit — no one else could be able to assess it."
>
> Truth Wisdom said, "This person's merit, compared to the merit of an enlightened being who has just determined to realize enlightenment, does not amount even to a hundredth, not even a thousandth, a hundred thousandth, a millionth, a hundred millionth, a billionth, a hundred billionth, a trillionth, a hundred trillionth, a quadrillionth, a quintillionth — that merit does not amount to the smallest imaginable fraction of the merit of determination for enlightenment."...
>
> Truth Wisdom said, "This person's merit, compared to the merit of an enlightened being who has just determined to realize enlightenment, does not amount to a hundredth part, not even a

[Samādhi] Sūtra and the *Avataṃsaka Sūtra*. These illustrate just the historical life [of a Buddha]; how much more so [is it true] for the other [stages]!

Previously, after [discussing] the two contemplations [of emptiness and conventionality], I summarized the deconstruction of dharmas as explained above. Now, with regard to the correct contemplation of the Middle Way, [I can summarize by saying that you should] contemplate ignorance and Dharma-nature without relying on the two extremes nor relying on the four options [of the tetralemma], [and know] ultimate purity and that there is nothing on which to be dependent or attached. Therefore the *Vimalakīrti Sūtra* says, "I pay homage to you who, like empty space, have no place on which you rely." When this wisdom [of the Middle] is fully disclosed, [you realize that] the destruction of one [affliction or delusion] is the destruction of all. Since there is no place that this does not pervade, this is called the universal destruction and deconstruction of dharmas.

thousandth, a hundred thousandth, or even the small fraction thereof. Why? Because when the Buddhas first set their minds on enlightenment, they do not do so just to provide the beings of innumerable worlds in all directions with all the comforts for a hundred eons or a hundred thousand quadrillion eons. They do not set their minds on enlightenment just to teach that many beings to cultivate morality and goodness, just to teach them to abide in the four meditations, four immeasurable minds, and four formless concentrations, just to teach them to attain the stages of the stream-enterer, once-returner, non-returner, saint, and independently enlightened one. Rather, they set their minds on enlightenment to cause the lineage of the enlightened ones not to die out, to pervade all worlds, to liberate the sentient beings of all worlds, to know the formation and disintegration of all worlds, to know the defilement and purity of beings in the world, to know the inclinations, afflictions, and mental habits of all sentient beings, to know where all sentient beings die and are born, to know expedient means appropriate to the faculties of all sentient beings, to know the mentalities of all sentient beings, to know all sentient beings' knowledge of past, present, and future, and to know all realms of Buddhas are equal.

The historical life 示八相: lit., "the eight aspects" or phases of the historical life of a Buddha.

I summarized the deconstruction of dharmas as explained above 已結成破法遍如上說: see the section above at *Mo-ho chih-kuan* 80a28–b16.

I pay homage to you who, like empty space, has no place on which you rely 稽首如空無所依: see the final line of verses concerning paying homage in the *Vimalakīrti Sūtra*, T 14.538a14. Boin (*Vimalakīrti Sūtra*, 14) translates:

> You have eliminated signs *(nimitta)* in all their aspects *(ākāra)*; you have no wishes *(praṇidhāna)* regarding anything. The great power *(mahānubhāva)* of the Buddhas is inconceivable *(acintya)*. All homage to you, who are as unsupported *(asthita)* as space *(ākāśa)*!

3. Deconstructing Dharmas Horizontally [83b17–84b24]

Second[, after the exposition of deconstructing dharmas vertically in terms of non-arising] is to clarify the deconstruction of dharmas [horizontally] in terms of the other [three] gates [of arising, both arising and non-arising, and neither arising nor non-arising]. In the above [section] we discussed the universal deconstruction [of dharmas] in terms of the one gate of non-arising, the vertical cultivation of the three contemplations, and the thorough illumination of the threefold truth. [Next we will discuss] the immeasurable gates or options as pursued through the gate or teaching of non-arising, that is, the horizontal aspect of the other gates or teachings. By analogy, it is like numerous gates built on a straight road [heading into the royal capital]. [If looked at straight on, it looks like one gate;] this is called the "vertical" [perspective]; [if looked at from the side] all lined up straight or in a winding path, [you perceive their multiplicity;] this is called the "horizontal' [perspective]. Whether considered vertically or horizontally, they all lead to an audience with the king. Therefore here I will make differentiations concerning the universal deconstruction of dharmas and discuss contemplation in horizontal terms.

The horizontal gate or teaching is like the eight negations of the *Middle Treatise*: not arising 不生, not perishing 不滅, not eternal 不常, not severed 不斷, not one 不一, not different 不異, not coming 不來, and not going 不去. Thus one treatise clarifies eight gates or teachings; the sūtras and treatises [as a whole] thus [clarify] immeasurable [gates or teachings] such as not Being 不有, not nothing 不無, not defiled 不垢, not pure 不淨, not abiding 不住, not attached 不著, not experienced 不受, not grasped 不取, not void 不虛, not real 不實, not bondage 不縛, and not liberation 不脫. In this way there are many gates of teachings and practices, whose number is immeasurable. They can all be penetrated, and therefore they are called "gates." The *Middle Treatise* says, "If you profoundly contemplate [the ideas] 'not eternal' and 'not severed', you will realize the meaning of 'not arising' and 'not perishing.'" Why is this so? Because "not arising" is the same as "not different,"

Eight negations 八不: see the *Middle Treatise*, T 30.1b–c, as referred to many times already in the *Mo-ho chih-kuan*, especially the opening lines (1b14–15). Bocking (*Nāgārjuna*, 103) translates: "No arising and no ceasing / No permanence and no severance / No identity and no difference / No arriving and no departing."

Penetrated 通: or, they all consist of "penetrating" insight?

If you profoundly contemplate 'not eternal' and 'not severed', you will realize the meaning of 'not arising' and 'not perishing' 若深觀不常不斷: see the *Middle Treatise* at T 30.1c19–2a2. Bocking (*Nāgārjuna*, 103) translates the context:

> Since no fixed characteristic of arising is tenable, there is no arising. As for 'no

and "not perishing" is the same as "not one." "Arising" implies coming to be through accumulation [of causes], which also implies the meaning of "difference." "Perishing" implies dissipation and destruction, which also implies the meaning of "one." "Not arising" is "not eternal," "not perishing" is [83c] "not severed," "not arising" is "not coming," "not perishing" is "not going," "not arising" is "not undefiled," "not perishing" is "not pure," "not arising" is "not increasing," "not perishing" 不滅 is "not decreasing" 不減, "not arising" is "not bondage," "not perishing" is "not liberation," "not arising" is "not existent," "not perishing" is "not nothingness." Thus by profoundly contemplating "not arising" and "not perishing," you will [realize] the meaning of all [the other] gates or teachings [horizontally].

As you contemplate [the objects of] the skandhas, [sense] entrances, and [sense] realms, progressively and not progressively, and so forth up to the three obstacles and four demonic forces through the gate of non-arising, you should also [contemplate these] through the other gates in the same way.

As you contemplate that "the mind is like an artist," it draws with the five skandhas; in all the world, there is nothing that is not produced by the mind; that one skandha, sense entrance, and sense realm includes all skandhas, sense entrances, and sense realms; that one appearance, nature, essence, or power [and so forth] includes all appearances, natures, essences, and powers [and so forth], through the gate of non-arising—so you should also [contemplate these] through the other gates in the same way.

As you arouse the true and correct aspiration for enlightenment *(bodhi-*

ceasing'; if there is no arising, how can there be ceasing? Since there is no arising and no ceasing, the remaining six are also negated.

Question: If "no arising and no ceasing" imply a comprehensive negation of all dharmas, why does he repeat the exposition with regard to the other six things.

Answer: It is in order to bring out the meaning of "no arising and no ceasing." There are some people who do not accept no arising and no ceasing, but do believe in no permanence and no severance. A deep inquiry into no permanence and no severance shows them to be the same as no arising and no ceasing.... This is why he teaches "no permanence and no severance," to lead into the meaning of "no arising and no ceasing."

Accumulation 集: presumably since something that arises through "accumulation" involves more than one factor, that is, different factors.

Perishing implies dissipation and destruction 滅名散壞: presumably since after something is destroyed, it no longer involves multiplicity.

The mind is like an artist 心如工畫師 ...: see the *Avataṃsaka Sūtra*, T 9.465c26–27, which has been quoted numerous times already in the *Mo-ho chih-kuan*; see notes at 8b23. Chih-i has modified the quote slightly.

Appearance, nature, essence, power 性相體力: the first four of the ten suchlike characteristics; for details, see at *Mo-ho chih-kuan* 53a10–54a18 and *Fa-hua hsüan-i*, T 33.694a10–696a3.

citta) and arouse the Four Universal Vows through the gate of non-arising—so you should also [arouse them] through the other gates in the same way.

As you peacefully calm your thoughts through cessation-and-contemplation, practice for yourself and to save others, practice faith [in the Dharma teachings] and Dharma [meditation], and switching and spinning between them, and skillfully use the [four] methods of instruction (*siddhāntas*) through the gate of non-arising—so you should also [practice these] through the other gates in the same way.

As you come to know [the real meaning of] Being and non-being, you should deconstruct the [mistaken] views [in their various aspects] as individual, multiple, combined, and beyond verbalization, realize that each and every [mistaken view] involves the three conventionalities and four contemplations, and [realize the four options of the tetralemma that the arising of dharmas is] not from oneself, not from another, not from both, and not without a cause. [This is done] through the gate of non-arising; you should also [come to know and realize this] through the other gates in the same way.

As you destroy or deconstruct [mistaken] views involving seventy-two thousand three hundred and eighty-four (72,384) [types of] cessation-and-contemplation through the gate of non-arising—so you should also [do this] through the other gates in the same way.

As you contemplate the wisdom obstacle and [realize that] things that [appear to] arise from themselves do not arise from themselves, and therefore it is taught that self-arising is empty; that the emptiness of self-arising is not a [total] self-emptiness and therefore the conventionality of self-arising is taught; that this self-conventionality is not [merely] conventionality and this self-emptiness is not [mere] emptiness and therefore self-arising is taught as the Middle; and that this "Middleness" of self-arising is not merely a [contrastive or compromising] Middle but is the dual illumination [of the true meaning] of emptiness and conventionality; therefore the "threefold contemplation in a single thought" 三觀一心 is taught through the gate of non-arising—so you should also [realize this] through the other gates in the same way.

As you contemplate the wisdom obstacle and [realize that] arising from others 他生 is not an arising from others, that arising from both 共生 [self and others] is not an arising from both, that arising from no cause 無因生

Four Universal Vows 四弘誓願: see above at *Mo-ho chih-kuan* 55c26–56b12.

Calm your thoughts 安心: see above at *Mo-ho chih-kuan* 56b12–59b7.

Individual, multiple, combined, and beyond verbalization 單複具足無言說: see above at *Mo-ho chih-kuan* 62b4ff.

72,384 types of cessation-and-contemplation 七萬二千三百八十四止觀: see *Mo-ho chih-kuan* 76c2.

is not an arising from no cause, and so forth [as in the previous example], therefore the "threefold contemplation in one thought" [is taught] through the gate of non-arising—so you should also [realize this] through the other gates in the same way.

As you contemplate the wisdom obstacle and [realize that] self-perishing is not self-perishing and therefore it is taught that self-perishing is empty; that the emptiness of self[-perishing] is not a [total] self-emptiness and therefore the conventionality of self-perishing is taught; that this self-conventionality is not [merely] conventionality and this self-emptiness is not [mere] emptiness and therefore self-perishing is taught as the Middle; and that this "Middleness" of self-perishing is not merely a [contrastive or compromising] Middle but is the dual illumination [of the true meaning] of emptiness and conventionality, and therefore [realizing] self-perishing through "threefold contemplation in a single thought" is taught through the gate of non-arising—so you should also [realize this] through the other gates in the same way.

As you [contemplate and realize] that which is in relative contrast to itself 自待 is not in relative contrast to itself and therefore this relative contrast to itself is taught as an emptiness of self-contrast; that this emptiness of self[-contrast] is not a [total] emptiness of self[-contrast] and therefore it is taught as a conventional self-contrast; **[84a]** that this self-emptiness is not [ultimate] emptiness and this self-conventionality is not [ultimate] conventionality and therefore self-contrast is taught as the Middle; and that this "Middleness" of self[-contrast] is not merely a [contrastive or compromising] Middle but is the dual illumination of the two truths, and therefore "threefold contemplation in a single thought" is taught through the gate of non-arising—so you should also [realize this] in the same way through the other gates.

As you [contemplate and realize] that which is in relative contrast to others 他待 is not in relative contrast to others, that which is in relative contrast to both [self and others] is not in relative contrast to both, and that which is in relative contrast through no cause is not in relative contrast through no cause, and so forth [as in the previous example], and thus "threefold contemplation in a single thought" [is taught] through the gate of non-arising—so you should also [realize this] through the other gates in the same way.

As you [realize] through the gate of non-arising that threefold contemplation consummates the universal deconstruction of dharmas—so you should also [realize this] through the other gates in the same way.

If you enter and realize the other gates as you realize all the Dharmas through the gate of non-arising as explained above, you will be unobstructed both vertically and horizontally, as a diamond-like (vajra) sword [cuts through all things] without obstruction.

If you realize the intent [of the above], you can penetratingly interpret the sūtras and treatises and "spin" [their contents] in accordance with this meaning; the text and its meaning will be harmonized, and there will be no context that does not fit. What does this mean? If[, for example,] you use this meaning to interpret the *Sūtra of Non-activity*, you can "spin" the meaning of non-arising to realize the gate of non-activity 無行, that is, the non-activity of truth, the non-activity of wisdom, the non-activity of *bodhicitta*; the non-activity of practicing a calm mind through cessation-and-contemplation; the non-activity of the destruction of [mistaken] views, conceptual attitudes, non-cognizance, and ignorance; the non-activity of samsara, nirvana, and the interim state [between death and the next rebirth]; the non-activity of activity, the non-activity of levels [of attainment], and the non-activity of teachings; in this way, all things can be realized through the teaching of the gate of non-activity, and are ultimately contained therein.

If you were to interpret *The Diamond Sūtra* by applying the meaning of non-arising and applying the gate of "non-abiding" 不住 [in this sūtra, we can see that] there are various types of non-abiding, such as giving that does not abide in [and becoming attached to] visible form *(rūpa)*, giving that does not abide in sound, odor, taste, or touch, [and this can be expanded to the ideas of] giving that does not abide in the objects of wisdom, giving that does not abide in compassion, giving that does not abide in [mistaken] views and conceptual attitudes, giving that does not abide in non-cognizance and ignorance; this is called the perfection *(pāramitā)* of giving. [This can be

Spin 迴轉: lit., "turn" or "spin," or "apply" as in "putting a spin on" by interpreting something in a certain way?

The text and its meaning will be harmonized and there will be no context that does not fit 文義允當無處不合: Ikeda (*Gendaigoyaku*, 427) translates freely to read, "If you realize this intent, you will be able to freely interpret any teaching of the sūtras and treatises, and there will be no text for which you do not understand the meaning."

Sūtra of Non-activity 無行經: see, for example, T 15.750aff.

Giving that does not abide in visible form 不住色布施: see, for example, the phrase in *The Diamond Sūtra* (T 8.749a12–14) which reads, "giving that does not abide in visible form, giving that does not abide in sound, odor, taste, or touch."

Diamond Samādhi 金剛三昧: see the section in the *Jen-wang ching* at T 826a–827c. The *Shiki* (BT–IV, 291) points to passages that "extinction is diamond-like, and is also called samādhi" (T 8.826a22–23) refers to the mindfulness of the first *bhūmi* stage, "first realizing the unconditioned, diamond-like forbearance" (T 8.827c14) refers to the seventh *bhūmi* stage, and "first realizing the diamond-like universal and full [wisdom]" (T 8.827c23) refers to the tenth *bhūmi* stage.

expanded in terms of all the perfections:] the keeping of the precepts that does not abide in visible form [and the other sense objects], and so forth, up to *prajñā*-wisdom that does not abide in visible form [and the other sense objects]; [it can be expanded in terms of the stages of attainment:] you should not abide in the first stage up to the tenth stage. Although you do not abide in the dharmas, you abide in *prajñā*-wisdom through the dharma of non-abiding: this is to realize emptiness. Through the dharma of non-abiding you abide in the worldly truth; this is to realize conventionality. Through the dharma of non-abiding you abide in the true aspect [of reality]; this is to realize the Middle. This wisdom of non-abiding is the Diamond Samādhi, which is able to break up the rocks and stones [of afflictions or obstacles to wisdom] to ultimately reach the fundamental limits [of reality]. Thus there are three places in the *Jen-wang ching* that clarify the Diamond Samādhi, that is, [the sections] on the seventh *bhūmi* stage, on the first *bhūmi* stage, and on [the stage of] the first abode; this is an example of interpreting the meaning of the levels of the three Teachings [of Shared, Distinct, and Perfect] in terms of diamond-like non-abiding. [The *Jen-wang ching*] also says, "Śākyamuni entered the great quiescence and concentration of the Diamond Samādhi." If this is so, then it is not appropriate, as is the general opinion, that the "unobstructed path" *(ānantarta-marga)* does include the Diamond [Samādhi] and the "path of severance" *(prahāṇa-marga)* does not include the Diamond [Samādhi]. A sūtra says that "the Buddha realizes [the Diamond Samādhi]," so how can it be said that the "path of severance" does not include the Diamond [Samādhi]? How can the treatises by Vasubandhu and Asaṅga [on the *Diamond Sūtra*], expansively interpreted by [Chi-tsang

Śākyamuni entered the great quiescence and concentration of the Diamond Samādhi 釋迦牟尼入大寂定金剛三昧: a rephrasing of a passage at the beginning of the *Jen-wang ching* (T 8.825b9–11):

> At that time the Buddha Śākyamuni — he of ten titles, three illuminating insights, the truth of great extinction, and diamond-like wisdom — in the first month of the first year [since his enlightenment?] sat at the tenth *bhūmi* stage for eight days, entered the room of the quiescence of samādhi, and through his intention released a great ray of light that illuminated the triple world.

General opinion 常途: the *Kōgi* (BT–IV, 292) points to a passage in *The Meaning of Mahāyāna* (T #1851), section 9–14 (T 44.637c–641a) which "discusses the Diamond [Samādhi] as the severing and overcoming of the delusions of being and non-being" and that Chih-i is criticizing the position of this text.

Unobstructed path 無礙道 **and path of severance** 斷道: these paths are part of the "four paths" scheme of the Yogācāra tradition.

A sūtra says 經云: it is not clear which sūtra Chih-i is referring to here; perhaps the *Jen-wang ching*?

Treatises by Vasubandhu and Asaṅga 天親無著論: the *Kōgi* (BT–IV, 293) suggests

of the] K'ai-shan [temple], go beyond the meaning of non-arising and non-abiding? [They cannot.]

In brief, I have taken up two sūtras [the *Sūtra of Non-activity* and the *Diamond Sūtra*] to illustrate **[84b]** one side of applying [the insight as outlined above]. If you realize this intent, you will have lucid and unobstructed [understanding] concerning the thousands of sūtras and the tens of thousands of treatises. This is the first "chapter" in learning contemplation, the foundation for conceiving the meaning, the sublime wisdom for interpreting the different [teachings], the signpost for entering and realizing the path. Its structure is vast and great, and includes both phenomena and the principle [of reality]. If one [aspect] is understood, then [understanding] the thousands [of other aspects] follows, and you have mastery over the teachings.

Question: If the one gate of non-arising proclaims all Buddha Dharmas, then why do you utilize the other gates or teachings?

Answer: "Dharma marks" must be understood in two senses. Different people are not the same [in their needs and abilities], and each must use various gates or teachings to practice individually. It is like in the *Vimalakīrti Sūtra*, where the thirty-two bodhisattvas each explain their own understanding of the teaching of non-duality. If you say that "arising and perishing" is the duality of the cycle of birth-and-death, and "neither arising nor perishing" is non-duality, this [interpretation] is the gate or teaching of emptiness; how can this be related to the Middle Way? In this interpretation "arising" refers to the cycle of birth-and-death (samsara) and "perishing" refers to nirvana; these are taken as two. If you can concurrently avoid [one-sided attachment to] these two extremes, you can attain the realization of the Middle Way. Here, in the "entry into the dharma gate of non-duality" [chapter of the *Vimalakīrti Sūtra*,] these bodhisattvas give their own interpretation, and are not concerned with other teachings. [As another example,] the

that this refers to the commentaries on the *Diamond Sūtra* by Vasubandhu (translated by Bodhiruci, T #1511) and Asaṅga (translated by Dharmagupta, T #1510).

Commentaries by [Chi-tsang of the] Ka'i-shan 開善廣解: these are not extant.

"Dharma marks" 法相: this term can also be translated, "the features of the teachings," the "appearance of reality," the "marks of phenomena," and so forth.

Two senses 二義相: that is, the universal application of "non-arising," and the particular application of all the various teachings?

The thirty-two bodhisattvas each explain their own understanding of the teaching of non-duality 三十二菩薩各説已入不二法門: see the famous "Entry into the Dharma Gate of Non-duality" chapter) of the *Vimalakīrti Sūtra* at T 14.550b2–551c27, where thirty-two bodhisattvas attempt to explain the teaching of "non-duality," only to be topped by Vimalakīrti's thundering silence. This has been referred to already in the *Mo-ho chih-kuan*; see note at 59c10–11.

Avataṃsaka Sūtra says, "I only know this one gate." If each and every person explains their own understanding of the gate or teachings, there are immeasurable [interpretations of this one] gate. Again, the conditions [for saving] other [beings] are not the same [for all], and there is not just one way to guide and save them. Even if one person is able to attain awakening through the teaching of non-arising and non-perishing [that is, of emptiness], others cannot [attain awakening even] through being told [this teaching], and it is of no benefit to them. Next, if a bodhisattva further teaches [the idea of] no defilement and no purity as the realization of non-duality, [perhaps] some by hearing this teaching can attain awakening. Such horizontal gates and teachings are immeasurable. If eight thousand bodhisattvas each teach individually, how can you criticize this and say that only one gate or teaching is sufficient?

Again, practitioners rely on the gate of non-arising to cultivate the Four Samādhis. At this time they may listen with joy, or arouse thoughts of faith and goodness, or destroy the attachments of evil notions, or [arouse] a delirious desire for awakening. If this happens, then this gate of non-arising is the gate to the path; if this does not happen, then [the teaching of non-arising] is not the [right] gate. If you follow and enter the gate of "non-perishing," and through this joy arises, goodness is aroused, attachments are destroyed, and you approach the path, then you should know that "non-arising" is the [correct] gate for realizing [the path]; if these things do not happen, then this is not the [correct] gate [for you]. In this way you should traverse various gates and teachings, and examine and test each and every one, until you encounter the one that is the most appropriate. This is like spreading a net widely in order to catch the bird of one's thoughts. This is why the horizontal perspective is expounded as well as the vertical perspective in order to manifest penetrating the gates [of teaching].

I only know this one gate 知此一門: see the *Avataṃsaka Sūtra* at T 9.691c9, which reads, "Good son, I only know this one Dharma gate."

Eight thousand bodhisattvas 八千菩薩: there is no explanation of why the number 8000 is used here. Perhaps it is an oblique reference to an unidentified source?

Four Samādhis 四三昧: see the explication in the *Mo-ho chih-kuan* at 11a21–20a24.

Spread a net widely to catch the bird of one's thoughts 張羅既廣心鳥自獲: the traditional commentaries do not speculate on the possible origin of this image.

4. The Non-duality of the Vertical and the Horizontal [84b24–86a9]

The third part [of the exposition on the universal deconstruction of dharmas] is to clarify cessation-and-contemplation in terms of the horizontal and vertical [both included] in one single thought 一心 [or "single-mindedly"]. As explained above, if you horizontally and vertically, deeply and broadly, destroy or deconstruct all harmful attachments, cultivate all contemplative practices as stated in all the sūtras and treatises, persist in all your [potential] capabilities and conditions, your turnings will be endless, such that [this situation] is troublesome to describe and difficult to perceive. Now I should consolidate [these complicated matters] and divulge the correct intent [of the Middle]. The gate of non-arising has thousands and tens of thousands of overlapping layers, and yet a single ignorant thought is a "dharma that arises through causes and conditions" that is simultaneously empty, conventional, and the Middle 即空即假即中; this is the inconceivable threefold truth 不思議三諦, threefold contemplation in a single thought 一心三觀, universal wisdom 一切種智, [84c] the Buddha eye 佛眼, and so forth. It is such for the [single] gate of non-arising, and it is also the same for the other [immeasurable] horizontally-viewed gates or teachings. Although these things are taught in their multifarious variety, they are all [included] in the threefold contemplation of a single thought. Thus there is no horizontal or vertical, but only the cultivation of cessation-and-cultivation in a single thought. Again, this [topic] involves two parts: first, the general clarification of "one thought"; and second, the successive passing through of other [dharmas] in a single thought.

1. *General Clarification of Single-mindedness, or in a Single Thought* [84c4]

For a general discussion, I will present this in terms of a single momentary thought of ignorance in the mind 無明一念心. This thought or mind includes the three truths [of emptiness, conventionality, and the Middle], so if you

Cultivate all contemplative practices as stated in all the sūtras and treatises 一切經論修一切觀行: or, "state or interpret all the sūtras and treatises and cultivate all the contemplative practices."

Dharma that arises through causes and conditions 因緣所生法: this, of course, refers to the first line of the famous verse 24:18 of the *Middle Treatise*, the basis for the threefold truth pattern.

The cultivation of cessation-and-cultivation in a single thought 一心修止觀: or, "the single-minded cultivation of cessation-and-cultivation." Ikeda (*Gendaigoyaku*, 430) breaks the sentences differently, putting in a paragraph break:

> Thus there is no horizontal or vertical.
>
> Merely, single-mindedly [or, "with a single thought"] cultivate cessation-and-contemplation....

have penetrating insight into one contemplation [such as the emptiness of ignorance], this contemplation includes all three contemplations [and insights]. If you have not attained the previous explanations of the horizontal and vertical [aspects of non-arising], then how can you understand this sort of [understanding] of objects and wisdom?

Earlier it was taught that one thought of ignorance combines with Dharma nature to bring forth all of the hundreds and thousands of dream-like phenomena [of our experiential world]; that one skandha or sense entrance or sense field includes all skandhas and sense entrances and sense fields; that there are immeasurable individual, multiple, combined, and beyond-verbalization [mistaken] views; that there are all of the conceptual attitudes of the nine levels of each of the three worlds; and that there are various Dharma teachings such as the sixteen gates for destroying or deconstructing [negative dharmas]. Previously you have already heard about the gradual and progressive [ways of practice] and the horizontal and vertical [aspects of the teachings and practices]. Now you hear about a single thought as "a dharma that arises through causes and conditions," as far transcending all the previous [teaching of] gradual and progressive [realization of] "the arising of dharmas through causes and conditions," and you come to know "the arising of dharmas through causes and conditions" as inconceivable. [This is the first option of "causal arising."]

Earlier you were taught that all dharmas involve the three conventionalities and the four options [of the tetralemma]; that even if you seek the real through these options, they are all unobtainable; the individual and multiple [mistaken] views are all empty; the nine levels of conceptual attitudes are all empty; and the sixteen gates are all empty. Since you have previously heard this already, now when you hear of "one thought," you can realize that it is empty, and, transcending the previous [teaching of] gradual and progressive [realization of] emptiness, you can know inconceivable, ultimate, and sublime emptiness. [This is the second option of "emptiness."]

Earlier you went through the clarification of [the various aspects of] conventionality such as defeating the scattered [delusions (through practice for the self)] and entering [the realm of] perversions [to save others], and discriminating medicines, diseases, and the application of medicines. Since you have already heard these Dharma teachings previously, now when you

Immeasurable individual, multiple, combined, and beyond-verbalization views 無量單複具足無言等見: see the section on deconstructing mistaken views in the *Mo-ho chih-kuan* above at 62b4ff.

Conceptual attitudes of the nine levels of each of the three worlds 三界九地一切諸思: see the section on deconstructing conceptual attitudes in the *Mo-ho chih-kuan* above at 70a1ff.

hear of the conventionality of a single thought you can transcend the previous [teaching of] gradual and progressive conventionality, and know conventionality as the double illumination of the two truths. [This is the third option of "conventionality."]

Now when you hear [the phrase] "neither emptiness nor conventionality," you can transcend the previous [teaching that] "all that is empty is not empty" and "all conventionalities are not conventional," and the previous distinctions that "all is neither being nor non-being" 非有非無, that the individual [mistaken] views neither exist nor do not exist, that the multiple [mistaken] views neither exist nor do not exist, that the combined [mistaken] views neither existent nor do not exist, the Tripitaka [Teachings] neither exist nor do not exist, the Shared Teachings neither exist nor do not exist, and the Distinct Teachings neither exist nor do not exist. Since you have already heard this earlier, now when you hear of "neither being nor non-being" [in the context of the Perfect Teaching, the Middle, of "one thought"], you can transcend these earlier [teachings] of neither being nor non-being and know the inconceivable [meaning of] "neither being nor non-being" of the Middle Way.

In this way, it is very difficult to come across people who understand [the meaning of] the threefold truth in a single thought 三諦一心中. Why is this so? Suppose you discuss ignorance in terms of thoughts or the mind. If you discuss "the arising of dharmas through causes and conditions" in terms of thoughts, you have the previous [position] that all dharmas exist [as causally arisen]. If you [discuss that these dharmas] are empty in terms of thoughts, you have the previous [position] that all is emptiness. If you discuss conventionality in terms of thoughts, you have the previous [position] of emerging in conventionality and so forth. Again, if you discuss the Dharma realm in terms of thoughts, you have the Middle Way of neither [merely] emptiness nor conventionality. The threefold truth is mutually inclusive 三諦具足, and is present in a single thought. You can discriminate the appearances **[85a]** [as manifold and various] as a gradual and progressive teaching, or you can discuss the principle of the path as present in a single thought, that is, as simultaneously empty, conventional, and the Middle. It is like the three aspects [of arising, abiding, and perishing] in a single moment *(kṣana)*: these three aspect are not the same—the arising, abiding, and perishing are different. Threefold contemplation in a single thought is also like this. "Conventional existence" is analogous to "arising"; "emptiness" and "nothingness" are analogous to "perishing"; "neither existent nor non-existent [nothingness]" is analogous to "abiding." [The individual aspects of] the threefold truth [of emptiness, conventionality, and the Middle] are not the same, and are present in one thought, as arising, abiding, and perishing are different and yet are present in one *kṣana* moment. Threefold contemplation 三觀, the three wisdoms 三智, threefold cessation 三止, and the three eyesights 三眼 can all be known [in the same way] from this example.

If you contemplate in this way, then "sentient beings will expose the Buddha's knowledge and insight." "Sentient beings" refers to those with thoughts [of the three poisons] of greed, anger, and ignorance and who all conceptualize that they have a "self." This [mistaken notion of a] "self" is [the defining feature of] a sentient being. This [notion of a] "self" arises through the mind, and these thoughts arouse the three poisons [of greed, anger, and ignorance]; thus those [who give rise to such thoughts] are called "sentient beings." When these thoughts arise, they are simultaneously empty, conventional, and the Middle; and as such thoughts arise in the mind, they also include [the powers and potential insight of] cessation-and-contemplation. "Contemplation" is called the Buddha's knowledge, and "cessation" is called the Buddha's insight. Cessation and contemplation will then be manifest from thought to thought; this is [what is meant by] "sentient beings exposing the Buddha's knowledge and insight." The fulfillment of this contemplation is called the first grade [of the five preliminary grades of the disciples of the Perfect Teaching] of "joy." Reading and chanting [the sūtras] assists this contemplation, to turn you towards clear insight, and you fulfill the second grade. As you practice and teach [the Dharma], your thoughts are nurtured and turned toward clarity, and you fulfill the third grade. As you add [preliminary] practice of the six perfections, your good qualities become deep, and you fulfill the fourth grade. As you fully practice the six perfections, [your understanding of] phenomena and the principle [of reality] does not perish, and you fulfill the fifth grade. From the fifth grade you turn and realize the purification of the six senses, which is called the level of "resemblance." Therefore the *Lotus Sūtra* says, "Although you have not yet attained [the state of] non-defilement, your mental faculty is pure and as if [you have

The Buddha's knowledge and insight 佛知見: a famous phrase from the second chapter of the *Lotus Sūtra*, T 9.7a21–28, which speaks of "exposing, signifying, awakening, and realizing" the knowledge and insight of the Buddha. This passage has been used many times already in the *Mo-ho chih-kuan*; see the note at 26b27.

The level of "resemblance" 相似: the fourth of the Six Identities; see Chart 1 in Volume 3.

Although you have not yet attained non-defilement, your mental faculty is pure and as if [you have attained non-defilement] 雖未得無漏而其意根清淨若此: a phrase, slightly changed, from the nineteenth chapter of the *Lotus Sūtra*, T 9.50a26–27. Hurvitz (276 [253]) translates the context:

> If a good man or good woman after the extinction of the Thus Come One accepts and holds this scripture, whether reading it, reciting it, interpreting it, or copying it, he shall attain a thousand two hundred virtues of the mind. With this pure mental faculty, by hearing so much as a single gāthā or a single phrase, he shall

attained non-defilement]." From the level of "resemblance" you progress to realize [the stage of] the copper *cakravartin*, where you destroy ignorance and attain the forbearance of the non-arising [of dharmas], and [fulfill] all of the forty-two stages. Therefore the *Lotus Sūtra* says, "You thus attain in this way the resultant reward of undefiled purity." Again, [it is said in the *Jen-wang ching* that] "Those of the three levels of erudition and ten noble stages abide in their resultant reward, but only the Buddha alone dwells in the Pure Land." From this example [we can see that] the reward of a Buddha, compared to that of those of [the thirty stages of] erudition and the [ten] noble [stages], is that of sublime awakening 妙覺.

The *Mahāparinirvāṇa Sūtra* speaks of "attaining the supreme reward." [For a Buddha] there is a manifestation of the reward [in this world] and therefore this is called the "supreme reward"; there is none after this life, so it is said that the Buddha experiences no [negative] retribution. The

> penetrate incalculable, limitless meanings;… In the thousand-millionfold world, among the living beings of the six destinies, the actions they perform in thought, the motions they make in thought, and the frivolous assertions to which they resort in thought are all known to him. *Though he shall not yet have attained knowledge without outflows, yet his mental faculty shall be as pure as this.*

Copper cakravartin 銅輪: equivalent to the level of "partial realization," the fifth of the Six Identities. See the notes on this term at *Mo-ho chih-kuan* 18b10 and 67a16.

You thus attain in this way the resultant reward of undefiled purity 得如是無漏清淨之果報: a reference to a passage from the twentieth chapter of the *Lotus Sūtra*, T 9.51a4–7. Hurvitz (281 [258–59]) translates the context:

> This bhikṣu, when faced with the end of his life, in open space heard distinctly twenty thousand myriads of millions of gāthās of the Scripture of the Dharma Blossom previously preached by the Buddha King of Imposing Sound, which he was able fully to accept and hold, and *straightway he attained the above-mentioned purity* of ocular faculty and purity of aural, nasal, lingual, bodily, and mental faculties. Having attained this purity of the six faculties, he increased his lifespan yet further by two hundred myriads of millions of nayutas of years, broadly preaching to others this Scripture of the Dharma Blossom.

Three levels of erudition and ten noble stages 三賢十聖: in the T'ien-t'ai scheme, these refer to forty stages in the Perfect Teaching: the "three levels of erudition" refer to the three groups of the ten abodes, ten levels of practice, and the ten levels of merit transference, and the "ten noble stages" refer to the ten bodhisattva *bhūmi* stages. For details, see above in the *Mo-ho chih-kuan* at 53a8–9 and 67a15–16.

Only the Buddha dwells in the Pure Land 唯佛一人居淨土: A phrase from verses in the *Jen-wang ching*, T 8.828a1; the section just prior to this phrase was quoted above in the *Mo-ho chih-kuan* at 84a24–25.

Attaining the supreme reward 得無上報: a phrase from the *Mahāparinirvāṇa Sūtra*, T 12.612b27: "I now attain a manifestation of my reward; in a supreme and most sublime place."

Mahāparinirvāṇa Sūtra also speaks of the "fruit of the seed" and the "seed of the fruit." Since there is a manifestation of reward, this is called the "fruit of the seed," and since there is no later retribution [for a Buddha in another rebirth], it is not called a "seed of the fruit."

Again, the *Suvarṇaprabhāsa Sūtra* speaks of the "manifestation body" as the mutual correspondence of objects and wisdom. These are called "Dharma body" 法身 with respect to objects, "body of recompense" 報身 with respect to wisdom, and "manifestation body" 應身 with respect to the arising of function [and activity in this world]. By attaining the Dharma body you become permanent, constant, and unchanging; the Dharma body is pure, so [your insight is] as extensive as the Dharma realm and as ultimate as emptiness, and exhausts the limits of the future. The *Ratnagotravibhāga* says that "permanent" means "non-arising," "constant" means "no old age,"

"Fruit of the seed" and the "seed of the fruit" 子果果子: see the *Mahāparinirvāṇa Sūtra*, T 12.768b–769a, which discusses the causes and conditions and fruit of Buddha-nature?

Manifestation body 應身: see the expanded translation of the *Suvarṇaprabhāsa Sūtra* (T #664) at 16.363b19–c5:

> Therefore Buddhas are endowed with three bodies. Good son. Because ordinary people are not yet able to extract and remove three mental states, they are far removed from the three bodies [of a Buddha] and are not able to reach them. What are these three? First is the mind of arousing [delusional] phenomena; second is the mental state of relying on the fundamental mind; third is the fundamental mind. Through the path of overcoming [the afflictions] you exhaust the mind of arousing [delusional] phenomena; through the path of severing [negative] dharmas you exhaust the mind of relying on the fundamental mind; through the superior path of extracting [suffering] you exhaust the fundamental mind. If you extinguish the mind of arousing [delusional] phenomena you manifest the transformation body. If you extinguish the mind of relying on the fundamental mind you manifest the manifestation body. If you extinguish the fundamental mind you reach the Dharma body. Therefore all Tathāgatas are endowed with three bodies.
>
> Good son. All Buddhas share the same phenomena with [other] Buddhas with regard to the first body. They share the same intent with [other] Buddhas with regard to the second body. They share the same essence with [other] Buddhas with regard to the third body.
>
> Good son. This first Buddha body is of many varieties, in accordance with the intents/wills of sentient beings; therefore various appearances are manifested, and therefore there are many teachings. This second Buddha body is a disciple of one intention, and therefore it is manifested in one appearance and its teaching is one. This third Buddha body goes beyond all manifold appearances, and is not attached to the appearances of objects; therefore it's name is taught as neither one nor two.
>
> Good son. This first body depends on the manifestation body in order to be manifested. All the manifestation bodies depend on the Dharma body in order to be manifested. The Dharma body is truly real, and does not depend on anything.

"Permanent" means "non-arising" … 常卽不生。恒卽不老。清淨卽不病。不變卽不

"purity" means "no disease," and "unchanging" means "no death." The Dharma body has the virtuous quality of purity 淨. To be vast and great like the Dharma realm is the virtuous quality of the self 我. To be ultimate like the empty sky is the virtuous quality of bliss 樂. To exhaust **[85b]** the limits of the future is the virtuous quality of permanence 常. Thus you should know that the Dharma body [realized] at the first abode is endowed in this way with permanence, bliss, selfhood, and purity, and the lack of birth, old age, [sickness,] and death.

2. *Passing Sucessively through Other Dharmas in a Single Thought* [85b2]

The threefold contemplation of a single thought while passing successively through other [dharmas is as follows]. If in general [you contemplate] ignorant thoughts but are not yet very good at it, you should [contemplate] other thoughts successively. Whether thoughts of [covetous] desires, thoughts of anger, thoughts of pride—when these thoughts arise [you should contemplate them] as simultaneously empty, conventional, and the Middle. In turn, [the rest] is as explained in the general discussion [above].

The earlier explanations were teachings that focused only on contemplating the skandha of consciousness. [Teachings concerning] the other four aggregates are likewise, and it is also likewise for the twelve [sense] entrances and the eighteen [sense] realms[, but I will not go into all the details here.] This is called the universal deconstruction of dharmas through contemplating the objects of the [five] aggregates (*skandha*), [twelve sense] entrances (*āyatana*), and [eighteen sense] realms (*dhātu*).

Question: When presenting the realization of conventionality you explained the causes and conditions, but why was this missing in [your presentation of] realizing emptiness? [In response to your presentation of] realizing emptiness there were questions and answers concerning the four gates, but why was this missing in [your presentation of] realizing conventionality?

Answer: [The teaching of] causes and conditions is included in the realization of emptiness, but I abbreviated and did not explain it. Why? [Because emptiness is taught] for the sake of liberation [of oneself], for the sake of liberating others, for the sake of [attaining] the life-force of wisdom, for the

死: these terms seem to be taken from the *Ratnagotravibhāga*, T 31.830b1–c5. This passage has been referred to previously in the *Mo-ho chih-kuan*; see the endnote at 30a11–12 for Takasaki's translation.

Contemplating the objects of the aggregates, sense entrances, and sense realms 觀陰入界境: see the opening of this section at *Mo-ho chih-kuan* 51c20.

Life-force of wisdom 慧命: on this term see the glossary, and the note at *Mo-ho chih-kuan* 19a29.

sake of [attaining] non-defilement, and for the sake of attaining the levels of the Dharma [teachings?] 法位. The bonds and attachments of samsara plague our spirits, and cannot be unraveled [and understood] without [realizing] emptiness. How is it possible to unravel the bonds of others when you are in bondage yourself? You must realize emptiness yourself in order to liberate others. The erudite and noble have wisdom as their life-force, and this life-force of wisdom cannot be established without [the realization of] emptiness. Of all the supranormal powers, the supranormal power of no outflows is the most superior, and you must certainly realize emptiness in order to [attain] this most superior supranormal power. Again, you cannot realize the levels of the Dharma [teachings] without wisdom, and you are able to realize the levels of the Dharma quickly with the wisdom of emptiness. There are very many causes and conditions for realizing emptiness, but following the later example [of the causes and conditions for realizing conventionality], five are taught.

[Next, with regard to the question concerning the handling of conventionality:] The contemplation of emptiness is common to both the Hīnayāna 小 and Mahāyāna 大, to [both] the one-sided or incomplete 偏 [Tripitaka, Shared, and Distinct Teachings] and the Perfect 圓 [Teaching]; if we wish to distinguish between these [understandings of emptiness] without disorder, they must be inquired into in terms of the four gates. However, the Hīnayāna is not included within [the purview of] conventionality, so [the categories of the four gates] are not used. There are two types of contemplating emptiness: analytical emptiness is used exclusively in the Hīnayāna, and [achieving direct insight into] emptiness as the essence [of reality] is common to both the Hīnayāna and the Mahāyana. The inquiry here concerned a distinction between [these two uses of] essential emptiness; although the same term "essence" is used [in both Hīnayāna and Mahāyāna], it was necessary to inquire into it to make a distinction in its application. The teachings [lit. "that which allows the penetrating" 能通] of the Distinct and Perfect [Teachings] each involve the four gates, but the objective [lit., "the place to which one penetrates" 所通] is the same, so the inquiry was closed [for this section].

There are different understandings and disagreements concerning the

The erudite and noble 賢聖: or, "those on the three [times ten] stages of erudition and the [ten] noble stages"; see note above.

Supranormal power of no outflows 無漏通勝: presumably the sixth of the six supranormal powers, that is, the ability to remove one's passionate afflictions.

Five are taught 說五: the five "conditions" of compassion, vows, wisdom, means, and diligence; see above at 75c11–76a19.

Different understandings and disagreements 異解不同: Chih-i does not give many examples of these "different

"wisdom obstacle" 智障. Here I will present the interpretation of *Dharmauttara.

Passionate afflictions *(kleśa)* are deluded thoughts, therefore passionate afflictions are an obstacle [to attaining the path]. Wisdom is clear understanding 明解, so why is it said that wisdom is an obstacle? [Answer] There are two types of wisdom: the wisdom of illumination 證智, and the wisdom of [human, conceptual] consciousness 識智. The wisdom of consciousness involves discrimination; it differs from an essential [understanding of emptiness] and corresponds to conceptual understanding. Since it corresponds to conceptual understanding, it is called "wisdom" [in a worldly sense]. Since it differs from essential [understanding] and involves discrimination, it hinders the wisdom of illumination. Therefore "wisdom" is called an obstacle.

Also, [the sūtras say that] the Buddha attains liberation from two obstacles. The *Mahāparinirvāṇa Sūtra* says, "By severing passions you attain the mind of liberation. By severing ignorance you attain the wisdom of liberation." The *Bodhisattva-bhūmi* says that "passion is the head 首 of afflictions *(kleśa)*; therefore the mind of liberation is the antidote for the obstacle of passionate afflictions *(kleśāvaraṇa)*. To be far removed from all ignorance and defilement, and to know all there is to know 所知 *(jñeya)* **[85c]** without obstruction, is called pure wisdom. Pure wisdom is the wisdom of libera-

understandings and disagreements," and there are few extant pre-Chih-i texts that allow us to trace the early development of Buddhist ideas in China. An indispensable text is *The Meaning of Mahāyāna* by Hui-yuan, which discusses the "two obstacles" *(kleśajñeyāvaraṇa)* at T 44.561–564.

Dharmauttara 達摩鬱多羅: identity uncertain. Chan-jan (BT–IV, 315) identifies him as an arhat who lived eight hundred years after the death of the Buddha, and who took three hundred verses from the *Abhidharma-mahāvibhāṣā-śāstra* (T no. 1546) to compile to an abbreviated *Samyukta-abhidharma-śāstra* (T no. 1552). The *Shiki* disagrees, pointing out that the *Samyukta-abhidharma-śāstra* does not contain any reference to *jñeyāvaraṇa*, and that the name of this text's author (Dharmatrāta 達磨多羅) is different. In any case, Chih-i's source is unclear.

By severing passions you attain the mind of liberation. By severing ignorance you attain the wisdom of liberation 斷愛故得心解脱。斷無明故得智解脱: see the *Mahāparinirvāṇa Sūtra*, T 12.835b15–17:

> One attains two liberations: by removing and severing passions you attain the mind of liberation, and by severing ignorance you attain the wisdom of liberation.

Note that the sūtra uses 慧 for "wisdom," whereas Chih-i uses 智, perhaps to make his text more consistent.

Passion is the head of afflictions … Pure wisdom is the wisdom of liberation 愛爲煩惱首故心解脱對治煩惱障也。遠離一切無明穢汚於一切所知知無障礙名智淨。智淨卽慧解脱: a paraphrase from an early version of the *Bodhisattva-bhūmi* section of the *Yogācāra-bhūmi* translated into Chinese by Dharmakṣema in the early fifth century. Chih-i's reference is to the Bodhipaṭalam chapter of the first section of this work (T 30.901b15–21).

tion." If we say that the hindrance to the knowledge *(jñeya)* of wisdom is the wisdom obstacle, then ignorance is the obstacle to wisdom. Thus, truly, ignorance is the essence of the wisdom obstacle. The *Introduction to Mahāyāna* says that "transworldly ignorance is the wisdom obstacle.... The erudite and noble are already far removed from [the activity of] worldly ignorance." That is to say, they first sever the obstacle of passionate afflictions.

What is *bodhi*-wisdom? In brief there are two types of severance and two types of wisdom, and this is called *bodhi*-wisdom. The two types of severance are the severance of the obstacles of passionate afflictions *(kleśāvaraṇa)*, and the severance of the wisdom obstacle *(jñeyāvaraṇa)*. The two types of wisdom are [first] the severance of the obstacles of passionate afflictions, to be separate from defilements and to purify all passionate afflictions that are not continuous with wisdom, and the severance of the wisdom obstacle, that is, all knowables that do not obstruct or hinder wisdom. Again, pure wisdom, all-wisdom *(sarvajñā)*, and unhindered wisdom, extinguish all the habitual traces of passionate afflictions, purifying them, clearly penetrating them, and forever severing them without remainder; this is called supreme *bodhi*-wisdom. This is called wisdom that ultimately severs all traces of passionate afflictions; this is called "pure wisdom." Wisdom that is unobstructed in all realms by all things and all types in all times is called "omniscience" *(sarvajñā)*.

For a full English translation of this section from the Sanskrit see John Keenan's translation of Hakamaya Noriaki's paper on "The Realm of Enlightenment in *Vijñāptimātratā*: The Formation of the 'Four Kinds of Pure Dharmas'" (*Journal of the International Association of Buddhist Studies* 3/2: 33). For Hsüan-tsang's translation of this section see T 30.498c20–27.

Ikeda (*Kenkyūchūshaku*, 392) points to an earlier section of the text, at T 30.888c, which discusses the attachments of passions and covetousness.

Hindrance to the knowledge of wisdom 以智所知礙名智障: here Chih-i uses the term 所知, later used by Hsüan-tsang to translate *jñeya* as the content of the obstacle (the "obstacle of knowledge"). Here 所知 is used to refer to the content of that which is known by wisdom, the goal to be achieved that is obstructed by ignorance; hence it is ignorance that is the obstacle, not "knowledge" or "knowables."

Transworldly ignorance is the wisdom obstacle.... The erudite and noble are already far removed from worldly ignorance 出世間無明是智障。世間無明賢聖已遠離: phrases from the *Introduction to Mahāyāna* at T 32.45c9–12. This text, as the title suggests, is a short introduction to basic Mahāyāna doctrine. It was translated into Chinese between 397 and 439 by Tao-t'ai, but is not extant in Sanskrit. The full context (T 32.45c2–13) reads:

> The arhat first severs passionate afflictions; later he removes the wisdom obstacle, cultivates the *bodhi* path, and attains perfect awakening. Among arhats there are those who sever a few wisdom obstacles, who have not severed [wisdom obstacles], who have attained the concentration of non-contentiousness *(araṇā-samādhi)*, who have not attained the concentration of non-contentiousness, who have attained the five supranormal powers, who have not attained the five supranormal powers, who have attained the four fluencies *(catuṣpratisaṃvid)*, who have not attained the four fluencies, who have attained the mastery of entering and coming out of meditation, who have not attained the mastery of entering and coming out of meditation.

The two obstacles [of passionate afflictions and ignorance] are both afflictions; why, then, do we say that ignorance is [the content of] the wisdom obstacle? Because[, in the case of the wisdom obstacle,] ignorance is the delusion with reference to wisdom. Wisdom is the essence [of the wisdom obstacle] and it is in reference to this wisdom that you speak of an obstacle. For example, when you speak of "unconditioned samsara" *(asaṃskṛtaḥsaṃsārah̤)*, it is in reference to the unconditioned [that is, nirvana] that you use the term samsara, and being "unconditioned" is the defining term. [On the other hand,] "passion" refers [in general] to the four categories of passionate afflictions that are able to obstruct wisdom. Although these [passions] are delusions [that involve] different mental activities, and are not the same with regard to [the content of their] understanding and delusion, in essence they are passionate afflictions. Therefore, because of their essence they are called the "obstacle of passionate afflictions."

Again, passions lead all phenomenal existence to continue, inflame the mind, and make the mind troubled. Although ignorance is covered and hidden, the impetus for its arising is watered and strengthened by the passions. Therefore passions are called "the obstacle of passionate afflictions." [On the other hand,] ignorance is something incomplete; it is truly the opposite of liberation. The nature of passion, though it is different [from ignorance], has ignorance as its basis. The nature of ignorance is delusion; it is clear how this is a wisdom obstacle[, that is, an obstacle to wisdom]. Therefore, because it is an obstacle, it is called a "wisdom obstacle."

Ignorance is of two types: first, delusions concerning the principle [of reality], and second, delusions concerning phenomena. Which of these can be called the wisdom obstacle? The *Bodhisattva-bhūmi* says that for those of the two vehicles who are undefiled [by passions], the wisdom of the non-

Why is this so? Because they have not severed all wisdom obstacles. Question: what is that which is called "wisdom obstacle"? Answer: *Transworldly ignorance (loka-uttara-avidya?) is the wisdom obstacle.*

It is as *Balaruci explains in a verse in the Jataka tales:

There are two types of ignorance:
The worldly and the transworldly.
Those who are wise have long ago parted
From the activities of worldly ignorance.
Those who are foolish do not have subtle understanding
And are not able to know this truth.

Unconditioned is the defining term 以無爲爲名也: Chan-jan (BT–IV, 318) explains that samsara is not really unconditioned, just as ignorance is not really wisdom. It is only in reference to the wisdom obstacle, that is, a relative ignorance as the obstacle to wisdom, that one speaks of ignorance in this way. Or, in other words, some forms of "ignorance" are closer to "wisdom" than others.

For those of the two vehicles who are undefiled ... this is the wisdom obstacle 二乘無漏人無我智為煩惱障淨智。佛

substantiality of the self is the wisdom purified of the obstacles of passionate afflictions; for Buddhas and bodhisattvas, the wisdom of the non-substantiality of phenomena or dharmas is the wisdom purified of the wisdom obstacle. If this is so, then both are a "delusion concerning principle," and this is the wisdom obstacle. On the other hand, if hindrance to the knowledge 所知 *(jñeya)* of wisdom is the wisdom obstacle, then, since the knowledge [of a Buddha] is unobstructed concerning all phenomena, only the "delusion concerning phenomena" is the wisdom obstacle. What, then, can be taken as a rule? Wisdom illuminates both phenomena and the principle [of reality]. Though in this sense there are two wisdoms, there is no [ultimate] distinction in the essence [of phenomena and principle]. Thus the wisdom obstacle and ignorance do not have two [different] natures; though they are said to be two, they are not two.

Again, if we say that the mind or thoughts of wisdom 心智 is the obstacle, then [this refers to] discriminatory wisdom *(vikalpajñāna?)* which in the final analysis conceptualizes [the objects of experience]. This [conceptualization] hinders [insight into] the way things truly are 如實, so that you cannot attain the wisdom of illumination. This [discriminatory wisdom] also is a kind of wisdom that is nevertheless an obstacle. By extinguishing conceptual thoughts you extinguish thoughts; thus you have the meaning of "wisdom of severance." If you abandon this discriminative [wisdom], then you are facing toward [the goal of] purifying the wisdom obstacle.

菩薩法無我智為智障淨智: a summary of the analysis of *kleśajñeyāvaraṇa* in the *Bodhisattva-bhūmi* found at T 30.893a, 900a, and 901bff. (see note above), though I could not locate a passage which makes such a tidy identification of the idea of non-substantiality of the self with *kleśāvaraṇa* and the idea of non-substantiality of dharmas with *jñeyāvaraṇa*. For a discussion of the development of the identification of these ideas, see Funahashi, "*Kleśajñeyāvaraṇa* and *Pudgala-dharma-nairātmya*" (1980), and Muller 2004.

Both are a "delusion concerning the principle," and this is the wisdom obstacle 二俱是迷理爲智障: both those of the two vehicles, and the bodhisattvas and Buddhas; or the content of the delusions they overcome, that is, the substantiality of the self and the substantiality of phenomena or dharmas.

Discriminatory wisdom that conceptualizes 究(竟)尋(求)分別智: although Chih-i does not identify the source of this phrase, later T'ien-t'ai commentaries (BT-IV, 321) refer to Vasubandhu's *Treatise on Consciousness Only* (T no. 1588).

Wisdom of severance 斷智: that is, the "discriminative wisdom" that involves conceptualization and is not the highest wisdom. This serves as an example of "wisdom" that is an obstruction to higher wisdom and must be overcome.

... purifying the wisdom obstacle 智障清淨: as I have explained in the article mentioned above (1983), Chih-i's rationale in this section is at times unclear. It appears that he is attempting to deal with the problem of having both ignorance and (imperfect) wisdom as that which obstructs the highest, perfect wisdom of a

Again, these matters are not so orderly; thus [it can be said that the "inferior"] wisdom is not severed. Therefore a sūtra says that "virtues [and their rewards] are not lost," and the *Treatise in a Hundred Verses* quotes the teachings of the Buddha that "those who have no fear with regard to virtue should practice them as auxiliaries to the path." People tend to produce exclusivistic theories, such as the two [extreme] paths of "severance" [or "annihilationism"] or "no severance" [or "eternalism"]. Upon examination [with the threefold truth as outlined above], these [two positions of the two obstacles] are not contradictory, and you should not arouse attachment to one side [or the other] and dispute [concerning them].

Question: The *Ying-lo ching* says that the third contemplation [of the supreme truth of the Middle Way] is made manifest at the first *bhūmi* stage. Why is it sometimes taught **[86a]** as arriving at the eighth *bhūmi* stage, or sometimes taught as arriving at [the stage of] the first abode?

Answer: These are taught according to context. Sometimes the higher is used to indicate the lower, as when they speak of the eighth *bhūmi* stage; or

Buddha, as well as attempting to deal with various interpretations of *jñeyāvaraṇa* (many unidentified and unexplained) as found in various texts and theories of his time. His solution—an application of the threefold truth—is that a certain level of wisdom is attained upon severing the passionate afflictions *(kleśāvaraṇa)*. However, a more fundamental ignorance, or what is at times called the "habitual traces" or "propensities" of ignorance *(avidyavāsanā)*, still remains. This acts as an obstacle to the highest wisdom of a Buddha, which is the wisdom of the Middle Way. Also, if one clings to the imperfect wisdom (of one-sided realization of emptiness and conventionality) already attained by severing the afflictions, this can also be an obstacle to attaining the highest wisdom. Thus both ignorance and imperfect wisdom are obstacles to the highest wisdom that is being obstructed; the "wisdom obstacle" is both "obstacles *to* wisdom" and "obstacles *of* wisdom."

Not so orderly 條然: this is a rather literal rendering; Ikeda (*Gendaigoyaku*, 435) extrapolates to read "The wisdom obstacle and the wisdom of the Middle are not matters that can be clearly distinguished."

A sūtra says that virtues are not lost 經有失之福言: The traditional commentaries (BT–IV, 322) admit that the source of this quote cannot be identified.

Those who have no fear with regard to virtue should practice them as auxiliaries to the path 福莫畏者助道應行: this phrase cannot be found in the text of the *Treatise in a Hundred Verses* at T no. 1569.

The third contemplation is made manifest at the first *bhūmi* stage 第三觀初地現前: see the *Ying-lo ching* at T 24.1021c20–23:

> The mind of the supreme truth of the Middle Way involves quiet extinction thought by thought, and realizing the clear gate of the myriad dharmas, [advancing] from the ten levels of faith to the ten levels of merit transference; naturally flowing into the path of equality and the unattainable, single-marked, true contemplation; thus singly illuminating and entering the path of the first *bhūmi*.

sometimes the lower is used to indicate the higher, as when they speak of the first abode. The *Ying-lo ching* clarifies the Distinct Teachings, and therefore it speaks of the first *bhūmi* stage.

Question: The two contemplations of conventionality and the Middle clarify the levels of cultivation according to three [different] roots or faculties [that is, inferior, middling, and superior]. Why do we not see such a classification of levels of cultivation for the first contemplation [of emptiness]?

Answer: The later contemplations all involve entering the levels [of attainment] and then cultivating [the realization of] conventionality and the Middle; therefore I have classified three shallow and deep faculties with regard to [their possible] levels [of attainment]. The first contemplation [of emptiness] begins at the stage of an ordinary person [where everyone is ordinary and ignorant], so there are no levels to classify as shallow or deep. On the other hand, the *Ying-lo ching* has a text that says "The fourth stage is called that of the stream-enterer." This corresponds to those of inferior faculties. Also, when it identifies the stream-enterer at the third stage, this corresponds to those of middling faculties. Or, when it identifies the stream-enterer at the first stage, this speaks of those of superior faculties.

[end of fascicle six]

The fourth stage is called that of the stream-enterer 四地名須陀洹: the traditional commentaries (BT–IV, 323) admit, and an online search of the SAT database confirmed, that this text cannot be found in the *Ying-lo ching*.

5. Knowing What Penetrates and What Obstructs the Path [86a17–87c8]

Fifth is "knowing what penetrates and what obstructs" [the path]. This is also called "knowing what is attained and what is deficient," and also called "knowing what is [in accord with] the verbal [teachings] and what is not [in accord with] the verbal [teachings]." You should penetratingly realize [the meaning of] non-arising as [explained] above [in the previous section four] on "deconstructing dharmas universally." If you have not realized this, then you should inquire after what is attained and what is deficient; [you should see that] you must be entangled in [the extremes of] affirmation and negation, and are singularly unable to attain understanding. Why is this so? If, in the same way as the non-Buddhists, you are passionately attached to the wisdom [gained from] the contemplation of emptiness, you should use the tetralemma to universally deconstruct [this passionate attachment], [emptying] the destroyer with the destroyed, and penetrate all obstructions. If you are not attached to the wisdom [gained from] the contemplation of emptiness, so that the destroyer is not like the destroyed, you have destroyed the obstacles and have penetrating [wisdom]. This is like removing a membrane to cultivate a pearl, or destroying bandits to guard the general. If you succeed, you are like a great guide who knows well how to [penetrate and over-

Penetration and obstruction 通塞: these terms have various nuances in Chih-i's work. 通 can be translated, according to context, as "penetrating," "understanding," "conducive," "passing through," "supranormal powers," "shared," "common," and so forth. The most important technical sense is as the "Shared Teachings" 通教, the second of the Fourfold Teachings in Chih-i's doctrinal classification system. 塞 can be translated "obstacle," "to stop up," "to block," or "a pass or border between frontiers," etc. Here the phrase refers to the parable of the conjured city in the *Lotus Sūtra*, T 9.25c28, and how many *yojanas* have been traversed; see explanation in the following notes.

Removing a membrane to cultivate a pearl, or destroying bandits to guard the general 如除膜養珠破賊護將: the classical commentaries do not give a source for these images. Chan-jan (BT–IV, 328) points out that these are both partial, half-measures: it is not enough just to remove the membrane to finally attain a pearl, and it is not enough just to destroy bandits to protect the general, just like destroying obstacles is necessary but not sufficient to penetrate to and attain the Path.

Great guide 大導師: see the parable of the conjured city and the guide who leads the people through the desert, in the *Lotus Sūtra*, T 9.25c26–26a24. Hurvitz (148 [136]) translates:

> There is a steep, difficult, very bad road, *five hundred yojanas* in length, empty and devoid of human beings—a frightful place. There is *a great multitude* wishing to traverse this road to arrive at a cache of precious jewels. There is *a guide*, perceptive and wise, of penetrating clarity, who knows the hard road, its *passable and impassable features* 通塞, and who, wishing to get through these hardships, *leads the multitude*.

come obstacles and] get through the pass 通塞, and can lead many people [to the goal] beyond [the great distance of] five hundred *yojanas*.

In the ancient [texts] it says that "the [mistaken] views and conceptual attitudes are exhausted at the sixth *bhūmi* stage; this is [equivalent to reaching] three hundred [*yojanas*]. [Realizing] the seventh and eighth *bhūmi* stages is [equivalent to reaching] four hundred [*yojanas*], and [realizing] the ninth and tenth *bhūmi* stages is [equivalent to reaching] five hundred [*yojanas*]." This interpretation conflicts with that of the *Ta chih tu lun*. This treatise says that [the attainments of] those of the two vehicles is [equivalent to] four hundred [*yojanas*], but that the path of the two vehicles does not [reach] the seventh and eighth *bhūmi* stages.

The scholars of the *She-lun* say that the three realms are [equivalent to reaching] three hundred [*yojanas*], and that adding the two samsaras of "means" and "causes and conditions" reaches to five hundred [*yojanas*], but this theory does not sufficiently exhaust the [numerous] possibilities. There is the samsara after existence 有後生死, and the samsara after non-existence 無後生死; to which of the hundred [*yojanas*] do these apply? **[86b]**

Scholars of the *Ti-lun* say that the [groups of] ten levels each of faith, abodes, practice, merit transference, and *bhūmi* stages correspond to the five hundred [*yojanas*]; this conflicts with the *Lotus Sūtra*. The *Lotus Sūtra* says that upon passing three hundred *yojanas*, the conjured city is produced,

This figure of "five hundred *yojanas*" thus symbolizes the long and difficult path to Buddhahood. This passage also provides the compound 通塞 ("through the pass") that serves as the subject of this section.

Ancient [texts] 舊云: or, "in the past it was said"; perhaps this interpretation is from a commentary to the *Lotus Sūtra* that is not extant? The traditional commentaries do not identify the source.

This treatise says that those of the two vehicles … eighth *bhūmi* stages 論以二乘爲四百二乘之道非七地八地: see the *Ta chih tu lun*, T 25.526b4–10:

> Concerning this Śāriputra gave his own interpretation of the parable, saying, with regard to people wishing to pass a dangerous road, "a dangerous road" refers to this mundane world, "one hundred *yojanas*" refers to the realm of desires, "two hundred *yojanas*" refers to the realm of form, "three hundred *yojanas*" refers to the formless realm, and "four hundred *yojanas*" refers to the paths of the śrāvakas and pratyekabuddhas. Again, four hundred *yojanas* is the realm of desires, three hundred *yojanas* is the realm of form, two hundred *yojanas* is the formless realm, and one hundred *yojanas* is [the realms of] the śrāvakas and pratyekabuddhas.

Two samsaras of "means" and "causes and conditions" 方便因緣兩生死: The source and exact meaning of these ideas and terms are not known. As pointed out previously, there is much that is not known about the texts and interpretations of the "scholars of the *She-lun*" in Chih-i's time.

Upon passing three hundred *yojanas*, the conjured city is produced 過三百由旬作化城: see the parable of the conjured city at T 9.26a4–5. Hurvitz (148 [136]) has:

while this [interpretation of the *Ti-lun* scholars] would mean that the conjured city is produced at two hundred [*yojanas*].

Again, there are people who understand [realizing] the triple world [up to the formless realm] as [equivalent to reaching] three hundred [*yojanas*], and adding [the realms of] the two vehicles reaches to five hundred [*yojanas*]. This interpretation has three faults. The first is that it establishes the conjured city as beyond and outside the triple world. How can those of the two vehicles transcend the triple world without entering the [conventional reality of the conjured] city, and advance further to four hundred and five hundred [*yojanas*]? There is no "conjured city" outside [the levels of] the four hundred and five hundred [*yojanas*], so where or what are those of the two vehicles suppose to enter and realize? Second, it is by extinguishing the conjured city [that is, by realizing its conventionality and its provisional role as a pointer to, or temporary substitute for, a higher attainment] that you attain progress [to the levels beyond], so how can those of the two vehicles abruptly advance to the four hundred and five hundred [*yojanas* level] when the [conjured] city is not yet extinguished? Third, those of the two vehicles share a common realization of the conjured city; how can the śrāvakas be assigned to [the level of] four hundred [*yojanas*] and the pratyekabuddhas to [the level of] five hundred [*yojanas*]?

Some people identify the passionate afflictions of the five levels [of delusions] with five hundred [*yojanas*]. If so, [it means that] those of the two

> The guide, being a man of many skillful devices, thinks, "These wretches are to be pitied! How can they throw away a fortune in jewels and wish instead to turn back?" With his power of devising expedients he conjures up on that steep road, *three hundred yojanas away* 過, a city, then he declares to the multitude, "Have no fear! There is no need to turn back! Here is the great city."

The Threefold Lotus Sutra (162) translates:

> … in the midst of the perilous road, he mystically makes a city over three hundred yojanas in extent.

Note that Hurvitz translates 過 as distance "away," *The Threefold Lotus Sutra* translates it as "extent," and Chih-i takes it to mean "distance traversed."

Two hundred [*yojanas*]: that is, at the stages of abodes?

There are people who understand the triple world as three hundred [*yojanas*] 有人解三界爲三百 …: the details of this theory, and the identity of the people who proposed it, are unknown.

Extinguishing the conjured city 滅化城: in short, if they have already realized the conventional nature of the conjured city, they have "extinguished" it and, having advanced to the path of Buddhahood, are no longer śrāvakas or pratyekabuddhas.

Some people identify the passionate afflictions of the five levels with five hundred [*yojanas*] 有人以五住煩惱爲五百 …: the details of this theory, and the identity of the people who proposed it, are unknown.

All of these theories may have been floating around in Buddhist circles during

vehicles have already severed the [first] four levels [of delusions], [but this cannot be because] this means that the conjured city is established beyond [the level of] four hundred *yojanas*.

Some people identify the severance of the conceptual attitudes of the triple world with three hundred [*yojanas*], [severance of] the minute dust-like [delusions] with four hundred, and [severance of fundamental] ignorance with five hundred. This also cannot be. The term *yojana* is basically used symbolically for the passionate afflictions. Why, then, are the more numerous [mistaken] views not counted, and the numerically fewer "conceptual attitudes" identified with [the level of] three hundred [*yojanas*]?

The meaning of these terms [such as "five hundred *yojanas*"] are based on [the parable of the conjured city in] the *Lotus Sūtra*. The *Lotus Sūtra* presents "five hundred [*yojanas*]" as the basic analogy, to illustrate the "perilous path" of samsara and the insightful knowledge of the guide. We should present three categories to clarify the meaning of "five hundred" as found in the sūtra: first, with regard to the "place" of samsara; second, with regard to passionate afflictions; and third, with regard to wisdom. The interpretations of the various teachers [as outlined above] are like trying to put a square [peg] in a round [hole], and like movement [contrasted with] stillness—they do not fit with the text. [These interpretations are] like taking a key for a single hole and trying to open three locks. The first interpretation establishes the conjured city at four hundred [*yojanas*] in terms of the levels of the Shared [Teachings]. The *She-lun* scholars interpret it in terms of samsara and divides that beyond and outside [three hundred *yojanas*] into two types. The *Ti-lun* scholars interpret it in terms of the levels of the Distinct [Teachings] and establishes the conjured city within the [triple] world. The next interpretation takes a shortcut and, without waiting for the disclosing of the tentative [meaning], directly manifests the real. [The interpretations of various] teachers are faulty in this way.

How about the interpretation of the *Ta chih tu lun*? This treatise contains two references [on this matter]. The first identifies those of the two vehicles with four hundred [*yojanas*] and stops without proceeding to five hundred. The later reference identifies those of the two vehicles with one

Chih-i's time, but records of their content and context are not extant.

Parable of the conjured city: see the *Lotus Sūtra*, T 9.25c–26a, as explained above.

Taking a key for a single hole and trying to open three locks 持一孔之匙開三須之鑰: Chan-jan (BT–IV, 332) adds that this illustrates trying to explain three things with the one-sided interpretation of one teacher.

The first interpretation: See above at 86a24–26.

Interpretation of the *Ta chih tu lun*: See T 25.526b4–10, as translated in the note above at 86a26–27.

hundred [*yojanas*]. What does this mean? The treatise is clarifying the intent of the Shared [Teachings]. Those of the Shared [Teachings] take [the realization of] the real truth *(paramārtha-satya)* [of emptiness] as the ultimate [attainment], so they do not deconstruct the conjured city even though they go beyond the triple world, and merely seek to enter and realize nirvana. Therefore they identify nirvana with [the level of] four hundred [*yojanas*]. The later section that identifies [the level of] the two vehicles with one hundred [*yojanas*] refers to clarifying [the idea of] emerging in conventionality, that is, bodhisattvas going beyond emptiness to emerge in conventionality without [remaining in the aforementioned] nirvana; this corresponds to one hundred. Entering the triple world [of desire, form, and formlessness] corresponds to three hundred. If we resolve the texts in this way, there is no problem with [the interpretations of] the sūtras and treatises.

[As for the three categories for clarifying the meaning of "five hundred *yojanas*,"] first, with regard to the place of samsara, the resultant retribution [of rebirth] in the triple world corresponds to three hundred. **[86c]** [Rebirth in] the "land where skillful means remain" and the "land of true recompense without obstruction" corresponds to the place of five hundred *yojanas*. Next, with regard to passionate afflictions [that are severed at different levels], [deluded] views concerning the truth correspond to one hundred [*yojanas*]; the five [afflictions that bind you to the] lower parts [of the threefold world, that is, the realm of desires] correspond to two hundred; the five [afflictions that bind you to the] upper parts [of the threefold world, that is, the realms of form and no-form] correspond to three hundred; the minute dust-like [delusions] correspond to four hundred; and ignorance corresponds to five hundred [*yojanas*]. Next, with regard to contemplative wisdom, [realizing]

Those of the Shared Teachings: the Taishō text here has "Taoist" 道家, but this is corrected in the *Bukkyō Taikei* (IV, 335) to 通家.

Land Where Skillful Means Remain 方便有餘土 **and Land of True Recompense** 實報無礙土: these two "lands" are the second and third of the "Four Lands" as taught in the T'ien-t'ai tradition. Those of the Shared Teaching, arhats, and pratyekabuddhas, who have severed the delusions of mistaken views and conceptual attitudes and have transcended the triple world, dwell in the "land of skillful means"; those of the Distinct Teaching, bodhisattvas, dwell in the "land of true recompense."

Five lower parts 五下分[結]: the various afflictions that bind people to the lowest of the three realms of existence, that is, to the everyday realm of desires. The five are greed or covetousness 欲貪, hateful anger 瞋恚, the view that the body is substantially real 有身見, the views that come from attachment to precepts 戒禁取見, and doubt 疑.

Five upper parts 五上分[結]: the various afflictions that bind people to the higher of the three realms of existence, that is, to the realms of form and no-form. The five are covetousness for visible form 色貪, covetousness for no-form 無色貪, restlessness 掉擧, pride 慢, and ignorance 無明.

the wisdom from the contemplation of emptiness is to know three hundred, [realizing] the wisdom from the contemplation of conventionality is to know four hundred, and [realizing] the wisdom from the contemplation of the Middle is to know five hundred [*yojanas*]. This [interpretation] matches the text and avoids the faults [of the interpretations] of the above-mentioned teachers. Again, the classification of levels [of attainment] by the various [above-mentioned] teachers makes [the goal] seem too distant, so that beginning practitioners who have not yet severed [mistaken] views will wonder how they can ever advance to [the full] five hundred *yojanas*.

What I have discussed above is the "horizontal" [perspective on] penetrating and obstructing [the path], but there is also a "vertical" [perspective on] penetrating and obstructing [the path]. The horizontal [perspective] includes three Dharma teachings: [first,] "obstacles" consist of suffering and the causes of suffering, and "penetration" consists of the path and extinction; [second,] "obstacles" consist of the twelvefold causes and conditions of ignorance, and "penetration" consists of the extinction of ignorance; [third,] "obstacles" consist of the six obscurations that cover the mind, and "penetration" consists of the six perfections. The vertical [perspective] of penetrating and obstruction [also includes three Dharma teachings]: [first,] "obstacles" consist of the [mistaken] views and conceptual attitudes of ordinary constituent samsara, and "penetration" consists of realizing the contemplation of entering emptiness from conventionality; [second,] "obstacles" consist of the samsara of not knowing [skillful] means 無知方便生死, and "penetration" consists of realizing the contemplation of entering conventionality from emptiness; [third,] "obstacles" consist of the samsara of the causes and conditions of ignorance 無明因緣生死, and "penetration" consists of realizing the correct contemplation of the Middle Way.

Now we should examine "penetrating and obstructing" with an interweaving of the horizontal and vertical [perspectives]. As you "enter emptiness from conventionality," you destroy all [mistaken] views and conceptual attitudes—the individual, multiple, combined and beyond-verbalization [mistaken] views and the nine times nine or eighty-one conceptual attitudes. Such delusions are fundamentally defiled; they cause passionate afflictions to increase and grow, and hinder and obstruct the practitioner. Why should you abruptly become attached [to these delusions] and affirm this or deny that, arousing various karmic bonds, fall into a defiled cycle of birth-and-death, and perceive only suffering and the causes of suffering and not perceive the path and extinction? [If you do this,] then you are not aware of the Four [Noble] Truths with regard to [mistaken] views and conceptual attitudes; if you do not know these things, [you are caught up in the twelvefold cycle of causes and conditions] that is known as "from ignorance to old-age-and-death." By constructing these causes and conditions, you cannot extinguish ignorance. If you do not extinguish [ignorance], you will be firmly attached to [your delusions] and will not be able to abandon them. You will stay on this shore [of samsara] and not reach the other shore [of awakening]. The *Mahāparinirvāṇa Sūtra* says, "A child who is starving will pick up fruit found in the midst of feces. A wise person will scold [the child], and [the child] will blush and be ashamed." Thus, losing the pure Dharma teachings is called an obstruction 塞. If[, on the other hand,] you arouse a [correct] thought concerning these [mistaken] views even for an ephemeral moment, and know that they are without a substantial nature, without permanent existence, and without a substantial subject, the perverted views are destroyed and there will be no residual karma. If there is no karma, there will be no effect; this is called [advancing on] the path. Since it is the path, there is extinction. If you are aware of the Four [Noble] Truths, there will be no ignorance, and thus no old-age-and-death. If these causes and conditions are destroyed, all existences are abandoned and you will reach the other shore [of awakening]. You should utilize this intent [of emptiness] to successively [contemplate] your thoughts one by one 歷一一心, to successively [contemplate] the subjects [of the contemplations] one by one 歷一一能, and to successively [contemplate] the objects [of the passionate afflictions] one by one 歷一一所. If these three arise as obstacles, you should deconstruct them and thus penetrate [beyond] them. If these three arise as penetrating 通 [understanding], you should nurture them to fulfill [awakening]. [The Tripitaka Teachings]

Again, if you realize the essential emptiness of [mistaken] views, then [you should realize that] the subject [who contemplates the views] is also essentially empty. This is like the mind of an arhat, who is said to be of

A child who is starving will pick up fruit found in the midst of feces. A wise person will scold, and [the child] will blush and be ashamed 童子飢時取糞中果智人呵之赧然有愧: see the *Mahāparinirvāṇa Sūtra* at T 12.677b12–20:

> Again, Kāśyapa, it is like a young Brahman *child who is near starvation who sees some mango fruit in a person's feces and then picks it up. A wise person sees this and scolds* [the child] saying, "You are of the pure lineage of the Brahmans. Why do you pick up this defiled fruit that was mixed with feces?" When the child hears this he *blushes and feels ashamed*, and he answers, "I have not eaten it. I only wish to wash it and then throw it away." The wise person said, "You are a great fool. If you planned to throw it away, you shouldn't pick it up to begin with." Good son, a bodhisattva-mahāsattva is like this. He neither takes up nor abandons this life [in samsara]. Like the wise person he scolds the children [who pick up defiled things]. Ordinary [ignorant] people revel in life and consider death evil, and like this child they take up this fruit only to throw it away [later].

The Tripitaka Teachings: This paragraph describes the approach of the Tripitaka Teachings, that is, reaching an understanding of causes and conditions and emptiness through analytical reasoning.

undefiled skandhas. [87a] But if our contemplation has not yet truly [realized emptiness], how can it be said to have no [defilements from] skandhas? If we make [mistaken] conjectures concerning the real [essence] of skandhas, this will result in the karmic bonds of samsara. If we are unaware of the Four [Noble] Truths with regard to skandhas, this is ignorance. If we are passionately attached to the wisdom of the contemplation of emptiness, we will not be able to abandon it. Use this meaning of emptiness to successively [contemplate] your thoughts one by one, to successively [contemplate] the subjects [of the contemplations] one by one, and to successively [contemplate] the objects [of the passionate afflictions] one by one. If these three arise as obstacles, you should deconstruct them and thus penetrate [beyond] them. If these three arise as penetrating [understanding], you should nurture them to fulfill [awakening]. Thus you can skillfully go beyond the obstacles of [mistaken] views and conceptual attitudes, and well penetrate to three hundred *yojanas*. [The Shared Teachings]

Next, in utilizing the horizontal perspective to know the vertical perspective, is to carefully examine things with the contemplation of realizing conventionality from emptiness, in order to penetrate obstacles. This is easy to understand [and has been outlined above]. Concerning each of the Dharma teachings of disease, medicine, and applying the medicine, and with regard to each and every one of the Dharma teachings, each and every one of the subjects [of contemplations], each and every one of the objects [of afflictions], you should clearly know [and apply] the [Four Noble] Truths, [twelvefold causes and] conditions, and [six] perfections. If these three arise as obstacles, you should deconstruct them and penetrate [beyond] them. If these three arise as penetrating [understanding], you should nurture them to fulfill [awakening]. Thus you will go beyond the obstacles of non-cognizance, and will penetrate to four hundred *yojanas*. [The Distinct Teachings]

Next, utilizing the horizontal perspective to know the vertical perspective is to carefully examine things with the correct contemplation of the Middle Way. Concerning ignorance and the Dharma nature, [the practice of] true cultivation 眞修 and deliberate [conditioned] cultivation 緣修 and so forth, and with regard to each and every dharma, each and every one of the subjects [of contemplations], and each and every one of the objects [of

The Shared Teachings: this paragraph describes the approach of the Shared Teaching, that is, directly reaching an understanding of the essential emptiness of all things.

The Distinct Teachings: this is the approach of the Distinct Teaching, which involves participation in the conventional world after having realized emptiness.

"Deliberate [conditioned] cultivation": the conscious and deliberate practice of gradual-and-successive contemplation, in contrast to the "true" spontaneous practice of contemplation; see Glossary.

afflictions], you should clearly know [and apply] the [Four Noble] Truths, [twelvefold causes and] conditions, and [six] perfections. If these three arise as obstacles, you should deconstruct them and penetrate beyond them. If these three arise as penetrating [understanding], you should nurture them to fulfill [awakening]. Thus you will go beyond the obstacles of ignorance and will penetrate to five hundred *yojanas*. [The Perfect Teaching]

If "penetration and obstacles" are discussed in this way, then progressively you can discuss the vertical perspective of the sixth *bhūmi* stage [of the Shared Teachings] and the first *bhūmi* stage [of the Distinct Teachings], and after advancing for numerous kalpas can achieve penetration of the obstacles. The *Mahāparinirvāṇa Sūtra* says, "The stream-enterers arrive after 80,000 kalpas; pratyekabuddhas arrive after 10,000 kalpas," that is,

The Perfect Teaching: this is the approach of the Perfect Teaching, which involves the direct, complete, and immediate insight of the Middle Way.

Progressively you can discuss the vertical perspective 次第竪論六地初地: That is, this is the level at which those of the Shared and Distinct Teachings can advance to the insight of the Perfect Teaching?

The stream-enterers arrive after 80,000 kalpas; pratyekabuddhas arrive after 10,000 kalpas, 須陀洹者八萬劫到乃至支佛十千劫到: a very short summary of a much longer passage in the *Mahāparinirvāṇa Sūtra:* at T 12.673a22–b14:

> Kāśyapa, there are five types of people mentioned in the Mahāyāna *Mahāparinirvāṇa Sūtra* who are involved in the "practice of disease" and are not Tathāgatas. What are these five?
>
> The first severs three bonds and attains the fruit of the stream-enterer. They do not fall into [the destinies of] hell, beasts, or hungry ghosts. After being human or divine beings for seven times, they forever sever all suffering and enter nirvana. Kāśyapa, these are called the first type of person who is involved in the practice of disease. *Such people will, in the future, pass through 80,000 kalpas* before they surely attain supreme enlightenment.
>
> Kāśyapa, the second type of person severs three bonds, decreases covetousness, anger, and ignorance, attains the fruit of the once-returner, forever severs all suffering, and enters nirvana. Kāśyapa, these people are called the second type of people who are involved in the practice of disease. These people will, in the future, pass through 60,000 kalpas before they surely attain supreme enlightenment.
>
> Kāśyapa, the third type of person severs four lower bonds and attains the fruit of the non-returner, and will not be reborn any more. They forever sever all suffering and enter nirvana. These people are called the third type of people who are involved in the practice of disease. These people will, in the future, pass through 40,000 kalpas before they surely attain supreme enlightenment.
>
> Kāśyapa, the fourth type of person forever severs covetous desires, anger, and deluded ignorance, attains the fruit of the arhat, has no remaining passionate afflictions, and enters nirvana, but does not practice alone like the unicorn 麒麟. These people are called the fourth type of people who are involved in the practice of disease. These people will, in the future, pass through 20,000 kalpas before they surely attain supreme enlightenment.
>
> Kāśyapa, the fifth type of person forever severs covetous desires, anger, and deluded ignorance, attains the path of

they arrive at the stage of a bodhisattva's first aspiration. This [passage in the *Mahāparinirvāṇa Sūtra*] discusses [the complicated gradual] stages of a noble sage, but what benefit is this to the practitioner who has experienced the first aspiration [of a bodhisattva]?

Next is to discuss "penetrating and obstructing" with regard to the horizontal perspective of the Distinct [Teachings]. As it says in the *Pañcaviṃśati Sūtra*, "There are bodhisattvas who, from the time of their first aspiration, have a rapport with omniscience *(sarvajñā)*," that is, has a rapport with emptiness. If, at the time of your first aspiration, you do not yet have this rapport, you should use [the teachings of] the [Four] Truths, [twelvefold] conditions, and [six] perfections to examine each and every thought. If these three present obstacles, you should deconstruct them and penetrate beyond them. If these three present [an opportunity for] penetration, you should nourish them to fulfillment, and thus pass beyond three hundred *yojanas*. Again, [the *Pañcaviṃśati Sūtra*] says, "There are bodhisattvas who, from the time of their first aspiration, are able to have supremacy in supranormal powers and purify a Buddha land." This corresponds to the meaning of "[re-]emerging in

> the pratyekabuddha, has no remaining passionate afflictions, and enters nirvana. They truly practice alone like a unicorn. These people are called the fifth type of people who are involved in the practice of disease. These people will, in the future, *pass through 10,000 kalpas before they surely attain supreme enlightenment.* Kāśyapa, these are the five types of people who are involved in the practice of disease and are not Tathāgatas.

There are bodhisattvas who, from the time of their first aspiration, have a rapport with omniscience 有菩薩從初發心即與薩婆若相應: see the *Pañcaviṃśati Sūtra* at T 8.226a6–15:

> Śāriputra, there are bodhisattva-mahāsattvas who, from the time they first arouse their aspiration [for enlightenment], practice the six *pāramitās*, ascend the bodhisattva stages, and attain the state of non-retrogression *(avaivartya, avaivartika)*. Śāriputra, there are bodhisattva-mahāsattvas who, from the time they first arouse their aspiration, also attain supreme enlightenment *(anuttarasaṃyaksaṃbodhi)*, turn the wheel of the Dharma, provide benefits for immeasurable incalculable sentient beings, and enter nirvana without remainder. After this Buddha enters *parinirvāṇa*, his Dharma teachings remain for one kalpa and perish after one kalpa. Śāriputra, *There are bodhisattva-mahāsattvas who, from the time they first arouse their aspiration, have a rapport with prajñā-pāramitā* and, along with innumerable hundreds of thousands of millions of bodhisattvas, from one Buddha land to another Buddha land, purify these Buddha lands.

Note that the sūtra speaks of "rapport with *prajñā-pāramitā*," not with *sarvajñā*.

There are bodhisattvas who, from the time of their first aspiration, are able to have supremacy in supranormal powers and purify a Buddha land 有菩薩從初發心即能遊戲神通淨佛國土: see the *Pañcaviṃśati Sūtra* at T 8.225c24–26:

> Śāriputra, *there are bodhisattva-mahāsattvas who have supremacy in supranormal powers, and go from one Buddha land to another Buddha land*, to places where there are no śrāvakas or

conventionality." If you cultivate conventionality from the time of your first aspiration, also use [the teachings of] the [Four] Truths, [twelvefold] conditions, and [six] perfections to examine each and every thought, deconstruct obstacles, and nourish penetration; thus you will go beyond four hundred *yojanas*. Again, [the *Avataṃsaka Sūtra*] says, "There are bodhisattvas who, from the time of their first aspiration, are able to sit on the seat of enlightenment *(bodhimaṇḍa)* and fulfill perfect awakening *(saṃbodhi)*." This corresponds to the meaning of the Middle. If you cultivate the Middle from the time of your first aspiration, also use [the teachings of] the [Four] Truths, [twelvefold] conditions, and [six] perfections to examine each and every thought, deconstruct obstacles, and nourish penetration, then you will go beyond five hundred *yojanas*.

If these matters are taught in this way [in terms of the Distinct Teachings], you can discuss "penetration" and "obstacles" in terms of the first aspiration, but the three dharmas [of emptiness, conventionality, and the Middle] are each distinct. The *Ta chih tu lun* uses three analogies [to illustrate these three abilities]: [**87b**] the first is like walking on foot, the second is like riding a horse, and the third is like [flying through the air with] supranormal powers. You should know about [the gradual and progressive types of] "penetration" and "obstruction" in the sense of the two activities of "walking" and "[riding] a horse" [as explained above]. Supranormal powers[, on the other hand,] are unobstructed, and so "obstacles" provide no hindrance; even a mountain-like wall is empty. What is there, then, to "penetrate"? The first

pratyekabuddhas, and nobody with the name of those of the two vehicles.

Note that the phrase about "purifying" Buddha lands is not found explicitly in this passage, but in the previous quote; see the last phrase at 226a15.

Note also that this phrase has been quoted above at *Mo-ho chih-kuan* 2c5-6, though with different wording.

There are bodhisattvas who, from the time of their first aspiration, are able to sit on the seat of enlightenment and fulfill perfect awakening 有菩薩從初發心即能坐道場成正覺: this phrase is from the *Avataṃsaka Sūtra*, T 9.449c14–15, though the pattern is from the *Pañcaviṃśati Sūtra* sections quoted above. This passage has been quoted previously in the *Mo-ho chih-kuan*; for details, see note at 62a27.

***Ta chih tu lun* uses three analogies** 大論引三喻: see T 25.342c2–7:

> What is this like? First, those who accumulate immeasurable merits, with clever faculties and a firm mind, and hearing the Dharma directly from the Buddha, are like those who travel far. Some go by riding a sheep, and some go by riding a horse, and some go by using supranormal powers. Those who ride a sheep take a long time to reach the goal. Those who ride a horse are relatively faster. Those who go by supranormal powers arrive at the same instant they arouse the intent [to leave].

Note that Chih-i substitutes "walking on foot" for "riding on a sheep" as the slowest method for advancing on the path.

contemplation [of emptiness] is analogous to walking; the next contemplation [of conventionality] is analogous to [riding] a horse; the last contemplation [of the Middle] is analogous to flying [with supranormal powers]. The three meanings are distinct and separated [in the Distinct Teachings]; this is not the [final] content of what I teach here [in the *Mo-ho chih-kuan*].

If we discuss the three contemplations [of the Distinct Teachings?] from the vertical perspective, the first two contemplations [of emptiness and conventionality] involve penetration of their respective stages and involve obstructions for those who seek the higher [levels]. The final contemplation [of the Middle] is superior to the lower [two contemplations] and in this sense involves penetration, and is separate from the Hīnayāna and in this sense involves "blocking" 塞 [the obstacles of the inferior teaching]. If we discuss the three contemplations [of the Distinct Teachings] from the horizontal perspective, they each can be differentiated with regard to penetration, but they are not mutually binding and thus involve obstruction. There is penetration or obstruction in accordance with the shallow or deep characteristics of these dharmas [of contemplation]. This even involves arousing suffering, the causes of suffering, ignorance, the obscurations, and so forth within [the contemplation of] the Middle. Thus all [the contemplations, from the perspective of the Distinct Teachings] involve obstructions and does not [ultimately] provide penetration [to the highest goal].

[In contrast,] if we were to examine the marks of these dharmas in terms of the three contemplations in a single thought, you can deconstruct the vertical "penetration" and "obstruction" of the Middle. The three contemplations in a single thought deconstruct horizontal penetration and obstruction. The three contemplations involve emptiness, and therefore they deconstruct the penetrations and obstructions of three hundred [*yojana*s], like walking over a mountain-like wall. The three contemplations involve conventionality; they deconstruct the penetrations and obstructions of four hundred [*yojana*s], like riding on a horse. The three contemplations involve the Middle, and deconstruct the penetrations and obstructions of [five hundred *yojana*s, like using] supranormal powers. Truly a single thought is simultaneously empty, conventional, and the Middle. All mountains and rivers, rocks and cliffs, and the paths of the hordes of demons, are all like empty space; you can freely and without obstruction [penetrate] them all with the three contemplations in a single thought. Finally, you do not have to leave the low [areas] to cross the heights, or abandon the mountains to

Obstructions for those who seek the higher levels 望上為塞: Ikeda (*Gendaigoyaku*, 443) translates, "the first two contemplations involve penetration, but, from the perspective of the higher [levels], involves obstruction."

follow the valleys; whatever obstacles you come in contact with, they can all be penetrated without obstruction. "They are able go beyond to five hundred *yojana*s and reach the place of treasures." This is called "penetrating," and "penetrating" is basically in contrast with "obstructing." However, everything that you come in contact with is empty and thus without obstruction, so if there is no "obstruction" there is no "penetration." If there is no obstruction and no penetration, and yet suffering, the causes of suffering, ignorance, obstacles and obscurations arise, you will not only lose the supranormal powers, you will also lose [the abilities that are analogous to] riding a horse and walking, and [the contemplation] that does the destroying is also destroyed, and verbal [teachings] 字 become that which is not [in accord with] the verbal [teachings of the Dharma] 非字. This is like the paths of insects [gnawing on wood] coincidentally carving the letters of the three contemplations. These insects do not know whether these are letters or not letters 字非字. If you realize that for each and every Dharma [teaching], each and every subject [of contemplation], and each and every object [of affliction], all are simultaneously empty, conventional, and the Middle, and endowed with the [Four Noble] Truths, [twelvefold causes and] conditions, and [six] perfections, this is called being without penetration and without obstruction, and illuminated concerning both penetration and obstruction. Those who are wise know what is [in accord with] the verbal [teachings] and what is not [in accord with] the verbal [teachings], as a good physician knows what is gained and what is lost.

This is the clarification of penetration and obstruction from the perspective of the gate of non-arising. It is the same for the other gates [or teachings]. This is what it means for the beginner to pass beyond to five hundred *yojana*s. This should be clarified by reference to the Six Identities.

They are able to go beyond to five hundred *yojana*s and reach the place of treasures 能過五百由旬到於寶所: phrases from the parable of the conjured city in the *Lotus Sūtra*, T 9.25c–27b; see note above.

Insects carving letters: see this simile in the story of the "good doctor" in the *Mahāparinirvāṇa Sūtra*, T 12.618b2–7. Chih-i has used this image many times already in the *Mo-ho chih-kuan*; for details, see note at 10b27.

Knows what is gained and lost 知得知失: Or, to give a more interpretive translation based on the source of this phrase in the *Mahāparinirvāṇa Sūtra*, "a good physician knows what is a useful and what is a harmful [remedy or medicine]." See the story of the "good doctor" in the *Mahāparinirvāṇa Sūtra*, T 12.618a–c, especially 618c3–4.

Six Identities 六即義: Chih-i does not go into further detail, but it is assumed that one could apply the categories of the Six Identities to these categories of "penetration" and "obstructions" based on the pattern of what Chih-i has already explained.

Question: Do the categories "penetration and obstruction" 通塞, "attainment and loss" 得失, and "verbal and not verbal" 字非字 have the same meaning, or are they different?

Answer: They have the same meaning, but with different interpretation. There are distinctions to be made: "penetration and obstruction" refers to understanding; "attainment and loss" refers to practice; "verbal and not verbal" refers to teachings. The *Suvarṇaprabhāsa Sūtra* says, "Hear correctly, listen correctly, discriminate correctly, understand conditions correctly, and be fully awakened correctly." To know the "verbal and not verbal" [teachings] is to "hear correctly and listen correctly." To know "attainment and loss" is to "discriminate correctly and understand conditions correctly." **[87c]** To know "penetration and obstruction" is to "be fully awakened correctly." However, despite these distinctions, these [categories] are the same in what they manifest.

Question: Do the "horizontal" obstacles obstruct the "vertical" penetrations, or not? Do the "vertical" obstacles obstruct the "horizontal" penetrations, or not? Do the "horizontal" penetrations penetrate the "vertical" obstacles, or not? Do the "vertical" penetrations penetrate the "horizontal" obstacles, or not?

Answer: In one sense, yes, but in another sense, no. As for "yes," ignorance *is* the [mistaken] views and conceptual attitudes; in what sense are these not horizontal obstructions? The wisdom of the Middle heals all; which of the horizontal obstructions are not penetrated? [And so forth ...] These are the content of the first sense, that is, the meaning of [the answer] "yes." The second interpretation [that is, the sense of "no,"] is as follows. The horizontal obstructions are obstacles that are "near," and are not able to obstruct the vertical penetrations. The power of the horizontal penetrations are weak, so they are not able to penetrate the vertical obstructions. The vertical obstructions are deep and distant, and do not become horizontal obstacles. The vertical penetrations are distinct according to their contrastive object 對當, so they do not penetrate the horizontal obstructions.

Hear correctly, listen correctly, discriminate correctly, understand conditions correctly, and be fully awakened correctly 正聞正聽正分別正解於縁正能覺了: see the *Suvarṇaprabhāsa Sūtra* at T 16.346c5–6: World Honored One, with regard to the Dharma I understand correctly and contemplate correctly, and have attained correct discrimination, correct understanding of conditions, and correct full awakening.

6. Cultivating the Steps on the Path [87c9–91a5]

Sixth is to clarify the regulation and fulfillment of the steps on the path. There are four [categories] of the steps on the path: first, their "limited distinctions" 當分; second, their "interweaving" 相攝; third, in terms of the levels [of attainment] 約位; and fourth, that of their "mutual arising" 相生.

1. Four Categories of the Steps on the Path [87c10]

First is to clarify the "limited distinctions." It is not necessary to consummate all the steps in order to attain the path. There are three [categories of] four [that is, the four mindfulnesses 四念處, four proper endeavors 四正勤, and four supranormal powers 四如意足], two of five [the five good roots 五善根 and the five powers 五力], one of seven [the seven components of awakening 七覺支], and a single eight [the eightfold noble path 八正道]. These are the limited distinctions concerning the path. Therefore it is said that "you should rely on mindfulness to attain the path." Again it is said, "These [thirty-seven

Steps on the path 道品: That is, the "thirty-seven steps on the path" *(bodhipākṣikadharma)*: the four mindfulnesses, four proper endeavors, four supranormal powers, five good roots, five powers, seven components of awakening, and the eightfold path. Chih-i does not give the details concerning these thirty-seven categories, which are assumed as part of the context of his discussion. For a good discussion of these details, see Hurvitz, *Chih-i*, e.g. 344–46. See the long section in *Ta chih tu lun* on the thirty-seven steps on the path, T 25.196b–205c, which gives the background detail for this section by Chih-i. Most of the quotes below from the *Ta chih tu lun* are from this section.

You should rely on mindfulness to attain the path 當依念處得道: see the *Ta chih tu lun* at T 25.198a9–17; Lamotte (*Le Traité* 3, 1143) translates:

> Question. — Les quatre fixations-de-l'attention *(smṛtyupasthāna)* étant suffisantes pour obtenir le chemin *(mārga)*, pourquoi parler de trente-sept auxiliaires? Serait-ce pour *abréger (saṃkṣiptena deśanā)* que vous parlez de quatre fixations-de l'attention, et pour vous étendre *(vistareṇa deśanā)* que vous parlez de trente-sept auxiliaires? Alors, ce n'est pas exact *(ayukta)*, car si on voulait s'étendre, il y aurait d'innombrables auxiliaires *(apramāṇapakṣa)*.
>
> Réponse. — 1. Bien que les quatre fixations-de-l'attention soient suffisantes pour obtenir le chemin, il faut aussi prêcher les quatre efforts corrects *(samyakpradhāna)* et les autres dharma auxiliaires.

Chodron (3, 941) translates:

> Question. Since the four foundations of mindfulness suffice to obtain the path, why talk about thirty-seven auxiliaries? Would it be for the sake of abridgment that you speak of the four foundations of mindfulness and for the sake of expansion, that you speak of the thirty-seven auxiliaries? Then that is not correct because, if one wants to expand, there would be innumerable auxiliaries.
>
> Answer. 1. Although the four foundations of mindfulness are sufficient to attain the path, the four right efforts and the other auxiliary dharmas must also be preached.

These [thirty-seven steps on the path] are the seat of enlightenment 是道場: see

steps on the path] are the seat of enlightenment." Again it is said, "These are [the content of] Mahāyāna." The [four] mindfulnesses are like this, and so are the others [of the thirty-seven] steps. These are limited distinctions concerning the steps on the path, but this [in itself] is not the regulating and stopping [of afflictions and so forth that obstruct attainment of the path].

Second is to clarify the "interweaving" [of the steps on the path]. All the steps [on the path] are encompassed in one dharma of mindfulness[, that is, in one thought]. To quote the text of the *Ta chih tu lun*, "One thought of mindfulness already encompasses the other steps; the other steps also encompass the thoughts of mindfulness." This is the interweaving of the steps on the path, but this [in itself] is not the regulating and stopping [of afflictions and so forth that obstruct the path].

Third is [the steps on the path] in terms of the levels [of attainment]. As [you cultivate] mindfulness, you should attain the appropriate level. The level of "heat" corresponds to "proper endeavors." [For example,] the level of "summit" corresponds to "supranormal powers." The level of "patience"

the *Vimalakīrti Sūtra*, T 14.542c26; Boin (*Vimalakīrti*, 97) translates: "It is the seat of the thirty-seven auxiliary dharmas of enlightenment *(bodhipākṣikadharma)* because it destroys conditioned dharmas *(saṃskṛtadharma)*."

These are Mahāyāna 是摩訶衍: see the *Ta chih tu lun*, T 25.406a–b, which explains each of the categories of the thirty-seven steps on the way as part of "the Mahāyāna of the bodhisattva-mahāsattva." Note that this section is actually a quote of the *Pañcaviṃśati Sūtra*, not from the commentary of the *Ta chih tu lun*; see the *Pañcaviṃśati Sūtra* at T 8.254b–c.

One thought of mindfulness already encompasses the other steps; the other steps also encompass the thoughts of mindfulness 念處既攝餘品餘品亦攝念處: a brief summary of a long section in the *Ta chih tu lun*, T 25.197b–205b; for details, see chapter XXXI on "Les trente-sept auxiliares de l'illumination" in Lamotte, *Le Traité* 3, 1119–207. The section at 198a9-16 reads:

> Question: The four mindfulnesses are sufficient (or include) the [steps for] attainment of the path. Why are thirty-seven explained?
> Answer: If you wish an abbreviated explanation, the four mindfullnesses (are enough). If you wish an expanded explanation, there are thirty-seven.
> [Question:] This is not right. Why? Because if you give an expanded explanation, there would be immeasurable [steps].
> Answer: Although the four mindfulnesses are sufficient for attaining the path, one should also know the various methods of the four proper endeavors, and so forth. Why? Because the minds of sentient beings are various and not the same. The afflictions that bind them are also not all the same. Their joy and understanding are also various. Although the reality and mark of the Buddha Dharma is one, for the sake of sentient beings there are the 84,000 collections in 12 sections of Dharma teachings, and thus various distinct explanations are made.

Appropriate level 當其位: That is, the levels of the five meditations or contemplations, and the distinct and general states of mindfulness. See Chart 1 under the Tripitaka Teaching.

corresponds to the "five [good] roots." The level "supreme in the world" corresponds to the "five powers." The levels of "insight into the truths" correspond to the eightfold right [path]. The levels of the path of cultivation *(bhāvanā-mārga)* correspond to the seven [components of] awakening. These are [the steps on the path] in terms of the levels [of attainment of the Tripitaka Teachings], but this [in itself] is not the regulating and stopping [of afflictions and so forth that obstruct the path].

Fourth is the mutual arising [of the steps on the path]. As you cultivate mindfulness, you will be able to give rise to proper endeavors. Proper endeavors arouse the supranormal powers. The supranormal powers give rise to the five [good] roots. The five [good] roots give rise to the five powers. The five powers give rise to the seven [components of] awakening. The seven [components of] awakening lead to entering the eightfold right path. This is the good and skillful control and fulfillment [of the steps on the path]. The precepts, concentration [samādhi], and wisdom are equal and "right" [as in the eightfold right path]. If you have pure thoughts that are constantly focused, then you will be able to perceive *prajñā*-wisdom. This is the "mutual arising" and the regulating and fulfillment [of the steps on the path].

Precepts, concentration, and wisdom are equal and right 戒定慧等皆名爲正: Or, if 等 is to be taken as a plural marker, rather than as meaning "equal," the phrase would read: "the precepts, concentration, and wisdom are all called 'right' [as in the eightfold right path]."

The *Kōgi* (BT–IV, 373) traces this sentence to a section in the *Ta chih tu lun*, T 25.203a23–25, which identifies different parts of the eightfold path with the precepts, concentration, or wisdom, though the connection with this statement by Chih-i is not obvious. Lamotte (*Le Traité* 3, 1183–84) translates:

> Ces huit chemis corrects *(samyagmārga)* se rangent en trois classes *(skandha)*:
> a. Trois d'entre eux [la parole correcte *(samyagvāc)*, l'action correcte *(samyak-karmānta)* et la manière de vivre correcte *(samyagājīva)*] forment la classe de la moralité *(śīlaskandha)*.
> b. Trois autres [l'effort correct (*samyagvyāyāma*), l'attention correcte *(samyaksmṛti)* et la concentration correcte *(sam-yaksamādhi)* forment la classe de la concentration *(samādhiskandha)*.
> c. Deux enfin [la vue correcte *(samyagdṛṣṭi)* et la conception correcte *(samyaksaṃkalpa)* forment la classe de la sagesse *(prajñāskandha)*.

Chodron (3, 971) translates:

> These eight right paths are arranged into three groups:
> a. Three of them, [right speech, right action, and right livelihood], make up the class of morality.
> b. Three others, [right effort, right mindfulness, and right concentration], make up the class of concentration.
> c. Two, finally, [right view and right thinking], make up the class of wisdom.

Pure thoughts that are constantly focused 清淨心常一 **...**: This phrase is also found in verses from the *Ta chih tu lun*; see T 25.190b21–23. These verses have been quoted previously in the *Mo-ho chih-kuan*; see note at 16c15. The verses quoted in full reveal a different meaning that the impression given by the shortened quote

The reasons why you must practice these [steps on the path] is that, although above [I have explained concerning] the universal deconstruction of dharmas and knowing the penetration and obstructions [of the path], if you do not control the steps on the path to stop [the afflictions and so forth], how will you be able to quickly attain a rapport with the true Dharma? The true Dharma is called "undefiled" [by passions]; the steps on the path involve defilement, but defilement can be a means for producing non-defilement. If there is no place for such means, then it is difficult to encounter the true Dharma. This is like the method for brewing spirits—if the [amount of] materials for fermentation and the heat [applied] is appropriate, the water changes into spirits. If the yeast loses the heat, then the flavor [of the spirits] will not be realized. The *Ta chih tu lun* says, "The 'thirty-seven steps' is a way of practicing the path; **[88a]** there are three gates for [entering] the city of nirvana." The three gates are a near [and direct] cause [for realizing Buddhahood]; the steps on the path are a distant cause [which requires a long gradual practice]. In this sense the [thirty-seven] steps on the path are necessary for controlling and stopping [the afflictions and so forth].

Question: The [thirty-seven] steps on the path are [Hīnayāna] teachings for those of the two vehicles. Why are they presented as part of the bodhisattva path?

Answer: The *Ta chih tu lun* denounces this sort of question, [saying], "whose words are these? Neither the Tripitaka nor the Mahāyāna makes

here. In the above context the verses are translated: "when all the immeasurable offences are removed, the pure mind [remains (or "is revealed")] in its eternal oneness. A noble and wonderful person such as [has attained] this is able to perceive *prajñā*-wisdom."

The 'thirty-seven steps' is a way of practicing the path; there are three gates for [entering] the city of nirvana 三十七品是行道法涅槃城有三門: see the *Ta chih tu lun*, T 25.206a11–13. Lamotte (*Le Traité* 3, 1210) translates:

> Les trente-sept auxiliaires sont le chemin *(mārga)* qui conduit au Nirvāṇa. Quand on a suivi ce chemin, on arrive à la ville du Nirvāṇa *(nirvāṇanagara)*. La ville du Nirvāṇa a trois portes *(dvāra)*: la vacuité *(śūnyata)*, la sans-caractère *(ānimitta)* et la non-prise en considération *(apraṇihita)*. Aussi, après avoir parlé du chemin [au chap. XXXI], faut-il parler ici des portes auxquelles il aboutit.

Chodron (3, 993) translates:

> The thirty-seven auxiliaries are the path leading to nirvana. When one follows this path, one reaches the city of nirvana. The city of nirvana has three gates, emptiness, signlessness, and wishlessness. Thus, after having spoken about the path [in chapter XXXI], it is necessary to speak of the gates that lead into it.

Whose words are these? ... 大論呵此問誰作是語。三藏摩訶衍皆不作是説那 得獨云是小乘法: A brief reference to a long passage in the *Ta chih tu lun*, T 25.197b21–c8. This refers to the opening of the section entitled "Why are the auxiliary steps [of the path] relevant to the Mahāyāna?" Lamotte (*Le Traité* 3, 1138–39) translates:

> Question. — Les trente-sept auxiliaires

(pākṣika) sont le chemin *(mārga)* des Śrāvaka et des Pratyekabuddha; les six perfections *(pāramitā)* sont le chemin des Bodhisattva-Mahāsattva. Pourquoi donc, à propos du chemin des Bodhisattva, parler de choses concernant [seulement] les Śrāvaka?

Réponse. — 1. Le Bodhisattva-Mahāsattva doit exercer tous les chemins de tous les bons dharma. C'est ainsi que le Buddha a dit à Subhūti: "Le Bodhisattva-Mahāsattva qui pratique le Prajñā-pāramitā doit s'exercer *(śikṣitavyam)* dans tous les chemins de tous les bons dharma, depuis la terre de la sagesse sèche (*śuṣka-* ou *śukla-vipaśyanābhūmi*) jusqu'à le terre des Buddha *(buddhabhūmi)*. Les neuf premières terres, il doit les exercer *(śikṣitavyam)*, mais ne pas les attester *(sākṣātkartavyam)*; quant à la terre des Buddha, il doit et l'exercer et l'attester."

2. En outre, où est-il dit que les trente-sept auxiliaires soient seulement des qualités de Śrāvaka et de Pratyekabuddha et ne constituent pas le chemin des Bodhisattva? Dans ce *Prajñāpāramitā-sūtra*, au chapitre intitulé Mahāyāna, le Buddha dit que [les trente-sept auxiliaires], *depuis les quatre fixations-de-l'attention (smṛtyupasthāna) jusqu'aux huit membres du noble chemin (āryāṣṭāṅgamārga), sont contenus dans la Triple Corbeille (tripiṭaka) du Grand Véhiclule; mais il ne dit pas que les trente-sept auxiliaires soient exclusivement (kevalam) des choses concernant le Petit Véhicule.*

Le Buddha, par grande bienveillance *(mahāmaitrī)*, prêche les trente-sept auxiliaires qui sont chemin du Nirvāṇa. Selon les voeux *(praṇidhāna)* des êtres, selon les causes et conditions karmiques *(hetupratyaya)* des êtres, chacun trouve son chemin. L'homme qui cherche *(paryeṣate)* à être Śrāvaka, trouve le chemin des Śrāvaka; l'homme qui a planté les racines de bien *(kuśalamūla)* des Pratyekabuddha trouve le chemin des Pratyekabuddha; l'homme qui cherche la Bodhi des Buddha, trouve le chemin du Buddha.

Selon ses voeux antérieurs *(pūrva-praṇidhāna)* et le degré aigu *(tīkṣṇa)* ou obtus *(mṛdu)* des ses facultés *(indriya)*, l'homme possède la grande compassion *(mahākaruṇā)* ou ne possède pas la grande compassion. De même, quand le roi-dragon *(nāgarāja)* fait tomber la pluie *(vṛṣṭi)*, il pleut partout sur terre et il pleut partout indistinctement *(nirviśeṣam)*; les grands arbres *(mahāvṛkṣa)* et les grandes herbes *(mahātṛṇa)*, parce que leurs racines *(mūla)* sont grandes, reçoivent beaucoup de pluie; les petits arbes *(alpavṛkṣa)* et les petites herbes *(alpatṛṇa)*, parce que leurs racines sont petites, en reçoivent peu.

Chodron (3, 938–39) translates:

Question. The thirty-seven auxiliaries are the path of the śrāvaka and pratyekabuddha; the six perfections are the path of the bodhisattva-mahāsattva. Then why speak of things concerning only the śrāvaka when dealing with the bodhisattva?

Answer. 1. The bodhisattva-mahāsattva must practice the paths of all the good dharmas. Thus the Buddha said to Subhūti: "The bodhisattva-mahāsattva who practices the Prajñāpāramitā should practice the paths of all the good dharmas, from the level of sharp wisdom up to the level of the Buddhas. He must practice the first nine levels but not realize them; as for the level of the Buddhas, he must practice and realize it."

2. Moreover, where is it said that the thirty-seven auxiliaries are the qualities of śrāvakas and pratyekabuddhas alone and do not constitute the path of the bodhisattva? In this *Prajñāpāramitāsūtra*, in the chapter entitled Mahāyāna, the Buddha says that [the thirty-seven auxiliaries], from the four foundations of mindfulness up to the eight members of the noble path are contained in the Three Baskets of the Greater Vehicle; but he does not say that the thirty-seven auxiliaries are things exclusively concerning the Lesser Vehicle.

In his great loving-kindness, the Buddha preached the thirty-seven auxil-

such a statement. How can it be said that these [steps on the path] are the Hīnayāna Dharma alone?" The *Vimalakīrti Sūtra* says, "The steps on the path are good friends; through these you attain correct awakening.… These [thirty-seven] steps on the path are the seat of enlightenment." Again, these are Mahāyāna [teachings, not Hīnayāna]. The *Mahāparinirvāṇa Sūtra* says, "If you are able to cultivate the eightfold right path, you can perceive Buddha-nature.… This is called the attainment of ghee." *The Great Collection*

iaries that are the path to nirvana. In accordance with the vows of beings, in accordance with karmic causes and conditions, each finds his own path. The person who seeks to be a śrāvaka finds the śrāvaka path; the person who has planted the roots of good of the pratyekabuddha finds the pratyekabuddha path; the person who seeks the bodhi of the Buddhas finds the Buddha path.

According to his previous vows and the sharpness or dullness of his faculties, the person has great compassion or does not have great compassion. Similarly, when the nāga king) makes rain to fall, it rains on the earth everywhere indiscriminately the big trees and the large plants receive a lot of rain because of their big roots; the small trees and the small plants receive but little because of their small roots.

The steps on the path are good friends; through these you attain correct awakening.… These steps on the path are the seat of enlightenment 道品善知識由是成正覺。道品是道場: see verses in the seventh chapter (in Kumarajīva's translation) on "the steps on the path" in the *Vimalakīrti Sūtra*, T 14.549c7. Boin (*Vimalakīrti Sūtra*, 180–81) translates:

For pure Bodhisattvas, their mother *(mātṛ)* is the perfection of wisdom *(prajñāpāramitā)*, their father *(pitṛ)* is skillfulness in means *(upāyakauśalya)*: the Leaders of the world *(nāyaka)* are born of such parents.

The joy of the Law *(dharmapramuditā)* is their wife *(bhāryā)*; goodwill *(maitri)* and compassion *(karuṇā)* are their daughters *(duhitṛ)*; the Law and truth *(satya)* are their sons *(putra)*; the contemplation of emptiness *(śūnyatārthacintā)* is their house *(gṛha)*.

All the passions *(kleśa)* are their disciples *(śiṣya)*, who bow to their will. *Their friends (mitra) are the limbs of enlightenment (bodhyaṅga): it is through them that they achieve excellent awakening (pravarabodhi).*

The last phrase, on the "seat of enlightenment," already quoted above at 87c12, is from an earlier section at T 14.542c26.

These are Mahāyāna 是摩訶衍: as pointed out above (see note at 87c12–13), this idea appears in the *Ta chih tu lun* (T 25.406a–b) and the *Pañcaviṃśati Sūtra* (T 8.254b–c).

If you are able to cultivate the eightfold right path, you can perceive Buddha-nature.… This is called the attainment of ghee 能修八正道者卽見佛性名得醍醐: see the *Mahāparinirvāṇa Sūtra*, T 12.784a26–28:

The Buddha said, "Good son, the Buddha-nature of sentient beings is neither one nor two. The Buddhas have equanimity, like empty space. All sentient beings are the same in having this [Buddha-nature]. *If you are able to cultivate the eightfold noble path, you should know that this person will attain clear insight [into Buddha-nature]*. Good son, there is a [type of] grass in the Himalaya mountains that is named 'patience', and if a cow eat this it *will produce ghee*. The Buddha-nature of sentient beings is also like this."

Part of this passage was quoted above in the *Mo-ho chih-kuan* at 34a10–11.

of Sūtras says, "The thirty-seven steps [on the path] are the treasure-torch *dharaṇi* of the bodhisattvas." In this way all of these sūtras clearly show that the [thirty-seven] steps on the path [are part of Mahāyāna teachings]; why do they say that it is Hīnayāna alone?

The *Mahāparinirvāṇa Sūtra* says, "The thirty-seven steps [on the path] are a cause of nirvana, but not a cause of great nirvana. Dharmas that assist in [attaining] *bodhi*-wisdom over immeasurable, incalculable kalpas are the causes for great nirvana," but there are no steps on the path distinct from the [thirty-seven] steps on the path, as there is no fifth "truth" outside of the Four [Noble] Truths. One type of suffering and the causes of suffering is like the [small amount of] soil on your fingernail. If we distinguish [all] the

The thirty-seven steps are the treasure-torch *dhāraṇī* 三十七品是菩薩寶炬陀羅尼: See verses in *The Great Collection of Sūtras*, T 13.25c9– 26b12, part of which [25c–26a] reads :

> Accepting and singly remembering the four mindfulnesses,
> Diligently obtaining the four proper endeavors,
> And being adorned with the four supranormal powers;
> This is called the treasure-torch *dhāraṇī*.
>
> Perfecting the five [good] roots and the five powers,
> So that all the evil winds [of passions] are immobile,
> And cultivating the supreme seven components of awakening;
> This is called the treasure-torch *dhāraṇī*.
>
> Perfecting the two wings of samādhi and wisdom,
> Soaring over the level eightfold right paths,
> And facing supreme wisdom and liberation;
> This is called the treasure-torch *dhāraṇī*.

Different verses from this section were quoted previously in the *Mo-ho chih-kuan*; see at 41b2.

The thirty-seven steps are a cause of nirvana, but not a cause of great nirvana. Dharmas that assist in *bodhi*-wisdom over immeasurable, incalculable kalpas are the causes for great nirvana 三十七品是涅槃因非大涅槃因。無量阿僧祇助菩提法是大涅槃因: see the *Mahāparinirvāṇa Sūtra* at T 12.736a2–5:

> Good son. "Giving" is a cause of nirvana, but not a cause of great nirvana; when it attains the name of "the perfection of giving" *(dānapāramitā)*, then it is a cause of great nirvana. *The thirty-seven steps [on the path] are a cause of nirvana, but not a cause of great nirvana;* it is the dharmas of *bodhi*-wisdom [practiced] for immeasurable, unlimited, incalculable kalpas that deserve the name of "a cause for great nirvana."

Soil on your fingernail 爪上土: See the *Mahāparinirvāṇa Sūtra*, T 12.809c4–13, which contains the following passage:

> Then the World Honored One reached down to the earth and took up a little soil on his fingernail, and said to Kāśyapa, "Is this very much soil? Is it as much as the soil in the worlds of the ten directions?"
>
> The bodhisattva Kāśyapa said to the Buddha, "World Honored One. The soil on your fingernail cannot compare with the soil in the ten directions."
>
> "Good son. There was a person who abandoned his body and then returned [to be reborn] in a human body. He abandoned the bodies of the three evil [destinies] to receive a human body, and was born in the Middle Kingdom with all physical organs complete. Endowed with

sufferings and causes of suffering there are immeasurable aspects, which are [as immeasurable] as the soil in all the ten directions. The direct clarification of a single "thirty-seven steps [on the path]" is a cause for nirvana, but to have an immeasurable [repetitions of] the thirty-seven auxiliary steps on the path is called a cause for great nirvana. Why is it called "immeasurable"? Because, there are [numerous variations, such as] the four types of the Noble Truths, that is, the sixteen gates [or meditations on the Four Truths]. Again, "the defiled [practice of the] steps on the path consists of twenty-two in the realm of desires, thirty-six for the [stage of] pre-dhyāna preparations, and [all] thirty-seven for the first dhyāna stage." All of these [types of] defiled

right faith he was able to cultivate the path, and by cultivating the path he was able to attain liberation. By attaining liberation he was able to enter nirvana. This is like a little soil on the fingernail. [On the other hand,] suppose someone abandons the human body to take on a body of one in the three evil [destinies], and abandons this body in the three evil [destinies] to [again] take on a body of one in the three evil [destinies], is born in a faraway [rustic] place and not fully endowed with all physical organs [i.e., "physically challenged"?], believes in perverted views and cultivates mistaken views, and is not able to attain liberation or the constant bliss of nirvana. This is like the soil of the worlds in the ten directions.

Twenty-two in the realm of desires 欲界二十二: that is, the thirty-seven steps on the path, not counting the seven components of awakening and the eightfold path.

Thirty-six for the pre-dhyāna preparations 未(至)到(地定)三十六: that is, the thirty-seven steps on the path, not counting the single component of "joy."

... All thirty-seven for the first dhyāna stage 初禪三十七: see the *Ta chih tu lun*, T 25.203b3–9 (in a section entitled "Répartition des auxiliaires dans les terres") soon after the passage quoted at 87c23 above. Lamotte (*Le Traité* 3, 1185–86) translates:

1. Les trente-sept auxiliaires de l'illu-mi-nation *(bodhipākṣikadharma)* sont au complet dans la terre de la première extase *(prathamadhyāna)*.
2. Dans la terre de l'*anāgamya* [recueillement liminaire de la première extase], il y a trente-six auxiliaires, en écartant le membre de l'illumination appelé joie *(prītisaṃbodhyaṅga)*.
3. Dans la deuxième extase *(dvitīya-dhyāna)*, il y a aussi trente-six auxiliaires, en écartant [le membre du chemin] appelé conception correcte *(samyak-saṃkalpamārgāṅga)*.
4. Dans l'extase intermédiaire *(dhyānā ntara)* [subdivision de la première extase], dans la troisième extase *(tṛtīya-dhyāna)* et dans la quatrième extase *(catur-thadhyāna)*, il y a trente-cinq auxiliaires, en écartant le membre de l'illumination appelé joie et en écartant le [membre du chemin appelé conception correcte.
5. Dans les trois [premiers] recueillements immatériels *(ārūpyasamāpatti)*, il y a trente-deux auxiliaires, en écartant le membre de l'illumination appelé joie et conception correcte, parole correcte *(samyagvāc)*, action correcte *(samyak-karmānta)* et manière de vivre correcte *(samyagājīva)*.
6. Dans le Sommet de l'existence *(bhavāgra)*, [ou quatrième recueillement immatériel], il y a vingt-deux auxiliaires, en écartant les sept membres de l'illumination *(saṃbodhyaṅga)* et les huit membres du noble chemin *(āryamārgāṅga)*.

[practices of the] steps on the path are like milk. The steps on the path of the Tripitaka [Teachings] are like cream, the steps on the path of the Shared Teachings are like curds, the steps on the path of the Distinct Teachings are like butter, and the steps on the path of the Perfect Teaching are like ghee. This comparison matches the meaning of the text [with regard to the analogy of the five flavors] in the *Mahāparinirvāṇa Sūtra*; there are no "steps on the path" outside of and distinct from these [thirty-seven] auxiliary methods.

Some say that the thirty-seven steps are "auxiliary practices of the path" and others say that they are the path proper. The *Ta chih tu lun* says that this is the bodhisattva path. This text favors [the interpretation that the thirty-seven steps are the path] proper. The *Vimalakīrti Sūtra* says "The steps on the path are good friends; through these you attain correct awakening." This texts favors [the interpretation that the steps are] auxiliary. Again, if we say that the thirty-seven steps are still defiled [by the outflow of passions], then how can we say that the seven components of awakening correspond to the path of cultivation *(bhāvanamārga)*? The *Lotus Sūtra* says, "The undefiled

7. Dans le Monde du désir *(kāmadhātu)*, il y a aussi vingt-deux auxiliaires [en écartant également les *sambodhyaṅga* et les huit *mārgāṅga*].

Ces précisions valent pour le système des Śrāvaka.

Chodron (3, 974–75) translates:

1. The thirty-seven auxiliaries of enlightenment are all present in the stage of the first dhyāna.
2. In the stage of the ānāgamya [preliminaery absorption of the first dhyāna], there are thirty-six auxiliaries, excluding the member of enlightenment called joy.
3. In the second dhyāna, there are also thirty-six auxiliaries, excluding [the member of the path] called right thinking.
4. In the intermediate dhyāna [subdivision of the first dhyāna], in the third dhyāna and in the fourth dhyāna, there are thirty-five auxiliaries, excluding the member of enlightenment called joy and excluding the [member of the path called] right thinking.
5. In the [first] three formless absorptions, there are thirty-two auxiliaries, excluding the member of enlightenment called joy and [the members of the path called] right thinking, right speech, right action and right livelihood.
6. In the summit of existence [or fourth formless absorption], there are twenty-two auxiliaries, excluding the seven members of enlightenment and the eight members of the noble path.
7. In the desire realm, there are also twenty-eight auxiliaries [excluding the *sambodhyaṅgas* and the eight *mārgāṅgas*].

This information is valid for the system of the śrāvakas.

Five flavors: see the analogy of the five flavors in the *Mahāparinirvāṇa Sūtra*, T 12.690c–691a.

This is the bodhisattva path 是菩薩道: see the section of the *Ta chih tu lun* (T 25.197b21–c8) quoted above at 88a3–4.

The steps on the path are good friends; through these you attain correct awakening 道品善知識由是成正覺: see the verses in the *Vimalakīrti Sūtra* at T 14.549c7, quoted above at 88a5–6.

Path of cultivation 修道: presumably the *bhāvanamārga* is supposed to be "undefiled" or does not involve any outflows of passionate afflictions.

faculties [or "roots"] and powers are the treasures of the path of awakening." Why should the eightfold path come before the seven components of awakening?

Three points should be distinguished here [with regard to the idea of involvement with the defiled and undefiled]. The first is that the thirty-seven steps all are "defiled." The second in that all are "undefiled." The third is that they are "defiled" and "undefiled."

As the *Ta chih tu lun* says, if you cultivate the eightfold right path, you will attain the first [level of] good yet defiled [body of] five skandhas. The "good yet defiled [body of] five skandhas" refers to [the stage of] "heat." So before [attaining] the stage of "heat," you must cultivate the eightfold right

The undefiled faculties and powers are the treasures of the path of awakening 無漏根力覺道之財: a phrase from the parable of the pearl in the king's top-knot in the fourteenth chapter of the *Lotus Sūtra*, T 9.39a5; note that the *Lotus Sūtra* has "all dharmas" instead of "path of awakening," and the context gives quite a different nuance that what appears to be Chih-i use of the phrase. Hurvitz (218–19 [200]) translates the context:

> The Thus Come One is also like this. Having gained the Dharma-realm with the power of dhyāna-concentration and wisdom, he reigns over the three spheres, yet the Māra kings will not consent to obey him. The wise and saintly generals of the Thus Come One do battle with them. With those who are successful he is also delighted at heart, and among the fourfold multitude it is to them that he preaches the scriptures, causing their hearts to rejoice. He confers upon them *the precious Dharma-gifts* of dhyāna-concentration, deliverance, *faculties without outflows, and powers.*

Why should the eightfold path ... 何八正在七覺前: I am not sure of the intent of this rhetorical question. Since the eightfold path involves dealing with the defiled world, should not the eightfold path come before the seven components of awakening? But it does not, perhaps because the eight elements all involve both the defiled and undefiled, and are thus Mahāyāna?

The stage of "heat" 煖法: see the *Ta chih tu lun*, T 25.226b9–11; Lamotte (*Le Traité* 3, 1411) translates the context:

> Il concentre sa pensée sur les quatre vérités, sans se laisser distraire. Il évite de la diriger vers les concentrations matérielles et immatérielles *(rūpārūpyasamādhi),* mais tend de tout son esprit vers le Nirvāṇa. Ceci s'appelle la concentration correcte *(samyaksamādhi).*
>
> Au début [au cours du Chemin préparatoire], le yogin obtient [ces racines de bien] bonnes-impures *(kuśalasāsrava) nommées Chaleur (uṣmagata),* Têtes *(mūrdhan)* et Patience *(kṣānti),* lesquelles se développent en pensées initiales, intermédiaires et finales.

Chodron (3, 1154) translates:

> He concentrates his mind on the four Truths without being distracted. He prevents it from being led toward the form and formless meditative stabilizations, but wholeheartedly moves toward nirvana. This is called right meditation.
>
> At the beginning [during the preparatory Path], the yogin obtains the good-impure good roots called heat summits and patience, which are developed in beginning, intermediate and final minds.

path. How should it be cultivated? First, you receive the Dharma teachings from a teacher and fix your thoughts **[88b]** in concentrated remembrance; this is called "mindfulness." If you seek this Dharma diligently, this practice is called "proper endeavor." If you cultivate this in a single thought [or, "singlemindedly"] 一心, this is called "supranormal powers." Then the five good faculties arise; this is called the "roots." The roots grow and increase; this is called "power." One is able to function by discriminating among [the steps of] the path, this is called the seven [components of] awakening. Practicing the path peacefully and calmly is called the eightfold right path. If you are able to cultivate [the path] in this way, you will attain the "good yet defiled [body of] five skandhas." You should know that this is the [thirty-seven] steps of the path [in the sense that] all are defiled.

For all [of the steps on the path] to be undefiled is as follows: that is, all the practices of the steps on the path that involve insight into the truth and [intellectual, conceptual] pondering are "undefiled." This is the intent of the text of the *Lotus Sūtra* [in general]. In the past it was said that you cultivate the eightfold right path and seven components of awakening in the midst of defilement, but there is no textual evidence for this [interpretation]. The *[Abhidharma-]vibhāṣā-śāstra* says, "If [the practice of] the eightfold right path comes after that of the seven components of awakening, this involves attaining defilement and attaining non-defilement." Why? Because you realize insight into the truth by relying on the eightfold right path, and this involves non-defilement. [The *śāstra* also says,] "If the eightfold right path is present before the seven [components of] awakening, you face solely toward non-defilement." This should be understood in this way. Quoting the text

If the eightfold right path comes after that of the seven components of awakening, this involves attaining defilement and attaining non-defilement 若八正在七覺後。亦得是有漏亦得是無漏 **... If the eightfold right path is present before the seven [components of] awakening, you face solely toward non-defilement** 若八正在七覺前一向是無漏: see the *Abhidharma-vibhāṣā-śāstra* at T 28.362c11–14, which is a bit different from Chih-i's "quote":

> In this Abhidharma [text], "being/existence" is the determining feature. If the components of awakening come after the teaching of the components the [eightfold] path, you should know that the components of the path are solely facing toward non-defilement. If the components of the path come after the teaching of the components of awakening, you should know that the components of the path involve both defilement and non-defilement. If the components of the Middle Way come after the teaching of the components of awakening, you should know that the components of the path involve both defilement and non-defilement.

See *Shiki* (BT–IV, 381–83) for an extended discussion of this text; it tries to deal with the anomaly that Chih-i is not quoting the text accurately, saying that "here he must be referring to the [deeper] meaning or intent 義 of the author" (381).

of the *[Abhidharma-]vibhāṣā-śāstra* affirms two meanings—that of both defiled and non-defiled, which place them in opposition.

2. The Thirty-Seven Steps on the Path as "Spontaneous" [88b12]

I cannot give a detailed explanation here concerning each of the thirty-seven steps of the various types of the Truths of the path. I will clarify only the thirty-seven steps of the Truth of the path as spontaneous, to consummate the meaning of threefold contemplation in a single thought.

1. The Four Mindfulnesses [88b14]

The *Pañcaviṃśati Sūtra* says, "If you wish to use all types [of practice] to cultivate the four mindfulnesses, [you should know that] a mindful thought is the Dharma realm and encompasses all dharmas [or, Dharma teachings]; all dharmas incline toward a mindful thought and do not go beyond this inclination." The *Avataṃsaka Sūtra* says, "This is analogous to the great earth, which is one and yet is able to give rise to various sprouts." The earth is the seed[-bed] of all sprouts. The *Lotus Sūtra* says, "All types of appearances, essences, natures, [and so forth] are all one type of appearance, essence, and nature." What is this "one type" [or, lit., "one seed" 一種]? It is the appearance,

Place them in opposition 是對位意: Ikeda (*Gendaigoyaku*, 447) gives an expanded, interpretive translation: "Again, to say that [this involves] both defilement and non-defilement is to take the meaning of the contrasting levels of the eightfold path and the levels of insight into the Four Noble Truths *(darśana-mārga)* 見道."

Various types of the Truths of the path 諸道諦: That is, the truth of the path as arising, non-arising, immeasurable, and spontaneous, corresponding to the positions of the Fourfold Teachings? See Chart 1 in Swanson, *Foundations*, 358–59.

Spontaneous 無作: Corresponding to the position of the Perfect Teaching.

... A mindful thought is the Dharma realm and encompasses all dharmas; all dharmas incline toward a mindful thought and do not go beyond this inclination 念處是法界攝一切法一切法趣念處是趣不過: a rephrasing of a passage from the *Pañcaviṃśati Sūtra* at T 8.333c12-14:

All dharmas incline toward [the thirty-seven] components of the path from the four mindfulnesses to the eightfold noble path, and do not go beyond this inclination. Why? The components of the path from the four mindfulnesses to the eightfold noble path are ultimately unobtainable. How can they be said to incline or not incline?

This is analogous to the great earth, which is one and yet is able to give rise to various sprout 譬如大地一能生種種芽: see the *Avataṃsaka Sūtra* at T 9.428a16 and 428b1; this phrase has already been quoted above in the *Mo-ho chih-kuan* at 50c19 and 75b1.

All types of appearances, essences, natures, are all one type of appearance, essence, and nature 一切種相體性皆是一種相體性: a summary of a passage from the fifth chapter of the *Lotus Sūtra* at T 9.b26–c3. Hurvitz (103 [96]) translates:

What is the reason? Only the Thus Come

essence, nature [and so forth] of the seed of Buddhahood *(buddha-gotra)*. It has always been said that the *Lotus Sūtra* does not clarify Buddha-nature. But the sūtra does clarify [the idea of] "one type" [or "one seed"] 一種. What is meant by this "one type"? [The parable of] the various types of grasses and trees in the forest is an analogy for the seven preparatory stages, and the one great earth is [analogous to the one] true reality, and this is called the "Buddha-seed." [This is the meaning of "one type," that is, "Buddha-nature."]

The arising of a single thought in the mind is beyond conceptual understanding. All types [of thoughts and experiences], the skandhas and senses of the ten realms, do not mutually obstruct each other. If you contemplate Dharma-nature [or, the nature of phenomena], [you realize that] they arise

> One knows these beings, their kinds, *their signs, their substance, their nature*, what things they think back on, what things they think ahead to, what things they cultivate, how they think back, how they think ahead, how they practice, by resort to what dharmas they think back, by resort to what dharmas they think ahead, by resort to what dharmas they practice, what dharma they gain and by resort to what dharma they gain it. The living beings dwell on a variety of grounds. Only the Thus Come One sees them for what they are and understands them clearly and without obstruction. Those grasses and trees, shrubs and forests, and medicinal herbs do not now themselves whether their nature is superior, intermediate, or inferior; but the Thus Come One knows this Dharma of a single mark and a single flavor....

Buddha-nature 佛性: the classical commentaries (BT–IV, 386) point to the discussion of this issue in *The Meaning of Mahāyāna* (T 44.466a26–b4) 大乘義章, an interpretation of Fa-yün 法雲 of the Kuang-chai ssu 光宅寺. The context reads:

> It has been said that the *Lotus Sūtra* does not teach Buddha-nature, and so [presents] a shallow nirvana, but this interpretation is not right. As sūtras teach about "nature" as the one vehicle, the *Lotus Sūtra* also clearly explains about the one vehicle. How can you say that it does not [teach about Buddha-]"nature"? Again, in the *Lotus Sūtra* there is the story of the Bodhisattva Never Disrespectful. When he sees the four assemblies of beings he cries out in a loud voice, "You will become a Buddha! I will not disparage you." Thus we know that [all] sentient beings have the Buddha-nature, because [this bodhisattva] said that all will become [Buddhas]. To say that all will become [Buddhas] is to say that they will manifest this [Buddha-]nature.

Grasses and trees in the forest 卉木叢林種種: see the parable of the grasses and trees—how they all grow according to their capacities in response to the same rain—at the beginning of the fifth chapter in the *Lotus Sūtra*, T 9.19a–c (see Hurvitz, 101–3 [95–97]). It seems to me, however, that this parable would signify difference and variety of natures and abilities, rather than proving that all beings have the same "Buddha-nature."

Seven preparatory stages 七方便: that is, the seven stages prior to becoming an arhat: the three levels of acquiring erudition, and the four stages of good roots.

Buddha-seed 佛種: Ikeda (*Gendaigoyaku*, 448) adds, "Therefore it can be understood that the *Lotus Sūtra* does indeed teach Buddha-nature."

Dharma-nature 法性: this term could be taken as "the nature of reality (Dharma),"

through causes and conditions, and one type is [the same as] all types, and one visible form *(rūpa)* is [the same as] all visible forms. If Dharma-nature is empty, then all visible forms are [the same as] one visible form, that is, the emptiness of one is the emptiness of all. If Dharma-nature [the nature of phenomena] is conventionally existent, then one visible form is [the same as] all visible forms, and one conventional existent is all conventional existences. If Dharma-nature is the Middle, then it is neither one nor all, yet both one and all are illuminated. Again, [the Middle] can be said to be neither empty nor conventional, yet both emptiness and conventionality are illuminated. That is, "all" is neither empty nor conventional, yet both emptiness and conventionality are illuminated 雙照空假. The visible forms of the nine dharma realms are also, in this way, simultaneously empty, conventional, and the Middle 即空即假即中. This is called "mindfulness of the body" [or of "visible forms"].

If you contemplate the sensations *(vedanā)* in terms of Dharma-nature [the nature of phenomena], [you realize that since] Dharma-nature arises though causes and conditions, one type is [the same as] all types, and one sensation is [the same as] all sensations. [**88c**] The Dharma-nature of sensations is empty, and therefore all sensations are one sensation, and the emptiness of one is the emptiness of all. The Dharma-nature of sensations consists of conventional designation, therefore one sensation is all sensations, and the conventionality of one is the conventionality of all. The Dharma-nature of sensations consists of the Middle, there is not one sensation and there is not all sensations; it is neither empty nor conventional, and so both emptiness and conventionality are illuminated. All are neither empty nor conventional, and so both emptiness and conventionality are illuminated. The sensations of the nine dharma realms are also, in this way, simultaneously empty, conventional, and the Middle. This is called the "mindfulness of sensations."

If you contemplate the Dharma-nature [the nature of phenomena] of thoughts, [you realize that] since dharmas arise through causes and conditions, one type is [the same as] all types; one thought is [the same as] all thoughts. Dharma-nature is empty, therefore all thoughts are [the same as] one thought, and the emptiness of one is the emptiness of all. Dharma-nature involves conventionality, and therefore one thought is [the same as]

or "the nature of phenomena (dharmas)." In either case it refers to the emptiness and non-substantiality of all things.

Mindfulness of the body 身念處: the first of "four mindfulnesses"; more specifically, "to be mindful that this physical body is impure."

Mindfulness of sensations 受念處: the second of "four mindfulnesses"; "to be mindful that all sensations are ultimately painful."

Thoughts 心: Or, "the mind"; or in terms of the five skandhas, consciousness 識.

all thoughts, and the conventionality of one is the conventionality of all. Dharma-nature is the Middle, therefore it is neither one nor all; it is neither emptiness nor conventionality, and so both emptiness and conventionality are illuminated. The thoughts of the nine dharma realms are also like this. This is called the "mindfulness of thoughts."

If you contemplate the Dharma-nature of the two skandhas of conceptions and volitions, [you realize that] since dharmas arise through causes and conditions, one type is [the same as] all types; one volition is [the same as] immeasurable volitions. Dharma-nature is empty, therefore all volitions are [the same as] one volition, and the emptiness of one is the emptiness of all. Dharma-nature involves conventionality, and therefore one volition is [the same as] all volitions, and the conventionality of one is the conventionality of all. Dharma-nature is the Middle, therefore it is neither one nor all, it is neither emptiness nor conventionality, and so both emptiness and conventionality are illuminated. All are neither empty nor conventional, and so both emptiness and conventionality are illuminated. The [conceptions and] volitions of the nine dharma realms are also like this—simultaneously empty, conventional, and the Middle. This is called the "mindfulness of phenomena (dharmas)."

In this way, the powers and functions of mindfulness are wide and extensive. Their meaning is concurrent with both Hīnayāna and Mahāyāna; together they involve destroying eight perversions, both [together] manifesting [four of] flourishing and [four of] decaying, and both [manifesting] [four of] "not flourishing" and [four of] "not decaying." It is in the midst of this that one enters *parinirvāṇa*; this is called "the seat of enlightenment," this is also called "Mahāyāna," and this is also called the "Dharma realm."

Mindfulness of thoughts 心念處: the third of the "four mindfulnesses"; "to be mindful that thoughts are impermanent."

Mindfulness of phenomena 法念處: the fourth of the "four mindfulnesses"; "to be mindful that phenomena (dharmas) are without substantial reality."

Eight perversions 八倒: that is, the four perverted views of the world as permanent, blissful, having selfhood, and pure; four each for Hīnayāna and Mahāyāna. The Mahāyāna, based on the *Nirvana Sutra*, posits the permanence, bliss, selfhood, and purity of nirvana, so the "perversion" of this would be to see the unconditioned as impermanent, involving suffering, having no selfhood, and impure.

Flourishing and decaying 榮枯: T'ien-t'ai teaches "four kinds of flourishing" and "four kinds of decay" in addition to the traditional "four kinds of perverted views." See Kuan-ting's commentary to the *Mahāparinirvāṇa Sūtra*, T 38.44b24–26:

> The Śāla tree, translated as "solid," has two trunks in each direction with eight trunks in the four directions, four flourishing and four decaying. Below the roots intertwine, and above the branches merge with each other. Thus [the trunks] mutually share their intertwining being, and they reciprocally yield to each other through flourishing and decaying.

What are the features of this concurrent [with both Hīnayāna and Mahāyāna] and extensive meaning [of Dharma-nature, the true nature of phenomena]? The visible form of Dharma-nature is truly not pure, but ordinary [ignorant] people misconceptualize it as pure; this is called a "perversion." [On the other hand,] truly it is not impure, but those of the two vehicles misconceptualize it as impure; this [also] is called a "perversion." Now [you should] contemplate the skandha of visible form *(rūpa-skandha)* as empty. Everything is empty. Within emptiness there is no purity; how can there be any defiled attachment? [Realizing] this is called "destroying the perverted views of ordinary people who conceptualize purity," and "fulfilling the mindfulness of 'decaying.'" [Then contemplate] the skandha of visible form as conventional. Everything is conventionally existent. The discrimination of names and appearances can never be exhausted. The wisdom of conventionality is constantly pure, and does not involve defilement by the dust-like delusions of non-cognizance. Why, then, would you become entangled in emptiness and be attached to [a Hīnayāna nirvana that is merely] an extinction to ashes, or say that visible forms are not pure? [Realizing] this is called "destroying the perverted views of impurity of those of the two vehicles," and "fulfilling the mindfulness of 'flourishing.'" This is called "destroying together the eight perversions," and "establishing both decaying and flourishing."

[Next,] contemplate visible form [in terms of the Middle] in its fundamental reality, as neither empty nor conventional, and that therefore all is neither empty nor conventional. Since it is not empty, there are no impure perversions, and since it is not conventional, there are no pure perversions. Since there are no pure perversions, there is no flourishing of the [Śāla] tree, and since there are no impure perversions, there is no decaying of the [Śāla] tree. **[89a]** Since there is no flourishing nor decay, there are no two extremes. There is no extreme and no middle; this is called being "in the midst" 中間. The Buddha encountered this principle; therefore this is called nirvana. Again, this is neither pure nor impure. The eight perversions do not arise;

What are the features 其相云何 **...**: from here Chih-i follows the same pattern as above, discussing Dharma-nature in terms of the four mindfulnesses (and five skandhas) of body (or visible form *[rūpa]*), sensation, thoughts (or consciousness), and dharmas.

Visible form 色: this is inferring the first mindfulness—to be mindful that the physical body is impure.

Śāla tree: see note above on the eight intertwining trunks of the Śāla tree, with four trunks flourishing and four trunks decaying, in Kuan-ting's commentary to the *Mahāparinirvāṇa Sūtra*.

Nirvana is called the secret treasury 涅槃名祕密藏: phrases from the *Mahāparinirvāṇa Sūtra*, 616b9–10. This passage has been quoted many times above in the *Mo-ho chih-kuan*; see note at 20c1–2.

this is called nirvana. This nirvana is called the "secret treasury." Having placed his children in the secret treasury, the Buddha himself dwells therein; therefore it is said that he "enters" [nirvana].

The sensations of the Dharma-nature [the nature of phenomena] are fundamentally not blissful, but ordinary people misconceptualize them as blissful; this is called a perversion. Truly they are not suffering, but those of the two vehicles misconceptualize them as suffering. Now [you should] contemplate the skandha of sensations *(vedanā-skandha)* as empty, that all [sensations] are empty. In emptiness there is no bliss; how can it give rise to defilement? Thus ordinary people can destroy their perverted views; this is the fulfillment of the mindfulness of "decay." [Next, contemplate] the skandha of sensations as conventional, that all [sensations] are conventional. But there is nothing [substantial] to sense and experience, even though all sensations are experienced. This is called "hearing of discriminations" but not arousing a weary cynical fear. Why should you abandon this and become mired in emptiness and a severance [nirvana] that is [merely a reduction of the body to] ashes? [Realizing] this is the destruction of perverted views by those of the two vehicles, and the fulfillment of the mindfulness of "flourishing." These [together] are called "the destruction of two [types of] perverted views" and "establishing both decaying and flourishing." [Next,] contemplate sensations [in terms of the Middle] in its fundamental reality, as neither [merely] empty nor conventional. Since they are not [merely] empty, they do not "decay"; since they are not [merely] conventional, they do not "flourish." Thus the extremes of perverted views do not arise; this is called "nirvana." Thus the principle of the Middle is manifested; this is called the "secret treasury." All [the details are] as explained above.

The thoughts or mind of Dharma-nature [the nature of phenomena] are fundamentally not permanent, but ordinary people misconceptualize them [as permanent]; this is called the perverted view of "eternalism." Dharma-nature is truly not transient, but those of the two vehicles misconceptualize it as transient. [This is the perverted view of "annihilationism."] Now [you should] contemplate the skandha of consciousness *(vijñāna-skandha)* as empty, that all [consciousness] is empty. Within emptiness there is no constancy; how can you say that there is continuity in the mind from thought to thought? [Realizing] this is called "destroying the ordinary person's perverted view of eternalism," and "fulfilling the mindfulness of decaying." [Next, contemplate] thoughts as conventional designations, that all [thoughts] are conventional. If mind [or thoughts] are [merely] transient, then how can you attain discrimination [as to which are good and important] among the features of immeasurable thoughts? [Realizing] this is called "destroying the perverted view of transience of those of the two vehicles" and "fulfilling the mindfulness of flourishing." Again, thoughts are neither [merely] empty nor conventional. Since they are not [merely] empty, they are not transient. Since they are not [merely] conventional, they are not permanent. They do not [merely] flourish nor decay; thus the extreme perverted views do not arise. This is called entering nirvana. The principle of the Middle Way is manifested; this is called the "secret treasury." Having placed his children [in the secret treasury, the Buddha] himself enters therein, and so forth [as explained above].

The phenomena of Dharma-nature are fundamentally without selfhood, but ordinary people misconceptualize them as having [substantial] selfhood. [This is a perverted view.] Fundamentally it is not that they have no selfhood [of individuality], but those of the two vehicles misconceptualize this as the lack of selfhood or individuality. [This also is a mistaken view.] Now [you should] contemplate Dharma-nature as empty, that all [dharmas] are empty. Within emptiness there is no selfhood; [realizing] this is called "destroying the perverted views of ordinary people" and "fulfilling the mindfulness of decay." [Next, contemplate] Dharma-nature as conventional, that all [dharmas] are conventional constructions. [Those who realize this] have a mastery [over their actions in the conventional world] without becoming entangled [in it], including the meaning of "selfhood." [Realizing] this is called "destroying the perverted views of those of the two vehicles" and "fulfilling the mindfulness of flourishing" [in the conventional world]. [Next,] contemplate dharmas in their fundamental reality [as the Middle Way], that is, as neither [merely] empty nor conventional. Since they are not [merely] empty, it is not that they have no selfhood [or individuality]; since they are not [merely] conventional, it is not that they have [substantial] selfhood. Thus the extreme perverted views do not arise, and this is called "entering nirvana" This principle of the Middle [Way] is manifested; this is called the "secret treasury." **[89b]**

In this way the perversions are subdued by the medicines of the Dharma, which number four [as outlined above]. The wisdom for contemplating Dharma-nature is called a "mindful thought" 念. There is one truth, that is, a threefold truth 一諦三諦; this is called the "object" [of wisdom]. All is empty: of all the perversions of flourishing and decaying, there is none that is not empty and quiescent. All is conventional: it is not that the two extremes [of the trunks] of the [Śāla] tree [that flourish and decay in turn] do not ensue [and play their provisional part]. All is the Middle: it is not that Dharma-nature is nothing. It is just that a single thought of the mind 一念心

It is not that Dharma-nature is nothing 非無法界: or, as Ikeda (*Gendaigoyaku*, 451) interprets, "there is nothing that is not the realm of the Buddha [= Dharma-nature]."

is vast and extensive in this way. If you are able to profoundly contemplate the objects of these thoughts, [realizing] this is the seat of enlightenment, it is the Mahāyāna, and it is both [aspects of flourishing and decaying] of the [Śāla] tree and the realization of nirvana. Both the beginning and the end are included herein, and it is not necessary to further cultivate any other method.

2. *The Four Proper Endeavors* [89b7]

If you do not realize [nirvana through cultivating the four mindfulnesses], you should further exercise the other steps [on the path]. If you diligently contemplate mindfulness, this is called "proper endeavor." When [mistaken] views and conceptual attitudes originally arise, this is called "evil" that has already arisen. Contemplate these [evil afflictions] as empty, and strive diligently so that those that have already arisen do not arise again. The [minute] dust-like [afflictions] and ignorance are called "evil" that has not yet arisen. Contemplate conventionality and the Middle, and strive diligently so that these [evils] that have not yet arisen do not arise. Do your best to practice the Four Samādhis, so that these two types of evil are obstructed. "Omniscience" *(sarvajñā)* refers to good that has already arisen. This "good" arises easily, so it can be said that the path to nirvana is easily attained. "The wisdom of the path" and "universal wisdom" refer to good that has not yet arisen. This discriminatory wisdom is difficult to arouse. You must strive diligently so that this wisdom of emptiness [that is, "omniscience"] will increase and grow. The wisdom of the Middle has not yet arisen, so you must [strive diligently] for it to develop and be aroused. There is no gap between these three wisdoms, so these [later] two wisdoms will arise [spontaneously from the first wisdom of emptiness]. These are the four proper endeavors, through which you are also able to attain the path of awakening. Therefore it is said that

Proper endeavor 正勤: for details, see Glossary under "four proper endeavors."

Evil that has already arisen 生惡: this refers to the second of the four proper endeavors, that is, "producing a desire for extinguishing evil that has already arisen."

Evil that has not yet arisen 未生惡: this refers to the first of the four proper endeavors, that is, "producing a desire for the non-arising of evil that has not yet arisen."

Do your best 竭力盡誠: lit., "exhaust your powers and your will."

"Omniscience" 一切智: in this context, to realize the emptiness of all things.

Good that has already arisen 生善: this refers to the fourth of the four proper endeavors, that is, "producing a desire for the duration, increase, non-loss, and fulfillment of favorable good things that have already arisen."

Good that has not yet arisen 未生善: This refers to the third of the four proper endeavors, that is, "producing a desire for the arising of favorable good things that have not yet arisen."

because you singlemindedly strive diligently, you can attain correct wisdom *(saṃbodhi)*, and the other steps are not necessary.

3. The Four Supranormal Powers [89b16]

If you do not realize [correct wisdom through the practice of proper endeavors], you should not exert yourself [for a while]. If the mind is excessively [diligent], it can become distracted and restless, and you need to realize a good quiescence. Inquire into and contemplate the nature of mind [and thoughts]; this is called "superior concentration." Within this superior concentration, cultivate the [four] supranormal powers, that is, [the powers endowed with the forces of concentration and exertion of] the will *(canda)*, diligent effort *(vīrya)*, the mind *(citta)*, and discursive reasoning *(mīmāṃsa)*. [First,] "will" refers to solely facing this [Buddha] Dharma, and is also called "being adorned" with this [Buddha] Dharma. From within concentration, contemplate wisdom as a flame in a closed room illuminates things fully. Through this "full illumination" you can fulfill the severance [of all afflictions and so forth] and cultivate supranormal powers. [Second,] "diligence" refers to fulfilling this Dharma. Dharma-nature is immobile, and yet you strive diligently in quiescence. You can thus, without gaps and without confusion, fulfill the severance [of all afflictions and so forth] and cultivate supranormal powers. [Third,] "mind" refers to [single-mindedness, or] proper abiding [in focused concentration]. You should thoroughly contemplate this [Buddha] Dharma. If the objects of a single thought are kept [through concentration] in a single place, there is nothing that cannot be accomplished. Thus you can fulfill the severance [of all afflictions and so forth] and cultivate supranormal powers. [Fourth,] "discursive reasoning" refers to being well able to discriminate this [Buddha] Dharma and [skillful] means. If you discursively reason in this way, you will not be restless and distracted. Because of this concentrated discursive reasoning, you can fulfill the severance [of all afflictions and so forth] and cultivate supranormal powers. In this way, by cultivating a concentrated mind, you can realize [awakening], and the other steps are not necessary.

Singlemindedly strive diligently 一心勤精進: the traditional commentaries do not identify this as a quote from a sūtra. Note that here I have translated 一心 as "singlemindedly," which has a somewhat different nuance than the translation "one thought."

A good quiescence 善寂: settle down and "just be quiet and be calm."

[Four] supranormal powers [四]如意足: see Glossary for details.

Single thought 一心: note that Chih-i shifts in his use of this term as "single-minded" concentration, and specifically to that of a "single thought."

4. The Five Good Roots [89b27]

If you cannot realize [awakening] through cultivating supranormal powers], you should cultivate the five [good] roots 五[善]根[, that is, faith 信, diligence 進, mindfulness 念, concentration 定, and wisdom 慧]. [First,] have faith that the principle of the threefold truth is the mother of the Buddhas of the past, present, and future, and that it is able to give rise to all the ten powers, [four] fearlessnesses, [three] liberations, and [three kinds of] samadhis. To cultivate only [the four types of] mindfulness and not seek the other steps, [believing that this is sufficient to attain Buddhahood,] [**89c**] is called the "root of faith." [Second,] "diligence" refers to [believing that] all Dharma teachings are encompassed in this faith. Because you believe in all these Dharma teachings, therefore you redouble your diligence. [This is called the "root of diligence."] [Third,] "mindfulness" refers to being mindful of both the path proper and the auxiliary parts of the path, and not being led astray by, or allow to enter, any mistaken [views] or delusions. Again, it refers to the diligent practice of this [Buddha] Dharma. Since this Dharma is not forgotten [even for a moment], this is called the "root of mindfulness." [Fourth,] "concentration" refers to single-minded and quiescent concentration, which is nonetheless practiced diligently. Again, this Dharma is encompassed in [one] thought [or, "in mindfulness"]. This Dharma is not forgotten, nor are you agitated[, even for a moment]; therefore this is called the "root of concentration." [Fifth,] "wisdom" refers to the wisdom of mindfulness, which is encompassed by the dharma [practice] of concentration. Your inner nature is spontaneously illuminated; it does not follow from someone else's knowledge. This is called the "root of wisdom." Merely by cultivating these five [good] roots, you can realize the path and fulfill the Mahāyāna.

5. The Five Powers [89c8]

If you are not able to realize [the path through cultivating the five good roots], you should diligently cultivate the five powers[, that is, of faith, diligence, mindfulness, concentration, and wisdom]. When the [five good] roots increase and grow, this hinders the passionate afflictions, and this is called "power." [First, the power of] faith destroys all doubt, and makes you immovable [or "unflappable"]. [Second, the power of] diligence removes lethargy, so that you can fulfill all that you originally vowed to attain. [Third, the power of] mindfulness destroys [mistaken] conceptualizations, so that the destructiveness of passionate afflictions does not occur. [Fourth, the

Powers, fearlessnesses, liberations, samādhis, dhyāna stages: For details on these and following terms, such as the four dhyāna stages, see the Glossary.

power of] concentration destroys distracted confusion, and takes you far from troubled disturbances. No matter what is said, the first dhyāna stage is not obstructed; even if you abide in conceptual examination *(vitarka)* and reflection *(vicāra)*, the second dhyāna stage is not obstructed; even if you arouse joyful thoughts, the third dhyāna stage is not obstructed; even if you teach and save sentient beings, the fourth dhyāna stage is not obstructed. Even if [the attainment of] the four dhyāna stages is hindered, this does not mean that all concentration is hindered, nor that you should abandon [the practice of] concentration, nor that you should not pursue [the practice of] concentration. This is called the "power of concentration." [Fifth, the power of] wisdom destroys harmful attachments, so that both all attachments and all wisdom are illuminated together. This is called the "power of wisdom." In this way the five powers are called "Mahāyāna."

6. The Seven Components of Awakening [89c16]

If you are not able to realize [the path through the cultivation of the five powers], you should use the seven components of awakening to regulate [all things] with equanimity. When your thoughts are "hovering," you should use the component of "removing" to remove the dust-like [afflictions] of body and speech, use the component of equanimity (or "abandonment") to abandon [attachment to] the wisdom of contemplation, and use the component of concentrated thoughts to enter dhyāna meditation. When your thoughts are depressed, [use the components of] diligence, discernment, and joy to arouse [your thoughts]. [The component of] mindfulness is a common condition for both situations. Cultivate these seven [components of] awakening, and you will realize the path. The *Ta chih tu lun* says, "If you are to be free from the five impediments, you should singularly cultivate the seven [components of] awakening, and there will be none who cannot realize [the path]."

Hovering 浮動: unfocused, "high," overly excited.

Removing 除覺: This must refer to the component of "serenity" or "making light" 輕 *(praçrabhisaṃbodhyāṅga)*, the fifth component of awakening as listed by Hurvitz (*Chih-i*, 345).

"Equanimity" or "abandonment" 捨: note the confusion in Chinese terms between "equanimity" 等 and "abandonment" 捨; this seems to stem from an inconsistency in interpreting and translating the Sanskrit term *upekṣā*.

If you are to be free from the five impediments, you should singularly cultivate the seven [components of] awakening, and there will be none who cannot realize 若離五蓋專修七覺不得入者無有是處: ***Ta chih tu lun***: See T 25.237a26–27, a section in the middle of a discussion of the "ten powers." Lamotte (*Le Traité* 3, 1525) translates:

> Et si celui qui a une mauvaise conduite ne peut renaître dans les cieux, comment

7. The Eightfold Right Path [89c21]

If you cannot realize [the path through cultivating the seven components of awakening], you should cultivate the eightfold right path. By means of the transworldly and most supreme "right views" 正見, contemplate the principle of the threefold truth. Arouse this contemplation by means of "right discrimination" 正思. To teach the marks of dharmas [or the Dharma] as they are and thus benefit both oneself and others is "right speech" 正語. [The *Mahāparinirvāṇa Sūtra* says,] "If you do black [evil] deeds, you will obtain black [evil] retribution. White [good] deeds result in white [good] recompense. Mixed [good and evil] deeds result in mixed retributions. Neither white nor black [neutral] deeds result in retribution that is [neutral, that is,] neither white nor black." This is the interpretation given in terms of Hīnayāna. Here, [since we are interpreting it in terms of the Mahāyāna Perfect Teaching,] "black deeds" refers to being mired in emptiness, and emerging in conventionality is "white deeds." Both of these together is [the content of] "mixed deeds," and the Middle Way is "neither white nor black deeds." All of these are called a "wrong" [or at least "not perfect"] way of life; but if your karmic deeds are all exhausted, this is called "right deeds" 正業. If you practice according to this [understanding], this is called "right deeds." "Right deeds" means that you are not entangled in either of the two extremes. If you see others gaining benefits and do not become mentally

> alors pourrait-il obtenir le Nirvāṇa? En effet les cinq obstacles *(pañcāvaraṇa)* recouvrent la pensée, on est distrait *(vikṣipta)* et, sans cultiver les sept membres de l'illumination *(saṃbodhyaṅga)*, il est impossible d'obtenir le Nirvāṇa. Lorsque les cinq obstacles recouvrent la pensée et qu'on ne cultive pas les sept membres de l'illumination, il est impossible d'obtenir la Bodhi des Śrāvaka et, à fortiori, la Bodhi des Buddha.

Chodron (3, 1246) translates:

> And if the person who is of bad conduct cannot be reborn in the heavens, how then could he obtain nirvana? In fact, the five obstacles cover the mind, one is distracted and, without developing the seven factors of enlightenment, it is impossible to attain nirvana. As long as the five obstacles cover the mind and one does not cultivate the seven factors of enlightenment, it is impossible to attain the Bodhi of the śrāvakas, not to speak of the Bodhi of the Buddhas.

Black deeds 黒業 **and white deeds** 白業 …: a summary of a much longer passage in the *Mahāparinirvāṇa Sūtra*, T 12.833a10–12ff.:

> There are four types of results and retributions. First is black [evil] results and retributions of black [evil deeds]. Second is white [good] results and retributions of white [good deeds]. Third is mixed results and retributions of mixed [deeds]. Fourth is neither black nor white results and retributions of neither black nor white [deeds]. Black results and retributions of black [deeds] refer to … [and so forth].

agitated and "heated" [with envy], [90a] and if you yourself gain benefits but know and stop with what is sufficient 知止足, this is "right livelihood" 正命. If you well realize the right truth, this is called "right diligence" 正精進. If your thoughts are immovable, and you are straightforward 正直 in not forgetting [your original aspirations and vows], this is called "right mindfulness 正念. To abide in the right with certainty is "right concentration" 正定. With this eightfold right path as the cause, you will realize the principle [of reality, that is, the threefold truth]. The *Mahāparinirvāṇa Sūtra* says, "If you are able to cultivate the eightfold right path, you will attain ghee."

In this way the [thirty-seven] steps on the path do not correspond to the levels [of attainment]; it is just that the contemplation of the principle of Dharma-nature as a beginner already includes the attainment [of all the levels]. The *Ta chih tu lun* says, "To strive diligently within the four mindfulnesses is called the 'four endeavors.' Four types of concentrating the mind [or, concentrated thoughts] 定心 is called the 'four supranormal powers.' The arising of the five good roots is called the '[five good] roots.' For these roots to increase and grow is called the '[five] powers.' To discriminate the path of the four mindfulnesses is to use that called the '[seven components of] awakening.' To rest peacefully in the path of the four mindfulnesses is called the 'eightfold right path.'" Thus we know that when beginners

... Will attain ghee 若有能修八正道者即得醍醐: see the *Mahāparinirvāṇa Sūtra*, T 12.784a26–28. This passage has just been quoted above; see note at 88a6–7.

To strive diligently ... is called the 'eightfold path.' 四念處中四種精進名四正勤。四種定心名四如意足。五善根生名爲根。根增長名爲力。分別四念處道用名爲覺。四念處安隱道中行名八正道: from the section in the *Ta chih tu lun* on "The order of the thirty-seven components" in the chapter on *bodhipākṣika*, T 25.198b18–c10. This is a long quote, but I give it in full as it shows the importance of the *Ta chih tu lun* for Chih-i exposition. Lamotte *(Le Traité* 3, 1147–50) translates:

> Question. — Il faudrait d'abord parler des [membres] du chemin *(mārgāṅga)*. Pourquoi? Parce que c'est seulement après avoir parcouru le chemin que l'on obtient les bons dharma. Ainsi un homme parcourt d'abord une route et, après, arrive à destination. Ici, par quelle méprise *(viparyāsa)*, parlez-vous d'abord des quatre fixations-de-attention *(smṛtyupasthāna)* et, à la fin seulement, des huit membres du chemin *(mārgāṅga)*?
> Rèponse. — Ce n'est pas une méprise. Les trente-sept auxiliaires sont en question dès qu'on veut entrer dans le Chemin.
> 1. Ainsi, quand le yogin s'est rendu auprès du maître *(ācārya)* et a entendu de lui l'enseignement relatif au Chemin *(mārgadharma)*, il utilise d'abord sa mémoire *(smṛti)* pour retenir *(dhāraṇa)* cet enseignement: ce moment-là est appellé "fixation-de-l'attention" *(smṛty-upasthāna)*.
> 2. Quand il a retenu et suivi cet enseignement, le yogin qui en cherche le fruit *(phalaparyeṣin)* s'exerce énergiquement *(vīryeṇa prayuñjate)*: ce moment-là est appellé "effort correct" *(samyak-pradhāna)*.
> 3. A la suite de cette dépense d'énergie *(bahuvīrya)*, sa pensée est distraite *(vikṣipta)*. Il concentre sa pensée *(cittaṃ pragṛhṇāti)* et la dompte *(damayati)*:

ceci est appelé "fondement du pouvoir magique *(ṛddhipāda)*.

4. Sa pensée étant domptée *(dānta)*, il produit les "cinq facultiés" *(pañcendriya)*;

a. Le Vrai caractère *(bhūtalakṣaṇa)* des dharma est très profond *(atigambhīra)* et difficile à sonder *(durvigāhya)*, mais par la faculté de foi *(raddhendriya)*, il y croit: ceci est appelé "faculté de foi."

b. Il n'épargne pas la vie de son corps *(kāyajīvita)* et, de tout son coeur *(ekacittena)*, recherche l'illumination *(bodhiṃ paryeṣate)*: ceci est appellé "faculte d'énergie" *(vīryendriya)*.

c. Il pense toujours à la Bodhi des Buddha et ne pense pas à autre chose: ceci s'appelle "faculté de l'attention" *(smṛtīndriya)*.

d. Toujours il concentre sa pensée sur la Bodhi: ceci s'appelé "faculté de concentration" *(samādhīndriya)*.

e. Il considère *(samanupaśyati)* les quatre vérités et le Vrai caractère *(bhūtalak-ṣaṇa)*: ceci est appelé "faculté de sagesse" *(prajñendriya)*.

5. Lorsque ces cinq facultés se sont développées *(vṛddha)*, elles peuvent intercepter les passions *(kleśa)*: c'est comme la force d'un grand arbre *(mahāvṛkṣa)* pouvant intercepter l'eau. Ces cinq facultés, quand elles se sont développées, peuvent graduellement pénétrer le dharma profond *(gambhīradharma)*: ceci est appelé "force" *(bala)*.

6. Ayant obtenu les forces, le yogin distingue les dharma du chemin [de la méditation *(bhāvanāmārga)*]:

Il y a trois membres *(aṇga)*: 1. le [deuxième] membre-de-l'illumination appelé descernement des dharma *(dharmapravicayasaṃbodhyaṇga)*; 2. le [troisième] membre-de-l'illumination appelé énergie *(vīryasaṃbodhyaṅga)*; 3. le [quatrième] membre-de-l'illumination appelé joie *(prītisaṃbodhyaṅga)*. Si la pensée s'affaisse *(avalīyate)* au moment où l'on pratique le Chemin, ces trois membres *(aṅga)* la relèvent *(samutthāpayanti)*.

[Il y a trois autres membres]: 1. le [cinquième] membre-de-l'illumination appelé relaxation *(praśrabdhisaṃ-bodhyaṅga)*; 2. le [sixième] membre-de-l'illumination appelé concentration *(samādhisaṃbodhyaṅga)*; 3. le [septième] membre-de-l'illumination appelé indifférence *(upekṣāsaṃbodhyaṅga)*. Si la pensée est distraite *(vikṣipyate)* au moment où l'on pratique le Chemin, ces trois membres la fixent *(pragṛhṇanti)* pour qu'elle se concentre.

[Quant au membre restant, à savoir: le premier] membre-de-l'illumination appelé attention, il intervient dans les deux cas [quand la pensée s'affaisse et quand elle est distraite]. Il peut réunir les bons dharma et arrêter les mauvais: c'est comme un portier *(dauvārika)* qui introduit ce qui est utile *(arthavat)* et écarte ce qui est inutile *(anarthaka)*.

Si la pensée s'affaisse, l'attention *(smṛti)* et trois members [2–4] la relèvent. Si la pensée est distraite, l'attention et trois membres [5–7] la fixent.

Ces sept choses, parce qu'elles marchent *(gāmitvāt)*, sont appelées "membres" *(aṅga)*.

7. Lorsque le yogin a obtenu ces choses et que sa tranquillité *(kṣema)* est partaite *(saṃpanna)*, il veut entrer dans la Ville inconditionnée du Nirvāṇa *(nirvāṇā-saṃskṛtanagara)*. C'est pourquoi il pratique les dharma [du *mārgāṅga*]: ce moment-là-est appellé "Chemin" *(mārga)*.

Chodron (3, 945–47) translates:

Question. First we must speak about the [factors] of the path. Why? Because only after having traveled the path are the good dharmas acquired. Thus, a person first travels over a road and later arrives at his destination. Here, by what mistake do you first speak of the four foundations of mindfulness and only at the end, of the eight factors of the path? Answer. It is not a mistake. The thirty-seven auxiliaries are involved as soon as one wants to enter onto the Path.

1. Thus, when the yogin goes to the teacher and hears the teaching on the Path from him, first he uses his mindfulness to retain

practice the path, they utilize the thirty-seven steps to regulate and nourish cessation-and-contemplation and the Four Samādhis and thus enter the bodhisattva levels. In this sense these [thirty-seven] steps on the path are "near causes" for [attaining] great nirvana, and other steps on the path should be called "distant causes."

8. *Analogies* [90a12]

Now I will use some analogies to manifest the meaning [of the thirty-seven steps on the path].

this teaching: that moment is called 'foundation of mindfulness.'

2. When he has retained and followed this teaching, the yogin who is looking for the fruit practices with exertion: this is called 'right effort.'

3. As a result of this expenditure of energy, his mind is distracted. He concentrates his mind and controls it: this is called 'foundation of magical power.'

4. His mind being tamed, he produces the 'five faculties.'

a. The True nature of dharmas is very profound and difficult to probe, but by means of the faculty of faith, he believes in it: this is called the 'faculty of faith.'

b. He does not spare his own life and seeks enlightenment wholeheartedly: this is called 'faculty of exertion.'

c. He constantly thinks about the Bodhi of the Buddhas and does not think about anything else: this is called the 'faculty of mindfulness.'

d. He always concentrates his mind on Bodhi: this is called the 'faculty of concentration.'

e. He considers the four truths and the True nature: this is called the 'faculty of wisdom.'

5. When the five faculties have been developed, they are able to intercept the afflictions: this is like the power of a big tree that is able to block off water. These five faculties, when they have been developed, are able to gradually penetrate the profound Dharma: this is called 'power.'

6. Having obtained the powers, the yogin distinguishes the dharmas [of the path of meditation]:

There are three factors: 1) the [second] factor-of-enlightenment called discernment of dharmas; 2) the [third] factor-of-enlightenment called exertion; 3) the fourth factor-of-enlightenment called joy. If the mind sinks when you are practicing the Path, these three factors raise it up again.

[There are three other factors]: 1) the [fifth] factor-of-enlightenment called relaxation; 2) the [sixth] factor of enlightenment called concentration; 3) the [seventh] factor-of-enlightenment called equanimity. If the mind is distracted when you are practicing the Path, these three factors settle it so that it is concentrated.

As for the remaining factor, namely: the [first] factor-of-enlightenment called mindfulness, it operates in both cases [when the mind sinks and when it is distracted]. It can unite the good dharmas and stop the bad ones; it is like a gatekeeper who allows what is useful to enter and sends away what is useless.

If the mind sinks, mindfulness and the three factors [nos. 2–4] raise it up. If the mind is distracted, mindfulness and the three factors [nos. 5–7] settle it.

Because these seven things work, they are called 'factors.'

7. When the yogin has obtained these things and his tranquility is complete, he wishes to enter into the unconditioned city of nirvana. This is why he practices the dharmas: that moment is called 'Path.'

1. The analogy of a plant [90a12]

If you plant seeds in the ground, first some sprouts will emerge, then it will put down roots [into the ground], and branches and leaves will spread out above; its flowers will stretch out and flourish, and as a result bear fruit. Dharma-nature and the Dharma realm are like the great earth. Mindfulness and contemplation are like planting seeds. The four proper endeavors are like the putting forth of sprouts. The five [good] roots are like putting down roots. The five powers are like the increase and growth of the stems and leaves. The seven [components of] awakening are like the blossoming of the flowers. The eightfold right [path] is like bearing fruit. "Bearing fruit" is like realizing the level of the copper *cakravartin*, and illuminating the forbearance [from realizing that dharmas] do not arise; again, it is called "reaching the place of treasures," and is also called "entering the secret treasury," and is also called "attaining ghee," and is also called "perceiving Buddha-nature," and is also called "the Dharma body manifesting the eight phases in the [historical] life of a Buddha." This is the meaning of [the saying in the *Vimalakīrti Sūtra* that] "the steps on the path are good friends; through these you attain correct awakening."

2. The analogy of the Bodhi tree [90a20]

If we interpret this crossing of the path in terms of [the analogy of] the Bodhi tree 道樹 [in terms of its leaves, flowers, and fruit], it is as clarified in the *Pañcaviṃśati Sūtra*: "To be free from the three evil destinies is called 'the

Level of the copper *cakravartin* 銅輪: that is, equivalent to the level of "partial realization of the real truth," the stage just before full Buddhahood. The term is from the *Jen-wang ching*, (T 3.826b–829a) and *Ying-lo ching* (T 24.1016a22). Chih-i has used this term in the *Mo-ho chih-kuan* previously; see at 18b10 and 67a16.

Reaching the place of treasures 至寶所: as in the parable of the conjured city, *Lotus Sūtra*, T 9.26a24.

Entering the secret treasury 入祕藏: as in the *Mahāparinirvāṇa Sūtra*, T 12.616b11.

Attaining ghee 得醍醐: as in the *Mahāparinirvāṇa Sūtra*, T 12.784a26–28. This passage was just quoted; see note at 88a6–7.

Perceiving Buddha-nature 見佛性: as in the same passage in the *Mahāparinirvāṇa Sūtra*, T 12.784a28–29.

Eight phases in the life of a Buddha 八相作佛: it is not clear which, if any, specific classical text Chih-i is reflecting with this phrase.

The steps on the path are good friends ... 道品善知識由是成正覺: see the *Vimalakīrti Sūtra*, T 14.549c7. This phrase was just quoted above; see note at 88a5–6 for details.

Leaves 葉益, flowers 花益, fruit 果益: see the *Pañcaviṃśati Sūtra* at T 8.377a14ff.

> Subhūti, what is the "benefit of leaves" for sentient beings? To attain separation from the three evil destinies by means of a bodhisattva-mahāsattva; this is called the "benefit of leaves" for sentient beings. What is the "benefit of flowers" for sentient beings? To attain the status

benefit of leaves.' To attain the body of a human or divine being is called 'the benefit of flowers.' To attain the fruits of the four paths [from stream-enterer to arhat] is called 'the benefit of fruit.'" This is an interpretation that is one-sided from the perspective of emptiness. To avoid the stages of the two vehicles is the "benefit of leaves"; to attain the body of transformation 變通身 is the "benefit of flowers"; to be endowed with the wisdom of the path is the "benefit of fruit"—this is an interpretation that is one-sided from the perspective of conventionality. To avoid being shackled by the two extremes is the "benefit of leaves"; to experience the body of the Dharma-nature is the "benefit of flowers"; to illumine and realize Buddha-nature is the "benefit of fruit"—this is an interpretation that is one-sided from the perspective of the Middle. If we were to take these three contemplations together, "simultaneously empty" 即空 refers to the "benefit of leaves," "simultaneously conventional" 即假 refers to the "benefit of flowers," and "simultaneously Middle" 即中 refers to the "benefit of fruit."

3. The analogy of the city with three gates [90a27]

Next, to practice the thirty-seven steps on the path is [analogous to] arriving at the undefiled city. This city has three gates. If you enter by these gates, you attain an arising of the true [that is, a realization of emptiness]; these are the [three] gates of emptiness *(śūnyata)*, formlessness *(ānimitta)*, and actionlessness *(apraṇihita)*. These are also called [**90b**] the "gates of the three liberations," and are also called the "three kinds of samādhi." If you enter concentration through "right views" and "right discrimination," non-defilement is aroused from this concentration. At that time the wisdom of right views is called the "great minister," and right concentration is the "great king" [of the city with three gates]. From this we can derive the names of

of a *kṣatriya*, brahman, rich layperson, a divine ruler in the four heavens, or to dwell in the state of neither-conceptions-nor-non-conceptions, by means of a bodhisattva; this is called the "benefit of flowers" for sentient beings. What is the "benefit of fruit" for sentient beings? This is for bodhisattvas to attain universal wisdom; to lead sentient beings to attain the [four] fruits of the stream-enterer, once-returner, non-returner, and arhat, and the path of the pratyekabuddha, and the path of the Buddha. Sentient beings gradually, through the dharma [teachings] of the three vehicles, attain nirvāṇa without remainder and *parinirvāṇa*. This is the "benefit of fruit" for sentient beings.

Three gates 三門: see the analogy of the "city with three gates" in the *Ta chih tu lun*, T 25.206a10–17. This passage was quoted above; see the note at 87c29.

Great minister 大臣 **and great king** 大王: see the continuation of the explanation of the analogy of the "city with three gates" in the *Ta chih tu lun*, T 25.207a5–10. Lamotte (*Le Traité* 3, 1221–22) translates:

> La *śūnyatā*, l'*ānimitta* et l'*apraṇihita* sont par nature *(svabhāva)* des concentrations *(samādhi)*. La pensée et les mentaux

the three kinds of samādhi. "If there is no wisdom, there is no dhyāna"; this is the meaning here. If right views arise through right concentration, and non-defilement is aroused through right views, then this right concentration is [like] the "great minister" and wisdom is like the "great king." From this we can derive the names of the three kinds of liberation. "If there is no dhyāna, there is no wisdom"; this is the meaning here. Or, samādhi is the path of overcoming 伏道, and liberation is the path of severance 斷道 and the

associés à ces concentrations *(samādhi-saṃprayuktacittacaitasika-dharma)*, les actes corporels *(kāyakarman)* et les actes vocaux *(vākkarman)* qui naissent à leur suite, les formations dissociées de la pensée *(cittaviprayuktasaṃskāra)* qui y surgissent forment un complexe *(sāmagrī)* qui est appelé concentration. Ainsi quand le roi *(rājan)* arrive, il a nécessairement avec lui un grand ministre *(mahāmātya)* et des soldats *(sainika)*. Ici la concentration *(samādhi)* est comme le roi, la sagesse *(prajñā)* est comme le grand ministre, et les autres dharma sont comme les soldats. Même si ces autres dharma ne sont pas mentionnés, ils doivent nécessairement être présents. Pourquoi? La concentration ne naît pas seule, elle ne peut pas avoir à elle seule toute l'activité. Les autres dharma naissent avec elle, durent avec elle, périssent avec elle et réalisent avec elle en collaborant au bien *(hita)*.

Chodron (3, 1002) translates:

Śūnyatā, *ānimitta* and *apraṇihita* are concentrations by nature. The mind and mental events associated with these concentrations, bodily actions and vocal actions that arise following them, the formations dissociated from the mind that come forth, form a complex called concentration. Thus, when the king arrives, with him, of necessity, come the prime minister and some soldiers. Here concentration is like the king, wisdom is like the prime minister, and the other dharmas are like the soldiers. Even if these other dharmas are not mentioned, they must necessarily be present. Why? Concentration does not arise by itself; it is unable to have all the activity by itself. The other dharmas arise along with it, endure with it, perish with it, and collaborate with it in realizing the good.

From this we can derive the names of the three kinds of samādhi 此得名名三三昧: that is, the three types of emptiness, formlessness, and actionlessness. It is not clear how the names or meaning are derived from the preceding statements. Perhaps "non-defilement" is emptiness, the "great minister" is formlessness, and the "great king" is actionlessness?

If there is no wisdom, there is no dhyāna 非智不禪: see the verses in the *Udānavarga*, T 4.766b29–c1:

Without dhyāna there is no wisdom;
Without wisdom there is no dhyāna.
It is through the path of [both] dhyāna and wisdom
That one approaches nirvana.

Ikeda (*Kenkyū chūshaku*, 399) points out that a similar saying occurs in the **Dharmatara-dhyāna-sūtra* 達摩多羅禅禪經 (T no. 618, 15.300c24-25): "If dhyāna does not include wisdom, it cannot reach quiescence; if wisdom does not include dhyāna, it cannot illuminate profoundly." See also the opening statements in *Hsiao chih-kuan* comparing the balance of wisdom and samādhi, teaching and practice, and so forth, to the two wheels of a cart and two wings of a bird (T 46.462b).

If there is no dhyāna, there is no wisdom 非禪不智: see the quote from the *Udānavarga* in the preceding note.

path of attestation 證道. Or, concentration [samādhi] and wisdom should be merged, so samādhi is indivisible from liberation, and liberation is indivisible from samādhi.

1. Tripitaka Teachings [90b8]

[These three gates] for the Tripitaka Teachings are as follows. The "gate of emptiness" consists of two lower [aspects of the sixteen meditations on the Four Truths] of "emptiness" and "without selfhood" *(anātman)*. The "gate of formlessness" consists of the four lower meditations on [the Truth of] extinction [as extinct, quiescent, sublime, and separate]. The "gate of actionlessness" consists of the lower eight meditations on [the Truths on] the cause of suffering [as cause, arising, birth, and conditions] and the path [as path, thusness, practice, and liberation], and two other lower [aspects of the Truth of] suffering [as transiency and suffering]. These sixteen meditations correspond to the "king" and "minister" [of the city].

2. Shared Teachings [90b11]

If [the three gates are discussed from the perspective of] the Shared Teachings, it clarifies that the "gate of emptiness" consists of [the realization that the Truths of] suffering and the causes of suffering are all like a magical apparition. The old text of the *Ta chih tu lun* says, "If you contemplate

Sixteen meditations 十六行: For details, see "sixteen meditations on the Four Truths" and the "sixteen truths" in the Glossary.

Old text of the *Ta chih tu lun* 古釋論本: This "old" text is probably an early version of Kumarajīva's translation, edited later by Seng-jui 僧叡, and not extant. The *Shiki* (BT–IV, 412) comments:

> Question: There is only one text of the *Ta chih tu lun*. Why does this refer to both an "old" and "new" text?
>
> Answer: Although there is only one text of the *Ta chih tu lun*, there are many variations in the fascicles and texts which are not the same. Presumably it was edited many times, and therefore the texts are not the same. A catalogue of the scriptures says that the *Ta chih tu lun* consists of one hundred fascicles, or of seventy fascicles. The first section of the *Commentary on the Vimalakīrti Sūtra* [by Chih-i] in interpreting the names of the bodhisattvas, says, "The old text [of the *Ta chih tu lun*] translates this [that is, "bodhisattva"] as 'a man of excellence' (Kao-shih 高士)." The *Xian* 暹 says, "The 'old text' presumably refers to an older translation of the *Ta chih tu lun*." Some person has said that "Mr. Yüan 遠公 [Hui-Yüan 慧遠] says that Kumārajīva [or, "Mr. Jī" 什公], in the seventh year of Hung-shih (A.D. 404 or 405), produced the *Ta chih tu lun* in one hundred and ten fascicles. Here and there were transliterations or interpretations in which the text was not easy [to understand]. This was edited in the tenth year of Hung-shih (408) into a one-hundred-fascicles [version] and a seventy-fascicles [version]. The former [one-hundred-fascicle version] is called the 'old' [text]."

However, the edition in the Taishō canon consists of one hundred fascicles, and contains the variant reading that

extremely minute forms 極微色, there are eighteen types of emptiness." The current text [of the *Ta chih tu lun*] says, "If you contemplate a single fragment of a fine piece of cloth, there are eighteen types of emptiness." These expressions are different in that [the translation] "fine piece of cloth" expresses [the sense of] "conventional designation," and "extremely minute [forms]" expresses [the sense of] "real dharmas." But if you understand the meaning, [you will realize that] the "conventional" and the "real" are all empty. If you still do not realize emptiness, [consider that] emotional conceptualization 情思 [or, "feelings and conceptualizations"] and meaningless disputation *(prapañca)* [lead you to] conceptualize that there are marks of emptiness 有空相; [however,] to know that there are no marks of emptiness 無空相 is called the "gate of formlessness." Although the marks of emptiness are empty, you still conceptualize a contemplative wisdom [of emptiness]. Yet there is no subject [who contemplates] nor object [that is contemplated], so who is it that does the contemplation of emptiness? This is called the "gate of actionlessness." There is no one who does the action; who, then arouses the vow to save [oneself and others]? This is called "vowlessness." These are the three kinds of samādhi, [the three liberations,] the king and the minister [of the city of three gates], and so forth.

3. *Distinct Teachings* [90b19]

If [the three gates are discussed from the perspective of] the Distinct Teachings, this clarifies [the idea] that entering or realizing emptiness from conventionality illuminates the real truth; this is called the samādhi

Chih-i refers to as the "new text"; thus, at least in this case, this one-hundred-fascicle version cannot be the "old text." The "one-hundred-fascicles and seventy-fascicles versions" probably refer to a version that included both the commentary and the sūtra text (in 100 fascicles) and a version that consisted of only the commentary (in 70 fascicles) [for details, see studies by Yinshun 印順]. Most likely the "old text" here refers to an earlier edition that was later edited by Seng-jui with some modifications of translation terms. This issue is worthy of further investigation, with an examination of Dunhuang manuscripts to see if any early, pre-edited versions are extant. See also studies by Chou 2004 and Shih 1981.

On the other hand, a sub-commentary (on Chih-i's *Commentary on the Vimalakīrti Sūtra*) written by Chih-yuan 智圓 and compiled by Chan-jan (T no. 1779, 38.729b28–c1) interprets this to mean "What is called 'the old text translating ["bodhisattva"] as a man of excellence refers to an old translation of this [*Vimalakīrti*] sutra" 古本翻高士者古翻此經也, rather than referring to an old version of the *Ta chih tu lun.*

If you contemplate a single fragment of a fine piece of cloth, there are eighteen types of emptiness 若觀一端疊則有十八空: See the *Ta chih tu lun*, T 25.148a20–21. This phrase has been quoted previously; for details and a translation of the context see the note at *Mo-ho chih-kuan* 32c6–7.

of emptiness. Those of the two vehicles only illuminate this emptiness, and think that there are marks of emptiness. Bodhisattvas know that emptiness is not empty [nothingness] and thus emerge in conventionality to teach and transform beings. [They also know that] there are no marks of emptiness; this is called the "samādhi of formlessness." If you progress and cultivate the Middle Way, [you realize that neither] the Middle nor the extremes have any marks, and that one should not seek either the Middle nor the extremes. This is called the "samādhi of actionlessness." This is the three wisdoms of contemplation, the king and the minister [of the city of three gates], and so forth.

Again, to interpret the meaning of "emerging in conventionality" in terms of the Distinct [Teachings] is as follows. Discriminating among immeasurable medicines and diseases is all a part of [the realm or aspect of] "conventional designation." Conventional designations have no [substantial] reality; since they have no [substantial] reality, they are empty. This is called the "gate of emptiness." Emptiness has no marks of emptiness; how could it have conventional marks? This is the "gate of formlessness." Emptiness and conventionality have no marks; again, there is no making of vows to save [beings] by knowing about diseases and having discrimination concerning medicines. Therefore this is called "vowlessness." This is the wisdom of emerging in conventionality, the king and minister [of the city of three gates], and so forth.

4. Perfect Teaching [90b27]

A distinct interpretation in terms of the Perfect [Teaching] is as follows. Although the names are the same as in the previous [paragraph(s)], the meaning is greatly different. The *Ta chih tu lun* says, "The śrāvakas cultivate the three liberations through [contemplating and realizing] emptiness; the bodhisattvas cultivate the three liberations through [contemplating and

The śrāvakas cultivate the three liberations through emptiness; the bodhisattvas cultivate the three liberations through the true aspect of all dharmas 聲聞緣空修三解脫。菩薩緣諸法實相修三解脫: see the *Ta chih tu lun* at T 25.207c16–22. Lamotte (*Le Traité* 3, 1231–32) translates:

> Dans le système de lAbhidharma, la porte-de-délivrance Vacuité *(śūnyatāvimokṣamukha)* a pour objet *(ālambate)* la vérité sur la douleur *(duḥkhasatya)* et comporte *(saṃgṛhṇati)* cinq agrégats *(skandha)*. La porte-de-délivrance Sans-caractères *(ānimittavimokṣamukha)* a pour objet un unique dharma: le *pratisaṃkhyānirodha* [ou disjonction d'avec les dharma impurs à obtenir par la compréhension des vérités]. La porte-de-délivrance Non-prise en considération *(apraṇihitavimokṣamukha)* a pour objet trois vérité sur l'origine de la douleur *(samudayasatya)* et la vérité sur la destruction de la douleur *(nirodhasatya)*; elle renferme cinq agrégats *(skandha)*.
>
> Dans le Mahāyāna, ces trois

realizing] the true aspect of all dharmas." [The *Mahāparinirvāṇa Sūtra* says,] "Wisdom is to perceive both emptiness and non-emptiness. **[90c]** This 'emptiness and non-emptiness' is also called the Middle Way. If you perceive this emptiness, you perceive Buddha nature." Again, those of the two vehicles contemplate eighteen kinds of activities in a dream, and [for them] the unobtainability of matters within a dream is called "the emptiness of internal dharmas," the unobtainability of matters outside a dream is called "the emptiness of external dharmas," and the unobtainability of eighteen kinds of existences within a dream is called the "eighteen kinds of emptiness." Now, those of the Perfect [Teaching] contemplate that the dharmas of sleep are unobtainable, so there are no [substantial] "internal dharmas." The dharmas that arise from sleep are all internal dharmas, and they are all unobtainable; this is called "the emptiness of internal dharmas." All dharmas incline to this internal emptiness. Sleep does not involve external dharmas, so all the "external" dharmas that arise from sleep are unobtainable. This is "the emptiness of external dharmas." All dharmas incline to this external

> portes-de-délivrance *(vimokṣamukha)* portent sur le Vrai caractère *(bhūtalakṣaṇa)* des dharma. Par ces trois portes-de-délivrance, l'ascète voit que le Saṃsāra est identique au Nirvāṇa. Pourquoi? Parce que le Nīrvāṇa est vide *(śūnya),* sans caractères *(ānimitta),* indigne d'être pris en considérations *(apraṇihita),* et le Saṃsāra également.

Chodron (3, 1010) translates:

> In the system of the Abhidharma, the emptiness gate of liberation has as its object the truth of suffering and comprises) the five skandhas. The signlessness gate of liberation has as its object a single dharma, the *pratisaṃkhyānirodha* [or disjunction from impure dharmas obtained by understanding the truths]. The wishlessness gate of liberation has as its object three truths [a part of the truth of suffering, the truth of the origin of suffering, and the truth of the cessation of suffering]; it comprises five aggregates.
>
> In the Mahāyāna, these three gates of liberation pertain to the true nature of dharmas. By means of these three gates of liberation, the ascetic sees that samsara and nirvana are the same. Why? Because nirvana is empty, without characteristics, not worthy of being taken into consideration, and samsara likewise.

This section in the *Ta chih tu lun* (T 25.206c–208a) contains many of the phrases and concepts used by Chih-i in his analysis of the "three gates." See the paragraph (207c4–10) that appears shortly before the above quote; for full translation see note at *Mo-ho chih-kuan* 59b21–22:

Wisdom is to perceive both emptiness and non-emptiness. This 'emptiness and non-emptiness' is also called the Middle Way. If you perceive this emptiness, you perceive Buddha nature 智者見空及與不空。此空不空亦名中道。若見此空即見佛性: see the *Mahāparinirvāṇa Sūtra* at T 12.767c19–20. This passage has been quoted many times already; for the translation of the full context, see note at 28a6–8. The first part of the quote is directly from the sūtra, but the second sentence is a reworded summary of the sūtra passage.

Within a dream 夢中: "internal emptiness" and "external emptiness" are the first two of the eighteen kinds of emptiness as listed in the *Ta chih tu lun,* 285b7–10.

emptiness, so the eighteen types of existence of the dharmas of sleep are unobtainable; this is called "the eighteen kinds of emptiness." All dharmas incline to the eighteen kinds of emptiness and traverse through eighteen objects; this is called "the eighteen kinds of emptiness." These are all one emptiness. A Vaipulya [sūtra] says, "The great emptiness [of Mahāyāna] and the small emptiness [of Hīnayāna] all return to one emptiness. 'One emptiness' is Dharma nature, the true mark [of reality], and the real Dharma of the Buddhas." The *Pañcaviṃśati Sūtra* speaks of a "lone emptiness." As with the previous contemplations of ignorance, this [ultimate truth] is unobtainable through the four options [of the tetralemma], and the emptiness of one is the emptiness of all. It cannot be perceived even through the discriminatory features of the four gates, and no one can obtain it either through deliberate [conditioned cultivation] 緣[修] or through true [spontaneous and intuitive cultivation] 眞[修]. This is the king and minister [of the city of three gates], and so forth.

3. Closing Summary [90c14]

In this way emptiness is formless and actionless, and applies to all dharmas. All dharmas are also like this. You should know that one gate of liberation includes the three gates of liberation, and the three gates of liberation are one gate of liberation. Again, within the four gates [of the Fourfold Teach-

The great emptiness and the small emptiness all return to one emptiness. 'One emptiness' is Dharma nature, the true marks, and the real Dharma of the Buddhas 大空小空皆歸一空一空卽法性實相諸佛實法: source unknown.

Lone emptiness 獨空: see the *Pañcaviṃśati Sūtra*, T 8.326c26–29ff.

> Next, Subhūti, *prajñāpāramitā* signifies the lone emptiness of the realm of the Buddha. How does it signify the lone emptiness of this realm? It signifies the lone emptiness of the realm of the five skandhas, and so forth up to signifying the lone emptiness of the realm of universal wisdom.

This statement is preceded by many statements of the same type, with the only difference being that the phrase "lone emptiness" is replaced by phrases such as "ultimate emptiness," the "nature of emptiness," "the emptiness of existent dharmas," "the emptiness of both existent and non-existent dharmas," and so forth.

Previous contemplations 前觀: see the discussion in the *Mo-ho chih-kuan* at 82a.

Four gates 四門: The fourfold structure of the Fourfold Teachings and other categories which form the structure of much of T'ien-t'ai discourse. See the discussion above.

Emptiness is formless and actionless, and applies to all dharmas 是空卽無相無作及一 切法: Ikeda (*Gendaigoyaku*, 457) has "this emptiness … is [the content of] all Dharma teachings."

All dharmas are also like this 一切法亦如是: That is, they are empty, formless, and actionless.

ings], all cultivate the three liberations and are mutually unhindered and unobstructed. In this way the meaning of the three gates [for the Perfect Teaching] is not gradual and successive. That of the Distinct [Teachings] is gradual and successive, even though it involves coming in [direct] contact 緣 with [or, "being linked with"] the true marks [of reality]. Again, it [the Perfect Teaching] is different from the Shared Teachings in that [the Shared Teachings involve] coming in contact with [or, "being linked with"] the principle of emptiness [but not that of conventionality]. Again, it is different from the Tripitaka [Teachings] in that the Tripitaka [Teachings involve] coming in contact with [or, "being linked with"] the wisdom of the Four Truths. Therefore you should know that there are various differences in the details [between the Fourfold Teachings] with regard to the three liberations, the [thirty-seven] steps on the path, and so forth.

Again, the *Avataṃsaka Sūtra* says, "When the sun rises, first it illuminates the tall mountains." This is inclined to emphasize the "four types of flourishing"; the Tripitaka [Teachings] of the Deer Park are inclined to emphasize the "four types of decay." The Vaipulya and Prajñāpāramitā [sūtras] involve emphasizing realizing [the aspect of] "flourishing" by regulating the [aspect of] "decay"; they lead those of the Hīnayāna to return to the Mahāyāna. At the Crane Grove [with the preaching of the *Mahāparinirvāṇa Sūtra*] the granting of transformation was completed, and you enter nirvana through a middle [balance] of "flourishing" and "decaying." For the sake of those who are extremely dull and difficult to save, both aspects of the [Śāla] tree were consummated [in the Nirvana teachings], and the meritorious qualities were accomplished for the first time. Those of clever faculties can attain and realize a clear awakening step by step, as Śāriputra and others "entered the secret treasury" and "attained insight into Buddha-nature" through the

When the sun rises, first it illuminates the tall mountains 日出先照高山: See the *Avataṃsaka Sūtra*, T 9.616b14–15. This passage serves as an important source for Chih-i's classification system of the Five Periods—the *Avataṃsaka Sūtra*, the Deer Park Āgama teachings, the Vaipulya sūtras, the Prajñāpāramitā sūtras, and the *Mahāparinirvāṇa* and *Lotus* sūtras. It has been quoted in the *Mo-ho chih-kuan* already; see note at 2c25–27 for a translation of the full context.

Flourishing and decay: See the analogy of the Śāla tree above—with its four trunks that "flourish" and four trunks that "decay"—at 88c17. In other words, the teachings of the *Avataṃsaka Sūtra* emphasize the positive aspects of the Dharma and how to grow in and advance in virtuous qualities such as wisdom and compassion, while the Tripitaka Teachings emphasizes the negative aspects, such as getting rid of passionate afflictions and extinguishing the flames of samsara.

Crane Grove 鶴林: Kuśinagara, the place of the Buddha's demise, and the location for preaching the *Mahāparinirvāṇa Sūtra*.

Secret treasury, Buddha-nature: These phrases are from the *Mahāparinirvāṇa*

Lotus [teachings]. In the *Mahāparinirvāṇa Sūtra*, eight thousand śrāvakas are pointed out from a distance who, in the *Lotus* [teachings], have [already] attained the prophecy that they will become Buddhas, as [the harvest is] gathered in the fall and stored in the winter, without any more production. According to this one [text], the "granting of transformation" had been completed earlier [through the *Lotus Sūtra*], without having to wait for the *Mahāparinirvāṇa Sūtra*. Again, [the *Mahāparinirvāṇa Sūtra*] asks, "Who is able to adorn the Śāla tree?" and proffers six people including Śāriputra, and also proffers the Tathāgata. Those who perceive Buddha-nature are able to

Sūtra (T 12.616b8–9), not the *Lotus Sūtra*. They have been quoted many times already; see above at 89a4. For a full translation of the context see note at *Mo-ho chih-kuan* 20c1–2. The *Mahāparinirvāṇa Sūtra* does not mention the *Lotus Sūtra*.

Eight thousand śrāvakas are pointed out from a distance who, in the *Lotus*, have attained the prophecy that they will become Buddhas, as [the harvest is] gathered in the fall and stored in the winter, without any more production 遙指八千聲聞於法華中得記作佛如秋收冬藏更無所作: see the *Mahāparinirvāṇa Sūtra* at T 12.661b3–10:

> [The teachings of the *Mahāparinirvāṇa Sūtra* are] like the rain from heaven which blesses all seeds with moisture and causes them to increase and grow and bring forth fruit. It eliminates all famine and provides bountiful delight. The immeasurable rain of the Dharma of the secret treasury of the Tathāgata is also like this. It is able to remove and extinguish all of the eight types of feverish diseases. This sūtra appears in this world and, like the fruit [produced through rain], is able to benefit many and bring peace to all; it can lead sentient beings to perceive the Tathāgata nature. *This is like the eight thousand śrāvakas within the Lotus attaining the prophecy that they will fulfill the great fruit [of Buddhahood], and like [the harvest that is] gathered up in the fall and stored in the winter, without any more production.*

Who is able to adorn the Śāla tree 誰能莊嚴娑羅雙樹: A brief reference to a much longer passage in the *Mahāparinirvāṇa Sūtra*, T 12.791a2–b16:

> The bodhisattva Lion's Roar said to the Tathāgata, "World Honored One. What does it mean for a bhikṣu to adorn the Śāla tree?
>
> [The Tathāgata replied,] "Good son. If there is a bhikṣu who accepts, reads, and chants the twelvefold scriptures; correctly has penetrating insight into the profound meaning of these texts; attains liberation for the sake of others and is good at the beginning, middle, and end; wishes to benefit immeasurable beings; and preaches noble conduct—such a bhikṣu is able to adorn the Śāla tree."
>
> Lion's Roar said, "World Honored One. If I understand the meaning of the Buddha's teachings, [we could say that] the bhikṣu Ānanda is one of these people [who can adorn the Śāla tree]. Why? The bhikṣu Ānanda accepts and reads and chants the twelvefold scriptures, expounds their true words and true meaning for the sake of people. Ānanda is like a person who replaces an empty vessel with another one [filled with water]. Since he has heard [the Dharma] from the Buddha, he transmits it as he has heard it [that is, accurately]."
>
> "Good son. if there is a bhikṣu who attains the pure divine eye, and can see the trichiliocosm in the ten directions as [clearly as] contemplating a mango *(ārma)* fruit in your hand. Such bhikṣu are able to adorn the Śāla tree."

adorn the Śāla tree, [91a] and within this, realize nirvana. The six people, including Śāriputra, are already able to adorn [the Śāla tree]; how could it be that it is not the case that they perceive Buddha-nature, and within this,

Lion's Roar said, "World Honored One. If this is the case, then the bhikṣu Aniruddha is one of these people. Why? Aniruddha, with the divine eye, was able to see the whole trichiliocosm, including the intermediate states, clearly and fully, without obstruction."

"Good son. If there are bhikṣus, with few desires and who know what is sufficient; whose mind is always quiescent; who strives to practice diligence, mindfulness, concentration, wisdom, and liberation; such bhikṣus are able to adorn the Śāla tree."

Lion's Roar said, "World Honored One. If this is the case, then the bhikṣu [Mahā] kāśyapa is one of these people. Why? The bhikṣu Kāśyapa is good at cultivating the dharmas [that lead to] few desires and knowing what is sufficient."

"Good son. If there are bhikṣus who, for the sake of benefiting sentient beings and not for their own benefit and nurturing, cultivate a penetrating understanding, the samadhi of non-disputation, noble conduct, and the practice of emptiness, such bhikṣus are able to adorn the Śāla tree."

Lion's Roar said, "World Honored One. If this is the case, then the bhikṣu Subhūti is one of these people. Why? The bhikṣu Subhūti is good at cultivating [the samādhi of] non-disputation, noble conduct, and the practice of emptiness."

"Good son. If there are bhikṣus who are good at cultivating supranormal powers, and in a single thought are able to perform various supranormal deed and transformations, and singlemindedly and in a single samādhi/concentration are able to attain the two fruits—that is, of water and fire—such bhikṣus are able to adorn the Śāla tree."

Lion's Roar said, "World Honored One. If this is the case, then the bhikṣu Maudgalyāyana is one of these people. Why? The bhikṣu Maudgalyāyana is good at cultivating supranormal powers and immeasurable transformations."

"Good son. If there are bhikṣus who are good at cultivating great wisdom, beneficial wisdom, the wisdom of adornments, the wisdom of liberation, profound wisdom, broad wisdom, unlimited wisdom, unsurpassed wisdom, and true wisdom, and is endowed with the fulfillment of the root of wisdom; so that even when in the midst of angry relations his mind does not discriminate; even when he hears of the eternal nirvana of the Tathāgata his mind does not waver; if he hears of the eternity of nirvana and that it is not something one enters, he does not rejoice—such bhikṣus are able to adorn the Śāla tree."

Lion's Roar said, "World Honored One. If this is the case, then Śāriputra is one of these people. Why? Śāriputra is good at fulfilling and being endowed in this way with great wisdom [and so forth]."

"Good son. If there are bhikṣus who are able to teach that all sentient beings have Buddha nature; can attain the diamond-like vajra body; that there are no limits to reality; [that nirvana is] permanent, blissful, selfhood, and pure; that the body and mind are unobstructed and can attain the eight masteries—such bhikṣus are able to adorn the Śāla tree."

Lion's Roar said, "World Honored One. If this is the case, then only the Tathāgata can be such a person. Why? Because the Tathāgata's body is diamond-like and unlimited; [he realizes that nirvana is] permanent, blissful, selfhood, and pure; his body and mind are unobstructed; and he is endowed with the eight masteries. World Honored One. Only the Tathāgata is able to adorn the Śāla tree [in this way]."

realize nirvana? Even śrāvakas are like this; so it should be known that [of course] bodhisattvas can gradually attain this realization. If they realize nirvana, they fulfill five liberations. [As the *Mahāparinirvāṇa Sūtra* says,] "Neither identical with the six dharmas [or perspectives] nor apart from the six dharmas [or perspectives] " This is the meaning of "threefold Buddha-nature."

Fulfill five liberations 成五解脱: liberation from the five skandhas?

Neither identical with the six dharmas nor apart from the six dharmas 不即六法不離六法: A phrase from the parable of the blind people each touching a different part of the elephant and extrapolating the whole from their limited knowledge. See the *Mahāparinirvāṇa Sūtra*, T 12.802a–c (for a translation of the parable, see note at *Mo-ho chih-kuan* 80b1). This phrase is found in 802b29–c2:

> Good son. These blind people each explain the elephant [from their limited perspective and knowledge]; they have neither attained the [full] truth, nor have they misspoken about the elephant [in the sense that their description is partially true]. Speaking about Buddha nature is also like this. *It is neither identical with the six dharmas [or perspectives], not is it apart from the six dharmas [or perspectives]*

7. Controlling and Healing through Auxiliary Methods [91a5–97b17]

Seventh is to control or heal [the passionate afflictions and so forth] through the auxiliary practices of the path. The *Ta chih tu lun* says that three kinds of samādhi are the basis for all samādhis. If you enter these three kinds of samādhi, you are able to perfect the Four Samādhis. Those with clever

Control or heal through the auxiliary practices of the path 助道對治: the compound 對治 can be translated many ways: "antidote," "regulate," "therapeutic" (as is one of the four *siddhāntas*); in this section I usually use the dual "control or heal."

Three kinds of samādhi: the samādhis of emptiness, formlessness, and actionlessness.

Three kinds of samādhi are the basis for all samādhis. If you enter these three kinds of samādhi, you are able to perfect the Four Samādhis 三三昧爲一切三昧作本也。若入三三昧能成四種三昧: see the *Ta chih tu lun* at T 25.268b4ff, The text does not actually say this but rather lists the various types of possible samādhis starting with this list of three samādhis. Lamotte (*Le Traité* 4, 1869ff.) translates:

> Les Samādhi "concentrations" sont de deux sortes: 1. Samādhi appartenant au système des Śrāvaka; 2. Samādhi appartenant au système du Mahāyāna.
>
> Les Samādhi appartenant au système des Śrāvaka sont les trois Samādhi: [samādhi de vacuité *(śūnyatā)*, de sans caractère *(ānimitta)* et de non-prise en considération *(apraṇihita)*].
>
> Il y a ensuite trois Samādhi: *śūnyatāśūnyatāsamādhi, ānimittānimittasamādhi, apraṇihitāpraṇihitasamādhi.*
>
> Il y a encore trois Samādhi: avec enquête et avec jugement *(savitarkasavicāra)*, sans enquête et avec jugement seulement *(avitarkavicāramātra)*, sans enquête ni jugement *(avitarka-avicāra)*.
>
> Il y a encore le Samādhi à cinq membres *(pañcāṅga)*, le Samādhi inhèrent aux cinq savoirs *(pañcajñāna)*: tous sont appelés samādhi....
>
> [a. Listes de concentrations mahāyānistes.]
>
> Les Samādhi mahāyānistes vont de la Concentration de la marche héroïque *(śūraṃgamasamādhi)* jusqu'à la Concentrations détachée, libérée, non-souillée comme l'espace *(ākāśāsaṅgavimuktinirupalepasamādhi)*, our de la Concentration voyant tous les Buddha *(sarvabuddhadarśisamādhi)* jusqu'à la Contemplation de la délivrance de tous les Tathāgata *(sarvatathāgatavimuktisamanupaśyanā)*, l'Étirement d'échine du lion *(siṃhavijṛmbhita)* et les innombrables et incalculables concentrations de Bodhisattva....

Chodron (4, 1536–38) translates:

> The samādhis belonging to the śrāvaka system are the three samādhis: i. [samādhi of emptiness, ii. of signlessness, and iii. of wishlessness].
>
> There are also three samādhis: i) *śūnyatāśūnyatāsamādhi*, ii) *ānimittānimittasamādhi*, iii) *apraṇihitāpraṇihitasamādhi.*
>
> There are also three other samādhis: i. with examination and analysis, ii. without examination and with analysis only, iii. with neither examination nor analysis.
>
> There is also the five-membered samādhi, the innate samādhi of five knowledges; all are called samādhi.
>
> Moreover, all the absorptions are sometimes called samāpatti and sometimes samādhi. The four trances are sometimes called dhyāna, sometimes samāpatti and sometimes samādhi. The other absorptions with the exception of the four trances are sometimes called samāpatti and sometimes samādhi, but not dhyāna. The absorptions coming under the ten levels [of the śrāvaka] are called samādhi....

faculties and with no hindrances can easily enter the pure and cool pond [of enlightenment], and do not need to heal or control [passionate afflictions and so forth through these auxiliary practices]. Those with clever faculties who have some hindrances should concentrate only on these three gates of liberation [of the three kinds of samādhi], and the hindrances will not be able to obstruct [such people] and they do not need the auxiliary practices of the path. Those with dull faculties and with no hindrances should use only the [thirty-seven] steps on the path for regulation and fulfillment; that is, they can convert their dullness into cleverness, and they also do not need the auxiliary practices of the path. Those with dull faculties and heavy hindrances [need the auxiliary practices]. Because of the dullness of their faculties, they are unable to open the three gates of liberation. Because their hindrances are heavy, their contemplation 觀心 is constrained and broken. For this reason, [these people] must make use of the auxiliary practices of the path to control and break the hindrances and obstacles [to enlightenment] and attain peace and enter the three gates of liberation. The *Ta chih tu lun* refers to the [methods for] control and healing as the auxiliary methods for opening the gate [to enlightenment], and it is this meaning that is referred to here.

Noble people who have attained the first fruit [of the stream-enterer] are undefiled [with regard to passionate afflictions] and have sharp faculties, so that they can clearly perceive the principle [of reality]. However, they are hindered and obstructed by passionate afflictions within their phenomenal activity, and so they cannot be called good people. The once-returners have defeated [the passionate afflictions of] the lower part [of the three realms, that is, the realm of desires] but still cannot be called "good people." Although they are not yet "good people," they truly are not ordinary [ignorant] people *(pṛthagjana)*. If they sever delusions by means of worldly wisdom, they have no phenomenal obstacles, but still they are not truly "Noble Ones." In this way, both of these types of people must utilize the auxiliary practices of the path. How much more so for those whose faculties are dull, and whose hindrances are heavy; if they do not cultivate the control [and

[a. Lists of Mahāyānist concentrations.] The Mahāyānist samādhis go from the concentration of the Heroic Progress up to the detached liberated unstained concentration like space, or the concentration of seeing all the Buddhas, up to the contemplation of the deliverance of all the Tathāgatas, the stretching of the lion's spine and the innumerable incalculable samādhis of the bodhisattva....

See the section on the Four Samādhis in the *Mo-ho chih-kuan* at 11a21–20a24.

Control and healing as the auxiliary methods for opening the gate 對治是助開門法: see the *Ta chih tu lun* at T 25.206a11–14, quoted earlier in *Mo-ho chih-kuan* at 87c29–88a1.

healing of passions through auxiliary practices of the path], how can they ever attain the realization [of nirvana]?

1. The Six Perfections [91a19]

The auxiliary practices of the path are immeasurable. In the section above on the meaning of penetrating and obstructing [the path], the hindrances were clarified in terms of the six obscurations, and the six perfections *(pāramitā)* were used for controlling [and healing] them; so these [categories] will be used for discussing the auxiliary practices of the path.

Suppose people cultivate the Four Samādhis to regulate and fulfill the steps on the path but cannot realize liberation, and instead greedy covetousness suddenly arises and their contemplative thoughts become agitated; they become protective and attached to their body, life, and material riches; and they have greedy covetous notions and conceptions that give rise to desirous thoughts. Even though they deliberately try to stop them, these [thoughts of] greedy covetousness repeatedly arise. At these times you should utilize [the virtue of] abandoning [these things] through *dāna* [the perfection of giving] to control [these matters].

Suppose that when you cultivate samādhi you are subject to the sudden arising of thoughts of breaking the precepts; you become lax in maintaining a noble demeanor and do not seek to maintain [the precepts], your physical and verbal [actions] become deviant, you oppose the system [of moral rules], and you do not maintain purity with regard to the pure prohibitions, so it becomes difficult to arouse samādhi. At these times you should utilize [the virtue of] *śīla* [the perfection of keeping the precepts] to control [and heal] [these matters].

Suppose that when you cultivate samādhi you experience a burst of anger, always show malice and bear a grudge, speak evil and deceitfully, and get involved in [useless] disputes over what is to be affirmed and denied. This poison [of anger] obstructs [the realization of] samādhi. At these times you should cultivate patience *(kṣānti)* to control [these matters].

Suppose that when you cultivate samādhi you become self-indulgent and lazy; you become selfish in your physical, verbal, and mental [activity], you become profligate and idle, without shame and without remorse,

Penetrating and obstructing 通塞: see the *Mo-ho chih-kuan* at 86a10–87c8. However, the six perfections are not a dominant theme of this previous section.

Lax in maintaining a noble demeanor 威儀: Ikeda (*Gendaigoyaku*, 459) translates, "you become hasty and careless in following [proper] procedure."

Speak evil and deceitfully 惡口兩舌: lit., "with two tongues," that is, "with a forked tongue," or "speak out of both sides of your mouth."

[**91b**] not able to show any fidelity in adversity, as one who repeatedly strikes sparks for a fire but stops before the flame catches. A person who has little perseverance cannot accomplish even worldly duties, how much less realize samādhi. At these times you should utilize [the virtue of] diligence *(vīrya)* to control [these matters].

Suppose that when you cultivate samādhi you become distracted and do not concentrate—physically you [spin] like a top, verbally you [croak] like a frog, and mentally you [flutter] like a candle in the wind. Because you are agitated and distracted, the Dharma does not become manifest. At these times you should utilize dhyāna meditation to control [these matters].

Suppose that when you cultivate samādhi you become deluded and confused, become attached to the two extremes of eternalism and annihilationism, and believe that there is a substantial self or life force within sentient beings, so that with regard to these matters you face a wall 面牆, make no progress, and always come up short. Thus you cannot respond to the needs of other beings; you are obstinate and clumsy in your thinking, and without any signs of wisdom. At these times you should utilize [the virtue of *prajñā*] wisdom to control [these matters].

Various obscurations cover the mind, and among these some are thick and some thin. When they are "thin," they agitate the mind [or mental functions], but do not necessarily agitate your physical and verbal [functions]. When they are "thick," they will agitate your physical and verbal [functions], but your mind will certainly be agitated first. When an internal disease is strong, its features will be manifested externally. If you use these methods for controlling [and healing] and successfully removing [passionate afflictions and so forth], then [you know that] these [practices] are appropriate for these diseases. If they are not removed by these methods, then you should rely on the "four appropriate methods" in turn to apply the auxiliary practices of the path. In the case of controlling or healing a single [experience of] greed, you may wish to cultivate giving, or not wish to cultivate giving, or give rise to good thoughts or not give rise to good [thoughts], or cultivate giving that destroys greed or does not destroy greed, or cultivate giving that discloses the auxiliary practices or does not disclose them. You should carefully consider [various] good and skillful means [according to the situation]—either in response [to what is appropriate], or in turn, or combined,

Physically you [spin] like a top 身如獨落: Ikeda (*Kenkyūchūshaku*, 401) concludes that the character 落 should be 樂, giving the phrase 獨樂, meaning a "top."

Four appropriate methods 四隨: equivalent to the four *siddhāntas*: to teach in accordance with the desires and needs of sentient beings, to teach in accordance with what is appropriate, to teach in accordance with what is therapeutic, and to teach in accordance with the truth.

or in accordance with the supreme [truth]. It is the same for cultivating the control or healing of the other [obscurations].

With regard to applying the six perfections as auxiliary practices, merely accomplishing an understanding of one matter does not mean you have fulfilled the auxiliary practices of the path. You should contemplate these auxiliary practices as beyond conceptual understanding and as encompassing all dharmas, as I will explain later. There is a person who says that "to teach the six [perfections] is to penetrate the teachings, and to teach the ten [perfections] is to penetrate to the gist," but this is not the case. The *Mahā-parinirvāṇa Sūtra* clearly states that the six perfections are Buddha-nature. The *Pañcaviṃśati Sūtra* says "this is Mahāyāna." One perfection encompasses all Dharmas, how much more so for the six [perfections]! If you realize the meaning of "exposing and merging" [the six and ten perfections], then there is no [sense of] "leaving behind" or "taking away" 去取 [some of the perfections]. For example, [the perfection of] dhyāna

In response 對, in turn 轉, combined 兼, and in accordance with the supreme truth 第一義: these do not appear to simply match the categories of the four *siddhāntas*. For later detailed T'ien-t'ai subdivisions of these categories, see the commentary of the *Kōgi* (BT–IV, 430–33).

There is a person who says 有人言: Chan-jan and later commentators (BT–IV, 434–35) trace this saying to an anonymous "man of old" and his interpretation of a passage in the *Laṅkāvatāra Sūtra*, but the context and details are unclear. For the passage in the sūtra see T 16.503a–b.

Ten perfections: an expansion of the traditional six perfections by adding that of vows 願 *(praṇidhāna)*, power 力 *(bala)*, means 方便 *(upāya)*, and wisdom 智 *(jñāna)*.

The six perfections are Buddha-nature 六度是佛性: the *Kōgi* (BT–IV, 436) points to a passage in the *Mahāparinirvāṇa Sūtra* at T 12.777c21–26, which seems to say the opposite of Chih-i's claim:

> If a person has achieved samādhi, why does the practitioner need to perceive the suffering, birth, old age, sickness, and death of the three evil destinies, and give birth to retrogressive thoughts? Again, such people do not need to cultivate the six pāramitās in order to attain *anuttarasaṃyaksaṃbodhi*. This is like milk turning into cream without any conditions. But it is not that there is no cause provided by the six *pāramitās* for the attainment of *anuttarasaṃyaksaṃbodhi*. According to this meaning, you should know that sentient beings all lack Buddha-nature.

The passage immediately preceding this quote (T 12.777c18–21) was quoted above in the *Mo-ho chih-kuan* at 11a20.

This is Mahāyāna 是摩訶衍: see the *Pañcaviṃśati Sūtra* at T 8.250a6–7: "the six *pāramitā*s are the Mahāyāna of the bodhisattva-mahāsattvas."

Exposing and merging 開合: this text is ambiguous, and the subject is not clear, but the comments that follow suggest the six and ten perfections. Ikeda (*Gendai-goyaku*, 463) attempts a much freer rendering: "The difference between the six perfections and the ten perfections is only in the degree of disclosing and merging; it is not that the ten perfections are fuller and the six perfections are insufficient."

includes [the perfection of] vows, wisdom[, and power], which discloses *praṇidhāna-pāramitā* [the perfection of vows]; having supranormal powers [through the practice of dhyāna] discloses *bala-pāramitā* [the perfection of power]; and these [in turn] support the perfection of dhyāna meditation. *Prajñā*-wisdom includes the wisdom of the path, and this discloses *upāya[-pāramitā]* [the perfection of means]; again, [*prajñā*-wisdom] includes universal wisdom, which discloses *jñāna-pāramitā* [the perfection of wisdom]; [finally,] omniscience is the basis on which *prajñā* is so-called. If we separate [these aspects] in this way, we have ten [perfections]; if they are bundled together, we have six [perfections]. If we consider them in expansive or abbreviated terms, we can classify them as Mahāyāna or Hīnayāna.

Now I will clarify the idea that the six perfections as auxiliary practices of the path exhaustively encompass all dharmas. In brief I will show that they encompass all the [thirty-seven] steps on the path. [The six perfections encompass] the regulating and overcoming of the six sense faculties, the ten powers, the four fearlessnesses, the eighteen unique qualities (of the Buddha), six supranormal powers, the three illuminating insights, the four inducements, the four [unobstructed] eloquences, *dhāraṇī*, the thirty-two major and eighty minor [physical] marks [of a Buddha], and so forth including all dharmas.

1. The perfection of giving (dāna-pāramitā) or "abandoning" [91b29]

How do [the six perfections] encompass all the steps on the path? [First, let us look at the perfection of giving.] All of the steps on the path each **[91c]** include the component of abandonment [or "equanimity"; *upekṣa*], which is encompassed by [the perfection of] *dāna* [giving]. Even if the component of abandonment by those of the Tripitaka [Teachings] does not involve realizing the principle [of reality], still they abandon their bodies, life, and

Praṇidhāna 泥滓: Here Chih-i uses an awkward transliteration for the perfection of vows. In this section I will give the Sanskrit equivalent in cases where Chih-i uses a transliteration. It is not clear why Chih-i uses unusual transliterations in this section instead of the usual Chinese translations.

Upāya-pāramitā: Here, instead of the transliteration for *pāramitā*, the text has 俱舍羅, perhaps a transliteration of *kuśala*?

***Prajñā*-wisdom includes the wisdom of the path** 般若有道種智: hence the interlocking connections and mutual interpenetration of the three wisdoms, *prajñā-pāramitā*, and *jñāna-pāramitā*.

Six sense faculties … thirty-two major and eighty minor marks 六根。十力。四無所畏。十八不共法。六通。三明。四攝。四辯。陀羅尼。三十二相。八十隨形好等: for details on these categories see the Glossary.

Abandonment 捨: one of the "seven components of awakening," the component of "equanimity." See above on the translation of *upekṣa* as "equanimity" or "indifference" 等 rather than "abandonment."

material riches [for the sake of the Buddha Dharma]. The *Ta chih tu lun* says, "Kindness *(maitri)*, compassion *(karuṇā)*, and joy *(muditā)* bring benefit to sentient beings; abandonment [or equanimity] *(upekṣā)* encompasses the six perfections and widely benefits sentient beings. This is called 'great benefit.'"

Kindness, compassion, and joy bring benefit to sentient beings; abandonment encompasses the six perfections and widely benefits sentient beings. This is called "great benefit" 慈悲喜於衆生有益。捨何所益捨能具足六度廣利衆生是名大益: see the *Ta chih tu lun:* at T 25.210b4–14. Lamotte (*Le Traité* 3, 1258–59) translates this section (entitled "Raisons de pratiquer l'équanimité") as follows:

> Question. — Si on aime les êtres aussi profondément, pourquoi pratiquer en outre la pensée d'équanimité *(upekṣācitta)*?
> Réponse. — Le yogin voit les choses de la manière suivante: jamais il n'abandonne les êtres et il songe seulement à abandonner les trois pensées [de bienveillance, de compassion et de joie]. Pourquoi cela? D'abord pour mettre un terme à d'autres dharma.
>
> Ensuite, par la pensée de bienveillance *(maitrīcitta)*, il désirait que les êtres fussent heureux, mais il ne parvenait pas à leur fair trouver le bonheur. Par la pensée de compassion *(karuṇācitta)*, il désirait que les êtres échappassent à la douleur, mais il ne parvenait pas à leur faire trouver l'exemption de la douleur. Quand il pratiquait la pensée de joie *(muditācitta)*, il n'arrivait pas non plus à ce que les êtres éprouvassent une grande joie. Tout cela n'était donc qu'élucubrations *(manaskāra)* sans aucune réalité vraie *(bhūtārtha)*. Aussi, voulant faire en sort que les êtres trouvent la vérité vraie, le yogin produit-il la résolution *(cittam utpādayati)* de devenir Buddha. Il pratique les six perfections *(pāramitā)* et perfectionne en lui les attributs des Buddha pour que les êtres trouvent le bonheur vrai. C'est pourquoi le yogin abandonne les trois pensées [de bienveillance, de compassion et de joie] pour entrer dans la pensée d'équanimité *(upekṣācitta)*.
>
> Enfin, les pensées de bienveillance, de compassion, et de joie sont d'un amour si profond qu'il est difficile d'abandonner les êtres. [Au contraire] si on entre dans la pensée d'équanimité, il est facile de s'en séparer.

Chodron (3, 1033) translates:

> Question. If one loves beings so deeply, why practice the mind of equanimity in addition?
> Answer. The yogin sees things in the following way: he never abandons beings and he thinks only of abandoning the three minds [of loving-kindness, compassion and joy]. Why? First of all, to put an end to other dharmas.
>
> Then, by the mind of loving-kindness, he wished that beings be happy, but he did not succeed in making them happy. By the mind of compassion, he wished that beings could escape from suffering, but he did not succeed in making them free of suffering. When he practiced the mind of joy he did not succeed in causing them to experience great joy either. All of that was mere mental activity without any real reality). And so, wishing to make beings find the real truth, the yogin makes the resolve to become Buddha. He practices the six perfections and perfects within himself the attributes of Buddha so that beings may find true happiness. This is why the yogin abandons the three minds [of loving-kindness, compassion and joy] so as to enter into the mind of equanimity.
>
> Finally, the minds of loving-kindness, compassion and joy are minds of love so deep that it is hard to abandon beings. [On the other hand], if one enters into the mind of equanimity, it is easy to separate from them.

Again, "abandonment" [that is, the perfection of giving] is like an ointment that is able to augment the brightness of the [other] five perfections. Therefore you should know that the perfection of giving encompasses the component of abandonment [equanimity]. The component of abandonment for those of the Shared Teachings is to abandon the body, life, and material riches because these three things are all empty, like an illusion or [magical] transformation. This [sense of the] component of abandonment is also encompassed by the perfection of giving. The component of abandonment for those of the Distinct Teachings involves abandoning ignorance concerning the body, life, and material riches, and this "abandonment" is also encompassed by the perfection of giving.

The component of abandonment for the Perfect Teaching involves abandoning the physical body of the ten dharma realms, abandoning the continuous life in the ten dharma realms, and abandoning the environment of the ten dharma realms. In this way [those of the Perfect Teaching] do not accept the two extremes with regard to the body, life, and material things [of this world]. Why? Material riches are called the six sense objects. If you suppose that the objects of the six senses should be abandoned and that you should give away [these things] to the people in front of you, and give away even your own body, this kind of giving can involve taking the six sense objects in the extreme sense of "[substantially] existing" 有邊. If you take these three things as all empty, you can fall into the extreme of "nothingness" 無邊. Now [in the Perfect Teaching] you contemplate material riches as empty so that you do not take [the extreme view of] Being, and you contemplate material riches as conventional so that you do not take the extreme view of emptiness 空邊 [as nothingness]. Non-dualistic abandoning is equivalent to attaining the limits beyond the cycle of birth and death [of samsara]; to be separate from old age, sickness, and death, and attain the indestructible constant abiding [of nirvana]. The extreme of existence refers to samsara and corresponds to that before the limits [of this world]; the extreme of emptiness [or nothingness] refers to nirvana and corresponds to that beyond the limits [of this world]. Everything included in these two [categories] is empty and unobtainable; therefore they are called equal 等 *(upekṣa)*. To be separate

Environment 依報: Lit., the "circumstantial recompense" which is the world in which we dwell due to past karma.

Non-dualistic abandoning 不二之捨: abandonment that avoids two extremes.

Non-dualistic … constant abiding 不二之捨與生死後際等離老病死得不壞常住: the *Kōgi* (BT–IV, 443) claims that this is from the *Aṅgulimāla Sūtra* (T 2.536a), but the connections are tenuous.

Constant abiding 常住…: These phrases are from the *Mahāparinirvāṇa Sūtra*, T 12.627c15–16. They were referred to above in the *Mo-ho chih-kuan* at 23b27–28.

from old age and death means to be separate from the old age and death of (ordinary) constituent samsara, since what is before the limits [of this world] is empty, and to be separate from the old age and death which involve transformation beyond understanding, since what is beyond the limits [of this world] is [also] empty. It is called "separate from" because you are forever exempt from these two types of death. To attain indestructible and constant abiding refers to the Dharma nature of the Middle Way. This is the teacher of all Buddhas; since the Dharma is constant, the Buddhas are also constant. This constantly-abiding material [wealth] cannot be broken or lost. This constantly-abiding body cannot be fixed or bound. This constantly-abiding life cannot be severed or extinguished. To perfectly fulfill the ultimate perfection of giving is to adorn yourself [with these best qualities]. Therefore *The Diamond Sūtra* says, "Even if you offered bodies [as numerous] as the sands of the Ganges River in the early, middle, and later part of the day, this does not compare with [the merit from] receiving and upholding one four-line verse of [this sūtra concerning] *prajñā*-wisdom." You should know that the abandonment that is the contemplation of the principle [of reality] in the Perfect [Teaching] involves a [unifying] encounter with the steps on the path, and [these are all] encompassed by the perfection of giving.

In this way [for those of the Perfect Teaching] the component of abandonment for the steps of the path consists of contemplation of the principle [of reality] deeply and minutely, and does not involve phenomenal practices. In the Tripitaka [Teachings], the giving of phenomenal things is vigorous and fierce; they cut and burn [their bodies] in exchange for salvation, or [abandon] their country, city, wife, and children. However, if they do not

Even if you offered bodies [as numerous] as the sands of the Ganges River in the early, middle, and later part of the day, this does not compare with receiving and upholding one four-line verse of *prajñā*-wisdom 初中後日分悉以恒河沙身布施不如受持般若一四句偈: see *The Diamond Sūtra*: at T 8.750a23–26:

> Subhūti, if there are good sons or good daughters who make an offering of their physical lives as much as the sands of the Ganges River, or if there are people who receive and uphold a four-line verse from this sūtra for the sake of other people, the blessings [to be gained] from this are exceedingly many.

Phenomenal practices 事行: or, more literally, "for those of the Perfect Teaching, phenomenal activities do not exist."

Cut and burn in exchange for salvation 剜燈救貿: The *Kōgi* (BT–IV, p. 446) identifies this phrase as coming from the *Sūtra of Recompense*, T no. 156, 3.134c7.

Country, city, wife, and children 國城妻子:these phrases are found in various stories in the *Ta chih tu lun*, e.g., T 25.146b1–6ff. Lamotte (*Le Traité* 2, 712–13) translates:

> Question. — Qu'entend-on par Perfection de vertu du don appartenant au corps né des liens et des actes?
> Réponse. — Sans avoir obtenu le Corps de la Loi *(dharmakāya)* et sans avoir brisé ses entraves *(kṣīṇasaṃyojana)*, le Bodhi-

have even a minute particle of the contemplation of the principle [of reality], they are at fault in both aspects. Now I am clarifying the giving of phenomenal things as an auxiliary practice that assists in destroying the obscuration of avarice or covetousness, to progress and fulfill the contemplation of the principle [of reality]. Why, then, should the two be considered separately? Even if people [abstractly] understand the contemplation of the true aspects of abandonment in the Perfect [Teaching], they just "rub their chests" [with self-satisfaction?] and discuss **[92a]** the practices [without actually doing them], avarice prevails in their involvement with phenomenal matters, and they are protective of their material treasures and do not abandon or give away even one minute amount. They shirk from stressful exertion, weighing their physical power and measuring their strength. They are not able to humble themselves and perfect others. They are avaricious with regard to their own lives. How can they contend with death and give up their own lives? When coming in contact with phenomenal things, they are parsimonious and grasping, but stubbornly do not take action; they merely "understand" without practicing. In such cases, how is it possible to destroy such heavy obscurations, and how can the gates of the three liberations be opened?

Now [in such cases] you should enter the meditation hall and repent bitterly; arouse a determination and a great vow [to attain Buddhahood]; abandon your body, life, and material riches; and resolve that you will have no passionate grudges. Establish the vow that "I myself will practice this perfection of giving and I will teach of it to others; I will praise the Dharma of giving, and rejoice in giving," and call on the Buddhas of the ten directions to

> sattva est capable de donner sans réserve tous ses biens précieux *(ratnadravya)*, sa tête *(śiras)*, ses yeux *(nayana)* sa moille *(majjā)*, son cerveau *(mastaka)*, son royaume *(rājya)*, ses richesses *(dhana)*, son épouse *(dāra)*, ses enfants *(putra)*, ses possessions internes *(ādhyātmika)* ou externes *(bāhya);* et cela, sans que son coeur éprouve de l'émotion.

Chodron (2, 566) translates:

> Question. What is meant by virtue of generosity belonging to the body born of bonds and actions?
>
> Answer. – Without having attained the Dharmakāya and without having broken his fetters, the bodhisattva is able to give all his precious goods unreservedly, his head, his eyes, his marrow, his skull, his kingdom, his wealth, his wife, his children, his internal or external possessions, without his mind feeling emotions.

At fault in both aspects 兩皆有過: that is, they have no insight into the nature of reality, and their "phenomenal practices" are ultimately of no benefit either.

Do not give away even one minute amount 一毫不捨: that is, if they accept the idea that a direct insight into the nature of reality is sufficient for attaining the wisdom of Buddhahood without a truly profound comprehension of what that means, they will mistakenly abandon other, "lower" forms of practice as unnecessary?

I myself will practice … rejoice in giving 自行此檀又以教他。讚歎檀法隨喜檀: see

bear witness and save you. If your thoughts are true and without deceit, the Buddha will respond by sending forth a ray of the light of giving, to illumine and remove the obscuration of avarice, as it says in the *Viśeṣacintibrahma-paripṛcchā.*

By receiving this light you establish a rapport with the component of abandonment and all the steps on the path, and should be able to interpret and understand each and every one of them. If the phenomenal and principle are both perfected, and your giving and abandonment are taken to their ultimate end, then material riches will be to you like dung, and your physical body like a vessel of poison, and your life like the drifting clouds; you can then discard these three things [as easily] as you spit. The obstacle of avarice will be destroyed; this is the fulfillment of the meaning of the path of healing, and you will attain liberation. Even if you are not [blessed] with these causes and conditions, you should practice the path according to these instructions; you should experience benefit even if your abandonments are

the *Pañcaviṃśati Sūtra*, T 8.281c11–24:

> Good sons and good daughters and people who have been taught [the Dharma] should all believe and accept [this Dharma]. They should be intimate with it and hold hard to it, and not teach words that are of no benefit. They should not be covered with anger, nor with the coverings of pride, greed, and jealousy. These people should themselves not take life, and should teach people not to take life, and praise the not taking of life, and rejoice in the not taking of life. They should themselves avoid taking things that they are not given, and should teach people to avoid taking things that they are not given, and praise the avoidance of taking what is not given, and rejoice in the avoidance of taking what is not given. They should themselves not indulge in illicit lust, and should teach people not to indulge in illicit lust, and praise not indulging in illicit lust, and rejoice in not indulging in illicit lust. They should themselves not speak falsely, and teach people not to speak falsely, and praise not speaking falsely, and rejoice in not speaking falsely. The same is true for speaking duplicitously, speaking evil, and using words that are without benefit. They should themselves not be covetous, teach people not to be covetous, praise that which is not covetous, and rejoice in that which is not covetous. The same is true for not being greedy and not have mistaken views [and so forth]. They should themselves practice the perfection of giving, teach people to practice the perfection of giving, praise the Dharma of the perfection of giving, and rejoice in and acclaim the practice of the perfection of giving. They should themselves practice the perfection of keeping the precepts, teach people to practice the perfection of keeping the precepts, [and so forth].

To bear witness and save you 爲證爲救: Or, "to enlighten and save you."

Buddha will respond by sending forth a ray of the light of giving, to illumine and remove the obscuration of avarice 能感如來放檀光明照除慳蔽: see the *Viśeṣacintabrahma-paripṛcchā* at T 15.33c29–34a2:

> Again, the light of the Tathāgata is called "abandonment"; the Buddha, by means of this light, is able to destroy the avaricious and covetous thoughts of sentient beings and lead them to practice giving.

as small as a mustard seed. Thus the oil of phenomenal [practices] will assist in increasing the clear light of the path, opening the three gates of liberation, and attaining the insight of Buddha nature. If you are unable to do this, you will not benefit from the auxiliary practices for healing and controlling [obstacles to the path].

2. *The perfection of upholding the precepts (śīla-pāramitā)* [92a16]

If you cultivate [these practices] in this way, you should attain awakening. If you are not awakened [through the practice of giving], you should ponder the steps on the path of contemplating the principle [of reality], and have right deeds, right speech, and right livelihood. This corresponds to, and is encompassed by, the perfection of *śīla* [upholding the precepts].

For the Tripitaka [Teachings], "right deeds" and so forth means to carefully maintain [the upholding of the precepts in the sense of] "no breaking, no fault, no rupturing, not mixed" [and so forth]. For the Shared Teachings, "right deeds" and so forth are physically and verbally "unobtainable" [because they are "empty"]; they are truly [empty] and yet phenomenal; and correspond to the precepts as "in accordance with the path" and "without attachment." For the Distinct Teachings, "right deeds" and so forth correspond to the precepts as "praised by the wise" and "mastery." For the Perfect Teaching, "right deeds" and so forth are all part of the contemplation of Dharma-nature, and corresponds to the precepts as "complete" [and integrated and all-inclusive]. The *Vimalakīrti Sūtra* says that if you are able to act in this way, "this is called 'honoring the Vinaya,'" and this is the meaning intended here.

Mustard seed 遺芥: Ikeda (*Gendaigoyaku*, 463) interprets this quite differently and translates: "Even if you have benefits, these should be abandoned like the dust." 芥 can mean either "mustard seed" or "dust."

No breaking 不破, **no fault** 不缺, **no rupturing** 不穿, **not mixed** 不雜 ...: these are the first four of the "ten types of upholding the precepts" as discussed in detail above in the *Mo-ho chih-kuan* at 36a13–38a15. The list is from the *Ta chih tu lun*, T 25.225c28–226a1, which is commentary on the passage from the *Pañcaviṃśati Sūtra*, T 8.386a3–8. For details, see expanded note at *Mo-ho chih-kuan* 36a15.

"In accordance with the path" 隨道 **and "without attachment"** 無著: the fifth and sixth of the "ten types of upholding the precepts."

"Praised by the wise" 智所讚 **and "mastery"** 自在: the seventh and eighth of the "ten types of upholding the precepts." It is not clear whether the ninth type, "in accordance with concentration" 隨定, should be included here or with the Perfect Teaching.

"Complete" 具足: the tenth of the "ten types of upholding the precepts."

Honoring the Vinaya 奉律: the phrase is from the *Vimalakīrti Sūtra*, T 14.541b28. This passage, though not this phrase, has been quoted in the *Mo-ho chih-kuan*

The precepts as contemplation of the principle are completed in the mind, but if you achieve this understanding [mentally] and are deficient in many physical and verbal [aspects of actual practice], your present life will be undeveloped and your future lives full of obstructions. If you do not repent [of these shortcomings], these [faults] will cover [and obstruct attainment of] the three types of samādhi, and you will not be able to open the [three] gates of liberation. Ponder [and reflect on] these things, and you should pity yourself and arouse a deep sense of reform [and repentance], that from this day, first you will sever mental continuity [with past evil deeds], vow to uphold the precepts of prohibition, not have any flaws in your actual [practices], "guard and uphold [the precepts] with loving care, as [a person trying to cross the sea] carefully holds onto a floating bag," so that until the end with your whole body you do not violate the precepts. As the poisonous dragon sought to save the ant even at the cost of his own

previously at 22b17 and 63b27. Boin (*Vimalakīrti Sūtra*, 73) translates:

> All dharmas are born of imagination *(parikalpotpanna)*, like the moon in the water *(udakacandra)* and a reflection in a mirror *(ādarśapratibimba)*. *Those who know this are called the true guardians of the discipline (vinayadhara)*; those who know this are well-disciplined *(suvinīta)*.

Carefully holds a floating bag 保浮囊: a phrase from the *Mahāparinirvāṇa Sūtra*, T 12.674a3–4. This refers to the analogy of a man "jealously protecting" a floating bag in order to cross the sea, who will not give up even a tiny bit of it, just as a person seeking to cross to the other shore of enlightenment should not give up on even a small part of keeping the precepts. For a full translation of this passage (*Mahāparinirvāṇa Sūtra*, T 12.673c18–674a29), see the note at *Mo-ho chih-kuan* 38a17–19.

Poisonous dragon sought to save the ant even at the cost of his skin 毒龍輸皮全蟻: see the story in the *Ta chih tu lun*, T 25.162a10–b2, used to illustrate the perfection of keeping the precepts. Lamotte (*Le Traité* 2, 853–55) translates:

> Certains disent que la vertu de moralité est la moralité du Bodhisattva qui préfère perdre la vie plutôt que de violer la plus petite défense. Comme on l'a dit plus haut dans le *Sou t'o sou mo wang king* (Sutasomarājasūtra), le Bodhisattva sacrifie sa vie pour garder les défenses. [*Jātaka du Nāga écorché*]. — De même, le Bodhisattva, dans une existence antérieure, était un dragon venimeux *(viṣanāga)* très puissant. Tous les êtres périssaient devant lui: les faibles devant son regard, les forts devant son souffle.
>
> Ce nāga, ayant pris la Moralité d'un jour *(rātridivasaśīla)*, sortit de la maison, se mit en quête d'une retraite et pénétra dans la forêt. Étant resté longtemps à méditer *(manasikāra)*, il s'endormit de fatigue. Or, c'est une loi chez les nāga, quand ils dorment, de prendre la forme *(saṃsthāna)* d'un serpent. Le corps du nāga portait une inscription, et les sept joyaux *(saptaratna)* y mêlaient leurs feux. Des chasseurs *(vyādh, lubdhaka)*, qui le virent, en furent surpris et dirent: "Une telle peau *(tvac-)* est extraordinaire *(ad-bhuta)* et rare *(durlabha)*; ne faudrait-il pas l'offrir au roi de notre pays en guise d'ornement?" Aussitôt, il écrasèrent la tête du serpent avec un bâton et lui enlevèrent la peau avec un couteau. Le nāga se dit: "Ma force est miraculeuse *(ṛddhika)*; si je la répandais sur ce pays, il serait retourné comme la main. Comment ces hommes, choses minuscules, peuvent-

ils m'entreprendre? Mais aujourd'hui que j'observe la moralité, je ne me soucie plus de la vie; je suivrai les enseignements du Buddha *(buddhavacana)*." Sur ce, s'armant de patience, il ferma les yeux et ne regarda plus; il retint son souffle et ne respira plus, car, plein de compassion *(anukampā)* pour ces hommes, [il voulait les épargner]. Pour garder la moralité, il subit résolument *(ekacittena)* le supplice de l'écorchement, sans éprouver de regret. Il perdit donc sa peau, et ses chairs sanglantes jonchaient le sol. Quand le soleil, très ardent, entrprit sa révolution autour de la terre, le nāga voulut gagner une grande étendue d'eau [pour s'y rafraîchir'; il vit alors de petits insects *(kṛmi)* s'approcher de lui afin de le manger; pour garder la moralité, il n'osa point remuer [de peur de les écraser]. Il se disait: "Aujourd'hui, je fais don de mon corps aux insectes; c'est pour arriver à l'état de Buddha que je donne ma chair et que je sacrifie ma vie; plus tard, quand je serai un Buddha, je poursuivrai cette [bonne] résolution en pratiquant le don de la Loi *(dharmadāna)*." Après qu'il eut fait ce serment *(praṇidhāna)*, son corps se dessécha et il mourut. Il renaiquit alors dans le deuxième ciel *(svarga)*: celui des Trāyastriṃśa.

Le dragon venimeux de ce temps-là était le buddha Śākyamuni; les chasseurs étaient Devadatta et les six maîtres hérétiques; les petits insectes étaient les 80,000 deva qui trouvèrent le Chemin *(mārga)* quand le buddha Śākyamuni fit tourner pour la première fois la roue de la Loi.

Le Bodhisattva, pour garder les défenses, sacrifie sa vie; il est ferme *(niyata)* et sans regret. C'est cela que l'on appelle vertu de moralité.

Chodron (2, 668–69) translates:

Some say that the virtue of morality is the morality of the bodhisattva who prefers to lose his life rather than break the smallest precept. As was said above in the *Sutasomarājasūtra*, the bodhisattva sacrifices his life to keep the precepts.

[*Jātaka of the flayed Nāga*]. – In a previous lifetime, the Bodhisattva was a very powerful poisonous dragon. All beings perished before him, the weak merely at the sight of him, the strong, at his breath.

Having undertaken the discipline of one day, this nāga started to look for a retreat and entered the forest. Having remained in meditation for a long time, he tired himself out and fell asleep. Now it is the rule among the nāgas, when they sleep, to take the form of a snake. The body of the nāga bore an inscription in which the seven jewels mingled their brilliance. Some hunters, seeing him, were astonished and said: "Such a skin is extraordinary and rare; should we not offer it to the king as an adornment?" Immediately they crushed the snake's head with a stick and cut off his skin with a knife. The nāga said to himself: "My strength is miraculous; if I spread out over this land, it would be turned over like your hand. How can these men, tiny things, engage me? But today when I am observing the discipline, I have no care for my life; I will follow the teachings of the Buddha." Thereupon, fortifying himself with patience, he closed his eyes and did not look; he held his breath and did not breathe for, out of compassion for these men, [he wanted to spare them]. To keep the discipline, he resolutely suffered the torture of flaying, without feeling any regret. Thus he lost his skin and his bloody flesh was scattered on the ground. When the hot sun started its journey around the earth, the nāga wanted to get to a large expanse of water [to cool off]; he then saw that small insects were coming to eat him; to keep the discipline, he dared not move [out of fear that he would crush them]. He said to himself: "Today I give the gift of my body to the insects; it is in order to reach buddhahood that I give my flesh and sacrifice my life; later, when I am a Buddha, I will follow this [good] resolution by practicing the generosity of the Dharma." After taking this oath, his body dried up and he died. He

skin [and life], as the king Sutasoma lost his kingdom to keep a verse [from the sūtras], you [should uphold] the precepts yourselves and teach others,

was then reborn in the second heaven, that of the Trāyastriṃśa.

The poisonous dragon of that time was the Buddha Śākyamuni; the hunters were Devadatta and the six heretic masters; the little insects were the 80,000 devas who found the Path when the Buddha Śākyamuni turned the wheel of Dharma the first time.

In order to keep the precepts, the bodhisattva sacrifices his life; he is steadfast and without regret. That is why it is called the virtue of morality.

King Sutasoma lost his kingdom to keep a verse 須陀摩王失國獲偈: another illustration of the perfection of keeping the precepts from the *Ta chih tu lun*, T 25.88c28–89b11. Lamotte, (*Le Traité* 1, 260–63) translates:

En n'épargnant pas sa vie quand il s'agit de garder les pures défenses *(viśuddhaśīla)*. Ainsi le roi Sutasoma, à cause du grand roi Kalmāṣapāda alla jusqu'à offrir sa vie, mais ne viola pas les défenses.

Il y avait autrefois un roi nommé Sutasoma, énergique *(vīryavat)*, observateur des défenses *(śīladhara)* et toujours fidèle à la parole donnée *(satyavādin)*. Un matin, il monta sur un char avec ses courtisanes *(gaṇikā)* et entra dans un jardin *(ārāma)* pour s'y promener. Au moment où il franchissait les portes de la ville, un certain brâhmane, venu pour mendier, dit au roi: "Le roi est très puissant *(mahāprabhāva)* et moi je suis un pauvre *(daridra)*. Qu'il ait pitié de moi et me donne quelque chose." Le roi répondit: "J'y consens. J'estime les enseignements des saints *(tathāgata)* [comme toi]; mour mous ferons mutuellement des cadeaux. Je dois sortir, mais je reviendrai." Après cette promesse, le roi entra dans son jardin où il se baigna et prit ses ébats.

A ce moment, un roi à deux ailes nommé "Pieds de gazelle" (Kalmāṣapāda) arriva à tire-d'aile et, au milieu des courtisanes, s'empara du roi et s'enfuit avec lui: on eût dit l'oiseau aux ailes d'or *(garuḍa)* s'emparant d'un serpent *(nāga)* en pleine mer. Les femmes se lamentaient et criaient; dans le jardin et dans la ville, au dedans comme au dehors, c'était l'émoi et la consternation.

Kalmāṣapāda, portant le roi, fendit l'espace *(ākāśa)* et arriva à sa demeure où il déposa Sutasoma parmi les quatre-vingt-dix-neuf rois [qu'il avait déjà capturés]. Le roi Sutasoma se mit à pleurer à sanglots: Kalmāṣapāda lui dit: "Grand roi kṣatriya, pourquoi pleures-tu comme un petit enfant? Tout homme qui naît doit périr; les composés doivent se dissocier." Le roi Sutasoma répondit: "Je ne crains pas la mort, mais je crains fort de manquer à mes promesses. Depuis ma naissance je n'ai jamais fait de mensonge *(mṛṣāvāda)*. Aujourd'hui matin, comme je franchissais les portes, un certain brâhmane est venu me demander une aumône, et je lui ai promis de revenir pour lui donner la charité. Je ne doute pas de l'impermanence *(anityatā)*, mais si je frustre ce [brâhmane] dans son attente, je commets un péché *(āpatti)* de tromperie. Voilà pourquoi je pleure." Kalmāṣapāda lui dit: "Ton désir sera satisfait. Pousque tu crains de manquer à ta promesse, je t'autorise à rentrer [chez toi]; tu as sept jours pour faire la charité au brâhmane; après, tu reviendras ici. Si, passés ces sept jours, tu n'es pas revenu, moi, avec la force de mes ailes, j'irai te reprendre sans difficulté."

Le roi Sutasoma put donc rentrer dans son pays natal et y faire l'aumône à sa guise. Il établit sur le trône le prince héritier *(kumāra)*. Réunissant son peuple, il s'excusa en ces termes: "Je sais que je n'ai pas réglé toutes les affaires; mon gouvernement n'était pas [toujours] conforme au Dharma. Je reconnais votre loyauté. Si je ne suis pas mort aujourd'lui, je reviendrai directement." Dans tout le pays, son peuple et ses parents frappaient la terre du front pour le retenir: "Nous voulons, disaient-ils, que le roi fasse attention et continue au pays sa bienveillante protection. Qu'il ne se soucie plus de Kalmāṣapāda, roi des Rākṣasa. Nous établirons une maison de fer *(ayogṛha)* avec des soldats d'élite. Si puissant que soit Kalmāṣapāda, nous ne la craignons pas." Mais Sutasoma qui n'était pas d'accord dit cette stance:

> La fidélité à la parole *(satyavāda)* est le premier des commandements;
> L'homme de parole gravit l'échelle du ciel.
> L'homme de parole, si petit soit-il, est grand;
> Le menteur entre en enfer.
>
> Je veux aujourd'hui garder ma promesse.
> Plutôt perdre la vie que d'y manquer.
> Mon coeur n'éprouve aucun regret.

Ayant réfléchi de la sorte, le roi partit et s'en retourna auprès de Kalmāṣapāda. Celui-ci, l'apercevant de loin, se réjouit et lui dit: "Tu es un homme de parole qui ne manque pas à ses promesses. Tous les hommes cherchent à épargner leur vie. Tu as eu l'occasion d'échapper à la mort, mais tu es revenu pour accomplir ta promesse. Tu es un grand homme *(mahāpuruṣa)*.

Alors le roi Sutasoma fit l'éloge de la fidélité à lo parole: "Celui qui respecte sa parole, disait-il, est un homme; celui qui y manque n'en est pas un." De toutes manières il loua la véracité *(satyavāda)* et flétrit le mensonge *(mṛṣāvāda)*. Kalmāṣapāda, en l'entendant, conçut une foi pure *(śraddhāviśuddhi)* et dit au roi Sutasoma: "Tu as bien parlé; en retour, je te relâche; tu es libre. Je t'accorde aussi les quatre-vingt-dix-neuf rois [prisonniers avec toi]. Qu'ils retournent, chacun selon son désir, dans leur pays d'origine." Quand il eut ainsi parlé, les cent rois s'en retournèrent.

C'est dans les Jātaka de cette sorte que le Bodhisattva remplit la vertu de moralité.

Chodron (1, 220–22) translates:

> Question. How does the Bodhisattva fulfill the virtue of discipline?
> Answer. By not sparing his life when it is a question of keeping the pure precepts. Thus king Sutasoma, for the sake of the great king Kalmāṣapāda went so far as to offer his life, but did not violate the precepts.
>
> There was once a king called Sutasoma, full of energy, observer of the precepts and always faithful to his given word. One morning he mounted his chariot with his courtesans and entered a garden to walk about. When he left the gates of the city, a certain brahmin who had come to beg said to the king: "The king is very powerful and I am a poor man. May he have pity on me and give me something." The king replied: "I agree. I value the teachings of saints such as yourself; we will make mutual gifts to one another." Having made this promise, the king entered his garden where he bathed and disported himself.
>
> Then a two-winged king named 'Gazelle's Foot' (Kalmāṣapāda) came swiftly and, from the midst of his courtesans, seized the king and flew away with him: one would have said it was the golden-winged bird seizing a serpent in mid-ocean. The women lamented and wept; in the garden, in the city, within and without, there was turmoil and consternation.
>
> Kalmāṣapāda, carrying the king, traveled through space and came to his home where he set Sutasoma down amidst the ninety-nine kings [whom he had already captured]. King Sutasoma began to weep. Kalmāṣapāda said to him: "Great kṣatriya king, why are you crying like a baby? Every man must die; everything composite must decay." King Sutasoma replied: "I am not afraid of death, but I am afraid of not fulfilling my promises. From the time that I was born, I have never lied. This morning, as I was leaving the gates, a certain brahmin came

praise the Dharma [of the precepts] and praise people [who uphold it], be unmovable in your great vows, [92b] call on the names of the Buddhas as your witness and to save you. If your mind is sincere, you will experience the Buddha emitting a ray of the pure light of the precepts, which is able to lead those who have slandered the precepts to be purified. When you encounter this light, the offences of the past and the present are extinguished. This means that "contemplation of the principle" and "right deeds" are in mutual rapport, and each single instance should be analyzed. If phenomenal matters and the principle [of reality] are in perfect harmony 圓, then ultimately you will uphold the precepts, enter the three gates of liberation, and perceive

to me to ask for alms and I promised to return to give him charity. I do not doubt impermanence, but if I disappoint this [brahmin] in his expectation, I am committing a sin) of deception. That is why I am weeping." Kalmāṣapāda said to him: "Your wish will be satisfied. Since you are afraid to break your promise, I allow you to return; you have seven days in which to give alms to the brahmin; after that time, you will return here. If you have not come back in that time, by the power of my wings, I will easily bring you back."

King Sutasama was able to return to his native land and give alms to the brahmin as he wished. He set the crown prince on the throne. Calling his people together, he excused himself in these words: "I know that I have not settled everything; my governing was not [always] according to the Dharma. I recognize your loyalty. If I am not dead by tomorrow, I shall return directly." Throughout the whole country, his people and his family struck their foreheads to the ground trying to keep him, saying: "We want the king to mind his country and to continue his kind protection. He should not worry about Kalmāṣapāda, king of the rākṣasas. We will build an iron castle surrounded by choice soldiers. No matter how powerful Kalmāṣapāda is, we are not afraid of him." But Sutasoma, who disagreed, spoke this stanza:

Faithfulness to your word is the foremost of the commandments;
The man of his word ascends the stairway to heaven.
The man of his word, no matter how small, is great;
The liar goes to hell.
I wish to keep my promise today.
Rather lose your life than break it.
My heart feels no regret.

Having reflected in this way, the king departed and returned to Kalmāṣapāda who, seeing him from afar, rejoiced and said to him: "You are a man of your word who does not break his promises. Every man seeks to save his own life. You had the chance to escape from death, but you came back to fulfill your promise. You are a great man."

Then Sutasoma praised faithfulness to one's word: "The one who keeps his word is a man; he who breaks it is not a man." He praised truth in every way and disparaged falsehood. Listening to him, Kalmāṣapāda developed pure faith and said to king Sutasoma: "You have spoken well; in return I will release you; you are free. I grant you also the ninety-nine kings, [your co-prisoners]. May they return, each as he will, to their own countries." When he had spoken thus, the hundred kings returned [to their homes].

It is in Jātakas such as this that the Bodhisattva fulfills the virtue of discipline.

See also the story of King Śrutasoma as explained in Chappell, *Tien-t'ai Buddhism*, 115.

Buddha-nature. This is called the oil of auxiliary practices for increasing the clear light of the path.

3. The perfection of patience (kṣānti-pāramitā) [92b5]

If you cultivate the precepts in this way, but still do not realize [enlightenment], you should again ponder as follows. These steps on the path each involve the [good] root of mindfulness, the power of mindfulness, mindfulness as a component of awakening, correct mindfulness, and so forth; this is the meaning of [the perfection of] "patience" [or forbearance] 忍. *Kṣānti* [the perfection of patience] encompasses [all of these].

"Right mindfulness" and so forth for the Tripitaka Teachings means forbearance from overcoming [passions] 伏忍. "Right mindfulness" and so forth for the Shared Teachings means the "forbearance from pliantly following [the path]" 柔順忍. "Right mindfulness" and so forth for the Distinct Teachings means "the forbearance of the non-arising [of dharmas]" 無生(法)忍. "Right mindfulness" and so forth for the Perfect Teaching means "the forbearance of quiescent extinction" 寂滅忍.

If a person is strong and steadfast in the power of mindfulness, the bandits of anger cannot gain entrance. If [anger] does gain entrance, this is due either to a lack of mindfulness, or that your mindfulness is not strong enough and so the obscuration of anger is able to arise. [Anger arises in various ways:] it arises either in this life or it arises in your previous life; or you are angry at a companion or guardian, or angry at some current affair; or you persist in a dislike toward some condition in the past; or when [anger] first arises it is a trivial matter, or when [anger] first arises it flames up intensely. If you give rein to this poison of anger, it will subvert you and leave you nothing. If you do not master it, you will be like a snake that bites itself. Anger obstructs hundreds of thousands of Dharma teachings. How can it be that you give rein to it and do not renounce it? You should know that merely understanding the principle [of anger] does not give you the power of patience [to overcome the anger].

Root of mindfulness 念根: one of the "five good roots," part of the thirty-seven steps on the path.

Power of mindfulness 念力: one of the "five powers."

Mindfulness as a component of awakening 念覺分: one of the "seven components of awakening."

Correct mindfulness 正念: one of the parts of the "eightfold noble path."

Forbearance: compare the four types of "forbearance" as they appear previously in the *Mo-ho chih-kuan*, 57b9–11:

> … [various kinds of patience such as] the forbearance that comes from faith 信忍, the forbearance from [pliantly] following [the path [柔] 順忍, [the forbearance of] non-arising無生[忍], and [the forbearance of] quiescent extinction 寂滅[忍],…

If you already know this you should have already deeply awakened repentance and aroused the great [bodhisattva] vows. Humble yourself, as the rivers through which turbid defilements return to the sea, or as a bridge which is trampled on by people and horses. You should [patiently] endure troubles and suffering, as in collecting arrows to shoot them from the firing mound. You should not be hateful or resentful, but be like Pūrṇa, who rejoiced when he was disparaged because his hands were spared, or rejoiced at his early extinction when he was cut with the sword. Those who are without fault 辜 but are still troubled increase even more in the strength of their patience, as wiping gold or polishing a mirror [makes it brighter]. Be like the "Sage of Patience" *(kṣānti-ṛṣī)*, who with staunch tenderness calmly endured [his persecution], be patient yourself and teach others, praise the Dharma

Turbid defilements return to the sea 江海穢濁歸之: or, this could refer specifically to the muddy waters of the Yangtze River flowing to the sea.

Pūrṇa 富樓那: one of the ten major disciples of the Buddha, known for his eloquence in preaching the Dharma. For further details, see the story of Pūrṇa (or Puṇṇa) in the *Miscellaneous Āgama*, T 2.89b17–c18.

Sage of Patience 羼提仙人: see the story of "Kṣāntiṛṣi" in the *Ta chih tu lun*, T 25.166c3–20. Lamotte (*Le Traité* 2, 889–90) translates:

> Le ṛṣi *Tch'an t'i* (Kṣāntiṛṣi), dans une grande forêt, cultivait la patience *(kṣānti)* et pratiquait la bienveillance *(maitrī)*. Un jour, le roi *Kia li* (Kali), suivi de ses courtisanes *(gaṇikā)*, entra dans la forêt pour s'y promener et s'y divertir. Son repas terminé, le roi s'arrêta pour dormir un peu. Les courtisanes se promenant dans la forêt en fleur, aperçurent le ṛṣi, lui présentèrent leurs hommages *(vandana)* et se placèrent de côté. Alors le ṛṣi leur fit l'éloge de la bienveillance et de la patience; ses paroles étaient si belles que ces femmes ne se lassaient pas de l'entendre et restèrent longtemps près de lui. Le roi Kali s'éveillant et ne voyant plus ses courtisanes, saisit son épée *(asipattra)* et suivit leurs traces. Lorsqu'il les vit debout à côté du ṛṣi, sa jalousie amoureuse déborda; les yeux furieux, brandissant son épée, il demanda au ṛṣi: "Que fais-tu là?" Le ṛṣi répondit: "Je suis ici pour cultiver la patience et pratiquer la bienveillance." Le roi lui dit: "Je vais aussitôt te mettre à l'épreuve. Avec mon épée, je te couperai les oreilles *(karṇa)*, le nez *(nāsa)* et jusqu'aux mains *(hasta)* et aux pieds *(pāda)*. Si tu ne t'irrites pas, je saurai que tu cultives la patience." Le ṛṣi répondit: "Fais à ta guise." Alors le roi tira son épée et lui coupa les oreilles, le nez, puis enfin les mains et les pieds, tout en lui demandant: "Ton esprit est-il agité." Le ṛṣi répondait: "Je cultive la bienveillance et la patience, mon esprit n'est pas agité." Le roi lui dit: "Ton corps agit là sans force; tu dis bien que tu n'es pas agité, mais qui pourrait te croire?" Alors le ṛṣi fit ce serment: "Si je cultive vraiment la bienveillance et la patience, que mon sang *(śoṇita)* devienne du lait *(kṣīra)*." Aussitôt son sang se changea en lait; le roi tout stupéfait s'en alla avec ses courtisanes. Mais alors, dans la forêt, une divinité-dragon *(nāga)*, prenant parti pour le ṛṣi, fit tonner, éclairer et lança la foudre; et le roi, atteint par son venin, s'écroula et ne rentra pas à son palais. *C'est pourquoi nous disons qu'il faut exercer la patience envers ses persécuteurs.*

Chodron (2, 694–95) translates:

> The ṛṣi (Kṣāntiṛṣi) was practicing

[of patience] and praise people [who practice it], be unmovable in your great vows, call on the Buddhas of the ten directions as your witness and to save you. The Buddha will emit a ray of the pure light of patience, which can erase and extinguish the many layers of offences and the obstacles of anger from the past and the present, and you can attain a rapport of mindfulness concerning [both] phenomena and the principle [of reality], and fulfill the power of patience with regard to all the different [sense] realms. This is the oil of auxiliary practices for increasing the clear light of the path.

4. The perfection of diligence (vīrya-pāramitā) [92b24]

If you cultivate [the perfection of patience] in this way but still do not realize [enlightenment], then you should again ponder as follows. Four categories of the steps on the path each contain eight diligences. These are all encompassed by *vīrya[-pāramitā]* [the perfection of diligence]. The *Ta chih tu lun* says, "The first three [perfections of giving, upholding the precepts, and

patience and loving-kindness in a great forest. One day, King Kali with his courtesans went into the forest to walk about and amuse themselves. His meal being finished, the king stopped to sleep. The courtesans, who were wandering in the flowering forest, noticed the ṛṣi and went to pay their respects to him. Then the ṛṣi praised loving-kindness and patience to them; his words were so fine that the women could not get enough of them and stayed with him for a long time. King Kali woke up and, not seeing his courtesans, seized his sword and followed their footprints. When he saw them standing by the ṛṣi, his jealousy broke out; with furious eyes and brandishing his sword, he asked the ṛṣi: "What are you doing here?" The ṛṣi replied: "I am here to cultivate patience and practice loving-kindness." The king said: "I will put you to the proof at once. With my sword, I will cut off your ears, nose, hands, and feet. If you do not get angry, I will know that you are cultivating patience." The ṛṣi answered: "Do as you will." Then the king took his sword and cut off his ears, nose, hands and feet, asking him: "Is your mind disturbed?" The ṛṣi answered: "I am cultivating loving-kindness and patience, my mind is not disturbed." The king said: "Your body lies there powerless; you are speaking the truth when you say that you are not disturbed, but nobody would believe you." Then the ṛṣi made this vow: "If I am really developing loving-kindness and patience, may my blood become milk." At once his blood changed into milk; the king was astounded and went away with his courtesans. But then in the forest, a nāga took pity on the ṛṣi, made thunder and lightning and let loose his thunder-bolt; struck by its poison, the king collapsed and died before he reached his palace.

This is why we say that it is necessary to exert patience toward your persecutors.

See also the story of "Kṣāntivādi-ṛṣi" as explained in Chappell, *T'ien-t'ai Buddhism*, 115–16.

Eight diligences 八精進: that is, "diligence" is one of the "five good roots," one of the "five powers," one of the "seven components of awakening," and one of the parts of the "eightfold noble path." It is not clear how "diligence" is taken as of eight types [or, are these related to the eight kinds of forbearance?] [See BT–IV, 456].

The first three are easy to fulfill, and do

patience] are easy to fulfill, and do not require diligence. The later two [perfections of dhyāna meditation and wisdom] are difficult to fulfill and definitely require diligence." It is due to diligence that you attain *bodhi*-wisdom *(saṃbodhi)*. [The *Ta chih tu lun* tells of the time when] "Ānanda taught [the component of] the perception of diligence, and the Buddha arose from his seat"; and [promoted diligence] like that of the [Bodhisattva] Great Giving who scooped up the sea [in search of the wish-fulfilling jewel].

not require diligence. The later two are difficult to fulfill and definitely require diligence 前三易成不須精進後二難成必須精進: see the *Ta chih tu lun*, T 25.172b21–26; Lamotte (*Le Traité* 2, 929–30) has:

> Pour les atteindre, il faut un effort corporel et mental *(kāyikacaitasikābhoga)*, et un empressement sans relâche *(asraṃsana)*. Aussi le Buddha a-t-il dit: "Que mon sang, ma chair, ma graisse et ma moelle se dessèchent, que j'en sois réduit à la peau, aux os et aux muscles; jamais je n'abandonnerai l'énergie." C'est ainsi qu'on parvient à acquérir l'extase et la sagesse; quand on possède ces deux choses, on possède tout. C'est pourquoi l'énergie vient en quatrième place; elle est la racine de l'extase et de la vraie sagesse. Dans les trois premières vertus [don, moralité et patience], il y a bien un peu d'énergie, mais si peu, qu'on n'en parle point.

Chodron (2, 722–23) translates:

> In order to attain them, bodily and mental effort and unrelaxing eagerness are needed. Thus the Buddha said: "May my blood, flesh, fat, and marrow dry up, may I be reduced to skin, bone, and tendons, but never will I abandon exertion." This is how one acquires rapture and wisdom; when one has these two, one possesses all. That is why exertion is in the fourth place; it is the root of rapture and true wisdom. In the first three virtues [generosity, morality and patience], there is indeed some exertion, but so little that we do not speak of it.

Ānanda taught the perception of diligence, and the Buddha arose from his seat 阿難說精進覺佛即起坐 **...**: see the *Ta chih tu lun*, T 25.173c4–8; Lamotte (*Le Traité* 2, 942) translates:

> En outre, lorsque Ānanda prêchait aux bhikṣu les sept Pensées de l'éveil *(sambhodhyaṅga)* et était arrivé à la Pensée de l'éveil nommée énergie *(vīrya)*, le Buddha dit à Ānanda: "Tu parles de la Pensée de l'éveil nommée énergie?" Ānanda répondit, "Oue, *je parle de la Pensée de l'éveil nommée énergie.*" Trois fois [le Buddha posa] la même question, et [Ānanda fit] la même réponse. *Alors le Buddha, s'étant levé de son siège*, dit à Ānanda: "Les hommes qui sauront aimer et pratiquer l'énergie, il n'est rien qu'ils ne peuvent obtenir; ils parviendront infailliblement à l'état de Buddha." C'est ainsi qu'en considérant de toutes manières les avantages de l'énergie, on parvient à augmenter cette énergie.

Chodron (2, 733) translates:

> Moreover, when Ānanda was preaching the seven minds of awakening to the bhikṣus and had come to the mind of awakening called exertion, the Buddha said to Ānanda: "Are you talking about the mind of awakening called exertion?" Ānanda replied "Yes, I am speaking about the mind of awakening called exertion." Three times [the Buddha asked] the same question and [Ānanda made] the same reply. Then rising from his seat, the Buddha said to Ānanda: "People who know, love and practice exertion, there is nothing that they cannot obtain; they will infallibly succeed in reaching buddhahood." It is thus by considering the benefits of exertion in many ways that one succeeds in increasing this energy.

However, now you are dissipated and indolent and indulgent, forgetting your original mind[fulness] and not having [**92c**] any stamina. Even though you are in the hall of meditation [and practicing contemplation], [your thoughts are] filled with miscellaneous evil perceptions; this is called "defilement." A day [of practice] without progress; this is called a "retrogression." Retrogression is the opposite of progress, and defilement is the opposite of purification; how, then, are you able to accord with the principle [of reality]? If your mind is covered with the obstacles of idleness from previous lives, you are like "a crazy drunk elephant running wild without a hook in its nose-holes." In the early, middle, or late evening you do not seek to overcome yourself [through self-denial] or "compete with" [that is, make good use of] your time, and you become more and more lethargic and waste the days and months away. You should then arouse the [bodhisattva] vows, carving them into your bones and engraving them into your heart, dedicating your physical life to the path, thus pushing away death and advancing [closer to enlightenment]. For immeasurable eons you have vainly loved, guarded, and cared for [your physical life], but now to seek samādhi you should be determined to abandon it. In the evening and through the day you should renounce your faults and mistakes *(ādinava)*. Practice the Dharma without indolence, and straighten your body, without thinking that it is dif-

Scooped up the sea 杼海: Ikeda (*Kenkyūchūshaku*, 405) points to a passage in the *Ta chih tu lun*, T 25.174c12–14, which tells of a "Bodhisattva Who Loves Giving" and his dedicated action in trying to scoop up the sea in his search for the wish-fulfilling jewel, as an example of the "perfection of diligence."

Chodron (2, 738) translates:

> Thus the bodhisattva Mahātyāgavat seeking the philosopher's stone (*cintamaṇi*), filtered the water of the ocean using his nerves and his bones, and did not stop working before having found this philosopher's stone; he gave it to beings to ease their sufferings. The bodhisattva thus accomplishes difficult things; this is his virtue of exertion.

A day without progress; this is called a "retrogression" 日不如日名之爲退: lit., "a day [of practice] is not like a day [of practice]," that is, it is without results and as if one has not practiced at all.

Purification 精: note that this is the first character in the compound that translates *vīrya* (diligence) 精進.

A crazy drunk elephant running wild without a hook in its nose-holes 穴鼻無鉤狂醉越逸: see the *Ta chih tu lun*, T 25.184c7–8. These phrases have appeared previously in the *Mo-ho chih-kuan* at 57b13; see note at this passage for details. See also the analogy of the drunk elephant in the *Mahāparinirvāṇa Sūtra*, T 12.756a23–26. This analogy has been referred to previously in the *Mo-ho chih-kuan*; for details and a full translation see note at 49a17.

Early, middle and late evening … waste the days and months away 初中後夜不克己競時蓮復遷延稽度日月: these phrases are ambiguous, and I have given a rather free paraphrase; I follow Ikeda's interpretation (*Gendaigoyaku*, 466; *Kenkyūchūshaku*, 405) rather than Chan-jan (BT–IV, 457–58).

Straighten your body 端直: that is, keep

ficult or troublesome. If you suffer from some disease, do not be troubled by it. Even if you cannot overcome it within one lifetime, [determine that you will] not rest throughout the ages. Be diligent yourself and teach others [to be diligent], guard the Dharma [of diligence] and praise people [who practice it], call on the Buddhas of the ten directions as your witness and to save you. Experience the Buddha's light of diligence, and attain a rapport with the eight kinds of diligence of the contemplation of the principle [of truth]. If you have a rapport with the Tripitaka [Teachings], you will realize the diligence of the "arising of arising." If you have a rapport with the Shared [Teachings], you will realize the diligence of the "non-arising of arising" [that is, emptiness]. If you have a rapport with the Distinct [Teachings], you will realize the diligence of the "arising of non-arising" [that is, conventionality]. If you have a rapport with the Perfect [Teaching], you will realize the firm and strong diligence of the "non-arising of non-arising" [that is, the Middle], open the gate of nirvana, and perceive Buddha nature. This is the oil of auxiliary phenomenal practices for increasing the clear light of contemplation. [Note that] "diligence" has both a shared essence and a distinct essence.

5. *The perfection of dhyāna-meditation (dhyāna-pāramitā)* [92c15]

If you cultivate [diligence] as explained above, but do not attain awakening, you yourself should ponder as follows. The steps on the path of contemplating the principle [of reality] each involve eight kinds of concentration, which are encompassed by the perfection of dhyāna meditation. However, if you just understand this [in the abstract] and really do not yet attain enlightenment, although you speak of the "fully realized meditative states" of the [four] basic [dhyāna concentrations], then the actual practice of concentration is not realized, and although you speak of "spontaneous" [or "actionless"] concentration, the [more basic] Śūraṅgama [Samādhi] is not realized. Those who have no concentration are like people who stumble and fall [even] on flat ground. Or, it may be that you cannot open samādhi because of distractions and restlessness from your past or present life. For this reason

a proper posture, such as sitting with your back straight.

Eight kinds of diligence of the contemplation of the principle 理觀八進: Chan-jan (BT–IV, 459) identifies these eight kinds of diligence with the four options of "arising of arising," "the non-arising of arising," "the arising of non-arising," "the non-arising of non-arising," and the four options of subject and object.

Shared essence and distinct essence 通體列體: the Taishō edition has 列, but the *Bukkyō Taikei* (IV, 459) and Ikeda (*Teihonkundoku*, 502) correct it to 別.

Eight kinds of concentration 八定: Chan-jan (BT–IV, 459) identifies these as the "four dhyāna stages" and the "four realms of formlessness."

you should singlemindedly determine [to attain] the fruit [of Buddhahood], and [meditate] in the early, middle, and late evening with your body straight and your mind quiet. If tired, tormenting, or false conceptions arise, they should be extinguished quickly. Practice dhyāna meditation yourself, and teach it to others, praise the Dharma [of meditation] and praise people [who practice it], be unmovable in your great vow, and keep it until your life is exhausted, and into the next life do not stop if you are not enlightened. Call on the Buddhas of the ten directions as your witness and to save you. Experience the Buddha's light of concentration, and destroy the obstacles of distraction and restlessness. Then you will expose and arouse [the fruits of] the actual practice of dhyāna meditation 事禪, and attain a rapport with the fourfold contemplations. The *Ta chih tu lun* comments on the perfection of dhyāna meditation, first listing the various methods of dhyāna meditation, then clarifying that it is unobtainable and thus manifesting the features of these virtues *(pāramitā)*, and then widely discussing the nine considerations [of decaying corpses], the eight mindfulnesses, and so forth as all proceeding forth from [the practice of] dhyāna meditation. The methods of dhyāna meditation are exceedingly numerous; here I will only take up five categories as [examples of] auxiliary practices of the path.

1. Counting your breaths [92c27]

If, when you practice dhyāna meditation, your mind is full of [negative] notions and perceptions and you are surrounded by contact with the three poisons [of greed, anger, and delusion], you should use [the method of] counting your breaths to control [and heal] them. If you cannot count, you know that you have lost [control of] your thoughts. If you lose [control], then seek to regain it by starting to count again from the beginning. This prevents distraction and focuses the mind, **[93a]** so that these matters can be well controlled. By making the thoughts abide in this way, people can arouse the concentrations of the realm of desires, and so forth up to and including being able to realize the concentration of the seventh level. If you

Fourfold contemplations 四觀: that is, of the Fourfold Teachings of the Tripitaka, Shared, Distinct, and Perfect.

***Ta chih tu lun* comments on the perfection of dhyāna** 大論釋禪度 **...**: this refers to the long section in the *Ta chih tu lun* which discusses the perfection of dhyāna meditation at T 25.180b–190a; see the chapter on "La vertu d'extase" in Lamotte, *La Traité* 2, 984–1057.

Five categories 五門: the following five methods (counting the breaths, the contemplation of impurity, compassion, and causes and conditions, and mindfulness of the Buddha) are the same as the "five contemplations for putting the mind at rest." These are discussed again later in the *Mo-ho chih-kuan* at 117b.

Concentration of the seventh level 七依定: Ikeda (*Gendaigoyaku*, 467) translates

are not able to attain *prajñā*-wisdom and [skill in] means, you will realize the Dharma of ordinary people; if you attain [skill in] means, you will realize the Mahāyāna. Therefore the *Sūtra on Petitioning Avalokiteśvara* says, "If you concentrate your mind by counting your breaths, you can see a Buddha in the pore of a hair, dwell in the Śūraṅgama [Samādhi], and attain the state of non-retrogression." By means of counting your breaths you can open the gate of liberation, and gain a rapport with the eight kinds of concentration of the Tripitaka [Teachings], up to and including a rapport with the eight kinds of concentration of the spontaneous [Perfect Teaching]. These actual practices are like the oil of auxiliary practices for increasing the light of the path.

2. Contemplation of impurity [93a6]

If you become fixated on the female [or male] form [in an erotic sense] and besotted with it in your thoughts, with deluded attachments so that you will not let them go, then you should use the "contemplation of impurity" to control and heal [these matters]. Contemplate the person you lust for as having the features of the first stage after death.

You have just been talking agreeably [with this person], but suddenly he or she is gone; his or her body becomes cold and changes color, worms and pus flow out, it stinks of impurity, and overflows with defilements. [Such corpses] are thrown away onto funeral mounds, like rotting wood. What was formerly loved passionately is now nowhere to be seen. Such a foul thing has caused you much grief. When you realize the error of your desires, your lustful thoughts will cease. The remaining eight considerations [of a decaying corpse] will also help you control and heal your lustful desires.

this as the "samādhi of the place of nonexistence" (*ākiṃcanyāyatana*) 無所有処定, the third level of the formless realm. In other words, all the levels of the triple realm of desires, form, up to the third (of four) levels of the formless realm.

If you concentrate your mind by counting your breaths, you can see a Buddha in the pore of a hair, dwell in the Śūraṅgama, and attain the state of non-retrogression 若數息心定毛孔見佛住首楞嚴得不退轉: see the *Sūtra on Petitioning Avalokiteśvara:* at T 20.36c7ff. mentions counting the breaths while practicing meditation, but not the other aspects quoted here.

Fixated 緣: or, "come in contact with," not necessarily physically but in the broader sense of "experiencing," including seeing or imagining.

Contemplation of impurity 不淨觀: to contemplate the impurity of various aspects of life, such as the impurity of the female (and male) body, the impurity of a corpse, and so forth, so as to overcome sexual lust and attachment to the physical body.

Stage after death 初死之相: as in the "nine considerations" of a decaying corpse. The first stage is to contemplate the corpse as it begins to bloat, then it turns a bluish hue, and so forth.

The *Ta chih tu lun* says that those who are full of lust should contemplate the nine considerations [of a decaying corpse]. If you do not gain mastery over these things due to your conditions, you should contemplate the [eight] liberations [or renunciations] *(vimokṣa)*; if you cannot apply these conditions broadly, you should contemplate [the eight levels of] domination *(abhibhu)*; if you are not able to convert and change [with these levels], you should contemplate the ten spheres of the totalization of objects *(ālambanakṛtsnaspharaṇāt)*. If you are fearful, you should cultivate the eight mindfulnesses *(anusmṛti)*. These all require the [contemplation of] impurity as the first step, and they all involve controlling and curing the fires of lustful passion, opening the gate of liberation, and realizing a rapport with the four types of eight concentrations. These are the oil of auxiliary practices for increasing the clear light [of contemplation and the path].

3. Contemplation of compassion [93a17]

If you become fixated on hateful anger, you should constantly use compassionate thoughts to control and heal this. Above we discussed the perfection of patience in general for controlling [and healing], but now [I will discuss] distinctly the boundless demeanor of friendliness 慈無量心 *(maitrī)*. The other three [boundless demeanors of compassion, joy, and equanimity] can be applied [in the same way] as you wish.

Those who are full of lust should contemplate the nine considerations 多婬者令觀九想: see the extended discussion of the "nine considerations" in the *Ta chih tu lun* at T 25.217a–218b. For details, see Lamotte (*Le Traité* 3, 1311–26), which is too long to quote here, as are the detailed explanations of the various categories that follow. This again demonstrates the reliance on the *Ta chih tu lun* for Chih-i's teachings.

[Eight] liberations 背捨: see the extended discussion in the *Ta chih tu lun*, T 25.215a1–216a3. For details, see Lamotte, *Le Traité* 3, 1291–99.

[Eight] levels of domination 勝處: these are the levels of contemplation, after attaining the eight liberations, wherein one increasingly attains mastery and domination over pure and impure realms. See the extended discussion in the *Ta chih tu lun*, T 25.216a3–b29. For details, see Lamotte, *Le Traité* 3, 1299–1304.

The ten spheres of the totalization of objects 十一切處: contemplations or meditations for becoming free of the passionate afflictions of the triple world; meditations on earth, water, fire, wind, blue, yellow, red, white, emptiness, and consciousness; the totality of contemplations; follows the attainment of the eight liberations and eight dominations. See the extended discussion in the *Ta chih tu lun*, T 25.216b29–217a4. For details, see Lamotte, *Le Traité* 3, 1304–7.

Eight mindfulnesses 八念: see the *Ta chih tu lun*, T 25.218c–228c; for details, see Lamotte, *Le Traité* 3, 1329–1429. For T'ien-t'ai definitions and lists of these various categories of contemplations, see the *Introduction to Graded Themes of the Dharma Realm* (T no. 1925).

To control and heal through the boundless demeanor of friendliness is as follows. When you come in contact with the suffering of sentient beings, you should deeply arouse pity [with regard to their] pain and wish to extract their suffering. Enter into concentrated samādhi with these [friendly] thoughts in mind, and realize a rapport with compassion 悲. "Friendliness" 慈 means to wish that sentient beings attain bliss; with these thoughts enter into and realize a rapport with a concentration of friendliness. "Thoughts of joy" mean to wish that sentient beings attain bliss. Give rise to great joy, and with these thoughts in mind enter into a rapport with a concentration of joy. "Thoughts of abandonment" means to abandon thoughts of passionate hate and dwell in the contemplation of equanimity 平等觀. With these thoughts in mind, enter into and realize a rapport with a concentration of abandonment [or equanimity]. Attaining these four samādhis means that you will not arouse any angry thoughts toward sentient beings. This will be discussed again below.

4. Contemplation of causes and conditions [93a25]

If you become fixated on mistaken perverted views, you should utilize the contemplation of causes and conditions 因緣觀 to control and heal these matters. The Abhidharma says to destroy [the notion of] the self by means of [analyzing] the sense realms, but here [in the T'ien-t'ai Mahāyāna tradition] we destroy [the notion of] the self by means of [contemplating the arising and perishing of] causes and conditions. Through the three times [of the past, present, and future], deconstruct [the two extremes of] eternalism and annihilationism; in the two times [of the present and future] deconstruct [the notion of] the self; and in a single thought deconstruct [and destroy] [the notion of a substantial self-]nature. If you realize this concentration, you attain a rapport with the contemplation of the principle [of reality], and this is an auxiliary practice to open the gate of nirvana.

5. Contemplation of mindfulness of the Buddha [93a29]

If the offence of [too much] sleep arises and obstructs [your progress on] the

As you wish: but Chih-i goes ahead and discusses all four of the boundless demeanors—friendliness, compassion, joy, and abandonment or equanimity—rather than specifically that of "friendliness."

Abandonment 捨: or "equanimity." See note above on the translation of *upekṣa*.

Discussed again below: see the discussion of the "contemplation of friendliness" at *Mo-ho chih-kuan* 124c–125c.

Abhidharma: Chan-jan (BT–IV, 465–66) points to a passage in the *Abhidharma-vibhāṣā-śāstra*, T 28.908b, but this could be just a reference to the way things are done in the "Abhidharma" tradition, not necessarily a reference to this specific text.

path, you should use the contemplation of mindfulness of the Buddha 念佛觀 to control and heal [these matters]. [**93b**] By coming in contact with the featureless features 無相之相 of the Buddha of transformation, the features of these conditions [that is, the obstructions of the path] will become clarified, and you can destroy the offences that obstruct the path, perceive the Buddhas of the ten directions, achieve rapport with the contemplation of the principle [of reality], and open the gate of nirvana.

6. The perfection of prajñā-wisdom (prajñā-pāramitā) [93b2]

If you cultivate [these five contemplations] as explained above, but still do not realize [the path], or if they are not appropriate for you, then you yourself should ponder as follows. The contemplation of the principle [of reality] includes[, from among the thirty-seven steps on the way,] the four mindfulnesses, the root of wisdom, the power of wisdom, the components of awakening of discernment and joy, right views and right discrimination—in this way, ten dharmas are encompassed by the perfection of wisdom.

Ten dharmas are encompassed by the perfection of wisdom 如是十法智度所攝: see the *Ta chih tu lun*, T 25.198b8–18, although the list of ten is somewhat different. Lamotte (*Le Traité* 3, 1145–47) has:

> Ces trente-sept auxiliaires ont dix choses *(dravya)* pour racines *(mūla)*. Quelles sont ces dix? 1. La foi 信 *(śraddhā)*, 2. la moralité 戒 *(śīla)*, 3. la conception 思惟 *(saṃkalpa)*, 4. l'énergie 精進 *(vīrya)*, 5. l'attention 念 *(smṛti)*, 6. la concentration 定 *(samādhi)*, 7. la sagesse 慧 *(prajñā)*, 8. la relaxation 除 *(praśrabdhi)*, 9. la joie 喜 *(prīti)*, 10. l'indifférence 捨 *(upekṣa)*.
>
> 1. La foi constitue: a. la faculté foi *(śrad-dhendriya)*; b. la force de foi *(śradd-hā-bala)*.
>
> 2. La moralité constitue: a. la parole correcte *(samyagvāc)*; b. l'action correcte *(samyakkarmānta)*; c. la manière de vivre correcte *(samyagājīva)*.
>
> [3. La conception constitue: la conception correcte *(samyaksaṃkalpa)*.]
>
> 4. L'énergie constitue: a. les quatre efforts corrects *(samyakprachāna)*; b. la faculté d'énergie *(vīryendriya)*; c. la force d'énergie *(vīrtyabala)*; d. le membre-de-l'illumination appelé énergie *(vīryasaṃbodhyaṅga)*; e. le [membre-du-chemin] dit effort correct *(samyag-vyāyāma)*.
>
> 5. L'attention constitue: a. la faculté d'attention *(smṛtīndriya)*; b. la force d'attention *(smṛtibala)*; c. le membre-de-l'illumination appelé attention *(smṛtisaṃbodhyaṅga)*; d. le [membre-du-chemin] dit attention correcte *(samyaksmṛti)*.
>
> 6. La concentration constitue: a. les quatre fondements du pouvoir magique *(ṛddhipāda)*; b. la faculté de concentration *(samādhīndriya)*; c. la force de concentration *(samādhibala)*; d. le membre-de-l'illumination appelé concentration *(samādhisaṃbodhyāṅga)*; e. le [membre-du-chemin] dit concentration correcte *(samyaksamādhi)*.
>
> 7. L sagesse constitue: a. les quatre fixations-de-l'attention *(smṛtyupasthāna)*; b. la faculté de sagesse *(prajñendriya)*; c. la force de sagesse *(prajñābala)*; d. le membre-de-l'illumination appelé discernement des dharma *(dharmapravi-caya-saṃbodhyaṅga)*; e. le [membre-du-chemin] dit vue correcte *(samyagdṛṣṭi)*.
>
> [8. La relaxation constitue le membre-de-l'illumination appelé relaxation *(praśrabdhisaṃbodhyaṅga)*.

1. Contemplation of the four perverted views [93b5–94a8]

As for this contemplation of the principle [of reality], the reason that your understanding is not clear is because of your habit of wandering in deluded ignorance in the past and present, with your spirit covered in darkness. Therefore you have not been able to manifest [the realization of] samādhi. You should repent and reform, and arouse the great [bodhisattva] vows, make your contemplation of [actual phenomena] clear, and destroy the four perverted views.

1. The perverted view of purity [93b8]

[How do you destroy the perverted view that the things of this world are pure?] Contemplate your body precisely, from your head to your feet, and realize that [it is impure, from] your seeds being impure up to and including [the body] being ultimately impure [in death], [all together] five types of impurity. That is, this physical body is produced by other bodies, through

9. La joie constitue la membre-de-l'illumination appelé joie *(prītisaṃbodhyaṅga)*.
10. L'indifférence constitue la membre-de-l'illumination appelé indifférence *(upekṣsāsaṃbodhyaṅga)*].

Chodron (3, 944–45) translates:

These thirty-seven auxiliaries have ten things as roots. What are these ten? 1. faith, 2. morality, 3. thought, 4. exertion, 5. mindfulness, 6. concentration, 7. wisdom, 8. relaxation, 9. joy, 10. equanimity.
1. Faith constitutes: a. the faculty of faith; b. the power of faith.
2. Morality constitutes: a. right speech; b. right action; c. right livelihood.
3. Thought constitutes: right thinking.
4. Exertion constitutes: a. the four right efforts; b. the faculty of exertion; c. the power of exertion; d. the factor-of-enlightenment called exertion; e. the [factor-of-the path] called right effort.
5. Mindfulness constitutes: a. the faculty of mindfulness; b. the power of mindfulness; c. the factor-of-enlightenment called mindfulness; d. the [factor-of-the-path] called right mindfulness.
6. Concentration constitutes: a. the four foundations of magical power; b. the faculty of concentration; c. the power of concentration; d. the factor-of-enlightenment called concentration; e. the [factor-of-the-path] called right concentration.
7. Wisdom constitutes: a. the four foundations of mindfulness; b. the faculty of wisdom; c. the power of wisdom; d. the factor-of-enlightenment called discernment of dharmas; e. the [factor-of-the-path] called right view.
8. Relaxation constitutes the factor-of-enlightenment called relaxation.
9. Joy constitutes the factor-of-enlightenment called joy.
10. Equanimity constitutes the factor-of-enlightenment called equanimity.

Four perverted views 四顛倒: the mistaken beliefs that the things of this world are permanent, blissful, selfhood, and pure, rather than transient, full of suffering, without selfhood, and impure. The following section analyzes these issues.

Five types of impurity 五種不淨: of the human body are 1. impurity of the place of birth 生處, 2. impurity of seeds 種子, 3. impurity of its nature 自性, 4. impurity of its features 自相, and 5. ultimate 究竟 impurity (in death). The list is from the *Ta chih tu lun*, T 25.198c22–24. Lamotte (*Le Traité* 3, 1151) translates the context:

the disgorging of red and white fluids and the merging of two drops of liquid, in which a consciousness is entrusted, and which then develops its own character. This is called the "impurity of seeds."

While dwelling in the womb, [the fetus] is steeped in defiled fluid, suddenly suspended or suddenly under pressure, at times hot and at times cold, [completely] changing every week, thus nursed [in the womb] for ten months. When the "six protrusions" are actualized, the form and features

> Question. — Comment obtenir ces quatre fixations-de-l'attention?
> Réponse. — Le yogin établi sur la moralité pure *(viśuddhaśīla)* et exerçant l'énergie *(vīrya)* de tout son coeur *(ekacittena)*, considère *(anupaśyati)* la quintuple impureté du corps *(kāyāśuci)*. Quelles sont ces cinq impuretés? 1. L'impureté de l'endroit de la naissance *(jātisyhānāśuci)*; 2. l'impureté de la semence *(bījāśuci)*; 3. l'impureté de la nature propre *(svabhāvā-śuci)*; 4. l'impureté des caractères propres *(svalakṣaṇāśuci)*; 5. l'impureté de l'aboutissement final *(paryavasānāśuci)*.

Chodron (3, 947) translates:

> Question. How does one obtain these four foundations of mindfulness?
> Answer. The yogin who is established in pure morality and is practicing exertion wholeheartedly considers the fivefold impurity of the body. What are these five impurities? 1. The impurity of birthplace; 2. the impurity of seed; 3. the impurity of intrinsic nature; 4. the impurity of intrinsic characteristics; 5. the impurity of the final outcome.

The impurity of seeds 種子不淨: this entire section is based on the section on the five types of impurity of the body already quoted above from the *Ta chih tu lun*, T 25.198c–199a, although many of the details vary. The explanation of the "impurity of seeds" is found at 199a2–8; Lamotte (*Le Traité* 3, 1153–54) translates:

> L'impureté de la semence *(bījāśuci)*. — Le père et la mère *(mātāpitṛ)*, par le vent *(vāta)* des conceptions trompeuses *(mṛṣāvikalpa)* et des réflexions fausses *(mithyāmanasikāra)*, soufflent sur le feu *(agni)* du désir sexuel *(rāga)*; le sang *(rudhira)*, la moille *(majjan)* et la graisse *(vasā)* s'écoulent, s'échauffent et se transforment en sperme. La connaissance-germe *(vijñānabīja)* conditionnée par les actes antérieurs *(pūrvakarman)* se fixe dans le sang *(śoṇita)* et le sperme blanchâtre *(śukra)*. Voilà ce qu'on appelle la semence du corps *(kāyabīja)*. C'est ainsi qu'il est dit:
>
> La semence du corps est impure,
> Elle n'a rien d'une substance précieuse,
> Elle n'est pas issue d'une pure blancheur,
> Elle sort seulement des voies urinaires.

Chodron (3, 950) translates:

> The impurity of the seed. – By means of the wind of deceptive concepts and wrong thoughts, the father and mother blow upon the fire of sexual desire; blood, marrow, and fat escape, get hot and are changed into sperm. The seed-consciousness conditioned by previous actions settles in the blood and whitish sperm. That is what is called the seed of the body. Thus it is said:
>
> The seed of the body is impure,
> It is not a precious substance,
> It has not come from pure innocence,
> It has come only from the urinary pathways.

Six protrusions 六皰 lit. "six pimples" The six limbs or six physical features that indicate the completion of the human form; the head, two feet, two arms, and the belly as listed in the *Ta chih tu lun*, 198c25? (Lamotte, however, translates these as numbering five.)

[of the human body] are complete, and the days and months are full [and the pregnancy reaches its full term], [the fetus] turns and faces the "birth canal" [to be born]. The *Ta chih tu lun* says that this [human] body is not born through a magical transformation, nor is it born on a lotus flower [as in a pure land], but merely emerges from the urinary tract. This place is vile and obscene 卑猥, in the lower and base parts [of the body]. This is called the "impurity of the place of [the fetus's] place of abiding."

After birth, having emerged [from the womb], [the fetus] lies sleeping in defiled excrement. [The child] is nurtured at the mother's breast, and as it grows from a child to an adult, the ear collects clumps of wax, the eyes flow with tears and grow dim, the holes of the nose drip with snot, the mouth stinks with bad breath, the grime from the head piles up like a shallow bog of manure. The piquant juice [that flows] from the buttocks and armpits is like

Emerges from the urinary tract 從尿道出: this is not biologically accurate, but I give a literal translation. See the *Ta chih tu lun*, T 25.198c28 and 199a7. The case for the impurity of the fetus seems to rely heavily on its proximity to the urinary tract.

Impurity of [the fetus's] place of abiding 住處不淨: In the *Ta chih tu lun* this is called the "impurity of the place of birth" 生處不淨. The explanation for this impurity is found at 198c25–199a2; Lamotte (*Le Traité* 3, 1151–52; see for detailed notes) translates:

> Qu'est-ce que l'impureté de l'endroit de la naissance *(jātisthānāśuci)*? Tête *(śiras)*, pieds *(pāda)*, ventre *(udara)*, dos *(pṛṣṭha)*, flancs *(pārśva)*, c'est un ensemble de choses impures *(aśuddhavastusāmagrī)* qu'on dénomme corps de la femme *(strīkāya)*.
> Intérieurement *(adhyātmam)*, il contient un estomac *(āmāśaya)*, un ventre *(pakvāśaya)*, des excréments *(viṣ)*, de l'urine *(mūtra)* et [autres] impuretés *(aśuci)*. Extérieurement *(bahirdhā)*, il y a un vent *(vāta)* conditionné par les passions *(kleśa)* et les actes *(karman)*, vent qui souffle sur la connaissance-germe *(vijñānabīja)* et l'introduit à l'intérieur des deux viscères. Et durant huit ou neuf mois, la connaissance-germe séjourne dans une fosse d'excréments et d'urine *(niṇmūtragarta)*. C'est ainsi qu'il est dit:
>
> Ce corps est fétide et infect:
> Ce n'est pas d'une fleur qu'il est né,
> Il ne provient pas non plus du Campaka,
> Et il ne sort pas d'une montagne de joyaux.

Chodron (3, 948) translates:

> What is the impurity of the place of birth? Head, feet, belly, back, thighs, that which is called a woman's body is a collection of impure things.
> Inwardly, it contains a stomach, a belly excrement, urine and [other] impurities. Outwardly, there is a wind conditioned by the afflictions and actions, a wind that blows on the seed-consciousness and introduces it within the two viscera. During eight or nine months, the seed-consciousness dwells in a pit of excrement and urine. Thus it is said:
>
> This body is foul and revolting:
> It is not from a flower that it is born,
> Neither does it come from Campaka,
> And it does not come from a jewel mountain.
>
> This is what is called the impurity of the place of birth.

the dripping of urine. When you put clothes on your body, they are [soiled] as if smeared with oil. This is called the "impurity of its features."

Inside [the human body] is only an accumulation of excrement and urine, an accumulation of pus, an accumulation of blood, accumulations of fat and marrow and so forth. The large and small intestines, the fat, the flesh that sticks to the bones, and the muscles are bound up together and smeared with blood; it is base to expose it, it is a place that stinks, and a place where worms gather. Even if you use all the water in the ocean to wash it, you cannot purify it. The *Ta chih tu lun* says of this [human] body that it is not like Mount Malaya, from which you are able to produce sandalwood. From when it is small until it is big, it is by nature impure. It is analogous to defiled excrement, which stinks whether there is a lot of it or only a little. This is called the "impurity of its nature."

Impurity of its features 自相不淨: the explanation for this impurity is found at 199a15–21; Lamotte (*Le Traité* 3, 1154–55) translates:

> L'impureté des caractères propres *(svalakṣaṇāśuci)*. — Ce corps, par ses neuf portes *(navadvāra)*, secrète toujours l'impureté: les yeux *(akṣi)* versent la chassie *(akṣigūthaka)* et les larmes *(aśru)*; les oreilles *(karṇa)* produisent le cérumen *(karṇagūthaka)*; le nez *(nāsā)* contient la morve *(siṃghāṇaka)*; la bouche *(mukha)* laisse passer la salive *(lālā)* et le vomi *(vāntīkṛta)*; l'anus *(guda)* et l'urètre *(mūtramārga)* évacuent constamment les excréments *(viṣ)* et l'urine *(mūtra)*; et les pores des poils *(romakūpa)* suintent l'impureté. C'est ainsi qu'il est dit:
>
> Toutes sortes de choses impures
> Remplissent l'intérieur de corps.
> Toujours il coule sans arrêt,
> Pareil à un sac-filtre contenant des saletés.

Chodron (3, 951) translates:

> The impurity of intrinsic characteristics. – This body with its nine gates is always secreting impurity: the eyes spill out rheum and tears; the ears produce wax; the nose contains snot; the mouth has saliva and vomit; the anus and the urethra constantly empty out excrement and urine; and the hair-pores sweaty impurity. Thus it is said:
>
> All kinds of impure things
> Fill the interior of the body.
> It flows ceaselessly
> Like a filter-sack containing dirt.

Flesh that sticks to the bones 膕膜: following the explanation of the *Kōgi* (BT–IV, 470). The terms could also be understood as "brain tissue," but the *Kōgi*'s explanation fits better in context.

Mount Malaya 摩羅延山: a mountain in south India known for the production of sandalwood; see *Ta chih tu lun*, T 25.191b27–29. This has been referred to previously; see the note at *Mo-ho chih-kuan* 23c23.

This is explained further in the *Mahāparinirvāṇa Sūtra*, T 12.840b2:

> Great King, it is like the waxing and waning of the moon, the salty taste of the ocean, and Mount Malaya; these are not matters that have been produced by someone.

The section that follows (840b3–6) has been quoted previously in the *Mo-ho chih-kuan* at 80a24. However, it does not seem to fit the context here. Ikeda (*Kenkyūchūshaku*, 407) merely states: "this is a mountain known for the production of sandalwood."

Impurity of its nature 自性不淨: The

Once life comes to an end, the provisional [body] returns to its original form [of the four basic elements]. Its "wind" [or spirit, breath] is gone, its "fire" [or heat] is cooled, its "earth" is broken apart, and its "water" flows away. It is chewed on by worms and pecked apart by birds, the head and hands are torn apart [from the torso] and [the innards] flow outside [the body]. Even if you are upwind, the stench can be perceived at a distance of three or five *li*. This malignant humour is rancid and fetid and is an affront to people's noses and breath. The malignant color of dark and bloody [flesh] defiles people's eyes. This is worse than a dead dog. This is called the "ultimate [final] impurity" [of death].

explanation for this impurity is found at 199a8–15; Lamotte (*Le Traité* 3, 1154) has:

> L'impureté de la nature propre *(svabhāvāśuci)*. — Des pieds à la tête et par les quatre côtés, le corps est unc vile guenille. Tout ce qui est en lui est rempli d'impuretés. Ornez-le d'habits, baignex-le d'eau parfumée, nourrissez-le de mets supérieurs et d'aliments aux multiples saveurs, au bout d'une nuit, tout cela sera impur. À supposer même que vous le vêtissiez d'habits célestes *(divyavastra)* et que vous le nourrissiez d'aliments célestes *(divyāhāra)*, tout cela, à cause du corps lui-même, deviendra impur. Que dire alors si vous ne lui donnez que des vêtements et des aliments humains? C'est ainsi qu'il est dit:
>
> Formé de terre, d'eau, de feu et de vent,
> Il transforme tout en impuretés.
> Videz la mer pour en baigner le corps.
> Vous serez incapable de le nettoyer.

Chodron (3, 950–51) translates:

> The impurity of intrinsic nature. – From head to toe and on all four sides, the body is a lowly rag. Everything in it is full of impurities. Decorate it with garments, bathe it with perfumed water, nourish it with the best dishes and food of many flavors, at the end of one night all of it will be impure. Even if that you clothe it in celestial garments and feed it with celestial food, because of the body itself, all of it will become impure. Then what can be said if you give it only human garments and human clothes? Thus it is said:
>
> Formed from earth, water, fire and wind,
> It transforms everything into impurities.
> Empty the sea to bathe the body,
> Still you will be unable to clean it.

Original form 還本: that is, the four basic elements (wind, fire, earth, and water), of which the human body is composed. These decompose and return to their original, basic state: "ashes to ashes, dust to dust."

Ultimate impurity 究竟不淨: the explanation for this impurity is found at 199a22–28; Lamotte (*Le Traité* 3, 1155) translates:

> L'impureté de l'aboutissement final *(paryavasānāśuci)*. — Jeté au feu *(agni)*, le corps devient cendre *(bhasman)*; dévoré par les ensectes *(kṛmi)*, il devient fumier *(purīṣa)*; placé en terre, il pourrit, se décompose et devient terre; mis dans l'eau, il enfle et pourrit, ou il est mangé par les insectes aquatiques. Entre tous les cadavres *(kuṇapa)*, celui de l'homme est le plus impur: ses impuretés *(aśucidharma)* seront exposées au long à propos des neuf notions *(navasaṃjñā)*. C'est ainsi qu'il est dit:
>
> Examinez minutieusement ce corps:
> Il aboutit nécessairement à la mort.
> Difficile à ménager, il ne rend rien en retour,
> Ingrat comme un vil personnage.

Chodron (3, 952) translates:

In this way [contemplating] the five types [of impurity] in all cases involves the contemplation of real [actual things], and is not a matter of contemplation for attaining an abstract understanding. How can you conclude that there is anything pure in [the human body]? You wear attractive clothes and eat delectable food to lovingly protect and nourish [your body] [**93c**]; you stroke your head and wipe your neck to sustain this poisonous body. This is analogous to dung beetles rolling up crude excrement into a ball. People [who fuss over their bodies] are also like this. They love and care for their physical body and do not weary of it, nor can they escape it, until they die. Because they nurture their physical body, they produce various offences. If you know these faults and diseases and that [these things] are impure from beginning to end, then you are able to destroy the perverted view [that things of this world are] pure.

2. *The perverted view of bliss* [93c4]

Again, [how do you destroy the perverted view that the things of this world are blissful?] You should know that the body is made up of the four great elements [of earth, water, fire, and wind]. Two [fire and wind] rise, and two [earth and water] sink, and their characteristics are mutually opposing. Earth restrains water, and water brightens earth. Wind scatters earth, and earth obstructs wind. Water extinguishes fire, and fire boils water. Thus they mutually intrude on each other, like four snakes placed together in a box. It is like a thorn in a wound, causing constant suffering. Where is there any bliss in this? In addition, there is hunger and thirst and cold and heat, and it is as if you are beaten with a whip and bound by shackles [as you pass] from birth through old age, sickness, and death. This is the "suffering of suffering." For the four elements to mutually intrude on each other, and mutually destroy each other, is called the "suffering of destruction." For things to flow

The impurity of the final outcome. (Thrown on the fire), the body becomes ash; devoured by insects it becomes dung; placed in the earth, it decays, decomposes, and becomes earth; put into the water, it swells up and decays or it is eaten by water-insects. Of all corpses, that of man is the most impure: his impurities will be explained at length in reference to the nine concepts. Thus it is said:

> Examine the body minutely:
> It ends up necessarily in death.
> Difficult to control, it gives nothing in return,
> Ungrateful like a lowly individual.

Four snakes 四蛇: this image is from the *Ta chih tu lun*, T 25.145b9–13, which was quoted above at *Mo-ho chih-kuan* 49b10. This passage compares the four elements to four poisonous snakes.

Suffering 苦: these are the traditional "three types of suffering" 三苦 *(tri-duḥkhatā)*: suffering from coming in contact with what is unpleasant, suffering from losing that which is pleasant or dear to you, and the suffering you feel from experiencing constant change.

and flare up [uncontrollably] from thought to thought is called the "suffering of activity" *(saṃskāra-duḥkha)*. You may arbitrarily give rise to thoughts of bliss within the world of suffering, but if you clearly perceive these features of suffering, [you will realize that] this [situation] is like a thorn sticking in a wound that constantly throbs with pain, and it should not be possible, with this body, to arouse even a single thought of the perverted view [that this world is] blissful.

3. The perverted view of permanence [93c12]

Again, [how do you destroy the perverted view that the things of this world are permanent?] You should contemplate as follows. Your ignorance from the past and your good and evil deeds spur or constrict your mind-consciousness, compelling it to reenter the womb [for another rebirth]. Like a bird that is captured and put in a cage, you may wish to escape, but cannot. Your mind-consciousness is also like this. The four elements are its cage, and it is as if bound with ropes. The mind has a cage of form *(rūpa)* but is not limited in the places that it reaches. However, as long as it has not severed the ropes of karmic deeds, it returns again [to this world] as soon as it has left. If the cage is broken open and the bonds severed, it can leave without returning, but the empty cage still remains so this [cage should be] destroyed and these [bonds] released. If you keep leaving the cage and entering the cage, you should destroy the "seal" 印 [that is, the cage itself] and fulfill the text [of the Dharma teachings] and not dwell there for even a single thought. Again, the spirit of the wind [or "breath"] is dependent on the body; this is called the inhaling and exhaling of the breath. When this breath is removed and fades, it is exhaled and the inhaling cannot be maintained. The Abhidharma says that "life is neither a dharma of matter *(rūpa)* nor mind." *The Great Collection of Sūtras* says, "The exhaling and inhaling of breath is called 'life-force.'" If even one breath does not "return," this is called the end of life. [It is said that] a bhikṣu said to the Buddha, "One cannot maintain [your own life alone] for seven days, and cannot maintain the exhaling and inhaling of your breath," and the Buddha replied, "Well said. This is to well cultivate [the truth of] transience."

Spur or constrict your mind-consciousness 驅縛心識: this phrase is very terse and vague. Ikeda's translation (*Gendaigoyaku*, 471) is also very interpretive and free.

The Abhidharma says that "Life is neither a dharma of matter nor mind" 命是非色非心法: the source for this Abhidharma teaching is not known.

The exhaling and inhaling of breath is called "life-force" 出入息名壽命: a phrase from *The Great Collection of Sūtras*, T 13.164b9–10.

One cannot maintain … cultivate the truth of transience 比丘白佛。不保七日乃至不保出入息。佛言。善哉。善修無常: see the

Again, contemplate karmic deeds as your enemy, as crows fight over meat. A sūtra says, "Evil that arises even for a brief moment *(kṣana)* [results in] the misfortune of falling into [the lowest] Avici hell." A short passing of time can bring about heavy karma; how much more so a long night of evil thoughts. Karma is unlimited; karma is like a hateful debt that is always stalking the person for relief. If you rightfully repay this debt, this does not draw in the other remaining karma. As the repayment comes to an end, the other karmic debts vie for attention. As you go, another remains, without end. The murderous demon of transiency does not make distinctions as to the vigorous or wise; [life, and the things of this world] are fragile, infirm, and unreliable. How can you calmly hope [to live] for one hundred years, galloping around in all directions in search of accumulating material riches? These accumulations [of wealth] are [always] insufficient, and when you die, even after a long life, all of your belongings become the possessions of others. As you pass alone through the dark regions [of death], who can inquire about the right and wrong [or positive and negative] 是非 [aspects of your life?]? There may be home-departed ones whose chests overflow with wisdom and [rational] understanding, or who diligently strive to extinguish the fire [of passionate afflictions], [**94a**] but are not aware of [the truth of] transiency. There is a proverb that says: "As you should pity those who are attractive but without the five kinds of allure, so should you [pity] those who practice with diligence without the [proper] aspiration for the path *(bodhicitta)*." This is what is being said here. If you perceive [the truth of] transiency, [you realize that] it is more [powerful] than raging waters and howling hurricane winds and swifter than lightning; there is no place to escape from it, in mountain, sea, sky, or city. If you contemplate in this way, your mind will be full of fear, you will not be able to sleep peacefully, your food will not be sweet in your

long passage in the *Expanded Āgama*, T 2.741c–742b, concerning the practice of the contemplation of death. The passage does not contain the term "transience" 無常, though certainly the idea is there.

Avici hell 無間: the *Kōgi* (BT–IV, 477) suggests that this refers to a phrase in the preface to the *Fan wang ching*, T 24.1003a26: "An offence produced for just one brief moment [results in] the misfortune of falling into Avici hell."

Who can inquire? 誰訪是非: the implication being that only the karmic influences of your past actions will be your "judge."

Proverb that says, As you should pity … aspiration for the path 諺云可憐無五媚精進無道心: the source of this proverb is unknown, as well as the specific content of the "five kinds of allure." A global search in the SAT online *Daizōkyō* text revealed that the phrase occurs only in the *Mo-ho chih-kuan* and its commentaries. The character 媚, however, clearly implies the coquetry of a woman.

Mountain, sea, sky, city 山海空市: See the Buddha's extensive exposition on transiency in the first sections of the Chinese *Dharmapada* 法句譬喩経, T 4.576c–577a.

mouth, and [you will strive diligently] as if seeking [relief from] a feverish head. As a white horse or crow or rabbit races competitively day and night, you should seek a basic transcendence *(nisaraṇa)* [of this world of transmigration]. Why should you again covet worldly riches, become bound up in worldly matters, perform deeds that have no benefit, and thus create karma [for further rebirth] in samsara? Immediately sever the chains that bind you; transcend them and directly leave them behind, "as the herder fled [from a lion that meant to eat him]," and "strive to escape the burning house" [of samsara], quickly seeking to be saved. This is what it means to destroy the perverted view of permanence.

[end of fascicle seven, part one]

Like seeking [relief from] a feverish head 如救頭然: this last phrase is from the *Treatise on the Ten Stages*, T 26.41a19, in a section discussing the auxiliary practices of the path. The context reads:

> If a person arouses a vow and wishes to seek supreme enlightenment but has not yet attained the stage of non-retrogression *(avaivartya)*, during this period he should not begrudge his physical life but should strive diligently both day and night, *as one who seeks to recover from a feverish head*. As it says in the verses on the auxiliary practices of the path.
>
> A bodhisattva who has not yet attained
> The stage of non-retrogression
> Should constantly strive diligently
> *Like one who seeks [relief] from a feverish head.*

White horse or crow or rabbit races competitively day and night 白駒烏兎日夜奔競: "white horse" 白駒 can refer to a sunbeam, and "crow-rabbit" 烏兎 can be taken as a compound meaning "sun and moon." Thus this could be translated, as by Ikeda (*Gendaigoyaku*, 472), "Day by day and month by month, one practices seriously both day and night ..."

The herder who fled 野干絶透: see the story of a herder chased by a lion in the *Sūtra on Previously Unheard-of Causes*, T 17.576c21–23ff. This story has been referred to earlier in the *Mo-ho chih-kuan*; for details, see the note at 45b28–29.

Ikeda (*Gendaigoyaku*, 472) translates this phrase "as a fox seeks to escape a trap." 野干 could be taken to refer to a wild animal, but in the context of the story from the sūtra, I believe it refers to a human being (a "herder"), since after he is chased into a well by a lion, he composes a famous verse on the significance of transiency.

Strive to escape the burning house 争出火宅: a phrase from the famous parable of the burning house in the *Lotus Sūtra*, T 9.12c13. Hurvitz (*Lotus Sūtra*, 59 [56]) translates the context:

> Accordingly, [the father] proclaims to them: "The things you so love to play with are rare and hard to get. If you do not get them, you are certain to regret it later. Things like these, a variety of goat-drawn carriages, deer-drawn carriages, and ox-drawn carriages, are now outside the door for you to play with. Come out of this burning house quickly, all of you! I will give all of you what you desire." The children hear what their father says. Since rare playthings are exactly what they desire, the heart of each is emboldened. Shoving one another aside in a mad race, all together *in a rush they leave the burning house.*

4. *The perverted view of selfhood* [94a16]

Again, [how do you destroy the perverted view that the things of this world have substantial selfhood?] You should contemplate as follows. For immeasurable eons you have presumed that people have a [substantial] self in the midst of their conventional [physical] form and mental functions. If you are attached to your activities, as soon as you hear praise or criticism you think, "I am being praised or criticized." Whether you move, stay, sit, or lie down, a "self" is presumed for all activity; it is like when you smear glue on your hands, whatever they touch sticks to them. A sūtra says that "it is not the case that ordinary people are ever free of their self-centeredness." If they are poor, they lose their "original mind" and count on their "selves" without ceasing. If they become rich, they capriciously use their power and scatter their poisonous influence to bring harm upon the world, and when their anger flares up they maliciously oppress the innocent. The arousal of such karma is all due to your "self" [or, self-centeredness]; who can take [the retribution] on your behalf? If you take up fire from upwind, how can you not burn your hand? "It is like in the [dark] evening thinking that there is a demon in the house, but when the skies brighten [in the morning], [you see that] it is only the 'old' [familiar] person who was there originally." Again, since they do not

Presumed that people have a self in the midst of their conventional form and mental functions 多約名色及以想行而計我人: lit., in terms of "name-and-form" *(nāma-rūpa),* and "conceptions and volitions." Or, as Ikeda (*Gendaigoyaku*, 473) translates, "Both physically and mentally you have acted self-centeredly."

Move, stay, sit, lie down 行住坐臥: four types of activity, which are supposed to cover all possible types of human activity.

It is not the case that ordinary people are ever free of their self-centeredness 凡夫若離我心無有是處: the *Kōgi* (BT–IV, 485) admits that the source of this quote is unknown.

Count on their selves 計我: Or, "always take themselves into consideration."

In the evening thinking that there is a demon in the house, but when the skies brighten, it is only the "old" person who was there originally 彼夜房謂言有鬼。天明照了乃本舊人: see the humorous story in the *Ta chih tu lun*, T 25.704c29–705a14:

> It is like [the story of] the Buddhist temple complex in the mountains, within which there was a detached residence, and within this residence was a demon who would come and frighten the monks. The monks all abandoned this residence and fled. There was a visiting monk who came and was assigned to live in this empty building and serve as an administrator. He was told that there was a demon living in this building who took pleasure in bothering people, but that if he was able to dwell in this building, he could stay here. The visiting monk was virtuous in keeping the precepts and was very learned, and so he said, "What can a little demon do? I will overcome him." So he entered and dwelt in this building. Later another monk came seeking to dwell here [in the temple complex], and he also was assigned to this building as an administrator. He, also, was told about

have wisdom, people presume and say that there is a self. If you contemplate with wisdom, [you will realize that] truly there is no [substantial] self. Where is this "self"? Contemplate your limbs precisely one by one, from your head to your feet, and comprehend that there is no "self" to be seen. There is no place within people and sentient beings [for a substantial "self"]. [What we mistake for a "self" is only] the power of karma that acts on the conventional yet empty collection [of aggregates that make up the human being, like an "empty village"], arising through [the interplay of] various conditions, which does not involve a controlling subject. It is like two demons inhabiting an empty room and fighting over corpses. When you contemplate in this way, the perverted view of a [substantial] self will cease.

the demon who liked to trouble people. He, also, said, "What can a little demon do? I will overcome him." The first person to enter [the building] had closed the door and was sitting in meditation, waiting for the demon. The later person came in the night and pounded on the door seeking entrance. The first person, thinking that it was the demon, would not open the door. The later person pounded on the door with all his might. The monk inside strove with all his might to resist, but the person outside prevailed, and removed the door and gained entrance. The person inside struck him, and the person from the outside punched back with all his might. This continued until dawn, and when they were able to see what had happened, and that they were both fellow monks, they both apologized to each other. All the members of the community laughed at this strange happening. Sentient beings are also like this. The five skandhas are empty, without a self and without personhood. They grasp phenomenal forms and fight with each other....

Two demons inhabiting an empty room and fighting over corpses 宿空亭二鬼爭屍: see the sixth example in the *Ta chih tu lun*, T 25.148c4–27, in the section that gives numerous examples of the "non-existence de l'ātman." Lamotte (*Le Traité* 2, 738–39) translates:

6. En outre, il est des circonstances *(samaya)* où l'on conçoit l'idée du Moi par rapport à autrui.

[L'homme dont les membres sont remplacés par ceux d'un cadavre]. — Ainsi, un homme, qui avait été chargé d'aller au loin, se trouvait passer seul la nuit dans une maison déserte. Au milieu de la nuit, un démon qui portait sur ses épaules un homme mort, vint le déposer devant lui; puis un autre démon accourut à la poursuite du premier et lui fit des reproches avec colère, disant, "Cet homme mort m'appartient; comment serait-ce toi qui l'as apporté moi-même." Le second démon reprit: "C'est bien moi qui ai apporté ici cet homme mort." Ces deux démons, empoignant chacun le cadavre par une main, se le disputèrent. Le premier démon dit: "Il y a cici un homme que l'on peut interroger." Le second démon se mit à l'interroger: "Qui a apporté ici cet homme mort?" L'homme se fit la réflexion suivante: "Ces deux démons sont très forts; que je dise la vérité ou que je mente, ma mort est certaine et, dans l'un et l'autre cas, je ne saurais l'éviter. A quoi bon mentir?" Il déclara donc que c'était le premier démon qui avait apporté [le cadavre].

Aussitôt le second démon, très en colère, lui saisit la main qu'il arracha et jeta à terre, mais le second démon prit un bras du cadavre dt le lui adapta en frappant dessus. De même il substitua à son

> corps les deux bras, les deux pieds, la tête et les côtes [du cadavre]. Puis les deux démons dévorèrent ensemble le corps de l'homme qu'ils avaient remplacé [par celui du cadavre], et, après s'être essuyé la bouche, ils s'en allèrent....
>
> Ainsi donc, il est des circonstances où l'on conçoit l'idée du Moi par rapport à autrui. Mais, sous prétexte qu'il est des distinctions entre "celui-là," on ne peut pas dire qu'il y a un Moi.

Chodron (2, 585–86) translates:

> 6. Moreover, there are circumstances where the idea of self is conceived in reference to another.
>
> [*The man whose limbs were replaced by those of a corpse*]. Thus, a man who had undertaken to go on a long journey spent the night alone in a deserted house. In the middle of the night, a demon, carrying a dead man on his shoulder, was about to set the corpse down in front of him; then another demon angrily chased the first one saying: "That dead man belongs to me; why are you bringing him here?" The first demon replied: "He is my property; it is I who took him and brought him here myself." The second demon continued: "No, it was I who brought that dead man here." Each seizing the corpse by one hand, the two demons argued with each other. The first demon said: "There is a man here and we can ask him." The second demon began to question him. The man thought: "These two demons are very strong; whether I tell the truth or I lie, my death is certain; in either case, I can't escape. What is the use of lying?" Then he answered that it was the first demon that had brought [the corpse].
>
> Immediately, very angry, the second demon seized the man by the hand which he tore off and threw on the ground; but the second demon took an arm of the corpse which he fitted onto the man by slapping it on. In the same way he substituted the two arms, the two legs the head and the sides [of the corpse]. Together, the two demons devoured the man's body which they had replaced [by that of the corpse], and after wiping their mouths, they went away.
>
> Then the man thought: "With my own eyes, I saw the demons devour the body which my mother and father gave to me; now my present body consists completely of another's flesh. Do I really have a body now, or am I only a corpse? If I think I have body, it is entirely another's body; if I think I don't have one, there is, however, a body that is visible." Having had these thoughts, he was very worried and became like a man who has lost his mind.
>
> The next morning, he resumed his journey. Having arrived at the kingdom that was his destination, he saw an assembly of monks around a Buddhist stūpa, and he asked them whether his body existed or not. The monks asked him: "Who are you?" He answered: "I don't even know if I am a man or not." He told the assembly all that had happened. The bhikṣus said: "This man knows for himself the non-existence of a self; he will easily be liberated."
>
> Speaking to him, they said: "From the very beginning until today, your body was always without ātman, and it is not just coming to the present moment [that that is so]; it is simply because the four great elements were combined that you thought: 'This is my body.' There is no difference between your previous body and that of today." The bhikṣus converted him to the Path; he cut through his passions and became an arhat.
>
> Thus there are circumstances where one conceives the idea of self in reference to another. But under the pretence that there are distinctions between "that" and "this," one cannot say that there is a "me."

This story raises contemporary issues as well, such as, how much of a human body can be replaced by mechanical parts before one is no longer "human," or (from the opposite perspective) at what point can an android (by adding organic parts or attaining "consciousness") become "human"?

2. The role of fear [94a28]

If you cultivate these four contemplations to destroy the four perverted views, [it is possible that] your aspiration for the path will flare up and you will give rise to great fear, [**94b**] as if you are chased by enemies or while using a dangerous path to escape enemy territory. With each thought you glance all around in fear, and seek only to escape from the path. [This is as when] a young deer learns that it is surrounded by hunters, and dashes out in

As if you are chased by enemies, use a dangerous path to escape enemy territory 如爲怨逐如叛怨國如行險道: on this image see note at *Mo-ho chih-kuan* at 56a8, though the point seems to be different.

Young deer learns that it is surrounded by hunters, and dashes out in fear and trembling 獐聞獵圍霍驚絶走: the following section, starting with "[This is as when] a young deer,..." seems to be based on the *Ta chih tu lun*, T 25.295b7–22. However, Chih-i refers only to the deer and elephant, and not the rhinoceros: Lamotte (*Le Traité* 4, 2139–40) translates:

> 7. *Le Buddha adopte son enseignement aux préférences et aux capacités des étres*
> En outre les êtres *(sattva)* sont de deux sortes: 1. ceux qui s'attachent au monde *(lokāsakta)*; 2. ceux qui recherchent le supramonde *(lokottaraparyeṣin)*. Parmi ceux qui recherchent le supramonde, il en est de supérieurs *(agra)*, de moyens *(madhya)* et d'inférieurs *(avara)*.
>
> Les êtres supérieurs sont les êtres de facultés vives *(tīkṣṇendriya)* et de grande pensée, qui recherchent la Bodhi des Buddha.
>
> Les êtres moyens sont des êtres de facultés moyennes *(madhyendriya)*, qui recherchent la Bodhi des Pratyekabuddha.
>
> Les êtres inférieurs sont des êtres de facultés faibles *(mṛdvindriya)*, qui recherchent la Bodhi des Śrāvaka.
>
> A ceux qui recherchent la Bodhi des Buddha, le Buddha prêche les six perfections *(pāramitā)*, et la Vacuité des choses *(dharmaśūnyatā)*.
>
> A ceux qui recherchent la Bodhi des Pratyekabuddha, il prêche les douze causes *(dvādaśanidāna)* [de la production en dépendance *(pratītyasamutpāda)*] et le comportement des solitaires *(ekacārin)*.
>
> A ceux qui recherchent la Bodhi des Śrāvaka, il prêche la Vacuité des êtres *(sattvaśūnyatā)* et les quatre vérités saintes *(āryasatya)*.
>
> [*Prosopapée du cerf, du rhinocéros et de l'élephant.*] — 1. Les Śrāvaka craignant le Saṃsāra et entendant prêcher la vacuité des êtres, les quatre vérités saintes, l'impermanence *(anitya)*, la douleur *(duḥkha)*, le vide *(śūnya)* et le non-moi *(anātman)*, s'abstiennent de vain bavardage *(prapañca)* sur les dharma. Exemple: dans un parc, le cerf *(mṛga)* qui, frappé d'une flèche empoisonnée *(viṣeṣu)*, cherche uniquement son salut sans songer aux autres.
>
> 2. Les Prayekabuddha, tout dégoûtés qu'ils soient de la vieillesse *(jarā)*, de la maladie *(vyādhi)* et de la mort *(maraṇa)*, considèrent un peu la profonde production en dépendance *(pratītyasamutpāda)* et sauvent un peu les êtres. Exemple: le rhinocéros *(khaḍgaviṣāṇa)* dans un parc qui, bien que frappé d'une flèche empoisonnée, se préoccupe encore de ses jeunes.
>
> 3. Les Bodhisattva, tout dégoûtés qu'ils soient de la vieillesse, de la maladie et de la mort, contemplent le Vrai caractère *(bhūtalakṣaṇa)* des dharma, s'enfoncent complètement dans la production-en-dépendance à douze causes, pénètrent la Vacuité des choses *(dharmaśūnyatā)* et entrent dans l'immense élément fondamental *(dharmadhātu)*. Exemple:

fear and trembling. Although it comes across water and grass, it has no time to drink or eat, yearning [only] to escape. The Śrāvakas are like this.

If a deer clears the perimeter [of hunters] and thus is able to escape danger a little, [it still] glances back as it dashes away, crying out and bleating as it painfully yearns for its home herd. As it hesitates with indecision, it realizes that there is no benefit [in yearning for what is left behind]. It "sucks in its wind and swallows its voice," controls its grief, and proceeds forward. The Pratyekabuddhas are like this. They themselves can escape [the cycle of] birth-and-death and pity [other] sentient beings, but even though they compassionately grieve and sympathetically ache [for other sentient beings], they are not able to save and extract them [from their suffering].

In the case of a great king of the elephants, although it discovers that it

> le roi des éléphants blanc en rut *(śveta-gandhahastin),* dans un parc de chasse: bien que frappé d'une flèche empoisonnée, il a souci du chasseur *(vyādha),* n'éprouve aucune crainte *(bhaya)* et, à la tête de son troupeau, s'éloigne à pas lents.
>
> C'est pourquoi, dans le Tripiṭaka, on ne parle pas beaucoup de la Vacuité des choses *(dharmaśūnyatā).*

Chodron (4, 1757–58) translates:

> 7. The Buddha adapts his teaching to the preferences and capacities of beings
>
> Moreover, there are two kinds of beings: i. those who are attached to the world; ii) those who seek the supramundane. Among those who seek the supramundane, there are the superior, the middling and the inferior.
>
> The superior beings are the beings with sharp faculties, who are of great mind and who seek the bodhi of the Buddhas. The middling beings are beings of medium faculties who seek the bodhi of the pratyekabuddhas. The inferior beings are beings of weak faculties who seek the bodhi of the śrāvakas.
>
> To those who seek the bodhi of the Buddhas, the Buddha preaches the six perfections and the emptiness of things.
>
> To those who seek the bodhi of the pratyekabuddhas, he preaches the twelve causes [of dependent origination] and the conduct of the hermit.
>
> To those who seek the bodhi of the śrāvakas, he preached the emptiness of beings and the four noble truths.
>
> [*Prosopopeia of the deer, the rhinoceros and the elephant.*] 1. The śrāvakas fear samsara and, hearing about the emptiness of beings, the four noble truths, impermanence, suffering, emptiness and non-self, they abstain from proliferation about dharmas. Example: in a park, the deer, struck by a poisoned arrow, seeks only its own safety without thinking about others.
>
> 2. Completely disgusted as they are by old age, sickness and death, the pratyekabuddhas consider somewhat the profound dependent origination and save a few beings. Example: the rhinoceros in a park which, although struck by a poisoned arrow, still busies itself with its children.
>
> 3. Completely disgusted as they are with old age, sickness and death, the bodhisattvas completely sink into the twelve-membered dependent origination, penetrate the emptiness of things and enter into the immense fundamental element. Example: The king of the white elephants in rut in a hunting park: although struck by a poisoned arrow, he cares about the hunter, has no fear and, at the head of his troupe, walks away with slow steps.
>
> This is why not much is said in the Tripitaka about the emptiness of things.

is surrounded [by hunters], it cannot bear to leave by itself; knowing that its own power is great and that it can endure in overcoming the swords and arrows [of the hunters], it [remains behind and] guards and protects its young, and leads its herd to safety and saves them from harm. The bodhisattvas are like this. When you have enlightened insight concerning [the truths of] transience and nonself, fear is severed from your mind, as in dousing fire with water. Again, the arousing of compassion [by bodhisattvas] is like a mother thinking of her child. Sentient beings are blind, and do not realize that they are burned by suffering. [You should think,] how can I abandon them and leave by myself? Calmly persevere in samsara, using the wisdom of means to teach and transform [beings] to attain maturity, and create for them the causes and conditions for crossing [to the other side of enlightenment]. For you yourself, convert [your mind] and increase in virtue and the wisdom-life of the Dharma body, and when your conditions and capacities mature, you will sit on the seat of enlightenment *(bodhimaṇḍa)* and attain Buddhahood, and escape from the triple world together with [other] sentient beings. This is like a great elephant who provides peace for both itself and others [by saving them from the hunters].

In the case of a small child elephant, although it could ward off the swords and arrows [of the hunters to some extent], eventually it will surely be taken in [and wounded] [by these attacks] and will be of no benefit to itself or others. [In the same way, if] a novice bodhisattva wishes to [re-]enter samsara, when he comes in contact with samsara he will lose and retrogress from his good faculties, and the Dharma body will be destroyed. Even so, the virtue from arousing thoughts of great compassion are praiseworthy. Therefore bodhisattvas, even though they fear [the suffering and delusions of] samsara, should constantly seek a basis for goodness and bear the burdens of sentient beings, and not be the same as those of the two vehicles [who are concerned only with their own enlightenment]. Even though [bodhisattvas] dwell in samsara, they do not covet [the objects of] the five [sense] desires; [they dwell in samsara] merely for the sake of the concurrent salvation [of both themselves and others], so they are not the same as ordinary [ignorant] beings. A sūtra says, "Do not abide in regulating and overcoming, and do not abide in not regulating and overcoming. Even though you know [the truth of] nonselfhood, do not grow weary of admonishing people; even though

Do not abide in regulating and overcoming … weary abandonment 不住調伏不住不調伏。雖知無我而誨人不倦。雖知涅槃而不永滅。雖知不淨不說厭離: a rephrasing of a passage from the *Vimalakīrti Sūtra*, T 14.545b25–c3ff. Boin (*Vimalakīrti*, 128–29) translates the context:

> Mañjuśrī, although a bodhisattva should thus subdue his mind, he cannot adhere *(sthātavyam)* to either the control of

you realize nirvana, do not [take this as] permanent extinction; even though you realize [the truth of] the impurity [of this world], do not teach weary abandonment [of this world like that of an ascetic]." This is the meaning [intended] here. Much cultivation of the six perfections and the virtues of the basis of goodness resembles the physical fattening of sheep. To diligently contemplate [the truth of] transience so that all evil karma is destroyed is like sheep that have no [extraneous] fat because they are constantly afraid of the wolves. This is called the "features of cultivating *prajñā*-wisdom in deed." To practice yourself and to teach others, to praise the Dharma [of *prajñā*-wisdom] and praise the people [who pursue *prajñā*-wisdom], calling upon the Buddhas of the ten directions; this is witness and salvation. The majestic power of the Buddhas will liberate you and free you from obstacles, so that you will have a rapport with the four types of the ten wisdoms. Thus the oil of phenomenal [practices] will assist in increasing the clear light of the path, and so forth.

If you are completely without insight into the principle [of reality] [or, "have no realization of the contemplation of reality"] and also have no [expe-

the mind *(cittaniyama)* or the license of the mind *(cittāniyama)*. And why? Because to adhere to the license of the mind is characteristic of fools (*bāla*), and to adhere to the control of the mind is characteristic of the Listeners *(śrāvaka)*. This is why a Bodhisattva cannot adhere to either the control or the license of the mind. Not to adhere to either of these two extremes *(antadvaya)*, such is the domain of the Bodhisattva *(bodhisattva-gocara)*.

1. That which is neither the domain of the worldly *(pṛthagnanagocara)* nor the domain of the holy *(āryagocara)*, such is the domain of the Bodhisattva.

2. A domain of the round of rebirth *(saṃsāragocara)*, but not the domain of the passions *(kleśacogara)*, such is the domain of the Bodhisattva.

3. A domain where Nirvana is known *(nirvāṇaprekṣaṇāgocara)*, but not the domain of definitive and full Nirvana *(atyantaparinirvāṇacogocara)*, such is the domain of the Bodhisattva....

This passage was also quoted above in the *Mo-ho chih-kuan* at 73b23–24. Note that once again these phrases follow the pattern of the four perverted views: that the world is pure, blissful, permanent, and involves selfhood.

Sheep that have no fat because they are constantly afraid of wolves 恒被狼怖如羊無脂: these images are from the *Ta chih tu lun*, T 25.169b6–10, where "fat" refers to the "glut of passionate afflictions." For a translation of the full passage, see note at *Mo-ho chih-kuan* 79a20–23.

Features of cultivating *prajñā*-wisdom in deed 修事般若相 ...: the *Inyō* attributes these phrases to the passage in the *Pañcaviṃśati Sūtra*, T 8.281c11–24, quoted above at 92a6–7.

Four types of the ten wisdoms 四種十慧: that is, the ten wisdoms understood in the fourfold pattern of arising (Tripitaka), non-arising (Shared), immeasurable (Distinct), and spontaneous (Perfect)

And so forth: this follows the pattern of set phrasing at the end of each of the expositions of the six pāramitās, indicating that this is the end of the exposition on the perfection of *prajñā*-wisdom.

rience of] actual repentance, but still seek the sign of [approval from] the Buddha 佛印, you are wishing for [personal, worldly] benefit and plotting [to acquire] fame. The sign of [approval from] the Buddha cannot be had from such a situation. If there is no gap in your insight into the principle [of reality], [**94c**] and you apply actual practice to destroy the obscurations, and repent with a true [sincere] mind, the sign [of the Buddha's approval] is to be found here.

The reason people should actually practice the auxiliary practices of the path [is as follows]. It is as if you strung together pearls at the place of two tens of thousands of millions of Buddhas, and through this forgot the Mahāyāna, and thus could not teach [beings] with the Mahāyāna [Dharma]. [As a result] you had to arouse this [Mahāyāna] by means of Hīnayāna [practices] through six hundred kalpas, leading to a fear of samsara and "gradually facing towards your father's house." Therefore know that you should appropriate the Hīnayāna [practices and teachings] to assist in [attaining] the Mahāyāna. Again, the Buddha first wished [to use] the Mahāyāna to teach [beings], but various Buddhas did not approve, and thought it good that he consider [other, provisional] means, as a rich family used yellow dragon potion [to treat] their child's disease. It is not that the parents were stingy with tasty medicine, but [realized] that a strong [remedy] was needed. [Indeed,] when this was applied, the disease was healed. The Buddha has

No gap 無間: or, "in your realization of the contemplation of reality." Then again, if 無間 refers to the Avici hell, "If you contemplate the reality of the Avici [hell] …"?

String together pearls 繫珠: Chan-jan (BT–IV, 492) explains that "in the past the meaning of 'stringing pearls' was like that of the 'right path,'" implying that this refers to Hīnayāna practices that lead you to forget or abandon the Mahāyāna.

Six hundred kalpas 六百劫: the *Shiki* and *Kōgi* (BT–IV, 492) both say that this refers to sixty kalpas for a śrāvaka and a hundred kalpas for a pratyekabuddha.

Gradually facing towards your father's house 漸向父舍: this phrase appears in the parable of the poor son in the *Lotus Sūtra*, T 9.16c11, which tells of the son, at first fearful, gradually becoming accustomed to his true status through the skillful means utilized by his father. Hurvitz (85 [79]) translates the context:

> At that time, the poor son, hiring himself out as a laborer in his wanderings, by chance reached his *father's house*, where, stopping by the gate, he saw in the distance his father seated on a lion throne, [and so forth] …

Did not approve 不印: lit., "did not give their sign," "did not stamp their approval."

Yellow dragon potion 黄龍湯: The *Kōgi* (BT–IV, 493) refers to a passage in the *Mahāparinirvāṇa Sūtra*, T 12.736b25–26: "Good son, this is analogous to a sick person removing the suffering of the disease and attaining peace by eating impure food." This phrase doesn't seem to apply directly here. On the other hand, Chih-i has used the example of the "yellow dragon potion" previously in the *Mo-ho chih-kuan*; see the note under 19a22.

an original vow to lead sentient beings to be like himself. How could he be stingy about [and hold back] the Mahāyāna? [It is just that sometimes] the situation is not advantageous, and must be responded to in accordance with the capacities of beings. Thus he discloses the teaching of the auxiliary practices of the path [as appropriate]. This is the meaning here.

3. The Steps on the Path and the Six Perfections [94c9]

Question: If you cannot realize samādhi [of actionlessness] without cultivating the auxiliary practices of the path, then are not the six perfections superior to the steps on the path?

Answer: There are three options: [1] [The practice of] the six perfections destroys [the need for] [the practice of] the steps on the path, and [the practice of] the steps on the path destroys [the need for] [the practice of] the six perfections; [2] [The practice of] the six perfections involves cultivating the steps on the path, and [practicing] the steps on the path involves the six perfections; and [3] the six perfections are indivisible from the steps on the path, and the steps on the path are indivisible from the six perfections.

[1] [The practice of] the steps on the path as [explained] above are not able to "provide a link" 契 with the true [i.e., to realize emptiness]. If you cultivate the six perfections, you are able to destroy the [six] obscurations. [In this sense,] how can it not be that [the practice of] the six perfections destroys [the need for] the steps on the path? Sometimes one is not able to reach the other shore [of enlightenment] by means of the six perfections, but if these cultivate the steps on the path, they can attain awakening and realization. This means that the steps on the path destroy [the need for] the six perfections.

[2] Suppose you cultivate the six perfections, first destroying the six obscurations, and then advancing to cultivate the steps on the path, and thus naturally realizing [enlightenment]: this is to cultivate the steps on the path as [included in] the six perfections. The [practices] I have just explained above consist of cultivating the six perfections as [included in] the steps on the path.

[3] The mutual inclusiveness of [the practices of] the six perfections and the steps on the path is [as follows]. "*Dāna* [the perfection of giving]

Six perfections superior to the steps on the path 六度應勝道品: Ikeda (*Gendaigo-yaku*, 476) gives an expanded translation based on the discussion of these matters above [see previous section; 88b12ff.]:

If you cannot realize the samādhi of actionlessness unless you cultivate in deed the auxiliary practices of the path, then are not [the practice of] the six perfections in deed superior to the "actionless (spontaneous)" [practice of] the steps on the path? See 87c–91a.

is Mahāyāna," and "the four mindfulnesses are also Mahāyāna." *Dāna* [the perfection of giving] and the steps on the path are neither two nor distinct, because they are [both] unobtainable.

If we discuss in general concerning all the teachings, [we should say that] if there is no benefit from a [certain] practice, this is mutually destructive 相破 [for both the perfections and the steps on the path], and if there is benefit from a [certain] practice, then both should be cultivated mutually 相修. In terms of the principle [of reality], both are mutually indivisible 相即. With regard to the Four [Noble] Truths or [twelvefold] causes and conditions, [you should consider whether in "practicing" or contemplating these matters] there is [benefit] or there is not [benefit], or there neither is nor is not [that is, it is indivisible from reality and thus "unobtainable"]. In broadly considering all dharmas [teachings and practices], they all [should be considered as] having these three options. If you realize this meaning, you will be able to teach with mastery.

How can [the practice of] the six perfections encompass the meaning of controlling and overcoming all the sense organs?

1. Tripitaka Teachings [94c23]

[1] If the six sense organs do not accept the six sense objects, this corresponds to the components of abandonment [or equanimity] *(upekṣa-saṃbodhyana)* and removal [of afflictions] among the steps on the path; this is the controlling and overcoming of all sense organs through the perfection of giving. [2] If the six sense organs are not harmed by the six sense objects, this corresponds to right deeds, right speech, and right way of life among the steps on the path; this is the controlling and overcoming of all sense organs through the perfection of [upholding] the precepts. [3] If the odious six sense objects are pacified and endured without agitation, this corresponds to

***Dāna* is Mahāyāna** 檀即摩訶衍: see, for example, the *Ta chih tu lun*, T 25.393b6–7: "The six *pāramitā*s are the Mahāyāna of the bodhisattva-mahāsattvas," a phrase from the *Pañcaviṃśati Sūtra*, T 8.250a5–6. This passage was quoted above in the *Mo-ho chih-kuan* at 91b19.

Four mindfulnesses are also Mahāyāna 四念處亦即摩訶衍: see the *Ta chih tu lun*, T 25.402c18–19: "The Buddha said to Subhūti, 'The Mahāyāna of the bodhisattva-mahāsattva includes the four mindfulnesses.'" This, also, is a phrase from the *Pañcaviṃśati Sūtra*, T 8.253b19–20.

In general 通: or, should this be understood as referring to the perspective of the "Shared Teachings," which would imply understanding all teachings from the perspective of emptiness? Since each of the Four Teachings are discussed in turn, here it probably just means "general."

Abandonment and removal 捨除: this must correspond to the component of "serenity" or "making light" 輕 *(pracrabhi-saṃbodhyāṅga)*, the fifth component of awakening.

the four types of mindfulness among the steps on the path; this is the controlling and overcoming of sense organs through the perfection of patience. [4] If you are on guard with regard to the sense organs and sense objects, and never lax, this corresponds to the eight types of diligence among the steps on the path; this is the controlling and overcoming of all sense organs through the perfection of diligence. [5] If your thoughts are concentrated and undisturbed, [**95a**] and are not deluded by the six sense objects, this corresponds to the eight types of concentration among the steps on the path; this is called the controlling and overcoming of all sense organs through the perfection of dhyāna-meditation. [6] If you know that the six sense objects are transient, consist of suffering, are empty, and are quiescent, this corresponds to the ten types of wisdom among the steps on the path; this is called the controlling and overcoming of all sense organs through the perfection of wisdom. This is the Tripitaka [teaching and practices] for controlling and overcoming the senses and fulfilling the six perfections.

2. *Shared Teachings* [95a4]

Again, [1] know that the eye [organ] is empty, and does not experience [substantive] sights. The visible forms [that are the sense objects of sight] are empty, and these visible forms are not experienced [substantively]. Since both the sense organs and objects are [realized as] empty, this is called the practice of constant abandonment [of attachment to empty things]. [The same is true for all the skandhas,] up to and including consciousness; they are empty, and consciousness is not experienced [substantially]. Phenomena [the objects of consciousness] are empty, and phenomena are not experienced [substantively]. This is called the practice of constant abandonment. This corresponds to the components of abandonment [or equanimity] and removal [of afflictions] among the steps on the path, and is called the controlling and overcoming of all the sense organs through the perfection of giving. [2] The emptiness of visible forms [the objects of sight] is not able to harm the emptiness of the eye. The emptiness of the eye is not able to harm the emptiness of visible forms. [The same is true for all the skandhas]

Four types of mindfulness 四種之念: not the "four mindfulnesses," but mindfulness as one of the four supranormal powers, one of the five good roots, one of the five powers, and one of the components of awakening [or, one of the eightfold path]?

This is the Tripitaka 此乃三藏: two components for the perfection of giving, three aspects of the eightfold path for the perfection of precepts, four mindfulnesses for the perfection of patience, eight diligences for the perfection of diligence, eight concentrations for the perfection of dhyāna-meditation, and ten wisdoms for the perfection of wisdom, for thirty-six of the thirty-seven steps on the path. Which one is missing?

up to and including [consciousness]. The emptiness of phenomena is not obtained by relying on consciousness, and the emptiness of consciousness is not obtained by relying on phenomena. This corresponds to right speech, right deeds, and right way of life among the steps on the path; this is called the controlling and overcoming of all sense organs through the perfection of [upholding] the precepts. [3] Again, because the eye organ and its sight objects [visible forms] are empty, it is not a matter of them being odious or acceptable, and not a matter of [patiently] enduring or not enduring [them as empty]. [The same is true for all the skandhas] up to and including [the option that] because consciousness and its objects (dharmas) are empty, it is not a matter of them being odious or acceptable, and not a matter of enduring or not enduring [them as empty]. This corresponds to the four types of mindfulness among the steps on the path; this is called the controlling and overcoming of sense organs through the perfection of patience. [4] The eye and its sense objects [visible forms] are always empty, and there is never a time when they are not empty, as the latent [delusions] and *prajñā*-wisdom mutually correspond. [This is true for all the skandhas,] up to and including [the option that] the consciousness and its objects [dharmas] are always empty, and there is never a time when they are not empty; this is called the mutual rapport of the latent [delusions] and *prajña*-wisdom. This corresponds to the eight types of diligence among the steps on the path; this is called the controlling and overcoming of all sense organs through the perfection of diligence. [5] Because the eye and its sight objects are empty, they are neither agitated nor concentrated. [The same is true for all the skandhas,] up to and including [the option that] because consciousness and its objects are empty, they are neither agitated nor concentrated. This corresponds to the [eight] types of concentration among the steps on the path; this is called the controlling and overcoming of all sense organs through the perfection of dhyāna-meditation. [6] Because the eye and its sight objects are empty, this involves neither delusion nor wisdom. [The same is true for all the skandhas,] up to and including [the option that] because the consciousness and its objects are empty, they are neither delusions nor wisdom. This corresponds to the ten types of wisdom among the steps on the path; this is called the controlling and overcoming of all sense organs through the perfection of wisdom. These are the Shared Teachings for controlling and overcoming the senses and fulfilling the six perfections.

Mutual rapport of latent [delusions] and *prajñā*-wisdom 如是習應與般若相應: a phrase summarized from the *Pañcaviṃśati Sūtra*, T 8.222c9–11.

Neither agitated nor concentrated 不亂不味: the Taishō text has 味 ("flavor") but I have taken this to be 昧 (from samadhi 三昧).

3. *Distinct Teachings* [95a21]

[1] If the eye and its sight objects [of visible form] include the ten dharma realms [from hell to Buddhahood], the ten dharma realms each are different with regard to superior and inferior fruits and recompense, and each of them have differences of profound and shallow causes for cultivating [the path]; [thus] they involve immeasurable causes and results such that they cannot be exhausted, so that even if people remove their ignorance and can discriminate among the features of phenomena, there is no place to which they can be attached [because they are empty]. [This is true for all the skandhas,] up to and including [the option that] consciousness and its objects include the ten dharma realms, which can be discriminated but have [no substance] to be attached to. This corresponds to the components of abandonment [or equanimity] and removal [of afflictions] among the steps on the path, and is called the controlling and overcoming of all the sense organs through the perfection of giving. [2] If you discriminate concerning the eye and its sight objects and [all the other skandhas up to and including] consciousness and its objects, their features are immeasurable. If you do not make errors concerning someone's potential and harm someone else's good roots, and you yourself are not harmed by the immeasurable senses and their objects, this corresponds to right deeds, speech, and way of life among the steps on the path, and this is called the controlling and overcoming of all sense organs through the perfection of [upholding] the precepts. [3] Again, with regard to the sense objects and organs of the ten realms, whether you find them odious or acceptable, if your thoughts are not agitated [**95b**] and you abide calmly within their conventional [reality or existence] and are able to patiently endure until you perfect the deeds of the path, this corresponds to the four types of mindfulness among the steps on the path, and this is called the controlling and overcoming of sense organs through the perfection of patience. [4] Again, when you discriminate among all the sense organs and their objects, if you experience thoughts of difficulty and suffering yet do not retreat from among them, and have courage while within samsara, this corresponds to [the eight types of] diligence among the steps on the path, and this is called the controlling and overcoming of all sense organs through the perfection of diligence. [5] Again, when you discriminate among all the sense organs and their objects, if your thoughts are not broken and disturbed, neither agitated nor biased, this corresponds to [the eight types of] concentration among the steps on the path, and this is called the controlling and overcoming of all sense organs through the perfection of dhyāna-meditation. [6] Again, when you discriminate among all the sense organs and their objects, prescribe medicine appropriately with the power of the wisdom of the path, using good and skillful means yet not becoming

defiled by nor attached to [the senses]. This corresponds to all [the ten types of] wisdom among the steps on the path; this is called the controlling and overcoming of all sense organs through the perfection of wisdom. These are the Distinct Teachings for controlling and overcoming the senses and fulfilling the six perfections.

4. *Perfect Teaching* [95b9]

Again, as it says in the *Aṅgulimāla Sūtra*, "these so-called 'eye organs,' with the constant [gaze] of the Tathāgata, are complete and without lacking in cultivation, and see fully and clearly." This indicates [the limits of] the sight organs of [those of] the nine dharma realms [outside the realm of Buddhahood]. "The constant [gaze] of a Tathāgata" refers to the idea that the nine realms, in themselves, [seem] each individually to be not truly [real], but when a Tathāgata contemplates them they are, from [the perspective of] the dharma realm of the Buddha, [seen to be] neither different [lit. "two"] nor distinct. "Without lacking in cultivation" means to perceive all sense organs as with the Buddha eye; this is the threefold truth in a single thought, in which the perfect causes are complete, and there is no lack or decrease [in your cultivation of the path or realization]. "Seeing fully and clearly" means to be fully illuminated concerning the real, and to be clearly illuminated concerning the conventional. Since the three wisdoms are included in a single thought, the five kinds of eyesight are all included and with perfect illumination. This is called "fully perceiving [seeing] Buddha-nature." "Seeing" 見 depicts "perfect realization" 圓證 [of enlightenment] and "cultivation" 修 depicts "perfect causes" 圓因. Again, "complete cultivation" 具足修 refers to [the practice of the six perfections, as follows]: to contemplate the

These so-called "eye organs," with the constant [gaze] of the Tathāgata, are complete and without lacking in cultivation, and see fully and clearly 彼眼根於諸如來常具足無減修了了分明見: see the *Aṅgulimāla Sūtra*, T 2.531c24–25; the meaning of the quote is close to the original verse, but with significant differences in terminology and order:

> These so-called "eye organs," with the constant [gaze] of a Tathāgata,
> Sees determinately and with discrimination [or "clarity"] 決定分別 (or 明) 見,
> complete and without decrease or loss 具足無減損 (or 修).

Chih-i's quote follows both the variants of 明 instead of 別 and 修 instead of 損, indicating that he was in possession of the variant text rather than the version in the Taishō edition. However, there is no indication as to why he uses the phrase 了了 instead of 決定; he could have been following a variant reading, or he may have been "quoting" creatively from memory. The context of this quote is not supplied here, but Chih-i uses the "out of context" phrase as a springboard to extract the meaning of his Perfect Teaching. See his analysis of the phrases in this quote as they follow in this paragraph. See also the use of this passage later at *Mo-ho chih-kuan* 100c25–27.

sight organ [the eye] and abandon the defilements of the two extremes is called *dāna* [the perfection of giving]; for the eye not to be harmed by [the afflictions of] the two extremes is called *śīla* [the perfection of upholding the precepts]; for the eye to be quiescent and not be agitated by [the afflictions of] the two extremes is called *kṣānti* [the perfection of patience]; for [all the senses from] the eye to consciousness to naturally flow into the sea of *sarvajñā* [that is, "omniscience"] is called [the perfection of] diligence; to contemplate the eye in its true nature is called superior concentration [the perfection of dhyāna meditation]; to illuminate the Middle Way concerning the eye by means of universal wisdom is called [the perfection of] wisdom. This is what it means [to practice] the "cultivation that is not lacking" for the eye. Since there is no lack, one "sees fully [and clearly]," and one can perceive the dharma realm of the eye. This can be applied [to all the skandhas], so that [all the senses] up to and including consciousnesses "with the constancy of a Tathāgata, complete and without lacking in cultivation, sees fully and clearly." Each individual sense organ is simultaneously empty, conventional, and the Middle. This threefold contemplation in a single thought is called "cultivation that is not lacking." The eye of wisdom, the Dharma eye, and the Buddha eye are realized and attained in a single thought; this is called "seeing fully." [The details are] all as explained above. This is so for the sense organs; the same is true for the sense objects, and the same is also true for all the Dharma teachings. This is the Perfect Teaching for controlling and overcoming the sense organs and fulfilling the six perfections.

In this way, the auxiliary practices of the path assist [in realizing] the ultimate path. [95c] You should know that [the practice of] the six perfections is able to universally control and overcome all [the passionate afflictions and delusions of] the sense organs. The *Pañcaviṃśati Sūtra* says, "The one who gives, the one who receives, and the material wealth [itself] are all 'unobtainable'; this is the fulfillment of the perfection of giving." Denying

The same is true for sense organs, sense objects, and all teachings: based on Chih-i's explanation above, one should be able to extrapolate all of the details regarding the rest of the senses and the sense objects, and for all the rest of the Buddhist teachings.

The one who gives, the one who receives, and the material wealth are all unobtainable; this is the fulfillment of the perfection of giving 施者受者財物不可得故具足檀波羅蜜: see the *Pañcaviṃśati Sūtra* at T 8.245b2–8:

> Again, Śāriputra, when the bodhisattva-mahāsattva practices *dāna-pāramitā*, he should give with the mind of *sarvajñā*, contemplate all phenomena as illusory. [That is,] the giver is unobtainable, the thing given is unobtainable, and the recipient is unobtainable. This is called practicing *dāna-pāramitā* when it is adorned with *prajñā-pāramitā* and the great vow. In this way, Śāriputra, a bodhisattva-mahāsattva has the mind of *sarvajnā*, that the marks of

these three things and not being attached to them is the essence of *dāna* [the perfection of giving]. That one should "fulfill" this means that one should practice giving both of material wealth and the Dharma; thus *dāna* is completely fulfilled. The phenomena and the principle [of giving] are both perfected, and both oneself and others are benefited; this is called "fulfillment." "Phenomenal" [giving] refers to destroying the actual phenomena of parsimony and the abandoning of material wealth. The "principle" [of giving] refers to destroying parsimonious thoughts and "abandoning" [that is, "giving away"] the Dharma [teachings]. This twofold destroying and twofold abandoning means that [both] the essence and function [of giving] are fulfilled; this is called the "perfection" *(pāramitā)* [of giving].

3. The Steps on the Path, the Six Perfections, and the Noble Demeanor of the Buddha [95c7]

How do the six perfections encompass the noble demeanor of the Buddha? The Buddha is endowed with noble demeanors such as ten powers, [four] fearlessnesses, and [eighteen] unique qualities. To cultivate the four [types of] steps on the path within a single thought is called "cultivating the noble demeanor of the Buddha." To realize the Buddha eye and the Buddha's wisdom is called "attaining the noble demeanor of the Buddha."

1. Encompassing the Ten Powers [95c10]

For verbal convenience let us clarify the encompassing of the ten powers [and so forth] in terms of the steps on the path.

[1. The power of knowing whether a position or place is suited to the

the *pāramitās* cannot be grasped or attained. It should be known that this bodhisattva-mahāsattva is adorned with the great vow.

Phenomena and principle 事理 : that is, the principle of giving is fully and perfectly known, and the practice of actually giving things is carried out.

Ten powers 十力**, fearlessnesses** [四]無畏**, and unique qualities** [十八] 不共法: these categories have appeared previously in the *Mo-ho chih-kuan*; see Glossary.

Ten powers 十力: this is one of the eighteen unique characteristics of the Buddha. The list given by Chih-i in his *Introduction to Graded Themes of the Dharma Realm* (T 46.694a21–23), probably based on the discussion in the *Ta chih tu lun*, T 25.235–247, has the ten powers as the knowledge of: 1. whether a place or position is suited to the path or not 是處非處力; 2. deeds and their respective retributions 業力; 3. meditative states and techniques 定力; 4. differences in the faculties of sentient beings 根力; 5. the range of beings' hopes or desires 欲力; 6. dharmas and their natures 性力; 7. the different destinies or abodes of existence, or the places where the paths lead 至處道力; 8. your own past existences 宿命力; 9. karmic destinies of other beings, or of your own for the future 天眼力; and 10. the exhaustion of the outflow of defilements 盡漏力.

path or not.] The four types of the steps on the path are determined in their causes and effects by the wisdom [or knowledge] of the four types of the Four [Noble] Truths. Knowing [the Noble Truth of] the causes [of suffering] as arising and perishing determines the experiencing of suffering in the triple world, this has its place; if [knowing the Noble Truth of] the causes [of suffering] as arising and perishing leads to the [Hīnayāna] nirvana of no remainder, this has no place. If [knowing the Noble Truth of] the path as arising and perishing is able to exhaust suffering and [lead to] the realization of nirvana, this has its place; if [knowing] the path as arising and perishing leads to [rebirth in] the triple world, this has no place. [The same is true for the other four aspects of the Four Noble Truths] up to and including [the Truths as "spontaneous"]. [If knowing the Noble Truth of] the causes as spontaneous penetratingly leads to [rebirth in] the world of transformations, this has its place; if it penetratingly leads to supreme nirvana, this has no place. If [knowing the Noble Truths of] the path and extinction as spontaneous penetratingly leads to [gaining] universal wisdom, this has its place; if it penetratingly leads to [the wisdom of] the two vehicles, this has no place. To know these four types of [knowing] causes and results within a single thought, and be able to clearly distinguish and determine them, is called [the first] "power of [knowing whether] a position [or place] [is suited to the path] or not." Therefore the Tathāgata's preaching of the Dharma is like a lion's roar, [and he says] "It is only within my Dharma that the four fruits of the *śrāmaṇa* are [possible]." This is the meaning here.

[2.] The power of the knowledge of karmic deeds and retribution is as follows. To know the four types [of the Noble Truth] of the causes [of suffering] is to know karmic deeds. To know suffering is to know the retribution [from karmic deeds]. The same is true for [the Noble Truths of] the path and extinction. To distinguish between the four types of karmic deeds and retribution, and not be mistaken concerning their shallowness or profundity, is the second power.

[3.] The power to know dhyāna meditation is as follows. The four types of the Truth of the path include eight types of concentrations. To distinguish

Four types of the Four Truths 四種四諦: that is, they follow the same pattern of the fourfold structure that is the basis of T'ien-t'ai hermeneutics: arising-and-perishing (Tripitaka), non-arising (Shared), immeasurable (Distinct), and spontaneous (Perfect).

This has its place 是處: in the sense that it is appropriate and useful and something to be sought? Ikeda (*Gendaigoyaku*, 480) translates 是處 as "in line with the truth."

It is only within my Dharma that the four fruits of the *śrāmaṇa* are [possible] 獨我法中有四沙門果 ...: the traditional commentaries do not give a source for this claim. Perhaps it is too common to attribute to any one source?

between shallowness and profundity and to be clearly illuminated concerning them without any error, is the third power.

[4–6.] The power to know the faculties, desires, and natures [of beings] is as follows. To know that the sufferings and causes [of suffering] of the past are not the same [for all sentient beings] is called "the power of [knowing] the faculties [of beings]." To know that the present sufferings and causes [of suffering], and the desires for pleasure, are not the same [for all sentient beings] is called "the power of [knowing] the desires [of beings]." To know that the future suffering and causes [of suffering], and the attainments and losses, are not the same [for all sentient beings] is called "the power of [knowing] the natures [of beings]." These are the fourth, fifth, and sixth powers.

[7.] The power to know the places where the paths lead is as follows: to know the places to which the four truths of the path lead is called the seventh power.

[8–9.] The power to know your own past lives and the destinies of other beings [lit., "divine insight"] is as follows. To be illuminated concerning the various potentials in the past, whether good or evil, in one life or many, and of the length or shortness of your life span: this is called the power of [knowing] your past existences. To be illuminated **[96a]**concerning the attractive or repulsive places one could be born in the future is called the power of divine insight. These are the eighth and ninth powers.

[10.] The power to exhaust [defiled] outflows refers to the liberation of undefiled mind or thoughts of wisdom and so forth that is illumined through the four types of the Truth of extinction.

One dharma teaching thus includes four types. As a king speaks with veiled words but a wise minister can understand his intent, so the Buddha teaches ten powers that apply to these four types of potentials, so that those of the Hīnayāna are not led to slander the Mahāyāna and thus harm their [potential] good qualities, and those of the Mahāyāna are not led to attain [merely] the Hīnayāna and thus constrain their good roots. Each individual is alone in what he hears, and each benefits individually. Because [the Buddha] has such uncontrived skill in tentative [means] he has the title "Humane One" [that is, Śākyamuni]. Bodhisattvas are the wise ministers who profoundly understand [the Buddha's] veiled words. If they know that his intent is to be found in the Tripitaka [Teachings], they will ask for [the standpoint of] "arising-and-perishing." They inquire earnestly, and lead those with [proper] conditions to quickly realize awakening. [The same is true for the others of the Fourfold Teachings,] up to knowing that [the

Humane One 能仁: The characters are a translation of "Śākyamuni" (sage of the Śākya clan), one of the titles of Gotama Buddha.

Buddha's] intent is to be found in the Perfect [Teaching]; they will at times commend [the standpoint of] "spontaneous" or ask for [the standpoint of] "spontaneous," thus leading others to attain understanding. A single sound of varied chants is heard by many and all rejoice. The oral mysteries [of the Buddha] are unlimited, and the meaning cannot be exhausted. As above, there are four interpretations [of the Fourfold Teachings]; how can one doubt that this is sufficient?

Question: The ten powers are the noble demeanor of the Buddha. How can they be learned by beginners, and how can they be attained?

Answer: The *Ta chih tu lun* says, "When bodhisattvas practice *prajñā*, they do not [yet] dwell in the ten powers or the [four] fearlessnesses. Since the Buddha is not lacking in any of the Buddha Dharmas, he can surely dwell [in them]. Since bodhisattvas do lack [some] Buddha Dharmas, how can it be asserted that they dwell [in the ten powers and so forth]?" Let me explain this. When bodhisattvas cultivate the good qualities of a Buddha, for many, grave attachments still arise. They must destroy these grave mental states, and therefore it is said that they do not [yet] dwell [in the ten powers and so forth].

[Question:] If this is so, then first you cultivate [the path] but do not yet attain [these qualities], and later it is said that you realize the levels [of a Buddha]. What, then, does this have to do with beginners?

[Answer:] If we rely on the chapter on the ten abodes in the *Avataṃsaka Sūtra*, it says that "bodhisattvas attain the portion of the ten powers due to arousing the first aspiration [for enlightenment]." [Later in the sūtra it says]

Single sound of varied chants 一音殊唱: "One sound" is representative of the Perfect Teaching, and the idea that ultimately there is only one truth even though it is represented in many different ways.

As above: or, to follow the variant reading of 止 instead of 上, "[Although the teachings and their meanings are immeasurable], we stop at four interpretations."

When bodhisattvas practice *prajñā*, they do not dwell in the ten powers or fearlessnesses 菩薩行般若十力無畏不應住: the *Kōgi* (BT–IV, 512) admits that such a passage cannot be found in the *Ta chih tu lun*.

Bodhisattvas attain the portion of the ten powers due to arousing the first aspiration 菩薩因初發心得十力分: a phrase from the *Avataṃsaka Sūtra* at T 9.445a7–8. Cleary (*The Flower Ornament Scripture*, vol. 1, 385) translates the context:

> What is the enlightening beings' abode of initial determination? The enlightening beings, seeing the magnificence of the Buddha, which people like to see, rarely encountered, having great power; or seeing their spiritual powers, or hearing predictions of enlightenment, or listening to their teachings and instructions, or seeing sentient beings suffering sever pains, or hearing the far-reaching teaching of enlightenment of the Buddhas, develop the determination for enlightenment, to seek omniscience. *The enlightening beings arouse determination with ten difficult-to-attain objectives*: the knowledge of what is so and what is not; knowledge of

"The divine being Right Mindfulness said to [the bodhisattva] Dharma Wisdom, 'Beginning bodhisattvas cultivate the [provisional] means of the

consequences of good and bad actions; knowledge of superiority and inferiority of faculties; knowledge of the differences of various understandings; knowledge of the differences of various realms; knowledge of where all paths lead; knowledge of all meditations, liberations, and concentrations; knowledge of past lives; clairvoyance; knowledge of the universal end of indulgence for all time.

The divine being Right Mindfulness said ... this enlightenment does not rely on others: a summary of the twelfth chapter of the *Avataṃsaka Sūtra* on "Noble Conduct" 梵行, T 9.449a12–c15. The way Chih-i picks up phrases here and there from the text to produce an abbreviated running text can be somewhat misleading; for a full translation of this chapter see Cleary, *The Flower Ornament Scripture*, vol. 1, 401–3:

> Then the godling Right Mindfulness said to the enlightening being Truth Wisdom, "In all worlds, enlightening beings, following the teaching of the Enlightened Ones, dye their clothing and leave home to become mendicants: how can they attain purity of religious practice, and from the state of enlightening reach the path of unexcelled enlightenment?"
>
> Truth Wisdom said: Great enlightening beings, when performing religious practice, should attentively contemplate ten things objectively: the body, physical action, speech, verbal action, mind, mental action, Buddha, the Teaching, the religious community, and the precepts. They should contemplate in this way: Is the body religious practice? And so on, down to: Are precepts religious practice? *If the body were religious practice*, then religious practice would be not good, it would not be the true teaching, *it would be defiled*, it would be impure, it would be foul, it would be unclean, it would be a corpse, it would *be a mass of microbes. If physical action were religious practice, then religious practice would be walking, standing, sitting, lying down, looking around, up and down.* If speech were religious practice, then religious practice would be sound and breath, chest, *tongue, lips*, exhalation and inhalation, constriction and relaxation, high and low, clear and unclear. *If verbal activity were religious practice, then religious practice would be greetings*, summary explanations, extensive explanations, metaphorical explanations, direct explanations, praise, criticism, definitions, explanations accommodated to conventions, clear explanations.... *If the precepts are religious practice, is the ordination altar the precepts? Is asking about purity the precepts?* Is teaching proper manners the precepts? *Is the threefold repetition the precepts? Is the instructor the precepts?* Is the tutor the precepts? *Is shaving off the hair the precepts?* Is putting on the monastic garb the precepts? *Is begging the precepts?* Is right livelihood the precepts?
>
> Having contemplated thus, having no attachment to the body, no clinging to practice, no dwelling on doctrine, the past gone, the future not yet arrived, the present empty, there is no doer, no receiver of consequences; this time doesn't move, another time doesn't shift — what thing is therein to be called religious practice? *Where does religious practice come from? Where is it?* Who is the body? By whom is it performed? Does it exist? Does it not exist? It is form? Is it not form? Is it sensation? Is it not sensation? Is it conception? Is it not conception? Is it action? Is it not action? Is it consciousness? Is it not consciousness? Contemplating in this way, because the reality of religious practice cannot be apprehended, because *the things of*

ten powers. How do they know that their [worldly] home is not [their true] home, so that they can leave home and learn the path? How do they use means to cultivate noble conduct, become endowed with the path of the ten abodes, and quickly attain *bodhi*-wisdom?' [Dharma Wisdom] answered, 'Bodhisattvas first should distinguish ten types of dharmas, that is, the three deeds [of six dharmas], the Buddha, the Dharma, the Sangha, and the precepts. If the body [itself] was noble conduct, then noble conduct would be defiled, like a mass of worms. If physical deeds [themselves] were noble conduct, then [noble conduct would be] the four activities [of going, stopping, sitting, and lying down], glancing around, and lifting and lowering your feet. If the mouth [itself] were noble conduct, then [noble conduct would be] sounds, breath, lips, teeth, and the movement of the tongue. If verbal deeds [themselves] were noble conduct, then [noble conduct would be just] words. … [And so forth,] up to, if the precepts [themselves] were noble conduct, the [noble conduct would be] the precepts platform, the questions on purity by

past, present, and future are all empty, because the intellect has no attachment, because the mind has no obstruction, because the sphere of operation is nondual, because expedient means are free, because of acceptance of formless truth, because of contemplation of formless truth, because of knowing the Buddha's teaching is equanimious, because of *fulfilling all qualities of Buddhahood*, is such practice called pure religious practice.

Ten things should also be cultivated: knowledge of what is so and what is not; knowledge of past, present, and future consequences of actions; knowledge of all meditations, liberations, and concentrations; knowledge of superiority and inferiority of faculties; knowledge of all kinds of understandings; knowledge of all kinds of realms; knowledge of where all paths lead; unhindered clairvoyance; unhindered knowledge of past lives; knowledge of the eternal cancellation of habit energy. *Contemplating each of these ten powers of the enlightened, in each power are innumerable meanings*; one should ask about them, and after having heard about them should arouse a mind of great kindness and compassion and observe sentient beings without abandoning them, reflect on the teachings unceasingly, carry out superlative deeds without seeking rewards, comprehend that objects are like dreams, like illusions, like reflections, like echoes, and like magical productions. *If enlightening beings can unite with such contemplations, they will not entertain a dualistic understanding of things and all enlightening teachings will become evident to them: at the time of their first determination they will immediately attain complete perfect enlightenment, will know all things are the mind's own nature, and will perfect the body of wisdom and understand without relying on another.*

The last part of this section has been quoted already in the *Mo-ho chih-kuan*; see notes at 62a27 and 87a25–26.

Beginning bodhisattvas 初心大士: or, "great beings who have just aroused the thought of, or aspiration for, enlightenment."

Three deeds 三業: involve six dharmas: body, physical deeds, mouth, verbal deeds, mind, and mental deeds.

Questions on purity by the assembly of ten [witnesses], the precept master, the fourfold motions 十衆問清浄戒師白四

the assembly of ten [witnesses], the precept master, the fourfold motions [of the ordination ceremony], shaving the head, begging, and so forth? None of these are noble conduct. Where is noble conduct? Who possesses noble conduct? The three times [of past, present, and future] are undiscriminated, like emptiness. This is called [skillful] means. Again, further cultivation and an increase of these ten dharmas results in the ten powers that are exceedingly **[96b]** profound and immeasurable. Those who contemplate in this way will quickly attain all the virtuous qualities of the Buddhas. At the time of their first aspiration they will already perfect correct awakening, know the true nature of all dharmas, and be fully endowed with the body of wisdom, and this enlightenment does not rely on others." In light of this clear text, how can it be said that a beginner does not cultivate and realize the ten powers?

Again, as the *Bodhisattva-bhūmi* says, "Bodhisattvas know the *tathāgata-garbha*. They cultivate the dhyāna of self-nature before they [even] hear or ponder [the Dharma], and attain the realization of universal dhyāna. There are three types of 'universal dhyāna'. First is that of the bliss of manifesting the Dharma. Because of this bliss of manifesting the Dharma, this is called the 'stage of joy.' Second is giving birth to the

羯磨: these three items describe the fourfold ordination ceremony for becoming a monk or nun, which involves stating your intent and asking and receiving approval three times, and requires the presence of three previously ordained masters and seven additional witnesses. See also above at *Mo-ho chih-kuan* 36b4.

Bodhisattvas know ... benefiting sentient beings: see the *Bodhisattva-bhūmi* at T 30.921b29–c10. The context, which gives a number of lists of various types of dhyāna, reads:

> What is the content of the bodhisattva's *dhyāna-pāramitā*? In brief, there are nine types. First is the "dhyāna of self-nature" 自性禪. Second is "universal dhyāna" 一切禪. Third is "difficult dhyāna." Fourth is "all categories of dhyāna." Fifth is "the dhyāna of good people." Sixth is "the dhyāna of all practices." Seventh is "the dhyāna of removing passionate afflictions." Eighth is "the dhyāna of this realm and the other realm." Ninth is "the dhyāna of being free from mistaken views."
>
> What is the "dhyāna of self-nature"? By nature 藏 the bodhisattvas practice worldly and transworldly good [deeds] before they hear or ponder 聞思 [the Dharma]. They singlemindedly dwell peacefully, either in cessation 止, or in contemplation 觀, or in these two in the same way, or in these [two] integrated. This is the "dhyāna of self-nature."
>
> What is the "universal dhyāna" of the bodhisattvas? In brief there are two types: first are the worldly, and second are the transworldly [dhyānas]. Again, depending on the place, there should be three types for each. First is the dhyāna of dwelling in the bliss from manifesting the Dharma. Second is the dhyāna of giving birth to the virtuous quality of the samādhi. Third is the dhyāna of benefiting sentient beings.

The nine types of dhyāna have appeared previously in the *Mo-ho chih-kuan* at 30c19–20.

Bliss of manifesting the Dharma 現法樂 or, "the manifestation of Dharma bliss"?

samāpatti (concentration) of the potential *(gotra)* of the ten powers, and to the removal [of afflictions] and realizations of those of the two vehicles. Third is the dhyāna of benefiting sentient beings." [Being at the stages of] the ten abodes is called "hearing and pondering" [the Dharma], and [being at the stages of] the ten levels of practice is called "wisdom through hearing" [the Dharma]. By cultivating [the dhyāna of] self-nature before this "hearing and pondering" [the Dharma], you realize the universal dhyānas, the attainment of which includes these three dharmas.

How, then, can it be said that these [dharmas] are not for the beginner to cultivate or to realize? The evidence of these three [texts] is clear. The steps on the path, the six perfections, and the ten powers of the Buddha are mutually involved and encompass each other, as I have explained above. If you cultivate the steps on the path and the six perfections, this is to cultivate the ten powers of the Buddha. If you regulate and overcome the six sense faculties and fulfill the six perfections, you will have fulfilled the ten powers, which is no different from dwelling in the noble demeanor of the Buddha.

The *Treatise on the Ten Stages* says, "[The ten] powers are all supporting aids, and their energy cannot be exhausted." The *Bodhisattva-bhūmi* says, "The attainment of something superior and the ability to endure it is called 'power.'" These ten "places" [that is, the ten powers?] are like reality; they involve freedom from empty delusions and victory over the demons. It involves practice on your own; therefore it is called "the attainment of something superior." It involves the ability to benefit sentient beings through [skillful] means; therefore it is called "the ability to endure."

[Question:] The power of the Buddha is immeasurable. Why is it limited to ten [types]?

[Answer:] In reality there is only one wisdom, but we say there are ten with relation to ten matters. These ten are sufficient for transforming sentient beings. When ten are provided, the rest should also be known. The *Aṅgulimāla Sūtra* says, "The 'ten powers' are a teaching for śrāvakas, and are not of the

Powers are all supporting aids, and their energy cannot be exhausted 力名扶助氣力不可窮盡: a phrase from the *Treatise on the Ten Stages*, T 26.82b6–7.

The attainment of something superior and the ability to endure it is called "power" 得勝堪能名爲力: See the *Bodhisattva-bhūmi*, T 30.896b28–c7, although the phrasing is different:

> What is "power"? In brief, there are three types. The first is for Buddhas and bodhisattvas to *attain* mastery over samādhi, and by this mastery over samādhi *be able to endure* all with regard to your desires. This is called "noble power."

The "ten powers" are a teaching for śrāvakas, and are not of the Mahāyāna. The Mahāyāna involves immeasurable powers 十力是聲聞宗非摩訶衍。大乘有無量力: verses in the *Aṅgulimāla Sūtra*, T 2.532b5–7:

> The so-called nine-sectioned sūtras

Mahāyāna. The Mahāyāna involves immeasurable powers." These two interpretations more fully manifest the meaning of the four types of the ten powers.

2. Encompassing the Four Fearlessnesses [96b20]

How do the parts of the way encompass the four fearlessnesses? [1] Fearlessness from [having attained] omniscience refers to completely knowing the four types of the [Noble] Truth of suffering and making [conventional] distinctions [concerning this truth] for the sake of others, to clearly indicate their faults, to be determined and roar like a lion, without even a trace of fear, and to have no difficulty in affirming this teaching [as right] or denying that teaching [as wrong]. [2] Fearlessness [in teaching] the obstacles to the path refers to being determined and roar like a lion even if the four types of the [Noble] Truth of the causes [of suffering] obstruct the four [types of the Noble Truths of] the path and extinction, and to have no difficulty in saying that this does not [really] obstruct the path. [3] Fearlessness in [teaching] exhaustively of suffering and the path refers to [knowing] the four types [of the Noble Truth] of the path and being able to practice the path, attaining the exhaustion of suffering and transcending this [mundane] world, being determined and roar like a lion, without even a trace of fear. [4] Fearlessness from having no outflows [of defilements] refers to the four types of the [Noble] Truth of extinction each having something to be realized and each having something to be extinguished, to be determined and roaring like a lion, without even a trace of fear. Thus the steps on the path and [the four] fearlessnesses are mutually involved and encompass each other. If you cultivate the steps on the path and the six perfections, this is to cultivate fearlessness, **[96c]** and to dwell in the noble demeanor of the Buddha.

Are of the śrāvaka vehicle;
They are not of the Mahāyāna.
The Mahāyāna consists of a single vehicle.
The Tathāgata's wisdom is unobstructed;
Why are ten named?
The so-called ten types of power
Belong to the śrāvaka vehicle;
They are not of the Mahāyāna.
The Mahāyāna involves immeasurable powers.

Four fearlessnesses 四無所畏: the *Introduction to Graded Themes of the Dharma Realm* lists four fearlessnesses as follows: 1. fearlessness from [having attained] omniscience 一切智, that is, the Buddha is without fear because he is knowledgable about all things; 2. fearlessness from having exhausted all defilements 漏盡, that is, the Buddha is without fear because he has exhaustively severed all passionate afflictions and defilements; 3. fearlessness in teaching the obstacles to the path 説障道, that is, the Buddha teaches without fear about the causes of suffering and the delusions and so forth that are obstacles to the path; 4. fearlessness in exhaustively teaching about suffering and the path 説盡苦道, that is, the Buddha teaches exhaustively and without fear about how to resolve suffering in this world (T 46.694c14–695a20).

The *Ta chih tu lun* says, "To be fully endowed [with good qualities] within your mind is called 'power'; to function externally without being afraid is called 'fearlessness.'" The *Treatise on the Ten Stages* says, "Why is it said that there are 'four' for the single matter (dharma) called fearlessness? It is because you have no doubt concerning four matters that there are said to be four [types]." [On the other hand,] the Buddha has no fear with regard to all dharmas. Why, then, are there only four [types of fearlessness]? [Because] this raises the essential matters and reveals the details [concerning these four types of fearlessness]; then you will not have fear concerning other matters.

To be fully endowed [with good qualities] within your mind is called 'power'; to function externally without being afraid is called 'fearlessness' 內心具足名爲力外用無怯名無畏: see the questions on the resemblances between the ten powers and the four fearlessnesses at T 25.242a29–b26, following the section on the ten powers (235a–241b). Many of the phrases in this section by Chih-i seem to have been taken from this section in the *Ta chih tu lun*. Lamotte (*La Traité* 3, 1573–75) translates:

> Question. — Les dix forces *(bala)* sont des savoirs *(jñāna)* et les quatre assurances *(vaiśāradya),* elles aussi, sont des savoirs. Quelles sont donc les ressemblances et le différences?
>
> Résponse. — Quand on expose au long *(vistareṇa)* les qualités *(guṇa)* du Buddha, il s'agit de *bala*; quand on les expose en bref *(saṃkṣepeṇa)*, il s'agit de *vaiśāradya.*
>
> En outre, là où il y a activité *(kriyā),* il y a *bala*; là où il n'y a ni doute *(saṃāśaya)* ni difficulté *(duṣkara)*, il y a *vaiśāradya.*
>
> Là où la sagess *(prajñā)* s'accumule, il y a *bala*; quand on disperse les ignorances *(avidyā)*, il y a *vaiśaradya.*
>
> Accumuler les bons dharma *(kuśala-dharma),* c'est *bala*; détruire les mauvais dharma *(akuśaladharma),* c'est *vaiśāradya*....
>
> Question. — Qu'appelle-t-on assurance *(vaiśāradya)*?
>
> Réponse. — L'absence de doute *(niḥsaṃśaya),* l'absence de crainte *(nirbhaya),* le non-recul de la sagesse, ne pas se décourager *(anālīnatā),* ne pas s'horripiler *(aromaharṣa),* en toutes choses agir comme on l'a dit *(tathāvādī tathākārī),* voilà le *vaiśāradya.*

Chodron (3, 1288–89) translates:

> Question. – The ten powers are knowledges and the four fearlessnesses are also knowledges. What are the similarities and the differences?
>
> Answer. When the qualities of the Buddha are explained at length, this is power; when they explained in brief, this is fearlessness.
>
> Furthermore, when there is activity, this is power; when there is neither doubt nor difficulty, this is fearlessness.
>
> When wisdom is accumulated, this is power; when ignorance is dispersed, this is fearlessness.
>
> Accumulating good dharmas is power; destroying bad dharmas is fearlessness....
>
> Question. – What is fearlessness called?
>
> Answer. – The absence of doubt, the absence of fear, the non-decline of wisdom, not becoming discouraged, not becoming exasperated, acting in all ways as has been said, all that is fearlessness.

Why is it said that there are "four" ... said to be four: 一法名無畏云何言四。於四事中無疑故名四: see the *Treatise on Ten Stages* at T 26.82a9–11:

> Question: [There is] one dharma called 'fearlessness'. Why, then, are there four?
>
> Answer: It is within four matters that one has no doubt or fear; therefore there are four [types].

3. *Encompassing the Eighteen Unique Qualities* [96c5]

[For the steps on the path] to encompass the eighteen unique qualities is as follows.

Eighteen unique qualities: see the discussion of the eighteen unique qualities of the Buddha in a long section of the *Ta chih tu lun*, T 25.247b11–256b4 (Lamotte, *Le Traité* 3, 1625–1701). The *Ta chih tu lun* (247b11–19) lists them as follows (Lamotte, 1625–1626):

Voici les dix huit attributs exclusifs *(aṣṭādaśāveṇikadharma)*:
1. Le Tathāgata n'a pas de faute corporelle *(nāsti tathāgatasya skhalitam)*.
2. I'l n'a pas de faute vocale *(nāsti ravitam)*.
3. I'l n'a pas de mémoire défaillante *(nāsti muṣitasmṛtitā)*.
4. I'l n'a pas notion de variété *(nāsti nānātvasaṃjñā)*.
5. I'l n'a pas de pensée non-concentrée *(nāsty asamāhitaṃ cittam)*.
6. I'l n'a pas d'indifférence inconsidérée *(nāsty apratisaṃkhyāyopekṣa)*.
7. I'l n'a pas perte de zèle *(nāsti chanda-parihāṇiḥ)*.
8. I'l n'a pas perte d'énergie *(nāsti vīrya-parihāṇiḥ)*.
9. I'l n'a pas perte de mémoire *(nāsti smṛti-parihāṇiḥ)*.
10. I'l n'a pas perte de sagesse *(nāsti prajñā-parihāṇiḥ)*.
11. I'l n'a pas perte de déliverance *(nāsti vīmuktiparihāṇiḥ)*.
12. I'l n'a pas perte du savoir et de la vision de la déliverance *(nāsti vimuktijñāna-darśanaparihāṇiḥ)*.
13. Tout acte corporel du Tathāgata est précédé du savoir et accompagne le savoir *(sarvaṃ tathāgatasya kāyakarma jñānapūrvaṃgamaṃ jñānānuparivarti)*.
14. Tout acte vocal est précédé du savoir et accompagne le savoir *(sarvaṃ vākkarma jñānapūrvaṃgamaṃ jñānānuparivarti)*.
15. Tout acte mental est précédé du savoir et accompagne le savoir *(sarvaṃ manaskarma jñānapūrvaṃgamaṃ jñānānu-parivarti)*.
16. Il a sur le temps passé un savoir et une vision sans attache et sans obstacle *(atīte 'dhvany asaṅgam apratihataṃ jñānaṃ darśanam)*.
17. Il a sur le temps futur un savoir et une vision sans attache et sans obstacle *(anāgate 'dhvany asaṅgam apratihataṃ jñānaṃ darśanam)*.
18. Il a sur le temps présent un savoir et une vision sans attache et sans obstacle *(pratyutpanne 'dhvany asaṅgam apratihataṃ jñānaṃ darśanam)*.

Chodron (3, 1335–36) translates:

Here are the eighteen special attributes:
1. The Tathāgata has no bodily defect.
2. He has no vocal defect.
3. He has no failure of memory.
4. He has no notion of variety.
5. He does not have an unconcentrated mind.
6. He does not have thoughtless indifference.
7. He has no loss of zealousness.
8. He has no loss of exertion.
9. He has no loss of mindfulness.
10. He has no loss of wisdom.
11. He has no loss of liberation.
12. He has no loss of the knowledge and vision of deliverance.
13. Every bodily action of the Tathāgata is preceded by knowledge and accompanies knowledge.
14. Every vocal action is preceded by knowledge and accompanies knowledge.
15. Every mental action is preceded by knowledge and accompanies knowledge.
16. He has non-attached and unobstructed knowledge about past time.
17. He has non-attached and unobstructed knowledge about future time.

First is to be [1] physically and [2] verbally without fault. These two qualities correspond to [the aspects of] the four types of the steps on the path of right deeds, [right] speech, and [right] way of life.

Not being haughty when receiving offerings, and not becoming dejected when being subject to slander is called [5] "complete meditative concentration." 無不定心. To constantly maintain concentration in the four proper activities [of going, stopping, sitting, and lying down] is called [6] "not being indifferent to or abandoning anyone" 無不知已捨. These two qualities correspond to the aspects of the four types of the steps on the path of the eight types of concentration.

To cultivate the precepts physically and [to cultivate] wisdom mentally without becoming exhausted is called [7] "not lacking in zeal" 欲無減. To compassionately save others, and to abide calmly in quiescent extinction that neither increases nor decreases, is called [8] "not lacking in diligence" 精進無減. To experience suffering for immeasurable kalpas for the sake of all sentient beings is called [9] "not lacking in mindfulness" 念無減. These three qualities correspond to the aspects of the four types of the steps on the path of the eight types of diligence.

To constantly illuminate the minds of sentient beings in the three times [of past, present, and future], without contemplating anything else, and to preach the Dharma for their sake without losing the previous mindfulness, is called [10] "not lacking wisdom" 慧無減. To keep in mind the [mundane] matters of the three times and not forget them is called [11] "not lacking in liberation" 解脫無減. To spontaneously attain awakening, unlike those of the two vehicles, is called [12] "not lacking in the knowledge and insight of liberation" 解脫知見無減. To have as your basis the wisdom of all physical deeds, and to attain unobstructed wisdom to preach without exhaustion, is called [13] "physical deeds accompanied by the action of wisdom" 身業共智慧行. [14–15] The action of wisdom accompanied by verbal and mental [deeds] is also like this. These eleven qualities correspond to the ten types of wisdom within the four types of the steps on the path.

The summation of the encompassing of these qualities [by the steps on the path] is as explained above.

18. He has non-attached and unobstructed knowledge about the present time.

Eleven qualities 十一法: Presumably including the five qualities that are not specifically mentioned here (though alluded to in the descriptions of other of the eighteen qualities), that is, [3] to be without fault mentally 心無失, [4] equanimity with regard to sentient beings 無異想, and [16–18] to be unobstructed in wisdom and knowledge with regard to all that was in the past 智慧知過去世無礙, present 智慧知現在世無礙, and future 智慧知未来世無礙.

4. Encompassing the Four Unobstructed Eloquences [96c19]

[For the steps on the path] to encompass the four unobstructed wisdoms [or "eloquences"; *pratisaṃvid*] is as follows. To be unobstructed with regard to the Dharma teachings refers to the names and words of the Dharma teachings with regard to the four types of the Four [Noble] Truths. Names and words are discriminated by the mind; if there is no mind [or thoughts, or mental process], then what will produce names? Since we already realize that one thought 一心 is immeasurable thoughts, we can also know that one name is immeasurable names. "Names" are inexhaustible. This is called "to be unobstructed concerning the Dharma teachings."

To be unobstructed with regard to the meaning [of the Dharma] refers to [realizing that] all Dharma teachings and all names return to one meaning, that is, the meaning of truth as it is. This is called "to be unobstructed with regard to the meaning."

To be unobstructed with regard to words refers to fully understanding all [verbal expressions], even though the words and expressions of the sentient beings of the ten dharma realms are not the same. The sounds and words of the ten realms are realized in one sound and word, so if you know [the words of] one realm, you understand [the words of all] ten realms, without any obstructions. This is called "to be unobstructed with regard to words."

Again, the "Dharma teachings" consist of the Dharma gates of the Four [Noble] Truths, the "meaning" consists of the four types of the Truth of the path, and the "words" consist of the four types of the Truth of suffering.

To be unobstructed with regard to eloquence in preaching refers to be skillful in using the four types of the Four Truths as applied to the capacities and conditions [of sentient beings]. To turn and join [the immeasurable variations of the teachings] and to preach without exhaustion, leading others to the bliss of hearing [the Dharma], preaching all words within one word, **[97a]** with all meanings expressed in all sounds; this is surely the way to be imbued with benefits individually, each according to one's spiritual capability.

The summation of the encompassing [of these by the steps on the path] is as explained above.

Four unobstructed wisdoms [eloquences] 四無礙智(辯): see the long section on four eloquences *(catuṣ-pratisaṃvid)*, T 25.246a22–247b3 (Lamotte, *Le Traité* 3, 1614–24), between the sections on the four fearlessnesses and eighteen unique dharmas. The four are: unobstructed wisdom concerning the meaning 義, the Dharma (teachings) 法, words 辭, and eloquence in preaching 樂說.

5. *Encompassing the six supranormal powers* [97a2]

[For the steps on the path] to encompass the six supranormal powers is as follows. The three supranormal powers of the [divine] eye [天]眼, [divine] ear [天]耳, and appearing wherever you wish 如意 are as explained above in the section on regulating and overcoming the sense faculties. [The three supranormal powers of] reading other minds 他心, knowing past lives 宿命, and exhausting defilements 漏盡 are as explained in [the section on] the ten powers.

6. *Encompassing the three illuminating insights* [97a3]

[For the steps on the path] to encompass the three illuminating insights is as explained under the six supranormal powers.

7. *Encompassing the four inducements* [97a4]

[For the steps on the path] to encompass the four inducements is as follows. If you give, this is encompassed by the components of awakening of abandonment [or equanimity] *(upekṣasaṃbodhyana)* and removal [of afflictions] among the four types of the parts of the path. "Loving words" are included in right deeds, [right] speech, and [right] way of life among the four types of the parts of the path. "Beneficial action" and "help through affinity" correspond to the eight concentrations among the four types of the parts of the path. Concentration (samādhi) involves supranormal power, and therefore you are able to perform beneficial actions and to help through [feeling] affinity [for others].

Six supranormal powers 六(神)通: for details, see the lengthy treatment in the *Ta chih tu lun*, T 25.264a21–265b16 (Lamotte, *Le Traité* 4, 1809–27).

Regulating and overcoming the sense facuties 調伏諸根: see above at *Mo-ho chih-kuan* 84c–95c.

Ten powers: see above at *Mo-ho chih-kuan* 95c–96b.

Three illuminating insights 三明: the three supranormal insights attained by arhats: 1. the ability to see the conditions and events of the past and thus know the faults of oneself and others; 2. the ability to see the results that are to come in the future, and thus be able to sever mistaken views; and 3. the ability to know and thus exhaust all the passionate afflictions of the present.

Four inducements 四攝: four methods used to induce people to convert to the Buddhist path: 1. *dāna* 布施: "giving" (preaching) the Dharma, and giving things that people need; 2. *priya-vādita* 愛語: inducing people through "loving" words; 3. *artha-caryā* 利行: "beneficial action"; helping people through physical, verbal, or mental conduct; and 4. *samānārthatā* 同事: "help through affinity"; to help others by putting oneself in their position, and being able to help through the affinity thus experienced.

8. Encompassing dhāraṇī [97a7]

[For the steps on the path] to encompass *dhāraṇī* is as follows. Holding good qualities is like a vessel filled to the brim with water; inhibiting evil qualities is like building [a fence of] thorns to protect the fruit. This corresponds to the four proper endeavors among the aspects of the four types of the steps on the path. One endeavors to hinder two evil [qualities], and endeavors to arouse two good [qualities]. Therefore the *Treatise on the Ten Stages* says,

Encompassing *dhāraṇī* 攝陀羅尼: see the *Ta chih tu lun*, T 25.268a1–b4 (Lamotte, *Le Traité* 4, 1854–69). The functions of *dhāraṇī* as described in this section include helping one to "hold" or "retain" 持 what you have heard (268a2–7) and to bring out the "good qualities" 善法 of a bodhisattva (268a29–b4). Lamotte (*Le Traité* 4, 1865 and 1869) translates:

> Auiconque veut retenir ce qu'il a entendu doit y songer attentivement de façon à développer sa mémoire *(smṛti)*. D'abord il doit songer à une chose analogue [déjà connue de lui] et y lier sa pensée de façon à découvrir une chose qu'il n'a pas encore vue. Ainsi *Tcheou-li-p'an-t'o-kia* (Cūḍapanthaka) mit tant d'attention à nettoyer des chaussures de cuir *(upanāha)* que son esprit *(manas)* se concentra et qu'il élimina les souillures de sa pensée *(cittamala)*. Telle est, chez le débutant *(ādikarmika)*, la Dhāraṇī retenant ce qu'on a entendu.…
>
> Le Bodhisattva que obtient toutes les concentrations du triple temps (*tryadhvasamādhi*), — concentration de l'éclat sans obstacle *(ānantaryaprabhā)*, etc. — obtient en chacune de ces concentrations d'innombrables et incalculables Dhāraṇī. Mises ensemble elles portent le nom de *Pañcaśatadhāraṇīmukha* "Les cinq cents moyens de mémorisation" et constituent le trésor des bons attributs et qualités du Bodhisattva *(bodhisattvakuśaladharmaguṇakośa)*.

Chodron (3, 1533–35) translates:

> Whoever wishes to retain that which he has heard must think of it attentively so as to develop his memory. First he should think of an analogous thing (already familiar to him] and to join that to his mind so as to discover a thing that he has not yet seen. Thus Cūdapanthaka paid so much attention to cleaning leather shoes that his mind became concentrated and he eliminated the stains of his mind. In the beginner, this is the dhāraṇī of retaining what one has heard.…
>
> The bodhisattva who acquires all the concentrations of the three times - concentration of unhindered brilliance, etc., - acquires each of these innumerable incalculable dhāraṇīs. Together, they are given the name of *pañcaśatadhāraṇīmukha*, "the five hundred means of memorizing"'and constitute the treasury of the good attributes and qualities of the bodhisattva.

In other sections of the *Mo-ho chih-kuan* Chih-i discusses the use of *dhāraṇī* as a way to control or overcome evil qualities; see the section on the Vaipulya Samādhi, 13a29–14a5.

Inhibiting evil qualities 遮諸惡法: in his description of the Great Vaipulya Dhāraṇī, one of Chih-i's definitions of *dhāraṇī* is "the great secret essence for inhibiting evil and sustaining good" 遮惡持善, in turn based on a definion of *dhāraṇī* as "securing good qualities" and "preventing unwholesome propensities" in the *Ta chih tu lun*, T 25.95c10016. For details, see note at *Mo-ho chih-kuan* 13b23.

Building [a fence of thorns] to protect fruit 棘援防果: or, "apply thorns to hinder [the development of evil] fruit"?

Severing evil qualities that have already arisen
is like removing a poisonous snake.
Severing evil qualities that have not yet arisen
is like making a dike for flowing water [in anticipation of a flood].
Bolstering good that has already arisen
is like irrigating plants that produce sweet fruit.
[Encouraging] good qualities that have not yet arisen
is like boring on wood to produce a fire.

9. *Encompassing the Thirty-two Major Marks* [97a15]

[For the steps on the path] to encompass the thirty-two major marks [of the Buddha] is as follows. The *Treatise on the Ten Stages* says that "In the chapter on the thirty-two marks in the Abhidharma, each individual mark is distinguished as having three types, that is, the essence of the mark, the karmic deeds [or causes] of the mark, and the results of the mark." The *Ta chih tu lun* says that "Over a hundred kalpas, [the Buddha] plants the seeds of the thirty-two marks." This is the meaning here.

Hinder two evil and arouse two good qualities 勤遮二惡勤生二善: That is, one strives to hinder the arising of evil qualities that have not yet arisen and extinguish evil qualities that have already arisen, and one strives to arouse good qualities that have not yet arisen and maintain good qualities that have already arisen.

Treatise on the Ten Stages: verses quoted from the *Treatise* at T 26.106c17–20.

Thirty-two major marks 三十二相: for a list of the thirty-two major physical marks of a Buddha, see Hurvitz, *Chih-i*, 353–55. Following the pattern in this whole section of taking up themes in order from the *Ta chih tu lun*, see also the long section on the thirty-two major marks and eighty minor marks in the *Ta chih tu lun*, T 25.273a10–276b20 (Lamotte, *Le Traité* 4, 1905–30).

… each individual mark is distinguished as having three types, that is, the essence of the mark, the karmic deeds [or causes] of the mark, and the results of the mark 一一相三種分別謂相體相業相果: see the *Treatise on the Ten Stages* at T 26.6bc27–29:

> In the chapter on the thirty-two marks in the Abhidharma, each individual mark is distinguished as having three types. They should all be known in this way. Question: What are the three types with which each individual mark is distinguished? Answer: the first is taught as the essence of the mark 相體; the second is taught as the result of the mark 相果; the third is taught as the activity [karmic deeds] of the mark 相業.

This passage has already been quoted above: see *Mo-ho chih-kuan* 13a4.

Over a hundred kalpas, [the Buddha] plants the seeds of the thirty-two marks 百劫種三十二相: see the *Ta chih tu lun* at T 25.87b24–27, where it says that it takes only takes ninety-one kalpas, if all goes well. See Lamotte (*Le Traité* 1, 252); Chodron (1, 213) translates:

> Question. During how long a time does the Bodhisattva accomplish the [actions producing] the thirty-two marks?
> Answer. During a hundred kalpas if he goes slowly, during ninety-one kal-

If we step back and examine this [encompassing of the thirty-two marks] in terms of the aspects of the six perfections of the steps on the path of the Tripitaka [Teachings], [we should say that] in the final analysis it does not go beyond giving, [upholding] the precepts, and wisdom. I will not go into a troublesome explanation, but you should be able to know the meaning of encompassing [in this context].

The essence, activities, and fruit of the [thirty-two] marks for the Shared Teachings are not the same as the above [for the Tripitaka Teachings]. If we were to seek the Buddha [only] with regard to these [physical] marks, then a world ruler (Cakravartirāja) would [the same as] a Tathāgata. People [who think] in this way practice a heterodox way. The Buddha taught that "the thirty-two marks are not [substantial] thirty-two marks." Each and every one is purified by the mind of emptiness; that which corresponds to emptiness is called a [true] mark. The *Treatise on the Ten Stages* again says, "Bodhisattvas single-mindedly cultivate the deeds [that cause] the thirty-two marks, and all have wisdom as their basis." This refers to the wisdom of emptiness. If so, then the thirty-two marks are all encompassed by the perfection of wisdom and the ten wisdoms that are the aspects of [the steps on] the path. This is the meaning [in the context] of the Shared Teachings.

Again, the two previous [Tripitaka and Shared] Teachings of the steps on the path clarify the causes so that you can attain [the thirty-two marks] through cultivating the karmic deeds for the marks, and discuss the fruits so that you can attain the essence of the marks. However, though these marks are a little superior to those of the world ruler *(cakrarāja)*, Māra is also able to transform himself [to possess them]; therefore they are not particularly unique [to the Buddha]. [Also,] when you enter nirvana without remainder, these marks are extinguished forever. This is like obtaining a bronze [mirror], but not being able to see your face [in it]. Those of the two vehicles

pas if he goes quickly. The Bodhisattva Śākyamuni realized the thirty-two marks in ninety-one kalpas.

It is not clear how these two passages illustrate the point Chih-i is making here.

Cakravartirāja is the same as a Tathāgata 轉輪聖王即是如來: because a world ruler is also endowed with these physical marks of a "great man."

Thirty-two marks are not thirty-two marks 三十二相卽非三十二相: A phrase from *The Diamond Sūtra*, T 8.750a22–23:

You cannot perceive the Tathāgata by means of the thirty-two marks. Why? The Tathāgata teaches that the thirty-two marks are not [substantial] marks, [therefore] they are called thirty-two marks.

Bodhisattvas single-mindedly cultivate the deeds [that cause] the thirty-two marks, and all have wisdom as their basis 菩薩一心修習三十二相業皆以慧爲本: a phrase from the *Treatise on the Ten Stages*, T 26.65c24–25, from the beginning of its explanation of the "karmic deeds" that cause the thirty-two marks.

and the Buddha of the Tripitaka [Teachings] can both realize true [emptiness], but this is not the [ultimate] image of the Dharma realm. You should know that the two previous [**97b**] [understandings of the] steps on the path are not the [true, ultimate] cultivation of the [thirty-two] marks. The latter two [interpretations] of the steps on the path [of the Distinct and Perfect Teachings] are the [true, ultimate] cultivation of the [thirty-two] marks. The *Lotus Sūtra* says, "Having profoundly mastered the features of offences and goodness, and universally illuminating all ten directions, [the Buddha's] extremely subtle and pure Dharma body is endowed with the thirty-two marks." If you realize the Middle Way, then the Middle Way is endowed with these [thirty-two] marks. As we see in the *Lotus Sūtra*, if those of the two vehicles are exposed to, signified concerning, awakened, and enter the sublime [Dharma] and encounter the Middle Way, they receive the prediction of the eight phases of a Buddha's life. This is analogous to acquiring a mirror in which myriad images will certainly be reflected; those of the Mahāyāna attain the Middle [Way] and so there is nothing that they cannot manifest. The "marks of the Dharma body" are called the "true marks." The *Vimalakīrti Sūtra* says, "[The Buddha] has already abandoned the marks and characteristics of worldly existence." The world ruler and Māra adorn their bodies with worldly marks, but these are all empty delusions; therefore it is said that [the Buddha] "has already abandoned" them. The Middle Way is like a clear mirror; originally it has no marks [but only reflects images]. To

Having profoundly mastered ... is endowed with the thirty-two marks 深達罪福相遍照於十方。微妙淨法身具相三十二: these verses from the *Lotus Sūtra*, T 9.35b28–29, have been quoted many times already in the *Mo-ho chih-kuan*. See note at 6c2–3; see also above at 40b26, 41c29–42a2, and 49c28–29.

Expose, signify, awaken, enter 開示悟入: these famous phrases from the *Lotus Sūtra*, T 9.97a22–b1, have been used many times already in the *Mo-ho chih-kuan*. For details, see note at 26b27, and use at 31a8–9, 34a21, 81b26, and 85a6.

Receive the prediction of the eight aspects of a Buddha 八相佛記: that is, they will receive the assurance that they will experience the various aspects of a Buddha's historical life—from descending from the Tuṣita heaven and entering his mother's womb, to turning the wheel of the Dharma and entering final nirvana. In short, they will become Buddhas.

Those of the Mahāyāna attain the Middle and so there is nothing that they cannot manifest 大乘得中靡所不現: or, "the Mahāyāna [teachings] consist of the Middle, so there is nothing that is does not manifest"?

True marks 眞相: In contrast to the temporary and conventional physical marks of the historical Buddha?

Has already abandoned the marks and characteristics of worldly existence 已捨世間所有相好: a phrase from the opening passage of the *Vimalakīrti Sūtra* at T 24.537a18. Rather than "marks and characteristics" 相好, however, the sūtra has "adorning marks" 相飾. This is given as a variant reading in the Taishō text.

have no [substantial] marks and yet [to manifest] marks means that [having] somewhat attractive or ugly [features] depends on this—more or less [manifesting them] in response to conditions. Such a universal manifestation of a physical body are "true marks." The *Contemplation of the Buddha of Immeasurable Life* says "The Buddha Amitāyus has eighty-four thousand marks, and each individual mark contains eighty-four thousand secondary marks." The *Satya Sūtra* and the *Avataṃsaka Sūtra* all say, "The [thirty-two major] marks are like a sea of great marks, and the [eighty] secondary marks are like a sea of minor marks." This is called a "sea of marks"; why should it be limited to thirty-two marks? Conditions are not the same, and there are more or less depending on the person. These are the truly real marks, and are encompassed by the steps on the path of the Distinct and Perfect [Teachings]. This meaning should be known, and does not require going into details.

4. Summary [97b14]

You should thus know that the auxiliary practices of the path of the six perfections encompass all good dharmas, which are immeasurable and unlimited, as I have taken up above in twelve sections to indicate only a fragment of the meaning. You should know that the remaining [elements that are not explicitly discussed] are also encompassed. Since the auxiliary practices of the path are like this, how much more is it so of the path proper.

The Buddha Amitāyus has eighty-four thousand marks, and each individual mark contains eighty-four thousand secondary marks 彌陀佛八萬四千相一一相八萬四千好: see the *Contemplation of the Buddha of Immeasurable Life* at T 12.343b24–25, which continues, "Each individual secondary marks contains eighty-four thousands rays of light. Each individual ray of light illuminates the worlds in the ten directions."

The [thirty-two major] marks are like a sea of great marks, and the [eighty] secondary marks are like a sea of minor marks 相爲大相海好爲小相海: the *Satya Sūtra* discusses the thirty-two major marks and eighty minor marks at T 9.342a–345c, but there is no mention of marks being like a "sea." The *Avataṃsaka Sūtra* discusses the thirty-two major marks in Chapter 29, the "Sea of the Tathāgata's Marks," at T 9.601a22–606c25

Twelve sections 十二條: it is not clear how this chapter is to be divided into twelve sections. Ikeda (*Kenkyūchūshaku*, 412) interprets this as referring to the explication of 1. regulating and overcoming the six sense faculties, 2. the ten powers, 3. the four fearlessnesses and the eighteen unique qualities, 4. the four unobstructed [wisdoms or eloquences], 5. the six supranormal powers, 6. the three illuminating insights, 7. the four inducements, 8. *dhāraṇī*, 9. the thirty-two major marks (and eighty minor marks), and 10. all dharmas. However, this still does not add up to twelve sections, unless items 3. and 9. are each counted as two.

8. Knowing the Graded Levels of Attainment [97b17–99a29]

Eighth is to clarify the graded levels [of attainment]. There are two types of levels, the true [levels] and those of resemblance. Those who have the knowledge and insight of liberation can clearly discriminate between [true] vermilion and the violet [color that resembles it]. They will not make the mistake of saying that they have attained what they have not yet attained, or presume that [attaining] the four good roots is [the same as attaining] the first fruit [of the stream-enterer], or that [attaining] the first fruit is [the same as attaining the level of] one who has nothing more to learn. They will themselves know what they have severed, and realize what they have not yet severed or realized. Although the names of the levels are different for the four gates [of the Tripitaka, Shared, Distinct, and Perfect Teachings], there is not even a slight difference in [the objects of] what is to be severed and in the principle of truth [to be realized].

1. The Levels in Terms of the Fourfold Teachings

1. Tripitaka Teachings [97b21]

[The teaching of] the two vehicles discusses in detail the severing of the bonds [of passionate afflictions] in a single lifetime, so the time frame is hurried. Their teachings are clear, being largely the same with minor differences, so mistakes can be avoided. The bodhisattva teachings involve not only a long time and practice with a distant [goal], but [the content of] their wisdom and severance is distinct. The pathways are different, but the goal to which they return is one. [The bodhisattvas of] the six perfections [of the Tripitaka Teachings] do not yet realize Buddhahood after their first incalculable *(asaṃkhyeya)* kalpa [of practice]; after their second incalculable kalpa they realize [Buddhahood] but do not yet preach; after their third incalculable kalpa they realize [Buddhahood] and preach. For a hundred kalpas they plant the seeds of the marks of a great person, become endowed with five good qualities, and [attain] the stage called "non-retrogression." These are all levels of "resemblance." To sit on the seat of enlightenment and become a Buddha is called the "true level." These [Tripitaka] Teachings are at first shallow, but involve graded levels; how can it be said that ordinary people, with minds that create [delusions], are at a high level? If this is not overweening arrogance, what is?

Their wisdom and severance is distinct 智斷亦別: distinct from the two vehicles; or from that of the other Teachings?

Five good qualities 五功德: the five good roots or faculties. For details see notes above and the Glossary.

2. *Shared Teachings* [97b28]

As for the levels of the true and resemblance in the Shared Teachings, [the content of] wisdom is different than that of the Tripitaka [Teachings], but the levels of severance are not different. The bodhisattva levels [**97c**] are clearly not the same. The common and distinct meanings of the terms are as [explained] in the *Fa-hua hsüan-i*.

3. *Distinct Teachings* [97c1]

The levels of delusions to be severed and [attaining] wisdom for the Distinct Teachings are as follows. Those of the two vehicles are as deaf and dumb, and are not a part of this realm; therefore this is called "distinct." Generally, the clarification of the levels and stages [of these Teachings] are from the *She-lun (Summary of the Great Vehicle)* and *Avataṃsaka Sūtra*, and the meaning [of these stages] are found therein. However, the meanings of the Distinct [Teachings] are manifold, with different explanations in accordance with the capacities [of the listeners]. Horizontally there are the four gates that are not the same, and vertically there are [the differences of] steps to be climbed, and deep and shallow [teachings and practices]. You cannot fix and cling to one sūtra [as the only true one], or mutually affirm or deny [the sūtras in general on the basis of one]. Again, bodhisattvas have produced treatises of the Shared [Teachings] to interpret the sūtras, or have produced treatises of Distinct [Teachings] to interpret the sūtras. For example, Nāgārjuna produced a thousand treatises, and the treatises produced by Vasubandhu and other bodhisattvas are beyond measure. There are few who can master [all of] these [works]. How, then, can you be at pains to take only one sense and criticize the rest of the teachings? If, indeed, you insist on making such judgments, you will forfeit the Buddha's [skillful] means, and invite calumny upon yourself. Wishing to proclaim the path, you will instead choke and obstruct it.

Now I will clarify the Distinct levels. There are different explanations of the four gates which are various and not the same. [However,] although

Levels of severance 斷位不殊: see Chart 1 in Volume 3.

Fa-hua hsüan-i 法華玄[義]: see the section on the stages in the fifth fascicle of the *Fa-hua hsüan-i*, T 33.732b21–746c6.

The levels of delusions to be severed and [attaining] wisdom 惑斷智位: or, "the delusions, severance, wisdom, and levels."

Nāgārjuna produced a thousand treatises 千部論: or, "a treatise in a thousand sections"? This could refer to the *Ta chih tu lun*, which was rumored to originally be ten times the length of the current one-hundred fascicles.

Four gates 四門: that is, the fourfold pattern of the tetralemma, the four aspects of the Fourfold Teachings, and so forth.

there are ways and paths in every direction, that to which they lead is one. There are not yet so many treatises in this place [that is, in China, compared to India], but if we infer on the basis of the previous four gates, if [you realize] the various levels as taught by the Shared Teachings you will know that this is the same as [realizing] the real truth *(paramārtha-satya)*, and if [you realize] the various levels as taught by the Distinct Teachings you will know that this is the same as [realizing] the Middle Way. The *[Lotus] Sūtra* says, "Although various paths are taught, there is really only one vehicle" [and] "the dharmas that are taught are all for reaching the stage of omniscience [of a Buddha]." If you understand this meaning, it is easy to put an end to suspicious doubts, and conflicts will not arise. The various levels have already been summarily explained above in the section on "deconstructing the conventionality of conceptual attitudes." If you wish to know [the details concerning these matters], you should check this [passage].

Ten meanings of adaptations to the Buddha Dharma [97c17]

Again, there are ten meanings to adapting the Buddha Dharma.

1. First is to clarify the principle of the path, that is, [the principle of reality is that all things are] absolutely quiescent and apart [from all verbal expression] and beyond conceptual understanding. [There are attempts to express it] such as with Four [Noble] Truths, three [truths], two [truths], one [truth], or no [truth], in accordance with the feelings [of sentient beings] or wis-

Although various paths are taught, there is really only one vehicle 雖說種種道其實爲一乘: a rephrasing of a basic teaching of the *Lotus Sūtra*. See, for example, the verses at T 9.9b6–7; Hurvitz (41 [38]) translates:

> The Buddhas of ages to come,
> Though they shall preach hundreds of thousands of millions
> Of numberless gateways to the Dharma,
> Shall, in fact, be doing it for the sake of the One Vehicle.

The dharmas that are taught are all for reaching the stage of omniscience 其所說法皆悉到於一切智地: the phrasing is closest to a passage at the beginning of the chapter on "Medicinal Herbs" at 19a24–25; Hurvitz (101 [95]) translates:

> He sets forth all dharmas by resort to wisdom and practical expedients. Without exception, the dharmas he preaches all reach to the ground of All-Knowledge.

Already been summarily explained: see the *Mo-ho chih-kuan* at 71b29–73b25.

Adapting 融通: that is, "adapted" or "fused" teachings is a characteristic feature (in terms of the classification of the Five Periods) of the fourth Prajñā Period, where distinctions such as "great" and "small" are removed, or fused, and the intention is to "integrate" the teachings with the idea of emptiness.

Four truths, three, two, one, none 四諦三二一無: this pattern is followed in the *Fa-hua hsüan-i*, T 33.700a–705b. For an annotated translation and lengthy discussion of these sections, see Swanson, *Foundations*, especially Chart 1 on pp. 358–59. The frequent reference to the *Fa-hua hsüan-i* in this section of the *Mo-ho*

dom [of the Buddha], by exposing or merging [the teachings]. If you know this meaning, the tentative and real [aspects] of the principle of the path, [these things will be] naturally ["coolly"] and spontaneously illuminated.

2. Second is to establish the structure and framework of the doctrines, embracing the secret and the exposed [teachings], and to "straighten the flow" of the large [Mahāyāna] and the small [Hīnayāna]. This involves [applying the hermeneutical categories of] gradual, sudden, variable, and secret, and Tripitaka, Shared, Distinct, and Perfect [Teachings]. If you realize this meaning, you should know the exposing and merging of the vocal teaching, and how to teach the path of transformation [for saving others].

3. Third, [some of the contents of] the sūtras and treatises are contradictory, and their words and meanings are mutually opposed. They cannot be reconciled by [ordinary] emotional beings, and a commonality cannot be found even by those with broad understanding. Debates have raged from ancient times, with no resolution [or "thaw"] from generation to generation. If you realize the meaning of the four *siddhāntas*, however, you can expose and adapt these binding entanglements, get them off your chest, and freely be rid of them, so that you will not be in a quandary or have doubts about this and that.

4. Fourth, if you know that you wrongly grasp [things and concepts], but still give rise to the obstacles of attachments, you [should] skillfully destroy and exhaustively purify [these attachments]. Totally expel [all the mistaken views and conceptual attitudes that are] individual, multiple, integrated or combined, and beyond words. [Also know that] the one who does the destroying is [empty,] just like that which is being destroyed; what is there to be attained?

5. Fifth is to become bound to the true Dharma teachings, and be matched with the [appropriate] level of practice. Cultivation [of the path] involves means, and realization involves steps. [If you realize the proper balance of] the tentative and real, and the Mahāyāna and Hīnayāna, and do not go to excess with regard to [the levels of] the erudite and the noble, then how can you give rise to the offence of overweening pride?

chih-kuan (and the literary nature [the use of many unusual compounds]) may indicate that it is the result of considerable editing by Kuan-ting, or just that Chih-i was "cribbing" from his earlier work.

Secret and exposed 密露: Ikeda (*Gendaigoyaku*, 488) translates these concepts with the later-developed concepts of 密教 (Jpn. *mikkyō*, "esoteric teachings") and 顯教 (Jpn. *kengyō*, "exoteric teachings"), but I hesitate to read these categories into this earlier work.

Individual, multiple, integrated, beyond words 單複具足無言: see the discussion of these four categories above in the *Mo-ho chih-kuan* at 62b8ff.

Erudite and noble 賢聖: that is, the "three levels of erudition and ten noble

6. Sixth, [**98a**] be unobstructed both vertically and horizontally with regard to one Dharma gate. Progressively connect the threads and indefatigably realize [the meaning of] the text.

7. Seventh, reveal [the meaning of] the text in stages, as in mutually fastening hooks and chains, and show a devotion for [the context and] the relationships [among the texts].

8. Eighth, gradually settle the interpretation of the sūtras with agreeable embellishments. In general, use the various methods [explained] above [in the *Mo-ho chih-kuan*] and finally interpret [the Dharma] in accordance with the words [of the texts]. The meaning should then follow, and the text should [then be understood].

9. Ninth, in translating the Sanskrit into Chinese, find words that share and combine [the meaning of both], and in using the vernacular do not conceal [the meaning].

10. Tenth is, with each and every phrase and verse, as you hear it and cultivate it, enter it into your mind, and contemplate it. If your contemplation harmonizes with [the meaning of] the sūtra, your contemplation will receive a seal [of approval]. If you contemplate with such a seal [of approval] in your mind, this is not like counting someone else's treasure [because it is your own experience].

I do not have the time to broadly examine the [ninth] issue of translating words [from Sanskrit to Chinese], but with regard to the [other] nine issues I am not in agreement with either the textual scholars of this world, nor in agreement with meditation masters who [merely] practice dhyāna-meditation. There is a type of meditation master who is concerned

stages,"—the three groups of ten stages of abodes, practice, and merit transference, and the ten *bhūmi* stages.

In translating Sanskrit to Chinese, find words that share and combine, and in using the vernacular do not conceal 翻譯梵漢名數兼通使方言不壅: that is, find a balance between being too literal and too free? Ikeda (*Gendaigoyaku*, 489) translates: "In translating Sanskrit to Chinese, find a common meaning between the two languages, and do not leave any points unclear in translating the meaning."

Counting someone else's treasure 数他[財]寶: this analogy (e.g., from the *Avataṃsaka Sūtra,* T 9.429a3) has been used many times in Chih-i's work. See, for example, the *Hsiao shih-kuan*, T 46.462b29–c1:

> If, however, you pointlessly cling only to the text and the words, and your disposition is to resist the teachings, then the days and months [of practice] will be spent in vain, and you will not be able to attain enlightenment. This is like a poor person counting another person's treasures; what benefit is there in this?

Textual scholars 文字法師: does this mean other Buddhist textual scholars, or non-Buddhist scholars? The context would indicate that he is referring to other Buddhist scholars. The implication is that these two groups do not maintain a proper balance between teaching and practice.

only with the single intent of contemplation. Or, some are shallow and some are spurious [even with regard to meditation], and are completely lacking with regard to the other nine [issues]. This is not a false charge. Those who have the eye of a later [stage] of erudition should realize and know this.

4. *Perfect Teaching* [98a10]

Next [it should be known that the category of] "graded levels" are [merely] one of the ten meanings. Suppose we examine the graded levels in terms of the Perfect Teaching. Vast distinctions are to be made within [the section on] bodhisattvahood as the object [of contemplation]. There I will discuss the realization [of enlightenment], but now [I will discuss only] the cultivation [of the path], and so I should be brief. If you cultivate the means of the Four Samādhis, this is as I have explained above. However, in the *Fa-hua san-mei ch'an-i* I have provided another explanation of the means [for this practice] in terms of "fivefold repentance in the six times," so now I will clarify the features of the levels in terms of the fivefold repentance.

2. The Graded Levels in Terms of the Fivefold Repentance [98a14]

First, know the ten kinds of mind that go against and with [the flow of samsara], and fix the true aspect [of reality] as the object [of your contem-

Vast distinctions 應廣分別: this indicates that Chih-i indeed did plan on giving a detailed exposition of the tenth of the ten objects of contemplation, that is, of bodhisattvahood. Alas, the *Mo-ho chih-kuan* ends at section seven, and the eighth through tenth sections are missing.

Cultivate the means of the Four Samādhis 四種三昧修習方便: see the section on the Four Samādhis in the *Mo-ho chih-kuan*, 11a21–20a24.

Fivefold repentance in six times 五悔六時: "fivefold repentance" refers to the fivefold ceremony for repenting of the sins committed by and through the six senses or sense organs; the five kinds of confession practiced by those cultivating the Lotus Samādhi: 1. repentance 懺悔 of the offences committed through the six senses, which includes (a) universal confession and (b) specific confession; 2. petitioning 勸請 the Buddhas to remain in the world and preach the Dharma, 3. rejoicing appropriately 隨喜 in the good of others, 4. transferring 回向 your own merit to others, and 5. vowing 發願 to save or benefit all beings.

The "six times" refer to the six periods in a day: early morning, mid-day, sunset, early evening, mid-night, and late night. See Chih-i's short exposition on the practice of "Lotus repentance," T no. 1941, 46.949–955; see especially 952a28–953b29. See the partial translation in Volume 3, and Daniel Stevenson's work listed in the Bibliography.

Ten kinds of mind that go against and with 逆順十心: see the extended discussion of these states of mind earlier in the *Mo-ho chih-kuan* at 39c26–40c5, as part of the "purification through repentance" that is the fifth of the five conditions in the preparation for practicing contemplation.

plation] 繫緣實相. This is the first [step of] repentance. This means that you are constantly repenting, and there is no time when you are not repenting. However, the thoughts of the principle [of reality] are minute and obscure, so if your practice of contemplation is superficial, dark evil will cover and obstruct them, making it difficult to quickly disclose the dawn [of awakening]. [In order to] repeatedly act physically and verbally [in ways that] assist the arousal of [proper] mental deeds, so that [your thoughts] will quickly reach a rapport [with the principle of reality], you should in addition practice the fivefold repentance [as follows].

1. Repentance [98a17]

[The first character of the compound for "repentance"] "to confess" 懺 refers to stating and exposing your previous evil [deeds]. [The second character] "to regret" 悔 refers to [the intent to] reform [the evil of] the past and [look forward] to cultivate [the path] in the future. [You should chant,] "The Buddha's wisdom is universally illuminating, and the Buddha's compassion is universally embracing. I, physically and verbally, cast myself at the feet of the Buddha. May the eyes of the whole world witness my repentance. I have, from beginningless time, committed immeasurable offences that obstruct the path of the Buddha. I have been confined by my ignorance to not know about the correct and true [Buddha Dharma]. Acting physically, verbally, and mentally [with my attention] fixed on the triple world, I have aroused the ten evil offences; done things that are not enriching or beneficial to the three treasures [of Buddha, Dharma, and Sangha], the six relations, things born in four ways, and those in the five destinies [from hell to human being]; [I have] disturbed the people who have aroused the mind of the three vehicles [of śrāvaka, pratyekabuddha, and bodhisattva]; and have performed the five [or seven] heinous offences. May I do [good] myself, teach others, and rejoice in seeing [others] do [good]. After this life I should experience various sufferings and afflictions [as a result of my evil deeds], but, as the

Repentance 懺悔: it should be pointed out that 懺 is a character created to transliterate the Sanskrit *kṣama*, the Buddhist term for repentance, but Chih-i parses it here as representing the "exposing" or "making public" aspect of repentance. Note that 懺悔 is a "mixed binome," in which the first character is a transliteration for *kṣama*, and the second character indicates the meaning of "regret" and repentance. On the significance of mixed binomes, see my essay (2004) on "Bodhidharma, wall-contemplation, and Sanskrit-Chinese mixed binomes."

Six relations 六親: father and son, elder and younger brother, and husband and wife. Or, father and mother, elder and younger brother, and wife and child.

Things born in four ways 四生: that is, born from an egg, from a womb, from moisture, and through some sort of transformation. In other words, all beings.

bodhisattvas of past, present, and future repented when they sought the path of the Buddha, I also do likewise. I grieve that I have sunk into dark confusion and do not have the eye of wisdom." As you state these words, your voice should fall along with your tears, and with real and true sincerity prostate yourself with your five limbs on the ground, as a tree that is felled. Obliterate your self, and eradicate all evil; this is called "repentance."

2. *Petitioning the Buddhas* [98a27]

"Petitioning" is [also] called "entreaty" 祈求. Śrāvakas [rely on the idea that they can] save themselves, so they only confess their own offences. Bodhisattvas practice the path because they pity sentient beings, and therefore they must make an exhortation [as follows]: "I now know my offences, but cannot become **[98b]** liberated. Sentient beings do not know that they will pass through the current of transmigration for many kalpas. I do not have the power to save them, so I petition the Buddhas of the ten directions [to help]. May the Buddhas pity the sentient beings without regard to great or small. May this vow be fulfilled without fail." The *Ta chih tu lun* clarifies [the issue of] petitioning and not petitioning, that is, to petition [the

***Ta chih tu lun* clarifies petitioning and not petitioning** 大論明請不請: see T 25.109b–c, which is more about specifically asking the Buddha to preach the Dharma than a general petition for help. Lamotte (*Le Traité* 2, 415–20) translates:

> *Sūtra*: Ils excellaient à inviter d'innombrables Buddha *(aparimitabuddhādhyeṣaṇakuśalaiḥ)*.
>
> *Śāstra*: Les invitations [qu'ils adressent aux Buddha] sont deux sortes:…
>
> C'est ainsi que les Bodhisattva invitent d'innombrables Buddha.
>
> Question. — Les Buddha ont une règle et, selon cette règle, ils doivent prêcher la loi et sauver en masse les êtres. Qu'on les invite ou non, cette règle reste la même. Pourquoi faudrait-il les inviter? D'ailleurs, s'il est possible d'inviter les Buddha qui sont à proximité, comment pourrait-on inviter les Buddha des innombrables *buddhakṣetra* les dix régions? On ne les voit même pas!
>
> Réponse. — 1. Bien que les Buddha soient dans l'obligation de prêcher la loi et n'ont que faire d'une invitation humaine, celui qui les invite peut gagner des mérites *(puṇya)* en les conviant. De même, bien que le roi trouve chez lui en abondance des mets délicats, il y a encore des gens qui l'invitent pour obtenir ses faveurs et recueillir ses avis.
>
> 2. D'ailleurs, si on éprouve de l'amitié *(maitrīcitta)* pour les êtres et qu'on leur veut du bonheur, on gagne de grands mérites, même si ces êtres n'obtiennent rien. Il en est ainsi quand on invite les Buddha à prêcher la loi.
>
> 3. En outre, il y a des Buddha qu'on n'avait pas invités à prêcher et qui sont entrés directement dans le Nirvāṇa sans avoir prêcher et qui sont entrés directement dans le Nirvāṇa sans avoir prêché la loi. Ainsi, dans le *Saddharmapuṇḍarīkasūtra*, le Bhagavat Prabhūtaratna, que personne n'avait invité [à prêcher], entra directement dans le Nirvāṇa, mais, dans la suite, son corps de buddha fictif *(nirmāṇakāya)* et son stūpa formé des sept joyaux *(saptaratna)* apparaissaient simultanément pour confirmer les prédictions du *Saddharmapuṇḍarīkasūtra*.…

Buddha] to turn the wheel of the Dharma. To exhort 勸, signify 示, and attest [to the truth] 證 in order to lead [beings] to realize the Four [Noble] Truths, so that they give birth to the clear awakening of the eye of wisdom: this is called the "three turnings" [of the Four Noble Truths]. There is a person who said that "petitioning [the Buddha] to teach the three vehicles is called the 'three turnings.'" If the Buddha preaches the Dharma, sentient beings will attain the enlightenment of nirvana. If there are those who do not yet attain [enlightenment], he leads them to experience worldly bliss. If the Buddha universally allows it, then all will attain the peace [of nirvana]. I am one of these, so my offences and suffering will be removed; this is as when one asks for the rain to fall everywhere, and I have a small field; naturally [my field] will be watered by the sweet moisture. Suppose you petition [the Buddha] to dwell in the world. [Usually] life gains an abode [in this world] through karmic deeds [in the past], but [a Buddha's body of] transformation can come to abide in this world through mental [deeds or intention], and when the thought ceases, the transformation disappears. [Thus you should intone] "I now petition the Buddhas, that they may enrich and benefit sentient beings like a great torch [that illuminates the darkness]. Do not cease your thoughts

Chodron (2, 335–36) translates:

Sūtra: They excelled in inviting innumerable buddhas.
Śastra: The invitations [which they address to the Buddhas] are of two types ... Question. The Buddhas have a pattern according to which they must preach the Dharma and save all beings. Whether they are invited or not, this pattern remains the same. Then why must they be invited? Besides, although it is possible to invite the Buddhas who are close by, how is it possible to invite the Buddhas of the innumerable buddha-fields of the ten directions? They cannot even be seen!
Answer. i. Although the Buddhas are obliged to preach the Dharma and need no human invitation, the person who invites them gains merit by doing so. In the same way, even though the king finds plenty of delicacies to eat at home, many people still invite him in order to gain his favor and obtain his advice.
ii) Moreover, if one feels friendship for beings and one wishes them happiness, one gains great merit even though these beings do not get any. It is the same when one invites the Buddhas to preach the Dharma.
iii) Furthermore, there are Buddhas who have not been invited to preach and who have entered directly into nirvana without having preached the Dharma. Thus, in the *Saddharmapuṇḍarīkasūtra*), the Bhagavat Prabhūtaratna, whom nobody had invited [to preach], entered nirvana directly but, later, his fictive *nirmāṇakāya* and his stūpa made of the seven jewels appeared simultaneously in order to confirm the prediction of the *Saddharmapuṇḍarīkasūtra*.

Three turnings 三轉: to be distinguished from the general "three turnings of the wheel of the Dharma." These are the three "turnings" (exhorting, signifying, and attesting) Śākyamuni gave in his exposition of the Four Noble Truths. See the *Miscellaneous Āgama*, T 2.104a; NAKAMURA, 483b.

A person who said 有人言: the source of this quote is not known.

of transformation, but abide [in this world] for a long time, to bring peace and liberation to all." This is called "petitioning" [the Buddhas].

3. Appropriate joy in the good of others [98b11]

"Appropriate joy" is [also] called "congratulating others" 慶彼. [You should chant as follows:] "The Buddha has already turned the wheel of the Dharma thrice, sentient beings have benefited in the three times [of the past, present, and future], and I rejoice that others have been helped. Again, I should encourage [others] and lead them to give birth to goodness, and I rejoice if that goodness arises spontaneously. I rejoice in the good of the fortunes and meritorious qualities of sentient beings of the past, present, and future; [rejoice] in the undefiled good of those of the three vehicles in the past, present, and future; and [rejoice] in all the good from their first aspiration to their entering the extinction of the Buddhas in the past, present, and future. I rejoice appropriately for all, and also teach others to rejoice." As three people—the seller and buyer of incense, and the bystander who watches [the transaction]—can smell the incense in the same way, the goodness is equal for these three: the one who teaches, the one who receives the teaching,

Three people— the seller and buyer of incense, and the bystander who watches [the transaction] — can smell the incense in the same way 如買賣香傍觀三人同熏: this example is from the *Ta chih tu lun*, T 25.269c6–14, where it gives the definition for "rejoicing appropriately." Lamotte (*Le Traité* 4, 1880–81) translates:

> Sur la pensée de complaisance *(anumo-danācitta)*, voir le *Souei-hi p'in* (Anumo-danāparivarta).
>
> Voice un exemple de complaisance. Quelqu'un exerce les qualités [en question: don, moralité, etc.]; un spectateur s'en réjouit *(anumodate)* et le félicite en disant: "C'est bien; en ce monde impermanent *(anityalokadhātu)*, enveloppé par les ténèbres de l'ignorance *(avidyāndhakāra)*, vous fortifiez la grande pensée [de Bodhi] et vous y plantez ce mérite *(puṇya)*."
>
> *Supposons un vendeur (vikretṛ) et un acheteur (kretṛ) en toutes sortes de parfums (gandha) merveilleux; un tiers s'en approche et se tient à côté. Lui aussi respire l'air parfumé; pourtant le parfum ne diminue en rien, et les deux trafiquants n'y perdent rien.*
>
> Supposons encore un donateur *(dāyaka)* et un bénéficiaire *(pratigrāhaka)*; un tiers, se tenant à leur côté, se complaît dans la bonne action. Il en jouit avec eux, mais les deux autres n'y perdent rien.
>
> Telle est la caractéristique de la complaisance *(anumodanā)*.
>
> Ainsi donc le Bodhisattva, rien que par une pensée de complaisance, surpasse les adeptes des deux Véhicules. Que dire alors *(kaḥ punarvādaḥ)* s'il exerce lui-même [les qualités dans lesquelles il se complaît]?

Chodron (4, 1544–45 translates:

> For the mind of sympathetic joy, see the *Anumodanāparivarta*.
>
> Here is an example of sympathetic joy. Someone is practicing the qualities [in question, viz., generosity, morality, etc.]; a spectator rejoices in it and congratulates him, saying: "That is good; in this

and the one who rejoices appropriately [over these circumstances]. If you contemplate the delusions of sentient beings, this should be exceedingly distressing. If you contemplate the good of sentient beings, we should pay them reverence. Like [the bodhisattva] Never Disrespectful, know deeply that sentient beings are endowed with [threefold Buddha-nature, that is,] the direct [cause] 正, the conditions 緣, and the complete 了 [cause of Buddha-nature], so that even if they have not yet aroused [the aspiration for enlightenment], they will encounter and certainly give rise to [Buddhahood eventually]. [At the sound of] the poisonous drum, those near and far will certainly die; therefore you should respect them as [you do] the Buddha. Why? Because

impermanent world enveloped in the shadows of ignorance, you are strengthening the great mind [of bodhi] and you are planting this merit."

Imagine there is a seller and a purchaser of all sorts of wonderful perfumes; a third person comes near and stands to one side. He also breathes the perfumed air; the perfume, nevertheless, does not diminish at all and the two people doing business lose nothing.

Imagine also a donor and a beneficiary; a third person, standing beside them, is joyful in the good action. He rejoices with them, but the other two lose nothing. Such is the characteristic of sympathetic joy.

Thus, just by a mind of sympathetic joy, the bodhisattva surpasses the practitioners of the two Vehicles. What more could be said if he himself practices [the qualities in which he is rejoicing]?

Bodhisattva Never Disrespectful 常不輕: see the story of Sadāparibhūta, who paid respect to everyone because they are all future Buddhas, in chapter 20 of the *Lotus Sūtra*, T 9.50b–51c.

Threefold Buddha-nature: the *Lotus Sūtra* does not use the term "Buddha-nature," but here Chih-i connects Sadāparibhūta's recognition of everyone as a future Buddha with his categories of threefold Buddha-nature or the three causes for attaining Buddhahood, analyzed as having three aspects: the "direct cause," that all beings are endowed with the nature of Buddhahood by their participation in reality; the "complete cause," the wisdom that illumines this nature; and "the conditional causes," the practices or conditions that bring about wisdom.

Poisonous drum 毒鼓: this image has been used above in the *Mo-ho chih-kuan* at 44a12–13. See the passage in the *Mahāparinirvāṇa Sūtra*, T 12.661a20–28:

> Again, good sons, it is as if a person took various poisons and rubs them on a great drum, and beats it to make a sound in the midst of people. Even though people do not wish to hear, those who hear will all die. There is only one [kind of] person who will not fall over and die. This Mahāyāna sūtra, the *Mahāparinirvāṇa Sūtra*, is also like this. People in various places doing various activities hear the sound [of this sūtra], and their greed, anger, and delusions all are extinguished. For even those who are not attentive among them, the power [of this sutra] as a cause for attaining great nirvana is able to extinguish their passionate afflictions, and their bonds extinguish on their own [self-destruct?]. Those who have offended against the four grave prohibitions and the five heinous [offences], when they hear this sūtra, they also will attain the causes for supreme wisdom and gradually sever their passionate afflictions. Only the icchāntika will not fall over and die.

the number of Tathāgatas in the future cannot be measured. This is the meaning of deeply rejoicing appropriately. The *Lotus Sūtra* [teaches about] appropriate joy with regard to the Dharma, and the *Pañcaviṃśati Sūtra* about appropriate joy with regard to people.

4. Transferring your own merit to others [98b22]

"Transferring" 迴向 refers to "turning" 迴 your good and "facing" 向 *bodhi*-wisdom. [You should chant as follows:] "The virtue and merit of all the wise and noble ones is expansive and great, and the appropriate joy of good fortune I now experience is also expansive and great. Sentient beings have no good—I shall give of my good, and after I finish giving to sentient beings, then I will properly face toward 向 [the attainment of my own] *bodhi*-wisdom." As when a sound is twisted as it enters a horn, and the sound [is magnified and] can be heard from afar, so there is great benefit from "turning back" [and transferring merit to others.] Correct "transferring" [of merit] consists of "severing the destinies of the triple world, extinguishing meaningless disputes *(prapañca)*, draining the swamp of passionate afflictions, putting an end to the forest of thorny troubles, removing your heavy burden." [You should realize that] there is nothing to grasp, nothing to be

Lotus Sūtra: see chapter 18 on "The Merits of Appropriate Joy," T 9.46b21–47c1, which tells of the "appropriate joy" experienced by those who hear the teaching of the *Lotus Sūtra*. For example, the prose section concludes (T 9.47a20–23; Hurvitz, 261 [239]):

> ... how great is the merit of him who encourages but one man to go and listen to the Dharma! How much the greater is that of one who single-mindedly listens to the preachings, reads and recites, and in the great multitude explains them to others, practicing as he preaches.

Pañcaviṃśati Sūtra: See chapter 39 on "Appropriate Joy," T 8.297b21–302aff, which tells of the "appropriate joy" of transferring or sharing supreme wisdom with all sentient beings. This leads into the fourth aspect of the fivefold repentance, that of "transferring" your merit to other beings.

The virtue and merit of all the wise and noble ones 一切賢聖功德: or, "of all those on the [thirty stages of] erudition and the [ten] noble [*bhūmi* stages]"?

Severing the destinies ... removing your heavy burden 斷三界道滅諸戲論乾煩惱泥滅棘刺林捨除重檐: Ikeda (*Teihonkundoku*, 531) substitutes 擔 for 檐, following the "original" in the *Treatise on the Ten Stages* (T 26.46b21). Although not identified here as a quote, these phrases are found just prior to the same passage quoted and identified from the *Treatise on the Ten Stages* a few lines below (*Moho chih-kuan* 98c5–6); see next note. The context (T 26.46b19–22) reads:

> If there are bodhisattva-mahāsattvas who wish to have appropriate joy and transfer their merit, they should be mindful of the Buddhas, *sever the continuity of destinies of the triple world, extinguish meaningless disputes, drain the muddy swamp of passionate afflictions, put an end to thorny troubles, and remove heavy burdens*, thus attaining self-benefit.

mindful of, nothing to perceive, and nothing to attain. There is no distinction between the one who does the transferring [of merit], and the object of the transferring; all dharmas are deluded conceptions that exist only as the harmonious merging [of causes and conditions]. Dharmas truly do not arise. There is no arising in the past, present, nor inevitably [in the future] 已今當, [**98c**] and there is no extinction in the past, present, nor inevitably [in the future]. All phenomena are like this[, that is, empty], so I should have appropriate joy and transfer [merit] in accordance with [this emptiness of] all dharmas. This is what is known, perceived, and granted by the Buddhas of past, present, and future. This is called the truly real transference [of merit]. Again, this is called "being supremely endowed with great transference [of merit]." [Such a person] does not slander the Buddha, has no fault, has no fixation, has no poison [of greed, anger, and delusion], and has no defect. It is not just the transfer of merit that is like this; the previous three and later one [aspects of fivefold repentance] are also like this. The *Treatise on the Ten Stages* says, "Offences should be repented of in this way: petition [the Buddhas] and have appropriate joy for your [good] fortune, and transfer [merits] toward [the goal of attaining] *bodhi*-wisdom."

5. *Arousing a vow to save or benefit all beings* [98c6]

"Arousing a vow" refers to "making an oath" 誓. Suppose you entrust something to a person; if you do not have a note [to that effect], [the status of] that thing cannot be determined. When you give of your good to sentient beings, if you do not have the necessary thoughts [of a vow], you may retract and regret it later, so [your resolve should be] reinforced with a vow. Again, if there is no vow, this is like a cow without a handler not knowing where to go. Making a vow supports your practice, so that you can reach your goal. This [vow] is also called a *dhāraṇī*, that is, [it is a device for] upholding good and hindering evil. [A vow is] like firing a clay bowl, which makes it able to become a vessel for holding [other] things. Those of the two vehicles exhaust

Offences should be repented of in this way: petition [the Buddha] and have appropriate joy for your [good] fortune, and transfer [merits] toward *bodhi*-wisdom 罪應如是懺勸請隨喜福迴向於菩提: see the verses in the *Treatise on the Ten Stages* at T 26.46c14–15:

> Offences should be repented of in this way:
> Petition [the Buddhas], have appropriate joy for [good] fortunes,
> Transfer [merits] toward [attaining] the supreme path.

Ikeda (*Gendaigoyaku*, 492) has: "You should not only repent of your offences in this way, but transfer [the merits of] your good fortunes from petitioning the Buddhas and having appropriate joy toward [the goal of attaining] *bodhi*-wisdom."

***Dhāraṇī* as upholding good and hindering evil** 陀羅尼持善遮惡: see the discussion of *dhāraṇī* at *Mo-ho chih-kuan* 97a7–14.

their births, so they have no need of vows. Bodhisattvas go from one birth to another to [teach and] transform beings, so they need general vows and specific vows. The Four Universal [Bodhisattva Vows] are general vows. The vows of Dharmākara, those taught in the *Avataṃsaka Sūtra*, and each individual good deed and *dhāraṇī* are all specific vows.

6. The practice of fivefold repentance [98c13]

Now, in the meditation hall, practice this repentance at the six times of day and night and destroy the great evil of karmic offences; petition [the Buddhas] and destroy the offence of slandering the Dharma; [practice the experience of] appropriate joy and destroy the offence of jealousy; [practice] transferring merit and destroy the offences done for the sake of this existence. If [you repent] in accordance with a vow based on [the truths of] emptiness and no marks, the merits you attain will be unlimited—they cannot be analogized, counted, compared, calculated, or explained.

If you are able to diligently practice the means of this fivefold repentance, this will help to open the gate of contemplation, and the threefold truth in a single thought will be lucid and clear. Just as you can fully perceive all visible forms when gazing in a spotless mirror, you will attain perfect understanding in a single thought. Even without the addition of special powers, you can spontaneously attain clear [wisdom]. If your correct faith is firm, you will remain unmoved. This is called "the profound faith of a mind with appropriate joy," and corresponds to the first grade [of the five preliminary grades] of the disciple. The chapter on "Discrimination of Merits" [in the *Lotus Sūtra*] says, "As for those sentient beings who hear of the Buddha's long life-span and are able to give rise to a single thought of faith and understanding, the

General vows 總願 **and specific vows** 別願: "general vows" are all-inclusive and universalistic vows, such as the famous Four Universal Vows of a bodhisattva; "specific vows" are more limited to a specific or distinct focus or situation, such as the forty-eight vows of Amitābha and the five hundred vows of Śākyamuni in the *Karuṇā-puṇḍarīka Sūtra*, T no. 157. See Nakamura, 877a and 1207a

Dharmākara 法藏: a bodhisattva who makes forty-eight vows and eventually becomes the Buddha Amitābha. See the larger *Sukhāvativyūha*, T no. 360, 12.267c–269b6. For an English translation see Gómez, *The Land of Bliss*, 162–74.

Avataṃsaka Sūtra see the "vows" or ideals listed in chapter on "Purifying Practice" at T 9.430c1–432c14. For an English translation of this section see Cleary, *The Flower Ornament Scripture*, 313–29.

First grade of the disciple 初品弟子位: the lowest level of the stages of the Perfect Teaching. The five degrees or grades are 1. appropriate joy, 2. reading and reciting the sūtras, 3. preaching the Dharma, 4. the preliminary practice of the six perfections, and 5. the proper practice of the six perfections. See Chart 1 in Volume 3.

As for those sentient beings who hear

merit they attain has no limit and no measure.... They are able to arouse the supreme wisdom of the Tathāgata.... If they hear this *[Lotus] Sūtra*, do not malign it, and arouse thoughts of appropriate joy, it should be known that this is because they already have the mark of profound faith and understanding." This is a text [illustrating] the first grade [of "appropriate joy"].

Again, cultivate the practice of fivefold repentance with the contemplation of perfect understanding, adding [the practice of] reading and reciting. The good words and sublime meaning [of the sūtra text] will coalesce with your mind, as grease helps fire [to burn brightly]. At this time your contemplation is clear and bright. This is called the second grade [of "reading and reciting the sūtras"]. The text [of the *Lotus Sūtra*] says, "How much more so for those who read and recite, accept and receive [this sūtra]. Such a person carries the Tathāgata on his head."

Again, cultivate the practice of fivefold repentance to an expanded degree with a triumphant mind, adding further [the practice of] preaching the Dharma, turning your inner understanding to guide and benefit **[99a]** the people in front of you. Through this vast salvific activity, the merits of these transformations will return to yourself. Turn your mind once, and double your previous triumphs. This is called the third grade [of "preach-

of the Buddha's long life-span ... already have the mark of profound faith and understanding 其有衆生 聞佛壽長遠。乃至能生一念信解。所得功徳不可限量。能起如來無上之慧。若聞是經而不毀呰起隨喜心: a collection of phrases from the chapter on "Discrimination of Merits," in the *Lotus Sūtra* at T 9.44c19–45b24. The phrases are at 44c19–21, 45b12–13, and 45b23–24. Hurvitz (249–52 [229–32]) translates the context:

> At that time the Buddha declared to the bodhisattva-mahāsattva Maitreya, "O Ajita! *Whatever living beings, hearing that the Buddha's life-span is as long as this, can produce as much as a single moment of faith and understanding shall gain merit that shall have no limit, no measure....*
>
> Further, O Ajita, if there is anyone who, hearing of the great length of the Buddha's life-span, understands the import of the words, the merit gained by that man shall have no limit or measure, for *he shall be able to produce the unexcelled knowledge of the Thus Come One.* How much the truer shall this be of one who broadly hears this scripture, or writes it down himself, or causes others to write it,...
>
> Again, if after the extinction of the Thus Come One *anyone hears this scripture and without maligning it raises up thoughts of appropriate joy, be it known that this is a mark of his having already achieved profound faith and understanding.* How much truer is this of one who reads and recites, accepts and keeps it! For such a man thereby carries the Thus Come One on his head.

How much more so for those who read and recite, accept and receive. Such a person carries the Tathāgata on his head 何況讀誦受持之者斯人則爲頂戴如來: the phrase immediately following the phrases of the *Lotus Sūtra* quoted above; see T 9.45b23–24. See Hurvitz's translation in the previous note.

ing the Dharma"]. The text [of the *Lotus Sūtra*] says, "If there are those who receive and uphold, read and recite, preach for the sake of others, copy it themselves, teach others to copy it, thus honoring the sūtra scrolls, it is not necessary for them to go further and erect stupas and temples as offerings to the multitudinous Sangha."

Again, cultivate the practice of fivefold repentance with increased diligence, concurrent with the cultivation of the six perfections. The power of such good blessings and merit will double and assist in your contemplation, which will advance to an even deeper level. This is called the fourth grade [of the "preliminary practice of the six perfections"]. The text [of the *Lotus Sūtra*] says, "If there are people who are able to uphold this sūtra, concurrent with the practice of the six perfections, these merits are most supreme, immeasurable, and unlimited, like space, and [these people] will attain universal wisdom."

Again, cultivate the practice of fivefold repentance with these thoughts [of practicing the six perfections] and properly cultivate the six perfections. Practice for yourself and teach and transform others, endowed with both the actual [practice] and the principle [behind the practice], and with your mind contemplating without obstruction, turn [to a level] more superior than before, such that it is incomparable. This is called the fifth grade [of the "proper practice of the six perfections"]. The text [of the *Lotus Sūtra*] says, "[Those who are] able, for the sake of other people, to [lead them to

If there are those who receive … offerings to the multitudinous Sangha 若有受持讀誦爲他人説自書教人書供養經卷不須復起塔寺供養衆僧: a passage from the *Lotus Sūtra*, T 9.45c12–14, a few lines after the passage quoted above. Hurvitz (253 [233]) translates:

> For that reason I say: if after the extinction of the Thus Come One there is *anyone who accepts and keeps, reads and recites, preaches to others, or writes down himself, or instructs others to write, and thus honors the scriptural roll, he need not go further and erect stūpa or monastery* or build saṃgha-cells *as offerings to the multitudinous saṃgha.*

If there are people … attain universal wisdom 況復有人能持是經兼行六度其德最勝無量無邊譬如虛空至一切種智: selected phrases from a passage in the *Lotus Sūtra*, T 9.45c14–17, immediately following the quote above. Hurvitz (253 [233]) translates:

> If, then, *there is a man who can keep this scripture and at the same time practice the spreading of gifts, the keeping of the prohibitions, forbearance in the face of humiliation, vigorous perseverance, single-mindedness, and wisdom,* how far superior his excellences shall be, *how incalculable, how limitless! Just as open space*, eastward, westward, southward, northward, as well as in the four intermediate directions, upward, and downward, is incalculable and limitless, so shall this man's merit, too, be incalculable and limitless, *leading quickly to Knowledge of All Modes.*

Able, for the sake of other people … close to supreme wisdom 能爲他人種種解説清淨持戒忍辱無瞋。常貴坐精進勇猛利根智慧。當知是人已趣道場近三菩提: a

experience] various liberations, uphold the precepts purely [and stay with gentle and agreeable people], have gentle forbearance without anger, [and with a firm will and mindfulness] constantly esteem sitting in dhyāna meditation [and attain deep concentrations], with persevering diligently and courageously[, embracing good dharmas], and being of sharp faculties and wisdom.… It should be known that such people already sit on the seat of enlightenment and are close to supreme wisdom *(saṃbodhi)*."

In this way [for the Perfect Teaching] the levels of the five grades [of the disciple] come before the ten levels of faith. According to *The Contemplation of Samantabhadra*, these five grades are five mental states of the ten levels of faith, but the Buddha's intent is difficult to know, and this is a different explanation for [people with] a certain capability. If this explanation can be appropriated to reveal understanding, then why should we take the trouble to painfully dispute over it?

3. The Graded Levels in Terms of Contemplating the Sense Fields [99a15]

Again, this current chapter is about contemplating the objects of the sense fields, so we should classify the graded levels in terms of the sense fields. The so-called "black" [or evil] aggregates *(skandha)*, sense entrances *(āyatana)*, and sense realms *(dhātu)*, are the levels of the three evil destinies, and the "white" [or good] aggregates, sense entrances, and sense realms are the lev-

paraphrase of the passage immediately after that quoted above; see T 9.45c21–25. Hurvitz (253–54 [233–34]) translates:

> If a person shall read and recite, accept and keep, this scripture and preach it to others, or write it down himself, or instruct another to write it; if, again, he can erect stūpas and build saṃgha-cells, making offerings and singing hymns of praise to the multitudinous saṃgha of voice-hearers; if also, having recourse to a hundred thousand myriads of millions of modes of praise, he lauds the merits of bodhisattvas; if he also, by various means, preaches to others, in accord with its meaning, this Scripture of the Dharma Blossom; if again, *he can purely keep the prohibitions* and dwell with gentle and agreeable persons, *enduring humiliation without anger*, his will and presence of mind hard and firm, *ever attaching great weight to sitting in dhyāna*, attaining to the deep concentrations, *persevering vigorously and with heroic courage*, gathering all good dharmas to himself, *being of keen faculties and wisdom*, skilled at answering queries and objections; if, O Ajita, after my extinction the good men and good women who accept and keep, read and recite this scriptural canon also have good merits like these, *be it known that these persons have already turned toward the Platform of the Way, that they are close to anuttarasaṃyaksaṃbodhi* and seated under the Tree of the Path.

The passages in brackets are given in the Taishō text as variant readings, and in effect fill in the quote from the *Lotus Sūtra*.

The Contemplation of Samantabhadra: Chan-jan and the *Inyō* admit that this interpretation is not to be found in *The Contemplation of Samantabhadra*. Perhaps it was a theory based on the sūtra that was known in Chih-i's day?

els of the three good destinies. The aggregates, sense entrances, and sense realms of good means are the "levels of resemblance" of the Hīnayāna. The undefiled aggregates, sense entrances, and sense realms are the true levels of those of the two vehicles. The aggregates, sense entrances, and sense realms that involve a transformation beyond conceptual understanding are the levels of the people of five types [of stages, that is, bodhisattvas]. The Dharma-nature's constant form, and constant sensations, conceptions, volitions, and consciousness, that is, the aggregates, and the [twelve] sense entrances and [eighteen] sense realms [of the Dharma-nature (or, "the true nature of reality")], is the level of the Buddha.

4. Closing Summary [99a21]

Again, [those who advance in] the five grades [in terms] of conventional designation will turn clear and pure, and spontaneously realize wisdom through hearing [the Dharma], have penetrating wisdom that is not entangled [with defilements], and have deep faith that is difficult to move; this is the mind of faith. In this way you gradually become endowed with the ten [levels of] faith — mindfulness, diligence, concentration, *dhāraṇi* [wisdom], moral life, preserving [the Dharma], merit transference, vows, and so forth. This is the "purification of the six senses," the levels of resemblance, where the four categories [of passions] are severed. The *Jen-wang ching* says, "The bodhisattvas of the ten good deeds arouse the great thought [of *bodhi*-wisdom, or aspiration for enlightenment] and for a long time disengage from the sea of transmigrating in the sufferings of the triple world." This is the meaning here. Next, they enter the first [stage of] abodes, where they destroy ignorance and perceive Buddha-nature. The *Avataṃsaka Sūtra* says, "When he first aroused the thought [of *bodhi*-wisdom, or aspiration for

People of five types 五種人: that is, those people on the five categories of ten stages of the Perfect Teaching: the ten levels of faith, ten abodes, ten levels of practice, ten levels of merit transference, and ten *bhūmi* stages. See Chart 1 in Volume 3.

The bodhisattvas of the ten good deeds arouse the great thought and for a long time disengage from the sea of transmigrating in the sufferings of the triple world 十善菩薩發大長別三界苦輪海: a phrase from verses in the *Jen-wang ching* at T 8.827b14.

When he first aroused the thought, he had already perfected correct awakening, knew the true nature of dharmas,... and this enlightenment did not rely on others 初發心時便成正覺眞實之性不由他悟: almost word for word from the *Avataṃsaka Sūtra* at T 9.449c14–15: "*At the time of his first aspiration he had already perfected correct awakening, knew the true nature of all dharmas,* was fully endowed with the body of wisdom, *and this enlightenment did not rely on others.*" This phrase has been quoted above in the *Mo-ho chih-kuan*; see notes at 62a27 and 87a25–26.

enlightenment], he had already perfected correct awakening, knew the true nature of dharmas,… and this enlightenment did not rely on others." This is the meaning here. In this way [by examining the sūtras and following their teachings], gradually and successively we have forty-two levels, until ultimately [you realize the highest level of] sublime awakening without going to excess. This is called "knowing the graded levels."

9. Resting in Patient Forbearance [99a29–99c14]

Ninth, resting in patient recognition, is to "be able to patiently perfect [**99b**] the matters of the path without being moved, and without retrogressing. This mental attitude is called [that of a] *[bodhi]sattva*." Beginning with the contemplation of the sense realms to knowing the graded levels [of attainment], [I have explained modes of contemplation concerning] eight obstructions to the Dharma and [the way] to turn these around and reveal wisdom. Some have not yet realized any degree [of attainment], but some have entered the first degree and their supranormal wisdom is keen. Suppose there is a sharp blade that is like "flying frost" and severs anything that it touches; the astute wisdom of beginners [that is, those who have their first aspiration for enlightenment] can be compared to this [sharp blade]. Even if they have not yet heard or studied [the Dharma], they are able to understand [the teachings of] the sūtras and śāstras. Upon reading other people's commentaries, they penetratingly understand its gist. If they wish to interpret one clause, their eloquence is inexhaustible. If you hold such a treasure in your hand and store such a jewel [within yourself], hoard your understanding and hide your name, and secretly strive diligently, and you will certainly realize the levels of attainment, or progress to deeper levels. Have a firm will, and do not be easily distracted, and you will attain an even more superior ability. However, if you "do not put away your awl in its bag" and you find

This mental attitude is called [bodhi-]sattva 心名薩埵: part of a verse from the section on the definition of a bodhisattva in the *Ta chih tu lun*, T 25.86a19–20. Lamotte (*Le Traité* 1, 241) translates:

Tous les attributs *(dharma)* de Buddha,
Sagesse *(prajñā)*, moralité *(śīla)* et concentration *(samādhi)*,
Qui sont profitables à tous,
Sont nommées Bodhi.
La Pensée inébranlable *(akṣobhya)*,
Capable d'accomplir avec patience les choses du Chemin,
Indestructible (aheya) et enfrangible (acyuta),
Cette Pensée est nommée Sattva.

Chodron (1, 205) translates:

All the Buddha-attributes,
Wisdom, discipline and meditation
That are profitable to all
Are called 'bodhi'.
The unshakable mind,
Able to patiently accomplish the dharmas of the Path,
Indestructible and infrangible,
This mind is called 'sattva'.

Beginning with the contemplation of the sense realms to knowing the graded levels 始觀陰界至識次位: that is, the first eight of the ten modes of contemplation as explained previous to this section; see sections 7.1.1 through 7.1.8 (*Mo-ho chih-kuan* 50c20–99a29).

Flying frost 飛霜: or, "like snow blowing in the wind"? Ikeda (*Gendaigoyaku*, 495), following Chan-jan, translates, "a sharp blade with the *fei-shuang* 飛霜 crest."

Hide your name 匿名, that is, "avoid fame" or "act anonymously."

Do not put away your awl in its bag 錐不處囊: refers to a saying from the *Shih-chi* 史記; "an awl in a bag" 囊中之錐 refers to the idea that one who is truly talented will

it difficult to hide and instead easily expose [your talents], when you see a lecturer [whose teachings] are not in line with reason, or see a practitioner whose [practice] is not appropriate, and compassionately point this out, you will then become surrounded [by followers]. You will be asked to lecture, or exhorted to become a leader of the multitude, so that internally you are irritated and externally agitated. You are able to preach only a small part of the Dharma, or teach only a small portion of dhyāna practice. At first you respond one-on-one, but [your work] spreads quickly and broadly without end. At first this seems beneficial, but the benefit for others is miniscule, and your own practice is impaired. It is not just that you do not advance on the stages [of attainment], but instead obstacles to the path are aroused even further. This is like a baby elephant whose strength is miniscule, and swords and arrows are thrust into its body [to weaken it further]; or, if you scoop up warm water and throw it on top of ice, you are left with even more ice. The *Treatise on the Ten Stages* calls such people "defeated bodhisattvas."

In the past there were meditation masters in Yeh and Lo-yang whose fame spread throughout the land. Wherever they went [the people] crowded around them like clouds from all directions to venerate them; and when they left, hundreds and thousands would follow them. Such roaring and rumbling; what benefit is there in this!? They will all regret it at the time of death. Wu-tsin lamented, "In my life I sought to realize [the stage of] the

find that it naturally comes to the fore, just as an awl in a bag tends to stick its pointed end out of the bag's opening.

Leader of the multitude 勸爲衆生: or "to exhort the masses." I follow the variant reading here, 主 instead of 生.

Obstacles to the path are aroused 障道還興: Chih-i seems to be speaking from his own experience. He abandoned a "successful" teaching career in the capital at Chin-ling to go to Mt. T'ien-t'ai, ostensibly to escape the increasingly unsatisfactory results of his work and to devote himself to contemplative practice. As Hurvitz (*Chih-i*, 116) points out, "the longer he remained in the Capital and the larger the number of his disciples the fewer were the hearts in which he was striking a responsive chord. Eight years in the metropolis had convinced him that here he could never achieve that religious development toward which he felt himself inclined, and he decided, after the manner of his own master, to betake himself to a mountaintop."

Defeated bodhisattvas 破敗: a phrase from the *Treatise on the Ten Stages*, T 26.38c29.

Masters in Yeh 鄴: Chan-jan (BT–IV, 576) writes, "Yeh is in the province of Hsiang 相州, the capital of the Ch'i 齊 and the Wei 魏. The Buddha Dharma prospered greatly there, and one of the Ch'an patriarchs converted the King [or, "had a great civilizing influence"]. In order to protect the intensions of the people of that time I will not give the names."

Throughout the land 河海: lit., "the rivers and seas."

Wu-tsin 武津: that is, Chih-i's teacher Nan-yüeh Hui-ssu.

copper wheel, but I started directing [other] people too quickly, and was not able to prevail in what I sought [for myself]." In the *[Establishment of] Vows* he wrote, "pick and choose, pick and choose." You should use the example of this lofty and superior [teacher] as a mirror. When your practice advances to this level, examine yourself and carefully consider [these things]. If your power of wisdom is strong and vigorous, you should broadly benefit [other beings], as a great elephant pushes [and leads] the herd. If your [wisdom] is not like this, then you should rest in patient forbearance [of your limited attainments] and deeply cultivate samādhi. It is not too late to teach others after you have perfected your practice and made manifest your power [of wisdom]. The *Ta chih tu lun* says, "The task of the bodhisattvas is to save people. Why, then, are they deep in the mountains [practicing] for their own good? Answer: This is like taking medicine to help your body [when you are sick], and then when you are physically healthy, you can act [for the sake of others] again. [When they are in the mountains,] although their bodies are far away [from the people they seek to save,] their thoughts are not far away."

Stage of the copper wheel 銅輪: that is, in terms of the Six Identities, equivalent to the level of "partial realization of the real truth."

Not able to prevail in what I sought 所求不克: see the biography of Hui-ssu in the *Biographies of Eminent Monks, Part 2*, T 50.563b10, which contains only the phrase "I attained the level of the ten levels of faith, the iron wheel."

Pick and choose 擇擇擇擇: this is the last line of Hui-ssu's *Establishment of Vows*, T 46.792b5.

The task of the bodhisattvas is to save people.... Their thoughts are not far away 菩薩以度人爲事云何深山自善。答曰。如服藥將身體康復業身雖遠離心不遠離: a summary from the *Ta chih tu lun* at T 25.180b17–26. Lamotte (*Le Traité* 2, 984) translates:

> Question. — Pour le Bodhisattva, la règle est de sauver tous les êtres; pourquoi se tient-il à l'écart dans les bois et les marais, la solitude et les montagnes, préoccupé seulement de sa propre personne et abandonnant le êtres?
> Réponse. — Bien que le Bodhisattva, corporellement, se tienne à l'écart des êtres, sa pensée ne les abandonne jamais. Dans la solitude *(śāntavihāra)*, il cherche la concentration *(samādhi)* et conquiert la véritable sagesse *(bhūtaprajñā)* pour sauver tous les êtres. Quant on prend un médicament *(bhaiṣajya)* pour raison de santé, on interrompt temporairement ses affaires familiales; puis, quand les forces se sont affermies, on reprend ses affaires comme auparavant. Le repos que prend le Bodhisattva est de cette nature-là. Par la force de l'extase *(dhyāna)*, il avale le médicament de la sagesse *(prajñā)*; quand il a obtenu la force des supersavoirs *(abhijñābala)*, il retourne chez les êtres, et devient, parmi eux, père, mère, épouse ou fils, maître, serviteur ou chef d'école, dieu, homme ou même animal; et il les guide par toutes sortes d'enseignements *(deśanā)* et de moyens salvifiques *(upāya)*.

Chodron (2, 762) translates:

> Question. The rule for the bodhisattva is to save beings; why does he dwell apart in forests and swamps, solitudes and mountains, preoccupied only with himself and abandoning beings?
> Answer. Although the bodhisattva stays

If you reach [the level of] the purification of the six senses, this is called the "earliest [level] where you become reliable to [other] people," and people can believe and accept what such a person teaches. A single sound [from such a person] pervades everywhere, and those who hear it rejoice. This is the "level of transforming [and saving] others." At this time the two bandits of strength [or "overconfidence"] and weakness do not appear, so there is nothing [to fear]. Your own practice will be perfected, and you will be eloquent [in teaching] for the sake of others. A great elephant protects [the herd] so that they are not subject to swords and arrows. If the rays of the sun illuminate the world, even long-term ice will melt. This is the power of "resting in patience."

If you are enfolded in the gauzy nets of fame, or in the hairy cords of profit, and, as a group of harmful insects gathering in a tree, corruption eats at you from within until finally [this damage appears] externally as on the branches [**99c**] and leaves [of the tree], you should quickly deduce [what is happening] and do not accept it and do not become attached to it. If you deduce this but do not get away and instead [fame and profit] become affixed to you, you should "shrink" your virtues and expose your flaws, exhibit your delusions and hide your true [qualities], as one secretly covers money so that it will not be seen and stolen. If you can conceal your traces but [still] cannot escape, you should in one fell swoop go 10,000 *li* to a secluded and faraway place, cut off all contact with acquaintances, and gladly practice the path, like Guṇabhadra. If the entourage of fame and profit follow you from

away from beings physically, his mind never abandons them. In solitude, he seeks concentration and gains true wisdom to save all beings. When you take a drug for health reasons, you temporarily interrupt family affairs; then when your strength has been recovered, you resume business as before. The rest that the bodhisattva takes is of that nature. He swallows the drug of wisdom by the power of meditation; when he has obtained the power of the superknowledges, he returns to people and, amongst them, becomes a father, mother, wife or son, master, servant or school-teacher, god, human or even an animal; and he guides them with all sorts of teachings and skillful means.

Perhaps a modern equivalent would be the ubiquitous instructions when an airplane is about to take off, that if there is an emergency and the oxygen masks are released, you should be sure to fasten your own before you attempt to help others?

Single sound 一音: or, "the singularity of their teachings." "One sound" is a characteristic of the Perfect Teaching.

Acquaintances 諳練: or, "have no connection with that with which one is accustomed"?

Guṇabhadra 求那跋摩: a famous translator of Buddhist texts; a brahman from central India who arrived in Canton in 435. See the biography in the *Biographies of Eminent Monks*, T 50.340a14–342b10, especially 340b4, which says that he "went alone into the mountains and fields, to avoid the traces of the world of people."

the outside and come to destroy you, remember these three techniques [for avoiding fame], grit your teeth, and patiently endure it, so that even thousands and tens of thousands of petitions cannot lure you away. Yield [to your good instincts]! Hide away! Leave [the mundane world]! If passionate afflictions, karmic deeds, concentrations, [mistaken] views, arrogance, and so forth come forth from inside and [threaten to] destroy you, remember these threefold techniques: [the contemplations of] the simultaneous identity of emptiness, conventionality, and the Middle. Even if your flesh is to be butchered and cut to pieces, you should not be mentally agitated; even if you are to be swallowed up by the great earth, you should not be overwhelmed by it; [even if faced with] hurricane-like winds, you will not be lightly [blown away]; frigid ice will not chill you; intense flames will hardly heat you. Straighten your thoughts and contemplate correctly; why should you rejoice with only a shallow attainment of a partial dhyāna meditation, or be despondent when barely seeing a little evil. Unfired [clay] vessels are easily [broken and thrown into] a pile, and it is difficult for the flower of an *āmra* (mango) [tree] to reach fruition. The *Pañcaviṃśati Sūtra* says, "Immeasur-

Three techniques 三術: according to Chan-jan (BT–IV, p. 579), the three "techniques" of 1. not accepting or becoming attached to corrupting influences, 2. "shrinking" your virtues and expose your flaws, and 3. going far away. This matches the pattern below of "yielding," "hiding," and "leaving."

Unfired vessels are easily [broken and thrown into] a pile 坯器易堆: the *Bukkyō Taikei* edition (BT–IV, 579) substitutes the character 搥 ("break") for 堆 ("pile up"). The image is probably based on a passage in the *Pañcaviṃśati Sūtra*, T 8.330a1–10:

> Subhūti, suppose there were men or women who carried an unfired [clay] bottle to fetch water. You should know that this bottle will not last long but will break. Why? Because the bottle is not yet maturated; it will return to the earth. Like this, Subhūti, are good sons and good daughters who, although they have the thought of *anuttarasaṃyaksaṃbodhi*, faith, patience, a pure mind, a profound mind, desire [for enlightenment], understanding, charity, and diligence, but do not maintain *prajñā-pāramitā* and the power of means; do not maintain *dhyāna-pāramitā, vīrya-pāramitā, kṣānti-pāramitā, śīla-pāramitā,* and *dāna-pāramitā*; and do not maintain [the various kinds of emptiness] from internal emptiness to the emptiness of nonexistent and existent dharmas, from the four mindfulnesses to the eightfold path, and from the ten powers of the Buddha to universal wisdom.

Fruit of the *āmra* [tree] 菴華: see the verses in the *Ta chih tu lun*, T 25.88a10–11; Lamotte (*Le Traité* 1, 257) translates:

> Des Bodhisattva qui produisent la Grande pensée,
> Des oeufs de poisson et *des fleurs de manguier*:
> Voilà trois choses assez communes,
> *Mais il est rare qu'elles portent des fruit.*

Chodron (1, 217) translates:

> Bodhisattvas who produce the Great Mind,
> Eggs of fish and flowers of the mango tree:
> These three things are rather common,
> But it is rare that they bear fruit.

able people arouse the thought of *bodhi*-wisdom [or, "the aspiration for enlightenment"], but many fall into the stages of the two vehicles." In order to accomplish the Great Matter [of Buddhahood], it is necessary to rest patiently. If you realize this meaning, you do not need [to contemplate] the other nine objects. For those who do not yet comprehend, we should clarify [these subjects] further and more broadly.

Immeasurable people arouse the thought of *bodhi*-wisdom, but many fall into the stages of the two vehicles 無量人發菩提心多墮二乘地: see the *Pañcaviṃśati Sūtra* at T 8.357c2–4:

> As there are few places in the great earth which gives forth gold, silver, and precious jewels, Subhūti, sentient beings are also likewise. There are few people who are able to learn *prajñā-pāramitā*, and many who fall into the stages of the śrāvaka and pratyekabuddha.

10. No Passionate Attachments to Dharmas [99c14–100a3]

Tenth is to have no passionate attachments to dharmas. If you practice the above nine matters and pass beyond the internal and external obstacles, then you should attain a realization of the true [that is, emptiness]. However, if you do not yet realize it, you may be unable to progress because you are passionately attached to these dharmas. The *Abhidharma-vibhāṣā-śāstra* says, "You can retrogress from the stage of 'heat,' but once the five sense faculties are established on [the stage of] patience and arouse [a realization of] the real [at the stage of 'supreme in the world'], there is no more discussion of retrogression. If you arouse passionate attachments at the stage of 'the summit,' you will not realize what you should realize, but will retrogress to perform the four serious and the five heinous offences." The idea of falling back from the stage of the summit applies to those of the Shared and Distinct [Teachings, as well as those of the Tripitaka Teachings.] If they cannot enter these levels, neither can they fall back into [the status of] those of the two vehicles. The *Ta chih tu lun* says, "The three kinds of samādhi resemble the levels of the path. When you have not yet aroused [a realization of] the true, you rejoice and have attachments to these dharmas. This is called 'falling back into [the stage of] the summit.'"

No passionate attachments to dharmas 無法愛: it is not clear whether this refers to "phenomena" or "teachings," or both, so I have kept the ambiguous "dharmas."

Nine matters: the first nine of the ten modes of contemplation.

You can retrogress … four serious and the five heinous offences 煖法猶退五根若立上忍發眞則不論退。頂法若生愛心應入不入退爲四重五逆: a summary of a passage in the *Abhidharma-vibhāṣā-śāstra* at T 28.19a23–c21, which discusses retrogressing from the stages of "heat" and "summit."

The stage of "heat" 煖: the first stage of the "four good roots" in the Tripitaka Teachings. See Chart 1 in Volume 3.

The stage of patience 忍: the third of the stages of the "four good roots."

The stage of "the summit" 頂: The second of the stages of the "four good roots."

The idea of falling back from the stage of the summit 頂墮之義: see the passage on "falling back into the stage of the summit" in the *Ta chih tu lun*, T 25.262b4–12. Lamotte (*Le Traité* 4, 1791–93) translates:

> Question. — Qu'est-ce que tomber des Sommets *(mūrdhabhyaḥ pāta)*?
> Réponse. — Comme Subhūti l'a dit à Śāriputra: "Lorsque le Bodhisattva-Mahāsattva dépourvu d'habileté en moyens salvifiques *(anupāyakuśala)*, mais pratiquant les six perfections, est entré dans [les concentrations] de la vacuité, du sans-caractère et de la non-prise en considération, il ne peut accéder au Bodhisattva-niyāma, mais ne tombe pas non plus au rang de Śrāvaka ou de Pratyekabuddha."
>
> Il s'attache *(abhiniviśate)* aux qualités *(guṇa)* et aux attributs; dans les cinq agrégats *(skandha)*, il saisit les caractéristiques *(nimittāny udgṛhṇāti)* d'impermanence *(anitya)*, de douleur *(duḥkha)*, de vide *(śūnya)*, d'impersonnalité *(anātman)* et y attache sa pensée; il déclare: "Ceci est le Chemin, cela n'est pas le Chemin; ceci doit être pratiqué, cela ne doit pas être pratiqué." Quand il saisit ainsi

Currently, of people who practice the path, the great majority does not reach [these levels of attainment]. If you attain [these levels], take care to guard yourself. There are no internal or external obstacles at this level [because they have been removed], but there is [still the possibility of] passionate attachment to dharmas. Passionate attachments to dharmas are difficult to sever, and if you are detained [by them], this is not an insignificant matter. This is analogous to having the same type of sailboat [in the water] yet one [of them] moves forward and one stays put; the one stays put because it has "attachments." Again, even if it is not stuck in the sand, or not attached to the shore, it stays because the wind has ceased. "Not stuck in the sand" is analogous for having no internal obstacles. "The shore" is analogous to the external obstacles. To arouse passionate attachments to dharmas even when the winds of non-abiding have ceased, and neither progress nor retrogress, is called "falling into [the level of] the summit."

If you do destroy the passionate attachments to dharmas, you will realize the three [types of] liberation and arouse the true Middle Way. The body of wisdom thus attained does not depend on others for its awakening. You will spontaneously flow into the sea of omniscience *(sarvajñā)* and dwell in the patient forbearance of [knowing] the non-arising of dharmas. Again, this is called the "forbearance of quiescent extinction." By means of the Śūraṅgama [Samādhi] you will have supremacy in supranormal powers, and be endowed with **[100a]** great wisdom, like the waters of the great sea. The virtuous qualities that you possess are known only by a Buddha.

The means for progressing in cessation-and-contemplation have now been put forth here. The virtuous qualities of the stages to be realized will not be expounded here, but I will elucidate them later.

> de telles caractéristiques et fait de telles distinctions *(vikalpa)*, le Bodhisattva est "tombé des Sommets" *(mūrdhabhyaḥ patitaḥ)*.

Chodron (4, 1473–74) translates:

> Question. What is falling back from the summits?
> Answer. As Subhūti said to Śāriputra: "When the bodhisattva-mahāsattva who is without skillful means but is practicing the six perfections has entered [the concentrations] of emptiness, signlessness and wishlessness, he cannot accede to bodhisattvaviyāma, but neither does he regress to the rank of śrāvaka or pratyekabuddha."
>
> He becomes attached to the qualities and the attributes; in the five aggregates he grasps the characteristics of impermanence, suffering, emptiness, non-self and attaches his mind to them; he says: "This is the Path, that is not the Path; this should be practiced, that should not be practiced." When he grasps such characteristics in this way and makes such distinctions, the bodhisattva has "fallen from the summits."

See this theme at T 25.664b13ff.

Elucidate them later 後當重辨: presumably in the tenth section on the realm of the bodhisattvas, a section which remained unfinished.

11. Summary of the Ten Modes of Contemplation: The Parable of the Great Cart [100a3–b16]

These ten methods [of contemplation] are called Mahāyāna (Great Vehicle) contemplations, and those who learn this [great] vehicle are called Mahāyānists. What is this "Great Vehicle"? As the *Lotus Sūtra* says, "Each of the children was offered equally one great cart. This cart was high and wide, and adorned with a multitude of jewels, surrounded by posts and handrails, with bells suspended on all four sides. Also, on its top were spread out parasols and canopies. Again, it was splendidly adorned with a rare assortment of jewels, intertwined with jeweled cords and hung with flowered tassels, having layers of carpets decorated with strips of cloth, placed with vermilion-colored pillows, yoked to a white ox which was well-fed and of great strength, whose skin was pure white and physical form was lovely, whose muscular strength was great and whose tread was even and proper and quick like the wind. Again, there were many attendants serving and guarding [this ox]."

The [practice of] cessation-and-contemplation of the Great Vehicle is also like this. Contemplate each thought-moment in the mind 念念心; there is nothing that is not Dharma-nature and the true aspect [of reality]; this is expressed as "equally [offered] one great cart." Each single thought 一一心 is simultaneously empty, conventional, and the Middle 即空即假即中; this is expressed as "each was offered a great cart." To be permeated with the basis of the threefold truth is expressed as "high." To embrace the ten dharma realms is expressed as "wide." The immeasurable steps on the path

Each of the children was offered equally one great cart 各賜諸子等一大車 **... serving and guarding**: see the parable of the burning house in the third chapter of the *Lotus Sūtra*, T 9.12b–16c. See especially the passage at 12c18–28; Hurvitz (60 [56]) translates:

> Śāriputra, at that time the great man gives to each child one great carriage. The carriage is high and wide, adorned with a multitude of jewels, surrounded by posts and handrails, little bells suspended on all four sides. Also, on its top are spread out parasols and canopies. Further, it is adorned with an assortment of rare and precious jewels. Intertwined with jeweled cords and hung with flowered tassels, having heaps of carpets decorated with strips of cloth, as well as vermilion-colored cushions, it is yoked to a white ox, whose skin is pure white, whose bodily form is lovely, whose muscular strength is great, whose tread is even and fleet like the wind. [This ox] also has many attendants serving and guarding it. What is the reason? Because this great man, of wealth incalculable, his various storehouses all full to overflowing, has this thought: "My wealth being limitless, I may not give small, inferior carriages to my children. Now these little boys are all my sons. I love them without distinction. I have carriages such as these, made of the seven jewels, in incalculable numbers. I must give one to each of them with undiscriminating thought."

are expressed as "adorned with a multitude of jewels." The four endeavors to hinder evil and uphold good, and to enact vows and maintain practices—to secure with nails and fasteners—is expressed as "surrounded by posts and handrails." Eloquently exposing the meaning of the Dharma and proclaiming it to bring out awakening [in people] is expressed as "bells suspended on all four sides." Covering all with compassion, with nothing left out and no limits, is expressed as "spread out with parasols and canopies." For the steps on the path to encompass the ten powers, fearlessness, and the eighteen unique qualities that cannot be replaced with others, is expressed as "splendidly adorned with a rare assortment of jewels." For the mind to be [focused on] the essentials and not retrogress through [maintaining] the Four Universal Vows is expressed as "intertwined with jeweled cords." Embracing beings through the four inducements so that there is none who does not rejoice is expressed as "hung with flowered tassels." Arousing the six supranormal powers through the various dhyāna meditations and samādhis is expressed as "layers of carpets decorated with strips of cloth." For the four gates [or teachings] to "return to the gist" and for all practices to come to rest is expressed as "placed with vermilion-colored pillows." Destroying and removing the darkness of the eight perversions through the four mindfulnesses is expressed as "yoked to a white ox." To increase and grow in the two types of good through the four proper endeavors is expressed as "well-fed and of great strength." To hinder and sever the two types of evil, and to exhaust and purify the two types of evil, is expressed as "the skin was pure white." Mastery in the four supranormal powers and the four [unobstructed] eloquences is expressed as "the physical form was lovely." To be firm in the five [moral] faculties so that you are not agitated is expressed as "muscle." To increase and grow in the five powers so that evil dharmas are hindered is expressed as "power." Selecting [matters] with regard to the seven [components of] awakening is expressed as your "tread." To rest peacefully in the eightfold path is expressed as "even and proper." All dharmas being encompassed [in the practices of] controlling and healing through the auxiliary methods of the path is expressed as "many attendants serving and guarding." Destroying ignorance and the passionate attachments to dharmas, entering the sea of omniscience *(sarvajña)*, and quickly arousing [a realization of] the true, is expressed as "quick as the wind." Thus [this vehicle] carries [**100b**] and gives a ride to all the children, who rejoice and are happy. This Mahāyāna contemplation is a Dharma gate that accommodates crossing [to the other shore of enlightenment], and cor-

Two types of good 二善: that is, maintain good that has already arisen, and arouse good that has not yet arisen.

Two types of evil 二惡: that is, evil that has not yet arisen, and evil that has already arisen.

responds with this *[Lotus] Sūtra*. Therefore it is called the Mahāyāna [Great Vehicle] contemplation.

Again, all Dharma teachings are of the one [single] vehicle 一乘, so among those who have thoughts [that is, everyone], there is none that is not already endowed with it. This "sublime Dharma" 妙法 is called "the vehicle as principle." If the Tathāgata does not preach it, then it cannot be known, and by hearing the teachings, [people] rejoice and humbly accept it. Thus this is called "the vehicle as verbal expression" 名字乘. By hearing these words, people come to rely on the teachings, cultivate practices, and enter the levels of the five grades [of the disciple]. This is called "the vehicle as contemplative practice" 觀行乘. Attaining the purity of the six senses is "the vehicle as resemblance [to enlightenment]" 相似乘. Transcending the triple world and reaching omniscience *(sarvajña)* and abiding therein, yet not abiding therein and entering [the bodhisattva stages] from the first abode to the tenth abode, means attaining "the vehicle as truly real." This is to "play" in the east. [Realizing] the ten [stages of] practice is to "play" in the south; [realizing] the ten [stages of] merit transference is to "play" in the west; [realizing] the ten *bhūmi* stages is to "play in the north." There are no borders to the circumference of the wheel [of existence], but it stops when you realize emptiness, and you stop in the middle. This is sublime awakening. This is the meaning of [the *Lotus Sūtra* when it says that one goes] "directly to the seat of enlightenment."

People of these days think that abandoning evil and accepting emptiness is [the content of] Mahāyāna. You are not able to escape the sixty-two [mistaken] views—and the individual and multiple evil [of these views]—with this [view of] emptiness. How, then, can you move [and progress to the final goal] with this vehicle? Even if this vehicle is used, this is only one [limited] stripped-down vehicle, and it is not a Dharma-gate that accommodates [the universal] crossing [of all beings to the other shore of enlightenment]. The correct Dharma *(saddharma)* is a great city, a treasure-store of diamonds *(vajra)*, which contains all and is not lacking in anything. How can you admit this stripped-down emptiness [as comparable to this complete

Vehicle as principle 理乘: Starting with this term, Chih-i applies the terms of the Six Identities to the idea of a "vehicle."

The vehicle as truly real 眞實乘: this must correspond to the fifth of the Six Identities of "partial realization."

Sublime awakening 妙覺: equivalent to the sixth level of the Six Identities, that is, "ultimate identity."

Directly to the seat of enlightenment 直至道場: see the *Lotus Sūtra*, T 9.15a14, towards the end of the parable on the burning house. This phrase has been quoted already in the *Mo-ho chih-kuan*; see note at 31a9–10 for a full translation of this section.

Mahāyāna emptiness]! If you affirm this "mere" [emptiness], this is like riding on the vehicle of deviant views, and you enter a dangerous and evil path. This is like a defective donkey cart.

Defective donkey cart 壞驢車: or, "ass-mobile"? In contrast to the "white ox cart" that is symbolic of the single and great vehicle of the Mahāyāna. The term is from the *Mahāparinirvāṇa Sūtra*, T 12.724c16 (and 481c8).

3. Contemplating the Sense Realms while Responding to Objects as Conditions Arise [100b16–101c23]

[Contemplating] the sense realms while sitting properly [in meditation] 端坐 is as explained above. Contemplating the sense realms while responding to objects as conditions arise 歷緣對境 is as follows. "Conditions" refer to the six actions, and "objects" refer to the six sense objects.

1. Contemplation and the Six Actions [100b17]

The *Ta chih tu lun* says, "There is the arousing of activity within conditions, and the arousing of accepting [the experience of] sense objects." This is as explained in [the section on the Samādhi of] "following one's own thoughts." The Pratyutpanna [Samādhi] of the constantly-walking [samādhi], and the Lotus [Samādhi] and Vaipulya [Samādhi] of the both-walking[-and-sitting samādhi], all include the activities such as "cleaning away" or attending to [various activities], but this [participation in activity] is most frequent within [the samādhi of] "following one's own thoughts." If you do not learn to contemplate within the activities [of daily life], how can you quickly attain a rapport with the principle of the path?

To briefly discriminate the features [of contemplating the sense realms

As explained above: see the long section just expounded above at *Mo-ho chih-kuan* 52b17–100b16 (about a third of the entire text). This previous section is not identified explicitly as contemplation to be performed while sitting in meditation until here, where it is identified as such in contrast to the contemplation of objects in everyday life as one carries out various activities (that is, "responding to objects as conditions arise").

Six actions 六作: a general term for all possible activities carried out by humans: walking or going, standing or staying, sitting, laying down, speaking and silence, and general movement or activity. At times "speaking" and "being silent" are divided up into the fifth and sixth activities.

There is the arousing of activity within conditions, and the arousing of accepting sense objects 於緣生作者於塵生受:: the text is ambiguous, and the *Kōgi* (BT-IV, 589) admits that this cannot be found in the *Ta chih tu lun*. It is not clear what Chih-i intends to convey here. Ikeda (*Gendaigoyaku*, 502) translates, "There is the one who performs actions within the six conditions, and the one who accepts [experience] within the six sense objects."

Explained in … following one's own thoughts 隨自意: see the section at 15c17–17b16 under the discussion of the practice of neither-walking-nor-sitting samādhi.

Cleaning away 掃灑: Lit. "sweeping away and sprinkling."

Samādhi of following one's own thoughts: or, the neither-walking-nor-sitting samādhi, the type of practice that involves the most activity and contact with sense experiences, since it involves contemplation within the activities of daily life rather than within a specified time and place limited to sitting or walking in meditation.

by responding to objects as conditions], I will follow the previous example of ten [modes of contemplation].

1. Objects as Inconceivable [100b21]

The first type, that is, "contemplating objects [as inconceivable]," is as follows. [For example, in the case of walking,] whether you raise your feet or lower your feet, this involves [dealing with] the phenomena of visible form *(rūpa)*. These forms are handled through mental processes [or, by the mind] for you to get from here to there. These thoughts rely on the forms [to arise]; this is the [first] skandha of "form" 色陰. To make these actions [of walking] your own is the skandha of "sensation" 受陰. To presume a self within these actions is the skandha of "conception" 思陰. To make good actions or bad actions is the skandha of "volition" 行陰. The thoughts within the actions [of walking] is the skandha of "consciousness" 識陰. If the sense objects of this action [of walking] become the object of your consciousness, you have the sense realms [that is, the twelve sense entrances and eighteen sense realms]. [This is so for all the sense realms,] from the visible forms seen by the eye 眼色 to the objects of consciousness [experienced in the mind] 意法. These sense fields—the skandhas, sense entrances, and sense realms—are all included in the span of raising and lowering [your feet while walking]. In this way the sense realms are the merging of ignorance with volition, which gives rise to the sense realms within the activity of walking. The sense realms are not different from emptiness. Ignorance is indivisible from Dharma-nature. Dharma-nature is indivisible from the Dharma realm *(dharmadhātu)*. All phenomena are included in the activity of walking, and do not go beyond this inclusion. [**100c**] One sense realm is all sense realms. The one and the many are neither one nor many; they do not mutually obstruct each other. This is called "[contemplating] objects as inconceivable while walking." [Contemplating in this way while performing other activities other than "walking" is to be understood in the same way.]

2. Arousing Compassion [100c2]

When you penetrate [and understand] these objects [in this way], compassion will arise concurrently, and you will feel pained that you have sunk

The previous example of ten [modes of contemplation] 例前爲十: see the list in the *Mo-ho chih-kuan* at 52b2–4.

Raising or lowering feet 擧足下足: this phrase is from the *Vimalakirti Sūtra*, T 14.543a6, quoted more fully below; see note at *Mo-ho chih-kuan* 100c16.

Merging of ignorance with volition 行陰: the Taishō text has 行緣, "activities and conditions," but, like the *Bukkyō Taikei* text and Ikeda, I follow the variant reading.

deeply and have constantly, for immeasurable kalpas, been deluded and deceived concerning the sense realms. When you become aware for the first time that all sentient beings without exception [ride on] the one vehicle, you should feel great pity for them [as they are still] in their deep intoxication and perverted understanding. [Therefore,] vow to destroy ignorance and to become something on which all [sentient beings] can rely.

3. Peaceful Mind [100c5]

Have a peaceful mind of concentration and wisdom, of quiescent illumination.

4. Deconstructing Mistaken Views and Attitudes [100c6]

If your thoughts are already peaceful, then universally deconstruct [mistaken] views and attitudes, and non-cognizance and ignorance, so that the obstacles to the threefold truth, both vertical and horizontal, are exhausted.

5. Knowing What Penetrates and What Obstructs the Path [100c7]

Again, know well what penetrates and what obstructs [the path], so that finally you do not have to take up medicine for disease while on [the path].

6. The Steps on the Path [100c8]

Know well the steps on the way—the parts that flourish and decay, and the [four] mindfulnesses—and enter *parinirvāṇa* between the Śāla trees.

7. Controlling and Healing through Auxiliary Methods [100c9]

Again, know well the antidote [for controlling and healing delusions and so forth] of the six perfections through the activity of walking, thus assisting in opening the gate of nirvana.

8. Knowing the Stages [100c10]

Be deeply conscious of the gradual stages, so that you know your own actions [of walking] are not yet the same as those of the superior noble ones.

9. Resting in Patient Forbearance [100c11]

Humbly repent and diligently cultivate [the path] without any respite.

Śāla tree: see the section above on the four mindfulnesses within the steps on the path, *Mo-ho chih-kuan* 88b14ff., especially the part which uses the image of the "flourishing" and "decaying" parts of the Śāla tree, 88c16ff.

Within your actions [of walking], externally defeat any fame and [worldly] benefit, and internally overcome the three obstacles, so that you rest in patience without agitation.

10. No Passionate Attachments to Dharmas [100c12]

Do not retrogress from [the stage of] "the summit" through entangling and grasping attachments to dharmas.

11. Summary [100c13]

Fulfill these ten methods and thus enter [the stage of] the copper *cakravartin*; realize the forbearance from [knowing that dharmas are] non-arising; attain "the one great cart that is high and wide, splendid and pure, adorned with a multitude of jewels, and quick as the wind," … "and playing and rejoicing … mount this jeweled vehicle and go directly to the seat of enlightenment *(bodhimaṇḍa)*." This is what it means to contemplate in terms of the conditions of your activities [of walking]. Control the chaff of ignorance and manifest the grain of dharma-nature. "Raising your feet and lowering your feet,… you arrive at the seat of enlightenment and are endowed with the Buddha Dharma." This should be known as in the examples given previously.

Retrogress from the stage of "the summit" 頂墮: for an explanation of this idea, see the section above on "passionate attachments to dharmas" at *Mo-ho chih-kuan* 99c14–100a3.

The one great cart that is high and wide, splendid and pure, adorned with a multitude of jewels, and quick as the wind 一大車高廣嚴淨衆寶莊校。其疾如風: a summary of the passage from the parable of the burning house in the *Lotus Sūtra* (T 9.12c18–28) quoted in the section above. See note at *Mo-ho chih-kuan* 100a4.

Playing and rejoicing … mount this jewelled vehicle and go directly to the place of enlightenment 嬉戲快樂乘是寶乘直至道場: excerpts from the verses on the parable of the burning house in the *Lotus Sūtra*, T 9.14c18 and 15a13–14. Hurvitz (71–74 [66–68]) translates the context:

These lovely carriages
He gave equally to all the children.
The children at this time,
Dancing for joy
And mounting these jeweled carriages,
Cavorted in all four directions,
Playing and enjoying themselves,
Completely at ease and feeling no encumbrances.…
If they can gain this kind of Vehicle,
I enable these children
Night and day, for a number of kalpas,
Ever to amuse themselves,
With bodhisattvas
And the multitude of voice-hearers
To mount this jeweled Vehicle
And to arrive directly at the Platform of the Way.

Raising your feet and lowering your feet,… you arrive at the seat of enlightenment and are endowed with the Buddha Dharma 擧足下足道場中來具足佛法: these phrases are from the *Vimalakīrti Sūtra*, T 14.543a6. For a translation of the context see note at *Mo-ho chih-kuan* 16b15–16.

This is how it is for [contemplating the sense realms with regard to] the conditions or activity of walking. [Contemplating while in the activities of] staying, sitting, laying down, speaking, and miscellaneous activity should be understood as in the previous example.

Three [of the Four] Samādhis do not involve the "activity" of lying down, but it is included in "following one's own thoughts" [that is, the fourth samādhi of neither-walking-nor-sitting]. [As it says in the *Ta chih tu lun*,] in the past there was a king who became awakened as a pratyekabuddha as he was lying down. Thus it should be known that the practice of contemplation can be realized while lying down.

A king who became awakened as a pratyekabuddha as he was laying down 昔國王於臥中悟辟支佛: see the story of the king who awoke from his sleep to find the flowers and forest around him in ruins, and realized the truth of transiency, and became a pratyekabuddha; in the *Ta chih tu lun* at T 25.191a22–b5; Lamotte (*Le Traité* 2, 1068) translates:

> Question. — S'il en va de même pour l'état de Pratyekabuddha, pourquoi établissez-vous une distinction entre Śrāvaka et Pratyekabuddha?
> Réponse. — Bien que l'état final soit du même genre, les savoirs utilisés sont différents. A une époque où les Buddha n'apparaissent pas et où la Loi du Buddha a disparu, les Pratyekabuddha, en raison des causes antérieures *(pūrva-janmahetupratyaya)*, produisent seuls la sagesse, sans l'avoir entendue des autres; c'est par leur propre sagesse qu'ils obtiennent le Chemin.
>
> *Ainsi, le roi* d'un pays était sorti se promener dans son jardin. Dans le matin clair, il vit combien les fleurs et les fruits des arbres de la forêt étaient beaux et désirables; il en mangea et *s'endormit*. Ses femmes et ses courtisanes, procédant ensemble à la cueillette des fleurs, saccagèrent les arbres de la forêt. Le roi s'étant réveillé, vit cette destruction et se dit en lui-même: "Le monde entier est transitoire *(anitya)* et périssable comme cette forêt." Dès qu'il eut fait cette réflexion, la pensée du Chemin pur *(anāsravamārga)* naquit en lui; il trancha toutes les entraves *(saṃyojana) et obtint l'état de Pratyekabuddha*. Muni des six supersavoirs *(abhijñā)*, il se rendit en volant dans une forêt solitaire. — Il est encore d'autres histoires de ce genre. Les mérites *(puṇya)* et les voeux *(praṇidhāna)* des existences antérieures activent un fruit de rétribution *(vipākaphala)* et, dans l'existence présente, il suffit au Pratyekabuddha de voir un événement minime pour réaliser l'état de Pratyekabuddha. En cela consiste la différence.

Chodron (2, 829) translates:

> Question. If it is the same for the state of pratyekabuddha, why do you make a distinction between śrāvaka and pratyekabuddha?
> Answer. – Although the final state may be of the same type, the knowledges used are different. At the stage where the Buddhas do not appear and the Buddhadharma has disappeared, the pratyekabuddhas, by reason of previous causes, alone produce wisdom without having heard it from others; it is by means of their own wisdom that they obtain the Path.
>
> Thus the king of a country had gone for a walk in his garden. In the cool morning, he saw how the flowers and fruits of the forest trees were beautiful and desirable. He ate some and fell asleep. His wives and courtesans, walking together to gather flowers, wrecked the forest trees. The king woke up, saw the destruction and said to himself: "The entire world

2. Contemplation and the Six Sense Objects [100c20]

[Contemplating] by responding to objects 對境 is as follows. With regard to the eye [and seeing], for example, you presume that there is a self and say that it is the self that experiences [visual phenomena]. One sense object involves three aspects, thus all together there are eighteen aspects of experience. The eye sees visible form, which involves the five skandhas, three [of the eighteen] sense realms, and two [of the twelve] sense entrances, as explained above. Again, the *Maitreya Sūtra on [the Consideration of] the Features of Bones* says, "One thought-instant of seeing color involves three hundred millions of arising and perishing of the five skandhas, and each and every one of the five skandhas are themselves the sentient beings." If this is so, then when the eye responds to color, how could this involve only the five skandhas, three of the sense realms, and two of the sense entrances [instead of all eighteen sense realms and twelve sense entrances]? If you contemplate color through the eyes in this way, this is called "lacking in cultivation," and

is transitory and perishable like this forest." As soon as he had this thought, the mind of the pure path arose in him; he cut all the fetters and attained the state of pratyekabuddhahood. Endowed with the six superknowledges he went flying to a solitary forest. – There are other stories of this kind. The merits and vows of previous lifetimes activate a fruit of retribution and, in the present lifetime, it is enough for a pratyekabuddha to see a very minor event in order to realize the state of pratyekabuddha. This is what he difference consists of.

One sense object involves three aspects 一塵有三: that is, the phenomenal object (for example, things that have color and form), the sense organ (for example, the eye), and the sense consciousness (that is, the mental process that analyzes the sight experience).

Eighteen aspects of existence 合十八受: the eighteen sense realms *(dhātu)*: the three aspects multiplied by the six senses of sight, sound, scent, taste, touch, and thought.

Sense realms and sense entrances: that is, out of the eighteen *dhātu*, the eye (sense organ), the sight objects, and the sight consciousness; and out of the twelve *āyatana*, the eye and the sight objects.

As explained above: it is not clear which "above" section is being referred to here. The *Kōgi* (BT–IV, p. 593) refers back to "the text on the ten modes [of contemplation]."

The *Maitreya Sūtra on the Features of Bones* 彌勒相骨經 says, One thought-instant of seeing color involves three hundred millions of arising and perishing of the five skandhas, and each and every one of the five skandhas are themselves the sentient beings 一念見色有三百億五陰生滅一一五陰卽是衆生: the identity of this text is unknown. Chan-jan (BT–IV, 592) admits that "this text is not in the canon," and points to passages in the *Bodhisattva Womb Sūtra* 菩薩處胎經 (T no. 284), one of which says, "Maitreya said, 'The moment of a clap or snap of the fingers contains thirty-two million and a hundred thousand thought-moments'" (T 12.1024b21–23), and another passage in which the Buddha speaks to Maitreya of his bones forming in the womb (1033b18ff.).

Through the eyes in this way 如此觀眼色: that is, as involving only the sense

is not that of Mahāyāna. If you contemplate color through the eyes "as the Tathāgatas constantly do, complete and without lacking in cultivation, so that the eye consciousness [sees] the gate to be entered," then [you realize that] this arises in a single moment of thought [in conjunction] with the eye and visible form. This is the Dharma realm, this encompasses all phenomena, and this is simultaneously empty, conventional, and the Middle.

If you seek [to explain it] through the tetralemma, it is "unobtainable"; therefore it is called "empty."

As Maitreya [considers] the features of visible forms, the five skandhas arise and perish three hundred million times in a single thought-moment, and one [101a] stage is ten stages; this is the way it is for the features of color-and-form, and it is again likewise for [the other skandhas of] sensations, conceptions, volitions, and consciousness. Again, [as it says in the Āgamas,] "the heterodox man pounded on a skull and made sounds, and by hearing this knew where it was born and knew immeasurable other things," with the same for smelling, tasting, and touching [the skull], and so forth. Therefore this is called "conventional."

experiences of seeing, instead of involving all of the sense realms and incalculable phenomena.

Without lacking in cultivation 無減修: see the verses in the *Aṅgulimāla Sūtra*, T 2.531c22–532b6, which speak of the Tathāgata's qualities as being "without decrease or loss" 無減損, or, in a variant reading, "without lacking in cultivation" 無減修, and concluding that certain qualities are those of the śrāvaka vehicle and not Mahāyāna (532b1–6), though they are contained in or encompassed by the Mahāyāna. See the notes at *Mo-ho chih-kuan* 95b9–11 and 96b18–20.

The eye consciousness [sees] 眼識: the Taishō text has 明識, with 眼識 as a variant reading. The *Bukkyō Taikei* text and Ikeda follow the variant reading. See also below (101a16), where this phrase is quoted again, this time in the same way as the sūtra, with the compound 明見 instead of 明識 or 眼識.

The gate to be entered 來入門: see the verses in the *Aṅgulimāla Sūtra*, T 2.532a7–8:

> The so-called sense-entrance of the eye,
> With the constant [gaze] of the Tathāgata,
> Clearly sees 明見 the gate to be entered,
> Completely and without and lack or loss.

Once again, see the note on this text at 95b9–11, and the discussion of this passage that follows as it relates to the Perfect Teaching.

Single moment of thought 一念心: here we have the interplay of the three aspects of the sense organ (eye), the sense object (visible form), and the sense consciousness (thought) in a single momentary thought.

Maitreya 彌勒: see the quote attributed to the *Maitreya Sūtra* above.

The heterodox man pounded on a skull and made sounds, and by hearing this knew where it was born and knew immeasurable other things 外道打髑髏作聲聽知生處知無量事: see the story in the *Expanded Āgama*, T 2.650c12–652b12. Perhaps these "worldly skills," such as knowing that the skull belonged to a man and not a woman just by hitting or smelling the skull, is representative of being familiar with the "conventional" world?

The conventional [dharmas] are not a fixed conventionality 定假; the empty [dharmas] are not a fixed emptiness 定空, and thus are neither conventional nor empty 非空非假. If a single dharma [perceived by] the eye is neither empty nor conventional, then all dharmas are neither empty nor conventional. This is like space, where existence and non-existence are eternally quiescent. Or again, this is like [the rays of] the sun and moon — there is no darkness that is not illuminated. [This is called the "Middle."]

[The Five Eyes and the Threefold Truth] Even though there is no [fixed] emptiness or conventionality, that which illumines [and perceives] both the empty and the conventional [dharmas] and illumines [and perceives] the coarse visible forms [that arise through] causes and conditions is called the "physical eye" 肉眼. That which illumines [and perceives] the minute visible forms [that arise through] causes and conditions is called the "divine eye" 天眼. That which illumines [and perceives] the emptiness of visible forms [that arise through] causes and conditions is called the "eye of wisdom" 慧眼. That which illumines [and perceives] the conventionality of visible forms [that arise through] causes and conditions is called the "Dharma eye" 法眼. That which illumines [and perceives as the Middle] visible forms [that arise through] causes and conditions is called the "Buddha eye" 佛眼. These five eyesights are included within one thought 一心. However, [all five eyesights] are not included in the physical eye of pus and blood of the ordinary person; they also are not [included in] the divine eye possessed by divine beings; they also are not [included in] the eye of wisdom mired in emptiness of those of the two vehicles; they also are not [included in] the [Dharma] eye of discrimination [of conventionality] of the bodhisattvas. It is the Buddha eye alone that includes [the powers of all] the five eyes. As when the various streams enter the sea [and become one], the original names [of the first four eyes] are lost [when subsumed in the Buddha eye]. [*The Diamond Sūtra* says,] "Therefore the Buddha asked Subhūti, 'Does the Tathāgata have the

Like space 如虛空: this illustrates the "empty" side of the equation or the Middle?

Like the sun and moon 如日月無幽不照: this illustrates the "conventional" side of the equation or the Middle?

Physical eye 肉眼: the first of the "five eyes" or "five eyesights."

It is the Buddha eye alone that includes all five eyes 但以佛眼具有五力: the Taishō edition has "five powers" 五力, with "five eyes" 五眼 as a variant reading. I have combined both variants in my translation.

Original names are lost 失本名字: That is, all the powers of the five different eyes or eyesights are included in the Buddha eye, and the Buddha eye alone. And, although the Buddha eye includes the abilities of the other eyes, the other names (such as "physical eye" and so forth) are not needed, because they are all subsumed under the Buddha eye. This is also true of the "Middle"; it includes and subsumes one-sided emptiness and conventionality.

Does the Tathāgata have the five

five eyes or not?' He answered, 'He does. The Tathāgata possesses them all.'" How can it be compared to the eyes of ordinary people and those of the two vehicles? The *Sūtra on Petitioning Avalokiteśvara* says, "Endowed with the five eyes and having perfected *bodhi*-wisdom." Thus the threefold contemplation in a single thought is expressed [in the *Aṅgulimāla Sūtra*] as "cultivation that is not lacking." The one [Buddha] eye includes the five powers [of all five eyesights]; this is expressed as "clearly seeing the gate to be entered." Again, this is perfect enlightenment [or, the realization of the Perfect Teaching 圓證]. Through the eye one has mastery over both internal [thoughts] and external [objects]. "The eye enters right concentration (samādhi)," and the nose arouses samādhi; or one enters [right concentration through] the nose and arouses [samādhi through] the eye. Although you move you are

eyes or not?' He answered, 'He does. The Tathāgata possesses them all 如來有五眼不。答云有皆稱如來有: see the *The Diamond Sūtra* at T 8.751b14–28, where Subhūti questions the World Honored One about each of the five eyes. (see also Conze, *Buddhist Wisdom Books*, pp. 59–60):

> Subhūti,... the thoughts of the past are unobtainable. The thoughts of the present are unobtainable. The thoughts of the future are unobtainable.

Endowed with the five eyes and having perfected *bodhi*-wisdom 五眼具足成菩提: a phrase from verses in the *Sūtra on Petitioning Avalokiteśvara*, T 20.37b28. The context reads:

> I, from the past and as innumerable Buddhas,
> Have heard the spell *(dhāraṇi)* for eliminating poison and restraining harm,
> Have extinguished and removed the three obstacles and have no evil,
> *Am endowed with the five eyes and have perfected bodhi-wisdom.*

Clearly seeing the gate to be entered 明見來入門: see the verses in the *Aṅgulimāla Sūtra*, T 2.532a7–8, quoted above. These verses are quoted more accurately here, using the compound 明見 instead of 明識 or 眼識.

Mastery over both internal and external 內外自在: for a longer explication of this idea, see the section on the "adornment of perfect mastery," and on "entering and leaving concentration" in various sense realms, above in the *Mo-ho chih-kuan*, 2a23–b7.

The eye enters right concentration and the nose arouses samādhi; or one enters through the nose and arouses through the eye 眼入正受鼻三昧起。鼻入眼起: these phrases are found in the *Avataṃsaka Sūtra*, T 9.438c2ff., within a long passage of verses on "entering right concentration within the various sense realms. This passage was quoted above in the *Mo-ho chih-kuan*, 2a24–b3, to illustrate mastery in concentration within all sense realms. Cleary (*Flower Ornament*, 356–59) translates the context:

> Entering right concentration in the eye-organ,
> Emerging from concentration in the field of form,
> Showing the inconceivability of the nature of form,
> Unknowable to all gods and men;
> Entering right concentration in the field of form
> And emerging from concentration in the eye, without disturbing the mind,
> Explaining the eye is birthless and has no origin,

quiescent; although quiescent, this does not hinder movement. Although quiescent, you move; although you move, this does not hinder quiescence. This is called "clearly seeing the gate to be entered."

Question: The Buddha is endowed with the five eyesights, and should clearly see the five sense realms. But a sūtra says, "I, by means of the five eyesights, do not see the three groups of sentient beings. The deluded have no eyesight, and yet they say that they see." Again, it is said [in the *Vimalakīrti Sūtra*] that "seeing visible forms is the same as being blind." If this [perception] is already the same as being blind, then how are you able to see the coarse and minute [objects of] visible form?

Answer: The five sense objects are all obscure [manifestations] of the true aspect [of reality]. The true aspect [of reality] cannot be seen. Because they cannot be seen [in this sense], this is compared to being blind. Although it cannot be seen [in this sense], there is no decrease or reduction in being able to see [in other ways]; with the five eyesights you have penetrating and thorough [insight] and [can see] the sense objects clearly. Although it is said that the five [eyesights] illumine [and perceive the five sense objects], just because they are illumined does not necessarily mean that they exist [substantially]. Although it is said that this is like being blind, this "blindness" doesn't necessarily mean that there is nothing [to be perceived]. The *Vimalakīrti Sūtra* says, "You have come without the mark of coming, and see

> By nature empty, null, and doing nothing....
> Entering right concentration in the nose faculty
> And emerging from concentration in the field of scent ...
> Emerging from concentration in space, mind undisturbed;
> This is called the inconceivable freedom of concentration.

I, by means of the five eyesights, do not see the three groups of sentient beings. The deluded have no eyesight, and yet they say that they see 我以五眼不見三聚衆生。狂愚無目而言見耶: The source of this quote is unknown.

Seeing visible forms is the same as being blind 見色與盲等: a phrase from the *Vimalakīrti Sūtra*, T 14.540b3. Note that in the sūtra the context concerns Vimalakīrti's instructions on how a bodhisattva should act and see, not about the lack of sight of deluded beings. Boin (*Vimalakīrti Sūtra*, 52) translates the context:

> It is in not taking anything that the food should be taken: 1. *to see forms (rūpa) as those blind from birth (jātyandha) see them*; 2. to hear sounds *(śabda)* as one hears an echo *(pratiśrutkā)*;...

You have come without the mark of coming, and see without the mark of seeing 不來相而來不見相而見: a phrase from the *Vimalakīrti Sūtra*, T 14.544b13–14, where Mañjuśrī comes to visit Vimalakīrti to inquire about his illness. Boin (*Vimalakīrti*, 116) translates the context:

> Then the Licchavi Vimalakīrti perceived Mañjuśrī the crown prince and, having perceived him, said to him: Mañjuśrī, you are welcome *(sugata)*, Mañjuśrī, you are most welcome. *You had not come and you come; you had not seen and you see*; you had not heard and you hear.

without the mark of seeing." This is the meaning here. This is [contemplating] the inconceivable realm.

[2] [If you consider that] my eyes and the eyes of sentient beings are neither dual nor distinct, [and wonder] why sentient beings are not awakened and do not know [the truth], then you will arouse compassion and vow to save and liberate them. [3] Wishing to complete this vow, you will rest **[101b]** your thoughts in concentration and wisdom. [4] By means of cessation-and-contemplation you will be able to universally deconstruct all [negative] dharmas. [5] With the eye [sight faculty] and [sense objects of] visible form, you will clearly know what penetrates and what obstructs [the path], so that this will not be like the way of the inchworm [which makes ineffectual progress]. [6] With the skandhas of the eye you cultivate [the steps on the path such as] the four mindfulnesses as neither pure nor impure, knowing both aspects of decaying and flourishing, and thus entering nirvana. [7] Learn the methods for controlling and healing as aids to open the three liberations. [8] Clearly be aware of [the levels of your attainment such as] the Six Identities without going to excess. [Know that] although your eye and that which is contemplated are endowed [potentially] with [the powers of] the five eyesights, you are merely [at the level of] verbal [identity] or [identity in] contemplative practice. If, gradually, you can see from outside these obstacles, later you will be able to perceive [universally, all the Buddhas] in the ten directions, as [it is expounded] in *The Contemplation of Samantabhadra*;

> Mañjuśrī replied: It is indeed so, O householder, it is indeed as you say. He who has already come comes no more; he who has already left leaves no more. Any why? Because he who has come no longer comes, he who has left no longer leaves, he who has seen no longer sees, and he who has heard no longer hears.

The inconceivable realm 不思議境 this is the first of the ten modes of contemplation. Chih-i goes through the rest of the ten in the next paragraph.

Inchworm 蝨: Ikeda (*Gendaigoyaku*, 506) interprets this using the image from the *Mahāparinirvāṇa Sūtra* of insects gnawing on wood (and sometimes accidentally and unconsciously carving meaningful characters). Thus he translates, "you will not be like insects who do not know the meaning of words." This is the interpretation given in the *Kōgi* (BT–IV, 600) and so it is a more traditional interpretation, but I believe my translation and interpretation is also possible.

Going to excess 叨濫: see the last line in the section on "Knowing the Graded Levels," *Mo-ho chih-kuan*, 99c29.

The Contemplation of Samantabhadra: see at T 9.390c1–6. *The Threefold Lotus Sutra* (352) translates this passage:

> Then the follower, hearing Universal Virtue preach the profound Law, will comprehend its meaning and keep it in his memory without forgetting it. As he does like this day by day, his mind will gradually acquire spiritual profit. The Bodhisattva Universal Virtue will cause the follower to remember the buddhas in all directions. According to the teaching of Universal Virtue, the follower will rightly

or, like [the bodhisattva] Never Disrespectful, will suddenly perceive the great chiliocosm. Both perceptions, gradual and sudden, involve the mutual functioning of the six sense faculties. [9] [However,] since you have not yet ascended all these stages [of attainment], you should not be arrogant but should practice diligently with shame and remorse. If you build up virtuous qualities and establish the terms [of the teachings], you should patiently recognize the internal and external obstacles [to the path], and be calm [and steady] as Mount Sumeru. [10] Do not arouse passionate attachments to dharmas, and [your practice will] not be entangled [with defilements]. In this way, "quick as the wind," realize a true and real eyesight, "ride on the one great cart" and "go directly to the seat of enlightenment."

If, through the eye, you are able to attain realization [of the path], then you can perform many deeds of a Buddha widely through the eye [or the sense of sight], [such as] constantly emitting golden rays of light to splendidly illuminate all things. The *Vimalakīrti Sūtra* says, "Or, there are Buddha lands where deeds of a Buddha are done with rays of light." The single sense experience of [the merging of] the eye and [the skandha of] visible form is

> think and remember everything, and with his spiritual eyes he will gradually see the eastward buddhas, whose bodies are gold colored and very wonderful in their majesty. Having seen one buddha, he will again see another buddha. In this manner, he will gradually see all the buddhas everywhere in the eastern quarter, and because of his profitable reflection, *he will universally see all the buddhas in all directions.*

The bodhisattva Never Disrespectful: see the story in chapter 20 of the *Lotus Sūtra*, especially T 9.51a3–7. Hurvitz (281 [258–59]) translates:

> This bhikṣu, when faced with the end of his life, in open space heard distinctly twenty thousand myriads of gāthās of the Scripture of the Dharma Blossom previously preached by the Buddha King of Imposing Sound, which he was able fully to accept and hold, and straightway he attained the above-mentioned purity of ocular faculty and purity of aural, nasal, lingual, bodily, and mental faculties. Having attained this purity of the six faculties, he increased his lifespan yet further by two hundred myriads of millions of nayutas of years, broadly preaching to others this Scripture of the Dharma Blossom.

Shame and remorse 慚愧: the Taishō text has 漸愧 ("gradually feel shame"), but I follow the emendation in the *Bukkyō Taikei* text (BT-IV, 601) and Ikeda (*Teihon-kundoku*, 546).

Quick, realize, ride, go directly to the seat of enlightenment: phrases from the *Lotus Sūtra*, T 9.12c18, 23 and 15a13–14. See the long discussion of this passage above at *Mo-ho chih-kuan* 100a3–b16.

There are Buddha lands where deeds of a Buddha are done with rays of light 有佛土以光明爲佛事: see the *Vimalakīrti Sūtra* at T 14.553c17. Boin (*Vimalakīrti Sūtra*, 223–25) translates:

> *There are Buddhakṣetras which actuate Buddha deeds (buddha-kārya)*: 1. through Bodhisattvas, 2. *through lights (prabhā)*, 3. through the tree of enlightenment *(bodhivṛkṣa)*, 4. through the vision of beauty *(rūpa)* and physical marks *(lakṣaṇānuvyañjana)* of the Tathāgata,...

like this; it is also the same for the other two sense experiences, as well as the other five sense organs, five sense objects, and fifteen sense experiences. A detailed explanation would go as explained above [for the one sense of sight]. Follow the previous explication and apply it to realize enlightenment through the six sense faculties. However, destroy the passionate afflictions and make them go away, and do not [necessarily] adhere to the usual "classifications." If it is through the ear that you attain the great cart, then you can perform many Buddha deeds through the use of sound; if it is through the nose, [Buddha deeds can be performed through] the use of odors; if through the tongue, the use of tastes, if through the body, the use of a celestial garment; if through consciousness, the use of quiescence. Buddha deeds done with one sense faculty mutually penetrate all the sense faculties. Use [skillful] means to benefit beings; at times [the applications] will be different, but [in all cases the purpose is to] lead sentient beings to attain ultimate bliss.

[Summary] If you are able to diligently practice as outlined above, you will certainly not pass your single life in vain. On the other hand, if you hear [these teachings] but do not put them to use, you are like a black snake clutching a [precious] jewel. What benefit is this [jewel] to a snake? Now I will give three analogies to illustrate the [possible] benefits and losses [of this practice]. [1] Suppose there is a brave husband who is trained in the use

Two sense experiences 二受: that is, of the sense entrances *(āyatana)* and the sense realms *(dhātu)*.

If through the body, the use of a celestial garment 身中用天衣: why "the body" instead of "touch." Perhaps because a "celestial garment" is so soft and comfortable for the body?

Black snake clutching a jewel: perhaps equivalent to "casting pearls before swine" (see Matthew 7:6)? The image of a black snake clutching a pearl is from the *Ta chih tu lun*, T 25.119b15–16. Lamotte (*Le Traité* 1, 492–93) translates:

> La cause en est à la rétribution des actes *(karmavipāka)* qui varie pour chaque cas. Certains hommes remplissent les causes et les conditions voulues pour voir un Buddha, mais ne remplissent pas les causes et les conditions voulues pour manger et pour boire. D'autres remplissent les causes et les conditions voulues pour manger et pour boire, mais ne remplissent pas les causes et les conditions voulues pour voir un Buddha. *C'est comme le serpent noir (kālasarpa) qui se couche en étreignant son Bijou du sommet de la tête (cūḍāmaṇi).* Il y a des Arhat qui mendient leur nourriture et n'obtiennent rien.

Chodron (1, 3919–2) translates:

> The cause of it is retribution of actions which varies for each case. Some people fufill the causes and conditions required to see a Buddha but do not fulfill the causes and conditions required to eat and drink. Others fulfill the causes and conditions required to eat and drink but do not fulfil the causes and conditions required to see a Buddha. It is like the black snake that sleeps while clasping the jewel at the top of its head. There are arhats who beg for their food and get nothing.

of a sword and an arrow, slays one or two bandits, and receives as a reward a piece of gold or a piece of silver, and uses this compensation to support his wife and child. Such a person merely uses his skill with a weapon to go forth and risk his life to earn cash. What need is there for him to be broadly learned in the military arts? [2] If there is a man who wishes to become yeast, a boat and oar, seasoning, and bountiful rain for the sake of his country, he should be well-versed in the literary and military arts, and make plans behind curtains to defeat enemies in all directions. That which he learns is profound, that which he destroys is also great, the rewards he obtains are weighty, and his compensation can support very many [people]. [3] [Finally there are those who,] although they have knowledge do not use it, or use it but are frequently defeated. Such [people] are not able to save their own bodies, much less assist other people.

Those who learn the contemplation of dhyāna-meditation are also like this [that is, they can be of three types]. [1] Those who know only one method, [such as] either cessation or contemplation, can arrange to destroy a little evil, quiet [**100c**] the mind and practice the path, and attain a little meditative concentration, and gather together a few followers. One who is satisfied with this [or, "thinks that this is sufficient"] is like [the first example of] the man who fights [alone in a limited way]. [2] Those who wish to become a great meditation master, destroy a great amount of passionate afflictions, make manifest immeasurable good dharmas, and benefit immeasurable conditions[, that is, sentient beings], should learn the ten modes of cessation-and-contemplation. With penetrating insight into the inclinations of the mind *(ābhiprāyika)*, [such a person will] be able to apply this to their practice and appropriately respond to the six conditions and the six types of sense experience. As soon as a passionate affliction arises, this is immediately contemplated [for what it is], and this contemplation subdues the delusion;

Boat and oar 舟楫: or, "the rudder of a boat." As Mathews (181) points out, this refers to "one who comes to assist in a crisis of State."

... Bountiful rain 霖雨: lit., "a long raining spell." Ikeda (*Kenkyūchūshaku*, 419) points out that these four (yeast, boat, seasoning, rain) are a classic group of terms from the 書經 indicating people who make notable contributions to governing the country.

Six conditions 六緣 **and the six types of sense experiences** 六受: if we follow the definitions given at the beginning of this section, the "six conditions" would refer to the "six actions," and the "six sense experiences" would refer in general to the totality of experiences that involve the six senses. See Nakamura, 1454b. Ikeda (*Gendaigoyaku*, 506), following the "quote" from the *Ta chih tu lun* at the beginning of this section (101b17–18) translates, "the six sense objects and the six consciousnesses," which captures the same idea.

thus one can bravely persevere over difficult matters, and "release the knot and attain the jewel" [of enlightenment]. [3] If you "release" 解 [and understand] yet do not use this [understanding], or use it unsuitably and instead take deluded thoughts as your teacher, how can you triumph on the path?

Again, [1] it is like a rustic shaman who only understands 解 one technique. He may be able to save some person and gain a side of meat [in compensation], so why should he study Shen Nung's [*Catalogue* of] basic herbs [and prescriptions]? [2] If you wish to be a great physician, you should widely examine various remedies, broadly heal all diseases, "turning the pulse and turning the spirit," frequently using [your knowledge and skill] and frequently making examinations, so the favor of your saving [activities] is widespread. Those who learn [only] dhyāna meditation are also like this. They focus exclusively on one method to subdue delusions and make them go away, so there is only a temporary and miniscule benefit; this ultimately is not the all-encompassing intent of the great path. Again, they are not able to destroy the passionate afflictions and realize the patient forbearance [of the idea that dharmas are] non-arising. Even though the medicine is good, if it is not applied as prescribed, how can the disease be cured? The performance [lit., "reading and reciting" 讀誦] of cessation-and-contemplation is very

Release the knot and attain the jewel 解髻得珠: this image is from a parable in the fourteenth chapter of the *Lotus Sūtra* (T 9.39a–b) about the king with a priceless pearl tied in his top-knot. Hurvitz (220 [202]) translates the context:

If there is a brave and stout fellow
Able to do difficult things,
The king *separates from his top-knot*
A bright pearl, which he gives to him.

Rustic shaman 野巫: Chan-jan (BT–IV, 605) explains that this term refers to a male shaman, and that the term 覡 is used for a woman (though the terms are reversed in the version of the Taishō text [388c18–19]). A shaman 巫 is defined as one who uses spells, or words of praise spoken by a priest or leader of a festival 祝者祭主申讃辭者. Ikeda (*Gendaigoyaku*, 506), following the explanation in Nakamura (1374d), translates as "a town magician or sorcerer." Nakamura adds that this term in the *Mo-ho chih-kuan*, pronounced *yabu* in Japanese, is the origin of the common put-down *yabu-isha*, or "quack" ("incompetent doctor").

A side of meat 脯胖: for the second character the Taishō has 柈, but I follow Ikeda's suggestion that this be substituted with 胖. Ikeda also suggests that this refers to the "half-side" of meat left from an animal's sacrifice, presumably used as payment for the shaman.

Shen Nung 神農: the legendary founder of medical arts in China and the compiler of the *Catalogue of Herbs* 本草綱目 that set the standard for herbal prescriptions. See note above at *Mo-ho chih-kuan* 78a15 and references to this figure at 78b17–21.

Turning the pulse and turning the spirit 轉脈轉精: traditional terms in Chinese medicine for effecting a healing change.

beneficial, but if your thoughts are not applied to your practice, [the realization of a patient forbearance of] non-arising will not be manifested.

Again, it is like [specialized scholars] who study the meaning [of texts], merely wishing [to pursue] one question and one answer [at a time] and momentarily show off [their knowledge]; why should they broadly seek [and study] the sūtras and treatises? [On the other hand,] if you wish to become a lord of the Dharma *(dharmasvāmin)*, you should be well versed in [many] different texts. However, even if you are acquainted with and understand many passages, but do not go out in public, you will be timid and weak and not be worthy of any reward. If you are not afraid you can give a hundred responses in accordance with the situation, not being limited to a set answer, and answer all sorts of questions. This is what it means to be a great Dharma master. It is the same for those who practice contemplation. If your practice of contemplation is clear, you are able to respond to objects as conditions arise and to function in response to objects as you come in contact with them. If you are not able to do this, how will you destroy the demonic hordes? How will you remove the heavy diseases of passionate afflictions? How will you manifest the profound meaning of Dharma-nature? If you cannot accomplish these three matters, you will be vexed by trifling matters. This is [the fate of] an ordinary ignorant being in samsara, and it does not involve carrying out of the means of the path of learning.

[end of fascicle seven]

Do not go out in public 不曾出衆: to share your knowledge through giving lectures, participating in debates, and so forth.

Not worthy of any reward 不任酬往: Ikeda (*Gendaigoyaku*, 548) translates, "you will not be able to answer questions."

All sorts of questions 縱横之問: lit., "both vertical and horizontal questions."

The means of the path of learning 學道方便: or, "not learning the path and carrying out the means (to help others)"?

2. CONTEMPLATING THE OBJECTS OF PASSIONATE AFFLICTIONS [102a1–106a19]

The second [of the ten objects of contemplation] is contemplating the objects of passionate afflictions. If you are not awakened through [contemplating the objects of the sense fields, that is,] the aggregates, sense entrances, and sense realms [as explained] above, then this [method of contemplation] is not suitable for you. If you do not put an end to this contemplation [of the objects of the sense fields], you may be pummeled by passionate afflictions and arouse greed and anger. Then you should abandon [contemplating the objects of the sense fields, such as that of] the aggregates and sense entrances, and you should [instead] contemplate the passionate afflictions.

Previously [I taught about] "renouncing the five [sensual] desires" in order to know about [sensual] faults and offences and "rejecting the [five] impediments" in order to abandon regular everyday [attachment to objects of the] sense fields, and to seek understanding by contemplating the recompense [that come from such desires and impediments]. Now you should contemplate [passionate afflictions such as] intense greed and anger as they arise in full force. You should be like steel, which merely remains black unless it is combined with fire, yet burns bright red when forged in the fire.

Again, the phenomena of karmic recompense are constant, and there is no time when they are not present, so it is easy to renounce and reject them, but if passionate afflictions arise abruptly, they are difficult to control. Why? Even if you are innately angry, you can put an end to it through disciplined enlightenment. [However,] that [actual anger] which arises now in the immediate moment is boisterous and should be feared. Innately, perverted conceptions arise abruptly and perish abruptly. [However,] those [perverted thoughts] that arise now in the immediate moment harass you and do not pass away [quickly, but seem to hang on forever]. Innate sensual desires can be controlled and stopped, but those that arise now in the immediate moment do not allow you to be choosy even about a dead horse, let alone the type [of horse]. When such deluded temptations arise in force and burn within you, seeing such external objects [such as the female form] causes the

Contemplating the objects of passionate afflictions 觀煩惱境: the second of the ten modes or objects of contemplation, following the long section on "Contemplating the Sense Fields" (51c20–101c23) which has taken up more than a third of the total contents of the *Mo-ho chih-kuan*.

Faults and offences 過罪 Or, "the fault of [sensual] excess." On "renouncing the five desires" 呵五欲 see the section above at 43c10–44c5.

Rejecting the impediments 棄蓋: see the section above at 44c6–47a24.

Dead horse 死馬: This phrase refers to a story concerning the power of sensual lust at the beginning of the *Vinaya in Ten*

mind to be obsessed and the eyes to darken. This is analogous to not knowing how quick is the flow of a river, and you measure it by throwing in a piece of wood and seeing how the ripples and spray splash up. Or, it is like touching a healthy person without knowing how strong he is, and he responds with anger. Passionate afflictions that are dormant are seemingly present yet seemingly not present. When you perform repentance at the meditation chamber and contemplate the sense realms, this can be like touching a sleeping lion, who awakes with an earth-shaking roar. Those who do not know this can be led into performing grave offences, so that they not only fail in [fulfilling their] cessation-and-contemplation, but also increase in their evil karmic deeds, fall into a dark pit, and are unable to extract themselves. For this reason it is necessary to contemplate passionate afflictions as the objects [of contemplation].

[The explanation of] this contemplation consists of four parts: 1. a brief clarification of the marks [of passionate afflictions]; 2. clarification of their causes and conditions; 3. clarification of different [methods for] healing [passionate afflictions]; and 4. cultivating contemplation [with regard to passionate afflictions].

1. Clarifying the Marks of Passionate Afflictions [102a24–c5]

First is to clarify the marks [of passionate afflictions (*kleśa*)].

First I will interpret the term. "Passionate afflictions" are phenomena that are dark and troublesome 昏煩, and which cause vexing disturbances 惱亂 to the heart and spirit 心神. Also, they cause the mind to be troubled 煩, and lead the heart to be vexed 惱. In short, they are the [ten] sharp and dull [afflictions] of [mistaken] views and attitudes. This is just one way to count

Recitations, T 23.2c29–3a: The Buddha tells the story of a mendicant who goes into town for his morning begging rounds. After eating his meal he enters the forest and spreads out his mat (*nisidana*) under a tree to sit in meditation. A female demon appears and, aiming to seduce the monk out of his samādhi, changes her form into a human body and stands in front of him. Since his dhyānic concentration is insufficiently firm, the monk arises out of his samādhi and arouses lust for this female body. When the female form gradually begins to walk away, the monk "arises" further by standing and following after her. Within the forest there happens to be the body of a dead horse, and when the demon in female form arrives at the place where the dead horse lies, she disappears. The monk, however, overcome by lust and his body burning with desire, performs sex with the body of the dead horse.

The phrase "dead horse" is found at 3a8.

Interpret the term 先釋名: Here Chih-i parses the meaning of passionate afflictions 煩惱 (*kleśa*) in terms of the two Chinese characters that translate the term into a Chinese compound: 煩 "trouble, confusion, annoyance, anxiety" and 惱 "vexation, irritation."

them, for the five dull [afflictions] are not limited just to greed and anger [but also incorporate the "sharp" afflictions]. This is like the wriggling of insects, which is not a rational matter; crabs raise their nippers, horses shake their manes 張鬐 [or, "fish spread their fins"], and [some animals open wide their] angry eyes, in order to make themselves look large. Why are base and mediocre people attached to views? Because whether they walk, stand, sit, or lie down, they always arouse self-centered thoughts 我心. Therefore you should know that the "sharp" [afflictions] are not absent from the five "dull" [afflictions]. [**102b**] And how can it be said that the five "sharp" afflictions are limited to the delusions of [mistaken] views, since it cannot be that they do not include anger and desires [which are "dull" afflictions]. You should know that the terms "dull" and "sharp" are shared by [the afflictions of] both [mistaken] views and attitudes.

Now I will classify these [passionate afflictions] according to levels [of attainment] so that there is no confusion. For those who have not yet begun to practice meditation, even if they have worldly wisdom and are eloquent in thinking rationally, they are weak with regard to their views and attitudes, and their ten afflictions are all "dull." If they arouse [mistaken] views through [meditative] concentration, so that their thoughts of [mistaken] views are prominent, then their ten afflictions, because of their strength, should be considered as "sharp." It is like two scholars, one of whom grasps the meaning of the Dharma teachings and becomes [argumentative and] "strong" in disputation. The other [merely] hears the words [of the Dharma teachings] and is "weak" in disputation [and that is his virtue]. The one who [merely] hears the words is like one who has not yet practiced dhyāna meditation, and the one who has grasped the meaning is like one who has aroused [dhyāna] concentration but has also given rise to passionate afflictions. This is exactly what is to be contemplated here.

If there are dull [afflictions] within the sharp, [while at the level of] "insight into the [Four] Truths" you should attempt to sever the sharp [afflictions], and leave the dull [afflictions] as they are. The Abhidharmists say that the dull [afflictions] above the sharp [afflictions] are called "background

Sharp and dull afflictions 見思利鈍: These are the "five dull afflictions" of the obvious passions—covetousness or passions, anger, ignorance, pride or arrogance, and doubt—and the "five sharp afflictions" of every-day unconscious mistaken views and passionate afflictions: 1. the mistaken view that the body is substantial, 2. extreme views, 3. deviant views, 4. attachment to mistaken views, and 5. excessive attachment to the precepts. See above at *Mo-ho chih-kuan* 49c.

Insight into the [Four] Truths 見諦: the level of attainment at which one perceives and has insight into the Four Noble Truths.

Abhidharmists 毘曇人: the source of this position is unknown.

afflictions" 背上使, and when the severance [of afflictions] occurs through "insight into the [Four] Truths," truly the sharp [afflictions] are already gone, and thus the background afflictions are also gone. The [afflictions] of [mistaken] views and attitudes are also likewise.

If we expand on these sharp and dull [afflictions], there are 84,000 of them. Now I will merely summarize them in four parts. The individual arising of the three poisons [of greed, anger, and delusion] has three parts, and these arising together is the [fourth] "plural" part. The three poisons arising individually are the "[negative] notions and perceptions" *(vitarka-vicāra)*, but they are not numerous; the three poisons arising together should be called the [negative] notions and perceptions that are numerous. Whether few or many, they involve distraction and restlessness, and are a hindrance to concentration. Neutral [actions] are a distraction in [the realm of future] recompense, so they are not a hindrance to concentration [samādhi]. A sūtra says, "When emerging from the samādhi of extinction, you enter into a distracted mind, and while in a distracted mind you return and enter into various samādhi." Thus [in this sense] distractions are not a hindrance to concentration [samādhi]; this is the meaning here. Followers of the *Ch'eng shih lun (Satyasiddhi)* say that "distraction is concurrent with non-cognizance, so ignorance hinders concentration [samādhi]." If this is so, since distraction is concurrent with [the two poisons of] anger and [greedy] desires, then how can they not hinder concentration? But the interpretation I am now giving has a separate meaning, as I have explained above in the section on "rejecting the impediments."

However, the features [and influence] of passionate afflictions are extensive and cannot be exhausted. If you fully make distinctions [concerning them], this will obstruct the practice of contemplation. The *Lotus Sūtra* says,

When emerging from the samādhi of extinction, you enter into a distracted mind, and while in a distracted mind you return and enter into various samādhi 從滅定出入散心中。散心中還入諸定: see the *Pañcaviṃśati Sūtra*, T 8.368b17ff., which gives a long list of emerging from this or that samādhi into a [regular] distracted mind, and then returning and entering into various samādhis.

Distraction is concurrent with noncongnizance, so ignorance hinders concentration 散兼無知癡能障定: the source for this interpretation is unknown, except for the attribution to those associated with the study of the *Ch'eng shih lun*.

Explained above: see the section on "Rejecting the Five Impediments in Practice" (45a28ff.), especially the section on "Do the five impediments all obstruct samādhi, or not?" (45c12–25), where it is emphasized that the strength of impediments is different for each person.

Cannot be exhausted 不可盡: this could mean that the afflictions themselves are too many to be [easily] extinguished, or, as Ikeda (*Gendaigoyaku*, 512) translates, "they cannot be exhaustively explained."

"For twenty years, he constantly removed dung." "Dung" refers to the defiled dharmas of passionate afflictions. If you can abandon and exhaust them, this will be of value for a day, but if you dwell on making distinctions of many or few [concerning the afflictions], finally [in the long term] you have not attained anything of value. Now you should contemplate the dung of passionate afflictions, seeking the coinage of wisdom, and not wish to make [numerous] discriminations concerning the [innumerable and inexhaustible] marks of [mistaken] views and attitudes.

[Question:] Why, then, did the five hundred arhats make such [numerous] distinctions?

[Answer:] In order to maintain the Buddha Dharma teachings, provide leadership to the masses, and get through many hardships, it was necessary to make such comprehensive distinctions [at that time]. But now if you are to correctly 正 enter the Path, there is no time to leisurely struggle [with such details]. Again, such [details] are not an urgent matter when it comes to contemplation [of emptiness]. It is enough to know in general the four categories of [passionate afflictions as] defiled dung, and strive to abandon them. When you [re-]enter conventional reality from emptiness, then you should be concerned with all of these distinctions.

Again, the sharp and dull [afflictions] merged together into individual bundles comprise four categories, and in the same way [the afflictions] within this [worldly] realm [of delusions] are severed along with those of the two vehicles; this is the passionate afflictions of the Shared [Teachings]. The four categories [of afflictions] of the realm beyond [delusions] **[102c]** that are not severed by those of the two vehicles is called the passionate afflictions of the Distinct [Teachings]. If you consider their mutual relationship, it is not the case that [the afflictions of] the Distinct [Teachings] exist apart from those of the Shared [Teachings]. The delusions [and afflictions] of the Shared [Teachings] are like the branches, and the delusions of the Distinct

For twenty years, he constantly removed dung 二十年中常令除糞: a phrase from the parable of the poor son in the *Lotus Sūtra*, T 9.17a27, where the poor son works for his father by sweeping away dung, as part of the process whereby the father uses various means to help his son mature and realize his true nature. Hurvitz (*Lotus*, 87–88) translates: "The poor son first took his pay, then swept the dung with them.... for twenty years he was kept constantly at work clearing away dung."

Five hundred arhats 五百阿羅漢: the disciples of the Buddha who gathered at the "first council" after the Buddha's death to, among other things, determine the content of the Buddha's teachings.

The *Kōgi* (BT–V, 16), identifies these as "the noble ones who compiled the Abhidharma four hundred years after the death of the Buddha." In any case, for Chih-i, therefore, these represent the Hīnayāna approach of the Tripitaka Teachings of "analyzing dharmas."

[Teachings] are like the trunk [or roots]. When you attain the wisdom of the truth [of emptiness, and advance from the Shared to the Distinct Teachings], you sever the branches; when you attain the wisdom of the Middle [and advance from the Distinct to the Perfect Teaching], you sever the trunk. From the perspective of the "inconceivable" [that is, the Perfect Teaching], overcoming the passionate afflictions within the realm [of this mundane world] requires *bodhi*-wisdom; how can you say that this is not the case also for the delusions of the Distinct [Teachings], as I have already explained previously?

2. Clarifying the Causes and Conditions for the Arising of Passionate Afflictions [102c5–c28]

Second is clarifying the causes and conditions for the arising of passionate afflictions. The causes and conditions are three [types: latent, karmic, and demonic], as explained below. The marks of their arising are fourfold: 1. deep yet not sharp; 2. sharp yet not deep; 3. both deep and sharp; and 4. neither deep nor sharp. The fourth phrase [of neither deep nor sharp] corresponds to the marks of delusions of the fruits and recompense of the common pathways 通途 [of everyday life], which are constantly present, and therefore are neither deep nor sharp. The third phrase [of both deep and sharp] refers to [afflictions] that arise and move 起動, and are different from those that are constantly present, that is, they correspond to the marks of passionate afflictions that are aroused. When they are aroused they are deep and grave, and cannot be denied. When contact is made with the objects [of the senses], they increase all the more so that you are unable to control them; therefore they are characterized as deep. As they arise more and more, they become deeper with each arising; therefore they are characterized as "sharp." The phrases "deep yet not sharp" and "sharp yet not deep" should be known along these lines.

The "causes and conditions" [for the arising of passionate afflictions] are [of three types]: 1. latent [repetitive] causes as "seeds" 習因種子; 2. the powerful influence of karma 業力擊作; and 3. demonic temptations 魔所扇動.

1. Latent [Repetitive] Causes as "Seeds" [102c13]

"Latent" [causes are as follows]: from immeasurable kalpas in the past, passionate afflictions have been repeatedly stacking up. When these "seeds" mature, their latent tendencies carry on continuously. As when you ride along with a fast current you are not aware of its speed, but know its raging speed if you measure it, so a practitioner who goes along with the flow of passionate afflictions and rides on the sea of samsara is not fully aware of these [afflictions]. If he cultivates the steps on the path, and resists the flow of existence, passionate afflictions will arise with a vengeance. All you can do is to redouble your efforts day and night and strive diligently to extract [the afflictions].

2. The Power of Karma [102c17]

[The power of] karma [is as follows]: from immeasurable kalpas in the past you have brought to pass evil deeds and added to the burden of grudging responsibilities, so that [you despair and think], how can you cultivate the path and attain deliverance [from these afflictions]! Thus you arouse even more evil karma and destroy the mind of contemplation, and are not able to establish good dharmas. As you are not aware of the flowing waves when the river is quiet, but a sudden gust of wind can result in waves like a range of mountains, and if you lose control of the rudder and sails, surely you will be destroyed. You must concentrate your mind and properly follow things in order, so that you can avoid a shipwreck.

3. Demonic Temptations [102c22]

Demonic [temptations are as follows]: if there is demonic activity, since such are things done by those of this ilk, you should not be agitated by it. If you practice the path and transcend this world, leave this [shore] behind and advance to that [shore of enlightenment], the ten legions [of demonic forces] will try to capture you, thereupon deep and sharp delusions will engulf you. It is like when the waters of the great sea are not disturbed by wind, but then

Waves like a range of mountains 波如連山: Chan-jan (BT–V, 21) attributes this phrase to the book "Pirates" (*Hai-fu* 海賦) by 木華 and adds: "'Waves like a range of mountains' refers to when the realm of the senses is quiet like a river, but when you cultivate contemplation it is like the wind arising, and the arousing of delusions are like great waves."

Ten legions 十軍: see the verses in *Ta chih tu lun* at T 25.99b24–c10; Lamotte (*Le Traité* 1, 341–43); Chodron (1, 279) translates:

> Desires *(kāma)* are your first army *(senā)*,
> The army of sadness *(arati)* is the second,
> The army of hunger and thirst *(kṣutpipāsā)* is the third,
> The army of greed *(tṛiṣṇā)* is the fourth.
> The fifth is the army of languor and torpor *(styānamiddha)*,
> The army of fear *(bhaya)* is the sixth.
> Doubt *(vicikitsā)* is the seventh army
> The army of anger *(krodha)* and hypocrisy *(mrakṣa)* is the eighth.
> The ninth army is covetousness *(labdhā)*
> And attachment to vain glory *(mithyāyśaś)*,
> The tenth army is self-praise *(ātmotkarṣa)*
> And distrust of others *(parāvajñā)*.

Chih-i has quoted the passage just prior to these verses in his earlier exposition of the four demonic forces; see notes at *Mo-ho chih-kuan* 12a1, and the section on demonic forces below (114c22–117a23).

Makara sucks up the water so that all things are pulled into it, and you cannot resist its power. Singularly chant the Buddha's name until you can escape [lit. "attain liberation"] [from these forces]. If fire is used as an analogy, then the latent [afflictions] are like the firewood, karma is like the wind from a fan, and the demonic forces are like tossing oil [on the fire]. Demonic actions are as explained below. The contemplation of passionate afflictions as latent [causes] is that which is to be contemplated now.

3. The Methods for Controlling the Passionate Afflictions [102c28–103a19]

Third, the methods for controlling [and healing the passionate afflictions] are not the same [for everyone]. [The methods for] controlling by those of the Two Vehicles are five: matching, turning, not turning, combining, and integrating. These five [are ways to] control the four categories of passionate afflictions. The arising of hindrances to the path are as explained below under "the objects of karma." **[103a]**

[First,] control by matching 對治 [afflictions is as follows.] [Each] one of

Like the waters of the great sea: a summary of a passage in *Ta chih tu lun* at T 25.109a13–25, illustrating the benefits to be gained from the samādhi of contemplating the Buddha 念佛三昧 (*buddhānusmṛtisamādhi*). See Lamotte (*Le Traité* 1, 409–15) and Chodron (1, 331–34):

> The *buddhānusmṛtisamādhi* is able to destroy sins quickly, better than all the other samādhis. Here is proof of it: Once there were five hundred merchants who had gone to sea to search for precious stuffs. They encountered *Mo k'ie lo* (Makara), king of the fish *(matsyarāja)*. The water of the sea rushed into its gaping mouth and the ship was about to be engulfed. The captain *(karṇadhāra)* asked the man in the look-out: "What do you see?" He answered: "I see three suns *(āditya)*, ranges of white mountains *(avadātaparvatarāji)* and a waterfall *(jalaprapāta)* at the entrance to a cave." The captain shouted: "It is the Makara, the king of the fish; he is holding his mouth agape; the first sun is the real sun, the other two suns are his eyes *(akṣi)*; the white mountains are his teeth *(danta)*: the waterfall is the sea water that is rushing into his mouth. Let each of you call upon the gods for help." Then each of the men called upon the god whom he worshipped, but with no success. Among them there was an upāsaka who observed the five precepts *(pañcaśikṣāpadaparigṛhīta upāsaka)* who said to the others: "We should all cry out together *Na mo fo (Namo buddhāya)*; the Buddha is unsurpassable *(anuttara)*; he will know how to help us." All the passengers unanimously *(ekacittena)* agreed and with one voice *(samaraveṇa)* they cried: *Namo buddhāya* (Homage to the Buddha). Now in an earlier lifetime *(pūrvajanma)*, this fish had been a bad disciple of the Buddha *(duḥśīlaśrāvaka)*; he still had the memory of his former lifetimes *(pūrvanivāsānusmṛtijñāna)*. Hearing the name of the Buddha pronounced, he felt remorse, closed his mouth and the sailors were saved.

Makara 摩竭[羅]: mythical sea monster, in the form of a great fish, whale, or turtle.

As explained below 魔業如下說: see the section on demonic forces at 114c22–117a23.

The objects of karma 如下業境: see the section below at 111c22–114c23.

the [four] categories of passionate afflictions has three types, giving a total of twelve [as explained above]. As a match to these, there are twelve [methods, that is, there is a matching method for controlling each of the types of afflictions]. This is like planning your strategic battle array in response to your enemy. This is called "control by matching."

[Second,] control by turning [is as follows]. For example, [the contemplation of] impurity is used [to control] covetous desires, but sometimes this matching [method of] controlling is not appropriate. Then the [opposite] contemplation of purity allows you to attain liberation [from the afflictions] by turning to the cultivation of a mind of compassion, by being mindful of pure dharmas and peaceful repose, without including defiled humiliations. This is called "control by turning."

If an angry person is taught [the contemplation of] impurity, an ignorant person is taught to consider what is limited and what is unlimited, those who are restless and distracted are taught to use wisdom to make distinctions, this involves not "turning" the disease but "turning" [i.e., changing the method of] control. These are all called "control by turning."

[Third,] controlling by not turning [is as follows.] Even though the disease is "turned," the [method for] controlling is never changed. Cultivate a method and only this [method for] controlling. This involves turning the disease without turning the method of control. Therefore it is called "control without turning."

[Fourth,] control by combining [is as follows.] Diseases [arise] in combination, so medicine is also combined. For example, covetous desires combined with anger require a combination of [the contemplation of] impurity and a compassionate mind. If one or two diseases are combined, one or two medicines should be combined. This is called "control by combining."

[Fifth,] controlling by integrating [is as follows]. Integrate all of the above methods to control [and heal] one disease [of the passionate afflictions].

Those of the Hīnayāna first use these five [methods of] controlling, and later use the wisdom of the [Four Noble] truths 諦智 to attain realization of the true [that is, emptiness].

As for clarifying [the meaning of] controlling [passionate afflictions] for those of the Mahāyāna, it is neither matching, nor combining, and so forth, but is a "control of supreme meaning." It is like the *agada* panacea that

Turning the disease without turning the method of healing 是病不轉而治轉: The *Kōgi* (BT–V, 25) suggests reversing the characters 治 and 病, and my translation follows this reading. Following the order in the *Mo-ho chih-kuan* text would give "turning the method of healing without turning/converting the disease."

is able to heal all diseases. Those of the Hīnayāna use to a great extent the [first] three [of the four] *siddhāntas* [of worldly, individual, and therapeutic], and those of the Mahāyāna for the most part use the [fourth] *siddhānta* of supreme meaning for controlling [and healing passionate afflictions]. From the perspective of emptiness and non-arising, who experiences passionate afflictions, and who is it that controls [and heals] them? [There is no substantial self that does these things.] Again, there are no [substantial] passionate afflictions, so what "thing" is there to turn? Since there is nothing to turn, there is nothing to combine or integrate. There is just "non-arising," in which all is controlled [and healed]. This is an extremely abbreviated [explanation], but you would do well to extact the meaning [from it].

4. Cultivating Contemplation [103a19–106a19]

Fourth is cultivating cessation-and-contemplation [with regard to passionate afflictions], which consists again of ten meanings [of the ten modes of contemplation].

1. Objects as Conceivable and Inconceivable [103a20]

First is to discuss "objects as conceivable" 思議境. A single thought of a desirous notion, when it first arises, is exceedingly minute, but if it is not immediately stifled, it will gradually grow and expand, so that such desires will entice you to go off the path and eventually [commit] the four grave and five heinous offences. These are called passionate afflictions that lead you to be born in hell. Due to these desires you know no shame, and you are ignorant and abrasive, have no courtesy, and have lost your humanity. This is called the covetous desire that leads you to be born in the realm of the beasts. Again, due to these desires you are stingy and protective, and begrudge [giving to] others [lit. "other households" 他家]. This is called the covetous desire that leads to birth in the realm of the hungry ghosts. Due to these desires you arouse jealousy, and becoming defensive with envy, you constantly wish to triumph over others, using any and all means to defeat them. This is called the covetous desire that leads to birth in the realm of the

***Agada* panacea** 阿竭陀藥: see the *Avataṃsaka Sūtra*, T 9.461c23–25; for details, see the note at *Mo-ho chih-kuan* 9b20.

Four *siddhāntas*: see the Glossary under "Four methods of instruction."

Ten modes of contemplation: most of the discussion centers on the contemplation of objects as conceivable and inconceivable, and the other nine modes themselves are referred to somewhat obliquely.

Ignorant and abrasive 魯扈觝突: a phrase from the *Sūtra of Immeasurable Life*, T 12.277a7–8. It has been used previously in the *Mo-ho chih-kuan*, 40a6.

asura. Again, due to these desires you arouse a deep passion for present pleasures, marry out of concern for custom, place a high premium on economy, carefully follow [the virtues of] humanity and duty, and keep the five [basic] precepts [of a layperson] for the sake of desiring pleasure in the future. This is called the covetous desire **[103b]** that leads to birth in the realm of humans. Again, when desires arise, you may despise human desires as being crude and seek after the desires of heavenly beings, diligently cultivating the ten goodnesses and striving to block [the ten evil deeds] so that they naturally do not arise. This is the contemplation of covetous desires that leads to birth in the six heavenly realms. Again, contemplating desirous thoughts, you can renounce them and be pure, thus being able to arouse meditative [dhyāna] concentration. This is the heavenly realm in the realms of form and no-form. Again, contemplating desires as [a kind of] "collecting" and that this collecting invites suffering, leads you to be weary of these causes of suffering and to cultivate the essentials for escaping them. This is the realm of the śrāvaka. If you contemplate desires in terms of ignorance, and that it is due to ignorance that all [karmic] actions are produced and that this leads to unlimited transmigration, and that if you put a stop to desires then ignorance and [karmic] actions will all come to an end, this is the realm of the pratyekabuddha. If you contemplate desires as being a hindrance and arouse compassion, practice the abandonment [of desires], have a [healthy] fear of transiency, and so forth up to realizing that desires are a matter of deluded ignorance, this is the realm of the six pāramitās [that is, of the bodhisattva]. If you contemplate desires as [lacking in] fundamental selfhood 本自 and not [truly] arising, and not abiding, nor perishing, that is, that desires are empty, and that emptiness is nirvana; this is the realm of the Shared Teachings. If you contemplate desirous thoughts as having immeasurable features, and the collection [of the causes of suffering] is not just one; and that suffering is also immeasurable, and know the roots of the nature of desires are all caused by desirous thoughts, and you discriminate them fully; this is the realm of the Distinct Teachings. The other parts of the three categories of passionate afflictions and the arising of all phenomena [related to them] are also likewise. [Contemplating] them gradually and successively is called [contemplating] objects as "conceivable."

Economy 撙節: Ikeda (*Kenkyūchūshaku*, 420) and the *Inyō* refer to a classical phrase in the 礼記 and interprets this as "propriety" or "manners."

Ten goodnesses 十善: to avoid the ten evil deeds; for details, see Glossary.

Six heavenly realms 六[欲]天: six heavenly realms, but still in the realm of desires. For details, see Glossary.

Collecting 集: this is the character used to express the second of the Four Noble Truths, that suffering has causes.

Objects as inconceivable [103b14]

[Second is] objects as "inconceivable" 不思議. The *Sūtra on Non-Activity* says, "Covetous desires are nirvana [or 'the Path' 道]; as it is so for anger and ignorance. Within these three dharmas are included all Buddha-dharmas." In this way, the four categories [of passionate afflictions] are indivisible from the Path, but that does not mean that you should follow after them. Following after [passionate afflictions] leads people to the evil destinies. Neither is it the case that you sever them; [thinking that] you have severed [the passionate delusions] leads to arrogance. To arouse all enlightening liberations without severing ignorance and passions; this is called the Path. Do not dwell in overcoming, nor in not overcoming. If you dwell in [the state of] "not overcoming" [passionate afflictions], this is a characteristic of a foolish person. If you dwell in [the state of] "overcoming," this is the way of the śrāvaka. Why is this so? Ordinary ignorant people are defiled by greed and follow after [the passionate afflictions of] the four categories, pile up [rebirth in] samsara, become fiercely regressive 狼戾 and difficult to tame; therefore

Covetous desires are nirvana; as it is so for anger and ignorance. Within these three dharmas are included all Buddha-dharmas 貪欲卽是道恚癡亦如是。如是三法中具一切佛法: a phrase in the *Sūtra on Non-Activity* from verses at T 15.759c13–14:

Covetous desires are nirvana;
As it is so for anger and ignorance.
Within these three matters
Is the immeasurable Buddha path.
If a person discriminates
[Between the Path and] covetous desires, anger, and ignorance,
This person is far away from the Buddha
As the heavens are from the earth.
Bodhi-wisdom and covetous desires
Are one, and not two.
All enter into the one Dharma Gate
And are equal and without difference.

A similar passage is found in the *Ta chih tu lun*, T 107c21–25, where the verses are attributed to Prasannendriya 喜根:

Erotic desires are the Path
As it is so for anger and ignorance.
Within these three dharmas
Is the immeasurable Buddha Path.
If a person makes a distinction
Between the Path and greed, anger, and ignorance,
That person has departed from the Buddha Path,
As far as the heavens are from the earth.
The Path and greed, anger, and ignorance;
These are equal and are one Dharma.

Prasannendriya appears again below; see note at 104a18.

To arouse all enlightening liberations ... 不断癡愛起所明脱: a phrase used frequently by Chih-i. A possible source is the *Vimalakīrti Sūtra*, T 14.540b24–25, which uses 滅 instead of 断. The following passage is full of various phrases and images from this section of the *Vimalakīrti Sūtra*.

Do not dwell in overcoming ... the way of the śrāvaka 不住調伏不住不調伏。住不調伏是愚人相。住於調伏是聲聞法: see a passage in the *Vimalakīrti Sūtra*, T 14.545b23–26

Mañjuśrī, bodhisattvas with a disease should overcome it in this way, by not dwelling in those thoughts. Again, do not

this is called "not overcoming" [passionate afflictions]. Those of the two vehicles fear [rebirth in] samsara, as if they were being pursued by an angry enemy, and rush to escape this triple world. Arhats are among those who do not overcome [afflictions]; since they have exhausted the delusions of the triple world, there are no delusions for them to overcome. In this way they do not overcome [anything further], but this could be called a kind of "overcoming." Thus their seeds are "burnt" and do not give birth [to higher realization], and their roots are defeated and useless. Bodhisattvas are not like this. They remain in samsara and are courageous; they are in nirvana but are not [consumed by] its flavor: courageous yet in samsara, non-arising yet arising, undefiled by the phenomena of arising, like a [lotus] flower that [thrives] in the mud, like a physician who heals diseases, not tasting of nirvana, knowing both emptiness and non-emptiness, and not taking emptiness as the sign of enlightenment. As a bird flies in the [empty] sky but does not dwell in the sky, [the bodhisattva] enters nirvana without severing passionate afflictions, and without severing [**103c**] the fivefold passions he purifies his roots. This is the meaning of neither dwelling in "overcoming" nor dwelling in "not overcoming."

The ignorant people in this [corrupt] latter age 末代 hear that the fruit of the *āmra* [mango] is very sweet to the taste, so they break open the core and lick it, [only to discover that the core] is very bitter, so they lose all taste

> dwell in thoughts of overcoming. What does this mean? Dwelling in thoughts of not overcoming is the state of a foolish person. One who dwells in thoughts of overcoming is the state of a śrāvaka. Therefore a bodhisattva should not dwell in neither the thoughts of overcoming nor not overcoming. To be free from these two states is the practice of a bodhisattva.

Roots are defeated 根敗: see *Vimalakīrti Sūtra*, T 14.549b20: "It is like those whose roots are defeated, and they are not able to recover with regard to the five desires."

Flower in the mud 如花在泥: a very common analogy in Buddhism, it appears [along with the previous and following images], in the *Vimalakīrti Sūtra*, T 14.549b6–10: "It is like a lotus flower that does not flourish in land on a high plain, but this flower will grow in the wet mud.… it is within the mud of passionate afflictions that the sentient beings arouse the Buddha Dharma. Again, it is like planting seeds in space: it will not grow. It is in soiled ground that it is able to grow."

Physician who heals diseases 如醫療病: another very common analogy. The *Inyō*, perhaps superfluously, refers to a passage in the *Ta chih tu lun*, T 25.224a.

Emptiness and non-emptiness 空不空: Ikeda (*Teihonkundoku*, 558) reads this as "knowing the non-emptiness of emptiness."

As a bird flies in the sky 如鳥飛空: note the play of words on 空 as "sky" and "empty." Also, see a similar phrase in the *Vimalakīrti Sūtra*, T 14.547b10.

Enters nirvana without severing passionate afflictions 不斷煩惱而入涅槃: this exact phrase is also found in the the *Vimalakīrti Sūtra*, T 14.539c25.

for the sweetness of the fruit. Since they are without wisdom, they break open the core and make a great mistake in this way. [In a similar way] people hear [the teaching] that there is neither overcoming nor not overcoming, and that overcoming is "unobstructed" 無礙, and non-overcoming is also unobstructed, and that being unobstructed is the "unobstructed path" 無礙道 *(ānantarta-marga)*, and due to [misunderstanding the idea of] being unobstructed [to mean licentiousness], their lustful desires flare up and they act without restraint in public, showing no shame, just like the wild animals. This is like consuming too much salt and suffering from thirst and disease [like high blood pressure]. A sūtra says, "If you become covetously attached to the teaching of non-obstruction, this person is far away from the Buddha, like the heavens from the earth." The *Mahā[parinirvāṇa] Sūtra* says, "I say that to cultivate no-marks is to not cultivate no-marks." These people are practicing the anti-path [that is contrary to the Buddha Path],

The fruit of the *āmra* 菴羅果: see the story in the *Mahāparinirvāṇa Sūtra*, T 12.667a23–26:

> It is like a person who eats an *āmra* fruit and spits out the core on the ground, and then says, "The sweet flavor should be in the core of this fruit." He then picks it up, breaks it open, and licks it. But the taste is very bitter, and he becomes angry and resentful.

Too much salt 噉鹽太過: see *Ta chih tu lun*, T 25.193a18–26; Lamotte (*Le Traité* 2, 1094). Chodron (2, 848) translates:

> [The fool who swallowed pure salt]. – A peasant was unfamiliar with salt. Seeing a nobleman put salt on his meat and vegetables before eating them, he asked why he did so. The nobleman replied that salt gave a good taste to food. The peasant thought that if salt gave a flavor to food, by itself it should be even better. So he took some pure salt, put it in his mouth and ate it. But a nasty pain hurt his mouth and he asked the nobleman: "Why did you say that salt has a good flavor?" The nobleman relied: "Fool! You have to measure out the amount of salt and mix it with the food to give it a good taste. Why did you eat pure salt?"
>
> In the same way, the ignorant person who hears of the door of liberation called emptiness *(śūnyatāvimokṣamukha)* and does not develop the qualities *(guṇa)* but wants only to obtain emptiness: that is a wrong view that destroys all the roots of good *(kuśalamūla)*. This is what should be understood by the 'teaching on emptiness'.

A similar phrase is also found at *Ta chih tu lun*, T 25.480c28: "It is like an ignorant person who does not know much about eating and drinking, but hears about [the benefits of] adding salt for flavor, and so he makes salt his main dish, and [as a result] he loses the flavor [of food] and becomes sick."

If you become covetously attached to the teaching of non-obstruction, this person is far away from the Buddha, like the heavens from the earth 貪著無礙法是人去佛遠譬如天與地: from the *Sūtra on Non-Activity*, a phrase from verses at T 15.759c13–14. see the note above at 103b15.

I say that to cultivate no-marks is to not cultivate no-marks 言我修無相則非修無相: The *Kōgi* (BT–V, 36) admits that this phrase cannot be found in the *Mahāparinirvāṇa Sūtra*.

Practicing the anti-path 行於非道:

wishing to attain the Buddha Path. Instead they throw up obstructions and become ordinary and rustic. This is [what it means to] dwell in [and become attached to] non-overcoming, and is not [the meaning of] "not dwelling" [in the sense of non-attachment].

Again, there are practitioners who hear of "not dwelling in overcoming nor dwelling in non-overcoming," but are afraid of the two extremes, work hard at self-control, and wish to cultivate the wisdom of the Middle and thus sever and destroy the two extremes. Such people are not realizing [the true meaning of] "the covetous desires are the Path." [They think that] severing the covetous desires is the way to attain the Path. This also is [a kind of] "dwelling in the thoughts of overcoming [passionate afflictions]," and is not [the true meaning of] "not dwelling." In the north both of these kinds of misunderstandings have become rampant.

Again, suppose you first study the contemplation of the Middle and sever covetous desires but are not able to attain any benefits, but then absentmindedly practice something that is beyond your control and yet from the very beginning of this practice you slightly attain some benefit. [And suppose that] due to this [experience] you then constantly practice this without ceasing, and even if no further benefit is to be gained, you continue this practice without any rectification. Just on the basis of this previous benefit, you teach others to do this practice, and also quote sūtras as a witness. Those followers who accept this teaching merely covet desirous pleasures, and there is not even a minute mustard seed's worth of benefit to this path. It leads to destructive fluctuations and addiction [to pleasures] so that [indulging in covetous desires] becomes a habitual custom, making the precepts impure and defiling the three treasures [of the Buddha, Dharma, and Sangha]. The House of Chou persecuted the Buddha Dharma for these reasons[, that is, corruption among Buddhists]. People dwelt in the [state of] non-overcoming [of passionate afflictions], and also dwelt in overcoming [that is, were satisfied with severing passionate afflictions without advancing further]. What does this have to do with not dwelling in either "overcoming" or "not overcoming"? This should be called a "great obstacle" 大礙 and has nothing to do with [the idea of] "non-obstruction." It encourages growth in the anti-path; how can it be said to be the Buddha Path? In this case both

a phrase from the *Vimalakīrti Sūtra*, T 14.549a1–2: "The bodhisattva practices the anti-path, and in this way attains the Buddha Path."

In the north 北方: these matters have been discussed in more detail earlier in the *Mo-ho chih-kuan*, 18c20ff., in the section on "Warnings against Teachers of Libertinism."

House of Chou 周家: for details on the persecution of Buddhism and the corruption among Buddhists at this time, about 17 years previous to Chih-i's lectures, see *Mo-ho chih-kuan* 19a.

"overcoming" and "not overcoming" should be classifed as "not overcoming." Why is this so? Because they all involve ordinary passions, and not [attaining the stages of] the wise and the noble.

What I am saying now is, do not dwell in [and become attached to] overcoming [passionate afflictions], do not dwell in the non-overcoming [of afflictions and become licentious], do not dwell in neither overcoming nor not overcoming, do not dwell in both overcoming and not overcoming. Again, dwell in overcoming [passionate afflictions and sever them], dwell in the non-overcoming [of afflictions by knowing that they are empty], dwell in neither overcoming nor not overcoming, and dwell in both overcoming and not overcoming. Why is this so? Passionate afflictions are indivisible from emptiness 煩悩即空, and so you should not dwell in non-overcoming; **[104a]** passionate afflictions are indivisible from the conventional 煩悩即假, and so you should not dwell in the overcoming [of afflictions]; passionate afflictions are indivisible from the Middle 煩悩即中, and so you should not dwell in "both overcoming and not overcoming." They all illuminate passionate afflictions, so you should not dwell in "neither overcoming nor not overcoming." Although [it is said] "do not dwell in overcoming, not overcoming, and so forth," in fact we dwell in overcoming [and try to sever passionate afflictions], not overcoming [by avoiding arrogance over our achievements], and so forth. Although we in fact dwell in overcoming, not overcoming, and so forth, we truly do not dwell in overcoming, not overcoming, and so forth. Why is this so? Because we should not one-sidedly contemplate just one option [of the tetralemma of a, non-a, both, or neither]. Although one option is indivisible from all the options, all phenomenal dharmas incline toward covetous desires, and passionate desires become the focus of all phenomena. If this meaning is used to apply all the options [of the tetralemma], then if covetous desires are understood in terms of being 有, this is called "dwelling in non-overcoming"; if it is understood in term of non-being 無, this is called "dwelling in overcoming." In this way, you can freely explain [all the various options].

In this way, if you have [penetrating] insight into the essence [of emptiness], this is called "the unobstructed Path" *(ānantarta-marga)*. "All unobstructed people escape from [the cycle of] samsara on the One Path." How do they escape? At times you have penetrating insight that covetous desires are ultimately pure, neither binding nor defiling, like empty space, and you awaken to [spontaneously] escape from samsara. This is called "dwelling in overcoming" and attaining benefit.

All unobstructed people escape from samsara on the One Path 一切無礙人一道出生死: from the *Avataṃsaka Sūtra*, T 9.429b19; see also *Mo-ho chih-kuan* 9b23.

At other times, with a deliberate mind you contemplate these covetous desires and their causes and conditions from beginning to end—which are diseases and which are medicines—like [the beautiful and wise woman] Vasumitrā, who was liberated from desires and able to save [other] sentient beings. When you perform this contemplation, you awaken to [spontaneously] escape from samsara. This is called "dwelling in non-overcoming" and attaining benefit.

At other times you attain benefit by denying both [overcoming and non-overcoming]. At other times you attain benefit by contemplating both together. In this way, through good and skillful [means] you should [at times] dwell, and you should [at other times] not dwell, and thus benefit both oneself and others. Thus there is neither gain nor decrease in the dharma of the bodhisattva, and by means of the four *siddhānta* [methods of instruction] you should act appropriate to the situation.

[For example,] it is like when Prasannendriya taught the Dharma to various laymen using skillful means and all of them attained the forbearance of non-arising (*anutpattikadharmakṣānti*), but the bhikhu Agramati practiced the [Hīnayāna] way of "clumsy deliverance" 拙度 and did not accomplish anything. Later he visited the village [where Prasannendriya and

Vasumitrā 和須蜜多: one of the fifty-three "friends" met by Sudhana on his journey to enlightenment described in the *Avataṃsaka Sūtra*, T 9.716c3–717b27. For details, see note at *Mo-ho chih-kuan* 17c15.

Prasannendriya 喜根 **and Agramati** 勝意: see the section on "saving with appropriate means" in the *Ta chih tu lun*, T 25.107b13–108a19 (Lamotte, *Le Traité* 1, 398–402). Chodron (1, 323–25) translates:

> There were, at that time, two bodhisattva bhikṣus named Hi ken (Prasannendriya) and Cheng yi (Agramati). The Dharma teacher Prasannendriya, of frank and simple manner, had not renounced the things of the world *(lokadharma)* and did not distinguish good from evil. His disciples were intelligent *(medhāvin)*, loved the Dharma and understood admirably the profound meaning *(gambhīrārtha)*. Their teacher did not recommend moderation in desires *(alpecchāsaṃtuṣṭi)* to them or the observance of the precepts *(śīlacaryā)* or the practice of the dhūtas. He spoke to them only of the true nature *(satyalakṣaṇa)* of the dharmas which is pure *(viśuddha)*. He said to them: "The dharmas are characterized by desire *(rāga)*, hatred *(dveṣa)* and delusion *(moha)*, but all these characteristics *(lakṣaṇa)* may be reduced to the true nature *(satyalakṣaṇa)* of the dharmas which is without hindrance *(apratihata)*." It was by these soteriological means (*upāya*) that he instructed his disciples and introduced them into the knowledge of the unique nature *(ekalakṣaṇajñāna)*. Thus his disciples felt no hostility *(pratigha)* or affection *(anunaya)* for people and, as their minds were unperturbed, they had obtained the patience towards beings *(sattvakṣānti)*; provided with the patience towards beings, they acquired the patience relating to the dharmas *(dharmakṣānti)*. In the presence of the true doctrine, they remained motionless *(acala)* like a mountain.
>
> By contrast, the Dharma teacher Agramati, clinging to the purity of the precepts *(śīlaviśuddhi)*, practiced the twelve dhūtas, had acquired the four

his disciples lived] and heard [the teaching] that covetous desires were indivisible from the Path, and became angry at Prasannendriya and said, "Why do you teach to others a way that hinders the Path?" not realizing his own exclusiveness. Prasannendriya responded by teaching some verses, [hoping that thereby Agramati might avoid] falling further. A bodhisattva knows that if one does not believe, then one will fall into hell. Therefore he [Prasannendriya] forcefully taught [these matters], producing causes [for Buddhahood] in a later time [even though at first Agramati fell into hell]. Thus you should skillfully contemplate the [four] *siddhāntas*—whether for oneself or others, whether [the goal of Buddhahood is] near or far—and dwell in overcoming, or dwell in non-overcoming, and so forth [as is appropriate for the situation], all without any fault. [The same could be said for] not dwelling in overcoming nor non-overcoming, again all without any fault. If you do not realize the intent of the four *siddhāntas*, whether you dwell or do not dwell [in overcoming or not overcoming afflictions], you will weave a web of passions for yourself and arouse slander and arrogance toward others,

dhyānas and the formless absorptions *(ārūpyasamāpatti)*. His disciples were of weak faculties *(mṛdvindriya)* and clung to distinguishing the pure *(śuddha)* [practices] from the impure *(aśuddha)* ones; their minds were always disturbed [by qualms]....

Agramati rose from his seat, saying: "[Your teacher] Prasannendriya deceives many beings and clings to wrong ways *(mithyāmārga)*." This bodhisattva Agramati did not know the *ghoṣapraveśadhāraṇī*; he was happy when he heard the speech of the Buddha and grieved when he heard a heretical *(tīrthika)* word; he was sad when he heard speak of the three evil *(akuśala)* things and rejoiced when he heard speak of the three good things (*kuśala*); he hated speaking about saṃsāra and loved to speak about nirvāṇa. Leaving the dwellings of the vaiśya, he went back to the forest and returned to his monastery (*vihāra*). He said to his bhikṣus: "You should know that the bodhisattva Prasannendriya is an impostor who leads people to evil. Why? He claims that the nature of desire, hatred and delusion *(rāgadveṣamohalakṣaṇa)* as well as all the other dharmas is not an obstacle."

Then the bodhisattva Prasannendriya had this thought: "This Agramati who is so fierce is covered with faults and will fall into great sins *(mahāpatti)*. I am going to teach him the profound Dharma *(gambhīradharma)*. Even if he cannot grasp it today, this teaching will earn him buddhahood later." Then gathering the saṃgha together, Prasannendriya spoke these stanzas:... [*see note above*]

Prasannendriya spoke seventy more stanzas of this kind and at that moment, 30,000 devaputras found acquiescence in the doctrine of non-production *(anutpattikadharmakṣānti)*; 18,000 śrāvakas, detached from all dharmas, found deliverance *(vimokṣa)*. The bodhisattva Agramati fell into hell (*niraya*) where he suffered torments for 10,000,000 years; then he was reborn among humans where he was exposed to ridicule for 740,000 lifetimes....

The verses from this section were just referred to above, see note at 103b15.

Falling further 便身陷: or, "whereupon [Agramati] physically fell even further [that is, into hell].

thus obstructing yourself and obstructing others, and not [attain the goal of] non-obstruction.

If a single thought of passionate afflictions arises in the mind, it includes the hundred dharmas of the ten realms [from hell to Buddhahood] that are mutually unobstructed. Although they are many, they do not exist substantially; though they are one, they are not nothing 不無. Though many, they do not accumulate; though one, they are not dispersed. Though many, they are not different; though one, they are not the same. The many are indivisible from the one; the one is indivisible from the many 多即一一即多. A sūtra says, "The shadow of a tree in darkness cannot be [**104b**] seen because of the darkness, but the divine eye can perceive it." This is to say that there is perception within the darkness. The wisdom obstacle 智障 is exceedingly blind and dark; it is darkness in the midst of light. Again, it is like when a flame is first lit, it dwells along with the darkness. In this way light and darkness do not mutually obstruct each other, nor do they mutually destroy each other. Why is this so? In everyday life, when you see a flame light up a room, you do not know where the darkness has gone, and when the flame is extinguished, where the darkness comes from. There is no "original source" to its coming, and no footprints to its going. You should know this about darkness; it is the same for light. Seeking darkness, there is no "darkness"; there is nothing that the light destroys. Seeking light, there is no "light"; there is nothing that the darkness hinders. Although there is no [substantial] light and darkness, yet we find destruction [of darkness by light] and hindrance [of light by darkness]. There is no accepting 不受, no attachment 不着, no thoughts 不念, no discrimination 不分別. With regard to that which newly arises, there is no accepting. With regard to that which has already arisen, there is no

Hundred dharmas of the ten realms 十界百法: each of the ten realms includes the other, so ten times ten makes one hundred combinations.

The shadow of a tree in darkness cannot be seen because of the darkness, but the divine eye can perceive it 闇中樹影闇故不見。天眼能見: see the *Mahāparinirvāṇa Sūtra*, T 12.622c25–b2:

> Good sons, it is like a tree is the cause for there being a shadow of the tree. The Tathāgata is also like this. There is a constant Dharma, and therefore people rely on it, and it is not transient. If you say that the Tathāgata is transient, then the Tathāgata is not something the heavenly and human beings can rely on.
>
> The bodhisattva Kāśyapa said to the Buddha, "World Honored One. It is like in the darkness there is a tree but no shadow.
>
> [The Buddha said:] "Kāśyapa, you should not say that there is a tree but no shadow. It is just that the physical eye cannot see it. Good sons, the Tathāgata is also like this. His nature constantly abides without changing, even though the wisdom eye cannot perceive it, like not being able to see the shadow of the tree in the darkness. Again it is like ordinary ignorant people who, after the death of the Buddha, say that the Tathāgata is a transient dharma.

attachment. With regard to what is internally experienced, there is no thought. With regard to what is externally experienced, there is no discrimination. Sublime wisdom is translucent; for this reason it is called "inconceivable," and things are not mutually obstructed nor mutually removed. If the flame of worldly wisdom is extinguished, the darkness of delusions will come again. In the case of the light of the wisdom of the Middle Path, it constantly abides and is immovable. This is like a divine jewel that constantly illuminates, so the darkness does not come. Contemplate the darkness of the passionate afflictions as indivisible from the light of great wisdom, and manifest the *bodhi*-wisdom of the Buddha, and the delusions will not come.

[The analysis of the rest of the] aggregates *(skandha)*, sense entrances, *(āyatana)*, and sense realms *(dhātu)* [as objects of contemplation] should be known in accordance with previous [explanations].

2. Arousing Compassion [104b14]

In this way, when you contemplate, strive to feel pain over your own transgressions, and have a broad compassion toward [other] sentient beings. Why? The principle is not limited to [either] light or darkness; it is due to delusions that the darkness of suffering and the causes of suffering arise, and it is due to the methods of understanding and healing that there is the light of the path and the extinction [of suffering]. It is in the context of darkness that there is pity 約闇故悲, and in the context of light that there is compassion 約明故慈. The mind of [making] a great vow arises along with [contact with the passionate afflictions of] the sense objects.

3. Skillful Means for a Peaceful Mind [104b18]

It is to complete these vows that you must establish essential practices. As for what is essential practice, there is nothing that takes precedence over cessation-and-contemplation. To realize that the four categories of passionate afflictions are empty [in their essence] is called "cessation as realizing the truth [of emptiness]" and entering the contemplation of emptiness. To contemplate all passionate afflictions and the ways and medicines [to heal these] diseases is called "cessation as [the realization of conventional reality as that which] arises through conditions" and the contemplation of [re-]entering conventionality. To contemplate all passionate afflictions

In accordance with previous explanations: see the analysis of the contemplation of the inconceivable at 52c–55c.

Suffering and the causes of suffering 苦集: the first two of the Four Noble Truths.

The path and the extinction [of suffering] 道滅: the third and fourth of the Four Noble Truths.

as being the same as reality-as-it-is, is called "cessation as putting an end to the two extremes" and entering the contemplation of the realization of the Middle Path. If you skillfully and with a peaceful mind cultivate this threefold cessation-and-contemplation, you realize and perfect the three eyes and the three wisdoms in a single mind (and thought).

行之要者莫先止觀。
四分煩惱體之即空。名體眞止入空觀也。
觀諸煩惱藥病等法。名隨緣止入假觀。
觀諸煩惱同眞際。名息二邊止入中道觀。
善巧安心修此三止三觀成一心三眼三智也。

4. Deconstructing Dharmas [104b22]

If the [three] eyes and [three] wisdoms have not yet been opened, strive in all ways to destroy the obstacles [to this attainment]. Contemplate the four categories of passionate afflictions thought by thought in their three [types of] conventionality. [Realize that they arise] neither on their own, through others, through both [self and others], apart from [any causes], single, multiple, or through inclusion, and that [mistaken] views and concepts do not [substantially] arise. Know the diseases and discern the medicine [to heal them], and noncognizance does not arise. [Know that they are] neither true [that is, merely empty] nor conditioned [that is, merely conventional], and ignorance will not arise. This is the universal deconstruction [of all passionate afflictions] both horizontally and vertically.

It is to complete these vows that you must establish … the three eyes and the three wisdoms in a single mind and thought: this paragraph is marked in bold and the Chinese added in full in order to highlight it as one of the best summaries of Chih-i's threefold truth. But it was only when the Chinese was extracted from the Taishō text and formatted by line that the sublime and exquisite balance of the Chinese was fully revealed: Note how the threefold pattern is reflected in the way the terms line up: the threefold truth itself 空假中, with terse summary of its content, as well as the threefold cessation and threefold contemplation, and the final summary including other threefold categories such as "three eyesights" and "three wisdoms." The balanced repetition and cadence makes for what could be called a poem, or even perhaps "poetic scholasticism." One could even say that this passage encapsulates the essentials of T'ien-t'ai thought and practice.

Thought by thought in their three [types of] conventionality 念念三假: that is, 1. as causally arisen 因成假, that things are conventional because they are the result of a confluence of causes and conditions; 2. as continuous 相續假, they exhibit some continuity of characteristics, though no permanence; and 3. as relative 相待假, they have their meaning or existence relative to other things.

5. Knowing What Penetrates and What Obstructs [104b25]

If even with [the realization of] emptiness there is still the conversion and buildup of suffering and the causes of suffering, this is called "knowing the obstacles." If even within suffering and the causes of suffering you achieve [realization of] emptiness, this is called "knowing penetrating insight." If even with various prescriptions there is still the buildup of diseases, this is called "knowing the obstacles." If within various diseases you are able to know the [proper] medicine, this is called "knowing penetrating insight." For Dharma-nature to be "converted" into ignorance; this is called an "obstacle." For ignorance to be turned and changed into insight; [104c] this is called "penetrating insight."

6. Steps on the Path [104c1]

Again, contemplate the passionate afflictions and cultivate the steps on the path. If the four categories [of passionate afflictions] arise in the mind, these are the defilements of the five aggregates *(skandha)*. One aggregate [such as that of form] contains immeasurable aggregates, and [the other aggregates of] sensations, conceptions, volitions, and consciousness are also immeasurable. All aggregates are empty; this [realization] destroys the perverted [views] of ordinary ignorant beings that gives rise to a small but decaying tree. All aggregates are conventionally existent; this [realization] destroys the perverted [views] of those of the two vehicles, giving rise to a great and flourishing tree. All aggregates are the Middle; this [realization] deconstructs the teaching of flourishing and decaying; the two extremes are quiescent, and you realize great nirvana, and so forth up to opening the three liberations and entering the pure and cool pond [of enlightenment].

7. Auxiliary Methods [104c6]

When the hindrances and obstacles [of passionate afflictions] are heavy, you should cultivate the auxiliary practices of the path. If your understanding is mixed with delusions, you should seek assistance. If external covetous desires arise, seek assistance through [the contemplation of] impurity. If internal covetous desires arise, seek assistance through [the eight] renunciations. If both external and internal covetous desires arise, seek assistance through [the eight levels of] domination. If anger that is contrary to the

Decaying tree 枯樹: see the note and detailed discussion of "four types of flourishing and decay" at *Mo-ho chih-kuan* 88c18.

Contemplation of impurity 不淨: such as contemplating the impurity of the physical body, or the stages of the decay of a corpse.

Dharma arises, seek assistance through compassion for sentient beings. If anger that is in line with the Dharma arises, seek assistance through compassion that is based on the teaching that all things are interconnected. If anger based on meaningless disputes arises, seek the assistance of unconditioned compassion. When the discriminations of [the two extremes of] eternalism and annihilationism arise, seek assistance through [realizing] the causes and conditions of the three times [of past, present, and future]. When the discrimination of a self arises, seek assistance through [contemplating] the two realms [of sentient beings and the natural world they live in]. When the discrimination of a [substantial] nature arises, seek the assistance of [the deconstructive analysis of] the causal arising of a single thought. When bright and beneficial notions arise, seek assistance through counting your breaths. When dark and depressing notions arise, seek assistance through contemplating your breaths. When partially depressing and partially bright notions arise, seek the assistance of following after your breaths. These auxiliary [practices to the] path are very strong, so through them you are able to open the gates to nirvana.

8. Graded Stages of Attainment [104c13]

Even if you have not yet realized [full enlightenment], there are times when you attain a type of understanding, or attain a type of meditative concentration; if so, you should consider this carefully. You should not deludedly mistake grass, trees, tiles, or stones for lapis lazuli jewels. If your attainment is a positive one, [you should consider] which passionate afflictions were extinguished, or which [mistaken] views 見, [mistaken] conceptions 思, minute [delusions] 塵沙, or [fundamental] ignorance 無明 [overcome]? If you are completely unaware of these various levels [of attainment], and mistakenly take these [attainments for what they are not], this is like the squeaking of a mouse [that doesn't mean anything] or taking the chirping of birds in the

Anger that is in line with the Dharma 順法瞋: perhaps a kind of "righteous indignation"?

Eight renunciations [八]背捨: eight stages of "liberation" leading to complete cessation *(nirodha-samāpatti)*.

Eight levels of domination [八] 勝處: after attaining the eight liberations, the levels of contemplation wherein you increasingly attain mastery and domination over pure and impure realms.

Compassion that is based on the teaching that all things are interconnected 法緣慈[悲]: that is, if you realize that all things are interconnected through various causes and conditions, you will spontaneously arouse compassion for all things. For details, see *Ta chih tu lun*, T 25.350b26ff.

Chirping of birds 空空如空鳥空: there are a number of puns at work here. First, the "chirping" is indicated by a double repeat of the character for "emptiness" 空空 (*k'ung-k'ung; kong-kong; kū-kū*), and

empty sky as a pronouncement of [the truth of] emptiness. If you do not know of these [basic] graded levels [of attainment], you will have no affinity with [the more sophisticated levels of the six identities such as that of] "contemplative practice" and "resemblance." If you are confused over these higher levels, this will give rise to suspicion.

9. Resting in Patient Forbearance [104c19]

If inner and outer obstacles arise, you should give preference to resting in patient forbearance. If your patience runs out, [you will become] like a bodhisattva who is defeated and broken. If you have restful forbearance that is unmovable, you will be able to become a bodhisattva and attain the prize of meditative [concentration] and the wisdom of one who has attained the path.

10. No Passionate Attachments to Dharmas [104c21]

If you attain this prize, be careful not to arouse passionate attachment to dharmas; such passionate attachment hinders the true path. If there is no falling from this pinnacle [of attainment where you are free from the afflictions of the triple world], then you will spontaneously be unobstructed, like the wind blowing through the sky. Your level of attainment will be like that of the stage of the copper *cakravartin*: you will destroy the delusions of [fundamental] ignorance and attain the forbearance of non-arising.

11. Summary [104c23]

If you attain "the one great vehicle, tall and vast with many servants attending and guarding it," "riding on this jeweled vehicle you will directly attain the

then the same character is used for "the birds in the *sky*." The puns, of course, do not work in English translation. See note above at 103b29, and a similar phrase in the *Vimalakīrti Sūtra*, T 14.547b10.

"Contemplative practice" and "resemblance" 觀行相似: the two levels in the categories of the "six identies" that contain most of the detailed levels of attainment in the fourfold teachings, and the afflictions that are severed thereby. For details, see Chart 1.

Defeated and broken bodhisattva 敗壞菩薩: see note above at 103b about bodhisattvas whose "roots are defeated"; see *Vimalakīrti Sūtra*, T 14.549b20.

Falling from the pinnacle 頂墮; retrogressing to a lower level after having attained freedom from the afflictions of the triple world at the level of the "summit." See *Ta chi tu lun*, T 24.262b4.

The stage of the copper *cakravartin* 銅輪: equivalent in Chih-i's scheme to the level of "partial realization of the real truth," the fifth of the "six identities."

One great vehicle, tall and vast with many servants attending and guarding it 一大車高廣僕從而侍衛之: From the parable

Buddha Path." This is also referred to as [realizing that] "the four categories of passionate afflictions completely include all Buddha Dharmas." It is also said, "by practicing the anti-path, you have penetrating attainment of the Buddha Path." It is also said that "passionate afflictions are *bodhi*-wisdom." It is also said, "one enters nirvana without severing passionate afflictions."

1. Thirty-six Options on Entering and Leaving Nirvana [104c27]

If we explain this extensively, there are thirty-six options, but first I will establish four options: [1] not severing passionate afflictions and not entering nirvana; [2] severing passionate afflictions and entering nirvana; [3] both severing and not severing [passionate afflictions] and both entering and not entering [nirvana]; [4] neither [**105a**] severing nor not severing [passionate afflictions] and neither entering nor not entering [nirvana].

The first option refers to [the state of] ordinary ignorant beings, the next refers to those who have nothing more to learn, the third refers to those with more to learn, and the fourth refers to the principle itself. These are the fundamental four options.

1. Sixteen options on entering nirvana [105a2]

Each option also involves four options. The four variations of the first option are [1] to not sever [afflictions] and not enter [nirvana], [2] sever but not enter, [3] both sever and not sever yet not enter [nirvana], and [4] neither sever nor not sever yet not enter [nirvana]. The first refers to ordinary ignorant beings who arouse evil. The second refers to non-Buddhists who attain meditative concentration. The third refers to non-Buddhists who attain

of the burning house in the *Lotus Sūtra*, T 9.12c18–24, referred to many times previously. Hurvitz (60 [56]) translates:

> At that time the great man gives to each child one great carriage. The carriage is high and wide, adorned with a multitude of jewels,... [and] has many attendants serving and guarding it.

Attaining this one great vehicle is, for Chih-i, synonymous with attaining the highest level of enlightenment.

... directly attain the Buddha Path 乘是寶乘直至道場: another phrase from the *Lotus Sūtra*, T 9.15a13–14, referred to many times previously. Hurvitz (74 [68]) has:

> To mount this jewelled Vehicle
> And to arrive directly at the Platform on the Way.

Practicing the anti-path 行於非道: A phrase also quoted earlier (103c) from the *Vimalakīrti Sūtra*, T 14.549a1–2: "The bodhisattva practices the anti-path, and in this way attains the Buddha Path."

Enters nirvana without severing passionate afflictions 不斷煩惱而入涅槃: another phrase quoted above (103b28), also found in the the *Vimalakīrti Sūtra*, T 14.539c25.

meditative concentration yet also arouse [mistaken] views. The fourth refers to people who are neutral.

The four variations of the next [second] option are [1] severing and entering, [2] not severing yet entering, [3] entering with both severing and not severing, and [4] entering with neither severing nor not severing. The first refers to those who have [mastered the Tripitaka method of] analyzing dharmas and have nothing more to learn. The second refers to those who have [realized] the essence of dharmas [as empty] and have nothing more to learn. The third refers to those who learn both the analyzing of dharmas and the essence of dharmas [as empty]. The final [fourth] refers to those who have realized the nature of the truth, and thus enter [nirvana].

The four variations of the third option are [1] both severing and not severing and both entering and not entering, [2] severing yet both entering and not entering, [3] not severing and both entering and not entering, [4] neither severing nor not severing and both entering and not entering. The first refers to those who learn both the analyzing of dharmas and realizing the essence of dharmas. The second refers to those who learn the analyzing of dharmas. The third refers to those who study the essence of dharmas [as empty]. The fourth refers to the truth that is shared by those who are learning and those who have nothing more to learn.

The four variations of the fourth option are [1] neither severing nor not severing and neither entering nor not entering, [2] severing yet neither entering nor not entering, [3] not severing yet neither entering nor not entering, [4] both severing and not severing yet neither entering nor not entering. The first is the principle applicable to both ordinary and noble people. The second is the noble principle for those who analyze dharmas. The third is the noble principle for [those who realize] the essence of the dharmas [as empty]. The fourth is the principle of those who learn [both] the analyzing [of dharmas] and [realize] the essence [of dharmas as empty].

This is an explanation of sixteen options based on the basic four options, which provide a total of twenty options concerning entering nirvana.

2. *Sixteen options on leaving nirvana* [105a18]

Again, there are sixteen variations concerning leaving nirvana. First are the basic four options: [1] Not severing passionate afflictions and not leaving nirvana; [2] severing passionate afflictions and leaving nirvana; [3] both severing and not severing passionate afflictions and both leaving and not

Twenty options 二十句: the original four options, plus sixteen variations.

leaving [nirvana]; neither severing nor not severing [passionate afflictions] and neither leaving nor not leaving [nirvana].

Each of these options also involves four options. The first four variations are: [1] not severing passionate afflictions and not leaving nirvana; [2] not severing passionate afflictions and leaving nirvana; [3] not severing passionate afflictions and both leaving and not leaving [nirvana]; [4] not severing passionate afflictions and neither leaving nor not leaving [nirvana]. The first refers to those of the two vehicles who [realize] the essence of dharmas [as empty]. The second refers to bodhisattvas who realize the essence of dharmas [as empty] and then reemerge in the conventional [world]. The third refers to bodhisattvas who realize the essence of dharmas as both empty and conventional. The fourth is the truth of the essence of dharmas.

The second of the four variations are: [1] severing passionate afflictions and leaving [nirvana]; [2] severing passionate afflictions and not leaving [nirvana]; [3] severing passionate afflictions and both leaving and not leaving [nirvana]; and [4] severing passionate afflictions and neither leaving nor not leaving [nirvana]. The first refers to those who have analyzed dharmas and have nothing more to learn, and who [remain in the world to] help the Buddha benefit sentient beings. The second refers to those who have analyzed dharmas and have nothing more to learn, and immediately enter extinction. The third **[105b]** refers to those who have learned to analyze dharmas and benefit both self and others. The fourth refers to the truth.

The third of the four variations are: [1] both severing and not severing, and both leaving and not leaving; [2] both severing and not severing, and leaving; [3] both severing and not severing, and not leaving; [4] both severing and not severing, and neither leaving nor not leaving. The first refers the bodhisattva who realizes emptiness by utilizing both analyzing and [realizing] the essence [of dharmas]. The second refers to the bodhisattva who reemerges in the conventional [world] and utilizes both analyzing and [realizing] the essence [of dharmas]. The third refers to those of the two vehicles who utilize both analyzing and [realizing] the essence [of dharmas]. The fourth refers to the true principle of the essence [of dharmas].

The fourth of the four variations are: [1] neither severing nor not severing, and neither leaving nor not leaving; [2] neither severing nor not severing, and leaving; [3] neither severing nor not severing, and not leaving; [4] neither severing nor not severing, and both leaving and not leaving. The first refers to the principle of the essence [of dharmas]. The second refers to bodhisattvas who realize the essence of dharmas and reemerge in the con-

Reemerge in the conventional 出假: that is, those who transcend the realization of emptiness by "returning" and focusing on the conventional world.

ventional [world]. The third refers to those of the two vehicles who [realize] the essence of dharmas. The fourth refers to bodhisattvas who [realize] the essence and enter emptiness.

If we establish these eight basic options [of four options each] for leaving and entering [nirvana], [along with sixteen variations for each,] we have forty options. If we take just the basic four options [only one time], we have thirty-six options.

2. Thirty-six Options for the Four Gates of the Four Teachings [105b12]

Question: These thirty-six options are limited to the Tripitaka and Shared [Teachings]. Can they be applied to the Distinct and Perfect [Teachings]?

Answer: There is no place that the meaning of the "essence of dharmas" cannot be applied. If we make further distinctions, it can be applied to the four gates of the Distinct and Perfect [Teachings]. These further distinctions are as follows.

The basic four options are: [1] "neither severing nor entering" is the gate of emptiness [Shared Teachings]; [2] "severing and entering" is the gate of existence [as causal co-arising, the Tripitaka Teachings]; "both severing and not severing and both entering and not entering" is the gate of both emptiness and existence [as conventional, the Distinct Teachings]; and [4] "neither severing nor not severing, and neither entering nor not entering" is the gate of neither emptiness nor existence [as the Middle Path, the Perfect Teaching].

Each of these gates has a further four variations. [1] "neither severing nor entering" is the worldly 世界 *[laukika-]siddhānta*; [2] "not severing yet entering" is the individual 為人 *[prātipauruṣika-]siddhānta*; [3] "not severing and both entering and not entering" is the therapeutic 對治 *[prātipākṣika-]siddhānta*; and [4] "not severing and neither entering nor not entering" is the supreme 第一義 *[paramārthika-]siddhānta*.

Again, each gate in return produces four gates. [First, with regard to the Tripitaka Teachings,] [1] "neither severing nor entering" is the gate of emptiness; [2] "not severing yet entering" is the gate of existence; [3] "not severing and both entering and not entering"is the gate of both emptiness and [conventional] existence; [4] "not severing and neither entering nor not entering" is the gate of neither emptiness nor existence. This is how it should be understood for one gate or Teaching; distinctions concerning each of the other three gates or Teachings should be understood in the same way.

Entering nirvana by the four gates is explained thusly. How about the sixteen options for leaving nirvana [and coming back to the conventional world]? [First there are four variations:] [1] not severing and not leaving; [2] not severing yet leaving; [3] not severing and both leaving and not leaving; [4] not severing and neither leaving nor not leaving. The first [variation] is the gate of emptiness. The second is the gate of existence. The third is the gate of both emptiness and existence. The fourth is the gate of neither emptiness nor existence. [105c] Each gate having four variations is like this; and the other three gates should be understood likewise. The thirty-six or forty variations should be known in accordance with the previous explanation. This is the universal application of small and large [Hīnayāna and Mahāyāna], both the analytical [approach] and [realizing] the essence [of dharmas]. If you understand this meaning, you can apply it to all dharmas in the same way.

3. Thirty-six Options for *Prajñā*-wisdom [105c3]

Question: If the Buddha, nirvana, and *prajñā*-wisdom are contemplated according to [the proper] method, these three share a unity of features. You have already clarified the thirty-six options for nirvana; how about *prajñā*-wisdom?

Answer: If nirvana is indivisible from *prajñā*-wisdom, why is it necessary to even ask this question? But now I will repeat my explanation. [1] Dharmas arise and *prajñā*-wisdom arises; [2] dharmas do not arise and *prajñā*-wisdom does not arise; [3] dharmas both arise and do not arise, and *prajñā*-wisdom both arises and does not arise; [4] dharmas neither arise nor do not arise, and *prajñā*-wisdom neither arises nor does not arise. These are the basic four options.

The first option [of dharmas arising] opens up four further variations: [1] dharmas arise and *prajñā*-wisdom arises; [2] dharmas arise and *prajñā*-wisdom does not arise; [3] dharmas arise and *prajñā*-wisdom both arises and does not arise; and [4] dharmas arise and *prajñā*-wisdom neither arises nor does not arise. This first option refers to mundane objects and the arising of the *prajñā*-wisdom of the path (*marga-anvaya-jñā* 道種智). The second refers to mundane objects and the arising of the *prajñā*-wisdom of omniscience (*sarvajñā* 一切智). The third refers to mundane objects and the mutual arising of both types of *prajñā*-wisdom. The fourth refers to mundane objects and the arising of the *prajñā*-wisdom of universal wisdom (*sarva-ākāra-jñatā, sarvajñatā* 一切種智).

[The four variations of] the second option [of dharmas not arising] are: [1] dharmas do not arise and *prajñā*-wisdom does not arise; [2] dharmas do not arise yet *prajñā*-wisdom arises; [3] dharmas do not arise and *prajñā*-wisdom both arises and does not arise; [4] dharmas do not arise and *prajñā*-wisdom neither arises nor does not arise. The first refers to true [empty] objects and the arising of the *prajñā*-wisdom of omniscience. The second refers to true [empty] objects and the arising of the *prajñā*-wisdom of the path. The third refers to true [empty] objects and the mutual arising of both types of *prajñā*-wisdom. The fourth refers to true [empty] objects and the arising of the *prajñā*-wisdom of the wisdom of the Middle Path.

[The four variations of] the third option [of dharmas both arising and not arising] are: [1] dharmas both arise and do not arise, and *prajñā*-wisdom both arises and does not arise; [2] dharmas both arise and do not arise, and *prajñā*-wisdom arises; [3] dharmas both arise and do not arise, and *prajñā*-wisdom does not arise; and [4] dharmas both arise and do not arise, and *prajñā*-wisdom neither arises nor does not arise. The first variation refers to both [mundane and true] objects and the arousal of the two wisdoms [of the path and omniscience]. The second refers to both objects accompanied by the arousal of the wisdom of the mundane 俗智. The third refers to both objects accompanied by the arousal of the wisdom of the true [emptiness] 眞智. The fourth refers to both objects and the arousal of the wisdom of the Middle 中智.

[The four variations of] the fourth option [of dharmas neither arising nor not arising] are: [1] dharmas neither arise nor do not arise, and *prajñā*-wisdom neither arises nor does not arise; [2] dharmas neither arise nor do not arise, and *prajñā*-wisdom arises; [3] dharmas neither arise nor do not arise, and *prajñā*-wisdom does not arise; and [4] dharmas neither arise nor do not arise, and *prajñā*-wisdom both arises and does not arise. The first refers to objects as the Middle [between two extremes] and arousing the wisdom of the Middle. The second refers to objects as the Middle and arousing the wisdom of the mundane. The third refers to objects as the Middle and arousing the wisdom of the true. The fourth refers to **[106a]** objects as the Middle and arousing the two wisdoms [of the mundane and the true].Thus I have already explained sixteen options and variations.

Next is the explanation [of four variations on the arising of *prajñā*-wisdom]: [1] *prajñā*-wisdom arises and dharmas arise; [2] *prajñā*-wisdom arises and dharmas do not arise; [3] *prajñā*-wisdom arises and dharmas both arise and do not arise; [4] *prajñā*-wisdom arises and dharmas neither arise not do not arise. The first refers to the wisdom of the path illuminating mundane objects. The second refers to the wisdom of the path illuminating true [empty] objects. The third refers to the wisdom of the path illuminating both [mundane and true] objects. The fourth refers to the wisdom of the path illuminating the objects as the Middle.

Next I will clarify [the four variations on the non-arising of *prajñā*-wisdom]: [1] *prajñā*-wisdom does not arise and dharmas do not arise; [2] *prajñā*-wisdom does not arise and dharmas arise; [3] *prajñā*-wisdom does not arise and dharmas both arise and do not arise; and [4] *prajñā*-wisdom does not arise and dharmas neither arise nor do not arise. This clarifies how the wisdom of the true [emptiness] illuminates all objects, and should be known in accordance with the above.

Next is the clarification of four variations of *prajñā*-wisdom as both arising and not arising. This refers to the wisdom on the Middle Path illuminating the four [variations of] objects, which should be known [as explained above], and so forth. This gives sixteen variations, which along with [the above sixteen and] the basic four options gives a total of thirty-six variations.

4. Thirty-six Options for the Dharma-body [106a12]

Question: How about with regard to the Dharma body?

Answer. *Prajñā*-wisdom is indivisible from the Dharma body, so why is it necessary even to raise the question? If you wish for the distinctions to be made [I will do so, but] if you know the intent [of these matters explained above], there is no need for troublesome textual [explanation].

Again, there are basically the four bodies [of the Buddha] of Dharma 法, reward 報, manifestation 應, and transformation 化. Each of these bodies gives rise to four bodies. That is, from the Dharma body there arises the reward [body], the manifestation [body], and [the body of] transformation, together giving rise to three bodies [in addition to the Dharma body as Dharma body, giving a total of four]. It is the same for the other bodies, thus giving a total of sixteen bodies. Again, from the four bodies you enter one body, and likewise with each of the bodies, thus giving [another] sixteen [variations]. Thus, together with the original basic [four bodies], there are thirty-six [variations] of bodies. Each body includes the Dharma realm 法界 (*dharmakāya*), and thus they all arise together and therefore all are able to enter [nirvana] together, and so forth.

Four bodies of the Buddha 四身: the most common theory of Buddha bodies in Mahāyāna Buddhism is of three bodies, but here Chih-i distinguishes between the "reward" and "manifestation" bodies to make four bodies.

3. CONTEMPLATING THE OBJECTS OF DISEASE [106a19–111c22]

The third [of the ten objects of contemplation] is contemplating the objects of disease 病患. Those who have [physical] bodies will [suffer from] disease. The four snakes [of the four elements] differ in their natures; water and fire are mutually opposed, so they are like kites and owls sharing a nest, or a python and rat sharing a hole; [the physical body] is a poisonous vessel, a heavy burden, and a marsh of suffering. [The four elements are] like four neighboring countries always invading and attacking [each other]; if there is a balance of power there may be some peace for a while, but as soon as there is a sign of weakness [an "empty ride" 虛乘], they try to swallow up the other. You should know that the vagaries of the four elements [and thus our physical bodies] are like these analogies. A standard greeting among the Buddhas is "May you have little disease and little suffering," which shows that the

Four snakes 四蛇: the Soothill-Hodous *Dictionary of Chinese Buddhist Terms* explains this metaphor:

> The *Fanyimingyi* [*Suvarṇaprabhāsa Sūtra*] under this heading gives the parable of a man who fled from the two bewildering forms of life and death, and climbed down a rope (of life) 命根, into the well of impermanence 無常, where two mice, night and day, gnawed the rattan rope; on the four sides four snakes 四蛇 sought to poison him (i.e., the four elements 四大 of his physical nature); below were three dragons 三毒龍 breathing fire and trying to seize him. On looking up he saw that two elephants 象 (darkness and light) had come to the mouth of the well; he was in despair, when a bee flew by and dropped some honey (the five desires 五欲) into his mouth, which he ate and entirely forgot his peril.

Differ in their natures 性異: see the *Suvarṇaprabhāsa Sūtra*, T 16.340b2–8:

> [The four elements of] earth, water, fire, and wind, merge together and establish [things]. Sometimes they increase and decrease, and share the marks of residual harm. They are like four snakes, together in one box; four large serpents, each with different characteristics, two above and two below, and two in each direction. In this way the large snakes extinguish everything without exception. The two snakes of earth and water have the characteristic of sinking; the two snakes of wind and fire have the characteristic of lightness and rising. The two natures of mind and consciousness, always moving without stopping, receive recompense according to their deeds. People and heavenly beings in their courses, act in accordance with their place, and fall into various [states of] existence, of water, fire, and wind; dispersed at the time of their extinction.

Chan-jan (BT–V, 71) refers also to a passage in the *Mahāparinirvāṇa Sūtra*, T 12.743a17–20:

> Bodhisattva-mahāsattvas are able to hear and keep the *Mahāparinirvāṇa Sūtra*; they contemplate the body as like a box [containing] earth, water, fire, and wind like four poisonous snakes. They see poison, touch poison, feel poison, and gnaw on poison. All sentient being encounter these four poisons, and mourn their life. The four elements of sentient beings are also like this.

May you have little disease and little suffering 少病少惱: a stock greeting that appears in many contexts. See, for example, the *Lotus Sūtra* at T 9.44a27 and

Buddhas are the same [in suffering such illness] as other people. People will suffer disease; even if temporarily [it seems that] you are without [disease], it just means that it is only "less" [than others and not apparent].

There are two meanings of "disease": the first is "real" disease 實病 from causes, and the second is "tentative" disease 權病 as a result [of certain conditions calling for compassion]. [As for "tentative disease," there is the example

b1; Hurvitz (227 [207–8]) translates the context:

> These four bodhisattvas ... inquired after him, saying, "O World-Honored One! *Are you in good health and free of pain?* Are you conducting yourself in comfort or not? ... At that time, the four great bodhisattvas proclaimed gāthās saying:
>
> O World-Honored One! Are you in comfort?
> *Are you in good health, free of pain?*
> When teaching and converting living beings,
> Do you contrive to do so without fatigue or disgust?
> Also, do the living beings
> Accept conversion with ease, or do they not?
> Are they not causing the World-Honored One
> To experience fatigue or labor?

A search of the SAT Taishō digital canon reveals a host of references in numerous texts. The *Ta chih tu lun*, T 25.131a–b. deals with this phrase at length, touching on the same themes as Chih-i. Chodron (1, 455–57) translates:

> Sūtra: [Samantaraśmi] said to the Buddha [Śākyamuni]: "The tathāgata Ratnā-kara asks you if you have but little anguish *(alpābādhatā)* and but little suffering *(alpātaṅkatā)*, if you are healthy *(yatrā)* and alert *(laghūtthānatā)*, if you are strong *(bala)* and if you are enjoying your ease *(sukhavihāratā)*;...
>
> Śāstra: Question. The Buddha Ratnākara is omniscient *(sarvajñā)*; why does he ask if the Buddha Śākyamuni has but little anguish and but little suffering, if he is healthy and alert, strong and in a joyful state?
>
> Answer. 1. It is customary for the Buddhas to ask about what they already know....
>
> Question. Why does he ask him if he has but little anguish *(alpābādhatā)* and but little suffering *(alpātaṅkatā)*?
>
> Answer. There are two kinds of torments *(alpābādhatā)*, those having an external cause *(bāhyahetupratyaya)* and those having an internal cause *(ādhyhātmika-hetupratyaya)*. The external torments are cold *(śīta)*, heat *(uṣna)*, hunger *(kṣudh)*, thirst *(pipāsā)*, armies *(caturaṅgabala)*, swords *(asi)*, knives *(śastra)*, clubs *(daṇḍa)*, catastrophes *(patana)*, ruins *(avamardana)*; all these external accidents of this kind are called torments *(ādādha)*. The inner torments are the 404 illnesses *(vyādhi)* that come from improper food or irregular sleep; all the sicknesses of this kind are called inner sicknesses. Corporeal beings *(dehin)* all have to suffer from these two kinds of illnesses. This is why [Ratnakāra] asks Śākyamuni if he has but little torments and suffering.
>
> Question. Why does he not ask him if he has no torment and suffering instead of asking if he has but little torment and little suffering?
>
> Answer. The wise *(ārya)* know very well that the body *(kāya)* is a source of suffering *(duḥkhamūla)* and that it is never without sickness. Why? Because the body is an assemblage *(saṃghāta)* of the four great elements *(caturmahābhūta)* and the earth *(pṛthivī)*, water *(āpas)*, fire *(tejas)* and wind *(vāyu)* that compose it are naturally in disharmony and struggle with one another.

of Vimalakīrti who,] while in repose at Vaiśālī, took the opportunity of his illness to teach [the Buddha Dharma]. Through [the appearance of] his physical illness he was able to clarify the teachings for ordinary, mundane [people], rejecting the Hīnayāna and rebuking the [inadequate] Mahāyāna [interpretations], and along with Mañjuśrī broadly clarified the causes of illness and the three types of regulating and overcoming them, and [also] broadly clarified the results of illness and the four types of healing. Again, when the Tathāgata approached his [physical] extinction [by death], he expounded on the permanent [in the *Mahāparinirvāṇa Sūtra*], and of [ten] powers with regard to disease. These all refer to tentative and skillful entering into disease for the sake of teaching the Dharma and guiding people in disease and suffering. These kinds of "tentative disease" [**106b**] are not what is to be contemplated now.

What is to be contemplated now is the physical body that is the result of retributive karmic actions. When the four snakes [of the four elements] are active and produce [their harmful effects and you suffer from disease], you abandon cultivating the Noble Path. If you are able to thoroughly contemplate [the disease], you will gradually benefit from this mental discipline. People of sharp [good] faculties with superior wisdom understand the "resting in forbearance" [as explained previously] and have penetrating insight with regard to the objects of disease, so I will not complicate matters

Vimalakīrti in repose 偃臥 **at Vaiśālī:** see the famous opening (Chapter 2) of the *Vimalakīrti Sūtra*, T 14.539a7ff., on Vimalakīrti's "illness," which serves as a skillful means for people to gather to hear him explain the Dharma. Luk (2002, 17) translates:

> Thus Vimalakirti used countless expedient methods (*upāya*) to teach for the benefit of living beings. Now using upāya he appeared ill, and because of his indisposition kings, ministers, elders, upāsakas, Brahmins, etc., as well as princes and other officials numbering many thousands came to enquire after his health.
>
> So Vimalakīrti appeared in his sick body to receive and expound the Dharma to them.…

Rejecting the Hīnayāna 斥小: see in particular the section of the *Vimalakīrti Sūtra*, T 14.539c14–542a25, chapter 3 on "The Disciples."

Rebuking the [inadequate] Mahāyāna 大呵: see in particular the section of the *Vimalakīrti Sūtra*, T 14.542a26–544a18, chapter 4 on "The Bodhisattvas."

Along with Mañjuśrī: see chapter 5 on "Mañjuśrī's Questions on Illness" in the *Vimalakīrti Sūtra*, T 14.544a26–546a2.

Three types of regulating and overcoming 調伏 **and four types of healing** 慰喩: see the last half of chapter 5 in the *Vimalakīrti Sūtra*.

Expounded on the permanent 談常: the eternal Dharma, and nirvana as constant or permanent, is a major theme of the *Mahāparinirvāṇa Sūtra*.

Powers with regard to disease 因病説力: see the long exposition in the *Mahāparinirvāṇa Sūtra*, T 12.670b22–c29, which discusses the vagaries of disease and the varying strengths of the physical body.

with repeated explanations. But for those without understanding I will now make some further distinctions. As felling a great tree requires ten thousand [swings of an] axe before it falls, and as sculpting a great stone requires a million bores, therefore I will repeat my explanations.

A long disease and traveling afar are [both] great hindrances to dhyāna meditation. If your body is stained with illness and you have lost the benefits of cultivating [the path], you may arouse immeasurable offences. A sūtra tells of "breaking the floating bag [of the precepts that keeps you afloat], and removing the beams of a bridge [of patience]" so that your true concentration is forgotten and lost. Breaking the precepts because of disease is like the bursting of the floating bag, and breaking dhyāna meditation [through loss of patience] is like removing the beams of a bridge. Arousing a deviant and perverted mind and holding dear a pus-filled and bloody body and destroying the pure Dharma body is [the result of] losing your true concentration. For these reasons you should contemplate the objects of diseases.

Again, there are people who leisurely loiter and are lazy when they are healthy, but when they suddenly become sick, have a change of heart and are able to accomplish many things. Again, the capabilities are not the same [for all people], and some are enlightened because they become sick. Thus the four methods of instruction *(siddhānta)*, in accordance with causes and conditions, should be used [to contemplate] the objects of diseases.

Contemplating disease has five sections: [1] Clarification of the marks of disease; [2] the causes and conditions that give rise to disease; [3] clarification of the methods for healing [disease]; [4] clarification of losses and benefits;

Long disease and traveling afar 長病遠行: phrases from the introduction to the *Abhidharma-vibhāṣā-śāstra*, T 28.3c20–22:

> As has been taught at one time, there are five reasons for an arhat to retrogress [from the path]: 1. working hard on business matters; 2. too much chanting of the sutras; 3. getting into arguments; 4. *travelling afar;* and 5. *a long disease.*

See also the appearance of this phrase at the beginning of the section on "the objects of dhyāna meditation," 117a24–26.

Breaking the floating bag 破壞浮囊, **and removing the beams of a bridge** 發撤橋梁: the *Kōgi* (BT–V, 76) says that this quote has not been identified 文未検, but the full phrase appears in the *Mahāparinirvāṇa Sūtra*, T no. 374, 12.437a12, the "Northern version" translated by Dharmakṣema 曇無讖, and also in the "Southern version" revised by Huiyan 慧嚴 (T no. 375, 12.678b27–c4; references to a "floating bag" can be found at, 12.674a3–4 and 673c19–22). These images, identified as from the *Mahāparinirvāṇa Sūtra* (at least the floating bag), have been used previously by Chih-i to illustrate the virtues of keeping the precepts and of patience; see their appearance and notes at 92a27 and 92b17, as well as earlier at 38a17–19. This indicates that Chih-i accessed both of these versions of the sutra, though he favored no. 375. It is strange that the quote remains unidentified in the commentaries, since it appears frequently and prominently in the *Mahāparinirvāṇa Sūtra.*

and [5] clarification of [the practice of] cessation-and-contemplation [with regard to disease].

1. The Marks of Disease [106b15]

First is the marks of disease. If you have good medical techniques and skillful knowledge of the four elements [of earth, water, fire, and wind], a superior doctor will listen to the voice [of the patient], a middling doctor will [observe] the marks of the color [of the patient's face or body], and an inferior doctor will examine the pulse. It is not necessary now to make fine distinctions with regard to medical methods, but I will provide some summary information.

The method of [examining] the pulse is a matter for medical specialists, so I should not speak in detail about it. [Instead] I will summarize the marks of disease in terms of the five [internal] organs 五藏 [of lungs, heart, liver, kidneys, and spleen]. If the pulse is like a deluge and direct 洪直, this is a mark of the disease of the liver 肝; if light and floating 輕浮, this is a mark of the disease of the heart 心; if acute 尖鋭 and sharp 衝刺, this is a mark of the disease of the lungs 肺; if like a string of jewels 連珠, this is a mark of the

A superior doctor will listen to the voice, a middling doctor will [observe] the marks of the color, and an inferior doctor will examine the pulse 上醫聽聲中醫相色下醫診脈: see the summary of ancient Chinese medicine by Paul Unschuld (1998, 26–27), which matches Chih-i's statement:

> The diagnostic instructions of the systematic tradition of Chinese medicine underwent an effective elaboration in the first century A.D., the effects of which lasted until the present. Since antiquity, it had been established that the patient had to be examined by four methods, namely inspection, listening and smelling, inquiry, and pulse-taking. Consequently, the best doctor was the one who could see a disease in the patient by mere observation, say, of changes in the complexion. According to the doctrine of the five phases, each organ sphere was externally associated with a particular coloring and a particular area of the face; particular changes in the coloration of the face made it supposedly possible to draw conclusions about morbid changes within the body.
>
> A doctor who did not have the ability to make a diagnosis on the first inspection could draw his conclusions from listening and smelling. Each organ sphere was associated with a particular smell and particular quality of voice; the healer could determine where the evil was located in the body from particular body odors and mouth smells as well as from crying, weeping, or other sounds emitted by the patient.
>
> If this method failed to identify the underlying disease, the doctor could also resort to inquiry. He could ask about the dietary habits, ability to sleep, digestion, pain in the body, and many other factors in order to form a picture of the condition resulting from disease within the body. Only when the hints gleaned by these methods provided no conclusive diagnosis could the doctor then resort to the fourth diagnostic method, pulse-taking.

disease of the kidneys 腎; if heavy 沈重 and slow 遲緩; this is a mark of the disease of the spleen 脾. The details are as explained by specialists in healing the body.

If the physical body is suffering and heavy, stiff 堅結 with many aches and pains, withered and numb 枯痺 and feeble 痿瘠, these are marks of disease of the element of earth. If swollen 虛腫 and bloated 脹脖, these are marks of the disease of the element of water. If the whole body is feverish 洪熱 and the bone joints have hardened 酸楚 so that breathing has become labored 頓乏, these are marks of disease of the element of fire. If the mind becomes anxious 懸 or suddenly ecstatic 忽悅, or anguished 懊悶 and forgetful 忘失, these are marks of disease of the element of wind.

Again, if the face has no shine 光澤 and the hands and feet are [dry] without sweat, these are marks of disease of the liver. If the face is pale and swollen 青肥 these are marks of disease of the heart. If the face is yellowish-black, these are marks of disease of the lung. If the body is listless and lacking in energy 無氣力, these are marks of disease of the kidney. If the body is astringent like barley bran, these are marks of disease of the spleen.

[The liver] If there is some white matter on top of the liver, this will cause a reddishness in the pupils of the eye, the pulse will be extended 脈曼 and you will suffer from leukoma 白翳, or the pupils will burst, or there will be boils above and below [the eyes], or tears will flow when [the eyes are] struck by the wind, or there will be itching or a sharp pain, or the pupils will sink in, so that when you come in contact with something you become angry. These are diseases that arise when the lung is harmed by the liver. **[106c]** They should be healed by using the *chi*-energy of rebuke 呵氣.

[The heart] If the heart is inflamed, and the hands and feet in contrast are cool, and the heart is in agony and weak, the lips and mouth dry and chapped, and below the navel there is an obstruction of the bowels 結癥 so that you cannot eat hot food, yet you feel an aversion to cold food, you are dizzy and distressed 眩懊 and like to sleep, you become forgetful and the heart is swollen 瘇, the head gets dizzy 眩, the mouth stutters, the shoulder-blades become stiff, the four limbs often ache, the heart is fatigued and the body inflamed, you are suffering from malaria 瘧, or have an obstruction of the bowels 癥結, or incontinent bladder 水僻[癖], or eyes with cataracts or nearsighted; these are caused by the kidney harming the heart, and should be healed through breathing [exercises].

If the lungs swell and the chest is constricted, there is pain in both

Specialists in healing the body 體治家: it is not clear who this refers to, whether to specific specialists or just in general.

Nearsighted 見近不見遠: lit. "see near but not far"; a rare case where the English is more concise than the original Chinese.

underarms, the shoulder blades hurt as if carrying a heavy weight, the head and nape of the neck feel pinched 急, the breath 氣 is gasping and labored so that you can exhale but not inhale, sores appear all over the body, the throat itches as if [infested by] insects or worms but unable to cough them out, sores appear in the throat and the jaw is affected, or sneezing bloody mucus from out of the nose, the eyes are dark and the nostrils painful, there are meaty growths in the nose so that the air (*chi* 氣) cannot pass through and you cannot distinguish between good scents and bad smells; these are caused by the heart harming the lung, and you should drink cold water and eat hot food. Coming in contact with these marks causes disease, and these should be healed through the use of slow breathing *chi*-energy 嘘氣.

If the hundred pulses 百脈 are not flowing and the joints are painful, the body is swollen, the ears deaf, the nose obstructed, the lower back in pain, the back stretched, the heart and belly swollen, the upper air 上氣 in the chest obstructed, the four limbs heavy, the face black and thin, the bladder in acute pain and agony, the urinary tract either just dripping or not working, the feet and knees feeling cold; these are caused by the spleen harming the kidney. Again, the demon of this disease is like the lord of the hearth 竈君; without a head or a face, appearing suddenly and covering people 掩人. These should be healed through the use of "bright" breathing *chi*-energy 熙氣.

If on the body and on the face there are measle-like 風痒 spots appearing here and there so that the whole body itches agonizingly, these are caused by the kidney harming the spleen. If the color [of the face or the body] is [yellow] like a basket or a bucket, or you feel like a small child pounding on his crib 擊櫪, or like a tornado churning things around 欒轉, these [symptoms] should be healed through the use of "poetic" breathing *chi*-energy 嗜氣.

Again, [1] if you are sorely confused, this means that there is no soul 無魂 in the liver. [2] If you are frequently forgetful of what is before or after, this means that there is no spirit 無神 in the heart. [3] If you are full of fear and the afflicted with dementia 癲病, this means that there is no soul 無魄 in the lungs. [4] If you vacillate between sadness and laughter, this means that there is no will 無志 in the kidneys. [5] If you are tossed around and perplexed by delusions, this means that there is no ambition 無意 in the spleen. [6] If there is much despair and discontent 悵怏, this means that there is no vitality 無精 in the body and mind 陰. These are called the six psychological marks of disease 六神病相.

Jaw is affected 牙關強: the meaning is ambiguous; lit. "mandibular joint is strong." Ikeda (*Gendaigoyaku*, 532) paraphrases this as "the gums and joints become painful."

Color is [yellow] like a basket or a bucket 籠桶: the *Kōgi* (BT–V, 82) identifies the color as "yellow" 黄.

2. The Causes and Conditions that Give Rise to Disease [106c23]

Second is the clarification of the causes and conditions that give rise to disease. There are six [categories]: [1] disease caused by an imbalance of the four elements; [2] disease caused by intemperance in drinking and eating; [3] disease caused by unregulated sitting in meditation; [4] [disease] caused by demons and spirits; [5] [disease caused by [the evil demonic activity of] Māra; and [6] disease caused by [the results of] karmic activity.

1. Disease Caused by an Imbalance of the Four Elements [106c26]

[Disease cause by] an imbalance of the four elements refers to when your practices are irregular, you have taken on too strong a burden, and do not take care for cold or heat. Outer heat assists [the element of] fire; if [the element of] fire becomes strong, water is destroyed; an increase in this leads to diseases of fire. Outer cold assists [the element of] water, and an increase in water harms fire; this leads to diseases of water. Outer wind assists air/*chi*; air blows [out] fire and fire moves water, which leads to diseases of wind/air. Or three elements [of fire, water, and wind] harm [the element of] earth; this is called **[107a]** diseases equal [to all the elements]. Or if the body increases and harms the three elements, these are also diseases equal [to all the elements], but belong to the diseases of the earth. In this way the four [elements] are in motion and through this competitiveness give rise to various sufferings.

Six categories 一四大不順故病二飲食不節故病三坐禪不調故病四鬼神得便五魔所爲六業起故病: this list is quoted by Paul Unschuld in the chapter on Buddhism in his authoritative *Medicine in China: A History of Ideas*, 1985 (2010). Although not naming Chih-i or the *Mo-ho chih-kuan*, and relying on an essay in the *Hōbōgirin* 1929, he identifies this list as one that combined and summarized previous developments in Chinese medicine, especially among the Buddhists. This analysis by Chih-i shows his talent for synthesizing vast amounts of teachings and ideas, Unschuld (2010, 143) writes:

> Toward the end of the sixth century, one author [that is, Chih-i] combined these [Buddhist ideas] and other concepts into a six-part etiology, which differentiated among:
>
> 1. illnesses caused by disharmony among the four elements;
> 2. illnesses caused by imbalanced nutrition;
> 3. illnessess caused by excessive meditation;
> 4. illnessses caused by demons;
> 5. illnesses brought about by evil gods (Mara);
> 6. illnessses caused by improper conduct during a previous existence.
>
> Accordingly, there were various types of appropriate therapy. These were, for illnesses from categories one and two: medicinal and dietetic measures; for illnesses from category three: an improvement of ascetic and meditative routine, as well as close regulation of breathing; for illnesses from categories four and five: amulets, incantations, introspection; and for illnesses from category six: introspection, confession, contrition, and penitence.

2. Disease Caused by Intemperance in Drinking and Eating [107a2]

Second, intemperance in drinking and eating can also cause disease. Ginger, cinnamon, and other spicy foods cause an increase in [the element of] fire. Sweets like sugar and honey are cool and cause an increase in [the element of] water. Pears cause an increase in wind, greasy fat causes an increase in earth, and cucumbers lead to feverish diseases. Since these are [diseases brought about by] foods with an unstable taste, those who eat them should [be careful to] make distinctions concerning their nature. If you eat them, after they are eaten they enter your stomach and are digested, the crude [materials] become feces and urine, and the fine [materials] are digested, and from the

The crude become feces and urine … become meat 麁者為糞尿細者融鎖。從腰三孔溜入四支。清變為血潤澤一身。如塵得水。若身血不充枯癖焦減。濁者變為脂膏。故諸根滅而成垢。新諸根凝而成肉: a summary of a long passage on the impurity of, and revulsion toward, food from the *Ta chih tu lun*, T 25.231b15–29. See Lamotte, *Le Traité* 3, 1453–54; Chodron (3, 1191–92) translates:

> When one notices that food arises from disgusting causes and conditions *(aśubhahetupratyaya)*, this is the notion of revulsion toward food *(āhāre pratikūlasaṃjñā)*.
>
> Thus, meat *(māṃsa)* comes from sperm *(bīja)*, blood *(śoṇita)*, and urine *(mūtra)*; it is the seat of pus *(pūya)* and worms *(kṛmi)*. Ghee *(ghṛta)*, milk *(kṣīra)*, and curdled milk *(dadhi)*, products of a transformation of blood, are nothing but rottenness.
>
> The cook also adds to it his sweat and all kinds of dirt. When food is put into the mouth, the throat *(mastaka)* secretes disgusting saliva *(siṅghāṇaka)* that runs down from two channels, joins with the mucus *(kheṭa)* and then produces flavor *(rasa)*. The food is thus formed like vomit *(udara)* where it is solidified by the earth [element] *(pṛthivī)*, moistened by the water *(ap)*, stirred by the wind *(vāyu)* and cooked by the fire *(tejas)*. In the same way, when boiled rice *(yavāgū)* is cooked in a pot *(sthālī)*, the dirt sinks to the bottom and the clean part stays at the surface. By means of a process similar to wine-brewing, the impurities are changed into excrement *(viṣ)* and the cleanliness into urine *(mūtra)*.
>
> The kidneys have three orifices. By means of the [internal] wind, the fatty juice spreads throughout the hundred veins *(asirā)*, joins with the blood, coagulates and is changed into flesh *(māṃsa)*. From this new flesh arise fat *(meda)*, bone *(asthi)* and marrow *(majjam)*.
>
> From that comes the organ of touch *(kāyendriya)*. From the union of the recent flesh and the new flesh arise the five sense organs *(pañcendriya)*. From the five sense organs arise the five consciousnesses *(pañcavijñāna)*. From the five consciousnesses arises the mental consciousness *(manovijñāna)* which analyzes and grasps characteristics *(nimittāny udgṛhṇāti)* and distinguishes the beautiful from the ugly.
>
> Next there arise the ideas of "me" *(ātman)* and "mine" *(ātmīya)*, negative emotions *(kleśa)* and bad actions *(nigha)*.
>
> This is how the yogin meditates on food, the first and last causes of which involve many impurities *(aśubha)*. He knows that his internal *(ādhyātmika)* four great elements *(mahābhūta)* are not different from the external *(bāhya)* four great elements, and it is only from the wrong view of the self *(ātmadṛṣṭi)* that the existence of the "I" is created.

three orifices at the waist they drip into the four limbs. The pure [materials] change into blood and enrich the whole body, like dust when it is watered. If the body does not have enough blood, it withers and loses weight. The turbid [materials] change into oily fats, the old roots decrease and become dirt, and the new roots coagulate and become meat.

Again, if the fire in the body is in the lower part, it [promotes] digestion by the organs, so that food and drink is digested and distributed throughout the body. A worldly proverb says, "If you wish to attain long life, you should heat your feet and cool your neck." If the fire of the body is in the upper regions and you eat food that is unsettling to the body, you will be troubled by disease.

Next, if you eat of the five flavors 五味 [of acidic 酸, bitter 苦, spicy 辛, salty 鹹, and sweet 甜], your organs will increase or take a loss accordingly. Acidic flavors cause an increase in the liver and a loss in the spleen. Bitter flavors cause an increase in the heart and a loss in the lungs. Spicy flavors cause an increase in the lungs and a loss in the liver. Salty flavors cause an increase in the kidneys and a loss in the heart. Sweet flavors cause an increase in the spleen and a loss in the kidneys. If you know about the hindrances to the five organs, you will avoid those that are harmful [and cause a loss], and consume those that are healthy [and cause an increase], and act appropriately to the situation.

3. Disease Caused by Unregulated Sitting in Meditation [107a16]

Third is [disease caused by] unregulated sitting in meditation 坐禪, for example, relying [inappropriately] on a wall or a pillar or clothing, or lying down when the multitude of people have not yet left [and are still practicing meditation]. This reveals an arrogant and lazy mind, which Māra can take advantage of so that the human body, [especially] the back and the joints, will suffer pain. This is called a disease of [the inability to control] the "flow" [of the mind], which is most difficult to heal.

1. The Eight Tactile Sensations and Counting Breaths [107a19]

Next is unregulated counting of breaths, which often leads people to [suffer from] chronic malarial fever 痁癖 and contraction of the tendons 筋脈攣縮.

Three orifices at the waist 腰三孔: The *Kōgi* (BT–V, 85) adds, "This is difficult to understand and should be rethought," perhaps because it is not clear what these "three orifices" are? Perhaps it refers to the three orifices of the kidney, as in the *Ta chih tu lun* passage just quoted.

A worldly proverb 世諺云欲得老壽當溫足露首: this is not identified in the classical commentaries.

If the eight tactile sensations 八觸 [of heavy 重, light 輕, cold 冷, hot 熱, rough 澁, smooth 滑, soft 軟, and coarse 麁] are aroused, and your breathing is inappropriate to the tactile sensations, this can cause disease. The eight tactile sensations are [as follows]: the mind and the four elements merge to form the four proper physical tactile sensations 四正體觸 and also the four dependent tactile sensations 四依觸; together these are the eight tactile sensations. "Heavy" is like sinking down. "Light" is like rising up. "Cold" is like being in an ice house. "Hot" is like in an oven. "Rough" is like resisting ["pulling against"] 挽逆 [the natural flow of things]. "Smooth" is like grinding fat 磨脂. "Soft" is like being boneless 無骨. "Coarse" is like husky flesh 糠肌. Of these eight tactile sensations, four go upward and four go downward. [That is,] breathing in in accordance with the element of earth is "heavy." Breathing out in accordance with the element of wind is "light." Again, breathing in in accordance with the element of water is "cold." Breathing out in accordance with the element of fire is "hot." Again, breathing in in accordance with the element of earth is "rough." Breathing out in accordance with the element of wind is "smooth." Again, breathing in in accordance with the element of water is "soft." Breathing out in accordance with the element of fire is "coarse." If [for example] the tactile sensation of "heavy" arises, and you count the breaths as you exhale but they are not in alignment with the tactile sensations, this will cause disease to arise. The other combinations should be known in the same way.

2. Cessation [107a29]

Again, if you use only [the methods of] cessation 止 [for meditation] without other means, this will cause disease. **[107b]** If you constantly stop 止 your thoughts in the lower [regions], often diseases of earth will be aroused. If you constantly stop your thoughts in the upper [regions], often diseases of wind will be aroused. If you constantly stop your thoughts too quickly, often diseases of fire will be aroused. If you constantly stop your thoughts too slowly, often the diseases of water will be aroused.

3. Contemplation [107b3]

Next, if the use of contemplation is unregulated and one-sided, this can cause disease. When one is first entrusted to the womb [as a fetus], conceptions and thoughts arise and [the fetus] is moved and calls out to its mother, and the mother thinks of the five [sensations] of color, sound, smell, taste, and touch. A trifle of *chi*-energy 一毫氣 is activated and becomes water, water becomes blood, blood becomes flesh, and flesh becomes the five sense organs and the five [internal] organs. Now, a person who sits in meditation

who does too much conceptualizing during contemplation damages the five organs and arouses disease. If there are many conditions of "color," the liver is affected. If there are many conditions of "sound," the kidneys are affected. If there are many conditions of "smell," the lungs are affected. If there are many conditions of "taste," the heart is affected. If there are many conditions of "touch," the spleen is affected.

Again, next for the eye, if there are many conditions of blue-green, this affects the liver. If there are many conditions of red, this affects the heart. If there are many conditions of white, this affects the lungs. If there are many conditions of black, this affects the kidneys. If there are many conditions of yellow, this affects the spleen.

For the ear, if there are many conditions of calling out 呼喚, this affects the liver. If there are many conditions of verbiage, this affects the heart. If there are many conditions of crying out 哭, this affects the lungs. If there are many conditions of muttering 吟, this affects the kidneys. If there are many conditions of singing, this affects the spleen.

For the nose, if there are many conditions of rancid smells 臊, this affects the liver. If there are many conditions of scorched smells 焦, this affects the heart. If there are many conditions of fishy smells 腥, this affects the lungs. If there are many conditions of stinky smells 臭, this affects the kidneys. If there are many conditions of fragrant smells 香, this affects the spleen.

For the tongue, if there are many conditions of sour tastes 醋, this affects the liver. If there are many conditions of bitter tastes 苦, this affects the heart. If there are many conditions of spicy tastes 辛, this affects the lungs. If there are many conditions of salty tastes 鹹, this affects the kidneys. If there are many conditions of sweet tastes 甜, this affects the spleen.

For the body, if there are many conditions of hardness, this affects the liver. If there are many conditions of warmth, this affects the heart. If there are many conditions of lightness, this affects the lungs. If there are many conditions of coldness, this affects the kidneys. If there are many conditions of heaviness, this affects the spleen.

In this way the five organs arise mutually, and if conditions are excessive [and imbalanced], this gives rise to disease.

If these interact adversely [it will be as follows]: If there are many condi-

For the eye … 復次眼緣青多動肝: various connections between the senses and the organs and how they affect your health, such as Chih-i lists here, are outlined in the classic *Inner Canon of the Yellow Emperor*. See the *Huang-ti nei-ching su-wen* 黃帝內經素問, compiled between the second century BC and the eighth century AD. Paul UNSCHULD provides a partial translation of this text in his *Medicine in China* (2010, 273–96), a detailed study in UNSCHULD 2003, and a complete, annotated translation in UNSCHULD 2011.

tions of white color, this subdues the liver. If there are many conditions of black, this subdues the heart. If there are many conditions of red, this subdues the lungs. If there are many conditions of yellow, this subdues the kidneys. If there are many conditions of blue-green, this subdues the spleen. The other items such as sound and so forth should be known as explained above.

If the diseases of the five organs are hidden and difficult to know, they can be prognosticated through sitting in meditation and dreams. If during meditation or in a dream there are many sights of the color blue-green, or [pale] blue-green people, or beasts like lions, tigers, or wolves, and you are filled with fear, these are diseases of the liver. If during meditation or in a dream there are many sights of the color red, fire burning, red people or beasts, red [bloody] battles with swords, red [sexual scenes of] young men and women embracing intimately, or of father, mother, brothers and so forth giving rise to joy or fear; these are diseases of the heart. The other items can be known in accordance with the various colors [and so forth].

Again, an imbalance in contemplation can affect the four elements. If the objects of contemplation are unsettled, with these conditions or those conditions so that the mind is quarrelsome, and because of this conflict a wild wind arises, resulting in diseases of wind. In such cases you should take a walk with steps like a little child, and let it be. If you rush and try to solve it quickly, you will become sick.

Again, if you focus solely on one object and arouse a hopeful mind, but the winds of retribution and powerful heat [of passionate afflictions] are not extinguished, the result is diseases of heat.

[107c] When you are contemplating objects and thoughts are arising but you think they are perishing, or when they are perishing you think they are arising, so that your thoughts and the marks [of disease] are in opposition, this leads to painful itching and results in diseases of earth.

Again, if you cannot "taste" the objects of your contemplation but you force yourself [to continue anyway], the element of water will increase and result in diseases of water. [And so forth …]

4. Disease Caused by Demons and Spirits [107c3]

Fourth, diseases [caused by] demons 鬼 [are as follows]: The four elements and five [internal] organs are not demons, and demons are not the four

Five organs arise mutually … 此乃五藏相生 …: The *Kōgi* (BT–V, 89) gives a detailed chart outlining the relationships between all of these fivefold categories: five voices, five sounds, five emotions, five colors, five flavors, five smells, five tactile sensations, five senses, five elements/phases, five organs, and so forth, some of which may be developments and analyses that postdate that of Chih-i.

elements and five organs. If they enter the four elements and five organs, this is called the diseases [caused by] demons. You may say that there are no diseases caused by demons, but there are times when evil shamans 邪巫 succeed in controlling demons. You may say that there are no diseases caused by [disharmony among] the four elements, but there are times when medical specialists succeed in healing them with liquid medicine. There was once a ruler of a country who suffered from a disease of demons that dwelt in his orifices, and repeatedly used needles [through acupuncture] to kill them. The king of demons himself came and dwelt above his heart, so that the acupuncturist had to submit [and could not continue treatment]. Therefore it should be known that diseases caused by demons do exist [and therefore exorcistic methods may sometimes be required]. But demons are not rampant in making people diseased. Rather it is because people arouse perverse thoughts with regard to various matters, or seek to know about sorcery [concerning good and bad fortune] 吉凶. The demon Tu xi luo [*Hidda] causes many changes, so that if colors such as blue-green and yellow enter the body from the five sense organs, the consciousness will make mistaken interpretations about good and bad fortune 吉凶, or matters of good or bad fortune of one body, or one family, or one village, or one country. These are not to be considered "noble knowledge." If these [diseases] are not healed and continue for a long time, it will kill the person.

5. Disease Caused by Māra [107c13]

Fifth is diseases caused by Māra. These are different from those [caused by] demons. Demons merely [cause] diseases of the body; Māra destroys the contemplative mind, destroys the wisdom-as-life 慧命 of the Dharma body, arouses deviant thoughts, and robs people of their virtues, so this is different from [the effects of] demons. Again, depending those who are practicing sitting in meditation, if they have evil thoughts of personal profit Māra will appear [and offer] various clothing, drink and food, the seven jewels, and other material things, and people will accept them and rejoice. Thus [Māra]

A ruler of a country 有一國王: Chan-jan (BT–V, 91) points out that the phrase "ruler of a country" does not appear in variant texts, and this "ruler" remains unidentified.

The demon Tu xi luo 兜醯羅鬼: transliteration of "Hidda"? Chan-jan (BT–V 92) identifies this demon as a five-colored demon who causes the diseases of the five organs that have just been listed above.

Diseases caused by Māra 魔病: in Buddhist tradition, Māra is the evil one, the tempter, the personification of evil desires and passions and the temptations of this world, and demonic forces that hinder contemplation.

enters the mind and causes disease. These diseases are difficult to heal; below I will explain the way of healing [these matters].

6. Disease Caused by Karmic Activity [107c18]

Sixth is disease caused by karmic activity [in the past]. Sometimes it is only the karmic activity from previous lives, or sometimes it is from breaking the precepts in your current life which affects the karma from previous lives, and this karmic power causes disease. You should know about these offences [that cause bad karmic effects] in terms of the five sense organs.

If you commit the karmic action of the offence of taking life, this [leads to] diseases of the liver and the eyes. The karmic actions of the offence of drinking intoxicating beverages [leads to] diseases of the heart and mouth. Karmic actions of the offences of illicit lust [lead to] diseases of the kidneys and ears. Karmic actions of offences of deluded speech [lead to] diseases of the spleen and tongue. Karmic actions of the offences of stealing [lead to] diseases of the lungs and nose. Karmic actions of breaking all [of these] five precepts arouse diseases of the five [internal] organs and the five sense organs, and if these karmic actions decline, [their effects] will go away.

If in your current life you keep the precepts, this can also affect the karma and cause disease. Therefore it is said that [there are cases where] if you have committed a grave offence, a headache may remove it, and grave offences for which you should fall into hell may be lightly recompensed 輕償 during your lifetime as a human being. These are karmic actions that you wish would disappear, but cause disease. There are many types of diseases caused by karmic action: tumors 腫, congestion 滿, jaundice 黄, and depletion 虛. Any and all manner of diseases should be minutely and closely examined. Knowing the root causes of diseases can later lead to healing them.

3. Clarification of the Methods for Healing Disease [107c27]

Third is clarifying the methods [for healing disease]. These should be appropriate [to the situation] and are not the same [for everyone]. If your work or your eating and drinking leads to sickness, this should be treated with medicine, and with regulated care this [disease] will end. If your sitting in meditation is unregulated and this leads to sickness, this should **[108a]** in

Below I should explain: for details, see section 7.5 of the *Mo-ho chih-kuan* on "Contemplation of the Objects of Demonic Forces," 114c22–117a20.

Therefore it is said: the source of this phrase or idea is unknown.

Karmic actions that you wish would disappear, but cause disease 業欲謝故病: or, "These are karmic actions for which one desires to repent and therefore becomes ill [in the process of eradicating karma]."

turn require further sitting in meditation. Well regulated contemplation of breaths should make this [sickness] end. Liquid medicine is not appropriate in this case. As for the two types of diseases caused by demons and Māra, these should be treated with the power of the practice of deep contemplation and the use of great spells 大神呪, and you can make them end. As for diseases caused by karma, you should internally use the power of contemplation, and externally make confession and repentance, and these will come to an end. All of these [methods of] healing are not the same [for everyone and every situation], and you should be aware of this meaning. You should not take up a knife or wield a blade and thus hurt yourself.

Now, in terms of sitting in meditation, in sum there are six [ways of] healing [disease]: [1] cessation 止, [2] *chi*-energy 氣, [3] breathing 息, [4] conventional conceptualization 假想, [5] contemplation of the mind 觀心, and [6] divination techniques 方術.

1. Using Cessation [108a7]

[First,] using [the practice of] cessation to heal [disease]: Master Wen says, "Link your mind [and concentrate] on your navel as if it were a large bean, unfasten your robe and clearly apprehend your situation, then close your eyes and arrange your mouth and teeth, lift your tongue toward the palate, and regulate and calm your breathing (*chi*). If your mind runs wild and wanders to external matters, contain it and make it return. If your thoughts become imperceptible, rearrange your robe and look at [your navel to regain your concentration] and carefully apprehend your situation, and repeat as before." This [practice] is able to heal various diseases, and also is able to arouse various dhyāna concentrations. When this contemplation is performed, it has immeasurable characteristics. At times there is pain like the piercing of needles; or acuteness like being pulled with ropes; or itching like being bit by bugs; or cold like being doused with water; or hot like being broiled with fire. In this way, when various tactile sensations arise, diligently continue [your practice] singlemindedly, without retreating or giving up. If you can be free of these tactile sensations, you will be able to arouse various dhyāna concentrations; if your psychological condition 神意 is quiescent, this is the mark of lightning-like concentration. Through this you are able to attain dhyānic concentrations; how can you not heal diseases?

Not take up a knife: could this be a pre-modern warning against the use of unnecessary surgery, or merely an injunction against suicide?

Master Wen 温師: the identity of this Master is not known. Chih-i quotes him also in his "Questions on Dhyāna" 天台智者大師禪門口訣. T no. 581, 46.581b13ff.

Bit by bugs 蟲嚙: or perhaps "eaten by worms."

The reason you "link the mind to the navel" is that [in meditation] the breath goes out through the navel and then enters from the navel, and the going out and coming in [of the *chi*-breath] is limited to the navel, which makes it easy to realize [the truth of] transiency.

Again, when you are entrusted to the womb [as a fetus] and your conscious spirit 識神 first coalesces with blood, the navel cord forms a connection, and the link [to the mother] is through the navel. Again, this [navel] is the source of the stomach and intestines, so if you investigate the source you are able to perceive the impurity [of the physical body] and are able to stop covetous desires. In terms of the four mindfulnesses, contemplating the navel is the "mindfulness of [the impurity of] the body." In terms of the "six subtle gates," [concentrating on] the navel is the gate of cessation. Both of these [practices] enable you to enter the path, and are therefore used often.

A proper use [of these practices] for healing disease [also involves] the "cinnabar field," which is a sea of *chi*-energy, able to lock up and contain all diseases. If you "stop" [and focus] the mind on the cinnabar field, your *chi*/breathing is regulated and calm, and thus you will be able to heal disease. This is the meaning here.

Again, a certain master said, "An excess of upper *chi*-energy; congestion in the chest; pain on both flanks [of the body]; pressure on the spine and back; pain in the shoulders; vexing heat in the heart; troublesome pain that cause loss of appetite; swelling of the heart; chill in the lower abdomen [below the navel]; heat in the upper and cold in the lower [parts of the body]; a disharmony of yin and yang; coughing: these twelve types of disease should all be dealt with by focusing on the cinnabar field." The "cinnabar field" is two-and-a-half inches below the navel. Or, if the pain is acute, shift your attention to face the three *li* [below the navel]. If the pain is not removed, shift to face the [acupuncture] point at the side of the nails on the big toes of both feet, and try to put an end to it.

A certain master: the identity of this person is unknown.

Cinnabar field 丹田: also translated as "elixer field": these are important focal points (or "dantian") throughout the body for internal meditative techniques. In Chinese medicine and also martial arts, the navel area is particularly important as the focal point for breathing techniques. In Buddhist meditation, focusing on the navel, or the "cinnabar field" in the lower abdominal area (or, "two-and-a-half inches below the navel"), helps to control thoughts and emotions and is an important step to attaining samādhi. See Chih-i's explanation that follows.

Three *li* 三里: the *Shiki* (BT–V, 97) points out that this refers to the area about two-and-a-half or three inches below the navel.

The [acupuncture] point at the side of the nails 大拇指爪横文上: the exact meaning of the text here is not clear, as 文 means "script" or perhaps "vein," but may refer to

If you have a headache and your eyes itch and are red, your lips and mouth are hot, [**108b**] spores 胞子 form around the nose, there are sudden pains in the abdomen, both ears become deaf, and the neck is tight 強: for these six diseases, you should make the area between your legs the object of your focus and link your thoughts to it. When suddenly you suffer acute pain from abdominal dropsy 水腹, just singlemindedly focus on this area. If the mind is troubled you should take short breaths, and if possible arise and repeat the previous practices. If you experience a little relief, you should continue to use these methods for healing. If these [practices] cause acute pain in the waist and/or legs, imagine and conceive of a ten-foot chasm below your feet and shift the focus of your attention to the bottom of this pit, and focus your thoughts primarily on this until [the pain] naturally comes to an end. This must be done in a quiet room.

Again, by constantly stopping [and focusing] 止 your thoughts on your feet, you are able to heal all manners of disease. Why is this so? The five consciousnesses [of sight, sound, scent, taste, and touch] are in the head, and the mind thus often has connections with this upper region, so the mind follows [the element of] wind, wind affects fire, fire melts water, and water moistens the body. Therefore even if the upper region is regulated, if the lower regions are disturbed this will lead to various diseases, such as chronic swelling of the legs and feet, and so forth. Again, the five [internal] organs are like lotus blossoms that bloom extravagantly but face downward, but since consciousness usually has connections to the upper region, if the *chi*-energy is strong in pressing against the bowels, this can in turn be destructive and cause disease. If the mind has connections to the lower region, fire will blow and slide to the lower region, drink and food will be digested [properly], and the five organs will be in balance. Stopping and focusing on the feet is thus the best for healing disease. So now if you constantly and repeatedly use [this method], there will be profound benefit. Through this you can heal others, as has already been tested [and proven] many times over. Chiang, Wu, and Mou are examples of such people [who have verified these medical methods].

an acupuncture point. Another possible reading is "horizontal patterns on the toenails" or the lateral markings at the base of the nail. In any case, the place to which one should focus attention—the nails of the big toes—is clear.

Chiang, Wu, and Mou 蒋呉毛: Chiang T'ien-wen/Jiang Tianwen 蒋添文, Wu Ming-che/Wu Ming-che 呉明徹 (512–578; [Ikeda has 523–589?]), and Mou Hsi/Mouxi 毛喜 (516–587): three historical military figures in Chih-i's time. For details on these three men see Ikeda, *Kokusei hyakuroku no kenkyū*, chart on pp. 43–45.

These three figures also appear in Chih-i's *Biography* (T 50.192c, 197b, and 197c), and in the *Hundred Records of the Kuo-ch'ing Temple*, T 46.807c12–808a3.

Again, if in accordance with the place of the disease you clarify the mind and stop and focus on this [place]; before three days have passed, surely conditions will have improved, and you can put an end [to the disease]. Why is this so? As the wind will blow through when a gate is opened, or be still when a fan is closed, the mind responds to the conditions of external objects, like the opening of a gate, and if the mind stops and focuses on the place where there is pain, this is like the closing of a fan. This is just the way things naturally are 理數然. Again, the mind is like a king, and diseases are like bandits; if the mind is calm, the bandits will disperse and be destroyed.

Again, you do not necessarily and exclusively stop and focus the mind on the [physical] place which is diseased. The *Secret Methods of the Emperor* says, "The two *chi*-energies from heaven and earth merge, and each has the five phases, [thus producing] metal, wood, water, fire, and earth. These circulate and thus metal is transformed and water arises, water flows and wood grows, wood moves and fire is lit, fire burns and earth is chaste; thus do they mutually arise. Fire meeting water means an extinction of light; water meeting earth becomes immobile; earth planting wood produces tumors; wood meeting metal brings about wounds; thus do they interact adversely." As metal overcomes wood, if the lungs are strong and the liver weak, you should stop and focus the mind on the lungs and gather white *chi*-energy, and the disease of the liver will end. The other four organs should be understood in the same way.

Again, using "stopping" to heal [the diseases of] the four elements [is as follows]: a quick stopping heals [the diseases of] water; slowly stopping heals [the diseases of] fire, stopping [and focusing] on the head heals [the diseases of] earth; stopping [and focusing] on the feet heals [the diseases of] wind; [and so forth].

2. Using *Chi*-Energy [108b27]

Second is using *chi*-energy to heal [diseases], that is, [the six *chi*-energy breaths of] sharp exhaling 吹 (*chui*), exhaling softly 呼 (*hu*), "bright" 熙

***Secret Methods of the Emperor* says, "The two *chi*-energies ..."** 如皇帝祕法云。天地二氣交合各有五行。金木水火土如循環。故金化而水生。水流而木榮。木動而火明。火炎而土貞。此則相生。火得水而滅光。水遇土而不行。土值木而腫瘡。木遭金而折傷。此則相剋也: the *Kōgi* (BT–V, 98) identifies this as a quote from the "Classic of Difficult Issues in the *Su-wen*" 素問難経, a commentary on the *Huang-ti nei-ching su-wen* 黄帝内經素問, and the related "Eighty-one questions of the Yellow Emperor" 黄帝八十一難 compiled in the mid- to late Han (239 A.D.). For details, see UNSCHULD 1986 on *Nan-Ching: The Classic of Difficult Issues*.

Six *chi*-energies: this list appears to be a combination of reliance on traditional indigenous lists of "six breaths," with some

(*xi*), rebuking 呵 (*he*), sighing 嘘 (*xu*), and "poetic" 呬 (*shi*). All of these are formed by the lips and mouth, converted by the teeth and tongue, and carefully applied in the mind and conceptualized, thus producing *chi*-energy [breaths]. When cold use "sharp exhaling," as in exhaling [**108c**] fire. When hot use "exhaling softly." When the hundred joints itch and are painful, use "bright" [*chi*] and heal [the diseases of] wind. If there is troublesome swelling and the upper air/*chi* 上氣 [in the chest is obstructed], use "rebuking." If too much mucus, use "sighing." If exhausted, use "poetic"[*chi*].

The six *chi*-energies for healing [diseases of] the five [internal] organs are: "rebuking" heals the liver, "exhaling softly" and "sharp exhaling" heals the heart, "sighing" heals the lungs, "bright" heals the kidneys, "poetic" heals the spleen. Again, the six *chi*-energies together heal one organ. If the organ is cold, use "sharp exhaling." If hot, use "exhaling softly" If painful, use "bright." If troubled by swelling, use "rebuking." If there is mucus, use "sighing." If

significant variations perhaps introduced by Chih-i himself or from the Buddhist tradition. See Catherine Despeux's essay on "The Six Healing Breaths" (2006), especially p. 40:

> The technique of the six breaths follows the ancient vision of "blowing out the old and drawing in the new," i.e., it proposes inhalation through the nose and exhalation through the mouth. Each breath is associated with a particular character, defined in some detail in ancient dictionaries, notably the *Shuowen jiezi zhu* 說文解字注 (Annotated Character Explanation) of the Han dynasty and the *Kangxi zidian* 康熙字典 (Kangxi Dictionary) of the eighteenth century. They are:
>
> 1. Si 四 is a gentle, relaxed exhalation that lets the breath escape between slightly opened lips
> 2. He 呵 or xu 昫 is a strong breath with open mouth that is accompanied by a guttural rasping through tightening of the throat at the base of the tongue. Also described as a hot breath, it may serve to expel burning or heat.
> 3. Hu 呼, the standard term for "exhale," indicates a blowing out of breath with rounded lips.
> 4. Xu 嘘 is a gentle expulsion of breath. The mouth is wide open and the air is released from the bottom of the lungs. When placing a hand in front of the mouth, one gets a feeling of lukewarm air.
> 5. Chui 吹 indicates a sharp expulsion of air, with lips almost closed and the mouth barely open. It is a puffing out of air that creates the feeling of a cold draft.
> 6. Xi 嘻/唏 is traditionally the sound of sighing. It describes a soft exhalation with the mouth slightly open that comes deep from within the body (see Maspero 1981, 497–98).

Comparing this list with that of Chih-i, as well as the explanations and uses of these six items, reveals many commonalities, as well as many interesting differences, e.g., two of the items (1. and 6.) appear in Chih-i's list with different Chinese characters. Also, though the translation "six breaths" seems to fit the Daoist context, Chih-i uses the term 息 for "breath/breathing," and *chi* 氣 for forces and actions beyond (though including) breathing, so I use the translation "*chi*-energy," though at times the context calls for translating *chi* as "air" or "breath."

weary and lacking [energy], use "poetic." It is the same for the other four organs.

Again, by exhaling with the mouth you get rid of a chill, and [exhaling] through the nose removes internal heat. Inhale calmly and carefully so that there is no clashing [between the breaths or energies]. Once you have been seated [for meditation], repeat [this cycle of breathing] seven times, then calm your mind, and after calming your mind for a little while, again utilize the *chi*-energies. This is what it means to use [*chi*-energy] for healing [diseases]. Usually it is enough to spew out defilements [through exhaling the breath] once or twice. Inhaling through the mouth gets rid of heat; [inhaling] through the nose brings pure and cool [air] inside.

"Bright" [*chi*-energy breathing] through the mouth gets rid of pain by removing [the element of] wind, through the nose brings internal peace.

"Rebuking" [*chi*-energy breathing] through the mouth gets rid of annoyances, and *chi*-energy in the lower regions [of the body] disperses mucus. As for mucus in the chest, that in the upper regions should be spit out through the mouth, and that of the lower regions smoothed out through breathing. Therefore it is not necessary to supplement [by blowing with] the nose.

"Sighing" helps get rid of swelling, and lets in calm assurance through the nose.

"Poetic" [*chi*-energy breathing] gets rid of fatigue, and lets in harmonious supplements [of *chi*-energy] through the nose. Carefully inhale and exhale [*chi*-energy] without any in excess. If this is done with discretion, with increases and decreases appropriate to the situation, you will not only be able to heal your own diseases, but also help save others.

3. Counting the Breaths [108c15]

Third is using [counting of] the breaths to heal [disease]. The body-and-mind 色心 are mutually dependent and involve breathing, like firewood and fire rely on each other to produce smoke. By observing the purity or turgidity of the smoke, you can know the rancidness or dampness of the firewood; so by examining the strength or weakness of the breaths, you can verify the health or disease of the [human] body. If the [element of] wind blows in the body as it pleases, then pain and itching will give rise to disease; you should not take time to attend to it but should quickly heal it. First you should be conscious of your breathing as having four associations. [1] If [the breath]

Four associations 伴: see the explanation of the four kinds of breathing during meditation in the *Shorter Manual*, T 46.466a1ff:

The method for regulating your breathing when you first enter meditation: There are four types of breathing: first, [blowing like the] wind 風; second, gasp-

makes a sound, this is called [blowing like] the wind 風; if you follow this, your [thoughts] will be dispersed. [2] If [the breath is] stagnant 結滯, this is called *chi* 氣; if you follow this your [thoughts] will be obstructed. [3] If the inhaling and exhaling is not exhausted, this is called "gasping" 喘; if you follow this you will be fatigued. If [the breathing] neither makes a sound nor is stagnant, and the inhaling and exhaling are both exhausted, this is called [proper, correct] breathing; if you follow this you will attain concentration.

You should seek a quiet place, sit in the lotus position and straighten your body and be calm. Let the body relax, spread out the four limbs and stretch the bones and muscles. You should see to it that the joints are in harmony, neither leaning [unbalanced] nor bent. Loosen your belt, lean to

ing 喘; third, coarse 氣; and fourth, restful 息. The first three are the marks of unregulated [breathing]; the final one is the mark of regulated [breathing].

Seek a quiet place, sit in the lotus position and straighten your body … 當求靜處結跏平身正直 …: more concrete and easy-to-follow instructions are given in the *Shorter Manual*, T 1915, 46.462–474, with the instructions for twenty-five preparations for practicing meditation; see especially the section at 466b12–26:

> When you reach the platform [on which you sit in meditation], you should first compose the place where you sit, so that everything is calm and relaxed, and there are no distracting hindrances for a long time.
>
> Next, you should sit in a cross-legged position. If you sit in a half-lotus position, the left leg should be placed on top of the right leg and drawn close to the torso. The toes of the left foot should be aligned with the right thigh, and the toes of the right foot aligned with the left thigh. If you wish to sit in a full lotus position, then the right leg should [also] be placed on top of the left leg [after the left foot is placed on the right thigh].
>
> Next, loosen the belt of your robe and fix it properly [that is, comfortably loose, but not too loose], so that it [the robe] does not fall off while you are sitting. Then you should arrange your hands by placing the left hand palms-up on [the palm of] the right hand. Straightaway place the overlapping hands aligned with and on top of the left leg, and draw them close to the torso. The mind should be calm and relaxed.
>
> Next, you should straighten the body. First you should shake your body and limbs seven or eight times like a masseur, [to relax the body] so that there is no unbalanced strain left in [the joints of] the arms and legs. When this is done, straighten your back so that your backbone is neither curved nor bent. Next, straighten your head and neck so that your nose is aligned with your navel, neither to the side or at a slant, neither facing downward nor upward, but staying perfectly level.
>
> Next, exhale all impure air through your mouth. The way you should exhale air is as follows: open your mouth to expel air, neither too roughly or quickly, deliberately discharging the air continuously, exhaling the breath and discharging the air until you think that there is no corner of the body which is not discharged [of impure air]. Then close the mouth and inhale fresh air through the nose. Go through this process three times. If the body and breath are regulated and harmonious, one time is sufficient.

Stretch the bones and muscles 布置骨解: I follow the variant reading of 筋 instead of 解.

the side and turn [the body] to adjust it [into a comfortable position]. Place your left hand on the top [palm] of your right hand, and lightly touch the tips of the thumbs. Make your cheeks vertical, open the mouth slightly, and exhale deeply four or five times. Next, gradually straighten the head and slowly close your eyes. Do not close your eyelids with great haste, but always in darkness [as in a cage] 籠籠, and then use your breathing.

Using your breathing to heal disease through being in accordance with and in opposition to the eight tactile sensations is [as follows]. If the sensation of "heavy" is the cause and this gives rise to the great diseases of [the element] earth, mostly use the exhaling of breath to heal it. If the sensation of "lightness" is aroused and gives rise to diseases of wind, mostly use **[109a]** the inhaling of breath to heal it. If the sensation of "cold" is aroused and gives rise to diseases of water, mostly use the exhaling of breath to heal it. If the sensation of "heat" is aroused and gives rise to the diseases of fire, mostly use the inhaling of breath to heal it. The others should be understood in the same way. If you attain regulated harmony and equanimity, follow the workings of your mind to put this to use. Constantly count your breaths, and do not produce other kinds of breaths.

Next are distinctions concerning the application of twelve [types of] breathing 十二息, that is, [1] upper 上, [2] lower 下, [3] scorched 焦, [4] full 滿, [5] increasing and growing 增長, [6] decreasing and extinguishing 滅壞, [7] cold 冷, [8] hot 煖, [9] rushed 衝, [10] maintained 持, [11] harmonious 和, and [12] supplemental 補. These twelve types of breathing outline the thoughts of temporary conceptions 假想心. What does this mean? When there is the first thought [of the fetus] upon entering the womb, there are [already] the [natural, inborn] breaths from [karmic] recompense 報息. [At first the breaths are] in accordance with the *chi*-breaths 氣息 of the mother; the child gradually grows, the wind passages become smooth, the inhaling and exhaling of the child is no longer in accordance with that of the mother. It is born and becomes apart from [the mother], so that each have their own [separate] breaths. This is called "breaths from [karmic] recompense." "Dependent breathing" 依息 refers to that which relies on the mind to arise; for example, at a time of anger or desire, the breathing becomes aroused. This is called "dependent breathing." The six *chi*-energy [breathing] discussed

Always [shutting out the light] as in a cage 常使籠籠: the *Shiki* (BT–V, 103) points out that in the Chan tradition of Baizhang 百丈禪師, "the eyes should stay open to avoid falling asleep. If you attain dhyāna-concentration, this power is most supreme. From of old it has been the practice of meditation among esteemed monks to always keep their eyes open during meditation." Ikeda (*Kenkyūchūshaku*, 425) points out that keeping your eyes open during zazen meditation was a central tenet of Dōgen's instructions, and it is the most common practice in Japan today.

above are [of the type] of "breaths from [karmic] recompense" and involve conceptualization. These twelve [types of] breathing belong to "dependent breathing" and involve conceptualization, and therefore they are not the same as the previous. The previous [types of breathing] were explained in terms of the five colors and their relation to the diseases of the five [internal] organs. These depend on the organs to arouse disease, and therefore you should now use "dependent breathing" to heal them. [1] Upper breathing heals the sinking and heavy diseases of earth. [2] Lower breathing heals the empty suspended 虛懸 diseases of wind. [3] Scorched breathing heals pressure from swelling 脹滿. [4] Full breathing heals withered emaciation 枯瘠. [5] Increasing and growing breathing is able to give rise to the growth of the four elements. Non-Buddhist ways for applying *chi*-breathing merely use the application of these [kinds of] growing and increasing of *chi*-energy or breathing. [6] Decreasing and extinguishing breathing dissipates diseases of the heart membrane 癃膜. [7] Cold breathing heals fever. [8] Hot breathing heals the chills. [9] Rushed breathing heals bowel obstructions and swelling from poison 癥結腫毒. [10] Maintained breathing heals the shakes and instability 掉動不安. [11] Supplemental breathing heals whatever is lacking 虛乏. [12] Harmonious breathing blends 通融 the four elements.

When producing these [kinds of] breaths, each is accompanied by conceptual thoughts that bring them to fruition. Know the diseases in detail, using the [various types of] breathing, and do not error in their application.

4. Healing by Conventional Conceptions [109a20]

Fourth, healing [diseases] through conventional conceptions: in the previous [sections on] *chi*-energy and breathing [methods], these involved using conceptualizations, but now [I am referring to methods that] use only conventional conceptualizations, such as the "debate masters" who have methods for [getting rid of] warts, such as [acupuncturists] using needles for people suffering from sickness, such as using warm resuscitative techniques for relieving fatigue like that found in the *Āgama*s, such as the method of "swallowing snakes," and so forth.

Debate masters 辯師: or, "Master Bian"? Identity unknown. Chan-jan (BT–V, 103) mentions Korean masters who know of ways to cure warts, but this may refer just to general home-style cures known at the time? Also, could be a variant for 論師.

Found in the *Āgamas* 如阿含中: see, for example, the passage in the *Miscellaneous Āgama*, fascicle 44 (T 2.319b27–c12), which tells of using a full bowl of curd, a bottle of oil, and a bottle of honey, along with some warm water, to relieve back pain. The oil was rubbed on the Tathāgata's back, washed with warm water, and he drank the curds and honey, and the Tathāgata was relieved of his back pain.

5. Healing by Contemplation of the Mind [109a23]

Healing [disease] by contemplation does not involve [non-Buddhist] conventional conceptions nor breathing [techniques], but is a direct contemplation of the mind. Whether you seek internally or externally, the "mind" cannot be obtained, so even if disease comes, who does it afflict, and who experiences this disease? [That is, it should be contemplated that there is no "self" that experiences disease.]

6. Healing by Divination Techniques [109a25]

Sixth is healing [disease] by divination techniques. These techniques may seem far away if you do not know of them, but if you know of them they are quite close to home, such as methods for healing hiccups, methods for fixing toothaches, healing the liver by twisting the thumbs, and so forth. These techniques are shallow and common, and are often based on illusions. They should not be used by home-departed ones [of the Buddhist Sangha]. Basically they need not be studied, and if they have been studied, should be quickly rejected. If you cultivate the Four Samādhis, the physical body that is weak like a water bubble has uncertain increases and decreases. If [these divination techniques] can be borrowed and used to heal diseases [**109b**], it may make it easier to stay on the path [of practice to enlightenment], so you should not despise them. However, if they are used to invite fame or to gain profit, and thus provoke or stir up the mundane people of the times, this is a

Somehow it is comforting to know that the Buddha [as with the Christ] suffered in the same ways as us.

Swallowing snakes 如吞蛇法: see, for example, the *Secret Essential Methods for Healing Disease through Meditation* 治禪病秘要法, T 15.338b8–21:

> Next, Śāriputra, suppose those of the four assemblies enter the water samādhi and water emerges from their entire body, so that you cannot see their body or mind, like the great sea. When they emerge from samādhi they should not eat or drink sweets, or their minds will become sick and their lower regions feverish, their pulses increase, and their sickness does not stop. This disease must be healed. The method for healing is to conceptualize a bird with golden wings, with a monk riding it, flying fearless above the great sea, and the dragons *(nāga)* and demons *(rākṣasa)* are all surprised and run away. The bird can capture and eat the dragon, and therefore the dragons are fearful, so they suck up and exhaust the water. They change into four snakes. The king of the golden-winged birds holds the four snakes in its mouth. The monks on their seats seek water but do not obtain it. The king of the golden-winged birds emits fire from its eyes and burns the snakes, and the snakes are frightened.…

Hiccups 如治咽法: I follow the variant 噦, instead of 咽, "to swallow."

Four Samādhis: see Chih-i's exposition of these earlier in the *Mo-ho chih-kuan*, 11a21–20a4.

Used to invite fame or to gain profit, and thus provoke of stir up the mundane

delusion and farce of Māra and should be quickly rejected, [I repeat,] quickly rejected 急棄急棄.

When the thirty-six types of beasts surround a person, you should chant these spells three times:

bo-ti-tuo 波提陀 *pi-ye-duo* 毘耶多 *na-mo-na* 那摩那 *ji-li-bo* 吉利波 *a-wei-po* 阿違婆 *tui-mo-tuo* 推摩陀 *nan-tuo-luo* 難陀羅 *you-tuo-mo* 憂陀摩 *ji-li-mo* 吉利摩 *pi-li-bo* 毘利吉 *zhe-tuo-mo* 遮陀摩.

At first be carefully attentive, and when you come in contact with outside objects [such as the thirty-six beasts] the mind will be alarmed, and because of this *chi*-energy will increase and the stomach will feel full, the chest will be troubled, the head ache, and the heart feel oppressed. Six psychological conditions 六神 parade through the entire body, causing surprise and a loss of your guard. Externally there will be evil spirits 惡神 that enter the body and snatch away your place of abode, thus guiding you in this way. The method to heal this is to close your mouth and plug your nose and do not let your *chi*-energy or breath escape. Maintain the *chi*-energy or breath until it permeates your body, and then release the *chi*-energy or breath long and far away. Conceptualize its expulsion throughout the body, from your head to the feet. Pull until it is exhausted. Do this three times, and then chant these spells:

zhi-bo-zhou 支波晝 *wu-su-bo-zhou* 烏蘇波晝 *fu-liu-bo-zhou* 浮流波晝 *qian-qi-bo-zhou* 牽氣波晝.

After chanting these three times, then regulate the breath and from one to ten command the exhaling and inhaling of breaths, saying, "*a-na-bo-na* 阿那波那 *a-zhou-bo-zhou* 阿晝波晝," and the diseases will come to an end. If you suffer from dysentery 赤痢 or white diarrhea 白痢, sudden bad health or "apoplexy" 卒中惡, a pale face, "reversal" of the eyes, blackening of the lips, and are not able to distinguish between people, [then you should] twist the

people of the times 若用邀名射利喧動時俗: this is a very typical Vinaya attitude, warning against the use of divination for gaining fame or for commercial purposes. See, for example, the *Ten Precepts for Monks and their Deportment* 沙彌十戒法并威儀, T. 24. 927a6–10. The *Ta chih tu lun* includes divination among the "five evil livelihoods" 邪命, T 25. 203a14ff. (My thanks to Esther-Maria Guggenmos for this information.)

Thirty-six beasts 三十六獸: the animals associated with the various times of the day, with three animals for each of the twelve periods of two hours. For details, see *Mo-ho chih-kuan* 115b5ff.

Spells 誦呪: the sources and meaning of these spells is unknown.

"Reversal" of the eyes 眼反: possible renditions are Calmette's reaction; conjunctival reaction; oculoreaction, ophthalmic reaction; ophthalmoreaction; Wolff-Calmette reaction, or Wolff-Eisner reaction.

cinnabar field [under your navel] with your hand until it hurts, and surely [these diseases] will end. Again, in accordance with the place on your body that hurts, hit the diseased place with a staff in your hand until it hurts, up to forty or fifty times. What is the meaning of this? Just this: diseases are products of the mind [lit. "there is none that is not produced by the mind" 無非心作]; the mind has thoughts of depressing misery, and thus introduces perverse *chi*-energy. Now if you attack it with pain, there is no room for extraneous conceptions, so the perverse *chi*-energy will go away and the disease will be removed.

4. Clarification of Losses and Benefits [109b23]

Fourth is to clarify the losses and benefits [from healing disease]. There are gradual and sudden aspects to each of such losses and benefits. If there are great excesses taken in using breathing [to heal disease], the five [internal] organs may suddenly change. Or, even if there is not yet any change, there may be gradual dramatic [changes] that result in sudden changes. Some people may skillfully cultivate [proper practices] and immediately and suddenly attain benefits, or some may have the symptoms of a disease for a while and later gradually be healed. This is like taking hot liquid medicine 湯藥 over a period of months or years until finally benefit is attained. Internal healing [of the mind] is also like this. For people whose minds are sharp and the disease light, or the mind is sharp and the disease heavy, or the mind is dull and the disease light, or the mind dull and the disease heavy: all are the same in being gradual or sudden [in being healed].

The medicines of this [secular] world may cost a fortune and take time to prepare. Also, they may be bitter and hard to swallow, and come with a variety of prohibitions, but [**109c**] those who rely on them for their lives continue to take them until they die. But now [I present a method that] does not cost a cent, does not waste even a half-a-day of effort, is not bitter to the taste, and can be eaten and drunk as you wish. Nevertheless people do not seek to practice it, and ordinary people are not aware of its value. Perhaps its charm is too high, and few can appreciate it 韻高和寡; this causes me great distress.

If you are able to be endowed with ten characteristics, you will certainly have a good result. That is, [1] faith 信; [2] utilization 用; [3] diligence 勤; [4] constancy 恒; [5] distinctions among diseases 別病; [6] means 方便; [7] a long time 久; [8] selecting and rejecting 取捨; [9] protecting 將護; and up to [10] to know the obstacles 遮障.

[1] Faith is the basis of the Buddhist path, the first gate [for entering]

Faith is the basis of the path 信是道元: see the *Avataṃsaka Sūtra*, T 9.433a26, that "faith is the basis of the path, the mother of virtue" 信爲道元功德母.

the Buddha Dharma. It is like, in order to heal someone with leprosy you must believe that blood is milk, and revere a camel's bone as a true relic. A firm faith in these methods is able to heal these diseases, so you should not give rise to a single doubt. [2] If you believe but do not actually use [these methods], such a person will gain no benefit. It is like taking up a sharp sword but not using it against bandits; this will instead lead to harm [as the bandits respond in kind]. It is the same with not [actually] utilizing [the practices]. [3] How about the necessity for "diligence"? You should practice diligently from the beginning, middle, and late night to the morning and to the sunset in the evening, your sweat showing the degree [of your commitment]. In starting a fire, if you quit in the middle it will be difficult for you to get a fire. It is the same for not being diligent. [4] How about constancy? This means constancy in utilizing the methods for healing, making [the right] conditions with every thought, and not being moved or agitated. [5] What is "distinctions among diseases"? You should make distinctions among diseases as to the causes for their arising, as I have explained above. If you do not know about diseases and yet practice the methods of healing without restraint, since the actions do not match the purpose there will be no benefit in this. [6] What is "means"? You should skillfully utilize healing [methods], and if the inhaling and exhaling [of breaths] is proper, and the carrying on of thoughts is completed [properly], the purpose will not be lost. It is like tuning a harp with the strings adjusted loose or tight at its bridge, and lightly or heavily [strumming it] with your fingers in order to tune and balance the sound. [7] What is "a long time"? If you utilize these methods but have not yet gained any benefit, you should not be concerned with the passing of days or months but practice without resting or abandoning [the quest]. [8] What is "selecting and rejecting"? If there is benefit, you should diligently use [that successful method]; if there is loss, you should change your [methods for] healing. [9] What is "protecting"? You should have a good knowledge of the prohibitions and warnings [associated with various medicines] so that your activities and eating and drinking does not infringe against it. [10] What is "knowing the obstacles"? If you find something effective, do not brag about it publicly, and if you find something ineffective, do not slander or cast doubt on it. In discussing these things with other people, [admit that at times]

Believe that blood is milk 信血是乳: from *Brief Essentials for Meditation* 思惟要略法, T 15.298c20–299a2, as part of a discussion of the "contemplation of white bones," one of the contemplations or considerations of impurity and dead bodies.

Revere a camel's bone as a true relic 敬駱駝骨是眞舍利: lit. *śarīra* 舍利, a bone left from the cremation of Gotama Buddha's body after his physical death.

As I have explained above: see the section on the "causes and conditions that give rise to disease," *Mo-ho chih-kuan*, 106c17–c27.

[diseases] that have not yet come to an end or may not come to an end; those that seem to have come to an end may reappear; those that seem to be healed may not have ended; and bringing them to an end again may require the redoubling of effort.

If you are able to be completely endowed with these ten characteristics, utilize the various healing [methods explained] above, and have no doubts about the benefits of concentrated meditation, I guarantee to you that these things will not be done in vain. [end of fascicle eight, part one]

[110a] If you well cultivate the Four Samādhis and attain a balanced harmony, given the power of the Path you will certainly be free from diseases. Even if you are a little unbalanced, with the assistance of the "dark blade" 冥刀 [of your practices], you yourself should be able to dissolve and heal [the diseases]. Even if various obstacles arise like a mountain peak, you should face death and sacrifice your life and [remaining] breaths, vow to stay to the end in the meditation chamber, and be determined to stay detached. What offence cannot be extinguished, and what karma cannot be overturned? Chen Zhen and K'ai-shan [were exemplars of this ideal].

How can it be that the four elements and five [internal] organs cannot be balanced and [the diseases] brought to an end? It is like a small demon respectfully avoiding the halls of Indra; the spirit 神 of the meditation chamber is so great that no delusions can invade it. Again, if the lord of a castle is

Chen Zhen 陳鍼 **and K'ai-shan** 開善: Chen Zhen was Chih-i's elder brother. It is said that the *Shorter Manual* (T no. 1915, 46.462–473) was compiled for and presented to Chen Zhen to help him recover his health, and that it was indeed effective (see the introduction at 462a9–11) in prolonging his life.

"K'ai-shan" refers to Chih-tsang of the K'ai-shan ssu 智藏開善寺 (458–522), a prominent scholar of the *Ch'eng shih lun* and *Mahāparinirvāṇa Sūtra*, famous for his lectures on Buddhist doctrine. For details on Chih-tsang see Swanson, *Foundations*, 89–93. Chih-tsang's emphasis on conventional reality, not as illusory phenomena that needs to be denied but as a positive interpretation of the meaning of emptiness which is to be incorporated into the Middle Path, makes him a worthy precursor to Chih-i and the development of the threefold truth.

Small demon respectfully avoiding the halls of Indra 帝釋堂小鬼敬避: see, for example, the *Miscellaneous Āgama*, fascicle 40 (T 2.291a27–b23) where the Buddha tells an anti-racist story about a *yakṣa* demon who sat in a high seat in the heavens. He was so ugly and of an "evil color" that the "thirty-three devas" became angry and insisted to Indra that the demon be removed. Indra politely approached the demon, who agreed not to appear anymore. Indra, and the Buddha, then used this as an opportunity to scold the thirty-three devas and preach about the dangers of harboring anger, hatred, and ill-will (not to mention judging someone on the basis of their "color").

See also other *Āgamas*, such as the passage at T 2.772c.

determined and hard as a rock, the guards are also strong; and if the lord of the castle is timid, then the guards will be busy [or, "hasten to run away"]. The mind is the lord of the body. "[Two] gods of the same name and same birth are spirits who guard a person." If your mind is firm, then you are strong; the same is true for the body and its [guardian] deities. How much more so for the spirit of the meditation chamber. [The importance of being determined and patient] is as the *Ta chih tu lun* explains about diligence and getting stuck to a demon in five places, and so forth. Just single-mindedly cultivate samādhi, and the diseases will melt and come to an end.

5. Clarification of Cessation-and-Contemplation [110a13]

Fifth is cultivating cessation-and-contemplation [for healing disease, which, as before, involves ten [modes of contemplation].

Gods of the same name and same birth are spirits who guard a person 同名同生天是神能守護人: see the *Avataṃsaka Sūtra*, T 9.680b29–c2:

> It is like a person, from birth, having two types of gods constantly waiting over and guarding him. First, they are born the same, and second they have thc same name. The gods always watch this person, though the person cannot see the gods. The supranormal apparitions 神變 of the Tathāgata are the same.

Stuck to a demon in five places 鬼黏五處: see the section of the *Ta chih tu lun* on "the features of diligence or exertion," T 25.174b2–9. See Lamotte, *Le Traité* 2, 946ff.; Chodron (2, 1191–92) translates:

> In a former lifetime, the Buddha Śakyamuni was once a merchant chief; at the head of some merchants, he went into a mountainous and difficult region where a rākṣasa demon stopped him, saying: "Stop! Do not move; I won't allow you to proceed." The chief of the merchants struck him with his right fist, but his fist remained glued to the demon and could not be detached; then he struck him with his left fist but it, too, could not be disengaged; next, he kicked him with his right foot, but the foot remained stuck; he kicked him with his left foot, but the same thing happened; he butted him with his head, but his head was stuck also. The demon asked him: "Now what are you going to do? Will you give in finally?" The bodhisattva answered: "Although the five parts [of my body] are fettered, never will my mind give in to you. I will fight you by the power of my exertion and never surrender to you." The demon, amused, said to himself: "This man's courage is very great," and speaking to the merchant, said: "The power of your exertion is very great; you definitely will not give in; I will let you go."

Is it possible that there is some connection with the story told by Uncle Remus about Br'er Rabbit and the tar-baby, e.g. through Indian folk tales and Aesop's fables?

Ten modes of contemplation: again, the ten modes themselves are taken up one by one in order, with the main emphasis on contemplating objects as inconceivable. The section headers have been added to clarify the structure of the section, and are sometimes ambiguous, as often one section flows into the next.

1. Objects as Conceivable and Inconceivable [110a14–111b10]

First, with regard to conceivable [objects] [that is, objects that can be conceptually understood]. The causes and conditions of disease also give rise to the ten dharma realms [from hell to Buddha], and it is due to disease that you retreat from and lose your fundamental mind [for seeking enlightenment], reject dhyāna meditation, slander the three treasures [of Buddha, Dharma, and Sangha], do not consider that previous offences are inviting calamity and instead say that cultivating good has no benefit, and thus arouse great perverse views. Again, you hold dear the physical body and nourish this life, partaking of fish and meat, spicy food, and alcoholic beverages, without regard for the time [of day] and without any moderation 非時無度. Or, when disease comes to an end and the body is robust, you indulge freely in the five desires so that your good thoughts are all exhausted and evil karma blazes up, you give rise to serious, middling, and minor offences, and then disease becomes a cause for producing conditions for the **three evil destinies** [of hell, beasts, and hungry spirits].

But if people are personally aware that these diseases cause suffering and that they are all brought about by the lack of good [deeds] of past days, they should be profoundly contrite and do not presume to be critical [of the Buddha's teaching?]. Then even if you give birth to illness, if you do not give up on a mind of goodness and [instead] arouse superior, middling, and minor good [deeds], then disease becomes a cause for producing the **three good destinies** [of pretas, humans, and divine beings].

If you encounter disease, and this causes you to fear [the cycle of] birth and death, know that this diseased body is a retribution for previous karmic actions, that if you construct [the causes for] birth and death, in the future how will you avoid the extreme pain of transmigrating again? Suffering and the causes of suffering make you weak and perilous; they continue from life to life and lead you to experience afflictions. You should seek after quiescent extinction and featureless nirvana. Then disease becomes a cause for arousing the **realm of the śrāvaka**.

Again, contemplate these diseases [in this way]: my body and mind are diseased, and these diseases lead to old age and death. Death results from birth, and birth results from past existence, [past] existence arises from grasping [**110b**], grasping comes from the arising of passion, passion comes from the arising of experience, experience comes from the arising of contact, contact comes from the arising of the six senses, the six senses come from the arising of name-and-form (*nāma-rupa*), where "form" is exactly the four elements and five sense organs [of the physical body] and "name" refers to the four mental [skandhas of sensation, conceptions, volitions, and consciousness]. Contemplate, where do these sense organs and elements arise from? The color blue-green arises from wood. The color yellow arises from earth. The color red arises from fire. The color white arises from wind. The color black arises from water. Again, contemplate that wood arises from water, water arises from wind, wind arises from the *yang*-positive *chi*-energy of earth, earth arises from fire, fire arises from wood, and wood in turn arises from water. In this way you realize that things go in a circle and return to the beginning. Nothing arises from itself [alone].

Contemplating the five external phases is as already explained. The five internal organs and colors are also likewise. The liver arises from blue-green *chi*-energy. The heart arises from red *chi*-energy. The lungs arise from white *chi*-energy. The kidneys arise from black *chi*-energy. The spleen arises from yellow *chi*-energy. Does this organ of the liver arise from itself, or does it arise from something else? You should know that the liver arises from the kidneys, the kidneys arise from the lungs, the lungs arise from the spleen, the spleen arises from the heart, the heart arises from the liver, and the liver does not arise on its own, but arises from the kidneys. In this way if we seek [the truth about] internal matters such as the four elements and five organs, we see that they are without a [substantial] essence. Why, then, are they indestructible? The four mental [skandhas] maintain them. The mental skandha of consciousness maintains earth. The mental skandha of conceptions maintains wind. The mental skandha of sensations maintains fire. The mental skandha of volitions maintains water. Therefore they are indestructible [and do not pass away completely].

Do these four mental [skandhas] arise on their own, or not arise on their own? You should know that volitions arise from sensations, sensations arise from conceptions, conceptions arise from consciousness, and consciousness arises from volitions from the past, volitions from the past arise from ignorance, ignorance arises from deluded conceptions, and deluded conceptions in turn arise from deluded conceptions. As a sūtra says, "Deluded conceptions give rise to deluded conceptions; this is the turning of the twelve conditions." It is like a person crazed with thirst mistaking a flame-like mirage for water and heading south in search of it, but it is not to be found; he shouts

Liver arises from blue-green *chi*-energy 肝從青氣生 … the spleen arises from yellow *chi*-energy 脾從黃氣生: as explained above, these connections between internal organs and colors are spelled out in the *Inner Canon of the Yellow Emperor*. See Unschuld 2011.

Deluded conceptions give rise to deluded conceptions; this is the turning of the twelve conditions 妄想生妄想輪迴十二緣: see the *Suvarṇaprabhāsa Sūtra*, T 16.340a–b, which contains the phrase (at 340b16–17), "The causes and conditions of deluded conceptions 妄想因緣, merge and come into existence 和合而有; they do not really exist [on their own] 無所有故, but are conventionally named and [based on] ignorance 假名無明."

out "water!" in a loud voice so that the sky trembles, and then thinks that he has come too far south and that water must be in the north, so he runs to the north, and in this way goes to all the four directions but is unable to find [water] anywhere. In great distress he then thinks that water is in the ground and so scratches at the earth and cries out; his body becomes exhausted until he is lost in the darkness, never being able to find water. Running south is like the tongue seeking tastes; running north is like the ears seeking sounds; running west is like the nose seeking scents; running east is like the eyes seeking color. Scratching at the earth is like the body seeking contact; "reaching darkness" is like the consciousness seeking ignorance. In this way the six sense organs run around [seeking] the various sense objects but are not able to [really] obtain even one. Again, such a one is not able to obtain [understanding] of how causes and conditions merge, thus merely suffering and becoming fatigued. If you can become aware of and know [about these things], you will not run around [in confusion] any more; if you do not "run around" [in confusion], the mind will become stable; if the mind is stable you will be open to enlightened understanding and arouse the causes and conditions for true wisdom, and you will know that the body and mind and so forth are originally **[110c]** and in essence quiescent, neither arising nor perishing, and that it is due to deluded conceptions and perverted views that you think that there is [real] arising and perishing. If you do not go along with these deluded conceptions, then [the twelvefold chain of dependent arising] from ignorance to old-age-and-death will be extinguished, these [causes and conditions] will come to an end and new ones will not be produced. It is like when there is no longer any fire, there will be no smoke. If you are not subject to [the cycle from] ignorance to old-age-and-death, then who is it that suffers disease? This is called the contemplation of disease for arousing the **realm of the pratyekabuddha.**

Again, contemplate these diseases [in this way]: everything is due to passionately caring for the physical body, life, and material wealth, so that you experience various afflictions. Again, you are not perfect in keeping the precepts, and so you suffer many diseases and a short life. Again, if your mental resolution is inferior and weak, you are not able to have a calm forbearance, and your body and spirit are unguarded. Again, if your power of diligence is light, you cannot be good at averting misfortune. Again, if you do not have the power of dhyāna meditation, you are affected by disease. Again, if your mind has little wisdom and does not have penetrating understanding of [the truths of] transience, suffering, emptiness, and no-self, you finally end up [suffering from] these illnesses. Now, if your own disease leads you to pity other people for their disease, this arouses compassion and leads you to take action and make a vow [to help others], to abandon [everything] without regret, and in accordance with the principle [of things] attain calm endurance, diligently increasing in correct intentions and awakening to [the truth of] transiency. These are the causes of diseases that arouse the **realm of the [Tripitaka] bodhisattva of the six perfections.**

Again, contemplate these diseases [in this way]: know that [diseases] arise from deluded conceptions, perverted views, and passionate afflictions in previous lives, In this way, deluded conceptions do not have true reality. The self and nirvana both are empty. This is called the causes of diseases that arouse **the realm of the bodhisattva of the Shared Teachings.**

Again, contemplate these diseases [in this way]: disease is ultimately empty. "Empty" means that there is no "place" [self] that experiences [disease], and yet all experiences are [conventionally] experienced. Without being fully endowed with the Buddha Dharma, you cannot extinguish experience and accept enlightenment. These are the causes of disease that arouse the **realm of the bodhisattva of the Distinct Teachings.**

In this way various methods are the causes of disease and gradually, step by step, give rise [to various levels of attainment]. This is called the "conceivable realms" and are not what is to be contemplated here.

Objects as Inconceivable [110c18]

The inconceivable realm is [as follows]. A single thought of the mind of disease is neither real nor does it exist [substantially], but partakes in the nature of reality 法性法界. All phenomena are involved in disease, and there are none that go beyond this involvement. There is only this reality (*dharmadhātu*), and there is no distinction [in this matter] between the nine realms [of hell to bodhisattva]. It is like the wish-fulfilling jewel, neither empty [nothingness] nor [substantially] existent, neither before nor after; disease is also like this. It is ultimately beyond verbal expression, quiescent and pure. Therefore it is called "inconceivable." If you penetrate to the limits of reality with regard to disease, what is there to rejoice about, and what to be sorrowful? When you contemplate in this way, then suddenly [diseases] will disappear and come to an end. The *Suvarṇaprabhāsa Sūtra* says, "Directly listen to these words, and disease will be removed and healed." This is the meaning of the first [of the

***Suvarṇaprabhāsa Sūtra* says, "Directly listen to these words, and disease will be removed and healed"** 金光明云。直聞是言病卽除愈: see the section on "Removing Disease" at T 16.352b2–8:

> At one time there were hundreds of thousands of immeasurable sentient beings who had encountered grave diseases. They directly heard these words and rejoiced in their minds, and thereupon the various diseases were removed and came to an end.…
>
> Again, there were immeasurable hundreds of thousands of sentient beings whose diseases and suffering was pro-

ten modes of] contemplation [of objects as inconceivable]. Again, [the sūtra says], "if there are deep and serious [diseases] that are difficult to remove and put an end to, you should go to an elder who has medicine at his disposal, and thus put an end to the diseases"; this refers to the meaning of the other nine [of the ten modes of] contemplations.

All sentient beings are endowed with this principle [of reality], but they are not able to know it. They follow the flow of mistaken views and conceptions, and drown in the sea of ordinary constituent [samsara]. If you deeply arouse compassion, and wish to share the bliss of [knowing the two truths] of the path and extinction which are emptiness and not [substantial] Being, a bodhisattva who is experiencing illness can overcome this [mistaken] mind with the contemplation of emptiness. **[111a]** Since this mind is overcome, real disease is removed and healed [for this bodhisattva], but due to compassion he arouses a tentative illness, and thus experiences this ordinary constituent realm [of samsara], where he perceives the people of this constituent realm as his only child. When a child is sick, the mother and father are also sick. Because they share this disease, they can heal it. When the child's disease is healed, the parents are also healed. This is called a **bodhisattva [of the**

found and heavy and difficult to remove and put to an end. Together they visited the elder. At that time the elder used sublime medicine and gave it to them to take. After taking [this medicine], [the diseases were] removed and put to an end.

When a child is sick ... parents are also healed 子既有病父母亦病。因以身疾而慰喻之。子病若愈父母亦愈: see the *Vimalakīrti Sūtra*, T 14.544b15–28, where Mañjuśrī visits Vimalakīrti, who is "feigning" illness; Luk (50–51, modified) translates:

When entering the house Mañjuśrī saw only Vimalakīrti lying on a sick bed, and was greeted by the upāsaka who said, "Welcome, Mañjuśrī, you come with no idea of coming and you see with no idea of seeing."

Mañjuśrī replied, "It is so, Venerable Upāsaka, coming should not be further tied to [the idea of] coming, and going should not be further linked with [the concept of] going. Why? Because there is neither whence to come nor whither to go, and that which is visible cannot further be (an object of) seeing. Now, let us put all this aside. Venerable Upāsaka, is your illness bearable? Will it get worse by wrong treatment? The World Honoured One sends me to enquire after your health, and is anxious to have good news of you. Venerable Upāsaka, where does your illness come from, how long has it arisen, and how will it come to an end?"

Vimalakīrti replied: "Delusion leads to passion which is the origin of my illness. Because all living beings are subject to illness I am ill as well. When all living beings are no longer ill, my illness will come to an end. Why? A bodhisattva, because of [his vow to save] living beings, enters the realm of birth and death which is subject to illness; if they are all cured the bodhisattva will no longer be ill. For instance, when the only son of an elder falls ill, so do his parents, and when he recovers his health, so do they. Likewise, a bodhisattva loves all living beings as if they were his sons; so when they fall ill, the bodhisattva is also ill, and when they recover, he is no longer ill."

Tripitaka Teachings] who has disease and heals by "analyzing the essence" [of things as empty].

Again, one contemplates these diseases as empty and quiescent, but not all sentient beings can attain liberation simply by realizing emptiness. Therefore you should know the various ramifications of the emptiness of disease. Śrāvakas and those of the two vehicles do not know these matters, so they follow the flow of ignorance and non-cognizance and drown in the sea of the ever-changing [world of transmigration]. They are unable to make distinctions concerning diseases, and are therefore unable to make manifest the Buddha Dharma, and so cannot help sentient beings attain the Pure Land. It is for this reason that you should arouse compassion, extract the suffering of non-cognizance, and share the bliss of making distinctions with the wisdom of the path. This is called a **bodhisattva [of the Distinct Teachings] who has disease and is able to regulate and overcome that mind [of disease] by the contemplation of conventional [reality].**

Since this mind [of disease] is overcome, actual disease 實疾 is removed and healed, but then due to compassion there is the arising of "tentative" disease 權病, and you are born in the realm of [tentative] means,[and dwells among] people [using skillful, tentative] means and perceive them "as his only child, and when this child is sick, the mother and father are also sick. Because they share this disease, they can heal this child." When the child is healed of its non-cognizance, the parents are also healed. [One like this] is called a **bodhisattva who has disease and is able to heal [others] with the Distinct Teachings.**

Again, contemplate disease [as follows]: everything is part of the Dharma-realm 法界, but sentient beings do not realize this Middle Path, and are not yet aware of this principle [truth], so they follow the flow of ignorance and drown in the sea of the ever-changing [world of transmigration]. A sūtra says, "those of the three levels of erudition and ten noble stages dwell

Mañjuśrī asked, "What is the cause of the bodhisattva's illness?

Vimalakīrti replied, "A bodhisattva's illness comes from [his] great compassion."

Realm of [tentative] means 方便土: the "land where skillful means remains" 方便有餘土; the second of "four lands" that the Buddha "creates." In other contexts, this is the state of arhats and pratyekabuddhas, who have severed the delusions of views and thoughts and have transcended rebirth in this triple world, yet are still a step away from the enlightenment of a Buddha.

As the third of these four lands is mentioned below, the two previous categories probably fit with the first of the four lands: the "co-dwelling land" 凡聖同居土, the land where ordinary people and sages dwell together.

Those of the three levels of erudition and ten noble stages dwell within the fruit of their reward 三賢十聖住果報: a phrase from the *Jen-wang ching*, T 8.828a1. This passage in the *Jen-wang ching* has

within the fruit of their reward," that is, the real recompense of the causes and results of disease. For this reason you should arouse compassion, extract the suffering of ignorance, and share the ultimate bliss [of Buddhahood]. Such a one is a **bodhisattva who has disease but uses the contemplation of the Middle Path to overcome this mind.** If this mind is overcome, actual disease is removed and healed. Due to compassion, tentative disease arises, and you are born in the realm of true recompense, and perceive people in this ever-changing world "as your only child, and when this child is sick, the mother and father are also sick. Because they share this disease, they can heal this child." When the child is healed from ignorance, the parents are also healed. Such a one is called a **bodhisattva who has disease and is able to heal [others] with the Perfect Teaching.**

2. Arousing Compassion [111a23]

In this way three types of diseases all arise in a single thought 一心, and in this way can be overcome by a single contemplation of overcoming [through compassion]. Such compassion is a perfect and universal compassion 圓普慈悲, and such a manifestation is a manifestation of the universal teachings [of the Buddha]. Such a healing is an "exposition of one sound" [and is thus

been quoted and used by Chih-i many times; see *Mo-ho chih-kuan*, 53a8–9.

Realm of true recompense 實報土: this is the third of the "four lands": the "land of true recompense without obstruction" 實報無障礙土; this is the state of the bodhisattva who has realized the truth of the Middle Way.

Universal teachings 普門: a phrase from the closing paragraph of the 25th chapter (on Avalokiteśvara) of the *Lotus Sūtra*, T 9.58b6. Hurvitz (319 [294]) translates the context:

> O World-Honored One! If there is a living being who shall hear this Chapter of the Bodhisattva He Who Observes the Sounds of the World, the deeds of self-mastery, the manifestation of *the gateway to everywhere*, the powers of supernatural penetration, be it known that that person's merit shall not be slight.

Chih-i has quoted this section before; see *Mo-ho chih-kuan*, 53a3.

Exposition of one sound 一音演說: a phrase that appears three times in verses from the opening chapter of the *Vimalakīrti Sūtra*, T 14.538a2–7; Luk (7) translates as follows (note that the translation for "one sound" shifts from "unchanging voice" to "one voice"):

> When He proclaims the Dharma with *unchanging voice*
> All beings understand according to their natures
> Saying the Bhagavat speaks their own languages;
> 'Tis one of His eighteen characteristics.
> When He expounds the Dharma in *one voice*
> They understand according to their versions
> Deriving great benefit from what they have gathered;
> This is one more of His eighteen characteristics.
> When He expounds the Dharma in *one voice*

internally consistent even though it may appear to have various aspects]. I have made many distinctions above in order to make it easy to understand, but truly this is the expounding of inconceivable compassion. This teaching is included in the *Vimalakīrti [Sūtra]*. The three [types of] actual [diseases are perfectly removed, and the three [types of] tentative [diseases] are made manifest; therefore it was difficult to face this Upāsaka [Vimalakīrti]. Kings and elders all had actual diseases and were not able to attend to the life [of Vimalakīrti]. Those of the two vehicles, though they had removed the marks of grasping, quit [**111b**] without being able to bear going [to visit Vimalakīrti]. Bodhisattvas had removed the adventitious afflictions but always submitted [to the superior teaching of Vimalakīrti], and only Mañjuśrī had [sufficient] power in the Path to stay by his side. He was able to rise to the occasion and make his intention known, and asked, "Upāsaka, what are the causes of your disease? Has it been long since they arose? How can they be extinguished?" The Upāsaka answered, saying, "My disease comes from the arising of great compassion. Because sentient beings have diseases, so I have disease. When sentient beings are healed of their diseases, then I will be healed."

The actual diseases of sentient beings arise from [their passionate afflictions such as] doubt and passions. The arising of even a smidgen of doubt and passion arouses [some] great compassion. The extinction of even a smidgen of doubt and passion leads to the extinction of [some] great compassion. If sentient beings are healed or not healed, bodhisattvas will have disease or not have disease. If [the child] has no disease, know that the child is healed; if [the child] has disease, you do not rest from [taking action on] the way to save it. Therefore the questions [to Vimalakīrti] in the ten-foot square hut about his disease, and the back pain [of Śākyamuni] at Kuśāgrapura, all have this meaning[, that is, they are "tentative" diseases for the sake of saving others]. Thus the noble vows [of bodhisattvas] are equivalent to emptiness, and so it is with disease and also the Dharma realm [of reality]. This is called "inconceivable compassion."

Some are filled with fear, others are joyful,
Some hate it while others are from doubts relieved;
'Tis one of His eighteen characteristics.

What are the causes of your disease 此疾何所因起 ...: see the *Vimalakīrti Sūtra*, T 14.544b15–28 quoted in full above.

The ten-foot square hut 方丈: said to be the dimensions of the room in which Vimalakīrti rested in repose and where he greeted his visitors, including Mañjuśrī. This is the origin of the title for the famous collection of essays *Hōjōki* 方丈記 (1212) by Kamo-no-Chōmei 鴨長明.

Kuśāgrapura 茅城: the capital of the kingdom of Magadha, a flourishing economic and cultural center at the time of the Buddha, near the Vulture Peak. The back pain may be referring to the *Āgama* passage referenced earlier at 109a22.

The power of compassion is great, and when bodhisattvas first arouse these thoughts [of compassion], disease is immediately removed and healed, so there really is no need to further cultivate the rest of the methods [from the third to tenth modes of contemplation], [as shown by] Fa-hsi and T'ien-t'ai [Chih-i], and so forth. If this arousal of compassion is not true, this is being deceitful toward sentient beings, and you need [to take refuge in] the three treasures [of Buddha, Dharma, and Sangha], for the diseases that you seek [to heal] will not come to an end. But if you are true and sincere, you will have great strength.

3. Skillful Means for a Peaceful Mind [111b14]

[Third, skillful means for] a peaceful mind: if people become sick when they are [practicing] in the meditation chamber, as explained above you should understand the essence [of emptiness] and arouse the aspiration [for enlightenment], straighten the body and focus your thoughts, practicing only cessation or only contemplation, and with good and skillful [means] use the [four] methods of instruction [*siddhānta*] to properly regulate [your practice] and attain the goal. Once you are seated [in meditation] you will experience a pure and cool awakening. You may lose [the disease] suddenly, or you may lose it gradually. This is called "great medicine," so you do not need to confuse the matter by cultivating other healing methods.

4. Deconstructing Dharmas [111b17]

[Fourth,] the universal deconstruction of dharmas. When one who is practicing becomes sick, [he should] contemplate that disease as follows: is the cause of the disease physical, or is the cause of the disease mental? If the cause of the disease is physical, then the outside world such as the mountains and forest and so forth should also be sick, and dead people likewise should be sick. But corpses and mountains and forests have never experienced such afflictions. You should know that disease is not a physical matter. Then consider that these diseases come from mental conceptions. Now contemplate mental disease [in terms of the tetralemma] as not [arising] from itself or

Fa-hsi 法喜 **and T'ien-t'ai** 天台: Chan-jan (BT–V, 129–30) points out that this phrase, referring to Chih-i in the third person, must have been added by Kuan-ting. Fa-hsi was the most prominent of the twenty-seven monks who accompanied Chih-i when he left his master Hui-ssu and traveled from Mt. Ta-su to the Chen capital of Chien-yeh. According to Chan-jan, Chih-i was still thirty-seven years old, and Fa-hsi was over sixty, but Fa-hsi followed Chih-i as his disciple. See also *The Biography of T'ien-t'ai Chih-che* (T 50.192b6, 194a12, and 197b24–c1) and the biography of Chih-i in *Further Biographies of Eminent Monks*, T 50.564b.

from another [or both or neither], and that all four options are unobtainable. It is neither internal nor external, yet ultimately pure. The mind is like the empty sky, so who is it that has disease? The *Vimalakīrti Sūtra* says, "It is not the element of earth, nor apart from the element of earth, nor a matter of merging with the body, for the marks of the body are unobtainable. It is not a matter of merging with the mind, because the mind is like an illusion." The arising of disease as mental is unobtainable, the non-arising of disease as mental is unobtainable, [the same is so for] both arising and non-arising and neither arising and non-arising. [Arising and non-arising] as single, multiple, complete and so forth are all as explained above in the section on the deconstruction of the sense fields.

5. Knowing What Penetrates and What Obstructs [111b27]

[Fifth,] knowing what penetrates and what obstructs. Contemplate the methods for [healing] disease, and in terms of each phrase [of the tetralemma], and know the [four noble] truths, [the twelve-linked chain of] conditioned co-arising, and the [six] perfections. Contemplate the methods of [healing] diseases in terms of each phrase [of the tetralemma] and know the [four noble] truths, [the twelve-linked chain of] conditioned co-arising, and the [six] perfections fully and clearly, and without doubt or delusion, understanding the verbal and non-verbal [meaning], and knowing what is obtained and what is lost. This is as explained [**111c**] above.

It is not the element of earth,… It is not a matter of merging with the mind, because the mind is like an illusion 非地大不離地大。非身合身相不可得故。非心合心如幻故: see the *Vimalakīrti Sūtra* at T 14.544c10–17, following the passage quoted above. Luk (52) translates:

> Mañjuśrī asked: "What form does the Venerable Upāsaka's illness take?"
> Vimalakīrti replied: "My illness is formless and invisible."
> Mañjuśrī asked: "Is it an illness of the body or of the mind?"
> Vimalakīrti replied: "It is not an illness of the body for it is beyond body, and it is not that of the mind for the mind is like an illusion."
> Mañjuśrī asked: "Of the four elements, earth, water, fire, and air, which one is ill?"
> Vimalakīrti replied: "It is not an illness of the element of earth but it is not beyond it; it is the same with the other elements of water, fire and air. Since the illnesses of all living beings originate from the four elements which cause them to suffer, I am ill too."

As explained above in the section of the deconstruction of the sense fields 如上破陰入中說: see the detailed exposition of "Deconstructing Dharmas Vertically in Terms of Non-Arising" at *Mo-ho chih-kuan* 62a22–83b17.

This is as explained above: see the exposition of "Knowing What Penetrates and What Obstructs the Path" at *Mo-ho chih-kuan* 86a10–87c8.

6. Steps on the Path [111c1]

[Sixth,] regulating the steps on the path. If you contemplate disease and that the diseases of the four elements are impure; or [contemplate] disease as separate from the four elements and thus pure; or [contemplate] disease as neither the four elements nor separate from the four elements; [contemplate] disease as neither pure nor not pure; as existing, true, or neither existing nor true; as empty, conventional, or neither empty nor conventional; as decaying, flourishing, or neither decaying nor flourishing; in this way the common meaning is that all are non-dual and not distinct [as realized] through mindfulness of the body. In this way [it is known that] the sensations of disease are neither that of suffering nor pleasure. The conceptions and volitions of disease are neither those of self nor non-self. The mind of disease is neither constant nor transient. This is as explained above. The thirty-seven steps [of the path] can all be realized while you are at your pillow [suffering from disease]. Understand that suffering is not suffering, and you will enter the pure and cool pond [of awakening].

7. Auxiliary Methods [111c8]

[Seventh,] auxiliary methods for the path. If you cultivate proper contemplation, but have not yet attained an end [to disease], borrow the above six modes for healing and by using these [six] proper [contemplations] along with auxiliary practices you should be able to realize the path. How can it be that the diseases of the body will not be extinguished and removed?

8. Graded Stages of Attainment [111c11]

When you practice this contemplation, although you may be sluggish at your bed and pillow [with disease], know deeply the graded stages. Contemplate your disease and the true principle will become clear. This is like a lapis lazuli jewel that is deep under water, and with your perception and wisdom it is known only in the abstract [lit., "only name and word" 名字], thus the cause of disease is not yet removed, and the result of disease is still apparent. If you advance to the level of "approximate understanding," the causes of disease will become a little lighter, and your aspiration for the path will turn mature. The results of [actual suffering from] disease are still heavy, and you are not exempt from various misfortunes. If you realize the forbearance from [knowing] the non-arising of dharmas, the causes of diseases will be extinguished, but you will still [suffer from] the results of diseases. You should be

As explained above: see the exposition in the section above on "Cultivating the Steps on the Path" at *Mo-ho chih-kuan* 87c8–91a5.

careful not to think [you have attained] a grade [that you have not reached] and become arrogant, and say that your practice of disease is equal to that superior person [Vimalakīrti].

9. Resting in Patient Forbearance [111c16]

[Ninth,] resting in patient forbearance. Just diligently practice the proper and auxiliary practices, and do not let internal and external hindrances and conditions obstruct or make you rest and stop [your practices]. If you consider taking a break from the proper and auxiliary practices, disease will appear and the path will be abandoned. Have a calm mind in the midst of your disease, without being moved nor retreating, well discerning your actions.

10. No Passionate Attachments to Dharmas [111c19]

[Tenth, no passionate attachments to dharmas.] If you attain some lessening of disease, and your contemplative practice becomes clear and pure, do not give rise to covetous attachments, and do not arouse defiled passions.

11. Summary [111c20]

Perfecting these ten methods for [healing] disease and realizing the flow of these methods is called cultivating the contemplation of the Great Vehicle, acquiring the forbearance from [realizing] the non-arising of dharmas, and attaining the One Great Cart with regard to the objects of diseases. This should be known as [explained] previously.

Discerning 辨: I follow the alternate 辨 instead of 辦 "handle, manage."

One Great Cart 一大車: from the parable of the burning house in the *Lotus Sūtra*, see the original summary at 100a–b.

This should be known as [explained] previously: see the summary of the "Ten Modes of Contemplation" above in terms of the parable of the Great Cart at *Mo-ho chih-kuan* 100a3–100b16.

4. CONTEMPLATING THE OBJECTS OF KARMA [111C22–114C22]

The fourth [of the ten objects of contemplation] is contemplating the objects of the marks of karma. Suppose a practitioner has been producing good and bad karma for immeasurable kalpas; some have already experienced the recompense [from these karmic actions] and some have not yet experienced recompense. If your mental processes are undifferentiated, these marks [of karma] will not become manifest. If you now cultivate cessation-and-contemplation, this will affect karma, so that good and bad marks will become manifest.

A doubter asks, given the Mahāyāna [teaching of] equality [and emptiness], what marks are there to be discussed? [There are none?] Now I say that this is not so. [On the contrary,] if the mirror of equality [emptiness] is pure, then karma will be reflected and made manifest. The *Suvarṇaprabhāsa Sūtra* says, "When you seek enlightenment on the ten *bhūmi* stages, the marks will all be made manifest." The *Āgama* says, "When you seek to realize the first fruit [of the path to enlightenment], eighty-eight snakes will die in front of you." There are a great many such texts, both Hīnayāna and Mahāyāna. The *Lotus Sūtra* speaks of "Having profoundly mastered the marks of offences and merit, and universally illuminating the ten directions." These "offences

When you seek enlightenment on the ten bhūmi stages, the marks will all be made manifest 將證十地相皆前現: this phrase appears repeatedly in the *Suvarṇaprabhāsa Sūtra* for each of the ten stages at T 16.374a16–b17:

When you seek to realize the first fruit, eighty-eight snakes will die in front of you 將證初果八十八頭蛇於其前死: not an *Āgama* text per se, but see the *Secret Essential Methods for Meditation* 禪祕用法經, another short text on dhyāna meditation whose translation is attributed to Kumārajīva. See T no. 613, 15.261c6–12:

> Again, contemplate your own body as black earth, and see within this black earth there are four black snakes. Their eyes are red like fire, and the snakes come and threaten you physically, spitting out poison and wishing to harm you, but they are not able to harm you, so they are transformed into fire and burn up their own bodies. At that time from up in the sky there is a spontaneous voice constantly teaching the truths of suffering, emptiness, transiency, non-self, and so forth. When you see this, each of the poisonous snakes, eighty-eight of them, will be burned in the fire. When you see this, water will fall spontaneously from the sky and be sprinkled on the bodies of the poisonous snakes, and the fire will be extinguished. The eighty-eight snakes will all disappear.

Having profoundly mastered the marks of offences and merit, and universally illuminating the ten directions 深達罪福相遍照於十方: from the Devadatta chapter of the *Lotus Sūtra*, T 9.35b28, spoken by the daughter of the dragon king. This has been quoted many times already in the *Mo-ho chih-kuan*. See Hurvitz, *Lotus Sūtra*, 200 [183].

> Having profoundly mastered the marks of sin and merit,
> Universally illuminating all ten directions,

and merits" are none other than good [112a] and bad karma. The *Vimalakīrti* says, "Being unmoved within the supreme [teaching], you are well able to make distinctions among all marks of phenomena." Thus your criticism is unwarranted.

Clarifying the marks of karma consists of four [sections]: [1] the causes and conditions for the arising of the marks [of karma]; [2] the proper arising of the marks [of karma]; [3] commentary with questions and answers; and [4] cessation-and-contemplation.

1. The Causes and Conditions for the Arising of the Marks of Karma [112a3]

[First,] the cause and condition [for the arising of the marks of karma]: there are internal and external [causes and conditions]. As for the internal, [the practice of] cessation-and-contemplation polishes the mind, so the mind gradually becomes clear and pure, and all good and evil are illuminated. Or, [the practice of] cessation is used to stop evil, and evil tends to perish; or [the practice of] contemplation is used to contemplate what is good, and good tends to arise. Or, in using cessation to stop evil, quiescence causes [something] evil to arise; or in using contemplation to contemplate good, contemplation causes [something] good to perish. Thus immeasurable marks of karma emerge from [the practice of] cessation-and-contemplation. It is like a mirror that has been polished; all images are manifested [therein] spontaneously. As for the external [causes and conditions], the compassion of the Buddhas is constantly manifested and offered to all, but sentient beings do not have the capacity [to accept it] and are not able to see it. By the power of cessation-and-contemplation you are able to communicate with the Buddhas. Through dhyāna meditation that reveals good and evil, all karma will be made manifest, like holding up a garland of flowers before a crowd. These are called the internal and external causes and conditions.

If you understand this meaning, you can minutely determine offences and merit and not have an excess of black or white, and can bear [the burden of] becoming a teacher of the Vaipulya [Mahāyāna teachings] and subdue others [in debate]. Now just polish the mind through cessation-and-contemplation, cause karma to disappear, and fulfill your practices. Singlemindedly take the path, and then what need is there to make convoluted distinctions

The subtle and pure Dharma-body
Has perfected the marks thirty-two,
Using the eighty beautiful features
As a means of adorning the Dharma-body.

Being unmoved within the supreme [teaching], you are well able to make distinctions among all marks of phenomena 於第一義而不動善能分別諸法相: a phrase from the opening section of the *Vimalakīrti* at T 14.537c13.

concerning the marks [of karma]? [But for the sake of those who are unable to follow what has already been explained, I will go ahead and make further detailed explanations.]

2. The Proper Arising of the Marks of Karma [112a14]

Second is clarifying the arising of the marks of karma. The arising [of karma] has no [necessary order such as] before or after, but for the sake of explanation I will first clarify the arising of good [karma]. These marks have six [aspects]: [1] the manifestation of the marks of resultant recompense 報果; [2] the manifestation of the marks of habitual causes 習因; [3] first the manifestation of recompense and later the manifestation of the habitual; [4] first the manifestation of the habitual and later the manifestation of recompense; [5] the simultaneous manifestation of recompense and the habitual; and [6] the before and after undetermined. Thus the manifestation of karma is irregular and of myriad types. If you know these six meanings, you can make distinctions without error.

What is that called "habitual causes and habitual results"? The Abhidharma people say that "habitual causes" (*vipāka-hetu*) are those that have themselves as the cause, and "habitual results" (*niṣyanda-phala*) are those that are dependent on the results. Again, "habitual" 習 refers to "habitual continuity" 習續 which gives rises to its own seeds [and to further results that are similar to itself]. Later when further thoughts arise, they are a habitual continuation of the previous thoughts, and previous thoughts are the cause for the resultant later thoughts. This meaning should be common to all three natures [of good, evil, and neutral], but the [Abhidharma] scholars apply it only to good and evil [actions], and say that there is no habitual continuity to neutral [action].

"Causal recompense and resultant recompense" 報因報果 refer to [the causes and results] in different times. All of the previous "habitual causes and results" are called "causal recompense," and these bring about future results; since they bring about [karmic] "recompense," they called "causal recompense." The later experience of physical [rebirth] on the five destinies [from hell to human] is called "resultant recompense." As for our current

Abhidharma people 阿毘曇人: it is not clear who this refers to, whether a specific person specializing in Abhidharma, or to the position taken by a school of Abhidharma studies.

Habitual causes and habitual results 習因習果: see the notes on these terms at *Mo-ho chih-kuan* 20a1. That is, that which causes a result or further causes that are similar to itself, such as good thoughts causing more good thoughts, and a result which is the same as its cause, such as an evil thought resulting in more evil thoughts.

bodies of resultant recompense [from past lives and deeds], we again give rise to a habitual continuity of good and evil [action and deeds], and these habitual causes and results—the sum total from a previous life—become the habitual continuity of the results [in this life], and looking forward to a later life, become the habitual continuity of causes [for the next life]. The Abhidharma scholars say that taking on the body of a pigeon or sparrow is a resultant recompense, and too much lust is its habitual cause. Scholars of the *[Ch'eng shih] lun* say that taking on the body of a pigeon and much lust is the resultant recompense, and that lust causes covetous desires to arise, and these covetous desires are the habitual results. Again, they say that the passionate afflictions that arise in this life are called "habitual [**112b**] causes," which become karma (that is, causal recompense), and the passionate afflictions that arise in a later life are called "habitual results," and the pain and suffering [that results] is called the "resultant recompense."

If while you are sitting in meditation you merely perceive the various marks [of karma], this is called "the manifestation of marks as resultant recompense," but since they are also coming from causes in the past, they are also called "causal recompense." Again, the arising causes induce the later recompense, thus mutually receiving their names. Here we merely distinguish the marks of resultant recompense.

If while you are sitting in meditation you do not perceive the various marks [of karma], and thoughts arise spontaneously, this is the arousal of habitual causes that are able to induce future results, and therefore are also called "habitual results"; they are the compensation for past causes, therefore they mutually receive these names. Here we merely distinguish the "habitual causes."

1. The Marks of Good Karma [112b7]

The marks of good [karma] are various and numerous, but I will summarize them with the six perfections (*pāramitā*).

1. The Perfection of Giving [112b8]

Arousing the marks of giving (*dāna*): [1] If while you are sitting [in meditation] and in an instant perceive the superior realm of the fields of merit, that

Abhidharma scholars 數家: lit., "those concerning with enumeration." It is not clear who this refers to specifically.

***[Ch'eng shih] lun* scholars** 論家: it is not clear who this refers to specifically.

Fields of merit 福田: *puṇya-kṣetra*, that which is worthy of receiving offerings; "suitable recipients." Namely the three treasures of Buddha, Dharma, and Sangha, but also your teachers, parents,

is, the images of the three treasures [of Buddha, Dharma, and Sangha], the noble assembly and their virtues, parents and teachers, and people who are practicing, and you yourself receiving offerings; or if you perceive the field of compassion and of you receiving offerings; or perceive both fields and everyone rejoicing even though they are not receiving offerings; or do not perceive the field [of merit] with people receiving or not receiving [offerings]; or just see the place of giving which is full with rows of donations; or do not see the donations [but] just see the pure place (*śuddha-bhūmi*) [where monks are practicing]; [2] or [perceive] the manifestation of the marks of rewards for giving in this life; or the manifestation of the marks of rewards for giving in a past life; [3] or perceive the people who enjoy the practice of giving who come before you and praise the sacrificial act of giving 檀捨; in this way these are all the arising of the marks of resultant rewards [for giving]. Next, [4] even if you do not perceive these marks, but in your mind you suddenly wish to practice charity and respectfully make offerings to the three treasures and to your parent and teachers; [5] or feel compassion toward those who are injured, poor, or suffering and wish to save them; [6] or have a penetrating and clear understanding particularly toward the teaching of the perfection of giving, these are all thoughts of the arising of the marks [of karma] from habitual causes. Or, first there is the arising of these thoughts and later you perceive the marks of the recompense; or first you perceive the marks of recompense and later these thoughts arise; or they arise together or arise in an indeterminate way. This meaning [for the rest of the six variations] should be known in this way.

2. The Perfection of Precepts [112b20]

When the marks of [keeping] the precepts arise, again there are six meanings [as listed above]. [1] If you perceive the ten masters [required for a proper ordination], your robe and begging bowl, the ordination platform 壇場, and the motions 羯磨 [of the ordination ceremony], and rejoice and have loving thoughts; [2] or even if you do not see these marks but see yourself in a robe

the poor, and so forth. These provides a "fertile field" for one to practice the perfection of giving and plant seeds of good karma. Ikeda (*Kenkyūchūshaku*, 429) gives a list of "eight fields of merit": Buddhas, noble ones (arhat 聖人), priests 和尚, teachers (*ācarya* 阿闍梨), monks, father, mother, and sick people.

Field of compassion 悲田: one of the "fields of merit." Those who are in need of pity and compassion, and offer an opportunity for charity and practicing the perfection of giving.

Six variations: it is not clear how to specify these variations into six categories. I have added numbers in brackets in the section above, and each of the following sections supposedly have these six variations.

of purity 淨潔 [having taken the precepts] and with the dignity 威儀 covering the assembly [of monks]; [3] or seeing the people who constantly maintain the precepts, their faces and eyes radiantly shining, their conduct solemn and steadfast, who come and praise the precepts; these are all the marks of the arising of the rewards and fruits of keeping the precepts. [4] At times all of these marks cannot be seen, but suddenly thoughts of keeping the precepts arise, and you yourself proclaim [an intent] to be pure in the precepts and not fail to keep [all the precepts in] the two categories [of precepts]; [5] or you wish to correct and rectify those who break the precepts and lead them to act in accordance with the Dharma; [6] or [wish] to understand yourself the precept texts and become an expert and have a thorough knowledge of the Vinaya; these are the marks of the arising of habitual causes [of good karma]. Before [the marks arise], after, together, or undetermined; these variations should be known as explained above.

3. The Perfection of Patience [112b28]

Arousing the marks of [the perfection of] patience: if you perceive a person who is patient, or see some physical practice that involves patience; or see yourself with your body in a proper position and pure, with your hands and feet [**112c**] strictly in order ["neat and tidy" 嚴整], such as is rarely seen in this world; or see a person who is proper and patient come and praise [the virtue of] patience; these are the marks of the resultant rewards of patience. Or if there is an immediate arising of the thoughts of patience, or an understanding of the teachings of patience, these are called the arising of the marks of the habitual causes of patience. Before [the arising of the marks], after, together, and indeterminate; the meaning of these [variations] should be known [as explained above].

4. The Perfection of Diligence [112c3]

The marks of [the perfection of] diligence: if you see a person who is diligent; or see yourself performing deeds with diligence; or perceive your body with much energy and accomplishing abundant heroic deeds, or see someone who constantly practices diligently both day and night without fail and praises [the virtues of] patience; these are the marks of the resultant rewards of diligence. Or if you do not see such marks but only arouse the thoughts

Two categories of precepts 篇聚: the complete [fivefold] precepts (具足戒, 五篇) plus a sixth and seventh category added to make a total of seven parts 七聚.

Physical practice that involves patience 身行忍事: Ikeda (*Gendaigoyaku*, 559) translates: "or if you yourself practice patience."

of diligence [on its own], and [diligently practice] from the early, middle and late evening without sparing your body, or have penetrating understanding into the teachings of diligence, these are called the marks of the habitual causes of diligence. Before [the arising of the marks], after, together, and indeterminate; the meaning of these [variations] should be known [as explained above].

5. The Perfection of Dhyāna Meditation [112c9]

The marks of dhyāna meditation are explained extensively in a later section.

6. The Perfection of Wisdom [112c9]

The marks of [the perfection of] wisdom: this should be explained extensively in the section on "the objects of bodhisattvahood."

7. General Comments on Good Dharmas [112c10]

The habitual rewards of the six perfections have already been given in six types. All good dharmas are also likewise. If we were to examine these dharmas in detail for a long time, this would become increasingly clear. But I do not want to make many troublesome explanations, nor do I wish to explain too much. Accept the oral explanations you have been faced with, and these should be discussed broadly in accordance with the thoughts [and capacity of the listener].

The transmission of the Vaipulya [Mahāyāna] masters says that when the marks from owing a debt to the three treasures [of Buddha, Dharma, and Sangha] become apparent, recompense must surely be paid. Master Nan-yüeh [Hui-ssu] said, "If you have something, it is good to use it to pay recompense, and if you do not have anything you may have to abandon your practice and run around in circles [to find a way to pay recompense]." This has

Later section: see the extensive section on "Contemplating the Objects of Dhyāna Concentration" at *Mo-ho chih-kuan* 117a24–131c24.

The objects of bodhisattvahood 菩薩境中: section 10 of this chapter VII on "Contemplation Proper," which was left unfinished. Perhaps the fact that Chih-i goes on to explain this topic in some detail here indicates that he was aware that this section would ultimately be left unfinished?

The Vaipulya masters 諸方等師: the identity of these masters is unknown.

If you have something, it is good to use it to pay recompense, and if you do not have anything you may have to abandon your practice and run around in circles 若自有物償者善。若自無物欲廢行法四方馳求: the source of this saying attributed to Chih-i's teacher is unknown. It is unclear how long this "quote" continues. In Ikeda's *Teihonkudoku* (607), the end-quote does not appear until just before the next quote.

two meanings. The offences that sentient beings have committed in the past are beyond measure; the debt owed to the three treasures does not end with just one item. [One should be] like an arhat who first directly takes up the path without rushing to compensate for his [past evil] karma; therefore this is called "resisting responsibility" 觝責. If a practitioner abandons the meditation chamber and instead practices the clamor of begging, and continues this confused activity for many years, how can this not become a [demonic] matter of Māra? For now do not concern yourself with compensation [for evil karma], but merely be determined in cultivating the true teachings of the Buddhas and exhibit the culmination of your own [practice]. "Culminating" 成 means maintaining the destruction of passionate afflictions and realizing the forbearance that comes from [the realization of] non-arising, and within the realm of the Dharma Body to extensively pay homage to all of the three treasures. Then you return and reenter [the cycle of] birth and death and pay recompense for sentient beings [through compassionate actions]. The bodhisattvas at this stage are no longer accused of "resisting responsibility." Again, "culminating" 立 means waiting for your work to reach its fullness so that both the teaching and practice are established, and the resultant rewards spontaneously arrive; at that time the three treasures can be compensated. Thus it is not the case that you are "resisting responsibility" and do not intend to pay compensation. Rather, you are seeking for a little "extension" [on the loan, as it were], which will certainly be covered [eventually]. How can this not be an admirable matter? If you abandon your practice and leave the meditation chamber, there will certainly be a price to be paid. Without reading or chanting [the sutras] or listening or studying, or running your own private business, you will certainly have to use various means to seek material wealth to pay recompense. This interpretation is in line with that of the *Upāsaka-śīla Sūtra*. The sūtra says that if one is indebted in material things to the three treasures, that person should cultivate the path, and those who seek to attain [the levels of] a stream-enterer to that of an arhat should not be required to pay recompense. Those who do not study the path

In his *Gendaigoyaku* (560), the quote is only one line, with the rest commentary by Chih-i. I follow the short quote.

Upāsaka-śīla Sūtra: see the passage at T 24.1046c15–1047a2, which tells of lay bodhisattvas and lay disciples attaining immeasurable merit even while maintaining their lay lives. The "quote" that follows here is at best a very free paraphrase of the sūtra content.

Again, it is not clear how far the quote continues. In Ikeda's *Teihonkudoku* (608), the end-quote continues to the end of the paragraph. In his *Gendaigoyaku* (561), the quote stops at "an arhat should not be required to pay recompense." I have left off the quotation marks to indicate that it is a paraphrase and that it is not clear how much of the text is attributed to the sūtra itself.

should quickly pay recompense [by other means]. If arhats use things [that belong to] the Buddha, this should not be considered an offence.

2. The Marks of Evil Karma [113a1]

[**113a**] Next is clarifying the marks of evil [karma]. There are a great many types of evil, but for now [we will look at them] in terms of the six obscurations. All have six variations [as above].

1. The Obscuration of Parsimony [113a2]

[First is] the marks of the obscuration of parsimony. [1] If you see the three treasures, your teacher, monks, father, or mother, their appearance emaciated, or their bodies naked, or their clothing of [plain] blue thread, or suffering from hunger, or their temples and houses in ruins; and see that all [material] things have been guarded, sealed up, and closed off [instead of being given away to help the people in need], this is different from [in fact, the opposite of] the previous [content of the good dharmas]. The previous people [who practice the six perfections] rejoice in handling things [to give it away], but here [those who are parsimonious, stingy, and covetous] are like beggars who get angry and abusive with regard to [material] things. For the previous [type of person], things are a tool for expressing giving; for these [who are parsimonious], things are a tool for expressing stinginess. [2] Or, you perceive a stingy person come and appear in front of you, [and so forth]. These are called the arising of the marks of the resultant recompense from the obscuration of parsimony. All together there are six variations that should be known as explained previously.

2. Breaking the Precepts [113a8]

The marks of breaking the precepts: If you see that the images of the three treasures, as well as your teachers, monks, elders, and including your parents, have been beheaded and have fallen to the earth, unable to arise, or their bodies have been broken and have suffered from being whipped; or you see that their bodies and heads are in different places, and the temples and houses scattered and in ruins; or see your parents being reviled and the three treasures being rebuked; or you see people rejoice in killing, or butch-

Six obscurations 六蔽: the six defilements that "cover" the mind (*saḍvipakṣa*), the opposite of the six perfections: parsimony/stinginess/covetousness/greed 慳貪 *(mātsarya)*, immorality/breaking the precepts 破戒 *(duḥśīla)*, anger 瞋恚 *(vyāpāda)*, indolence/sloth 懈怠 *(kusīda)*, distractedness/lack of concentration 散乱 *(vikṣepa)*, stupidity/ignorance 愚癡 *(mūḍha)*

ers of babies come and dwell in your midst. Again, [you see] evil birds and poisonous insects become connected to your body and neck. These are all marks of recompense from the obscuration of hatred [and thus breaking the precepts]. These also have six variations as explained above.

If you see impurities [such as] feces, urine, corpses, and other stinking objects blocking the path, or deep water across the road so that you are unable to proceed; or see a person with whom you have had a licentious relationship in the past, again indicating impure features and defilements that you should be ashamed of; or you perceive that your own body is a place that stinks; or see many licentious people come and speak of the indulgent life; or see birds, beasts, and people involved in sexual intercourse; these are all marks of recompense from the offences of lust. These also have six variations.

If you see during your single life things being stolen, or [see] the owner of stolen material come and angrily take back those things, or see someone who likes to steal come and encourage others to steal things; these are all the marks and resultant recompense of stealing. These also have six variations as explained above.

If you see your father, mother, teacher, monks, or outsiders quarreling with poisonous anger, making various criticisms and denigrating themselves; or you see someone coming who has many verbal faults, these are the marks of the resultant recompense from the four verbal faults [of lying, slander, harsh words, and frivolous speech]. These also have six variations.

If you see a drunk person vomiting or laying down or in disarray, or see your own body sunk in darkness [from intoxication], these are all marks of the resultant recompense from drinking intoxicating beverages. These also have six variations.

These are all marks of the resultant recompense from the obscurations of breaking the precepts

3. The Other Four Obscurations [113a25]

The other four obscurations should be known as with the above examples, so it is not necessary to list them all.

Again, if you have internal mental suffering, this comes from the habitual [effects] of killing; if you have internal mental depression, this comes from the habitual [effects] of stealing; if you have internal mental agitation, this comes from the habitual [effects] of lust; if they all arise together, this is from the habitual [effects] of them all.

3. Commentary with Questions and Answers [113a28]

Third is commentary on the appearance of the marks of good and evil [karma] and how they are not the same in being an obstacle [to the path]. [There are four options:] [1] not an obstacle and yet an obstacle; [2] an obstacle and yet not an obstacle; [3] an obstacle and not an obstacle both being an obstacle; and [4] an obstacle and not an obstacle [**113b**] both not an obstacle.

"Not an obstacle and yet an obstacle" means: If a person first arouses good marks and at that time rejoices, but later arouses passions and arrogance and is scornful of others, and depending on these [limited] marks of enlightenment make them the basis for pride, gradually becoming defiled with [desire for] fame, his faults and mistakes will be repeated, his mind will retrogress and the Dharma be destroyed, he will abandon the precepts and return to lay life, and produce evil [karma]. Certainly at first this was a cause for good that was not an obstacle, but later became evil that was a great obstacle [to the path].

"An obstacle and yet not an obstacle" means: suppose at first there is the arousal of evil marks but through shame and fear you strive to repent of this evil, to sever the mental continuity [with past evil deeds] and for a long time do not give rise to evil, striving to do various good [deeds] until you accomplish the great matter [of enlightenment]. Certainly at first this was a cause for obstacles, but latter became something that was not an obstacle [to the path].

"Both being an obstacle" and "both not an obstacle" should be known in the same way.

"Not an obstacle and yet an obstacle" [also] means, when good [karma] is about to perish and yet its marks are [still] manifested, this perishing of good makes the arising of evil appear. "An obstacle and yet not an obstacle" [also] means, when evil [karma] is about to perish and yet its marks are [still] manifested, this [perishing of] evil makes the arising of good appear. "An obstacle and not an obstacle both not an obstacle" refers to marks in which good appears and is not perishing, and evil is not arising. "An obstacle and not an obstacle both an obstacle" refers to evil appearing and not perishing, and good not arising. These are expressions in terms of the early [appearance] of good [karma], where good is not an obstacle and evil is an obstacle [to the path], as analyzed above. If expressed in terms of the real truth (*paramārtha-satya*) [that is, in terms of emptiness], the above-mentioned "good" and "evil" are all obstacles [to the path]. Therefore it says in the *Sūtra*

Sūtra on the Obstacles of Pure Karma 淨業障經云。一切惡障一切善障: a very short Vinaya text referred to here for the first and only time in the *Mo-ho chih-kuan*. Rather than a strict quote, it is a succinct summary of the main point of the sūtra; see T 24.1097b8–16 for a passage that reflects Chih-i's quote:

> The Buddha said to Mañjuśrī, "As for obstacles 障礙, covetous desire is an obsta-

on the Obstacles of Pure Karma that all evil is an obstacle and all good is an obstacle. If expressed in terms of conventionality, good and evil [at the level] of the real truth are all obstacles. If expressed in terms of the Middle, good and evil [at the level] of conventionality are all obstacles. Therefore obstacles are never exhausted.

Next, the arising in the mind of the habitual causes of good and evil are easy to know. The arising of the marks of the resultant recompense of good and evil [on the other hand] are difficult to know. If the marks of the rewards of good are helped by the arising of thoughts of good habitual causes, or are manifested before or after them, in many cases these are the marks of the nature of goodness. If they arise alone and spontaneously, in many cases these are the marks of unproduced goodness. If the marks of the resultant recompense of evil are helped by the arising of thoughts of evil habitual causes, before or after, in many cases these are [the marks of] the nature of evil. If they are not helped by the arising of habitual [causes], in many cases they are different from unproduced evil.

Again, if the resultant recompense of good and evil arise alone and spontaneously, although these are classified as "unproduced," their reality is difficult to clarify, and in many cases they tend to mix with the demonic marks of Māra. If you wish to discriminate these further, they must be examined with great care. You should use emptiness to clarify good and evil and the ten destinies and test them thoroughly. If there are faults or inadequacies, these are the marks of Māra. If not, then they are [truly] unproduced. Again, test them thoroughly with the three phases [of arising, changing, and perishing]. That is, do they abide for a long time, or come frequently? Again, do they destroy the mind of dhyāna meditation? If they have these three [marks], they are the marks of Māra. If they do not have these three marks, they are unproduced.

Again, when the marks of evil are manifested, the first time you may be angry, the next time you may be composed, and the third time you may be joyful, some people may feel admonished, and some people may reject [the marks]. You should know that all [113c] these are marks of evil about to perish.

cle, hateful greed is an obstacle, ignorance is an obstacle, giving is an obstacle, keeping the precepts is an obstacle, patience is an obstacle, diligence is an obstacle, dhyāna meditation is an obstacle, wisdom is an obstacle, conceptualizing the Buddha is an obstacle, conceptualizing the Dharma is an obstacle, conceptualizing the Sangha is an obstacle, conceptualizing emptiness is an obstacle, conceptualizing no marks is an obstacle, conceptualizing spontaneity is an obstacle. conceptualizing non-action is an obstacle, conceptualizing non-arising is an obstacle. Mañjuśrī, the gist of the matter is, all dharmas involve both binding and liberation. You should know in this way everything is a [possible] obstacle [to the path].

If your aspiration [for enlightenment] is right and true, and your understanding of wisdom is clear, you should know well the various marks [of karma], each and every one without error. Do not be deluded by various obstacles; discipline your mind and realize the truth and grow further in clarity. When you attain extra strength in your practice, you can discriminate the various aspects of karma with penetrating mastery, and thus also save others. Even if you are not able to discriminate the marks of karma [in minute detail] with all its threads and fragments, if you know in general that it is an obstacle, and there is nothing to become attached to, and discipline your mind and contemplate the truth [of emptiness], then karma will not be able to obstruct you [in attaining the path]. If basically you do not have an understanding mind [of wisdom], and instead arouse a perverse aspiration, when you see these marks [of karma] you will give rise to passionate attachments, and Māra will take advantage of this to enter and bring about various fortunes and misfortunes, and because of these you will arouse further [passionate attachments], you will barter for material wealth and food, and when you die you will be reborn in the realm of the hungry ghosts. Who would say that this is not a "demonic dhyāna"?

If you are to "correct yourself and correct others," you must attain the intent [of enlightenment], so earnestly do your practice for enlightenment yourself. Again, it is through the oral transmission of your teacher that the words [of teaching] are clarified, so do not therefore become boastful and delude yourself into [thinking that you can easily judge between] hot and cold, which would be a great disaster. I urge you deeply, [again] I urge you deeply, that those who come after us be very careful [in these matters].

Question: if the spirit of the meditation chamber 道場神 is guarding it from malice, why should one be perturbed?

Answer: It is as you say. It is like in the [secular] world, a friendly army has a police officer who only keeps watch for trouble and protects against evil. The responsible person is careful with [material] things so that [others] are unhindered. When [the marks of] karma appear and you are faced with retribution, you should understand them in accordance with this.

Correct yourself and correct others 自正正他: although this is not identified as a quote, it probably reflects a passage in the *Mahāparinirvāṇa Sūtra*, T 12.625b4ff, which begins:

> The Buddha said to Kāśyapa, "Good son. A bodhisattva-mahāsattva discriminates in revealing great *parinirvāṇa* with four meanings: 1. correcting oneself; 2. correcting others; 3. responding well to questions and answers; and 4. well understanding the meaning of causes and conditions…"

A police officer 虞候: this translation follows the explanation by Chan-jan (BT-V, 173), that is, an officer who is in charge of handling trouble, perhaps the chief of Military Police?

Again, the various names, teachings, and features of the essence of karma are as [explained in] the Abhidharma and the *Ch'eng shih lun* treatises. If you wish to perform contemplation and destroy karma, this is explained in detail in the *Middle Treatise*. These two traditions each have their strengths and weaknesses, but the current intent [in the *Mo-ho chih-kuan*] is different than these. With regard to clarifying good and evil, they are sufficient if not taken in excess. If used to discriminate broadly, they may hinder the true path, and if you are merely aiming to directly destroy [karma], they do not provide full knowledge of the proper and auxiliary steps on the path and how to mediate them, and so their methods are not complete. The current [teaching of] cessation-and-contemplation [in the *Mo-ho chih-kuan*] may be insufficient in clarifying [all the details of] the marks of karma, but the methods of contemplation [provided] are more than enough.

4. Cultivating Cessation-and-Contemplation [113c19]

Four, cultivating cessation-and-contemplation [with regard to the marks of karma also] involves ten [modes of contemplation].]

1. Objects as Conceivable and Inconceivable [113c20]

What are the objects of karma as "conceivable"? [The *Ta chih tu lun* explains that] if karma is able to beckon retribution [of rebirth] in the three evil destinies, these involve upper, middle, and lower [of the realms of hell, beasts, and hungry ghosts], and if karma is able to beckon the reward [of rebirth] in the three good destinies, these involve upper, middle, and lower [of the

Abhidharma and *Ch'eng shih lun*: 毘曇成實論: the *Inyō* and Ikeda (*Kenkyū-chūshaku*, 430) point to specific passages in Abhidharma texts and the *Ch'eng shih lun*: see T 28.579b–584c T 28.812b–815b; and T 32.289c–308c.

Middle Treatise: see the seventeenth section on "Contemplating Karma" at T 30. 21b20–23c14.

***Ta chih tu lun* explains that if karma ...**: this is a summary of a longer passage on "The Various Categories of Beings" at T 25.279c6–18; see Lamotte, *Le Traité* 4, 1951–52, translated into English by Chodron (4, 1601–2):

> Beings *(sattva)*. – The name *(prajñapti)* of "being" is given to the five skandhas *(skandha)*, to the eighteen elements *(dhātu)*, to the twelve bases of consciousness *(āyatana)*, to the six elements (dhātu) [of the human body], to the twelve causes *(nidāna)* and to a quantity of dharmas; they are gods *(deva)*, humans *(manuṣya)*, cows *(go)*, horses *(aśva)*, etc.
>
> There are two kinds of beings: mobile *(cala)* or still *(śānta)*: the mobile ones produce physical and mental actions *(kāyavākkarman)*, the still ones are unable to do so; material *(rūpin)* or immaterial *(arūpin)*; with two feet or without feet; four-footed or multi-footed; worldly *(laukika)* or supraworldly *(lokottara)*; big *(mahat)* or small *(alpa)*; noble *(bhadrārya)* or ordinary *(pṛthagjana)*.

realms of asuras, humans, and divine beings], and nonpropelling karma beckons the reward of [birth in the realms of] form and no-form. In this way karma beckons [rebirth as] body-and-mind 色心, and by returning to the delusions of [a life with] body-and-mind, you arouse the four warped views [that the world is permanent, full of pleasure, having selfhood, and pure *(nitya-sukha-ātma-śuci)*], and you are unable to sever [rebirth in this cycle of] birth and death; truly this is how it happens. Now contemplate karma as non-karma [that is, as empty], and that perverted delusions do not [truly] arise, and through this extinguish the defilements [of passionate afflictions]. This is called the contemplation of karma by **śrāvakas.**

If you contemplate karma as [arising] from ignorance, and that karma is a result of ignorance, and [the rest of the twelvefold chain of causality from] name-and-form up to [the cycle of] birth-and-death is a result of karma, and that if you know [the truth about] ignorance and do not arouse a grasping for existence, then ignorance wil perish and therefore all [karmic volitional actions will perish. This is the contemplation of karma by **pratyekabuddhas.**

If you contemplate karma and volitional actions as illusory phantasms, and that these illusory phantasms are empty, and this emptiness is nirvana, this is called the contemplation of karma by **those of the Shared Teachings.**

There are beings predestined to damnation (*mithyātvaniyata*), predestined to salvation (*samyaktvaniyata*) or without predestination (*aniyata*); unhappy (*duḥkha*), happy (*sukha*) or neither unhappy nor happy (*aduḥkhāsukha*); higher (*agra*), middling (*madhya*) or lower (*avara*); still practicing (*śaikṣa*), no longer practicing (*aśaikṣa*) or neither one nor the other (*naivaśaikṣanāśaikṣa*); conscious (*saṃjñā*), unconscious (*asaṃjñā*), or neither conscious nor unconscious (*naivasaṃjñināsaṃjñin*); belonging to the desire realm (*kāmadhātu*), to the form realm (*rūpadhātu*) or to the formless realm (*ārūpadhātu*).

Beings belonging to the desire realm are of three kinds: as a result of their roots of good (*kuśalamūla*), they are higher (*agra*), middling (*madhya*) or lower (*avara*). The higher ones are the six classes of the gods of desire (*kāmadeva*); the middling ones are those among humans who are wealthy and noble; the lower ones are those among humans who are vile. The four continents (*dvīpaka*) are distinguished by differences in face. Bad beings are also of three categories: the higher are the damned (*naraka*); the middling ones are the animals (*tiryañc*), the lower are the pretas.

Nonpropelling karma 不動業 **beckons the reward of [birth in the realms of] form and no-form**: the *Inyō* identifies this phrase as from the commentary to the *Abhidharma-kośa*, T 29.237a21. The DDB has: "activity (karma) that is neither negative nor positive. Karma which is neither felicitous 福 (*puṇya*) nor evil 罪 (*apuṇya*), but is also not simply a matter of being 'neutral.' In most cases it is a more refined function of karma, since both the good and bad forms occur within the desire realm, while 'inactive [or nonpropelling] karma' is a result that is related to existence in the two upper realms of form and formlessness. One of the three kinds of karma 三業. (Skt. *āniñjyaṃ karma, ānaiñjya, āneñja, acalakarma*)."

If you contemplate karma as like the great earth, able to give birth to various sprouts, and that the ten dharma realms [from hell to Buddha] all arise through karma, this is called [114a] the contemplation of karma by **those of the Distinct Teachings.**

These are all [contemplations of] objects that are conceivable, and are not what is used here [in the *Mo-ho chih-kuan*].

Objects as Inconceivable [114a1]

[The contemplation of] objects as inconceivable is [as follows]. As the [*Lotus] Sūtra* says, "Having profoundly mastered the marks of offences and merit": "offences" refers to [rebirth in] the three evil [destinies], and "merit" refers to [rebirth in] the three good [destinies]. If you merely understand the marks of karma for the three evil destinies, and do not have penetrating understanding of the three good [destinies including that] of human and divine beings, this cannot be "profound mastery." Penetrating [both] evil and good is truly "profound mastery." If you penetrate the marks of good and evil karma only in the sense of [identifying] good and evil, this is not called "profound mastery." Again, "good" and "evil" [as opposites of each other] are both evil; to be free from good and free from evil are both "good"; this is "profound mastery." Again, penetrating good and evil in the human and divine realms involves extremes of [the realm of] birth and death; the penetrating of nirvana by those of the two vehicles is free from good and free from evil, but this is emptiness as an extreme [that is, emptiness in contrast to being or non-emptiness]; this merely involves [the duality] of two extremes, so it is not called "profound mastery." Again, everything involving [the duality of] two extremes is evil, and is not called "profound mastery." **Bodhisattvas of the Distinct Teachings** are able to penetrate [beyond] the shallowness of two extremes and gradually advance to profound mastery; therefore this is called "profound mastery." However, [bodhisattvas of] the Distinct Teachings gradually [and not immediately] advance [to profundity], so this is not [ultimate] "profound mastery." **Those of the Perfect Teaching** have penetrating understanding of deep karma even with regard to shallow karma, and therefore they deserve [to be described as] "having profoundly mastered the marks of offences and merit, and universally illuminating the ten directions." In this way they have profound mastery of reality, can

Having profoundly mastered the marks of offences and merit 深達罪福相: from the Devadatta chapter of the ***Lotus Sūtra***, T 9.35b28; this has been quoted many times already in the *Mo-ho chih-kuan*; see note at 111c27.

And universally illuminating the ten directions 遍照於十方: the second part of the phrase from the *Lotus Sūtra*, T 9.35b28; see previous note.

discern the three realms without a warped view, and can realize emptiness [directly] without any shortcuts. This is the meaning here.

Contemplate a single thought as it arises, that it includes [all] the ten dharma-realms [from hell to Buddha], which is [also] called the "ten directions" [or, is the same as "everywhere"]. The "ten directions" refer to the "circumstantial recompense" [of our environment]; the "ten destinies" refer to the "direct karmic recompense" [of our specific minds and bodies]. If there is no "circumstantial recompense" there is no "direct karmic recompense"; if there is direct karmic recompense, we already have the hundred dharmas [from the interaction of the ten suchlike characteristics] such as your nature, appearances, and beginning-and-end-ultimately-equal [and so forth]; this is also called "one hundred directions." [All of] these dharmas are included in the karma of one single thought; therefore it is said that one karmic deed includes all karmic deeds. The *Avataṃsaka Sūtra* says: "Son of the Buddha. The nature of the mind is one; how is it that various karma arises?" The answer is: it is analogous to the great earth which is one but is able to give rise to various sprouts. If the earth receives rain, [both] poisonous and medicinal [herbs] spring forth simultaneously. Now, when the ground of the Dharma-nature 法性地 receives the rain that comes from practicing the path 行道雨, the sprouts of good and evil karma compete to arise in a single thought. "Karma" is thus called the "dharma realm" 法界, and includes all dharmas. Therefore this is called "objects as inconceivable."

Shortcuts 徑侹: The *Kōgi* (BT-V, 176) identifies this phrase as appearing in the "Enjoyment in Untroubled Ease" chapter 逍遙篇 of Chuang-tzu.

If there is no "circumstantial recompense," there is no "direct karmic recompense" 若無依報亦無正報: or, if there is no environment, there is no birth with a personal body and mind?

Hundred dharmas 百法: see the analysis of the interpenetration of the ten destinies and ten suchlike characteristics into a hundred and then a thousand dharmas, *Mo-ho chih-kuan* 52c9ff.

Son of the Buddha. The nature of the mind is one; how is it that various karma arises? 佛子心性是一云何能生種種諸業: see the *Avataṃsaka Sūtra* at T 9.427a3–9, the opening question of a long chapter on "Clarifying Difficulties." For a translation of this section see Cleary, *Flower Ornament Scripture*, 298–311.

The great earth is one but is able to give rise to various sprouts 大地一能生種種芽: the answer to the question appears later in the chapter of the *Avataṃsaka Sūtra* at T 9.428a16–17, b1–2 (Cleary, 303):

> It is analogous to the great earth being one but is able to give birth to various sprouts; the nature of the earth is not different or distinct. All dharmas are also like this.... It is analogous to the great earth being one but is able to give birth to various sprouts without either enmity nor intimacy. The Buddha's fields of merit are also like this.

2. Arousing Compassion [114a21]

Thus if you have profound mastery [and penetrating understanding] of the objects of karma, including both good and evil, then compassion will arise. The principle of offences and merit is neither a matter of being "contrary" nor being "in accord" 非違非順, but being contrary [to the principle] results in offences and being in accord with [principle] results in merit.

For example, in terms of the worldly truth, the names and forms and various material things also are not a matter of being "contrary" or "in accord," but if you steal [some material thing] this is an offence that will result in the evil karma of the three [evil] destinies. If you abandon [material things], this will produce merit that will result in karma [for birth] in the three good destinies. Bodhisattvas have profound mastery in this way concerning being contrary or in accord, arousing pity with regard to that which is contrary, and arousing compassion with regard to that which is in accord.

In terms of the real truth of emptiness, the path is taught without words, so it involves neither being "contrary" nor "in accord." "Contrary" in this context refers to the karma from the defilements of the six destinies [from hell to the realm of gods], and "in accord" refers to the undefiled karmic reward [of enlightenment] of those of the three vehicles. Bodhisattvas have profound mastery [of the truth] of emptiness that does not involve being "contrary" or "in accord," and so with regard to what is "contrary" **[114b]** they arouse pity, and with regard to what is "in accord" they arouse compassion.

The truth of the Middle Path also does not involve being "contrary" or "in accord." "Contrary" in this context refers to the karma of the extremes of defiled and undefiled, and "in accord" refers to the karma of the Middle Path that is neither defiled nor undefiled. When the *Lotus Sūtra* says, "Attained after cultivating karmic deeds for a long time," this is the karma [that is meant here]. Bodhisattvas have profound mastery of the true aspect [of reality] of the Middle Path that do not involve being "contrary" or "in accord," and so arouse pity with regard to what is "contrary" and arouse compassion with regard to what is "in accord." If you have profound mastery [and penetrating understanding] that a single thought of the mind involves neither being "contrary" nor "in accord" [with the principle of karma], does not involve threefold distinctions [with regard to emptiness, conventional-

Attained after cultivating karmic deeds for a long time 久修業所得: a phrase from verses in the *Lotus Sūtra* chapter on "The Lifespan of the Tathāgata," T 9.43c221; Hurvitz (244 [225]) has:

Such is the power of my knowledge,
The rays of my wisdom having an incalculable glow,
My life-span being of numberless kalpas,
Gained after cultivation of long practice.

ity, and the Middle], and that this single thought of compassion has neither before nor after, this is called "true and correct aspiration for enlightenment (*bodhicitta*)."

3. Skillful Means for a Peaceful Mind [114b7]

A peaceful mind [by realizing] the emptiness of karma involves being in accord with good and stopping evil. "Stopping evil" is also called "cessation" 止, and being in accord with good is also called "contemplation" 觀. A peaceful mind [by realizing] the conventionality of karma involves stopping evil and being in accord with good. A peaceful mind [by realizing] karma as the Middle involves stopping evil and being in accord with good. Since it is "in accord," it is called "contemplation"; since it is "stopping [evil]," it is called "cessation." This is called "contemplation of karma as skillful means for a peaceful mind."

4. Deconstructing Dharmas [114b10]

The universal deconstruction of dharmas [with regard to the marks of karma] are as follows: The Abhidharma says, "Karma returns and enters [from?] the past, and the practitioner is restricted as if bound by shackles, so that he receives karmic recompense in the future." The *Ch'eng shih lun* says that karma goes from the present and enters the future, so that you receive karmic recompense in the future. Now you should contemplate this karma

True and correct aspiration for enlightenment 眞正菩提心: this is the phrase used in the original section explaining the arousal of compassion and the aspiration for enlightenment as the second of the ten modes of contemplation; see *Mo-ho chih-kuan* 55c26–56b12.

Abhidharma says, "Karma returns ... in the future" 阿毘曇云。業謝入過去得繩繫屬行人。未來受報: the source for this interpretation is unknown.

Bound by shackles 繩繫: a phrase also used at 93c14.

***Ch'eng shih lun* says "karma goes from the present and enters the future, so that you receive karmic recompense in the future"** 成實云。業從現在入未來未來受報: a summary of a passage at T 32.297b26–c1.

Question: In the sūtras the Buddha explains three kinds of karma: the karma of present recompense, arising recompense, and later recompense 現報生報後報業. What does this mean?

Answer: If this body produces karma, then this body must receive [the resultant karmic effects]. This is called "the karma of present recompense." Karma produced in this world can [arouse karmic effects] in the coming world. This is called "arising recompense." Karma produced in this world can effect faults in the following worlds. This is called "later recompense."

The three types of karma are also defined as follows (DDB): "The three kinds of recompense, i.e. in the present life for deeds now done 現報; in the next rebirth for deeds now done 生報; and in subsequent lives" 後報.

[as follows]: suppose karma [arises] in the past, but the past is already gone, and therefore how can we say that karma exists [in the past]? Suppose karma [arises] in the future, but the future does not yet exist, so how can we say that there is karma [in the future]? Suppose karma [arises] in the present, but the present does not abide from thought to thought, and once a thought passes on it is part of the past. If a thought has not yet arrived, it is part of the future. [Thoughts] arise and perish; what is the "present"? If we say that karma exists when it passes on 去 and that this is the "present," then what passes on is karma. If [we define] karma in terms of what passes on, then the time that it passes on [that is, the present] passes on, so the passing on passes on, and so the "present" does not exist. Thus "karma" cannot be attained [or explained rationally]. If examined through the three times [of past, present, and future], and analyzed both horizontally and vertically, the karma of good and evil cannot be obtained [or verbally or conceptually explained]; it is ultimately pure. Moreover, to speak [verbally] of good and evil karma is merely using mundane words and conventional names to make distinctions; you should not upon hearing names assume that [what they refer to] is real. Why is this so? We basically seek the truly real, and do not seek [that which is merely] vain and empty designation. [That which is merely] a vain and empty designation has no [substantial] nature, and though distinctions are made forcefully, it is like pointing at empty space. [Thus you should know that] karma is neither [really] produced nor received; the threefold truth [of emptiness, conventionality, and the Middle reveals that] all are quiescent. Therefore this is called "the universal deconstruction of dharmas" [of the marks of karma].

5. Knowing What Penetrates and What Obstructs [114b24]

Knowing what penetrates and what obstructs [with regard to the marks of karma] is as follows: you should know about suffering and the causes of suffering within the four options of karma, not-karma, both-karma-and-not-karma, and neither-karma-nor-not-karma, and completely know about the path and the extinction [of the causes of suffering] within each and every

The passing on passes on: 爲當去時去去者去: see the second chapter on "Coming and Going" in the *Middle Treatise*, T 30.3c5ff., esp. 4a1–6. Brian Bocking (Ph.D. thesis, vol. 2, 16–17) translates:

> In the already-gone there is no going
> And in the not-yet-gone there is no going
> Apart from the already-gone and the not-yet-gone
> The moment of going also has no going.
> … If someone asserts that there is going in a moment-of-going,
> This person is in error.
> The moment-of-going exists without any separate "going"
> Since the moment of going "goes" in itself.

[thought] in the mind. You are accomplished in all these matters, so this is not like words made by insects [chewing on wood]. Therefore this is called "knowing what penetrates and what obstructs."

6. Steps on the Path [114b27]

Adjusting the steps on the path [is as follows]: The scholars of the *Ch'eng shih lun* say that mental karma arising on its own is not yet [functional] karma. When the mind obtains real dharmas, concepts attain a conventional name, and volitional activity makes connections, then mental karma attains fruition. That is, there are the three bases of thought; the two types of physical [**114c**] and verbal karma are [involved in] physical form *(rupa)*, which we call the mindfulness of [the impurity of] the body 身念處. The scholars of the Abhidharma say that mental activity and consciousness [lit, the "mind-king"] arise simultaneously. This "king" [of consciousness] is [what we refer to as] "the mindfulness of thoughts [as impermanent]" 心念處. "Sensations" 受數 is [what we refer to as] "the mindfulness of sensations [as ultimately painful]" 受念處. Conceptions and other mental activity are all part of the skandha of volitional activity, which is [what we refer to as] "the mindfulness of dharmas [as being without substantial reality] 法念處. The consciousness and mental activity depend on physical form *(rupa)* to arise, which is [what we refer to as] the mindfulness of the body 身念處. Whether at the same time or at a different time, all things have these four mental aspects.

Now, contemplate this karma as including the five aggregates [from physical form to consciousness] of the ten dharma realms [from hell to Buddha], and that each includes all of the four types of mindfulness. All karma involves the same type of physical form; this is the mindfulness of the body. This body is neither pure nor impure. The other four [mental] aggregates involve [the other] three types of mindfulness [of thoughts, sensations,

Words made by insects: a reference to a passage in the *Mahāparinirvāṇa Sūtra*, T 12.618b2–6 which points out that insects do not know whether or not the marks they happen to make from chewing on wood are words having meaning or not. This image has appeared many times in the *Mo-ho chih-kuan*; see note at 10b27.

Scholars of the *Ch'eng shih lun* say that mental karma arising on its own is not yet karma 成論人云。意業單起未得成業: it is not clear who precisely this refers to.

Three bases of thought 三念處: of sensation 受, body 身, and dharmas/phenomena 法? Or, this could refer to "three kinds of mindfulness"? In any case Chih-i's use of these three categories is not clear here, especially when he brings up the "mindfulness of the body," which in the T'ien-t'ai context is one of four types of mindfulness. The rest of the four types follow, with no clear reference to these "three bases."

Scholars of the Abhidharma say "mental activity and consciousness arise simultaneously" 心數心王同時而起: it is not clear who precisely this refers to.

and dharmas]. These three involve neither suffering nor bliss, neither self nor non-self, neither permanence nor transience; they involve neither flourishing nor decaying, yet with both [aspects] involved in [the attainment of] nirvana and the three kind of liberation. This is called [adjusting to] the steps of the path.

7. Auxiliary Methods [114c9]

Controlling and healing through auxiliary methods for the path are [as follows]: you should be mindful of the thirty-two marks of the Buddha of manifestation 應佛 [in his historical body], and be mindful of the immeasurable virtues of the Buddha of recompense 報佛 [enjoying the rewards of his good karma], who have both destroyed the habitual causes of evil karma; be mindful of the Dharma-teachings Buddha that destroys habitual causes [of karma] and its thirty-two marks which destroy the resultant recompense [of karma], and so forth. Being mindful of the Dharma-teachings Buddha assists in destroying the resultant recompense of evil karma. Due to the power of being mindful of the Buddha, the obstacles of evil karma can be converted, and you can enter the gate of nirvana.

8. Graded Stages of Attainment [114c14]

When you contemplate in this way, there is no need to garrulously explain the upper noble 上聖 [stages of attainment].

9. Resting in Patient Forbearance [114c14]

Again, you should rest in patient forbearance with regard to internal and external obstacles, being without obstructions.

10. No Passionate Attachments to Dharmas [114c1]

Even if you arouse [the level of] resemblance to the path, you have not yet realized true understanding, so you should not arouse passionate attachments to dharmas. If you do not arouse passionate attachments to dharmas

Neither flourishing nor decaying 非榮非枯: see the note and discussion of "four types of flourishing and decay" above at *Mo-ho chih-kuan* 88c18.

Dharma-teachings Buddha 法門佛: this unusual rendering seems to refer to the teachings [Buddha Dharma] itself, so it is somewhat different than the usual "Dharma Body" which rounds out the list of the triple body of the Buddha, which is given in its more common form a few lines below. Chih-i sometimes uses this form of Buddha-body, which makes it difficult to give a consistent interpretation of his theory of the three [or four] bodies of the Buddha.

you will be spontaneous and unobstructed, and flow naturally to the pure and cool ground [of enlightenment].

11. Summary [114c17]

These are the ten [modes] of contemplation of the Mahāyāna, by which you attain the immeasurable, undefiled, and pure resultant rewards [of good karma], obtains the unsurpassed reward [of enlightenment], and obtains the karmic reward of mastery. Through profound mastery you are ultimately undefiled by offences or merit, and therefore this is called "pure." This is the Dharma Body. Turning back to the basis and returning to the source 反本還源, wisdom is illuminated and perfected. Therefore this is called "unsurpassed"; this is the Body of Recompense. These forms are let down in the nine realms [from hell to bodhisattvahood] and manifested universally. Therefore this is called "mastery," and is the Body of Manifestation. In this way these three bodies [of the Buddha] are the high and broad way of Mahāyāna, the direct way to the seat of enlightenment. The rest is as explained above.

Manifested universally 普門示現: a phrase from the closing paragraph of the 25th chapter (on Avalokiteśvara) of the *Lotus Sūtra*, T 9.58b6; see note at 11a25.

Direct way to the seat of enlightenment 直至道場: a phrase from the verses in the second chapter of the *Lotus Sūtra*, T 9.15a14. This phrase has been quoted many times already; see note at 31a9–10.

As explained above: see the summary after the original exposition on the ten modes of contemplation at 100a3–b16.

5. Contemplating the Objects of Demonic Forces [114c22–117a20]

The fifth [of the ten objects of contemplation] is contemplating the objects of demonic matters [of Māra]. When a practitioner cultivates the Four Samādhis, leaving behind evil and wishing to give birth to good, then Māra fears that this person will turn away and escape from his realm, and furthermore save others, so that he [Māra, thinks], "I will lose the people who belong to me and my palace will become empty." Again, he anxiously thinks, "If this [person] attains great supranormal powers and the power of great wisdom, he will engage in a great battle against me, will overcome and restrain me, and be a great vexation for me." [Māra] thereupon rushes to keep him from attaining [enlightenment] and to destroy his good roots. Therefore these are called "demonic matters" [of Māra]. When the practitioner is still weak with regard to the path, [the demonic powers of] Pāpīyas are not yet put in motion, but [as you advance along the path and attempt to leave behind the realm of desires,] all of the demons and spirits associated with the six heavenly realms [of desire] will try to protect this realm and will certainly put these [demonic forces] into motion. A sūtra says, "Not speaking of demonic matters and the demonic offences **[115a]** is for a bodhisattva to be a bad friend." If you have a penetrating understanding of the deviant and correct [matters concerning demonic forces], the yearning to embrace them will pale. Know that the suchness of the demonic realm and the suchness of the Buddha realm are of one suchness and not two, undiscriminated and of one mark 平等一相, so do not mourn concerning the demonic, or rejoice over the Buddha, but rest peacefully in true reality. If you are able to be this

Demonic matters [of Māra] 魔事: see also the shorter analysis of this topic in the *Shorter Manual*, T 46.470b1–471b1.

Pāpīyas 波旬: the lord of demons, another name for Māra. "Transliteration of the Sanskrit; also Pāpīyān, meaning 'devil' 'evil demon,' 魔 or 'demon king;' 魔王, the Evil One 惡者, the Murderer 殺者, Māra, because he strives to kill all goodness" (DDB).

Not speaking of demonic matters and the demonic offences is for a bodhisattva to be a bad friend 魔事魔罪不説者是菩薩惡知識: see a passage in the *Pañcaviṃśati Sūtra*, T 8.241a–c, which includes the following:

> Subhūti, bodhisattva-mahāsattvas can also be bad friends, if they do not teach about demonic matters and do not teach about demonic offences or speak of them. A demon can take the form of a Buddha and appear in this guise, kill [the spirit of the] bodhisattvas, and make them depart from the six perfections.

The suchness of the demonic realm and the suchness of the Buddha realm 魔界如佛界如: see the *Śūraṅgama Samādhi Sūtra*, T 15.639c15, which has the phrase, "The suchness of the demonic realm and the suchness of the Buddha realm are neither two nor distinct."

This has been referred to above in the *Mo-ho chih-kuan*, see note at 50a4–5 for a translation of the context.

way, perverse [evil] will not obstruct the right [path], and even if vexations arise from the presence of Māra, this is still exceedingly good.

Now the clarification [of matters] concerning Māra consists of five [parts]: 1. Distinctions concerning similarities and differences; 2. Clarification of the marks of the arising [of demonic influences]; 3. Clarification of their obstructions and disturbances; 4. Clarifying ways to control [demonic matters]; and 5. Cultivating cessation-and-contemplation.

1. Distinctions concerning Similarities and Differences [115a6]

Similarities and differences [are as follows: there are four categories of demonic forces.] [1] the demons of the skandhas 陰魔 are those associated with the objects of the [five] aggregates *(skandha)*, the [twelve] sense entrances *(āyatana)*, and the [eighteen] sense realms *(dhātu)* 陰入界; [2] the demons of passionate afflictions 煩惱魔 are those associated with the objects of the passionate afflictions; [3] the demon of death 死魔 refers to disease as the cause of death, and is associated with the objects of disease; here we will clarify [4] the supernatural demons 天子魔.

The difference between the four warped [views that the world is permanent, full of pleasure, endowed with selfhood, and pure *(nitya-sukha-ātma-śuci)*] and the four demonic forces is as follows. The four warped views are all a part of the demons of passionate afflictions; because of the demons of passionate afflictions there are the demons of the aggregates, sense entrances, [and sense realms]; because of the demons of the aggregates and senses, there is the demon of death; and one speaks of the supernatural demons because one has not yet escaped this triple world.

As for the similarities and differences [in demonic forces] in the realm beyond [delusions] 界外, having destroyed the four warped views within the [triple] realm 界内 (of desire, form, and no-form) you can get past all of the demons of [ordinary] constituent [samsara], but if [vestiges of] the four warped views such as [the world is] impermanent and so forth remain, these become the demons of passionate afflictions in the realm beyond [delusions]. Because of these demons of passionate afflictions, there are the visible forms

If [vestiges of] the four warped views such as [the world is] impermanent and so forth remain 唯有無常等四倒: Usually the "four perversions" or "warped views" are to be attached to the world as "permanent, blissful, with selfhood, and pure," but in the realm beyond delusions, the vestiges of the four warped views are to be attached to the opposite views of impermanence, suffering, non-selfhood, and impurity?

This may refer to a passage from the *Mahāparinirvāṇa Sūtra*, T 12.761a–b, which speaks of the demon Pāpīyas and our attachments to objects of the five desires of the senses. This has been referred to above in the *Mo-ho chih-kuan*, see note at 20b13.

that are "equal with the unequalled," which are the demons of the skandhas of the realm beyond [delusions]. Due to the demons of the skandhas, there is death. As for the resultant recompense of those in the three levels of erudition and ten noble stages, up to the level of "equivalent to awakening," these people have already passed beyond three types of demonic forces [of the skandhas, passionate afflictions, and the supernatural] and are only faced with one: the demon of death. These are the three demonic forces [of the skandhas, passionate afflictions, and death] of the realm beyond [delusions]; there are no demons of the sixth heavenly realm, but since the Red-colored

Visible forms that are "equal with the unequalled" 無等等色: Skt. *asamasamarupa*), "equal to the unequalled (Buddha)." In the realm beyond delusions, one who is seen as equal to the ideal (of Buddhahood) can be a "demon" that distracts from enlightenment?

Resultant recompense of those in the three levels of erudition and ten noble stages 三賢十聖住果報: a phrase from the *Jen wang ching*, T 8.828a1. This phrase has also been referred to many times already in the *Mo-ho chih-kuan.*

Passed beyond three types of demonic forces 三魔已過 ...: although the context seems quite different, see the *Ying lo ching* at T 24.1012c27–1013a14:

> Son of the Buddha, the bodhisattva with the necklace of Maṇi jewels is one of those with the nature of [the level] equivalent to awakening. His name is Vajra-wisdom Banner Bodhisattva. He dwells at the peak of quiescent concentration, and with the power of great vows dwells alive for a hundred kalpas, cultivating a thousand samādhis and entering the Vajra Samādhi, simultaneously merging with the marks of all dharma-nature, the two truths, and the one truth. Again, he dwells for a thousand kalpas studying Buddhahood with dignity, like the king of elephants carefully watching the ambulating lions. Again, he cultivates Buddhahood with immeasurable, inconceivable, supranormal, and transformative methods, and therefore all Buddha-dharmas appear before him. He enters the Buddha's place of practice and sits on the Buddha's seat of enlightenment, and *conquers the three [types of] demons.* Again, he dwells for 10,000 kalpas and is transformed and becomes a Buddha, entering great quiescent concentration, *with awakening equivalent to the Buddhas* and [realizing] the two truths of the realm beyond [delusions]. neither existent nor non-existent, without thoughts and without form, without any remaining habitual causes or effects, appearing the same as the Buddhas of old, but having a name of a Manifestation [Body of a Buddha?]. Appearing with various forms and thought, he teaches and saves sentient beings, appearing the same as the Buddhas of old, constantly practicing the Middle Path. He has great bliss and is without action, but has the differences of arising and perishing.... Constantly staying on the Middle Path and transcending all dharmas, he overcomes the four [types of] demons.

Sixth heavenly realm 第六天: the sixth of the six heavenly realms of desire; the heaven where one enjoys objects of bliss created by other divine beings (*paranirmita vaśavartin* 他化自在天). The DDB has: "The sixth of the six heavens of desire, or affliction heavens, the last of the six *devalokas* 六欲天, the abode of Mahêśvara (Śiva), and of Māra. The beings there enjoy a good environment created by others. Also where Pāpīyān, the King of the Māras, resides."

Samādhi has not yet been fulfilled, there are still the supernatural demons. If sublime awakening has been perfected, ignorance is extinguished and therefore there are no passionate afflictions. You do not dwell with any resultant recompense, and therefore there is no death. The Red-colored Samādhi is complete, so demonic matters are ultimately ended. The *Avataṃsaka Sūtra* clarifies ten types of demonic forces, but they do not go beyond the meaning here.

2. Clarifying the Marks of the Arising of Māra [115a19]

Second is clarifying the marks of the arising of Māra. In general, whether in charge or affiliated 管屬, all of these take the name of "demon" Māra 魔; if examined in detail with regard to their differences as branches, there are no more than three types: 1. Fearful nerve-racking demons 媞惕鬼; 2. Form-shifting demons of the time periods 時媚鬼; and 3. the demon Māra 魔羅鬼. Each of these three types are different in the marks that they arouse.

1. Nerve-Racking Demons [115a22]

The arising of "nerve-racking" [demons] [is as follows]: when a person sits [in meditation], [these demons may] make contact with your head or face,

Red-colored Samādhi 赤色三昧: the fourteenth of the twenty-five Samādhis, during which one transcends the six heavenly realms of desire (see Glossary). See the list of twenty-five Samādhis in the *Mahāparinirvāṇa Sūtra*, T 12.690b2–23, esp. line 14: "The Red-colored Samādhi allows you to sever [passionate attachments], save others, and allow mastery of existence in the heavens."

Ten types of demonic forces 十魔: see the list of ten demonic forces in the *Avataṃsaka Sūtra* at T 9.663a6ff.:

> Son of the Buddha, the bodhisattva-mahāsattva deals with ten types of demons. What are these ten? They are [1] the demons of the five skandhas 五陰魔, which are due to the covetous attachments of the five aggregates.[2] The demons of the passionate afflictions 煩惱魔 are the defilements of the passionate afflictions. [3] The demons of karma 業魔, because they are able to obstruct you. [4] The demons of the mind 心魔, because of your arrogance. [5] The demon of death 死魔, because it means separating from life. [6] The heavenly demons 天魔, because they arouse arrogance and indolence. [7] The demons of losing your good roots 失善根魔, because the mind is unrepentant. [8] The demons of samādhi 三昧魔, because you become attached to its flavor. [9] The demons of good friends 善知識魔, because you become attached to this life. And [10] the demons of not knowing bodhi-wisdom and the true Dharma 不知菩提正法魔, because you are unable to arouse great vows. Son of the Buddha, these are the ten types of demonic forces of the bodhisattva-mahāsattva....

Nerve-racking demons 媞惕鬼: Soothill-Hodous has "A demon of the nerves who troubles those who sit in meditation. Also 堆惕鬼; 埠惕鬼."

When a person sits ... with four eyes and two mouths: more details on these demons are found in the closing section

or make contact with your body, falling or rising repeatedly without end. Although this does not cause pain, it is insistent and difficult to endure. Or they drill into people's ears, eyes, or nose, or embrace or attack so that you feel as if invaded by something, but you cannot get hold of it, and even if it seems you have driven it away, it appears again, or there is a ringing in your ears like the busy chirping of birds or insects. The faces of these demons are like a flat lute 琵琶, with four eyes and two mouths, and so forth.

2. Form-Shifting Demons of the Time Periods [115a26]

Form-shifting demons of the time periods [are as follows]: *The Great Collection of Sūtras* explains about the twelve beasts who dwell in the mountain of treasures and cultivate compassion conditioned by Dharma teachings. These

of the *Secret Essential Methods for Healing Disease through Meditation*, T 15.341a23–342b14, which appears to be an independent sūtra:

> Methods for healing for the beginner sitting in meditation who is unable to attain concentration due to various anxieties and attachments by demonic forces (questions by Ānanda). Thus have I heard. At one time the Buddha dwelt in Vaiśālī, in the Jetavana Park.… Mahākāśyapa taught the thousand monks saying, "In counting your breath [during meditation] at a quiet place, demonic forces 鬼魅 can become attached [to you], and you will see a demonic spirit, whose face is like a flat lute, with four eyes and two mouths, light shining from its face, with its hands holding weapons, as well as under both armpits and other parts of its body, its mouth chanting the words 'be anxious, be anxious' 埠惕埠惕, so that one feels locked in a ring of fire, attacked by lightning, sometimes arising and sometimes perishing, making the practitioner feel unstable and anxious. If you see this, you should quickly try to control it.…

The text continues with suggestions for controlling the situation and further questions along this line, which is referred to below at 116a12–20.

The twelve beasts who dwell in the mountain of treasures and cultivate compassion conditioned by Dharma teachings 十二獸在寶山中修法緣慈: see the long section in *The Great Collection of Sūtras* at T 13.167c–168a, concerning the twelve animals associated with the twelve periods of a day, the twelve months, and the twelve-year cycle, but the point seems quite different from Chih-i's application. See especially 168a5–11:

> These twelve animals move constantly day and night within [our world of] Jambudvīpa, and divine and human beings respect them, and they bring about benefits. When a Buddha makes a profound vow for a day and night, he constantly leads one animal on a journey of teaching and transformation, and the other eleven to peacefully dwell in cultivating compassion. This cycle is then repeated. [For example,] on the first day of the seventh month of the rat a journey begins, and with the śrāvaka vehicle all sentient beings with the body of a rat are taught to be free from their evil deeds and encouraged to cultivate good deeds. In this way you pass through thirteen days, and there is also a return for the rats [of another 13 days?]. In this way twelve months are exhausted; the same cycle is repeated over twelve years.

are the lords of the form-shifting [demons]. Those that appear tentatively in response [to conditions] do not necessarily cause afflictions, but those that appear in reality are able to trouble the practitioner [of meditation]. Sitting in meditation with deviant conceptions often results in possession by these form-shifting [demons]. At times [**115b**] they will appear as young boys or young girls, or as an old man or old woman, or in the form of a beast. They appear in various forms which are not the same. At times they entertain people, and at times they seem to teach or command people.

Now I wish to distinguish the various beasts of the time periods. By examining the twelve time periods and at what time these [demons] come, you can tell which beast it is by the time it comes. If it is the time of the tiger 寅 [3:00–5:00 AM], it is a tiger 虎 [that appears], and so forth up to the time of the ox 丑 [1:00–3:00 AM], when a bull 牛 [that appears]. Again, each time period has three [associated animals], so that for twelve time periods there are [a total of] thirty-six animals. The time of the tiger has three: the first is a badger 貍; the second is a panther 豹; the third is a tiger 虎. The time of the rabbit 卯 [5:00–7:00 AM] has three: fox 狐, rabbit 兎, and raccoon 貉. The time of the dragon 辰 [7:00–9:00 AM] has three: dragon 龍, scaly dragon or shark 蛟, and fish 魚. These nine are associated with the direction of the east and with [the element of] wood. These nine appear in order from the first of the month, to the middle, and through the seasons 孟仲季. The time of the snake 巳 [9:00–11:00 AM] has three: cicada 蟬, carp 鯉, and snake 蛇. The time of [the horse at] noon [11:00 AM–1:00 PM] has three: deer 鹿, horse 馬, and roebuck deer 獐. The time of the goat 未 [1:00–3:00 PM] has three: sheep 羊, wild goose 雁, and hawk or eagle 鷹. These nine are associated with the direction of the south and with fire. The time of the monkey 申 [3:00–5:00 PM] has three: gibbon 狖, ape 猿, and monkey 猴. The time of the rooster 酉 [5:00–7:00 PM] has three: black crow 烏, crow 雞, and pheasant 雉. The time of the dog 戌 [7:00–9:00 PM] has three: dog 狗, wolf 狼, and jackal 豺. These nine are associated with the direction of the west and with metal. The time of the pig 亥 [9:00–11:00 PM] has three: pig 豕, hog 貐, and wild boar 猪. The time of the rat [11:00 PM–1:00 AM] has three: cat 猫, mouse 鼠, and bat 伏翼. The time of the ox 丑 [1:00–3:00 AM] has three: bull 牛, crab 蟹, and tortoise 鼈. These nine are associated with the direction of the north and with water. The middle direction and earth are the kings of the four seasons, so if you go in the four directions you should use [the element] earth, which [in terms of animals] are fish, wild goose, jackal, and tortoise. If each [of the three time periods] has three options, this gives [a total of] thirty-six [animals]. If each are given a further threefold variation, there are one hundred and eight animals for the time periods. If you deeply consider these meanings, and depending on the time call out the names [of the animals], their enchanting forms should vanish, If you are possessed by them for a long time, it can cause you to go mad or fall into a trance, mistakenly teach about divination, and fail to avoid [the dangers of] water and fire, and so forth.

3. The Demon Māra [115b17]

Next is to clarify [concerning] Māra. In order to destroy the two types of goodness 二善 [of the already good and future goodness] and cause an increase in the two types of evil 二惡 [of the already evil and future evil], he delights in working his destruction through the [five] senses, appearing in [both] strong/hard and soft 強軟 [guises]. The *Ta chih tu lun* says, "Māra is called the 'floral arrow' and 'the five arrows.'" Each [of the arrows] is "shot"

Demon Māra 魔羅: the lord of demons, the personification of death, also called "the murderer" and "the tempter" because he uses various temptations and strives to hinder Buddhist practice and kill your aspiration for enlightenment. In accounts of the life of the Buddha, he is the one who tried all desperate measures in a final attempt to keep Gautama from attaining enlightenment under the Bodhi tree.

The "floral arrow" 花箭 **and "the five arrows"** 五箭: "floral arrow" presumably because his temptations are disguised as being attractive, like flowers, especially to the desires of the five senses, which are the target of the "five arrows." See the extensive section at *Ta chih tu lun*, T 25.99b17–100a8 ("arrows" are mentioned at 99c21). See Lamotte (*Le Traité* 1, 339–46); Chodron (1, 282) translates:

> Question. Why is he called Māra?
> Answer. He is called Māra because he carries off *(harati)* the *āyuṣmat* and because he destroys the good root of the dharmas of the Path and of the qualities *(guṇa)*. The heretics *(tīrthika)* call him *Yu tchou* 欲主 (Kāmādhipati [Lord of Desires]), *Houa tsien* 華箭 (Kusumāyudha [Flower Arrows]) or also Pañcāyudha [Five Arrows 五箭]). In the Buddhist texts, he is called Māra because he destroys all good works.
> His actions and works are called *māra-karman*.
> Question. What are the works of Māra?
> Answer. 1. They are defined in the chapter of the *Mārāvabodhaparivarta*.
> 2. Furthermore, if people have had to undergo happiness and misfortune in the course of successive lifetimes, the causes are the fetters *(samyojana)* as well as king Māra, who is called the enemy of the Buddha *(buddhavairin)*, the thief of the holy ones *(āryacaura)*. Because he destroys the actions of all who are ascending the current *(pratisrotagāmin)*, because he has a horror of nirvana, he is called Māra.
> 3. Māra has three types of actions: a. play *(līlā)*, laughter *(hāsya)*, idle chatter *(ālapā)*, singing *(gītā)*, dancing *(nṛtya)*, and everything that provokes desire *(rāga)*; b. iron fetters *(bandahana)*, beating *(ghaṭṭana)*, whipping *(kaśa)*, wounds *(prahāradāna)*, spikes *(kaṇtaka)*, knives *(śastra)*, slashing *(saṃchedana)* and everything that is caused by hatred *(dveṣa)*; c. [demented mortifications] such as being burned, being frozen, tearing out your hair *(keśolluñcana)*, starving, jumping into the fire, throwing oneself into the water, falling onto spears and everything that results from stupidity *(moha)*.
> 4. Finally, the great hindrances *(ādīnava)*, impure attachments to the world, that is all the work of Māra. Hatred of the

at the five sense organs and together they destroy the mind. The five senses each last only a single moment and if it "turns" for only a moment it becomes associated with the mental faculties, so if the mind is destroyed, how can the other five senses continue [to act as they should]? If the eye sees visible forms that [arouse] passionate attachment, this is called a "floral arrow," and this is like a "soft" bandit. If the eye sees visible forms that arouse fear, this is called a "poisonous arrow" and this is like a "hard or strong" bandit. If you see visible forms that are "flat" [and do not arouse passions and so forth], these are "bandits" that are neither soft nor hard. The rest of the four senses are likewise, giving a total of eighteen "arrows," also called the "eighteen experiences." Based on this, you should not arouse attachments [through the senses]; attachments arouse disease, and diseases are difficult to control or heal, and will obstruct dhyāna meditation for a long time, and when you die you will fall into the path of Māra. Again, even if Māra's shots [of arrows] do not enter internally, he can externally agitate your donor, master, colleagues, and disciples and thus shoot out eighteen arrows. In the past many monks suffered internal afflictions due to Māra but received praise or blame from donors, and the strong/hard and soft [bandits of desires] were not victorious, and Māra left in tears. The practitioners [of meditation] should well heed their masters and donors. Or, sometimes the strange words of a Dharma master will anger the disciples, and the bitter words [**115c**] of the disciples will cause the Dharma master to be bewildered. These stories are as taught extensively in the *Pañcavimśati Sūtra* [and *Ta chih tu lun*].

Again, Māra uses skillful tactics first to have people act contrary to good and arouse evil, and if they do not go along, simply leads them to "fall" into [being distracted by] performing good [deeds], to put up stupas and build temples, and thus hinder and disperse their practice of meditation. If even then they do not go along [with Māra], he leads them to follow [the way of] the two vehicles. Māra does not truly understand the two vehicles, but by leading people in this way hopes to lead them to not practice Mahāyāna. [Māra hopes that] like an ignorant child these people will [become attached

good, scorn of nirvana and of the path to nirvāṇa are also the work of Māra. Plunging into the ocean of suffering without ever awakening and innumerable errors of this kind are all the work of Māra. When one has rejected and abandoned these, one is *mārakarmasamatikrānta*.

Pañcaviṃśati Sūtra: Ikeda (*Kenkyū-chūshaku*, 424) and *Inyō* (74) point to a passage at T 8.320b–323a, but the contents do not match very well. Perhaps Chih-i was referring to the sūtra (or, as is often the case, the *Ta chih tu lun*) in general rather than to a specific passage. The *Kōgi* (BT–V, 198) points to "section 69/7" of the *Ta chih tu lun*, which likely refers to the passage in fascicle 69 at T 25.541a9–542c2, which explains how Māra can take on the form of a monk and work to destroy the perfection of wisdom.

to] the practice that they were first exposed to and thus abandon the Mahāyāna and cultivate Hīnayāna, and after much effort they would have many regrets and no benefit. One who practices hard, however, truly does not make distinctions between Mahāyāna and Hīnayāna. Again, in trying to save others, some may use emptiness without [skillful] means, saying there is no Buddha and no sentient beings, falling into a one-sided emphasis on emptiness, or into a one-sided [emphasis on] conventionality, and take various shortcuts that do not lead to realizing the Perfect [Teaching]. Even [respected disciples such as] Ānanda and Gupta, when they were [at

The brief nature and unclear meaning of these sentences, however, indicate that they refer to specific stories that would clarify what Chih-i is trying to say here. Numerous searches of the SAT database with various phrases from this passage, however, did not provide any clues.

Ānanda and Gupta 笈多: on Ānanda see the story in the *Mahāparinirvāṇa Sūtra*, T 12.848c13–845a21:

> At that time the World Honored One knew already but spoke to Ājñāta-kauṇḍinya saying, "Where is the bhikṣu Ānanda now?" Ājñāta-kauṇḍinya said, "World Honored One, the bhikṣu Ānanda is outside the *śāla* forest, twelve yojanas away from this assembly, being harassed by 640 billion demons 魔. Each and every one of these demons has transformed its body into the form of the Tathāgata, some preaching that all dharmas arise from causes-and-conditions, some preaching that all dharmas do not arise from causes, some preaching that all causes and conditions are [based on] eternal dharmas, but the arising from conditions is transiency, [and so forth] ... Or again they are manifested as a bodhisattva who takes seven steps when he is first born, dwells in the [royal] palace and experiences the five desires, leaves home and cultivates ascetic practices, sits in samādhi under the Bodhi tree and destroys the host of Māra, turns the wheel of the Dharma teachings, shows great supranormal powers, and enters nirvana. The bhikṣu Ānanda sees these things and has these thoughts. 'In this way magical transformations occurred in the past but were not seen. Who did this? It cannot be the World Honored One Śākyamuni who did this.' Thus desires were aroused and desires were expressed so that finally he was not able to follow the intent [to reach enlightenment]and the bhikṣu Ānanda fell into Māra's noose. He also thought, 'The teachings of all the Buddhas are not the same; whose words should I accept now?' World Honored One. Ānanda now is at an extreme in experiencing great suffering. Although he is mindful of the Tathāgata, he is not able to be saved. For these reasons he cannot come to be in this great assembly."

On Gupta (the fourth patriarch in the T'ien-t'ai lineage, after Ānanda and Śāṇavāsa) see note at *Mo-ho chih-kuan* 1a15. See also *The Transmission*, T 50, 306b10–cff.

> Śāṇavāsa [younger brother of Ānanda, third T'ien-t'ai patriarch, and teacher of Gupta] said, "The records of the Buddha say that you [Gupta] will appear one hundred years after [the Buddha's death], will be foremost in sitting in meditation and great in saving sentient beings. Now is surely that time to perform benefits and lead the masses to partake of the taste of ambrosia." Upagupta said, "Whoever accepts these teachings must deal with the attacks of Māra like clouds over the assembly."... The Demon King Papīyas also arouses great fear and thinks, "Upagupta will teach and lead the great assembly to leave my territory.

high levels of achievement such as] learning about non-retrogression 阿鞞跋 (*avaivartika*), are all afflicted by the influence of Māra; how much more so [is it difficult] for beginners to avoid the thirty-six arrows [used by Māra to obstruct the practices] for self-benefit and saving others! However, if you know that both the Buddha and Māra are a part of reality-as-it-is, you will have no fear. The *Mahāparinirvāṇa Sūtra* says, "For the sake of the śrāvakas the overcoming of Māra is taught; but in the case of those of the Mahāyāna, the overcoming of Māra is not taught." If you single-mindedly realize the principle [of the truth], who would debate over [matters concerning demons such as their being] "strong/hard" or "soft"?

3. Clarifying Their Obstructions and Disturbances [115c13]

Third is clarifying the obstructions and disturbances [caused by demons]. When the hard and soft arrows [of Māra] first are shot at the five sense organs, there are three kinds of torments: 1. causing human disease 令人病; 2. losing the contemplative mind 失觀心; and 3. attaining deviant dharmas 得邪法.

1. Causing Human Disease [115c14]

[First,] disease has various marks: disease that enters through the eye leads

> I should surely destroy this intent." So when [Gupta] preached the Dharma he [Māra] caused gold and jewels to rain down [and other distractions] so that not even one person could attain the Path. The Demon King rejoiced and was deeply satisfied with himself. Upagupta thereupon entered samādhi and perceived who had done these things. The Demon King also placed a garland of pearls and flowers around his neck, but the Noble One [Gupta] perceived that this was Māra's doing and thought, "The evil demon is jealous and wishes to destroy the true Dharma."… [and so forth].

For the sake of the śrāvakas the overcoming of Māra is taught; but in the case of those of the Mahāyāna, the overcoming of Māra is not taught 爲聲聞人説有調魔爲大乘者不説調魔: see the *Mahāparinirvāṇa Sūtra*, T 12.638a27–b12:

> Again, good sons, it is like the nature of a dragon is to be exceedingly evil. Wishing to harm people, it sometimes uses its eyesight and sometimes its [fiery] breath. Therefore all [creatures such as] lions, tigers [and so forth] arouse fear.… It is likewise with śrāvakas and pratyekabuddhas. When they see the demon Papīyas, they are all afraid, and the demon Papīyas is not afraid and proceeds to perform demonic deeds. Those who learn the Mahāyāna are also like this. Seeing the śrāvakas being fearful of demonic deeds, and not arousing faith in this Great Vehicle, first they use skillful means to overcome all demons, so that all are led to receive good and accept this [Great] Vehicle. This is the reason for extensive teachings and various sublime dharmas for śrāvakas and pratyekabuddhas to see and overcome demons and not arouse fear. But within this Great Vehicle—the unsurpassed true Dharma and the way to arouse faith—it can be said that we now follow this and do not need [the instructions concerning demons], and within the true Dharma they can [in turn] be an obstruction.

to disease of the liver, and so forth should be known for the rest of the sense organs. When the physical body encounters disease and suffering, the mind becomes deluded and reckless; dhyānic concentration disappears and the end is death.

2. Losing the Contemplative Mind [115c16]

[Second,] losing the contemplative mind: basically what you cultivate is contemplating good dharmas and attaining calm tranquility, but after you see and hear through the five sense organs [that are the conduit for temptations from Māra], the basis of the mind suddenly becomes dark and disordered.

3. Attaining Deviant Dharmas [115c18]

[Third,] deviant dharmas [are as follows]. We should consider ten types of true dharmas [in dualistic pairs] to examine deviant marks.

[1] "Being or existence" 有: when visible form enters through the eye you see mountains and rivers, stars and planets, sun and moon, houses and palaces, but if you also perceive in the obscure [darkness] various wild forms and faces in their direction, this is an excess of "being." "Non-being or nothingness" 無: when visible form enters through the eye [and you see things] but further [take the extreme view] that all phenomena are empty as if annihilated, and that phenomena are void and [nirvana merely a reduction to] ashes, this is exceedingly fearful. This is an excess of "non-being or nothingness."

[2] "Brightness or clarity" 明: after visible form enters [the eyes], if things are too open and constantly bright, as if the sun and moon are shining [in your eyes, this is an excess of brightness.] "Darkness" 闇: a dark gloom like black varnish obscures everything so that it is as if you are not awake[; this is an excess of darkness].

[3] "Stability" 定: after visible form enters [the eyes], the mind is like wood or a rock, stiff and straight[; this is an excess of stability]. "Disruption" 亂: after visible form enters [the eyes], you [lose control and] get thrown around and dragged about[; this is an excess of disruption].

[4] "Foolishness" 愚: after visible form enters [the eyes], you become dull and short-sighted, vulgar and superficial, so that you feel no shame at being naked. "Wisdom" 智: after visible form enters [the eyes], you become too clever, and quick to fall ill.

Should be known: as explained above in the section on Contemplating the Objects of Disease [106A19–111C22].

Empty as if annihilated 斷空: implies the mistaken extreme view that nirvana is merely being reduced to ashes with nothing left, and that "emptiness" means a nihilistic nothingness.

[5] “Sorrow” 悲: after visible form enters [the eyes], you are vexed by misery, and tears flow. “Happiness” 喜: after visible form enters [the eyes], you indulge in song and are always [excessively] happy.

[6] “Suffering” 苦: your hundred joints are in great pain, as if you were being burnt with fire. “Pleasure” 樂: your physical body is intoxicated with happiness, as if enjoying the five desires.

[7] “Misfortune/calamity” 禍: you constantly invite misfortune upon yourself, and also causes misfortune for others, and knowingly bring about misfortune to others. **[116a]** “Fortune” 福: you constantly invite [good] fortune for oneself, and also you are able to bring about [good] fortune for others.

[8] “Evil” 惡: you do not avoid producing evil [yourself], and also lead others to do evil. “Good” 善: you perform [good deeds such as] giving and so forth yourself, and also lead others to perform giving [and so forth].

[9] “Animosity” 憎: to not have the patience to see [and put up with] people and to dwell alone far from others. “Love” 愛: to cleave heavily [to persons and things] and be afflicted with attachments.

[10] “Strong or hard” 強: for your mind to be hard and strong so that you do not easily go in and out freely, like tiles or stones that are difficult to move about or change, and so you are not in accordance with the good path. “Soft or weak” 軟: your mind and resolution is soft, and is easily beaten or broken. If the clay is too soft, it cannot be used to make a vessel.

In this way, if things are in excess or insufficient, they are all called the marks of deviance.

One sense organ has three sensations; each sensation has twenty deviant dharmas [as just explained above], so the three sensations together add up to sixty deviant dharmas. The five sense objects together give a total of three hundred deviant dharmas. There are ninety-five varieties of various heterodox and deviant teachings, but it is certain that they first enter [your mind or consciousness] through the five sense organs, and if they are examined in detail, they are no different from the three hundred [deviant dharmas].

The nerve-racking demons often can cause your dhyānic contemplation to disappear or be lost, and the form-shifting demons of the time periods often can lead people to attain deviant dharmas, but it is Māra who can bring about both of these damages.

Three sensations 受: good, evil, and neutral?

Ninety-five varieties of various heterodox and deviant teachings 九十五種種種異邪: a general grab-bag of “non-Buddhist” teachings.

4. Clarifying Ways to Control Demonic Influences [116a12]

Fourth is clarifying ways to control [demonic influences].

[1] If you are to control the nerve-racking [demons], you should know that at the time of the Buddha Konāka[muni] there was a bhikṣu of the Latter [degenerate] Dharma 末法比丘 who delighted in afflicting and disturbing the assembly of monks, and so he was expelled [from the Sangha]. He immediately aroused an evil vow, that he would constantly trouble those who sit in dhyāna meditation. This was the original ancestor of these demons. His karmic recompense has already come to an end, but those who perform the same deeds [and become demons] can afflict and disturb us. Now you should rebuke this patriarch [of the demons], and hearing this he will be ashamed and leave. Rebuke him, saying, "I know your name! You are the nerve-racking evil yakṣa demon! At the time of the Buddha Konāka[muni] you broke the precepts and stole some dried meat, and [like the demon]

Control 治 the nerve-racking demons: this content is based on the closing section of the *Secret Essential Methods for Healing Disease through Meditation*, T 15, 341b24–c1, following the passage referred to above at 115a26:

> How, then, should these [demons] be controlled? The Buddha said to Ānanda, "Listen well. Listen well! Contemplate well on these things, for I will teach them for you. There are four groups of disease [caused by] demons. I should teach for you the methods for controlling these demons. These nerve-racking demons have sixty-three names. In the past, in the time of the Buddha Kanakamuni 迦那含牟尼佛 there was a bhikṣu who was approaching the stage of a stream-winner, but because of his deviant life-style was expelled from the Sangha, and in anger put an end to his life. He vowed to become a demon and up to this day he afflicts the members of the four assemblies [of monks, nuns, laymen, and laywomen]. His lifespan is one kalpa, and when the kalpa is over his life is over, and he falls into the Avici hell. You should today proclaim "I know your name," and singlemindedly fix your attention on him, so that he cannot disturb you.

Apparently the secret to controlling the demons is to know their name and be aware of their powers. Chih-i extrapolates further on what should be done to control these demons.

The Buddha Konākamuni 拘那含佛: or, "Kanakamuni." The DDB explains:

> Lit. the golden recluse 金寂, or golden *ṛṣi* 金仙; Brahman of the Kāśyapa family, native of Śobhanavatī, second of the five buddhas of the present bhadrakalpa, and the fifth of the seven ancient Buddhas 七佛; possibly a sage who preceded Śākyamuni in India. Also abbreviated as 拘那含, 俱那含, and 拘那牟尼, and further transliterated as 迦那伽牟尼, and 迦諾迦牟尼, as well as written with the buddha character at the end 拘那含牟尼佛.

Stole some dried meat 偸臘: there seem to be various ways to interpret this phrase. The character 臘 can also refer to the sacrifice to the gods three days after the winter solstice, to a "monastic year," or to the end of the annual summer retreat. Chan-jan (BT–V, 204–205) suggests that this refers to "cheating on monastic years" 盜增法歲 [seniority?] in order to avoid monastic duties, and that the name derives from a covetous desire for food. He also

Kicci covetously desired food to smell its aroma. I am now keeping the precepts and am not afraid of you!" If you rebuke [the demons] in this way, they should depart. If they do not depart, you should secretly chant the introduction to the precepts and the precepts [themselves], and the divine [guardian of] the precepts 戒神 will protect you and the precept-breaking demon will depart.

[2] Controlling the form-shifting demons of the time periods. You should know well the twelve time periods and thirty-six animals of the time periods. Be aware of the time and chant their [appropriate] names, and the form-shifting [demons] will depart. Hermits and mendicants *(dhūta)* often place a square mirror suspended on the backs of their seats; the form-shifting demons are not able to change [their shape] when their forms are [reflected] in a mirror. When they see the mirror they realize this, and should take their leave on their own. These are both internal and external [Buddhist and non-Buddhist] methods for controlling [demons]

[3] Controlling Māra consists of three [methods].

1. First is to rebuke him as soon as you become aware of him, like a gatekeeper will block [something] evil and not allow it to proceed. As the Buddha warned the bhikṣus not to accept any other thing [except the teaching of the Buddha?], you should not accept anything, and with this technique [of not accepting any other thing from Māra] you will be able to control all demonic forces with regard to yourself and others.

2. If you have already accepted something, you should contemplate precisely one by one [your entire body] from your head to your feet. [Realize

suggests that the character 臘 can be substituted with 獵, "to hunt," because during this month one hunts for animals that are offered at the festival rituals for the ancestors.

The demon Kicci 吉支 [Ji-chih, Ji-zhi]: Chan-jan (BT–V, 205) explains that this is the name of a demon whose origin can be traced to the breaking of precepts, and therefore when he hears the listing of the precepts he feels ashamed, and the "god of precepts" 戒神 will guard you and cause the precept-breaking demon to depart.

Secretly chant the introduction to the precepts and the precepts 密誦戒序及戒: this advice is also found in the *Secret Essential Methods for Healing Disease through Meditation*, T 15, 341b8–9:

> If you are a home-departed one, you should chant the introduction to the precepts and also chant the three refuges, the five [major] precepts, and the eight precepts.

Ikeda (*Kenkyūchūshaku*, 435) adds that this refers to chanting the introduction to the bodhisattva precepts in the *Fang wang ching* (T no. 1484, 24.997ff.), which includes ten major and forty-eight minor precepts.

Hermits and mendicants … in a mirror 隱士頭陀人多畜方鏡挂之座後: The Inyō identifies this as a classical reference from the 抱朴子·内篇·登涉篇.

Not accept any other thing 一切他物不受: the *Kōgi* (BT–V, 206) points to a passage in the *Expanded Āgama*, T 2.562a14–b7, but Chih-i's source is not clear.

that] in seeking Māra he is not to be found [in the body], and if you search your mind he is not to be found there [either]. From where, then, does Māra come, and how does he desire to afflict you? This is like an evil [thief] who, upon entering a house, is faced with illumination everywhere so there is no place to him to stay [and hide].

3. If he does not depart even [when faced with] such contemplation, resist him with a strong mind, even unto death [**116b**], and do not allow him to dwell with you, using various skillful techniques.

In this way there are three ways to control [demons], and there should be no need to explain further.

5. Cessation-and-Contemplation [116b2]

Fifth is [cultivating] cessation-and-contemplation [with regard to demonic activity]. As before, there are ten categories [that is, the ten modes of contemplation].

1. Objects as Conceivable and Inconceivable [116b2]

[Contemplating] "objects as conceivable" is as follows: if demonic matters arise and you follow after these demonic actions and perform evil deeds, you will experience the **three [evil] destinies**. If you follow Māra and yet perform good, such as practicing giving while being affiliated with the other [that is, under Māra's influence], although you may be born in the [three] good destinies, you will be defiled by the marks of the world, at times having attachments that rely on verbal expression. Even if you abandon your body and life, you will receive recompense [for your past evil deeds], and even if you wish to cultivate the path there will be obstacles at every turn. A sūtra says, "There are bodhisattvas who have demons and who do not have demons." This is the meaning here. This is [objects as conceivable] in the **three good destinies**. Māra also tempts people to enter nirvana by themselves [instead of remaining in this world to help others], saying, "Why do sentient beings need to rely on you? Instead of experiencing pain and suffering for naught, why don't you accept enlightenment [for yourself]?" This is the realm of the **two vehicles**. Māra also leads people to use roundabout and clumsy [practices] that are not quick ways to enter the path of *bodhi*-wisdom. In this way, going from shallow to profound with distinct levels 淺深歷別 is the way of [contemplating] objects as conceivable.

There are bodhisattvas who have demons and who do not have demons 有菩薩有魔無魔: a phrase from the *Pañcaviṃśati Sūtra*, T 8.228a15, and found also in the *Ta chih tu lun* at T 25.349a25.

Objects as Inconceivable [116b11]

If you [contemplate] these demonic matters as the ten destinies and the hundred realms interpenetrating [each other], as [all] existing in a single thought, that all dharmas have an inclination toward Māra and the demonic, as one dream includes all things, one demon is all demons, all demons are one demon, it is neither one nor all, and it is both one demon and all demons, and one Buddha is all Buddhas. There is nothing that is apart from the Buddha realm, so it is indivisible from the realm of demons; [the realm of Buddhas and of demons] is neither two nor distinct. If you contemplate in this way, you will conquer Māra and this is your seat of enlightenment. Those of superior faculties and sharp wisdom can control Māra and be clear concerning the [true] principle, and even if attended by Māra are not afraid of Māra, like firewood benefits from a fire. With deliberate cultivation you are not able to attain quiescent illumination, just like the Bodhisattva Ruler of the World was not aware of the deceit of the demon, and welcomed him.

Conquer Māra and this is your seat of enlightenment 降魔是道場: see the phrase in the *Vimalakīrti Sūtra*, T 14.543a1; Luk (*Vimalakīrti*, 40) translates, "The defeat of demons is the bodhimaṇḍala, for it is imperturbable."

Deliberate [conditioned] cultivation 緣修: the conscious and deliberate practice of gradual, successive contemplation; in contrast to the "true" intuitive and spontaneous 眞修 practice of contemplation.

Bodhisattva Ruler of the World 持世菩薩: see the chapter on bodhisattvas who were not qualified to visit Vimalakīrti in the *Vimalakīrti Sūtra*, T 14.543a9–27ff.; Luk (*Vimalakīrti*, 41–42) translates:

> The Buddha then said to the Bodhisattva Ruler of the World, "You call on Vimalakīrti and enquire after his health on my behalf."
>
> Ruler of the World replied, "I still remember that once as I was staying in a vihāra, a demon like Indra appeared followed by twelve thousand goddesses (*devakanyā*) playing music and singing songs. After bowing their heads at my feet they brought their palms together and stood at my side. I mistook the demon for Śakra and said to him, 'Welcome, Śakra, although you have won merits, you should guard against passions (arising from music, song, and sex). You should look into the five desires (for the objects of the five senses) in your practice of morality. You should look into the impermanence of body, life, and wealth in you quest of indestructible Dharma.'
>
> "He said, 'Bodhisattva, please take these twelve thousand goddesses who will serve you.'
>
> "I replied, 'Śakra, please do not make to a monk this unclean offering which does not suit me.'
>
> "Even before I had finished speaking, Vimalakīrti came and said, 'He is not Śakra; he is a demon who comes to disturb you.' He then said to the demon: 'You can give me these girls and I will keep them.'
>
> "The demon was frightened, and being afraid that Vimalakīrti might give him trouble, he tried to make himself invisible but failed, and in spite of his use of supernatural powers he could not go away. Suddenly a voice was heard in the air, saying, 'Demon, give him the girls and then you can go.' Being scared, he

True [intuitive] cultivation leads to quiescent illumination, so that you can see as if in a mirror even without seeing or contemplating, so [Vimalakīrti] knew that the demon was not Indra/Śakra. Those [bodhisattvas] of the Distinct Teachings cannot put up with negative dharmas [teachings] 非法, and therefore say "this is not something that I approve." But those of the Perfect Teaching rest in true reality, and therefore say, "I can accept this," are not afraid of non-human beings and courageously face the cycle of birth and death. This is called [contemplating] objects as inconceivable.

2. Arousing Compassion [116b21]

The realm of demons and the realm of Buddha are indivisible 魔界即佛界, but sentient beings do not know this. They are deluded with respect to the Buddha realm and perversely arouse the realm of demons; while having *bodhi*-wisdom, they arouse passionate afflictions. Therefore you should arouse compassion and wish to lead sentient being to encounter the realm of Buddha within the realm of demons, and encounter *bodhi*-wisdom within passionate afflictions. This is the arousing of compassion. Have the kindness 慈 of immeasurable Buddhas, and pity 悲 the immeasurable demons, and this immeasurable compassion will become the one great compassion that is without conditions.

3. Skillful Means for a Peaceful Mind [116b26]

If you wish to complete this vow [of arousing compassion] and to clearly understand the principle [of truth], you should make the conquering of demons your place of enlightenment (*bodhimaṇḍa*). For an assembly of eighty-four billion [demons] to be unable to perturb your mind is called "cessation" 止, and to reach penetrating understanding that the realm of demons and the realm of Buddha are indivisible is called "contemplation." However, you must use the four methods of instruction *(siddhānta)* to attain the peaceful mind of cessation-and-contemplation.

4. Deconstructing Dharmas [116b28]

If you are faced with the arising of demonic forces, use the four options of the tetralemma to deconstruct them. Horizontally and vertically, singly and plurally, deconstruct them all without obstruction.

gave the girls to Vimalakīrti who said to them, 'The demon has given you to me. You can now develop a mind set on the quest of supreme enlightenment.'"

Vimalakirti then expounded the Dharma to them urging them to seek the truth.

In the Tripitaka [Teachings], [**116c**] first the four types of demons were overcome [by Śākyamuni] sitting under the Bodhi tree. [1] He destroyed the demon of passionate afflictions and attained the path of *bodhi*-wisdom. [2] Again, he attained the body of Dharma-nature 法性身 and destroyed the demons of the skandhas. [3] Through both of these together he destroyed the demon of death. [4] Under the Bodhi tree he attained the immovable concentration of samādhi 不動三昧. He transformed the three jeweled female [temptresses], destroyed the eighty-four billion soldiers [of Māra], and caused the crowns, coverings, and swords each to fall away. Thus he destroyed the supernatural demons.

In the Shared [Teachings], you first attain the forbearance that comes from [realizing] non-arising, and so forth up to reaching the sixth bhūmi stage and attaining the path of *bodhi*-wisdom, as explained previously. To be current in both the path and contemplation at the eighth *bhūmi* stage is equivalent to the immovable samādhi and destroying the supernatural demons. The śrāvakas of both [Tripitaka and Shared Teachings] are limited only to destroying three types of demons [and not the supernatural demons]. For example, Gupta was always being afflicted [by demonic forces] and though he later attained supranormal powers, he was able to control but not destroy them.

Those of the Shared Teachings on the ten *bhūmi* stages have already destroyed the four demons of this world. In ascending the *bhūmi* stages they partially attain the path of *bodhi*-wisdom and destroy the demons of passionate afflictions. By partially attaining the Dharma Body they destroy the demons of the skandhas. By partially attaining the Red-colored Samādhi they destroy the supernatural demons. The *Ying-lo ching* says that [those

In the Tripitaka Teachings ... the supernatural demons: on the four types of demons see the *Ta chih tu lun*, T 25.99b11–20. For a full translation see note at *Mo-ho chih-kuan* 12a1.

The *Inyō* (74) and Ikeda (*Kenkyū-chūshaku*, 436), point to a long passage in *The Great Collection of Sūtras*, T 13.130a–143c as the source for this section.

Under the Bodhi tree 道樹下: for details, see the various legends concerning Śākyamuni conquering the final temptations brought about by Māra, before he attained enlightenment, such as turning away the various desires that appeared in the form of beautiful women, the slings and arrows threatened by the host of Māra's army, and so forth.

Gupta: the fourth patriarch in the T'ien-t'ai lineage; see *The Transmission*, T 50, 306b10–cff., full translation given in the note above at *Mo-ho chih-kuan* 115c8–9.

Red-colored Samādhi 赤色三昧: the fourteenth of the twenty-five Samādhis, during which one transcends the six heavenly realms of desire. See note at 115a16.

***Ying-lo ching* says**: appears to be a summary of the passage at T 24.1013a5–14, which claims that those who have attained the stage "equivalent to awakening" 等覺諸

who have attained the stage of] "equivalent to awakening" have already extinguished three types of demonic forces, and only the demon of death remains. But it cannot be that you first extinguish three [types of demons] and are left only with the one [of death], so this must be a teaching of skillful means of the Shared Teachings.

Those of the Perfect Teaching at the first *bhūmi* stage have already destroyed the eight demons, having attained the path of *bodhi*-wisdom and destroyed the demons of passionate afflictions, and so forth up to reaching [the ultimate stage of] sublime awakening where the eight types of demonic forces are ultimately and forever extinguished. Though it is said that these are destroyed at the first *bhūmi* stage, it is not that they are destroyed at the first *bhūmi* stage; although it is said that later [upon attaining sublime] awakening they are destroyed, it is not that they are destroyed upon later [attaining sublime] awakening. On the other hand, [destroying the demonic forces] is not separate from the first *bhūmi* stage and later [sublime] awakening. This is what is meant by "universally deconstructing all dharmas."

5. Knowing What Penetrates and What Obstructs [116c15]

Through the above methods of destroying demons one by one, all should know [the Four Noble Truths such as] suffering and the causes of suffering, [twelvefold dependent co-arising starting with] ignorance, and the hindrances to the [six] perfections, and know them literally and non-literally.

6. Steps on the Path [116c17]

The steps on the path [with regard to demonic forces are as follows]: the

佛 have overcome three types of demons, and those who have attained "sublime awakening" 妙覺 have overcome all four types of demons.

Eight demons 八魔: Chan-jan (BT–V, 211–12) points out that these eight are the four types of demons described above plus the "four perversions" of transciency, non-blissfulness, no-self, and impurity.

The DDB defines them as: "The eight destroyers: the māras of the afflictions 煩惱魔; the skandha-māras 陰魔; death-māra 死魔; the māra-king 他化自在天魔. The above four are ordinarily termed the four māras: the other four are the four Hīnayāna delusions of śrāvakas and pratyekabuddhas, i.e. impermanence 無常; joylessness 無樂; selflessness 無我, and impurity 無淨."

The *Mahāparinirvāṇa Sūtra* defines these at T 12.740b26–29:

> Suppose there are good sons and good daughters who wish to see me and wish to pay respect to me, wish to have the same dharma-nature and see me, wish to attain the concentration of emptiness, wish to see the true marks of reality, wish to attain the Śūraṅgama Samādhi and the Lion Samādhi, and wish to destroy the eight demonic forces. The eight demonic forces are the so-called four demonic forces plus transiency, non-blissfullness, non-self, and impurity 無常無樂無我無淨.

realm of demons includes all visible forms. Visible forms are empty, so visible forms are impure; but visible forms have conventional [reality], so they are called pure. Visible forms are the Middle, so they are neither pure nor impure. The other four skandhas are also likewise. Also, what is called one mindfulness is all mindfulness, up to [and including] the three gates of liberation [of emptiness, formlessness, and actionlessness].

7. Auxiliary Methods [116c20]

If a gate does not open, there is certainly something obstructing it. Since long eons past you have been manipulated by demonic forces, giving offerings (*dāna*) to Māra in order to receive recompense. You have kept demonic precepts, in order to gain benefits. You have practiced a demonic patience, due to a fear of others. You have cultivated a demonic diligence, in an effort to seek fame. You have attained a demonic dhyāna-concentration by tasting demonic methods [of meditation]. Seeking to enjoy demonic wisdom, you have discriminated with the net of mistaken views. In this way these six methods [parallel to the six perfections] can be called "doing good," but truly they are demonic. Due to these deviant hindrances, the three gates of liberation are obstructed. Now you should use the proper [six] perfections [of giving, keeping the precepts, patience, diligence, concentration, and wisdom] in order to heal and control the six obscurations [that are the opposite of the six perfections, that is, parsimony, immorality, anger, indolence, distractedness, and stupidity]. If the obscurations go away and the virtues are perfected, it will be like oil [added to a lamp and the flame] burning brighter. If these are mixed with passionate afflictions, you should use the previously explained four types of [mindfulness] contemplation as auxiliary methods. If they are mixed with karma, use the mindfulness of two Buddhas as an auxiliary method.

Since long eons past 久遠劫來: note that the binome 久遠 used here is the same as that used for the so-called "Eternal Buddha" (or, more precisely, "Buddha awakened since the inconceivably distant past") in the *Lotus Sūtra*, one of its basic and unique teachings. The term "eternal" is not appropriate in the Buddhist context.

Tasting demonic methods 味於鬼法: I follow the revised text in BT–V, 213, and substitute 味 for 昧 in the Taishō text.

Should use the previously explained four type of contemplation 當用前四分觀助治: see the explanations in the section on "Controlling and Healing through Auxiliary Methods" at 91a5–97b17, and on "Contemplating the Objects of Passionate Afflictions" at 102a1–106a19.

Mindfulness of two Buddhas 念二佛: I was unable to find any commentary to identify these "two Buddhas."

8. Graded Stages of Attainment [116c28]

For the Hīnayāna, completing the path of overcoming [mistaken views and attitudes] is called [the level of] "wisdom through hearing [the Dharma]," and so forth up to the Perfect Teaching, where the five preliminary grades are equivalent to the level of "wisdom through hearing [the Dharma]." At this level you have not yet perfected [enlightenment], so how can you boast of [knowing and attaining] the true [way and awakening]; this will arouse arrogance. **[117ac]**

9. Resting in Patient Forbearance [117a1]

If you wish to enter the true [way and awakening], you should singlemindedly rest in patient forbearance and avoid further [contact with] the instability and disturbances of demonic forces. Contemplate them clearly in extreme detail, and with a strong mind rebuke and resist them.

10. No Passionate Attachments to Dharmas [117a2]

If you enter the level of "[Identity in] Resemblance" and are rewarded with [a certain] attainment of the Dharma, you should not give rise to a haughty and passionate mind. This would be like a person who expects to be rewarded with a great medal but is instead dismissed to a minor district, or loses his job, or even loses his life. If you arouse passionate attachments to dharmas, this is a grave offence. But understanding at [the level of] "Resemblance" is like [being assigned to] a minor district, and losing the understanding of [the level of] Resemblance is like losing your job, and falling onto the ground of those of the Two Vehicles is like losing your life, because it extinguishes the foundations of the household duties of the Mahāyāna. If there are no passionate attachments to dharmas, you can advance from [the level of] Resemblance and realize the truly real [awakening], tame the demonic forces and make them your servants, and directly reach the place of enlightenment.

The level of wisdom through hearing 聞慧: in Chih-i's scheme, this is the level of attainment equivalent to the third of the Six Identities, the "Identity in Contemplative Practive." For those of the Shared Teachings it is at the level of the first two of the ten *bhūmi* stages, and for those of the Distinct Teachings it is at the "Ten Levels of Faith" (the first ten of the fifty-two stages of a bodhisattva). See Chart 1 on "Levels of Attainment and the Fourfold Teachings" in Volume 3.

Household duties 家業: the responsibilities transferred to the prodigal son by the rich father in the parable of the *Lotus Sūtra*. Symbolic of the teachings of emptiness transferred to the śrāvakas by the Buddha in the Prajñā Period 般若時, during the fourth of the Five Periods of T'ien-t'ai classification.

Again, retreating in wisdom is like losing a medal, retreating in meditative concentration is like losing your job, and retreating in both is like losing your life.

11. Summary [117a9]

Again, in general you should contemplate with a singular intent; if the practitioner's faculties are dull, you should first understand the meaning of the Shared [Teachings of emptiness] and, with a roundabout [attainment of the] perfections, enter the Distinct [Teachings]. For example, the *Middle Treatise* has a distinct intent in each chapter, but together they combine [to clarify the teaching of] non-arising. [In this way] the mutual advancement of the Shared and Distinct [Teachings] attain the intended meaning [of the Dharma] and mutually perfect [the teachings with regard to demonic forces].

Question: When demonic forces finish moving and then favorable dharmas arise, is this the natural way of things, as when the cold [of winter] passes with the coming of spring?

Answer: This is not necessarily the case. There are times of misfortune when favorable dharmas do not arise. Demonic forces arise from feeling evil conditions, and good comes from the power of the mind. [On the other hand,] the *Ta chih tu lun* says, in the past Śākyamuni dwelt in an evil world, a world with no Buddha. He sought the Dharma diligently, but finally was not able to attain it. Māra transformed himself into a Brahman and cunningly said, "I know one verse of a Buddha. If you provide your skin as paper, your bones for a brush, and your blood as ink, I can show it to you." The bodhisattva sought joyfully for the Dharma, so he cut off his own skin and dried it in the sun to make paper for the verse. Then Māra immediately

In the past Śākyamuni dwelt in an evil world 釋迦往昔在惡世 …: a story found in the *Ta chih tu lun* at T 25.412a12–20:

> When Śākyamuni Buddha was originally a bodhisattva named Joy in the Dharma 樂法, at the time there was no Buddha in the world and he could not hear the good words [of the Buddha-Dharma]. He sought the Dharma in all four directions, diligently and without respite, but finally was unable to attain it. At that time Māra transformed himself into a Brahman and spoke, saying, "I have one verse that was taught by a Buddha. If you can take your skin for paper, your bones for a brush, and your blood as ink, I can write and copy this verse [to the skinpaper] for you." Joy in the Dharma immediately thought to himself, "In this world I will lose my body [anyway] and there are innumerable benefits that I will not attain [if I do not accept this offer]." So he cut off his own skin and dried it in the sun, wishing that it could be used as a scroll book for the verse. But Māra then extinguished his body [as a Brahman]. At that time a Buddha knew about [Śākyamuni's] sincere mind and arose from under the ground and taught this profound Dharma [to him], and he attained the forbearance [from realizing] the non-arising of dharmas.

hid himself. A Buddha knew his [Śākyamuni's] mind and rose up from below the ground and taught him the profound [contents of the] sūtra, and he attained the forbearance that comes from [realizing the] non-arising [of dharmas]. This is testimony [to the converting of demonic forces to good]. [end of fascicle eight]

6. CONTEMPLATING THE OBJECTS OF DHYĀNA MEDITATION [117a21–131c21]

The sixth [of the ten objects of contemplation] is contemplating the objects of dhyāna meditation. Now, long disease and traveling afar are obstacles to dhyāna meditation. The *Treatise on the Worldly-established Abhidharma* says that much quarreling and much [involvement in] business affairs are also obstacles to dhyāna meditation, and that again, much reading and chanting [of the sūtras] can also be an obstacle to dhyāna meditation. *The Questions of Mañjuśrī* says that **[117b]** dhyāna meditation involves thirty-six impurities. "Impurities" are obstacles.

For those who have been able to realize [enlightenment] through the above [five types of contemplation of] objects [of the sense fields, passionate afflictions, disease, karma, and demonic forces], and have reached the pure and cool pond, and finally entered the stream [of wisdom or awakening], it is not necessary to contemplate the objects of dhyāna meditation. If even after the demonic forces have passed away. But you have not yet aroused true enlightenment, even though you do not use the cultivation of the Distinct [Teachings] but use the cultivation of the Shared [Teachings], habits from the past will be aroused and confused dhyāna [states] will appear. You should set aside demonic forces and contemplate these dhyāna [states]. What does this mean? The bliss of dhyāna [states] is sublime, and you can joyfully become obsessed with their flavor, so that impurities [like dirt and grease on human skin] increase daily. Although this [dhyāna meditation] is part of the path, you can fall into arrogance[, thinking that you have attained

Long disease and traveling afar 長病遠行: Chan-jan (BT–V, 219) points out that traditionally there are five matters that hinder meditation and attaining the fruit of the arhat: 1. long disease 長病, 2. traveling afar 遠行, 3. indulging in disputes 諫諍, 4. business affairs 營事, and 5. too much reading and chanting 多讀誦.

The Treatise on the Worldly-established Abhidharma 立世阿毘曇: this seems to refer to the *Loka-prajñaptyabhidharma-śāstra* 佛説立世阿毘曇論, T no. 1644, 32.173–226, attributed to Paramārtha, but as the classical commentaries point out (BT–V, 219–20), these phrases do not appear in this text. Instead see the *Abhidharma-vibhāṣā-śāstra*, T 28.3b23–25: "As it has been taught, there are five causes and conditions for an Arhat to retreat from attaining liberation: 1. working hard on business affairs 營事勤勞, 2. too much chanting of the sūtras, 3. quarreling 諍訟, 4. traveling afar, and 5. long disease."

Thirty-six impurities 三十六垢: Chan-jan (BT–V, 219) points out that this phrase does not appear in *The Questions of Mañjuśrī* (T no. 468, 14.492–509), and a search of the SAT Text Database showed that this phrase appears only once in the Taishō canon, at this passage in the *Mo-ho chih-kuan* and in the classical commentaries to this passage. A search for "thirty-six obstacles" 三十六障 also gave no hits.

Do not use the cultivation of the Distinct but use the cultivation of the Shared 雖無別修以通修故: or, "do not use a distinct cultivation but use a general cultivation"?

enlightenment]. However, if you reject and abandon this [dhyāna meditation], you would lose [skillful] means [for attaining enlightenment]. These sorts of mistakes need not be recorded [here] fully. Even though you have avoided harm from demonic forces, there may be bonds from [dhyāna] concentration. It is like avoiding fire and falling into water; this does not help in attaining samādhi. It is for these reasons that you should contemplate the objects of dhyāna meditation. However, the constituents of dhyāna 禪支 and various concentrations provide powerful auxiliary methods for the path [of contemplation]. The Mahāyāna and Hīnayāna sūtras all agree in praising their beauty. The *Abhidharma* and *Ch'eng shih lun* clarify in detail the four dhyāna [stages] and eight concentrations. On the nine dhyānas such as that of self-nature and so forth, the *Bodhisattva-bhūmi* and *Daśabhūmika* give exceedingly clear classifications. Now I will summarize them and signify the marks of their arising roughly with four meanings: 1. clarifying their expansion and merging 明開合; 2. the causes and conditions of their arising 發因緣; 3. clarifying the marks of their arising 明發相; and 4. [in terms of] cultivating cessation-and-contemplation 修止觀.

1. Clarifying the Presentation of Dhyāna [117b13]

First is to clarify the expanding and merging [of dhyāna]. The gates of dhyāna are immeasurable, but can be summarized into ten gates or categories: 1. the basic four dhyānas 根本四禪; 2. the sixteen superior [meditations] 十六特勝; 3. the [six] supranormal powers and [three illuminating] insights 通明; 4. the nine considerations 九想 [of decaying corpses]; 5. the eight liberations or renunciations 背捨; 6. [contemplation of] great impurity 大不淨; 7. a compassionate mind 慈心; 8. causes and conditions 因緣; 9. mindfulness of the Buddha 念佛; and 10. supranormal powers 神通.

Are these ten gates the same or different than [the categories of] the five

Like avoiding fire and falling into water 如避火墮水: or, in more common English parlance, "from the frying pan into the fire"?

Four dhyāna [stages] 四禪 **and eight concentrations** 八定: for details on the four dhyāna stages see the *Abhidharma-vibhāṣā-śāstra*, T 28.307cff. and 324cff. For further details on these see also the *Ch'eng shih lun*, T 32.335c–344c.

Nine dhyānas 九禪: a list of nine dhyāna meditations, starting with the dhyāna of self-nature 自性禪, ways of cultivating single-mindedness and another name for *śamatha-vipaśyanā*. As mentioned previously in the *Mo-ho chih-kuan*, these are listed in the *Bodhisattva-bhūmi*, T 30.921b29-c3. As for the **Daśabhūmika-vibhāṣa-śāstra* (T no. 1521, 26.20–122), however, it is not clear to which passage Chih-i is referring; the *Shiki* (BT–V, 222) adds that in the *Daśabhūmika* the nine dhyānas are explained in terms of the ten *bhūmi* stages.

gates and the fifteen gates [of dhyāna meditation]? The only differences are in presentation [in being expanded or merged]. Expanding five into ten is as follows: "Counting your breaths" is expanded to include [the sixteen] superior meditations and the supranormal powers. "[Contemplation of] impurity" is expanded to include the [eight] renunciations and [contemplation of] great impurity. "A compassionate mind" and "causes and conditions" stay as they are. "Mindfulness of the Buddha" in the *Abhidharma-hṛdaya-śāstra* is called "worldly means," and in Dhyāna sūtras is called "mindfulness of the Buddha," and this also stays as it is. "Supernatural powers" are a part of the other nine [types of] dhyāna and do not "belong" to a single category [of the five gates].

Merging fifteen into ten is as follows: "Counting the breaths" and "impurity" each have three parts that are not merged [which gives six categories]. "A compassionate mind" also has three parts, but are merged into one, that is, compassion for sentient beings. The reason that the other two categories [of compassion in dharmas and "unconditioned compassion"] are dropped is that the gate of dhyāna practice is an orderly and practical method 詮次事法. [Contemplation of compassion] in connection with phenomenal dharmas 法緣 is a contemplation for realizing the principle [of truth] for those of the two vehicles, and "unconditioned" 無緣 [compassion] is a con-

Five gates 五門: that is, the five contemplations for putting the mind at rest 五停心觀: of counting your breaths, impurity, compassion, causes-and-conditions, and mindfulness of the Buddha.

Fifteen gates 十五門: the above five types of contemplation with each expanded to three types: "counting your breaths" includes the four basic dhyānas, the sixteen superior meditations, and the supranormal powers; "the contemplation of impurity" includes the nine considerations of the decaying of corpses, the eight renunciations, and the contemplation of great impurity; "the contemplation of a compassionate mind" includes that in connection with sentient beings, dharmas, and unconditioned; "the contemplation of causes and conditions" includes that of the past, present, and future; "mindfulness of the Buddha" includes mindfulness of the three bodies of Dharma Body, Recompense Body, and Body of Transformation/Enjoyment (see Ikeda, *Kenkyūchūshaku*, 437; BT–V, 223–24, and Chih-i's exposition that follows.)

Worldly means 界方便: see the *Abhidharma-hṛdaya-śāstra*, T 28.908b1–21, which teaches three kinds of contemplation: the contemplation of impurity, counting the breaths, and being mindful of the means of this world. This last one involves contemplating all conditioned things as all being "dispersed" [and thus empty?]. It is not clear how this relates to being mindful of the Buddha.

Dhyāna sūtras 禪經: see, for example, the *Sūtra of the Secret Essential Methods for Meditation*, T 15.255a22–b6ff., which explains "mindfulness of the Buddha" 念佛 first by explaining in general the proper way to sit in contemplation, and then specifically in terms of contemplating the thirty-two major marks and eighty minor marks of the Buddha's body.

templation for realizing the principle [of truth] for those of the Mahāyāna. By dropping the [abstract] matters concerned with the principle [of truth], two are left behind and only one [category] of practical matters remains. If we expanded [this category], it could be included in the two objects of the bodhisattvas of the two vehicles. "Causes and conditions" also have three gates or categories: transmigrating in the three times [of past, present, and future] is the "rough" [interpretation], and clarifying the meaning of resultant recompense in a single mind is the "fine" [interpretation]. Since the "fine" involves the [abstract] principle [of truth], and the "rough" involves practical matters, for now we will drop the fine and keep the rough, and just call this the gate or category of the three times [of past, present, and future]. "Mindfulness of the Buddha" also involves three [Dharma Body, Body of Manifestation, and Body of Recompense], but here we take only [the one of] being mindful of the Buddha of Manifestation. "Supranormal powers" refers only to the five [supranormal] powers.

Thus if we limit ourselves to five gates or categories, some things cannot be included. If [117c] we use fifteen gates or categories, the meaning will overflow into [contemplation] of the principle [of the truth], and therefore we will set aside [for now abstract matters of] the principle and concentrate on the practical matters. Therefore, even though the presentation is different [by expanding or merging categories], each of them has the same intent.

1. Clarifying in Terms of Defiled and Undefiled [117c2]

Next is clarifying [contemplating the objects of dhyāna] in terms of "defiled" and "undefiled" 漏無漏. If we rely on the Abhidharma, it classifies them into ten dhyānas, all of which are called "defiled." To cultivate wisdom in connection with the truth 緣諦智修 is called "undefiled" dhyāna. Unlike this, to cultivate in connection with practical matters 緣事修 is called "defiled" dhyāna. [The teachings in] the *Ch'eng shih lun* are also likewise. It claims

Rely on the Abhidharma 若依毘曇: see the *Abhidharma-hṛdaya-śāstra*, T 28.924a–b, which contains an extensive description of the four dhyānas in terms of being "defiled" and "undefiled."

In the *Ch'eng shih lun*: see the passage at T 32.340a18–29:

> Question: these various natures depend of the attainment of what kind of concentrations?
> Answer: In the sūtras it is explained that from the nature of enlightenment through to the nature of neither-conceptualized-nor-non-conceptualized, all are the result of attaining concentration through your own practices. That is, this is an attainment that results from practicing on the conditioned path 行緣有爲道. This is a result of a first [level of] wisdom from connections to color-and-form, and is called "the nature of enlightenment." The second nature also involves grasping visible form. By grasping it and then making discriminations [about it], you are led [to realize] emptiness.

that the [four] basic dhyānas involve defilement [through contact with the phenomenal world], but [in contrast] cultivating a mind of emptiness and no-marks is called "undefiled."

Now, [the explanation here in the *Mo-ho chih-kuan*] is a little different. The essential mark of the ten [categories of] dhyāna is that of being "defiled" [through connection with phenomenal dharmas]. In general these are the practical [aspects of] dhyāna. [The *Mahāparinirvāṇa Sūtra* says] that [eating] cucumbers can cause a feverish disease, because it produces [certain] causes and conditions; these small matters must be differentiated [clearly]. The four [basic types of] dhyāna were present in the world [before the time of the Buddha] and are shared with the heterodox [non-Buddhist] paths of ordinary people. To practice only these [four dhyāna] will merely arouse defiled [dharmas or results] from practicing the twelve gates for yourself. If you [work to] save others and praise the Dharma, this is what the *Mahāparinirvāṇa Sūtra* calls [the expertise acquired from practicing for] "forty-eight years"; this is the meaning here.

As for the sixteen superior meditations and [six] supranormal powers and [three] illuminations, ordinary people of sharp faculties can cultivate these dhyāna meditations even if a Buddha does not appear in the world,

In this way up to the nature of neither-conceptualized-nor-non-conceptualized, the nature of extinction, the nature of entering extinction, are all attained due to [realizing that] all conditioned phenomena are empty. All conditioned things are included in this extinction, and therefore you should know that within the explanation of extinction this is called the nirvana of undefiled exhaustion.

Question: These various liberations occur at what *bhūmi* stage?

Answer: A practitioner who wishes to destroy visible form, or relies on the concentration linked to the realm of desires, or relies on the concentration of the realm of visible form, and able to attain [realization of] the emptiness of visible form, and can attain a mind of emptiness within all *bhūmi* stages.

Question: How many of these liberations are "defiled" and how many are "undefiled"?

Answer: Since they involve the nature of emptiness, all are "undefiled."

Cucumbers 胡瓜: see the *Mahāparinirvāṇa Sūtra*, T 12.768b12–13:

> It is like cucumbers can bring about a feverish disease. Why is this so? It is able to bring about a feverish disease through producing certain causes and conditions. The twelvefold causes-and-conditions are likewise.

Various passages from this section on the relation between Buddha nature and causes-and-conditions have been quoted previously, such as *Mo-ho chih-kuan* 74c24 and 75a16.

Forty-eight years 四十八年: see the *Mahāparinirvāṇa Sūtra*, T 12.618a2, at the beginning of the parable of the doctor who prescribes various medicine according to the disease, and not always just milk, and who prefaces his remarks by pointing out that it took him forty-eight years of training to attain his expertise. For a full translation of this section see the note at *Mo-ho chih-kuan*, 10b27.

but without arousing undefiled [dhyāna]. If a Tathāgata teaches it, you can arouse the undefiled. Compared to other dhyānas, its power is weak, but they are superior to the four basic dhyānas. Due to this meaning, we speak of both the "defiled" and the "undefiled."

As for the nine considerations [of a decaying corpse] and so forth, these are all methods that transcend those [dhyānas] of the world [and are thus specifically Buddhist methods]. Although they involve various practical methods, they are able to counter the excesses of desires. Without waiting for [attaining] the wisdom of the [Four Noble] Truths, you are able to arouse undefiled [dhyānas]. It is like Kaṭhina and the five hundred arhats: even though each of them explained the Four [Noble] Truths seven times, he still was not able to attain the path of awakening, but when the Buddha taught about impurity, he aroused undefiled [dhyānas]. The power of disillusion is

Kaṭhina and the five hundred arhats 迦絺那五百羅漢: see the story at the beginning of the *Sūtra of the Secret Essential Methods for Meditation*, T 15.242c29–244b20:

> At that time in Vaiśāli there was a monk named Mahākaṭhina, wise and with much knowledge, who came to the Buddha's place and circumambulated the Buddha seven times. At that time the Buddha was in a state of deep dhyānic concentration, and was silent, without speaking a word. At that time Kaṭhinananda saw the Buddha enter samādhi while dwelling with Śāriputra. Putting his head to the ground he said, "Śāriputra of great merit, I only ask that for my sake you extensively preach the essentials of the Dharma." At that time Śāriputra explained the Four Noble Truths and discriminated its meaning, from one time up to six times. Then Kaṭhinananda still had a doubt in his mind and in this way went around to the feet of five hundred arhats, seeking that they teach the essence of the Dharma. All the śrāvakas each explained the Dharma of the Four Noble truths seven times for his sake. Then Kaṭhinananda, his mind still confused, again returned to the Buddha's place and bowed to the Buddha.
>
> Then the World Honored One arose from his dhyānic concentration, saw Kaṭhinananda bowing his head at the Buddha's feet, weeping tears like the pouring rain, and beseeching the World Honored One. "I only ask that for my sake you turn the wheel of the True Dharma." Then the World Honored One again taught extensively the Dharma of the Four Noble Truths, not only once but up to seven times, but Kaṭhinananda still did not understand....
>
> The Buddha said to Kaṭhinananda, "You should accept my words and do not fear. From this day you should cultivate the way of the śrāmaṇa. The way of the śrāmaṇa is to be in a quiet place with a teacher, sit in a full-lotus position, properly arrange your clothing, sit with your body properly erect, bare your right shoulder, place your left hand on top of your right hand, close your eyes and place your tongue at the roof of you mouth, concentrate your mind and do not let it be scattered. First fix your thoughts on the big toe of your left foot, [and so forth ...]."

The passage ends, "He gradually cultivated and attained the fruits of the four śrāmaṇa, and became fully endowed with the three illuminations and the six supranormal powers."

strong, therefore it is judged to be associated with the undefiled. But even if we say this [disillusion] is not undefiled, we should not call it the noble [three learnings of Buddhist] precepts, concentration, and wisdom. The Noble words [of the Buddha] are true 正, so how could it be a mistake [to call these practical aspects] undefiled? The *Mahāparinirvāṇa Sūtra* says, "Noble practices are all part of the realm of the Buddhas, and not something to be known by those of the two vehicles. The Buddha teaches this Dharma and those of the two vehicles practice it with reverence, and therefore it is called 'noble practice.'" Now the Buddha is teaching the Noble Dharma and those of the two vehicles are practicing it; how can this not be "undefiled"? Again, the *Pañcaviṃśati Sūtra* says, that the basic [dhyānas] are worldly Dharma offerings, and [the contemplations of] impurity and so forth are

Noble practices 聖行 **are ...**: see the *Mahāparinirvāṇa Sūtra*, T 12.690a16–21:

> The bodhisattva Kāśyapa said to the Buddha, "World Honored One, what is the meaning of 'noble practices'? World Honored One, if these are practices of the Buddhas, then they should not be cultivated by śrāvakas, pratyekabuddhas, and bodhisattvas." [The Buddha answered:] "Good son, the World Honored Ones dwell peacefully in great Nirvana and in this way expose and discriminate these meanings in their sermons. In this sense they are called 'noble practices': śrāvakas, pratyekabuddhas, and bodhisattvas in this way hear [of these practices] and respectfully practice them. Therefore they are called 'noble practices.'"

***Pañcaviṃśati Sūtra* says that the basic [dhyānas] are worldly Dharma offerings, and impurity and so forth are transworldly Dharma offerings** 根本是世間法施。不淨等是出世法施: see a passage at T 8.394b3–c9:

> Subhuti, by what kinds of offerings of Dharma should a bodhisattva engage sentient beings? Subhuti, there are two kinds of Dharma offerings. The first is worldly, and the second is transworldly. What is the worldly Dharma offering? It is to teach and manifest the worldly Dharma, that is, the contemplation of impurity, counting the breaths, the four basic dhyānas, the four immeasurable mindfulnesses, and the four concentrations of no-form. These are worldly dharmas, along with other various practices of ordinary people common [to those in Buddhism]. These are called worldly Dharma offerings. When a bodhisattva is this way finishes with worldly Dharma offerings, with various causes and conditions he leads people to depart far from the worldly Dharmas. After they depart far from the worldly Dharmas, with the power of skillful means he attains the noble, undefiled Dharma and the noble undefiled fruit of the Dharma....
>
> Subhuti, a bodhisattva-mahāsattva through causes and conditions of the worldly Dharma offerings attains the transworldly Dharma offerings. In this way, Subhuti, a bodhisattva-mahāsattva teaches sentient beings and leads them to attain worldly Dharmas, and with the power of skillful means teaches and leads them to attain transworldly Dharmas. Subhuti, what are these bodhisattva transworldly Dharmas? They are the same as those that are not in common with ordinary ignorant people: that is, the four mindfulnesses, the four proper endeavors, four supranormal powers, five good roots, five powers, seven components of awakening, the eightfold noble path, the three gates

transworldly Dharma offerings. If they are said to be transworldly, how can they not be "undefiled"? Again, it is said that the nine considerations [of a decaying corpse] open to impurity, impurity opens to mindfulness of the body, mindfulness of the body opens to the other three [of the four] mindfulnesses, and these three mindfulnesses open to the thirty-seven steps on the path, and the thirty-seven steps on the path open to nirvana. How can it be that the first step to attaining nirvana is not "undefiled"? If it is said that the practical matters of dhyāna should always be considered "defiled," that is like having two rocks, one hot and one cold. The same with the practical matters of dhyāna: there should be a difference between the defiled and the undefiled. If we are to call undefiled conditions as "undefiled," since you sever the mistaken views at the sixth *bhūmi* stage and the mistaken conceptions at the seventh *bhūmi* stage, then these conditions should be "undefiled." For the mistaken views and conceptions to be severed at the sixth and seventh

of liberation, the eight renunciations, the nine gradual concentrations, the Buddha's ten powers and four fearlessnesses and four unobstructed wisdoms and eighteen unique characteristics and the thirty-two major and eighty minor physical marks and five hundred gates of *dhāraṇī*.

The nine considerations open to impurity ... open to nirvana 九想開不淨。不淨開身念處。身念處開三念處。三念處開三十七品。三十七品開涅槃: see the *Ta chih tu lun*, T 25.218b9–18 (see Lamotte, *Le Traité* 3, 1325–26) Chodron (3, 1084–85) translates:

Question. What is the intrinsic nature *(svabhāva)* of these nine notions, what is their object *(ālambana)* and where are they contained *(saṃgṛhīta)*?

Answer. As their nature, they have the grasping of characteristics *(nimittodgrahaṇa)*; they are contained in the aggregate of form *(rūpaskandha)*.

They are also contained in a small part of the foundation of mindfulness on the body *(kāyasmṛtyupasthāna)*, in the desire realm *(kāmadhātu)* or also in the first, second and fourth dhyāna.

The person who has not yet renounced desire *(avītarāga)* and who has a distracted mind *(vikṣiptacitta)* belongs to the domain of the desire realm *(kāmadhātvavacara)*; the person who has renounced desire *(vītarāga)* belongs to the domain of the form realm *(rūpadhātvavacara)*.

Eight notions, those of the bloated corpse *(vyādmātaka)*, etc., are contained in kāmadhātu and the first and second dhyānas. The notion of pure bone *(asthisaṃjñā)* is contained in kāmadhātu, the first second and fourth dhyānas. As there is a great deal of happiness *(sukha)* in the third dhyāna, this one is exempt from the notion of horror.

These nine notions open the gate of the foundation of mindfulness on the body *(kāyasmṛtyupasthāna)*. Mindfulness of the body opens the gate of the other three foundations of mindfulness. The four foundations of mindfulness open the gate of the thirty-seven auxiliaries to enlightenment *(bodhipākṣhika dharma)*. The thirty-seven auxiliaries to enlightenment open the gate to the city of nirvana. Entering into nirvana, the suffering of sadness, sorrow, etc. *(śokadaurmanasyādiduḥkha)* are eliminated and, as the process of interdependency of the five aggregates *(pañcaskandhapartītyasamutpāda)* has been destroyed, one enjoys the eternal bliss of nirvāṇa *(nirvāṇanityasukha)*.

bhūmi stages, finally it is not that you use only the basic [four dhyānas], but must encounter the wisdom of the [Four Noble] truths [**118a**] and arouse [the undefiled dhyānas] at these levels, and merely using only the basic [four dhyāna] is not an undefiled condition. [The contemplation of] impurity and so forth are not like this; a direct use of [the contemplations] of impurity can bring about the conditions [for the undefiled].

2. Categories Not Covered [118a2]

[There are categories that are] not taken up here. The ten considerations 十想 are [as follows]: the first three [considerations of impermanence, suffering, and no-self are for those with] "insight into the truth" 見諦. The middle four [considerations of (4) the impurity of what we eat; (5) the impossibility of finding true happiness in this world; (6) death; and (7) the impurity of our physical bodies, are for those at the level of] "pondering." The final three [considerations of (8) severing passions and delusions, (9) becoming free of desires; and (10) exhausting our karmic bonds are for] those who have no more to learn. All of them correspond to [the abstract] principle [of the truth], and therefore we do not take them up [here].

Again, we do not take up the eight mindfulnesses 八念 [of Buddha, Dharma, Sangha, the precepts, equanimity, heavenly matters, the inhaling and exhaling of your breath, and death] because if you have cultivated the nine considerations [of decaying corpses], you are [already] fearless.

Again, the gate of mindfulness of the Buddha 念佛門 is already included, and therefore it is not taken up here.

The contemplation of a compassionate mind corresponds to both [defiled and undefiled]. If you arouse compassion through the basic [four dhyānas], this corresponds to "defiled." If compassion is aroused through [the contemplation of] impurity and so forth, this corresponds to "undefiled." Compassion is not [linked to any particular] level of stages [of your own attainment], but depends on the stages of others. Those who rely on the [four] basic [dhyānas] arouse [compassion] through connection with sentient beings; those who rely on the [eight] renunciations or liberations arouse [compassion] through connections with the Dharma. The causes and conditions [of compassion] are also unrelated to the level of stages. Mindfulness of the Buddha and the five supranormal powers all depend on the stages of others. In this way the mind of compassion corresponds to both [defiled and undefiled], and so forth.

Stages of others 他階級: the Taishō text has 地階級 "stages of stages," but I follow the BT–V (237) and Ikeda (*Teihonkundoku*, 637) in substituting 他 (other) for 地 (stage).

3. Differences in the Gist Compared to the *Tz'u-ti ch'an-men* [118a10]

Next, concerning that the gist is not the same [for the *Mo-ho chih-kuan* and the *Tz'u-ti ch'an-men*].

Question: Among these ten categories, how are they the same or different and how should you deal with them as presented in the *Tz'u-ti ch'an-men*?

Answer: The *Tz'u-ti ch'an-men* focuses on attaining the perfection of dhyāna meditation (*dhyāna-pāramitā*). Since [for that audience] the good roots of dhyāna meditation were sharp, first [I taught] arousing the gate or practice of dhyāna meditation and later examined good and evil. In this [exposition of the *Mo-ho chih-kuan*] the focus is on *prajñā*-wisdom for those whose roots of dhyāna meditation are dull, so first we obstruct passionate afflictions, encounter karma and demonic forces, and only later arouse dhyāna. [The section on] "Controlling and Healing [through Auxiliary Means]," [teaches how to] cultivate the path of auxiliary means [such as the six perfections and so forth] for the sake of destroying obstacles. Now in this [text of the *Mo-ho chih-kuan*] the focus is on contemplating objects naturally and spontaneously 任運自發. Although [both texts are] the same in [expounding] the gate of dhyāna meditation, each has its own intent.

4. Clarifying in Terms of Deep and Shallow [118a16]

Next is to clarify the differences between [the categories of dhyāna meditation in terms of] deep and shallow. [1] The four dhyānas are basic, and involve [attachment to] the flavor of dhyāna 味禪 and dark enlightenment 闇證. It is common to both ordinary and noble people, and even a shallow cultivation will provide attainment. [2] The [sixteen] superior meditations include a little of contemplative wisdom but involve no [attachment to the] flavor [of dhyāna] nor dark enlightenment. Horizontally they contrast with the mindfulnesses, and vertically contrast with the basic [four dhyānas]; therefore first there is the flavor [of dhyāna] and then the purity [of dhyāna]. [3] The contemplative wisdom of the [six] supranormal powers and [three] illuminations is profound and fine in its features of enlightenment, and is next among the general [categories]. These [first] three [that is, the four basic dhyānas, the superior meditations, and the supranormal powers and illuminations] are the same in being the foundation of real contemplation

Tz'u-ti ch'an-men 次第禪門: An earlier exposition by Chih-i on the "gradual method," which focused on expounding the gradual-and-successive practice of dhyāna meditation. See especially the section at T 46.508a18ff. See also the exposition earlier in the *Mo-ho chih-kuan* in the section on "Controlling and Healing through Auxiliary Methods," 91a5–97b17, especially section 5 (92c15–93a29) on "the perfection of dhyāna meditation (*dhyāna-pāramitā*)."

實觀, but they are weak in their power to control delusions. [4] The nine considerations [of decaying corpses] are truly the first gate of conventional conceptualization. With a sharp point 前鋒 they overcome desires, and therefore they are listed next. [But] the nine considerations merely make you weary and disillusioned of the external realm, and do not yet heal the mind. Therefore [they come before] the next [category] of the eight renunciations. [5] The [eight] renunciations: although these destroy the internal and external covetous desires, they are still general and not yet specific, so you are not yet able to attain mastery within conditions. [6] Therefore next we clarify [contemplation of] great impurity, which can destroy covetous desires among sentient beings and the world in which they dwell. Although these involve controlling covetous desires both generally and specifically, they do not yet involve great meritorious virtue. [7] Next is a compassionate mind. Although again this involves internal control of grave covetous desires and external cultivation of meritorious virtue, you do not yet realize [the fundamental truth concerning] causes and conditions, so it is not a true perception of the world. [8] Therefore next [in line] is [contemplation of] causes and conditions, [wherein you realize that] transmigration in the three times [of past, present, and future] has no subject 無主 and no self, and you attain a true perception of the world. [9] Although you have a true perception of the world, your power of virtue is still weak [with regard to helping] people below you on the causal stages, so you should try to come in contact with [the Buddhas who have attained] a higher fruit, and expand your virtuous power [through being mindful of the Buddha]. [10] Even though you have the concentrations explained above, you do not yet have the power and mastery in performing transformations 轉變, **[118b]** and therefore the next [on the list] is the supranormal powers.

5. Differences in Mutual Arising [118b1]

Next is the gradual mutual arising [among the ten categories of dhyāna meditation]. There are eight ways in which these mutually arise, which should be known from the explanation [in the section on] "The Contemplation of the Sense Fields."

Next among the general [categories] 次於總: Ikeda (*Gendaigoyaku*, 587) translates this ambiguous phrase rather freely as "it is thus different from the supreme [contemplations]."

Eight ways in which these mutually arise, which should be known 有八種例陰界境可知 …: see, for example, the section on "Ten Ways the Ten Objects of Contemplation Arise" (49c3–50c2), which gives nine pairs and one sevenfold category of how they "mutually arise." The precise content of "eight ways" is not clear.

2. The Causes and Conditions of the Arising of Dhyāna [118b2]

Second is to clarify the causes and conditions of the arising of dhyāna. The *Mahāparinirvāṇa Sūtra* says, "all sentient beings without exception have the first stage of the flavor of dhyāna, and whether they cultivate or do not cultivate [dhyāna], they can certainly attain [some form of] concentration." If your recent conditions are [inauspicious such as] that of the end of a kalpa, or you have not cultivated [dhyāna or the path], but then if you do practice for a long time, you may encounter [an opportunity to be] free from the coverings [of desires]. This is analogous to chanting the sūtras: if you have only recently stopped [reciting] then it is easy to practice [again], and if it has been a long time [since you last chanted] then it will be difficult to practice [again]. You should know that if you have gradually practiced in the past, then [results will] gradually be aroused, and so forth up to, if you have cultivated the practical matters [of dhyāna] then the practical [results] will arise, and so forth. This is like the great earth being endowed with all varieties of seeds, and if it is blessed with the moistening from rain, each [of the seeds] will open and grow; their growth will be different, and their fruit not [ripen] together. The plum will take four [years], the peach seven, the pear nine, and the persimmon ten. Although the conditions of the rain are the same [for all], the arising of fruit is different. Your conditions from previous lives are like these seeds, and [the practice of] cessation-and-contemplation is like the rain. The arising of dhyāna is like the fruit, which matures irregularly 參差. Therefore it is said that there are eight types [of mutual arising]. This is called the arising of internal causes and conditions [in your own mind].

Again, although there are [various] good factors that should be aroused, it is certain that [the Buddha's] majestic power [or "spiritual vitality" 威神] will be a conventional factor in arousing [dhyāna]. Even if there are seeds in the ground, without the sun they will not sprout. The Buddha [like the sun] benefits all universally according to their conditions, and without passionate attachments. As conditions [improve] gradually, so the influence [of the Buddha] is gradually added 加, and so forth until the conditions of actual cultivation produce actual [results]. The way a great bell is struck depends on whether the stick is large or delicate. The added assistance 加 [of the

All sentient beings without exception have the first stage of the flavor of dhyāna ... 一切衆生皆有初地味禪。若修不修必定當得: this probably refers to Buddha nature? See the *Mahāparinirvāṇa Sūtra*, T 12.760c17–19:

> It is like sentient beings in the realm of desires, who all without exception have the first stage of the flavor of dhyāna. Whether they cultivate or do not cultivate, they will always have it, and so when they encounter [the proper] conditions, they can attain even more.

Growth will be different 生亦前後: lit. "arise before and after [each other]."

Buddha] is always undiscriminating; the shallowness or depth depends on the one who hears and practices. The *Ta chih tu lun* says, "The flowers in a pond must have sunlight or without a doubt they will wither and die. [One who has] good [virtues] without receiving the added [help of the Buddha] will sink and drown and no longer appear." The *Sūtra of Pure Salvation* says, "[Someone said,] 'Sentient beings save themselves; the Buddha does not benefit them in this matter.' But the bodhisattva Pure Salvation said, 'If sentient beings do not hear the twelvefold sūtras of the Buddha, how can they be saved?'" These two quotes may appear contrary to each other, but together they have the same intent. This is called the arising of external conditions [of assistance from the Buddha].

3. The Marks of the Arising of Dhyāna [118b19–130b10]

Third is clarifying the marks of the arising of all the [ten categories of] dhyāna [from the four basic dhyāna to the supranormal powers].

1. The Four Basic Dhyānas [118b20]

The [four] basic [dhyānas] may play a small part of the Pratyutpanna [Samādhi of the constantly-walking Samādhi] and so forth [of the other

Flowers in a pond must have sunlight or without a doubt they will wither and die 池華不得日翳死無疑。善不被加沈溺未顯: see the *Ta chih tu lun*, T 25.63a28–c. Chodron (1, 68) translates the opening to this section:

> It is like the lotus *(utpala)* in the water: some are born, some ripen, some remain within the water without emerging. If they do not have sunlight *(sūryaprabhā)*, they do not expand *(vikasanti)*. The Buddha is like [the sunlight]: sent forth by his great loving kindness and great compassion *(mahāmaitrīkaruṇā)*, that he might have pity for beings and preach the doctrine." The Buddha recalled the qualities *(dharma)* of the buddhas of the three times *(tryadvan)*, past *(atīta)*, future *(anāgata)* and present *(pratyutpanna)*, all of whom preached the doctrine in order to save beings: "I too," said he, "must do the same."...
>
> Thus the great disciples Devadatta, Kokālika, etc., not having faith in the Dharma, fell into the evil destinies *(durgati)*. These men had no faith in the Buddha's doctrine and were unable to discover it by their own wisdom *(prajñā)*.

Sūtra of Pure Salvation 淨度經: this text is not extant today, but Chan-jan (BT–V, 248) adds:

> The final fascicle of this sūtra says, "[Someone says,] 'In this way people are not saved by a hundred million Buddhas, let alone one Buddha. Therefore people must save themselves.' But the bodhisattva Pure Salvation said, 'Sentient beings must hear the twelvefold sūtras.'"

The [four] basic [dhyānas] may play a small part 根本而少: Chan-jan (BT–V, 428) adds, "The constantly-walking [Samādhi] has the least [occurrence of the four basic dhyānas] and the constantly-sitting [Samādhi] has the most, and therefore the two are contrasted with each other. It is not that they do not occur at all, but merely that it is less."

Samādhis of both-walking-and-sitting and neither-walking-nor-sitting], but it is very common for the constantly-sitting [Samādhi], so now I will discuss it in terms of "sitting" [in meditation]. If your body is straight, your mind collected, and your breathing balanced and harmonious, so that you are awake to the pathways of your mind [or, "mental road (to Buddhahood) 心路]—passive, clear, and still 泯然澄靜, quiet and tranquil 怗怗安隱—treading gingerly to enter [meditation]; this mind sets the conditions so that [your thoughts] will not be scattered. This is called [the preliminary] "rough dwelling" 麁住. From this mind you will later quietly advance to superior [stages]; this is called "fine dwelling" 細住. For both of these mind sets—before and after and in between—there are methods for maintaining the physical body. When these methods are used, the body naturally straightens itself and does not become tired or painful, and it is as if there is something that is helping your physical power. If there comes a time when you are bad at maintaining [this quietude and stability], you will suddenly feel a powerful pain, or when you arise [from meditation] this will cause sluggishness and fatigue. This is a rough and bad way to maintain [meditation]. A good way to maintain [meditation] is to maintain both the "rough dwelling" and "fine dwelling" [as explained above], without excessive leniency or quickness, sometimes for one or two hours, or for one or two days, or for one or two months, so that you gradually awaken to that which is deeper and finer and the mind becomes lucid and achieves a partial **[118c]** opening of enlightenment 開明. Your body is like the clouds, like a shadow, shining bright and pure. If applied in mutual rapport with the methods of concentration and the mind is maintained immobile, yearnings will be purified and removed, so that you will be cool and pure. Although you have thus realized the purity of emptiness, you still have mistaken views concerning the marks of the body and mind, and do not yet have the [more advanced] dhyānic constituents of virtuous qualities. This is called "the concentrations of the realm of desires" 欲界定.

The *Ch'eng shih lun* calls these "the ten good minds associated with [afflictions]" that sparkle brightly but do not last for long. Now I say that the

Dhyānic constituents of virtuous qualities 支林功德: the *Tz'u-ti ch'an-men* at T 46.511a17 contains the phrase, "dhyāna is called a 'forest of constituents' 禪名支林." These are defined below, at 119b3–7, as having ten constituents.

The ten good minds associated with [afflictions] 十善相應心: this phrase does not appear in the *Ch'eng shih lun*, only in a few texts related to Chih-i. Chan-jan (BT–V, 249) explains that these are "ten goodnesses in the realm of desires. When you attain concentration or dhyāna within desires, that means to be in rapport with ten good dharmas." The *Kōgi* (BT–V, 249) adds that "There is no such text in the *Ch'eng shih lun*; it must be a teaching of one of it's masters."

concentrations [or dhyānas] of the [realm of] desires are brittle like bricks that have not yet been fired and are not secure, so they are referred to as a twinkling [of an eye]. They are not steady like the flame of a lamp. Again, they are called a flash of lightning. This *[Ch'eng shih] lun* says, "Apart from the seven dependent [concentrations], are there any further concentrations that are aroused undefiled, or not? The answer is: there are concentrations of the realm of desires that are able to arise undefiled. But the arising of the undefiled is quick and sudden like a flash of lightning. If there is no arising of the undefiled, then it can dwell for a long time." The *I chiao ching* says, "If you see a flash of lightning, momentarily you will be able to see the path." It is like Ānanda, who disciplined his mind but could not attain arising [of dhyāna], but when he released his mind and took his pillow [to lie down] he had [an experience like] a flash of lightning. A flash of lightning is also like a Vajra [Samādhi?]; a Vajra [Samādhi?] does not arise alone but you enter the undefiled through the realm of desires. The undefiled arises quickly, like a flash of lightning. The samādhis of the realm of desires do not deserve this name [of a "flash of lightning"]. Dwelling in the samādhis or concentrations of the realm of desires can last for months or years. These methods of concentrations should be maintained in the mind without negligence and without pain, not emerging from them for consecutive days, and then they will be attained.

Following after this mind[set] you turn and rest [in dhyāna concentration], and within the concentration of [the realm of] desires become

***Ch'eng shih lun* says, "Apart from … for a long time"** 七依外更有定發無漏不。答云。有欲界定能發無漏。無漏發疾倏如電光。若不發無漏住時則久: see a long passage at T 32.338c18–339c27, which mentions "seven dependencies" and of "lightning-like samādhis" 如電三昧.

***I chiao ching* 遺教, "If you see …"** 若見電光暫得見道: see T 12.1112b2, "Hearing the Buddha preach, everyone attained liberation, like lightning flashing in the night and seeing the path."

Ānanda's flash of lightning 電光: see the *Ta chih tu lun*, T 25.69a7–15; Chodron (1, 96) translates

> At that moment, Ānanda reflected [on the nature] of dharmas and sought to exhaust his last impurities *(āsrava)*. During the night, he sat in dhyāna, walked to and fro, and sought the Path *(mārga)* anxiously and zealously. Ānanda's wisdom *(prajñā)* was great, but his power of samādhi was weak. That is why he did not obtain the Path immediately. If his power of concentration had been equal to his wisdom, he would have quickly obtained [the Path]. Finally, when the night was almost over and he was very tired, he lay down. Now, on lying down to reach his pillow *(bimbohana)*, just as his head touched it, suddenly he attained enlightenment. As a bolt of lightning drives away the shadows, he saw the Path. Then Ānanda entered the diamond-like *(vajra)* samādhi and crushed the mountain of all the afflictions *(kleśa)*. He obtained the three knowledges *(vidya)*, the six superknowledges *(abhijñā)*, complete liberation *(vimokṣa)* and became an arhat of great power.

oblivious to your own body, clothes, meditation mat [and so forth]. This is like the void, brightly shining and peaceful. The body is an obstacle to actual deeds, and these are an obstacle for future [attainment], but when the obstacles pass and the body is empty, attainment [of dhyāna] will arise in the future. This is called "the marks of the stage of incomplete attainment." People without knowledge attain this concentration and [mistakenly] think they have attained the forbearance of [realizing] the non-arising [of dharmas], but they still have the nature of obstructions [of the delusions of the realm of desires] and have not yet entered even the first dhyāna. How could you mistake this for the concentration of [realizing the forbearance of] non-arising? This is like ashes covering burning coals and an ignorant person frivolously stepping on them [and getting burned]. According to the *Ch'eng shih lun*, there is no "future [as yet incomplete] dhyāna," and therefore says "The 'future dhyāna' of which you speak; is this not my 'concentrations of the realm of desires'?" The Abhidharma contains this teaching [of a 'future dhyāna'] by the honorable Ghoṣa. The *Ta chih tu lun* explains these in detail. The Buddha taught both of these explanations [of the concentrations of the

Stage of incomplete attainment 未到地: "preparatory practice done prior to the entry into the first concentration 初禪定. It is the type of incomplete concentration accessible to practitioners in the realm of desire 欲界定. (瑜伽論 T 1579.30.590c3) (Skt. *anāgamya-samādhi, anāgamya, anāgamya-bhūmika*.) Abbreviation for 未至到地定" (DDB).

Ashes covering burning coals 如灰覆火: a phrase from a section on the icchantika in the *Mahāparinirvāṇa Sūtra*, T 12.660a10–b16 (the phrase appears at 660b6: "If there are ashes covering burning fire [or coals] and you foolishly and frivolously step on them, such a person is called an icchantika."

See also T no. 374, 12.419a3–b7.

***Ch'eng shih lun* and "future dhyāna"** 未來禪: see the passage at T 32.339a4–7:

> Question: Some people say that relying on the limits of the first dhyāna and the stage of incomplete attainment 未到地 you can attain the fruit of the arhat. What do you think of this?
> Answer: This is not so. If you rely on the stage of incomplete attainment, this is a mistake. If you are able to attain the stage of incomplete attainment, how can you not realize the first dhyāna. Therefore it is not the case [that you attain arhatship at this stage?].

The Abhidharma 毘曇: the classical commentaries say that the source for this is unknown.

The honorable Ghoṣa 尊者瞿沙: the "name of a famous dialectician and preacher who is accredited with restoration of sight to Dharmavivardhana, i.e. Kuṇāla, son of Aśoka, 'by washing his eyes with the tears of people who were moved by his eloquence.' (Eitel) Also author of the *Abhidharmāmṛta śāstra*, which is called 瞿沙經" (DDB).

***Ta chih tu lun* explains in detail**: see T 25.248b3–22 (Lamotte, *Le Traité* 3, 1636–37); Chodron (3, 1084–85) translates:

> Question. The concentrations go from the *anāgamya* [preliminary concentration of the first dhyāna] on up to the absorption of cessation *(nirodhasamāpatti)*. When one enters into these absorptions,

it is impossible to assert any physical action *(kāyakarman)* or vocal action *(vākkarman)*. Hence, if the Buddha is always concentrated *(samāhita)* and has no non-concentrated mind, how can he travel through the kingdoms, take up the four positions *(īryāpatha)* and preach the Dharma to the great assemblies with all kinds of nidānas and avadānas? Whether these actions are of the domain of the desire realm *(kāmadhātvavacara)* or of the Brahmā world, the Buddha cannot enter into concentration if he wants to accomplish them.

Answer. When we said that he has no non-concentrated mind, that can have several meanings. Being concentrated means being fixed on the good dharmas with a mind that is always absorbed *(sadāsaṃgṛhītacittena)*. Now the Buddha is fixed on the true nature *(bhūtalakṣaṇa)* of dharmas and never strays from that. Therefore he does not have a non-concentrated mind.

Furthermore, in the desire realm *(kāma-dhātu)* there are some concentrations where those who have entered into them are able to preach the Dharma. Thus, in the Abhidharma it is a question of [concentrations] belonging to the desire realm *(kāmadhātvavacara)*, such as the four levels of saints *(āryavaṃśa)*, the four foundations of mindfulness *(smṛtyupasthāna)*, the four right efforts *(samyakpradhāna)*, the four bases of magical power *(ṛddhipāda)*, the five faculties *(indriya)*, the five strengths *(bala)*, the concentration preventing being attacked by others *(araṇā-samādhi)*, the knowledge resulting from aspiration *(praṇidhijñāna)*, and the four unhindered knowledges *(pratisaṃvid)*. There are marvelous qualities of this kind in which the Buddha is established while entering into the world of desire: this is why he has no non-concentrated mind.

When the śrāvakas and pratyekabuddhas emerge from concentration *(samādher vyuthitāḥ)*, they enter into an undefined mind *(avyākṛtacitta)*, they enter into a good mind *(kuśala-citta)* or they enter into a defiled mind *(samalacitta)*. But when the Buddha comes out of concentration and enters into a concentration of the desire realm *(kāmadhātusamādhi)*, he has not a single moment of distracted mind *(vikṣiptacitta)*: this is why he has no non-concentrated mind.

On the "incomplete or preliminary attainments" 未到地 *(anāgamya)* see also T 25.187a2–26; (Lamotte, *Le Traité* 2, 1036–38); Chodron (2, 803–5) translates:

When the disciple of the Buddha wishes to abandon the desires *(kāma)* and passions *(kleśa)* of kāmadhātu, by means of meditation he cuts the nine categories of passions, strong *(adhimātra)*, medium *(madhya)* and weak *(mṛdu)*, namely: 1. strong-strong, 2. strong-medium, 3. strong-weak, 4. medium-strong, 5. medium-medium, 6. medium-weak, 7. weak-strong, 8. weak-medium, 9. weak-weak.

Having cut these nine categories, the disciple of the Buddha can try to obtain the first *dhyāna* by the *sāsravamārga*. In this case, in the *anāgamya* (preliminary concentration preceding the first *dhyāna*), in the course of nine *ānantaryamārga* (successive abandonments of the nine categories of passions of the lower level) and eight *vimuktimārga* (taking possession of these successive abandonings), he first practices the *sāsravamārga*, then the *sāsrava* or *anāsravamārga*. In the course of the ninth *vimuktimārga*, in the *anāgamya*, he first practices the *sāsravamārga*; then the *sāsrava* or *anāsravamārga* of the *anāgamya*, and the *sāsrava* of the *sāmantaka* of the first *dhyāna*. If he wishes to attain the first *dhyāna* by way of the *anāsravamārga*, he will do the same.

If he abandons the passions of the first dhyāna by means of the *sāsravamārga*, in the *sāmantaka* of the second *dhyāna*,

realm of desires and the stage of incomplete attainment?], but the treatises [of the Abhidharma and *Ch'eng shih lun*] only give a one-sided [presentation]. Now I am following various people in making distinctions. There are those who have themselves attained the concentrations of the realm of desires, spent many months dwelling in [the stage of] incomplete attainment, and before long enter the first dhyāna. This is only what is called [the concentrations of] the realm of desires, and is not what is meant by the "[stage of] incomplete attainment." Some people dwell in [the concentrations of] the realm of desires for a short time and dwell in [the stage of] incomplete attainment for about a third of a month 旬, and therefore this is called "[the stage of] incomplete attainment" and not [the concentrations of] the realm of desires. Some people dwell in both types of concentrations for a long time, and therefore cannot be said to be one-sided. Here [in the *Mo-ho chih-kuan*] I depend on the detailed explanation of the *Ta chih tu lun*. A section-by-section account concerning the mistaken and correct features [of these matters] is given in detail in the text on "cultivating enlightenment" [in the *Tz'u-ti ch'an-men*]. However, [the stage of] the first dhyāna is close to the realm of

during nine *ānantaryamārgas* and eight *vimuktimārga*, he first practices the *sāsrava* of the *sāmantaka* of the second *dhyāna*, then the *sāsravamārga* of the *sāmantaka* of the second *dhyāna* as well as the first *anāsrava dhyāna* and its sequel. During the ninth *vimuktimārga*, in the *samantaka* of the second *dhyāna*, he first practices the *sāsravamārga* of the *sāmantaka* of the second *dhyāna*, then the *sāmantaka* of the second *dhyāna*, then the *anāsrava* of the first *dhyāna* and its sequel, the second *śuddhaka* or *anāsrava dhyāna*.

If he abandons the passions of the first *dhyāna* by means of the *anāsravamārga*, during the course of nine *ānantaryamārga* and eight *vimuktimārga*, he first practices the *anāsravamārga* of his own level, the *sāsrava* or *anāsrava* of the first *dhyāna* and its sequel. In the course of the ninth *vimuktimārga*, he first practices the *anāsravamārga* of his own level, then the *sāsrava* or *anāsravamārga* of the first *dhyāna* and its sequel.

It is the same in the practice of the other concentrations from the second *śuddhaka* or *anāsrava dhyāna* up to the abandonment that characterizes the *ākiṃcanyāyatana*. In the abandonment that characterizes the *naivasaṃjñānāsaṃjñāyatana*, during the nine *ānanataryamārga* and eight *vimuktimārga*, he practices just the universal *anāsravamārga*. In the course of the ninth *vimuktimārga*, he practices the roots of good of the threefold world (*traidhātukakuśalamūla*) and the *anāsravamārga*; thus he drives out absorption without mind (*acittaka-samāpatti*).

The text on "cultivating enlightenment" 修證 [in the *Tz'u-ti ch'an-men*]: see the section at T 46.509b23ff.:

Third is clarifying the marks of enlightenment through dhyāna. Generally "enlightenment" is discussed through means, which involves three stages: 1. enlightenment as the marks of the concentrations of the realm of desires 證欲界定相; 2. enlightenment as the marks of the concentration of incomplete attainment 證未到定相; and 3. a correct clarification of enlightenment at the marks of the first dhyāna 證初禪相.

desires, and as crossing a boundary presents many difficulties, it is necessary to know about it in general.

Starting from the [stage of] "rough dwelling" until finishing at the [highest] stage of [the concentration of] "non-conceptions," generally there are four aspects, that of "retrogressing" 退, "protecting" 護, **[119a]** "dwelling" 住, and "advancing" 進.

[1.] The aspect of "retrogressing" also has two meanings: 1. "natural 任運 retrogressing"; and 2. "retrogressing through contact with conditions [of tactile sensations]" 緣觸. [For this second category] there are internal and external conditions. The loss of external [conditions for practicing concentration] such as the twenty-five [preparatory] means and breathing [exercises] [and so forth] are called "retrogressing through contact with external conditions." [As for internal conditions,] within a quiet [concentrated] mind there are three obstacles [of karmic recompense, passionate afflictions, and karmic deeds] and four demonic forces [of skandhas, passionate afflictions, death, and the supernatural demons] which give rise to sorrows and passions; [if you give in to these temptations] this is called "retrogressing through contact with internal conditions." Later you may again cultivate and attain [concentration], or may cultivate and not attain [concentration]. There are very many people like this.

[2.] The aspect of "protecting": this refers to when good [is obtained] through internal and external means, and you protect this concentrated mind and do not allow it to be lost.

[3.] The aspect of "dwelling": by protecting and maintaining the peaceful calm [of concentration] without losing it, or by dwelling in it naturally, this is called the aspect of "dwelling."

[4.] The aspect of "progressing": there is "natural" progressing, and progressing through diligent planning. Each has horizontal and vertical aspects. Each horizontal and vertical aspect has gradual and sudden aspects. If we were to take up each of the twelve gates [of the four dhyānas, four boundless demeanors, and four concentrations on emptiness] one by one, this would be called a "gradual [vertical] progression." If they are all included at once, this is called a "sudden [vertical] progression." If discussed with regard to the

First, the clarification of enlightenment as the concentrations of the realm of desires has two meanings: 1. correct clarification of the marks of enlightenment, and 2. clarification of what is attained and lost.

Now I will explain [the concentrations of] the realm of desires, which have three parts: 1. the mind of rough dwelling 麁住心; 2. the mind of fine dwelling 細住心; and 3. enlightenment as the concentrations of the realm of desires....

The twenty-five [preparatory] means 方便二十五種: see the detailed explanation of these in Chapter VI of the *Mo-ho chih kuan*, 35c1–48c29.

arisings [of concentration in] each category such as the superior meditations and supranormal powers and illuminations [and so forth], this is a horizontal gradual [progression]. Their arising together at one time is a horizontal sudden [progression]. Again, each of these aspects of the four aspects have four parts. These are given in detail in the text on "cultivating enlightenment" [in the *Tz'u-ti ch'an-men*].

Now I will discuss the aspect of "progressing" from the vertical perspective [of making progress up a series of stages]. From [the stage of] incomplete attainments of concentration, you gradually become awakened to the empty quiescence of your body and mind. Internally you do not perceive your body, and externally you do not perceive [material] things. This concentrated mind may last without breaking for a day, or up to a month or a year. Within this concentration you are aware of the body and mind as subtle and quiescent in movement, and yet arousing [the tactile sensations such as] movement [or restlessness], itching, lightness, heaviness, cold, heat, roughness, and smoothness. A person has said, "The functioning of the mind becomes subtle and fine, and the pure visible forms of the realm of form come in contact with the body of the realm of desires. For example, this is like the pure visible forms of the realm of desires appearing before the sense organs so that you are able to see and hear them." If we rely on this meaning, objects [of "contact"] are external. But if we say that all sentient beings without exception have the first stage of the flavor of dhyāna 初地味禪 [= Buddha nature, as in the *Mahāparinirvāṇa Sūtra*], this is like a very rich but blind child knowing that bamboo has within it [the potential to burn with] fire. The passionate afflictions within the mind do not arise in order, and the dhyāna [concentrations] are also likewise. The crude obstructions of the obstacles of phenomenal or actual deeds make you unable to attain arising. Now, cultivate [a concentrated] mind and gradually [attain] benefit; the obstacles of the nature [of reality] are removed and fine dharmas arise.

In detail in the text on "cultivating enlightenment" 具如修證中説 **[in the *Tz'u-ti ch'an-men*]**: see, for example, the section at T 46.512b20–c3.

A person has said 有人言: the source of this quote cannot be identified.

Pure visible forms of the realm of desires 欲界淨色: the material objects themselves of our senses and desires (not yet conceptualized and thus "pure")?

Very rich but blind child knowing that bamboo has within it fire 如大富盲兒竹中有火: this sounds like it could be an analogy or parable from the *Mahāparinirvāṇa Sūtra* or *Ta chih tu lun*, but the classical commentaries do not identify its source, and a SAT search did not turn up any pre-Chih-i sources.

The crude obstructions of the obstacles of actual deeds 事障麁礙 **...**: for a more detailed discussion on the effects of these earlier levels of meditation, see the section on "the realm of forms" at 70c8ff.

How can it be said that these come externally [when it is clear that they arise internally]? Why is this so? [The practice of] counting the breaths is able to turn 轉 the mind; the mind turns fire; fire turns wind; wind turns water; water turns earth. Thus the four great elements [gradually] become finer, and therefore we have the eight contacts [or tactile sensations of movement, itchiness, lightness, heaviness, cold, heat, roughness, and smoothness]. This is like barley turning into malt, malt turning into distilled grain, and distilled grain turning into beer. The distilled grain is an analogy for the concentrations in [the realm of] desires, and the beer is an analogy for the first [stages of] dhyāna. The barley is the basis or origin [for the resulting beer], and this does not come from something external. If you become determinedly attached to [either extreme of thinking that things] emerge [internally] from themselves, or come [externally] from the outside, this is to fall into the mistaken excess of [establishing] a fixed nature [that things arise from] "self" or "other" 自他性. Now, if we rely on the *Middle Treatise*, we can deconstruct all four options [of arising from self, other, both, or neither]; what need is there to discuss [further the duality of] emerging internally or coming from the outside?

Again, the eight contacts [of tactile sensations] are [indivisible from] the four great elements. Movement and lightness are wind; itching and heat are fire; cold and smooth are water, heavy and crude are earth. The essence and function [of the four elements] intersect and we have the eight tactile sensations. When there is contact with movement, whether in the head, back, **[119b]** hips, ribs, or feet, and [this sensation] gradually spreads throughout the body, there are no external marks of such movement even though you are aware of movement inside your body. Therefore [the sensation] arises like the wind [from where, nobody knows,] and moves delicately from the head to the feet, often resulting in a retrogression [in concentration]. But if these [sensations] arise from the hips, this may result in "dwelling" [in concentration]; if they arise from the feet, often this will result in "progressing" [in concentration].

The tactile sensation of movement has constituent virtuous qualities 支林功德, and these virtues can be summarized in ten types: 1. empty 空; 2. clear 明; 3. stable or concentrated 定; 4. wisdom 智; 5. good mind 善心; 6. flexibility 柔軟; 7. joy 喜; 8. bliss 樂; 9. the realm of liberation 解脱境界; and 10. correspondence 相應.

[1.] "Empty": when the tactile sensation of movement arises, the empty

Rely on the *Middle Treatise* to deconstruct four options 依中論破四性: see the deconstructive arguments using the tetralemma at, for example, T 30.2a–b.

mind opens up, which is not the same as before when the obstacles of the nature [of reality] have not yet been removed.

[2.] "Clear": [the mind is] shining and pure, beautiful and subtle beyond compare, like the light of the moon.

[3.] "Stable or concentrated": single-minded and peacefully calm, without any distractedness.

[4.] "Wisdom": no dark delusions or nets of doubt; the understanding of the mind is quiet and piercing.

[5.] "Good mind": [a mind that is] conscientious, [has proper] shame, is trustful and respectful. Embarrassed that you have not yet encountered and attained this Dharma, you think with shame, "I am still like this," and believe that all wise and noble ones are endowed with the profound and sublime Dharma, and bows [to them] with immeasurable respect.

[6.] "Flexibility": to be free from the realm of desires, with its imbalance and coarse harshness, as with [the use of]brain matter a cow's hide can be stretched and wrapped at will.

[7.] "Joy": to give rise to ecstatic joy in the dharmas that have been attained.

[8.] "Bliss": to find pleasure in your contact with the dharmas, with a tranquil cheer and sublime beauty.

[9.] "The realm of liberation": to not return to the five impediments [of covetous desires, hateful anger, drowsiness and sleep, restlessness and remorse, and doubt].

[10.] "Correspondence": for the sensation of movement to be in correspondence with the virtues and not agitating [each other]. Again, it means a correspondence in maintaining mindfulness so that it is not lost, for a day, a month, or a year. Peaceful calm dwells for a long time, so that if you gather your thoughts, then [concentration] will come.

Such pervasive discipline and cultivation for a long time will [increase] the class and level of the tactile sensation of movement and turn it deeper. This is called vertical arising [through stages], and the other seven tactile sensations [from itchy to smooth] should be known as in this example.

After the tactile sensation of movement arises, whether it ends or does not end, contact with the tactile sensation of "cold" arises. When the sensation of "cold" ends or does not end, the other tactile sensations arise, and they interact horizontally as explained above for the eight tactile sensations. This is called "horizontal arising."

Brain matter 腦: Chan-jan (BT-V, 261) explains: "a pharmaceutical that heats or tans hides, called 'brain.' 'Brain' refers to the marrow 髓 within the head."

Again, "vertical" and "horizontal" [arising] may happen one after the other, but if you examine them in terms of the five [preliminary] constituents [of meditation] of the ten virtuous qualities of the eight tactile sensations, there should not be any confusion.

Again, the arising of these [tactile sensations] together in one mind or thought is not attainable. Why is this so? The eight tactile sensations are like the four elements; water and fire are mutually incompatible, and cannot arise at the same time.

In this way the eight tactile sensations are adorned with eighty virtuous qualities; although their names are the same, the enjoyment of each is different. It is like when the flavor is different and the enjoyment special for each of [the hot dishes of] boiled soup and roasted meat, and [the cold dishes of] raw mackerel and chilled plum. Such distinctions apply also for the other six tactile sensations.

If the eight tactile sensations arise within the concentrations of the realm of desires, these are all perverse sensations, sensations of disease and passionate afflictions. These are explained in detail in the text on "cultivating enlightenment" [in the *Tz'u-ti ch'an-men*], so I will not discuss it here. However, in terms of the eight tactile sensations and the first dhyāna, I should distinguish between "perverse" and "correct." Why? First, because this is a borderline area where you are close to departing the realm of desires, and second, if you become wrapped up in the mental state of the realm of desires, perverse matters will enter accordingly. It is like opening a gate: bandits can enter thereby. If demonic forces should enter into your dhyāna meditation, [this is to be avoided because] dhyāna should not include demonic forces. If you do not know about these matters, proper tactile sensations will be broken, leaving only perverse and evil [sensations] remaining.

Perverse sensations, in terms of the ten good virtues of the eight tactile

Five [preliminary] constituents of meditation 五支: in the Abhidharma tradition there are five constituents of meditation, which in T'ien-t'ai are considered "preliminary" constituents: [1.] *vitarka* 覺, "a process of positioning, implying examination leading up to judgment and decision"; [2.] *vicāra* 觀, "the steadily moving reflection, the quiet and serious consideration and study of that which has been brought into the circle of interest by the gross *vitarka*." These first two constituents are "the cognitive aspect of the process of concentration," and are followed by; [3.] *prīti* 喜, joy, "an agreeable sensation," and [4.] *sukha* 安樂, bliss, which together are the "emotive aspect which is never absent in any of our mental processes." Finally, there is [5.] *cittāikāgratā* 心一境性, concentration.

In detail in the text on "cultivating enlightenment" 具如修證中說 **[in the *Tz'u-ti ch'an-men*]**: see the extensive section starting at T 46.509b22, also referred to above at 118c28.

sensations, [119c] are either an excess or insufficiency of these. For example, when the tactile sensation of movement arises, if immediately you become moody and your physical movements neither slow nor fast, but your actions become [too] quick, and you scratch your hands and feet, this is [a sign of] excess. If, on the other hand, you become immobile, like someone who is tied up, this is [a sign of] insufficiency. It is the same for other tactile sensations like cold and heat.

Again, the ten virtuous qualities such as "empty" and "bright" for the tactile sensation of movement, if discussed in terms of excess or insufficiency [are as follows:] [1.] "Empty": to be open yet unobstructed, this is right and proper emptiness. If for a long time you are cut off in quietude and unaware of all things, this is an excess. If you are hard like a clod [of dirt] and obstructed, this is an insufficiency. [2.] "Bright": to shine like the full reflection of the moon in a mirror. If it is [too] bright like the sun, or you can see various rays of light, this is an excess. If all cannot be seen, this is an insufficiency [of brightness]. [3.] "Stable or concentrated": the clear quietude of single-mindedness. If you are bound by attachments and immobile, this is an excess. If you chase after all sorts of things, this is an insufficiency [of concentration]. It is the same for [the remainder of the ten virtuous qualities] up to that of "correspondence." Thus in one sensation of movement there are twenty types of perverse marks. Along with the other seven virtuous qualities [in addition to the three described here], together there are one hundred and sixty perverse phenomena.

Originally, proper dhyāna should not have anything to do with perverse [matters]. When it does, it is like taking calamus [myrtle] grass 菖蒲 as a medicinal herb and becoming very angry, or taking the "essence of yellow" 黄精 to gain strength and becoming full of [lustful, erotic] desires. It is not that these medicinal herbs caused these [perverse feelings], but that the herbs stimulated your "rough dharmas" [of desires], and these "rough dharmas" [of desires] were brought forth and stimulated. If you are just in the realm of desires, then there are only perverse sensations, which increases disease and increases hindrances so that there are no proper virtuous qualities. If you enter the concentration of [only] visible form [beyond the realm of desires] and initiate the ten virtuous qualities such as "empty" and

One hundred and sixty perverse phenomena 百六十邪: twenty for each of the eight tactile sensations.

Wind is able to arouse rain, and wind is able to destroy rain 有風能成雨有風能壞雨: see the *Ta chih tu lun*, T 25.234a29, in a passage on the three types of samādhi:

> Conceptual examination and reflection *(vitarka-vicāra)* 覺觀 is able to arouse samādhi, and conceptual examination and reflection is able to destroy samādhi, like the wind is able to arouse rain, and it is able to destroy rain.

"bright" of the eight tactile sensations, again there are one hundred and sixty perverse sensations of which you should not be ignorant. The *Ta chih tu lun* says, "Wind is able to arouse rain, and wind is able to destroy rain." Clouds collect in the northeast, and clouds disperse in the southwest. Dhyāna is also like this. If you awaken 覺 the ten virtuous qualities of the eight tactile sensations, you will arouse dhyāna [concentration]. If you awaken the one hundred and sixty perverse [sensations], this will destroy dhyāna. If there is even one dharma-sensation that is perverse, this will defile all the rest; this is like when even one of your companions is a bandit, the rest of you will all be branded as evil friends. If from the beginning there are no perverse sensations, then the rest of the dharmas will all be good.

[Next, as for] the five [preliminary] constituents of proper dhyāna, when the body comes in contact with the first tactile sensation [of movement] and becomes a "condition," this is [the first constituent of] "examination" *(vitarka)* 覺. When the mind makes finer distinctions concerning the eight tactile sensations and its ten associated [virtuous qualities], this is called [the second constituent of] "reflection" *(vicāra)* 觀. Rejoicing at now attaining that which you have not yet attained in the past is called [the third constituent of] "joy" *(prīti)* 喜. Calm pleasure [in these attainments] is called [the fourth constituent of] "bliss" *(sukha)* 安樂. Such quiescence is called [the fifth constituent] of "single-mindedness" 一心. The Abhidharma teaches twenty-three mental factors that appear at one time, taking the five strongest for deciding on the five constituents. The five constituents are all [said to be] the essence of concentration. The various means before [attaining] the essence are as explained above [as the "incomplete attainments"]. The *Ch'eng shih lun* clarifies that of the five constituents that arise one after the other, the

Clouds collect in the northeast, and clouds disperse in the southwest 東北雲屯西南雲散: Chan-jan (BT–V, 265) explains:

> In the first book [of the *Mo-ho chih-kuan* or *Ta chih tu lun*?] it says, "The northeast wind collects clouds, and the southwest wind disperses the clouds and leads to a clear [sky]." This is an explanation of the analogy of the wind.

A search for the phrase "northeast wind" 東北風 in the SAT database did not result in any hits.

The Abhidharma teaches twenty-three mental factors that appear at one time 毘曇二十三心數一時而發: the *Abhidharma-vibhāṣā-śāstra*, T 28.13b, gives a summary of *vitarka-vicāra*. As the *Kōgi* (BT–V, 267) points out, however, the number twenty-three is found in an explanation in *The Meaning of Mahāyāna*, T 44.725a18–25, which assigns twenty-three mental states (out of eighty-six) to the first dhyāna stage.

***Ch'eng shih lun* clarifies that of the five constituents ... "single-mindedness" is the essence of concentration** 成論明五支前後相次而起。四支為方便。一心支為定體: again, as the *Kōgi* (BT–V, 267) points out, rather than the *Ch'eng shih lun* see the explanation in *The Meaning of Mahāyāna*, T 44.725b1–3, 18–21.

[first] four are [skillful] means, and the constituent of "single-mindedness" is the essence of concentration. The *Great Collection* says that "the mind of silence" is the essence of concentration. Some people say that the five constituents are [the content of] the ninth mental state in the realm of desires. Others say [**120a**] that they are [mental states] previous to the concentrations of the realm of desires. However, these are not the "five constituents."

Now I will give my interpretation: [the constituents of] "examination" *(vitarka)* and "reflection" *(vicāra)* [and so forth] are together a part of dhyāna and properly contribute to the determining of the first dhyāna, so how can you accept these [just-outlined theories]? The five constituents arise together, but there are strong and the weak [influences] shading into each other, and those aspects that are fulfilled are taken up and made into the five constituents. This is like a mallet hitting a temple bell; there are differences in that at first the sound is rough but gradually it becomes finer. The five constituents are also like this. At first there is abundant contact with the aspect of "examination," but this does not hinder [the presence of] the other four constituents such as "reflection." If "examination" is strong, then "reflection" is not yet complete; when "examination" ceases, "reflection" becomes clear. "Joy" is already present from the beginning, and when "reflection" ceases, the constituent of "joy" is perfected. "Bliss" is already present from the beginning though that bliss may not yet be full; when "joy" ceases, then "bliss" is perfected. "Single-mindedness" is already present from the begin-

The *Kōgi* adds, "If we rely on the *Ch'eng shih lun*, the five constituents of the first dhyāna appear one after the other and not at the same time, because it teaches that the mental factors are not simultaneous."

***Great Collection* says that "the mind of silence" is the essence of concentration** 大集以第六默然心爲定體: the *Kōgi* (BT–V, 267) points out that the attribution to "the *Great Collection [of Sūtras]* must be a mistake, and it should be [attributed to] that written in the *Ying-lo ching*." See the passage in the *Ying-lo ching* at T 24.1015a2–13:

> Sons of the Buddha, third is entering samādhi like an illusion 入如幻三昧, that is, the twelve gates of dhyāna. The five preliminary constituents of examination, reflection, joy, bliss, and single-mindedness are the causes. The sixth [constituent] of the "mind of silence" is the essence of concentration. [Or,] joy and bliss rely on single-mindedness, so the [first] four constituents are the causes and the fifth "mind of silence" is the essence of concentration. . . .

Some people, others say 有人言: the identities of the advocates of these positions are unknown.

Mallet hitting a temple bell 如一槌撞鐘: see the *Ta chih tu lun*, T 25.186a13–16. Chodron (2, 797) translates:

> Question. Are *vitarka* and *vicāra* one and the same thing or are they two different things?
> Answer. They are two different things. *Vitarka* is the first moment of a coarse mind *(sthūlaprathamakṣaṣa)*, *vicāra* is a more subtle *(sūkṣma)* analysis. Thus, when a bell is struck, the first sound is strong, the subsequent sound is weaker; this is *vicāra*.

ning in the movement of the [first] four constituents, but now when "bliss" ends, "single-mindedness" is perfected. It is like when you first open a store of treasures, you "examine" the treasures. Then, knowing it is precious, you feel joy and bliss at this certain conception [of having treasure], even though you do not yet know exactly what this treasure is. Next, you sort out the gold and silver, and after sorting it out and receiving it, you feel joy. Because of this joy you experience bliss, and rest pleasantly in single-mindedness. This is like [the sensation of] a person who is sated with food and does not need any more. Again, it is like being extremely sleepy from [indulging in] the five kinds of desires. Therefore the *Ta chih tu lun* says, "This is like a person who has found a store of treasures."

If the four dhyānas are all the same in having the constituent of single-mindedness as the essence [of concentration], then how are there differences among the four [dhyānas]? What distinguishes the first dhyāna is the presence 家 of single-mindedness in [the constituents of] "examination" and "reflection"; therefore you can distinguish four [dhyānas]. If we advance to the second dhyāna, this involves only rebuking "examination" and "reflection," and the first dhyāna is destroyed; this should in turn clarify the meaning that they are distinct. What is common is that they all have single-mindedness as the essence. The interpretation of the five constituents in terms of name, meaning, marks, and so forth are provided in detail in the text on "cultivating enlightenment" [in the *Tz'u-ti ch'an-men*].

Next, when the eight tactile sensations begin moving, the virtuous qualities are still crude, and when their arising becomes more numerous,

Like a person who has found a store of treasures 如人得寶藏: see the *Ta chih tu lun*, T 25.186a8–13. Chodron (2, 797) translates:

> The [five] characteristics of the first dhyāna are: examination *(vitarka)*, judgment *(vicāra)*, joy *(prīti)*, happiness *(sukha)* and one-pointedness of the mind *(cittaikāgratā)*.
>
> It is '*savitarka* and *savicāra*': by acquiring the good dharmas *(kuśaladharma)* and the qualities *(guṇa)* not previously acquired, in the first dhyāna the mind experiences great fear. When [a person] who has ceaselessly been burned by the fires of desire attains the first dhyāna, it is as if he were entering a pool of cold water. *Or else he is like a poor man (daridra) who suddenly finds a treasure:* the ascetic, who has meditated and analyzed the disadvantages of *kāmadhātu* and who sees the importance of the benefits and qualities of the first dhyāna, feels great joy *(prīti)*: this is why it is called *savitarka* and *savicāra*.

Extremely sleepy 極睡: though not a direct quote, see the passage following the two quoted above; see the *Ta chih tu lun*, T 25.186a29. Chodron (2, 798) translates:

> When a tired and weary man regains his breath and wants to sleep, when his neighbor calls him, that makes him very annoyed. It is for all these reasons that he condemns *vitarka* and *vicāra*.

In the text on "cultivating enlightenment" [in the *Tz'u-ti ch'an-men*]: see the section at T 46.511a–512a.

they turn deeper and sharper. Their varieties are said to be three, or said to be nine, or to be immeasurable varieties. They are enjoyed mutually and the virtuous qualities become crowded or "busy" so that you cannot attain single-mindedness, like the constant playing of musical instruments [or courtesans], or like looking after many guests so that when you are finished taking care of one, another one appears. When you come out of and disperse [the state of concentration], this [busyness] disappears for a while, but when trying a little [to enter dhyāna again], it appears again. If you wish to get away from this [busyness], just reject "examination" and "reflection." Then when the first dhyāna comes to an end, an intermediate and simple concentration will arise, which is called "the converted quiescent mind," and also called a "receding dhyāna," and also called "the mind of bamboo shavings." In this mind of "simple quiescence," you have already lost the lower [dhyāna concentration] and not yet aroused the higher, so if you arouse regret or remorse, you can lose this mental [concentration]. If you do not have any regret, an inner purity will arise, and you will no longer experience or discriminate the eight tactile sensations; therefore this is called a "concentration of single consciousness" 一識定. The visible forms of the four elements are mixed into one pure visible form; illumination of the mind will turn pure and arise along with joy; there will be no demonic and evil marks, and since you are no longer in a borderline realm, after joy there arises bliss, and when that ends you attain single-mindedness.

If in this [first] dhyāna [the constituent of] joy is too moving, and [the constituent of] bliss unstable, then you should discipline this joy, and when

Said to be three or nine 或言三或言九: see the *Tz'u-ti ch'an-men* at T 46.512b3–5:

> It is as the *Treatise* says, when the disciple of the Buddha cultivates dhyāna, there are inferior, middling, and superior: these are called three levels. Aside from the three levels, each level also has three, therefore there are nine levels, with the marks of shallow and deep. If discussed in detail, there are immeasurable levels.

Intermediate and simple concentration 中間單定: Chan-jan (BT–V, 273) explains that this means one goes beyond the first dhyāna and extinguishes the five constituents, that the "single-mindedness" explained previously was a single-mindedness that came after the other four constituents, and that this "simple concentration" refers to a single-mindedness that is attained later: "after the constituent of single-mindedness there is a further single-mindedness," and therefore it is called "converted quiescence" 轉寂.

Receding dhyāna 退禪: Chan-jan (BT–V, 273) adds that here "receding" refers to liberating renunciation, not "retrogression."

The mind of bamboo shavings 篾屑心: Chan-jan (BT–V, 273) explains that this means that "the previous virtuous qualities are now gone," which is not really helpful in explaining this image; "bamboo shavings" must have some special implication that is not explained here.

joy comes to an end you will enter [the stage of concentration of] incomplete attainment, quickly arouse the [other] three dhyānas, along with the arising of their accompanying bliss. On the other hand the dharmas of visible form will turn subtle, but it is not that bliss arises based on joy, so this properly-attained bliss is experienced throughout the body. Noble Ones **[120b]** are able to abandon [this bliss], but ordinary people find it difficult to abandon it. These [later three dhyānas] have five constituents: abandonment, mindfulness, wisdom, bliss, and single-mindedness. Their order, before or after, depends on the sūtra or treatise, but only because there are minor differences according to the ways of cultivation.

This [constituent of] bliss is in contrast to suffering. If you discipline the bliss so that it comes to an end, again you enter [the stage of the concentration of] incomplete attainment. When this "incomplete attainment" comes to an end, you arouse an immovable concentration. In turn the dharmas of visible form will turn subtle, and you will not be moved by suffering or bliss. This is called "immovable concentration." The concentration is calm and tranquil, and there is no inhaling or exhaling of breath, no suffering, no bliss, and its constituents are liberation, mindfulness, purity, and singlemindedness.

Even so, these are still phenomena of visible form, so you should discipline the three types of visible form and extinguish the three types of visible form, attain concentration through contact with emptiness, and never again perceive visible form. If the mind is liberated from visible form, like a bird escaping from a cage, this is called "the concentration of emptiness" 空定. When this concentration comes to an end, again you realize [the concentration of] incomplete attainment 未到; the concentration that arises from contact with consciousness is called "the abode of consciousness" 識處. When this concentration comes to an end, there is no more contact with existence, and you realize the non-existence [or non-Being] of dharmas and their correspondence [as emptiness], which is called [the concentration of] "the abode of no functioning" 不用處. In the past it was said that [at this stage of concentration] there is still a small contact with consciousness. But if this is so, then this is still within the realm of existents or of functioning; how could it be said to be [the abode of] no function or non-existence? When this concentration is past and done, immediately [the concentration of] "neither conceptions nor no-conceptions" 非想非非想 arises. This concentration has no contact with the abode of consciousness, and therefore is "non-conceptual" 非想; it has no contact with the abode of no functioning, and therefore is "not non-conceptual" 非非想. Further, there is no higher dharma to be attained; it is the ultimate dhyāna in the triple world. In the world it

In the past it was said: the attribution for this position is unknown.

is considered to be ultimately sublime, so non-Buddhists consider it to be nirvana, but truly it is a "dark enlightenment." It still involves suffering and the causes of suffering, so when the three kinds of existence [in the realms of desire, form, and no-form] are extinguished, you again fall into the three [evil] destinies.

One who wishes to know more to clarify the [four] basic [dhyāna] should examine the text on "cultivating enlightenment" [in the *Tz'u-ti ch'an-men*].

2. The Superior Meditations [120b17]

Next is clarifying the arousing of [the sixteen] superior [meditations]. If you rely on the teachings of the Vinaya, these [meditations] come after [the contemplation of] impurity [such as observing the nine stages of the decaying of a corpse], but if we rely on the actual practice, they come before [the contemplation of] impurity. As it says in the Vinaya, the Buddha taught the contemplation of impurity for the sake of the monks, but they all became disgusted and were not able to abide together in their stinking bodies, and they used their robes and begging bowls to hire Mṛgala [to help them]

The text on "cultivating enlightenment" [in the *Tz'u-ti ch'an-men*]: see the section starting at T 46.508a17.

Sixteen superior meditations 特勝: sixteen supreme or extraordinary forms or grades of meditation or contemplation, arranged "vertically" (to be followed in order, from easy to difficult) in contrast to the "horizontal" (not to be practiced in any particular order) listing of the various forms of contemplation known as the "six subtle gates"; sixteen stages of dhyāna meditation from "regulating the mind" to attaining the concentration that is "neither conceptual nor non-conceptual. The list given in Chih-i's *Six Subtle Gates*:

1. knowing the inhaling of breaths;
2. knowing the exhaling of breaths;
3. knowing the length and shortness of breaths ;
4. knowing the breaths permeating the body [concentration of incomplete attainment];
5. removing the various physical actions [earliest of the first dhyāna stage];
6. for the mind to be joyful;
7. for the mind to experience bliss;
8. to experience all mental activity [highest of the first dhyāna stage];
9. for the mind to produce joy;
10. for the mind to produce inclusion [second dhyāna stage];
11. for the mind to produce liberation [third dhyāna stage];
12. to contemplate transiency [fourth dhyāna stage];
13. to contemplate escape from scattered [thoughts] [concentration of emptiness];
14. to contemplate freedom from desires [concentration of consciousness];
15. to contemplate extinction [concentration of non-existence];
16. to contemplate liberation [concentration that is neither conceptual nor non-conceptual].

As it says in the Vinaya 如律云: see, for example, a passage in the *Vinaya in Ten Recitations*, T 23.7b–8a.

Mṛgala 鹿杖: lit. "deer staff": the translation of the name Mṛgānandi,蜜利伽羅 or 勿力伽難提; "rejoicing deer; a śrāmaṇa called 鹿杖 Lu-chang, who was satisfied

commit suicide. So the Buddha abandoned [the teaching of contemplating] impurity and instead had them cultivate the [sixteen] superior meditations. If you consume too much rhubarb (*Rheum*) or [oil from the seed of] purgative croton (*Croton tiglium*) [as a laxative], this will weaken your physical strength and cause damage [rather than good], and you should use other medicinal herbs as a supplement. As a supplement they are endearing, and their use is a [more acceptable] method. As a method they are superior to the basic [four dhyānas], and they are more endearing than [the contemplation of] impurity. If used along with contemplation, they are called "undefiled," and if your control is weak it is called "defiled." It is like when a thrifty person eats [an expensive meat dish like] pork, he boldly eats it even though he knows that [the hog] was originally something that held dung, but he would not eat it if he knew that the meat had been rotting for six months and filled with worms and flies. The supreme [meditations] can be accepted as contemplations of reality, but [contemplating] impurity often cannot be tolerated even as a consideration of conventional [reality].

The arousing of the [sixteen] superior meditations are as follows: [1.–3.] perceiving in an instant the inhaling, exhaling, and long and short of the breaths, and knowing that they come from nowhere and go away to nowhere, and that though inhaled [the breath] does not accumulate [anywhere], and though exhaled [the breath] is not dispersed [anywhere]. In terms of the [four] basic [dhyānas], this corresponds to the crude and fine dwelling [in meditation]. [4.] If you perceive that the breaths come and go and permeate the body, in terms of **[120c]** the [four] basic [dhyānas] this corresponds to the [concentrations of] incomplete attainment. However, [in terms of] the [four] basic [dhyānas] enlightenment is not yet revealed, and even though you feel that the body and the meditation seat and pillow are "nothing," it is not that they are not real [in a conventional sense]. This is like ashes covering a fire, which an ignorant person will frivolously trample on [and get burned], like eating late in the evening, like blindly touching a woman; all of these are like not being able to communicate your passions. At this stage you have [some] contemplative wisdom and can perceive the breath permeating the body, with a concentrated mind that is clear, pure, and calm; therefore this is different from the "dark enlightenment" [of the four basic dhyānas].

Again, perceiving the thirty-six things within the body is like opening

with the leavings of other monks; also a previous incarnation of Śākyamuni, and of Devadatta, who are both represented as having been deer. Translated as 鹿喜. (四分律, T 1428.22.576a3)" (DDB).

Rhubarb 大黃: or, root of "great yellow."

Like not being able to communicate your feelings 不暢其情: that is, leave a sense of incompleteness?

Thirty-six things 三十六物: the various

a warehouse and seeing various grains, millet, hemp, and beans. In terms of the [four] basic [dhyānas], this corresponds to the first dhyāna stage. The previous eight tactile sensations [within the first dhyāna stage] are like touching the warehouse of the physical body; since the eye of the mind has not yet been opened, you cannot see the internal things. Since the superior meditations already include contemplative wisdom, "tactile sensations" in this case opens the warehouse of the body, and the eye of the mind can perceive the thirty-six [external and internal] things. That is, the liver is like green beans, the heart is like red beans, the kidneys are like bird beans, the spleen is like millet, the great and small intestines are like paths mutually leading to each other, the flowing of the blood vessels is like the currents of the great rivers. There are twelve internal items [or organs], such as the liver, heart, mucus, and inflammation. There are twelve intermediate items such as membranes, skin, and fat. There are twelve external items such as hair and so forth. The inhaling and exhaling of the breath integrates these spaces; [realizing that these are all] impure, transient, full of suffering, empty, and without a Self brings all physical activity to rest, and finally you do not create evil [deeds] with the body. This is called [5.] "removing all physical actions." In terms of the steps on the path, this is "mindfulness of the body." In terms of the [four] basic [dhyānas], these are the [first] two constituents of examination *(vitarka)* and reflection *(vicāra)*. The eye of the mind is first opened by the constituent of examination; to discriminate the thirty-two things without error is the constituent of "reflection."

For the mind to be joyful [6.] corresponds to the constituent of "joy." The previous constituent of joy [within the first dhyāna stage] had the flavor of being hidden and impure. Here joy does not have the flavor of being hidden or impure. Since this is joy in the Dharma it is not a mere experience of joy, [7.] The mind experiencing bliss is also like this; it is not merely the enjoyment of bliss. To know that the pleasures of the three types of experience [of pain, pleasure, and neither-pain-nor-pleasure] are all [painful and] without [true] pleasure, is called the constituent of bliss [here in the context of the

parts of the physical human body, divided into three groups of twelve items: 1. twelve external items, such as hair and nails; 2. twelve internal items, such as blood and bones, and 3. twelve organs, such as the heart and lungs (DDB).

Eight tactile sensations 八觸: see the exposition on the tactile sensations above at 107a and 119a–c.

Three types of experience 三受: "Pleasure 樂 (樂受), pain 苦 (苦受), and neither-pleasure-nor-pain 捨 (捨受). When things are opposed to desire, pain arises; when accordant, there is pleasure and a desire for their continuance; when neither, one is detached or free. (Skt. *sukha-duḥkhâdi, vitti-traya, trividhā vedanā, vedanā-traya, tri-vedanā*; Pāli *tisso vedanā*) (DDB).

All without pleasure 皆無樂: The

sixteen superior meditations. [8. The superior meditation of] "experiencing all mental activities" corresponds to the constituent of "single-mindedness." To know all mental activities as "single-mindedness" is not the same as [the single-mindedness] of the [first stage of] basic [dhyānas], which is a calculated [form of] true single-mindedness. [9.–10.] For the mind to produce joy and the mind to produce inclusiveness is as follows. The previous "joy" [of the first dhyāna stage] arises through the thirty-six items [of the physical body]; this [joy of the superior meditations] comes directly from the mind to produce joy. Therefore you should know that it corresponds to the second dhyāna. *The Great Collection of Sūtras* clarifies that the second [stage of] dhyāna has only three constituents but not inner purity. Now [with regard to the superior meditations] the meaning of the mind producing joy is similar to this. [The mind] "producing inclusiveness" is as follows: when you are moved by joy, there is [the danger of] scattered distraction, but if [the mind is inclusively] collected you can realize single-mindedness. The basic [dhyānas] merely involve an experience of joy through inner purity; the superior meditations involve contemplative wisdom and so there is a constant inclusion of joy. [11. The superior meditation of] the mind producing liberation corresponds to the third dhyāna. The bliss of the basic [dhyānas] involves joy permeating the body; an ordinary person will find it difficult to abandon this [bliss]. The superior meditations involve contemplative wisdom, and there is no flavor of the passions 愛味, and therefore there is liberation. From [the 9th superior meditation of] the mind producing joy to [the 11th of] the mind producing liberation, these all correspond to the mindfulness of thoughts [as impermanent] 心念處.

From [the 12th superior meditation of] contemplating transiency, these correspond to the fourth dhyāna. **[121a]** Other places also [teach] contemplating transiency, but they are not yet distinctly regulated. When you attain the unmovable concentration, this has [the danger of] the flavor of permanence. Now [with the superior meditations] there is contemplative wisdom,

Taishō text gives a variant addition of the character for "painful" 苦, which is added in the BT (V, 282) text.

The Great Collection of Sūtras: see the passage at T 13.161a18–23:

> What is [the constituent of] "joy" 喜? It is like knowing the truth and the mind being moved. This is called "joy." What is calm quietude 安? It is for the body to be calm and the mind to experience quietude. To experience the sensation/touch of bliss is called "calm quietude." What is "concentration" 定? If the mind dwells in a great dwelling without disturbance, and has no connection with error and has no perversions; this is called "concentration." The second dhyāna is the same in being free from five matters, that is, five hindrances. It includes three constituents: 1. joy, 2. quietude, and 3. concentration.

In other explanations, the second dhyāna involves four constituents, that of inner purity, joy, bliss, and single-mindedness.

and you know freedom from suffering and pleasure and have put an end to the phenomena of visible form and realize transiency, so there should be no defilement. Therefore this is called [producing an awareness of] transiency. [13.] To contemplate escape from scattered [thoughts] corresponds to the place of [the concentration of] emptiness. This is the extinction of the three types of visible form, and is like a bird escaping from a cage, and therefore it is called an "escape." [14. Contemplating freedom from desires:] Because there is a connection with emptiness it is called "scattered." Although there is a connection to emptiness, since there is contemplative wisdom, this contemplation to be free from desires corresponds to the place [of the concentration] of consciousness 識處. When there is an abundance of connection to emptiness, this can lead to scattered distraction, which becomes a "desire." The superior meditations involve contemplative wisdom and so you become free from these scattered thoughts. Therefore it is called "freedom from desires." [15.] The contemplation of extinction corresponds to the place of [the concentration of] non-existence 無所有處. The superior meditations involve contemplative wisdom and so whether there is much or little consciousness, [one realizes that] it is all nothing. Therefore this is called "the contemplation of extinction." [16] The contemplation of liberation corresponds to the place of [the concentration that is] neither conceptual nor non-conceptual 非想非非想處. Abandoning the place of [the concentration of] consciousness and the place of [the concentration of] non-existence and reaching a sublime concentration 妙定 is called [the concentration that is] "neither conceptual nor non-conceptual." Ordinary [ignorant] people erroneously call this "nirvana." The Buddha's disciples know that although crude passionate afflictions are gone, there still are fine passionate afflictions. But since there is no flavor of passions, this is called a dhyāna-concentration of purity. From the [12th contemplation of] transiency to the [16th contemplation of] liberation, these correspond to the mindfulness of dharmas 法念處 [as without substance].

These sixteen [superior meditations] can be [interpreted] horizontally [in succession] with regard to dharmas [of the four mindfulnesses] or vertically with regard to dharmas [of the four stages of dhyāna], with each aspect being different. The [four] basic [dhyānas] are a "dark enlightenment," and its merits are light, like eating a meal without salt. The merits of the superior meditations are heavy, like eating a meal with salt. For a complete discussion of the marks of the arising [of these superior meditations], the details are in [the section on] "cultivating enlightenment" [in the *Tz'u-ti ch'an-men*].

Details in the *Tz'u-ti ch'an-men*: see the section starting at T 46.525c.11.

3. The Dhyāna of the Six Penetrating Supranormal Powers and Three Illuminating Insights [121a16]

Next is the arising of the marks of the dhyāna of the [six] supranormal powers and [three illuminating] insights.

When you cultivate the above [sixteen] superior meditations, the contemplative wisdom [gained thereby] is still general, and the enlightenment gained from perceiving the thirty-six items [of the physical body] is also still general. When you cultivate the [six] supranormal powers and [three illuminating] insights, [the contemplative wisdom] is fine and subtle, and the enlightenment is distinct and clear. These terms are also found in the *Avataṃsaka Sūtra*. *The Great Collection of Sūtras* differentiates concerning the treasure-torch *dhāraṇī*, which is [a type of] dhyāna. The *Sūtra on Petitioning Avalokiteśvara* also contains this meaning. When you cultivate [these meditations], they are cultivated thoroughly in all three matters [of body, breath, and mind], so you are able to arouse the three illuminating insights and the six supranormal powers. Again, when you cultivate the treasure-torch [*dhāraṇī*] and up to entering the concentration of extinguishing sensations and conceptions, you should know that this gate involves the eight liberations, the three illuminating insights, and the six supranormal powers. Therefore it is called [the dhyāna of] penetrating powers and insights.

The Great Collection of Sūtras distinguishes these into five constituents or items. [1.] Contemplating the nature of the mind by examining the mind

Six supranormal powers and three illuminating insights 通明: the six supranormal powers are 1. the ability to appear anywhere one wishes 身如意; 2. the ability to see your own and others' future lives 天眼; 3. the ability to hear sounds that others cannot hear 天耳; 4. the ability to read other peoples' minds 知他心; 5. the ability to perceive your own and others' past lives 宿命; and 6. the ability to remove your passionate afflictions 漏盡. The three illuminating insights are 1. the ability to see the conditions and events of the past and thus know the faults of oneself and others; 2. the ability to see the results that are to come in the future, and thus be able to sever mistaken views; and 3. the ability to know and thus exhaust all the passionate afflictions of the present.

Avataṃsaka Sūtra: see the list of ten types of "pure dhyāna" possessed by bodhisattvas at T. 9.660b22–c5. The list includes the item "an internally pure dhyāna of supranormal powers and illuminating insight" 諸通明內淨禪.

Treasure-torch *dhāraṇī* 寶炬陀羅尼: see *The Great Collection of Sūtras (Saṃnipāta Sūtra)*, T 13.25c9–26b12. This has appeared previously in the *Mo-ho chih-kuan* at 41b2 and 88a8; see note at 41b2.

Sūtra on Petitioning Avalokiteśvara: see T 20, 36c–37c, which expounds on "cultivating the five gates of dhyāna."

Three matters 三事: these are identified specifically a few lines below as "the physical [body of visible form], the breath, and the mind 色息心."

The Great Collection of Sūtras: see the passage at T 13.161a, referred to above.

as it is 如心覺, as a great examination [or awakening] 大覺, and considering things as a great consideration 思惟大思惟; this is the constituent of examination (*vitarka*) 覺支. [2.] Contemplating mindful practice and great practice 心行大行 and pervasive practice 遍行 is the constituent of reflection (*vicāra*) 觀支. [3.] For the mind to know things as they truly are 如實知 and to have great knowledge 大知, and thus the mind being moved by joy, is the constituent of joy 喜支. [4.] For the body to be calm and the mind to be calm 身安心安 and thus to experience the sensation of bliss is the constituent of calm quietude 安支. [5.] For the mind to dwell in a great dwelling without being disturbed by conditions is called the constituent of [single-minded] concentration 定支.

[1. The constituent of examination 覺支.] If from the beginning you contemplate the three matters [of body, breath, and mind], they are all integrated; when you are enlightened, all three matters [of body, breath, and mind] are one. Therefore this is called "examining the mind as it is." If you examine [and are awakened] concerning the real truth, then you will see that the physical [body of visible form], the breath, and the mind are submerged into one and are not different.

Again, if you know [or are conscious of] the mundane truth, that skin, flesh, bones, and so forth all have ninety-nine layers, and examine [and become aware of] the five organs giving rise to five *chi*-energies, and again perceive through verbal descriptions that within the body **[121b]** worms come and go, then there is no detail that you cannot comprehend. Examine [and become aware of] the first aggregate [of life] taking residence in the womb, that the karmic influence of past ignorance is like wax, that the semen of the father and blood of the mother in the present is like mud. If the karmic influences of the past do not abide [and life does not come forth], this is like the breaking of a seal; if in the present a consciousness is implanted [and a life begins] with the completion of name-and-form, this is

Ninety-nine layers 九十九重: Chan-jan (BT-V, 290; T 46.417c15–20) explains:

There are three hundred sixty large and small bones, with ninety-nine layers of marrow. Between these bones there are many worms or bugs 蟲, with four heads and four mouths and ninety-nine tails. Their number is not limited to one.

The brain has four parts, and each part has fourteen layers. The five organs have overlapping "leaves," like a lotus flower. The orifices are open and pass to the inside and outside, and each have ninety-nine layers. Again, there are eighty thousand worms or bugs that dwell within, each supporting each other with sounds and words, coming and going and moving and breathing. Details are given in the *Tz'u-ti ch'an-men*.

Chan-jan's explanation is based on the the *Tz'u-ti ch'an-men* at T 46.530b18ff.

Past ignorance 過去無明: the first of the twelvefold chain of condition co-arising. The rest of the twelvefold links, name-and-form and so forth, follow as Chih-i describes the development of a new life.

like the completion of a [written] character. [This fetal life] dwells and grows beneath the stomach 生藏 and above the intestines 熟藏 and inside the womb 子腸, with a very delicate and fine form. It has only a deluded conception of a single thought, and the form and body are mutually dependent; somewhat existing and somewhat non-existing, like a dream. Through the power of karmic influences, spontaneously it is able to arouse a single thought of a conceptual mind 一念思心, feeling the call of the mother. The mother further conceptualizes [matters such as] the color blue-green, the sound of calling, the *chi*-atmosphere of oil, or the taste of vinegar, and due to the power of her thoughts gives rise to *chi*-energy [the size of] a single hair. The *chi*-energy changes to water, the water changes into blood, and the blood changes into flesh. The mother's *chi*-energy [breaths] go out and in, mutually supporting and moistening each other, so that we have the development of the liver. Facing upward there is the development of the eyes; facing downward there is the development of the thumbs on the hands and [large toes of] the feet. When there is the thought of the color white, the sound of weeping, the *chi*-atmosphere of stinky fish, and the taste of pungency, then there is the further development of the lungs. Facing upward there is [the development of] the nose, and facing downwards there are the second fingers and toes of the hands and feet. When there is the thought of the color red, the sound of words, the *chi*-atmosphere of burning, and the flavor of bitterness, there is the development of the heart. Facing upwards there is [the development of] the mouth; facing downwards there are the third fingers and toes of the hands and feet. When there is the thought of the color yellow, the sound of songs, the *chi*-atmosphere of incense, and the flavor of sweetness, then there is the further development of the spleen. Facing upward there is the tongue; facing downward there are the fourth fingers and toes of the hands and feet. When there is the thought of the color black, the sound of chanting, a stinky *chi*-atmosphere, and the flavor of salt, then there is the further development of the kidneys. Facing upward there are the ears; facing downward there are the fifth fingers and toes of the hands and feet. These are all examples from examining the distinct fine details of the body.

"Considering things as a great consideration" means to consider the real and mundane [truths], and to contemplate the nature of the mind as empty. Whether [considering] the real [truth] or the mundane [truth], it is the same in realizing the nature of the mind. The *Sūtra on Petitioning Avalokiteśvara* says, "Each and every one [practice] involves realizing the limit of reality."

Each and every one involves realizing the limit of reality 如實 一一入於如實之際: a phrase from the *Sūtra on Petitioning Avalokiteśvara* at T 20, 37a12. A search of

This meaning of the constituent of examination [or awareness] here is quite different from that [explained] above.

[2. The constituent of reflection [or contemplation.] Mindful practice and great practice previously referred to the understanding gained from the constituent of examination, but here refer to leaving behind the [previous] practice of mindfulness 心行 and practicing contemplation 觀行. The mind "practices" 心行 [being mindful of] the worldly truth, and therefore this is called "practice"; practicing the real truth is called "great practice." These are practiced together in all three matters [of body, breath, and mind]; therefore it is called "pervasive practice" 遍行. [3. … 4. …]

[5. The constituent of concentration.] "For the mind to dwell" 心住 refers to attaining single-mindedness with regard to the mundane truth; "great dwelling" refers to attaining single-mindedness with regard to the real truth. "Without being disturbed by conditions" refers to perceiving the immeasurable objects of the real and the mundane in the mind without error. A detailed clarification of these various aspects is contained in the section on "contemplating penetrating powers and illuminated insights" [in the *Tz'u-ti ch'an-men*].

When you arouse these concentrations, you perceive that the body, breath, and mind are all the same in that, like the banana tree, there is no firm [substantial] reality; this is the mark of the stage of incomplete attainment. To perceive these three matters [of body, breath, and mind] as the same in being [empty] like water bubbles or foam is [the mark of the stage of] the first dhyāna. To perceive these three matters as the same in being like floating clouds is the second dhyāna. To perceive these three matters as the same in being like a shadow is the third dhyāna. To perceive these three matters as the same in being like **[121c]** a reflection in the mirror is the fourth dhyāna. The extinction of these three matters is [the concentra-

the SAT database showed that this is the only sūtra in which this phrase, "the limit of reality" 如實之際, appears, which is then used in a number of works by Chih-i.

Constituent of examination [or awareness] 覺支; **constituent of reflection [or contemplation** 觀支: in the context of the five constituents, the character 覺 refers to "examination" *(vitarka)*, but as a Chinese character (especially in the Mahāyāna Buddhist context) it also implies "awareness, awakening, satori." Chih-i seems to be using the term in both ways here. Chih-i then does the same with the character 觀, which in the context of the five constituents is "reflection" (*vicāra*), but is also the character for "contemplation."

[3. … 4. …]: the explanation for the two constituents of "joy" and "bliss" is not spelled out.

The section on contemplating penetrating powers and illuminated insights 如通明觀中廣説 **[in the *Tz'u-ti ch'an-men*]**: see the section starting at T 46.530a.

tion of] emptiness. The extinction of emptiness brings you into contact with [the concentration of] consciousness. The extinction of [the concentration of] consciousness brings you into contact with [the concentration of] non-existence. The extinction of [the concentration of] non-existence brings you into contact with [the concentration of] neither-conceptions-nor-non-conceptions. The extinction of [the concentration of] neither-conceptions-nor-non-conceptions and the sensations and conceptions of the three matters [of body, breath, and mind], and becoming enlightened concerning the extinction of the sensations of the body, means the perfection of liberation. If this is a contemplation of the mundane [truth], this is called "defiled" 有漏, but if it is a contemplation of the real [truth], this is called "undefiled" 無漏.

These [interpretations of] dhyāna are concerned with both [actual] phenomenal [practice] 事 and [abstract] principle 理, and so they involve stages [of development]. Those of the *Ch'eng shih lun* utilize this [explanation of the dhyāna of penetrating powers and illuminating insights] to clarify the path and [the practice of] concentrations, and thus to realize the eight liberations. This interpretation is convenient, but I deliberately do not use it here. The Abhidharma teaches the attainment of both the [actual] phenomenal [practices] and [abstract] principle with regard to the eight renunciations. In this sense these are different from the heterodox non-Buddhist [teachings] and are called "those who attain liberation." The *Ch'eng shih lun* [itself] is concerned with the [abstract] principle and not the [actual] phenomenal [practices], so [technically it may be said that] it is not included in [teachings for] "those who obtain liberation." [But both of these traditions teach only dhyāna that is the same as non-Buddhist traditions.] If the practical aspects of dhyāna are given [only] in terms of heterodox non-Buddhist dhyāna, then [it could be said that the practical aspects of] the precepts are limited to the ten good deeds, and wisdom is limited to worldly wisdom. [However,] the [Buddhist] precepts and wisdom are different from the heterodox non-Buddhist, so how can it be said that [the practice of] concentration is the same [as the heterodox non-Buddhist]? "Each doctor does not have each concentration, so they do not perfect the eight techniques [of the eight liberations

Those of the *Ch'eng shih lun* 成論人: it is not known exactly to whom or what interpretation this refers, or if only in general to the "*Ch'eng shih lun* school."

The Abhidharma: it is not clear exactly to what interpretation this refers, or if only in general to the "Abhidharma tradition."

The *Ch'eng shih lun*: see the passage on "liberation" at T 32.358b–c.

Each doctor: probably a reference to the passage in the *Mahāparinirvāṇa Sūtra*, T 12.617c–618c, about how a good doctor prescribes different things for different diseases; see note at 10b27. In this case, however, the point seems to be that some doctors do not give the right prescription, as non-Buddhists do not give the right instructions for attaining liberation.

or renunciations]." A more detailed discussion on these aspects are in the text on "cultivating enlightenment" [in the *Tz'u-ti ch'an-men*].

4. Dhyāna Meditations on Impurity [121c12]

Next is clarifying the arousing of dhyāna[-meditations] on impurity. First, the nine considerations [of decaying corpses] has two types: 1. by those who [believe in the] destruction of dharmas, and 2. by those who do not [believe in the] destruction of dharmas.

[1.] As for the cultivation of the nine considerations [of a corpse] by those who [believe in the] destruction of dharmas, [the nine stages are:]

1. consideration of bloating	脹想
2. consideration of decay	壞想
3. consideration of blood smears	血塗想
4. consideration of rotting pus	膿爛想
5. consideration of turning blue	青瘀想
6. consideration of chewing [by birds and beasts]	噉想
7. consideration of scattering [of body parts]	散想
8. consideration of [white] bones	骨想
9. consideration of cremation	燒想

These people merely seek a severance from suffering [and escape from samsara] by cremating the bones of people, hasten to grasp on to [the level of] one who has no more to learn, and find no joy in contemplating [phenomenal mundane] matters. As mere people of bones, they have nothing to contemplate, and also do not [attain] dhyāna-concentrations, penetrating supranormal powers, transformations, vows, wisdom, or "peak meditations." Although it is said that they [have considered] extinction through cremation, truly they still have a body. This is just like [the fact that] you still have a physical body even after realizing the extinction of sensations and conceptions.

Such people tend to retrogress. The Abhidharma contains [explanations of] the aspect of retrogressing, that the fourth fruit [of the Arhat] is like sand at the bottom of a well. The *Āgamas* say that "those who have attained the

Tz'u-ti ch'an-men: see the section at T 46.533a–c.

Nine considerations 九想: To contemplate a corpse as it passes through nine stages of decay. For details, see the *Ta chih tu lun*, T 25.217a6–218c18.

Peak meditations 頂禪: "Synonymous with the transcending samādhi: 超越三昧 (Skt. **prānta-koṭika-dhyāna*)" (DDB).

Abhidharma and retrogressing: see, for example, the passage on the possibility of an Arhat retrogressing in the *Abhidharma-vibhāṣā-śāstra*, T 28.239a–241c.

***Āgamas* and retrogressing**: the *Kōgi* (BT-V, 301) points out that "the *Shiki* says that this is contained in section 35 of the

third fruit [of the "non-returner"] who rejects the precepts, returns to his [worldly] home, and abandons the moral discipline (and ceremonial observances) 律儀 [of the monk's life], still does not lose [the moral actions that] accompany the path. A worldly person may slander him and say that he no longer keeps the noble Dharma, but the Buddha says that [this person will] tire of desires and grow weary, and before too long will again return to seek [the status of] a home-departed one. Other monks may not forgive this person, but the Buddha will forgive him, and he will become an Arhat. Ānanda asked [the Buddha] saying, 'Oh you of great virtue, do people with more to learn retrogress, or do people with nothing more to learn retrogress?' [The Buddha] answered, 'Those with more to learn retrogress.'" If this is the case, this refers to the people who attain liberation through wisdom, by severing delusions through worldly wisdom, and that is why they retrogress. It is not the case that you will retrogress if through undefiled wisdom you sever a category of delusions and advance to a category of understanding. If you arouse these nine considerations [of decaying corpses] without having the virtuous qualities of the various dhyānas, then this is [what is meant by] "a person who [believes in the] destruction of dharmas."

[2.] As for the nine considerations for those who do not [believe in the] destruction of dharmas, [they advance] from the first consideration of bloating to dwelling in the consideration of [white] bones, but do not advance to the consideration of cremation. Instead they [seek to] attain [the concentrations of] "flowing light" 流光, the renunciations [of liberation] and [the levels of] domination, and [the four aspects of] contemplation, training, discipline, and cultivation 觀練薰修; **[122a]** penetrating supranormal powers and transformations, to be completely endowed with all virtuous qualities and become a person endowed with liberation.

As for cultivating [these virtuous qualities], when you have many sensual passions you should contemplate external [objects], and when you have many [mistaken] views you should contemplate the body, and when passions and mistaken views are equal, contemplate both the internal and

Expanded Āgama, but a search of the text revealed nothing."

Passions and mistaken views are equal 見愛等: see the passage on the eight liberations and contemplating internal and external objects, in the *Ta chih tu lun*, T 25.215a, containing the following passage (215a13–17); Chodron (3, 1058) translates:

> These two vimokṣas both contemplate the horrible *(aśubha)*: the first contemplates inner as well as outer visibles; the second does not see inner visibles and sees only outer visibles. Why is that?
>
> Beings *(sattva)* have two kinds of behavior *(pratipad)*: sensualism *(tṛṣṇācarita)* and rationalism *(dṛṣṭicarita)*. The sensualists *(tṛṣṇābahula)* are attached to happiness *(sukharakta)* and are bound *(baddha)* by outer fetters *(bāhyasaṃyojana)*. The rationalists *(dṛṣṭibahula)* are strongly attached to the view of the individual *(sat-*

external. When arousing these dhyāna meditations, you should know to follow these [instructions]. Suppose you are sitting in meditation and suddenly you see a corpse lying on the ground. Until a few moments ago you were speaking [with this person], but now suddenly he is gone, with his *chi*-breath extinguished and his body cold, his spirit departed and his color changed. [The law of] transiency occurs and he is no choice between the powerful and the humble, the rich and the poor, the old and the young, the beautiful and the ugly; there is no place to hide [from this fate]. Even a compassionate parent or filial child cannot take another person's place [in this matter]. The corpse lies stinking on the ground; the wind blows and it is exposed in the sun, and its original form is changed forever. Whether you see one corpse or many corpses, this is a contemplation of great impurity. Whether [corpses] litter a whole village or an entire country; whether one corpse changes color or many corpses change color, [the number of] corpses does not matter for the nine considerations. This is the basic idea for [the practice of] the various [nine] considerations, so it should be explained first.

These corpses have faces that are pitch black; the bodies lie stretched out straight, the hands and feet open like a flower, bloated and broken like a leather bag filled with wind, and extremely defiled and evil [odor and liquid] pour forth from the nine orifices. The practitioner thinks to himself, "My body is also like this; I am not yet free nor have I escaped it. In contemplating those that I love, [I see that] the same is true for them." When these aspects [of meditation] appear, you have attained a part of a concentrated mind, which is somewhat peaceful and pleasing. In the twinkling of an eye you see this corpse [1.] "bloat," blown by the wind and scorched by the sun, the skin and flesh destroyed, the body split open, the form and color changing beyond comprehension; this is called the mark of [2.] "decay."

Again, seeing where it has split open, blood spurting forth, scattering and smearing, making a motley mess here and there, pouring out into the ground, making a vigorous stench; this is the mark of [3.] "blood smears." Again, rotting pus pours out like sweat, like a candle on fire; this is the mark of [4.] "rotting pus." Again, you see the remaining skin and flesh dried by the wind and scorched by the sun, smelling rotten and falling apart, half blue and half bruised, breaking apart into pieces; this is the mark of [5.] "turning blue." Again, you see the corpse chewed on and eaten by foxes, wolves,

kāyadṛṣṭi), etc., and are bound by inner fetters *(adhyātmasaṃyojana)*. This is why the sensualists [usefully] contemplate the horrors of outer visibles *(bāhyarūpāśubha)*, whereas the rationalists [usefully] contemplate the horrors *(aśubha)* and corruption *(vikāra)* of their own body.

Nine orifices 九孔 **[of a man]:** the mouth, two eyes, two ears, two nose openings, the colon, and the urethra.

and birds, as they fight over the scattered pieces, tearing and dragging and pulling them around; this is the mark of [6.] "chewing." Again, you see that the head and hands are [scattered] in different places, and the five organs divided up so that they are unrecognizable; this is the mark of [7.] "scattering." Again, you see two types of bones, one still with clinging remnants of blood and fat, and others pure white. Or you see a complete skeleton, or scattered around in clusters. [This is the mark 8. of "considering bones."] In this way the various marks [of corpses] turn [and change] with time, and the concentrating mind should follow these changes, grow deeper in quiescence, discover a quiet subtlety and a peaceful joy that cannot be explained. This is the extent of what is contemplated by those who do not [believe in the] destruction of dharmas.

Those who have not yet seen these marks [of a decaying corpse] still have strong attachments to passions. But if they see these things, their desirous thoughts will come to an end, and they will not endure being attached to them. It is like you can eat food as long as you do not perceive dung, but as soon as you smell the stink [of the dung], you feel like vomiting. Again, it is like a Brahman who is attached to the rules of purity but eats cake smeared with tumorous marrow; he will **[122b]** pound his head and reproach himself saying, "this is the end of me!" Once you are enlightened concerning these

The Brahman who is attached to the rules of purity ... 捉淨法婆羅門而噉塗癰髓餅: see the *Ta chih tu lun* at T 25.231c9–22; Chodron (3, 1193) translates:

> There was a brahmin who practiced the rules of [alimentary] purity. Having to go to some unclean land on business, he thought: "How will I manage to avoid all this uncleanliness? It will be necessary for me to eat dry food and so I will be able to maintain my purity."
>
> He saw an old woman who was selling cakes of white marrow (meal, flour?) and said to her: "I have reason to stay here for about a hundred days. Make me these cakes regularly and bring them to me, I will pay you well." Each day the old woman made the cakes and brought them to him. The brahmin liked their taste and was happy with this plentiful food.
>
> At the beginning, the cakes made by the old woman were white, but later, little by little they lost their color *(rūpa)* and their taste. The brahmin asked the old woman what was the reason for this. She replied: "It is because the canker *(gaṇḍa)* is healed." The brahmin asked her what she meant by this and the old woman answered: "At my house, a prostitute contracted a canker on her privy parts and we applied flour *(saktu)*, ghee *(ghṛta)* and sweet herbs *(yaṣṭimadhu)* to it. The canker ripened, the pus *(puya)* came out and mixed with the poultice. This happened every day and I made the cakes that I gave you with this: that is why they were so good. Now that the woman's canker has healed, where am I going to find [the wherewithal to make them]?"
>
> Having heard this, the brahmin struck his head with his fists, beat his breast, vomited and shouted: "How can I say how much I have violated the rules of [alimentary] purity? But now my business is settled." Leaving all his affairs, he returned in haste to his native land.

marks [of a decaying corpse], even though again [you are faced with the supposed beauty of women with] high eyebrows, emerald eyes, white teeth, and cinnabar lips, they will be to you as if covered by a mass of urine and feces. Again, imagine a festering corpse temporarily wearing a silk fabric; you would not look at it with your eyes, let alone approach the body. If it is going to lead to hiring Mṛgala to [help you] commit suicide [out of disgust for your body], why would you cry for their embrace and [seek] erotic pleasure?

In this way these marks [of decaying corpses] are like [the remedy of] the great yellow [dragon] potion for [controlling] the disease of erotic desires. This is like people who desire food; they know that hogs were once filled with urine, and yet they still have a strong desire to eat [pork]; if they see the pig with its worms and stench, they would not be able to eat it. The power of the previous superior meditations are weak and so you cannot decisively remove [these desires], but the power of this contemplation [of the impurity of a decaying corpse] is strong and can extinguish the fire that is the disease of erotic passions. Therefore it is said [in the *Ta chih tu lun*] that when the

Hiring Mṛgala 雇鹿杖: see note above at *Mo-ho chih-kuan* 120b19–20.

Yellow dragon potion 大黄湯: made from excrement by mixing human feces and urine with wild boar and cat excrement and salt. See note at *Mo-ho chih-kuan* 19a22.

Therefore it is said: see, for example the *Ta chih tu lun* at T 25.218a9–23 (quoted previously at *Mo-ho chih-kuan* 70a27–b1); Chodron (3, 1082–83) translates:

> These nine notions [of the horrible] eliminate the seven types of lust *(saptavidha rāga)* in people.
>
> 1. There are people who are attached to colors *(varṇa)*, red *(lohita)*, white *(avadāta)*, reddish-white *(śvetarakta)*, yellow *(pīta)*, black *(kṛṣṇa)*.
>
> 2. There are people who are not attached to colors but who are attached only to shapes *(saṃsthāna)*, delicate skin, tapered fingers, expressive eyes, arched eyebrows.
>
> 3. There are people who are not attached to either colors or shapes, but who are attached only to postures *(īryāpatha)*, ways of entering, of stopping, sitting, rising, walking, standing, bowing, raising or lowering the head, raising the eyebrows, winking the eye, approaching, holding an object in the hand.
>
> 4. There are people who are not attached to colors or shapes or postures, but who are only attached to language, soft sounds, elegant words, speech appropriate to the circumstance, replying to a thought, honoring orders, capable of moving people's hearts.
>
> 5. There are people who are not attached to colors or shapes or positions or soft sounds, but who are only attached to fine smooth [furs], gentle to the skin, softening the flesh, refreshing the body in the heat and warming it in the cold.
>
> 6. There are people who are attached to all five things listed above at once.
>
> 7. There are people who are not attached to these five things but who are only attached to the human appearance, male or female. Even if they were to enjoy the five lusts *(kāma)* mentioned above, when they come to lose the loved person, they refuse to separate from them and they renounce the five objects of enjoyment *(pañcakāmaguṇa)* so esteemed by the world so as to follow their loved one in death.

contemplation of the nine considerations [of a corpse] is accomplished, the six bandits [of the six desires] are already removed, and you become aware that "passions are a bitter fraud," and know the vacuousness of temporary conventional reality. In this way you become weary [of fleshly desires] and you not only remove desires but also are able to arouse [the state of being] undefiled [by the outflows of passions], and you also perfect the Mahāyāna.

The *Ta chih tu lun*, after explaining the [nine] considerations of the changes [in a corpse] after death, proceeds to expound on the six perfections and the four mindfulnesses, and many teachers say that this is a mistake in translation [but this is not the case]. Here it clarifies that a bodhisattva who cultivates the first consideration [of a corpse] is endowed with the Mahāyāna, and is able to broadly expound the Dharma teachings. Later when it says that "[cultivating the other considerations] up to [the ninth] consideration of cremation," it is also the same [in being endowed with the Mahāyāna]. How can it be said that this is a failure [in translation]?

5. The Eight Renunciations [122b13]

Next is to clarify the eight renunciations [or liberations]. The first three items [of the four basic dhyānas, the sixteen superior meditations, and the six supranormal powers and three illuminating insights] correspond to the

Aware that passions are a bitter fraud 識愛怨詐: a phrase found in the *Mahāparinirvāṇa Sūtra*, T 12.744a7–21, a long passage that concludes: "based on the meaning of supreme ultimate wisdom, the bodhisattva-mahāsattva sees that these bonds of passionate attachments are like a fearful fraud of intimacy" 怨詐親.

***Ta chih tu lun* … proceeds to expound:** see the long passage at T 25.404b–406a,

Many teachers 諸師: it is not known specifically to whom this refers.

Eight renunciations 八背捨: Eight stages of "liberation" leading to complete cessation *(nirodha-samāpatti)*:

1. remove desires by concentration on and internalizing a certain external object 內有色相外觀色;
2. cultivate total concentration by focusing the mind internally 內無色相外觀色;
3. attain a state of mental and physical purity 淨背捨身作證;
4. maintain calm while freeing the mind from external objects 虛空處背捨;
5. focus on unlimited space and dissolve the distinctions of the external world 識處背捨;
6. attain both physically and mentally a realm without limits where there are no "existants" 無所有處背捨;
7. attain the foundation that transcends space and the mental realm, which is neither-conceptual-nor-non-conceptual 非有想非無想背捨; and
8. attain a state in which this foundation is constantly manifested, with a complete extinction of sensations and conceptualizations 滅受想背捨.

For details, and the basis of Chih-i's discussion, see the *Ta chih tu lun*, T 25.215a5–217a4, which is quoted extensively in notes that follow below.

basic flavor and purity [of contemplation]. The nine considerations [of a decaying corpse] reach to [the ten concentrations of] the totalization of objects 一切處. These are called "contemplations" 觀. The nine gradual-and-successive concentrations are called "training" 練. The "Lion of Resolute Speed [Samādhi]" is called "discipline" 薰. "Transcending" [your former state] is called "cultivation" 修. These four types [of contemplation, training, discipline, and cultivation] are concentrations of actuality.

Now I will first clarify "renunciations." These renunciations also have a "general" and "specific" meaning. The "general" is for those of the two vehicles, and the "specific" is for bodhisattvas. Again, the [eight] renunciations are not determined [in order]. At times the results are explained in terms of the causes, and renunciation becomes liberation. Or, the causes are explained in terms of the results, and liberation becomes renunciation. If we were to settle on a definition, it is "the ultimate severance of delusions" 斷惑究竟, which includes both the actual [practical matters] and the [abstract] principle 事理具足; therefore it is called "liberation." If delusions are not yet severed, your concentration is not yet complete; this is called "renunciation." [There are two parts to the term "renunciation":] "To be contrary" [lit. "turn your back"] 背 means to be weary of the lower stages [of attainment]

Basic flavor and purity 根本味淨: Chan-jan (BT–V 311) adds that the four basic dhyāna correspond to "flavor" [because it still involves "defilement" with the passions], and the superior meditations, supranormal powers, and illuminating insights correspond to "purity."

The nine gradual-and-successive concentrations 九次第定: the four levels of dhyāna meditative trance, the four concentrations on emptiness in the realm of formlessness, and the final concentration (samādhi) wherein all feelings and conceptions are extinguished *(nirodha-samāpatti)*.

The Lion of Resolute Speed 師子奮迅 **Samādhi**: A concentrated state realized by a Buddha in which he can manifest great power and compassion towards sentient beings, like an invigorated lion. The *Lotus Sūtra* speaks of "Buddha's power to move with the resolute speed of a lion." *Graded Themes* defines this in terms of being able to enter and leave samādhi quickly.

Concentrations of actuality 事定: DDB has "functional concentration. (Pāli *kiriyā-samādhi*) (T 1648.32.407b22). The material and immaterial concentrations as attained by the arahant, i.e., they are neither results nor giving result (*nevavipā kanavipākadhammadhamma*)."

Two parts: this is a breakdown of the two characters 背捨 that make up the Chinese term for "renunciations." A similar analysis is found in the *Ta chih tu lun*, T 25.215a8–9, indicating that at least this part was added to the *Ta chih tu lun* by Kumārajīva or one of his Chinese colleagues. Chodron (3, 1058) translates: "They 'turn the back' *(pei)* on the five objects of enjoyment *(kāmaguṇa)* and [they 'reject' *(chö)*] or eliminate the mind of attachment *(saṅgacitta)* towards them; this is why they are called 'turning the mind and rejecting' (*pei-chö*, in Sanskrit *vi-mokṣa*)."

and your own level, and [seek to] purify [oneself of] the five desires [of the senses]; "to abandon" 捨 means to forsake the mind of attachments. Therefore it is called "renunciation" 背捨.

If you are to destroy the abundance of passions, you should arouse the external marks [of attainment], as explained previously [in the section on the nine considerations of a decaying corpse]. If you are to destroy the abundance of mistaken views, you should arouse the internal marks [of attainment]. The "internal marks" are precisely the eight renunciations, that is, from the first [renunciation] of internalizing a visible form by contemplating an external visible form 内有色外觀色, to the eighth renunciation that is a complete extinction of sensations and conceptualizations.

[1. The first renunciation of] internally contemplating an external object involves neither destroying nor breaking any internal [formation of an object with] visible form, but is the internal contemplation of white bones and [decaying] flesh in contemplating an external object [such as] a corpse, and so forth. If you wish to cultivate these marks, see the details in the *Tz'u-ti ch'an-men*. Now I will briefly summarize the arousing of these marks.

A practitioner may suddenly perceive that the wrinkled skin on the toes of his own feet are like blisters, and gradually [contemplate] up to the shins and then to the hips and throughout the body until reaching the top [of the head], so that in a moment the whole body is deluged with sudden swelling, the five fingers open like flowers, both legs are like pillars, the hips and lower belly like a jar, the head like **[122c]** a bowl, and the swelling in various places is like the wind filling a leather bag; when these marks are aroused, or advance from the legs to the head, or from the head to the legs, so that the entire coarse cot [of a meditator] is filled; the skin becomes tight and the flesh torn so that it is about to split, and it bursts and pus flows out, and soaks and stains [the cot] with its dampness. Or from the head to the feet the skin and flesh start to peel off, so that only white bones remain. The joints sustain each other, but cannot move; the skin and flesh fall off and gather into one place, like a gathering of inchworms, defiling and ugly. If these marks arise, be deeply anxious about your body, and consider it disgusting, like dung. How can you spare regard for wife and child or material wealth? The Sattva [that is, Śākyamuni in a previous life] gave up his body [to save a starving

Details in the *Tz'u-ti ch'an-men* 具如禪門: see the section at T 46.541b3–542a29.

Sattva gave up his body 薩埵亡身: a well-known tale of the Buddha in a previous life who, as an ascetic in the wilderness, comes across a starving tiger who cannot feed her newborn cubs. He either cuts himself and feeds her with with blood and flesh, or jumps off a nearby cliff so that the tiger can feed on his corpse. See, for example, the version in the *Suvarṇaprabhāsa Sūtra*, T 16.354a–c.

tiger], and Mṛgala [is asked to help] harm [oneself]; these are all examples [of the results of] this contemplation. Internally there is no self to consider; externally there is nothing to passionately love. You should lower your head and be ashamed, and continuously have a mind that is weary [with the things of the world]. The *Mahāparinirvāṇa Sūtra* says, "Removing the skin and flesh, you truly contemplate the white bones." Fix your thoughts on each of the joints [between the bones], and contemplate them carefully forwards and backwards to purify the bones. This is called internalizing a visible form by contemplating an external visible form: externally you perceive corpses that are bloated and overflowing with pus, filling a village or the whole countryside; such is the previous nine considerations as the contemplation of impurity. Therefore it is called "the external contemplation of a visible form." As for the level [of meditative stages], this corresponds to concentrations in the realm of desires.

As this method progresses, you perceive the bones giving off four colors: blue, yellow, white, and red, bright and lucent, at times shining or not shining, a blue light from a blue color, and so forth to a red light from a red color. In form like flowing water, the light encompasses the skeleton [like a cage], like a mirror [obscured] by dust and the sun by mist. If your thoughts are connected to the feet, the light tends to face downward, and if your thoughts are connected to the head, the light tends to face upward. The power of the blue light is such that it shines over the ten directions, so that everything looks blue, like when looking in the direction of Mt. Sumeru it has one color. [The other colors, such as yellow and white] up to red are also the same; these colors give forth light rays, at times shining or not shining, The stage of this [phenomenon] is that of the concentration of incomplete attainment.

If this continues for a long time in this way, the light will arise spontaneously. If it does not arise, collect your thoughts and contemplate precisely, emitting [light] from between the eyebrows, and thus arouse [rays of light]. In form this is like blowing smoke from holes in bamboo; at first there is only a little, but later it is scattered widely. The four colors turn around as they are

See an earlier note at *Mo-ho chih-kuan* 59c26 which quotes the passage immediately before this story, introducing the section on the Buddha "abandoning the body."

Mṛgala: see note above at 120b19–20.

Removing the skin and flesh ... 除却皮肉諦觀白骨: see the *Mahāparinirvāṇa Sūtra* T 12.675b16–17: "The bodhisattva then removed the skin and bones, [revealing] only the white bones."

Blue, yellow, white, and red 青黄白鴿: the Taishō text has the character for "dove/pigeon" 鴿 for the fourth color, but Ikeda (*Gendaigoyaku*, 608) extrapolates to give the color red as the fourth. Chan-jan (BT–V, 316) admits that concerning the four colors "the sūtras and treatises are not the same; some say blue, yellow, red, and white."

emitted from between the eyebrows, and shine out everywhere in the ten directions, lucid and bright.

One color contains the marks of the ten virtuous qualities, the eight tactile sensations, the five constituents [of meditation], good and evil [or correct and deviant] 正邪, and so forth. When the colors first arise, this is [the first constituent of] "examination." When they are distinguished into eight colors (of earth, water, fire, wind, blue, yellow, white, and red], this is the constituent of "reflection." In the past although you knew that there were bones within your flesh, you did not know that within the bones there were eight colors. To perceive something that you did not yet know, and thereby celebrate and rejoice and yet be sad and ashamed [at your past ignorance], is called the constituent of "joy." When this color arises, there is an experience of pleasure, and the basis of the mind is tranquil and pleased; this is called the constituent of "bliss." [As for the fifth constituent of single-minded concentration,] a concentrated mind is profoundly peaceful, dwells calmly without moving, and is dark and profound. [It contains virtues such as] emptiness, illumination, wisdom, concentration, faith, respect, and conscientious shame, and is without the arousing of slander, is free from hindrances, and is in accordance with [the Dharma]. [As for the eight tactile sensations,] if there is cold or heat and so forth, they are gathered together without mistaken confusion; therefore this is called **[123a]** a "forest" [of virtues].

However, although within [these colors] there are the marks of [the sensations such as] restlessness and itchiness, [virtues such as] emptiness and illumination, and the five constituents, and the eye of the mind is open and clear, the Dharma-methods deep and the bliss profound, it is not the same as the basic [dhyāna], and it is also different from the supreme meditations and the supernatural powers and illuminating insights. In those [meditations] you are still wrapped in skin and flesh, and the tactile sensations do not peacefully penetrate. Now [with these eight renunciations] you can feel to the bone, and the Dharma-method is profoundly sublime.

If we discuss evil or deviant marks with regard to the eight colors, such as being able to see the color blue but not very clearly and instead as motley and unseemly, this is an evil or deviant mark. It is the same for the other seven colors. A dark enlightenment [such as that of the Hīnayāna] does not include contemplative wisdom; it is like the night that allows for [the activity of] many bandits. These dhyāna meditations [of the eight renunciations] include [the wisdom of] contemplation; just as there is little deception in the daylight, and if there is, it is easy to remove. A Tripitaka [master] says, "The

Tripitaka master 三藏云: identity unknown, though Chan-jan (BT–V, 319) identifies this person as "the Tripitaka Master Paramārtha."

eight colors are the phenomena of the realm of visible form, people with bones in the realm of desires come in contact with these sensations, and this leads to the arising of various virtuous qualities." However, this explanation relies on the basic dhyāna that still involve defiled [passions]. The Mahāyāna seeks to clarify the dharmas of the precepts, concentration, and wisdom, without being able to exhaust them all. Why is this so? Even if life decays and the precepts disappear, the "spontaneous" [or "actionless" precepts] are not extinguished. As for concentration, although you can subdue the delusions, this [state of] severance does not last forever; it is like having worms in your body that remain in your internal organs and harm your life, that is, even if you have not yet died, your activity will not last long. The path of wisdom, however, is not lost; the attainment of the first fruit [of entering the stream] continues through seven deaths [and rebirths], remaining undefiled. You should know that the precepts and concentrations are undefiled. If so, the light of the eight colors are also phenomenal dharmas of the transworldly realm. If these marks are aroused, this means that you have attained the first renunciation, and the level is that of the first dhyāna.

The *Ch'eng-shih lun* says that [the first] two renunciations are contained in the realm of desires; [the third] renunciation involving purity is contained in the realm of visible form; the fourth renunciation is contained in the realm of no-form; the renunciations of extinction transcend the triple realm [of desires, form, and no-form]. The Abhidharma says that the first two renunciations penetrate the realm of desires and the second dhyāna; the renunciation involving purity corresponds to the fourth dhyāna; the third dhyāna involves an abundance of bliss and so does not correspond to any of the renunciations. Some person has said, "The third dhyāna does not include the superior meditations, and the fourth dhyāna does not include the renunciations. These three traditions are all different [in their interpretations of the eight renunciations]. Here I rely on the *Ta chih tu lun*: the first

Ch'eng-shih lun 成論云: see the passage at T 32.340a25–29, which is not as specific as Chih-i's "quote":

> Question: On which stages are these various liberations?
>
> Answer: The practitioner wishes to destroy form, so he relies on the concentrations of the realm of desire. Then he relies on the concentrations of the realm of form to attain the emptiness of form. One can attain the mind of emptiness in all stages.
>
> Question: Of these liberations, which involve defilements and which are undefiled?
>
> Answer: Because of the nature of emptiness, all are undefiled.

Abhidharma 毘曇云: source unknown.

Some person 有人言: identity unknown, though the *Shiki* (BT–V, 323) attributes it to Chih-i's master Hui-ssu.

Rely on the *Ta chih tu lun* 今依釋論: see the passage at T 25.216c1–24; hereafter, following Chih-i's argument requires the background and careful consideration of the *Ta chih tu lun* exposition, which I will quote in detail. Chodron (3, 1068–71) translates this section:

> As for the ten kṛtsnāyatanas "spheres of totality of the object," we have already spoken of them in regard to the vimokṣas and the abhibhvāyatanas. They are called "spheres of totality" because they embrace their object in its totality *(ālambanakṛtsnapharaṇāt)*.
>
> Question: [Of the four formless spheres *(ārūpyāyatana)*], only the first two, ākāśānantyāyatana "sphere of infinite space" and vijñānānatyāyatana "sphere of infinite consciousness," are kṛtsnāyatanas. Why are [the other two formless spheres], namely, ākiṛcanāyatana "sphere of nothing at all" and naivasaṃjñānāsaṃjñāyatana "sphere of neither identification nor non-identification"] not kṛtsnāyatanas as well?
>
> Answer: The kṛtsnāyatanas are subjective views *(adhimokṣamanasikāra)* and, of the formless spheres, only two, those of infinity of space and infinity of consciousness, lend themselves of subjective extensions.
>
> "Safety *(yogakṣema)*, happiness *(sukha)*, vastness *(viśāla)*, immensity *(apramāṇa)* and infinity *(ananta)*, the sphere of space," said the Buddha. – Throughout all the kṛtsnāyatanas there is a consciousness *(vijñāna)* capable of quickly bearing upon all things and, faced with these dharmas, one determines the presence of consciousness. This is why the two spheres *(āyatana)* [of space and consciousness] constitute the kṛtsnāyatana.
>
> On the other hand, in the sphere of nothing at all *(ākiṃcanyāyatana)*, there is no substance *(dhātu)* capable of being extended; there is no happiness *(sukha)* there and, in regard to nothing-at-all, the Buddha said nothing about infinity, immensity.
>
> In the sphere of neither identification nor non-identification *(naivasaṃjñānāsaṃjñāyatana)*, the mind is dull *(mṛdu)* and it is hard for it to grasp a concept *(nimittodgrahaṇa)* and extend it to infinity, as is the case for the kṛtsnas.
>
> Furthermore, the ākāśāyatana is close to the form realm *(rūpadhātu)* and it can still be concerned with visibles *(rūpa)*. The vijñānāyatana also can be concerned with visible objects. Besides, coming out of the vijñānāyatana, one can leap into the fourth dhyāna and, on coming out of the fourth dhyāna, one is able to leap into the vijñānāyatana. On the contrary, the ākiṃcanāyatana and the naivasaṃjñāyatana [as the higher spheres of the ārūpadhātu] are very distant in formlessness: this is why they are not kṛtsnāyatanas.
>
> Every utilization of these three types of dharmas realizes a mastery over the object *(ālambanābhibhavana)*.
>
> 1. The kṛtsnāyatanas are impure *(sāsrava)*.
>
> The first three vimokṣas, the seventh and eighth vimokṣas are impure. The others are sometimes impure *(sāsrava)*, sometimes pure *(anāsrava)*.
>
> 2. The first two vimokṣas and the first four abhibhvāyatanas are contained *(saṃgṛhīta)* in the first and second dhyānas.
>
> The śubhavimokṣa (3rd vimokṣa), the last four abhibhvāyatanas and the first eight kṛtsnāyatanas are contained in the fourth dhyāna.
>
> 3. The first two kṛtsnāyatanas are called ākāśāyatana. The ākāśāyatana contains the vijñānāyatana. The vijñānāyatana contains the first three vimokṣas, the eight abhibhvāyatanas and the [first] eight kṛtsnāyatanas, all of which have as object *(ālambana)* the visibles of the desire realm *(kāmadhāturūpa)*.
>
> The four next vimokṣas (nos. 4–7) have as object the formless realm *(ārūpadhātu)*, the marvelous qualities of pure dharmas *(anāsravadharma)* and the good *(kuśala)* in [the four] fundamental [absorptions] *(maulasammapatti)*, because the fundamental formless absorptions *(ārūpamaulasamāpatti)* do not concern the levels lower than them.
>
> The absorption of the cessation of concepts and feeling *(saṃjñāvedita-nirodhasamāpatti)* constituting the

renunciation and the [first] two supreme meditations are contained in the first dhyāna. The presence of the five constituents confirm that this is the first dhyāna.

2. [The second renunciation of] contemplating external visible objects

eighth vimokṣa, being neither mind *(citta)* nor mental event *(caitasika-dharma)*, has no object *(anālambana)*.

The seventh vimokṣa, namely, the absorption of neither identification nor non-identification *(naivasaṃjñānanā-saṃjñāyatana)* alone has as its object the four formless aggregates *(ārūpya-skandha)* and the pure dharmas *(anāsrava-dharma)*.

The nine successive absorptions *(anu-pūrvasamāpatti)*:

Emerging from of the first dhyāna, the yogin then [directly] enters into the second dhyāna in such a way that there is no other intervening mind, whether good *(kuśala)* or defiled *(saṃkliṣṭa)*. [From the dhyāna into the samāpatti], the yogin continues in this way until the absorption of cessation of concept and feeling *(saṃjñāveditanirodhasamāpatti)*.

The second renunciation: On the first two renunciations (*vimokṣa*), see the *Ta chih tu lun*, T 25.215a11–b2. Chodron (3, 1058–59) translates:

B. The first two vimokṣas

The yogin has not destroyed inner and outer visibles: he has not suppressed the notion of both [his own] inner and outer visibles *(rūpasaṃjñā)* and he sees these visibles with a feeling of horror *(aśubhacitta)*: this is the first vimokṣa.

The yogin has destroyed the inner visibles and suppressed the notion of inner visibles *(adhyātmaṃ rūpasaṃjñā)*, but he has not destroyed outer visibles nor suppressed the notion of outer visibles *(bahirdhā rūpasaṃjñā)* and it is with a feeling of horror that he sees outer visibles: this is the second vimokṣa.

These two vimokṣas both contemplate the horrible *(aśubha)*: the first contemplates inner as well as outer visibles; the second does not see inner visibles and sees only outer visibles. Why is that?

Beings *(sattva)* have two kinds of behavior *(pratipad)*: sensualism *(tṛṣṇācarita)* and rationalism *(dṛṣṭicarita)*. The sensualists *(tṛṣṇābahula)* are attached to happiness *(sukharakta)* and are bound *(baddha)* by outer fetters *(bāhyasaṃyojana)*. The rationalists *(dṛṣṭibahula)* are strongly attached to the view of the individual *(satkāyadṛṣṭi)*, etc., and are bound by inner fetters *(adhyātmasaṃyojana)*. This is why the sensualists [usefully] contemplate the horrors of outer visibles *(bāhyarūpāśubha)*, whereas the rationalists [usefully] contemplate the horrors *(aśubha)* and corruption *(vikāra)* of their own body.

Furthermore, at the beginning of the practice, the yogin's mind lacks sharpness *(asūkṣma)* and at the start it is difficult for him to fix his mind on a single point [viz., outer visibles]. That is why he disciplines his mind and tames it by gradual practice *(kramābhyāsa)* consisting of the [simultaneous] consideration of both outer and inner visibles. Then he can destroy the notion of inner visibles and see only outer visibles.

Question. If the yogin no longer has the notion of inner visibles, why can he see outer visibles?

Answer. This is a matter of a subjective method *(adhimuktimārga)* and not an objective method *(bhūtamārga)*. The yogin thinks about his future corpse burned by the fire *(vidagdhaka)*, devoured by insects *(vikhāditaka)*, buried in the ground and completely decomposed. Or, if he considers it at present, he analyzes this body down to the subtle atoms *(paramāṇu)*, all non-existent. This is how "he sees outer visibles, not having the notion of inner visibles."

without internal visible forms and with an impure mind 内無色以不淨心觀外色 is as follows: human bones are made from semen and blood [or, "the essence of blood"], and you should critique and extinguish [attachment to the physical body] by analyzing the four subtle [colors] of the bones. Through the Mahāyāna method of realizing the essence of dharmas [as empty] you should know that bones arise through the mind, that the mind is like an illusion, that human bones are empty and [only] conventionally existent, that human bones perish naturally on their own. This is like a tame horse following the will of its master, and like good co-workers who come and go without getting in each others' way. If after [the internal image of] the human bones has left, and a new object [of purity, the third renunciation)] has not yet arisen, there is a danger of retrogressing through an abundance of joy; therefore, just contemplate an external visible form with thoughts of impurity. The "external visible form" refers to corpses; or "external" refers to the eight colors emitted by human bones. The reason that you contemplate external visible form is that you are close to leaving the realm of desires and should therefore contemplate external impurities. If you are to cultivate [contemplation of] the destruction of human bones, there is a separate contemplative method [for this], but now I will only discuss the method for arousing it.

Immediately you can perceive human bones as they naturally wear down, leaving only the eight colors and the external, impure objects. When the human bones are extinguished, the level is that of **[123b]** an intermediate [stage]. Again, when you perceive the eight colors, the internal pure dharmas arise simultaneously, and the blue, yellow, and so forth rays of light further increase in brightness. The four constituent virtuous qualities of internal purity, joy, bliss, and single-mindedness turn to be superior to the previous [contemplations]. This is the second renunciation; the level corresponds to the second dhyāna.

3. [The third] renunciation of attaining enlightenment through purity

Question. In the [first] two abhibhvāyatanas, the yogin sees inner and outer visibles; in the [last] six abhibhvāyatanas he see only outer visibles. In the first vimokṣa, he sees inner and outer visibles; in the second vimokṣa, he sees only outer visibles. Why does he destroy only the concept of inner visibles and not destroy the outer visibles?

Answer. When the yogin sees with his eyes this body marked with the marks of death (*maraṇanimitta*), he grasps the future characteristics of death; as for the actual body, in it he sees, to a lesser degree, the disappearance *(nirodhalakṣaṇa)* of the outer four great elements *(mahābhūta)*. Therefore, since it is difficult for him to see that they do not exist, the [Sūtra] does not speak of the destruction of the visibles. Besides, at the time when the yogin will have transcended the form realm *(rūpadhātu)*, he will no longer see outer visibles.

in body [and mind] 淨背捨身作證 is as follows: the first and second dhyānas do not involve bliss that permeates the body, and the fourth dhyāna involves no bliss, so what does enlightenment consist of [at this stage]? The scholars of the *Ch'eng-shih lun* say that the fourth dhyāna corresponds to the [third] renunciation that is purity. Here [I propose that] both [the third and fourth] dhyāna correspond to the [third] renunciation that is purity. Since it has already been said that the third dhyāna involves the permeation of the body with bliss, you should be enlightened about it first [at the third dhyāna] and this will be perfected at the fourth dhyāna, and include the superior meditations. Therefore know that the renunciation that is purity corresponds to the third dhyāna.

"[The third renunciation as] purity," according to the *Ta chih tu lun*, "is [renunciation as] purity because purity is its object." The eight colors are already pure dharmas [at the third dhyāna], they have not yet been polished to a luster; the purity of colors is ultimately realized at the fourth dhyāna. When these colors arise, the luster of the eight colors further turns clear and pure; therefore it is said "it is purity because purity is its object."

"The sensations [of bliss] permeating the body" 遍身受 means that, since ultimate bliss is available at the third dhyāna, in general it exists for these two [that is, the third and fourth] dhyānas, and so this is called "renunciation as purity."

Scholars of the *Ch'eng-shih lun* 成論人: identity unknown. Chan-jan (BT–V, 327) adds that "previously it was pointed out that the *Ch'eng-shih lun* classifies the third renunciation as within the realm of form; therefore it is known that the fourth dhyāna corresponds to the [third] renunciation that is purity."

Purity is its object 緣淨故淨: see the *Ta chih tu lun* at T 25.215b29: "Because purity is its object it is called 'renunciation as purity.'" Chodron (3, 1059–61) translates the context on the third renunciation (215b2–29); note that my translation "purity" 淨 is rendered by Chodron as "pleasant":

C. The third vimokṣa

"He actualizes the pleasant vimokṣa [of purity]" *(śubhaṃ, vimokṣaṃ kāyena sākṣātkaroti)*. – This is a pleasant meditation in regard to unpleasant things *(aśubheṣu śubhabhāvanā)*, as is said about the eight abhibhāyatanas.

The first eight kṛtsnāyatanas contemplate, in the pure state *(śuddha)*: 1. earth *(pṛthivī)*, 2. water *(ap)*, 3. fire *(tejas)*, 4. wind *(vāyu)*, and also 5. blue *(nīla)*, 6. yellow *(pīta)*, 7. red *(lohita)*, 8. white *(avadāta)*.

The [fifth] sees visibles as blue *(rūpāṇi nīlāni)* like the blue lotus flower *(nīlotpalapuṣpa)*, like the *kin-tsing-chan*, like the flax flower *(umakapuṣpa)* or like fine Benares muslin *(saṃpannaṃ vā vārāṇaseyaṃ vastram)*. It is the same for the visions of yellow *(pīta)*, red *(lohita)* and white *(avadāta)*, each according to its respective color. The entire thing is called "the pleasant vimokṣa."

Question. If all of that is the pleasant vimokṣa, it should not be necessary to speak of the kṛtsnāyatanas [under the pain of repeating oneself].

Answer. The vimokṣas are the initial practice *(prathamacaryā)*; the abhibhvāyatanas are the intermediate practice *(madhyamacaryā)* and the kṛtsnāyatanas are the long-standing practice.

The meditation of the horrible *(aśubhabhāvatana)* is of two types: i. unpleasant *(aśubha)*; ii. pleasant *(śubha)*. The [first] two vimokṣas and the [first] four abhibhvāyatanas are of the unpleasant type. One vimokṣa [the third], the [last] four abhibhvāyatanas and the [first] eight kṛtsnāyatanas are of the pleasant type.

Question. When the yogin takes as pleasant *(śubha)* that which is unpleasant *(aśubha)*, he is making a mistake *(viparyāsa)*. Then why is the meditation that he practices in the course of the pleasant vimokṣa not erroneous?

Answer. The error is in seeing wrongly as pleasant [or pure] a woman's beauty which is unpleasant, but the meditation practiced during the pleasant vimokṣa is not a mistake due to the extension *(viśālatva)* of all true blue color, [etc].

Moreover, in order to tame the mind *(cittadamanārtham)*, the pleasant meditation presupposes a lengthy practice of the meditation on the horrible *(aśubhabhāvana)* and on mental revulsion *(cittanirveda)*: this is why practicing the pleasant meditation is not a mistake and there is no desire *(lobha)* in it.

Moreover, the yogin begins by contemplating the horrors of the body and fixes his mind on all the inner and outer horrors in bodily things. Then he feels revulsion *(nirveda)*: [his negative emotions], lust *(rāga)*, hatred *(dveṣa)* and stupidity *(moha)* decrease; he becomes frightened and understands: "I do not possess these characteristics as a person at all: it is the body that is like that. Then why am I attached to it?"

He concentrates his mind and meditates so as not to commit mistakes. As soon as his mind becomes disciplined and gentle, he avoids thinking of the horrors of the body, such as skin *(tvac)*, flesh *(māṃsa)*, blood *(lohita)* and marrow *(asthimajjan)*: for him there are only white bones *(śvetāsthika)* and he fixes his mind on the skeleton *(kaṅkāla)*. If his mind wanders outward, he concentrates and gathers it back. Concentrating his mind deeply, he sees the diffused light of the white bones *(śvetāsthika)* like a conch-shell *(śaṅkha)*, like shells *(kapardaka)*, lighting up inner and outer things. This is the gateway of the pleasant vimokṣa.

Then, noting the disappearance of the skeleton, the yogin sees only the light of the bones *(asthiprabhā)* and grasps the characteristics *(nimitta)* of outer and inner visibles. For example:

1. diamond *(vajra)*, pearl *(maṇi)*, precious golden and silver objects *(hemarajataratnavastu)*,
2. very pure *(supariśuddha)* earth *(pṛthivī)* [first kṛtsna],
3. pure water *(ap)* [second kṛtsna],
4. pure fire *(tejas)* without smoke *(dhūma)* or kindling *(indhana)* [third kṛtsna],
5. pure wind *(vāyu)*, without dust *(rajas)* [fourth kṛtsna],
6. blue visibles *(rūpāṇi nīlāni)*, like the *kin-tsing-chan* [fifth abhibhu and fifth kṛtsna],
7. yellow visibles *(rūpāni pītāni)*, like the ginger flower *(campakapuṣpa)* [sixth abhibhu and sixth kṛtsna],
8. red visibles *(rūpāni lohitāni)*, like the flower of the red lotus *(padmapuṣpa)* [seventh abhibhu and seventh kṛtsna].
9. white visibles *(rūpāṇy avadātāni)*, like white snow *(hima)* [eighth abhibhu and eighth kṛtsna].

Grasping these characteristics *(nimittāny udgṛhṇan)*, the yogin fixes his mind on the pleasant meditation *(śubhabhāvana)* on the pure light *(pariśuddhaprabhā)* belonging to each of these visibles. Then the yogin experiences joy *(prīti)* and happiness *(sukha)* filling his entire body *(kāya)*: this is what is called the pleasant vimokṣa *(śubha vimokṣa)*. **Since it has pleasant [pure] things as object *(ālambana)*, it is called "pleasant" [pure] vimokṣa 縁淨故淨.**

"Purity" has four meanings. [1.] "The impurity of impurity" 不淨不淨 means, the physical body in the realm of desires is already impure, and now [as a corpse] it is bloated, and therefore it is said to be an impurity of impurities. [2.] "Impurity that is pure" 不淨淨 means, when the skin and flesh are removed and you precisely contemplate the [remaining] white bones, there are no longer any guts or sinew or blood, like a conch-shell or [other white] shell, and therefore it is called "impurity that is pure." [3.] "Impure purity" 淨不淨 refers to the rays of light in eight colors that emerge from between the eyebrows. The rays of light are pure, but have not yet been "polished," and therefore are called "impure purity." [4.] "Pure purity" 淨淨 refers to the third renunciation, where the objects are pure and polished; therefore it is called "pure purity."

4. [The fourth] renunciation through emptiness: going beyond all visible forms, the existent objects 有對 of visible form are extinguished [by realizing their emptiness] and you are not mindful of various visible forms. "All visible forms" are the internal or external visible forms of the realm of desires; "existent objects" are the objects of the five senses. These two types of visible form have already been extinguished in the first three renunciations, but there are still the eight colors that turn and change in accordance with the mind; therefore these are called "various visible forms." Rejecting the visible forms and embracing emptiness, you do not use any other method except only entering the concentration of emptiness. [As the *Ta chih tu lun* points out,] ordinary ignorant people have many defilements and become attached

Ordinary ignorant people ... 凡夫多染保著空定。聖人深心智慧利直去不迴: see the passage in the *Ta chih tu lun* at T 15.215c1–11, immediately following the passage in the previous note. Chodron (3, 1061–62) translates:

> As the yogin has not yet destroyed the impurities *(akṣīṇāsrava)*, it happens that, from time to time, passionate thoughts *(saṃyojanacitta)* arise in him and he becomes attached *(anusajate)* to pleasant visibles *(śubharūpa)*. Then he vigorously *(ātāpin)* and energetically *(vīryavat)* cuts this attachment *(tam āsaṣgaṃ samucchinatti)*. Actually, this pleasant meditation is a result of his mind. And just as a master magician *(māyākāra)*, in the face of objects that he has created magically, knows that they come from him, so the yogin is no longer attached *(āsaṅga)* and no longer pursues objects *(ālambana)*. Then the vimokṣa "liberation" changes its name and is called "sphere of mastery over the object" abhibhvāyatana.
>
> Although the yogin thus masters *(abhibhavati)* the pleasant meditation *(śubhabhāvana)*, he is still incapable of extending it *(vistārayitum)*. Then he returns to grasp the pleasant characteristics *(śubhanimitta)*:
>
> a. Using the power of the vimokṣas and the power of the abhibhvāyatanas, he grasps the nature of pleasant earth *(śubhapṛthivī)* and gradually extends it *(krameṇa vistārayati)* to all the empty space *(ākāśa)* of the ten directions. He does the same with water *(ap)*, fire *(tejas)* and wind *(vāyu)*.
>
> b. He grasps the nature of blue *(nīlanimitta)* and gradually extends it to all the

to this concentration of emptiness; Noble Ones have a profound mind of wisdom that is sharp, and so straightaway depart from and do not return to [attachments to anything]; therefore this is called a "renunciation."

If there is an abundance of contact with emptiness and [your thoughts become] scattered, this is a deceitful void and not real, so you should abandon [focusing only on] emptiness and take consciousness as your object; this is [5. the fifth] "renunciation through the abode of consciousness" 識處背捨.

Again, consciousness arises and perishes, is transient and a deceitful void, so [the objects of consciousness] should not be [grasped] as an object, but only a point of contact; therefore this is [6. the sixth renunciation] through [the concentration on] no existents 無所有處.

Again, the abode of consciousness is like a carbuncle, and the sphere of no existents is like a tumor; to abandon consciousness and no-consciousness is [7. the seventh renunciation] through [the concentration that is] neither-conceptions-nor-no-conceptions 非想非非想.

[The state of] no-conceptions also involves minute passionate afflictions, so now at this stage you abandon it by taking as the object "sensation and conceptions as no-conceptions" 非想之受想. Again, [because they are empty] there are no conceptions to be extinguished. The practice of concentration **[123c]** in the physical body is already "no-conceptions" just as it is; just like fish under the ice or worms in hibernation [they are there whether you are aware of them or not]. If we speak of it in terms of "what is extinguished," this involves climbing [stages] upward and being weary of what is below. What is different? Here you extinguish your own stage as well as extinguishing other stages; therefore this is called [8. the eighth renunciation that is] the extinction of sensations and conceptions 滅受想背捨. These are all explained in detail in the section on "cultivating enlightenment" [in the *Tz'u-ti ch'an-men*].

The Abhidharma clarifies that attaining the concentration of extinction is "liberation including both [wisdom and concentration]," and not attaining this concentration is called only "wisdom liberation" 慧解脫. The *Ch'eng-shih*

space of the ten directions. He does the same with yellow *(pīta)*, red *(lohita)* and white *(avadāta)*.

Now the abhibhvāyatanas are transformed and become the kṛtsnāyatanas "spheres of totality of the object."

These three, [namely the vimokṣas, the abhibhvāyatanas and the kṛtsnāyatanas], are one and the same thing *(ekārtha)*, with three name-changes.

Tz'u-ti ch'an-men: see the long section on the renunciations at T 46.540c5–543c9.

Abhidharma 毘曇明: source unknown.

Liberation including both [wisdom and concentration] 俱解脫: The DDB has "As distinguished from wisdom liberation 慧解脫, where one uses wisdom alone to accomplish freedom from the hindrances of affliction 煩惱障, one instead uses both

lun says that attaining [the samādhi of] flashes of lightning is called "wisdom liberation," and to attain this together with the worldly dhyānas is called "both [wisdom and concentration] liberation." The *Ch'eng-shih lun* also says that the later four [renunciations] are not distinct methods but should [all] be cultivated with an undefiled mind. This is fine, but what about the meaning of not having a distinct method for the first three [of the renunciations], which means they are interpreted only in terms of heterodox non-Buddhist dhyāna meditation? If in the past you have already attained the eight concentrations [of renunciations], you have therefore aroused conditions from previous lives. However, the concentration of extinction is one type that will not be perfected even if cultivated, unless you have attained [the state of] non-defilement [beyond passions]; therefore we do not discuss "conditions from previous lives" [in this context]. The nine gradual and progressive concentrations, [the samadhi of] transcendence, and so forth [are concentrations explained] in terms of the Tripitaka [Teachings]. There are no ordinary, ignorant people who cultivate these concentrations, so we do not discuss the arising of conditions from previous lives. If explained in terms of the Mahāyāna, this meaning should be included, but I will not discuss it here.

6. The Contemplation of Great Impurities [123c12]

Next is to clarify arousing the contemplation of great impurities, also called "great renunciation." In the previous contemplations and arisings, there was the removal of skin and flesh, and the precise contemplation of the human bones of a corpse and its impurity, whether one corpse or two [or multiple] corpses, in a city or village, spewing forth their impurity. Since this was done in terms of your own or another's [physical body that is the result of] karmic recompense; this was called a "minor" impurity. We discussed weariness [for things of the world] and abandonment in terms of this [minor impurity], so it was called renunciation [lit. "rejecting and abandoning" 背捨], with general and specific aspects.

wisdom and concentration to liberate oneself both from the hindrances of affliction, and the hindrances of liberation 解脱障. Due to this liberation, one attains the samādhi of total annihilation 滅盡定." See also the explanation of "the two obstacles" in the Glossary.

Ch'eng-shih lun: on the topic of "wisdom liberation" and "both liberations" see the passage at T 32.245c–246c. The phrases "electricity-like (or 'electric-light') 電光 samādhi" and "wisdom liberation," appear at T 32.339c17–26.

Nine gradual and progressive concentrations 九次第定: the progressive cultivation of concentration starting with the four dhyāna and continuing through the four concentrations on emptiness in the realm of formlessness 四無色定 and finally attaining the concentration of extinction 滅盡定.

This contemplation of great impurities, however, is not just about the outflows of impurity from [the physical body that is] your karmic recompense, but also involves the circumstantial recompense [of the world we live in], such as houses, monetary wealth, grain and rice, clothing, food and drink, and mountains, streams, parks, and forests, great rivers, lakes, and swamps. All things connected to visible phenomena are without exception impure. Worms and pus flow out, smelling stinky and rancid. Houses are like a mound of graves; money is like a dead snake [or, "a snake of death" 死蛇]; a meal of soup is like a gruel made of dung; rice is like white worms; clothes are like smelly hides; mountains are like a cluster of flesh; lakes are like rivers of pus; forested parks are like withered bones; the rivers and sea are like expansive pools of defilement. The *Mahāparinirvāṇa Sūtra* says that "delicious soup produces the conception of defiled juice"; this is what you should contemplate. While sitting in meditation, immediately perceive things as explained above. Perceive this great earth as not having any attractive or good features; the world we live in is not something we should covetously desire. This is called arousing [the contemplation of] great impurity. This is like when you first light a fire, preparations are made but there is only a little arousing of smoke and flames, but when the fire gains strength it will burn anything, even drying up the waters of a great river. When you first contemplate impurity, [the idea is to] stop [and focus on] one corpse or one country, destroying each lustful thought as it arises, but now [at this level] the power of concentration is such that weariness toward evil is abundant, and [one realizes that] both your body and environment are in no case without impurity, and thus desirous thoughts will cease forever.

Again, what set of marks do all things have? [There are none.] People feel and perceive things differently, according to their karmic influences. **[124a]** People with good karma experience pure visible forms; people with evil karma experience impure visible forms. It is like the jeweled lands and palaces of the gods, when compared to the riches of human beings; is like taking tiles and stones and turning them into silver and gold. When the power of good [karma] is induced, both the body and environment are pure. The

Delicious soup produces the conception of defiled juice 美羹作穢汁: see the *Mahāparinirvāṇa Sūtra* at T 12.696b2–4, which contains the phrase, "All that you eat produces the marks of worms, but in reality there are no worms. Contemplate bean soup as producing the conception of lower juice [from your anus?], but that in reality it is not dung." Or, if one follows the numerous variant readings in this passage in the Taishō text, which are closer to Chih-i's quote, we can translate this section: "Contemplate attractive and delicious soup as producing the conception of defiled juice, but that in reality it is not defiled."

A great river 江河: or, the Yangtze and Yellow rivers.

[conditions of] hells explained in the *Sūtra on Protecting the Sangha* shows that the features of hells are not all the same. Or you perceive that the flesh of the body becomes earth, and is tilled by someone else. Or you perceive that the physical body is like trees in the forest that are eventually broken down and rot. Or the body is like a mountain, or a hut, or clothing, all of which are subject to a hundred and twenty types [of exposure and suffering], all of which are experienced through evil karma and invite the visible forms of impurity. If you grasp the pure and pleasant visible forms, and maintain a hard and firm passionate attachment to them, you should destroy these thoughts of great attachment with the great power of contemplation. Overturn the great perversions and perfect the contemplation of great impurity.

Why is this so? Magical techniques of illusion are mostly matters of fraudulent deception, but through the penetrating supranormal powers you attain the principle 道理 [of things] and is able to transform all things. For example, wax, gold, and steel are transformed into liquid when exposed to fire, and water when exposed to cold becomes [hard ice like] earth. When you attain understanding through contemplation, you are in agreement with the path of transformations, because the power of concentration is like this. The [four] basic dhyānas only remove the attachments of the lower stages and are not able to remove the attachments of your own [present]stage. As the renunciations of great and small [impurity] are not yet undefiled [by passions], it is only a matter of removing the attachments of the lower stages and your own stage, but if you penetrate to where the objects [of contemplation] are undefiled, then you can remove all the attachments of the lower, your own, and the upper stages. If people arouse [the contemplation of] great impurity and realize the renunciations, this is a great [renunciation], and is contained in the first dhyāna. If you perceive that there are no bones internally, and contemplate the eight colors and your body and environment, this is a great condition, and is called the second great renunciation, and includes the second dhyāna. If through [contemplation of] great impurity you realize the [third] renunciation through purity, this also is "great." And so forth through the [eighth] renunciation that is extinction, these are also likewise. If we discuss this in terms of the great superior meditations, this is a further maturation of the renunciations and leads to a condition where there is mastery of transformations. The *Ta chih tu lun* clarifies that

Sūtra on Protecting the Sangha 僧護經: see the long section describing various aspects of hell in the *Sūtra on the Causes and Conditions for Protecting the Sangha* at T 17.567a6–572b13. This is the only place where Chih-i quotes this short sūtra.

Hundred and twenty types 一百二十種: I could not locate any explanation of these; perhaps it just means "a lot."

***Ta chih tu lun* clarifies …**: a summary of the passage on the impurity of external visibles, at T 25.216a29–b29, following the passages quoted in notes above. Chodron (3, 1066–68) translates:

Question. While having the notion of inner visibles *(adhyātmaṃ rūpasaṃjñā)*, how does the yogin see outer visibles *(bahirdhā rūpāṇi paśyati)*?

Answer. The eight abhibhvāyatanas can be attained *(prāpti)* by ascetics who have entered deeply into concentration and whose mind is disciplined and softened. Sometimes the yogin sees the horrible *(aśubha)* of his own body and also sees the horrors of outer visibles.

The contemplation of the horrible *(aśubhabhāvana)* is of two types: i. that which contemplates all kinds of impurities *(nānāvidhāśuci)*, such as the thirty-six bodily substances *(dravya)*, etc.; ii. that which, disregarding in one's own body as in others' bodies, the skin *(tvac)*, flesh *(māṃsa)* and the five internal organs, contemplates only the white bones *(śvetāsthika)*, like a conch-shell *(śaṅkha)*, like snow *(hima)*. The sight of the thirty-six bodily substances is called 'ugly' *(durvarṇa)*; the sight of the conch or snow is called "beautiful' *(suvarṇa)*.

C. The second abhibhu

At the time he is contemplating inner and outer [visibles], the yogin is distracted *(vikṣiptacitta)* and only with difficulty can he enter into dhyāna. Then he excludes notions of his own body *(ādhymatmikasaṃjñā)* and considers only outer visibles *(bāhyarūpa)*. As is said in the Abhidharma, the yogin who possesses vimokṣa contemplates and sees the dead body: after death, the latter is picked up and taken to the charnel-ground *(śmaśāna)* where, burned by fire *(vidagdhaka)* and devoured by insects *(vikhāditaka)*, it disintegrates. From then on, the yogin sees only the insects and the fire, but does not see the body: this is why the Sūtra says that "not having the notion of inner visibles, he sees outer visibles" *(adhyātmam ārūpasaṃjñī bahirdhā rūpāṇi paśyati)*.

In accordance with instructions, the yogin perceives and looks at the body as a skeleton *(kaṅkāla)*. When his mind is distracted outwardly, he brings it back and concentrates on the skeleton as object. Why is that? At the beginning of the practice, this person was unable to see subtle objects *(sūkṣmālambana)*, and that is why the sūtra said [in regard to the first abhibhu that the yogin sees only] visibles **"few in number"** *(rūpāṇi parīttāni)*. But now, this yogin, whose path of seeing is developing, deepening and broadening, uses this skeleton in order to see Jambudvīpa as skeletons everywhere, and this is why the Sūtra says here that he sees **"numerous visibles"** *(rūpāṇy adhimatrāṇi)*.

Then he concentrates his mind again and no longer sees a single skeleton; this is why the sūtra says that "he cognizes visibles by mastering them and sees visibles by mastering them" *(tāni khalu rūpāṇy abhibhūya jānāty abhibhūya paśyati)*.

And since, the yogin is able at will *(yatheṣṭam)* to master the concept of man and woman *(puruṇastrīsaṃjñā)* and the concept of beauty *(śucisaṃjñā)* in regard to the five objects of enjoyment *(kāmaguṇa)*, that is indeed a "sphere of mastering the object" *(abhibhvāyatana)*.

Thus a strong man *(balavat)* mounted on his horse who captures the enemy is able to destroy them is said to "master" them and, as he is also able to control his horse, he "masters" it. It is the same for the yogin: in the meditation on the horrible *(aśubhabhāvana)*, he is able to do a lot with just a little, and do a little with a lot: that is an abhibhvāyatana. He is also able to destroy his enemies, the five objects of enjoyment *(kāmaguṇa)*; that also is an abhibhvāyatana. When without destroying inwardly [the notion] of his own body, the yogin sees visibles outwardly, **numerous or few in number, beautiful or ugly,** that is a matter of the first and second abhibhvāyatanas.

D. The third and fourth abhibhus

When, no longer having the notion of

when dull people finish cultivating the eight renunciations, then they cultivate the superior meditations and the [ten] spheres of totality. Those of middling faculties cultivate the third renunciation, and then within the fourth dhyāna cultivate the superior meditations and so forth. Those of superior faculties fully cultivate the first renunciation, and thus cultivate all methods. Now I will explain this passage. "Whether numerous or few" refers to [contemplation] in terms of the environment. One corpse is "few"; two corpses [or more] is "many." The rest should also be understood in this way: one robe, one meal, one mountain and river, are "few." Immeasurable robes, meals, mountains, and rivers are "many." When you first cultivate [or practice], you start with the few and advance to the many. Now the arousing [of various contemplations] is also like this. "Whether beautiful or ugly" means: when good karma is the starting point, this is beautiful, and when evil karma is the superficial base, this is ugly. As for these two matters, what is good to me is "beautiful"; what is evil to me is "ugly." What comes from wisdom is beautiful; what comes from ignorance is ugly. What comes from wealth is beautiful; what comes from poverty is ugly. In this way, the beautiful and the ugly are both impure. The mountains, rivers, lands, clothing, food, houses, and so forth: their beauty and ugliness **[124b]** are both impure. Again, the body and environment are both ugly. The eight colors that are emitted from human bones are beautiful, but the eight colors can also be ugly; they should be polished to be beautiful. The beautiful and the ugly

visibles concerning his own body, the yogin sees visibles outwardly, **numerous or few, beautiful or ugly**, that is the third and fourth abhibhu.

E. The four last abhibhus

When, having concentrated his mind, the yogin deeply penetrates into the absorptions *(samāpatti)*, suppresses [the concept] of inner body *(adhyāymakāya)*, sees outer objects perfectly pure *(bāhya-pariśuddhālambana)*, blue *(nīla)* and blue in color *(nīlavarṇa)*, yellow *(pīta)* and yellow in color *(pītavarṇa)*, red *(lohita)* and red in color *(lohitavarṇa)*, white *(avadāta)* and white in color *(avadātavarṇa)*, this is a matter of the last four abhibhvāyatanas.

Question. What is the difference between the last four abhibhvāyatanas and the last four kṛtsnāyatanas of color, blue, etc., that are part of the ten kṛtsnāyatanas?

Answer. The kṛtsnāyatana of blue grasps absolutely everything as blue; the corresponding abhibhvāyatana sees a large number or a small number of objects only as blue, at will *(yatheṣṭam)*, without, however, eliminating foreign thoughts. Seeing and mastering these objects, it is called abhibhvāyatana.

Thus, for example, whereas the noble cakravartin king totally dominates the four continents *(cāturdvīpaka)*, the king of Jambudvipa dominates only a single continent. In the same way, whereas the kṛtsnāyatanas totally dominate all objects, the abhibhvāyatanas see only a small number of visibles and dominate them but are unable to include all objects.

This is a summary *(saṃkṣepeṇa)* explanation of the eight abhibhvāyatanas.

For the "ten spheres of totality" see also the section that follows (T 25.216c1–24), quoted above at *Mo-ho chih-kuan* 123a19.

are both impure. These two superior meditations are included in the first dhyāna. If the internal [bones] do not show the marks of color, contemplate the external visible forms, whether few or many, and whether beautiful or ugly. One with superior knowledge and superior insight will internally extinguish the human bones, and externally perceive the eight colors. Again, the matters of person and environment, few or many, and beautiful or ugly, are as explained previously. [end of fascicle nine, part one]

"Superior knowledge and insight" 勝知見 refers to [realizing that] the mental is superior to the [physical] visible forms, and not being fettered by visible forms. Instead, the mind in turn converts [and thus knows] the visible forms, and therefore this is called "superior knowledge." "Superior insight" refers to [realizing that] the pure and impure are all mastered within the mind, so that contemplative understanding is fulfilled; therefore it is called "superior insight." These two are included in the second dhyāna.

When this superior level is perfected, there is no more concern for [your own] body, not to mention material wealth or other bodies. Wise ones in the ancient past declined rank and gave up their country, and "returned the bulls and washed their ears." All of them in a past life had cultivated this contemplation, so they naturally had this disposition and were not defiled by passionate attachments. If this meaning is not realized, you will become covetous unto death, and how would you be able to abandon glory and reject [social] rank?

The final four of the superior meditations are realized in the fourth dhyāna [stage]. [The idea that] the third dhyāna still includes much bliss so

Wise ones in the ancient past 上古賢人 ...: A reference to cases "where an exemplar of rightness 義 declines a govermental position (usually the position of emperor) that is not rightfully his.... Much of this is based in early abdication literature where the tension between rule by lineage and rule by worth plays out." (personal note from Michael Ing). See also Sarah Allen, *The Heir and the Sage*, 1981, especially the chapter on Tang Yao and Yu Shun: "Xu You, in refusing the throne offered to him by Yao, is the first in a series of sages who either would not accept the throne or refused to serve under a king who had violated propriety by depriving the rightful heir of his throne" (p. 41).

See also the "Giving Away a Throne" chapter in the *Chuang Tzu* (Watson, *Complete Works*, 309–22), and the *Chou pen chi* 周本紀 section of the *Shih Chi* 史記.

Returned the bulls and washed their ears: [Ing:] "Xuyou/Hsu Yu 許由 declines Yao's attempt to give him the throne because he is a minister, not a son of Yao. The notion of washing the ears is something Xuyou is described doing after fleeing the scene, an attempt to purge his ears from hearing something so inappropriate. The idea of washing your ears is then used as a kind of trope for those who act like Xuyou." The story behind "returning the bulls" is unknown. See the story of Xuyou/Hsu Yu in the *Kao shih yun* 高士伝 section of the *Shih Chi* 史記.

you are not able to attain transformation [at this stage] is part of the teachings for the śrāvakas, but the teachings for the bodhisattvas is that there are transformations in each of the dhyānas, so why should it be said that there is no attainment [at the third dhyāna]? The *Ta chih tu lun* says, "[Whether] blue, yellow, red, or white," these are based on real dharmas 實法. The *Ying-lo ching* tells of "earth, water, fire, and wind" as being based on conventional names and being mutually interdependent. These [last] four superior meditations extinguish the internal and external visible forms, leaving only the eight colors; there are only [differences of] few or many transformations, but not any transformations in the sense of beautiful or ugly.

The ten spheres of totality 十一切處 are included in the fourth dhyāna. The first dhyāna involves much examination and reflection 覺觀; the second dhyāna involves [much] restless joy; the third dhyāna involves [much] restless bliss, and so the spheres of totality are not attained broadly and universally [in these first three dhyāna stages]. Only with the unmoving mindfulness of wisdom [of the fourth dhyāna] is there a broad and universal [attainment of these spheres]. When blue pervades the ten directions, everything in the ten directions is blue, and so forth for the other colors. Therefore it is called "the spheres of totality." "Entering the totality" 一切入 means that when blue pervades everything, yellow will be absorbed by blue and also pervade all places. **[124c]** Blue and yellow do not lose their basic marks, but mutually integrate [with each other] without being confused with each other. The mutual integration of the other colors is also the same. This is called "entering the totality." This involves your internal mind emitting color to pervade all places, not taking external [objects such as] trees and leaves as your objects to pervade all places. The internal mind, without dharmas, is able to transform the external [objects such as] trees and leaves; first the mind is transformed, and then the leaves are transformed. The *Ta chih tu lun* refers to the "blue lotus flower": since there is a fear that people will not understand, an external object is used as an analogy for an internal matter, but you should not become attached to the analogy and make that the correct meaning. If you contemplate with penetrating understanding, [you will

Blue, yellow, red, or white 青黄赤白: see the phrase "blue and blue in color, yellow and yellow in color, red and red in color, white and white in color, this is a matter of the last four abhibhvāyatanas," in the *Ta chih tu lun* at T 25.216b22–23.

Earth, water, fire, and wind 地水火風: see the *Ying-lo ching*, which contains a phrase on the emptiness of "the four elements [of earth, water, fire, and wind] and the four colors [of blue, yellow, red, and white]" at T 24.1013a27–28.

Blue lotus flower 優鉢羅華 (*utpala*): this appears in the *Ta chih tu lun* at T 25.215b5. For the full context see the note above at 123b8–9 under "the second renunciation." Chan-jan (BT–V, 349) adds that this refers to "a type of blue-green lotus flower."

realize that] it is not that you rely on the internal human bones or that these emit the eight colors, but when you cultivate these superior levels you may use an external condition, or you may not. Those who "do not [believe in the] destruction of dharmas" 不壞法人 [for their contemplation] naturally emit [the colors] internally, without relying on external objects.

Next, when the bodhisattva cultivates these superior levels, it includes all practices. If you do not have penetrating understanding of both your own person and environment, then you may arouse greed and stinginess. If you contemplate these things clearly, you will wish to abandon even your own body. How can you cling dearly to your material possessions, or covet the wealth of others? This is called [the perfection of] "giving" (*dāna*). By attaining this contemplation you are not tempted by wealth or [the attraction of] visible forms, or to break the precepts. Even if [there is the opportunity to] harm or kill a rich person and take his wealth for your own, or through a many-sided fraud gain all riches, you would never [abandon] your principles [and do such a thing]. This is [the perfection of keeping] the precepts 尸 (*vinaya*). When you attain this contemplation, even if you are disturbed and vexed by others, or are attacked, in the end you will not arouse anger, which would be like quarreling over defiled dung. This is called [the perfection of] patience. When your contemplation is perfected, you do not retrogress from a concentrated mind because of the impurity of a corpse or the impurity of the environment. This is called [the perfection of] diligence. When this contemplation includes all [the aspects of] contemplation, training, discipline, and cultivation, supranormal powers, transformations, vows, knowledge, and the summit [of concentration], this is called [the perfection of] dhyāna meditation. When you attain this contemplation, you realize that all subjective and objective dharmas are unobtainable, neither arise nor perish, and are ultimately pure. This is called [the perfection of] wisdom.

All the teachings of paths [of wisdom] and concentrations are transformed and perfected in these superior levels. The mind is concentrated and you have mastery over its turning and going and dwelling. You produce all Dharma teachings, and the mind follows them perfectly, like a nimble horse who breaks through the [enemy's] battle formation yet controls itself and stays steady. At this time the mind is clear and pure, with no demonic influences. The mind controls the demonic [influences] and the demons are not able to destroy the mind. If those who practice the Four Samādhis arouse these dharmas, many will turn and enter the five preliminary grades of the

Five preliminary grades of the disciple 五品弟子位: In the T'ien-t'ai scheme of the various stages on the path to Buddhahood, the five lowest or preliminary levels of practice and attainment (in the Perfect Teaching) for a disciple of the Buddha:

disciple. Why is this so? The power of the auxiliary practices of the path is great, and you are able to quickly approach the pure and cool pond [of enlightenment]. Equally you attain contemplative dhyāna 觀禪. Again, you arouse the marks of Mahāyāna dhyāna. As for the dhyāna [of the other three aspects] of training, discipline, and cultivation, ordinary ignorant people are not able to learn them, so I will not discuss their arising. If a separate [discussion is needed], it can be found in the sūtras and treatises, so I will not discuss it here.

7. The Arising of Compassion [124c27]

Seventh is to clarify the arising of compassion. A compassionate mind is at the beginning and end of the basic dhyāna. [Compassion means that when you] immediately come in contact with all sentient beings and perceive their marks of bliss, you do not get bitter or troubled, but have joyful thoughts in accordance with their intent; or, perceiving that they have attained bliss in the human realm, or perceiving that they have attained **[125a]** the bliss of the divine realm, through good cultivation you attain understanding and a lucid and concentrated mind, so that [you wish that] there is not even one sentient being who does not attain bliss. At the beginning you take small steps to attain a fine quietude, and later turn to a deep concentration. However, there are three types of coming in contact with objects [for a compassionate mind]. If you come in contact with [1.] intimate persons and [help them] obtain bliss, this is "vast"; [2.] if [in contact] with a middling [likable] person, this is called "great"; [3.] if [in contact] with a person you dislike, this [compassion] is "immeasurable." Again, coming in contact with sentient beings from one

appropriate joy 随喜品, reading and reciting of the sūtras 読誦品, preaching the Dharma 説法品, preliminary practice of the six perfections while practicing contemplation 兼行六度品, and the proper practice of the six perfections 正行六度品. The level of a practitioner before attaining the stage of "faith." This is the level claimed to have been attained by Chih-i.

Coming in contact with intimate persons ... this is immeasurable 若縁親人得樂名廣。中人名大。怨人名無量 ...: this whole section seems to be a summary of a passage in the *Ta chih tu lun* at T 25.209a29–b21. Chodron (3, 1066–68) translates:

"With a vast, expanded, immense mind." – This mind [of compassion, *maitrī*] is single, but as its magnitude differs, there are three attributive adjectives used.

This mind is vast *(vipula)* when it includes one single region, extended *(mahadgata)* when it goes far and high, immense *(apramāṇa)* when it includes the nadir *(adhastād diś)* and the other nine regions.

Furthermore, if it is low *(avara)*, *maitrī* is called vast *(vipula)*; middling *(madhya)*, it is called extended *(mahadgata)*; higher *(agra)*, it is called immense *(apra-māṇa)*.

Furthermore, if it bears upon the beings of the four main directions *(diś)*, *maitrī* is called vast *(vipula)*; if it bears upon the beings of the four intermediate directions *(vidiś)*, it is said to be extended

direction and obtaining bliss is called vast; with those of the four intermediate directions [of southeast, southwest, northeast, and northwest] is called "great"; with those of the ten directions is called "immeasurable."

This concentration [of compassion] is sometimes hidden and sometimes not hidden. If the mind comes in contact with sentient beings, it should be determined to produce thoughts of compassion; the mind should be exceedingly lucid; but if you do not perceive the obtaining of bliss by the sentient beings that are the object [of your compassion], this means that internally it is not hidden, even though externally it is hidden. Again, if internally the mind is clear and pure, and externally perceives the obtaining of bliss [by sentient beings through your compassion], then both internally and externally it is not hidden.

Suppose you first attain this concentration [of compassion], and then

(mahadgata); if it bears upon the beings of the zenith and the nadir, It is said to be immense *(apramāṇa)*.

Furthermore, if it destroys the minds of enmity *(vairacitta)*, *maitrī* is called vast *(vipula)*; if it destroys the minds of rivalry *(sapatnacitta)*, it is called extended *(mahadgata)*; if it destroys the minds of malice *(vyāvadhyacitta)* it is called immense *(apramāṇa)*.

Furthermore, all the defiled minds *(kliṣṭajñāna)* cultivated by vile individuals giving rise to evil things are called vile *(hīna)*. The most vile of them are enmity *(vaira)*, rivalry *(sapatnatā)* and malice *(vyāvadhya)*. Since *maitrī* destroys these vile minds, it is called vast *(vipula)*, extended *(mahadgata)* and immense *(apramāṇa)*. Why? Because great causes and conditions are necessary to destroy vile things. The "vast" mind *(vipulacitta)* that fears sin *(āpatti)*, that fears falling into hell, eliminates the bad dharmas from the mind; the "extended" mind *(mahadgatacitta)* that believes in the retribution of merits *(puṇyavipāka)* eliminates the bad thoughts; the "immense" mind *(apramāṇacitta)* that wants to attain nirvāṇa eliminates the bad thoughts.

Furthermore, when the yogin observes the purity of the discipline *(śīlaviśuddhi)*, this is a "vast" mind; when he is endowed with trance and absorption *(dhyāna-samāpattisaṃpanna)*, this is an "extended" mind; when he is endowed with wisdom *(prajñāsaṃpanna)*, this is an "immense" mind.

When the yogin, by means of this mind of loving-kindness *(maitrīcitta)*, thinks about the noble people *(āryapudgala)* who have found the Path, this is an "immense" mind because he is using immense means to distinguish these noble people. When he thinks about the noble abodes *(āvāsa)* of gods and men, this is an "extended" mind. When he thinks about lower beings *(hīnasattva)* and the three unfortunate *(durgati)* destinies, this is a "vast" mind.

When he thinks with loving-kindness about a being that is dear to him *(priyasattva)* and he extends this thought [to all dear beings], this is a "vast" mind. When he thinks with loving-kindness about people who are indifferent to him *(madhyastha puruṣa)*, this is an "extended" mind. When he thinks with loving-kindness about his enemies *(vaira)* and thus his merits *(guṇa)* are many, this is an "immense" mind.

The mind that bears upon a limited object is called "vast"; that which bears upon a small object is called "extended"; that which bears upon immensity is called "immense."

This is the meaning of these distinctions.

arouse the good qualities of the five [preliminary] constituents [of meditation of examination, reflection, joy, bliss, and single-minded concentration]. [1.] This means that at first you examine [and become aware of] 覺 all sentient beings, that all will attain bliss, that their thoughts and concentrations are merged, and your own mind is blissful, so that there is good cultivation [of the path] and attainment of understanding. This is called "the constituent of examination." [2.] You discriminate [through reflection] on the attainment of bliss, whether among humans or the gods above, so that the immeasurable discrepancy [in the amount of bliss] according to levels is clearly and fully known. This is called "the constituent of reflection." [3.] The hated and intimate [should be treated] equally [with compassion]; you should not fear what is hated, or be sorrowful over the suffering of your intimates. This is called "the constituent of joy." [4.] When the restlessness of the constituent of joy ceases, and the spirit of the mind rejoices, and the objects [of your compassion, that is, other sentient beings] attain the marks of bliss, this is called "the constituent of bliss." [5.] When your practice of concentration turns deep and profound, and you maintain a [concentrated] mind without moving, this is "the constituent of single-mindedness." These terms are the same as [those used in the context of] the basic [dhyāna], but they are different in the length of [maintaining] the flavor of the Dharma, as when honey is added to water, the coolness [of the water] is the same but the flavor is different. If you arouse only the first basic [dhyāna], you are limited to the rewards of Brahmā's assembly or the ministers of Brahmā, but if you attain the concentration of compassion your reward is [like that of] the Brahmā King; as the results are superior, the causes are also great. If you first attain the basic [dhyāna] and then later add the concentration of compassion, the benefits of the basic [dhyāna] becomes even more profound.

Again, if the concentration of compassion is aroused within the second dhyāna, the four constituents [of meditation] of inner purity[, joy, bliss, and single-mindedness] are perfected. Again, if it is aroused within the third dhyāna, bliss accompanied by the five constituents [of meditation] is perfected. Again, if aroused within the fourth dhyāna, each one [of the good qualities] correspond with all the dhyāna, including the [ten] constituent [virtuous qualities], so that the flavor of the Dharma doubles, as illustrated previously. However, a compassionate mind basically seeks conditions for others to attain bliss, so internally you experience blissful concentration, and

Ten constituent virtuous qualities 支林[功德]: these are outlined above at *Mo-ho chih-kuan* 119b3–7. The ten are: 1. empty 空; 2. clear 明; 3. stable or concentrated 定; 4. wisdom 智; 5. good mind 善心; 6. flexibility 柔軟; 7. joy 喜; 8. bliss 樂; 9. the realm of liberation 解脱境界; and 10. correspondance 相應.

externally you perceive the bliss of others. These features belong to the third dhyāna. At the fourth dhyāna you only perceive the attainment of bliss by others, and there is no internal experience of bliss [by oneself] because you have [dispassionately] abandoned both pain and pleasure [or "suffering and bliss"]. However, these sorts of distinctions are made for the sake of those of the Hīnayāna. The Buddha, at one time, in order to destroy attachments and in response to conditions, said "the merits of the mind of kindness *(maitrī)* lead to universal purity. The merits of the mind of compassion *(karuṇā)* lead to the place of emptiness. The merits of the mind of joy lead to the place of consciousness. The merits of the mind of abandonment lead to the place of no functioning." However, bodhisattvas are constantly accompanied by kindness and compassion; at what stage are they without kindness and compassion? Kindness and compassion permeate all good things; how could it be limited only to the [first] three dhyāna? [To say that bliss or compassion is missing in the fourth dhyāna] is only one way of speaking. If first you arouse the [four] basic [dhyāna] and then later the concentration of compassion, it is also the same. However, for those with a dark **[125b]** enlightenment, this remains hidden [both internally and externally], or, even if the internal is hidden, the external is hidden, and so forth.

If you arouse the concentration of kindness through the superior meditations or the [six] supranormal powers and [ten] insights, the concentration on which you rely is, on it's own, one extreme, and the kindness that relies on [the concentration] arises without overflowing. This concentration [of kindness] already includes the contemplation of compassion, and the concentration of kindness is not hidden, and the flavor of the Dharma of the five constituents are doubly superior to that of the basic [dhyāna].

Or, if the cause of the concentration of kindness is aroused by the superior

The merits of the mind of compassion ... place of no functioning 慈心福至遍淨。悲心福至空處。喜心福至識處。捨心福至不用處: a summary of a long passage in the *Abhidharma-vibhāṣā-śāstra* at T 28.324b8–c25 that begins:

> The Buddha explains in a sūtra that a broad cultivation of the mind of kindness is rewarded with an unmistaken universal purity; a broad cultivation of the mind of compassion is rewarded with an unmistaken place of emptiness; a broad cultivation of the mind of joy is rewarded with an unmistaken place of consciousness; a broad cultivation of the mind of abandonment is rewarded with an unmistaken place of non-existence 無所有處....

The concentration on which you rely ... arises without overflowing 所依之定自是一邊能依之慈附起不濫: see Ikeda (*Gendaigoyaku*, 621), based on commentary in the *Kōgi* (BT–V, 357), who gives a very loose translation of this ambiguous passage: "The marks of this concentration are not the same as the basic dhyāna, and the arising of the concentration of compassion is also different."

meditations and the powers and insights, this concentration of kindness is also not hidden, and the flavor of dhyāna-meditation is also profound.

Or, the concentration of compassion is the cause for arousing [contemplation of] minor and great impurity, [Question: The contemplation of] impurity involves destructive features for sentient beings, so sentient beings should not take this as the object [of contemplation]. Who would attain bliss [from this contemplation]? [Answer:] Although there is no bliss for sentient beings within the realm of defiled passions, there is bliss in nirvana [as a result of contemplating impurities]. This is the arousing of "compassion based on awareness of [the true nature of] phenomena."

Question: Kind compassion has as its object the marks of purity of sentient beings, and without anger or affliction focuses on their likable features; the contemplation of impurity [of a corpse] focuses on the [physical] destruction of sentient beings and their bad features. How can these arise together?

Answer: There is no hindrance here. Suppose you perceive impurity [such as an undisciplined and debauched person]; this does not hinder you from also perceiving a pure person with proper posture and attire. Again, even if you give rise to the concentration of kindness, this does not hinder [one from seeing] impurity. The concentration of kindness is a grand adornment for the [eight] renunciations and so forth, and lead to a doubling of the depth of good qualities, so it is superior to just arousing [the contemplation of] impurity. Or, they can arise one after the other, and so forth. The other three boundless demeanors also arise mutually, and should be known in accordance with [the explanation of] the concentration of kind compassion.

If the four boundless demeanors arise along with the basic dhyāna, this gives rise to defilement [from passions]. If they arise along with the superior meditations and the [six] powers and [three] insights, this gives rise to both defilement and non-defilement. If they arise along with [the contemplation of] impurity, this gives rise to non-defilement [from passions]. The causes and conditions are not the same, so the concentrations of kindness and so forth can be deep or shallow. There can be hundreds or thousands or millions of different types, such that they cannot all be explained. For example, it is like the visible forms of the four elements in the realm of desires produce various landscapes which are not the same [in their combination of] blue, yellow, red, and white, high or low, and so forth, producing various kinds of trees, grasses, and fruits that are sweet, bitter, spicy, or sour, medicinal or

The other three boundless demeanors 餘三無量心: that is, of the four immeasurable states of mind 四無量心 other than kindness (*maitrī*): that of compassion (*karuṇā*), joy (*muditā*), and abandonment or equanimity (*upekṣa*).

poisonous, fragrant or stinky; producing various people who are upright or mean, intelligent or dull, poor or rich, good or bad; producing various types of beasts, with hair or horns, which fly or run. In this way there is no limit to variety and differences, and yet there is no confusion. Each follows after their own nature in accordance with their own powers and abilities. It is like people with meagre fortune subside only on tares and millet, and cannot believe that there are such things as sugar cane and fruit such as peaches and grapes. The pure phenomena of the realm of visible form is also like this. The transformations of the [ten] constituent [virtuous qualities] all have various flavors of kind compassion, and though they mix with each other they are not convoluted.

In this way the four boundless demeanors [or immeasurable states of mind] are also vast and great. Why is this so? Sentient beings are immeasurable, and therefore conceiving their attainment of bliss is also immeasurable. Phenomena are immeasurable so the phenomena that is involved in the arising of the constituents [of virtuous qualities] is also immeasurable and cannot be calculated. Sentient beings with meagre merit cannot believe in [the beneficial results of] dhyāna meditation. They may believe in one Dharma teaching, but cannot believe in the immeasurable virtuous qualities [that result from such practice]. It is like [the rustic] people to the east of Mount Taihua who are not conscious of various delicacies, and the frog in the well which cannot comprehend the god [and vastness] of the ocean, and thus are greatly to be pitied. People who can believe know that the noble realm [of enlightenment] **[125c]** is difficult to comprehend, but you should never slander it.

8. The Arising of Causes and Conditions [125c1]

Eighth is clarifying the arising of causes and conditions. When a practitioner has great meritorious deeds, the Buddhas bestow the samādhi of dhyānic concentration, and due to conditions from past lives the concentrations of causes and conditions 因緣定 arise from beginning to end. While you are sitting [in meditation], you should directly ponder the objects [of conditions] that appear in the mind. Some objects or conditions will be good thoughts; some objects or conditions will be bad thoughts. Both the subject and object of conditions are part of the constituent of existence 有支 [as in

People to the east of Mount Taihua: lit. "to the left of the mountain" 山左, which Chan-jan (BT–V, 361) explains as "to the east of Tai-hua shan 太華山, where people do not know the various delicacies available in the Capital [of Xi'an]." Currently, this area is the province Shānxī 山西. Mount Taihua is one of the five sacred Taoist mountains in China, located about 120 kilometers east of Xi'an.

the twelvefold chain of dependent co-arising]. "Existence" involves results, and this "existence" is due to grasping 取. Because the mind grasps [dualistic concepts such as] "good" and "evil," there is "existence." If you do not grasp [these dualistic concepts], there is no "existence." Therefore you should know that "existence" comes from the arising of grasping. Also, you should know that grasping leads to the arising of passionate attachments 愛, and that there is grasping because of passionate attachments, like one who is passionately attached to visible forms and grasps after them until death. If there are no passionate attachments, there is no grasping. Passionate attachments cause the arising of sensations 受, and the acceptance of the sensations of good and evil lead to the arising of passionate attachments. If there is no acceptance of these sensations, then there is no arising of passionate attachments. Again, if you contemplate sensations as arising from contact 触, [you will see that] because of the contact of the six sense objects with the six sense organs, there is the sensation of "existence." If there is no "contact," there is no sensation. A sūtra says, "The causes and conditions of the six types of contact [of the six senses] gives rise to the sensations"; thus sensations are due to contact. Again, you should know that [sensual] contact is due to the various [six] sense gate-entrances 入門. If there were no six sense consciousnesses to control the six sense organs, you would not be able to traverse and enter the [sense] objects and give rise to contact. Thus contact is due to [sense] entrances, and sense entrances rely on name-and-form 名色. If there was only [external] visible form [and no sense organs or consciousness to experience it], then there could be no contact with visible form, like the case of a dead person. If there were only name-and-form, there could be no contact with such "names," like the case of a blind and deaf person. It is through the

Twelvefold chain of dependent co-arising: in this paragraph Chih-i works his way backwards through the twelve linked aspects of causation: ignorance 無明, volitional activity 行, consciousness 識, name-and-form 名色, the six senses 六入, contact 觸, experience/sensation 受, passion 愛, grasping 取, existence 有, rebirth 生, and decay-and-death 老死.

A sūtra says, "The causes and conditions of the six types of contact gives rise to the sensations" 六觸因縁生諸受故受由於觸: the *Miscellaneous Āgama* has a passage at T 2.50a:

Thus have I heard. At one time the Buddha dwelt in Jetavana grove in Śrāvastī. At that time the World Honored One said to the monks, "All things are transient. What is meant by 'all things'? The eye is transient. If color has visual contact with visual consciousness, then the causes and conditions of visual contact give rise to sensations. Whether suffering or bliss, or not suffering nor bliss, this is transient. The same is so for the ears, nose, tongue, body, and consciousness. If a dharma has mental contact with mental consciousness, the causes and conditions of mental contact gives rise to sensations. Whether suffering or bliss, or not suffering nor bliss, this is transient..."

merging of [external] visible form and [internal] mind that there is [sensual] contact. "Visible form" is the [first] aggregate (*skandha*) of "visible form" (*rupa*), and the "mind" refers to the other four aggregates [of consciousness, sensations, conceptions, and volitions]. It is the "aggregate of consciousness" 識陰 that makes distinctions concerning these visible forms, and that which receives them is called the "aggregate of sensations" 受陰. Volitional activity 行 arouses greed and anger, which belong to the two aggregates of conceptions 想 and volition 行. It is because of the coming together of the five aggregates that there is the experience of [sensory] contact. Therefore you should know that [sensory] contact is [ultimately] due to [the conventional existence of things with] name-and-form.

The name-and-form [of a human being] is due to the beginning of a consciousness entrusted to the womb. When first entrusted to the womb, this is called *kalala*. At this time it is endowed with three things: 1. life; 2. warmth; and 3. consciousness. Within these are the winds of karmic recompense 報風 and the winds of reliance [on the environment] 依風; this is called "life." The semen and blood neither smell nor fester; this is called "warmth." Within is mental activity 心意; this is called "consciousness." Due to a consciousness entrusted to the womb, there is a congealing of curds and thin cream, then an expansion of six blisters [or swellings], and the name-and-form [mind and body] merge. It should be known that name-and-form [mind and body] are not due to consciousness. Consciousness is due to karmic activity. If, in the past, one has kept the five precepts [of a basic moral life] and performed good deeds, karma will lead you to receive the name-and-form of a human being; if, in the past, you abandoned keeping the five precepts and performed evil deeds, karma will lead you to receive [rebirth in] the three evil destinies. Therefore you should know that consciousness is due to karma, and karma is [due to] volitional activity. Volitional activity is due to ignorance, delusion, and passionate attachments, which produce various volitional actions and lead the consciousness to transmigrate. From the past to the present, the current passions and attachments are the conditions for existence; existence contains the results that invite [the cycle of] birth and death in the future. The causes and conditions of the three times [of past, present, and future] are empty and without a substantial subject [or self].

When you ponder in this way and arouse contemplative wisdom, you

***Kalala* 歌羅邏**: the first week of the fetus in the womb. These ideas concerning the development of the fetus and the stages of human life have been outlined previously; see the context and notes at *Mo-ho chih-kuan* 52c27–29.

Six blisters [or swellings] 六皰: which develop into the head, body, two hands, and two feet. There is also a category of "twenty-four limbs, or blisters" that refers to the eyes, ears, nose, mouth, and twenty fingers and toes.

will destroy the mistaken imputation of a human self, your mind of concentration will quietly advance from [**126a**] crude to subtle, and the incomplete [concentrations] of the realm of desires [and so forth] up to the basic [four] dhyānas and five constituents of virtuous qualities will gradually arise. To examine and be aware of the emptiness of causes and conditions, that there is no subject [or self], is the constituent of examination. [To reflect that all things] transmigrate through the past, present, and future while mutually relying on each other, and to know this clearly without differentiation, is the constituent of examination. Attaining the wisdom of causes and conditions and profoundly knowing the past, present, and future, how can you not rejoice? This is the constituent of joy. To maintain the mind on the practice of concentration so that your joy is beautiful and subtle: this is called the constituent of bliss. For the concentrated mind to naturally be without conditions [or objects] and without thoughts: this is called the constituent of single-mindedness. This is the samādhi of [realizing the truth concerning] causes and conditions, which is the nature of wisdom. Because of this clarity of wisdom, you arouse the basic [dhyāna]. Or, basic [dhyāna] and [the realization of] causes and conditions mutually merge, and the flavor of the Dharma is pure and rich, and not the same as when you arouse only the five constituents [of virtuous qualities].

This samādhi of [realizing the truth concerning] causes and conditions is sometimes hidden and sometimes not hidden. If in your inner mind you understand only the Dharma of causes and conditions, and do not arouse the perversion of [grasping on to] a substantial self, this corresponds to only [realizing] the basic dhyānas. This understanding is "dark," so it is called "hidden." If, when this samādhi arises, your mind is clear and pure, you can perceive the *kalala* [fetus in the first week], the expansion of the five swellings [into human form], the place where it will be born and dwell, and also perceive good and evil karmic activity, and likable and ugly actions. Again, you can perceive the future [cycles of] birth and death, clearly distinguishing matters of the past, present, and future; these are aspects that are not hidden. However, these two matters [of hidden and non-hidden] all have the ten [virtuous] qualities of emptiness, clarity[, and so forth]; therefore it is said that the basic dhyānas arise due to [realizing] causes and conditions. The arising of the superior meditations, [six] powers and [three] insights, the renunciations, and so forth, are also likewise [both] hidden and not hidden and arise due to [realizing] causes and conditions.

The basic dhyānas can be the cause of arising [the contemplation and realization] of causes and conditions. Immediately within the concentrations, you ponder that the concentrations of the basic dhyānas all arise through causes and conditions, that things that arise through causes and conditions and that which brought about the causes and conditions makes up what is "existent." This [existence] includes both crude and fine abodes, including the existence of Yama and Tuṣita heavens.

If there is birth, there will certainly be death. The concentrations of the realm of desires also exist through causes and conditions; this existence contains the fruits that should lead to being transformed and reborn in a blissful heaven, but even if you are **born** 生 [in the heavens], there will [eventually] be **death** 死. The incompletely attained concentrations also exist through causes and conditions, and this existence contains the fruits that should lead to demonic or heavenly existence. Again, corresponding with the first dhyāna contains [the fruits of] this existence, and so forth up to and including the [concentrations of] "neither conceptions nor non-conceptions." In this way "**existence**" 有 is all due to "**grasping**" 取. "Grasping" [and becoming attached] to the marks of the first dhyāna was explained previously along with the twenty-five preparatory means. You have various hopes, and so grasp on to their various marks and features; therefore you should know that existence is due to grasping. Grasping, in turn, is due to **passionate attachments** 愛; through hearing people speak of the virtuous qualities of the first dhyāna, you give birth to the flavor of passionate attachments. Again, know that these passionate attachments are due to [the experience of] **sensations** 受; by hearing of their virtuous qualities you come under the control of these sensations, and arouse passionate attachments. Again, you should know that these sensations are due to the **sense entrances** 入, and these sense entrances are the [six sense] organs. Without the sense organs, no sensations will enter. Sensations are also due to **contact** 觸; because there is contact with the dustlike objects [of the senses], there is "entry" [of the sensations]. Contact is due to **name-and-form** [mind and body] 名色; The five skandhas [of physical and mental aggregates] merge, and therefore there is contact. Name-and-form [body and mind] are due to the three matters [of life, warmth, and consciousness] at the beginning of **consciousness** 識; these three matters are due to [the **volitional activity** of] karma, which in the future receives a body. Karma is due to **ignorance** 無明 **[126b]**, which leads to

Yama and Tuṣita heavens 炎魔兜率天: Yama could refer to the lord and judge of the realm of the dead, or to the third of the six heavens of the realm of desire. Tuṣita is the next, or fourth, of the six heavens. This is where the "next Buddha" dwells before being reborn in our world to become a Buddha; currently occupied by Maitreya.

If you are born, there will be death 生則有死 ...: again in this paragraph Chih-i works his way backwards through the twelvefold chain of dependent causation, from death and birth to existence, grasping, passion, and so forth finally to ignorance.

Explained previously along with the twenty-five preparatory means 如前二十五方便中: see the earlier section of the *Mo-ho chih-kuan* at 48a.

existence, giving rise to [the rest of the twelvefold chain] from consciousness to old-age-and-death.

Thus from the top [concentration of] neither conceptions [nor non-conceptions], to the bottom crude stages [of concentrations], all involve knowing about the twelvefold [chain of] causes and conditions, comprehending each and every one clearly. This includes the superior meditations, the [six] powers and [three] insights, and so forth, which can be the cause for arousing the [four] basic [dhyāna]. Each should be known [as explained above].

This contemplation [of causes and conditions] already destroys the perversion of [assuming] a substantial Self, just as the skillful teachings with regard to the [eighteen sense] realms [of the six sense objects, six sense organs, and six sense consciousnesses] destroy the idea of the "Self" in the same way. We rely only on a dhyāna sūtra for the term "the samādhi of causes and conditions." Although investigating [the causes and conditions] of the past, present, and future is the nature of wisdom, this is also called "putting the mind at rest." Attaining a restful dwelling of the mind is like being in a closed room with no wind, where you can produce the [four] contemplations of mindfulness [of body, sensation, mind, and dharma]. The perfection of the contemplations of mindfulness is called "wisdom through hearing" [the Dharma]. "Wisdom through hearing is the principle of contemplation. [In the *Mahāparinirvāṇa Sūtra*] Punya apprehended [the Dharma] and said "I finally understand and finally know." [The Buddha said,] "What is it that you know?" [Punya answered, "If you know [the truth about] ignorance, then grasping for existence does not arise." This is the meaning of "the wisdom of hearing [the Dharma]." This contemplation of causes and conditions

Rely only on a dhyāna sūtra 但依禪經: the *Kōgi* comments that "Having examined all of the dhyāna sūtras, this phrase is not found; one should look further."

Putting the mind at rest 停心: see the Glossary for "five contemplations for putting the mind at rest" 五停心觀; to put the mind at rest through compassion, counting your breaths, meditating on conditioned co-arising, meditating on impurities, and being mindful of the Buddha.

Punya apprehended ... 富那領解: Punya appears in the *Mahāparinirvāṇa Sūtra* at T 12.844c18–845b9, but the passage on understanding ignorance and not producing grasping and ignorance appears in the next section at 845b14–c5; see especially b23–c1:

> [The Buddha said,] "Good son, if a person abandons [attachments] and does not produce new karma, that person is able to know what is transient and not transient." The Brahman said, "I already know and perceive [these things]." The Buddha said, "Good son, What is it that you know?" [He answered:] "What was called 'ignorance' and 'passionate afflictions,' is newly called 'grasping' and 'existence.' If a person is far separated from ignorance and passionate attachments, he will not produce grasping and existence. That person truly knows what is transient and not transient."

comes before the mindfulnesses, and does not have its power, and therefore it corresponds to "practical contemplation" [in contrast to the principle of contemplation].

This gate [or teaching] of causes and conditions is not the same with regard to the capacities [of the listener or practitioner]. The *Ying-lo ching* clarifies ten types, and *The Great Collection of Sūtras* clarifies [the idea of] results and retributions in a single thought.

There are various masters who have transmitted [their teachings] throughout the three times [of the past, present, and future]. Nāgārjuna produced the *Middle Treatise*, and the first chapter clarified "causes and conditions." A master of [this] treatise says that this [teaching of causes and conditions] does not exhaustively include the [Buddha-]Dharma, and that [the idea of] causes and conditions is not the gist [of the Buddha's teachings]. This is only the worldly truth; exhaustively destroying [the idea of substantiality behind] causes and conditions is the real truth. Therefore the two truths are the gist [of the Buddha's teachings]. But now I say, which topic is not deconstructed exhaustively by the worldly truth? This is a general interpretation 通, and not the specific 別 intent [of the *Middle Treatise*]. The *Treatise* first gives a general [analysis of] the contemplation of causes and conditions, and in the chapter on defilements specifically deconstructs the constituents of passionate attachments and grasping. The chapter on the six senses specifically deconstructs the constituent of suffering. And so forth, such as the two last chapters that specifically discuss the contemplation of

The *Ying-lo ching* clarifies ten types 瓔珞明十種: see the passage at T 24.1015a22–28, which gives ten types of "twelvefold causality" 十二緣, that of 1. the mistaken view of the self 我見十二緣; 2. mental activity 心爲十二緣; 3. ignorance 無明十二緣; 4. conditioned by marks 相緣由十二緣; 5. arising of grasping 助成十二緣; 6. three types of karma (of word, thought, and deed) 三業十二緣; 7. three times [of past, present, and future] 三世十二緣; 8. three sufferings 三苦十二緣; 9. the nature of emptiness 性空十二緣; and 10. arousing bonds 縛生十二緣.

***The Great Collection of Sūtras* clarifies results and retributions in a single thought** 大集明果報一念: see the passage at T 13.164a10–11, which contains the phrase "In this way the twelvefold [chain of] causes and conditions are all included in a single thought of one person."

Nāgārjuna produced the *Middle Treatise*, and the first chapter clarified "causes and conditions." 龍樹作中論初明因緣品: see the opening chapter of the *Middle Treatise* at T 30b11–3c16.

A master of this treatise 論師: the identity of this master is unknown.

The chapter on defilements 染染品: see chapter six of the *Middle Treatise* at T 30.8a14–c22.

The chapter on the six senses 六情品: see the third chapter of the *Middle Treatise* at T 30.5c15–b17.

Two last chapters 後兩品: see the twenty-sixth chapter of the *Middle Treatise* on "Contemplating twelvefold causes

causes and conditions by the śrāvakas. Thus there are general and specific meanings, but all concern the contemplation of causes and conditions. How can it be said that [the teaching of] "causes and conditions" is not the gist [of the Buddha's teaching]? A master of the north takes the meaning of salvation in the final chapters, with six causes and four conditions, to be the gist [of the teachings], but this concerns only causes and conditions as arising and perishing [which is the perspective of the Tripitaka Teachings]. The meaning of the last two chapters is not the true gist of this *Treatise*. After the Buddha left this world, the faculties of the people who followed turned dull; they grasped and became attached to a fixed interpretation of [the teaching of] causes and conditions, and did not understand the intent of the Buddha. Therefore this [*Middle*] *Treatise* was composed to clarify the teaching of contemplating the twelvefold [chain of] causes and conditions.

1. The Ten Modes of Contemplation in Terms of Causes and Conditions [126b23–129b25]

Now I have already [explained] the teachings of arousing [the contemplation of] causes and conditions, and so I will now explain in terms of clarifying cessation-and-contemplation, with the usual ten meanings [of the ten modes of contemplation].

1. Objects as conceivable and inconceivable [126b23]

[Contemplating] objects as "conceivable" is as follows: Ignorance from the past in the mind produces "black" karma 黒業 [evil deeds] so that you cannot do good actions, and you are consigned to the three [evil] destinies. If you produce "white" karma 白業 [good deeds] or nonpropelling karma 不動業 [neither negative nor positive deeds], you will be consigned to the three good destinies. If you convert ignorance into a clear insight into the arising and perishing [of causes and conditions], this is called "the contemplation of inferior wisdom" attained with the *bodhi*-wisdom of the śrāvakas. If you convert defiled [passionate] actions into transworldly auxiliary practices of the Path, there are seven types of learners with residual karma that is not yet exhausted, but who are yet able to be born in a good destiny. If those with no more to learn still have a passionate attachment to undefiled karmic deeds

and conditions" and the twenty-seventh chapter on "Contemplating mistaken views" at T 30.36b17–39b29.

A master of the north 北師: the identity of this master is unknown.

Contemplation of inferior wisdom 下智觀: see the *Mahāparinirvāṇa Sūtra* at T 12.768c12–18. The four kinds of wisdom (inferior, middling, superior, and most supreme) with regard to twelvefold causes and conditions has appeared previously. See the *Mo-ho chih-kuan* at 5c24–27.

and attachment for the real truth, and still are imbued with fundamental ignorance, they can be born in the "land where skillful means remain" and experience that name-and-form [body and mind], give rise to passionate attachments [**126c**] and hate, and arouse a grasping for existence [or, "grasping and existence"]. This is the realm of the śrāvakas.

If you turn ignorance into a clear insight with regard to non-arising and non-perishing [of causes and conditions], this is a middling wisdom attained through the *bodhi*-wisdom of a pratyekabuddha. The *Sūtra on Petitioning Avalokiteśvara* says, "Contemplating twelvefold causes and conditions as [empty] like a dream, an illusion, or a banana tree, you realize the path of the pratyekabuddha." This is the meaning here. You convert defiled [passionate] actions to undefiled [practices] with the auxiliary steps on the path, and the exhaustion and non-exhaustion of the bonds of karma are the same as above. This is the realm of the pratyekabuddha.

If you convert ignorance into *prajñā*-wisdom, and convert activity that is not good into the other five perfections, but have not yet aroused the true [realization of emptiness], you will be endowed with [the understanding of] twelvefold causes and conditions within this world, which is the realm of [the Tripitaka bodhisattvas of] the six perfections.

If you convert ignorance into the wisdom of emptiness, and convert your actions to the six perfections, but have not yet exhausted and severed the delusions up to the sixth or seventh [bodhisattva] *bhūmi* stage, you are the same as in the previous [stages]. But one who exhaustively severs [the delusions] is born here [in the realm of the bodhisattva], with somewhat superior merits and wisdom. This is called "the contemplation of middling wisdom" attained through *bodhi*-wisdom [of bodhisattvas] of the Shared Teachings.

If you convert ignorance to a clear insight [into causes and conditions] gradually, converting your actions through a graded and specific practice, you have not yet exhaustively severed [the delusions of] the ten stages of "faith" and "abodes" 十信住, but exhaustively sever them at the ten stages of "practice" and "[merit] transference" 十行向, which are all the same as the

***Sūtra on Petitioning Avalokiteśvara* …** 請觀音云觀十二因緣如夢幻芭蕉成緣覺道: see the passage at T 20.37a18–21:

> Contemplating [twelvefold causes and conditions from] ignorance and volitional activity up to old-age-and-death, each and every nature and mark is [seen to be] unreal, like the emptiness of an echo in the valley, like a banana tree that has no real trunk, like the heat of a flame, like the actions of a horse in the wild, like the Gandharva spirits, like bubbles on the water, like an illusion, like a magic trick, like dew, and like a flash of lightning. Precisely contemplating each and every one of the twelvefold causes and conditions leads to realizing the path of the pratyekabuddha.

previous [stages]. This is called "the contemplation of superior wisdom," and therefore you attain the *bodhi*-wisdom of [the bodhisattva of] the Distinct Teachings.

Objects as inconceivable [126c12]

[As for the contemplation of objects as inconceivable,] if you convert ignorance into the clear insight of the Buddha's wisdom, from the first aspiration [to enlightenment] you know the twelvefold causes and conditions as threefold Buddha nature. If you penetratingly contemplate twelvefold causes and conditions as they truly are in reality, this is Buddha nature as the "direct cause" [of Buddhahood]. Contemplating twelvefold causes and conditions as wisdom is the Buddha nature as the "completing cause." Contemplating twelvefold [causes and] conditions in the mind while being endowed with all practices is Buddha nature as the "conditional causes" [of Buddhahood].

If you contemplate [each of the aspects of twelvefold causes and conditions] distinctly or specifically, [the aspects of] ignorance, passion, and grasping correspond to "Buddha nature as completing cause." [The aspects of] volitional activity and existence correspond to "Buddha nature as conditional causes." The seven constituents of consciousness and so forth [that is, name-and-form, the six senses, contact, sensation, birth, and old-age-and-death] correspond to "Buddha nature as direct cause." Why is this so? The path of suffering is this samsaric cycle of birth-and-death, but this body of [birth-and-]death is transformed into a Dharma body. Passionate afflictions are "dark" phenomena, but ignorance is transformed into clear insight 轉無明為明. Karmic actions are dharmas of bondage, but bonds are transformed into liberation. Thus the three paths [of suffering, passionate afflictions, and karma] are [transformed into] the three virtuous qualities [of Dharma body, *prajñā*-wisdom, and liberation]. The cause is that [these qualities are already inherent] in your nature, being neither vertical nor horizontal, like [the three

Threefold Buddha nature 三佛性: the three causes for attaining Buddhahood. The potential to attain Buddhahood, analyzed as having three aspects: the "direct cause" 正因, that all beings are endowed with the nature of Buddhahood by their participation in reality; the "completing cause" 了因, the wisdom that illumines this nature; and "the conditional causes" 緣因, the practices or conditions that bring about wisdom. For details, see my essay on "T'ien-t'ai Chih-i's concept of threefold Buddha nature: A synergy of reality, wisdom, and practice," 1990 (171–80).

The path of suffering 苦道: part of the circular "threefold path" 三道 of our samsaric existence in which illusion and passionate afflictions lead to karma, karma leads to suffering, and suffering leads to illusion and passionate afflictions.

Neither vertical not horizontal 不縱不橫: an image used by Chih-i to describe the symmetry and unity of various threefold concepts, such as the threefold truth, the three virtues of a Buddha, and so forth.

parts of the Siddham] letter "i" [∴]. This is called the Nirvana of three virtuous qualities. The *Vimalakirti [Sūtra]* says that all sentient beings are [indivisible] from Great Nirvana, from the Buddha, and from *bodhi*-wisdom; this is the meaning here. This is called "the contemplation of the most supreme wisdom" and the attainment of the *bodhi*-wisdom of the Buddha.

If you are at the five preliminary levels but have not yet severed [all delusions], you are the same level as that of the learners; if at the level of the copper *cakravartin,* long separated from the sea of suffering, you are at the same level as those with no more to learn. But even though you are again physically reborn with the five sense organs [in this samsaric world] in a transformation beyond conceptual understanding, your merits are far different [from those of the two vehicles]. The *Ta chi tu lun* says that those of the two vehicles experience the body of Dharma-nature, but their faculties are dark and dull, because they have taken a circuitous way to the Buddha Path. Those of the Distinct and Perfect [Teachings] are able to destroy ignorance and directly open the path of suffering to the true dharmas as they truly are and attain true reward; directly within your actions and existence be endowed with all practices; intuitively attain [understanding of] your body and environment without any obstacles; having sharp faculties and profound merits, not the same as those of middling **[127a]** and inferior [faculties].

Those at the three levels of erudition and ten noble stages dwell in their karmic reward, having perfectly realized these twelvefold causes and condi-

Siddham letter "i": the three-yet-one pattern of the letter; see text and notes at *Mo-ho chih-kuan*, 23a20.

All sentient beings are … 一切衆生卽大涅槃卽是佛卽是菩提: see the phrase in the *Vimalakīrti Sūtra*, T 14.542b 16–17: "All sentient beings are [indivisible] with the mark of *bodhi*-wisdom."

***Ta chih tu lun* says that those of the two vehicles …** 二乘受法性身諸根闇鈍以其於佛道紆迴故: see the passage at T 25.580a14–25. However, it should be noted that this passage discusses two types of bodhisattvas, not "those of the two vehicles" per se:

> There are two types of bodhisattvas: 1. those with a fleshly samsaric body and 2. those with the body of Dharma-nature, who attain the forbearance of non-arising, having severed all passionate afflictions, and having abandoned this [physical] body attain the body of Dharma-nature.
>
> Those with a fleshly body who have attain the level of non-retrogression (*avaivartika*) again are of two types. There are those who, in front of the Buddha, attain the prophecy [of eventual Buddhahood], and those who do not receive the prophecy in front of the Buddha. If one attains the forbearance of non-arising when the Buddha is not present in the world, this is one who does not receive the prophecy in front of the Buddha.…

Three levels of erudition and ten noble stages dwell in their karmic reward 三賢十聖: this phrase is found in the *Jen-wang ching*, T 8.828a1: "those of the three levels of erudition and ten noble stages dwell in their karmic reward, but only the Buddha alone dwells in the Pure Land."

tions. Those [whose attainment is] equivalent to awakening have only one life remaining within [the realm of] causes and conditions. [Those who attain] the final [subtle awakening of a Buddha] have reached the limit and ultimately exhausted the basis of ignorance as well as passionate attachments and grasping; therefore this is called ultimate *prajñā*-wisdom. The seven fruits of [the constituents of] consciousness and so forth [that is, name-and-form, the six senses, contact, sensation, birth, and old-age-and-death] are exhausted; therefore this is called the ultimate Dharma body. Volitional activity and existence are exhausted; therefore this is called ultimate liberation. Although it is said to be "exhaustively severed," there is no thing to be severed, so this is an inconceivable severance. Not severing ignorance, passionate attachments, and grasping, you enter perfectly pure nirvana 圓淨涅槃. Not severing the seven constituents [of twelvefold causes and conditions such as] name-and-form, you enter nirvana of the nature of purity 性淨涅槃. Not severing [the duality of] good and evil of volitional activity and existence, you enter the nirvana of purity of skillful means 方便淨涅槃. The *Vimalakīrti [Sūtra]* says that "with the marks of the five heinous offences you attain liberation; again, there is no bondage and no liberation." From this perspective you could say that the twelvefold causes and conditions are indivisible from all, immeasurable, Buddha Dharmas. This is called "the objects [of causes and conditions] as inconceivable."

Next, the correspondence of the twelvefold causes and conditions with the ten suchlikes of the *Lotus Sūtra* is as follows: "Suchlike nature" corresponds to ignorance. The *Vimalakīrti [Sūtra]* says that if you know the nature of ignorance, you know the nature of enlightenment. "Suchlike appearance" corresponds to "volitional activity." [Suchlike] essence corresponds to the seven constituents of "consciousness" and so forth. [Suchlike] power corresponds to passionate attachments and grasping. [Suchlike] activity corresponds to the causes of existence. [Suchlike] causes refers to the [habitual] repetitive causes of ignorance, passionate attachments, and grasping. [Suchlike] conditions corresponds to volitional activity and existence.

With the marks of the five heinous offences ... 以五逆相而得解脱亦不縛不脱: the phrase is found in the *Vimalakīrti Sūtra*, T 14.540b25, except that it ends with "no liberation and no bondage."

Ten suchlikes 十如: the ten "suchlike" characteristics of reality, based on Kumarajīva's translation of the *Lotus Sūtra*: suchlike appearances 相, nature 性, essence 體, power 力, activity 作, causes 因, conditions 緣, results 果, recompense 報, and "beginning and end ultimately equal" 本末究竟等. See the *Lotus Sūtra*, T 9.5c11–13.

If you know the nature of ignorance, you know the nature of enlightenment 若知無明性即是明性: the phrase as found in the *Vimalakīrti Sūtra*, T 14.551a16, goes: "The true nature of ignorance is enlightenment" 無明實性即是明.

[Suchlike] results correspond to the repetitive results where ignorance gives rise to wisdom. [Suchlike] reward corresponds to the five types of nirvana [that arise] from volitional activity and existence. [Suchlike] beginning corresponds to the three paths [of suffering, passionate afflictions, and karma] and threefold Buddha nature. [Suchlike] end corresponds to the nirvana of the three good qualities [of Dharma-body, *prajñā*-wisdom, and liberation].

Next, the correspondence [of the twelvefold causes and conditions] with the ten realms [from hell to Buddha] is as follows. The ten dharma realms as consisting of sense aggregates and sense entrances, and with regard to disease, correspond to the seven constituents [of the twelvefold causes and conditions] of consciousness and so forth. [The ten dharma realms as consisting of] passionate afflictions, mistaken views, pride, and so forth correspond to [the constituents of] ignorance, passionate attachments, and grasping. [The ten dharma realms consisting of] karma, demonic forces, dhyāna, the two vehicles, and bodhisattvas correspond to the constituents of volitional activity and existence.

Next, if the twelvefold causes and conditions, ten suchlikes, and ten realms are differentiated within the mind, this is [the understanding of] arising and perishing as conceivable. If they are [included] in one thought in the mind, this is [the understanding of] neither-arising-nor-perishing as inconceivable. The *Avataṃsaka Sūtra* says that twelvefold causes and conditions exist in one thought in the mind. *The Great Collection of Sūtras* says, "Twelvefold causes and conditions are all included in a single thought of one person." This text [here] is just a summary [of this meaning]. If you say that all the ten [dharma] realms, the ten suchlikes, and the twelvefold causes and conditions are all without exception included in a single thought of one person, this should be called the Mahāyāna, inconceivable [understanding of] twelvefold causes and conditions.

Question: In the *Treatise on Twelve Subjects* it says, "Conditioned phenomena in reality do not arise. If we were to say that they arise, do they exist in one thought, or do they exist in many thoughts." How can you say that they exist in one thought 一念?

Twelvefold causes and conditions exist in one thought in the mind 十二因緣在一念心中: see the phrase in the *Avataṃsaka Sūtra* at T 9.558c10–11, which actually reads: "The triple world is an empty delusion; it is only made/created by the mind. the twelvefold consituents of [causes and] conditions all rely on the mind" 十二緣分是皆依心. It could be said that the meaning is the same, but the text is missing the crucial phrase "one thought."

Twelvefold causes and conditions are all included in a single thought of one person 十二因緣一人一念: this phrase can be found in *The Great Collection of Sūtras* at T 13.164a10–11.

Conditioned phenomena in reality do not arise. If we were to say that they arise,

Answer: The *Avataṃsaka Sūtra* says "One is within the immeasurable, and the immeasurable is within one." The *Pañcaviṃśati Sūtra* says that all dharmas tend toward ignorance without exception, and so forth to all dharmas tend toward old-age-and-death. Now I say that one mind 一心 includes the twelvefold causes and conditions; so what is the problem? Also, what is called "one thought" 一念 is not the same as **[127b]** that of worldly people who grasp at and become attached to unities or differences as a set characteristic of a "single thought." [What I mean here by a "single thought"] is neither a unity nor difference, but is discussed as "one." It is analogous to when one is sleeping and the mind is covered [with drowsiness]: in a single thought one can dream of immeasurable things and worlds. This is as [explained] in the *Lotus Sūtra*.

does it exist in one thought, or does it exist in many thoughts 緣法實無生若謂爲生者爲在一心中爲在衆心中: this phrase can be found as a verse in the *Treatise on Twelve Subjects* at T 30.160a22–23, with slightly different characters: 緣法實無生若謂爲有生爲在一心中爲在多心中.

One is within the immeasurable, and the immeasurable is within one 一中無量無量中一: see the phrase in the *Avataṃsaka Sūtra* at T 9.423a1, which actually reads, "the immeasurable is understood within one, and the one is understood within the immeasurable."

All dharmas tend toward ignorance … 一切法趣無明是趣不過乃至一切法趣老死: a summary of a long passage in the *Pañcaviṃśati Sūtra* at T 8.332c–333c on the "tendencies" of categories such as the five aggregates and the eightfold noble path.

In the *Lotus Sūtra*: as Chan-jan suggests (BT–V, 385), see the verses at the end of fourteenth chapter on "Practices for Peace" at T 9.39c6–17; Hurvitz (*Lotus Sūtra*, 223 [205]), translates:

The Buddhas' bodies, of golden hue,
With a hundred happy marks shall be adorned.
He hears the Dharma and preaches it to others:
Such shall ever be this lovely dream.
He also dreams of becoming lord of a realm,
Of forsaking palace and retinue,
As well as the supremely wondrous objects of the five desires.
He goes to the Platform of the Path;
Under the bodhi-tree,
Seated on a lion throne,
His quest for the Path having passed the seventh day,
He gains the knowledge of the Buddhas.
Having achieved the Unexcelled Path,
He rises, and turns the Dharma-wheel.
To the fourfold assembly preaching Dharma
Throughout a thousand myriads of millions of kalpas.
Preaching the Fine Dharma without outflows
And conveying to salvation incalculable living beings,
Thereafter he is to enter into nirvana,
As smoke stops when the candle is extinguished.
If in the latter evil age
He preaches this prime Dharma,
This man shall achieve great profit,
Such as the merits told above.

2. *Arousing compassion* [127b3]

[Second, causes and conditions in terms of] the true and correct arousing of aspiration for enlightenment (*bodhicitta*) [and compassion] are as follows: if you rely on [the perspective of] arising-and-perishing [that is, causation], no-arising-nor-perishing [that is, emptiness], or conventional names for [understanding] twelvefold causes and conditions and arousing a vow of compassion, this is [still] not the true and correct [arousing of *bodhicitta*]. Therefore the *Avataṃsaka Sūtra* refers to "a demonic [aspect of] *bodhicitta*." This is the meaning here.

If [on the other hand] you rely on the inconceivable for [understanding] twelvefold causes and conditions and arousing compassion, you can cover and save all [sentient beings]. This is called "true and correct" [arousing of *bodhicitta*].

[Compassion or kindness 悲 as] "extracting suffering" 拔苦 is of two types. One is to extract the five types of the causes of suffering—that is, of ignorance, passionate attachments, grasping, volitional actions, and existence—in the ten dharma realms [from hell to Buddhahood]. Second is to extract the seven types of the results of suffering—that is, of consciousness, name-and-form [and so forth]—in the ten dharma realms. It is the same for the "granting of bliss" through [compassion as] pity 慈與樂. That is, [first,] contemplate ignorance, passionate attachments, and grasping in the ten dharma realms, and by perfecting the correct path of compassionate deeds, you convert [the two constituents of] volitional activity and existence, and fulfill the various auxiliary practices of the path. This is called "granting the cause of bliss" 與樂因. [Second,] contemplate the [other] seven constituents [of twelvefold causes and conditions such as] name-and-form [and so forth] as all having the nature of peaceful bliss; this is great Nirvana which cannot be extinguished again. This is called "granting the result or fruit of bliss" 與樂果. You arouse the four universal vows with respect to these four mean-

Demonic *bodhicitta* 菩提心魔: see the *Avataṃsaka Sūtra* at T 9.66c11 in the context of discussing ten types of "demonic forces." The tenth is "Not knowing *bodhi*-wisdom is truly a demonic dharma 不知菩提正法魔, because one is not able to accomplish all the great vows [of a bodhisattva]." Note that the phrase used in the sūtra is "*bodhi*[-wisdom]," not "*bodhicitta*."

Also note that this passage has been quoted previously in the *Mo-ho chih-kuan*; see text and notes at 43b28–29.

Four universal vows 四弘誓: here Chih-i explains a clear correspondence between the four universal vows and the four Noble Truths of suffering, the causes of suffering, the path, and extinction. For a detailed study on this relationship see Robert Rhodes, "The four extensive vows and four noble truths in T'ien-t'ai Buddhism" (1984).

This pattern can also be found in the opening of the fifth chapter on "Medicinal Herbs" of the *Lotus Sūtra* at T 9.19b11–13.

ings [of two types of extracting suffering, and two types of granting bliss]: [1.] to save those that are not yet saved, and saving those with the seven constituents of [twelvefold causes and conditions such as consciousness and so forth] in the ten dharma realms, from the sufferings of this samsaric cycle of birth-and-death; [2.] to understand that which is not yet understood, that is, understand the five constituents of ignorance, passionate attachments, grasping, volitional activity, and existence, as the cause of suffering; [3.] To lead to peace that which is not yet peaceful, that is, attain peace through the proper and auxiliary [practices] of the path with regard to ignorance, passionate attachments, grasping, volitional activity, and existence in the ten dharma realms; [4. to attain] the nirvana that is not yet attained by being led to attain peaceful nirvana with regard to the seven constituents such as consciousness and so forth.

3. *Skillful means for a peaceful mind* [127b17]

[Third, causes and conditions in terms of] skillful means for a peaceful mind are as follows. Skillfully contemplate the seven constituents [of the twelvefold causes and conditions such as] consciousness and so forth of the ten [dharma] realms as Dharma-nature, that the eight perversions and delusions of ignorance, passionate attachments, and grasping, do not arise. This is called the contemplation of putting an end to the various perversions of volitional activity and existence in the ten dharma realms. Therefore it is [also] called "cessation."

4. *Deconstructing dharmas* [127b19]

[Fourth, causes and conditions in terms of] deconstructing dharmas universally are as follows: Horizontal deconstruction of the twelvefold causes and conditions of the ten [dharma] realms is all in a single thought. A single thought does not arise from itself, nor from another, nor both together, nor without a cause. It should be known that the ten realms are all non-arising. Vertical deconstruction [involves realizing that] volitional activity, existence, mistaken views and conceptions, the minute dust-like delusions, non-cognizance, and ignorance of the ten realms do not arise, and so forth up to the forty-two levels [of ignorance] are a non-arising of non-arising. This is called "Great Nirvana."

Hurvitz (102 [96]) translates:

> Those who have not yet crossed over I enable to cross. Those who do not yet understand I cause to understand. Those not yet at ease I put at their ease. Those not yet in nirvana I enable to attain nirvana.

5. Knowing what penetrates and what obstructs [127b23]

[Fifth is causes and conditions in terms of] knowing well what penetrates and what obstructs [the path]. Having penetrating understanding 達 of the truth of causes and conditions is called "penetrating" 通; arousing the attachments of mistaken views and conceptions is an "obstacle" 塞. To sink before the truth is to be "not penetrating"; to understand causes and conditions of actual phenomena 事 is to be "not obstructed." To arouse passionate attachment of phenomena with regard to the three paths [of suffering, passionate afflictions, and karma] is an "obstacle"; to understand causes and conditions within the principle 理 [of truth] is "penetrating." If in turn there arise ignorance, passionate attachments, grasping, volitional activity, and existence, this is a loss 失. If in turn [concerning each of the twelvefold causes and conditions] there is wisdom concerning them all, this is an attainment. Or, you directly discuss as obstacles the four types of [the truths of] suffering and the causes of suffering, such as that of [the four noble truths] as conditioned 有作, or [discuss] the four types of [the truths of] the path and extinction as "penetrating [understanding]." Or, you directly approach the three types of conventionality [as causally arisen, continuous, and relative] and therefore this becomes an "obstacle"; or by deconstructing the three **[127c]** conventionalities as non-arising, this is "penetrating [understanding]." As this is so with the delusions in the Shared [Teachings], it is also likewise with the delusions in the Distinct [Teachings]. Or, directly approaching the four types of mistaken views and giving rise to ten kinds of afflictions is an "obstacle"; destroying mistaken views is "penetrating," and so forth.

6. Steps on the path [127c2]

[Sixth is causes and conditions in terms of] well cultivating the [thirty-seven] steps on the path. If discussed in general [in terms of the four mindfulnesses, the first of the thirty-seven steps], [1. contemplating] the visible phenomena of visible form within the causes and conditions of the ten realms is [mindfulness of] the physical body [as impure]. [2. Contemplating] all phenomena of sensations is [mindfulness of] sensations [as involving suffering]. [3. Contemplating] all phenomena of consciousness is [mindfulness of] thoughts 心 [as impermanent]. [4. Contemplating] all conceptualization and volitional actions is [mindfulness of] phenomena [as without substantial reality]. If discussed distinctly, [1.] that of "form" from the constituent of "name-and-form" [that is, the "body" part of "body and mind"], that of five sense entrances from [the constituent of] "the six sense entrances," and that of five [sensual] contacts and five sensations from [the constituent of] "contact," and two types of visible form from the constituents of "birth" and "death": all are encompassed in the mindfulness of the physical body. [2.] The part of consciousness from the constituent of "name-and-form" [that is, the "mind" part of "body and mind"], the [sixth] sense entrance of "mind" from [the constituent of] "the six sense entrances," and the consciousness parts of the constituents of "birth" and "death": all are encompassed in the mindfulness of thoughts. [4.] Conceptualizations and volitional activity from the constituents of "ignorance," "volition," and "name-and-form"; contact with phenomena from the constituent of "contact"; conceptualizations and volitional activity from the constituents of "passionate attachments," "grasping," "existence," "and "birth"; and also conceptualizations and volitional activity from the constituent of "death": all are encompassed in the mindfulness of phenomena. Sometimes it is said that "ignorance" is the "passionate attachments" from the past, and passionate attachments defile the five aggregates, but if we are to discuss it for the present, "ignorance" is encompassed in the mindfulness of phenomena, "volitional activity" is [also] encompassed in [the mindfulness of] phenomena, consciousness is encompassed in [the mindfulness of] thoughts, "name-and-form" is encompassed in both [mindfulness of] body and mind. The "six sense entrances" coming into contact with the six sense objects is encompassed in [the mindfulness of] dustlike phenomena. The [six] sense entrances are encompassed in [mindfulness of] the body. "Contact" is encompassed in [mindfulness of] phenomena. "Sensations" are also encompassed in [mindfulness of] phenomena. Passionate attachments are defiling, and are encompassed in both [mindfulnesses of] body and thoughts. "Grasping" is encompassed in [mindfulness of] phenomena. "Existence" is encompassed in [mindfulness of] phenomena. "Birth" arouses visible forms, and "death" extinguishes visible forms; these are encompassed in [mindfulness of] phenomena.

Question: Abhidharma scholastics teach that the samsaric cycle of birth and death is all a matter of [dharmas] not associated with mind, so they all should correspond and be encompassed in the mindfulness of phenomena. Why is it that in general some [are included] in the other three mindfulnesses?

Answer: The *Mahāparinirvāṇa Sūtra* says, "These five aggregates per-

"Existence" is encompassed in [mindfulness of] phenomena 有行攝: following the text this phrase would be translated as "existence is encompassed in volitional action 行," but I take the variant 法 for 行 as a better fit for the context.

Abhidharma scholastics teach that the samsaric cycle of birth and death is all a matter of not associated with mind 數人説生死皆是不相應行: see, for example, a passage in the *Abhidharma-vibhāṣā-śāstra* on "not-good karma" at T 28.83c1–20.

Five aggregates perish, and then the five aggregates are born. This is like pressing a wax seal into mud ... 五陰滅彼五陰續生如蠟印印泥印壞文成: see the *Mahāparinirvāṇa Sūtra*, T 12.780c5–8:

> When these aggregates perish, the aggregates [in turn] continuously arise, like when a flame arises, darkness perishes,

ish, and then [in turn] the five aggregates continuously are born. This is like when pressing a wax seal into mud, the seal is broken but the impression remains." Therefore you should know that the phenomena of the cycle of birth and death are not separate from the five aggregates [of body and mind], which supports this teaching [that they are also included in the mindfulnesses of body and thoughts].

If [we contemplate] the visible forms of causes and conditions both generally and specifically, they are all neither impure nor pure, but being able to illuminate both purity and impurity is called "the mindfulness of the body." Contemplating the sensations of causes and conditions both generally and specifically, they are neither suffering nor bliss, but both suffering and bliss are illuminated; this is called "the mindfulness of sensations." Contemplating consciousness and mind of causes and conditions both generally and specifically, they are neither permanent nor transient, but both permanence and transiency are illuminated; this is "the mindfulness of thoughts." Contemplating conceptualizations and volitions both generally and specifically, they are neither selfhood nor non-Self, but both selfhood and non-Self are illuminated; this is "the mindfulness of phenomena." These four [mindfulnesses] are able to destroy the eight kinds of perversions within the twelvefold chain of causes and conditions. The eight perversions are transformed into four kinds of "decaying" and four kinds of "flourishing," and also neither decaying nor flourishing, in the midst of which you enter nirvana and perceive Buddha nature. If you are diligent in contemplating these four [mindfulnesses], this is called the "[four] proper endeavors," and so forth [through the thirty-seven steps on the path] up to the eightfold [Noble] Path, as explained previously.

Contemplating fundamental non[-arising] in terms of the four options [of the tetralemma, [one realizes that] things do not arise and do not perish, and are ultimately empty. This emptiness includes eighteen types of emptiness, and all eighteen types of emptiness are in one emptiness. **[128a]**

and when the flame perishes [and goes out], the darkness is born. Good sons, it is like a wax seal pressed into the mud [when making pottery?]; the seal merges with the mud and though the seal perishes, [the impression of] the letters remains. Even though the seal does not change, it "remains" in the mud. The letters are not separate from the mud and removed to another place. Thus the seal is the cause and condition for giving rise to the letters.

Four kinds of decaying and four kinds of flourishing 四枯四榮: see the text and notes on the "four flourishing and four decaying" trunks of the Śīla tree as a symbol for the intertwining of arising and perishing, *Mo-ho chih-kuan* 88c18.

As explained previously: see the discussion of the thirty-seven steps on the path in the section on "Penetrating and Obstructing the Path" earlier in the *Mo-ho chih-kuan* at 87c10–91a4.

A Vaipulya [sūtra] says, "The small emptiness [of Hīnayāna] and the great emptiness [of Mahāyāna] all return to one emptiness." The *Pañcaviṃśati Sūtra* says "One, lone emptiness." This is called [1.] the "gate to liberation as emptiness." All who realize this emptiness will not grasp after the four marks of Dharma-nature [of permanence, bliss, selfhood, and purity], will not receive nor be attached to them, neither think of nor make discriminations about them as being [neither] new nor old, internal nor external, and so forth. If your thoughts are not reliant on these things, [and you realize that] there is nothing to be perceived, this is to perceive true Buddha nature. By not dwelling in phenomena, you dwell in Great Nirvana. This is called [2.] the "gate to liberation as formlessness." This Great Nirvana is neither cultivated nor produced; it does not arise by itself, so it is not caused; it does not arise from some other, so it is not conditioned; it does not arise from both [self and other] nor by their merging; it does not arise without a cause, and therefore it is not separate [from causes and conditions]. This lack of cultivation and lack of attainment is called [3.] the "gate to liberation as [spontaneous] actionlessness."

7. Auxiliary methods [128a8]

[Seventh is] controlling and overcoming through auxiliary methods. In the previous [practice of the thirty-seven] steps on the path you directly come in contact with the principle [of reality], and convert [the constituents of] ignorance, passionate attachments, and grasping into enlightened [wisdom]. Although you are endowed with proper wisdom 正慧, you are not able to attain realization [of Buddhahood]. Why is this so? Ignorance, passionate attachments, and grasping are the evil [side of] principle, and are in contrast with the wisdom [side of] principle. Again, [the constituents of] volitional activity and existence involve evil aspects that assist in obstructing the wisdom [side of the] principle [of reality]. It is like when there are many bandits and only one of myself [so that one can be easily overwhelmed]; therefore it is necessary to add the cultivation of the good aspects of volitional activity and existence to assist in opening the gate to nirvana. [1] If you arouse the

A Vaipulya [sūtra] says "Small emptiness and great emptiness all return to one emptiness" 小空大空皆歸一空: original source unknown. This quote has appeared previously in the *Mo-ho chih-kuan* at 90c10–11.

***Pañcaviṃśati Sūtra* says "one, lone emptiness"** 一獨空: see a passage at T 8.326c26–29:

> Again, Subhuti, the perfection of wisdom shown by the Buddha is that the world is only empty 世間獨空. How is it shown that the world is only empty? It is shown in the five aggregates that the world is only empty, and so forth up to the universal wisdom 一切種智 shows that the world is only empty.

activity and existence of covetousness, these should be converted into the activity and existence of giving; in other words, the perfection of *dāna* gives rise to good roots. [2] If you arouse the activity and existence of breaking the precepts, these should be converted into the activity and existence of keeping the precepts; [the perfection of] *śīla* gives rise to good roots. [3] If you arouse the activity and existence of hatred and anger, these should be converted to the activity and existence of patience; [the perfection of] *kṣānti* gives rise to good roots. [4] If you arouse the activity and existence of indolence, these should be converted to the activity and existence of diligence; [the perfection of] *vīrya* gives rise to good roots. [5] If you arouse the activity and existence of distraction, these should be converted into the activity and existence of meditative concentration; [the perfection of *dhyāna*] gives rise to the [ten dhyānic] constituents of virtuous qualities. [6] If you arouse the activity and existence of foolish delusions, these should be converted to the activity and existence of awakening concerning transience, suffering, and emptiness[; this is the perfection of wisdom]. Thus the actual aspects of wisdom are clearly illuminated, and assist in destroying delusions concerning the principle [of reality]. If there is even one obstacle, you cannot perceive the principle [of reality]; how much more so if there are six! Now if you [focus on] destroying only the strong [obstacles], the weak ones will follow in its wake.

If the power of these auxiliary [methods of the] path is strong, you can perfect all virtuous qualities, regulate and control all sense organs, complete the six perfections, and be endowed with the noble demeanor of the Buddha, that is, from the ten powers and [four] fearlessnesses up to the [thirty-two] major and [eighty minor physical] marks, as explained previously. Ponder this yourself, and then practice it.

Again, the "noble demeanor of the Buddha" refers to the Buddha sitting on the seat of enlightenment, turning the wheel of [and preaching] the Dharma, and entering nirvana, all in accordance with the twelvefold [chain of] causes and conditions. The *Pañcaviṃśati Sūtra* says "If you are able to deeply contemplate the twelvefold causes and conditions, you will sit on the seat of enlightenment." There are four types of the "seat of enlightenment."

Constituents of virtuous qualities 支林功德: these were listed above, at *Mo-ho chih-kuan* 119b3–7, as having the ten constituents of 1. empty; 2. clear; 3. stable/concentrated; 4. wisdom; 5. good mind; 6. flexibility; 7. joy; 8. bliss; 9. the realm of liberation; and 10. correspondence.

As explained previously: see the lengthy section on "Controlling and Healing through Auxiliary Methods" at *Mo-ho chih-kuan* 91a5–97b17.

If you are able to deeply contemplate the twelvefold causes and conditions, you will sit on the seat of enlightenment 若能深觀十二因緣即是坐道場: see the passage in the *Pañcaviṃśati Sūtra* at T 8.364b23–27:

> Subhūti, [the truth of] the twelvefold causes and conditions is the Dharma

[1] If one contemplates the twelvefold causes and conditions as ultimately arising and perishing, this is the [historical] Buddha [physically] sitting on the seat of enlightenment that is the grass seat under the Bodhi tree, of the Tripitaka [Teachings]. [2] If one contemplates the twelvefold causes and conditions as ultimately empty, this is the Buddha sitting on the seat of enlightenment that is the seat of celestial garments under the seven-jeweled tree [in a Pure Land?], of the Shared Teachings. [3] If one contemplates the twelvefold causes and conditions as ultimately conventional names, this is the Buddha [Vairo]cana sitting on the seat of enlightenment that is a seven-jeweled seat, of the Distinct Teachings. [4] If one contemplates the twelvefold causes and conditions as ultimately the Middle, this is **[128b]** the Buddha [Mahā]vairocana sitting on the seat of enlightenment, a seat that is an empty void. You should thus know that there are great [Mahāyāna] and small [Hīnayāna] seats of enlightenment, but they do not go beyond contemplating the twelvefold causes and conditions.

Again, the Buddhas all turn the wheel of [and preach] the Dharma through this contemplation [of causes and conditions]. [In terms of the Five Periods, first] if [we speak of] the "eight assemblies in seven places" which is the seat of enlightenment as quiescent extinction, then the twelvefold causes and conditions as neither-arising-nor-perishing is taught to bodhisattvas of sharp faculties. This is also called [the teaching of] conventional names, and is also called the meaning of the Middle Way. [Second,] if at the Deer Park, then the twelvefold causes and conditions as arising-and-perishing is taught for the sake of the disciples of dull faculties. [Third,] if the twelvefold scriptures of the Vaipulya sūtras, then the twelvefold causes and conditions

teaching [realized by] the solitary bodhisattva, who is able to remove all extreme perversions. When he sits on the seat of enlightenment, one knows that through this contemplation one should attain universal wisdom. Subhūti, if there is a bodhisattva-mahāsattva who is not able to gain extinction through emptiness, he should practice the perfection of wisdom by contemplating the twelvefold causes and conditions. Thus he will not fall back into the stages of the śrāvaka or pratyekabuddha, but dwell in the highest, supreme wisdom.

Vairocana 舍那佛 **and Mahāvairocana** 毘盧遮那佛: Chih-i makes a distinction here between the Vairocana of the Distinct Teaching and that of the Perfect Teaching, though in Sanskrit it is the same "Vairocana." Compare the passage on the "four Buddha lands" at *Mo-ho chih-kuan* 53a1–10, that "Tathāgatas dwell in the land of constant quiescent light."

Eight assemblies in seven places 七處八會: the places, or "seats of enlightenment," from where the sixty-fascicle *Avataṃsaka Sūtra* is said to have been preached. This corresponds to the first of the "Five Periods" in the T'ien-t'ai classification system. The five periods, in temporal order in the life of the Buddha, are that of [1] the *Avataṃsaka Sūtra*, [2] the Āgamas (Deer Park), [3] the Vaipulya sūtras, [4] the Prajñāpāramitā sūtras, and [5] the *Mahāparinirvāṇa* and *Lotus Sūtras*.

is taught as arising-and-perishing yet identical with emptiness, identical with conventionality, and identical with the Middle 卽空卽假卽中. [Fourth,] if the *Mahā-prajñāpāramitā* [sūtras], then the twelvefold causes and conditions are taught as identical with emptiness, identical with conventionality, and identical with the Middle. [Fifth,] if the *Lotus Sutra*, then the twelvefold causes and conditions are taught as identical with the Middle, rejecting the skillful means of the three [vehicles]. If the *Mahāparinirvāṇa Sūtra*, then the twelvefold causes and conditions are taught as including all four meanings [of the Fourfold Teachings of the Tripitaka, Shared, Distinct, and Perfect], and that all have Buddha nature, just like milk contains the nature of ghee and yet the five flavors of the Fourfold Teachings are not the same. Thus all [the Buddhas teach] with regard to the twelvefold causes and conditions, making distinctions with good and skillful means, and leading and guiding people in accordance with their capacities.

Again, "putting poison in milk" is an explanation of the twelvefold causes and conditions in the *Mahāparinirvāṇa Sūtra*, which clarifies the variable teachings. Also, the passage in the *Mahāparinirvāṇa Sūtra* says with regard to the twelvefold causes and conditions, "I taught that when I first attained the Path, the bodhisattvas of the ten directions had already asked about this meaning," was a "secret teaching." What does this mean? At first, for the sake of disciples with dull faculties, the twelvefold causes

Five flavors 五味: the analogy based on the *Mahāparinirvāṇa Sūtra* that compares the various teachings of the Buddha and the attainment of nirvana to the five progressive stages in the refinement of milk; used in T'ien-t'ai as an analogy for the five periods in the development of the Buddha's teaching. The five flavors are milk 乳, coagulated milk [cream] 酪, curds 生酥, butter 熟酥, and ghee 醍醐, corresponding respectively to the teachings of the *Avataṃsaka Sūtra*, the Tripitaka (the Āgamas), the Vaipulya sūtras, the Prajñāparāmitā sūtras, and the *Mahāparinirvāṇa* and *Lotus Sūtras*.

Putting poison in milk: an analogy from the *Mahāparinirvāṇa Sūtra*, T 12.784c9–10, which compares Buddha nature in all beings to putting poison in milk, in the sense that the poison will still be there when milk turns to ghee. See note at *Mo-ho chih-kuan* 31c21–26.

Variable teachings 不定教: one of the "four teachings according to method" 化儀四教 in the T'ien-t'ai classification system.

Bodhisattvas had already asked 十方菩薩已問此義: see the *Mahāparinirvāṇa Sūtra*, T 12.620a12–17:

> Good sons. when I sat on the seat of enlightenment under the Bodhi tree and first attained awakening, at that time bodhisattvas, from various Buddha realms as immeasurable and countless and as sands of the Ganges River, assembled and asked me about this exceedingly profound meaning. Their questions and words were virtuous, and everyone was the same without any difference. In this way these questions were able to benefit immeasurable sentient beings.

Secret teaching 祕密教: another one of the "four teachings according to method."

At first, for the sake of disciples with dull faculties … 初爲鈍根弟子說十二因

and conditions as arising-and-perishing were taught. But separately 別 there was a seat for bodhisattvas of sharp faculties, who secretly heard about the twelvefold causes and conditions as neither-arising-nor-perishing, and they were immediately awakened concerning Buddha nature, and attained the forbearance of realizing non-arising. This is the meaning of "secret." This is the turning of the wheel of the Dharma in the land [where ordinary people and sages] dwell together.

Again, all Buddhas have attained parinirvana through this contemplation [of causes and conditions]. If you have dull faculties, and contemplate [the twelvefold causes and conditions] from the perishing of ignorance to the perishing of old-age-and-death, and the explicit and latent [afflictions] are all extinguished, this is the nirvana-with-remainder and with-no-remainder of the Tripitaka Teachings. If you contemplate [the twelvefold causes and conditions] from the perishing of ignorance to the perishing of old-age-and-death as empty, this is the nirvana-with-remainder and with-no-remainder of the Shared Teachings. If you contemplate causes and conditions as conventional names and the Middle Path, from the perishing of ignorance to the perishing of old-age-and-death, this is the nirvana that is permanent, blissful, selfhood, and pure, and of the Buddha of the Distinct Teachings. If you [contemplate] the twelvefold causes and conditions in terms of the threefold path [of suffering, passionate afflictions, and karma] as indivisible from threefold Buddha nature and the three types of nirvana, then nirvana is called the Dharma-realm of the Buddhas; this is the nirvana of four virtues [of permanence, bliss, selfhood, and purity] of the Buddha Vairocana of the Perfect Teaching. This shows how there are four types of nirvana, from the perspective of the [Buddha-]land of [ordinary people and sages] dwelling together, as found in the *Sūtra on Clearing Doubts Concerning the Semblance*

緣生滅: see, for example, the chapter on "Contemplating Causes and Conditions" in the *Middle Treatise*, T 30.1b23–28:

> The Buddha, wishing that all mistaken views be severed in this way according to his knowledge of the Buddha-Dharma, at first as teachings for the śrāvakas explained twelvefold causes and conditions. Again, for the sake of those who had already cultivated and had a great mind and profoundly accepted the deep Dharma, with the teaching of the Mahāyāna explained the marks of causes and conditions, that is, that all dharmas neither arise nor perish, are neither one nor different, and so forth, are ultimately empty and have no place of existence, as it is taught in the Prajñāparāmitā.

See also a passage on the two extremes of annihilationism and eternalism in the *Mahāparinirvāṇa Sūtra*, T 12.768b3ff., a passage quoted above at 75a16.

Land of dwelling together 同居土: the land where ordinary people and sages dwell together 凡聖同居土, one of the "four Buddha lands" in the T'ien-t'ai scheme.

Three types of nirvana 三涅槃: that of innate purity 性淨, perfected purity 圓淨, and purity of skillful means 方便淨.

Dharma. Attaining the path, turning the wheel of the Dharma, and entering nirvana from the perspective of the two [Buddha-]lands of "skillful means" and "true recompense" should also be understood in the same way. This is called "encompassing the meaning of the Dharma in terms of the twelvefold causes and conditions."

8. Graded stages of attainment [128b28]

"Knowing the graded stages" is as follows. The lightness and heaviness of [birth in] the three evil [destinies], and which [destiny] you reach, all depend on your ignorance, evil actions, and passionate grasping [in the present and former lives] for non-good [deeds]. The height or lowness of [birth in] the three good [destinies] depends on **[128c]** your ignorance, good deeds, and passionate grasping for stable [non-karmic] actions 不動行. If you convert ignorance, passionate attachment, and grasping, and arouse wisdom concerning arising and perishing, you will [attain] the high and low levels of practice of the wise and the noble [that is, the "three levels of erudition and ten noble stages"], of liberation by wisdom, within the Tripitaka Teachings. If you convert your volitional actions and existence and arouse the virtuous qualities from each of the practices of contemplation, training, discipline, and cultivation, you will [attain] the high and low levels of practice of the wise and noble, of liberation by both [wisdom and concentration], of the Tripitaka Teachings. This type of person [that is, those who reach enlightenment on their own through realizing the truth of causes and conditions] for both Hīnayāna and Mahāyāna can be known in this way. By converting the [first] five perfections [from giving to dhyāna meditation] and perfecting your actions and existence, and with [the perfection of *prajña*-wisdom you convert ignorance, passionate attachments, and grasping, and thus regulate and control all sense organs, you attain the level [of the tenth *bhūmi* stage] that takes three incalculable eons [to reach]. [This corresponds to the Shared

Sūtra on Clearing Doubts Concerning the Semblance Dharma **像法決疑經**: these phrases are found in this sūtra at T 85.1337a. This is the only reference to this sūtra in the *Mo-ho chih-kuan*.

Lands of skillful means and true recompence 方便實報: the second and third of the "four Buddha lands."

This type of person: the text uses the unusual compound 迦羅, which is the transliteration of the Sanskrit *kalā*, meaning "minute part," "atom," or "short time," which seems out of place here. Given the context, Chan-jan (BT–V, 403) interprets it to refer to "awakening through causes and conditions" 因緣覺, or "awakening by oneself" 獨覺, the characteristics of a pratyekabuddha, and I have followed this reading in my translation.

The level that takes three incalculable eons [to reach] 三僧祇位: that is, through the fifty stages, from the ten stages of faith, ten abodes, ten practices, and ten of merit transference (which take one incalculable

Teachings.] If you convert ignorance, passionate attachments, and grasping by penetrating to the essence of its true [emptiness], and convert your actions and existence by cultivating the six perfections, like planting a tree in the empty sky 空種樹, you will attain the high and low levels of practice of the four forbearances [of the Distinct Teachings]. If you convert ignorance, passionate attachments, and grasping to give rise to the wisdom of the path, and convert volitional activity and existence and cultivate the six perfections for another incalculable eon, attain supranormal powers, purify a Buddha land, and perfect sentient beings, you will attain the high and low levels of practice of the "six rings" [of 1. the ten levels of faith, 2. ten abodes, 3. ten practices, 4. ten levels of merit transference, 5. ten *bhūmi* stages, and 6. "equivalent to awakening"]. If you convert ignorance, passionate attachments, and grasping into a flaming torch of perfect enlightenment (*saṃbodhi*), you have attained the high and low level of the Six Identities of the Perfect Teaching 圓教六卽.

[For the Perfect Teaching,] the twelvefold causes and conditions are all included in a single thought of a single person. Ignorance is like empty space, which cannot be extinguished, and so forth [for the rest of the twelvefold chain] up to old-age-and-death is like empty space and cannot be extinguished. To be empty means that there is no extinguishing nor non-extinguishing. [The teaching of] "emptiness" is Mahāyāna. *The Treatise on Twelve Subjects* says, "[The teaching of] emptiness is called 'Mahāyāna.' Samantabhadra, Manjuśrī, and [other] great men ride on it, and therefore it

eon), through the first seven *bhūmi* stages (which take a second incalculable eon), up to the tenth *bhūmi* stage (which takes a third incalculable eon).

The levels of the four forbearances 四忍位: the four levels of "forbearance" or "recognition" 認: 1. forbearance from overcoming [delusions] 伏忍; 2. forbearance from attaining faith 信忍; 3. forbearance from pliantly following [the path] 柔順忍; and 4. the forbearance of the non-arising of dharmas 無生法忍. In T'ien-t'ai classifications, these are levels of attainment for those of the Distinct Teachings.

The Treatise on Twelve Subjects 十二門論: a central text of the Chinese Mādhyamika tradition. See the opening section at T 30.159c14–24:

Question: Why is this called Mahāyāna?

Answer: Because Mahāyāna is superior to the other two vehicles it is called "the great vehicle." Buddhas are able to attain this greatest of vehicles; therefore it is called "great." Buddhas and great men ride this vehicle; therefore it is called "great." Again, it is able to extinguish and remove great suffering from sentient beings; therefore it is called "great." Again, bodhisattvas such as Avalokiteśvara, Mahāsthāmaprāpta, Manjuśrī, Maitreya, and so forth, these great beings ride it; therefore it is called "great." Again, this vehicle is able to extinguish all extreme dharmas; therefore it is called "great." Again, as it says in the Prajñāpāramitā sūtras, the Buddha himself taught the immeasurable and unlimited meaning of the Mahāyāna, and because of these causes and conditions, it is called "great."

is called a 'great vehicle.'" The *Pañcaviṃśati Sūtra* says, "This vehicle does not move or emerge. People may wish to use it to bring out the ultimate reality of Dharma-nature, but this vehicle [itself] does not move nor emerge." The *Mahāparinirvāṇa Sūtra* says, "All sentient beings correspond to the one vehicle."

In this way these [texts witness to] the [1.] "identity in principle" [of the Perfect Teaching]. Due to this "identity in reality," you attain [2.] "verbal identity" 名字卽, that is, from the time of your first aspiration [for enlightenment] you hear the teachings of Mahāyāna and thus know that sentient beings are indivisible from the Buddha, but since the mind erroneously grasps and has attachments, you are not able to practice contemplation, like inchworms who chew on wood and accidentally produce letters. But

> For the most part its profound meaning is found in "emptiness." If one is able to penetratingly understand this meaning, one will penetratingly understand Mahāyāna, including being unobstructed with regard to the six perfections. Therefore now I concentrate only on interpreting emptiness. To interpret emptiness involves twelve subjects to realize the meaning of emptiness.

This vehicle does not move or emerge ... 是乘不動不出。若人欲使法性實際出者是乘亦不動不出: see the passage in the *Pañcaviṃśati Sūtra* at T 8.259c17–22:

> The Buddha said to Subhūti, "You have asked about this [great] vehicle, 'where does it come from, and where does it dwell?'" The Buddha said, "This vehicle emerges from the triple world, and dwells in omniscience 薩婆若 (*sarvajña*), because it is a non-dualistic dharma. Why is this so? The two dharmas of Mahāyāna and omniscience are neither merged nor scattered, neither color nor form, and not in contrast with the mark of unity, that is, without marks. People may wish to use these to bring out ultimate reality, and these people may wish to use [the idea of] no-marks to bring out [the meaning of] dharmas. People may wish to use the nature of suchlike dharmas to bring out [the meaning of] the nature that which is inconceivable, and these people may wish to use [the idea of] no-marks to bring out [the meaning of] dharmas."

All sentient beings correspond to the one vehicle 一切衆生卽是一乘: the passage in the *Mahāparinirvāṇa Sūtra* at T 12.770b29 contains the phrase, "All sentient being are all of one vehicle."

Identity in principle 理卽: the first level of the "Six Identities." From the perspective of the Perfect Teaching, the basic state of sentient beings, in which they are inherently endowed with the three virtuous qualities of the Dharma Body, *prajñā*-wisdom, and liberation.

The analysis continues with the rest of the Six Identities to illustrate the "levels" of the Perfect Teaching: 2. verbal identity 名字卽, to hear the words concerning the dharma and reach an intellectual understanding; 3. identity in contemplative practice 觀行卽, to meditate on and practice reality as threefold truth; 4. identity in outer appearance 相似卽 (or resemblance), to become related, or have a semblance to, true enlightenment, to sever all obstacles of mistaken views and thoughts of this triple world; 5. identity in partial realization 分證卽, to have complete insight into the threefold truth and awake from all ignorance; and 6. ultimate identity 究竟卽. ultimate enlightenment.

Inchworms who chew on wood and accidentally produce letters 如蟲食木偶得成字: see the *Mahāparinirvāṇa Sūtra* at T 12.618b2–3. This image has appeared many

due to verbal [teachings], you can attain [3.] the practice of contemplation, as explained previously in the seven sections on the methods of contemplation; if you penetratingly understand without obstruction, this will be your locus of practice. Due to the practice of contemplation, you can attain [4.] a resemblance 相似 [to the Buddha]. When you arouse attainment of the first grade [of "appropriate joy" of the five preliminary grades], this stops at "faith" in the Perfect [Teaching]. The second grade of reading and chanting [the sūtras] helps by assisting the mind of faith 信心. The third grade of preaching the Dharma also assists the mind of faith. These three grades all involve a quick vehicle but laxity with regard to precepts 乘急戒緩. The fourth grade [of practicing the six perfections along with contemplation] involves a slightly more urgent [approach to the] precepts. The fifth grade involves urgency with regard to both the practical [practice] and the [abstract] principle. You thus advance to arouse various samādhis and *dhāraṇī*, attain the purity of the six senses, and enter [the stage of the] copper *cakravartin* [that is, the stage of "identity in partial realization"]. Due to [identity in] resemblance, you can attain [5.] "partial realization" 分證, that the threefold path [of suffering, passionate afflictions, and karma] is indivisible from the three virtuous qualities [of the Dharma body, *prajñā*-wisdom, and liberation], and you are spontaneously awakened, perceive threefold Buddha nature, dwell in threefold nirvana, and enter the secret treasury. The pure and sublime Dharma body profoundly and peacefully responds to all. Thus up to [the stage of] "equivalent to awakening" 等覺, all **[129a]** are part of "identity in partial realization." To convert ignorance and give rise to illuminating wisdom is like from the first day to the fourteenth day of the [phases of the] moon, and converting volitional actions and existence and

times already in the *Mo-ho chih-kuan*; for a full translation of the context see under *Mo-ho chih-kuan* 10b29.

As explained previously: see the seven preceding topics from "contemplation of the inconceivable" to "auxiliary methods on the path." I follow the interpretation of Chan-jan (BT–V, 407).

The first grade 初品: the first of the five preliminary grades of the disciple for the Perfect Teaching. In the T'ien-t'ai scheme of the various stages on the path to Buddhahood, the five lowest or preliminary levels of practice and attainment (in the Perfect Teaching) for a disciple of the Buddha: 1. appropriate joy 隨喜品, 2. reading and reciting of the sūtras 読誦品, 3. preaching the Dharma 説法品, 4. preliminary practice of the six perfections while practicing contemplation 兼行六度品, and 6. the proper practice of the six perfections 正行六度品. This is the level of a practitioner preceding the attainment of the ten stages of "faith."

First day to the fourteenth day of the moon 如初日月乃至十四日月: an analogy in the *Mahāparinirvāṇa Sūtra*, T 12.724b11–17, already used many times in the *Mo-ho chih-kuan*; for a full translation of the context see note at 10c14.

giving rise to liberation is like the sixteenth to the twenty-ninth day, and the gradual manifestation of the Dharma body through consciousness and name-and-form is like the full moon. Due to partial realization, you attain [6.] ultimate [identity], the three virtuous qualities are perfectly complete, with ultimate *prajñā*-wisdom 究竟般若, totally sublime Dharma-body 妙極法身, and mastery in liberation 自在解脱; it is like there are no letters to explain after the [final] letter *ḍha* 荼 [or the Greek *omega*]. Therefore you should know that the successive levels of the Hīnayāna and Mahāyāna are all explained in terms of the ten dharma realms [from hell to Buddha] and twelvefold causes and conditions.

[Question:] What sort of successive levels are there for thusness as quiescent extinction 寂滅眞如? If the first stage and second stage [and so forth] are indivisible, and the stages arise in this way, it is as if there is no arising, and if they perish in this way, it is as if there is no perishing. If all sentient beings are indivisible from great nirvana, there can be no perishing. How can there be high and low or great and small successive levels [of attainment]?

[Answer:] The non-arising of non-arising cannot be explained, but since there are causes and conditions, these can be explained. "The causes and conditions of the ten dharma realms produce causes for sentient beings." It is like drawing [a picture] or planting a tree in space as a [skillful] means. Therefore one teaches all [these various] levels [of attainment]. If people do not know of all of these successive levels [as explained] above, errors will give rise to grasping and attachments, resulting in arrogance, like the bodhisattva Candala.

9. *Resting in patient forbearance* [129a14]

Resting in patient forbearance [is as follows]. When you contemplate the causes and conditions of the ten types of destinies, there certainly arise various hindrances to the practice of the path, that is, various deviances such as

Causes and conditions of ten dharma realms 十因緣法 …: a phrase from the *Mahāparinirvāṇa Sūtra*, T 12.733c20 which has been quoted many times already in the *Mo-ho chih-kuan*; see, for example, 3a18–19 and 60a–61c.

Like drawing [a picture] in space or planting a tree as a [skillful] means 畫虛空方便種樹: see a phrase from the *Viśeṣa-cintibrahma-paripṛcchā*, T 15.42c12–13:

> This [attainment of a bodhisattva] is analogous to having a tree that does not rely on [being planted in] the earth but exists in space, and its roots, stalk, branches, leaves, flowers, and fruit are exceedingly mysterious.

Bodhisattva Candala 栴陀羅: or, "a *caṇḍāla* bodhisattva." Usually *caṇḍāla* is a discriminatory term for an "outcast." Chan-jan's somewhat forced explanation (BT–V, 411) is that here "candala refers to a murderer, or one who is obsessed with advancing in levels so he is 'killing' his life-force. Or, if teaching for the sake of others, he harms the wisdom-life of others."

the three obstacles [of karmic deeds, passionate afflictions, and karmic recompense] and four demonic forces [of passionate afflictions, five skandhas, death, and supernatural demons].

[1] The object of karmic deeds such as that of demons, dhyāna meditation, the two vehicles, the bodhisattvas, and so forth all arise from the two constituents of "volitional activity" and "existence." If you are able to rest in patient forbearance, you are able to perfect the virtuous qualities of the volitional activity and existence of a Tathāgata, that is, the karmic recompense from purifying the six senses.

[2] If the obstacle of passionate afflictions arises, that is, covetousness, hate, mistaken conceptions, the deep and sharp mistaken views and arrogance of those of the two vehicles, of the Tripitaka, Shared, and Distinct [Teachings], and the practice of wisdom by bodhisattvas and so forth; these all arise from the constituents of ignorance, passionate attachments, and grasping. If you are able to completely penetrate resting in patient forbearance, you can reveal the Buddha's knowledge and insight.

[3] If the obstacle of karmic recompense arises, that is, from the various aggregates, sense entrances, and sense realms, as well as the "eight winds" [that agitate the human mind: benefit, decline, ruin, honor, praise, slander, suffering, and pleasure], and various diseases; these arise from the seven constituents [of consciousness, name-and-form, the six senses, contact, sensation, birth, and old-age-and-death]. If you know that this is Buddha nature, you will not be agitated nor [inconsistently] grasp and reject, but will be [calm] like empty space; you will enter nirvana without severing samsara; you will manifest the true Dharma body without destroying the aggregates or senses.

If you have penetrating understanding in this way, you will not be obstructed by the three obstacles; "you will dwell on the ground of forbearance, tolerant and agreeable, and without fits of violence nor a mind that is alarmed." This is called "perfecting the mind that rests in patient forbearance." If those of the two vehicles dwell in this patient forbearance, they will never retrogress to commit the five heinous offences like an icchantika 闡提 [who is not able to attain Buddhahood]. If a bodhisattva dwells on the ground of such forbearance, he will never arouse obstacles to the path or commit grave offences.

You will dwell on the ground of forbearance ... nor a mind that is alarmed 住忍辱地柔和善順而不卒暴心亦不驚: a quote from the opening of the "Peaceful Practices" chapter in the *Lotus Sūtra*, T 9.37a15. Hurvitz (208 [191]) translates:

> If a bodhisattva-mahāsattva dwells on the ground of forbearance, if he is gentle, agreeable, good, and acquiescent, not given to fits of violence, not at heart becoming alarmed; ...

10. No passionate attachments to dharmas [129a28]

[Finally,] no attachment to dharmas while being in accordance with the path [is as follows.] First are those [at the level] of resemblance, and second are those [at the level] of the real [awakening]. From the first forbearance from overcoming [delusions] to realizing the [third] forbearance of pliantly following [the Path], you arouse **[129b]** [the stage of] the copper *cakravartin* and have a resemblance and understanding of the virtuous qualities [of Dharma body, liberation, and *prajñā*-wisdom], not being defiled by these three dharmas: that is, [the level of] resemblance to wisdom, virtuous qualities, and Dharma-nature. Since [at this level] this wisdom still involves [the constituents of] ignorance, passionate attachments, and grasping, and the virtuous qualities still involve [the constituents of] volitional activity and existence, and Dharma-nature still involves samsaric name-and-form, therefore you should not become attached to any of these. If these three dharmas give rise to passionate attachments, you cannot enter the level of the bodhisattva, nor do you fall back into that of the two vehicles. This is called "falling from the pinnacle" 頂墮, and is also called "being in accordance with the path" 順道. Contemplate ignorance, passionate attachments, and grasping in accordance with the path of the practice of [intellectual] wisdom 慧行, and contemplate [the constituents of] volitional activity and existence in accordance with the path of the practice of [experiential] practice 行行, contemplate [the seven constituents of] consciousness and so forth in accordance with the path of Dharma nature. Being in accordance with these three paths, you will not fall into the stage of the śrāvaka, but due to passionate attachment to these three paths, you do not enter the stage of the bodhisattva.

How do these passionate attachments arise? Like someone entering a *campaka* [magnolia] grove and not smelling any other scent, a bodhisattva becomes passionately attached to only the virtuous qualities of the Buddhas, and is not mindful of the existence of the two vehicles or the way of other skillful means; this is called [a kind of] passionate attachment. Because of these passionate attachments, you are not able to transform ignorance, passionate attachments, and grasping into true illuminated insight [*prajñā*-wisdom]; you are not able to transform volitional activity and existence into the sublime activity [of liberation]; and you are not able to manifest consciousness and visible forms as the Dharma body. Without transforming these three paths, how can you enter the level of a bodhisattva? If you are not attached

Entering a campaka grove and not smelling any other scent 如入薝蔔林不嗅餘香: a phrase from the *Vimalakīrti Sūtra*, T 14.548a25–26. For a translation of this context see the note at *Mo-ho chih-kuan* 2c20.

to these three dharmas of [the level of] resemblance, and do not have passionate attachments to being "in accordance with the path," then "all the immeasurable offences will be removed, the mind pure and always one, and in this way a noble and sublime person is able to perceive *prajñā*-wisdom." You are not attached to this *prajñā*-wisdom, not to mention the other dharmas [of virtuous qualities and Dharma nature]. Realizing the principle of *prajñā*-wisdom is called "dwelling"; that is, "from dwelling in the first aspiration [for enlightenment], you have already perfected correct awakening, know the true nature of all dharmas, are fully endowed with the body of wisdom, and do not rely on others for this enlightenment." "To perceive *prajñā*-wisdom" means to truly perceive the three paths of the three types of *prajñā*-wisdom. From here on, "the thoughts of the mind are quiescent and extinguished, and flow naturally into the sea of omniscience (*sarvajña*)," and immeasurable ignorance is destroyed. As the *Ta chih tu lun* says, why do various places teach a samādhi of the destruction of ignorance? The answer is, ignorance is of many types and of an exceedingly great number, from the first thought [of aspiration for enlightenment] to attaining the vajra crown [of awakening], all involves destroying ignorance and all manifests the nature of dharmas. If there is only one item [of ignorance] remaining, and if you remove this item, then this is called attaining Buddhahood. The body of the Tathāgata is [hard] like the essence of a diamond; when all evil has been severed, then all good is universally encountered, the three virtues are made ultimate [and are beyond verbal expression], like after the [final] letter *ḍha* 荼 [or the Greek "omega"] there is nothing left to explain.

All the immeasurable offences … 則無量衆罪除清淨心常一如是尊妙人則能見般若: a quote from the *Ta chih tu lun*, T 25.190b22–23. For a translation of the context see note at *Mo-ho chih-kuan* 11c15. Chodron (2, 821) translates:

> Immeasurable, free of any defect,
> Mind pure, always unified:
> This is how the venerable one
> Sees Prajñā

From dwelling in the first aspiration … 卽是初發心住時便成正覺。知一切法眞實之性。具足慧身不由他悟: phrases from the *Avataṃsaka Sūtra* at T 9.449c14–15 (already quoted above at 62a27, 87a25–26, and 99a26–27): "At the time of his first aspiration he had already perfected correct awakening, knew the true nature of dharmas, was fully endowed with the body of wisdom, and this enlightenment did not rely on others."

The thoughts of the mind are quiescent and extinguished … 心心寂滅自然流入薩婆若海: from the *Ying-lo ching*, T 24.1015a26–27; the context reads: "Passionate affliction are ultimately not experienced; the thoughts of the mind are quiescent and extinguished. Like dharmas flowing in water, it naturally flows to the sea of omniscience."

Why do various places teach a samādhi of the destruction of ignorance 何故處處説破無明三昧: a summary of a passage in the *Ta chih tu lun* at T 25.736b29–c14; for the full context see note at *Mo-ho chih-kuan* 46b13–14.

11. Summary [129b24]

[In sum,] this is called "riding the jeweled vehicle directly to the place of enlightenment," as explained above.

9. Mindfulness of the Buddha [129b25]

Ninth is clarifying [dhyāna] in terms of arousing mindfulness of the Buddha 念佛. You can arouse mindfulness of the Buddha and then arouse [the practice of] various dhyāna meditations, or dhyāna meditations can be the cause for arousing mindfulness of the Buddha.

[First is arousing mindfulness of the Buddha and then arousing various dhyāna meditations.] While sitting in meditation 坐禪 you can suddenly come to ponder the virtuous qualities of the Buddhas as immeasurable, unlimited, and beyond conceptual understanding, and you trust and respect [the Buddhas], have shame [concerning your own unenlightened state], and arouse a deep yearning [to be like the Buddhas]. You consider that all Buddhas have great supranormal powers, have great wisdom, have great meritorious virtue, [**129c**], and have great physical attributes, that from these physical attributes arise these virtuous qualities and from those [other] physical attributes arise those [other] virtuous qualities, that from these physical attributes there are these meritorious virtues and from those [other] physical attributes there are those [other] meritorious virtues. You come to know the essence of these attributes, to know the results of these attributes, and the karmic influence of these attributes. Each and every Dharma teaching is penetratingly illuminated and fully clarified, so that you deeply understand this sea of attributes, without any doubt or obstruction. Your concentrated mind is quiet and peaceful, with no agitation or confusion. Calmly dwelling in this concentration, it gradually turns more profound, until in an instant you arouse the crude and fine dwelling of the stage of incomplete attainment in the realm of desires, and progress to enter or realize the first dhyāna stages. "Being mindful of the Buddha" and "the [four] basic [dhyānas]" are each one "extreme"; if you are aware of this realm of mindfulness of the Buddha, this is called the [first] "constituent of examination" (*vitarka*). If you make distinctions concerning mindfulness of the Buddha, that there are various physical marks and various virtuous qualities and teaching so that all of them are clearly distinguished, this is called the [second] "constituent of reflection" (*vicāra*). In this way if you have already perceived [mindfulness of the Buddha], your mind will greatly rejoice so that internally you will be

As explained above: see the original extended "summary" of the ten modes of contemplation and the Great Cart at *Mo-ho chih-kuan* 100a3–b16.

filled with joy; this is called the [third] "constituent of joy." If you are single-minded and tranquil, so that your body is happy, this is called the [fourth] "constituent of bliss." If you are without connections and thoughts and realize [mindfulness of the Buddha] deeply and profoundly, this is called the [fifth] "constituent of mindfulness." In this way the five [preliminary] constituents [of meditation] and mindfulness of the Buddha arise together, perfumed with the Tathāgata's power of virtuous qualities, its flavor multiplied that of other constituents, such that it cannot be explained. Only those who are enlightened can know it. Only [know this, that] the virtuous qualities and attributes of the Buddha-Dharma are immeasurable; the samādhic concentrations to be attained are also immeasurable, and the five constituents [of meditation] to be aroused are also immeasurable, and are beyond words and cannot be explained. Each of the five constituents are all endowed with ten types of virtuous qualities, the retinue of virtuous qualities 支林 [empty; clear; concentrated; wise; good mind; flexibile; joyous; blissful; liberated; and corresponding]. These are the causes for the samādhi of mindfulness of the Buddha 念佛三昧, by which is aroused the attainments from the first dhyāna up to the four [concentrations of] emptiness [of the formless realm]. [Applying this to] the [sixteen] superior meditations, the [six] supranormal powers and [three illuminating] insights, [the concentrations on] impurity, the [eight] renunciations, compassion, and so forth, follows the same pattern.

How about dhyāna meditation as the cause for arousing the samādhi of mindfulness of the Buddha? Suppose a practitioner arouses various dhyāna meditations such as the [four] basic [dhyānas], and within a concentrated mind suddenly reflects on and is mindful of various Buddhas and Tathāgatas, is deeply moved by their meritorious qualities and by their physical attributes, that their good deeds are done through their physical attributes, and that these three attributes [of meritorious qualities, physical attributes, and good deeds] enter a correspondence with their mind that is amply successful and fully clear; when these phenomena appear, the subtlety of this dhyāna meditation and the constituents of meditation are multiplied. [Applying this to] the four dhyāna meditations, superior meditations, renunciations, and so forth, follows the same pattern.

This concentration of mindfulness of the Buddha also has two types: 1. hidden, and 2. not hidden. If you first attain the hidden, understand the virtuous qualities of the Buddha, and recollect them clearly and fully, and then later attain that which is not hidden, clearly perceiving the [physical] marks [such as] rays of light, paying respect to their mysterious contents, clearly and appropriately elucidating them, that these are not [the result of] demonic forces, and you are able to increase and progress in virtuous qualities, making support for good roots, these are causes for [attaining] mindfulness of the Buddha, and broadly penetrating the six Dharma gates of mindfulness. That is, being mindful of the Dharma teachings of the Buddha's virtuous qualities is [2] "mindfulness of the Dharma" 念法. For disciples to experience practice and be mindful of the marks, deeds, and essence of the fruit [of Buddhahood], and to harmoniously regulate these three matters, is [3] to be mindful of the Sangha 念僧. Through this mindfulness of the Sangha, mindfulness of the Buddha, and mindfulness of the Dharma, good **[130a]** overcomes all evil thoughts; this is [5] the mindfulness of renunciation 念捨. When you are mindful in this way and have trust and respect [for the Buddha] and shame [at your condition], this is [4] mindfulness of the precepts 念戒. To be mindful that within these concentrations the [ten] constituents of virtuous qualities is equal to that of all heavenly beings; this is [6] the mindfulness of the heaven realms 念天. Three [that is, the mindfulness of Dharma, of renunciation, and of the precepts] are mindfulnesses of the self; three [that is, the mindfulness of Buddha, Sangha, and divine beings] are mindfulnesses of others. Including these, if you penetrate all dharmas within the gate of mindfulness of the Buddha, you perfect the Mahāyāna. When Sadāprarudita encountered the Buddha, he attained immeasurable Dharma gates; this means that the internal and external [teachings] are all not hidden. If the internal [teachings] are dark and hidden, we cannot know even one part of the teachings of virtuous qualities, and if externally you see the [physical] attribute of rays of light such that it blinds the eyes, this is a demonic influence. It breaks the good sprouts and stalks [of attainment], and so you lose the flowers and fruits of the path. At this time people think they have seen the Buddha, but the Dharma teachings are not in their minds, and none of this is of the Buddha.

If you attain this meaning, you have grasped Dharma correctly. Merely seeing the visible forms is not the correct [mindfulness of the Buddha]. If you only grasp the visible forms, these may be forms created through

Six Dharma gates of mindfulness 六念法門: six types of mindfulness: 1. mindfulness of the Buddha 念佛, to be mindful of and want to become a Buddha; 2. mindfulness of the Dharma 念法, to be mindful of the Buddha's teachings and be committed to it; 3. mindfulness of the Sangha 念僧, to be mindful of cultivating the path of a home-departed one; 4. mindfulness of the precepts 念戒, to be mindful of keeping the precepts; 5. mindfulness of giving 念施 (or the "mindfulness of abandonment/renunciation" 念捨), to be mindful of giving to others; and 6. mindfulness of the divine realms 念天, to be mindful of the possibility of being reborn in the divine realms due to the merit accumulated from practicing the Buddhist path.

Sadāprarudita 薩陀波崙: for the story of this man and his various sacrifices for the sake of the Dharma, see the *Pañcaviṃśati Sūtra* at T 8.418c–420. For a translation and comments, see previous appearance in *Mo-ho chih-kuan* at 49a14–15.

demonic transformations. Also, [those visible forms made from] mud, wood, and drawings should all be the Buddha. Again, the manifestations of the Tathāgata are free and unobstructed, why should it be determined that they are made of a light-like ten-foot [statue of a Buddha] 丈光. The form of a light-like ten-foot [statue] is just a copy of a dignified person. The Buddha is universally manifested as a body of joy 喜身, universally manifested as an appropriate body 宜身, universally manifested as a body of regulated control 對治身, and universally manifested as a body of salvation 度身. Whether it be of a teacher or monk, father or mother, deer or horse or monkey, all statues of visible form, when they are perceived, contain the potential to arouse Dharma teachings. Again, that which is able to cause an increase in the basis of good roots is called the samādhi of mindfulness of the Buddha.

10. The Arising of Supranormal Powers [130a15]

Tenth is clarifying [dhyāna in terms of] the arousing of supranormal powers. In short, there are five: 1. the divine eye 天眼; 2. [the ability to read] other people's minds 他心; 3. the divine ear 天耳; 4. [the ability to perceive] past lives 宿命; and 5. [the ability] for the physical body to appear anywhere 身通. [The sixth, the ability to remove passionate afflictions and attain] non-defilement corresponds to the lower realms so will be discussed there [and so is not included here]. These are attained by arousing supranormal powers with dhyāna as the cause; it is not that the attainment of dhyāna is aroused with supranormal powers as the cause. The reason is that dhyānas are all practices of concentrated meditation and can arise mutually: dhyānas are the essence of the supranormal powers, and the supranormal powers are the functioning of dhyāna. Functioning follows essence; therefore supranormal powers depend on the essence [that is dhyāna meditation]. Functioning does not arise on its own, but depends for its arising on the essence [of dhyāna]. The *Lotus Sūtra* says, "Profoundly cultivate dhyāna meditation and attain the five supranormal powers." This is the meaning here.

Supranormal powers 神通: powers possessed by an enlightened person: 1. the ability to appear anywhere you wish 如意通 or 神足通; 2. the ability to see what ordinary people cannot see 天眼通; 3. the ability to hear sounds that others cannot hear 天耳通; 4. the ability to read other peoples' minds 他心通; and 5. the ability to perceive your own and others' past lives 宿命通. Usually a sixth, the ability to remove your passionate afflictions 漏盡, is added to make six supranormal powers.

Will be discussed there: however, the *Mo-ho chih-kuan* comes to an end after the section on "The Objects of Mistaken Views," so this topic remains unexplained.

Profoundly cultivate dhyāna meditation and attain the five supranormal powers 深修禪定得五神通: a phrase from the opening chapter of the *Lotus Sūtra* at T 9.3a22. Hurvitz (8 [9]) translates:

If we were to discuss the arousing [of supranormal powers] in general, each and every one of the dhyānas are all able to arouse the five supranormal powers. If we were to approach them in a convenient way and discuss them distinctly [it would be as follows]. As for the [four] basic dhyānas, for the most part [the supranormal powers] are not aroused, and even if they are aroused, they are not beneficial. For the superior meditations and [meditations of] supranormal powers and insights, there is much arousing of a light advance [in the ability] for the physical body to appear anywhere. For [the meditations of] renunciations and levels of domination, there is much arousing of the ability to be transformed as you wish and have mastery over the supranormal power for the body to appear anywhere. If you are within the concentration of a compassionate mind, you can attain [an understanding of] what will make him happy depending on a person's visible countenance. Through [observing] the visible forms you can know that mind, and become aware of that person's suffering and bliss. This arousing is the supranormal power of knowing another's mind. If you already have observed the visible form and [through this] knows the mind, you will also know [unspoken] words and sounds; this is the arousing the supranormal power of the divine ear. If you contemplate the causes and conditions of a person in the three periods [of past, present, and future], illuminating matters of the past often means arousing the supranormal power of perceiving past lives, and illuminating matters of the future often involves arousing the supranormal power of the divine eye. If within the concentration of mindfulness of the Buddha that is not hidden, this often involves the arousing of the divine eye.

Also, **[130b]** if these supranormal powers are very fine, they become the three [illuminating] insights, except for the [third] illuminating insight of non-defilement [through exhausting all passionate afflictions, which should be discussed below]. By analogy, this is like a blind eye or a deaf ear suddenly opening [to be able to see and hear]; this is a matter of great rejoicing. How much more so for the inner blindness of the five senses that had continued for immeasurable eons, but now the "five shades" [covering

Profoundly cultivating *dhyāna*-concentration [meditation, mystic trance]
And attaining the five supernatural penetrations (*abhijñā*)

Three illuminating insights 三明: three supranormal insights attained by arhats: 1. the ability to see the conditions and events of the past and thus know the faults of oneself and others; 2. the ability to see the results that are to come in the future, and thus be able to sever mistaken views; and 3. the ability to know and thus exhaust all the passionate afflictions of the present.

Five shades 五翳: lit. the "five shades" that block the light of the sun or moon: smoke, clouds, dust, fog, and the asura Rāhu (the mythological figure who causes eclipses), here used to illustrate the five senses that are "shaded" and cannot clearly perceive things are they truly are.

the five senses] are destroyed, and this purity arouses the five supranormal powers. Each and every supranormal power contains the five [preliminary] constituents [of meditation]. For example, when the obstacles to the eye are destroyed and the faculty of seeing becomes aware of 覺 visible forms and creates a correspondence with them, this is the "constituent of examination" 覺支. When you discriminate visible forms and so forth into immeasurable marks, this is the "constituent of reflection." When these supranormal powers are revealed, there is great rejoicing; this is the "constituent of joy." The internal mind experiencing this pleasure is the "constituent of bliss." For there to be no conditioned objects and no thoughts, but just spontaneity; this is the "constituent of single-mindedness." It is the same for the other four supranormal powers.

If we discuss these in terms of the essence of the dhyāna meditations, such as attaining an internal mental understanding but not clearly [perceiving] external marks, this is the meaning of being "hidden." But the supranormal powers are the functioning of the "house" of concentration 定家. The functioning must be clear and fully known, and therefore all [of the supranormal powers] are not hidden.

4. Cessation-and-Contemplation [130b10]

Fourth is to clarify [dhyāna meditation] in terms of the cultivation of cessation-and-contemplation. When practitioners arouse the attainment of various dhyānas without having skillful means, [they may become] "covetously attached to the flavor of dhyāna; these are the bonds of a bodhisattva." In accordance with this [attachment to] dhyāna they give rise to further transmigration in the cycle of birth-and-death. If you seek to escape [this fate], you should carefully contemplate the ten modes [of contemplation, as follows.

1. Objects as Conceivable and Inconceivable [130b13]

If you contemplate dhyāna as like a cucumber [that tastes good when you eat it but later causes problems], then you are able to realize that the ten dharma realms are created from causes and conditions. Although at first when you arouse [dhyānic] concentration you can pliantly overcome physical and verbal [afflictions], it is like having a snake in a tube; [one may stay straight and controlled] due to being in dhyānic concentration, but when you emerge from contemplation and are faced with various conditions and objects,

Covetously attached to the flavor of dhyāna 貪著禪味: a phrase from the *Vimalakīrti Sūtra*, T 14.545b5.

what had been controlled may again return to its twisted ways and give rise to passionate afflictions. What at first is like a few drops of water, later can cause a great vessel to overflow. When the practice of dhyāna meditation is lost, you may then break the precepts, act contrary to the Path, and produce unremitting karmic retribution [and be reborn in the *avīci* hell]. [It is said that] "when the Buddha was in this world, a bhikṣu who attained the four dhyānas [also] attained the fourth fruit" [of an arhat, but in fact he became arrogant and fell into the *avīci* hell]. Again, this is like the bear's child. Again, Agramati became attached to dhyāna and took it upon himself to slander Prasannendriya. Again, there may be no evil while you have entered concentrative meditation, but when you emerge from contemplation evil can arise and result in karmic recompense. For those who lose their concentration, the [resulting] evil will pull them into the evil destinies. Even for those who do not lose their concentration, evil karma will arise when the karmic recompense of their dhyāna meditation is exhausted, and they will "receive the body of a flying fox and chew on fish and birds." This is the meaning here. If

When the Buddha was in this world, a bhikṣu who attained the four dhyānas attained the fourth fruit 佛在世時得四禪比丘謂爲四果: see the story of the arrogant monk in *Ta chih tu lun*, T 25,189l1–29. For a full translation of this story see note at *Mo-ho chih-kuan* 38b18–21.

Like the bear's child 熊子: the meaning of this is unclear; could it refer to someone's name, as in Chuang-tzu? The *Shiki* (BT–V, 426) says that it refers to someone who has attained dhyāna but is destroyed by fame, and falls into hell (like in the *Ta chih tu lun* story). The *Kōgi* adds that "this matter needs to be examined further."

Agramati 勝意 **and Prasannendriya** 喜根: see the story of Agramati's arrogance in the *Ta chih tu lun*, T 25.107b13–108a19. See a discussion of this story and a full translation above at *Mo-ho chih-kuan* 104a18.

Receive the body of a flying fox 飛貍: see the story of Udraka in the *Ta chih tu lun*, T 25,189a1–11: Chodron (2, 814–15) translates:

> Thus, the ṛṣi *Yu t'o lo k'ie* (Udraka) who [possessed] the five superknowledges *(abhijñā)*, each day flew to the palace of the king where he took his meal. The king and queen, according to the custom of the land, greeted him by [placing their head at his feet *(pādau śirasābhivandana)*. The queen having touched him with her hand, the ṛṣi lost his abhijñās. [Unable to fly,] he asked the king for a chariot and drove away. Returning home, he went into a forest and tried to retrieve his five abhijñās. The concentration returned, but as he was about to regain the abhijñās, a bird perched on a tree suddenly began to sing and distracted him. Udraka then left the forest and went to the shore of a lake in search of concentration; there too he heard some fish that were fighting and disturbing the water. Not finding the concentration that he wanted, the ṛṣi became angry and said: "I would like to kill every last fish and every last bird." Long afterwards, by the power of meditation, he regained samāpatti and [after his death] he was reborn in the sphere of neither discrimination nor non-discrimination *(naivasaṃjñānāsaṃjñāyatana)*. When his life was over, *he was reborn as a flying fox and he killed all the fish and birds that he encountered.* Having com-

these people had not attained dhyāna, they would not have obtained fame [and fallen into hell], but by attaining dhyāna, this [eventually] became a cause for them to produce [rebirth in] the three [good] dharma realms.

If, while you are within dhyāna meditation, you become defiled with the marks of attachment to this concentration, but when you emerge from contemplation you arouse a mind of compassion, benevolence, and propriety 慈仁禮義 and do not lose this concentration, you will be reborn in the realm of human beings when the karmic recompense of dhyāna meditation is exhausted. If the contemplation of dhyāna is utilized so that you are perfumed with the ten goodnesses, then naturally and spontaneously, without further protection, you will gain the karmic recompense of [being reborn as] a divine being, and the karmic recompense of the four dhyāna stages and the four [concentrations of] emptiness in the two upper realms [of form and formlessness]. If you focus only on cultivating the [four] basic [dhyāna], this will result in increasing the length [of time] as a human or divine being, but you will never attain the going forth [of awakening]. This is like the time the Buddha Victorious in Penetrating Knowledge was told by the Brahma Kings that "for one hundred and eighty eons it has been empty and has passed without a Buddha, and the three evil destinies have been full," and not one person can attain escape from the cycle of birth and death. If you focus only on cultivating [the practices of] impurity, the renunciations, **[130c]** and so forth, and do not rely on the wisdom of the [mundane, worldly] truth, you can arouse [the state of] non-defilement and perfect the dharma realm of the

> mitted innumerable crimes, he fell into the three unfortunate destinies *(durgati)*. This [sad fate] was caused by his attachment to the dhyānas and samāpattis. It will be the same for heretics [immoderately attached to the dhyānas].

The story of Udraka has appeared previously; see *Mo-ho chih-kuan* 40c12.

The time of the Buddha Victorious Through Great Supranormal Powers ... 如大通智勝佛時諸梵自云一百八十劫空過無有佛三惡道充滿了無一人得出生死: Phrases from the chapter on the Conjured City of the *Lotus Sūtra*, T 923c5–19. Hurvitz (135–36 [125]) translates the context:

> At that time, the Brahmā god kings of five hundred myriads of millions of lands, together with their palace retinues, each putting divine flowers atop a cloth spread, went together to the northwest to seek this portent. They saw the Thus Come One Victorious through Penetrating Knowledge on the Platform of the Path under the bodhi tree.... Straightway the Brahmā kings with heads bowed worshipped the Buddha, circumambulated him a hundred thousand times,... then in the Buddha's presence with a single thought and with a common voice they praised him saying:
>
> The World-Honored-One is very rare,
> For only in long intervals of time does he appear; and but once
> One hundred and eighty
> Kalpas have gone by empty, without a Buddha,
> The three evil courses being full,
> The multitude of gods few and decreasing.

śrāvaka. If you cultivate all the dhyānas and are able to destroy the six hindrances—these hindrances are the causes [of suffering] which assemble and beckon the results of suffering—destroying them is the path; and the path leads to extinction. This again is the dharma realm of the śrāvaka, and is also the dharma realm of the bodhisattva of the six perfections [of the Tripitaka Teachings]. Again [in terms of the six perfections], dhyāna meditation will certainly involve abandoning sensual desires; this is [the perfection of] giving (*dāna*). If you do not keep the precepts, samādhi will not be manifested; this is [the perfection of] *śīla*. If you attain dhyāna you will have no hatred; this is [the perfection of] patience. If you attain dhyāna you will not have distracted thoughts; this is [the perfection of] diligence. This practice [being discussed here] is [the perfection of] dhyāna meditation. Knowing that all phenomena are transient is called [the perfection of] wisdom. This is called dhyāna as the cause for the arising of the dharma realm of the bodhisattvas of the six perfections.

Again, contemplating these dhyānas in terms of the arising of phenomena through causes and conditions: if you contemplate these dhyānas in terms of the constituent of existence, and that the constituent of existence relies on the constituent of grasping, and so forth up to [the constituent of] old-age-and-death, this is as explained above, and is the dharma realm of the pratyeka [buddha awakened through realizing the truth of causes and conditions] 緣覺. Again, contemplating these dhyānas in terms of "dharmas that arise through causes and conditions are empty," that the arising of phenomena is empty; this is the truth of the path of non-arising, which is the dharma realm of the śrāvakas and bodhisattvas of the Shared Teachings.

Again, contemplating these dhyānas in terms of "dharmas that arise through causes and conditions are empty, are conventionally existent, and are the Middle" means that the ten dharma realms arise through dhyāna and are extinguished through dhyāna. Why is this so? If you give rise to the dharmas of the three [evil] destinies or six paths [from hell to divine] with dhyāna meditation as the cause, and thus increase and lengthen the time in the twenty-five realms existence (in samsara), this gives rise to the six

The twenty-five realms of existence [in samsara] 二十五有: there are variant lists of these sub-realms of existence. Hurvitz (*Chih-i*, 339–43) gives a detailed explanation with a listing of the four continents (north, south, east, and west) 四州 [4], the four evil destinies 四惡趣 (hell, beast, preta, asura) [4], the six divine realms of desire 六欲天 [6], the Brahmā heaven 大梵天 [1], the four dhyāna stages 四禪天 [4], the four divine realms of emptiness 四空處天 [4], the divine realm of no-thought 無想天 [1], and the fivefold divine realms of the non-returner *(anāgāmin)* 五那含天 [1].

The DDB has what is perhaps a more commonly used list: "The division of the three realms that sentient beings transmigrate through into twenty-five sub-realms.

dharma realms [from hells to heavens] and extinguishes the four dharma realms [from śrāvaka to buddha]. If you give rise to the dharmas of the renunciations and so forth with dhyāna meditation as the cause, you overcome the twenty-five realms of existence [in samsara], and can break down and hide the six dharma realms [from hells to heavens]. If you contemplate the renunciations and so forth as transient, this functions as the "clumsy deliverance" 拙度 [of the Hīnayāna teaching] of arising-and-perishing, destroys the twenty-five realms of existence [in samsara], extinguishes the six [lower] dharma realms, and gives rise to the one Dharma realm *(dharmadhātu)* [of Buddhahood]. If you contemplate dhyāna in terms of "dharmas that arise through causes and conditions being empty," this functions as the "skillful deliverance" 巧度 of [the teaching of] non-arising[-and-non-perishing], destroys the twenty-five realms of existence [in samsara], extinguishes the seven [lower] dharma realms [from hells to śrāvaka], and gives rise to the one Dharma realm. If you contemplate dhyāna as indivisible from conventional reality, this functions as immeasurable "clumsy deliverance," destroys the twenty-five realms of existence and adventitious passionate afflictions, extinguishes the eight [lower] dharma realms [from hells to pratyekabuddha], and gives rise to the one Dharma realm. If you contemplate dhyāna as the cause of "dharmas arising through causes and conditions being indivisible from the Middle," this functions as the "skillful deliverance" of the one true reality, destroys the twenty-five realms of existence and the delusions of ignorance, extinguishes the nine [lower] dharma realms [from hell to bodhisattva], gives rise to the one Dharma realm [of Buddhahood], perfects the King of Samādhis, and universally includes all samādhis, so that all [practices and attainments] from the [four] basic [dhyānas] to the [eight] renunciations, and so forth, are included therein, like all rivers flow into the sea. The [four] basic [dhyānas], the renunciations[, and so forth], are transformed, and all perfect the Mahāyāna. The meaning of being "all-inclusive" is like all rivers flowing into the sea; the meaning of being "extinguished" is like its weak flavor becoming exhausted; the meaning of "arising" is for it to become salty. The perfection of dhyāna meditation transforms this

In the desire realm there are fourteen existences, in the form realm there are seven existences, and in the formless realm, four existences. The twenty-five are grouped into the four evil destinies 四惡道, the four continents 四洲, the six heavens of desire 六欲天, the four meditation heavens 四禪天, the heaven of the five pure abodes 五淨居天, and the four spheres of the formless realm 四空處天."

King of Samādhis 王三昧: another name for the contemplation of the Middle; as Chih-i says, "this is called the 'king of samadhis' because it involves attaining the samādhi of the threefold truth, and all samādhis are included within it."

concentration of compassion to perfect unconditioned compassion; transforms this mindfulness of the Buddha to perfect the great sea of mindfulness of the Buddha, so that the Buddhas of the ten directions are all manifested before you; and transforms these supranormal powers to perfect the Tathāgata's nonscheming and good tentative means [in saving other beings].

To take up and discuss the most important points: if in the nine dharma realms you realize the precepts, **[131a]** concentrative meditation, and wisdom and enter the King of Samādhis, these are transformed and called "noble practice." These noble practices form a covenant so that you calmly dwell in the principle of the truth; this is called "heavenly practices." These divine practices are of the same essence as unconditioned compassion, so they are "noble [compassionate] conduct." By solely illuminating mercy as identifying with passionate afflictions, you wish to extract the suffering [of others]; this is "the practice of disease." By solely illuminating kindness as identifying with "small acts of goodness," you wish to grant bliss; this is "parental practices." Through these five practices you give rise to the ten virtuous qualities, and so forth up to ultimately perfecting Great Nirvana. This is called the arising-and-perishing of the ten dharma realms, and the hidden and manifested threefold truth, with dhyāna meditation as the cause. Gradually you give rise to deliverance [from samsara], increasing and progressing in expanding and converting [towards awakening], and accomplishing the perfection of the Buddha Dharma, which are all included in being indivisible from the Middle and within the King of Samādhis. These all are the objects [of meditation] that are conceivable, and are not the focus of contemplation here [in the *Mo-ho chih-kuan*].

Five practices 五行: the practices of a bodhisattva as explained at length in the *Mahāparinirvāṇa Sūtra*, T 12. 673b–729b: 1. noble practice 聖行, the cultivation of precepts, meditation, and wisdom; 2. noble [compassionate] practice (or "noble conduct") 梵行, actions to relieve suffering and bring joy to sentient beings; 3. divine practices 天行, actions in accordance with divine principles; 4. parental practices 嬰児行, to act with compassion, as a mother to a child; and 5. the practice of disease 病行, to suffer pain in the same manner as other sentient beings, for their benefit.

After this long explanation, the topic is summarized, at T 12.730a5–10, as follows: At that time the World Honored One spoke to the Bodhisattva Mahāsattva Universally Illuminating Light and King of Noble Virtue, saying, "Good son. If there is a Bodhisattva Mahāsattva who cultivates [these five practices] in this way as [explained] in the *Mahāparinirvāṇa Sūtra*, he will attain ten virtuous qualities, not the same as the śrāvaka or pratyekabuddha, that are inconceivable. Those who hear of it will be amazed. These are neither internal nor external, neither difficult nor easy, neither with marks nor without marks, neither of this-worldly teachings nor having its attributes, and not of this world."

Objects as Inconceivable [131a8]

Contemplation [of the objects of dhyāna meditation] as inconceivable is as follows. If you arouse one single thought in a concentrated [dhyānic] mind, whether of flavor, or of purity, and so forth up to that of a supranormal power, you should know that this mind is [indivisible from] ignorance, the nature of reality (Dharma nature 法性), and the Dharma realm 法界; that the immeasurable concentrations and distractions of the hundred [interpenetrating] realms of the ten destinies are included in a single thought. Why is this so? It is due to delusions concerning Dharma nature that we have all the scattered distractions of evil dharmas; it is due to understanding Dharma nature that we have the various practices [and results] of [dhyānic] concentration. Concentration and distraction are indivisible from ignorance; ignorance is indivisible from Dharma nature. Delusion and understanding, concentration and distraction: these do not have two [different] natures. This is subtle and difficult to understand; it is beyond words and verbalization. It cannot be measured by emotion or concepts, which will only bring about fatigue. How, then, can [it be realized by] ordinary ignorant people and those of the two vehicles? Nevertheless, although it transcends [understanding through] ordinary feelings, it is not separate from the mass of living beings. A sūtra says, "All sentient beings have the concentration of complete extinction." Although this defines "concentration" in terms of [the nature of] the mind, it is not that sentient beings actually have this [concentration] from the beginning, nor that sentient beings do not have this [concentration] from the beginning. Why is this so? If it is [completely] separate from sentient beings, how can they seek [dhyānic] concentration? Therefore it is not that they do not have this from the beginning. [On the other hand,] if sentient beings had this concentration [of complete extinction from the beginning], they would not be sentient beings [rather than Buddhas]. Therefore it is not that they have this from the beginning. They do not have this [attainment] yet, therefore it is not immediately theirs 不即; it is not that they are completely without [potentially attaining it]; therefore it is not separate [from their possible eventual attainment] 不離. Neither identical nor separate 不即不離, the subtle [truth] is in the middle, difficult to measure, like emptiness. "Only a Buddha and a Buddha are able to exhaust it." A single thought in

All sentient beings have the concentration of complete extinction 一切衆生即滅盡定 (*nirodha-samāpatti?): probably from the *Viśeṣacintabrahma-paripṛcchā*, T 15.43a7–18, which claims that "all ordinary ignorant people" also have the "samādhi of complete extinction."

Only a Buddha and a Buddha are able to exhaust it 唯佛與佛乃能究盡: a famous phrase from the opening of the chapter on "Skillful Means" in the *Lotus Sūtra*, T 9.5c11. Hurvitz (22 [22]) translates:

dhyānic concentration is like this, and all objective realms are also like this. If you contemplate in this way, you will spontaneously attain awakening. "By directly hearing these words, you will heal the disease of passionate afflictions," without any need for the dharmas of the [lower] nine destinies.

2. Arousing Compassion [131a23]

If this contemplation does not yet result in awakening, then repeatedly arouse compassion. The principle is quiescent [and does not change], but sentient beings arouse delusions [concerning it]. Ignorance and frivolous disputes screen out the *tathāgata-garbha* and make the forest of passionate afflictions flourish. Therefore you should arouse mercy and extract the basic and heavy sufferings [of sentient beings]. Again, [you should realize that] ignorance is indivisible from Dharma nature, and passionate afflictions are indivisible from *bodhi*-wisdom. If you wish to lead sentient beings [to enlightenment], use practical phenomena to [clarify] the real [truth], and thus manifest the Dharma body. Thus you should arouse kindness and grant them ultimate bliss. In this way your vows should be clear, pure, true, and correct 清淨眞正. Above, seek the Path of the Buddha; below, save sentient beings. Do not mix in poison, nor rely on one-sided deviant [views], nor rely on any [attachments], but avoid the two extremes. This is called "arousing the mind of *bodhi*-wisdom." When this mind is aroused, **[131b]** you will spontaneously attain awakening, like a nimble horse that takes the right road just by glimpsing the shadow of a whip.

3. Skillful Means for a Peaceful Mind [131b1]

If you do not pass [to awakening even through the contemplation of compassion], you should calm your mind in cessation-and-contemplation and turn to the cultivation of good, skillful means. Whether cessation or con-

Concerning the prime, rare, hard-to-understand dharmas, which the Buddha has perfected, *only a Buddha and a Buddha can exhaust their reality*.

By directly hearing these words, you will heal the disease of passionate afflictions 直聞是言煩惱病愈: probably referring to a similar passage in the *Suvarṇaprabhāsa Sūtra*, T 16.352b2–4:

> At that time there were a hundred thousand sentient beings who had encountered extremely grave diseases. But by directly hearing these words [of the Buddha], their minds rejoiced and their various maladies were removed, and they again recovered their original full strength.

Arousing the mind of *bodhi*-wisdom 發菩提心: or, more commonly, "arousing the aspiration for enlightenment."

Nimble horse ... 如快馬見鞭影卽到正路: this simile has already appeared many times. For a full explanation and textual references, see the note at *Mo-ho chih-kuan* 19a23.

templation, if you contemplate a single thought in dhyāna meditation and the two extremes are quiescent, this is called "cessation as realizing the true [essence as empty]" 體眞止. To illuminate the Dharma nature [of reality] as pure, unobstructed, and unhindered is called "the contemplation of emptiness itself" 卽空觀. Again, to contemplate the mind of dhyāna meditation as itself both empty and conventional 卽空卽假 is to illuminate both [the mundane and real] truths, that is, the immovable and true reality 不動眞際; this is called "cessation as [the realization of reality as conventional existence] that arises through conditions" 隨緣止. To have penetrating understanding about medicine and diseases and apply them appropriately [in order to heal sentient beings] is called "the contemplation of conventional existence itself" 卽假觀. Again, to deeply contemplate mind of dhyāna meditation as itself simultaneously empty, conventional, and the Middle 卽空卽假卽中, neither two nor distinct 無二無別, is called "cessation of non-discriminatory conceptualizations" 無分別止. To penetrate the true marks [of reality], the *tathāgata-garbha*, and the supreme truth, neither two nor distinct, is called "the contemplation of the Middle itself" 卽中觀. This threefold cessation and threefold contemplation is in a single thought of the mind, and is neither before nor after, neither one nor different. It destroys the two extremes and is called "one" and is called "Middle" 名一名中; it destroys a one-sided attachment to arising-and-perishing, so it is called "perfect quiescent extinction" 圓寂滅. It destroys the gradual [progression through] three types of cessation and three types of contemplation, so it is called "threefold contemplation in a single thought or mind" 三觀一心. In reality there are no marks of concentration such as "Middle," "perfect," or "one mind." Therefore this cessation-and-contemplation [should be used for] calming the mind.

4. Deconstructing Dharmas [131b13]

If these two [practices of cessation and contemplation] do not prepare the mind enough to realize [awakening], you should know that as long as you do not yet arouse [a realization of] the real [truth of emptiness], all that is before you is delusion and confusion. Through single-minded threefold contemplation you should universally deconstruct both vertically and horizontally all delusions and confusions. When delusions pass away, wisdom arises; when confusion ceases, you perfect concentration.

5. Knowing What Penetrates and What Obstructs [131b15]

If still you are not awakened, that means you have obstructions and cannot penetrate [to awakening]. You should further contemplate, what is not penetrating, and what will not be an obstruction? If there are no obstructions, then you should be able to penetrate. If you [realize] what is not penetrating, you should further contemplate thoroughly, knowing what are true letters [or teachings] or not true letters [or teachings], thus through the fourfold truth becoming aware of what is attained and what is lost.

6. Steps on the Path [131b18]

If still you are not awakened, that means you do not understand how to regulate and control the steps on the path. What does this mean? A single thought in a dhyānic [concentrated] mind includes all the aggregates of the ten destinies [from hell to Buddha]. To realize that all the aggregates are empty is to destroy the four perversions in this world [of desires], and perfect the four kinds of decay; to realize that all skandhas are conventionally existent is to destroy the four perversions of the transworldly realm and perfect the four kinds of flourishing; to realize that all aggregates are the Middle is [to realize that these matters are] neither internal nor external [or, neither of this world nor of the transworldly realm], and neither flourishing nor decaying, and nirvana is realized in the midst of this. In this way the four mindfulnesses open the gate to the steps on the path, the steps on the path open the gate of the three liberations, and you enter nirvana and [the steps on] the path are endowed with the [dhyāna] concentrations.

7. Auxiliary Methods to Assist the Path [131b24]

Why is it that you are still not awakened? It is because, due to the manifestation of past obstacles and hindrances, and attachment to the flavor of dhyāna, you are not able to abandon them. Matters from the present and the past mutually support each other in arousing the hindrances of stinginess [and so forth], so how can the path be aroused? You should repent until it hurts, and abandon your physical body, life, and material wealth, abandon coveting the flavor of dhyāna, and cultivate the perfection of giving, and thus assist in controlling the obstacles of stinginess [and so forth].

Again, being attaching to the flavor of dhyāna destroys [the keeping of] precepts that are in accordance with the path 隨道戒, and so forth up to destroying the complete precepts 具足戒. The mutual support [of effect from

Four kinds of decay 四枯 **and four kinds of flourishing** 四榮: an image for the eight kinds of perversions. For details, see the note at *Mo-ho chih-kuan* 88c16–18.

Repent until it hurts 苦到: Chan-jan comments (BT–V, 439), "Since these things hinder the essence of dhyāna, it should be done 'until it hurts'. How much more so if passionate afflictions and karmic and demonic influences not be repented of? People of the world think that they have committed no offences and that it is not necessary to repent, but this is a mistake."

breaking the precepts] in the present and the past together forms the hindrance of destroying the precepts. You should repent until it hurts, carefully measuring various actual affairs, thus assisting in controlling the obstacles to [keeping] the precepts. **[131c]** It is like being in the Black-toothed Brahmā Heaven and still harboring anger, so now even if you arouse the actual phenomenal aspects of dhyāna, how can you get rid of anger?

Again, you may consider dhyāna concentration to exist, but if it "exists" this is neither [the forbearance of] non-arising nor quiescence; since it is neither of these two forbearances, you naturally become angry. The mutual support from matters in the past and present together forms this obstacle of anger. You should repent until it hurts, adding the cultivation of practical compassion, to assist in controlling these obstacles to forbearance.

Again, attachment to the flavor of dhyāna leads to negligence; blinded by ignorance you become distracted and confused. The mutual support of matters in the past and present together forms indolence. You should [repent] until it hurts, so that your diligence is unbroken and continuous, to assist in controlling the obstacles to progress 進 [or "diligence"].

Again, the marks of karma that are aroused within dhyāna may vex and confuse the mind of dhyāna, so that you cannot attain the deep unity [of concentration]. Those of the two vehicles merely sever passionate afflictions and seek to pass [into nirvana] while resisting karma and not discussing the severing of karma. Bodhisattvas sever passionate afflictions and experience the body of Dharma nature. Among the Dharma teachings there are those that are open and not open. You should know the obstacles due to karma, and should cultivate various good karma until it hurts. The same is true for the body of Dharma nature. And how much more should those with bodies in the cycle of birth-and-death [strive to achieve] the calm of attaining [the state of] no more karmic recompense. They should cultivate good [karma] to assist in controlling the obstacles to [dhyāna] concentration.

Again, [attachment to] the flavor of dhyāna means that you are completely uncomprehending of the transiency of arising and perishing, not to mention comprehending the non-arising-and-non-perishing of the flavor of dhyāna. The mutual support of matters in the past and present together forms the obstacles of ignorance. You should repent until it hurts to control and heal these matters of deluded perversity.

This is an abbreviated clarification of regulating and controlling [such

Black-toothed Brahmā Heaven 黒齒梵天: Chan-jan (BT–V, 438) notes that this appears during dhyāna meditation.

[The forbearance of] non-arising 無生 **and quiescent** 寂滅: the fourth and fifth of the "five kinds of forbearance."

matters], and even an extensive discussion could not exhaust it. The methods of contemplation for a practitioner reach their ultimate end here.

8. Graded Stages of Attainment, 9. Resting in Patient Forbearance, and 10. No Passionate Attachments to Dharmas [131c15]

If still you are not awakened, this is a matter of very dull faculties or [the result of] obstacles of heavy offences. I am afraid that such obstacles from offences will cause the production of further faults, so I should again clarify the following three items. [8.] Being aware of the graded stages [of attainment] internally protects against arrogance. [9.] Resting in patient forbearance externally protects against the eight winds [that agitate the human mind: benefit, decline, ruin, honor, praise, slander, suffering, and pleasure]. [10.] Removing passionate attachments to dharmas protects against "falling from the pinnacle" [and retrogressing to a lower level].

11. Summary [131c8]

Fulfill these ten modes [of contemplation] and you will quickly enter [the forbearance that comes from realizing the] non-arising [of dharmas], attain the one great vehicle, traverse the four directions, and directly reach sublime awakening, having destroyed the twenty-five realms of existence, realized the King of Samādhis, and be completely endowed from beginning to end with the practice [to benefit] oneself and save others. The rest is all as explained above. [end of fascicle nine]

7. Contemplating the objects of mistaken views [131c28–140c19]

The seventh [of the ten objects of contemplation] is contemplating the objects of mistaken views 諸見境. There is not [only] one, so they are multiple 諸; they involve a deviant understanding, so they are called [mistaken] views 見 *(dṛṣṭi)*. On the one hand, the meaning of a "view or perception" 見 is to "understand and know" 解知, but in speculating on the truth, [the results are] not what they should be. Instead, one-sided views come to the fore, and these are determined **[132a]** to be [the correct] understanding. Therefore they are called "mistaken views."

Those who [only] hear and study [the teachings without practicing contemplation] attain [an understanding of] names and characteristics [or, "verbal scholastic distinctions" 名相] through reciting or reading [the scriptures], but end up with merely a literal understanding of the texts. The eye of their mind is not opened, and they have absolutely no contemplation or insight into the principle [of reality]. They live relying [only] on texts, and die without enlightenment. Those who cultivate [just] dhyāna meditation, on the other hand, only esteem contemplation on the principle [of reality] and integrate tactile objects in their mind, but remain in the dark about [actual] names and characteristics [of phenomena] and are not aware of even one phrase [of scripture]. Those who recite or read the texts "guard the stump" [and become fixated on the literal details], but those who can penetrate beyond their passions can have a sublime awakening. Both types have their shortcomings, and upon being evaluated everyone has faults. Even if your views and understanding are not stagnant, and you are well versed in [the meaning and content of] names and characteristics, if you inquire after others with your [one-sided] understanding, you cannot exhaust their intent. This is like crookedly shooting [an arrow] at a meandering bird, and it flies away and its track is lost. Again, trying to interpret a difficult question involves extra care, like shooting an arrow into space so that the arrow passes without obstruction. You should know that if these things are not perfected through study, mistaken views will certainly arise.

These mistaken views may arise due to dhyāna meditation, or may arise through hearing [the teachings]. For example, when [the state of] non-

Guard the stump 守株: Chan-jan (BT–V, 442) explains, "In the [ancient] Sung period there was a farmer who had a field, and there was a rabbit that ran into a stump and died. After this he abandoned tilling the field and always kept his eye on the stump, hoping that another rabbit would come.... Therefore, in worldly sayings, a person who is attached to delusions is referred to as 'guarding the stump.'"

This story is included in the early classic *Han Feizi* 韓非子, and is the source of the idiom, "guarding the stump and waiting for the rabbit" 守株待兎.

defilement [from passions] arises, it is by means of faith in the Dharma, and by hearing and considering it. [Views] that are aroused through hearing [and studying the Dharma] are as follows: even if originally you do not hear much, by broadly applying it you turn toward awakening, so that your understanding becomes clear, and you can wisely discuss various questions. [Views] aroused through dhyāna meditation are as follows: first you cause a quieting of the mind, and later contemplation turns clear, until you have mastery over turning [to enlightenment] and you have sublime-like penetrating [understanding]. Those who cultivate dhyāna [in this way] in the south are few, so the number of people who arouse [mistaken] views [in this way] are minuscule, but in the north there are many who do these things. They are blind and do not realize it, and claim to have attained the true path, or to have attained *dhāraṇī*. Knowledge concerning these people is obscure, so sometimes they maintain a high rank, or sometimes they are not trusted, and they are rejected as being crazy or deluded. But now I say, these people are neither crazy nor are they noble sages. They are able to speak as if possessed by a demon, but when the demon passes they are just deluded. These things [they are saying] are not really their own, so they are not crazy. If we inquire after the reasons for their delusions, they have [problems with] greed and anger. In accordance with new delusions, they further increase in passionate afflictions; they become bound up in the fetters of the eighty-eight afflictions and mistaken views; therefore you should know that they are not noble sages. They have only aroused the wisdom of [mistaken] views 見慧.

If we were to discuss the arising of [mistaken] views in general, some arise through hearing [and studying the Dharma teachings], and some arise from [the practice of] dhyāna meditation, but mostly they are due to [one-sided reliance on] dhyāna meditation. Sometimes [mistaken] views are aroused when dhyāna meditation is finished, or sometimes [mistaken] views are aroused together with dhyāna meditation. It is rare that dhyāna meditation is attained after the [arousing of mistaken] views, but often with both together. For example, it is like after penetrating through the dhyāna meditations, you arouse [the state of] non-defilement [from passions]. It is rare that one arouses [mistaken views] at the level of "incompletely attained" 未到 [concentration], but it seems that there are many who arouse them at the sixth or ninth bhūmi stage. Because of this situation, I will discuss the various [mistaken] views right after [discussing] the objects of dhyānic concentration [see previous section].

In the south: Chan-jan (BT–V, 444) identifies this as referring to the land of the Chen 陳.

In the north: Chan-jan (BT–V, 444) identifies this as referring to the land of the Qi 齋.

When people arouse [mistaken] views, those with mature sharp and wise faculties are able to judge and correct them on their own, or inquire in the sūtras and treatises to consider and know their own faults, but such people are difficult to find. If you are not able to correct [these mistaken views] on your own, you should approach a "good friend" who can clarify matters and help you destroy these thoughts of [mistaken] views. This is also difficult to attain. Therefore it is said, "The true Dharma and one who can teach it, and those who hear it, are difficult to find." For those who cannot be awakened on their own, or who cannot encounter a teacher, their deviant views will increase daily, and their [bondage of suffering in the cycle of] birth and death will become more extreme by the months [and years]. "This is like wandering in a dense forest with a bent staff; how can you ever escape from it?"

Now, contemplating various [mistaken] views consists of four parts: 1. Clarifying the people and Dharma teachings of [mistaken] views 諸見人法; 2. Clarifying the arousing of causes and conditions for the [mistaken] views 諸見發因緣; 3. Clarifying the faults 過失 [of mistaken views]; and 4. Clarifying cessation-and-contemplation 明止觀 [with regard to mistaken views].

1. The People and Teachings of Mistaken Views [132a29]

First is **[132b]** clarifying the people and teachings of [mistaken] views. This also has two parts: 1. Differences among people of mistaken views; and 2. Differences in the teachings to which people of mistaken views are attached.

1. Differences among People of Mistaken Views [132b2]

The differences among people of mistaken views also has three parts: 1. Heterodox ways outside the Buddha Dharma; 2. Heterodox ways affiliated with the Buddha Dharma; and 3. Becoming heterodox after studying the Buddha Dharma.

Good friend 善知識: as pointed out earlier in the *Mo-ho chih-kuan* (43a18–c9), there are three kinds of such good friends: 1. external guardians who provide material support and external protection; 2. fellow practitioners; and 3. a teacher or master. In the current context Chih-i is probably referring to the second and mostly the third type.

The true Dharma and one who can teach it, and those who hear it, are difficult to find 真法及說者聽衆難得: see the *Middle Treatise*, T 30.39a16, with the characters 聽者 instead of 聽衆, to read: "The true Dharma and one who can teach it and one who can listen [to it] are difficult to find."

Wandering in a dense forest with a bent staff; how can you ever escape from it 如稠林曳曲木何得出期: a phrase from the *Ta chih tu lun*, T 25.316a6–7.

Heterodox ways outside the Buddha

1. Heterodox Ways outside the Buddha Dharma [132b2]

There are basically three heterodox ways that are external [to Buddhism]: 1. The heterodox way of Kapila, here translated as "Yellow Head." He considered that results were included in causes. 2. The heterodox way of Ulūka, here translated as "watchful." He considered that results are not included in causes. 3. That of Ṛṣabha, here translated as "the ascetic." He considered that results both are and are not included within causes.

Again, the *Introduction to Mahāyāna* says, "The teaching of Kapila makes the mistake of 'unity,' that the producer and what is produced are one, that attributes and he who has the attributes are one, that parts and he who has the parts are one. In this way it can be said that he considers [everything to be] one and the same. Ulūka [on the other hand] considers things to be different. Kakudha Kātyāyana considered things to be both one and the

Dharma 佛法外外道: The classical commentaries contain a long explanation of these three "non-Buddhist" teachings (BT–V, 447–59), or the "three famous *ṛṣi*" before the time of Śākyamuni, as Chih-i's analysis of them is rather perfunctory.

Kapila 迦毘羅**, or "Yellow Head"** 黄頭: "Founder of Sāṃkhya philosophy; also called 數論師. The meaning of *kapila* is brown, tawny, red; interpreted as red head, or yellow head; but it is chiefly used for the sage Kapila, founder of the classical Sāṃkhya philosophy and the school of that name" (DDB).

Ulūka 漚樓僧佉**, or "Watchful"** 休睺: founder of Vaiśeṣika philosophy. Ikeda (*Kenkyūchūshaku*, 457) adds that the nickname "watchful" comes from the meaning of his name as an "owl."

Ṛṣabha 勒沙婆**, or "The Ascetic"** 苦行: a patriarch of Jainism. "Described as one of three famous *ṛṣi*, before the days of Śākyamuni, of the Nirgrantha type of naked ascetics" (Soothill).

***Introduction to Mahāyāna* says, "The teaching of Kapila … do not go beyond these four heterodox ways:** see the passage at T 32.40b13–19:

> Question: Various heterodox ways do not understand causes and conditions, and thus arouse four attachments. What are these faults?
>
> Answer: The Sāṃkhya teaching has one fault, that the produced and the producer are one, that attributes and he who has the attributes are one, that parts and he who has the parts are one, and thus considers all things to be one and the same. Ulūka considers things to be different. Nirgraṇtha considered things as both one and different. Jñātiputra considered things to be neither one nor different. All heterodox ways, including Matala [Mahāllaka?, *see below*] 摩他羅 are different, but all of them do not go beyond these four types.

Kakuda Kātyāyana 迦羅鳩駄: according to Ikeda (*Kenkyūchūshaku*, 457), "he taught that all things depend on the actions of the gods; when the gods/heavens are happy, they grant peace to people, and when they are angry they cause people to suffer." The DDB adds:

> He taught that all the fortune and misfortune of living beings is created by the god Īśvara 自在天. When Īśvara is happy, people can enjoy security and happiness; when he is angry, people are beset with suffering and misfortune. Thus, there is basically nothing that people can do about their own fortunes. If one commits murder and feels no guilt, they need not

same and different. Nirgraṇtha Jñātiputra considered things to be neither one and the same nor different. All of the heterodox ways, as well as the teaching of Mahāllaka all seem to be different, but they do not go beyond these four options." Various branches and currents [of teachings] emerged from three or four heterodox ways. [As Kumārajīva explains,] until the Buddha [Śākyamuni] appeared in the world, there were six great teachers, as follows. [1.] Pūraṇa Kāśyapa: Kāśyapa was his family name. He considered things to neither arise nor perish. [2.] Māskārin Gośāliputra: considered all the pain and pleasures of sentient beings to be without causation, and arising naturally. [3.] Sañjaya Velaṭṭhiputta: considered that sentient beings attain the path when the time is ripe, after passing through 80,000 eons, or when your "number of beads on the string" has been exhausted. [4.] Ajita Kesakambharin: "Kambharin" refers to a deer-skin coat. He considered that the suffering from the retribution from past offences should be [atoned for] in this life by [ascetic deeds such as] throwing oneself against a wall or pull-

fall into hell; but if he does feel guilt, he will fall into hell. From the perspective of Buddhism, they are referred to as the Shameless Non-Buddhists 無慚外道 who are gripped by evil views 邪見.

Nirgraṇtha Jñātiputra: a founder of Jainism (see above). According to Ikeda (*Kenkyūchūshaku*, 457), "his original name was Vardhamāna. A founder of the Jina school. He reformed the Nirgrantha school that taught that the world was eternal and that the soul is unlimited, instead teaching a relative form of abiding and emphasizing that with ascetic practice the soul could escape the physical body and thus attain liberation."

Teaching of Mahāllaka 摩迦羅: according to Ikeda (*Kenkyūchūshaku*, 457) and Soothill, a term meaning "stupid and old."

Until the Buddha appeared ... cannot be reformed: this analysis of the six non-Buddhists teachers is a summary from Kumārajīva's commentary on the *Vimalakīrti Sūtra*, T 38.350c–351a.

Pūraṇa Kāśyapa 富蘭那迦葉: "One of the six major non-Buddhist philosophers contemporary with Śākyamuni 六師外道, distinctive for the fact that his teachings denied the law of cause-and-effect—that all was illusion, and that there was neither birth nor death; ergo, neither prince nor subject, parent nor child, nor their duties" (DDB).

Maskarin Gośāliputra 末伽梨拘賒梨子: "one of the six Tīrthikas 外道六師. He denied that the present lot was due to deeds done in previous lives, and the *Laṅkāvatāra Sūtra* says he taught total annihilation at the end of this life" (DDB).

Sañjaya Velaṭṭhiputta (or Sañjayin Vairāṭīputra) 刪闍夜毘羅胝子: a cynic or agnostic who "taught that there is no need to seek the right path 求道, as when the necessary kalpas have passed, mortality ends and nirvana naturally follows. One of the six non-Buddhist schools 外道六師 in ancient India" (DDB).

Ajita Kesakambharin (or Ajita-keśa-kambala) 阿耆多翅舍欽婆羅: "The unyielding one whose cloak is his hair. One of the six Tīrthikas, or brahmanical non-Buddhists 六外道, given to extravagant austerities; his doctrine was that the happiness of the next life is correlative to the sufferings of this life" (DDB).

ing out one's hair. [5.] Kakuda Kātyāyana 迦羅鳩馱迦旃延 considered things to both exist and not exist. [6.] Nirgraṇtha Jñātiputra considered that the results of karma are set and cannot be reformed. This [information] comes from Kumārajīva's commentary [on the *Vimalakīrti Sūtra*]. The names are the same in the *Mahāparinirvāṇa Sūtra,* but with regard to their teachings three are the same and three are different. There may be a mistake in translation, or there may be some other meaning, but I will not take it up in detail here. In general [these various teachings] transmit the lineage of Kapila and so forth, so basically there are three, or maybe four. These are the four [basic mistaken] views [of non-Buddhists].

2. Heterodox Ways Affiliated with the Buddha Dharma [132b22]

Heterodox ways affiliated with the Buddha Dharma refers to [heterodox ways that] arise of themselves among people like Vatsīputra or of the [Mahāyāna] Vaipulya. Due to their own acumen they read the Buddhist sūtras and texts and give rise to one [mistaken] view; since they aroused [this mistaken view] while affiliated with the Buddha Dharma, it is named in this way. [As it says in the *Ta chih tu lun*,] Vatsīputra read the Abhidharma of Śāriputra and came up on his own with a separate interpretation [of the Buddha Dharma], saying, "the self (*pudgala*) is a fifth category apart from the four options, an unexplainable phenomenon, contained in the scriptures (*piṭaka*)." These "four options" are [1] the self is indivisible from visible form;

Names are the same 名與大經同: see the long passage on this topic in the *Mahāparinirvāṇa Sūtra* at T 12.717b12–720a4.

Vatsīputra 犢子: "Vatsa (lit. 'calf' 子牛) the founder of the 犢子部, Vātsīputrīyas (Pali Vajjiputtakas), one of the main divisions of the Sarvāstivāda (Vaibhāṣika) school; they were considered schismatics through their insistence on the reality of the self; 'their failure in points of discipline,' etc.; the Vinaya as taught by this school 'has never reached China.' (Eitel)" (DDB).

Vatsīputra read the Abhidharma ... contained in the scriptures 犢子讀舍利弗毘曇自制別義言。我在四句外第五不可說藏中: see the *Ta chih tu lun* at T 25.61a22–27. This context has been referred to above; see note at *Mo-ho chih-kuan* 73b27–28.

Chodron (1, 55–56) translates:

> In the Vātsīputrīy-ābhidharma it is said: "The five aggregates *(skandha)* are not separate from the pudgala and the pudgala is not separate from the five aggregates. It cannot be said that the five aggregates are the pudgala nor that there is a pudgala apart from the five aggregates. **The pudgala is a fifth category, an ineffable *(avaktavya)* dharma, contained in the *piṭaka*.**" The adepts of the Sarvāstivāda say: "The pudgala is not established in any way, in any time, in any text *(dharmaparyāya)*. It is non-existent like the horns of a hare *(śaśaviṣāṇa)* or the hairs of a tortoise *(kūrmaroman)*. Furthermore, the eighteen elements *(dhātu)*, the twelve bases of consciousness *(āyatana)* and the five aggregates *(skandha)* truly exist, but the pudgala is not found among them."

[2] the self is separate from visible form; [3] there is a self within visible form; and [4] there is visible form within the self. It is the same for the other four [mental] aggregates, together giving a total of twenty [mistaken] views [of the self] with regard to the person. The *Ta chih tu lun* says, "if you destroy the twenty mistaken views regarding the body, you attain the level of a stream-winner." This is the meaning here. Now, what Vatsīputra considered to be "the self (*pudgala*)" is different from that of the six [non-Buddhist] teachers, but it is also contrary to the Buddha Dharma, and the various [Buddhist] treatises all [132c] reject his conjectures. In other words, he is affiliated with the Buddha Dharma, but the person and his teachings are heretical. Or, "four options" could refer to the three times [of past, present, and future] or unconditioned dharmas.

Again, [in contrast to the Hīnayānist Vatsīputra,] people of the [Mahāyāna] Vaipulya may rely on their own acumen, read the ten analogies [for emptiness] of the Buddha, and construct their own meaning, saying, "Neither-arising-nor-perishing is like an illusion and like a transformation, and the illusion of emptiness is the gist." But Nāgārjuna rejects this, saying, "This is not the Buddha Dharma." Therefore these conjectures of those of the

If you destroy the twenty mistaken views regarding the body, you attain the level of a stream-winner 破二十身見成須陀洹: see the *Ta chih tu lun* at T 25.148b20–22, which says: "Again, the five aggregates arise through causes and conditions, and are therefore empty and without selfhood. Through ignorance concerning causes and conditions, there arise twenty mistaken views regarding the body."

The various treatises all reject his conjectures 諸論皆推不受: see, for example, the discussion on "destroying the teaching of the self" in the *Abhidharma-kośa*, T 29.306b–c.

Ten analogies 十喻: that phenomena are like an illusion, a flame, the reflection of the moon in the water, space, an echo, an illusory castle, a dream, a shadow, a reflection in a mirror, and a magical transformation. Appears in the *Pañcaviṃśati Sūtra* at T 8.217a, and is discussed in detail in the *Ta chih tu lun*, T 25.101c–105c.

This is not the Buddha Dharma 非佛法: see the passage in the *Ta chih tu lun*, T 25.61b6–18, immediately after the passage just quoted above. Chodron (1, 56) translates:

> Question. If the views *(dṛṣṭi)* are all false, what is the absolute point of view *(paramārthika siddhānta)*?
>
> Answer. It is the path that transcends all discourse *(sarvadeśanātikrāntamārga)*, the arrest and destruction of the functioning of the mind *(cittapravṛttisthiti nirodha)*, the absence of any support *(anāśraya)*, the non-declaration of the dharmas *(dharmāṇāṃ anidarśanam)*, the true nature of the dharmas *(dharmāṇāṃ satyalakṣaṇaṃ)*, the absence of beginning, middle and end *(anādimadhyānta)*, indestructibility *(akṣayatva)*, inalterability *(avipariṇāmatva)*. That is what is called the absolute point of view. It is said in the *Mo ho yen yi kie* (Mahāyānārthagāthā?):
>
> The end of discourse,
> The arrest of the functioning of the mind,
> Non-arising and non-destruction,
> Dharmas similar to nirvana.

Vaipulya are also [contrary to the Buddha Dharma, and] these people and their teachings are heretical.

3. Becoming Heterodox After Studying the Buddha Dharma [132c5]

Third are those who take the heterodox way after studying the Buddha Dharma; because they are attached to the teachings of the Buddha and give rise to passionate afflictions, they are not able to realize the principle [of the truth]. The *Ta chih tu lun* says, "If you do not attain the skillful means of *prajñā*-wisdom but instead enter [the perspective of] the Abhidharma, you will fall into [a belief in substantial] existence [or 'Being'], by entering [a false understanding of] emptiness you will fall into [a belief in] non-existence [or 'nothingness'], and by entering the *Peṭaka Treatise* you will fall into [a belief in] 'both existence and non-existence.'" The *Middle Treatise* says, "Being attached to [the option of] 'neither-existence-nor-nothingness' is also called a foolish and deluded argument." Thus being attached to a correct Dharma

> Speaking about subjects promoting action (*abhisaṃskārasthāna*):
> Those are mundane systems.
> Speaking about subjects promoting non-action (*anabhisaṃskārasthāna*):
> That is the absolute system.
>
> Everything is true, everything is false,
> Everything is both true and false at the same time,
> Everything is both false and true at the same time:
> That is the true nature of the dharmas.
>
> In various sūtras of this kind, it is said that the absolute point of view *(paramārtika siddhānta)* has a profound *(gambhīra)* meaning, difficult to see *(durdṛśa)*, difficult to understand *(duravabodha)*. The Buddha preaches the *Mahāprajñāpāramitāsūtra* to explain [this meaning].

If you do not attain … fall into 'both existence and non-existence' 若不得般若方便入阿毘曇即墮有中。入空即墮無中。入昆勒墮亦有亦無中: see the *Ta chih tu lun* at T 25.194a29–b1; Chodron (2, 848) translates the context:

> The person who enters into the three teachings [of the Piṭaka, the Abhidharma, and Emptiness] knows that the teachings of the Buddha do not contradict one another. Understanding that is the power of the Prajñāpāramitā which encounters no obstacles *(āvaraṇa)* to any of the Buddha's teachings. Whoever has not understood the Prajñāpāramitā [will come up against innumerable contradictions in interpreting the Dharma]: if he approaches the Abhidharma teaching, he falls into realism. If he approaches the teaching on emptiness, he falls into nihilism; if he approaches the Piṭaka teaching, [sometimes] he falls into realism and [sometimes] into nihilism.

Peṭaka* (or *Piṭaka*)*Treatise 昆勒: "a distant echo of the Abhidharmic work carried out … by the Buddha's great disciple Mahākatyāyana" (Lamotte, *History of Indian Buddhism*, 188–89). This text has appeared previously; see full note at *Mo-ho chih-kuan* 73c25.

Being attached to 'neither-existence-nor-nothingness' is also called a foolish and deluded argument 執非有非無名愚癡論: a summary of the passage in the *Middle Treatise* on "contemplating dharmas" at T 30.25a–b. A more direct source is in the *Ta*

teaching can instead produce heterodox people and teachings. Even if you study the four gates of Mahāyana, but lose the intent of *prajñā*-wisdom, you will be burned by the fires of heterodoxy and instead produce heterodox people and teachings. Therefore the *Treatise in a Hundred Verses* deconstructs the deviance of heterodox ways. Now there are Mahāyāna masters who blaze up and refute the Abhidharma and *Ch'eng-shih* [teachings] saying that these are the heterodox ways of "Being" and "nothingness." How-

chih tu lun at T 25.170c15–29. Chodron (2, 714) translates the context:

> *To say that dharmas are both eternal and transitory is a foolish argument.* Why? It is both denying the denial of non-existence and denying the existence of that which is not denied. If one denies both of these, what is the dharma of which one will still be able to say anything? Question. In the Buddhadharma, characterized by eternal emptiness *(śūnya)*, there is neither existence *(bhāva)* nor non-existence *(abhāva)*. Emptiness *(śūnya)* excludes existence, and the emptiness of emptiness *(śūnyaśūnyatā)* prevents non-existence; this adds up to the fact that there is neither existence nor non-existence. Why accuse that of being a foolish argument?
>
> Answer. The Buddhadharma in its true nature transcends every belief *(grāha)* and every opinion *(abhiniveśa)*. By believing in dharmas that are neither existent nor non-existent, you are holding a foolish argument. To affirm both non-existence and not non-existence is a debatable and refutable thesis; it is a theoretical position *(cittotpādasthiti)* and an occasion for dispute *(vivādasthāna)*. The Buddhadharma is not like that. Even though there are reasons for affirming non-existence and not non-existence, the Buddhadharma does not express an opinion *(abhiniveśa)* on this subject; as it dos not express an opinion, it cannot be refuted or confounded. The Buddhist position is the same [for the other difficult questions]: are dharmas finite, infinite, both finite and infinite, neither finite nor infinite? Does the Tathāgata exist after death, does he not exist after death, does he exist and not exist after death, is it false that he exists and does not exist after death? Is the vital principle *(jīva)* the same thing as the body *(śarīra)*, is the vital principle different from the body? – All of that is futile. [The bodhisattva] also considers as wrong all the theories relating to the sixty-two views *(dṛṣṭigata)*. He avoids them all; he believes in the pure unalterable nature *(viśuddhāvikāralakṣaṇa)* of the Buddhadharma; his mind is free of regret and functioning. This is what is called *dharmakṣānti.*

Four gates of Mahāyana 摩訶衍四門: for an explanation of this pattern [e.g., being, emptiness, both, and neither], see earlier in the *Mo-ho chih-kuan* at 59b, 60a–62b, and 73b25–75b27, and Chart IV in Volume 3.

Burned by the fires of heterodoxy 邪火所燒: perhaps this is an echo of a passage in the *Ta chih tu lun* at T 25.190c23–24, quoted above at *Mo-ho chih-kuan* 74c7–8. Chodron (2, 714) translates the context:

> The Prajñāpāramitā
> Is like the flame of a great fire:
> Ungraspable from any direction,
> Without holding or not holding.
>
> Escaping from any grasp,
> It is called ungraspable.
> The taking of it when it is ungraspable
> Is what the grasping of it consists of.

Treatise in a Hundred Verses 百論: appears to be a statement of the theme of this text (T 30.168a–182a) rather than a specific quote.

ever, the *Ch'eng-shih lun* says that the true meaning of the Tripitaka is emptiness, even though it seems to resemble the meaning of "nothingness." Again, [those of the *Ch'eng-shih lun*] are the same as the *Hundred [Verses]* in what they affirm, and different from the *Hundred [Verses]* in what they deny. You can fall [into one-sided mistakes] by grasping their meaning [too literally]. Again, it is similar to the meaning [of taking the mistaken option] that there are both results and no results [already] within a cause. Again, this is similar to the intent of the *Peṭaka Treatise*. At the time that these discussions arose, people were all able to attain the path. Now, in our time, being attached to these teachings is a fault of the people [of our time], and does not mean that the teachings themselves are to be denied. You should follow these [Buddhist treatises] and not blindly follow [the non-Buddhist ways of] Kapila and so forth. Again, using the Mahāyāna to destroy the Hīnayāna is rejected in the *Vimalakīrti Sūtra*; if you grasp [a one-sided view] and do not perceive the principle of the Middle, then you are the same as those of the heterodox ways, but this does not mean that you take away the meaning of [skillful] means.

2. Differences in the Teachings to Which People of Mistaken Views Are Attached [132c19]

Second is clarifying the differences in the teaching to which heterodox people are attached. The "commentary from within the pass" says, "One teacher has three types of Dharma teachings: 1. attaining a teaching of omniscience [or "universal knowledge or wisdom" 一切智]; 2. attaining

True meaning of the Tripitaka is emptiness 三藏中實義空是: see the *Ch'eng-shih lun* at T 32.239b1–2 which contains the verse, "Various bhikṣu have different arguments, and the Buddhas listen to all of them; therefore I wish for the correct argument, the true meaning in the Tripitaka."

Different in what they affirm and deny 同百家之是異百家之非: Ikeda's translation (*Gendaigoyaku*, 654) extrapolates by adding that the Mahāyānists (or scholars of the *Ch'eng-shih lun*) are concerned with criticizing the Hīnayāna, while the *Hundred Verses* is concerned with criticizing non-Buddhist, heterodox ways. This follows the commentary of Chan-jan (BT–V, 471):

> The masters of the [*Ch'eng-shih*] treatise are the same as those of the *Hundred Verses* because they take Mahāyāna as their gist. Therefore it is said that they are the same as those of the *Hundred Verses* in what they affirm. The masters of the [*Ch'eng-shih*] treatise criticize the Hīnayāna, and therefore it is said that they are different from those of the *Hundred Verses* in what they deny.

Rejected in the *Vimalakīrti Sūtra* 淨名所斥: see the passage at T 14.540b29–c4, which lists the six non-Buddhist teachers and warns against following after them.

Commentary from within the pass 關中疏: this refers to Kumārajīva's commentary on the *Vimalakīrti Sūtra*, T 38.351a.15–19:

> These six teachers exhaustively arouse deviant views. The naked ascetic himself called it "universal wisdom." They are generally the same with minor differences. Together there are three types

supranormal powers; and 3. attaining the heterodox teaching of the Vedas 韋陀外道." [Attaining] "omniscience or universal knowledge" [in this context] means that each person arouses one type of [mistaken] view with regard to their reasoning, and their mental understanding becomes clear and sharp so that the wisdom based on this view is applied to all phenomena; therefore this is called the "omniscience or universal knowledge of a heterodox view." [Attaining] "supranormal powers" [in this context] means that you attain the five supranormal powers such as transforming a city into salt, turning Śakya into a sheep, stopping up a river into your ear, and stroking the sun and moon. These are called the supranormal powers of those of heterodox ways. [Attaining] the teaching of the "Vedas" refers to understanding and knowing well the various worldly writings such as that on astrology, medicine, military affairs, fortune-telling, and so forth; this is called the heterodox ways of the Vedas. One teacher thus has three types of teachings that may be attained, that are not all the same. [The teachings of people like] Vatsīputra or of the [Mahāyāna] Vaipulya are also like this. If you wish to know about attachments to the Buddha Dharma and heterodoxy in terms of the four gates of the Tripitaka [Teachings], each gate has three types: [1] directly arousing an understanding of the principle and then arousing [mistaken] views on the nature of wisdom; [2] attaining supranormal powers; and [3] having a literal understanding of **[133a]** [the teachings of] the Four Āgamas. In this way the four gates include twelve types of differences in teachings [to which people can become attached].

of each of the six teachers, for a total of eighteen. The first type calls itself "universal wisdom." The second attains the five supranormal powers. The third chants the four Vedas. The six teachers explained above are of the first type.

Supranormal powers 神通: some of these are listed in the *Mahāparinirvāṇa Sūtra* at T 12.840b3–11. The first part of this passage was referred to above at *Mo-ho chih-kuan* 80a24. The full passage reads:

> Great King, have you not heard of the sage Agastya, who for twelve years stopped up the waters of the Ganges River in his ear? Great King, have you not heard of the sage Gautama who manifested supranormal powers and for twelve years changed into the body of Śākyamuni? And also changed the body of Śākyamuni into the form of a sheep, and produced a thousand women's sense faculties into that of the body of Śākyamuni? Great King, have you not heard of the elderly sage who, in one day, drank up the water of the four seas and gave it to the parched earth? Great King, have you not heard of the sage Vasu who produced three eyes for the god Maheśvara? Great King, have you not heard of the sage Rāla who transformed the city of Kapila into salt? Great King, among the Brahmans there are those who, in this way, have great powers and can be manifestly compared to the sages.

Four Āgamas 四阿含: in Chinese translation, there are four sets of (Hīnayāna) Āgama texts: the Long Āgamas, the Middle Āgamas, the Expanded Āgamas, and the Miscellaneous Āgamas.

Again, the meaning of attainment includes the first three types of mindfulness within each and every one of the [four] gates: 1. mindfulness of [self-]nature 性念處; [2.] mindfulness of both [principle and actual] 共念處; and [3.] mindfulness of objects 縁念處. [Mindfulness of] "nature" means to directly come in contact with the principle of the [Threefold] truth 諦理. "Both" means cultivating both the principle and the actual together 事理合修. "Objects" means universally coming in contact with all phenomenal objects. Again, if we were to consider this in terms of the Tripitaka Teachings, when you later attain the fruit of enlightenment, this involves the three liberations: liberation through wisdom, liberation through both [wisdom and concentration], and unobstructed liberation [through the practice of concentration]. Therefore when the treasury of the Dharma was assembled

Each and every one of the gates there are the first three types of mindfulness 一一門中初有三種念處: see a passage in the *Ta chih tu lun* at T 25.200c29–201a12. Chodron (3, 961–62) translates the context (note that my translation of the three mindfulnesses from the Chinese is quite different):

> The four foundations of mindfulness *(smṛtyupasthāna)* are of three kinds: i) mindfulness in itself *(svabhāvasmṛtyupasthāna)*; ii) mindfulness by connection *(saṃsargasmṛtyupasthāna)*; iii) mindfulness as object *(ālambanasmṛtyupasthāna)*.
>
> i) What is mindfulness in itself *(svabhāva)*? The wisdom *(prajñā)* that considers the body *(kāyam anupaśyan)* is mindfulness of the body. – The wisdom that considers the feelings *(vedanā)* is mindfulness of feelings. – The wisdom that considers the mind *(citta)* is mindfulness of mind. – The wisdom that considers dharmas is mindfulness of dharmas. This is mindfulness in itself.
>
> ii) What is mindfulness by connection *(saṃsarga)*? When they consider the body at the head of the list, the dharmas of the Path [other than prajñā], coming from causes and conditions *(hetupratyaya)*, impure *(sāsrava)* or pure *(anāsrava)*, are mindfulness of the body. – When they consider feelings, the mind or dharmas as head of the list, the dharmas of the Path [other than prajñā], coming from causes and conditions, impure or pure, are mindfulness of feelings, mind or dharmas [respectively]. This is mindfulness by connection.
>
> iii) What is mindfulness as object *(ālambana)*? All dharmas with form *(rūpadharma)*, namely, the ten bases of consciousness *(daśāyatana)* and a small part of the *dharmāyatana* are mindfulness of body. – The six kinds of feelings, namely, feeling arising from contact with the eye *(cakṣuḥsaṃsparśajā vedanā)* and the feelings arising from contact with the ear *(śrotra)*, nose *(ghrāṇa)*, tongue *(jihvā)*, body *(kāya)* and mind *(manas)* respectively - The six kinds of consciousnesses, namely, consciousness of the eye *(cakṣurvijñāna)* and consciousnesses of the ear, nose, tongue, body and mind are mindfulness of mind. – The notion aggregate *(saṃjñāskandha)*, the volition aggregate *(saṃkāraskandha)* and the three unconditioned *(asaṃskṛta)* are mindfulness of dharmas. That is mindfulness as object.

Unobstructed liberation 無礙解脫: the Taishō text has "without doubt" 無疑, but the classical commentaries correct this to "unobstructed" 無礙.

When the treasury of the Dharma was assembled 故結集法藏時: that is, when the

[after the death of the Buddha], a thousand people were chosen, all whom could use their unobstructed liberation to universally interpret the internal and external sūtras and texts and overcome external enemies [in debate]. The *Abhidharma-vibhāṣā-śāstra* says that there is liberation from the obstacle of passionate afflictions, liberation from the obstacles to dhyānic concentration, and liberation from the obstacles to all dharmas. People who have liberation through wisdom attain the first kind of liberation [from the obstacle of passionate afflictions]. Those who have liberation from both [wisdom and concentration] attain the second kind of liberation [from the obstacles to dhyānic concentration], and only the Buddha attains the third liberation [from the obstacles to all dharmas]. In general these are called the "unobstructed liberations." [It is the same with regard to] losing the intent and becoming attached to [mistaken views of] the Mahāyāna and the four gates of the Shared, Distinct, and Perfect Teachings. Thus there are thirty-six different types [of attachments to mistaken views] of Dharma teachings.

2. The Causes and Conditions for the Arising of Mistaken Views [133a12]

Second, the arousing of mistaken views has two parts: 1. clarifying [the causes and conditions for] the arousing of mistaken views 明諸見發; and 2. the differences in [the causes and conditions for] the arousing of mistaken views 見發不同.

1. The Marks of the Arising of Mistaken Views [133a13]

First is clarifying the arousing of views. Sometimes the cause is dhyāna meditation, and sometimes the cause is hearing [the Dharma teachings].

teachings were recorded after the death of the Buddha. See the lengthy explanation of this scene in the *Ta chih tu lun* at T 25.67c–69b. Chodron (1, 89) translates the core point (67c12–17):

> All who had come to the assembly accepted this command and remained. Then Kāśyapa the Great chose a thousand individuals. With the exception of Ānanda, all were arhats, having acquired the six superknowledges *(abhijñā)*, liberation *(vimokṣa)* complete and without any doubt. All had acquired the three knowledges *(vidyā)*, mastery of samādhi *(samādhivaśitā)*. They could practice the samādhis in a forward or reverse direction *(pratilomānulomataḥ)*. All were without obstacles *(avyādhāta)*. They recited the three baskets *(tripiṭaka)* and understood the inner *(ādhyātmika)* and outer *(bāhya)* sacred scriptures. They recited and knew fully the eighteen kinds of great sūtras of the heretical sects *(tīrthika)* and all of them were able to conquer the heterodox *(pāṣaṇḍa)* in debate.

***Abhidharma-vibhāṣā-śāstra* says that there is liberation from the obstacle of passionate afflictions, liberation from the obstacles to dhyānic concentration, and liberation from the obstacles to all dharmas** 毘曇婆沙云。煩惱障解脫禪定障解脫一切法障解脫: the source of this quote is not known.

Sentient beings have been producing [bad karma] for long eons, and in the past habitually forming various views, yet through various lives forgetting about them, so that their offences veil their original understanding, and their minds cannot quickly open [to enlightenment]. Now if your obstacles [to enlightenment] are thin, you should be able to arouse various dhyāna meditations, or dhyāna and views can arise together, or views arise after [practicing] dhyāna, or views arise suddenly upon hearing someone else's exposition [of the Dharma]. It is like a spring of water that is obstructed by earth or rocks, but when the obstructions are removed it flows forth like a river. If the dark obstructions are removed, [false] discriminations also pass far away, so that if for a day or ten days you continue without stopping, so that one by one you question things yourself and one by one you understand them yourself, you begin to penetrate to the reality of things that you had been attached to, and even things that you had not been attached to are seen as empty and are spontaneously deconstructed. Again, you can skillfully explain your own [understanding of the] Dharma eloquently and without entanglement, adorned with appropriate words. If others attack you with difficulties, you are able to sublimely respond with an explanation.

Where does this "wisdom of views [or insight]" 見慧 come from? It comes from the constituent of reflection within dhyāna meditation. The constituent of reflection is the mental functioning of wisdom 慧數, which involves an excessive reflection on phenomena such that you do not know how to stop yourself. This is like a nimble horse that, when it starts sweating, cannot be restrained. If lecturers [on the Buddha Dharma] do not have their mistaken views moistened by the practice of dhyāna, from the beginning they desire to make [unwarranted] discriminations and thus will often be as though they were having their guts extracted or coughing up blood; in this way their lives will be restricted and finally, views [or insight] will not arise. If, however, the power of [dhyānic] concentration moistens their reflections, although the excesses make it difficult to control, you will not reach the point where [it feels like] your guts are being extracted, and often views [or insight] will arise.

If through this constituent of reflection you thoroughly study the principle of the path and conclude that, for all phenomena, results exist within the causes, this understanding becomes sharp and you can see meanings from afar, surpassing [the abilities of] other people. Because of this you criticize others for not understanding, and thus verbally abuse others, becoming attached **[133b]** to your own interpretation. When others are not able to criticize you, then you become more convinced of your own truth, thinking that this is the true wisdom of non-arising, and that you have attained the sublime mind of [insight into] the principle [of reality]. However, if this is inquired after in detail, it is seen to be merely a sharp-witted defense of mistaken views and delusions of worldly wisdom, including the eighty-eight afflictions, and a chain of perverted views and delusions. How can this be considered a "true understanding" 眞解? It should be known that this is the mark of the arousing of the views of Kapila [and the Sāṃkhya philosophy].

Suppose that through the constituent of reflection you inquire into all phenomena [and conclude] that results are not included in causes, and you clearly understand this view and your mind is ardently clever, so that even though there are many difficulties you are able to see through them and apply various proofs concerning the idea that there are no results within causes. Thus you are able to destroy [the viewpoints of] others so that others are not able to respond, removing them through verbal abuse. If others come to destroy you [or your arguments], you become even more attached to your views, thinking that they are the truth, always returning to verbally support only [the idea that] results are not included in causes. You should know that this is surely the arousing of the views of Ulūka [and the Vaiśeṣika].

Suppose through the constituent of reflection you consider that results both are and are not included within causes. The *Ta chih tu lun* says, "Existence disputes non-existence, and non-existence disputes existence," and that "Dīrghanakha was attached to [the view] both-existence-and-non-

Existence disputes non-existence, and non-existence disputes existence 有與無諍。無與有諍: see the passage in the *Ta chih tu lun* at T 25.61a3–14. Chodron (1, 55–56) translates:

> It is said that ordinary people depend on wrong views *(dṛṣṭi)*, on systems *(dharma)*, on theories *(updeśa)* and therefore stir up quarrels *(vivāda)*. Futile nonsense *(prapañca)* is the origin of quarrels and futile nonsense gives birth to wrong views *(dṛṣṭi)*. A stanza says:
>
> Because one adopts systems, there are quarrels.
> If no-one accepted anything, what could they discuss?
> By accepting or rejecting 'views'
> People are all divided.
>
> The yogin who knows this does not accept any system *(dharma)*, does not accept any nonsense *(prapañca)*, adheres to nothing and believes in nothing. Not really taking part in any discussion *(vivāda)*, he knows the taste of the ambrosia *(amṛitarasa)* of the Buddhadharma. To act otherwise is to reject the doctrine.

Dīrghanakha ("Long Nails") 長爪: Ikeda (*Kenkyūchūshaku*, 461) claims that this is a "nickname" for Śāriputra, who sported long nails as part of his persona, but the *Ta chih tu lun* passage (T 25.61b18–62a22) presents him as one who disagrees with the teachings of the Buddha as expounded by Śāriputra. For a translation of this section by Lamotte see note at *Mo ho chih kuan* 40c13. Chodron (1, 58–61) translates as follows;

> 17. Furthermore, the Buddha has preached the *Mahāprajñāpāramitāsūtra* because he wanted the brahmacārin Dīrghanakha and other great masters *(upadeśācārya)*, e.g., Śreṇika Vatsagotra and Satyaka Nirgranthīputra to have faith *(śraddhā)* in the Buddhadharma. These great masters of (Jambudvīpa) said that all the treatises can be refuted, all

the confused affirmations *(vāda)* and all the twisted beliefs *(grāha)*, and consequently, there is no true religion deserving of belief *(śraddhā)* or respect *(arcana, satkāra)*....

People asked him: "Brahmacārin, what are you looking for, what are you studying?" Dīrghanakha (Kauṣṭhila's surname) replied: "I want to study the eighteen great treatises in depth." They replied: "If you would dedicate your whole life to understand a single one, then how would you ever come to the end of all of them?" Dīrghanakha said to himself: "Previously, I acted out of [injured] pride because I was outshone by my sister; again today these men are covering me with shame *(gurulajjā)*. For two reasons, I take an oath henceforth not to cut my nails *(nakha)* before I have exhausted the eighteen treatises." Seeing his long nails, people called him the brahmacārin 'Long Nails' *(dīrghanakha)*. By the wisdom that he derived from treatises of all kinds, this man refuted *(nigṛhṇāti)* by every means Dharma and Adharma, compulsory and optional, true and false, being and non-being. He confounded the knowledge of his neighbors *(paropadeśa)*. Like an enraged mighty elephant *(gaja)* whose raging trampling cannot be directed, the brahmacārin Dīrghanakha, having triumphed *(abhibhavati)* over all the teachers by the power of his knowledge, returned to Magadha, to Rājagṛha in the public square *(naranigama)*. Having come to his birthplace, he asked people: "Where is my nephew *(bhāgineya)* now?" They said to him: "From the age of eight years, your nephew has exhausted the study of all the treatises *(śāstra)*. When he was sixteen, his learning triumphed *(abhibhavati)* over everybody. But a monk of the Śākya, called Gautama made him his disciple." At this news, filled with scorn *(abhimāna)* and disbelief *(āśraddhya)*, Dīrghanakha exclaimed: "If my nephew is so intelligent *(medhāvin)*, by what trick *(vañcana)* has this Gautama succeeded in shaving his head for him and in making him his disciple?" Having said this, he went at once to the Buddha.

At that moment, having been ordained a fortnight ago *(ardhamāsopasaṃpanna)*, Śāriputra was standing behind the Buddha, fan in hand *(vyajanavyagrahasta)*, fanning the Buddha. The brahmacārin Dīrghanakha saw the Buddha and having exchanged salutations with him *(kathāṃ vyatisārya)*, sat down to the side. He thought: "All treatises can be refuted, all refutation can be confounded and all beliefs can be overcome. Then what is the true nature *(satyalakṣaṇa)* of the dharmas? What is the absolute *(paramārtha)*? What is self nature *(svabhāva)*? What is the specific nature *(lakṣaṇa)*, the absence of error *(aviparyāsa)*? Such questions are tantamount to wanting to empty the depths of the ocean. He who attempts them will be a long time without discovering a single reality capable of affecting the intellect. By what teaching *(upadeśa)* was this Gautama able to win over my nephew?" Having reflected thus, he said to the Buddha: "Gautama, no thesis is acceptable to me *(sarvaṃ me na kṣamate)*." The Buddha said to Dīrghanakha: "No thesis is acceptable to you; then even this view is not acceptable to you?" The Buddha meant: You have already drunk the poison of false views *(mithyādṛṣṭiviṣa)*. Now expel the traces of this poison *(viṣavāsanā)*. You say that no thesis is pleasing to you, but this view does not please you? - Then, like a fine horse *(aśva)* which, on seeing the shadow of the whip *(kaśācāyā)*, rouses itself and goes back to the proper route, in the face of this shadow of the whip that is the Buddha's speech *(buddavāc)*, the brahmacārin Dīrghanakha collected himself and laid aside *(nisṛjati)* all pride *(darpa)*; shameful *(lajjamāna)* and with drooping head *(adhomukha)* he thought: "The Buddha is inviting me to choose between two contradictions *(nigrahasthāna)*. If I say that this view

existence, and disputed with those who taught [the views of] existence or non-existence." If you enter this [mistaken] view, you cannot exhaust the difficult problems [that will arise]. How can this not be the arousing of the views of Ṛṣabha?

Thus the reasonings of the six [heterodox] teachers are not the same, but surely if you understand well the attachments of the various teachers and their arousing of mistaken views and considers them carefully, although there are minor differences among them, they all resemble each other in essence, that is, the six teachers arouse [mistaken] views.

If through this constituent of reflection you reason that it is necessary for the self to exist, but that it cannot exist within the four options of the views of the physical body, not does it exist within the four options of the non-existence of the three times [of past, present, and future], and claims that it exists as a fifth option that is unexplainable but contained in the scriptures, when this view is aroused and the mind's understanding becomes sharp so

pleases me, that is a gross *(audārika) nigrasthāna* which is familiar to many people. Why then did I say that no thesis is pleasing to me? If I adopted this view, that would be a manifest lie *(mṛṣāvāda)*, a gross *nigrahasthāna* known to many people. The second *nigrasthāna* is more subtle *(sūkṣma)*; I will adopt it because fewer people know it." Having reflected thus, he said to the Buddha: "Gautama, no thesis is agreeable to me, and even this view does not please me." The Buddha said to the brahmacārin: "Nothing pleases you, and even this view does not please you! Then, by accepting nothing, you are no different from a crowd of people. Why do you puff yourself up and develop such pride?" The brahmacārin Dīrghanakha did not know what to answer and acknowledged that he had fallen into a *nigrasthāna*. He paid homage to the omniscience *(sarvajñāna)* of the Buddha and attained faith *(śraddhācitta)*. He thought: "I have fallen into a *nigrahasthāna*. The Bhagavat did not make known my embarrassment. He did not say that it was wrong, he did not give his advice. The Buddha has a kind disposition *(snigdhacitta)*. Completely pure *(paramaśuddha)*, he suppresses all subjects of debate *(abhilāpasthāna)*; he has attained the great and profound Dharma *(mahāgambhīradharma)*; he is worthy of respect *(arcanīya)*. The purity of his mind *(cittaviśuddhi)* is absolute *(parama)*."

And as the Buddha, by preaching the doctrine to him, had cut through his wrong views *(mithyādṛṣṭi)*, Dīrghanakha at once became free of dust *(viraja)* and defilements *(vigatamala)* and acquired the perfectly pure *(viśuddha)* Dharma-eye *(dharmacakṣus)*. Also at that moment, Śāriputra, who had been following this conversation, became an arhat. The brahmacārin Dīrghanakha left home *(pravrajita)* and became a monk *(śramaṇa)*; he became a very powerful arhat. If the brahmacārin Dīrghanakha had not heard the Prajñā-pāramitā preached, the powerful doctrine excluding the four alternatives *(cātuṣkoṭikavarjita)* and dealing with the absolute (*paramārthasaṃprayukta*), he would not have had faith. How then would he ever have been able to gather the fruit of the religious life *(pravrajitamārgaphala)*? Therefore it is in order to convert the great teachers *(upadeśacārya)* and men of sharp faculties *(tīkṣṇendriya)* that the Buddha preaches the *Mahāprajñāpāramitāsūtra*.

that you can question and give answers, so clever and quick that your ability to solve problems is like the pointed tip of a sword, so that you can overcome others and establish your own [view] in a certain and unshakable way. You should know that this is the arousing of the views of Vatsīputra.

If through this constituent of reflection you see all phenomena as an illusion or transformation, and arouse the marks of exhaustion which is emptiness, and see that even this understanding is empty, and there is no difference [in the emptiness] of both phenomena and the mind that understands [them] in that they are the same in being like an illusion or transformation, so that whoever understands this meaning can remove all deluded words, this is the arousing of the views of the [Mahāyāna] Vaipulya.

If through this constituent of reflection you surmise that all phenomena are transient, and arise and perish without abiding, that a personal self is unobtainable like the hairs of a tortoise or the horns of a rabbit, that there are only true dharmas, and by analyzing the dust-like objects of these true dharmas, whether crude or fine, all are contemplated as transient and without selfhood, though they appear to have some reality, the arousing of such views and understanding matches that of the Abhidharma. Many people of old have heard [this view] and although they have interpreted names and characteristics in this way, it does not penetrate to the mental road [to Buddhahood]. If these views are aroused, then even though you remain in the dark with regard to texts, you can advance a hundredfold in mysterious understanding 神解. Those who are not aware [of true understanding] think that such people are wise and noble [and have attained this high level], but in reality they are not. If such people are truly wise, their aspiration for enlightenment should be naturally luxuriant [in them] and arise together with understanding; they should be capable of overcoming passionate afflictions and attaining the level of skillful means. Now, however, even though they understand [the truth of] transience, they increase in disputing, so that their aspiration for enlightenment [133c] sinks and their passionate afflictions flare up. Therefore know that this is the arousing of the views of the "gate of Being or existence."

If through this constituent of reflection suddenly you arouse an understanding of emptiness—that is, the transience of arising and perishing is the "floating void" 浮虛 of the three types of conventionality [as causally arisen, continuous, and relative]—and by using various skillful means to analyze dust-like objects as empty, this view is sharp and clear. Thus your spiritual functions become quick, you have strength to overcome difficult problems, and you destroy [the mistaken views of] others and perfect your own. This truly removes delusions; it is the arousing of the views of the "gate of emptiness [or non-Being]."

If through this constituent of reflection you consider all phenomena as both existing and not existing and you enter this gate, then difficult problems will never be exhausted. This is the significance [of the views] of the *Peṭaka Treatise*. This treatise was not transmitted [to China], but there is no end to the arousing of its habits [and way of thinking]. This is the arousing of the view that things both exist and do not exist. It should be known that it is the same for the view that things neither exist nor do not exist.

It should be known that if you penetrate to the principle [of the truth] through these four gates [of Being, non-Being, both, and neither], you can attain correct views, but if you lose skillful means, you fall into the four [mistaken] views. Therefore this is called "mistaken views within the Buddha Dharma." How can it be said that only attachments among the four gates of the Tripitaka Teachings lead to mistaken views? You can study the Mahāyāna of the Shared, Distinct, and Perfect [Teachings] for immeasurable eons, and equally not realize the principle [of true reality]. If you insist that this[, that is, only your own views] are right, and grasp onto any of the four extremes, then mistaken views will burn you like a fire.

Now, with the constituent of reflection you can instantly arouse the previous understandings [of the four gates], and [advance further to see] that [1.] the illusion of existence is like flowers floating in space in a dream, and make this understanding of existence a clear and sharp mental understanding. [2.] Or make [an understanding that] these illusions basically have no reality, and to have no reality is to be empty, so that the understanding of emptiness is clear and sharp. [3.] Or, make an understanding of "both emptiness and existence," analogous to an illusion or transformation that can be seen but also cannot be seen. [4.] Or, make an understanding of "neither emptiness nor existence," denying that the illusion exists, and also that the illusion does not exist. The chapter on contemplation in the *Middle Treatise* says, "If you say that phenomena do not exist and do not not exist, this is called a foolish and deluded argument." People who are facing the path who can attain enlightenment upon hearing this teaching are called "those who attain [insight into] true reality." Those who with a deviant mind become attached [to this teaching or view] and give rise to vain disputes, belong to

Mistaken views will burn you like a fire 邪見火燒: a similar phrase is found in the *Ta chih tu lun*, T 25.190c23–24, which has already been quoted previously; see note at 74c7–8 and 132c10.

If you say that phenomena do not exist and do not not exist, this is called a foolish and deluded argument 若言諸法非有非無。是名愚癡論: see the *Middle Treatise* at T 30.25a–b and the *Ta chih tu lun* at T 25.170c15–29; for full quote see note above at *Mo ho chih kuan* 132c8–9.

the category of those who indulge in foolish and deluded arguments. These are the four views of the four gates of the Shared Teachings.

If through this constituent of reflection you ponder the understanding of the four gates of the Distinct Teachings, that things within this world are an illusory dream, that this dream arises from the phenomenon of sleep, and and sleep is ignorance, by contemplating this ignorance you realize Dharma nature [that is, the truth of reality]; this also involves the four gates [of Being, non-Being, both, and neither]. [1.] You could say that Dharma nature is like seven treasures in a well [that are there but out of reach]; or [2.] you could say that it is like empty space; or [3.] you could say it is like liquor or cream in a bottle; or [4.] you could say it is the Middle Path. These four understandings are clear and sharp; that is, they are the arising of the views of the four gates of the Distinct Teachings.

If through this constituent of reflection you instantly understand, [1.] that ignorance 無明 is transformed into clear enlightenment 明, and this enlightenment includes all dharma [teachings]. Or [2.] that ignorance is unobtainable and yet is transformed into enlightenment, so how can enlightenment be attained? Although it is unobtainable, it includes all dharma [teachings]. Or [3.] enlightenment concerning so-called "Dharma nature" is both attainable and not attainable, and [4.] it is neither attainable nor not attainable. One single gate or teaching is indivisible from the [other] three gates, and the [other] three gates are indivisible from a single gate. This understanding is clear and sharp. If something is deconstructed, there is nothing that is not destroyed; if something exists, there is nothing that is not established. You are not able to excel beyond this, **[134a]** again [believing] that you have attained the forbearance of non-arising. This is the arousing of the views of the four gates of the Perfect Teaching.

Thus the four gates of Mahāyāna all can result in [mistaken] views; true words 實語 can become vain words 虛語, because of the rise of [mistaken] views of words 語見, and because nirvana can give rise to the covetous desires of samsara. These four [mistaken] views are the basis for all

Seven jewels in a well 井中七寶: an analogy for things that are there (like bottles and trays of food in a dark room) but cannot be seen clearly or reached. See the analogy in the *Mahāparinirvāṇa Sūtra* at T 12.735b13–17; for the full quote see note at *Mo ho chih kuan* 47c15.

Liquor or cream in a bottle 酒酪瓶: an analogy from the *Mahāparinirvāṇa Sūtra* at T 12.635c8–26. This is explained earlier in the *Mo ho chih kuan*, 75a3–7, as "a bottle that is filled with water, liquor, or cream cannot be said to be empty, because it is not empty. This is called the gate of both emptiness and being [for the Distinct Teachings]."

These four [mistaken] views 四見: one of the classical formulations of the tetralemma; the four options 自他共無因 that something arises from itself, from

[mistaken] views: [the options of] "self" and "other" are the basis for [the options of] "both together" and "without a cause." Therefore after Nāgārjuna deconstructed [the two options of arising from] "self" and "other," he showed that [arising] "together" had both faults, and "without a cause" is impossible, [Arising from] self or other [causes] cannot be real, how much more so for [arising] without a cause! If the trunk is destroyed, the branches follow; this is the meaning here. If the options of [causation by] "self" and "other" are established, [the other options of] "together" and "without cause" are thereupon established. Now with regard to the arising of views from perverse attachments of the four gates of Hīnayāna and Mahāyāna, if we only clarify the meaning of [causation through] "self" and "other," then it is possible to know about the rest [of the options].

[1.] As for the Tripitaka Teachings, it clarifies that great arising gives rise to smaller arising, that all arise from ignorance and yet there is no true arising. If ignorance is extinguished, all volitional activity is extinguished, but this is not true extinguishing. If you become attached to this view [that things arise and perish], this is the mistaken view of "selfness."

[2.] The Shared Teachings clarifies that truly things do not arise [but are empty]. Because they do not arise [substantially], there is arising, and all delusions arise. If these delusions are extinguished, this in turn depends on their non-arising. The attachment to [this view] is the mistaken view of "otherness." Delusions within this [triple] world are [thought to be] self[-caused], and true [emptiness] is an other-cause, therefore we have this teaching.

[3.] For the transworldly realm, the Dharma nature is considered self-caused, and ignorance is other-caused, so the Distinct Teachings surmises an *ālaya* consciousness that gives rise to all delusions, and that ignorance is extinguished through the deliberate cultivation of wisdom. [Ignorance] arises and perishes, but has no connection with Dharma-nature. This attachment to "otherness" gives rise to mistaken views.

[4.] The Perfect Teaching expounds that the Dharma nature gives rise to all phenomena, and that the Dharma-nature extinguishes all phenomena; this reasoning can lead to the mistaken view of "selfness." The previous [Distinct Teachings is like the lord being weak and the ministers strong; this

"others" or a cause outside itself, from both self and others, and without a cause (or "neither"), all of which are "unobtainable."

Nāgārjuna deconstructed self and other ... 龍樹破自他竟。點共有二過無因則不可: see the verses in the opening of the *Middle Treatise*, T 302b6–7, already quoted many times already:

Phenomena do not arise by themselves,
And they do not arise from another;
Nor both together, nor without a cause.
Therefore know their non-arising.

Lord weak and ministers strong 君弱臣強: Chan-jan explains (BT-V, 491–92) that "lord" stands for the "true" or "principle," and "ministers" stand for "skillful means."

[Perfect Teaching] is like the lord being strong and the ministers weak. The other two can be known in the same way [that is, for the Tripitaka Teachings the lord is weak and the ministers strong, and for the Shared Teachings the lord is strong and the ministers weak].

When hearing [the teachings] is the cause [of views], usually you arouse views based of principle 理見, with fewer arousing of [views based on] supranormal powers or the Vedas. When dhyāna meditation is the cause, usually you arouse [views based on] supranormal powers or the Vedas, and fewer views based on principle. Those who arouse views based on principle can overcome scholars; those who arouse supranormal powers can overcome mundane worldly people. Mundane worldly people are attached to what is different and are not attached to understanding; scholars are attached to understanding and are not attached to what is different. Arousing [views based on] the Vedas can overcome both. If you can arouse all three together, this is most effective in overcoming both [worldly and learned people]. Arousing [of supranormal powers] due to dhyāna meditation is as explained above, so here I should explain about arousing due to hearing [the Dharma teachings].

A practitioner who, although he has attained dhyāna but has not yet aroused [mistaken] views will certainly have his thoughts instructed by those who are temporarily in front of him. Your mind is already quiet and sharp, so when you hear that results are included in the causes, your mind will spontaneously open and be enlightened to a deviant wisdom or knowledge, and a hundred thousand meanings will become deep and reach far, like [water released from] a spring [covered with] rocks. People who hear this will arouse the [heterodox] views of Kapila. It is the same for the other three [options, such as results not being included in causes, and so forth]. If you hear of a fifth [category apart from the four options] that is unexplained but [contained] in the scriptures, and hears of illusions and transformations [**134b**], you arouse the views of Vatsīputra. Of if you hear the four gates of the Tripitaka Teachings and understand one stanza, thoughts of views instantly arouse a deep understanding of transience, but the contemplative mind hurriedly leaps [to conclusions] and is not able to control it, and this hearing [of teachings] causes an arousal of the [mistaken] view of the gate of "Being." The other three gates [of non-Being, and so forth] are also like this. If you hear the twelvefold gates or teachings of Mahāyāna, each gate will give rise to its own understanding, and your understanding will become clear and sharp, so that you can go beyond what you have heard before. Although this

As explained above: see the exposition in the section on dhyāna meditation and supranormal powers at *Mo ho chih-kuan* 130a15–29.

understanding is aroused, if you do not use great [skillful] means, you cannot enter even [the level of] the wise ones of the Hīnayāna. Again, these are not [the same as] the deviant understandings of [non-Buddhists like] Kapila and so forth; therefore you should know about arousing the views of the twelvefold gates of Mahāyāna.

2. Differences in the Arising of Mistaken Views [134b7]

Second is to clarify the differences in arousing the phenomena [of mistaken views]. The heterodox path [of the Sāṃkhya philosophy] of Kapila directly arouses an understanding of [mistaken] views. This understanding is ferocious, and its deviant wisdom or knowledge is transcendent, such that it cannot be subdued, and you attain a kind of omniscience [or, a "universal knowledge concerning phenomena" 一切智法]. If you directly arouse supranormal powers, such as walking on water or fire, or can freely hide or manifest oneself, who would not call such people noble sages? The Tripitaka master Paramārtha said, "In the country of China there are two types of blessings," in attaining supranormal powers. If you directly arouse [knowledge of] the Vedas, and come to know worldly writings, then upon reading various texts you can understand them at a glance. Or if you furtively read the Tripitaka or Mahāyāna sūtras, you can know them at one reading 綷眼 and in turn with this knowledge you can adorn your Dharma teachings. If you are like this, you may confuse the inner and outer [Buddhist and non-Buddhist teachings] so that you can hardly tell the difference between them. Now there are many who have returned to lay life, dreading official duties,

Paramārtha 眞諦三藏: (499–569), "A scholar-monk of brahman background from Ujayinī in the Avanti region of Western India, who become one of the 'four great translators' in Chinese Buddhist history.... Among these translations were such influential scriptural texts as the *Suvarṇa-prabhāsa-(uttama)-sūtra* 金光明經, the *Mahāyāna-saṃgraha* 攝大乘論 and the *Madhyânta-vibhāga* 中邊分別論. He is also (problematically) attributed with the translation of the *Awakening of Mahāyāna Faith* 大乘起信論. His translation and study of the *Mahāyāna-saṃgraha* would cause that text to become very influential in helping Chinese clearly define the distinctions between the categories of Mahāyāna/Hīnayāna, and Paramārtha would eventually come to be regarded as the founder of the *Mahāyāna-saṃgraha* school (Shelun zong 攝論宗)" (DDB).

However, the source of this attribution in the *Mo ho chih kuan* is not known, and Chih-i rarely name-checks Paramārtha.

In China there are two types of blessings 震旦國有二種福: Chan-jan (BT–V, 495) interprets this to mean that in China there are no *rākṣasa* 羅刹 demons, and no heterodox teachings 外道, at least not like the ones in India.

There are many who have returned to lay life 今時多有還俗之者: see comments on the social and political situation of Chih-i's time at *Mo ho chih kuan* 19a2–8.

and have entered heterodox paths, stealing the meaning of the Buddha Dharma and pilfering it to understand Chuang-tzu and Lao-tzu, finally mixing them up so that beginners become confused as to who or what is correct and who or what is deviant. This is the arousing [of mistaken views] based on [becoming accomplished in] the teachings [of mundane knowledge such as those] of the Vedas.

Each single type of heterodox path includes attaining three types [of mistaken views]; with respect to people there are seven types [of mistaken views]. That is, there are three types of single [mistaken views], three types of multiple [mistaken views], and one type of [all-]inclusive [mistaken views]. It is the same for the other two heterodox paths, so together there are twenty-one differences that can be attained. With regard to the six [heterodox] teachers, each has three [types of mistaken views] for a total of eighteen. With regard to people they can attain many or few [mistaken views], but there are forty-two types of differences that can be attained.

There are differences in the arousing of views by people like Vatsīputra or of the [Mahāyāna] Vaipulya. Again there are three types of single [mistaken views], three types of multiple [mistaken views], and one type of [all-] inclusive [mistaken views].

As for the differences in arousing deviant views by those within [the Buddha Dharma], if we look at each and every gate or teaching and how it surmises with regard to the principle of the [Buddhist] path, and distinguish them carefully, we can say that [for those who arouse attachment to the gate of Being] there is the attainment of the [mistaken] view of mindfulness of [self-]nature, or the liberation through [imperfect] wisdom 慧解脱 [as explained above]. It is the same for the other [three] gates. Whether you attain only one or attain many supranormal powers, such as mastering [the power of] flight, there is the attainment of the views of the mindfulness of both [the principle and the actual], and liberation from both [wisdom and concentration]. If you master both supranormal powers and wisdom, but are not able to teach the Dharma, you should enquire into the sūtras and treatises, or listen to the teaching of others, and thus become proficient in the technical details [of the Buddhist teachings], whether at the bottom having a penetrating knowledge of [worldly information such as that of] the Vedas, or at the top having a penetrating knowledge of Mahāyāna, always using your own views to digest all the teachings, and using the teachings to adorn your own views. As for the four gates, each has three types [of mistaken views], and with regard to people again there are seven meanings. Whether [134c] for the Shared, Distinct, or Perfect [Teachings], the four gates each involves directly arousing the understanding or liberation of [imperfect] wisdom 慧解, and each involves the transformations of supranormal powers, and each involves knowledge of internal and external texts, so that you yourself claim to have the Path and the truth, and others say that this is a high achievement. Now, however, we must say that these are mistaken views. One gate has seven [variations], giving a total of eighty-four types [of mistaken views].

Again, previously we have discussed differences [in mistaken views] in general; now we should discuss each one of the differences [specifically]. The three heterodox paths and the six [heterodox] teachers may be the same in arousing [a kind of] universal wisdom or knowledge, whether it be a universal knowledge of the [mistaken] view of Being, or a universal knowledge of the [mistaken] view of nothingness. In this way these various types of universal wisdom or knowledge are distinct in what they reason about, and therefore the wisdom or knowledge of the views are different. Each affirms what it apprehends, and denies that of others. The *Lotus Sūtra* says, "The jackals are already dead." This clarifies that when the sharp afflictions arise, the dull afflictions have already sunk [out of sight]; therefore it is said that they "are already dead." It then says, "The great evil beasts compete to come and chew on them," that is, the single view that you are attached to is able to devour all [other] views. [The *Ta chih tu lun* says,] "[A Brahmin named] *Vivādabala [Great Debator] said that all of these teachers ultimately have an ultimate path, but Mṛgaśiras [Deer Head] was the most supreme." You

"The jackals are already dead" 野干前死 and **"The great evil beasts compete to come and chew on them"** 諸大惡獸競來食噉: phrases from the parable of the burning house. See the *Lotus Sūtra*, T 9.14a27–28. Hurvitz (67 [63]) translates:

> Since the bands of yeh-kan [jackals]
> Were already dead,
> The great malignant beasts,
> Racing to the spot, devoured them.

***Vivādabala said that all of these teachers ultimately have an ultimate path, but Mṛgaśiras was the most supreme** 論力云。一切諸師皆有究竟道鹿頭第一: see the *Ta chih tu lun*, T 25.193b8–29. Chodron (2, 841–45) translates:

> Moreover, in Vaiśālī there was a brahmacārin named *Vivādabala. The Licchavi granted him a large sum of money to go to debate with the Buddha. Having accepted the engagement, he prepared five hundred arguments during the night and the next day, accompanied by the Licchavis, he went to the Buddha. He asked the Buddha: "Is there one definitive Path *(ātyantikamārga)* or are there many?" The Buddha replied: "There is but one definitive Path and not many." The brahmacārin continued: "The Buddha speaks of only one single Path and yet the heretical teachers *(tīrthika)* each have their own definitive path; therefore there are many paths and not just one." The Buddha answered: "Even though the heretics have many paths, not one of them is the true Path. Why? Because all these paths that are attached to wrong views *(mithyādṛṣṭyabhiniviṣṭa)* do not merit the name of definitive path." Again the Buddha asked the brahmacārin: "[According to you,] did the brahmacārin Mṛgaśiras find the (true) Path?" Vivādabala replied: "Mṛgaśiras is the foremost of all those who have found the Path." Now at that time, the venerable Mṛgaśiras, who had become a bhikṣu, was standing behind the Buddha and was fanning him. Then

should know that such "universal knowledge" each has its own differences, up to and including the universal knowledge of the four gates of the Tripitaka Teachings, the universal knowledge of the gates of Mahāyāna, and each have their attachments due to [mistaken] views, and mutually swallow and devour each other. Each is different, and should be understood accordingly.

Next, differences in the phenomena of supranormal powers [is as follows]. Supranormal powers are attained with dhyāna as the cause, but there are differences in the attainment of dhyāna. Heterodox paths outside [of Buddhism] arouse supranormal powers always with the [four] basic dhyāna meditations as the cause, or [arouse them] with the first, second, third, or fourth [dhyāna]; the power and function [of the supranormal powers] are different depending on their causes. The internal [Buddhist] deviant views also have the [four] basic dhyāna meditations as the cause, or have "pure dhyāna" as the cause. The superiority or inferiority of the functioning of these supranormal powers depends on the shallowness or depth of their causes. The *Ta chih tu lun* says, "The functioning of supranormal powers is extensive when it is based on [proper] causes; the functioning of supranormal powers is inferior when there are not [sufficient] causes." Moreover, dhyāna meditation is the actual practice 事 and supranormal powers are its functioning 用, and both correspond to the "adornments of meritorious virtue," so there is

the Buddha asked Vivādabala: "Do you not recognize this bhikṣu?" The brahmacārin recognized [his friend] and, learning that he had become converted, bowed his head in shame. Then the Buddha spoke these stanzas of the *Arthavarga*):

Each person speaks of an Absolute
And is passionately attached to it.
Each one accepts this and not that;
But none of that is the Absolute.

These people enter into debate.
Discussing their reasons
They show their agreement and disagreement in turn
Vanquisher or vanquished, they feel sadness or joy.

Conqueror, they fall into the pit of pride,
Conquered, they fall into the prison of sadness.
This is why those who are wise people
Do not follow these antagonisms.

Vivādabala, you should know
That, for me and my disciples,
There is no mistake and no truth.
What are you searching for here?

Do you want to confuse my teaching?
In the end, you will not have the possibility to do so.
The Omniscient One is difficult to conquer
[To attack him] is to go down to your own defeat.

***Ta chih tu lun* says, "The functioning of supranormal powers is extensive when it is based on [proper] causes; the functioning of supranormal powers is inferior when there are not [sufficient] causes"** 大論云。所因處用通廣。所不因處用通劣: the classical commentaries admit that the source of this phrase is unknown, and SAT database searches yielded no hits in the *Ta chih tu lun*.

no place or reason for them to compete. But, if you compare their causes, they are all different in their functioning.

Next is differences in [various worldly learning such as] the Vedas. Those of heterodox paths outside [of Buddhism] arouse [views] and read texts on "regulating the home and aiding the world" 治家濟世. The books are not the same [for everyone], and each of their contents is different. Those who read much [of these texts] have an extensive knowledge, but those [who read] few have a narrow knowledge. They have a lasting pride and think themselves great, but all depend on different texts. As for those of heterodox views within [Buddhism] who do not arouse such views and do not read the texts of heterodox paths external [to Buddhism], their knowledge is narrow. Those who do read [these texts] have an extensive knowledge. Those who do not arouse [views] nor read the texts of the Tripitaka Teachings do not know [much] about the names and characteristics of this world, and so their knowledge and views are narrow. Those who do read [these texts] have an extensive knowledge. Those who do not arouse [views] nor read the texts of the Mahāyāna do not know about the names and characteristics of the transcendent world, so their knowledge is narrow. Those who do read [these texts] have an extensive knowledge. You should thus know that the teachings of [worldly knowledge such as] the Vedas all have differences, phrase by phrase.

Next is to summarize the difference among the deviant views. Both those internal and external [to Buddhism] clarify matters of wisdom concerning the principle [of the truth], of supranormal powers, and of various texts. If you establish virtues and regulate your mind, and respect others and humble yourself, then your voice will move others. But just as it is difficult to tell if the fruit of the *āmra* [mango] **[135a]** is mature, so [it is difficult to tell] what is good and bad [or fine and ugly] under the sun, and to measure wrong and right. But now it is very easy to judge [these mistaken views]. As for the seven types of different [views] of Kapila [and so forth], if you examine their root, they all arise from a deviant [or false] view of nothingness. Suppose you surmise that "results are included in the causes," denying all other teachings and only affirming this one option, and you manifest various supranormal powers and influence the mundane worldly people of the times, lead people to believe and accept [the view] that results are included in the causes, quote from different traditions of [worldly texts such as] the Vedas, so that [the understanding of various] names and characteristics [of things] are adorned with [the idea that] results are included in the causes, establish your practices on this basis and rely on this purport for the tendency [of your practice]. If [the idea that] "the results are included in the causes" is the ultimate teaching and you become attached to it, then you will be physically, verbally, and mentally moved to produce immeasurable offences, as explained below. Because of this you can examine and know that this is the heterodox path of Kapila. That of Ulūka and Ṛṣabha are likewise; they start by arousing the deviant view of nothingness, and finally return [to this purport] and become attached to it. Vatsīputra is also like this. The four gates of Hīnayāna and Mahāyāna should also be understood in accordance with this.

If these [mistaken views] are examined as to their original basis 元始, and are investigated by returning to their gist 歸宗, [their differences can be seen] as the flow of clear and muddy [waters] are distinct [from each other], and the varieties of beans and barley [can be distinguished]. How can you exaggerate and put [the teachings of] Chuang-tzu and Lao-tzu on a par with that of the Buddha Dharma, or mix up and confuse the deviant views from the correct!? [On what basis] can you extract the Mahāyāna as different from the Hīnayāna? If your own practice [for your own benefit] is not clear, how can you save others? Both the teacher and the disciple will fall together [into mistaken views].

3. The Faults of Mistaken Views [135a13]

Third is to clarify the faults [of mistaken views], in two parts: 1. Clarifying the faults, and 2. Lining up and determining [the true and the false].

1. Clarifying the Faults of Mistaken Views [135a13]

First is clarifying the faults [of mistaken views].

1. Mistaken Views of Non-Buddhist Paths [135a14]

In India there were basically three [types of mistaken views], and the same can be said of China. Chou Hung-cheng interpreted the three gists [of Chinese traditions] saying that the *[Book of] Changes* makes judgements based on the eight trigrams 八卦, and Yin-yang [reveals] good and bad fortune; these clarify the gist of things in terms of their existence. Lao-

As explained below: it appears that Chih-i meant to explain this in more detail in his final, tenth chapter, which remain unfinished. See also the discussion of this idea of "returning to the purport" in the final section of the opening summary at 21a25–b8.

The flow of clear and muddy 涇渭分流: this image is also known as a metaphor for distinguishing between good and evil.

Chou Hung-cheng (Zhou Hongzheng) 周弘政[正]: a contemporary (487–565) who passed away when Chih-i was thirty-three years old. *The Biography of T'ien-t'ai Chih-che*, T 50.192c, points out that he attended the lectures by Chih-i that became the *Fa hua hsüan-i*, and his name appears in many of the other classical Buddhist biographies.

tzu's "fusing with the void" 虚融 clarifies the gist in terms of nothingness. Chuang-tzu's "spontaneity" 自然 clarifies the gist in terms of both existence and nothingness. The various branches [of these traditions] all emerge from the original founders, so for now I will clarify their faults in these terms.

As Chuang-tzu said, "rich and poor, suffering and pleasure, right and wrong [or positive and negative], attainment and loss; all are spontaneous." To say that things are spontaneous is to deny [the idea of] results; to not discuss previous karma is to deny [the idea of] causes. The regulation of ritual propriety and the ideal of benevolence are for protecting our physical bodies and bringing peace to the country; if these things are not practiced, it will

As Chuang-tzu said, "rich and poor, suffering and pleasure, right and wrong, attainment and loss; all are spontaneous" 如莊子云。貴賤苦樂是非得失皆其自然: see the "Autumn Floods" section of the *Chuang-tzu*. WATSON (*Chuang Tzu: Basic Writings*, 97–100) translates the context:

"You can't discuss the ocean with a well frog—he's limited by the space he lives in. You can't discuss ice with a summer insect—he's bound to a single season. You can't discuss the Way with a cramped scholar—he's shackled by his doctrines. Now you have come out beyond your banks and borders and have seen the great sea—so you realize your own pettiness. From now on it will be possible to talk to you about the Great Principle...."

"Well, then," said the Lord of the River, "if I recognize the hugeness of heaven and earth and the smallness of the tip of a hair, will that do?"

"No indeed," said Jo of the North Sea. "There is no end to the weighing of things, no stop to time, no constancy to the division of lots, no fixed rule to beginning and end. Therefore great wisdom observes both far and near, and for that reason recognizes small without considering it paltry, recognizes large without considering it unwieldy, for it knows that there is no end to the weighing of things. It has a clear understanding of past and present, and for that reason it spends a long time without finding it tedious, a short time without fretting at its shortness, for it knows that time has no stop. It perceives the nature of fullness and emptiness, and for that reason it does not delight if it acquires something nor worry if it loses it, for it knows that there is no constancy to the division of lots...."

"Therefore the Great Man in his actions will not harm others, but he makes no show of benevolence or charity. He will not move for the sake of profit, but he does not despise the porter at the gate. He will not wrangle for goods or wealth, but he makes no show of refusing or relinquishing them. He will not enlist the help of others in his work, but he makes no show of being self-supporting, and he does not despise the greedy and base. His actions differ from those of the mob, but he makes no show of uniqueness or eccentricity. He is content to stay behind with the crowd, but he does not despise those who run forward to flatter and fawn. All the titles and stipends of the age are not enough to stir him to exertion; all its penalties and censures are not enough to make him feel shame. He knows that no line can be drawn between right and wrong, no border can be fixed between great and small."

For a detailed discussion of Chih-i's take on the Lao-tzu and Chuang-tzu traditions, see Ikeda Rosan's article "Tendai kyōgaku to rōsō shisō" in *Komazawa Daigaku Bukkyōgaku ronshū* 21 (1990).

lead to the extinction of the family and the death of the household [lineage]. However, they merely establish virtues for the current world, and do not provide guidance for retribution or reward in the next world, which means that results are denied, but causes are not denied. If it is said that felicitous matters flow over into the next life, then, if lined up with the previous [teaching], this means that there both are results [in future lives] and there are no results [in future lives].

Each single [tradition] has three practices. [First, in terms of the view of existence:] 1. by surmising existence, you practice good deeds; 2. by surmising existence, you practice evil deeds; and 3. by surmising existence, you practice neutral deeds. As it is said, the principle of the matter is as it should be 理分應爾: that is, riches should not be actively sought, poverty should not be bitterly avoided, and birth and life is not necessarily a matter for rejoicing, and why should death be dreadfully feared? With this "empty mind" 虛心 you can dwell in riches without being haughty, and can dwell in extreme poverty without discomfort. If your covetous and angry mind has ceased, and you have embraced a calm and peaceful [mind], you can instruct others in the way of natural spontaneity, and entice people to realize the principle [of the truth]. These are the [positive] attainments of this [view]. However, such attainments are of many types [and not all are positive]. If you say **[135b]** that there are never any desires and this sublimity is contemplated, then what are the desires that are missing? [In the past people have] declined [social] rank and rejected official posts, and "washed their ears and returned the bulls" in order to guard their lofty aspirations. This involves rejecting the desires of this realm of desires and aiming for the higher and superior goal of sublime liberation, that is, the sublime [attainment] of the first dhyāna meditations. How do you know that these are attained? In the *Chuang-tzu* the [Yellow] Emperor asks about the Way, and [learns that] by contemplating mysterious energies you can perceive the various things within your body.

Decline rank and reject official posts 忽玉璧棄公相: a reference to cases "where an exemplar of rightness 義 declines a governmental position (usually the position of emperor) that is not rightfully his" (personal note from Michael Ing; see also Sarah Allen, *The Heir and the Sage*). Also, see note at *Mo-ho chih-kuan* 124b17.

Washed ears and returned the bull 洗耳還牛: this saying has been used previously; see note at *Mo-ho chih-kuan* 124b17.

In the *Chuang-tzu* the Emperor asks about the Way, and by contemplating mysterious energies you can perceive the various things within your body 莊公皇帝問道觀神氣見身內羅物: see the dialogue between the Yellow Emperor 黃帝 and Guang Cheng-zi 廣成子 in the "Letting Be" 在宥 chapter of the *Chuang-tzu*. Legge translates:

> Huang-Di [the Yellow Emperor] had been on the throne for nineteen years, and his ordinances were in operation all through the kingdom, when he heard that Guang Cheng-zi was living on the

summit of Kong-tong, and went to see him. "I have heard," he said, "that you, Sir, are well acquainted with the perfect Dao. I venture to ask you what is the essential thing in it. I wish to take the subtlest influences of heaven and earth, and assist with them the (growth of the) five cereals for the (better) nourishment of the people. I also wish to direct the (operation of the) Yin and Yang, so as to secure the comfort of all living beings. How shall I proceed to accomplish those objects?" Kong Tong-zi replied, "What you wish to ask about is the original substance of all things; what you wish to have the direction of is that substance as it was shattered and divided. According to your government of the world, the vapours of the clouds, before they were collected, would descend in rain; the herbs and trees would shed their leaves before they became yellow; and the light of the sun and moon would hasten to extinction. Your mind is that of a flatterer with his plausible words—it is not fit that I should tell you the perfect Dao."

Huang-Di withdrew, gave up (his government of) the kingdom, built himself a solitary apartment, spread in it a mat of the white mo grass, dwelt in it unoccupied for three months, and then went again to seek an interview with (the recluse). Kong Tong-zi was then lying down with his head to the south. Huang-Di, with an air of deferential submission, went forward on his knees, twice bowed low with his face to the ground, and asked him, saying, "I have heard that you, Sir, are well acquainted with the perfect Dao—I venture to ask how I should rule my body, in order that it may continue for a long time." Kong Tong-zi hastily rose, and said, "A good question! Come and I will tell you the perfect Dao. Its essence is (surrounded with) the deepest obscurity; its highest reach is in darkness and silence. There is nothing to be seen; nothing to be heard. When it holds the spirit in its arms in stillness, then the bodily form of itself will become correct. You must be still; you must be pure; not subjecting your body to toil, not agitating your vital force—then you may live for long. When your eyes see nothing, your ears hear nothing, and your mind knows nothing, your spirit will keep your body, and the body will live long. Watch over what is within you, shut up the avenues that connect you with what is external—much knowledge is pernicious. I (will) proceed with you to the summit of the Grand Brilliance, where we come to the source of the bright and expanding (element); I will enter with you the gate of the Deepest Obscurity, where we come to the source of the dark and repressing (element). There heaven and earth have their controllers; there the Yin and Yang have their Repositories. Watch over and keep your body, and all things will of themselves give it vigour. I maintain the (original) unity (of these elements), and dwell in the harmony of them. In this way I have cultivated myself for one thousand and two hundred years, and my bodily form has undergone no decay."

Huang-Di twice bowed low with his head to the ground, and said, "In Kong Tong-zi we have an example of what is called Heaven." The other said, "Come, and I will tell you: (The perfect Dao) is something inexhaustible, and yet men all think it has an end; it is something unfathomable, and yet men all think its extreme limit can be reached. He who attains to my Dao, if he be in a high position, will be one of the August ones, and in a low position, will be a king. He who fails in attaining it, in his highest attainment will see the light, but will descend and be of the Earth. At present all things are produced from the Earth and return to the Earth. Therefore I will leave you, and enter the gate of the Unending, to enjoy myself in the fields of the Illimitable. I will blend my light with that of the sun and moon, and will endure while heaven and earth endure. If men agree with my views, I will be unconscious of it; if they keep far apart from them, I will be

To take this as the Way resembles the supranormal powers, insights, and contemplations that are aroused in the sublime attainments of the first [stage of] dhyāna meditations.

If we say that the causes of suffering have covetous desires as their basis, then being liberated from covetous desires is the attainment of nirvana. This means that there are no desires in the triple world, that this is the attainment of the sublimity of extinction and cessation 滅止妙 and the sublimity of liberation 離之妙. Again, this dharma is called "undefiled" [by attachments]; if this dharma is defiled [by attachments], then nirvana is defiled [by attachments]. If there are no such defiled desires, you have attained the One Path of subtle sublimity. If these desires are made sublime, then there is neither desires nor the sublime. What, then, is attained? Since they do not know the desires of the realm of desires, nor the sublimity of the first [stage of] dhyāna meditations, how can they know the sublimity that follows after desires [have ceased]? Even if we tentatively suppose that they will advance gradually in accordance with their capabilities, so that there can be a "veiled" discussion of desires and sublimity, they cannot attain a clear expression [of this] nor explain the full meaning. However, if you stop calculated desires, and contemplate the sublimity of spontaneity, then dangerously biased actions are already removed, and the wind of benevolence is present. These all surmise existence and spontaneity to perform good.

Again, if you surmise spontaneity and a natural, carefree spirit or energy, without any attempt to follow good, and even though you do not move to actively produce evil, if the spirit of harmony 神和 is wounded, this cannot be said to be "spontaneous." Even though there is no grasping or abandoning, this is merely acting "neutrally" [without good or evil], and since karmic actions are not yet extinguished, who can doubt that eventually you will receive [karmic] recompense? Those who surmise spontaneity and produce evil say that the myriad things are all spontaneous, and so they produce evil as they wish, and finally return to spontaneity. This, however, can hardly be considered a "lack of desire," but rather is unrestrained desire. This is the opposite of "sublime" and instead is "crude." Chuang-tzu rejected [the Confucian ideal of] benevolence and righteousness, saying that although promoting the ideal of benevolence and righteousness restrains minor rob-

unconscious of it; they may all die, and I will abide alone!"

See also the translation by Burton Watson, *Complete Works of Chuang Tzu*, 118–20.

Chuang-tzu rejected [the ideal of] benevolence and righteousness … overthrow the country 莊周斥仁義。雖防小盜不意大盜揭仁義以謀其國: see the chapter on "The Robber Kih" 盜跖 in which a great robber lectures Confucius on the inadequacy of his ideals. Here is an excerpt, from Legge's translation, at http://oaks.nvg.org/zhuangzi28-.html#29:

bery, it has no effect on major robbery, and this becomes a scheme that will overthrow the country. But basically [Chuang-tzu's idea of] stopping desires through spontaneity promotes a spontaneity that produces evil. This meaning should be known.

Next, with regard to mistaken views in India, the [mistaken] view of emptiness is the strongest, so now I will discuss advantages and faults with regard to this [mistaken view of emptiness]. There are three types of [mistaken] views of emptiness: 1. deconstructing the causes but not deconstructing the

"There is no greater robber than you are; why does not all the world call you the Robber Khiu, instead of styling me the Robber Kih?

"You prevailed by your sweet speeches on Tzu-lu, and made him your follower; you made him put away his high cap, lay aside his long sword, and receive your instructions, so that all the world said, 'Khung Khiu is able to arrest violence and repress the wrong-doer'; but in the end, when Tzu-lu wished to slay the ruler of Wei, and the affair proved unsuccessful, his body was exhibited in pickle over the eastern gate of the capital; so did your teaching of him come to nothing.

"Do you call yourself a scholar of talent, a sage? Why, you were twice driven out of Lu; you had to run away from Wei; you were reduced to extremity in Khi; you were held in a state of siege between Khän and Zhâi; there is no resting-place for your person in the kingdom; your instructions brought Tzu-lu to pickle. Such have been the misfortunes (attending your course). You have done no good either for yourself or for others; how can your doctrines be worth being thought much of?

"There is no one whom the world exalts so much as it does Hwang-Ti, and still he was not able to perfect his virtue, but fought in the wilderness of Ko-lu, till the blood flowed over a hundred li. Yao was not kind to his son. Shun was not filial. Yü was paralysed on one side. Tang banished his sovereign. King Wu smote Kâu. King Wän was imprisoned in Yu-li. These are the six men of whom the world thinks the most highly, yet when we accurately consider their history, we see that for the sake of gain they all disallowed their true (nature), and did violence to its proper qualities and tendencies: their conduct cannot be thought of but with deep shame....

"I cast from me, Khiu, all that you say. Be quick and go. Hurry back and say not a word more. Your Way is only a wild recklessness, deceitful, artful, vain, and hypocritical. It is not available to complete the true (nature of man); it is not worth talking about!"

Confucius bowed twice, and hurried away. He went out at the door, and mounted his carriage. Three times he missed the reins as he tried to take hold of them. His eyes were dazed, and he could not see; and his color was that of slaked lime. He laid hold of the cross-bar, holding his head down, and unable to draw his breath....

See also the translation by Burton Watson, *Complete Works of Chuang Tzu*, 325–31.

Three types of mistaken views of emptiness 空見為三: see the passage in the *Ta chih tu lun* at T 25.193c21–194a17, soon after the passage just quoted above. Chodron (2, 846–48) translates:

Question. There are three kinds of wrong view: i. Denying the retribution of sins and merits without denying sin and merit, denying the fruit of retribution of causes and conditions without denying causes and conditions, denying the future existence without denying the present existence; ii. Denying the retri-

results, and deconstructing the results but not deconstructing the causes; 2. deconstructing both causes and results, and not deconstructing all dharmas; and 3. deconstructing causes, results, and all dharmas. [In this context] "all

bution of sins and merits and also sin and merit, denying the fruit of retribution of causes and conditions and also denying the causes and conditions, denying the future lifetime and also denying the present lifetime; avoiding, however, the denial of all dharmas; iii. Denying all dharmas to the extent of rendering them non-existent (*asat*). [You], supporter of emptiness, who proclaim [all dharmas] to be empty of reality and non-existence, how are you different from this third wrong view?

Answer. – 1. The person of wrong view ends up at emptiness by suppressing all dharmas, whereas the supporter of emptiness considers dharmas as empty of any reality, indestructible and unchangeable.

2. The person of wrong view declares all dharmas to be empty and non-existent, but grasps the empty nature of these dharmas *(dharmāṇaṃ śūnyalakṣaṇam udgṛhṇāti)* and talks about it. The supporter of emptiness knows the emptiness of dharmas but does not grasp the characteristic and does not talk about it.

3. Furthermore, the person of wrong view, although he verbally professes universal emptiness, loves when he has the occasion to love, is angry when he has the occasion to be angry, is proud when he has the occasion to be proud, makes a mistake when he has the occasion to make a mistake; thus he is lying to himself. For the disciple of the Buddha, who truly knows emptiness, the mind is unshakeable *(āniñjya, akṣobhya)*, the fetters *(saṃyojana)* do not arise where normally they would arise. In the same way that space *(ākāśa)* cannot be tarnished by fire nor soaked by a shower, so no kinds of passions (*kleśa*) can become attached to the mind of the supporter of emptiness.

4. Furthermore, the person of wrong view talks about the non-existence [of dharmas], but the latter does not originate so much from desire *(tṛṣṇā)* as from cause and condition *(hetupratyaya)*; on the other hand, true emptiness comes from desire, and that is a difference. If the four boundless ones *(apramāṇacitta)* and pure dharmas *(viśuddhadharma)*, because their object *(ālambana)* is unreal, are thus unable to produce the true knowledge of emptiness, what can be said then of wrong view?

5. Furthermore, these (imperfect) views are called wrong views *(mithyādṛṣṭi)*; the correct seeing of emptiness is called right view *(samyagdṛṣṭi)*. The person who practices wrong views, in the present lifetime, passes as an evil person; later he will fall into the hells. The person who practices the true knowledge of emptiness acquires fame in the present lifetime, later he will become a Buddha. These two people differ from one another like water and fire, ambrosia *(amṛta)* and a poisonous drug *(viṣauṣadhi)*, nectar *(sudhā)*, the food of the gods, and rotten garbage.

6. Furthermore, in true emptiness there is the concentration of the emptiness of emptiness *(śūnyatāśūnyatāsamādhi)*. In emptiness wrongly perceived, there is indeed emptiness but not the concentration of the emptiness of emptiness.

7. Furthermore, the person who contemplates true emptiness possesses, from the beginning, immense [qualities] by way of generosity *(dāna)*, morality *(śīla)*, and dhyāna; his mind is soft and gentle *(mṛdutarauṇacitta)* and his fetters *(saṃyojana)* are light; later he will obtain true emptiness. These advantages are absent in [the person] of wrong view: he wants to grasp *(grahaṇa)* emptiness only by means of speculation, analysis and wrong concepts.

dharmas" refers to the three kinds of unconditioned [nothingness]. How is the third type of heterodox path different from the Buddha Dharma?

The *Ta chih tu lun* clarifies that the emptiness of the Mahāyāna and Hīnayāna are different in [directly realizing its] essence and [attaining it] analytically. Heterodox paths also [realize emptiness through] essence and

Three [kinds of] unconditioned [nothingness] 三無爲: three "things" that are unchanging and unconditioned: unconditioned empty space *(ākāśa)*, unconditioned chosen extinction (that is, nirvana) *(pratisaṃkhyā-nirodha)*, and unconditioned unchosen extinction *(apratisaṃkhyā-nirodha)*.

The emptiness of the Mahāyāna and Hīnayāna are different: see, for example, the *Ta chih tu lun* at T 25.147c21–148a22. Chodron (2, 576–81) translates:

> The Atomist. – It is impossible that every object *(drvaya)* exists indiscriminately only by virtue of the complex of causes and conditions *(hetupratyayasāmagrī)*. Thus, the ultimate atoms, because of their extreme subtlety *(paramaśukṣmatvāt)*, have no parts *(bhāga, avayava)* and, having no parts, have no complex *(samāgrī)*. Being coarse *(sthūla, audārika)*, cloth is susceptible to being torn *(rūpaṇa)*, but how could the ultimate atom, that has no parts, be broken?
>
> Answer: 1. The extremely tiny does not exist; this is said mistakenly. Why? Because coarseness *(sthūlatva)* and subtleness *(sūkṣmatva)* are relative concepts *(parasparāpekṣika)*. The subtle exists in contrast with the coarse and this subtle always has something more subtle than itself.
>
> 2. Moreover, if there existed a substance *(rūpa)* in the state of ultimate atom *(paramāṇu)*, it would entail tenfold spatial division *(daśadighbhāgabheda)*; but if it entailed the tenfold sparial division, it would not be a question of the ultimate atom. On the other hand, if there is not tenfold spatial division, it is not a question of matter.
>
> 3. Furthermore, if the ultimate atom existed, it would have spatial subdivision *(ākāśapariccheda)*; but if there is subdivision, it cannot be a question of the ultimate atom.
>
> 4. If the ultimate atom existed, color *(rūpa)*, smell *(gandha)*, taste *(rasa)* and touchable *(sparṣṭavya)* would occur as a function of the parts *(bhāga)*; but it cannot be a question of the ultimate atom there where color, smell, taste and touchable function as parts.
>
> Try as one may to argue about the ultimate atom, this is why it cannot be established. The sūtra says: "All matter *(rūpa)*, whether coarse *(audārika)* or subtle *(sūkṣma)*, inner *(adhyātman)* or outer *(bahirdhā)*, if considered generally, is transitory *(anitya)* and non-substantial *(anātmaka)*," but it does not say that ultimate atoms exist. This is called the emptiness of the division into parts.
>
> Moreover, for those who contemplate emptiness *(śūnyatādarśin)*, matter exists as a function of the mind *(cittanuparivartin)*. Thus these contemplatives *(dhyāyin)* see matter as being earth *(pṛthivī)*, water *(ap-)*, fire *(tejas)* or wind *(vāyu)*, as being blue *(nīla)*, yellow *(pīta)*, red *(lohita)* or absolutely empty *(atyantaśūnya)*. And in the same way they can contemplate the ten views of the object as totality of the object *(kṛtsnāyatana)*.
>
> [*Dārukkhandhakasutta*]. The Buddha, who was dwelling on Gṛdhrakūṭaparvata, went one day to the city of Rājagṛha along with the assembly of bhikṣus. Seeing a large piece of wood (change *ta houei* "great water" to *ta mou* "big piece of wood" or "*mahādāruskandha*") in the middle of the path, the Buddha spread out his mat *(niṣadana)*, sat down and said to the monks: "A bhikṣu entered into

analysis; how is this different [from Buddhism]? [The answer is that] heterodox paths follow deviant [understandings of] causes and conditions, or [teach] that there are no causes and conditions. Whether through analysis or [direct realization of its] essence, they may conclude that ultimately things are empty, but whether through analysis or [direct realization of] essence, the Buddha's disciples know from the causes and conditions of passionate attachments that things are ultimately empty. Someone has said, "Deconstructing words [through analysis] is not [the same as directly realizing] the essence." Now, to clarify this, **[135c]** the *Middle Treatise* from beginning to end has "deconstructing" as its theme, and "deconstructing" is a different way to express [realizing] the essence. Therefore we do not distinguish wrong and right and large [Mahāyāna] and small [Hīnayāna] in these terms. We rely only on the *Ta chih tu lun* to analyze the correct [understanding of] causes and conditions differently than that of heterodox paths, and to [directly realize] the essence of the correct [understanding of] causes and conditions differently than that of the Hīnayāna.

trance *(dhyānapraviṣṭa)* and, endowed with mastery of mind *(cetovaśiprāpta)*, would be able to change this big piece of wood (read *ta mou*) into earth *(pṛthivi)* and this would be real earth. Why? Because the earth element exists in the wood. He would also be able to change it into water *(ap-)*, into fire *(tejas)* into wind *(vāyu)*, into gold *(suvarṇa)*, into silver *(rājata)* and into all kinds of precious substances *(nānāvidharatnadravya)*; and they would all be real. Why? Because the elements *(dhātu)* of all these things exist in the wood (read *mou*)."

2. Moreover, it is the same as in the case of a beautiful woman; the voluptuous man *(kāmeṣu mithyācārin)* who sees her, takes her to be a pure wonder and his heart clings to her; the ascetic given to contemplation of the disgusting *(aśubhabhāvana)*, on looking at this woman, finds all sorts of defects without any beauty; her rival, when she sees her, feels jealousy *(īrṣyā)* hatred *(dveṣa)* and bad feelings; she does not want to look at her, as if she were ugly. On looking at this woman, the voluptuous man feels neither attraction nor repulsion: it is as if he was looking at a piece of wood. If this beauty were truly pure, the four men who were looking at it should all see it as fine *(śubha)*; if it were truly ugly, all should see it as ugly *(aśubha)*. But, [as this is not the case], we know that beauty and ugliness are in the mind *(citta)* and outwardly *(bahirdhā)* there is nothing fixed *(niyata)*. It is as if one were looking at the void *(śūnya)*.

3. Finally, because the eighteen emptinesses *(aṣṭadaśaśūnyatā)* are found in matter, it appears as empty *(śūnya)* on being examined; being empty, it is non-existent *(anupalabdha)*. In the same way, all wealth *(āmiṣadravya)* resulting from causes and conditions *(pratītyasamutpanna)* is empty *(śūnya)* and absolutely non-existent *(atyantānupalabdha)*.

Someone has said, "Deconstructing words is not the essence" 有人言。破語非體: it is not known to whom this refers.

Rely only on the *Ta chih tu lun* to analyze the correct … of the Hīnayāna 但依大論析正因緣異外道。體正因緣異小乘: see the passage at T 25.147c–1488b just quoted in the note above.

If you arouse a [mistaken] view of emptiness in terms of a wrong [understanding of] causes and conditions, again there are three types of actions [of good, evil, and neutral], but mostly evil is produced. Those who truly contemplate emptiness know that things arise from passionate attachments and do not produce good [deeds], let alone evil [deeds]. Those who arouse a [mistaken] view of emptiness do not argue over the fruits of their karmic rewards or wealth or status, but they do dispute over emptiness. They feel friendly and arouse passionate attachments toward those who agree with their own doctrine of emptiness, but they feud bitterly against those who praise [the idea of] existence and deny emptiness, and become angry and vexed, saying that people do not know emptiness, and so they arrogantly treat them like dirt. They do not have a proper awe toward the mind of emptiness and have no sense of propriety, and being unrestrained emotionally and indulging in desires, they destroy the correct view [of emptiness], proper demeanor, and a pure life, and after death they all should fall into hell.

The six teachers [of the heterodox paths] say those who feel shame should fall into hell, and those who do not feel shame should not fall into hell. [According to this mistaken view,] whether they use the back of a [statue of the Buddha as a cutting board to mince] fish, or use sūtra [paper to plaster folding] screens, or take a piss into a well during a thunderstorm, or rebel against their fathers and be arrogant toward their mothers, thus making advancing on the road [to enlightenment] more severe, they claim that

Six teachers say those who feel shame should fall into hell, and those who do not feel shame should not fall into hell 六師云。若有慚愧則墮地獄。若無慚愧不墮地: see the explanation of these "mistaken views" in the *Mahāparinirvāṇa Sūtra* at T 12.719b17–26:

> Suppose a person murders or harms all sentient beings, but he feels no shame in his mind and heart, finally he will not fall into hell, as empty space does not accept dust-like objects or water. Someone who feels shame [at doing evil deeds] will enter hell, like a great flood of water moistens the earth. All sentient being are subject to the actions of Īśvara 自在天. When Īśvara is happy, people can be calm and happy; when he is angry, people suffer and are troubled. Whether sentient being commit offences or have fortune, it is due to the actions of Īśvara, so why should we talk about people committing offences or having fortune. It is like when a craftsman builds a gate, who is to say how the lumber people will go, dwell, sit, or lie down? Sentient beings are also like this. Īśvara is like the craftsman; sentient beings are like the lumber people [who just follow instructions]. In this way things happen; who is to say that there is an offence [to be punished]?

The back of a [statue of the Buddha as a cutting board to mince] fish 背鱠: following the explanation by Chan-jan (BT–V, 511).

Use sūtra [paper to plaster folding] screens 經屏: again, following the explanation by Chan-jan (BT–V, 511). These are examples of terrible actions that would be done only by someone without a proper conscience.

these are not obstacles. But matters that are intimate are different from that which is unfamiliar, and they are not the same. If you yourself perform such debauched and evil deeds, and also teach them to others so that you perform these negative acts together, you will lose your propriety and be like a beast. How can you gain the approval of the world? [Those with this mistaken view] may say that there are no obstacles [created by evil deeds], but they do not dare to defy their lord or be arrogant toward their sovereign queen. They are begrudging of their own bodies, and so [the safety of] their physical bodies is [in fact considered] an obstacle. When such people directly arouse these [mistaken] views, these views [and their results] flame up, so that you cannot attain dhyāna [concentration] for a long time. If [these mistaken views arise] after you attain dhyāna, much of the results of dhyāna will be lost. The dhyāna [concentrations] after the arousing of these [mistaken] views are mostly demonic dhyānas 鬼禪 and demonic [supranormal] powers, such as prediction of good or bad fortune, or knowing the thoughts of others.

Again, if we expansively consider [various worldly teachings such as] the Vedas, and provide evidence for this view and lead people to believe and accept it, since [these mistaken views] destroy worldly and transworldly good, this is like a man-eating dog which is not satisfied if even one view is not yet deconstructed. The mind with such a view [of negative emptiness] is satisfied when all dharmas are deconstructed, but just when it is satisfied, it again flares up. Internally [in this mind] there is no action that accords with reality, but only empty disputation and calculation, like the howling [of dogs] seeking food. People become attached to emptiness and argue that it exists; they seek to deconstruct the marks of emptiness and existence like dogs showing their fangs. The way they praise themselves is like the baying of dogs. They destroy others by attacking them, and establish themselves by pulling down [others]. Again, the way they have doubts that are unresolved is like dogs showing their fangs. The way they make others fearful is like the baying of dogs. It is like a dog guarding his house and scaring others by barking.

Again, these people are always doing evil themselves and teaching others [to do the same] in four ways: 1. doing evil oneself but encouraging people to do good; 2. pretending to do good oneself and encouraging people to do evil; 3. both doing evil oneself and encouraging others [to do evil]; and 4. both doing good oneself and encouraging others [to do good].

1. Those who do evil themselves but encourage people to do good say that they have penetrated to the principle [of the truth] themselves and thus have no obstacles with regard to evil, but [think that] you are still shallow in your practice and therefore it is necessary for you to cultivate good deeds; so they teach and lead others to first do good deeds.

2. Those who [pretend to] do good themselves but encourage others to do evil say that they themselves are the teacher and should do good in order to "soften their light," **[136a]** but since you are practicing the correct [path], [it is not a problem that] you should do evil [deeds].

3. Those who both do evil themselves and encourages others to do so [think that] both [themselves and others] are practicing the true path.

4. Those who both do good oneself and encourage others to do so [think that] both [oneself and others] are practicing a tentative path.

These four options are different, but all involve evil at their basis, and will cause you to sink due to karmic retribution. Why should you follow these paths?

Again, having a [mistaken] view of emptiness yet doing good is as follows: in emptiness there is no "good" or "evil," but nevertheless you should practice good. As for those who do not practice good, the god Viṣṇu will be angry and cause [these] sentient beings to suffer, and due to suffering they will produce karma, and due to past karma they will receive retribution in the present life. But if in the present you keep the precepts and do ascetic practices, you can restrain the current appearance of evil karmic results, and even attain the exhaustion of passionate outflows. Therefore you should do good, such as keeping the precepts and regulating your body, minimizing your desires and knowing what is sufficient 知足, such as wearing rough clothing and eating grass or vegetables. But if you practice based on [a mistaken view of] emptiness, and give rise to [emotions such as] happiness or anger, this [mistaken view of] emptiness can result in hatred or passionate attachments, and become the place for calculated arguments. If you attain dhyāna and then arouse this [mistaken] view [of emptiness], the dhyāna concentration will disappear and [mistaken] views will flame up. If you attain dhyāna after you already have [mistaken] views, these will be demonic dhyānas and demonic [supranormal] powers. In this way for those with [mistaken] views of emptiness, there is one way to practice for oneself, and four ways for teaching others, as explained above. [In this case,] practicing for oneself and transforming others depend on your karma, and the world floats or sinks in accordance with your karma, so [in the final analysis] what connection does this have with the Way [of the Buddha]?

Next, being attached to the [mistaken] view of emptiness without doing

Soften their light 和光: A phrase from Lao-tzu's *Tao-te ching*: "[The tao] softens its light and joins the dust [of the mundane world]." Chih-i uses this phrase to illustrate the activity of the bodhisattva who chooses to remain in the "dust" of the samsaric realm in order to help other sentient beings. In this context, however, "softening their light" is an act of hypocrisy.

either good or evil means that you act naturally and remain cool and composed. Although you are said to be "cool and composed," if you are praised you becomes passionately attached [to your own importance], and if criticized becomes depressed [for not receiving "proper" attention]. If you seek to promote oneself through this "composure" 平平, then you should know that this "composure" is a basis for giving rise to passionate afflictions. If [in this situation] you attain dhyāna and then arouse this [mistaken] view [of emptiness], it is as explained above. Again, if through [worldly learning such as] the Vedas you penetrate to a pilfered understanding of the Buddha's teachings, and then adorned with [a karmically] neutral [view of emptiness begin to argue], this is like [dogs] showing their fangs and baying and barking; immeasurable bonds of afflictions will arise from these "neutral" [actions]. [As above,] there is one way to practice for oneself, and four ways for teaching others. If these people do not arouse dhyāna, karma will drag them into the evil destinies. If they do arouse dhyāna, they will experience rebirth in accordance with their dhyāna [concentrations]. If their karma [from dhyāna] is not yet mature, they will be pulled primarily by whatever karma was the strongest in their previous lives. You should know that these various [mistaken] views are not able to overcome delusions. How can it be said that they sever delusions!

The marks of attainment and faults [of mistaken views] with regard to [the belief that things] both exist and do not exist, should be known in accordance with this [previous explanation]. [end of fascicle ten, part one]

1. Internal Buddhist Mistaken Views [136a24]

Next is clarifying the attainments and faults of internal [Buddhist] deviant [views]. The four gates [of the options of Being/existence, non-being/emptiness, both, and neither] of the Tripitaka Teaching are basically for realizing the principle [of enlightenment], but some people become attached to vain argumentation, and obtain dhyāna while arousing [mistaken] views, both [thought to be] in accordance with the sūtras. If you become attached to these gates **[136b]**, you will surely arouse good [deeds], but you are associated with [mistaken] views and in turn arouse the three [karmic] actions [of word, thought, and deed]. These good deeds will consist mostly of producing karmic recompense for other beings, but if you grasp and become attached to the gate of Being, you will give rise to passions and anger. Those who are victorious will fall into the pit of pride, and those who fail will fall into the hellish prison of sorrow. Since [in this case] this gives rise to passionate

Acts naturally and remains cool and composed 騰騰平住: this paraphrase follows the explanation in the *Kōgi*, BT–V, 514.

afflictions, the gate of Being instead blocks [the way to enlightenment] so you cannot attain liberation.

As for those who perform evil [deeds], they become attached to [the idea of] Being or existence and affirm it, and reject all others as mistaken. On the basis of this gate of Being, there is no evil that they will not do. The demons of mistaken views enter their minds, and they only extend their negativity.

Of the ninety-six paths, three are in accordance with the Buddha Dharma; thus we have the Abhidharma paths and the paths of the sūtras. However, if the five hundred arhats attained liberation through this gate or teaching of existence, how can you say that it is a deviant view? People in the present time perversely grasp onto it [one-sidedly] and thus the demons [of mistaken views] enter their minds; therefore this is called the "Abhidharma demons." Or, they enter through mistaken views, or enter through [the practice of] dhyāna meditation. [As explained above,] there is one practice for the [sake of] oneself, and four for saving [other] people. The one gate [of existence] is such; the [other] three gates are also likewise.

As for the Shared, Distinct, and Perfect [Teachings], each have the four gates that may give rise to [mistaken] views. One view includes the three [karmic] actions. As for those who do good deeds, this should be known [as explained above]. As for those who do evil, they become attached [for example] to the Mahāyāna teaching that covetous desires are themselves the path, or that the three poisons [of greed, anger, and ignorance] encompass the entire Buddha Dharma. These types of true words [such as "passionate afflictions are indivisible from wisdom"] originally were meant to extinguish passionate afflictions [and not just mistakenly affirm them], but if they are one-sidedly grasped as attachments, instead they will give rise to karmic bonds; as you are praised or slandered, you will become depressed or passionately attached, become deceived and arrogant, get into verbal shouting matches, and compete [with others] over fame and fortune. [As before,] there is one practice for the [sake of] oneself, and four for saving [other] people. Since you are not yet without any defiled outflow [of passions], your ignorance smooths the way for karma, the power of karma incites rebirth, and where will it all end? I cannot explain in detail here, but [the details] should be known in accordance with the above [explanations].

Ninety-six paths, three in accordance with the Buddha Dharma 九十六道三順佛法: The *Shiki* (BT–V, 515) adds that "this reference cannot be identified; it must refer to a *Sūtra of Ninety-six Ways.*" The *Kōgi* (BT–V, 516) speculates that it refers to the various types of Buddhist teachings, but the content is not clear. Neither is it clear which "three paths" are in accordance with the Buddha Dharma.

Five hundred arhats 五百羅漢: the five hundred holy ones, led by Mahākāśyapa, who assembled at the First Council immediately after the death of the Buddha.

In this way, [mistaken] views are in opposition to the Noble Path, and also are able to give rise to and lengthen [the span of] various offences and faults. Those who are not aware of this become attached to [mistaken views] and say that these are the path. Even if they know that these are [mistaken] views, they follow these views and their actions lead to their own fall and oblivion. How can those who are moved and not moved by [mistaken] views still cultivate the steps on the Path [and attain enlightenment]? Thus have I summarized how [mistaken] views are aroused and give rise to various faults.

2. Lining Up and Determining the True and the False [136b20]

Second is to clarify the lining up and determining of the true and false [with regard to mistaken views]. First is to line up and determine with regard to the Dharma teachings that arouse [mistaken views], and second is to line up and determine the differences in the Dharma teachings on which they depend.

1. Determining with Regard to Teachings That Arouse Mistaken Views [136b21]

Now, in general, the names and numbers are the same for the four options of the heretical paths external [to Buddhism] up to the [mistaken] views of heretical paths in the four gates of the Perfect [Teaching], shared with [the worldly teachings such as] the Vedas through the gates of the Perfect Teaching of the three bases of thought [of sensation, body, and dharmas] and three liberations. The offences and fetters from the [mistaken] views that are aroused are not different. They are analogous to a chain with gold and steel links. Again, from the four options of the heretical paths to the four

Moved and not moved by views still cultivate the Path 見動不動而修道品: this may refer to a passage in the the *Vimalakīrti Sūtra*, T 14.539c24, "with regard to [mistaken] views, one remains unmoved yet cultivates the thirty-seven steps on the path."

Analogous to a chain with gold and steel links 金鐵二鎖: an analogy from the *Ta chih tu lun*, T 25.226a9–15. Chodron (3, 1152–53) translates:

> In the face of morality, the yogin does not undergo the fetter of lust *(rāga)*, pride *(māna)*, etc. He knows the true nature *(bhūtalakṣaṇa)* of morality *(śīlaninittani nodgṛhṇāti)*. If he grasps the characteristics of morality, he would be like a prisoner held by manacles who, even after having been pardoned, remains attached to his golden manacles. The person attached [to his own morality] by the passion of love is as if in prison: even if he manages to escape, he remains attached *(sakta)* to the morality like golden fetters. But the yogin who knows that morality is cause

types of [mistaken] views of the Perfect Teaching, although the words may be pure and beautiful, the essence of passionate afflictions that are aroused are defiled. This is analogous to a jewel and a rat both being called an unpolished gem. Again, from the four options of the heretical paths to the four types of [mistaken] views of the Perfect Teaching, although they are the same in having to be polished and tempered, some are perfected and some are not perfected, analogous to a cow and an ass both giving milk. Again, from the four options of the heretical paths to the four types of [mistaken] views of the Perfect Teaching, some are harmful and some not harmful. This is analogous to the two fruits of the Kālaka and Tinduka [trees]. The assumption of a spiritual soul [*ātman* 神我] is a teaching of bondage **[136c]** and is not the same as [the idea of] a self with mastery [over liberation]. Each person is attached to their own views and rejects the others as false speech;

and condition for purity *(anāsrava-hetupratyaya)* does not experience this attachment [to morality itself] and is liberated, free of fetters: this is what is called morality "without thoughtless attachment" *(aparāmṛṣṭa)*.

Jewel and rat both called an unpolished gem 玉鼠二璞: Chan-jan (BT–V, 518) points to a saying that "the Zhou people 周人 have a custom to call a dead rat an unpolished gem."

Cow and ass both giving milk 牛驢二乳: see the *Ta chih tu lun*, T 25.191c1–4. Chodron (2, 830–31) translates:

> It is like the milk of the cow *(gokṣīra)* and that of the ass *(aśvatarīkṣīra)*: they both have the same color, but the cow's milk when churned gives butter *(sarpis)* whereas the ass's milk when churned gives urine *(mūtra)*. It is the same for the words of the Buddha and the words of the heretics *(tīrthika)*: insofar as they teach non-killing, non-stealing, having loving-kindness and compassion for beings, concentrating the mind *(cittasaṃgrahaṇa)*, renouncing desires *(vairāgya)* and contemplating emptiness *(śūnyasamanupaśyanā)*, they are similar; but the heretics' words, seemingly excellent at the beginning, reveal themselves at the end to be completely false.

Fruits of the Kālaka and Tinduka 迦羅鎮頭二果: the fruit of the Kālaka tree is black, and though it looks like the fruit of the Tinduka ("persimmon"), it is harmful if eaten. The analogy is found in the *Mahāparinirvāṇa Sūtra* at T 12.641c4–642a2:

> It is like the Kālaka grove that has many Kālaka trees, but within that grove there is one tree called the Tinduka. Now, the two fruits of the Kālaka tree and the Tinduka tree are similar in features so that they cannot be distinguished. When the fruits matured, a certain woman gathered them up, with the Tinduka fruits in one part and the Kālaka fruits of ten parts. That woman was not aware [of the difference between the fruits] and brought them to sell in the market. An ignorant child also did not distinguish between them, and bought a Kālaka fruit, ate it, and his life came to an end. A knowledgable person heard of this incident and asked the woman to show the place where she got the fruit. Then the woman showed him the place. The people said, "This place has an abundance of Kālaka trees, and only one Tinduka tree." Upon knowing this, the people laughed and abandoned it....

they mutually reject each other, so how can they pass on to the truth? They claim that [only] their own [view] is the true path, but instead take the path of Being; seeking to attain nirvana, they sink into the cycle of birth-and-death. They say that they themselves have the truth as it should be, but end up deviant and one-sided. They give rise to passionate attachments with regard to objects of passion; they give rise to anger with regard to objects of anger. Even if they arouse compassion, is this not just pity based on their passions and [mistaken] views? Even if they calmly bear the anointing and cutting off [of their hands], this merely strengthens their forbearance with regard to arising and perishing. Although it may be called omniscience, it is only worldly speculation. Although they may think they have attained the transformations of supranormal powers of the [four] basic [dhyānas], these are still defiled transformations. They are worldly wisdom and explanations of what you have read in [worldly writings such as] the Vedas, and not [the true Buddha Dharma of] the powers of *dhāraṇī* nor the flow of the Dharma realm. Although they sever the dull afflictions, this is like the progress of an inchworm. The healing of a worldly physician lasts for a while but then [the disease] is aroused again. The eighty-eight afflictions gather [vast and

Take the path of Being 開有路: that is, follow the first of the "four gates." Ikeda (*Gendaigoyaku*, 675), however, interprets this as "taking the path of defilement/outflow of passions 有漏."

Anointing and cutting off [of their hands] 塗割: The DDB [from Soothill] explains: "To anoint the hand, or cut it off. An example made from the case of a person in a compassionate state of mind and a person holding resentment. The person in a compassionate state of mind daubs his other hand with perfume, while the person bearing grudge cuts off the hand of the other person." On the other hand, see also the *Mahāparinirvāṇa Sūtra* at T 12.620c25–621a20:

> The bodhisattva Kāśyapa again spoke to the Buddha, saying, "World Honored One. It is as the Buddha says, that this is like viewing all sentient beings without equanimity, or to consider them like Rāhula, your own son. World Honored One. Suppose there is a person who harms [and cuts] the Buddha with a sword, and there is another person who anoints the Buddha with sandalwood. If the Buddha maintains a mind of equanimity toward these two people, why should there be a call for regulation/punishment for breaking the precepts? If there is a regulation/punishment for breaking the precepts, this would be a mistake."…

Progress of an inchworm 歩屈蟲: The *Inyō* and Ikeda (*Kenkyūchūshaku*, 485) refer to a passage in the *Mahāparinirvāṇa Sūtra* at T 12.651b2–3, which compares the "severing of mistaken views" to the progress of an inchworm. But see also the earlier reference to an inchworm at *Mo-ho chih-kuan* 41b5 (and 65b20): "You realize [the extreme of] nothingness by getting rid of [lit., 'moving' the notion of] Being, like an inchworm who can attain [some] movement but is not able to cultivate the practices of the path," a reference to a passage in the *Mahāparinirvāṇa Sūtra*, T 12.410b22–24.

unquenchable] like the sea. The cycle of birth and death in the triple world is a ring of suffering without limit. If they fall into attachments for passions, they will not be able to escape for a long time. This is all due to the illusions and falsity of mistaken views. How can they be taken for the true path?

2. Determining with Regard to the Differences in the Teachings on Which They Depend [136c11]

Second, with regard to the differences in the teachings on which [mistaken views] depend: all [mistaken] views each depend on their own dharma teachings. The three [types of] heretical ways external [to the Buddha Dharma] rely on people who still have the outflow [of passions], arouse defiled phenomena [of passions], and with thoughts of defiled passions become attached to [Dharma] teachings. This attachment to teaching and attachment to thoughts 著法著心 is the essence of their argumentative quarreling. It does not stop with the initial "seizing of heads and pulling out of hair"; after arousing these mistaken views you claim that this is nirvana, and the attachment to these views is fierce, and its poison increases and the struggle vigorous. The teachings on which these depend are not true, and the views that are aroused are also false. Although these are deviant teachings, if you intimately attain their intent, you can realize the correct marks [of their teachings] by means of their deviant marks. This is just as the small causes and conditions such as the wafting of a flower [petal] or the drifting leaves can lead to the enlightenment of a pratyekabuddha; how much more so for the [potential benefit of] old [pre-Buddhist?] worldly teachings! However, even if [the enlightenment of] the pratyekabuddha is right, that does not mean that the flowers and leaves [themselves] are the "right [true] teaching." 正教. The heretical ways external [to Buddhism] can provide a "secret awakening" 密悟, but these teachings are merely a passage for mistaken views, and are not the true Dharma 正法. They all depend on a mind of attachment, and attachment to teachings of [passionate] attachments, in which the causes and results are in a mutual struggle. Surely there is no doubt that these deviant teachings give rise to deviant views!

As for the four gates of the Tripitaka Teachings, this is a transworldly Dharma teaching by transworldly noble people. Its essence is pure and it extinguishes the bases of passionate afflictions. It is not only the sūtras [with the sermons] of the Buddha that contain the true Dharma [teachings]; [the teachings] spoken by the five hundred [arhats] are also efficacious for

Seizing of heads and pulling out of hair 捉頭拔髮: presumably with a verbal argument turning into a physical brawl; a phrase from the *Mahāparinirvāṇa Sūtra* at T 12.725a5, illustrating arguing over mistaken views. See below at 137a11–12.

attaining the Path. *The Sūtra of Sublime and Supreme Samādhi* says, "After the Buddha left this world, in the next one hundred years there were one hundred thousand people who became home-departed ones, and ninety thousand people attained the Path. In the second one hundred years, one hundred thousand people became home-departed ones, and ten thousand attained the Path." You should know that by means of a mind of non-attachment, you do not become attached to teachings of non-attachment. With an aspiration [for enlightenment] that is right and true, an awakened awareness of the transience of all things, and of each thought as it arises and perishes, [knowing that what is there] in the morning may not last until the evening, seeking for escape [from the cycle of birth-and-death], you do not "close the gate" [to the true Dharma teachings] and give rise to defiled [passions] and arouse vain arguments. This is analogous to a person who wishes to quickly see the king, and having been granted an audience for an interview, can enter [the city] through [any one of] the four gates; why should he linger and stop, arguing over which [gate] is better or worse? You should know that a gate is a passageway [**137a**], and it is not necessary to quarrel or calculate [about which is better if they all allow entrance]. Again, it is like medicines for curing disease; [if they work] it is not necessary to distinguish between them. Quickly escape the burning house [of this world] and exhaust all suffering. When true clarity [or, "enlightenment concerning the truth" 眞明] is aroused, you are enlightened concerning the ultimate Path, so ultimately there is nothing to argue about. If there is no argument, there is no karmic [retribution]. If there is no karma, there is no [cycle of] birth and death [with its suffering and causes for suffering]. There is only the Path and extinction [of suffering]. There is only the repose of the basis of the mind; causes and con-

***The Sūtra of Sublime and Supreme Samādhi* 妙勝定[経] says, "After the Buddha ... attained the path"**: this text was once lost but rediscovered at Tun-huang. See the critical edition published by Sekiguchi in *Tendai shikan no kenkyū*, 379–402; see page 400, which says that eighty years after the death of the Buddha, out of one billion people, nine hundred million had attained the fourth fruit of the arhat; that after three hundred years, out of ten billion people, one billion had attained the fourth fruit, and so forth.

This text has already been quoted by Chih-i; see the notes at *Mo-ho chih-kuan* 26c20–21 and 39c15–16.

Quickly escape the burning house 速出火宅: a reference to the parable of the burning house in the *Lotus Sūtra*; see T 9.12b–15a, esp. 14b23–25. Hurvitz (69–70 [65]) translates:

> When the children heard him tell
> Of carriages such as these,
> Straightway, racing one another,
> They ran out at a gallop,
> Reaching an empty spot
> And getting away from woes and troubles.

ditions [for karmic retribution] do not exist, and argumentative quarrels are extinguished. There are only right views and no deviant [mistaken] views.

Again, although it is said that the four gates [of the Tripitaka Teachings] are the true Dharma, if you become attached to these four gates with a mind of attachment, then you give rise to deviant [mistaken] views, perceive the differences between the four gates, and arouse argumentative quarrels when cultivating the causes [for enlightenment]. This is analogous to a person who has dwelt for a long time within the city gates [and really knows the neighborhood], can distinguish among the tiles and the trees and evaluate what is fine and course, who then says that the southern [gate] is good and the northern is bad, or the eastern [gate] is fine and the western is crude, thus delaying himself and not making any forward progress; this is not a fault of the gate. It is the same for those who have attachments. They may distinguish among names and forms [and make verbal scholastic distinctions], have a broad knowledge of passionate afflictions, cultivate many steps on the path, gather together a large assembly for the sake of fame, boasting and seeking attention, beating their own drum and flying their own proud banners, acting pompously before others, "mutually arousing a quarrelsome spirit, grasping their heads and tearing out their hair," which vastly inflames the eighty-eight types of passionate afflictions such as anger and passionate attachments, all due to a mind of attachment. Although you have entered through the gate of the true Dharma, you still give rise to deviant [mistaken] views. The passionate afflictions that are aroused are not different from those of the heretical ways external [to the Buddha Dharma], even though the teachings that are discussed are as far apart [from these external ways] as the heavens from the earth. *The Great Vaipulya [Dhāraṇī Sūtra]* says, "A wise person rejects various [impractical] questions about a bridge." People should be the same way. For the sake of the [academic] path of learning, you cultivate [and studies the details concerning] the four gates [of teachings], spending thirty years making distinctions concerning one gate and not yet fully clarifying it; when your efforts begin to show a smidgen of results, "you

Mutually arousing a quarrelsome spirit, grasping their heads and tearing out their hair 互生鬪諍捉頭拔髮: a phrase from the *Mahāparinirvāṇa Sūtra* at T 12.725a5. The phrase has been quoted before in the same context of an argument over mistaken views turning into a physical brawl: see *Mo-ho chih-kuan* 62c8 and 136c14.

A wise person rejects various questions about a bridge: a summary of a long passage in the *The Great Vaipulya Dhāraṇī Sūtra*, T 21.655b–c, which speaks of a great bridge, and people who wondered how many people had crossed it, what wood from what forest and how many elephants had been used to build it, and so forth up to 7,800 questions. A wise man said they should abandon their questions and just cross the bridge and be on their way.

are already old and can no longer partake in the three flavors [of home-departing, reading and chanting (the sūtras), and sitting in meditation]." Birth is empty, death is empty, and one life has been thrown away in vain. This is like all those questions concerning a bridge; of what use is it all [if there are only questions and you do not cross the bridge]? This is due to a mind of attachment being attached to Dharma teachings of non-attachment, and thus giving rise to deviant [mistaken] views.

Next, as for the four gates of the Shared Teachings, the essence [of the Teachings] is the true Dharma, and [these teachings] penetrate close to the conjured city. The previous [teachings of the Tripitaka] were roundabout [ways to enlightenment]; this is direct. Although there are differences in being skillful or clumsy, they are not distinct in that they both penetrate to the place [of enlightenment], just as the Heavenly Gate [opening to the direct road to the emperor's palace] is straight and [gorgeous as a lotus] flower, and the other gates lead to a roundabout way and are plain. You should not dwell at either of these two gates, but both allow for penetrating and progressing [toward enlightenment]. But if you [stop to] count the tiles and the trees [at the gate], they can both act to delay and obstruct [your progress]. If you are not sluggishly delayed by these Dharma gates, then you will not be attached to arguing about what is the cause and what is the result; this is called the mind of non-attachment. If you are not attached to Dharma teachings of non-attachment, you will not give rise to deviant [mistaken] views.

Next, if with a mind of attachment you become attached to this direct gate [or teaching that leads directly to enlightenment], you will give rise to deviant [mistaken] views. If you make distinctions concerning the features of the gate for the sake of fame, for gathering a crowd, for victory [in debate],

You are already old and can no longer partake in the three flavors 年已老矣無三種味: see the *Mahāparinirvāṇa Sūtra* at T 12.678a9–16:

> Good sons, people also become frail and old and dried out. In their minds they constantly think of the times when they experienced the pleasures of the five senses, Again, Kāśyapa, it is like at the time of the autumn moon the lotus flowers have all been enjoyed and have wilted and yellowed, or taken by evil people. Good sons, the coloring of advanced age is also like this. All passionate pleasures, when one has reached old age, have become evil and despised. Again, Kāśyapa, it is like sugar cane that has already been pressed so there is no flavor left. The visible forms of advanced age are also like this. When you are already old, you cannot take part in the three flavors: first is the flavor of leaving home; the second is the flavor of reading and chanting; the third is the flavor of sitting in meditation.

Penetrate close to the conjured city 近通化城: that is, leads all the way to enlightenment; a reference to the "parable of the conjured city" in the *Lotus Sūtra*, T 9.22a–27b. Note that "penetrate" is a translation of the same character 通 used for the "Shared" Teachings.

or for [material] benefit, then the bonds of hatred, covetous passions, and pride will be the cause for the arising [of mistaken views]. This is analogous to adding poison to good medicine; you will die from it [even if the original medicine is good]. If the poison of attachment to mistaken views is added to the true Dharma, suffering and the causes of suffering will increase; this is not the fault of the Tathāgata [or his teachings]. Those of heretical paths with clever faculties may realize true marks [of the teachings] through deviant marks and thus cause their attachments to become non-attachment and become a child of the Buddha. Those with dull faculties on the internal path [of the Buddha] **[137b]** may enter deviant [mistaken views] by means of the true marks [of the Dharma teachings] and arouse attachments through [the teaching of] non-attachment, and thus become a deviant disciple [of the Buddha]. How sad this is!

As for the four gates of the Distinct and Perfect [Teachings], whether they are skillful or crude, sharp or dull, both [of these teachings] penetrate to ultimate nirvana. The cause is not dwelling in attachments, and the result is no argumentative quarreling. If you "close the gate" and arouse mistaken views, you will give rise to passionate afflictions, like [the heretical ways of] Ulūka. If you contemplate [the true Dharma] in this way, it is like a person with clear sight being able to distinguish between the [clear and muddy] waters of the Ching and the Wei [rivers]. Why should you be confused over names [and teachings] and not be able to be aware of [the difference between] the pure and the impure or muddy?

If we summarize the clarification of arousing [mistaken] views, there are five types. Each type has four [variants], giving a total of twenty gates [or teachings]. Each gate has seven [variants], giving a total of one hundred and forty different teachings of mistaken views. If we discuss these [views] extensively, they are immeasurable, and they all are exposed and aroused on the basis of causes and conditions. If you consider it well, it is due to the penetrating cultivation of cessation that you are able to arouse various dhyāna [concentrations], and it is due to the penetrating cultivation of contemplation that you are able to arouse various [correct?] views. The condition of penetrating cultivation is due to [the practice of] cessation-and-contemplation, but the basic and distinct cause [for the arising of mistaken views]

The heretical ways of Ulūka 漚樓佉: see the discussion of various heretical ways earlier in the *Mo-ho chih-kuan* at 132b2ff.

Distinguish between the waters of the Ching and the Wei 涇渭: the waters of these two rivers are so different, one muddy and the other clear, that 涇渭分明 ("clearly distinct as the Ching and the Wei") is a common aphorism meaning "completely or entirely different," and 涇渭不分 means "unable to distinguish between the clear and the muddy; unable to distinguish between good and evil."

is surely [karmic influences from] past lives. Or, [the cause may be] from learning heretical ways external [to that of the Buddha]; or, from becoming a disciple of the Buddha and learning about Mahāyāna or Hīnayāna; or the cause may be the arousing of views upon hearing of the "characteristics of phenomena"; or, the cause for arousing [mistaken] views may be sitting in meditation. It may be that [many] lives have passed and you have forgotten, or that [your former] understanding is not made manifest. Now [in the present life] by cultivating a quiet mind [through meditation], or by hearing the [Buddhist] sūtras and treatises, you may become suffused with the karmic influences of past lives and thereupon resuscitate [mistaken] views. That which has come to maturity in past lives can be aroused easily in this present life; that which has not matured in past lives is difficult to arouse in this present life. If far [and a lot of time] has passed, it will be difficult to arouse; if near [and not much time has passed], it is easy. If the maturation of heretical views external [to Buddhism] is near, then they will be aroused first; if the maturation of internal [Buddhist] views is near, these will be manifested first. Supranormal powers and [worldly teachings such as those of] the Vedas are practical matters, if there is a span of a lifetime [or more] it is easy to forget and difficult to arouse them. These views entail a certain [limited] wisdom, so they are difficult to forget and easy to arouse. It is like people who are separated for a long time; you may remember the name but forget the face. The difficulty and ease of [the arising of] matters of actual practice or of principle are also like this. If in a previous life you externally had contact with a demon, then demons [or demonic forces in your current life] may augment this by arousing demonic dhyānas and demonic views. If externally you had contact with a noble person [in a past life], then a noble person [in this life] may augment [your past good experiences] by arousing right dhyāna and views.

Next, if you are not aware of the faults of various [mistaken] views, you will arouse fear with regard to the views and rush too quickly to sever them. Now, if you are aware of these deviant [mistaken] views, you can cautiously sever them without acting too quickly. Just let them come about as they will, using the power of auxiliary practices of the path, which will surely have great benefit. It is like having poisonous worms in your stomach; you should wait until they grow white and over an inch long, and later they can be purged with pearl barley broth. The reason for this [warning] is that ignorant

Characteristics of phenomena 法相: this may refer to the East Asian Yogācāra tradition (which, strictly speaking, emerged as a specific school, the Fa-hsiang, after the time of Chih-i), or just in general to the focus on learning in detail about "the marks of phenomena."

Pearl barley broth 幹珠: Chan-jan (BT–

people of this world are stubborn, just like bulls and horses; if they suddenly hear the thundering Dharma-sounds [of the Buddha's teaching], or see the expansive spreading out of an embroidered brocade, hearing or seeing these things will bring no benefit to them. If you are obsessively attached to the five sense desires, this is the suffering of poisonous worms. If you arouse various [mistaken] views and are consumed by these dull afflictions, you are like a white inch-long worm. If the wisdom of mistaken views and that of true contemplation are set side by side, when you hear the Dharma it will be easy to be awakened, like using pearl barley broth [to flush out the worms]. In this sense, therefore, you should foster these [mistaken] views and polish the mind as a preparation for opening and being guided to [the right path].

If you enter [the teachings of] the two vehicles, the [mistaken] views will be moved and you will cultivate the steps on the Path. If you enter those of the Mahāyāna, you will cultivate the steps on the Path without being moved by mistaken views. [137c] This is like receiving a medal after conquering bandits, or [in the case of Mahāyāna], the fostering of heretical views is like [training] soldiers [for battle].

If you arouse the views of the clumsy four gates of the Tripitaka Teachings, or the views of the skillful four gates of the Shared Teachings, even though these views can be an obstacle, they can act as profound auxiliary aids to the path. Although the [worldly] teachings of fortune and merit may make it easy to ascend to the heavens, they make it difficult to attain the path. These views entail a certain [limited] wisdom, so it is easy to drown in them, or one may quickly become awakened to the path. The *Ta chih tu lun* says, "There are those who attain the path from the three evil destinies, but they are few, and therefore not mentioned. It is just as a white person with black spots or moles [on his body] is not called a black person." If you know about

V, 532) explains, "this is a broth made from boiling the root of the Adlay (Job's tears, Chinese pearl barley, *Coix lacryma-jobi*) plant, which can wash out white inch-worms. Also useful for controlling larvae."

There are those who attain the Path from the three evil destinies, but they are few, ... not called a black person 三惡亦有得道人少故不說。白人黑黶不名黑人耳: see the passage in the *Ta chih tu lun* at T 25.72c8–14. Chodron (124–25) translates:

> Question. The Buddha [does not save only gods and men]. He can save also the beings who have fallen into other destinies *(gati)* such as the nāgas, the asuras, etc. Why is it said only that he is the teacher of gods and men?
>
> Answer. 1. The Buddha rarely saves beings belonging to the other destinies, whereas he frequently saves those who are reborn among gods and men. [This is why it is said that he only saves gods and men.] Just as when a man is white in color, even if he has black stains on his face, he is not described as a negro, because the black is insignificant.
>
> 2. Furthermore, the fetters *(saṃyojana)* among men *(manuṣya)* are light and

these [mistaken] views, delusions will not arise, and you can appropriately discriminate concerning them. It is like those of the heretical teachings who first had a mind of mistaken views, but when they accepted the teachings of the Buddha, they were like a nimble horse who reacts just by seeing the shadow of a whip, and were able to attain awakening. If there were no views, a thousand chops of the ax would not cut down the tree [to attain enlightenment]. It would be like preaching to bulls and horses; you could not get them to understand. The Chao-liao 獵獠 [barbarians in the southwest] cannot even understand [simple] words; how can they be expected to discuss profound matters? That is why the Buddha did not appear in this world in order to preach to these types of people, but changed his form and dispersed his essence to become a teacher and a friend and give guidance concerning these teachings of views. When the sun of the Buddha first emerged, the conventional [teachings] led to a drawing out of the real [teachings], and those who heard the Dharma were awakened. The *Lotus Sūtra* says, "He secretly dispatched two people." With regard to the Dharma teachings this refers to the skillful means of two teachings; with regard to people this means that conventionally he becomes the same as those of the two vehicles. All of the Noble Ones bend over to guide and teach people concerning views; now that you have aroused views, why should you rush to remove them?

If in a previous life you have cultivated the eight gates of the Distinct and Perfect Teachings but have not yet severed the delusions of the Shared Teachings, these views are aroused with the same faults as those of the three types of heretical ways. If in a previous life you have already destroyed the delusions of the Shared Teachings but are not yet awakened concerning the principle of the Distinct Teachings, you are the same as those of the two vehicles; if you have already fostered the previous views [of the Shared Teachings], why not [foster] these views [of the Distinct Teachings]? Vimalakīrti said "to take away the faulty extremes of the two vehicles and

detachment (*nirvedacitta*) is easy to attain (*sulabha*). Wisdom (*prajñā*) is sharp (*tīkṣṇa*) among the gods. This is why the Path is easily found in these two states. This is not the case in the other destinies (*gati*).

Nimble horse 快馬: this example (from the *Miscellaneous Āgama*) of a nimble horse who reacts just upon seeing the shadow of a whip and does not need to actually be whipped, has appeared in the *Mo-ho chih-kuan* many times already. For details, see the note at 19a23.

He secretly dispatched two people 密遣二人: a phrase from the parable of the poor son, T 9.17a8. Hurvitz (87 [80]) translates the context:

> At that time the great man, wishing to entice his son, devised an expedient: *he secretly dispatched two men*, whose appearance was miserable and who had no dignity of bearing …

Take away the faulty extremes of the two vehicles and become affiliated with the heretical ways 取二乘過邊撥屬外道: a

become affiliated with the heretical ways," and "to take the extremes of the auxiliary [practices of the Path] and make them your servants." Understand

summary of a passage at the beginning of "The Disciples" chapter in the *Vimalakīrti Sūtra*, T 14.539c15–27 and 540b19–c21. Luk (*Ordinary Enlightenment*, 20, 25–26) translates:

> Vimalakīrti wondered why the great compassionate Buddha did not take pity on him as he was confined to bed suffering from an indisposition. The Buddha knew of his thoughts and said to Śāriputra, "Go to Vimalakīrti to enquire after his health on my behalf."
>
> Śāriputra said, "World Honored One, I am not qualified to call on him and enquire after his health. The reason is that once, as I was sitting in meditation under a tree in a grove, Vimalakīrti came and said, 'Śāriputra, meditation is not necessarily sitting. For meditation means that non-apearance of body and mind in the three worlds (of desire, form, and no form); giving no thought to inactivity when in nirvana while appearing (in the world) with respect-inspiring deportment; not straying from the Truth while attending to worldly affairs; the mind abiding neither within nor without; *being imperturbable to wrong views during the practice of the thirty-seven contributory stages leading to enlightenment;* and not wiping out troubles (*kleśa*) while entering the state of nirvana. If you can thus sit in meditation, you will win the Buddha's seal.'..."
>
> The Buddha then said to Subhūti: "You call on Vimalakīrti to enquire after his health on my behalf."
>
> Subhūti said, "World Honored One, I am not qualified to call on him and enquire after his health. The reason is that once when I went to his house begging for food, he took my bowl and filled it with rice, saying: 'Subhūti, if your mind set on eating is in the same state as when confronting all (other) things, and if this uniformity as regards all things equally applies to (the act of) eating, you can then beg for food and eat it. Subhūti, if without cutting off carnality, anger, and stupidity you can keep from these evils; if you do not wait for the death of your body to achieve the oneness of all things; if you do not wipe out stupidity and love in your quest of enlightenment and liberation; if you can look into (the underlying nature of) the five deadly sins to win liberation, with at the same time no idea of either bondage or freedom; if you give rise to neither the four noble truths nor their opposites; if you do not hold both the concept of winning and not winning the holy fruit; if you do not regard yourself as a worldly or unworldly man, as a saint or not as a saint; if you perfect all Dharmas while keeping away from the concept of Dharmas, then can you receive and eat the food. *Subhūti, if you neither see the Buddha nor hear the Dharma; if the six heterodox teachers, Pūraṇa-kāśyapa, Maskari-gośālīputra, Sañjaya-vairāṭīputra, Ajita-keśakambala, Kakuda-kātyāyana, and Nirgrantha-jñāti-putra are regarded impartially as your own teachers and if, when they induce leavers of home into heterodoxy, you also fall with the latter; then you can take away the food and eat it. If you are (unprejudiced about) falling into heresy and regard yourself as not reaching the other shore (of enlightenment);*... if you are discontented with all living beings, defame the Buddha, break the law (Dharma), do not attain the holy rank, and fail to win liberation; then you can take away the food and eat it.'"

Take the extremes of the auxiliary [practices of the Path] and make them your servants 又取助邊使之為侍: see the *Vimalakīrti Sūtra*, T 14.544c7–8, which reads, "all demonic forces and heretical ways can become servants of awakening 一切衆魔及諸外道皆吾侍也." See also the

this as you make progress or retrogress, and do not just face in one direction. If you cultivate the path now in this life and [mistaken] views are aroused, you may realize the true principle [of awakening] in this life; if views do not arise, it may be difficult to encounter the noble realm [of enlightenment].

beginning of the chapter on "The Buddha Path" (T 14.548c29–549a27); Luk (*Ordinary Enlightenment*, 81–85) translates:

Mañjuśrī asked Vimalakīrti, "How does a Bodhisattva enter the Buddha path?"

Vimalakīrti replied, "If a Bodhisattva treads the wrong ways (without discrimination) he enters the Buddha path."

Mañjuśrī asked, "What do you mean by a Bodhisattva treading the wrong ways?"

Vimalakīrti replied, "(In his work of salvation) if a Bodhisattva is free from irritation and anger while appearing in the fivefold uninterrupted hell; is free from the stain of sins while appearing in the (other) hells; is free from ignorance, arrogance, and pride while appearing in the world of animals; is adorned with full merits while appearing in the world of hungry ghosts; does not show his superiority while appearing in the (heavenly) worlds of form and beyond form; is immune from defilements while appearing in the world of desire; is free from anger while appearing as if he were resentful; uses wisdom ot control his mind while appearing to be stupid; appears as if he were greedy but gives away all his outer (money and worldly) and inner (bodily) possessions without the least regret for his own life; appears as if he broke the prohibitions while delighting in pure living and being apprehensive of committing even a minor fault; appears as if he were filled with hatred while always abiding in compassionate patience; appears as if he were remiss while diligently practicing all meritorious virtues; appears as if he were disturbed while always remaining in the state of serenity; appears as if he were ignorant while possessing both mundane and supramundane wisdoms; appears as if he delighted in flattering and falsehood while he excels in expedient methods in conformity with straightforwardness as taught in the sūtras; show arrogance and pride while he is as humble as a bridge; appears as if he were tormented by troubles while his mind remains pure and clean; appears in the realm of demons while defeating heterodox doctrines to conform with the Buddha wisdom; appears in the realm of śrāvakas where he expound the unheard of supreme Dharma; appears in the realm of pratyekabuddhas where he converts living beings in fulfilment of great compassion; appears amongst the poor but extends to them his precious hands whose merits are inexhaustible; appears amongst the crippled and disabled with his own body adorned with the excellent physical marks (of the Buddha); appears amongst the lower classes but grows the seed of the Buddha nature with all relevant merits; appears amongst the emaciated and ugly showing his strong body to the admiration of them all; appears as an old and ill man but is actually free from all ailments with no fear of death; appears as having all the necessities of life but always sees into impermanence and is free from greed; appears to have wives, concubines and maids but always keeps away from the morass of the five desires; appears amongst the dull-witted and stammerers to help them win the power of speech derived from the perfect control of mind; appears amongst heretics to teach orthodoxy and deliver all living beings; enters all worlds of existence to help them uproot the causes leading thereto; and appears as if entering nirvana but without cutting off birth and death; Mañjuśrī, this Bodhisattva can tread heterodox ways because he has access to the Buddha Path."

4. Cultivating Cessation-and-Contemplation [137c20]

Fourth is cultivating cessation-and-contemplation with regard to [mistaken] views. Previously we discussed in general the differences involved in attaining views, that is, that there are one hundred and forty types. If discussed distinctly with regard to the internal [Buddhist] deviant [views], there are one hundred and twelve types. If we clarify the meanings with regard to [various Buddhist] schools 宗, there are many different schools, based on treatises such as the *Daśabhūmika* 十地, the *Middle [Treatise]*, the *She[-lun]* 攝 (*Mahāyānasaṃgraha-śāstra*), the Abhidharma treatises 數論, [the *Ch'eng-shih lun* 成實論,] and so forth, which make distinctions concerning the features of such views. Here [is my analysis in the *Mo-ho chih-kuan*] the same or different? How is this different with regard to deviant or correct, the way or a rut, superior or inferior? If we understand this meaning, we will know that [the interpretation here and that of the other various treatises] do not match [completely]. If there are those who do not understand [these differences], how can they be said to know [the deeper meaning]?

The Buddha Dharma has two [methods of] teaching: you are to be comprehensive [and inclusive], and the other is to analyze [and make distinctions]. For example, there are the "peaceful practices" [in the *Lotus Sūtra*] that are neither long nor short; this is the meaning of the "comprehensive" [and inclusive approach]. The *Mahāparinirvāṇa Sūtra* speaks of "taking up the sword as a weapon and cutting off the head [of the enemy]"; this is the meaning of "analyzing." Although the methods of "positing or refuting" are different, they both lead to some benefit. If [mistaken] views lead to the flowing and turning [in samsaric transmigration], you should sever them until they are exhausted. If they assist in training mysterious clarity 神明, and in converting the mind to realize the true [Dharma teachings], these should all be embraced.

I have explained above about various views with regard to a great variety of people **[138a]**, but there is no one person who arouses all of these [views]. Even if it seems that all [views] are aroused, they will certainly be swallowed

Peaceful practices 安樂行: see chapter 14 of the *Lotus Sūtra*, especially the phrase "Nor is one to talk of the good and bad, the advantages and deficiencies of others" 不說他人好惡長短 at T 9.38a3–4.

Taking up the sword as a weapon and cutting off the head 執持刀仗乃至斬首: see the *Mahāparinirvāṇa Sūtra* at T 12.624a16–17, which reads, "Protecting the True Dharma may require taking up a sword as a weapon and becoming a defensive guardian Dharma master." The phrase "cutting off the head" 斬首 appears earlier at 618a20.

This passage could (and was) used to justify war or violence to "protect the true Dharma," but Chih-i clearly uses it in a metaphorical sense.

up in a single [view of] truth 一事實. If every one [of the one hundred and forty] views are each analyzed through the Dharma gates [of the ten modes of contemplation], a skillful explanation [of these alone] would require [the entire summer retreat of] ninety days. Even if we bundle each and every one [of the views] together and in the same way [explain them] in terms of one of the modes of contemplation, this would require including all dharmas, and again could not be exhausted, even if you had mastery over the many and of [each] one. Now I will take up one view, and [it should be known that the explanation] would be the same for the many [other views]. Among the many views, "emptiness" is able to deconstruct all [others], while all other [views] cannot deconstruct emptiness, so it is very beneficial for leading people [to enlightenment]. Therefore I should first [expound on] contemplating emptiness as an example, in terms of the ten modes [of contemplation].

1. Objects as Conceivable and Inconceivable

1. Objects as Conceivable [137a7]

[Contemplating views as] conceivable objects [is as follows]: the [mistaken] view of emptiness gives rise to the phenomena of the ten dharma realms [from hell to Buddha]. A cucumber that is not cooked [or "exposed to heat"] can be the cause of disease; the view of emptiness is not [the same thing as] the ten dharma realms, but it can produce causes and conditions [that gives rise to these destinies]. The *Ch'eng-shih lun* says that even a moment *(kṣaṇa)* of an extreme view arising in the mind is a not-good [matter]. The Abhidharma clarifies that a moment of an extreme view in the mind should not be considered good or evil, but as neutral, as "a mind that arises on a par with its causes," and that all good and evil arise and are caused by this. Now these views of emptiness [in these two traditions] have two meanings. If they are

***Ch'eng-shih lun* says that even a moment of an extreme view arising in the mind is a not-good [matter]** 成論云。刹那邊見心起卽是不善: the source of this reference is unknown, although the *Kōgi* (BT–V, 540) points to a passage in *The Meaning of Mahāyāna* 大乘義章, T no. 1851, 44.465–875, section "5-15."

Abhidharma clarifies that a moment of an extreme view in the mind should not be considered good or evil, but as neutral, as "a mind that arises on a par with its causes," and that all good and evil arise and are caused by this 毘曇明。刹那邊見心起不當善惡名為無記。因等起心一切善惡因之而起: the source of this reference is unknown, and may be a general extrapolation by Chih-i of the Abhidharma teachings.

A mind that arises on a par with its causes 因等起心: meaning not clear; the *Kōgi* (BT–V, 540) tries explaining this clause as meaning "the first thought of a neutral mind, its thoughts, and its accompanying phenomena are the causes for arousing later thoughts of good and evil." Perhaps the initial simple thought is neutral, but can become good or evil?

contemplated separately, [one could say that the view of emptiness] arises on a par with its causes [of good and evil] and thus the ten dharma realms arise with this as their cause. Why is this so? In the past the [mistaken] view of emptiness had not yet been encountered or practiced. Now if you have aroused the view of emptiness, there will be the three actions [of good, evil, and neutral], as explained previously. Those who create evil [deeds] due to [the mistaken view of] emptiness [mistakenly think that they] practice the unobstructed Dharma [that anything goes]. On the one hand they do not perceive that they should honor the Dharma (sūtras), Buddha, and Sangha [or, lit. "field of respect" 敬田], and on the other hand do not perceive the virtue of honoring their parents. They cultivate the way of naked beasts, cutting off and extinguishing both worldly and transworldly goodness. Icchantika [who have no "seeds" to attain Buddhahood] may be evil, but they still have the goodness of mercy and love. Those with the [mistaken] view of emptiness will not have [even these virtues] for long, but only [abide in] the three [evil] destinies: those who inflict harm are born in hell; those who have no conscience or shame are born in the realm of beasts; those who are covetous or break the monastic rules [such as not eating after noon] are born in the realm of hungry ghosts. Because they break the rules [of not eating after noon], they are always hungry; because they are impure they eat defiled [food]. As for those who do good with [the view of] emptiness as the cause, they keep the precepts, practice austerities, and are adorned with the ten good deeds, and when their threefold karmic activities [of word, thought, and physical deed] reach maturity, they will be reborn in the three good destinies [of asura, human, and divine]. Also, if they arouse the basic [four dhyāna meditative states], they will attain the realm of form [beyond the realm of desires].

1. *The View of Emptiness among the Śrāvakas* [138a22]

As for those who are born in the realm of the śrāvakas with [the view of] emptiness as the cause, although this is called "emptiness," in reality they are not aware of [the teaching of] emptiness within the four [noble] truths. Why is this so? If they are enlightened concerning Dharma nature, this [understanding of] emptiness is pure, but the [mistaken] view of emptiness is vacuous and deluded and is certainly dependent on resultant recompense [from past karma], and this resultant recompense is of a defiled visible form. The *Pañcaviṃśati Sūtra* says that whether visible form is [seen as] permanent or transient all depends on [the view of] visible form. If emptiness is affirmed

Whether visible form is permanent or transient all depends on visible form. If emptiness is affirmed you are correct; otherwise [your views are] wrong 色若常無常等皆依

you are correct, otherwise [your views are] wrong. Emptiness takes on imaginary form, but is different from phenomenal dharmas of existence. The three actions [of good, evil, and neutral] have emptiness as a condition [for arising]. To distinguish the mind of emptiness as superior to other Dharma teachings is called [the teaching of] the "five aggregates." If emptiness is the object of the mind, these are two sense entrances. And if you add consciousness, then we have the three realms [of desire, form, and no-form]. Thus sense realms *(dhātu)*, aggregates *(skandha)*, and sense entrances *(āyatana)* are [the object of] the truth of suffering.

The [mistaken] view of emptiness is a place for hateful anger, a place for passionate attachments, a place for pride. But those for whom the [mistaken] view of emptiness is weak are able to seize and deconstruct the dharmas of Being; they can draw on the principle [of the truth] **[138b]** and approach emptiness without arousing doubt. If upon seizing [the dharmas of Being] they do not deconstruct them, and upon drawing [on the principle of truth] do not come [to realize emptiness], they may become quarrelsome and give rise to doubt. Again, although they may not have doubt now, they will surely have great doubt later. Why is this so? If their [view of] emptiness is [in accordance with] the principle [of truth], they should be equal to the noble sages, but those who are not equal [to the noble sages] cannot but arouse doubt.

Who is it that has calculating considerations about emptiness? It is "I" [or "the Self"] that has such calculating considerations about emptiness. [It is thought that] the Self is not really empty, and that emptiness is not the Self, and that emptiness is a cause for the arising of the Self. This so-called "Self" acts, the Self understands, the Self is praised, and the Self is defamed. To be attached to this extreme [view of] emptiness is to not be able to abandon and be free from it. If you wish to penetrate to nirvana with the way of emptiness as the cause, then this emptiness will be your precepts; these are not the precepts of birds and dogs [that allow for anything], but it assumes as causes the

於色。受納空是餘者則非: not a direct quote, but see the passage in the *Pañcaviṃśati Sūtra* at T 8.237b21–27:

> Śāriputra, the emptiness of visible form is not visible form, but there is no visible form apart from emptiness, and no emptiness apart from visible form. Visible form is emptiness, and emptiness is visible form 色卽是空空卽是色. [The same is true for] sensations, conceptions, volitions, and consciousness. If empty there is no consciousness, but apart from emptiness there is no consciousness, and apart from consciousness there is no emptiness. Emptiness is consciousness, and consciousness is emptiness. It is the same up to the eighteen unique dharmas of emptiness. There are no eighteen unique dharmas; apart from emptiness there are no eighteen unique dharmas, and emptiness is the eighteen unique dharmas, and the eighteen unique dharmas are empty.

idea that [some things have] no causes. These "causes" rob [the true meaning of causes], so this is [the mistaken view of] "attachment to precepts." To take a calculating [mistaken view of] emptiness as [true] emptiness is truly not the principle of emptiness. This takes what is not the fruit [of enlightenment] to be the fruit. This is like stealing [the meaning of] a "fruit"; and is to be attached to a [mistaken] view. Such a [mistaken] view of emptiness is a one-sided prejudice, and is a deviant view.

In this way the ten [dull and sharp] afflictions arise from [a mistaken view of] emptiness: [the noble truth of] suffering includes [all] ten; [the noble truth of] the causes [of suffering] include seven, excluding [the afflictions of [the mistaken view of] the body [or the self], extreme views, and attachment to precepts 身邊戒取; [the noble truth of] the path includes eight, excluding [the mistaken view of] the body [or the self] and extreme views; and [the noble truth of] extinction includes seven, excluding [the mistaken view of] the body [or the self], extreme views, and attachment to precepts. This gives a total of thirty-two [varieties of afflictions with regard to the four noble truths in the realm of desires]. [The realms of] form and no-form exclude [the affliction of] anger in the four [noble truths], so each [of the two realms] include twenty-eight [afflictions], giving a total of eighty-eight [32+28+28] afflictions. This is called the [noble] truth of the causes of suffering. These causes [of suffering] arise in the midst of suffering, and suffering arises due to these causes. "Suffering and the causes of suffering flow through this samsaric world, unknown to Dīrghanakha." Again, even a demon who sets his head on fire [as an ascetic practice] while already in [the divine realm of] no conceptions does not escape [from transmigrating in samsara]. How can you attain [liberation] while having [a mistaken view of] emptiness that is not aware [of the real meaning of the noble truths] of suffering and the causes of suffering?

[The view of emptiness in terms of the four mindfulnesses:] [1] If you are aware of the [mistaken] view of emptiness with regard to [the Noble Truths

Truly not the principle of emptiness: Ikeda (*Kenkyūchūshaku*, 467) follows the revised reading proposed by the *Kōgi* (BT–V, 543) that "this is to take a calculating [mistaken view of] emptiness as the principle [of truth]; [such an] emptiness is truly not the principle [of truth]" 計空爲理空實非理. The basic point is the same.

Ten afflictions 十使: the "five dull afflictions" of mistaken view of the self 我見 or 身見, extreme views 邊見, deviant views 邪見, attachment to precepts 戒取, and attachment to mistaken views 見取, and the "five sharp afflictions" of passions 愛, anger 瞋, arrogance 慢, ignorance 癡 or 無明, and doubt 疑.

... unknown to Dīrghanakha 長爪不識: this refers to a long passage in the *Ta chih tu lun*, T 25.61b19–62a28, already quoted many times in the *Mo-ho chih kuan*; see notes at 40c13, 62c8–10, and the full English translation at 133b11.

of] suffering and the causes of suffering, [you realize that] suffering and the causes of suffering all depend on visible form. "All phenomena of visible form" are called the "physical body." This body of visible form is defiled [by passions]; to be defiled is to be impure. Those who are wise consider this evil, and destroy the perverse view that [the physical body] is pure. This is called "mindfulness of [the impurity of] the body" 身念處. [2] If you sense 受 the view of emptiness, this is to sense or experience no sense 不受 [or lack of substantial existence of sense experience], which is the second option [of the tetralemma]. If in accordance with emptiness, you sense pleasure or bliss; if contrary to emptiness, you sense pain or suffering; if neither contrary to nor in accordance [with emptiness], you sense neither pain nor pleasure. These three types of sensations are the same as the three types of suffering. If you consider suffering or pain to be pleasure or bliss, this is called a perversion; if you know that there is [ultimately] no pleasure [in this world] and destroy the perverted [view of] pleasure, this is called "mindfulness of sensations" [as ultimately painful and involving suffering] 受念處. [3] The dustlike objects of emptiness are the objects of the mind, and give rise to consciousness. [The thoughts of] this mind arise and perish, always new and flowing like a current. If there are conditioned objects, then the concept [of emptiness] will arise; if there are no conditioned objects, then the concept [of emptiness] will not arise. These [thoughts] arise and perish and are transient, but they are [mis]taken to be constant, so this is a perverted view. To be aware of the transiency of consciousness is to destroy the perversion of "eternalism." This is called "mindfulness of thoughts" [as impermanent] 心念處. [4] If you grasp on to the image of that which is [actually] empty, and then perform good and evil [deeds], you conceive of a [substantial] "self" within those actions. If there is a "self" that performs these actions, then there are good or evil volitional actions, and if there is a rise and fall in these volitional actions, then it is the same with the "self." Since there are immeasurable actions, then if the "self" pervades them all, then the "self" is also immeasurable. If [the "self"] does not pervade [all such immeasurable volitional actions], then a single volitional action is without a "self," and therefore all volitional actions are without a "self." If you insist on calculating and positing a "self," [it must be said that] this is a perverted view. If you

Three types of suffering 三苦: suffering from coming in contact with that which is unpleasant, suffering from losing that which is pleasant or dear to you, and the suffering you feel from experiencing the constant change of this phenomenal world. The DDB has "(1) 苦苦 the suffering one experiences from contact with unpleasant objects (as one experiences in the conditions of sickness or hunger); (2) 行苦 the suffering caused by change; (3) 壞苦 the suffering experienced due to the destruction of conditions pleasing to the subject. (Skt. *tri-duḥkhatā; duḥkha-traya*)."

know [the truth of] no-self (*anātman*), this will destroy [mistaken] conceptions and volitional action. This is called "mindfulness of phenomena" [as without a substantial self] 法念處. You could apply these four perversions [in the same way] to all of [the rest of] the aggregates, though [it can be said that] the positing of a [perverted view of a substantial] "self" is strong in [the aggregates of] conceptions and volitions **[138c]**, the positing of [a perverted view of] purity is strong in [the aggregate of] visible form, the positing of [a perverted view of] constancy is strong in [the aggregate of] the mind [or consciousness], and the positing of [a perverted view of] pleasure is strong in [the aggregate of] sensations. This is called a "distinct mindfulness" 別念處 [that is distinctly mindful of individual characteristics]. A comprehensive mindfulness 總念處 is not like this. Thus I have discussed the view of emptiness as it gives rise to contemplations of mindfulness.

[The view of emptiness in terms of the four proper endeavors and the rest of the thirty-seven steps on the path:] If you diligently destroy the perversions through contemplation, this is [the destruction of mistaken] views through the [four] proper endeavors 正勤. To cultivate these with a concentrated mind is called the [four] "supranormal powers" 如意足. To give rise to the five good roots is called the [five] "roots" 五根. To destroy the five delusions 五惑 [of passionate desires, anger, ignorance, pride, and doubt] is called the [five] powers 力. To function peacefully on the Path is called "the seven [components of] awakening" 七覺. To practice peacefully on the Path is called "the eightfold Noble Path" 八正道. This is how the view of emptiness is able to give rise to the [Noble] Truth of the Path.

Because the four perversions are removed, ignorance is extinguished. Because ignorance is extinguished, passionate attachments are extinguished. Because passionate attachments are extinguished, anger is extinguished. Because anger is extinguished, you know that the [mistaken] view of emptiness is not the [right] path. Because you hang your head in shame, therefore pride is extinguished. Since there is nothing to be attached to, therefore doubt is extinguished. Thus the view of emptiness includes the [Noble Truths of] suffering and the causes of suffering, but [the Noble Truths of] suffering and the causes of suffering are not [the same as] ultimate emptiness; if you destroy the mind that is attached to emptiness, you no long seek a [substantial] "self." If a "self" is not sought after, then you can destroy [1] [mistaken] views of the physical body. If [mistaken] views of the physical body are destroyed, you can destroy [2] [mistaken] views of the self. If [mistaken] views of the self are destroyed, you can destroy [3] extreme views [such as annihilationism and eternalism]. [To know that mistaken] views of emptiness are not the path is to destroy [4] attachment to precepts. [To know that mistaken] views of emptiness are not nirvana is to destroy [5] attachment to [mistaken] views. [To know that mistaken] views of emptiness do not correspond to the principle [of reality or truth] is to destroy deviant views. By destroying these ten afflictions, you destroy eighty-eight kinds of passionate afflictions. By destroying the eighty-eight afflictions, you destroy the bonds of afflictions. Because you destroy the bonds of afflictions, you are able to arouse the first fruit [of the stream-winner] and progress to achieve [the level of] one who has no more to learn. If the bonds to these fruits are destroyed, you enter nirvana-with-no-remainder. This is [the explication of] the view of emptiness that gives rise to the [Noble] truth of extinction, that is, the Dharma realm of the śrāvaka.

If by means of the view of emptiness you clarify and become aware of the Four [Noble] Truths, you will know the exhaustion of suffering and the true path. The true path overcomes [obstacles such as mistaken views] and severs [delusions] so that you can attain [the level of] the wise and the noble [that is, three levels of erudition and ten noble stages]. Up to one hundred and forty types of [mistaken] views—single, multiple, combined, and non-verbal [mistaken] views—all are known on the true path, and thus you are able to move among and emerge from the [mistaken] views. If this is not so, then you cannot perceive the true [meaning] of the Four [Noble] Truths, and for that reason would forever flow in the great sea of suffering that is the samsaric cycle of birth and death. If you are able to perceive the Four [Noble] Truths, then you can attain a severance of [suffering in the cycle of] birth and death; if the arising of existence is already exhausted, you no longer experience these existences. This is the meaning [of my explanation] here.

2. *The View of Emptiness among the Pratyekabuddhas* [138c22]

Next is to clarify the view of emptiness for the arising of the pratyekabuddhas. The [mistaken] view of emptiness is not [true] emptiness; a deluded [view] is said to be emptiness. This requires distinctions concerning perverted views. Perverted views are [the same as] ignorance[, the first of the twelvefold chain of causation, which is the focus for pratyekabuddhas]. Because of ignorance there is attachment to the view of emptiness. If you know [the truth concerning] ignorance, why would you be attached [to anything]? If you know [the truth concerning] ignorance, you do not arouse

[Mistaken] views of the physical body … attachment to [mistaken] views: these are the "five mistaken views" 五見: 1. the mistaken view that the body is substantial 身見 *(satkāya-dṛṣṭi)*, 2. extreme views 邊見 *(antagrāha-dṛṣṭi)*, 3. deviant views 邪見 *(mithya-dṛṣṭi)*, 4. attachment to mistaken views 見取見 *(dṛṣṭi-parāmarśa)*, and 5. excessive attachment to the precepts 戒[禁]取見 *(śīlavrata-parāmarśa)*.

attachment and [further birth in] existence, and ultimately will not produce new [causes for rebirth]. If you do not produce new [causes for rebirth], you will not arouse attachment and [further rebirth in] existence, and ultimately will not arouse ignorance. If there is no ignorance, you will perfect the clarity of wisdom. Since you have wisdom, at that time there will be no passionate afflictions. If there are no passionate afflictions, at that time ignorance is extinguished. If ignorance is extinguished, all volitional activity will be extinguished, and so forth up to old-age-and-death being extinguished. The *Middle Treatise* says, "Why do śrāvakas, when they contemplate the mean-

Why do śrāvakas, when they contemplate the meaning of twelvefold causation, then expound the sixty-two views of eternalism, transiency, and so forth 云何聲聞觀十二因緣義。乃說常無常等六十二見: see the *Middle Treatise,* chapters 25–27 on "Contemplating Nirvana," "Contemplating Twelvefold Causation," and "Contemplating Deviant Views," at T 30.36b–c, esp. 36b10ff.

> These sixty-two deviant views are ultimately empty and unobtainable; all existence and what is obtained cease; and vain argument perishes. Because vain argument perishes, one penetrates all dharmas and their true aspect, and attains the calmness of the Path....

The exposition continues in Chapter 26, "Contemplation of the Twelve Causes and Conditions" [T 30.36b20–c8]; Bocking (1995, 372–74) translates (with some modification in terms to fit my translation):

> Question: You have expounded the Way of the ultimate meaning according to the Mahāyāna. Now we want to hear you discuss how the Śrāvaka-dharma enters into this Way of the ultimate meaning.
>
> Answer: Living beings, obscured in delusion
> Subsequently give rise to the three actions
> And through producing these three actions
> According to their predispositions they fall into the six destinies.
> Conditioned by the predispositions
> Consciousness receives a body of the six ways
> When consciousness becomes attached
> Name and form develop.
> Name and form developing
> Cause the six entrances to arise
> When senses, objects, and consciousness combine
> There arises sixfold contact.
> On account of the six contacts
> The threefold sensations arise
> One account of the threefold sensations
> Craving is produced.
> On account of craving there are the four graspings
> And because of the grasping there is existence.
> If the grasper would not grasp
> There would be liberation, and no existence.
> From existence there is birth
> From birth comes old age and death
> Because of old age and death there are
> All the afflictions of sorrow and ill.
> All such things as these
> Arise from birth
> Only through these causes and conditions
> Does the great suffering of the skandhas accumulate.
> The basis of birth and death
> And predispositions just described
> Is created by the unenlightened man.
> The man of insight does not create it.
> When these thing cease
> They do not arise.
> This suffering assemblage of the skandhas
> Thus simply ceases.

ing of twelvefold causation, then expound the sixty-two [mistaken] views of eternalism, transiency [annihilationism?], and so forth." **[139a]** It may seem that this question and answer [from the Middle Treatise] has no bearing [on the issue at hand], but now I should point out that this "answer" identifies the [mistaken] views of eternalism and transiency [or annihilationism] as ignorance. That is, if you know [the truth about] ignorance, you will not arouse attachment and [further rebirth in] existence: this is the contemplation of twelvefold causes and conditions within the Dharma teachings of the śrāvakas. The *Lotus Sūtra* speaks of "[those who] find pleasure alone in good quietude, and seek wisdom naturally." This wisdom is well able to put to rest the sixty-two [mistaken] views.

Again, contemplating the view of emptiness for even a brief moment *(kṣaṇa)* already includes [insight into] the Four [Noble] Truths. This mind of the view of emptiness, does it exist 有 or not exist 無? When a momentary thought is aroused, this already includes the five aggregates. How can we say that it is nothing 無 [or, does not exist]? This is the constituent [of twelvefold causes and conditions] of "existence" 有支. "Existence" contains "results," so again this is the interpretation that results are contained within the causes. Even if we say that there are no results [within causes], the constituent of existence is already a cause, and contains the meaning of a cause. Where, then, does this "existence" arise from? If there is no grasping, then "existence" does not arise. [The constituent of] "grasping" is equivalent to the five mistaken views. If you become attached to emptiness, this is an extreme [view], and you [mistakenly] posits a "self" in the emptiness [and so forth]. What is [mistakenly] called "empty" is taken as the Path, as nirvana, and as correct. This is the constituent of "grasping" 取支. "Grasping" arises from passions, to rejoice in the passions, to be angry about that which is contrary [to your desires], and to be proud and doubtful. These called the constituent of passions 愛支. Passions are the cause of [the constituent of] sensations 受, and passions are aroused because of sensations. It is like experiencing a single phenomena, and becoming passionately attached to this flavor, and

Find pleasure alone in good quietude, and seek wisdom naturally 樂獨善寂求自然慧: see the description of the pratyekabuddha in the explanation of the parable of the burning house at T 9.13b22–23. Hurvitz (63 [59]), translates:

> ... who, earnestly striving and seeking the knowledge which is so of itself (*anācāryakaṃ jñānam*), desire the quietude which is content with its own goodness (*damaśamatham ākāṅkṣamāṇāḥ*), and are deeply aware of the causes and conditions of the dharmas (*hetupratyayānubodhāya*), these are called [Those Who Mount] the Vehicle of the Pratyekbuddhas.

Note that the two phrases are inverted in Chih-i's quotation.

Five mistaken views 五見: see above at 138c11–13.

continuing to seek after it. Knowing sensations is caused by [the constituent of] "contact" 觸; thus there is the faculty of consciousness, through which you come in contact with empty dustlike objects. A sūtra says, "Due to the causes and conditions of contact, various sensations arise." Due to contact, there are the entrances 入 [of the six senses]. When the sense organs come in contact with the dustlike objects, you attain the entrances [of the senses]. Due to the sense entrances, there is [the constituent of] name-and-form 名色, with the three [false] imputations [of self-nature, a "self," and thoughts] of *kalala* [and so forth], then taking visible form with the five limbs, being able to sustain life, and developing the four mental aggregates which are the "name" [of "name-and-form"]. Again, "name-and-form" acquires the three [false] imputations, and due to this the fetus first has consciousness 識 [and volition]. Consciousness is due to [past] karma, and karma is due to [the constituent of] ignorance 無明, and ignorance is from the perverted views of the past. Based on mistaken views it is said that these matters exist or do not

Due to the causes and conditions of contact, various sensations arise 觸因緣故生諸受: a similar phrase is found in the "Ten *Bhūmi* Stages" chapter of the *Avataṃsaka Sūtra* at T 9.558b21–22, a section that has been quoted frequently in the *Mo-ho chih-kuan*. The exact phrase is found in the *Sūtra of the Ten Bhūmi Stages*, T 10.502a22.

The *Kōgi* (BT–V, 550) identifies this phrase as from the *Miscellaneous Āgama*, T 2.50a–c, but since it is a quite simple construction, it could probably be traced to a number of sources.

Three [false] imputations 三事: there are a variety of "three items" in Buddhist thought, but probably this one refers to categories from the Yogācāra tradition. The DDB explains: "In the *Bodhisattva-bhūmi-śāstra*, the three are a categorization of the eight deluded conceptions into three groups:

1. false imputation of self nature 自性妄想, differences 差別妄想, and generic clusters 攝受積聚妄想
2. false imputation of 'I' 我妄想 and 'mine' 我所妄想
3. false imputation of a thought 念妄想 a non-thought 不念妄想, and the difference between the two 俱相違妄想.

"In the *Yogācārabhūmi-śāstra*, the 'three circumstances' are taught in connection with the eight kinds of deluded conceptualization 八種分別. The first three imputations, that of self-nature 自性分別, differences 差別分別, and generic compounds 若總執分別, are the grounds for the arising of the bases and objects of conceptualization 分別戲論所依緣. The bases and objects of conceptualization serve as the ground for the arising of the views of self, and pride 見我慢. The views of self and pride serve as a basis for the generation of greed, hatred and delusion 貪瞋癡. These three together serve as the basis for the appearance of all conditioned phenomena."

Kalala 歌羅邏: the first of five "stages" in the development of a human fetus, referring to the first five weeks in the womb; a categorization from the *Abhidharma-kośa*: *kalala, arbuda, peśī, ghana, praśākhā*.

For an outline of this theory of the development of the fetus in the womb, see the *Mo-ho chih-kuan* at 52c27.

Five limbs 五胞: that is, two arms or hands, two legs or feet, and the head.

exist, therefore giving rise to the discourse in the present world about a physical body. A sūtra says, "The seeds of consciousness, the field of karma, the water of passions, and the obstructing coverings of ignorance, give rise to the sprouts of name-and-form." Now again there are perversions so that you are deluded into the [mistaken] view of emptiness, arouses good and evil deeds, and plants the seeds for the future sprouts of name-and-form. Perverted views build on perverted views and ignorance builds on ignorance, acting mutually as causes and conditions, so that there seems to be no end to them.

If you know ignorance and perverted views, it is not necessary to speculate about whether something "exists" or "does not exist." If you have penetrating understanding about the essential nature [of emptiness and reality], [you know that] basically it has no reality in itself, but seems to "exist" because of deluded conceptions of the merging of causes and conditions. If you already know [the truth] about perverted views, then ignorance will be put to rest; since it is put to rest all actions [and constituents of twelvefold causation up to] old-age-and-death will all be put to rest. For those to whom the [mistaken] view of emptiness, ignorance, and old-age-and-death are put to rest, a hundred and forty [mistaken] views, ignorance, and old-age-and-death will be put to rest. Because they are put to rest, the twenty-five realms of [samsaric] existence are destroyed and their habitual traces removed. This is called [the analysis of] the view of emptiness that arises in the dharma-realm of the pratyekabuddha.

Seeds of consciousness ... sprouts of name-and-form 識種業田愛水無明覆蔽生名色芽: see the passage referred to above in the the *Avataṃsaka Sūtra* at T 9.558b15–26:

> All ordinary ignorant people constantly follow after deviant thoughts, practice deviant and deluded paths, are blinded by deluded ignorance, are covetously attached to a "self,"... Why is this so? They arouse seeds of passion in the mind. Because they have a mind that grasps after defiled passions, they arouse a samsaric body. This is called the "earth" of karma. Consciousness [provides] the seeds, ignorance is an obstructing cover, and the water of passions the moisture. A "selfish" mind cultivates the various mistaken views, which grow and give birth to the sprouts of name-and-form. Due to name-and-form, there is the birth of various sense organs. Sense organs merge [with their objects] to make contact, and from contact is born sensations. Sensations of pleasure give rise to passions, and passions grow and there is grasping. Grasping is the cause and conditions for there being "existence," and existence arouses the five aggregates, which is the arising of the physical body. The five aggregates are transformed and are [eventually] called "old age." The perishing of the five aggregates is called "death." With old-age-and-death as cause and condition, there is sorrow and afflictions, the assembly of suffering and the causes of suffering. This is twelvefold causality. This is the assembly of non-existence and existence, and the dispersal of non-existence and existence. When there is a merging of conditions, this is "existence." When the conditions disperse, this is "non-existence."

If you are aware of [the role of] ignorance in the [mistaken] view of emptiness, this ignorance should be extinguished. If you are not aware of this, you cannot escape from the [mistaken] view of emptiness, and will produce karma because of this [mistaken] view, "as a silkworm produces a cocoon." How can such a one become a pratyekabuddha? There are "nose-focused meditation masters" who attain the view of emptiness **[139b]**, but many fall into the trap [of other mistaken views, or a mistaken view of emptiness] and are not able to extricate themselves. There are [scholarly] Dharma masters with distracted minds who, though they can classify and distinguish all the various afflictions, do not themselves know about the faults of the [mistaken] view of emptiness, like an ordinary tortoise whose sight is darkened, or a blind dog barking wildly. Whether practicing for oneself or saving others, they have absolutely no sense of the Path.

3. *The View of Emptiness among the Bodhisattvas of the Six Perfections of the Tripitaka Teachings* [139b3]

The view of emptiness which gives rise to the dharmas of the bodhisattvas of the six perfections [of the Tripitaka Teachings] is as follows. You are already aware of [the role of] the [Four Noble] Truths and [twelvefold causes and] conditions with regard to the view of emptiness, so then you should know about diseases and be aware of the medicines [for healing these diseases]. If you are aware of the medicines, you will rejoice for yourself; if you know about diseases, you will sympathize with others, and wish to be liberated from suffering and seek bliss together with other sentient beings. [From the perspective of] the view of emptiness, the [five] aggregates and [eighteen]

As a silkworm produces a cocoon 蠶作繭; see the *Mahāparinirvāṇa Sūtra* at T 12.613a6, "The binding wrappings of passionate afflictions are like the cocoon of a silkworm." See also at 768c6–7:

> Good sons, all sentient beings are not able to perceive [the true way of] twelvefold causes and conditions, and therefore they transmigrate [in samsara]. Good sons, as a silkworm produces a cocoon, [sentient beings] are born of their own [karmic actions] and die of their own [karmic actions].

Nose-focused meditation masters 鼻隔禪師: this seems to be a jab at those who are concerned only with their meditation (focusing on the tip of their nose) at the expense of broader learning and insight.

Dharma masters with distracted minds 散心法師: this seems to be a counter jab (see previous note) against those who are overly concerned with learning and fail to achieve proper concentration through meditation.

Ordinary tortoise 凡龜: Chan-jan (BT-V, 552) points out that there are ten types of tortoises, from the divine to those who live in the mountains, swamps, water, or fire, and that those who live in the mountains, swamps, water, and so forth, are "ordinary" tortoises.

realms are [the truth of] suffering; the ten afflictions and so forth are [the truth of] the causes of suffering; mindfulness and so forth are [the truth of] the path; the destruction of the four perverted views are [the truth of] extinction. It is in accordance with this that you then arouse [the four universal bodhisattva] vows. [1] One single [mistaken] view of emptiness can, in one day and night, give birth to many hundreds of thousands of millions of aggregates, and each and every one of the [collection of] five aggregates is a sentient being. Each day and night is like this; how much more [the number of collections of aggregates and sentient beings produced] in one lifetime, not to mention immeasurable lifetimes: as it is with the view of emptiness, so is it also with the other [mistaken] views. What are produced from [mistaken] views are truly many, and the aggregates that are given rise to also cannot be calculated. This is so for one person; how much more so for many people! Therefore there is [the first universal bodhisattva vow that] "though sentient beings are unlimited, I vow to save them all" 衆生無邊誓願度. [2] One single view of emptiness, from thought to thought, involves eighty-eight types of afflictions; the other three types of mistaken views, or sixty-two types [of mistaken views], also [each] involve eighty-eight types of afflictions. This is so for one person; how much more so for many people! Therefore there is [the second universal bodhisattva vow that] "though passionate afflictions are immeasurable, I vow to sever them all" 煩惱無量誓願斷. [3] One single view of emptiness involves cultivating mindfulness and the steps on the path; removing all [mistaken] views involves the proper and auxiliary practices of the path, which are immeasurable and inexhaustible. This is so for one person; how much more so for many people! Therefore there is [the third universal bodhisattva vow that] "though dharmas are inexhaustible, I vow to study them all" 法門無盡誓願知. [4] One single view of emptiness extinguishes passionate afflictions; immeasurable views extinguish immeasurable passionate afflictions. This is so for one person; how much more so for many people! Therefore there is [the fourth universal bodhisattva vow that] "though the Buddhist path is supreme, I vow to perfect it" 無上佛道誓願成. If the suffering and causes of suffering among sentient beings are their true nature, then they cannot be saved, but since suffering and the causes of suffering arise from causes and conditions, they do not have a [substantial] self-nature (*svabhāva*), the sea of suffering can [some day] dry up, the basis of the causes of suffering can easily be exhausted, and therefore it is said that [sentient beings] can be saved. This is the explanation of contemplating emptiness and arousing the [bodhisattva] vows [in the Tripitaka Teachings].

Arouse vows: the following gives a brief presentation of the four bodhisattva vows. For a detailed analysis of these vows, see the *Mo-ho chih-kuan* at 8a7–10b7.

Arousing practices [of the six perfections] in terms of [the view of] emptiness is as follows. [1] If you become attached to the view of emptiness, and yet practice [the virtue of] giving, this is a demonic giving. If you know [the role of] the [Four Noble] Truths and [twelvefold causes and] conditions with regard to the view of emptiness, of its faults and that things are transient and without a "self" and so forth, then you can abandon the [mistaken] view of emptiness, can sympathize with others and encourage them to abandon the [mistaken] view of emptiness; this is the [true] practice of [the perfection of] giving.

[2] If you are attached to the view of emptiness and yet attempt to keep the precepts, how is this different from "precepts" kept by beasts such as birds and dogs? If you know the [mistaken] view of emptiness, of its faults, and transiency, and so forth, then the view of emptiness will not be harmful, you can have compassion for others and lead them not to be hindered by the [mistaken] view of emptiness. [This is the true practice of the perfections of keeping the precepts.]

[3] If you are attached to the view of emptiness and arouse anger and passions, but forcibly practice [the virtue of] patience, your power will be insufficient, and your "patience" will only be a fear of others. Now, if you know the [mistaken] view of emptiness, of its immeasurable faults and so forth, then you will be able to overcome the [mistaken] view of emptiness and the sixty-two types [of mistaken views] and encourage others to have a calm patience with regard to the view of emptiness. [This is the true practice of the perfection of patience.]

[4] If you cannot remove the [mistaken] view of emptiness but try to be diligent [**139c**], then since [this diligence] is "mixed" [with mistaken views] it is not "fine," and since it involves retrogressing into the three destinies it is not "progress." Now, if you know the [mistaken] view of emptiness, for this [mistaken] view of emptiness to not arise is called "fine," and for the view of emptiness to destroy karma and for you to attain transcendence is called "progress." Again, to encourage others [to reach the same attainment] is to cultivate [this perfection of] diligence.

[5] If you do not destroy the [mistaken] view of emptiness and yet attain [a state of] dhyāna meditation, usually this will be a demonic affair. Now, if you know the faults of [the mistaken view of] emptiness, and are not moved by the [mistaken] view of emptiness, thus perfecting correct dhyāna and

It is not fine 精**, … it is not progress** 進: note that Chih-i is playing with the two characters that make up the binome for the virtue of "diligence" 精進, which makes a smooth English translation impossible, and also makes for an interpretation that would not be possible with the original Sanskrit *vīrya*.

correct penetrating [supranormal powers], and not for the sake of flattery, to toady favor, for pride, or for [material] benefit, then you use supranormal powers to encourage and save sentient beings and lead them to abandon the dissipation of [mistaken] views and enter dhyānic [concentration]. [This is the true practice of the perfection of dhyāna meditation.]

[6] If you are attached to the [mistaken] view of emptiness and yet cultivate wisdom, this is a deluded and ignorant worldly wisdom. Now, if you are aware of the view of emptiness in terms of [the Four Noble] Truths and [twelvefold causes and] conditions, you will "use the wolf of transiency to frighten the sheep of the [mistaken] view of emptiness and thus melt away the fat of passionate afflictions." You should broadly arouse the practice of the [bodhisattva] vows, so the body of virtuous qualities is fattened, and you should have compassion on sentient beings and lead them to remove the fat [of afflictions] and extend the flesh [of good qualities]. [This is the true practice of the perfection of wisdom.]

Thus [the bodhisattvas of the six perfections of the Tripitaka Teachings] mature their capacities through such conditions, and come to sit on the seat of enlightenment, severing the bonds [of passionate afflictions], and become Buddhas. This is called [the explanation of] the view of emptiness that arouses the Dharma world [of the bodhisattvas] of the six perfections

4. *The View of Emptiness for the Bodhisattvas of the Shared Teachings* [139c10]

[The view of emptiness for the bodhisattvas of the Shared Teachings is as follows.] Contemplate the view of emptiness as indivisible from ignorance, and ignorance as indivisible from the view of emptiness, that all suffering and the causes of suffering arise from ignorance, and all are unobtainable.

Use the wolf of transiency to frighten the sheep of the view of emptiness and thus melt away the fat of passionate afflictions 以無常狼怖空見羊煩惱脂銷: see the passage in the *Ta chih tu lun* at T 25.169b6–12. Chodron (2, 708) translates:

> A king had a prime minister *(mahāmātya)* whose faults he himself concealed so that they remained unknown. He said to him one day: "Go and find me a big sheep but that has no fat; if you don't find one, I will inflict punishment on you." The prime minister was learned: he chained up a big sheep, fed it with grass and grains; but three times each day, he frightened it with a wolf. Thus the sheep, in spite of all the food that it received, was big but had no fat. The minister brought the sheep and presented it to the king who commanded his people to kill it; it was big but had no fat. The king asked how that was done, and the minister gave him the reason we have just described. The bodhisattva acts in the same way: he contemplates *(samanupaśyati)* the wolf of impermanence *(anityatā)*, suffering *(duḥkha)* and emptiness *(śūnya)* in such a way that the fat of the passions *(saṃyojanameda)* melts while the flesh of the qualities *(guṇamāṃsa)* becomes solid.

Why is this so? The four perverted views [that things involve permanence, bliss, selfhood, and purity] are all mistaken positing that things are a true [substantial] nature; these perversions that must be healed do not exist [substantially], nor do the mindfulnesses that perform the healing [exist substantially], and so forth up to the path of awakening. All, without exception, do not arise [substantially], and are therefore unobtainable. Therefore the *Pañcaviṃśati Sūtra* speaks of "habitually learning the emptiness of suffering," and so forth. Those of the two vehicles know [the first aspect of the threefold truth, which is] emptiness itself, sever suffering, and realize extinction. Bodhisattvas [also know the truth of] emptiness and arouse compassion and the practice of the vows to save sentient beings. Although sentient beings are saved, what is saved is empty. Although passionate afflictions are severed, it is like fighting against empty [space]. Although Dharma teachings are aroused, it is like arousing empty space. Although sentient beings attain extinction [in nirvana], truly there are no sentient beings who attain the salvation of extinction. This is [true] wisdom; this is [true] severance; this is the bodhisattva's forbearance of [realizing that] dharmas do not arise. This is called the view of emptiness that arouses the Dharma realm of the bodhisattvas of the Shared Teachings.

5. *The View of Emptiness for the Bodhisattvas of the Distinct Teachings* [139c20]

[The view of emptiness for the bodhisattvas of the Distinct Teachings is as follows.] Contemplate this view of emptiness as having immeasurable features. For example, the Four [Noble] Truths can be distinguished and examined and calculated in an inexhaustible way. This inexhaustibility arises from the view of emptiness; the view of emptiness arises from ignorance. If that which arises is immeasurable, that which produces the arising is also immeasurable. That which arouses is conventionally named; that which is aroused is also conventionally named. If you infer ignorance in this way, then [one must say that] it arises from the nature of reality [or Dharma-nature 法性]. It is analogous to searching after a dream and knowing that it is due to being asleep. Contemplate this view of emptiness and become aware of the true aspect [of reality] 實相. The true aspect [of reality] is the womb or treasury of the Tathāgata *(tathāgata-garbha)* 如來藏. The immeasurable adventitious afflictions cover this treasury of the principle [of reality], and cultivating the Dharma teachings that are as numerous as the sands of the

Habitually learning the emptiness of suffering 習應苦空: see the passage in the *Pañcaviṃśati Sūtra* at T 8.222c8–28, which speaks of the emptiness of the five skandha, the Four Noble Truths, twelvefold causation, and so forth.

Ganges River will manifest its pure nature. This is called the view of emptiness that arouses the Dharma of the Distinct Teachings.

6. The View of Emptiness for the Bodhisattvas of the Perfect Teaching [139c27]

The view of emptiness in the Perfect Teaching is as explained above and below.

7. Summary [139c20]

Next, "the delusions of mistaken views are vast and extensive, like the waters of forty *li*; the remaining power of the conceptual delusions is like a drop of water." The various means [explained] above together control and heal the delusions of mistaken views; to exhaust the delusions is called "entering the current [of the path to Buddhahood" spontaneously and without retrogression.[**140a**] The delusions of mistaken views are difficult to remove, so you should skillfully use [various] means. The *Ch'eng-shih lun* says that delusions are healed and controlled by emptiness. If through the healing control of emptiness you can attain the realization [of Buddhahood], you do not need to wait for other Dharma teachings. If you cannot realize [Buddhahood just through emptiness], then what other ways of controlling [delusions] should be established? This is just as when fire arises in the midst of water: the water is not able to extinguish it. How can emptiness heal and control the excesses that arise from the [mistaken] view of emptiness? Now [to deal with this] you should know the [mistaken] view of emptiness as a disease of [the truths of] suffering and the causes of suffering, and then use the wisdom of the [Four Noble] truths to heal and control it. Those of the Tripitaka Teachings [should use] the wisdom of transiency; those of the Shared [Teachings] [should use] the wisdom of emptiness itself. All of these should have removed the mistaken view [of emptiness] already. Those of the Distinct [Teachings] again have previously removed [mistaken] views [of emptiness] and realized [true] emptiness. Next, they should skillfully emerge in conventional reality, like planting trees in the empty sky 空中種樹. As for those of

The delusions of mistaken views are vast and extensive, like the waters of forty *li*; the remaining power of the conceptual delusions is like a drop of water 見惑浩浩如四十里水。思惑殘勢如一渧水: from the *Mahāparinirvāṇa Sūtra* at T 12.824c16–18: "The passionate afflictions severed by a stream-enterer are like an expanse of water whose length and breadth is forty *li*, and what remains is like a drop of water."

This passage has been quoted above at *Mo-ho chih-kuan* 69a17 and 77a8–9.

Delusions are healed and controlled by emptiness 以空治惑: see the extensive discussion on emptiness in the chapter on "extinguishing dharmas" in the *Ch'eng-shih lun* at T 32.332c7–333c16.

the Perfect [Teaching], they do not deliberately remove mistaken views, but mistaken views have already been spontaneously removed. Removing such firm and stable mistaken views requires various means of healing control; how can you agree [with the *Ch'eng-shih lun*] that they can be healed and controlled only through emptiness?

How can various [methods] for healing control [over mistaken views in the Four Teachings] together heal and control one mistaken view? It is like a patient with the chills who utilizes four types of medicine. When you take ginger, the disease will pass and you will recover your strength. When you take the "five stones," the disease will pass and the color [of your face] will improve. When you take *zhong-lou* 重婁, you will add to your lifespan and be able to fly. When you take gold elixer 金丹 you will become a great sage 仙人. Although the disease is the same, the type of medicine is different, and the powers attained are also different. The Four Teachings heal and control mistaken views, but the exhaustion of these views and their understanding is different. It is thus with healing and controlling mistaken views, and it is the same with healing and controlling the other [delusions].

[One way] for a healing control [of mistaken views] with these Four [Teachings] is with the four mindfulnesses [of the body, sensations, thoughts, and dharmas]. The *I chiao* suggests that by depending on the four mindfulnesses you can cultivate the Path and escape from the "burning house" [of this samsaric world]. What does this mean? One thought of the view of emptiness in the mind involves all three realms [of desire, form, and no form], and "the three realms are not distinct phenomena, and are only produced by one mind." The view of emptiness gives rise to the karma of the six destinies [from hell to divine], so that you experience a physical body

Utilizes four types of medicine 用四種藥: The Taishō text, followed in the critical edition in BT–V, 559, gives the variant "applies" 同服 instead of "utilizes" 用.

Five stones 五石: Chan-jan (BT–V, 560) identifies these five items as white crystal 白瑛, fluorite (lapis fluoris) 紫英, gypsum 石膏, stalactite 鐘乳, and "stone fat" 石脂.

Zhong-lou 重婁: I have been unable to identify this medicine.

By depending on the four mindfulnesses you can cultivate the Path and escape from the "burning house" 令依四念處修道得出火宅: this content is not found in the *I chiao ching* (T no. 389), and the parable of the "burning house," as noted many times already, is found in the *Lotus Sūtra*. The *Kōgi* (BT–V, 561) points to a passage in the *Mahāparinirvāṇa Sūtra* at T 12.901b–c, but this is a stretch, as it just contains the phrase "the great fire of the three realms" (901b26) and then mentions the four mindfulnesses.

The three realms are not distinct ... 三界無別法唯是一心作: see the chapter on the ten *bhūmi* stages in the *Avataṃsaka Sūtra*, a section that has been quoted frequently in the *Mo-ho chih-kuan*. The phrase is at T 9.558c10 and reads, "The three realms are an empty delusion, which are produced by [one] mind" 三界虛妄但是(一)心作.

in the six destinies and dwell in the place of the six destinies; this "place" is the "burning house." For the physical body to dwell there involves suffering, and the karma is that of demonic spirits, where they compete with and reject each other, trying to ride the three vehicles to escape from there. The "three vehicles" are the mindfulnesses of the three vehicles [of śrāvaka, pratyekabuddha, and bodhisattva] of the Tripitaka [Teachings], and also these three [types of] people in the Shared [Teachings] who share one type of the mindfulnesses. Again, this refers to three types of the mindfulnesses within the [skillful] means of those of the Distinct [Teachings], and one type of the mindfulnesses that is truly real [that is, not just a "means"]. Again, the Perfect [Teaching] involves one true mindfulness. In sum, then, there are nine types of the four mindfulnesses [for the Four Teachings]. If explained in detail we could discuss [a similar] nine types of the steps on the path, or even more expansively discuss nine types of the Four Noble Truths. All of these various types of the [four] mindfulnesses are able to heal and control mistaken views so that you can escape the "burning house" [of samsara]. This is the meaning of the passage from the *I chiao*. However, when Śākyamuni first appeared [in this world], he first signified [the teachings of] the three types of people [of śrāvaka, pratyekabuddha, and bodhisattva] who would utilize the four mindfulnesses. This is as taught in the *Lotus Sūtra* as "each escaping the burning house for the goat, deer, and ox vehicles."

For the physical body to dwell there involves suffering ... to escape from there 身居即苦具。業即鬼神。競共推排三車自運乃得出耳: see the parable of the burning house in the *Lotus Sūtra* at T 9.12b–c.

Nine types of the four mindfulnesses 九種四念處: that is, three for the Tripitaka Teachings, one for the Shared Teachings, four for the Distinct Teachings, and one for the Perfect Teaching. See Chan-jan's extensive discussion of these nine at BT-V, 561–65.

Each escaping the burning house for the goat, deer, and ox vehicles 羊鹿牛車各出火宅: see the *Lotus Sūtra* at T 9.13b; Hurvitz (62–63 [59]) translates:

> Śāriputra, if there are beings who within are wise by nature, who, having heard the dharma from the World Honored One, believe and accept it; who, earnestly striving and wishing to leave the three worlds, seek nirvana for themselves; these are named [Those Who Mount] the Vehicle of the Voice-Hearers They are like those children who left the burning house in quest of goat-drawn carriages.
>
> If there are beings who, having heard the dharma from the World Honored One, believe and accept it; who, earnestly striving and seeking the knowledge which is so of itself, desire the quietude which is content with its own goodness, and are deeply aware of the causes and conditions of the dharma, these are called [Those Who Mount] the Vehicle of the Pratyekabuddhas. They are like those children who left the burning house in quest of deer-drawn carriages.
>
> If there are beings who, having heard the Dharma, believe and accept it; who, vigorously practicing and striving, seek All-Knowledge, Buddha-Knowledge, the knowledge which is so of itself, knowledge without a teacher, the knowledge

Next is to explain how the three types of people are the same in cultivating one mindfulness. This is as [taught] in the *Pañcaviṃśati Sūtra*, that "this vehicle [allows you to] escape from the triple world and dwell in [the wisdom of] *sarvajñā*." Again, it is like the statement in the *Great Collection [of Sūtras]* that says, "People of the three vehicles are the same in severing passionate afflictions by means of the Path that cannot be verbalized."

Next I will explain how bodhisattvas cultivate mindfulness gradually. The *Pañcaviṃśati Sūtra* makes distinctions among the vehicles as to unique *prajñā*-wisdom and mindfulnesses that are not yet merged [with the practice and attainments of other vehicles], but later explains that all [vehicles] of Hīnayāna and Mahāyāna involve the same one mindfulness. This is like

and insight of the Thus Come One, his strengths, and his fearlessness; who, mercifully recalling and comforting incalculable living beings and benefiting gods and men, convey all to deliverance; there are named [Those Who Mount] the Great Vehicle. It is because the bodhisattvas seek this Vehicle that they are named Mahāsattvas [great beings]. They are like those children who leave the burning house in quest of ox-drawn carriages.

This vehicle [allows you to] escape from the triple world and dwell in *sarvajñā* 是乘從三界出到薩婆若中住: see the *Pañcaviṃśati Sūtra* at T 8.259c18–19 and 260b22–23, which reads "Subhūti, through causes and conditions the Mahāyāna leads one to escape from the triple world and arrive at [the wisdom of] *sarvajñā* (omniscience), and dwell there immobile." See also the *Ta chih tu lun* at T 25.420b16–c3ff.

People of the three vehicles are the same in severing passionate afflictions by means of the Path that cannot be verbalized 三乘之人同以無言説道: this passage cannot be found in *The Great Collection of Sūtras* 大方等大集經, T no. 397, and perhaps just refers to the "great collection" of all sūtras? This full phrase has been used in many contexts previously in the *Mo-ho chih-kuan*, without attribution to a specific sūtra; see at 24a7–8, 28a4, and 68a16.

Distinctions among the vehicles as to unique *prajñā*-wisdom and mindfulnesses that are not yet merged 不共般若諸念處乘別而未合: see the *Pañcaviṃśati Sūtra*, as quoted in the *Ta chih tu lun* at T 25.564a21–b5:

> Some person has said that there are two types of *prajñā*-wisdom: the first type is taught only to the bodhisattvas, and the second type is taught together to the those of all three vehicles. That which is taught in common to the śrāvakas and Subhūti, [is taught] along with the birth of the Buddha. That which is taught only to the bodhisattvas is not taught to Subhūti along with the birth of the Buddha. Why is this so? The great bodhisattvas have a body born of Dharma nature, and within this there is no body born from the bonds of karma, but only a body born from transformation that has extinguished the three poisons and escaped the triple world. They dwell in this world to save sentient beings and purify a Buddha world. There are no śrāvakas in this world. But the great merciful mind of the Buddha is the same for the bodhisattvas. This is called the birth of bodhisattvas in accordance with [the Buddha]. Subhūti only grasps on to nirvana, so this "being born in accordance with [the Buddha]" is not taught [to him]. But this *[Pañcaviṃśati] Sūtra* teaches it together to both vehicles.

the *Lotus Sūtra* [which teaches about all three vehicles being included] as the same vehicle as the "great cart" **[140b]** that goes directly to the place of enlightenment. The view of emptiness in these terms clarifies all delusions and clarifies all [means to] heal and control them, and that all sūtras and treatises are not in mutual opposition or contradiction. [The *Avataṃsaka Sūtra* says], "The billions of scrolls of sūtras are contained in one minute particle of dust." This is the meaning here.

2. Objects as Inconceivable [140b3]

Next is to clarify the objects [of mistaken views] as inconceivable. One thought of the view of emptiness includes all ten dharma realms [from hell to Buddhahood]. That is, it is the Dharma nature. The Dharma nature is not something that is far away, [and so it is with] this mind of the view of emptiness. The *Vimalakīrti Sūtra* says, "The liberation of the Buddhas should be sought within the mind and actions of sentient beings, and should be sought within the sixty-two types of mistaken views." These three dharmas [of liberation, sentient beings, and the mistaken views] are not different, but are pointed out [one by one] in turn. All sentient beings are indivisible from *bodhi*-wisdom, which is unobtainable yet is perfectly pure liberation. The five aggregates are indivisible from nirvana, which cannot be extinguished and yet is liberation as pure means. The suchness of sentient beings is indi-

The same vehicle as the "great cart" that goes directly to the place of enlightenment 同乘大車直至道場: see the *Lotus Sūtra* and the parable of the burning house at T 9.15a13–14; Hurvitz (73–74 [68]) translates:

> If they can gain this kind of Vehicle,
> I enable those children
> Night and day, for a number of kalpas,
> Ever to amuse themselves,
> With bodhisattvas
> And the multitude of voice-hearers
> To mount this jeweled Vehicle
> And to arrive directly at the Platform of the Way

The billions of scrolls of sūtras are contained in one minute particle of dust 一微塵中有大千經卷: see the *Avataṃsaka Sūtra* at T 9.624a6 and again at 625a6c10–1. This has been quoted previously; for a full translation and discussion of the context, see *Mo-ho chih-kuan* at 9a16.

The liberation of the Buddhas should be sought within the mind and actions of sentient beings, and should be sought within the sixty-two types of mistaken views 諸佛解脱當於衆生心行中求。當於六十二見中求: see the *Vimalakīrti Sūtra*, T 14.544c4–10; Luk (*Ordinary Enlightenment*, 51) translates:

> Mañjuśrī asked: "Where can emptiness be sought?"
>
> Vimalakīrti replied: "It should be sought in the sixty-two false views."
>
> Mañjuśrī asked: "Where should the sixty-two false views be sought?"
>
> Vimalakīrti replied: "They should be sought in the liberation of all Buddhas."
>
> Mañjuśrī asked: "Where should the liberation of all Buddhas be sought?"
>
> Vimalakīrti replied: "It should be sought in the minds of all living beings."

visible from the suchness of the Buddha; this is liberation as the nature of purity. The liberation of the Buddha is the five types of nirvana, such as the liberation of visible form. The mind of the view of emptiness is indivisible from the defilements of the five aggregates: sentient beings are made up of the five aggregates, and sentient beings have five aggregates. "Name and form" [that is, the mental and physical aggregates] and sentient beings are mutually bound together, and they cannot be mutually separated. Contemplating these five aggregates, they are indivisible from nirvana, and so they do not need to be extinguished. Originally there are no bonds or fetters [of afflictions]; this is liberation. Originally there is liberation, which encompasses all phenomena. Therefore it is said that liberation should be sought in the mind [of sentient beings].

Again, contemplate this mind of the view [of emptiness] and the five aggregates as indivisible from Dharma nature [or the nature of reality]. Again, there is no [substantial] mind of views or the five aggregates. By extinguishing visible form you attain the constant form and so forth of the five aggregates of Dharma nature. By extinguishing sentient beings, you attain constant dwelling as a sentient being of Dharma nature. One visible form is all visible forms; one consciousness is all consciousness; one sentient being is all sentient beings; these do not mutually obstruct each other, just as a clear mirror is pure and manifests all colors and images. This is called "the nature of purity." The three types of liberation cannot be mutually separated, are neither vertical nor horizontal, are inconceivable, are perfectly complete and inclusive, and so should be sought within the view of emptiness. This is called "the objects as inconceivable."

2. Arousing Compassion [140b21]

These objects [of mistaken views] have naturally been endowed with [both] ignorance and Dharma nature, and yet you have harmed yourself and sunk

Five types of nirvana 五種涅槃: see the section on "objects as inconceivable" earlier in the *Mo-ho chih-kuan* at 127a1–18, which mentions "perfectly pure nirvana" 圓淨涅槃, "nirvana of the nature of purity" 性淨涅槃, and "nirvana of purity of skillful means" 方便淨涅槃. From the context here, it seems that there is a "nirvana" that corresponds to each of the five aggregates, but they are not spelled out, nor their correspondence identified.

See, however, a passage in the *Mahāparinirvāṇa Sūtra* [T no. 374] at T 12.467b19–20 and [T no. 375] at 710a18–119, which mentions "the five types of nirvana, that is, the liberation of visible form up to the liberation [of the fifth aggregate] of consciousness."

Three types of liberation 三種解脱: that is, the three liberations of [1] liberation as the purity of means 方便淨解脱; [2] liberation as perfect purity 圓淨解脱; and [3] liberation as the [fundamental] nature of purity 性淨解脱.

into darkness, and now for the first time have become aware that all sentient beings are also like this. If you know Dharma nature [in this way], how can you not arouse kindness 慈? If you know ignorance [in this way], how can you not arouse pity 悲?

3. Skillful Means for a Peaceful Mind [140b24]

In contemplating this view of emptiness, [you realize that] your inherent original nature 本性 is empty and quiescent, and pure like space. You should polish these two dharmas [of cessation and contemplation] skillfully and with a peaceful mind.

4. Deconstructing Dharmas [140b25]

The view [of emptiness] of the [five] aggregates, and the view [of emptiness] of conventionality do not give rise to the four options [of the tetralemma, but should be universally deconstructed].

5. Knowing What Penetrates and What Obstructs [140b25]

The single and multiple [forms of] the various options, and each of the options [of the tetralemma], involve the obstacles of suffering, the causes of suffering, ignorance, and the obscurations [of afflictions]. Each of the options [of the tetralemma] involves the penetrating [insight] of the path and extinction.

6. Steps on the Path [140b27]

In contemplating the view of emptiness, one skandha is all skandhas. [Know that] the threefold truth is immobile [and does not change]; this is what it means to apprehend the Dharma Body. Contemplate the aggregates as neither pure nor impure, and so forth. This is the [final] nirvana [of the Buddha] under the twin [*śāla*] trees [at his death in Kuśinagara]; again, it is the seat of enlightenment. This contemplation is called "*prajñā*-wisdom." To destroy the eight perversions is called "liberation." To have one mindfulness **[140c]** is to arouse all mindfulnesses, which regulates and controls sentient beings. In this way these three dharmas [of the Dharma Body, *prajñā*-wisdom, and liberation] are neither cause nor result. They are not a cause, and yet mindfulness is a cause for [attaining] the seat of enlightenment. They are not a result, and yet the result of being in the midst of the twin [*śāla*] trees was to enter [final] nirvana. Although the view of emptiness is immobile [and does not change], you cultivate the inconceivable thirty-seven steps [on the path]. In this way you universally deconstruct [all dharmas]; the non-attaining of the view of emptiness is called "the samādhi of emptiness"; not perceiving the marks of emptiness is called "the samādhi of formlessness"; and that these samādhi do not arise from real conditions is called "the samādhi of actionlessness."

7. Auxiliary Methods [140c6]

If you have still not realized [enlightenment through the above contemplations], you should arouse a great vow, internally to abandon attachment to [mistaken] views, and externally to reject [worldly] life and treasure. If your view of emptiness is contrary to the principle [of truth], your keeping of the precepts is not pure, so vow that your view of emptiness will not offend against the Dharma Body. Maintain the seven components [of awakening] without flinching in your consciousness.

9. Resting in Patient Forbearance [140c9]

If your view of emptiness is clamorous and unsteady, patience will not be perfected. Now you should vow to suffer the view of emptiness with a peaceful mind, like a bridge [that allows people to walk over it] or the earth or the sea, taking on all [suffering] in your own body, while the mind remains unmoved. If your view of emptiness is troublesome, vow to focus purely and to flow from thought to thought. Again, if your view of emptiness torments you so that you are not able to focus calmly, then sincerely confess and put an end to the two aspects of [mental function and cognized objects in] the flourishing of conditions. If universal wisdom is not yet disclosed, then ignorance has not yet been destroyed, so vow to contemplate the view of emptiness so that Dharma nature will be made manifest. Make progress bravely with a firm conviction, and do not rest if you have not yet been enlightened. In this way control and heal [the afflictions] to assist in manifesting nirvana.

8. Graded Stages of Attainment [140c14]

Be deeply aware of the graded stages [of attainment] so that you will not be indiscriminate about the upper *bhūmi* stages [and think you have attained them when you have not].

10. No Passionate Attachments to Dharmas [140c15]

If you are not able to destroy the internal wind [of passions] and external dust-like objects, but are in accordance with the path, then attachment

Without flinching in your consciousness 不撓含識: or, "without yielding to sentient beings"?

Two aspects of the flourishing of conditions 二攀緣: (see DDB) "encountering cognized objects"; that is, the arising of consciousness due to contact with the external world, or, the mental function of cognizing objects and the cognized objects themselves.

to dharmas will not arise, and you will not fall from the pinnacle [and retrogress to a lower state]. The thoughts of your mind will be quiescent and extinct, and you will flow into the sea of [the wisdom of] omniscience *(sarvajñā).*

11. Summary [140c17]

Riding on the one great vehicle, you will traverse the four directions directly to the seat of enlightenment, and perfect right awakening. The rest is as explained above. [end of fascicle ten]

Riding on the one great vehicle, you will traverse the four directions directly to the seat of enlightenment, and perfect right awakening 乘一大車遊於四方。直至道場成得正覺: as before, from the *Lotus Sūtra,* T 9.15a13–14.

End of fascicle ten: here ends the exposition of the *Mo-ho chih-kuan*. As stated in the opening paragraph (1a7), Chih-i "completed only through [the section on the contemplation of] the objects of [mistaken] views." However, it is not difficult to extrapolate the possible content of the remaining sections (see comments by Chan-jan, BT–V, 572). The remaining three sections of this Chapter 7, that is, 8. Contemplating the Objects of Overweening Pride, 9. Contemplating the Objects of the Two Vehicles, and 10. Contemplating the Objects of the Bodhisattvas, should involve an analysis of these themes in terms of the threefold truth, Fourfold Teachings, and so forth, and a parsing of these topics through the ten modes of contemplation, especially on the details and levels of enlightenment. The final three chapters, that is, 8. Results and Recompense, 9. On Instilling the Teachings, and 10. The Ultimate Meaning, can also be extrapolated based on the final three sections ("Experiencing Great Results" [20a24–b4], "Rending the Great Net" [20b4–13], and Returning to the Great Abode" [20b13–21b9]) in the opening synopsis of the *Mo-ho chih-kuan*. Of course, no one knows what juicy insights Chih-i's genius would have come up with in the details.

There is some debate as to whether the exposition stops here because they had reached the end of the three-month summer retreat. In the *Mo-ho chih-kuan* itself, Chih-i states that "vast distinctions are to be made within [section 10] on bodhisattvahood as the object [of contemplation]. There I will discuss the realization [of enlightenment]…" (98a11–12) and "The virtuous qualities of the stages to be realized will not be expounded here, but I will elucidate them later" (100a2–3), indicating that Chih-i indeed intended to complete the final sections.

Chan-jan, on the other hand, claims that the last three chapters remain unspoken because "they go beyond the patience from realizing the non-arising of dharmas," presumably because this cannot be explained in words. However, this has not stopped Chih-i in other places from trying to explain what is "beyond verbalization."

Again, it is difficult to imagine that, if Chih-i had prepared some lecture notes for these remaining sections, Kuan-ting would not have incorporated (and expanded on) them during the long editorial process that resulted in this final text. The most reasonable conclusion is that Chih-i did not prepare an exposition of these final sections.